THE COMMITTEE ON STANDARDS IN PUBLIC LIFE
TRANSCRIPTS OF ORAL EVIDENCE

TABLE OF CONTENTS

VOLUME II
LIST OF WITNESSES

Where witnesses have submitted opening statements these have been included at the end of each days evidence.

Standards in Public Life

WITHDRAWN

Local Public Spending Bodies

FURTHER AND HIGHER EDUCATION BODIES (INCLUDING UNIVERSITIES)

GRANT-MAINTAINED SCHOOLS

TRAINING AND ENTERPRISE COUNCILS AND LOCAL ENTERPRISE COMPANIES

HOUSING ASSOCIATIONS

*Second Report of the Committee on
Standards in Public Life
Chairman Lord Nolan*

Volume 2 : Transcripts of Oral Evidence

Presented to Parliament by the Prime Minister by Command of Her Majesty

May 1996   Cm 3270–II   £34

LONDON : HMSO

TRANSCRIPTS OF ORAL EVIDENCE

LIST OF SUPPLEMENTARY MEMORANDA RELATING TO TRANSCRIPTS OF ORAL EVIDENCE

VOLUME II

The principal documents necessary to understand evidence given by witnesses in the transcripts of oral evidence are included at the end of this volume. Copies of other submissions received by the Committee, relating to local public spending bodies, may be consulted at the Public Records Office in Kew, the Public Record Office of Northern Ireland in Belfast, the Scottish Public Records Office in Edinburgh, and the National Library of Wales in Aberystwyth.

LIST OF ORGANISATIONS SUBMITTING WRITTEN EVIDENCE

LIST OF MEETINGS AND VISITS UNDERTAKEN BY THE COMMITTEE AND MEMBERS OF THE SECRETARIAT

TUESDAY 14 NOVEMBER 1995

Members Present:
The Rt Hon Lord Nolan (Chairman)

Sir Clifford Boulton GCB
Professor Anthony King
The Rt Hon Peter Shore MP
The Rt Hon The Lord Thomson of
 Monifieth KT DL

Sir William Utting CB
Dame Anne Warburton DCVO CMG
Diana Warwick

Witnesses:
Sir Geoffrey Holland KCB (Vice-Chancellor of Exeter University and former
Permanent Secretary at Department of Education and Department of Employment)
Sir William Stubbs, Chief Executive, Sir Robert Gunn, Chairman, Mr Roger
McClure, Director of Finance, Further Education Funding Council for England
Derek Betts, Head of Policy, Vicky Seddon and Peter Latham, National
Association of Teachers in Further and Higher Education
Keith Scribbens, Chair and Roger Ward CBE, Chief Executive, Colleges
Employers Forum and Ruth Gee, Chief Executive and Mike Thrower, Member of the
Council and Chair of the Ethics Committee, Association for Colleges

1. LORD NOLAN: It is not quite 10.30, but an extra two minutes is always welcome. We have the committee here and we have Sir Geoffrey Holland. So let me welcome you all to the first day of open hearings in this, the second study by the Committee on Standards in Public Life.

This study, as I am sure everyone present knows, is looking at what we have described as *"local public spending bodies"*. These are universities and other higher education bodies, further education colleges, training and enterprise councils—or local enterprise companies in Scotland—grant maintained schools and housing associations. In our Issues paper we said that they spent about £11 billion a year between them. I am told that in the current financial year it is in fact nearly £15 billion.

We chose to describe these bodies as local public spending bodies to reflect the fact that most of them have local rather than national roots and that they all, in one way or another, spend public money to deliver public services to individuals. The description has caused some controversy, and I hasten to make it clear that, for example, we know that universities have a role which goes much wider than their immediate locality, and we are not claiming that bodies such as housing associations are part of the public sector.

However, we have deliberately grouped this disparate collection of bodies into a single study in the hope that we can build on the ground work of our first study, where our recommendations on quangos have virtually all been accepted by government, and determine whether there are general principles and safeguards which can apply to all bodies providing public services, regardless of their precise position on the public/private sector spectrum.

The setting and the lay-out of this room will be familiar to all those who sat through our first hearings, though I suspect that the degree of day-to-day public interest may not be quite so intense. As a good lawyer should, I shall follow the precedent of those first hearings and begin by introducing our witnesses for today.

Our first witness, as I have indicated, is Sir Geoffrey Holland, a very distinguished figure in the world of education and training, former Permanent Secretary of the Departments of Employment and Education, although, unlike the present occupant, he held those posts in sequence. He is now Vice-Chancellor of Exeter University. I hope that, as our opening witness, Sir Geoffrey, drawing on the breadth of his experience, will range widely in his observations.

Our second witnesses are old friends. Sir Robert Gunn, Chairman, and Sir William Stubbs, Chief Executive, of the Further Education Funding Council, appeared during our first study to describe some of the good practice which they had adopted and which greatly informed our recommendations then. I have no doubt that they will be equally helpful today. Today they are accompanied by Roger McClure, the Director of Finance.

Unfortunately John Akker, General Secretary of the National Association of Teachers in Further and Higher Education, has had to stand down this morning. We shall instead look forward to hearing from Derek Betts, the association's head of policy. He will be accompanied by Vicky Seddon and Peter Latham.

Finally this morning, we shall hear jointly from the Colleges Employers Forum and the Association for Colleges, two organisations which I understand are in the process of merging. Keith Scribbens, Chair, and Roger Ward, Chief Executive, represent the former, while Mike Thrower, council member and Chair of the Ethics Committee, together with Ruth Gee, Chief Executive, represent the latter.

That concludes my opening statement. Before we go any further, may I ask members of the committee present today to declare their interests in the subject matter of our inquiry, the field of higher education. Dame Anne.

ANNE WARBURTON: Chairman, I serve currently on the council of the University of East Anglia.

DIANA WARWICK: Chair, I am the Chief Executive of the Committee of Vice-Chancellors and Principals of British Universities.

PROF ANTHONY KING: And I teach at a university, the University of Essex.

WILLIAM UTTING: I am the deputy chairman of the council of Goldsmiths College, which is one of the schools of the University of London.

2. LORD NOLAN: There is a glittering academic array in front of you, Sir Geoffrey. We shall begin our questions, if I may.

You of course are now presiding over an institution—Exeter University—which has always been, to a large extent, self-governing, but while you were at the Departments of Employment and Education you oversaw a process that moved training out of the realm of the Manpower Services Commission and into the training and enterprise councils, which are virtually private sector organisations, and at the same time moved colleges and many schools out of local authority control into self-governing status. Having seen the position from, so to speak, both sides, the public and the private side of the fence, what do you see as the main advantages of the self-governing form of organisation?

SIR GEOFFREY HOLLAND KCB

SIR GEOFFREY HOLLAND KCB (Vice-Chancellor of Exeter University and former Permanent Secretary at the Departments of Education and Employment): Chairman, could I right at the beginning say that I am going to answer all these questions as an individual and not as a representative of any body. Thank you for asking people to declare their interests. I will try to find my way through some of the minefields.

The policies that you refer to, Chairman, were of course determined by Ministers, but I think that there are clear advantages in the self-governing status, and quite a number of them. I quite agree, incidentally, with the general thrust of the Committee's document that there need to be safeguards on the way. But for the moment I just want to list some of the advantages.

It seems to me that, once one has a self-governing organisation, several things become much clearer to the great advantage of the operation. The objectives of the organisation are determined by the organisation, within no doubt a general framework of government policy, and they are clearer. I think the accountability—who is accountable for what and to whom—is clearer. I think that there are all the advantages of devolved management and responsibility for youth resources and recruitment and deployment of staff. I think there is a much clearer ability to focus upon the customer and services tailored to the customer. There is a much greater possibility, it seems to me, for local variations of provision and of organisation to suit the needs of a particular local area or, if I may say so, a wider market place. I personally think that, certainly in the fields of higher education and further education, and probably also in the field of schools, the increased element of competitiveness is a spur to efficiency and greater value for money. I think also, from the governmental and funding body end, that once one has that structure which you described, Chairman, there is pressure on the funding body to focus on the outputs, the purposes and the objectives rather than obsession with the processes.

Perhaps I could just tell a small story. I will not try the Committee's patience too long. When the Manpower Services Commission was first formed, it had a major

responsibility for training. The Ministry of Labour, and the Department of Employment before it, had had responsibility for something called training and a training policy. What one found in the Manpower Services Commission was that the Department and its officials knew a very great deal about processes and appointments to particular bodies like industry training boards but nothing at all about outputs, achievements or quality. It was that move towards pushing the Higher Education Funding Council, the Further Education Funding Council, the Funding Agency for Schools and, beyond that, the Government Department as it now is—the singular—to focusing on what we want to achieve in this country and whether we are achieving it rather than obsession with individuals, politics and processes.

3. LORD NOLAN: In the course of determining what we want to achieve in this country is there a danger of too much diffusion of ideas about what we want to achieve as you move away from political oversight and away from the area of central government?

GEOFFREY HOLLAND: The answer to that question must be yes. I would argue that it is a good thing in the local context, but I think the thrust of my last point in answer to your opening question, Chairman, is that government and others are pushed increasingly towards a framework of national objectives. For example, it is no coincidence in my view that, since some of the developments that you mentioned in your opening question, the thrust towards national education and training targets and an agreed framework nationally espoused has taken place. That is what we are trying to achieve as a national framework. It seems to me that any government of any complexion—any central government—has a responsibility for establishing and communicating, in partnership with others, what national objectives might be, but then, as it were, the variety of ideas about carrying those out, the translation of those objectives into what makes sense in a particular market place or locality, seems to me very much better done locally than centrally.

4. LORD NOLAN: I wonder if you could turn now with me to the question of how you recruit the boards of these various organisations, because, as we all know, a great deal of public money goes through their hands. They are not appointed by Ministers, they are not elected, they are not paid. What can you tell us, please, about what you see as the best practice and recruitment and also, as a rider to that, tell us whether you think there is any case for payment?

GEOFFREY HOLLAND: Let me turn to best practice first, Chairman, if I may. The danger is very clearly identified by the Committee: it is of self-perpetuating groups of people and it is of people who go on and on past their sell-by date and of, as it were, hidden and opaque processes and individuals which nobody can see, nobody knows quite who is there, why they are there or what they are doing. I think that the best practice is the kind of best practice which has been, I think, urged upon the committee by representative bodies from all the areas that you are investigating in this second series: that is to say, to have a nominations committee; to have an open process of advertisement, certainly within the institution, I hope more broadly in the locality, of any vacancies that arise; to have clearly stated, as it were, terms and conditions about how long an appointment is for. I think myself, though I would not want it to be too rigid, that there should be an upper age limit and an upper length of service. I think of all of that, as it were, needs to be open, as indeed does the membership of the appointing bodies and the decisions they have reached afterwards. I think that is the set of best practice, and I would apply that myself, certainly to higher education institutions. I would commend to the Committee the document and guidance of the Committee of University Chairmen, which in my view is an excellent document from beginning to end and which has had a considerable influence, I may say, on higher education institutions. All the things that I have just sketched out have, since the appearance of that document, actually been decided and are being implemented at my university, for example, and I believe that most of the universities are in that position at the moment.

"Is there a case for payment?"—the second half of your question. I hope not, Chairman. I think there is a lot to be said for the British voluntary tradition and for public service, and for giving to the community some of your time and effort, and I would be very sorry if, certainly in higher education, close at hand, but also in the other areas that you are investigating at the moment, there was a rate for the job and a salary. I do think that these people who give a very great deal of time—I will quantify the time in the case of my own institution in a moment—deserve to be paid some expenses, but I would not pay them a salary. The amount of time is very considerable for a lay member of a council of an older university. For example, the chair of our council gives at least a whole day a week, and so do many of the other lay members as well, because they are members of just about every university committee, along with the staff. We trade, as it were, on their good will, but I do think that it would be a terrible mistake to move to a kind of professional, paid class of appointees to these bodies.

5. LORD NOLAN: It was a question that we felt we had to raise, and of course these are early days of the inquiry, but what you have said has been echoed by many people, who say that the tradition of voluntary service and the ability of highly skilled and very experienced people to make themselves available whatever the difficulties is a precious resource. It must be used, of course, with the greatest care, because it is a limited resource, but as long as we can get along without the paid professionals, you would support that.

GEOFFREY HOLLAND: I think it follows from the first bit of my answer that one needs, as it were, the widest possible field from which to draw that resource, and I would like it to be wider. When I first went to Exeter University I asked the questions "Who are these council members, where do they come from and how did they get there?" Before the document of the Committee of University Chairmen came out it was the kind of process that I described. I think it is now very much more open. We have a nominations committee, we have the open advertisement of the vacancies, we have an agreed three-year term of office, which may be repeated up to but not beyond nine years, we have a presumed upper age now of 70, and I may say there was absolutely no difficulty about getting that change. It was recognised by the council members as overdue, timely and right that it should be open in that way.

6. LORD NOLAN: A number of the people we have seen in the different types of organisations have spoken of the increased freedom which they feel because of the absence of party political pressures. Particularly I think this is true of those who moved away from the local government sphere. Is this something which, in your experience, looking broadly at the field of education, is a plus factor, something that is to be welcomed?

GEOFFREY HOLLAND: I think you have to look at the three cases separately. Sorry, there are more than three cases.

As regards higher education, I do think it is important for the Committee, and I am sure it has, certainly with the membership that you have and the interests declared, to distinguish between the pre-1992 universities and the new universities and the set-up there. The pre-1992 have a structure which might be thought to be slightly bizarre in this day and age, but which I think works extremely well. Our council, for example, has 50 members, of whom 30 are lay, but half the lay members are, by the statute, representatives and nominees of local authorities. They are, therefore, councillors, and there is, as it were, that certain element of politics, both party and local, in what those members say and do, inevitably perhaps. But it does not obtrude, and it would be rather curious, I think, if, given that rather considerable weight of local authority representatives, the council did not look outside the local authority sphere for the other members, and that is indeed the case. We have at least one very distinguished ex-local government officer, but not a politician. The politicians reappear on our court super-structure—the Members of Parliament, for example, and representatives of every local authority in the south-west, as far as I can see.

As to the further education funding councils—you would have to ask the witnesses—I would have thought that all the things I said in answer to my first question, those being the concerns, there being the freedom of organisation of structure, of time and of responsibility to address what I will call the real output concerns and the other questions that I raise, would be regarded as entirely appropriate to those organisations, and I think that is probably true of grant maintained schools as well.

Having said that about grant maintained schools, it is important not to overlook the very significant changes in governance of other schools which have taken place beforehand—restructuring governing bodies, so that, for example, parents and local employers are represented. There have been these other changes outside those self-governing bodies.

7. LORD NOLAN: You will forgive me for asking what seem naive and uninstructive questions, because we are embarking on a fairly swift learning curve over a wide area, but am I right in thinking that the council system, if I may call it that, has not been generally adopted in the new universities?

GEOFFREY HOLLAND: That is, I would have said, the case. Firstly, the legislation establishing the new universities set a different framework, and I think the documentation the Committee will have received very clearly defines that, but in general terms there is a smaller body than the council, and it is one which I will describe as more a board of management than the collegiate council, if I could draw that distinction. If you will allow me to say so, I think you would have to inquire of a new university how that met.

8. LORD NOLAN: In the older universities such as Exeter the council is really separate from day-to-day management, is it not?

GEOFFREY HOLLAND: Yes and no, Chairman. I am sorry to be irritating in the form of that reply. Lay council members, including the chair, including the treasurer, including other senior members of the council, are members of every important university committee, so for example they are members of the finance committee, they are members of the planning and resources committee, they are members of the staff committees—the academic staff committee and indeed the other staffing committee. They are not members of the teaching committee or the research committee, but they are involved in just about everything else that goes on, and I do not think that they would regard themselves as outside the stream of what is happening in the university. Indeed, I think they would regard themselves as very much involved in that. Incidentally, in all the committees that I have mentioned the students are represented too.

Whereas the council as such meets only once or twice a term—that is five or six times in the course of a year—and is by and large receiving reports and taking final decisions about big resource allocation questions and big policy questions—for example we have drawn up a 10-year strategy document at Exeter since I arrived and it was for them to endorse that—they take the big decisions, with ultimate responsibility, about allocation of money to academic or non-academic activities in the university. Whereas that is true and therefore they are not, week in, week out, in that position, they are certainly involved. Having said that, the Vice-Chancellor is the chief executive of the outfit and absolute day-to-day management is very much in the hands of the Vice-Chancellor, the three deputies and the registrar. That is the top management structure.

9. LORD NOLAN: The structure you have described provides, it seems, an effective way of monitoring performance in the various departments of the university. Is that right?

GEOFFREY HOLLAND: Yes.

10. LORD NOLAN: I am little more concerned about other types of organisations. For example, take a training and enterprise council. If you have a board that is, shall we say, under-performing—not doing as well as it should—what is the remedy?

GEOFFREY HOLLAND: The remedy, I am sure the Department would say, is the abrogation of its contract. The monitoring of training and enterprise council activity is at the moment done by the Department. I do think that all that I have said about membership of bodies applies equally well to training and enterprise councils. Events, for example in the South Thames Training And Enterprise Council, and it is not the only one, suggest that there is variability of performance between the training and enterprise councils, and I think there is some case for a closer look at a tighter set of expectations about performance. I think it will be a bold moment when a contract of a training and enterprise council is revoked, but I think that it would be a very healthy shock to a system if there were a non-performing TEC.

11. LORD NOLAN: Is there room for a uniform system of supervision among these different kinds of bodies or is it better to treat each one as a separate case?

GEOFFREY HOLLAND: I would myself, Chairman, treat each one as a separate case and set of circumstances.

It seems to me that the world of higher education is the world of higher education, and you yourself in your opening remarks made some qualifying remarks about your terminology of local public bodies. For example, of the intake of new students to Exeter this year only 90 are local students out of 2,100, just to give a feel for it. I regard Exeter as serving the nation and internationally as well as being part of a local community. That seems to me to be a different situation from colleges of further education, which in general terms are not into, for example, residential education and residential provision. It seems to me that training and enterprise councils, grant maintained schools and the NHS bodies are a different case again.

12. LORD NOLAN: I wonder if I could take up your point on the students coming to Exeter and concentrate for this purpose on universities both old and new. Are there enough students to go round?

GEOFFREY HOLLAND: Most certainly, Chairman. Most certainly. You will know that the position at the moment is that about 30 per cent of young people are going into higher education, which is about two and a half to three times. I hope the committee is familiar with the CBI's urgings that that should be 40 or 50 per cent if we are going to be internationally competitive. The Pacific Rim countries are way beyond 50 per cent at the moment. I think that a very considerable demand is building for higher education. I think there is a demand, as it were, from the competitive international market in which we are now operating. A demand is undoubtedly building up through the expansion of further education, because a lot of young people who have moved from school at 16 or 17, or indeed of adults who have come in part time or full time, are finding themselves in further education engaged, enthused and making progress in the world of achieving qualifications or credits in a way they never have before, and they want to go on. I also think that there will be a rapidly increasing demand—you can see it now in the major professions—for what in the jargon is called "continued professional development", updating regularly. I have no doubt at all that the market place is very large indeed. Indeed I say on public platforms, and believe it, that all of us who are in the world of education are in the world's biggest and most rapidly growing market.

13. LORD NOLAN: I had two particular pieces of evidence or suggestions in mind when I asked that question. One was that there seemed in some instances to have been an element of competition between universities to get students. This may be a very healthy thing, I do not know, but it indicated that some universities were feeling that their numbers were not keeping up to the levels needed to maintain adequate funding.

GEOFFREY HOLLAND: I think competition has been extremely healthy for higher education, and I think that the change in the status of the polytechnics to new universities has been a very healthy shock indeed to the system, because in my view the polytechnics, and indeed many of the new universities, were the innovators in higher education, and I think it has been a very considerable stimulus. I think also that the development that there has been towards the assessment of teaching quality and research, the public grading of universities and the publication of league tables—we can argue about how some of those things are done—is enormously healthy. I must say that I would shed no tears for a university that could not attract students. I think it knows what it has to do nowadays to do it. I think that the pressures that there are, for example, on an older university, making us look towards changing our provision so as to make it more accessible to part-time adults, the modularisation of courses, the easy movement of students from one institution to another when pursuing qualifications and the fact that in many cases, and I think this is true of all the universities, sometimes departments in the ratings that I have just referred to discover they are not as good as they thought they were by comparison with others and with benchmarks, are very much for the good of the system.

14. LORD NOLAN: The other piece of evidence of the two I mentioned is unspecific, but it seemed quite important. That was to the effect that a survey of the current generation of students and of those eligible to go to university indicated that about 40,000 were not going to take up the opportunity because they felt that they could not get by on their grants, they would have to borrow money and they were not prepared, at their age, to saddle themselves with debt. Have you any experience of a substantial falling off in the number of students wanting to go to university?

GEOFFREY HOLLAND: No, Chairman. I do not want to sound smug, but Exeter still has 14 applicants for every place, but on the whole Exeter is the kind of place where the majority of students—this is a sweeping generalisation—come from a professional background and better-off families, so the incidence of student poverty at somewhere like Exeter is a great deal less than somewhere else. But what is certainly true is that students are not well off, they are poorer than they were, there is increased hardship among students and that position is driving students increasingly to look to their local university rather than around the country. I think you could argue whether that is a good thing or not. I personally think it is probably unfortunate for the country if choice is limited to the local university.

15. LORD NOLAN: I should perhaps have declared a common interest. One of my sons-in-law was at Exeter University and I have been left in no doubt what the attractions were.

GEOFFREY HOLLAND: I should have asked the Committee to put their hands up if they had a relative at Exeter. I have discovered one already.

16. LORD NOLAN: Sir Geoffrey, I am going to ask others now to take a turn, but I wonder if I could conclude by asking if there are any other points that you wish to raise, in particular about the relationship with government of universities in your experience and whether that is satisfactory, or anything else that comes to your mind.

GEOFFREY HOLLAND: I just want to make two or three points very briefly. Firstly, I think it is important for this Committee to recognise firstly that public funds are not the only funds that universities get, and in many cases are a minority of the funds and, secondly, that even within public funds, the funding council element is, though the largest, by no means the only. To give a figure for Exeter, we have an income per annum of about £70 million, but £26 million only comes from the funding council. So to put everything on the funding council seems to me to misread the position. Thirdly, I was going to reinforce the fact that we are looking for volunteers prepared to give a lot of time. Fourthly, although a university is serving a wider nation, I do think that, when it comes to council and governance, it is very much of its community. Therefore, I think myself that if one can introduce the kind of things I was talking about, which you led me towards, Chairman—the nominations committee, the open process, etc. etc.—I do not myself think that it would be helpful or indeed attractive to the volunteers to have, as it were, an outside, independent individual somewhere in the process.

I will stop there, because I am anxious to help members of the Committee.

LORD NOLAN: Thank you very much. Sir Clifford, have you any questions you would like to ask Sir Geoffrey?

17. CLIFFORD BOULTON: We are looking at governance of course from the point of view of standards of conduct, or maintenance or achievement of standards and their monitoring, so, although one is anxious to respect the different personalities and roles of different higher education institutions, it could be worth looking at whether there is uniformity of rules relating to standards and their monitoring, I suppose. I just have a technical question about the Privy Council, because a large number of the pre-1992 universities, if they want to amend their statutes or their charter, have to take the Privy Council route. It is not a body which most people are very familiar with and I simply wondered, for our own education at this stage of the inquiry, if you could describe how those Privy Council changes are examined and what the path towards their approval is. Is there some standing body within the Department of Education and all these universities know they start by going to them and sounding out what their prospects are?

GEOFFREY HOLLAND: Chairman, I have no direct experience of this. I want to preface my reply by saying that. Sir Clifford is entirely right. If for example the basic statutes, for example on the composition of the council that I described at an older university, were to be pursued, it would have to go to the Privy Council and it would have to be approved by it. Before it got to the Privy Council, it would first have to go through the council of the university and then, in the case of an older university, the court of the university. The court is a huge body, if ours is anything to go by, and I am sure that others who are associated with the older universities will say exactly the same. Ours is a body which, if everybody turned up, is about 200 strong. It contains every MP in the south-west, it contains at least one representative of every local authority, it contains everybody, as it were, including all the council members and so on. But the court would have formally to approve that. It would then, as I understand it, submit it to the Privy Council office, and the Privy Council office, I have no doubt, would then refer it towards the Department for advice in the particular set of circumstances.

I have to say that when I arrived at Exeter I did think that some of the structures looked archaic, but then actually experiencing them, for example the council and its workings, I thought that they were very much more effective than one could ever have imagined they would be, and the practical workings day to day seemed to be carried on perfectly satisfactorily. I therefore concluded, to be rather blunt in my answer to Sir Clifford, that it was not worth the candle of all the delay and all the hassle and all the local bodies that would have to be consulted and all the different views that would be expressed, leaving you almost in a position of irreconcilable conflict. It would also be utterly distracting of management time in the university. Therefore, for myself as it were, and incidentally being very strongly supportive of the quality of our council members, having observed them in action, I think the thing to do is to make the present systems work as much as possible. But Sir Clifford is entirely correct: it does disappear into the Privy Council. I understand that it takes a process of two or three years to get anywhere, and no doubt Sir Clifford has personal and direct experience of that.

18. CLIFFORD BOULTON: No, but I simply gather from what you say that if we were minded to try and introduce more uniformity into the way in which standards are maintained and monitored in the older universities, the Department of Education/Privy Council route is not likely to be a very helpful one, so to whom would we look? Would we look to the funding council to impose a bit of pressure to carry out certain reforms or changes, if they were felt to be desirable?

GEOFFREY HOLLAND: Just a couple of comments about that. Firstly, so far as the pre-1992 universities are concerned, and probably the polytechnics as well, although I know their world much less well, for obvious reasons, I think one needs to be a bit careful about the search for uniformity and imposing it, because the universities have roots. For example, Exeter, though serving the nation, and the international community as well, I hope, in terms of academia and so on, does have its roots in the city, there is local pride attached to it, and I think we would lose something valuable in terms of a university in the wider role it plays in its community, if we tried to impose too much from outside.

Secondly, I hope the funding council would not be the mechanism. In my view the funding council is imposing too much and too detailed mechanisms at the moment in the complexity of its funding arrangements, and making those more elaborate is causing some irresponsibility, if the truth be told, in universities, as they play around to try to fit the computer model of the funding council. I think we are in danger of stifling the individual character and the organic growth of particular institutions. I think the only route, if the Committee were minded to go that way, certainly with higher education and probably with the others as well, is the legislative route—centrally—but I hope very much that the Committee would not feel that necessary.

19. CLIFFORD BOULTON: As you are aware, I was talking about the desirability of openness, transparency—those kind of vogue words—which we cannot really dispute as being desirable, and simply a question of how they should be monitored, and also reluctance to live for ever perhaps with new universities and old universities, unless one of them is a false prospectus, which I trust it is not.

GEOFFREY HOLLAND: Could I just say, Chairman, that if you look at the higher education sector, let alone the others, and other witnesses will give you figures for that sector, the higher education sector, just to put two figures on it, has one million students at the moment and hundreds of thousands of staff. I think the number of instances of things that go wrong is very small

indeed in proportion to that totality. I think it is enormously important that the tail of some individual behaviours at some institutions does not wag the dog, when the dog is pretty well standing on its feet. Sorry to use a colourful analogy.

CLIFFORD BOULTON: Thank you.

LORD NOLAN: Sir William, would you like to ask some questions?

20. WILLIAM UTTING: That leads me on to asking Sir Geoffrey for his views on the role and responsibilities of the Secretary of State when things go wrong, because from my reading of the documentation it looks as though the Secretary of State has substantial powers of intervention and direction and that there may be a very short path from the individual institution in which things have gone wrong to the Secretary of State's desk. Is that right or could it be better managed?

GEOFFREY HOLLAND: That is right, Chairman. If we take the Huddersfield passage, for example, I may say that the path to the Secretary of State's desk was very fast indeed, and it was very fast indeed from the rest of the system, which could see that one incident could tarnish the whole sector. From the Secretary of State's desk it was a very short path indeed to the Committee of University Chairmen, who then produced their document. All within a year this has happened, and I may say, as far as I can make out from information made available to me from fellow vice-chancellors, that a very large number of universities have moved very swiftly to put things right. So I think that the informal path rather than the formal path has proved itself to be very effective.

21. WILLIAM UTTING: It seems rather strange though that, if something goes wrong in a grant maintained school, this should end up on the desk of the Secretary of State, who presumably has quite enough to do running national policy for education without having to direct what happens in individual establishments.

GEOFFREY HOLLAND: Yes. That may be to do with the terms of reference of the Funding Agency for Schools in that particular case. The Funding Agency for Schools is, as the name suggests, about funding and about planning of provision in particular parts of the country. I must say that when I was at the Department of Education a kind of recurrent nightmare was how the Department would deal with thousands of individual cases being raised with it from about the countryside. I think that if the number of grant maintained schools is to rise or does rise a good deal more, that is an area that somebody will have to look at.

22. WILLIAM UTTING: May I raise one other point, going back to the appointment of members of councils and boards of management? Looking at the criteria that are set out—for example for the appointment of the members of the boards of further education colleges—there is a definition of independent member there that appears to be restricted to people from business and professional backgrounds. I wondered whether that in a sense did not mean that groups like women, people from black and ethnic minorities or disabled people might also be excluded, because of that sort of definition.

GEOFFREY HOLLAND: I would hope very much not. Certainly a considerable preponderance of the independent members at Exeter—I know we are talking about further education colleges—are women. There are not too many blacks or ethnic minorities around Exeter, but we would hope very much that we would see one or two people from that community before we are very much older.

To come back and address myself more seriously to the college of further education situation, I think that a lot turns on whether there is a nominations committee, whether the process is open and to whom vacancies are advertised, and how much active encouragement is given to people to nominate in the community. I would hope very much that one would not go in for a lot of categorisation of, for example, gender balance, ethnic minority, disabled, etc. etc. I think it is a combination of vacancies being notified, a pretty regular turnover, so that there are vacancies, and a nominations committee which is induced to be open-minded. I dare say that if this Committee, Chairman, addressed itself to the Committee of University Chairmen and I dare say that if it addressed itself to some of the representative bodies of further education, they would find a great goodwill to push people in the direction we are talking about but I do think that some central stipulation is wrong in these circumstances because of different local circumstances.

23. WILLIAM UTTING: That may be but the Government's recently published *Guide to Public Appointments* did have quite a strong push on the equal opportunities front and I am curious as to whether that is going to be followed in the educational sphere.

GEOFFREY HOLLAND: Well, it certainly is in the case of my institution and, I think, of higher education. I think you would have to ask your other witnesses about the other sectors but I have not encountered anywhere in the education field any resistance to equal opportunities and promoting them. On the contrary, I have found all over the country in my journeyings around the education system people, as it were, waking up and moving as far as they can to—and I choose the words carefully, as the Chairman at least will recognise—positive action to ensure that things happen.

WILLIAM UTTING: Thank you, Chairman.

24. DIANA WARWICK: Chairman, could I just follow that question. It is quite interesting that you were very strong in your view that the volunteer element, the voluntary element, in most of the serving boards should be maintained when Lord Nolan addressed the issue of whether they should be paid but the groups that Sir William has referred to, women and ethnic minorities but also people of lower incomes as well, are usually the people who have most difficulty, for example, in getting paid time off work in order to undertake public duties. I wondered, given that in some of our evidence we have been urged to seek to broaden the range of representation, whether that would influence your judgment about whether members of such bodies, of all the bodies that we are dealing with particularly, I think, in grant-maintained schools which are the most locally based in a way, whether that would influence your judgment about whether they should be paid.

GEOFFREY HOLLAND: Thank you for the question. I think when one comes to the level of the governing body of a school, and particularly if we are

thinking about governing bodies of let us say inner city schools, there is a case actually for considering some payment to the governors. I think there is much less case in the further education college or higher education sphere and I certainly do not think there is a case in a Training and Enterprise Council sphere.

LORD NOLAN: Dame Anne, I think you wanted to——

25. ANNE WARBURTON: Chairman, thank you very much, a very brief question. I noted that Sir Geoffrey puts a lot of emphasis on nomination committee. I just wondered if he could say something to us about the composition of the nomination committee.

GEOFFREY HOLLAND: The composition of the nomination committee—there is the guidance from the Committee of University Chairmen, and I will not repeat that but for the record it is paragraph 4.29 and 4.30 of their document of June 1995 and I commend that to the committee. Ours follows almost exactly that. What we have is the Chair of Council, in our case, the other pro-chancellor, the Treasurer—all those are lay members of the council itself—we have myself and we have the senior deputy vice-chancellor, who is the senior academic, and then we have the Registrar as the secretary of that committee.

That is a small body. You might think that one should add a lay member or two, and actually it is slightly smaller than the Committee of University Chairmen urge in that respect, and we might think again about that at Exeter. What I think is important and cannot be stressed too much because it did not happen before, I think, in many an institution is the open advertising of a vacancy and encouragement of people to nominate. We are, for example, most definitely doing that and I understand from fellow vice-chancellors that increasingly other universities—indeed, the great majority—are doing that as well.

It is the knowledge that a vacancy is around and a belief that you can nominate and that your nomination will be taken seriously and feedback of the outcome of it so that this is not a mysterious, remote body with which you have, as a staff member for example or, let us say, a local employer absolutely no connection.

26. LORD NOLAN: Sir Geoffrey, you have been extremely helpful. I wish we could keep you for much longer but I am afraid our time is up and we must move on to our next witnesses. I am sure I speak for the whole Committee in sending you our warmest thanks for coming to us today and giving us the benefit of your experience. Thank you.

GEOFFREY HOLLAND: If I can help in any further way as you go on, I shall be happy to do so, Chairman. Thank you very much.

27. LORD NOLAN: That is very good of you, thank you.

Good morning, Sir Robert and Sir William and Mr McClure. I am going to ask Lord Thomson to lead the questioning, please. You have been kind enough to let us have an opening statement which we have all read. Lord Thomson and I thought perhaps it would be a little long to go right through and I think, Lord Thomson, you were thinking of asking if it could be highlighted.

28. LORD THOMSON: I wonder if Sir Robert could draw our attention to some of the principal features in his mind of the statement that would set the scene for us. We have all had the statement and personally I found it an extremely useful starting point for our discussion today.

SIR WILLIAM STUBBS, SIR ROBERT GUNN, AND ROGER McCLURE

SIR ROBERT GUNN (Chairman, Further Education Funding Council for England): I am not sure that there is a tremendous number of points that I would like to pull out. I think we have tried to address the main points that you gave us in your letter on the various topics in which you had an interest. I think we would be very happy to answer any questions you may have on the document and maybe elucidate a little further anything which you found perhaps not sufficiently explained to you.

29. LORD THOMSON: Sir Robert, that is extremely helpful. As always, time is of the essence for us in this matter. We have the document and that will be part of our record, of course, and if we can use that as the basis for our questions I think that will make the best use of our time. You have, of course, I think been able to listen to the evidence we have just been having?

ROBERT GUNN: Yes, we have.

30. LORD THOMSON: So perhaps I could move straight from that evidence into the important issue of the methods of appointment of members of the governing bodies of the further education colleges. I wanted, in particular, to ask you if you could tell us what your general impression is about how far the advice you give on these matters is being followed, particularly in terms of the widest possible advertising in order to obtain the widest range of choice for members of the governing council.

ROBERT GUNN: Let me say, first of all, that the colleges have been independent for only 2½ years and, therefore, it is very early days in the conduct of re-appointing for a second term and that sort of thing. It has not actually happened yet.

Our knowledge of what colleges do is also still not by any means complete because our evidence really comes not from a survey of how people appoint, because we do not actually do that at all, but our inspectorate look at the methods and the results of the appointment of governors and they do inspect governance and management within the colleges. Now, they are about half way through a four-year cycle of inspections so they have just completed maybe just a bit over half of the colleges so far. Our information that we have at the moment is that generally speaking the results of whatever methods that have been used have given a pretty well balanced governing body.

Of course, there are set down in regulations the sort of types of people who have to be on governing bodies in the further education sector and at least half of them have to be independent or business members. So, there is a restriction for the college to decide who actually goes on to their governing body but they have a lot of flexibility within that and their governing body can be anything from 10 people to 20 people and it is up to them to decide whether they have student representation, whether they have staff representation or other types of thing, but our evidence so far is—and we have given a lot of advice on this subject—that they do look at the needs of the locality as well as of the college's needs and appoint people accordingly.

We have recommended, and so have the associations for colleges, that there should be either what Sir Geoffrey was calling a nominations committee and which many of our people call a search committee and we think that is absolutely right and we would recommend that that continued to play a part. Whether or not too many colleges are advertising fully, I do not think I am in a position to say.

31. LORD THOMSON: Do you give advice, do you recommend that there should be some limit on the length of service?

ROBERT GUNN: No.

32. LORD THOMSON: I wondered on the question of the fact that it is laid down, of course, that 50 per cent, or more than 50 per cent, have to be independent or appointments from TECs, I wondered if you had any . . .

ROBERT GUNN: No, sorry. The appointments from TECs, they have to have at least one person. Half of them have to be business or commercial or independent but there only has to be one TEC nominated person on the board.

33. LORD THOMSON: I see, and is it normally one person or is it often more than one person from the TEC?

ROBERT GUNN: It can be more.

34. LORD THOMSON: Yes. Does that create any problems of conflict of interest in the sense that, in fact, further education colleges are very frequently main contractors to the TECs?

ROBERT GUNN: I do not think so. The relationships between the colleges and the TECs have been improving steadily and I think this framework has, in fact, helped that. One of the things that the TECs have a responsibility for is to approve the strategic plans of the colleges and, therefore, the fact that they are involved in the development of these strategic plans I think is helpful rather than the reverse.

35. LORD THOMSON: I expect you listened with interest, as I did, to the view of Sir Geoffrey about what I think he called the variability of the performance of TECs and whether, in fact, it might not be a healthy shock to the system if at some point one contract had to be brought to an end. I wondered if you had any overall impression of the role that the TECs play in terms of the effective operation of the further education colleges.

ROBERT GUNN: I think that our belief would be that the situation has improved quite substantially over the past two or three years. There are still very variable performances amongst the TECs and, of course, we were quite upset when one of them went bankrupt and a number of our colleges lost a lot of money.

36. LORD THOMSON: Yes, that was what I had in mind in asking the question. Can I move on to accountability arrangements. What fascinated me about studying your statement as a layman at the beginning of

what the chairman has called a pretty steep learning curve is the fact that on the face of it you have a funding role and it is the Secretary of State that has the regulatory role yet I was personally a little reassured, I think, to get the impression that somehow or other out of your reports they seem to be regulators' reports. Would you like to comment on that?

ROBERT GUNN: I think I would like Sir William to comment perhaps on that because it is quite true that we are not a regulatory body but because of our necessity to look after public funds we have introduced a number of safeguards, shall we say, which put us in a slightly regulatory situation, but I think Sir William will be able to explain that.

WILLIAM STUBBS (Chief Executive, Further Education Funding Council for England): Yes, thank you, Chairman. The arrangements for the instrument and articles of government which are the prime documents for the governance of colleges, those are made by the Secretary of State and the categories that the chairman has referred to within those are determined by her and if a college wishes to change those they need approval by the Secretary of State.

Turning to the Funding Council, there are three systems that you could consider the Funding Council operates with respect to colleges. The first is, as you say, regulatory. We make regulations with respect to the use of public funds, the financial memorandum. We attach, and can attach, conditions to our funds on an annual basis and we can also enter into funding agreements with colleges on use of recurrent funds or use of capital funds and those are binding on colleges.

Then we also require colleges to disclose certain information. For example, they must make their annual accounts publicly available. Those accounts, by the way, are externally audited and are open to scrutiny by the National Audit Office. We also publicly collect and publish ourselves certain key statistics about colleges that enable an interested observer to understand individual colleges and put that college in the context of the broader family of colleges.

Then, the third type of system is the scrutiny system in which the council ensures that there is audit and, indeed, I suspect that witnesses later this morning will certainly not be complaining about the extent of audit in further education. There are more levels of audit than there are tiers on most birthday cakes. There is internal and external audit. There is audit by the Funding Council. There is audit by the national office. For those that receive funds from the Training and Enterprise Council there is audit by the TEC and for those that are fortunate enough to receive European funds there is audit by the European Auditor and there is a reserve—if you think a reserve is necessary—that the Department for Education may also audit. So, I think in terms of systems of audit they are fairly robust.

Then the Council itself——

37. LORD THOMSON: Would you say you were over-audited?

WILLIAM STUBBS: I would hold back from saying that one was over-audited—there are some who always wish to see an extra dimension—but I think those who are

concerned about the proper use of public funds can be content that they are being properly husbanded, so to speak.

Then the third—I am talking about the system of scrutiny—the second system of scrutiny is inspection and the chairman has referred to that and the third system is that there is a complaints procedure for every college. So, our role as regulator, as you put it, has to be seen through those three different channels.

38. LORD THOMSON: Thank you very much, that is very helpful. Could I follow it up in this way. We are very conscious, I think here, particularly at this beginning stage of our enquiry, that we are dealing with public bodies in the education field whereas those who serve on the governing councils do so as unpaid, voluntary servers and that is a very great and positive feature.

In the cases that have gone wrong, of course, as always you get the massive publicity for where it goes wrong but, by and large, taking the situation as a whole, as far as I can see it, really the scandals are not unimportant but they are fortunately rare. In between, the real problem so often is an institution that is not really doing very well, it is not quite up to it. I just wonder to what degree your system of scrutiny and supervision is able to deal with that.

I mean, if you had a college that was perhaps in a rather isolated bit of the country and was really just under-performing, not dramatically but continuously, and the board were leaving it all to the principal and the staff were becoming a bit demoralised, would you know about that and if you did know about it what would you do about it?

ROBERT GUNN: That depends in which sphere you are talking about under-performance. We would certainly know whether——

39. LORD THOMSON: I am thinking about under-performing educationally.

ROBERT GUNN: Whether they were losing student numbers, we would certainly know that because we monitor the student numbers. If they were under-performing financially, we would also know about that.

40. LORD THOMSON: That would be clearly recorded, would it not?

ROBERT GUNN: And we would certainly do something about that. I think maybe Roger is the best person to say just how we would deal with a college which was getting into difficulty because he is the person who actually does it.

ROGER McCLURE (Director of Finance, Further Education Funding Council for England): Chairman, perhaps before I answer I should declare my interest as a member of the Council of King's College London. I would say, first of all, that the funding system which the council uses, which accounts for a very large proportion of the income of most colleges in the sector, has performance built into it so that put in simple terms, the survival of colleges depends on performing. It is not possible for a college to go along in a kind of easy way, not particularly attracting students or whatever because its performance in attracting students, in retaining them and helping those students to achieve are all built into the funding system and if a college is not managing to do that then it will very soon become evident in its income and in its financial position, which we monitor very closely. I think, in fact, that is the most powerful scrutiny system you can have because the survival of the institution depends on the level of performance.

Where a college gets into difficulty, perhaps because it is not attracting students, we have regular and systematic financial monitoring. We have heard about the audited annual accounts which are analyzed each year. We also have a system for three-year financial forecasting on a rolling basis each year, similar to that in the universities, with a mid-year update so we know on a regular basis where each institution is financially. Where it becomes apparent from those forecasts that the college is heading for financial difficulties or has already arrived in financial difficulties then we require the college to take action to extract itself from those difficulties and that can be a condition of funding. If the college is not taking appropriate action we can require it—compel it effectively—to take effective action to deal with the situation.

41. LORD THOMSON: What is your ultimate sanction in terms of ensuring that they do take the action? Is it the funding instrument?

ROGER McCLURE: The ultimate sanction would be that the college could close because the Council does not have a commitment to any particular individual college. Its statutory commitment is to the population of England and if a college is not attracting students to the extent that it can no longer be viable then it could close, although there are probably intermediate solutions which could also be explored, such as a closer association with a neighbouring institution, or whatever.

42. LORD THOMSON: But you do have the actual power to close a college if it is in——

ROGER McCLURE: No, we would have to recommend to the Secretary of State and the Secretary of State can, yes.

43. LORD THOMSON: I see, but it would be you who recommended to the Secretary of State?

ROBERT GUNN: Yes.

44. LORD THOMSON: Yes, that is very clear. Could I just ask a more specific point in terms of financial control. You mention, I think, somewhere in your papers about your scrutiny of severance settlements. You say that in your evidence to the Public Accounts Committee you have expressed support for the financial terms of severance settlements for senior staff to be contained in the college accounts and you have issued revised guidance to make this clear. Have you had a reaction to that and can you do more than guidance? Can you insist?

ROGER McCLURE: It is a requirement of our accounting policies. Perhaps our opening statement was slightly misleading there. Our initial accounting policies already required colleges to declare the full remuneration and emoluments of the senior managers of the college and the revised guidance simply made it clearer than we managed to make it first time round. But we already have

information from the first set of accounts on all the colleges in the land.

45. LORD THOMSON: Thank you. Associated with that, in terms of grievances, what is your machinery for dealing with grievances?

ROBERT GUNN: There is a complaints system under the further education charter. Each college is supposed to have a charter and have a complaints system. Under that, they can appeal. If the complaint has been going through the procedure and has not succeeded in that they can appeal to us or they can appeal direct to the Secretary of State and we have had a number of direct appeals from students and staff—I think something in the order of 50.

46. LORD THOMSON: 52 you mentioned in your report?

ROBERT GUNN: Yes.

47. LORD THOMSON: Are you able to deal adequately with these. Of the 52 could you tell us how many of them you felt were justified and required any action from you?

WILLIAM STUBBS: Yes, it may help the committee if I just give you some of the detailed background of the complaints. Half of them have been from students themselves. A third of them have been from parents and 10 per cent have come from college employees and the remainder have come from members of the public. Of the 34 complaints that have been concluded by the Council, 60 per cent have been upheld, or partly upheld, by the Council. A very small number have been upheld completely because there is usually a number of elements within them, but if you put upheld or partly upheld then that is the figure you get, and the remainder have been rejected.

The Council has started the practice of publishing for the whole sector details of the types of complaints that are received, although without specifying the colleges against which the complaints were registered.

48. LORD THOMSON: That is very interesting and useful information for us to have. Do you feel that the machinery is satisfactory? Do you feel there is a need for an Ombudsman in this field?

WILLIAM STUBBS: If you were saying an Ombudsman specifically with respect to complaints about colleges?

LORD THOMSON: Yes.

WILLIAM STUBBS: I think I would underline what Sir Robert has already said, that these colleges have been independent for 2½ years. You have referred, Chairman, to your own steep learning curve; the governing bodies themselves have had a steep learning curve and they have travelled a long way in a relatively short distance and I think prudence might say before changing that, are there very good grounds for changing it?

There is, as I said, much scrutiny taking place. You, yourself, have said that there are very few scandals so, in the main, the system is working in a way which I believe can command confidence. However, if the general conclusion was that there should be some office like an

Ombudsman I am sure that you would wish to be clear how those related to the many existing lines that a complainant has within either existing legislation or existing regulations.

49. LORD THOMSON: Thank you. Perhaps one final question before I hand over to other colleagues. I noticed, and was pleased to notice, that the Funding Council has an annual open meeting when its clients can question it. Is that meeting open in the sense of open to the public or is it by invitation only? Could you tell me something about it and how it goes?

ROBERT GUNN: We cannot give you the experience because it does not happen until Friday. We are holding an Annual General Meeting in the Queen Elizabeth II Conference Centre on Friday. We have invited to that Annual General Meeting all the chairmen of governors of all the colleges. We have also invited the TECs to send representatives and various other organisations such as the FC and the local authorities and we have advertised in the newspapers inviting people from the public if they wish to come as observers, or the press for that matter.

It is by ticket only because we wanted to have some indication of the numbers that we were likely to have to cope with but the press and the public are there as observers and we do not know yet but we think we will get about 300, 350.

LORD THOMSON: That should be a very interesting experiment indeed and we will follow the results with interest. Perhaps some of our hardworking secretariat might be invited to attend.

ROBERT GUNN: I have to say that it is also quite expensive to put on.

LORD THOMSON: I am sure it is. I think it does you great credit.

50. LORD NOLAN: I wonder if I could just pick up one of the questions that Lord Thomson was asking about the complaints procedure. As you know, many organisations now have a confidential system. Is yours confidential or is it open at the present stage?

WILLIAM STUBBS: Sorry, complaints to the Council after a complainant has complained to a college?

LORD NOLAN: Yes.

WILLIAM STUBBS: It is confidential insofar as we do not publish the college against which the complaint has been made, nor do we give the name of the individual. What we do is publish the type of complaint on an annual basis.

51. LORD NOLAN: Yes. Within the college the complainant, say a member of staff, he would complain openly, would he, without any secrecy being attached to it. Is that right?

WILLIAM STUBBS: The individual complainant complaining to the college, if they are a member of staff, I would expect within each college there is a formal grievance procedure. That is when I was saying earlier on, one needs to be careful as to where a new complaints

procedure is going to intertwine or cross with another, there would be a grievance procedure so that individual members of staff have a way of bringing to the attention of the college at different levels their concerns and, of course, that is not anonymous.

52. LORD NOLAN: There has been some pressure for a confidential system of complaint to perhaps a senior member of staff so that the possibly junior member complaining would not feel under any fear of being discriminated against if he raises a complaint which may turn out to be groundless.

WILLIAM STUBBS: I quite understand the concern; indeed, the Council itself has put in place arrangements for its own staff that a member of staff who has concerns about aspects of the way in which the executive of the Council were operating may contact an individual named member of the Council—as it so happens, it is the chairman of the audit committee—and may do so on a confidential basis guarding against that kind of arrangement. It would be possible, I suppose, for a college to put in place a similar arrangement if you thought necessary.

LORD NOLAN: Thank you very much. Now, I am going to ask Dame Anne if she would like to put any questions she has.

53. ANNE WARBURTON: Chairman, thank you. I had thought of questions on the lines that you were just pursuing yourself and I would like just to put one thought about it. The sort of complaints of which you have been speaking I think may have been mostly complaints of grievances, whereas, I think, we have been very much preoccupied with the question of complaints about propriety, perhaps other peoples' propriety. That may be why the Chairman was particularly pursuing the idea of whether in colleges there is an arrangement so that people do not jeopardise their position by complaining that things are not being done properly.

WILLIAM STUBBS: The complaints that we have received from, say, students or former students or members of the public, it would be difficult to say that they are a grievance and not about propriety; they are often the way in which the complainant feels the college has interpreted its own rule, either to do with fees or to do sometimes with suspension of students, and so forth. I can think of a parent who was concerned about those procedures.

If you are saying there may be in individual colleges one or more members of staff who are concerned about the general direction, management and governance of a college and that for them to bring it forward risks putting themselves at risk then it is open to them to bring it to the attention of the Funding Council and, as you will know from the last time we met Chairman, the Council did receive complaints about one individual college which, taken in context with other complaints we were receiving, ultimately led to an enquiry. If someone were to write to us and specify that it was confidential I have no doubt that the Council would respect that confidentiality. There is a route there which has occasionally been used.

ANNE WARBURTON: Thank you very much.

ROBERT GUNN: May I add something there? There are two other points that we have not properly brought out. The principal, who is the accounting officer for the institution, has an obligation under the financial memorandum to bring to our attention at any time when the governing body is not acting in accordance with the financial memorandum. It is his duty to come direct to Sir William.

We are about to publish, in addition to the *Guides to Governors* which we have done a guide to clerkship because we believe that the clerk is a very important person on the governing body and we are recommending that as a last resort that clerk should appeal to the Council if he believes that the governing body, having been fully informed that they are acting outside the law, or whatever, if they continue to do so he is obliged to consult the Council about it.

54. ANNE WARBURTON: Can I go on? Appointments: there are two aspects I wanted to ask you about. Is it correct that you see it as preferable if outside bodies were invited to nominate people for consideration as members of the governing body that those persons should specifically not be representatives of the bodies which put their names forward? I see you nodding. That is all I needed to check on.

ROBERT GUNN: I do not think we would wish them to be representatives and acting as representatives of governing bodies. I think they have to play a part as being a full member, a full governor, of the institution.

55. ANNE WARBURTON: Then, secondly, on appointments; I am a little surprised you did not take a stronger position in your paper about the representation of staff and students on governing bodies. I think you remark in the paper that tensions are perhaps eased if they are there—but I find it perhaps a little out of date not to have some acceptance that you must always have staff and student representatives.

ROBERT GUNN: We have not determined the composition of governing bodies. We do not really think that it is our position to do so. I think some colleges have found it helpful to have staff on, others maintain that they have much easier, free discussion if staff members are not present. I do not think, as long as the college operates efficiently and effectively, that we are particularly concerned whether they use their right to have them on or not to have them on.

56. ANNE WARBURTON: But really your position is that it is outside your remit?

ROBERT GUNN: Yes.

57. ANNE WARBURTON: One last thought. I was quite impressed at the amount which is happening, the various things which are being considered, registers and codes and those moves. I was almost left wondering when do you think that these will be a good vantage point, a good time space, to examine? How much has already been achieved? I had the feeling that perhaps you did not think that November 1995 was the perfect time to be looking at these things.

ROBERT GUNN: Well, Sir William appeared before the Public Accounts Committee and he made a certain recommendation to them so perhaps he should answer the question.

WILLIAM STUBBS: I did not intend to give the impression that it was not a sensible time to look at how well the colleges and the governing bodies were performing. Indeed, the National Audit Office carried out a survey and published a report on that and that was the basis for the hearing by the Public Accounts Committee that the Chairman has referred to.

What I was saying was that with particular respect to the Ombudsman proposal that there are considerable arrangements in place now to allow grievances and complaints about propriety, and so forth, to be considered and it may be rather early before significantly adding to, or changing, the existing arrangements. That is what I had in mind, Chairman.

ANNE WARBURTON: Thank you very much.

LORD NOLAN: Professor King, would you like to take up the questioning?

58. PROF ANTHONY KING: I was charmed, as I am sure some of my colleagues were, by paragraph 14 in your submission, "The underlying reasons for conflict between the governing bodies in institutions and the permanent staff", in the course of which you remark that——

"staff in some colleges seem suspicious of governors' motives believing them to be concerned more with financial efficiency than educational effectiveness."

Are all the members of staff in colleges who are thus suspicious wrong? Is that the inference I am to draw from this passage?

WILLIAM STUBBS: The basis for that, Chairman, derives from the observations of my inspectorate colleagues who, as part of their regular inspection system, look at governance and management and consult with those inside the colleges. That is the basis for it.

You say in those cases where they have found unease were there good grounds for it and I think frankly one has to say to you, Chairman, that the changes that have been brought forward, the extent of the changes and the rapidity of the changes, have undoubtedly left reasonable unease in some colleges. There is no getting away from that. What we were endeavouring to say to you this morning is that with respect to the proper use of public funds and propriety the Funding Council goes to considerable lengths to inform itself and look behind some of these concerns but, as the opening statement reminds you, that has to be seen in the context of a fairly long-running now and somewhat bruising negotiation over pay and conditions of service.

59. PROF ANTHONY KING: Could I ask you along the same lines about a previous paragraph in which you remark that the Council has established a range of systematic monitoring systems which record colleges outputs. What are colleges outputs?

WILLIAM STUBBS: Forgive me, Chairman, I can see the academic reproof lying gently behind that question from Professor King. If the rebuke is to do with the fact that we are perhaps inferring that students are outputs, I apologise for that, although certainly one would wish to see the success which students achieve in obtaining qualifications.

I think, unlike any other phase of education, students in the further education sector are there primarily to gain a qualification. It is the experience that is undoubtedly beneficial to them but the prime motive for being there is a qualification and, therefore, the Council has a series of performance indicators with the co-operation of the colleges. Can I say, Chairman, on the record that the extent to which colleges and their governing bodies and the principals have co-operated with the Council merits much support and recognition.

We have put in place five performance indicators, some relating to the extent to which students achieve their academic success, others the extent to which the individual college obtains value for money and indicators of that order, others to do with the extent to which students fail to complete the programme for which they are registered. That is what we had in mind when we are talking about outputs, even if we put it rather clumsily.

60. PROF ANTHONY KING: I take it that there is potentially, at any rate, a conflict between the financial carrot which you offer colleges and the inspection stick because if a college appears to be doing well it gets money, if it is not actually doing well you want to know that. Could you say just a little bit more than you do here about how you ensure that in your best judgment the academic standards are maintained? Is this largely the external bodies that award the qualifications?

WILLIAM STUBBS: It is the examining bodies and the awarding bodies who have the main responsibility as to whether colleges are fulfilling their requirements and regulations, with extent to the success of students in achieving their registered qualifications. By the way, may I say that as from last year it is now a requirement in every college that for every student registered and enroled in the college who will be indirectly a recipient of Council funds that they have a registered learning objective so it is clearly known from the outset the intention of the student in being enroled at the college.

We rely on our inspection colleagues for their evidence about not only individual subjects at departmental standards but also the cross-college provision to do with the way in which they counsel students and receive students. That, I believe, is systematically now looked at and commands widespread confidence. You will wish, I am sure, to ask others about that but I think the inspection procedure has surprised people with the extent to which it probes and can retain the confidence.

Then there are the performance indicators I have referred to, but lying behind those is the fact that if a college is falling short in a significant way in terms of students achieving their objectives, and as you have heard from Mr McClure there is a financial, some may say a marginal, sanction. Some ten per cent of the total fund is related to that. If the Inspectorate find that an area of college performance is falling into a category where it is giving serious cause for concern, our categories 4 or 5, the council requires of the college that they produce a recovery plan and requires that they admit no more students to that area until they have redressed matters, and has made it clear that in the event that the recovery plan was unsatisfactory the council would consider formally withdrawing money and making it a requirement that no further students are admitted. That is not necessary, but there have been a number of cases where

we have gone back to governors and said "you have got a category that has given us cause for concern, we will re-inspect within the year", and I am pleased to report to you, Chairman, that I think in all cases when the inspectors have gone back there has been significant progress.

61. LORD NOLAN: That is, I think, most interesting and encouraging. In other words, there has been no need to do more than use the threat of withdrawal of funds to produce the required improvement internally. It has not been necessary to find some mechanism for replacing the reward or bringing in new blood.

WILLIAM STUBBS: Not with respect to the particular question of Professor King on academic standards. But, as you will know, there have been two instances where matters got to such an unsatisfactory state that governors were replaced and there was recently a college where the inspection report revealed such comprehensive concern about the college that the college governors themselves resigned, and one feels that there was clearly a cause and effect there.

62. LORD NOLAN: In the former case was it the Secretary of State?

WILLIAM STUBBS: In the first two cases it was the Secretary of State who replaced the governing body on advice from the council following an inquiry. On the third case it was the governors who acted themselves in the light of the inspection report.

63. DIANA WARWICK: I just wanted to follow up the point and ask you whether you could say a little bit more about educational effectiveness. You said that this comment in your paper to us was based on inspectors reports. Is hidden in there a suggestion that the funding system and the mechanisms that Mr McClure talked to us about mean that there is rather too much emphasis on quantity and not on quality of educational provision? Could you say something about that because I wondered what it was that was prompting complaints or worries about educational effectiveness?

WILLIAM STUBBS: I certainly, Chairman, do not think that we put too much on quantity rather than quality. Indeed, the judgment of our inspectorate colleagues is the primary source of information and that is the judgment of involved experience and skilled peers that involve people who are now working in the area in industry as well as full time inspectors, and, indeed, those who are teaching in other colleges. So, it is a mixture of subjective and objective.

I think some of the concerns, Chairman, that one may hear from time to time about standards within the further education sector generally need to be seen in the context of the virtual revolution that has taken place in the way in which students' achievements are now assessed. No more does one rely on a formal set piece examination as might have been the experience of many of us. It is now very much to do with whether the student has achieved competencies, for example, with vocational qualifications, and those competencies are required to be assessed in a working context and require a value judgment from an experienced observer. That is a significant change in terms of assessment, and that has been taking place quite separate from the changes in governance and funding, but

I am sure influences, perhaps adds, to some of the concerns that you hear about.

64. WILLIAM UTTING: May I just make clear that you are responsible for inspecting colleges of further education and OFSTED is not?

WILLIAM STUBBS: That is correct, yes.

65. WILLIAM UTTING: The second point is, you do not have formal regulatory functions across all the responsibilities of colleges of further education, but it rather sounds as though you exercise regulatory functions on behalf of the Secretary of State at the request of the Secretary of State. Would that be fair?

ROBERT GUNN: We receive guidance from the Secretary of State on certain points, and each year when the financial settlement is announced we get a further letter of guidance, but there are very few occasions when that is really asking us to take a regulatory position. Most of the regulatory controls we have introduced are really following our insistence on the proper use of public money and value for money. We do not, for example, have any control over Health and Safety at Work Act or any of these other laws; we do not have a part to play in any of that.

66. WILLIAM UTTING: I appreciate that. It just seems to me to be extraordinarily difficult for the Secretary of State to exercise regulatory functions over 500 colleges without the active assistance of some intermediary body.

ROBERT GUNN: Yes, and she does ask us for advice from time to time.

WILLIAM STUBBS: If I may, Chairman. Let us say the register of interests of governance in which there was a clear procedure for them registering their financial and other interests, that stemmed not from a request formal or informal from the Secretary of State; that stemmed from the interest shown by the Public Accounts Committee about certain matters in which they then said to the council "What do you propose to do about it?"

WILLIAM UTTING: I did not mean to imply that we were restricted not to ask about the Secretary of State except in relation to the Secretary of State's own powers.

67. LORD NOLAN: Mr McClure, had you wanted to add something in answer to the previous question?

ROGER McCLURE: Chairman, it was about this question of educational effectiveness and volume and so on, and I think it is possibly worth pointing out that we have talked already about the main outputs, to use that phrase, being students with qualifications, colleges helping students to achieve qualifications, but of course there are quite a large number of intermediate outputs which the funding methodology is intended to bring the colleges' attention to, and therefore attaches also financial sanctions if those intermediate outputs are not met. An example is that much greater attention is being paid to initial assessment and guidance of students when they first arrive in the institution to try and make sure that they get onto an appropriate course, and of course that has a knock-on affect on whether they stay the course and achieve an appropriate qualification at the end of it.

Other examples would be the additional support which is offered to students who have learning difficulties like numeracy, illiteracy and so on, and fee remission for people on low incomes. All of these things are included within the methodology. Colleges get recognition where they deliver these things, and all of these intermediate outputs, as well as the main outputs, are audited by their external auditors when they actually come to settle up for the final reckoning of the bill, so to speak, from public funds at the end of the day. So I think the methodology is intended to be very much congruent with educational outputs.

LORD NOLAN: Thank all of you very much. I am afraid our time is up but it has been most helpful to hear you expanding on the paper you put before us and we are very grateful to you all for coming.

LORD THOMSON: Can I make a frivolous remark, Chairman? The FEFC is entirely prevented from dealing with Scotland, but I am glad to see that Scottish further education tradition seems to be thriving in England.

LORD NOLAN: Good afternoon all of you. Thank you very much for coming along to offer us your help. I understand that you have not prepared an opening statement that you wish to make, but you have, of course, supplied us with a substantial amount of material headed *"Opening up the Institutions"* and outlining your interests and concern in the governance of post school educational institutions.

I am going to ask Sir Clifford Boulton to take up the questioning please.

68. CLIFFORD BOULTON: Can I just, for the record, make clear where your membership lies. You say that the University and College Lecturers' union represents 70,000 staff delivering education and training programmes in the new universities, higher education colleges and further adult education colleges and services. Do you have any membership in the older universities or not really?

**DEREK BETTS, VICKY SEDDON,
AND PETER LATHAM**

DEREK BETTS (Head of Policy, National Association of Teachers in Further and Higher Education): No we do not.

69. CLIFFORD BOULTON: No, I understand for historical reasons how this division has come about, but it does help us to know whether you might have had experience across the divide.

We were set up to examine current concerns about standards of conduct. In our last report we found widespread concern about the things that we examined at that stage. Have you come to tell us that there is widespread concern in your world about standards of conduct? Are we more talking about a situation where we are more looking for preventive measures and reassurance rather than having to deal with a situation of deep concern?

DEREK BETTS: That is a rather value loaded judgment really. I think that we are concerned. I would not like the impression to be given that we just believe that we are about preventive action. I do think that there are a number of cases, they may not be large in number, yet we think there are enough cases that have hit the headlines for us to believe that we would like to have something in place that would prevent that. But, in response to a question one of your colleagues which was interesting, we are also concerned, not just about the headline cases which, of course, we are, but also whether the system that we have is sufficiently robust to ensure that measures of quality, standards of conduct and all the rest, are there for all potential cases even if they are slightly hidden at the moment.

70. CLIFFORD BOULTON: Thank you very much. Obviously we are looking at the question of governance as it relates to conduct and transparency and so forth. I see that you want to see the membership of governing bodies based on the principle of representation, and you want to achieve that by repealing Section 7 of the 1988 Act and substituting requirements for membership which would meet your points. At that point this would need, obviously a parliamentary intervention to achieve that. Would you look at that stage to perhaps introduce more uniform standards for this subject across the board of universities, or are you really thinking only in terms really of the new universities?

DEREK BETTS: We are responsible to our members for that sector, therefore our proposals are based in that area. I ought to add that it is Schedule 4 of the 1992 Act which would have applied to FE, and what we say in terms of HE should be read across into Schedule 4 of the 1992 Act because the same principles would apply. We would be looking for a wider representational base on governing bodies. We believe that the current definition in both of those Acts is too narrow. We are not afraid of the word "representation" because we think that it carries with it, accountability, and we think that those bodies that are prepared to put forward members to governing bodies should bear that "accountability" in mind.

71. CLIFFORD BOULTON: As you will have heard earlier, someone was expressing some anxiety about a member of a governing board who saw himself in a representational capacity, and your own paper, I notice on page 12 said, "It would be necessary for a governing body to recognise the special position of representative governors to allow for their relationship with their constituencies". So it is not an uncomplicated situation, is it, but on the other hand you did say, "There have been examples where governors, notably staff governors, have been removed or threatened with removal if they expressed dissent from the majority view". Do you want to fill that out at all? Is this a general problem or something that has a reason for it?

DEREK BETTS: It is not a general problem of removal, although we have to confirm what was said in the last session that there are certainly some FE colleges that have not sought to have staff representation on the governing bodies. We do know of one or two cases where staff governors have been removed, and there was one very important case which you know about. But there is also a feeling amongst our membership that staff governors are excluded from much of the work of the governing bodies; that they are excluded from committees and they are excluded from a lot of the discussion that we believe needs to be made more open. We fully accept that they have certain interests that they will have to declare in certain areas of the college's management, but we believe

there can be much more openness in the affairs of governing bodies and that staff governors and student governors can play a full and open part in that.

72. CLIFFORD BOULTON: Obviously you could not in the new rules that you wanted to provide be absolutely precise about whether the spirit of the new rules was being followed, so you would presumably favour some kind of monitoring to take place on the membership of these bodies. You appear to me to have great confidence in the funding councils in your paper. Is that the body you would see as keeping an eye on this?

DEREK BETTS: All funding councils have great power. The money is quite an important aspect of the system, and after all, they are one remove from government and in a position of power at the national level. We believe that you cannot, in the end, legislate for every eventuality. I think that what we are looking for in the legislation would be a framework for handling problems, but we believe that if the representational base was widened there would be an improvement in the checks and balances in the system. We have some confidence that it is the addition of greater checks and balances at college level which will prevent many of the problems that we have currently been grappling, with from occurring in the first place. So we do accept there is a limitation in terms of the legislation, but we do think that it will introduce a sort of checks and balances that would be valuable.

73. CLIFFORD BOULTON: I know this is not directly your concern, but have you had any experience of difficulty in recruiting lay governors in some areas?

DEREK BETTS: We certainly had feedback that there is. I am not sure that the colleges are operating what was said earlier about the search committees, and even if they are I am not sure that those search committees are formed in quite the balanced way which we would argue is necessary. We think that if the search committee is going to be of value, it should mirror the broad base of the parent body, the governing body. If it does not, I am not sure that it is of great value. From perhaps more anecdotal evidence, I am not sure that the majority of colleges are operating through search committees.

74. CLIFFORD BOULTON: Do you have any wish to see the possibility of some kind of compensatory remuneration introduced for people who perhaps were going to suffer financially by serving on these bodies, or are you more interested in preserving the voluntary principle?

DEREK BETTS: I think the voluntary principle is very important, but in our paper we do recognise that given the enormous responsibilities that governors are now being given, very different from three or four years ago, that perhaps a debate should be had about remuneration, not obviously more than perhaps the replacement of expenses and perhaps the replacement of salary lost as you might as a juror. We certainly do not want to go beyond that, and we think there ought to be a debate in that area. We are finding a lot of governors saying to us that frankly they did not come in to being governors to do the amount of work and take the amount of responsibility they are now being asked to do on top of the work that they currently have. I think they are finding it rather difficult.

VICKY SEDDON (National Association of Teachers in Further and Higher Education): Chair, if I might just add to what Sir Clifford was asking us about members of governing bodies and search committees, and I speak as somebody who works in a university and I am speaking for the university sector whereas my colleague here will speak for the FE sector. We do have a lot of concern about, for example, the very small numbers of women who serve on governing bodies, and the almost invisible numbers of members of the ethnic minorities who serve on governing bodies. We think if those governing bodies are to be truly representative of the communities they serve that that needs to be addressed in a serious fashion, and the current arrangements certainly have not addressed that issue either in higher education or in further education.

75. CLIFFORD BOULTON: Is there a shortage of enthusiastic advertising for vacancies and that sort of thing?

VICKY SEDDON: I think there is a shortage of enthusiastic looking to make sure that those bodies do reflect the community more widely. I think where there have been some attempts in some institutions that has been more successful, but I do not think enough attention has been given to it.

76. CLIFFORD BOULTON: I notice you are against the idea of extending the role of "visitor" at colleges as a kind of arms length adjudicator which exists very widely, of course, in the older universities. You obviously think that grievances and matters of that sort should be better tackled by a more in-house body. Is that your feeling about a "visitor" role?

DEREK BETTS: Again I think it is a little bit of a repeat of my very first answer. It is not opposition in a sense that we are opposed to it in quite that way. We have to operate within the legislation by which we are governed. The legislation that set up both further and higher education, is on the Statute Book and we believe that we could amend the legislation to give us the checks and balances and the preventative measures that we believe are important. So it is not an opposition in the sense that we think it should be taken away from where it is; we just think that it is most appropriate for our union and our members to be associated with amendments to the current legislation that we currently work under.

VICKY SEDDON: And that in fact having a robust system within the university itself is what is absolutely our first priority. Of course we need something but our emphasis is on the very great need for change within our own institutions rather than having a "visitor" would actually solve the problem. We do not think it would. We actually think that there is a need for change in how our governing bodies are set up, how they operate. They should be more open, they should be seen to be more accountable, the representative nature of them, who should serve on the sub-committees. The whole thing is about it being seen to be very open and reflecting the philosophy of education which is that things should be out in the open, available to challenge, available to reporting, so that the public can see what is happening in what are public institutions.

77. CLIFFORD BOULTON: There are some guidelines about procedure for committees reporting up, are there not, to the main body, they are fairly new. In your experience is there still quite a need for more of these executive committees to keep in closer touch with their parent body?

PETER LATHAM (National Association of Teachers in Further and Higher Education): Speaking from an FE perspective as staff governor of a college, I think there is a whole range of issues relating to the way in which governing bodies function, the procedures, the rules and regulations under which they operate. We have already referred to issues relating to how people become governors, and I think experience that I hear of is that in many colleges it is simply a question of the Chair and the Principal finding somebody they think has the skills and ability to be a governor. There is no search committee, there is no advertising, and there is only a rubber stamp by the full governing body which is given one name generally—no choice. There are issues relating to the way in which sub-committees function, as you have highlighted. A tendency to secrecy; a tendency to extreme unwillingness to report back to the full body; decisions delegated, and delegated quite properly, to the sub-committees but delegated in such a way that they are not supposed to be reported to the full governing body. Given that the sub-committees are in many institutions virtually entirely populated by the business governors plus the Principal, a large section of the governing body is effectively excluded from the decision making process, and even is not aware of decisions that are taken although when they ask questions they are told that they are responsible for collective decisions taken on their behalf by the sub-committees, and if they were to dissent from them they would be breaking the rules of collective responsibility.

78. CLIFFORD BOULTON: Yes. You mention business governors and, of course, one of the things that we have been reminded is that not all of the resources in higher education institutions come from the taxpayer, and that there are commercial activities increasingly being undertaken by these bodies. Do you have anything you want to say about any anxieties you have about the pressures which commercial considerations give rise to? Is there any strain on academic priorities or anything like that being brought about by commercial considerations? You did not mention it in the paper so is it not something that you had a particular attitude about?

PETER LATHAM: I think there are two orders of concern about this. I think there is a general concern amongst staff that the system is, in the global sense, too much driven by commercial or financial considerations at least, so that is a question of funding, what is vulgarly known as "bums on seats" I believe is the word that is used. There is also a concern that colleges may move into areas which they have not traditionally operated in and in which they are perhaps not sufficiently skilled and informed to operate successfully. I think it relates back again to the issue of the way the governing body is functioning; the quality and the detail of the reports which are given to the governing body, and the expertise which the governing body can bring to bear on those reports.

VICKY SEDDON: I think there is also the developing ideology of corporateness and corporate identity in our universities and colleges where members of staff (and we do mention this in our submission) are meant to be loyal to and look to the interests of their institution, rather than their academic subject area or to the interests of students. That has certainly led to situations in which people have felt gagged from making criticisms or making it appear that their university is less good than other universities. I think the competition that is now built up between local colleges competing for the same pool of students, and similarly in universities competing for students and competing for the better students. I think the funding mechanisms have been such that those elements of competition have actually been exacerbated, and then you get pressures within the institution for members of staff not to rock the boat. I think that is very clear to us.

In those circumstances we have found members of staff sometimes wanting to make complaints or to publicise those circumstances, and that has become extremely difficult. People no longer, very largely, have permanent status in their employment. More and more fixed term contracts, part time contracts, which are not renewable necessarily, are endemic in our institutions. Under those circumstances the pressures on people not to say things, not to rock the boat, those pressures are very clearly there and we as a union are in situations sometimes where we seek to defend those members who are making their complaints openly and we have very great difficulty in protecting their employment prospects under those circumstances. I think that is an indication of the way in which the culture of our institutions is changing and why all of our submission really has been about how we need good, robust, open, transparent systems of governance within the institution that can actually make sure that the governors do those jobs rather than expecting individual members of staff who may be vulnerable to actually pull the plug. That should be a responsibility of governors. They should have the time and space to be able to do that. They should have access to proper information within the institutions so that they can do that, and that is why we see the governing bodies as being of such great significance, and that that system is the one that needs to be seriously addressed and changed and improved. I think we have suggested ways that that could be done. I hope that has answered the question, Chair.

CLIFFORD BOULTON: Thank you very much, that is a very relevant answer to our concerns.

79. PETER SHORE: The composition of the governing bodies obviously is a cause of considerable dissatisfaction, but you refer in your paper to "small and narrow circles" that the governors are drawn from. Can you elaborate on that?

PETER LATHAM: There is a requirement in the Act that at least 50 per cent of the governing body should be drawn from business governors, and I think it would not be unfair to say that these are drawn from senior persons in local companies and tend not to be women, not to be black, and that not only do they preponderate in terms of numbers but they also have disproportionate power on the governing body because of the way many of the governing bodies operate their sub-committees. Coming from the north-east of England I find it strange in an area where there is very heavy unemployment that there are very seldom any representatives of unemployed people on governing bodies who might well be the people most interested in the training the college could provide. But we are concerned that a broad range of organisations in the community, whether it be the CBI or the Engineering Employers or the local Centre Against Unemployment, be represented on the governing body so it is, in some sense, representative of the community for which it is working.

80. PETER SHORE: This predominance of businessmen which you have made very clear, how does it really express itself in terms of the functioning of further education colleges and, indeed, the courses which they have to offer?

PETER LATHAM: I do not think that the preponderance of business governors means that the courses offered are any way skewed to their particular interests, but I think it does mean that a new (as somebody who has been on a governing body for 15 years) ethos, a new approach, has been brought in which talks much more about the real world and about business and commerce. Now, I think we all welcome the disciplines that we can acquire from the private sector. We need to know how much things cost and how we should use our resources effectively, but sometimes there is a lack of understanding of the educational process, particularly the further educational process which is obviously not the same as the university process which many of the governors would themselves have experienced, and also a tendency perhaps to not understand the complexity of delivering training and education to the range of students that there are in further education.

DEREK BETTS: Can I just add to that that the narrowness of governing bodies in terms of their representation is a matter of fact. We have carried out surveys and have described it as "male, middle aged managers", and they are white. We have to remember that this is an Act of 1992 and we are only in 1995, and changes in education policy or in terms of curriculum would take some time. I think we are expressing a fear that change may be distorted by that form of governing body in the longer term. Many, many students in further education come from groups such as students with learning disabilities and difficulties. There are many other sub-groups of students which actually require a great deal of money, probably more expensive than the norm. There is a fear that, if you have a college which is set down or looking at a more rigorous commercial route ensuring a maximum income at all times, the total community which is what most of us believe the colleges should be representing and serving, could be at a disadvantage if there were no voices from that community on the governing body. So it is not that the colleges would not necessarily be successful in what they are doing, it is just there is a debate about what they should be doing and whether they have got the balance right.

PETER SHORE: Thank you.

81. LORD NOLAN: I just had one short factual question going back to the question of payment. You spoke of reimbursement for loss of earnings. Would it be normal for the employers of those serving on governing bodies to restrict their earnings for time spent on the governing body, or are there other ways in which earnings are lost through service on such a body?

DEREK BETTS: I have no evidence that the earnings would be restricted. It is a little bit like the argument in terms of local councillors. Are you debarring certain people from putting their names forward because they might actually incur a loss of salary? I suspect that at the moment they are not, but then are we fishing in that very large pool that we would like to fish in, or are we fishing in a very narrow one?

LORD NOLAN: Yes, I follow. Thank you very much. I am afraid time is up, but may I on behalf of the

Committee thank all of you very much indeed for your help and for the very clear way in which you have expressed yourselves to us.

We look forward to your joint effort, and this is the herald, I think, of closer union to come, is that right?

KEITH SCRIBBENS, ROGER WARD CBE, RUTH GEE, AND MIKE THROWER

KEITH SCRIBBENS (Chair, Colleges Employers Forum): We are complete and we represent two organisations, as you know—the Colleges Employers Forum and the Association for Colleges. I am Keith Scribbens, next to me is Mike Thrower, next to him is Roger Ward and on my left is Ruth Gee. Both those organisations were set up after incorporation and I think we can proudly say we represent the interests of the governors of those colleges as well as the chief executives and we believe we have every eligible college in the country in membership of one or other and most are in membership of both—probably as many as ninety per cent in membership of both.

82. LORD NOLAN: I see. And they form the large part of the case for amalgamation, I take it?

KEITH SCRIBBENS: Indeed, we have consulted with our members, sir, and we have gained a good deal of views which have been incorporated in the evidence which we have put forward, which is not only in our statement to you but also we believe you have out latest information, a survey of the backgrounds and operations of governors which may answer some of the questions posed earlier in the day.

LORD NOLAN: Thank you very much indeed. I am going to ask Sir William Utting to take up the questioning, if you would, please, Sir William.

83. WILLIAM UTTING: Thank you, Chairman. May I thank you for the excellent documentation that you have given to us, not only your submission but the wealth of information that backs it up, your model register of members' interests, model terms of reference, research on nominations' committee, the analysis of questionnaires of your members, a model code of ethics for colleges and a model code of conduct for Corporation Members. You have certainly not been idling your time away in either of your associations since you were set up. And could I also say at the beginning that I quite take the point that has been made that these are comparatively new arrangements, they are still bedding down, and it would be premature to make precipitate judgments on a number of the issues that have been raised with us. But it perhaps will not surprise if I just wish to pursue this question about the appointment of governors a little further.

The thing I was raising with Sir Geoffrey Holland arose not so much from my concern about equal opportunities but from what appeared to me to be a rather curious definition of "independent" and the fact that the practical application of this might lead to a restrictive choice of people to go on boards of management for further education. And I wondered whether, although you yourselves are, in fact, now representing these sorts of people, whether you felt that that was a wholly satisfactory definition of "independent", if one is talking about business people, professional people, or people with other relevant employment experience. Are there

not others beyond those categories who might be thought of as independent who could make a useful contribution, or perhaps not?

KEITH SCRIBBENS: I think you must be right. There are others who we would wish to see the term "independent" applied to. The term comes from the instruments and articles of government—we have taken it, I think, for the most part to be a category which is relatively loose and whilst those who may come from the business interest—the "TEC" representative and the independent members form a particular category—I think the evidence shows that governing bodies have tried to recruit people who were perhaps not intended by that categorisation in the strict words of the legislation. We have to bear in mind, I think, the strong vocational aspect of further education institutions and the fact that, as Sir Geoffrey said, they are primarily, though not exclusively, local bodies and therefore I see governors today giving as much emphasis on gaining community representation which may be social as well as economic in its character and I do not see that decreasing over the years but increasing.

There is very much more difficulty in gaining community representation especially in some of the areas which have been described here this morning, where people from certain social backgrounds are under-represented. But many of the colleges have to live and work in those kind of communities so I believe they have gained knowledge about how to get community representation through the variety of community groups. And so I think it is very important that we retain both—the business perspective but in addition the social perspective that comes through community representation. I think the evidence shows that we are not perfect in that, but we are trying.

84. WILLIAM UTTING: That is very helpful. What about Local Authority members? I can quite see that when these colleges were reconstituted it was extremely important to demonstrate that Local Authority control had, in effect, been broken. But to remain in perpetuity with the statement that Local Authority members are not eligible as full members of the board but only as co-opted members in a sense seems to run counter to a desire to involve people from the local community in the management of the organisation. What are your feelings about the future for Local Authority representation?

KEITH SCRIBBENS: Well, of course, sir, in general we have had to work within the framework which was provided for us.

WILLIAM UTTING: You do, there is no question about that.

KEITH SCRIBBENS: But I think again we can see evidence that governors have found continuity and they have also found some skill being brought by the co-option of Local Authority members and officers of Local Authorities. After all, in our kind of communities the Local Authority may be a major employer and, therefore, there would be grounds on that account alone for their involvement in the process. Whether or not it was wise for the instrument and articles to create as it were a two-fold citizenship here of some who had extensive powers and some who did not, I think is now time for us to reappraise. But certainly, again, the evidence suggests that colleges have a close link with their Local Authorities, that often Local Authority councillors and officers have continued in membership of the governing body and I suppose in a way we would see that as equivalent to the TEC representation, which the Instrument and Articles require of us, whereas with Local Authority representatives, as it were, there is not that requirement.

85. WILLIAM UTTING: What about the staff and students? I mean, the regulations appear to allow up to two members of staff and one student. Do you recommend this, I mean as a means of at least incorporating some representatives of the "awkward squad" onto boards of management?

KEITH SCRIBBENS: You will see from our codes of conduct, from the proposals we have made to enable "whistleblowers" to blow whistles effectively, that we are keen that where people feel there is a need to act having exploited local arrangements above and beyond those, there is a facility for them to do so. We hold to all the principles of "Nolanism", I think it has been called, and we hold to that one too.

As far as whether or not there is need for statutory intervention to compel the existence of staff and student members on governing bodies we do not go that far. What we do do is recommend that in its local circumstances each governing body considers two things; first, whether or not to have staff and student representatives—and they are separate categories. And I think you have to bear in mind in our sector we are dealing with a much greater variety and type of student than is the case in the classical universities. Most of our students are part-time and attend the college therefore relatively infrequently. There is a large number of relatively young students matched, perhaps increasingly, by a wider age-range, but we do recommend that governors consider that question of staff and student representatives in their local situation. What we certainly recommend governors to do, if they take the decision not to admit staff and students into the governing body, is to contemplate other ways in which there is proper communication with them and not just through the industrial relations process but through all of the devices we have heard about this morning and some more besides.

Finally, can I say the evidence on this which is coming forward more and more as we survey what our members are doing, is that a large proportion—we think it will end up being over half—of the colleges have decided to have staff representation and student representation on their governing bodies.

86. WILLIAM UTTING: Thank you. You nail your colours to the mast for voluntary service as far as board members are concerned. I was left after our first enquiry, when we had been looking at the NHS, rather concerned that perhaps the management of public business by volunteers might be being eroded and that this was now being seen as a necessity in fact to pay people if they were to take management responsibility. Now, you certainly do not share that view?

KEITH SCRIBBENS: Certainly not. I think that we start with the view that representation, as it were, on our governing bodies is by local people. We like to encourage the notion that there is an ownership of what the college does by the local social and economic community and we therefore, whilst we regard it important that governors act

in a businesslike way, do not encourage them to think that what they are doing is running a business. But they are there to be widely, if not representational, carrying the culture and views of different elements in the community.

We have to balance that need—and particularly the need to attract those who may be self-employed and may genuinely lose income through involvement, the need to encourage greater participation from people who are in relatively low-paid jobs and may find it quite difficult to lose their hourly rates of pay that they might lose if they were involved, those from the community who may have child-care needs and for whom some kind of payment may be wise—we have to balance that against the inappropriateness of having people come forward as it were for the money or thinking that they are paid to be directors of a business in the sense that you might make directors' fees.

Our view comes to two things: first, we think this is an issue of social policy that goes far beyond further education and we would like to see this matter dealt with across local public spending bodies generally. What we find difficult to understand is variation in views, even one you heard this morning from Sir Geoffrey, that there may be grounds in certain institutions but not in further education. We find that difficult, we find it difficult to understand why hospital trusts may be in one situation and we are in another. But we are not as a body entering this fray by calling for the extension of fee payments, we would like to see a proper investigation of how far the absence of payments is excluding certain groups in the community and perhaps we might support a situation in which those who can demonstrate a loss have a pull or an opportunity to seek that loss recovered.

87. WILLIAM UTTING: And a corollary of voluntary service in your view is relief from individual liability as governors?

KEITH SCRIBBENS: That is a very important point and perhaps I could hand over to my colleague, Michael Thrower, from the AFC to address you on that, sir.

MICHAEL THROWER (Member of the Council and Chair of the Ethics Committee, Association for Colleges): Yes, thank you. I think one of the problems that we have is that, in giving more and more work to our governors, we are seeing governors now questioning just what would be the extent if financially that particular college ran into difficulty and despite best efforts we are not able to get a clear-cut explanation of their exact liability in such circumstances. Whilst it is not frustrating the recruitment of individuals at this stage, it will clearly have an effect if that uncertainty continues and we believe that it is quite unfair to have a group of individuals, particularly in voluntary service, who are suffering this uncertainty.

88. WILLIAM UTTING: Thank you. I almost have to declare an interest myself in that area as a trustee of a number of charities. Could I ask you, finally, for any observations you may have for actually improving things? How could everything be made to work better?

KEITH SCRIBBENS: I think the first improvement is the generation of more good practice and better self-regulation, which I believe the publications of the last few months, the publications which the FEFC have made, our own publications on code of conduct and all the rest of it are very important. So we would want to see the development of a generally good standard through that self-regulation and good practice.

Secondly, we would wish to see in relation to the search for members where we believe the deepest problem of this continuation of a clique, as it has been called by some, needs to be addressed, a rather more extensive use of the search committees which have been referred to. Our understanding from our survey is that more and more colleges—and, again, we believe over half—not only have search committees but have composed them to an extent of independent members and are using them well. We believe that advertising and the notification to bodies who might wish to nominate members is a strong way of achieving an avoidance of self-perpetuation and, of course, we understand you will need to look at the question of whether there should be an ultimate control on the number of years on which an individual is capable of sitting on a body. Sir Geoffrey mentioned nine years in their case. Our inclination was to say that two periods of four years was probably the right figure in our case because four years is the period prescribed in the Instrument and Articles of Government currently.

But we do believe that self-regulation in these matters is preferable to adding yet more inspectorial processes to which, as I think you will agree in the hearing this morning, are already very burdensome for us. We do not complain about it because we see that as being the exchange, if you like, for us being un-elected. But at the end of the day there has to be a proper balance given the cost that can be involved in responding to these initiatives between us being able to operate in a businesslike fashion and in an accountable one.

So self-regulation seems to be the way we would wish to go within a strong framework of accountability which we think increasingly is coming to be the case. But, again, we are not perfect. We hope that we are learning by our mistakes and might be excellent in the future.

LORD NOLAN: Good, thank you. Lord Thomson would like to ask one or two questions.

89. LORD THOMSON: Could I just follow up very briefly the question of liability? Like Sir William I declare a certain self-interest as a trustee of various bodies who are concerned about the problems here. In your case, would this require a change in the law?

MIKE THROWER: Unfortunately it would appear that the only way we can establish what the law is is through precedent and we have not yet had the test cases, I am afraid. In that instance I believe it would require a change of law, yes. Unfortunately we do not appear to fall within the law relating to companies, neither do we appear to fall within the law relating to trustees. So we are right in the middle and I believe it does require clarification.

90. LORD THOMSON: Thank you. Could I then ask also about the arrangements for a Register of Interests for the governors and for the procedure for declaration of interests? In the evidence we had earlier today from the FEFC they told us that they planned to survey the extent to which registers are in place by the end of this year and will consider in the light of that evidence whether it may be necessary for this to be made a condition of funding. I wondered what you could tell us about the situation and

more particularly, apart from the Register of interests, when it comes to dealing with contracts, do you have the impression that there is effective machinery in place in governing bodies for people to absent themselves from voting on matters on which they have a declaration of interest?

KEITH SCRIBBENS: We commissioned a specialist company in these matters of solicitors, Eversheds, to draft a model Register of interest. It has been circulated with advice and strong endorsement to every governing body. We believe that by the end of this year there will be no governing body that does not have a Register of interest and the only issue which we know to be troubling governors is whether or not the full declaration should apply to spouses, partners and children, as well as to them themselves as you might fully expect. But I think that debate shows a seriousness in the matter and we expect there to be registers in place. We fear not any inspection the FEFC may do of it but I do wonder whether or not people can be trusted to develop these things when they have a code of conduct which they have signed up to and perhaps may not need yet another inspection on that.

As far as declaration is concerned, a separate matter, again we have advised on the form in which individuals might declare an interest on the occasion of a debate or a consideration of a letting of a tender or a contract which might affect them personally. And we do see the two strands—the Register and the Declaration—as being equally important and one is not a substitute for the other. And, again, we have, as I have said, given advice to colleges how that may be pursued. I serve as Chair of a local college, I am also a member of governors of Fircroft College and I Chair a company which lies between the college and the local Training and Enterprise Council and I have to say, in that experience, I have never known of an occasion on which an individual has not been alert to the need to make it clear if they have a commercial connection with the matter in hand, and by and large are keen to withdraw rather than to have a presence.

I know this is where one of the areas of scandal lies from the reports which we have heard of and in this business an ounce of shame is worth a ton of virtue and praise and, of course, we want to see that everybody operates a common standard in that. So anecdotal evidence does not help when there is some against us. But, again, we are trying to spread the practice in that respect. I do not think it is a problem but we are about trying to make sure that it never is.

91. LORD THOMSON: Thank you. I think in the meetings that took place between some of you and our staff in preparation for this meeting very understandably some of you drew attention to the fact that this is a new situation, it is two years old, and inevitably there are stresses and strains in the adjustments—stresses that we heard about between the academic staff and governing bodies—and other problems, some of which were aired in the evidence we heard immediately before you. I just wondered what advice you give to your members about the kind of issues that were being raised a few minutes ago, which I think we are all familiar with from time to time and the way boards and committees operate—I mean the suggestion that it is possible for a governor, a chairman and a principal really to run the show and make sure that the sub-committees are organised in such a way—in fact the general body of governors find themselves rubber-stamping decisions that are taken elsewhere and, of

course, facing the liability for them if something goes wrong. I just wondered what your comments would be on these kind of complaints about the settling-in process for the new procedures.

KEITH SCRIBBENS: I think we would admit that bad practices can develop. I think that the enquiries show that in some cases bad practices have developed. What we also find—and quite a large number of governing bodies are so keen on the business that they repudiate the notion that there should be lots of committees in favour of the view that they should meet monthly themselves as a corporation and deal with all matters. And sometimes that can be ineffective as well. But the kind of evidence which you heard earlier, I think, falls into two parts. There is first of all how far governors are available to staff and students and other complainants and people who have got concerns, in order that if there seems to be the development of a clique that is acting as an inner cabinet and running things really, other governors can be alerted to it. And certainly we have encouraged in our documents to governors to make themselves accessible to all those who might have an interest in the business of the college, bearing in mind, of course, they are not there to represent any particular constituency.

The second aspect, I think, of your point relates to the industrial relations' situation, perhaps, that has developed as a consequence of rapid and sometimes dislocating change which we have had to be the proprietors of to some degree. I will perhaps ask Roger Ward, our Chief Executive, if he might like to comment on that aspect of the matter, sir.

ROGER WARD CBE (Chief Executive, Colleges Employers Forum): Simply to say that we inherited contracts of employment, sir, which had conditions within them that were too restrictive for us to successfully operate our colleges and part and parcel of very much the whole process that we have been talking about today, this period of rapid change, sadly has impacted on the industrial relations scene. But we feel now that that is really a matter that is more or less over and done with.

92. LORD THOMSON: Just one final point on this area: when you have finally merged your organisations, as I understand you are doing, will you have within your procedures some machinery for dealing with problem areas? Will you have some rights as the parent organisation of which the various colleges are members to deal with the problem as it arises and to intervene—are you proposing any machinery for this?

KEITH SCRIBBENS: One of the things we have to look at in the process of the merger discussions is what extra value can be created by the merger of our two organisations and certainly a function which neither organisation has heretofore sought to pursue has been the creation of a channel whereby they may be the expression of public concerns about what has happened in the case of an individual college. But certainly our sister organisation, the Association for Colleges, has a strong track record in enabling members of the public and groups of people to voice concerns and try to persuade the Association to take them forward to government and to other bodies, not about individual college cases but about the generality of the development of further education and whether or not it is sufficiently accessible to particular groups. So I will ask Ruth to comment on that in a moment. But certainly

we could not pretend that we have that in mind as an object at the moment, but we will be reviewing all our objects and if as a result of this enquiry and evidence which is given to it there seems to be a brokerage role which it would be possible for an organisation of governors and chief executives to play in dealing as a last resort with matters which have not been able to be dealt with locally, we would evidently be pleased to play it.

RUTH GEE (Chief Executive, Association for Colleges): We are, of course, two membership organisations and in that respect already our members seek advice from us and part of our role is quite critically to offer them informal advice, but the formal mechanisms that you allude to would be, indeed, a matter for the future.

I would like to take the opportunity, though, to comment on the role that we play in encouraging the training of all governors. For example, within the last two weeks we have held a national training event, almost exclusively for lay governors, not Chairs and not principals, specifically to ensure that they do understand the very complex nature of the social businesses for which they have got responsibility. It is our experience that people welcome that training; we have just evaluated that event and others and found that the training opportunities are very much welcomed and we see that whatever the framework in which we continue in the future, there will be an ongoing demand, both for new and experienced governors to keep up to date with what is happening in the sector.

LORD NOLAN: Thank you very much. Diana, do you want to ask anything?

93. DIANA WARWICK: Can I also thank you for the wealth of information that you gave us—it was enormously helpful and to me, at least, it indicated that you must be one of the most regulated parts of the education sector. Sir Bill Stubbs told us about the range of audits and the performance indicators and so on that you are required to work to. There must be a question for those—you have to both lead the institution and respond to the funding council but also to make sure that the academic standards of your institutions are maintained and your staff doing their jobs well—do you feel that you are over-regulated, or is there anything more you can say about the balance between responding to public concerns but also making sure that you can get on and do the job?

MIKE THROWER: Because the sector is a new one I can well understand why the audit procedures were put in place. In dealing with public money it is absolutely vital that people see that you are dealing with it properly. So anything that I say is not necessarily trying to argue for dismantling those procedures. But I think we have to recognise that there are compliance costs in those audit procedures and I wonder if perhaps at some stage in the near future we might look a little more at just how much all that is costing. That might give us a clue as to whether we are over-audited or under-audited from your point of view.

KEITH SCRIBBENS: Yes, I think if I could just add briefly to that. I did say earlier that the view of my colleagues is certainly that in a situation in which one does not have a constituency from which one is elected to this office one expects that there will be great openness and emphasis on that, there will be devices such as annual meetings which will enable us to simulate, if you like, a degree of accountability and that, finally, especially where government or state money is involved, there is going to be a degree of inspection. We have also got to see that there are two sorts of inspection by and large—one of a financial sort and one of a quality sort—and we generally welcome them all. But I think that we have to say that it would be welcome to have a degree of trust in us, being what we are and where we come from, that there is no self-seeking in this and therefore it is genuinely community contribution to balance against a desire perhaps to always fly to inspection as a means of regulating the process. I am sure that will settle down and I am sure that the procedures so far in place are model procedures for achieving the accountability with which we spend locally public money.

94. DIANA WARWICK: I am very conscious of the time—it is just a very brief question. So much emphasis has been placed, both by the union and by the funding council and by yourselves on the role of governors, the training that they require, and so on. Are you satisfied that the guidance that is available from a wide variety of sources provides governors with sufficient information to take what might be quite difficult decisions, not just in financial terms but also in terms of the academic standing of the institutions? Is the information that governors can require and obtain sufficient?

KEITH SCRIBBENS: I think that it is sufficient in abundance. The difficulty is communicating it in a way that busy men and women have an opportunity to absorb as a background to the decisions that they have got to make. So we are looking at ways in which we can express these things more conveniently to governors, through digests of published material, through our publications, such as the AFC publication, on further education, which goes to a wide number of people. The Funding Council's own circulars are available. Ultimately governors are not there to be experts in the business of managing or running a college; they are there as people who can carry the community, social and economic, into the life of the college and, therefore, they do not need to understand the detail in the sense that the Chief Executives do. But what we do say is that we have seen an improvement in the standard of papers that come before us over the years, with Chief Executives, I think, understanding more now how material needs to be presented to us, how decisions we have to make are highlighted and how recommendations, if there are any, come to us, not just from inside the college but from outside it as well.

But, yes, there is a surfeit of information, yes we struggle under it and I hope that we are providing methods in which our members can better easily understand it.

DIANA WARWICK: Thank you very much.

LORD NOLAN: You mention in your paper that there is little evidence to suggest that there is a demand for great openness from the public at large. Rather the experience of most colleges is the lack of interest in board activities—we have heard from more than one source of public meetings, widely advertised, and only a few members of the public turn up. What I think is very clear to us with your help is that there is a great desire for openness amongst college boards themselves and their representatives and we hope that our enquiry will enable them to learn from each other and from you about the best practices generally. We are certainly very grateful for your help this morning. Thank you all very much indeed.

TUESDAY 14 NOVEMBER 1995

OPENING STATEMENT

Opening Statement from Further Education Funding Council for England

Introduction

1. In its invitation to the Council to give evidence, the Committee gave an indication of issues in which it had a particular interest. This statement gives an outline of the Council's position on these issues. The Council has seen the evidence provided to the Committee by the Department for Education and Employment and jointly by the Association for Colleges and the Colleges' Employers' Forum.

2. The Council's role in relation to the governance of colleges is limited. Colleges are required to operate under instruments and articles made by the Secretary of State and the Secretary of State, not the Council, has powers to direct governing bodies where they act in breach of legal duty. The Council does, however, have a specific role in relation to governance through its responsibilities for quality assessment and through its responsibility for ensuring the proper use of public funds.

The merits of governance systems in the new FE system in ensuring proper conduct

3. The Council has available evidence from its inspectorate on the actual operation and effectiveness of governing bodies. What follows is largely based on that evidence. The mechanism of having a governing body to manage a public body such as a college itself has merit. Such arrangements permit members of the wider community to play a part in the organisation and running of colleges within the framework of regulations made by the Secretary of State in respect of the instrument and articles of government of each college. Within the limits prescribed each institution has the freedom to determine the precise composition of its governing body. Inspection evidence indicates that the majority of colleges made good use of this freedom to appoint governors with expertise and experience in areas which will be of particular value to the institution. Most governing bodies include individuals from a wide range of public and private sector organisations and, generally, reflect the college's provision and locality. The arrangements for the composition of governing bodies require independent and training and enterprise council members to be at least half of the membership and give independent governors certain reserve powers, for example, to appoint new independent members if the governing body delays doing so; and requiring business to be deferred if the independent and training and enterprise council members present are in a minority. These arrangements ensure that wider interests than those directly related to the college have oversight of the college's affairs.

4. There is evidence from inspection and audit that the governors of most colleges conduct their role and responsibilities conscientiously and aim for high standards. They are aware of their corporate responsibility for the financial health and good management of the college and for the proper use of public funds. As unpaid volunteers, governors meet their obligations out of a sense of public duty. Many of them devote substantial amounts of their time to governing body affairs and demonstrate willingness to improve their effectiveness through attendance at training events.

5. According to inspection evidence provided to the Council in most institutions governors have a clear understanding of the division of responsibility between themselves and the managers of the college and a high level of trust exists between governors and managers. At the same time, governing bodies expect to be kept fully and formally informed about developments in the college. In general, the expertise which governors possess ensures that reports received from college managers are understood and adequately scrutinised.

6. There are two checks on the system which are crucial. First, the Council requires through its financial memorandum with each college that the principal must inform the chief executive of the Council if he or she considers that the governing body is proposing to act in a way which is incompatible with the terms of the memorandum. Secondly, the clerk to the governing body has a responsibility for advising the governors on the legality and proper conduct of their decisions. The Council will soon publish guidance on clerking arrangements at colleges, which has been developed with advice from representatives of further education colleges. In cases where the clerk considers that the governing body may be proposing to act or has acted unlawfully, and if all avenues have been exhausted in bringing this to the attention of governors, the Council intends to advise the clerk to inform the Council.

The use of independent and flexible scrutiny systems

7. A number of independent scrutiny systems act as a check on the conduct of governors. Colleges are required to make publicly available papers and minutes of meetings subject to normal rules on confidentiality and to have a policy on public attendance at meetings. These requirements provide a check in the public interest. Colleges are also required to have their annual accounts audited and to make them available to the public.

8. In evidence to the Public Accounts Committee, the Council has expressed its support for the financial terms of all severance settlements for senior staff to be contained in the college's accounts and has issued guidance to colleges to make this clear.

9. The Charter for Further Education makes clear that colleges are expected to have in place formal procedures to deal quickly and effectively with complaints. The Charter includes arrangements whereby individuals can make complaints to the Further Education Funding Council (the Council) or the Secretary of State for Education and

Employment if they are dissatisfied with the outcome of the college's complaints system. The Council has received 52 complaints under this procedure.

10. Increasingly colleges have developed, and are using codes of conduct to which governors are asked to subscribe. The introduction of registers of governors' interests is also now firmly established as an issue which colleges are addressing. Guidance on these matters has been provided by the college representative bodies. The Council plans to survey the extent to which such registers are in place by the end of this year and will consider in the light of that evidence whether it may be necessary for this to be made a condition of funding.

11. The Council considers that accountability goes wider than propriety. It embraces also the effectiveness and efficiency with which public funds are used. The Council has established a range of systematic monitoring systems which record colleges' outputs, the amount of output they achieve for the public funds provided, the observed quality of their output, and their financial health. The information collected by these systems informs the Council's decisions and is published in summary form. Main systems developed by the Council to monitor colleges' performance are:

—analysis of each college's three year strategic plan

—college inspection

—audit systems

    external audit of annual accounts and student records

    colleges required to have internal audit and audit committee

—monitoring visits by Council's audit service

—financial monitoring

    three year financial forecasts and mid-year updates

    audited annual accounts

—college performance indicators

—data collections on students, staff and finance.

Best practice in appointments to governing bodies

12. The Guide for College Governors, published by the FEFC and developed by a working party including governors and senior managers of colleges recommended that colleges should plan the future membership of their governing body more formally than they do currently. The guide proposes that institutions should undertake a skills and experience audit to establish the ideal profile for the governing body. It suggests also that the process for appointing new governors should be as open as possible and that colleges should consider inviting applications in the local press for people with specified skills and experience.

13. The Council does not collect systematic information on colleges' appointment practices. Some information is available from a survey undertaken by the Colleges' Employers' Forum which indicates that colleges are addressing this issue. Regardless of how potential governors are identified, some institutions report difficulty in persuading individuals to take on the time-consuming role of college governor. Inspection evidence shows, however, that colleges generally have governing bodies with a broad and balanced membership. This was confirmed by the National Audit Office report, Managing to be Independent, published in February 1995.

The underlying reasons for conflict between the governing bodies in institutions and the permanent staff

14. In most colleges, the relationships between governors and senior managers appears good and the Council is not aware that this is a general difficulty. The Council has evidence from inspection which suggests that staff other than those senior managers tend to be fairly neutral towards their governing body. However, staff in some colleges seem suspicious of governors' motives, believing them to be concerned more with financial efficiency than educational effectiveness. The long-running national dispute over the contractual obligations of lecturers has strained the relations between teaching staff on the one hand and governors and senior managers of many colleges on the other. Again, according to inspection evidence, where teaching and support staff are included in membership of governing bodies, this has lessened the tension in colleges to some extent.

The importance of quality control in the provision of further education and the role of the FEFC as funder and regulator of further education system

15. The main responsibility for quality assurance and the development of appropriate quality control procedures lies with the colleges themselves. Control is exercised also through the various accreditation, validating and examining bodies, and through the standards set out in the Charter for Further Education. In addition, the Council has a statutory duty to ensure that satisfactory arrangements exist to assess the quality of the education and training which it funds.

16. The Council fulfils its responsibilities for quality assessment by inspecting and publishing reports on the quality of education colleges and through the regular collection and publication of statistical data to enable comparisons to be

made between the performance of colleges. The Council's chief inspector has a degree of independence in that the work of the inspectorate is overseen by a quality assessment committee, the membership of which is drawn from colleges and business. To emphasise this independence, the Council has specifically refrained from appointing any member of the Council to this committee. The inspectorate's judgments are not subject to review by the Council and the Council's chief inspector publishes his own annual report.

17. The inspection reports on colleges are published to a common format. A distinctive feature of the inspection process is that the reports set out and grade on a five point scale the strengths and weaknesses of both the subject provisions made by colleges and cross-college aspects, comprising responsiveness and range of courses, governance and management arrangements, procedures to recruit, guide and support students, teaching and the promotion of learning, achievements of the students, quality assurance arrangements, and physical and human resources. Inspection reports are published and disseminated widely including to college libraries and the national and local press.

18. Through the publication of its inspection reports and linking quality assessments to funding allocations, the Council is having a significant effect on the development of colleges' internal quality assurance arrangements and improving the quality of courses. Funding penalties are imposed on colleges when curriculum areas are judged by the inspectorate to have more weaknesses which outweigh the strengths. Re-inspection of 15 curriculum areas in 12 colleges following the award of low grades showed that 14 areas had improved sufficiently to allow funding penalties to be lifted. However, while significant progress has been made in a relatively short period of time, the arrangements in many colleges are not yet sufficiently robust to ensure in all cases that activities and outcomes are monitored comprehensively and actions to enhance quality are taken speedily.

19. Turning to the Council's role as funder, the Council is the principal source of funds for most colleges, providing overall 67 per cent of their income in the 1994-95 teaching year. In this context, the Council does have a regulatory role.

20. The Council has put in place regulatory and disclosure systems including:

—the financial memorandum with colleges, including an annual funding agreement and conditions of funding

—an accounts direction specifying the form and content of college accounts

—rules requiring the Council's consent for certain capital and borrowing transactions

—requirements for disclosure of accounts

—the collection and publication of data and monitoring of college strategic plans

21. These systems of regulation and disclosure, coupled with the system of external scrutiny and inspection set out in this paper are designed to ensure that value for money is obtained and that good use is made of the substantial public funds available to colleges.

WEDNESDAY 15 NOVEMBER 1995

Members Present:

The Rt Hon Lord Nolan (Chairman)

Sir Clifford Boulton GCB   The Rt Hon Lord Thomson of Monifieth KT DL
Professor Anthony King   Sir William Utting CB

Witnesses:

Dr Joanna de Groot, President and David Triesman, General Secretary, Association of University Teachers

Hadrian Southorn, Chairman, Ian Rule, Secretary, and Walter Ulrich, Information Officer, National Association of Governors and Managers Cecil Knight OBE, Chairman, David Meikle MBE, Secretary, and Pauline Latham, Governor Member, Grant Maintained Schools Advisory Committee

Sir Robert Balchin, Chairman, Andrew Turner, Director, Grant Maintained Schools Foundation, and Roger Sheffield, Headteacher, Langley Park School, Bromley

Dr Kevin Brehony, Senior Lecturer in Education, Department of Education Studies and Management, University of Reading and Professor Rosemary Deem, Department of Educational Research and Dean of Social Sciences, Lancaster University

95. LORD NOLAN: Welcome to the start of our second day of oral evidence. We are already into our familiar routine and I shall waste no time but go straight on to introduce today's witnesses. We shall hear first from the Association of University Teachers, represented by their President, Dr Joanna de Groot, and their General Secretary, David Triesman. We are then spending the rest of the morning on grant maintained schools. The National Association of Governors and Managers whose members are mainly State school governors but also include grant maintained school governors, will be represented by their Chairman, Hadrian Southorn, together with Walter Ulrich, their Secretary, and Ian Rule, their Information Officer.

By way of contrast, the Grant Maintained Schools Advisory Committee is also a membership body but its members are mainly drawn from heads and governors in the grant maintained sector. It will be represented by its Chairman, Cecil Knight, its Secretary, David Meikle, and Pauline Latham. Mr Knight is, I understand, a head master while Mr Meikle and Mrs Latham are both chairs of governors.

Next, we shall hear from Sir Robert Balchin, Chairman, and Andrew Turner, Director, of the Grant Maintained Schools Foundation. I hope I am describing the Foundation correctly as a body whose role is to promote the development of grant maintained schools. Certainly, Sir Robert is well known for the part he has played in developing the concept.

Our final witnesses this morning are Dr Kevin Brehony of the University of Reading and Professor Rosemary Deem of Lancaster University. I think all I need do to describe their area of expertise is to say that their research has been published in a book entitled, *Active Citizenship and the Governance of Schools.*

Now, I am afraid we are, by our usual Committee standards, depleted in number this morning. Both Dame Anne Warburton and Diana Warwick unfortunately are unwell and later on, although not until 11.45, Lord Thomson and I are going to have to leave to attend parliamentary functions across the road but we shall still

undoubtedly be quorate and I can assure those who may be concerned that all of us will have the transcripts and will carefully study them, as well as those of us who are here today being able to hear it live.

Dr de Groot and Mr Triesman, may I begin by thanking you very much for the extremely helpful and very comprehensive material that you have sent us, including a number of specific recommendations which is always a great help to us as a first draft to work on. Thank you very much for that. I am going to ask Sir Clifford Boulton to go through your evidence with you.

96. CLIFFORD BOULTON: Good morning. I notice that you end your paper by stating:

"We seek to blend independence and accountability, academic freedom and responsibility, openness and a professional ethic."

Thank you very much for mapping out the minefield for us so sympathetically because it is a very sensitive area that we are entering and all I can do really, I think, is to assure you that we do appreciate this and certainly we are not a review of the totality of governance of the universities. Our terms of reference are related to standards and their maintenance, as you appreciate.

As I read your paper, most of the supplementary questions that occurred to me I found dealt with on the following page and so my questioning will, I think, be more directed to giving you an opportunity to fill out some of the areas that you touched on in the paper so that you can perhaps express them more fully or, perhaps, less formally.

Can I just establish that your membership is pretty well confined to the pre-1992 universities. Is that the situation?

**DR JOANNA DE GROOT, AND
DAVID TRIESMAN**

DAVID TRIESMAN: That is generally true, although the membership of academic and related staff in some of the new universities, particularly in Scotland, have recently joined us.

97. CLIFFORD BOULTON: Thank you. And what will happen to movement of academic staff between the two types, if I can use that expression, of university. Will there be a continuing membership if a member of your Association moves into a new university in a teaching post? What happens then?

DAVID TRIESMAN: We tend to advise people to move to the association which is recognised for bargaining purposes in the institution but I must say that our recent experience, perhaps I should say happily, our recent experience is that our members choose to stay members of the Association of University Teachers.

98. CLIFFORD BOULTON: So there may be an increasing knowledge from direct experience among your members across the board?

DAVID TRIESMAN: Yes, I am sure that is true. One of the effects of competitiveness in research funding has meant that many of the new universities have been very active in what is sometimes these days called a transfer market in getting eminent researchers and academics from the old universities across to help boost often the beginnings of a serious research programme in new universities. So, there is a good deal more movement than there was and, I think, as you are saying, a great deal of cross-fertilisation in ideas.

99. CLIFFORD BOULTON: The reason I was asking these questions was really because your paper also seems to see an inconsistency between the systems of governance of the new and the old universities. Am I correct in saying that you would like all universities to have the equivalent of the charter status?

DAVID TRIESMAN: Well, Sir Clifford, we regard it as indispensable and I must say that those of our members who have gone to the new universities continue in the view that they had before they went to the new universities. Our reasoning is, in a way, very straightforward. We do not assert that nothing can go wrong in a university that has a charter. We are, from time to time, ourselves advised of things which staff, very senior staff, regard as problematic in universities which have charters, but what we do observe is that the structure of the charter, the pattern of rights that it establishes and the patterns of responsibilities that it insists upon, mean that it is almost impossible, so far as we can tell, for any malpractice to remain hidden. It is flushed out within that system and we regard that as essential. There should never be a hiding place for things that are going wrong.

I fear that in institutions which are incorporated, and I used to negotiate on behalf of staff in those institutions myself when Deputy General Secretary of NATFHE, when you have institutions which are incorporated the means of getting rid of the nuisance committee that keeps probing, keeps asking questions, is all too easy. There is not a robust enough structure of defence and that is what we believe charters give.

100. CLIFFORD BOULTON: And so, effectively, you would need to set about amending the 1988 and 1992 Acts probably, which provide a statutory framework for the governance of the new universities and set off down—now, what would you be doing then, you would be setting off down a Privy Council route, would you, for all these bodies?

DAVID TRIESMAN: We would. I think probably they can apply for charters to the Privy Council as matters stand, even with the current legislation, but we would certainly be happy if it were useful to take further advice on that ourselves. That has been our working assumption. May I say that our own experience of the Privy Council when, for example, it has altered some of the terms within a charter as a result of legislation is that they are very careful but they work reasonably quickly and to well established patterns. It is very hard to mistake what the officials in the Privy Council regard as good practice or how it should be achieved and we are reasonably confident it could be done quickly.

101. CLIFFORD BOULTON: You did express confidence in the Privy Council system but, to my knowledge, I do not think this work is done by staff in the Privy Council, is it? Are you experienced of who actually does the examination and vetting of these charter proposals?

DAVID TRIESMAN: There is certainly a good deal of work done within the Department for Education and now Employment. In the past when it was done, of course, it was the Department for Education and in the Scottish and Welsh Offices and in the Department of Education in Northern Ireland. They tend to look at some relatively formal matters and their advice to the Privy Council thus far has been on what is the proportion of post-graduate work done. Are post-graduate research degrees undertaken? What are the general standards in the provision of under-graduate degrees?

They have gone through a set of questions and I believe—I do not know whether Dr de Groot would take a different view—but I believe that the criteria that the Departments for Education would first address have all been addressed in granting university status to the new universities. So, that large chunk of work, I would suggest, has really been done. The real question would then be for the Privy Council to assure itself that the normal criteria of holding a charter had been met in the formal sense.

102. CLIFFORD BOULTON: And you are reasonably satisfied—I am sure none of us is thinking in terms of imposing a total consistency and uniformity in systems of government in universities—but are you reasonably satisfied within the charter universities that there are satisfactory controls because some of the systems of governance in, let us say, the ancient universities if we are sub-dividing or in London University which is an enormous body, they are very difficult to equate with some of the 20th century universities. By and large, you do not see any defects in openness, transparency in the old charter system?

DAVID TRIESMAN: Let me try to answer making a couple of points. Firstly, the charters are tremendously robust instruments in ensuring the independence of universities and, for that reason, I would say old or new they would be valued. Secondly, I do believe that many people find some of the structures under the charters less efficient than they would find in the governance, for example, of a private company.

It can be laborious to take decisions in universities on occasions but the reality is that the interleaving of responsibilities, the involvement of people from outside, the involvement of the membership of the university from inside has, in our experience, flushed out the kinds of things which I believe become very problematic in some of the new universities.

I could, although I would not want to pillory any particular university, I could think immediately of several examples of financial decisions which in an old university were regarded as questionable but could not be hidden and were resolved within the university under the terms of its charter.

103. CLIFFORD BOULTON: You favour the visitor system, do you not, of an arms length relationship with someone who can come and look at something from outside? We have met some resistance to that idea in some areas but would you like just to expand on that?

DAVID TRIESMAN: To put it at its briefest, the existence of a person who has considerable power in relation to the good governance of any university seems to us to be valuable and to be more valuable than some of the alternatives. I do not argue, I will not argue that it is inconceivable that an Ombudsman for universities could work but I think what we have observed is that the visitors of universities or the people who are usually asked to act for the visitor of the university where the visitor is a member of the Royal Family, for example, tend to get to know their institution very well.

The Sir Michael Davies report, and I do apologise for burdening you with very large amounts of it but it was quite a good example of the operation of a visitor, the Sir Michael Davies report shows the work of somebody who knew that institution inside out. There were not things that could be hidden from Sir Michael. My view is that it is on the balance of probabilities more likely that a single person or an office centrally trying to do the job for the whole of higher education would inevitably be at a disadvantage in knowledge of the systems within a highly diverse set of institutions. For those reasons we would like to be sure that the person who was asked in really did know the place, knew which questions to ask, knew how to carry on probing when they were really being given less than the whole information.

104. CLIFFORD BOULTON: I suppose there is a variety in the kind of sieving processes that have to be gone through before something could get to a visitor formally, is there? I mean, are you satisfied generally with the way that the route is prepared because obviously you do not want to burden your visitor with trivial or silly complaints?

JOANNA DE GROOT: Perhaps I can speak from experience as somebody who has worked in universities for over 20 years. I would say that within the framework that is created by charters and statutes there are structures of scrutiny, debate, appeal which mean that before any difficult issue reaches a visitor it has, as it were, already been very thoroughly tested and explored, if that is the question that you are asking.

Yes, I think it is precisely at the point at which, if you like, the openness and the informed externality needs to come in, if you want to put it that way, that the visitor can play, and does play—I have had one or two experiences in difficult situations—does play a very useful and constructive role.

I have heard people complain about many bits of systems. I do not think I can remember a time when

people have felt that the role of the visitor has been misplayed and, obviously, that is simply my own experience but I offer it for what it is worth because you take an interest in such things and I think we would have noticed if there had been real doubts emerging about the office and the way that it has been exercised and you have at least one example of where it has played a very positive role.

105. CLIFFORD BOULTON: Yes. What about cases where a complainant feels a great deal of personal sensitivity about complaining because they feel making a complaint could be very damaging. Do you have any thoughts on that?

JOANNA DE GROOT: I do and I think that is why we have views about whistle blowing, of course. I think now there is a lot of experience in a range of situations. I will just take an area I know a little bit about, which is the area of harassment, of where somebody with a complaint of harassment, with a problem of harassment, can be protected and the issue of victimisation can be openly and explicitly addressed. Oddly enough, it is the very knowledge that it can be, as you probably well know in other circumstances, that makes it the more difficult, I think, to mistreat a person in that situation.

If I can say something more general: I think the kinds of recommendations that we are making in this area are ones which would create a climate in which people would feel more confident and those who might want to behave in a less than totally scrupulous way would feel inhibited because they are operating within a certain culture.

My own experience of universities and other institutions is that it is where there is that common understanding backed by the proper codes and regulations that actually you can stop abuses most effectively because people feel so uncomfortable at the thought of it that, in a sense, it almost stops before it starts.

106. CLIFFORD BOULTON: You talk about ethics officers and ethics committees. Is there much UK experience of such bodies?

DAVID TRIESMAN: I think there is relatively little. Looking at the experience that I have read about, which is principally United States experience, there does seem to be a great deal of confidence built up in those bodies which operate in this way.

Universities, I think we feel, are very sensitive places. We say they should remain autonomous, that they should be self-governing in all principal ways and I think it is almost inevitable that when the public looks at a body which makes an assertion of that kind for itself that it should be really, really confident not just that its money is well spent—it certainly should feel that—but it should be really confident that the things that go on inside it meet standards which are explicit—no longer assumed standards but explicit standards—because that seems to me to be the only way in which in the long term Parliament representing the public is likely to accept that independence is the correct continuing pattern.

May I just add one word to what Joanna has said. We have—and, if it is helpful, would leave with the secretary—a brief note on how we believe the whistle blowing mechanism might operate which adds a little, I think, to the paper that we have put before you. I do not mean to burden you with even more paper but it might actually assist in explaining how we feel people might feel confidence that they will not suffer a penalty for behaving properly.

107. CLIFFORD BOULTON: Is there anything on the US experience of ethics committees and ethics officers that exists in print that you could let us have or that you are aware of?

DAVID TRIESMAN: I certainly would be happy to go back to some of the material that I have read and try and bundle it up if that is useful.

LORD NOLAN: Thank you.

108. CLIFFORD BOULTON: Just briefly, there are one or two areas where you might care to expand a little bit on the basis of your experience. You talk about wanting to open up some of the works of committees and sub-committees because this could be a device effectively for removing scrutiny from a wider body. You want to see a model way of opening up by way of model standing orders, or whatever it might be.

Are you aware—again, do not give us details of specific cases—but are you aware of real anxieties that have arisen or would they simply more or less be precautionary. Have you got experience of what you yourself call abuse?

DAVID TRIESMAN: I think we are aware, now in some volume, of two areas of very real anxiety. The first is that there are certainly—I was aware of it all the time with the former polytechnics and new universities because I used to get the detail across my desk literally day by day, I occasionally do nowadays in relation to the older universities—but we are aware of whole ranges of decisions about the resources that are being passed to departments, sudden changes in resources passed to departments, being taken in committees which have been syphoned off from the main committee structure and where, other than for a relatively small number of very senior members of the university, nobody seems to have the smallest idea of why the decisions were taken. That does not help.

One of the advantages is that in the final analysis in a chartered institution with a senate you can usually bang away at the information until you get it but sometimes that is a little late to do anything about it. I mean, you find the truth but sometimes the body is cold.

The second area which I am becoming myself increasingly concerned about—I think we are as an association—is that so many of the systems now are based on competition for funds. I understand that—selectivity and excellence issues do provide a context for competition—but many of the things which were discussed openly among academics and right across the whole of the university system are now not discussed at all because you reveal the competitive edge that you might have and people are very loath to do that. If they are developing a new course or a really significant area of new research they do not want another prestigious institution to lift that work or sometimes even to identify the academics who are doing it because in the transfer market that I referred to some extremely lucrative offers are made to people to come across with that work once you

can identify them. Neither of those are helpful to the openness within an institution and certainly not to academia as a whole.

CLIFFORD BOULTON: So you are saying it does produce some of the strains that I quoted right at the beginning that need to have some system.

DAVID TRIESMAN: Absolutely.

JOANNA DE GROOT: Discussions of difficulties would be an excellent example where people feel in a situation where a particular department is in difficulties and there might be a number of resolutions to its—financial difficulties I am talking about here—that one of those resolutions might be a change in staffing patterns, to put it neutrally, but where that cannot be discussed as one alternative among others openly because to do so would identify the department in the public arena let alone in the university as a whole. Therefore, what you get is a discussion which is much less than rational, that serves neither actually probably the interests of the best practical solution nor, indeed, the academic interests of the department.

I think it is that kind of failure to recognise the close relationship between the academic decisions and the academic personnel and, if you like, the financial and practical ones which perhaps is one of the distinctive things about university life that we are trying to address in our evidence.

109. CLIFFORD BOULTON: There is no simple answer to this, is there? If you see the benefits of competition you cannot reveal an awful lot of commercially sensitive information?

DAVID TRIESMAN: I do agree. It is a very, very difficult balance to strike. What I think we would suggest is that if the balance has to be adjusted it be adjusted in the direction of openness because the alternatives seem to us to be worse. I do think there is probably a great deal further that many universities could go in sharing information without undue risk of unfair competition than breaking out with other universities.

What I suspect has happened, and this could be no more than a suspicion, is that in attempting to embrace a more commercial ethos many colleagues have probably read the books about what commercial ethos' are like and they plunge into it in a very full-hearted sort of way and frequently probably go a lot further than they need to in the notion of secrecy.

In the new universities, my experience of the negotiations around the "gagging clauses" was that we were talking to heads of institutions who plainly believed their institutions would be stripped out, broken up, demerged almost instantly if things were revealed and it seemed to me to be unrealistic and I do suspect it took processes very much further than they needed to go.

110. CLIFFORD BOULTON: Thank you. I have just got one final question before asking colleagues for theirs. The membership of the funding councils and the research councils, I think that you want more information about—at least, I think I would like more information about how openness over membership of these bodies could be achieved. What are your proposals? Are you not

totally happy with the way these bodies come about? They are very, very powerful bodies.

DAVID TRIESMAN: The determination of membership seems to be exclusively a matter for whoever the Secretary of State of the day is and I think that we have looked on occasions at the lists of people appointed and you can see a significant number of very eminent people and you can understand what must have gone through the Secretary of State's mind and in some cases it is not at all clear. It may be that I, we, simply do not understand the criteria that have been used.

I have noticed increasingly, if I may say so to Lord Nolan since your Committee started its work, that a great many public bodies do now advertise when they have a vacancy in their most senior governing structures. That is a system which has not yet visited us and I think that is a very great pity. It may be that we would end up with exactly the same people after such a process but everyone would feel a great deal more confident about it.

JOANNA DE GROOT: I think it is the two elements. It is the element of selection that David Triesman has just spoken about and I think it is also some knowledge of what the criteria being exercised are, as it were, other than simply personal individual choice which, obviously, at the margin operates but in many walks of life, you know, what the criteria for appointments to particular hosts or bodies are is a perfectly familiar thing and I would have thought there was no reason, if we can assume that the decisions are at large sensible ones, why that should not be the case for the bodies that we are speaking about now like the funding councils.

111. CLIFFORD BOULTON: This is based really on the principle of how personnel are chosen rather than any specific complaints about their failure of performance, or anything like that?

JOANNA DE GROOT: Absolutely.

CLIFFORD BOULTON: Thank you very much.

LORD NOLAN: I am going to ask Lord Thomson if he has any questions to put to you.

112. LORD THOMSON: I would like to follow up immediately on the point that you have just left. Does the AUT have a policy in which they press for a certain code of behaviour in regard to advertising for membership of governing councils?

DAVID TRIESMAN: We do for all posts within universities and for all posts in the overarching bodies outside universities. Our belief is that it should be transparent, that it should be open to testing on equal opportunities and other criteria and that has been a very long-standing feature of our policy.

113. LORD THOMSON: Yes, and do you have any view as to how successful you are in seeking this?

DAVID TRIESMAN: Can I just make one very quick comment. Forgive me, Joanna. Within universities I think that we have been successful. I would not argue that we are the only force who have put these arguments. I have known members of the Committee of Vice-Chancellors

and Principals who have argued it just as fiercely as we have. I think there has been some success there although paradoxically the headhunting in the research area has meant that people are being brought across on a headhunted basis and without any advertisement and one of the things which I am told by a number of vice-chancellors rather than by our own members—actually, sorry, they are our own members but they are telling me as vice-chancellors of this—is that they believe that in many instances there has been no consideration given, for example, to the effects on equal opportunities of simply drawing staff across in that way.

114. LORD THOMSON: Thank you. We are a lay body, as must be quite obvious to you, and, of course, our point of entry really in this particular area of our enquiries is the public sector and, basically, the responsibility for public funds and that, of course, is a bigger consideration in some of the other educational areas we are looking at—the further education colleges, the TECs, and so on. I just wondered if you could help me with a figure of how far the university sector that you cover, what is the average percentage of your revenue that comes from public funding?

DAVID TRIESMAN: To answer it in the most helpful way I probably do need to divide it between the old and the new universities. There is very nearly now a balance in the old universities between public funds and funds which are drawn from other sources. In the new universities my belief is the figure is about 65 to 70 per cent of public funds, the remainder from other sources.

There is a complexity in this and, forgive me, I know that organisations like ours do have a habit of slipping into the obscure areas of funding formulae and I do apologise for that. The ways in which you count research funding are quite sensitive in this and my figures for the old universities, for example—well, for both sets but I can illustrate it with the old universities—deal with a great deal of the research funding as though it was not public money in the sense that a great deal of it is money that comes from industry, from charities, and so on, and some of it does come from the funding councils, which is public, of course, in the most direct sense. There is a mix in there.

115. LORD THOMSON: It would be quite helpful to me to be brought up to date on the sort of picture of the different categories of university. I got a little confused yesterday when we were discussing these matters with the simple category of new universities and old universities. It seems to me there are some new universities that are newer than others and some old universities that are a good deal older than others.

I was for 14 years a chancellor of a Scottish technical college that became a charter university. Does that count as an old university now?

DAVID TRIESMAN: It does. Yes, yours certainly does. Professor King's and my university which we share in common is an old university.

JOANNA DE GROOT: I was going to say that I think the term "new" in the public mind has been confusing because in the sort of Robbins era of the 1960s there were, of course, a number of new institutions that were founded which were then described as "the new universities" and they were new in a number of ways, partly physical so, partly that they organised their academic life in a somewhat different way. In some cases they grouped disciplines and patterns of study somewhat differently than the older universities of that time. I think now the term "new" is often being used for those universities that have emerged in the post-1991–92 era, what are sometimes referred to as the former polytechnics. I think that is probably where, in common parlance, the blurring starts to happen.

116. LORD THOMSON: Apart from the fact that the newest of the new universities are statute bound and the less new universities are charter bodies which is the major distinction which you are recommending to see abolished really in one way or another. Does that divide the teaching staff, the academic staff, in a serious way?

DAVID TRIESMAN: The principal division, I think, occurs not out of any choices made by the academic staff at all but because historically the burden of research funding has flowed to what we have been describing as the old universities, those that were in existence before 1991–92. As a consequence, both within the contracts of the academic staff in those universities and because of the availability of resources a very much higher proportion of their time and the resource that they use is given to research.

The new universities, if you take research funding as a whole, 92 per cent of it very nearly goes to old universities, by our definition; only about 3½ to 4 per cent goes to new universities. That is an extraordinary difference and that does produce differences of sorts between staff, although there is, in general, a belief that we would like to see all universities having the same opportunities in research.

117. LORD THOMSON: And if you take university teachers as a whole, roughly what proportion of them are members of the AUT?

DAVID TRIESMAN: It is about two to one. Within the old universities it is about 70 per cent; of all those who might join us it is about 70 per cent. We are in the fortunate position of there being no competition among unions within our sector so that there is not another unionised group.

Within universities taken as a whole, or higher education taken as a whole, we have roughly twice as many members in our membership as all of the others in the new universities have together.

118. LORD THOMSON: One final question. I remember the Jarrett Report as a milestone in trying to bring the new efficiency ethos into academic institutions and that has gone a great deal further since then and universities have to compete for students now worldwide really. University principals seem to spend a good deal of their time going off to faraway places to see what they can do in attracting students.

I wondered whether you had any feelings about any risks attached to this process in terms both of the standards of entry into universities and then at the other end of the standards of academic achievement. Has the pressure to bring in students from a much wider international catchment area produced the temptation to dilute standards in any way?

JOANNA DE GROOT: I wonder if I could respond, as somebody working within the system initially. I am sure

that David will have some things to say as well. I think there is a real difference between talking about opening up access to very differing groups of students, actually differing groups of students in the United Kingdom as well as, perhaps, growing numbers of students from overseas. The challenges that poses to the design, the delivery, the assessment of university level education and the creative changes, I would say at its best, that that stimulates and the pressures of funding regimes because the expansion of intake of differing groups of students has come partly from a commitment, which again I think we have shared on the whole with vice-chancellors, to opening access to, if you like, the fullest interpretation of the Robbins principle and other things where in the bigger political and commercial world funding systems have been designed that require universities to recruit students in a certain way in certain numbers.

I think AUT has—and, in fact, we have recently been trying to make some statements about this—recognised potential tensions there. I think if we would want to embrace what you call the competitive approach it would be much more about a competitiveness in the excellence and diversity of what is on offer rather than having to knock someone else out in order to succeed yourself. There is more than one version of what competition would be and in the field of education I do not think it is appropriate to see someone else's downfall as the condition of your own success. It is much more all striving for the best in different ways through emulation and also diversification.

I think when that is restricted by the constraints of funding rules, where money follows or does not follow students, that confusion occurs rather than in some general relaxation of standards, but you might have other things to say on that.

DAVID TRIESMAN: No, I just add this. I must say that I was very concerned by some of the reporting about the way in which some entry standards have been used this year and I know that it did cause a good deal of public concern. I think that the examples of where it had happened were actually really very limited but, nonetheless, they were disturbing and I thought that the CVCP was quite right to decide that it needed to ensure that standards did have a credible basis that the public could rely upon.

LORD NOLAN: Thank you. I think Professor King had a question.

119. PROF ANTHONY KING: Yes, I have one answer as well as a question. My answer to Lord Thomson's question, wearing my hat as a university teacher, is "yes".

My question is as follows, and I am really asking you here to extend your remit a bit. Right at the beginning, David Triesman paid tribute to the utility of the office of the visitor. There are more and more university-like institutions around the place—that is to say, bodies that are spending large amounts of public money, in toto at any rate, but which operate pretty autonomously. One has in mind grant maintained schools; one has in mind colleges of further education.

I will put it this way round: can you see any arguments against extending the device of the visitor to institutions like that? Would you off the cuff—and you have had no warning of this—would you off the cuff think there might be a case for extending that device to such institutions?

DAVID TRIESMAN: I think the answer is going to be yes but with the same brevity Professor King just answered the question. I am sure the answer to that is it could be extended. I do not think that any organisation that receives significant amounts of public money, or even perhaps relatively limited amounts of public money, where it is in general asked to have custody of its own ethics would ever be disadvantaged if there was somebody outside who enjoyed those kinds of powers. It should never be afraid of it.

PROF ANTHONY KING: Right.

120. LORD NOLAN: I wonder if I could go back to two aspects of competition which you have already touched on, the first being competition for resources. You say that there is a danger here—I am reading your letter—its consequences are that a lack of internal and external scrutiny, public funds, is justified by maintaining a competitive edge. I see that and you say, of course, it stifles the spread of knowledge.

Some of us recently visited one of the new universities where they were making a good deal of money by licensing the intellectual property which they have built up over the years. I did not ask who the licensees were but is this a way in which universities could share knowledge at a reasonable cost and, in this way, overcome both the grave disadvantages of undue confidentiality and, at the same time, enable universities to earn a legitimate bob or two from the work they have done. Is that happening?

DAVID TRIESMAN: It certainly is true that some universities have, for a long time, generated televisual materials, written materials—the Open University is a fine example of it—which have been marketed much more generally and have been used in other universities and other teaching institutions. We certainly have never seen a difficulty with that.

I think what has happened more recently, and certainly since the new universities made their contractual arrangements with their staff in 1990-91 is that the material that has become included within the area that is the property of the university rather than the property of the academic using it has increased enormously. I can say from first hand experience that in the negotiations over that universities—polytechnics as they still just were at that stage—polytechnics were arguing that they should own everything including the notes from which lecturers spoke in their lectures and be able to utilise those in order to generate commercial products.

At the end of the argument they did not quite end up owning the notes but they certainly got pretty close and I think that has now meant that they are very much more protective of a wide sphere of material than was ever the case in the past. I know of lecturers who would normally have sent materials in draft to colleagues for professional comment, which academics in the past and very much in the present do all the time, who now will not do that because they believe they are contractually forbidden from doing it, that it would interfere with the commercial purpose and would put them at risk in the general environment that is in operation now. Personally, I find it very hard to imagine university life being healthy on that basis.

121. LORD NOLAN: Yes, I follow that. It is the lure of money being the root of all evil, is it not? Funds are tight and here is an easy way of making some. We are also told of Cornell marketing on the Internet a whole course in, I think it was, advanced engineering and I think this is something that universities are going to have to grapple with, are they not, by way of competition.

DAVID TRIESMAN: Under the last Uruguay round of the GATT treaty—I have been talking with colleagues in organisations throughout the world in February this year when we were making an assessment of the effect of that—it is not lawful now in international law, as I understand it, to prevent the import of various kinds of intellectual products including courses. In the University of the South Seas, for example, which is a university run, I think, by seven different governments and spread across a very considerable area, they are finding it very hard to persuade students in their own island nations to take their courses when they can take CALTECH and MIT courses extra-terrestrially and by terrestrial means because of the prestige of the universities involved.

No one is going to close down satellite airwaves, or whatever, that is in part a world which we have to take proper account of but I remain profoundly concerned when academics behave as though their work should be secret for the sorts of reasons that I have given.

LORD NOLAN: I quite see that.

JOANNA DE GROOT: And the flip side of that coin would be that judgements would be made about the value of academic work which were not about its value but about its marketability. Now there is clearly an overlapping area sometimes, but there is clearly also not an overlapping area. I believe you have had the submission which we originally made to the Secretary of State about university work in which we emphasised that one of its characteristics is that it is critical, it is at the edge, it may sometimes be uncomfortable or unpopular and I do not need to spell out for any of the members of the Committee the consequences therefore of too great a concern on the part of university managements as to what is marketable for that core activity of university teaching and research.

122. LORD NOLAN: Yes. It is inimitable to the best type of university education, which most of us have been fortunate enough to experience, and which depends so much on a personal link between the student and his tutor and the confidence that knowledge will be shared.

JOANNA DE GROOT: That is right.

123. LORD NOLAN: I must not over-run, but you also touched with Lord Thomson on competition for students. We were told from one source that it is feared that many eligible students—a figure of 40,000 this year was quoted—are turning down the offer of university because they say they cannot get by on their grants and they are not willing to run up debt at their age. Is this an increasing tendency in your experience?

DAVID TRIESMAN: Absolutely so. One of the things which makes me most depressed about the system is when I get together with those of our members who are in charge of the student counselling services in universities. They tend to be very responsible, practical people. I do not think they are scaremongers by nature and they talk about the number of students they know who have problems about their funding once they are in, let alone those they know of who would not come in in the first place, and the proportion of the time of many academics whom they know which is now being absorbed in counselling people on very straightforward nuts and bolts questions such as "How do I get through next week?".

That has become a really worrying preoccupation and some student health centre reports last year and some of the reports done by some of the church organisations show the re-emergence of illnesses of malnutrition which the Victorians believed they had eliminated. I find it—well, I do not know how to put it—stunning, that in 1995 I should even be saying this, but it is well documented.

JOANNA DE GROOT: You will perhaps already have heard evidence that it is not only a question of potential students who do not take up places, but that some of the student drop-out can now be attributed to financial hardship.

LORD NOLAN: Yes.

JOANNA DE GROOT: That is quite well documented.

LORD NOLAN: And of course there is very great difficulty in recovering loans from those who take them out in many cases.

DAVID TRIESMAN: Yes.

LORD NOLAN: It is perhaps on the fringe of our terms of reference, but it certainly is a factor of which we are very conscious.

DAVID TRIESMAN: May I just add one very brief thought. One of the things that we ourselves would hope would be in the statement of ethics that we advise, is a statement about what the responsibility of the institutions is for trying to sustain students, often in increasing difficulty. I am aware that does not print any money, but it certainly might give much broader guidance through the university community about how to approach some of the issues which are in some senses new.

You mentioned the university experience perhaps some of us had. If I reflect for a moment on the period when I was an undergraduate, I suppose many things happened but I did not see many people suffering the kinds of hardship that we see today and I am not sure how many members of staff are really prepared with an understanding of how to deal with it.

124. LORD NOLAN: Thank you both very much indeed. We would like to talk a lot longer with you, but we must move on to the next witnesses. You have been extremely helpful.

At the moment we are short of one Committee member, Lord Thomson, but he will be back in a moment and so I think we will continue if we may by welcoming you and thanking you very much for coming along to help us.

It is Mr Hadrian Southorn, Chairman, Mr Ian Rule, Secretary and Mr Walter Ulrich, Information Officer of the National Association of Governors and Managers. In a democratic way, we tend to share out the questioning in this Committee and I am going to ask Professor King to take you through the evidence which you kindly sent us.

125. PROF ANTHONY KING: Can I first thank you very much for the evidence. I am not giving any secret away when I say that some of the opening statements of evidence we receive are pure rant. It was nice to have a balanced argument presented.

Could I indeed take you through it, not in enormous detail, but just to try to tease out some of the issues that you yourselves alluded to. One of them comes in your second paragraph when you refer to the new system and the legal framework. You say that this new system is entirely capable of securing high standards in this sector of public life. Then you say "Whether it does so in practice is likely to depend on how well it copes with certain inherent weaknesses." I have cut off the sentence at that point. Could you say what you think these inherent weaknesses in the new system are?

HADRIAN SOUTHORN, IAN RULE, AND WALTER ULRICH

WALTER ULRICH: Essentially that it pivots on 325,000 individuals in the State system, both LEA maintained and grant maintained, who, by any standards, are ordinary citizens who in many cases have considerable difficulty in measuring up to the very challenging demands of this public office. They do it unpaid as volunteers; they are always liable, if the going gets rough, to throw in their hand and there must therefore be inevitably question-marks as to how well such a system would operate in a pretty complicated legal framework involving a lot of quite difficult, and on occasions, stressful responsibilities.

126. PROF ANTHONY KING: You say in your document that these are inherent weaknesses. You have underlined that point in what you have just said. Given that school governors are going to be recruited in that way and given those responsibilities, it sounds as though this is something we just have to live with.

WALTER ULRICH: For the moment, certainly. We have always taken the view that this is a great experiment in participatory public service by ordinary citizens. It is an experiment: it is a very big step and there is a certain fragility about it. If everyone does their best to make it work, then we believe it will work and work pretty well.

If, for whatever reasons, it turns out that the inherent weaknesses are not remediable easily, or not surmountable, then maybe in five, 10, 15 years' time, who knows, the country will decide that something else has to be done.

127. PROF ANTHONY KING: Could I ask you a bit about the recruitment of these ordinary citizens who become school governors? Are you satisfied that boards of governors do the best job they can in perpetuating themselves in getting the right kinds of people to join them?

WALTER ULRICH: First of all, of course, some governors are elected by people over whom the governing body has little influence or control and this is true both of grant maintained schools and county, voluntary and special schools. There is an element there of the given. Where the governors have power to co-opt, in the case of those grant-maintained schools that have first governors and in the case of county and controlled schools, there is a real problem. Co-option is intended to bring in the community element, which is not otherwise provided for. It is a means very often of bringing in the obligatory governor who is a member of the local business community. It is a means by which the governing body, if it is wise and conscientious, tries to fill in gaps in its other membership.

128. PROF ANTHONY KING: I may not have been precise enough in my question. My question really was, given that those are the objects of the recruitment enterprise, in your best judgement is that recruitment enterprise now being conducted as well as it could be and if it is not, what suggestions might you have for how to change it.

WALTER ULRICH: In our experience it is a wide spectrum. Many governing bodies take co-option extremely seriously and do it in a systematic way. Others find it all rather difficult.

129. PROF ANTHONY KING: Given that spectrum, is there best practice that you know of in some schools, that you would like ideally to see adopted in most of them?

WALTER ULRICH: There is probably, as so often with governing bodies, no single best practice. It does depend on the school or the locality and so on. But the important thing from our point of view is that it should be a serious and structured process.

130. PROF ANTHONY KING: How would you structure it?

WALTER ULRICH: Well, the first thing to ask is "are we looking for particular aptitudes, skills, experience, background that we have not got"? The next is to see if there are sources from which recruitment might be made. The third is to pool all the ideas that people have. The fourth is, when ideas come forward, to have a look at the possible candidates in some formal way. For instance, the governing body might say "Well we think so and so, whom we know, or some governors know about, might be suitable. We will leave it to the chair and vice-chair to get in touch with them, ask them whether they would be willing to serve, talk it through with them and then give us a report.". That is the kind of thing that can be done.

Always there is the problem that it is a two-way street—that the governors may want somebody who looks very suitable, but very often the most obviously suitable people are not the ones that want to serve.

131. PROF ANTHONY KING: Can I ask you about rows, because in grant maintained schools, as in all schools—but we are particularly concerned about grant maintained schools at the moment—rows take place, members of the staff versus the headteacher, the headteacher versus the chairman of the governors or whatever. There was a recent case in the newspapers—and I will not refer to it by name, because that is neither here nor there—and one of the people involved in that particular row is said in the press to have remarked, "grant-maintained status gives schools freedom, but unfortunately there is no-one to turn

to for help when things go wrong". Certainly one comes across a lot of press reports of rows of an almost family character where there does not appear to be any kind of device or mechanism available for sorting it out before it goes nuclear. Are you conscious of this as a problem?

WALTER ULRICH: Yes. We are conscious of it. It comes up very much on our national help line. We get calls from people who say "What on earth do we do next?". In the case of LEA maintained schools, it is possible sometimes, provided the row is not with the local education authority itself, to use the good offices of the LEA, though governors do need to be careful not to get pushed into a situation where the LEA becomes a mere arbiter, say, between the governors and the head.

132. PROF ANTHONY KING: I know this is utterly arbitrary, but can we leave LEAs out of it because at the moment we are just focusing on grant maintained schools.

WALTER ULRICH: Yes, of course. In the case of grant maintained schools, we have always felt, right from the time of the legislation, that there was a problem for a state school not having access to some public body that, as it were, had the same point of view as they did, the same objectives, that was concerned in some way, if you like, with the quality assurance function that they themselves had and would help them with it. At the moment, in a grant maintained school where the governors feel that for some reason or another they cannot solve the problem, and it is in fact their problem, they have got to solve it, they may find themselves dealing on financial matters with the funding authority, but on other matters, and maybe even on financial matters, with the Secretary of State via this relatively little used, potentially enormously important channel of a request for a direction under Section 68 or 99 of the 1944 Act.

133. PROF ANTHONY KING: Does that strike you and your organisation as sensible? On the face of it, it seems rather silly, if there is some domestic row in a school in Huddersfield or somewhere in Cornwall that the only way in which some external force can be brought to bear on it, or some external mediation introduced, is for somebody to have to go to the Secretary of State down the road. That seems a little dotty on the face of it.

WALTER ULRICH: We do think that is something that should be seriously thought about in the case of grant maintained schools. We think that a public body like the LEA is needed for all State schools to exercise, if you like, the function of the critical friend.

134. PROF ANTHONY KING: What device might you have in mind?

WALTER ULRICH: We argued at the time when the legislation went through that the funding authorities should have that sort of quality-assurance/critical friend type function, but ministers were evidently determined not to, as they saw it, recreate the LEA under another guise and simply took the line that the governors must consume their own smoke. We thought that on the whole that was likely to be a mistake and we think that some of the developments since then have shown that we were right.

135. PROF ANTHONY KING: There is one specific kind of row that is inevitable in organisations of this

character and that is where somebody, it could be headteacher, a teacher or another member of the school staff, is dismissed under circumstances that cause controversy. Are you happy or unhappy with the present mechanism that deals with that?

WALTER ULRICH: On the whole that mechanism ought to be capable of working because there is the safeguard of the industrial tribunal. No governing body, knowing that it would have to answer in an industrial tribunal, would, unless they are very foolish take a dismissal lightly.

136. PROF ANTHONY KING: But you referred earlier on to the whatever it was, 350,000, ordinary human beings. In my experience, some proportion of those are likely to be foolish and there have been quite a number of instances, though not a huge number, where real difficulties have been caused under precisely these circumstances, and as we know industrial tribunals are very lengthy and inclined to be expensive. Might there not be a case for having some kind of in-house set of arrangements before going down that road?

WALTER ULRICH: I am not sure what you mean by in-house, Professor King, but if there were to be the creation, say, via the funding agency, of a public body that had more than financial responsibilities in relation to grant maintained schools, then it would be very reasonable to give them some kind of advisory locus. One of the possibilities would be, and here you would be recreating the situation that obtains in the LEA maintained sector, a situation where the funding agency for schools might refuse to stand behind the financial consequences of going down before an industrial tribunal. That is one of the checks on the other side of the fence.

The LEA has no power to stop a governing body from dismissing. All they can say is, "We have the right to advise you. We have exercised our right and we say to you, if you guys go on with this dismissal and you go down at an industrial tribunal as we think you will, don't expect us to foot the bill because we have the power not to. Normally we have to, but if we have good reason not to, then we don't.". One might consider that kind of arrangement, but then of course you would be bringing grant-maintained schools very much more into line with what is happening in the LEA sector.

PROF ANTHONY KING: Let me leave it there. I have two or three other questions, but my time is up.

LORD NOLAN: Lord Thomson, do you have some more questions for this witness?

137. LORD THOMSON: I was wanting to follow up your ideas on paragraph 18 of your submission to us. You make a case for the critical friend and you have the quite strong sentence, "Ministers, however, made it clear they do not want to see any ongoing support as part of their department's role.". There clearly is a big gap there, is there not? Would you like to expand on Professor King's question as to what would be the kind of body that could fill that gap that we might consider as one of our recommendations?

WALTER ULRICH: Simply on the principle of Ockham's razor there would be a lot to be said for giving the body which acts as the source of finance and the

custodian of financial propriety, responsibility, value for money and so on, the function also of the critical friend because on a wide view of——

138. LORD THOMSON: The FAS you are talking about?

WALTER ULRICH: Yes, that is right. On a wide view of value for money, value for money in schools depends not just on financial judgements but good educational judgements which are relevant to the educational performance of the school which, as we all know, is difficult to measure, but people can have a go at assessing it.

139. LORD THOMSON: Would that be also an over-centralised body for dealing with the wide variety of circumstances in a wide variety of areas throughout the country of individual schools?

WALTER ULRICH: That would certainly be a difficulty, though it might not be impossible to think of some kind of agency arrangement, a local regional system, with local offices, not only one in York, getting to know their parish really well. The alternative of giving the LEA some sort of a function is presumably to be ruled out of court on the grounds that the whole point of grant-maintained status is that you should not in some way be dependent on the LEA, except for those specific services of special educational needs and so on where it has a statutory responsibility.

140. LORD THOMSON: I agree with you about the likely view of government about bringing the LEA back into the act, but from your own experience as governors, would you feel that the LEA would have a role if the Government's doctrinaire objections could be overcome?

WALTER ULRICH: We are non-political on this and we do not want to get into politics. We also are very keenly aware that some LEAs discharge the function of the critical friend very much better than others. There are LEAs, and we will not mention them here, whom we would regard as critical, but not friendly in the way in which they deal with their schools and the attitude they have.

That in a way is possibly remediable, and LEAs are well placed to do this in relation to their own schools because they have a quality assurance function and it makes sense to give them the quality assurance function in relation to grant-maintained schools, but that would be a very big step. It would be going into an arrangement whereby much of the outside influence, the advice and so on, on grant-maintained schools would come from those LEAs from which they are now separated.

141. LORD THOMSON: I hope this will not be taken as a political remark from me, but looking at the papers about the present structure of grant maintained schools, with, I must confess, a virgin mind, it did strike me that the Government provides the funding for you, but having provided the funding through the FAS, it rather washes its hands of you. I was slightly shocked to note, for example, that you are working very hard to provide NAGM papers sold at modest prices to give the best guidance to governors and grant maintained schools.

Would it not be a good idea for government to fund that and take on some responsibility for providing the handbooks and guidance books as to the best practice for governors of grant maintained schools, instead of leaving it you to engage in flogging them yourself?

WALTER ULRICH: I do not think we want to denigrate what the Government is actually doing in the way of providing advice. There is advice which they issue or cause to be issued by others and so on, both of a specific kind on the law, and that is pretty good, and of a more general kind on what you might call good practice, some of which is apt and some of which is perhaps less apt. That is certainly as much available to grant maintained schools as it is to LEA-maintained schools.

The point we have always made is that you cannot expect, particularly in the political atmosphere, government, or, for that matter, local government, to provide advice which is wholly user friendly, and which sees things entirely from the point of view of the governors, which does not look sideways over what the Headteachers Associations might think or what Members of Parliament and so on might think. So there is a place for this user-friendly advice.

The trouble about having this Association subsidised by the Government is that it then reduces our independence and that is extremely valuable to us. Our papers are actually quite profitable. Our problem, and maybe our fault, is that we have simply not succeeded, being a small organisation run by volunteers, in opening up this market. We are having a go at that and we hope in the longer term to succeed. That way there would certainly be a lot of advice available to governors of the kind which we regard as the most valuable, not the kind which says "best practice, chaps, is so and so", but "there is a variety of good practice and a variety of situations. These are the possibilities and these are the considerations you ought to bear in mind".

Our model of the information and advice to governors is not telling governors what to do, but getting them to think.

142. LORD THOMSON: Just one purely factual question: can you give me an impression of what proportion of funding on average for grant maintained schools comes from the FAS? Is it nearly 100 per cent, 60 per cent or what?

WALTER ULRICH: If the grant maintained school is in an area where the FAS operates, it is the great majority of it, if not the whole amount. I think you have witnesses coming who will be able to answer that precisely, but certainly in those areas where the FAS operates, they are essentially the funders of the school, though the school may get something for special educational needs and so on from the local education authority.

LORD THOMSON: I see, thank you.

LORD NOLAN: I think Professor King had one more question.

143. PROF ANTHONY KING: Just one follow-up to my line of questioning and also Lord Thomson's. It is straightforwardly this: you acknowledge the need for a critical friend. LEAs are ruled out for reasons given, the Funding Agency for Schools probably would not be appropriate, too centralised. What about adopting the

practice that has been very common in British universities, and indeed in medieval monasteries it seemed to work pretty well, which is to have each grant maintained school required to appoint somebody called "a visitor" who might, ex officio, be the local mayor, but who would be in a position, if he or she could not do it, to appoint some kind of agent to make enquiries. It seems to work well in the university sector; why not do that in the grant maintained schools?

WALTER ULRICH: I cannot speak for universities. We were extremely worried when the Government first of all thought that their new inspection system should be conducted on the basis of the inspected choosing their inspectors. There are problems about that. There is a lot to be said for whoever is going to act as your critical friend not necessarily being the one that you appoint.

PROF ANTHONY KING: The system does not work quite like that. The person is normally designated ex officio. It is not a question of saying "we'll have Bloggs.".

WALTER ULRICH: I am so sorry. I thought you said they would choose them. It is an interesting idea. The problem is that it is not just a case of picking somebody who has lots of common sense, wisdom and so on. The critical friend function presupposes a real understanding of how schools work, of the problem of measuring or even assessing a school's performance, combined with a genuine built-in commitment to the objectives of high quality and so on. That may be quite difficult to do in a single person picked from the list of the great and good.

144. LORD NOLAN: I am sure we would all like to keep you here much longer, but I am afraid we have run out of time, so we can only thank you very much for being so clear and concise, as well as substantially helping us in our inquiry. Thank you very much.

Good morning, and thank you very much for coming along to help us. I should, before the last witness, have just enquired of members of the Committee whether they by any chance have connections with grant-maintained or, for that matter, local authority schools, either as parents or governors or whatever? No, the answer is no. I just like to clear these things up. In the Committee we take it in turns to start off the questioning and I am going to ask Sir William Utting to take you through your evidence.

145. WILLIAM UTTING: On the question of interest, though, I had better declare that my wife is the retired head of a primary school. That is my only connection and I am no more knowledgeable about the sector than that might imply. But I do not think we are knowledgeable, either, about the role and functions of your advisory committee. I am not proposing to go through your evidence in detail but I think it would be helpful if we entered on the record just the first paragraph of your evidence, which explains who you are and what you do. Would you care to read that in, or should I?

CECIL KNIGHT OBE, DAVID MEIKLE MBE, AND PAULINE LATHAM

DAVID MEIKLE, MBE (Grant Maintained Schools Advisory Committee) We are happy for that to stay in, Sir William, yes.

146. WILLIAM UTTING: May I just read it in then because I think it would help people, if we say that your

Grant Maintained Schools Advisory Committee represents equally all the 1,081 grant-maintained schools. You were set up by the Department for Education and Employment, you serve as a channel for consultation with grant-maintained schools as well as to enable those schools to make known to the Department and to other educational bodies the views and concerns of the sector. In order to achieve this there is no membership fee and your committee is funded by means of a grant from the Department, which is currently £90,000 a year.

PAULINE LATHAM (Governor Member, Grant Maintained Schools Advisory Committee): Could we just make sure that we add that it is a head teacher and governor organisation—it is the only one that exists in the country and it is a very important partnership and that is what grant-maintained schools are about, about the partnership between grant-maintained governors and heads.

WILLIAM UTTING: Good. Thank you very much.

CECIL KNIGHT, OBE (Chairman, Grant Maintained Schools Advisory Committee): Equal numbers of head teachers and governors on the committee.

LORD NOLAN: A unique balance.

PAULINE LATHAM: Yes, it is.

147. WILLIAM UTTING: We had evidence from Sir Geoffrey Holland yesterday in which he said that among the advantages of devolving responsibility for managing their own affairs to individual educational bodies was the fact that this enabled them to clarify both their objectives and their accountability. I confess I am in some confusion on this question of accountability. The DfEE. evidence to us about grant-maintained schools said that they account to their local communities for their performance. That seems to me—I mean, local community is a term of art and one needs to unpick this and decide what it is and what constitutes a local community and I would like to hear from you what elements in the local community you account to. You also have the Funding Agency for Schools which makes money over to you and you must account for that, presumably. And somewhere or other you have the Secretary of State who is called in to sort of referee and decide problems that cannot be sorted out locally. Could you say something more to us then about accountability and who accounts to whom for what?

CECIL KNIGHT: I think you have to bear in mind that the grant-maintained schools sector is a very broad church—we are talking about voluntary and aided and controlled schools as church schools, for example, as well as ex-Local Authority schools and the "community", so-called in inverted commas, of a voluntary school, a church school, is essentially a Christian community to whom it is responsible, although as the Christian community it obviously is there to serve the secular community with which it is surrounded. And in the case of ex-LEA schools, they may serve a very narrowly defined community—as, indeed, my own school where you have to live within ten minutes' walk of the school to get a place—or a slightly broader community. It depends very much upon the situation and where the school is placed.

But the accountability in its most powerful sense is to parents. They are represented on the governing body,

there are nine parents on a governing body of seventeen and those are elected—well, seven of them are elected by the parents, two are co-opted by the other governors. That does enable the governors to ensure a balance of representation to see that minorities and so on are represented whereas they might otherwise be overlooked. I am speaking there of the two co-optees.

Then, of course, there is an annual parents' meeting, there is the publication of accounts, there are the publication of exam results of OFSTED reports, so the whole conduct of the school is certainly remarkably transparent as far as parents are concerned. The majority of that data and information is equally open to other interested members of the school's community, however one may wish to define that, and there are abundant channels for anybody who has a particular interest and concern to make a direct approach to the governing body and no governing body of a grant-maintained school would be wise—indeed I doubt would be inclined—to disregard a serious approach made by a member of the local community who was not directly connected with the school. They can, of course, raise matters by approaching particular governors. The names of the governors have to be published by law—most grant-maintained schools, in fact, have their names and photographs with abundant information inside their front doors. I do not know whether my colleagues wish to add to that?

DAVID MEIKLE: I would like to add something. As a governor I think the one thing I would like to say above all else is that the clarity of purpose, the clarity of the responsibility that one has in a grant-maintained school is absolutely undiluted—I mean, you are responsible. You mention all these different sorts of accountability and we are very aware of all of them and understand that we must meet them and are very happy that should be the case. Because the clarity is there, we know what we have got to do. And in terms of the local community, as a governor, you cannot miss that accountability, it is there all the time. Every time you go outside the front door, you answer the telephone, you are about school business—whatever you are doing that accountability is there, you cannot go back to the Town Hall or the County Hall and vanish from it. There is nowhere to go. So the accountability is very clear indeed. We like the accountability nationally, which we understand because we are nationally funded. We like reporting through the FAS to the Secretary of State: we see that it is laid down; we know where we are going and we find that very acceptable.

PAULINE LATHAM: As far as financial accountability is concerned I think we are more accountable than any other sector of the educational system in this country because we are audited internally, we are audited externally by our auditors that we appoint, the Funding Agency for Schools scrutinises our accounts monthly, although now if you have got a good track record we only have to submit them quarterly. But our accounts are more accountable than any others. We also have the National Audit Office coming into schools and we have OFSTED.

WILLIAM UTTING: I am sorry, I did not hear that last sentence.

PAULINE LATHAM: We have the National Audit Office come in and look at a selection of schools. We have all sorts of people coming and looking at us and I think, whereas we have to stick in the black, unlike LEA schools, who are allowed to overrun and pay it back the next year—but I have doubts whether some of them ever do—we cannot do that, we have to have a good financial plan in place and I think we are much more accountable. And our parents see our accounts every year and see that they are audited thoroughly.

148. WILLIAM UTTING: I think the only body you have not mentioned is the Audit Commission actually.

PAULINE LATHAM: Yes, they look at us as well! Everybody looks at us.

CECIL KNIGHT: I think another dimension that we have not mentioned is that, of course, on the governing body by law and, indeed, from a genuine desire in any case, we have to have the local business community represented and that is obviously exceedingly important—they have a stake in the school—and obviously through those governors people who are engaged in commerce and industry within the school's local community can raise issues concerning the curriculum and any other matters that the conduct of the school might raise for them. In my own school, just to perhaps cite a particular example, which is in the inner ring of Birmingham, the fact that we have among our parent governors people who speak probably about eight different Asian languages, is a tremendous asset. They would have great difficulty, many of our parents, if they had a concern in finding their way to the education office in the centre of the city and, indeed, communicating the nature of their complaint. They know that they just have to go down the road.

149. WILLIAM UTTING: I quite take those points. Could I just raise something about business people on your boards? I quite see the importance and relevance of having business people on your boards but it is the only group that is specified, is it not, other than parents and staff and elsewhere in your submission you say that you are actually opposed to prescription of other groups? I mean, I wonder if business people are so separate and so important that they, so to speak, deserve special prescription and whether it is interpreted to meaning private business rather than employers generally when people are appointed.

PAULINE LATHAM: It could mean anything. I mean, "business people" means all sorts of things. It can mean solicitors, accountants, people in industry, in engineering —

150. WILLIAM UTTING: In public service? I mean, civil servants ——

PAULINE LATHAM: Yes, absolutely. And I think what grant-maintained schools do is look at a wide-range of expertise to fulfil the needs of their school and different schools have different needs and I think if it was to be more prescriptive what we would find is that we would stop being able to choose the people that would suit our school better.

DAVID MEIKLE: One thing that is certain about the business community is that it is a common thing to all areas. One of the problems about being too prescriptive is that the circumstances of different societies and communities are different and if, in fact, for instance

where Cecil works—it is important that he has members of the ethnic community as part of his governing body, it may not be a great issue at another area, it may be totally inappropriate. So that is the problem. We can say business community and we can all, whether it is farmers or British Gas or the Civil Service, we can accommodate the business community, but we want a bit of freedom to make sure that we do get together a governing body that does represent the community that we serve.

151. WILLIAM UTTING: Yes, I think as a Committee we are in favour of broad principles rather than detailed prescription so I do not think we will be pressing you on that particular point.

CECIL KNIGHT: I think identifying business community—the point you made originally in your question—is right and proper because schools must recognise and, indeed, do, have a stake in the economic well-being and future of society and it seems entirely justified on those grounds.

152. WILLIAM UTTING: Yes. Can I move over to the nature of the business. It seems to me that running a school is a very complex and difficult operation and the schedule of legal responsibilities that was appended to some of our evidence is really quite intimidating when one looks at what governors and head teachers are actually responsible for. We have also heard that there are three hundred thousand school governors in this country who all share these very onerous responsibilities. Are you happy that ordinary people can be brought into this system and equipped, so to speak, from day one, to discharge effectively and with personal liability these very onerous and difficult responsibilities?

DAVID MEIKLE: You cannot say that from day one, because let us be fair about it, there does have to be an element of induction and that is why there needs to be stability in governing bodies as they move along and there is a stable element that introduces the rest. But, yes, in fact we do not find this a major problem and one of the problems—we go back to this clarity thing—it is our responsibility, we do know exactly what our responsibility is. We also find that the decision-making is easier because we do not have to refer to somebody else because we are grant-maintained and self-governing. What is interesting is that in fact it is actually easier, it would appear, to find and appoint good quality governors to grant-maintained schools than it is to LEA schools, where they have quite some problems sometimes. We do not say that we do not have any vacancies but the National Audit Office report, which has just come out and which you must have reference to, actually says that going round the schools they found almost no vacancies at all on governing bodies. So it seems to work and people seem to accept that responsibility.

153. WILLIAM UTTING: You make a point about training in your submission. Is this something that you, as an advisory committee, are actually working on a sort of standard package of training for governors?

CECIL KNIGHT: We would regard it as our brief to advise training agencies if we see gaps in the provision. At the moment the market is so rich and flourishing in training opportunities that the likelihood of a niche or a gap arising, I think, is remote in the extreme.

154. WILLIAM UTTING: Who provides this training?

CECIL KNIGHT: Well, we might start, for example, with the Grant Maintained Schools Centre, which is based in High Wycombe and then there are university departments of education, there are companies set up by folks such as retired HMI—Her Majesty's Inspectors of Schools—all manner of folk are in the market.

155. WILLIAM UTTING: So it is local and bespoke?

CECIL KNIGHT: Yes.

WILLIAM UTTING: You would have a view yourselves about a sort of good model of training presumably, what the structure and the content would be——

PAULINE LATHAM: Except that schools are free to choose their own and I think the difference with grant-maintained schools is that we actually have money in our budget for training that is accessible to governors which did not happen in the LEA sector. So I think that governors can, if they choose, take up all manner of training which they just never would have done before because it was given by the Local Authority to Local Authority governors and this market did not exist before. It does now. And we can, of course, buy our services from the LEA, if we choose to, as well.

156. WILLIAM UTTING: Can I just conclude by asking about the role of the Secretary of State? Do you feel that there is unnecessary intervention by the Department in the affairs of individual schools if there are problems? Who trouble-shoots if there are problems? Do you have a potential role in this yourselves as an advisory committee?

CECIL KNIGHT: Our relationship with the Secretary of State is one in which the Department are fully informed of what is going on in our schools through the various mechanisms which apply, of course, to all schools, but if there are difficulties and problems within any particular grant-maintained school the Department sees it as the responsibility of the governing bodies to look after their own affairs. If it was felt that a governing body was not doing that adequately, either out of malice or out of ignorance, the Secretary of State, of course, is entitled to place on the governing body two governors of her own choice, who would make sure that these particular problems were addressed. So basically where a school is running well—and this applies and has applied over the last six years to the vast majority of grant-maintained schools—there is a very detached attitude, we have the funding, it is our job to get on, we are immediately accountable and that has provided a tremendous stimulus in raising the quality of education and educational achievement. Where there has been a need the Secretary of State has been able to intervene in that way but prior to that we do have a very strong network between our schools through our own committee and other organisations and where there are difficulties, advice is frequently sought and can be obtained—advice of a very high quality—from, for example, organisations which will send in experienced heads and inspectors, folk with a depth of experience and sound knowledge in the particular problems which might be affecting a school

PAULINE LATHAM: Can I add to that, that I actually think grant-maintained schools have a big

advantage over LEA schools because politics has been taken out of the governing body. We only have one reason to exist and that is to run our school for our pupils and provide the best quality education. Before, when we had LEA appointed governors, they did not necessarily have the same aim. Sometimes they had the party line, of whatever political colour it was, of their County Hall, Town Hall, or wherever, and they would go against the best interests of the school in order to do what they had been told to do by the people who have put them onto the school. And I feel very strongly that the criticisms that we have about power being centralised is wrong—power has not been centralised, although ultimately, yes, it has, on paper—we actually have one reason to exist and that is just for our school and that has been a powerful motivator of people working closely together without having pre-meetings, without having any sort of political element. I mean, I am involved in politics but there has never been any politics in our governing body since we went grant-maintained, there was before and it was awful. It just destroyed the whole reason for us carrying on with the school.

157. WILLIAM UTTING: I am sure we accept the genuineness of that motivation. I mean, it simply is not our business to comment on whether one way of running schools is better or worse than another way.

PAULINE LATHAM: No, but we feel very strongly about it.

WILLIAM UTTING: I am sure you do and you have made your point. Yes, thank you Chairman.

LORD NOLAN: Thank you very much. Sir Clifford?

158. CLIFFORD BOULTON: Perhaps I could follow up Mrs Latham's point, because I believe that in her own school, of the fifteen governors all but three are parents of pupils currently attending the school. Is that correct?

PAULINE LATHAM: They were, but it is less now—we have had a couple of vacancies and we have actually appointed somebody who will be a parent—I mean, he is a parent but he is a parent of a primary school child—and somebody else from local industry, from Rolls Royce, a graduate trainee, who is very interested in science in education, who has come onto the governing body. So I am not sure what the exact numbers are. But up until recently, yes, we have had more parents than anything else.

159. CLIFFORD BOULTON: Yes, I simply wanted to ask whether there can ever be a danger, as you are on your own—each school—and consist of, very often, very largely people who have been sufficiently interested to become governors because their own child is at the school, whether there is any risk you perceive of a sort of short-termism of governors being in a hurry to get facilities and things going while their own children are at the school and perhaps hurry on maybe capital expenditure, or something like that, which seen in a broader context a group of schools might have to wait their turn. I think we are very sensitive to the idea you do not want to be too prescriptive about the composition of governing bodies but do you sense ever that the brakes have to be put on sometimes—the enthusiasm of parent governors to spend money on their own institution?

PAULINE LATHAM: No, because if we have got money to spend on our own institution that is what we should be spending it for and if we have been given a capital allocation, which is judged on an independent criteria—we put in a capital bid but we do not determine it—and I think if parents could be criticised for short-termism, if what they are doing is improving the fabric and the facilities for the pupils in school, now that is going to benefit the pupils in time and as we get parents going through the system they will continue that push for better quality facilities and better quality education for the pupils and that can only help to raise standards. So I think one of the reasons why many schools went for more parents was as a reaction, probably, against having people imposed on them before and as we are maturing—and grant-maintained schools are maturing now because there is a history of them—I think we are looking at a wider balance probably than we had before. But the reason why parents were picked was not particularly because they were parents, it was because they had a specific interest. I mean, for instance, one is a consultant paediatrician in the area who happens to be a parent. Well, he will have more interest in our school being a governor than he would on another school, because he is a busy person, and so we looked at a wide range of expertise, not just because they were parents, it often was coincidental.

160. CLIFFORD BOULTON: And what is the general experience of the usefulness or success of parents' meetings? Are they regarded as a bit of a pain by governing bodies? I hope they are because ——

DAVID MEIKLE: You must remember that they are a basic part of the accountability and, I mean, when you have really got a full house you have quite likely got a problem and that is a good thing, there is this safety valve, and we realise that. But from a year to year basis, certainly in my own personal experience, these are a very useful business meeting when, having had the report of the governing body, those parents who are interested can come along, maybe fifty, seventy, a hundred of them or so, and they can have a discussion on their agenda about the way that the school is accountable to them and the educational provision that is at that school. And they are very useful meetings, but yes, we do not worry too much if we have not got the whole school parental body there.

161. CLIFFORD BOULTON: The general experience of them is that they are a useful tool and that they are working reasonably well?

CECIL KNIGHT: Very well. I think they fulfil a very valuable purpose and one should not judge the annual parents' meeting on the attendance figures which vary greatly from school to school because different schools use different devices sometimes to draw more parents in. I can get 90 per cent of parents into my own school, 95 per cent to a parents' evening where they are going to talk about the educational progress of their particular child. We might only get twenty parents to an annual parents' meeting, but I think the analogy here, perhaps, to the House of Commons, if I may dare make such an analogy to such an august body, if there is a time of national crisis the House is packed and that conveys a message in itself. In the conduct of everyday business there are varying degrees of numbers there and certainly within my own experience, both as a grant-maintained head and as a governor of an LEA school, when parents are concerned about an issue you will find the hall full to overflowing. When parents are satisfied, that satisfaction on that particular occasion is usually manifested by them staying away. They rarely come to give thanks!

162. LORD NOLAN: We hear this in many spheres. May I just mention one point? The places you tell us are filled by volunteers, although there are never enough of the ideal governors to go around you have succeeded so far on the basis of a voluntary system. The suggestion has been put to us that, perhaps not in all areas, but in some poorer areas, there may be very good governors who either are self-employed and unable to get off work or who cannot get time off from their work, who would suffer a loss of remuneration if they became governors. Do you see that as a matter that could be dealt with locally if it arise?

CECIL KNIGHT: I personally would deeply disagree with that. I come from one of the most under-privileged areas of the U.K.—in a particular inner ring part of Birmingham. I do not think, first of all, that our governors—many of our parent governors are unemployed,—that they would thank us for that kind of discrimination being exercised in their favour. There is a grace in giving and a grace in receiving and for them they have the commitment to the community which gives them a sense of meaning and a purpose and a status and a dignity within the community which is clearly ample payment and motivation for what they are doing.

In terms of the practical issues, of course, of being able to meet, those who are employed who do have to arrange for time off certainly do find their employers co-operative but the majority of the business of a governing body can be conducted at times which are suitable to the various folk involved. Governing bodies do not meet that often as a full body, it is very often sub-committees and so on, and it is a matter of finding convenient times.

PAULINE LATHAM: I do not think it is just in poorer areas. I am in what is seen as an affluent rural area and our governors cannot get time off with pay to come and one of them works for the Local Authority and she is not allowed to do it either. She can get it without pay, so I think it is not just because they are poorer areas, I think it is a widespread thing and, as Cecil said, we can arrange our meetings to suit most governors and most governors will give up some of their own time to go into schools during the day.

163. LORD NOLAN: Yes. In your experience it is not a problem and we all know, of course, that it is a wholly admirable feature of life in this country, that so much of our organisation and management is carried out by volunteers.

CECIL KNIGHT: It would be a retrograde step, I think, if ——

PAULINE LATHAM: It would, and we would be much poorer because I think what would happen is you would get people vying to have so many meetings, so that they could claim expenses and we would get back to Local Authority problems.

LORD NOLAN: May I on behalf of the Committee thank you all very much indeed. You have been most helpful and most interesting.

PAULINE LATHAM: Thank you.

164. LORD NOLAN: Now, I must offer apologies from Lord Thompson and myself to Sir Robert and Mr Turner and the remaining witnesses, because he and I

have to cross the road to fulfil Parliamentary obligations and so Sir Clifford Boulton is going to take the Chair for the rest of the meeting.

165. CLIFFORD BOULTON: Good morning, Sir Robert. I wonder if you would care to introduce yourself and your colleagues for the purpose of the record?

SIR ROBERT BALCHIN, ANDREW TURNER, AND ROGER SHEFFIELD

SIR ROBERT BALCHIN (Chairman, Grant Maintained Schools Foundation): Yes, indeed. I am Sir Robert Balchin, I am the Chairman of the Grant Maintained Schools Foundation. On my right is Andrew Turner, who is the director of the Grant Maintained Schools Foundation, on my left is Mr Roger Sheffield, who is the head teacher of Langley Park School for Boys in Bromley, which has been a grant-maintained school since 1991. And so he is an experienced grant-maintained school head.

166. CLIFFORD BOULTON: Thank you very much. We are grateful to you for the material you have supplied us with and the fact that you also very helpfully gave some information earlier to the secretariat. Professor King is going to open the questions to you this morning.

167. PROF ANTHONY KING: Before asking questions could I just make two points absolutely clear? One is that we are not here to discuss the principle of grant-maintained schools or whether grant-maintained schools are better or worse than LEA schools. That is a matter of public policy and is nothing to do with us. And, secondly, unless you care to disagree, it is not the view of the Committee that there are dreadful ethical problems and problems of malpractice in grant-maintained schools all across the country. In other words we are not here because we are persuaded that something is dreadfully wrong, we just want to find out a little bit more about how the thing works and whether there are some issues that could usefully be addressed. Can I first ask you a couple of questions arising out of your opening statement, which you kindly gave us. One of them does have to do with the business which we have come back to again and again about the way in which governors are recruited—and I think probably "recruited" is the right term. Clearly in grant-maintained schools you want governors who come from a wide variety of backgrounds, who are genuinely interested in the future of their school and the pupils within it. Are you yourself satisfied, from where you sit, that the great majority of grant-maintained schools go about the business of recruiting governors assiduously and thoughtfully as they ought to?

ROBERT BALCHIN: A year or two ago we conducted some research as far as governors were concerned amongst grant-maintained schools and the response indicated that well over 90 per cent of those grant-maintained schools that responded—and most did—found no difficulty about the recruitment of governors or the retention of good school governors.

168. PROF ANTHONY KING: That was not quite my point. I am sure that recruitment is not proving a difficulty. There is the danger obviously in any such body of self-perpetuation, of like reproducing like. It would be thought odd, for example, if the members of this Committee perpetuated themselves by choosing other members of the Committee as vacancies occurred. It is that kind of worry.

ROBERT BALCHIN: As you will be aware, a large proportion of the governing body of a grant-maintained school is in fact elected and other governors, yes, appear to be chosen by the governing body themselves. But first of all there is a clear end to the term of office, but secondly it is really quite hard work being a grant-maintained school governor, there is a lot to do, it is challenging work, I think people like doing it for the most part, and I think my impressions across the grant-maintained school sector are that the schools get in a wide variety of people to do their work, are not worried about that particularly, and that there is a reasonably constant flow. Of course, the grant-maintained sector has not been around for such a long time as yet—the first eighteen schools have been out for six years now—and I guess that we would not able to say that people have been staying on for ever, but my impression is that there is a good turnover and that schools for the most part are not concerned too much about the problems of getting people in.

169. PROF ANTHONY KING: In your written submission you say that a compulsory procedure could have the effect of excluding those with appropriate skills and experience but you also do say "while the publication of job descriptions and selection criteria would doubtless help". I mean, would it in practice be a good idea if, as a matter of routine, grant-maintained schools looking for new governors, did put a notice in the local paper to say that there were one or two vacancies, that they were looking for people and would people care to nominate potential governors? Would that be a good idea?

ROGER SHEFFIELD: Can I answer some of the points there, Professor King? If I can go back initially to one of the points you made about the self-perpetuating approach, I can give you a practical example from my own school where we had a parent governor who was an elected governor, whose term of office came to an end, who was not eligible to be reappointed because his son had by then left the school and who expressed a wish indeed to be a first governor of my school. That was considered by the governing body and it was rejected and it was rejected on the very grounds that they did not wish to seem to be engaged in that sort of activity, it was felt to be inappropriate that at that stage he should automatically simply shuffle across to a different category.

As far as the selection of first governors goes, very narrow guidelines, I think, would be counter-productive. There are occasions when a school will be looking ——

170. PROF ANTHONY KING: Incidentally, I did not suggest very narrow guidelines, I simply suggest putting a notice in the newspaper.

ROGER SHEFFIELD: A lot of schools do that.

171. PROF ANTHONY KING: But would it be a good idea if that became part of the standard operating procedure?

ROGER SHEFFIELD: I think that would depend upon circumstance. In my own school's case, for instance, I actually have a waiting list of people who have expressed an interest to be governors and they come from a wide range of backgrounds. I think it would depend very largely on the area. I mean, if I were to use —not strictly for governors, we are obliged by statute to advertise for members of Appeals panels which I had to do for the first time last year and we did advertise extensively in the area and we received one application and that was someone I already knew. You cannot assume, I think, that would necessarily bring forth the people you would require.

172. PROF ANTHONY KING: Could we move on to Appeals panels. Could you tell me precisely what they are? I have seen it in the papers but what is a "Governor's Appeal Panel"?

ROBERT BALCHIN: The one to which we refer here is really the last Court of Appeal as far as staff discipline is concerned and there has been expressed to me by, I think quite a considerable number of heads and governors, that they would feel more comfortable if that Appeal Panel were strengthened with the inclusion of two outsiders who could perhaps be a grant-maintained school head and a governor drawn from some special list, some way away, for instance. I think there are two reasons for that; that there are some staff who—and this, I think, is actually rather widespread amongst head teachers, whether they be in independent schools or in LEA school or in grant-maintained schools, there is a feeling that circumstances, the devolution of many more things to the school and the head, has caused in a few cases a frisson of difficulty between the head and the governing body and I think they would feel to a degree happier, whether this perception is correct, I do not know, but the perception is there, they would feel to a degree happier if there was just this modicum of independence pushed into the Appeals Panel.

173. PROF ANTHONY KING: And in your view would they be right to want such an independent element?

ROBERT BALCHIN: There is very little evidence about such panels being biased because there have been very few occasions that I know of, that have reached me, when they have reached decisions which perhaps were questionable. There is, of course —eventually there is an appeal to an industrial tribunal and other mechanisms, of course, which come after that, but that is the last one within the school.

174. PROF ANTHONY KING: Sure. Incidentally, I was not for a moment trying to suggest that these kinds of problems would arise frequently, but you do want the right mechanisms to be in place for the rare occasions when they do arise and on the face of it, if the source of the difficulty was a row between the governors and the head teacher, who had, say, for the sake of an example, been sacked, the head teacher might think it a little bit odd if the appeal body to which he or she could appeal was constituted largely by the opposite side in the row.

ANDREW TURNER (Director, Grant Maintained Schools Foundation): I think there is a misunderstanding there of who is the opposite side. It is not the governing body that has the power to sack a head, it is the staff disciplinary committee of the governing body and the appeal is to an appeal committee of the governing body—they are separate bodies.

175. PROF ANTHONY KING: I can see that but you can see how, if one were the aggrieved head teacher, it might not feel that there was all that much difference.

ROBERT BALCHIN: I think that Andrew is absolutely right, that they are separate parts of the governing body, but you are quite right that there is a

perception that —in fact governing bodies can be strengthened that way. Governors believe that too—I think they feel that it could help them in carrying out their duties and so this is something which I think I personally would be keen to see added to what we do already.

176. PROF ANTHONY KING: Could I ask about rows more generally, because there have not been many in grant-maintained schools but there have been a few well-publicised and pretty spectacular ones? Reading about them I have had the impression that the governors of the school, the members of the staff, whoever was involved in these rows, have been kind of left to their own devices, that there has not been somebody from outside who could give them a hand, except in a totally informal kind of way. One person who was involved in one of these rows said "grant-maintained school status gives schools freedom but unfortunately there is no one to turn to for help when things go wrong". Previous people who have appeared before us have suggested that was, indeed, a problem, and some of the written evidence suggests that is a problem. Is it a problem? If it is, what might be done about it?

ROBERT BALCHIN: I do not think it is so much of a problem because there are not so many upsets and I would be very reluctant indeed to try to legislate, to help out in some way when there are indeed so few problems to cope with. Having said that, though, there are a considerable number of private consultants out there who are able to give a good deal of advice to heads and governors under these circumstances and I know for certain of schools that have availed themselves very well of consultants. They might be consultants concerned with management or with finance or whatever, and so I do not think the imposition of some—if that is what you are getting at—of some new statutory structure would, in fact, help.

177. PROF ANTHONY KING: I was inviting you to —I was not getting at anything, these are questions, not veiled statements. I was just curious to know whether you thought there was a problem and if so how you would solve it.

ROBERT BALCHIN: I think on the whole the structures that are there are adequate for what happens with the possible exception of the suggestion which I have made already concerning the strengthening of the Appeals Committee.

178. PROF ANTHONY KING: Can I just put one point to you, at the risk of boring my colleagues, because I have raised this before? Universities, which in some ways are rather like grant maintained schools at the moment, in the sense that both sets of institutions operate pretty independently but both are largely funded indirectly by the government, have people appointed ex officio as visitors to the universities. My university has, I think—I can't remember—the Lord Chancellor or somebody rather grand like that, who is somebody whom the university can turn to in extremis, quite officially, properly, appropriately and publicly, if there is some internal dispute that cannot be solved internally. Might it be possible, might it be sensible, to have some such arrangement for grant maintained schools?

ANDREW TURNER: I am sure that all sorts of arrangements could be examined which compare with others in both the private and public sectors. My personal concern is: is there sufficient evidence of trouble to justify messing about with existing structures? The more levels you have, the more difficult it is to reach decisions, let's be absolutely clear, and one of the benefits of grant maintained status is the ability of schools to take decisions quickly.

To examine what happens to heads who lose the favour of their governors, one can only look at comparisons with local authorities, where heads are quite frequently, it seems to me, paid off with gagging clauses, of which I know no examples at all in the grant maintained sector. What we are looking at is a system which is able to make quick decisions, obviously appropriate decisions, but there is a great commitment in the sector, which I think would be diluted if it were felt that schools did not have to sort these problems out for themselves where they arise.

179. PROF ANTHONY KING: One of the things this committee is obviously concerned about is both real conflicts of interest and perceptions of conflicts of interest in the public sector. To what extent, as far as you know, is there a problem in grant maintained schools with regard to, to take an invented example, somebody who is in charge of purchasing computing equipment for the school and has access to the governors, and it turns out that his brother-in-law runs a local computer supply firm and, lo and behold, it is that company that supplies the computers. How does the grant maintained sector handle that?

ROBERT BALCHIN: First and foremost, the Funding Agency has now made a register of governors' interests a condition of grant. The NAO recently, as I am sure you are aware, talked to some 80 schools and, of those, 63 had that register in position already, and of course that was quite some time ago when they were carrying out this investigation. This is simply anecdotal evidence of course, but I believe that governing bodies of grant maintained schools actually bend over backwards for the most part to avoid any impropriety of that sort. Certainly very early on it was one of the things which we all discussed at the greatest length, and I believe that in the culture of grant maintained schools there is avoidance of anything which could give rise to that kind of criticism.

Of course that will not mean that very, very occasionally something like that just might not happen, but I believe that, first of all, the culture is right and, secondly, the current structures are right, and I believe therefore that we have enough there to pick that up. I can only bring to mind one minor occurrence that reached my desk, and it was revealed, and corrected, pretty quickly by the current structures.

ROGER SHEFFIELD: Can I also add, Professor King, that in practice to do that sort of thing would require a conspiracy of so many people as to render it unlikely. Within the context of my own school two people minimum have to sign the cheques; somebody else has to deal with the order. The whole thing has to be approved of by a finance committee which includes governors and somebody else, and so forth and so forth. There are so many people who must inevitably be involved with it that, unless we were all getting together on a fairly grand scale, it just could not happen.

The other point I would make is that, since we have gone grant maintained, it would be fair to say that my governors are far, far more conscious now of their public

accountability than they ever were as local authority governors. In fact one of the difficulties that we had in the early days was getting them to calm down and not assume that they had to check on every single thing in case they went to gaol. They really were very conscious of their public accountability and were over-cautious in seeing that they did not do anything that could be misconstrued publicly.

180. PROF ANTHONY KING: One final line of questioning, briefly. Can you, Sir Robert, map for us the grant maintained schools sector that you are involved in? Very quickly, what is the Grant Maintained Schools Foundation?

ROBERT BALCHIN: Perhaps I should start a little earlier. The Grant Maintained Schools Trust was founded in 1988 and it had two functions at that time. The first was to provide information and help to those local education authority schools that were considering grant maintained status. The second was to help, advise or support, as much as they required it, those schools which had gone grant maintained.

181. PROF ANTHONY KING: It was a government-funded body?

ROBERT BALCHIN: It was partly government funded at that stage, yes. Subsequently, those two areas of work have been divided into two separate organisations, both of which I chair, because of course I chaired the original organisation from which they are built. They are known as the Grant Maintained Schools Foundation, which is wholly government funded and which provides information and help to local education authority schools wishing to learn about grant maintained status, and the Grant Maintained Schools Centre, which undertakes the other duty of the original trust, which is to support grant maintained schools and advise them to the extent that they require it, and that exists not on a government grant but on subscription of the schools themselves. Both are non-profit companies limited by guarantee.

182. PROF ANTHONY KING: Finally, and you will forgive me if these things get a little confusing, there is also the Grant Maintained Schools Mutual Insurance Co. How does that fit into this to me unfamiliar picture here?

ROBERT BALCHIN: The Grant Maintained Schools Mutual Insurance Co. does not fit into the picture which I have just outlined for you. I believe that the collapse in early 1993 of the Municipal Mutual Insurance Co. which insured a large number of schools, meant that in a few cases it was impossible for schools to obtain insurance on the market. At that stage I and a number of heads and governors founded a mutual insurance company, which in fact was not a mutual in the true sense, although it has the ability to become one at some time in the future. But basically it is a group of schools getting together to use their aggregate power to buy a good insurance deal for their schools. Again, it is a non-profit company, limited by guarantee. It had the effect of stabilising the insurance market and stabilising premiums, so we think that it has saved a good deal of public money.

183. PROF ANTHONY KING: And you presumably receive some kind of remuneration, or "emolument" I think is the polite term.

ROBERT BALCHIN: I did when I was a director of the Grant Maintained Schools Mutual. I am no longer a director of it. I helped to start it. All directors received a small emolument at that early stage, which was agreed at the annual meeting by heads and governors.

184. WILLIAM UTTING: The job of your foundation then is to provide information to schools who might be interested in grant maintained status and to give them some practical advice and help up to the point at which they are established as grant maintained schools, and at that point your responsibility ends and the various jobs that you have done are taken on by some of the other bodies that you have mentioned. Is that roughly right?

ROBERT BALCHIN: That is correct. Of course the foundation keeps in close contact with heads and governors of grant maintained schools, because those local education authority schools who are approaching grant maintained status do like to go in and see a grant-maintained school that is actually working to talk to a local colleague. Governors tour the grant maintained schools, so it is very important for the foundation to keep in close touch with grant maintained schools so that customers, as it were, can be directed towards them, because obviously they can learn a great deal from going to a local school.

WILLIAM UTTING: So there is no abrupt severance of your interest when a school is established.

ROBERT BALCHIN: No.

185. WILLIAM UTTING: There is a kind of after-sales service, is there?

ROBERT BALCHIN: That might be said, yes.

186. WILLIAM UTTING: Could I ask about the kind of information and help that you afford in the preparative stage? You obviously give a great deal of practical advice. Would that include such nuts-and-bolts issues as how to hold fair elections for posts on the governing body? Would you be giving a package of advice, say, about the maintenance of propriety in schools, once they are independently established? Would you say something about the training that governors ought to undertake? Are those sorts of thing part of your brief?

ANDREW TURNER: The latter two not significantly, no. We very much take the view that those are issues for the schools to deal with, should they become incorporated. Certainly we would take the view that most schools know how to organise elections of parent governors, because they will have had to do so in the past, but certainly we would offer advice if that were sought. It tends to be more on how we can communicate effectively with parents on what are sometimes quite complex sounding issues, which it is very easy for others to misrepresent: how shall we go about recruiting first governors in the former county schools, because there is a requirement in general, which is sometimes not observed, to appoint first governors before parents ballot on whether the school should become grant maintained? I am frequently asked "What kind of people should we have as first governors?" So it is the mechanics, it is the law, it is general strategic and tactical advice, but on the presentation of the information which is available.

187. WILLIAM UTTING: I raised the point about training with our previous witnesses from the Advisory Committee because I have been struck by the extent and nature of governors' responsibilities when it comes to managing a school. Written down in cold print they are actually quite intimidating. I had assumed, almost as a matter of course, that it would be very desirable for somebody somewhere to be setting out in general terms the kind of training that ought to be provided to help people to discharge those responsibilities. Do you think that is a sensible approach or is that in fact teaching grandmothers to suck eggs who are perfectly capable of doing that on their own?

ANDREW TURNER: It is certainly far more like that than it was in 1988 and 1989, because of course most schools now have responsibility for 75, 80 or 85 per cent of their budgets. I believe the DFE and the Funding Agency give advice to governors on these sort of general issues, and we would certainly be prepared to say "There are a number of training bodies in the field and you would do well to consult one or more of those training bodies", but we would not issue that training ourselves.

ROGER SHEFFIELD: It would be fair to say that the number of bodies who offer their services to schools these days in the training area are like fleas on the back of a dog—probably more so. In practical terms we get a whole range of offers, including from the previous local authority, of training courses that they offer for governors. We make a point in my particular school of making these available to governors and we set aside funds to pay for governor training if they so wish, and they can choose what they feel is appropriate to them to learn about. We have in the past made use of Andrew's organisation for governor training, but we have also made use of other bodies as well.

188. WILLIAM UTTING: I am sure it is highly desirable that there should be a wide range of agencies providing choice, but there are questions about people's competence in this field. In some senses bad training is worse than no training at all. I do not know whether any systems for exchanges of information about the effectiveness of agencies or any system of accreditation exist in this area.

ROBERT BALCHIN: The Grant Maintained Schools Centre does indeed have a kind of accreditation system, in which trainers could apply to the centre. They would have to provide evidence from a number of schools to which they had given courses that the schools felt they had provided a good service and a useful service. Under those circumstances they could be included in one of the Grant Maintained Schools Centre's directories, so that schools could find their names and addresses. But as far as we are concerned it is caveat emptor. Grant-maintained schools are really very smart at finding the best people. Word gets around the grant maintained school community very quickly about who is good and who is useless. Quite a lot of governor training goes on, in my view, and I think the importance of the current system, if you can call it that, is that such governor training as goes on is governor training that the individual school considers necessary and not some kind of blanket imposition that comes from some outside body, which may not be necessary . As Mr Sheffield has suggested, it could be ad hoc. For instance, quite recently a governing body that I visited had taken some training on a specific area concerned with the sale of assets because it wanted to be absolutely clear that the decisions that it had to make were made in the light of the best possible advice. So I am pretty happy about the way things are going on at the moment as far as governor training is concerned.

WILLIAM UTTING: I appreciate that some of these matters are outwith your terms of reference.

ROBERT BALCHIN: Indeed.

WILLIAM UTTING: But you are knowledgeable about and interested in this sector——

ROBERT BALCHIN: And encourage that training to go on.

189. WILLIAM UTTING:—so I am really seeking your views on that. There is a slight sting in the tail as far as governors are concerned, in that they may carry a degree of personal liability if things go wrong. Is this actually so and, if so, how serious is this?

ROGER SHEFFIELD: The personal liability that a governor carries is the same as that carried by a member of a local authority. That is to say, if they fail to give proper consideration to advice or are wantonly negligent in the exercise of their responsibilities, they are personal liable, but otherwise they are only liable as part of the corporation of the school.

190. WILLIAM UTTING: That sounds like the degree of risk that I run as a trustee of a charity, for example—that would be par for the course—and there are means of insuring individuals, are there not, against that liability?

ROGER SHEFFIELD: "Insuring", yes.

ROBERT BALCHIN: Most of my governors are insured. Most governing bodies take care to get such insurance.

191. WILLIAM UTTING: Yes. May I, in the end, ask you about propriety? I did not have a chance to pursue with the Advisory Committee its views on propriety, and it has an impressive list of matters that ought to be covered in the interests of propriety—a register of interests containing all interests, financial and non-financial, standing orders for the governing body and its committees, terms of reference for each committee, the code of conduct for the governing body itself and for individual governors, agreed terms of employment for senior staff and good communication within the governing body. Do you think that any of this is taking a sledge-hammer to crack a nut or is this the sort of prescription that people should be following if they are to ensure propriety in the conduct of business?

ROBERT BALCHIN: I think most grant maintained schools have over the past years come across some very clear advice of this kind. I think it was in 1992 that the Grant Maintained Schools Foundation and Centre produced this book, *The Roles of Governors and Heads in Grant Maintained Schools,* which is being revised at the moment and will be reprinted within the month. It has references to precisely the kinds of codes of practice which you have mentioned. I think that most grant maintained schools have looked at this and have looked at the others which are available and have evolved their own codes based upon it. I am conscious that those are in place in every school that I have visited—I very frequently ask—but I would not want to have something which tried to encapsulate all these things and was a rigid, statutory code. I think that at the moment we are in a very

worthwhile position and that on the whole schools take these things very seriously indeed.

WILLIAM UTTING: Good. Thank you, Sir Robert.

192. CLIFFORD BOULTON: One of the points that we have come across frequently in the material that various sources have sent us is a recognition on paper of the key role that can be played by the clerk of a governing body, something that rings a bell with me, as I spent all my working life as a clerk in a self-administering body over the road, because there can be someone there, whose role is probably understood, who can be quite a safeguard against people losing their way or generally failing to get hold of this appropriate advice which it is their duty to get, in addition to complying with their obligations. There is a whole range of grant maintained schools, down to quite small bodies. Has there been a general understanding of what the clerk's job ought to be and can be, or has it sometimes just been a job which has been handed to someone who perhaps could not be expected to fulfil that role? What is the general feeling of satisfaction about the status of the clerks in post?

ROBERT BALCHIN: Of course schools have been used to having clerks for a long time.

193. CLIFFORD BOULTON: They were served up from the local authority though, weren't they, who often had a slightly different function?

ROBERT BALCHIN: Yes, indeed. In fact guidance to clerks is in here and is also the subject of conferences and training by the Grant Maintained Schools Centre, and indeed other bodies, who assist clerks to be sure that they know what their duties are. Once again, anecdotally, I would say that the governing bodies insist, and grant maintained schools insist, that their clerks are well up to scratch as regards all the legal implications of their job, so that the schools and the governing bodies are not let down.

ROGER SHEFFIELD: Indeed. We rely very much upon the activities of the clerk, because something can arise during a governors' meeting when we would want some advice, usually on some legal point centering perhaps on the articles and instruments of government, etc. and therefore there is an expectation on our part that the clerk is well up to that. Obviously, as grant maintained schools came into being, this represented a learning curve for them. In the case of big secondary schools—it would be wrong for me to comment on primary schools—many of them would have retained the clerks that they had, who were experienced clerks and who had access to the sort of information where they could engage in that learning curve, and others have become more so, now that it is a more common phenomenon. What I can say is that in the case of schools of my acquaintance locally this has not been a problem, but I could not speak for the primary sector.

194. CLIFFORD BOULTON: It could be an area where mutual help could be useful, because they could circulate information to each other, they could have model standing orders, and those sorts of thing, so one would hope that perhaps that sort of thing could be pursued.

ANDREW TURNER: Certainly there are examples of such sharing expertise in the primary sector, and I think it is fair to say that some of the clerking services that local authority schools have leave something to be desired. We deal with a lot of local authority schools, as you would expect, and we sometimes find that the clerking service owes more loyalty to the authority than to the school by whom they are notionally employed. Obviously grant maintained schools can also employ those services if the local authorities are willing to sell, but, as Roger has done, I would, I think, temper the impression that I am getting that running a grant maintained school is a terribly difficult job and requires governors of Olympian expertise. In some cases it is not a terribly difficult job and, while it requires someone who is abreast of the requirements, it does not require Superman.

195. CLIFFORD BOULTON: No, but it could be regarded as a lonely job, in that, just staying with the point of the clerk, it can be a very sensitive and difficult position for a clerk to feel that they must firmly advise the chairman that he or she is wrong and may not do what they want to do. There can be a situation where the committee clerk on loan from a local authority at least can go back to and get some comfort from a clerk on the main authority, or something. I was simply looking for a way of reinforcing existing structures without having to invent any external supervision, whereby maybe the strengthening of that kind of system and advice on legal, procedural and constitutional matters might be a strengthening, to give this reassurance. As has already been said, we are not dealing with a situation of great scandals but about the ability to give public reassurance that public money is being spent in an open and transparent way.

I think we have exceeded the time that we set aside and we are very grateful to you for coming in and speaking to us so frankly and co-operatively. Thank you very much indeed.

I should like to welcome our new witnesses, Dr Kevin Brehony and Professor Rosemary Deem, and to commiserate with you. I gather you have had a dreadful morning trying to get here. Have you had time to gather your thoughts?

DR KEVIN BREHONY, AND PROFESSOR ROSEMARY DEEM

KEVIN BREHONY: Yes, I think so.

ROSEMARY DEEM: Yes, thank you.

196. CLIFFORD BOULTON: It is something which I have a lot of personal sympathy with, as I come from the Midlands every day myself.

I should apologise, to start with, for the absence of Lord Nolan and other members of our Committee, who are involved in the opening of Parliament today, and we have two members who are ill as well. So I hope you will understand that we are a much attenuated body, but that all the members do receive the full transcript of evidence, so that none of it will be wasted. So thank you very much indeed for coming.

197. CLIFFORD BOULTON: Professor Deem and Dr Brehony, would you like to tell us your own posts at the moment first?

ROSEMARY DEEM: I am Dean of Social Sciences and Professor of Educational Research at Lancaster University.

KEVIN BREHONY: I am a senior lecturer in education at Reading University.

198. CLIFFORD BOULTON: And can you add to that by giving us the background to your interests and experience in the area of school governance?

ROSEMARY DEEM: Yes. In 1988 we embarked on what transpired to be a four-and-a-half year study of school governing bodies in local authorities, so we did not specifically research grant-maintained schools, because when we began the project there were not any such schools. That project was subsequently funded by the Economic and Social Research Council and involved a very, very detailed study of 10 governing bodies in two different local authorities in England. We were interested in the impact of the educational reforms, including the 1986 Education Act, which changed the composition of school governing bodies, and the 1988 Education Act, which significantly added to the responsibilities of governing bodies. It is largely on the basis of that study, which as far as I know is a unique study—I do not think any comparable study of that length of time has been made of the governing bodies after the period of reform to which the 1986 Act gave rise—that we submit what we wish to say today and what appeared in our written submission. But I was also, for a year, the chair of governors of a grant maintained school in Milton Keynes, so I have some personal experience of that sector, and although I am no longer living there and no longer have that post, I have kept in touch with the developments that have taken place in that sector since.

KEVIN BREHONY: My own personal experience was as a governor of a school prior to 1988, and I was chair of governors at that school. I have subsequently conducted research this year, not on this issue but on other issues in grant maintained schools.

199. CLIFFORD BOULTON: You say that, while there is little evidence of any impropriety, "the conditions under which governing bodies operate are such that impropriety could remain undetected for a considerable period of time". You will not be surprised to hear that our witnesses earlier today, and I am sorry that you have not been able to hear them, will be unlikely to accept that. They said that the mix of governors, the fact that the funding body requires a declaration of interest and these sorts of things mean that they are talking about a very healthy situation. Would you explain the reasons why you have a particular anxiety about these grant maintained schools?

ROSEMARY DEEM: I think there are a number of reasons. Firstly, one of the differences between LEA governing bodies and grant maintained governing bodies is that you do not have local authority representatives on grant maintained school governing bodies. Therefore there is less opportunity to spot problems, not just in things like the minutes, because I think the kinds of thing that we might be talking about are not things that will appear in minutes, they will not appear in audited accounts. So we are looking for ways in which things which potentially lead to misconduct or are actually misconduct are picked up. It seems to us that is less likely in a grant maintained school, because, for example, you do not have a representative of the local authority, there is not usually a representative of the Funding Agency for Schools present at meetings—that would, I imagine, be very, very unusual—so the only check on that governing body is the external checks that are made of things which are done very often on an annual basis, so they are things like the auditing of accounts.

That opens up the possibility that if something begins to happen, it is not picked up. It is not guaranteed that it will be picked up in a local authority governing body, but whether the clerks of local authority governed schools are members of the local authority that employs them or not, they do report to the local education authority. That line of reporting also exists, I assume, between clerks and the Funding Agency for Schools, but it is a much less close relationship, because it is not a local body. Also, it is not clear that many clerks of governing bodies, whether in grant maintained schools or in LEA schools where they are not employed by an LEA, have had any specific training. The clerk is a very key person, who may pick up issues to do with misconduct or potential misconduct, or something which may lead to misconduct.

200. CLIFFORD BOULTON: I ought to say straight away that, as a committee, we have to take the grant maintained system as given. We are not a constitutional body. We are concerned with openness and propriety and standards in the system as it exists. But what we are looking for, if you have anxieties about these things, is the way to improve it rather than to pack it in, unless you have come to tell us that it is incurable. But that is something specific that you did mention, that strengthening the role of the clerk is something that you would see as desirable. What degree of co-ordination and help is there in the grant maintained system to achieve uniformity of standards of advice, shall we say, and quality of administration performed by the clerks? Is there much positive help available to them?

ROSEMARY DEEM: There does not appear to be, no, and I think some consideration might be given to seeing whether that can be strengthened, because it seems to us that the clerk is a vital link and that if some kind of identifiable training, and perhaps even a system of accreditation for clerks of grant maintained school governing bodies, could be developed, I think that would improve the possibility of those clerks being significantly aware of the issues. As I am sure you know, in many schools, whether they are grant maintained or not, where a clerk is actually an employee of the school, they are very often someone who works in the school—they may be a school secretary or a school bursar or something of that kind—this is a job which is often done very much in their non-work time, or certainly not as part of their official role. So they may not have that wider knowledge which an LEA clerk will tend to have, because they will have gone to other governing bodies and will therefore be able to make some kind of comparison. This will be a clerk who is only servicing this particular governing body and therefore will not have any wider knowledge. Therefore, it is important that there is a framework in which that can be imparted.

201. CLIFFORD BOULTON: Who do you see providing that—a funding body or one of this plethora of bodies that take an interest in grant maintained schools, which we have been seeing this morning? Where would it come from?

ROSEMARY DEEM: I would have thought that it would be most appropriate for the Funding Agency for Schools or something of that kind to provide it, because they can be seen to be a statutory body concerned with the organisation and running of funding of grant-maintained schools, whereas the various other bodies to do with grant-maintained schools are much more in the nature of a pressure group. It seems to me that it is therefore less appropriate for them to run it, although of course if they wish to run a training programme, I am sure that will be quite helpful.

202. CLIFFORD BOULTON: Have you anything to add to that, Dr Brehony, or are you content with funding bodies?

KEVIN BREHONY: Yes.

203. CLIFFORD BOULTON: You expressed a bit of anxiety about governors being selected from a narrow section of the population, and I think in your opening statement you referred to that again. Do you have any suggestions about how that could be improved, how the balance of governors could be improved, as you see it?

ROSEMARY DEEM: Typically what happens both in grant maintained schools and in LEA schools when a new governor is needed, perhaps because somebody has resigned, is that informal networks are used to produce a person, or sometimes more than one person, but very often just one person. Certainly in our research we very seldom observed more than one candidate being put forward for a co-opted place, and I have no reason to suppose that is any different in the grant maintained sector. Of course informal networks will always influence the names that come forward, but one possible way in which to widen it would be to make it compulsory for grant maintained schools to advertise vacancies in local papers. That would at least open up the possibility that a wider range of people might be encouraged.

I also think that it might be helpful if governors had some kind of job description, and then that could be used not necessarily to put people off but to tell people what the job is about, because we found in our research, and this is supported by other research on governing bodies, that a lot of governors, even some who are quite experienced, often do not know the full depth and implications of the job. They see it simply as something to do with schools and they think it is quite important that they should do it, but many governors do not know fully what they have taken on.

PROF ANTHONY KING: Like the members of the Nolan committee!

ROSEMARY DEEM: Absolutely.

KEVIN BREHONY: I think that point is extremely germane to the point that we are trying to make here. We are aware of the difficulty that arises out of codes of practice or through statutory regulation and its actual enactment, and the gap that is often observable between the two. What we have tried to do, certainly in our submission, is to put forward a number of proposals that are designed to narrow that gap. But, as we saw it in the governing bodies that we were looking at, there was a considerable variation in the extent to which the governors of those particular bodies were aware of what the statutory situation regarding various practices actually was. Again we found in numerous instances that governing bodies were acting illegally. That is not to say that the result of that illegality would be something serious or even improper, but things like the requirement that a chair of governors be elected on an annual basis were ignored in a number of instances, and of course that kind of thing can take place equally in grant maintained schools.

ROSEMARY DEEM: Another example of that was that sub-committees of governing bodies are supposed to have minutes, which are then supposed to be presented to the full governing body. We observed a number of instances where that did not take place. It is something which should not happen, but it is not of itself misconduct, but in some cases such an instance could be a cover for misconduct or could potentially be such a cover. So there is a gap between what people are required to do and what exists in things like instruments and articles and their understanding of them. Although new governors are supposed to be provided with training, we found, and there is no evidence to suggest that this is different in the grant-maintained sector, that a lot of governors do not go on that training. Parent governors are the most likely to, possibly because they have a degree of humility about their role and feel that they do need to learn something about this demanding task that they are to take on, but other governors, particularly those who have been recruited perhaps for commercial or legal expertise or something of that kind, may feel that they do not need the training. But particularly for those individuals who work in the private sector, the transfer into being involved with the governance of an institution in the public sector is a different culture with a very different set of values and emphases, and it is not necessarily the case that people will automatically know what to do or how to do it.

204. CLIFFORD BOULTON: Some of the things that you mentioned as going wrong of course would go straight back to the role of the clerk.

ROSEMARY DEEM: Yes.

CLIFFORD BOULTON: But you are simply saying that also there is plenty of room for induction and training for new governors, to understand the importance of their role.

ROSEMARY DEEM: Yes.

KEVIN BREHONY: Yes.

205. CLIFFORD BOULTON: You mentioned parent governors—that is, governors who currently have a child or children at the school. Of course they will be bidding like fury for funds for the school to help it while their child is in school, and they can often seem perhaps, from a wider perspective, to have a rather short-term concern. Perhaps I could refer to a previous experience of mine, where I was a board member of a charity which owned seven schools, but I was also the chairman of governors of one of those schools, and I had to discipline myself to know what was appropriate in the way of planning. Is it the funding body that has to marry up these bids to decide how much the income per annum of a grant maintained school is, and how does it assess the relative size of the grants that will go to individual schools? Do you know how that works?

ROSEMARY DEEM: It depends whether you are talking about revenue or capital. Capital grants are done by competitive bid and revenue grants are done largely, although there are some variations to allow for the different route by which the funding comes, on the basis of a formula.

CLIFFORD BOULTON: I was thinking about capital when I asked the question.

ROSEMARY DEEM: Yes. That is done by the Funding Agency, yes, but obviously the parameters within which different governing bodies understand that and how they view it are a potential issue. You made the point that some governors may be governors of more than one institution. They may also be governors of other kinds of educational institutions which may have an interest. Although they may have business interests, they may also be involved with other local or community pressure groups, and that too can sometimes lead to a conflict of interest. So there is lots of potential there, not just over financial issues but over a whole range of things. Obviously some of those things have to be put on a register, but not all of those things.

206. CLIFFORD BOULTON: I think we are going to get information about the amount of registration that is required, and we can look into that. As academic students of this matter, have you come across any examples from overseas that would be helpful to our study?

ROSEMARY DEEM: I think the most powerful comparative evidence is that in those countries which have some kind of equivalent to school governing bodies, including North America, Spain, Sweden, which is just developing a system of this kind, and the Netherlands, governing bodies do not have the range of responsibilities that governors in this country have for things like finance, employment of teachers and so on. Clearly you are not in a position to alter the law on that, but if governing bodies have responsibility for those things which are about parents, about the community and about the students of the school, they do not necessarily get into issues to do with where the governing body's responsibility stops, where the head's starts, issues to do with the employment of staff, issues to do with ownership of land. Also, in most of the countries that I mentioned, although not all—in the United States it depends on the state—there is also student representation on governing bodies, obviously not in primary schools, but older students in secondary schools are represented. Again that is another check. It is not something which in itself will have a miraculous effect, but it is another interest group that should properly be represented.

CLIFFORD BOULTON: Yes. I sometimes get the impression that parent/teacher associations in the States are much more vociferous, better attended and more vigorously pursued than is the tradition in this country.

KEVIN BREHONY: But in some cases that is also true here, particularly with regard to the contrast that may be drawn between attendance at the PTA functions or the open evenings that schools run for parents and the annual meeting for parents, which is notoriously under-attended in both LEA and grant-maintained schools.

207. CLIFFORD BOULTON: Obviously we are only considering grant-maintained schools, but do you think that, generally speaking, not a very useful function is being performed by those annual meetings?

ROSEMARY DEEM: I think it is useful in one sense, but the fact that in most schools in England and Wales parents do not attend them in large numbers suggests that the majority of parents regard it very much as a kind of safety valve and will only go to those meetings if there is an issue that they want to raise, and very often when they do go the issues that they raise are not really to do with the governing body: they are to do with what someone in someone's class has done, or something that happened in the playground, or something that occurred on a school visit. There are things that impinge on the governing body, but they are not usually things directly relating to the activities of the governing body.

208. PROF. ANTHONY KING: Could I just intervene to say isn't that the way of the world?

ROSEMARY DEEM: Yes, sure.

PROF. ANTHONY KING: Everybody I have ever been involved with is—

ROSEMARY DEEM: Yes, absolutely, that is the case, but the point is that the claim is being made. Certainly the claim made by the Funding Agency for Schools and by most of the grant maintained school head teachers that I talk to is that the annual meeting for parents is an important form of accountability. What we are saying is that it is a form of accountability. It is not particularly effective, especially since we know from our research that a lot of the reports that the governors are supposed to write are often not written by governors, and much of what they contain does not necessarily relate to the activities of the governing body. They are actually reports by the school. There are exceptions to that, but I think that perhaps the guidance on that is not clear enough. One thing that might be done is to require governing bodies, when they present their annual report, to say how that report was written and who was responsible for it. Obviously the whole governing body has to approve it, but then we saw instances where the governing body simply rubber-stamped a report that had been written by the head teacher or members of staff.

CLIFFORD BOULTON: Would you like to carry on the questioning now?

209. PROF ANTHONY KING: Yes. Could I press you on this a little bit further? Clearly one would like to live in a perfect world. Change has costs attached to it—the issuing of new rules, for example to headmasters that they must say who they consulted before issuing the report—and often the costs are unpredictable. It may turn out that what the parents really want is a report on the school rather than a report on the activities of the board of governors. At several points in your submission you suggest not merely new rules but new bodies to help establish district consultation panels and so on. Given that there would be all kinds of costs, and I do not mean just financial costs—we are all university teachers and we know exactly what is happening in universities as, if I can put it like this, people like you come along and say we should do this, that and the other thing and fill in more forms and so on—are the actual problems in grant maintained schools sufficiently serious, are things going sufficiently awry in your view, to warrant the pretty major refurbishment of some of their ways of operating that you suggest in this document? The world jogs along. I have not yet been persuaded that things are sufficiently dire that this kind of slightly mechanistic intervention is required.

ROSEMARY DEEM: Obviously that is partly judgment, not only about what has already happened in the grant maintained sector. Clearly there have been instances where there have been severe problems. That in itself, given the size of the sector, suggests that the potential for those problems to develop in the future, as more schools become grant maintained, is quite considerable. Secondly, clearly it is public money, and therefore we should have a legitimate interest, as clearly this Committee does, in making sure that the mechanisms of accountability are as strong as possible. Thirdly, obviously different things that we have suggested have different levels of cost. The District Consultation Committee is one possible way of extending community accountability. That is a very difficult concept. I do not actually think it is very likely that anybody will do that, but nevertheless it is worth saying that it is something that is done in some other countries, where it works well. Some of the other things we have suggested, for example requiring the advertising of vacancies in local papers or drawing up a job description, are things that many people in the voluntary sector already do. Those things do not seem to me to have a large cost, but they have quite a significant pay-off in relation to greater accountability of grant maintained schools to parents and to the community, and not just to the immediate parents, because many parents who live in a community may be interested in a grant maintained school but may not currently have children at that school.

210. PROF ANTHONY KING: Can I just press you? I may not have made my central point clear enough. Many of the things you suggest not only seem to me to make good sense, but, as I was muttering to the assistant secretary, I actually agree with, but in my experience every silver lining has a cloud. What I am really centrally concerned about is not the desirability of some of the specific suggestions. But is it your judgment—you said it was a matter of judgment—that the situation in grant maintained schools, which is all we are looking at at the moment, is sufficiently serious at the moment, or is likely to become sufficiently serious, that we as a committee, as it were, need really to pull out all the stops and suggest a number of what in some cases would be fairly radical reforms? Is this a big deal? We are talking much too much in this Committee about sledge-hammers and nuts, but before employing a sledge-hammer, I want to have some idea what the size of the nut is.

KEVIN BREHONY: With respect, it is a question of judgment, isn't it? How many scandals do we require before it becomes a matter of public concern?

211. PROF ANTHONY KING: How many do you require? I do not mean to be contentious. I am just curious to know what is your judgment. How many scandals do you require?

ROSEMARY DEEM: I think there is an argument that once there has been one major one, and clearly there has been more than one major one in the grant maintained sector, one starts to have legitimate worries about the extent to which a sector of state education, which allegedly itself talks about the ethos of autonomy, of being able, within certain, often fairly voluntary, sets of guidance, although clearly some of it is statutory, can do what it wants. It actually suggests that there is a great deal of scope within that sector for public money to be misused or for people with conflicting interests to use it in ways which are not in the best interests of the school or the community or the children and teachers in the school. On those grounds I would say yes, there are strong grounds for thinking that, and obviously the bigger the sector becomes, the greater the potential for that, particularly since we know that some of the schools which have opted out—we do not know if this will be the case in the future—have done so because there are already questions about their financial viability, not their financial regularity but their viability because of the size of schools. Clearly those schools have chosen to opt out because they think that that will be a route to greater financial security. That actually puts governing bodies in a situation where they may be more willing than they would be if they were an LEA school to take various kinds of risk. Some of those risks may be financial, some will be other kinds of risk. That seems to me to pose an issue which says that it is worth while, it is not just a small nut and it is important that mechanisms of accountability are more firmly put in place.

212. PROF ANTHONY KING: Could I ask you one final question? You said there have been a number of instances in grant maintained schools of rows, impropriety, things going wrong. Could you put a number on it? You said "There have been a number". What number would you put on it?

ROSEMARY DEEM: I have not systematically collected it, but certainly there have been between seven and 10 incidents of that kind which I would say are fairly serious. Probably only two or three have been very serious, but then often the things that are revealed are only part of what is going on, just as the number of criminals that are convicted does not tell you about the amount of crime that is actually committed.

213. PROF ANTHONY KING: How could we as a committee find out about all these instances, apart from reading the newspapers?

ROSEMARY DEEM: It is not specifically on governing bodies, but there are three researchers, one based at the University of Warwick, one at the University of Wales, Cardiff and one at the Institute of Education, who have done quite a lot of research on the grant maintained sector, and I think they have quite a lot of evidence, not necessarily all of which they have published, which begins to give some insights into the sorts of things that might be going on, although I must emphasise that their projects have not specifically been on governing bodies, but they have certainly interviewed grant maintained school governors.

214. PROF ANTHONY KING: Could you give us the names and addresses?

ROSEMARY DEEM: Yes. We can certainly do that, yes.

215. WILLIAM UTTING: Just one point, if I might. It seems to me that the conversation is going in the direction of regretting the loss of the local authority as a parent for these schools, possibly not a very good parent, but a parent, and we now have a number of schools that have relationships with a variety of other bodies and are fulfilling some of the local authority functions, but certain of those functions are no longer there. What I am feeling for is some kind of advisory/exhortatory/monitoring/scrutinising role, which I do not see being performed. Nobody has mentioned OFSTED to me this morning, for example.

ROSEMARY DEEM: No. I think the point about OFSTED is an important point to make. Clearly OFSTED does inspect schools, and that inspection includes talking to governing bodies about the way in which they perform their role. But that is very much a kind of dipstick approach. First of all, it can potentially miss things. You can't compel the teaching staff to be there, they might be ill that week, but it is very difficult to compel the whole of a governing body to be present when OFSTED visits. In fact I understand there is some evidence that very often there are only a few members of the governing body present. Obviously because the visit takes place during the day, many governors cannot take time off work to attend it. But also OFSTED's main concern is teaching and learning, and they are interested in how governors relate to those specific things. They are not specialists in school governance, and the kinds of questions that they ask are not necessarily ones which in themselves will tell you all about the way in which a particular governing body performs that, although they will tell you something about it.

To go back to your starting point, which was whether this is a kind of regret for the disappearance of the LEA, we have to distinguish between the LEA as it has existed and what LEAs represent in a more generic sense, which is often an imperfect form. I do not think anyone would disagree with you on that. Certainly in our research we found lots of evidence of LEAs that were imperfect in all sorts of ways. But it is a democratic means of accountability and it does allow the possibility that people outside the immediate group of people involved with, running, being students at, being parents of students at or being governors of a grant maintained school will know what is happening in that school. Of course the Funding Agency for Schools does that in a very loose sense, but it does not have that local connection that an education authority has. So it is the democratic nature and the local or regional role which seem to some extent to have disappeared.

Of course there are many advantages for grant maintained schools in not having that. My own personal experience was precisely of a school which wanted, for all sorts of reasons, some of which are not necessarily typical of grant maintained schools, to escape from certain aspects of the local authority, so I am well aware of that side of it. But there is the issue of how we can ensure that those schools which are still using public money remain democratically accountable at the local level, and that seems to me to be at the crux of the issues as to how grant maintained schools and their governance differ from local education authority maintained schools and their governance.

WILLIAM UTTING: Thank you.

KEVIN BREHONY: I would just like to add to that statement, because I thought that was a very interesting metaphor, the metaphor of parent. Of course local education authorities, like parents, might occupy a position anyway between authoritarian and permissive. Indeed, there is plenty of research to suggest that is what they did. But what we would like to see alongside the democratic accountability is a locally available source of advice. That is the point that we would like to underline. I do not necessarily see that as a parental function, although it may well be.

216. CLIFFORD BOULTON: A friend, a helpful friend.

KEVIN BREHONY: Yes.

CLIFFORD BOULTON: Again, commiserations to you for the terrible journey that I understand you had this morning. I hope you feel that, in conjunction with all the written material that you have sent us, you have had an opportunity to give us such thoughts as you were anxious to get over to us verbally. I think my colleagues have extinguished the questions they had in mind, so thank you very much indeed for your helpfulness.

WEDNESDAY 15 NOVEMBER 1995
OPENING STATEMENTS

Opening Statement from the National Association of Governors' and Managers

Our Association, whose members are mainly State school governors in England and Wales who pay a modest subscription, does most of its work through an elected National Executive and Officers who are themselves governors and serve unpaid. It is a registered charity. Its aim is to improve the contribution made by governors to the quality of education. It serves both its members and governors generally by supporting them with information and advice and by seeking to speak for them nationally and locally.

Our response to the Committee's consultation paper "Local Public Spending Bodies" can be briefly summarised as follows.

1. The issues involved in applying the Committee's seven Principles of Public Life arise at grant-maintained schools in much the same way as at other State schools, which are also now largely autonomous.

2. The statutory framework within which State schools are managed provides safeguards against impropriety which are adequate in most situations.

3. But governors and others could and should do more, mainly by non-statutory means, to make more effective the overall management of State schools, so that these better fulfil their public purpose, secure better value for the public money with which they are entrusted and so better discharge their multiple accountability. To achieve these challenging objectives, it is necessary to address the intractable problems of assessing a school's performance, securing enough good governors and supporting them adequately.

Opening Statement from the Grant Maintained Schools Foundation

Background

Proper consideration of arrangements in grant-maintained schools cannot take place without a full understanding of the sector of schooling from which all grant-maintained schools (except two) have emerged. The opportunity to become grant-maintained was made available because it was felt (in retrospect with justification) that decisions on education are better made at the rim of the wheel than at its hub, and also because many LEA schools felt themselves unduly restricted in their activities by political as well as administrative interference and bureaucracy from town and county halls.

Despite the general success of Local Management of Schools (LMS), this interference continues. Schools are frequently given inadequate and partial information by LEAs, not only (and perhaps understandably) in the run-up to ballots on grant-maintained status, but also when exercising their rights under LMS to determine the source of supplies.

In my judgment grant-maintained schools have bedded down successfully in their existing constitutional arrangements and it would be unhelpful to change them without good reason, especially in view of the range of other changes and challenges which continue to face all schools. One of my strongest beliefs—reinforced by the Prime Minister in his Birmingham speech to heads of grant-maintained schools—is that grant-maintained schools are capable of exercising their powers appropriately without significant prescription of procedures, and that where possible the burden of such procedures should be relieved rather than strengthened. However, no system is incapable of improvement, and where a consensus exists—one which carries with its heads and governors of grant-maintained schools—improvements should be introduced.

Accountability

Governing bodies of grant-maintained schools are accountable principally to their customers: the pupils, parents and guardians. They are accountable through two mechanisms. You will be familiar with the formal ones—election of parent governors, annual report and annual parents' meeting. You may not have given due weight to the market mechanism—that is, the power of parents not to choose the school in the first place or, having done so, to withdraw or threaten to withdraw their children, a power which is seldom used but (and I speak with experience of the LEA and private sector as well as of the grant-maintained sector) which represents a more effective weapon in parents' hands than any number of appeal systems.

Your publication *Local Public Spending Bodies* (page 16) asserts that "the governing body [of a grant maintained school] is directly accountable to FAS... for the use of funding." There is no reference there to accountability to parents. Only later is there a reference: the requirement to hold an annual meeting and publish an annual report to parents.

I find the concept of accountability to "the local community" difficult. Where some schools have a clearly defined catchment area which the local community inhabits, it would be possible to have governors elected by the local community. For good or ill that is only infrequently the case: a county council is often too big (and such authorities often effectively delegate to their own members the power to appoint LEA governors in maintained schools); a school in a borough often admits many—if not a majority—of out-borough pupils.

Appointment of first governors

Schools have a variety of means of selecting and appointing first governors—while the publication of job descriptions and selection criteria would doubtless help, a compulsory procedure could have the effect of excluding those with the appropriate skills and experience who might be unwilling to submit to a formal application process.

One school which is currently considering grant maintained status (South Dartmoor Community College, in Devon) has tackled the perceived "unrepresentative" nature of first governors by enabling the parents to elect them as well as parent governors, but without a prerequisite that those nominated be parents themselves.

Division of responsibility between governors and heads

My organisation has published guidance agreed by a working party of grant-maintained heads, governors and representatives of head teachers associations and which sets out recommendations. While I am aware that some observers would like to see this division of responsibility incorporated into legislation on the lines of that of the Principals of FE colleges, my view is that greater flexibility would be permitted without legislative change if, when new heads were appointed, a division of responsibilities appropriate for that school were written into their contract.

Code of conduct

Most schools already have a Register of Interests and the FAS makes it a requirement before grant is paid.

Whistleblowing and independent scrutiny of staff grievances

I know of no restriction on "whistleblowing" (although it would not be appropriate for an employee to fail to go through established internal procedures or to apply to someone who does not have the duty to put things right). Whistleblowers are, of course, protected by Employment Protection legislation unless they have acted inappropriately.

In my view it would be helpful for Governors' Appeal panels (when considering staff issues) to include two independent members drawn from other grant-maintained schools.

Conclusion

The opportunity of making their schools self-governing is something entirely new for parents, teachers and governors. Its success depends on the enthusiasm and commitment of those who have undertaken the process as well, of course, as on their professionalism and skills. The National Audit Office report published a fortnight ago confirms that grant-maintained schools are run with efficiency and propriety, and it has been the Government's intention throughout, and one with which grant-maintained schools are wholly in accord, that as many as possible of the powers of LEAs are transferred to grant-maintained schools, not centralised either at FAS or DfEE level, and that no regulations should harness the working of grant-maintained schools that do not apply to LEAs and their schools.

Where there is a need for change it is important that each school be free to implement that change in its own way, taking into account, as do its competitors in the private sector, the desires of its customers. The light-touch model has worked well for the grant-maintained sector. Over regulation will be detrimental to the schools and their pupils.

Written Submission on School Governing Bodies from Dr Kevin Brehony and Professor Rosemary Deem

During the course of our study we found little evidence of governors or governing bodies who were involved in any financial or other kind of impropriety. On the other hand, we feel that the conditions under which governing bodies operate are such that impropriety could remain undetected for a considerable period of time. We are concerned by the lack of accountability of many governors, especially those who are selected rather than elected. School governors are also drawn from a relatively narrow section of the population.

Moreover, within a given locality, many governors are connected through political, business and/or social networks. This is not necessarily a problem, but it does mean that governing bodies do not always contain a plurality of views and ideas. Furthermore, in the event of a breach of that conduct, such close networks might mitigate against disclosure of that conduct or make dealing with it more difficult. This is particularly likely in grant-maintained school governing bodies, where the constituencies from which governors are drawn are fewer in number than in LEA schools.

In our submission we make several proposals regarding the ways in which school governing body accountability and openness may be enhanced. There are, however, two issues which are worthy of consideration in this context since they affect the framework within which governors operate. The first concerns the way that governors interpret and enact their roles. What was strikingly evident during our project was the extent to which these interpretations varied, in spite of being based upon statutory guidance such as instruments and articles of government. This was most noticeable in the LEA, which did not provide LEA-employed clerks for governing body meetings. The variations in interpretation of existing guidance tend to strengthen the argument for a compulsory code of conduct.

The second issue is one that is explicitly raised in the Issues and Questions document, and that concerns the status of governors as voluntary workers. While we saw many outstanding examples of selfless voluntary service, especially as carried out by the chairs, that standard is only attainable by those governors whose resources, including time, administrative experience and judgment, enable them to engage fully in the responsibilities attached to their office. Many governors are not in such fortunate situations.

Rather than diminish the role of voluntary service in the governance of schools, we feel that a reduction in their responsibilities would be beneficial to the governors and to the schools they govern. This would in turn reduce the possibilities for impropriety and would clarify further the distinctive roles of governors and headteachers.

WEDNESDAY 22 NOVEMBER 1995

Members Present:

The Rt Hon Lord Nolan (Chairman)

Sir Clifford Boulton	Sir William Utting CB
The Rt Hon Lord Thomson of	Dame Anne Warburton DCVO CMG
Monifieth KT DL	Diana Warwick

Witnesses:
Professor Brian Fender CMG, Chief Executive, Rob Hull, Secretary and Jane Henderson, Finance Director, Higher Education Funding Council for England
Professor Graham Zellick, Principal, Queen Mary and Westfield College
Lord Limerick, Chairman, Brian Heron, Chairman of the Council of UMIST, and Michael Shattock, Secretary, Committee of University Chairmen
Professor Peter Scott, Director of the Centre for Policy Studies in Education, University of Leeds
Sir Peter Swinnerton-Dyer, former Chief Executive of the Universities Funding Council

217. LORD THOMSON: Good morning, can I welcome you all to our third day of oral evidence and I have to begin with an apology from our Chairman, Lord Nolan, who, as a Law Lord, is off on an urgent judicial duty; in fact, instead of chairing the hearing of evidence he is giving evidence himself this morning to the Security Committee but he will join us as soon as he possibly can. Until then, you will have to put up with me in the chair, I am afraid.

The evidence that we are taking today will all be related to universities. It is our practice in these hearings just to put on record at the beginning the witnesses that we are going to have before us. So, first of all, we shall hear from the Higher Education Funding Council, from the new Chief Executive Professor Brian Fender, who was until recently the Vice-Chancellor of Keele University and, therefore, brings a very wide experience of the issues we are considering. He is accompanied by Rob Hull, the Secretary, and Jane Henderson, the Financial Director of the Council.

Our second witness this morning is Professor Graham Zellick, the Principal of Queen Mary and Westfield College. Professor Zellick is Deputy Vice-Chancellor of the University of London and is a member of the Council of the Committee of Vice-Chancellors and Principals and serves, or has served, on a number of other governing bodies. He is a lawyer and he has taken a special interest in the law relating to higher education and has considerable experience of drafting charters and statutes.

Thirdly, we hear from the Committee of University Chairmen who will be represented by a team led by Lord Limerick, Brian Heron and Michael Shattock. The committee is responsible for producing guidance for governing bodies of universities and colleges. Lord Limerick, as well as being chairman of the committee, is chairman of governors of London Guildhall University. Brian Heron is the Chairman of the Council of UMIST and Michael Shattock is Secretary to the Committee and Registrar of the university of Warwick.

Our fourth witness is Professor Peter Scott, the Director of the Centre for Policy Studies in Education at Leeds University. Professor Scott was a distinguished editor in the educational field before taking on this post and is much involved in research into patterns of

governance in higher education. Then, finally today, we hear from Sir Peter Swinnerton-Dyer. Sir Peter, as is well known, headed the old UGC and its successor, the Universities Funding Council, and is a great expert in the field. So, we have an array of expertise this morning, starting with the Higher Education Funding Council.

Do you wish to put on record an opening statement, Professor?

PROFESSOR BRIAN FENDER CMG, ROB HULL, AND JANE HENDERSON

218. LORD THOMSON: You have circulated one and we are also happy with that because it saves time. We share out the questioning and Lord Nolan was to have questioned you but I will take on the opening questions.

I think our central concern in many ways, in terms of the universities—many of which are old-established institutions though there is now an area of new universities with a different statutory background—one of our principal concerns is to get the best possible advice about the problems of good governance. You are a Funding Council and are at some pains to emphasis that you are not a regulator in any detail but I wonder if you could start off by giving us your impressions as to what sort of role you can play in good governance as distinct from good financial management.

PROF BRIAN FENDER: Perhaps it would be helpful if I just elaborated a little on the Funding Council's role. There are really three functions that the Funding Council exercises. The first relates to the programme, the overall programme that universities carry out in teaching in research and the advancement of knowledge. That, obviously, is our main concern but we have two other important concerns and one is as a regulator. One is acting as a conduit for accountability; we do not duck that function. The third is to give advice—advice about the aspirations and needs of higher education to government and to the general public, to give them information about the opportunities and achievements of higher education.

We always have to keep in mind these three functions. We are really concerned with this question of regulation at the moment and, for me, if it is helpful, I think the best way to express that is through audit because audit allows the expression of accountability but, at the same time, it is also a vehicle for exchanging good practice because the auditors themselves are aware not only of the practice in the institution that they are visiting but many of the other universities and colleges that they have come across in their work. So, audit is the main route.

There are some overlaps with these functions, of course. Basically, assessment is largely about finding out more about the programme and being in a position to give information to students and others interested in higher education as to the state of play in British higher education. Sometimes, this question of accountability and autonomy are put in opposition. There is talk of balance. I do not think that is really at all the right way to look at it. Autonomy is not, for me, jeopardised by accountability. There is no reason at all why one should not be open about what one is doing and, through that openness, express accountability. In fact, looking at the Nolan principles—I have an eighth principle I would like to suggest—but of the seven that are down there I think openness is the most important really in many ways. If openness exists then you are well on the way to satisfactory governance and good accountability.

I rather like the way the responsibilities and the autonomy are expressed in fact by Jane, sitting on my right here, at an induction meeting which we hold for new vice-chancellors and principals. We now invite them to Bristol and they spend a day with us. She puts them in this simple way that institutions are self-governing; they are academically autonomous—and that is a reference to the particular forms of autonomy which are written into legislation; they are classified as private sector,—which draws attention to the fact that their funding is multiple and public funding is only a part of that overall financial resource; and they are free to generate income and to retain surpluses—which, again, is another way of expressing independence. But, in addition to that, institutions must not—and if we had an overhead projector I could recreate exactly what we say to new vice-chancellors—institutions must not act unreasonably; they must not misuse public funds; they must not withhold information; and that includes information to the Funding Council; and they must not ignore value for money, probity or good governance.

It seems to me that in exercising those earlier elements of autonomy which I referred to just a moment ago, these acts of accountability do not in any way challenge the autonomy, they are simply elements of good practice which I would expect every university and college to exercise.

219. LORD THOMSON: That is very helpful. It might, in fact, be useful for us, without an overhead projector, if you have on paper the advice that you give to new vice-chancellors and Principals. I think that might be a useful bit of evidence for us.

PROF BRIAN FENDER: We would be happy to do that.

220. LORD THOMSON: Could I then follow that up by asking you very specifically—you mention the audit as one of the methods of openness and of being able to look at good governance as well as good financial management. How would that apply to the Huddersfield case that you mentioned in your written evidence to us. Was it after the

event that that was discovered and are there lessons to be drawn for the future out of that kind of arrangement and the severance payments that were regarded as excessive?

PROF BRIAN FENDER: For the exact history of it I may turn to Jane, but the important point from the Huddersfield exercise—the lesson, if you like—is that it did emerge and actions were taken and that seems to me part of the process.

221. LORD THOMSON: But they were taken, if I understood it, after the event and really after publicity had forced some action to be taken. Is that unfair?

PROF BRIAN FENDER: I think it is probably factually correct but I would want to say that we are talking about many, many years of universities and the number of instances of irregularity are tiny and we should really keep these things in proportion. I think there is a great danger that the one or two lapses of judgment are beginning to exaggerate the very good governance which I believe exists in all universities and colleges.

You cannot ever, it seems to me, write a set of rules which will deal with a lack of judgment. In the end, that will be inevitable whatever system you have. What you want where that occurs is to be able to spot it and to act effectively and that, I think, is what happened with Huddersfield.

LORD THOMSON: Yes, thank you.

JANE HENDERSON (Finance Director, Higher Education Funding Council for England): If I may come in, chairman. The fact about Huddersfield is we did prevent an unreasonable payment being made. As soon as untoward matters came to our attention, raised by the MP, our auditors immediately went in, investigated the situation, got hold of all the papers that were there to be got hold of, and we did, in fact, prevent that payment being made. So, although we may not have been the first movers I think it was a success story and an indication of one of the ways in which our audit service works. In addition to its routine rolling audits of institutions, it is also, if you like, a rapid reaction force in response to things that are brought to our attention.

222. LORD THOMSON: Yes, thank you. I fully take the point about seeing it in proper proportion against the overall record of the older universities over many years but could I follow up just one fairly narrow but specific point in relation to this area.

Do you have a view about what are popularly called "gagging" clauses in terms of the financial arrangements of universities? You talk about the importance of openness, which I am sure is right, but are not "gagging" clauses a direct contradiction of openness?

PROF BRIAN FENDER: Yes, we are against "gagging" clauses. I mean, very simply, one should not withhold information at all. Having said that, I will use the odd weasel word which is that there may be circumstances, particularly those which affect third parties, which require a degree of confidentiality but you should certainly start with the assumption that "gagging" clauses are bad.

223. LORD THOMSON: Yes, thank you. The second general question I wanted to ask you about and get the

benefit of your experience—the university sector now is divided really into two groups. What are called the old universities, though they include some comparatively new universities, but the charter universities is, I think, one way to describe them, and the new universities which are statute-based.

These are early days yet but I just wondered whether you had any judgments to make to us as to whether we ought to be thinking about recommending some kind of greater degree of harmonisation of arrangements and changes in the legislative basis of the new universities. What is the distinction and how does it work out from your point of view?

PROF BRIAN FENDER: I very much hope you would not be thinking of legislation to bring in a single form of governance. I think that would be a mistake. Of course, there are not just two forms of governance in universities. We have Oxford and Cambridge, we have variations on governance within the two broad sectors which you have described.

LORD THOMSON: London.

PROF BRIAN FENDER: Exactly, London, Wales, etcetera. I am sure Peter Scott later on in the morning will give you a flavour from his study of the differences of style between the old and new governances. I am pretty certain he will point to increasing convergence between the two systems. It is not surprising there are different forms of governance. They come out of different backgrounds and out of different histories, but if you look at the business of those governing bodies then they are—and here there is a high degree of overlap—they are primarily concerned with the strategic sense of direction of the institution and they are concerned with the matters of audit and propriety which we have talked about.

I think they also should be looking at the Executive in the sense that governing bodies, whether they are from new universities or old universities, have lay members and non-executives—and one of their functions, I am sure, is to judge the people who are carrying out the executive functions of the university. Those three functions are important aspects of governance which are shared by old and new universities.

After that, it is really a question of style and some differences in composition reflecting when they were created. I think one can see strengths in both of them. The strength of the old universities is, in fact, curiously enough the fact that they are rather large and that a variety of different interests come in to observe in quite close detail the major decisions of the university. So, you have the local government representation. You have staff in significant numbers. Most universities—all, I think—will try to balance those with a good representation of members from industry and commerce.

I think that really works rather well for a university which itself is a very open and critical organisation. It lives on criticism. You might be interested in a fact which perhaps illustrates that in a slightly humorous way. The pensioners of the university superannuation scheme write five times as frequently to the organisation as any other pension fund. I give that as an illustration simply to say that universities are used to debate, they are used to speaking up. Keele used to hold assemblies of all staff who

wanted to come, all kinds of staff who wanted to come, twice a year. There would be, effectively, a general question session. It was not just an ordered agenda. There would be ordered elements to it but there was plenty of time for free questioning. I could think of a number of organisations where if the Chief Executive stood up there would be a rather long silence if he asked his employees if they had any questions about the running of the organisation. The hands go up all the time and quite naturally within the university and that is a feature we always have to take into account. So, this larger body of councils of the pre-1992 universities is surprisingly effective.

It has also the safeguards of a court which effectively acts in many ways like a shareholders' meeting. A large group—very large, in some cases, generally speaking a good representation—will attend this annual meeting and there are important formal powers that the Court has.

Now, the new universities, smaller because the feeling at the time was that that would lead to a more managerial and more effective form of governance and, indeed, because the group is smaller—typically, 15 to 20—it does allow perhaps somewhat better discussions around the major issues. But, on the other hand, it does not touch parts of the community which the older universities do. I see strengths in both and I certainly would not want—I do not think we can foresee exactly what the challenges of higher education will be over the next decade or more and I would not want to prescribe the particular form of governance to deal with those challenges.

224. LORD THOMSON: Do I take it from what you say that since the new universities have a new Act of Parliament and have a different history that there is room for them to usefully widen their areas of governance of the councils of a wider range of people? Are they in some danger of becoming the cliche that we keep coming up against, self-perpetuating groups of cronies?

PROF BRIAN FENDER: They do have scope to widen their governing body if they wish to do so.

225. LORD THOMSON: Are you satisfied with what they do?

PROF BRIAN FENDER: I think increasingly the element which was missing—I mean, I now have to work on limited experience of one year on the governing body of a new university—the missing element in many ways on those governing bodies was a strong staff input. My impression is that the new universities started off with rather too big a separation between the management function and the academic staff carrying out the academic programme. That was a division which does not exist in the more collegiate, older university.

My impression is that the new universities recognise that it is important not to have too big a gap there, that that is not, in fact, the best way of getting the most out of the university and, as a result, I believe they are bringing staff into the governing body discussions in a more extensive way and I think that is a good thing.

ROB HULL (Secretary, Higher Education Funding Council for England): Can I add to that, chairman? It seems to me that the guidance from the Committee of University Chairmen is relevant here. They have advocated more open methods of recruitment to the governing bodies of universities, the use of nomination committees, the possibility of advertising, a more open approach to membership. It seems to me that that is absolutely right and if one does have an open approach to appointment of new members of the governing body that helps to guard against the risk of cronyism which you referred to.

226. LORD THOMSON: We shall, of course, follow that up later this morning with the chairmen of the universities. Could I follow up a different aspect of this which, I think, applies to some degree to both the old and the new universities, the concern does, I mean. Universities are primarily academic institutions and academic quality and the autonomy that is part of it, of course, is part of the essence of it, as you have been saying. But they are also operating in a world that has become increasingly competitive, competitive in the financial sense and, to some extent, in a quasi-commercial sense. My own experience of the university I know best is that they keep going off around the world to market themselves and to try to attract students.

Inside the universities there are increasingly quasi-commercial activities. Again, the university I know best does some very interesting distance learning in Hong Kong, for instance. Is there something to watch here from your experience about the effect on academic standards? In competitive managerial efficiency is there a threat to academic standards?

PROF BRIAN FENDER: No, I do not think there is. After all, competition implies—I mean, one of your strongest elements in a competitive environment is the quality assurance that you can describe and talk about and I think you will find that that becomes increasingly an element in a university's presentation of their programme. In a way, that carries a safeguard with it.

227. LORD THOMSON: We have had some evidence that the search for students tempts you to lower entrance standards and, equally, the search for financial prosperity tempts you to lower your exit standards. Do you share these concerns? Are you watchful about it?

PROF BRIAN FENDER: It is why I am keen that we should have a good quality assurance system. As you may know, there are discussions going on at the present time with a view to creating a single quality assurance agency where the elements of audit, assessment, enhancement and standards can be brought together. I think that is an extremely important development which we must all work hard to achieve over the next 12 months or so. If we do that, if we bring off that effective single agency, we will have done not only something rather good for British higher education but we will have addressed those nagging worries which you were expressing a moment or two ago, I think, to a large extent.

In terms of entry, I think there is a natural desire, and we can see all the good reasons, why we should maintain in our graduate population a largish proportion, or a large proportion of scientists and engineers. Now, the flow of those scientists and engineers is not as copious as we would like and the national need for those may cause the entry standards in one or two subjects to be a bit stretched.

228. LORD THOMSON: My successor as Chancellor at Heriot-Watt is the present Lord Chancellor, Lord Mackay. When he as a young lecturer at St Andrew's went off to higher things down in England he handed over all his lecture notes to his successor who later became a very distinguished professor in Heriot Watt. We had some very disturbing evidence the other day that in one of the new universities there was some attempt being made to suggest that lecturers' notes were the copyright property of the university and should not be handed on to anybody else at all.

If that allegation had substance in it, who would deal with it? How would that be corrected, apart from having a Nolan Committee to take this sort of evidence?

PROF BRIAN FENDER: That is a new suggestion to me on the whole. I have not come across that restrictive practice.

LORD THOMSON: It was given in serious evidence to us the other day.

PROF BRIAN FENDER: Was it? Was it? Have you got a way round the potential——

ROB HULL: I do not think I have the answer but I do want to draw the Committee's attention to the limits on the Funding Council's responsibility here in that questions of academic behaviour are not normally handled by us. It is the sort of thing I would have expected the higher education community collectively to address rather than us in the first instance.

LORD THOMSON: Thank you. Sir William?

229. WILLIAM UTTING: Yes, thank you, chairman. Professor Fender, I have a few, mainly clarifying questions, at least I think they are clarifying, they may lead on to other things. The first was just to clear up the position of the HEFCE itself. This is a non-departmental, public body and the members of that body are appointed by the Secretary of State for Education and Employment now.

Some concern has been raised with us about appointments to bodies like this, quangos, and specifically in relation to your council it has been suggested that people may be appointed to it who themselves have a considerable vested interest in the outcome of the financial allocation that you ultimately make. Could I ask if that is so and, if it is, what the sort of compensating advantages might be, if any, for that sort of system?

PROF BRIAN FENDER: A totally disinterested body may be an uninterested body and my eighth principle, if I were to be able to add a principle to the Nolan Committee, would be commitment. I think commitment to an organisation is one of the most important elements in looking at governors and, therefore, there has to be a balance struck between external objectivity, internal expertise and the hope that all, from their different perspectives, have a commitment.

I have only, of course, observed the board of the Higher Education Funding Council on two occasions but I have been impressed by the fact that all members do participate from a wide range of backgrounds and I have to say I do not see any signs of special pleading from those more involved with higher education directly. If I did, then I am sure the chairman would have spotted it before I did, or at least as quickly, and I am sure he would take action. I think governing bodies have to have the expertise which comes from direct involvement and as long as that is kept in reasonable proportion it is helpful.

230. WILLIAM UTTING: I agree with you that it is extremely difficult to find the completely independent person and I also agree that in jobs like this it is possible for people to separate different aspects of their roles and responsibilities. I think I was repeating, however, simply how this system appears to some other people to work and that, in itself, is actually a serious issue.

PROF BRIAN FENDER: I think openness in recruitment is one way to help that process. I rather hope that the Funding Council will advertise its vacancies. I hope it will, in other words, cast a trawl for potential members of that board as widely as possible.

WILLIAM UTTING: Good, that is very consoling.

PROF BRIAN FENDER: Rob, would you like to—you are the Secretary in this, after all.

ROB HULL: I just wanted to add a couple of points. One is about the nature of our work. The great majority of our money is distributed on the basis of a formula. It is not on the basis of individual judgments about individual institutions and, in that case, the debate on the council is about the operation of the formula at large, it is not about the needs of individual institutions. So, that in itself is some sort of safeguard.

Secondly, when we do deal with specific funding of individual institutions, when we are talking about bids for particular projects, this sort of thing, we require members to declare their interests and, if necessary, withdraw. We are conscious of that process. That is the other side of it.

231. WILLIAM UTTING: Good, thank you. Professor Fender, when you opened you spoke about the HEFCE being a conduit for accountability and since you are appointed by the Secretary of State and yourselves accountable to the Secretary of State I assume that it is the Secretary of State who would ultimately exact accountability in this sector. That is the position, is it not?

PROF BRIAN FENDER: In the areas determined by Parliament.

232. WILLIAM UTTING: In the areas determined by Parliament, yes, as far as your functions are concerned. It raises the question with me about what kind of information you pass on to DFEE and what sort of action might follow from that on the part of the Secretary of State.

Your implication of being a conduit is that you are no more than a vessel through which information passes. That is not actually my perception being on the council of a higher education body of the way in which you are perceived or actually behave.

PROF BRIAN FENDER: Perhaps a conduit was not the best possible word but what I meant was that the audit process allows accountability to be expressed and then made public. I think it is also worth pointing out though that in the accountability of universities as a whole the accountability to the Funding Council is only one of the accountabilities. I totted up that there are something like 17 bodies, or groups of bodies, which have the right to enter universities and report upon their activities. Quite a number of these, in fact, have come into being over the past five or 10 years so. The Funding Council's role in audit is to address the financial area—and we do that with the Funding Council audit which, of course, backs up other audits,—the external audit of the university, the internal audit procedures which have had to be in place since 1988—and, of course, there are then bodies like the National Audit Office which can take an interest in specific matters.

The process of assessment in research and in teaching gives also some measure of accountability through the performance in research and teaching respectively of institutions and that is what I meant when I said a conduit. We are setting up structures which allow universities' performance to be seen by whoever wants to look at it and, in that sense, we are a conduit.

233. WILLIAM UTTING: Yes, when financial monitoring leads on inevitably to a concern for more general management but also for the quality of the product?

PROF BRIAN FENDER: Of course.

234. WILLIAM UTTING: They are all linked. The Further Education Funding Council has its own inspectorate, I understand. You do not go that far. You do not have a separate core of professional officers who are going round and investigating in more detail the quality of the product?

PROF BRIAN FENDER: We have our own auditors and for the assessment of teaching we have a group specifically charged to do that.

235. WILLIAM UTTING: You have the equivalent?

PROF BRIAN FENDER: I would not actually call them inspectors.

WILLIAM UTTING: No, but you have the equivalent.

PROF BRIAN FENDER: They are fulfilling an inspection function in a way.

ROB HULL: I think the difference between us and the Further Education Funding Council is that we rely on peer review. The people who actually go out and assess the quality of teaching are contracted to us from higher education institutions. That is an important feature of what we do.

236. WILLIAM UTTING: I understand that there is work going on that may lead towards the setting up of a separate quality agency in this sector. Would you regard that as a good development? It seems to me to be actually quite difficult to separate consideration of quality from consideration of management and the resources that go into producing quality.

PROF BRIAN FENDER: They are inextricably linked, which is why I referred to the agency earlier on as being a broader assurance of the integrity of the programmes being proposed and carried out by individual universities and colleges. Yes, I think it is a very good thing. I would almost say it is necessary, not to guard against malpractice, though no doubt it will do that, or unsatisfactory performance, it will do that, but I see it much more as a vehicle for an enhancement of teaching and other matters. At the end of the day, the Funding Council funds and it funds, as I said, a programme but its aim must be to improve the quality of education and research in the country and quality assurance, or a set of quality assurance procedures, would enhance that, in my view.

237. WILLIAM UTTING: Just one further point about the actual operation of the audit service. There was a statement, I think, in your evidence that suggested that there is a three-year rolling programme for auditing these institutions but I could not quite make that square with some of the figures that were in the report that you had visited 40 institutions in the course of 1994-95 but I worked out there were something over 200 that you might actually be liable to visit. Could you just clarify that for me?

JANE HENDERSON: Yes, certainly. There are, in fact, some 150 institutions for which we have legal accounting responsibility. Those are the higher education institutions.

WILLIAM UTTING: Yes, it was the other 70 or so.

JANE HENDERSON: The other 70 or so, I suspect, are further education institutions which provide higher education and there is what you might call a back-to-back arrangement between ourselves and the Further Education Funding Council. Sir William Stubbs, as Accounting Officer for the FEFC, provides assurance on those institutions on our behalf and, reciprocally, we provide such assurance where further education is provided in higher education institutions.

WILLIAM UTTING: So, you have a tight, three-year rolling programme, then, for——

JANE HENDERSON: Yes, and, of course, it is not exhaustive in the sense that we also make return visits to institutions to see whether our recommendations have been implemented and we also respond to particular issues. So, the rolling programme is, as it were, the baseload activity of our audit service on which we superimpose special audits, audits for cause and, indeed, value for money studies which is another thematic strand of activity undertaken by our audit service.

238. WILLIAM UTTING: And the monitoring of the non-financial issues that you are concerned with would be undertaken in the course of these audit inspections?

JANE HENDERSON: The audits will look at the key control systems in an institution. Clearly, they will centre on the financial systems but they will also need to look at management information, personnel information, performance review, how the committees interact with the executive, really the whole panoply of supporting systems which give us the assurance that public money is being well used and safeguarded.

239. WILLIAM UTTING: Could I conclude by asking if you have any positive proposals that you may want to put to the Committee about how these systems could be improved, in particular those that promote propriety in the conduct of public business.

PROF BRIAN FENDER: If you were asking the question, could I see ways in which the advice which the Committee of University Chairmen has given could be extended, I think that is a very good document. Your own existence has made people think about the question of governance and that, I believe, is a good thing.

Would I want to go further? The answer is very little but in one or two areas I think I would want to go just a little bit further. First of all, I would want to see advice given to governing bodies—incidentally, the evidence coming in is that this advice is being well picked up by universities and colleges and I detect all round a general acceptance of the guidance—but, to go a little further, I would like to see advice given on induction of new members, new governors. I think that process really is a very important one. It also brings the governor rather quickly into the business of the governing body and I think that is good. Ideally, I would like to see all new governors spend a day in the institution before taking up office.

I would like to see the canvassing, as I said in connection with the Funding Council itself, I would like to see the canvassing of vacancies done as widely as possible and though I started—and now I am talking as a poacher, as a vice-chancellor, rather than as a gamekeeper—although I saw the immediate need for a remuneration committee, the nomination committee given that there are not enormous numbers of people willing and able to serve on governing bodies, I suppose I took a little longer to be persuaded about. Now I am rather strongly persuaded not only from the point of view of safeguards but from the systematic attempt to bring in the best possible governors which I think a nomination committee encourages and also to make sure that the representation is as wide as is reasonable to govern a higher education institution.

I was struck by some of the surveys that Peter Scott has done. In some ways, governors are perhaps drawn from rather too narrow a range of society and if nomination committees could find a way of encouraging a bit more breadth in those governing bodies then that would be a good idea.

WILLIAM UTTING: Thank you, chairman.

LORD THOMSON: Diana Warwick?

240. DIANA WARWICK: I have two questions and both relate to your emphasis on openness and one actually naturally follows on from what you have just said about induction for governors. Information is obviously key to openness. Are you satisfied that sufficient guidance exists for governing bodies, for governors, of the information that they can expect from an institution. Some of the evidence we have suggests that it is really very easy to withhold information from governing bodies precisely because they are not always clear what information might be appropriate. For example, some evidence has suggested that things like student progress and dropout, major capital expenditure items, the business plan or the corporate plan of the organisation not necessarily routinely being agreed with the governors or discussed with the governors.

Is this an area where the funding council would provide advice or is it an area where the advice already given to universities could be extended?

PROF BRIAN FENDER: I think the core of that advice is undoubtedly present in the committee's rather comprehensive document really—it does refer to that information—but, in particular, picking up the points you used by illustration, the university governing bodies need to be involved in the strategic plans of the university, covering all the aspects that you touched on, and also I would think it good practice—I hope it would be taken almost as read—that the strategic plans were accompanied by a statement of achievements over the past year against the aims of the strategic plan in the immediate past year and a clear statement of the targets for the coming year which would allow, of course, subsequent monitoring.

I think without that element of sharpness relating to the coming year—I am avoiding using the words "business plan" because I do not want to put a particular framework around it—but a clear identification of targets and how the university has performed against those targets is, for me, an essential bit of information.

241. DIANA WARWICK: I would like to pick up the point that Dr Hull made about the limits on the role of the Funding Council and you indicated that academic behaviour was off limits. I would like to link that to the whole question of whistle-blowing which has been raised with us in very many different contexts now.

Much of the evidence that we have had has talked about the problems for whistle-blowers in relation to the erosion of academic standards. That clearly is outwith, or appears to be outwith, the remit of the Funding Council. Are you satisfied—given what you said, for example, about Huddersfield which was not academic standards but, nonetheless, was a public airing of a problem—are you satisfied that the processes of appeal and of reassurance to whistle-blowers on the whole area of academic standards are satisfactory?

PROF BRIAN FENDER: She asked you!

ROB HULL: I do not think we have the evidence that they are not satisfactory, but nor do we have the evidence that they are satisfactory, because we would tend not to hear about those things. As I said earlier, I would see that as primarily a question for the academic community and I would have thought that it was a good question for them, first, whether within institutions there should channels created for whistleblowers' friends to be available and, secondly, whether the academic community more widely might be thinking about the existence of some channel outside the university, but I do see that primarily as a question for the academic community.

The legislation under which we operate, particularly Section 68 of the 1992 Act, specifically excludes the Secretary of State from questions about, academic staff, admission of students and so on and by extension I think the implication is that the Funding Council too does not have a primary responsibility in that area.

DIANA WARWICK: So we will raise it elsewhere. Thank you.

LORD THOMSON: Sir Clifford?

242. CLIFFORD BOULTON: You said that the future arrangements for securing quality assurance in higher education were currently under discussion. Have they reached the point where there is any paper you would be able to let us have? Are there any letters or invitations to consider these matters, a potential agenda or anything that you could supply us with to see what form it is going to take?

PROF BRIAN FENDER: Let me explain the stages. Currently there is a discussion group called a forum whose task is to set up a joint planning group. The joint planning group will have terms of reference to bring about a single agency. The nature of the role of the single agency will be determined by these terms of reference, which include specific requests by the Secretary of State and the outcome of extensive consultation.

What we have got is a process in which this planning group, charged with the responsibility of bringing the new agency into being, will start work in January, hopefully will conclude its work in the late summer and the proposals will go back to the various bodies involved with a view to setting up the agency on 1 January 1997. From what I have said about openness, any time there is anything we can give to the world about that whole process, we will be happy to do so.

CLIFFORD BOULTON: Thank you. We are in existence for another two years, so we will be waiting.

PROF BRIAN FENDER: You will have an opportunity I hope to see it all happen.

CLIFFORD BOULTON: Thank you.

LORD THOMSON: I am afraid time has run out on us, but thank you very much indeed for coming and giving us evidence. It has been very helpful to us.

Professor Zellick, we are very grateful to you for coming along. I am not sure whether you were here when the session opened and I explained that Lord Nolan hopes to be with us quite soon. Until then I am taking the Chair. We always allocate the lead question to one of our members and I think Sir Clifford Boulton is going to open the batting.

243. CLIFFORD BOULTON: Thank you very much for your typically clear paper, but would it be fair to deduce from it that so far as the chartered universities are concerned, you do not actually come to us in a white sheet? You think that by and large their systems of governance have got enough in-built checks and balances to be providing sufficient openness and reassurance about standards?

PROFESSOR GRAHAM ZELLICK

PROF GRAHAM ZELLICK (Principal, Queen Mary and Westfield College): I do believe that very strongly. There have been recent changes, as you know, which have strengthened that position and I have every confidence that those arrangements serve the public interest and the academic community extremely well.

244. CLIFFORD BOULTON: Even though there is certainly nothing very uniform about them, they have grown up in their own way very often and have got their own characteristics. There is no best that you would like to see more evenly distributed amongst the older universities?

PROF GRAHAM ZELLICK: Putting Oxford and Cambridge to one side—which are quite different and of which I have no direct experience other than as a student—the features that are similar across the chartered universities are more striking than the differences. I would maintain that they are sufficiently close in the salient features for us to be able to generalise and say that it is actually a single system of governance.

245. CLIFFORD BOULTON: To help us identify what particular characteristics you have in mind, you say in paragraph 7 of your paper, "It may be that the arrangements for the statutory universities need to be modified to bring them more into line with the chartered institutions.". What characteristics would you think of importing into the statutory universities?

PROF GRAHAM ZELLICK: Let me just make it clear that I am in no position really to comment on the efficacy of the arrangements in the new universities. I am, as I have indicated, a member of one governing body and I have been immensely impressed in every respect, both by the way the governing body conducts itself and by the quality of its senior management. There is nothing in my personal direct experience which leads me to suppose that there is a need for change.

The real point I was making there is that change should not be imposed upon the chartered universities to bring them into line with the new universities which, after all, have governance arrangements which are the product of more recent governmental consideration.

246. CLIFFORD BOULTON: They have often got quite small governing boards, which they claim lead to greater efficiency. That carries with it the suggestion that some of the governing boards of the chartered universities are very large indeed and have more of the nature of a meeting which gets addressed by a vice-chancellor or chairman than a genuinely governing body. Have you ever heard that said about large governing bodies?

PROF GRAHAM ZELLICK: I have indeed heard it said and I have heard it said that any principal or vice-chancellor would want as large a governing body as he could possibly have.

CLIFFORD BOULTON: Yes.

PROF GRAHAM ZELLICK: Size is not irrelevant, but in my view it is not terribly important. Efficiency of the body in the sense that here is in mind is not to my way of thinking the over-riding requirement. My Council of Queen Mary and Westfield College has just come down to 36 from 41. Many people would say that that is impossibly large for some kind of board of directors. It works perfectly well. Anything smaller would certainly suffer in terms of the representation it brings. It would certainly suffer in terms of its role in disseminating information, particularly through its internal members across the institution.

One has to remember that much of the detailed work that comes to the Council for further consideration or approval has to be done in the nature of things elsewhere in smaller groups—sub-committees, policy and resources committee, staffing committee and so forth. I am therefore not at all persuaded by the argument that these bodies are over large. I think that those who subscribe to

that view probably do so because they have a mistaken conception of the role of the governing body of the institution.

247. CLIFFORD BOULTON: Yes. You have had a bit of direct experience I imagine from the developments that have been taking place in the business of getting charter revision and going to the Privy Council. Are you satisfied with the way that works? Is it looked at by people who know what they are talking about? What advice does the Privy Council use in considering the amendments that go before them?

PROF GRAHAM ZELLICK: My own experience of the Privy Council in this procedure is on the whole a happy one and the Privy Council Office itself is admirable. My own contacts are mostly with the Deputy Clerk, who has enormous expertise in relation to charters and statutes of universities. We have only just completed both charter and statute revisions recently for my own college in relation to merger with the two medical schools.

CLIFFORD BOULTON: Yes.

PROF GRAHAM ZELLICK: And they could not have been more helpful. The system miscarries from my perception only when things have to leave the Privy Council Office and advice has to be taken from the appropriate department. That, of course, in practice is usually the Department for Education and Employment and that is usually where the difficulties begin, but then it is matters of policy—I have not always got what I wanted.

248. CLIFFORD BOULTON: But they have been to do with policy rather than matters which are directly related to our terms of reference to do with governance as far as standards and conduct and so forth are concerned?

PROF GRAHAM ZELLICK: Yes.

249. CLIFFORD BOULTON: On the question of governance, the possibility sometimes builds up of a tension between the vice-chancellor and the chairman of the governing body. You point to the role, in paragraph 14 of your paper: you say, "There is no doubt that the vice-chancellor or principal, as chief executive, has a duty to challenge inappropriate decisions by the Council and in appropriate cases, report the matter to the Funding Council. It would be difficult to require or expect the clerk or a secretary to the council to be able to perform a similar role and he/she should certainly advise the chairman and vice-chancellor". Elsewhere in the evidence we have received, we have been told that in some universities there is a strong, influential and excellent registrar, secretary or clerk to the council who does perform quite a powerful role as a person who ensures good and open government.

In your experience, is there an uneven approach to the role of that person and are some of them perhaps under-filled by the person who has been asked to do it? Is there scope, possibly, for having a more consistent role for that officer?

PROF GRAHAM ZELLICK: I think there is legitimate variation across the sector and it could not be otherwise. The management arrangements, even in the old universities, change. Not so many years ago one would have found someone called the Secretary and registrar or the Secretary of the university who would have been the head of the administration and the senior administrator under the vice-chancellor and who would have been able—and in most cases where those arrangements persist is still able—to fulfil the role you identify. But in many institutions, that monolithic structure has been supplanted by very different management arrangements where there is no single very senior head of the administration, where the Vice-Chancellor has quite properly assumed fully the role both of administrative and academic leader of the institution.

It has to be left to institutions to judge the most appropriate management arrangements. Ultimately it has to be the vice-chancellor who must be relied upon to alert public authorities to major problems. I do not say that the Secretary to the governing body has no role at all to play, and I hope that he or she in performing that role would be mindful of that public responsibility, but I think we should locate it unequivocally on the head of the institution.

250. CLIFFORD BOULTON: Well, of course, he or she is the accounting officer and I suppose to that extent it is inevitable that that should be the direct relationship with, for example, the Funding Council.

Can I just ask you about your experience of the function of the visitor? Those institutions which have them, by and large are telling us that they appreciate having them and that they have a very valuable function. People without them say they do not want one, by and large. What experience have you had of the use to which your visitor has been put?

PROF GRAHAM ZELLICK: Happily, very little—only one or two cases that I can recall. We have, on the advice of the Privy Council, just slightly simplified our arrangements and altered our charter accordingly so that the visitor ceases to be the Queen in Council and now becomes the Queen, acting through the Lord President, which does, I understand, offer some advantages in dealing with these matters.

One of the complications of course in recent years, as you, Chairman, will know, is that the extension of judicial review to decisions of the visitor has in some respects brought into question its value. Fortunately, the Law Lords drew back from the more extravagant claims of judicial review in respect of the visitatorial jurisdiction, but it is still there in some cases so that the advantage to institutions and, indeed, to complainants, of having not only a speedy and cheap system but also one that came to an end quickly and could not then by reopened in the courts, has been qualified. It seems to me that it is a very desirable arrangement to have in place.

I would not make extravagant claims for it, but to be able to offer an ombudsman type adjudication—which is what it is—of certain kinds of disputes, where the costs are not likely to be great, offers great advantages and it would be foolish to throw it over.

251. CLIFFORD BOULTON: Do you have an adequate filtering system for making sure that frivolous or vexatious complaints do not go forward?

PROF GRAHAM ZELLICK: No, indeed. We could not operate any kind of filtering system. Anyone can petition the visitor, as of right and it is then for the visitor to decide matters of jurisdiction and so forth.

252. CLIFFORD BOULTON: Have you had experience of complaints which the visitor chose not to pursue because they fell into some sort of category of vexatiousness?

PROF GRAHAM ZELLICK: I would like to think it is because of splendid management and attention to complaints and so forth, but I can think in my own College of only one case that has actually gone to the visitor in nearly 25 years. There may have been others, but I do not think so.

CLIFFORD BOULTON: No.

PROF GRAHAM ZELLICK: That was rejected on its merits. I think the University of London has had greater experience, simply because of the very large number—tens of thousands a year—of students it deals with, many of them external, but I do not think I can help you very much more on that.

253. CLIFFORD BOULTON: Have you been satisfied with your relationship with the Funding Council? Have there ever been times when you felt that they were trespassing a little beyond what they were supposed to be doing and taking an interest in the internal governance in an inappropriate way?

PROF GRAHAM ZELLICK: No, not in any serious respect. There is a very satisfactory process of dialogue between the Council and institutions and it is extremely rare for them to do anything or come to any conclusion on things without a very adequate—some might even say over-elaborate—consultation. I could not recall the details, but some proposals in the financial memorandum, for example, possibly some in relation to audit, have, I know, raised questions in the sector as to appropriateness. They have been put to the Council and as far as I know, agreement has then been reached on what the proper limits are, so I am not aware of any problems here.

254. CLIFFORD BOULTON: Does the university ever appear to be over-reaching itself in the extent to which it is interested in the internal affairs of the College?

PROF GRAHAM ZELLICK: The University of London?

CLIFFORD BOULTON: Yes.

PROF GRAHAM ZELLICK: There was a time when you would have had a very long and passionate answer on that question, but that is no longer the case because of the very far-reaching changes that have been made in the relationship between the University and the constituent colleges within the last year or two. The statutes have been entirely rewritten and in effect the Colleges of the University of London now operate indistinguishably from the unitary universities across the country, with the University of London itself performing a role in relation to a prescribed range of matters.

255. CLIFFORD BOULTON: Which would extend to the reputation attaching to the degree of the university?

PROF GRAHAM ZELLICK: Yes.

256. CLIFFORD BOULTON: So that if there was anxiety about colleges getting sloppy about admission

because it was lowering the standard of the University, would they have a look in there? Do they collect information about that sort of thing?

PROF GRAHAM ZELLICK: We have arrangements in place in which the Vice-Chancellor and the Academic Committee of the University receive the assessment reports and the audit reports and so forth. There can then be an exchange of views between the Vice-Chancellor and the Head of College. These are new arrangements so we do not have very extensive experience of them, but of course when you are dealing with very large and distinguished institutions such as Imperial College and University College, it would be very difficult to justify imposing upon them a whole layer of university supervision that, say, the University of Manchester or University of Birmingham did not have to experience—particularly as these things are not cost-free—and so what has been agreed is a fairly light layer of University oversight, which I think meets the collective University's interest in maintaining the quality of its degree.

CLIFFORD BOULTON: Thank you. Perhaps I ought to give colleagues an opportunity.

257. DIANA WARWICK: Could I perhaps follow up with you the point that I put to the Funding Council for England in relation to academic judgements and the role of whistle blowing. Sir Clifford raised reference to the visitor. That is obviously both not much used and an extremely grand answer to what might often be not a very huge problem, at least in the first instance. I imagine that every university would want to have internal procedures to be able to deal with those sorts of questions pretty quickly.

Do you have an internal appeal arrangement that would generally satisfy the requirements for whistle blowing to be exercised satisfactorily?

PROF GRAHAM ZELLICK: I think I shall have to ask you what we are really talking about here. You know we have the standard grievance procedures for example which were introduced into the statutes of all the old universities by the University Commissioners. We then have all sorts of other arrangements which any large organisation will have. Students obviously have channels through the Union and representation on committees and boards, staff through their own unions in ways both formal and informal.

I do not think one can generalise. One has to take particular areas or examples and I would be happy to respond.

DIANA WARWICK: I was thinking of the issue of academic standards that has been referred to by several of the people who have written to us, such as the whole question of Philosophy at Swansea.

PROF GRAHAM ZELLICK: Yes.

258. DIANA WARWICK: I suppose most of the academic profession knows a little bit about that. Do you feel that in your institution there are provisions in place that would ensure that any accusation of lowering of standards could be dealt with adequately?

PROF GRAHAM ZELLICK: I have no doubt at all. There are now really quite elaborate mechanisms—

reports from external examiners, every one of which is looked at at a very high level and is answered, Quality Standards Committee, which would certainly react to matters of that kind and ultimately the jurisdiction of the Academic Board. It would be quite impossible—as the example you mentioned shows—to sweep this sort of thing under the carpet. It would not work, so what any sensible institution would do would be to address the concerns properly.

There are areas, as you know I am sure, in academic life these days—and it may have been so for a long time—where academic views within particular disciplines can be very controversial and are not straightforward matters at all. Perhaps in the sciences it is on the whole straightforward, but it is not entirely absent there. I have seen experts with enormously different views about whether an individual member of the academic staff should be promoted: one Fellow of the Royal Society saying "This person should be a professor. He is doing wonderfully original work." and another Fellow of the Royal Society saying "This is complete rubbish and I am surprised you are even continuing to employ him.". But if one comes over into the social sciences and the humanities, there can be some very divergent approaches to disciplines—deeply ideological divisions and so forth. So these matters are not free of contention.

It is not a matter of saying "This is good academic quality; this is bad." and the world of experts in the discipline would line up behind one or other of those judgements. Would that it were that straightforward.

259. DIANA WARWICK: That leads me on to another question, which was raised in relation to HEFCE, but I think also can be raised in relation to organisations like the Royal Society and the British Academy and that is the whole problem, if you like, of self-perpetuating bodies or self-appointed members of such bodies. It has been argued to us that some of the bodies shape academic destinies quite substantially. Is there an argument for having much more open appointment to these bodies?

PROF GRAHAM ZELLICK: Which bodies?

260. DIANA WARWICK: We raised earlier the question of appointments to the Funding Council, but your mentioning of the Royal Society suggested that there were also bodies that had influence on universities and yet they were relatively closed organisations.

PROF GRAHAM ZELLICK: Yes. Let me be absolutely clear, or I shall get into a lot of trouble. I was referring to individuals who, it so happened, were Fellows of the Royal Society, as many eminent academics on the science side are and their counterparts on the other side are in the British Academy. Those bodies are nothing more or less than collections of distinguished scholars who do perpetuate themselves—and I have no problem with that at all. In the nature of things there are worthy people who will be overlooked, deliberately or otherwise and some perhaps less than distinguished people who get in. That does not cause me a great deal of concern.

When we turn to those outside for expert guidance in matters of appointments, promotions or course evaluation, we exercise individual ad hominem judgements. We look to individuals who may or may not be members of these bodies. I know they do perform some public functions as well in the distribution of public funds. I do not think it is a matter of serious concern. On the whole the selection process works reasonably well. I do not think it is a matter that ought to worry you too much.

261. DIANA WARWICK: Finally, does it worry you that on the Higher Education Funding Council for England—and I believe it is only England, I do not think this applies to the other two Funding Councils—there are, if you like, four insiders, four vice-chancellors, making judgements about the allocation of funds to other universities and, indeed, to their own?

PROF GRAHAM ZELLICK: That is an interesting point and, of course, as you will know it is a practice which was not followed previously, either in the old UGC or I think in its successor body. When the new Funding Council was set up and the sector was unified—I cannot remember in point of time whether this was the old small CVCP or the larger converged CVCP—I remember arguing that the old UGC practice ought to prevail in which there were no vice-chancellors on the Council, or the Board as we are now told to call it, of the Council.

We have had several years in which there have been several members on it. I must say I have never heard any criticism expressed of that. I have never myself had any reason to suppose that it had led to anything that could be criticised, but I would personally adhere to the original view. In a way there is something to be said for ensuring that the Council does have a real awareness of how difficult it is to manage institutions, which even the most distinguished academics from within the system might not have. Until you have actually done this job as a vice-chancellor, or possibly a deputy, you really do not have a full sense of some of the overall difficulties. So there is an advantage, but I think on balance I would prefer the old UGC practice, though I doubt if one could claim that it was a matter of great significance.

DIANA WARWICK: Thank you.

262. LORD THOMSON: We have come up to time. Thank you very much indeed for coming and for the way you have answered our questions. It has been very helpful.

PROF GRAHAM ZELLICK: Chairman, I know we are out of time, but would you like me to try to assist you on a matter you raised with Professor Fender, namely, the copyright of lecture notes?

LORD THOMSON: Yes, indeed. I would be most interested.

PROF GRAHAM ZELLICK: I was slightly amused by that exchange. In the first place, if I could express a legal view, I think it is most unlikely that a university could sustain the argument that it owned the copyright in the lecture notes. Indeed there is the dictum of a distinguished judge in an old case who was hypothesising about the lecture notes of the great Professor Maitland of Cambridge and said it was inconceivable that the University of Cambridge could own the copyright in the lecture notes.

However, I have never heard of any academic handing over his or her lecture notes to anybody else. You were troubled by the assertion by the University of a right in the intellectual property. I am more troubled by what I would

see as a rather questionable academic activity—namely, passing on secondhand lecture notes. I should say that that is not meant as any criticism of Lord Mackay, whom I have known and respected for many years. The basic legal position under the Copyright Act is that the employer does own the intellectual property of employees' work produced in the course of employment. In practice, universities in their contracts of employment with staff have handed over those rights to members of staff.

I do not believe that that is necessarily the optimal position and there could well be arguments for re-addressing that, but I do think that is a matter for either universities individually or collectively. If you felt that there was somehow some abuse here in the particular university throwing its weight around or misusing its authority—if that is the issue—then I would say, first of all—and it perhaps comes back to the whistle blowing analogy—the individual member of staff has the whole range of opportunities to raise the matter through the union, through the grievance procedure and if that is not effective, through the courts.

We cannot expect, and should not try, to provide universities with some kinds of mechanisms that do not apply to other organisations, whether commercial or non-commercial, whether in the private sector or the public sector. If there are perfectly proper opportunities, whether it is through the courts or otherwise, for the redress of grievances, that should satisfy us. Universities will sometimes act badly, either on the basis of mistaken legal advice or no legal advice, but there are mechanisms for correcting that.

LORD THOMSON: Professor Zellick, it is very fortunate for us to have such a highly expert legal opinion given to us on the matter. It was the witness who felt disturbed by some of the implications in relation, I think, to more general questions of academic freedom.

PROF GRAHAM ZELLICK: Yes.

LORD THOMSON: But it is very helpful to have your views. Thank you very much.

LORD NOLAN: Professor Zellick, I am very sorry to have missed the first part of your evidence. I was prevented by duties elsewhere from being here, but I shall read it with great interest. Thank you.

PROF GRAHAM ZELLICK: Thank you.

263. LORD NOLAN: Lord Limerick, you and I have met when I have been fortunate enough to be your guest on less formal occasions. Thank you all very much for being with us this morning and I wonder if I could begin by asking you this simple question: your organisation has produced guidance for members of university governing bodies, which is very comprehensive and carefully thought out and based on experience. Can you tell us, please, what the normal role of the Committee of University Chairmen is and its membership and how it relates to other bodies? Is the production of guidance the purpose for which you were formed?

LORD LIMERICK, BRIAN HERON, AND MICHAEL SHATTOCK

LORD LIMERICK (Committee of University

Chairmen): No, it is not. There were two separate bodies, one which brought together the Chairmen of the old universities and another which brought together the Chairmen of the polytechnics. So the obvious issue with the ending of the binary line was what should happen in relation to those two bodies. They very quickly agreed that the right thing to do was to bring them together, which has happened very quickly and really quite seamlessly, to the extent now that all of our procedures are informed by and Committees are manned by people virtually indifferently from the old and the new university sector.

There was a perception that the Chairmen of governing bodies with their particular responsibilities have matters which they would like to share with each other, which there is no other forum for doing. This gives them a separate voice to the Department of Education—to HMG—if that be appropriate. Without suggesting that we see things differently from the CVCP, which we hardly ever do, nevertheless we approach those subjects from a somewhat different standpoint with our responsibilities and experiences. It was seen as appropriate and, indeed, is I think seen to be working effectively, that we do therefore have these two voices. So the Chairmen were meeting already and were discussing matters such as the proper remuneration of chief executives and senior management members, or the appropriate mechanisms for getting more funding into higher education which they had in common. Then particular issues arose which brought a focus onto the governance and hence the production of the guide.

We saw the value of that as it was a field in which the lead was taken by the CUC, first with some general, rather targeted points in the wake of the Huddersfield affair, after this initial advice was issued in December. Brian Heron's working party expanded the advice into the guide which emerged which we think, hope and believe has been generally accepted as a model. Indeed, we have evidence of that because we did poll our members prior to our meeting in April, as to whether they accepted what was said and expected to implement it. Given that by then a number of them had not even had a governors' meeting in time to give us a definitive answer, the response was very positive—more than ninety per cent of our members said yes, they were looking at these matters and many of them said they had already done a lot of the things that were required, in so far as those were not already in place in their practices.

264. LORD NOLAN: Yes, thank you very much. I would like, if I may, to come back a little later to the incidents which gave rise to the production of the code of guidance and what lessons remain to be learned from them. But before doing that, could I continue, please, with some more general questions? Your guidance—it is by definition, it is not especially prescriptive—how important is self-regulation in the traditional concept of a university? Leave aside financial audit which, of course, everyone is subject to. What limits should be set on autonomy in order to guarantee accountability? For example, some universities have Visitors, the older universities in particular. For example, we have the Higher Education Funding Council exercising a degree of supervision. Are those, in your view, satisfactory safeguards on the public interests which do not interfere with the proper autonomy, or do they cause difficulties in practice for universities?

LORD LIMERICK: I will ask Michael Shattock to make the first comment on that, if I may, because he has got a background in these subjects.

LORD NOLAN: Yes, please.

MICHAEL SHATTOCK (Secretary, Committee of University Chairmen): Well, we are, of course, only in receipt of funds from the Funding Council, subject to our acceptance of the terms of the Funding Councils' Financial Memorandum. So we are quite strongly controlled by the Funding Council in the way we spend the resources that we receive from them. Also our books are open to the Comptroller and Auditor General and so, again, we are subject to the normal scrutiny by the National Audit Office and the Public Accounts Committee. More recently the Funding Council has introduced a quality assurance mechanism which again ensures—I think it is 917 departments have so far been quality assessed—that academic quality, so far as teaching is concerned is assessed. There is quite an extensive panoply of powers to ensure that universities are adequately accountable.

Internally universities have their own quite strong procedures. All universities now will have an audit committee and an internal audit service. That is a requirement arising from the financial memorandum, but most universities had them anyway. And, of course, the whole relationship between the governing body and the senate or the Academic Board guarantees that there is a great deal of internal monitoring of performance and quality which takes place. So I think one's view is rather that we are somewhat over-burdened by controls rather than the opposite.

265. LORD NOLAN: Yes. Is there much difficulty in recruiting members of governing bodies, in your experience?

LORD LIMERICK: I think there is always difficulty in recruiting the right members or the best members. Is this the moment to say a little bit about the procedure for the identification of independent members?

LORD NOLAN: By all mean, if you would, please, nominations for committees and so forth. Yes, please do.

LORD LIMERICK: Well, the nomination committee procedure is one that obviously is increasingly familiar in company life. It is being adapted and adopted, in the new universities particularly, they have come to it, of course, by a very different route from the old universities. I think one just has to remember that the universities, who came through the PCFC door, seven or eight years ago had really almost nothing by way of procedures themselves. These were provided through the local authorities, so all this change has come to them very quickly.

What most seek to do—and one can speak best from one's own experience—is to look very long and hard at the requirements of your particular university, its particular place in the market as well as the requirements for good governors and you then identify by type what you need to plug gaps in that particular array of experience and talent. At that point you start to look for individuals to fill them. It is, of course, an unremunerated office and it is capable of being onerous in terms of time and a responsibility, so that it is never easy to get the best people. Nevertheless, we have so far never failed to get more than adequate people in the fields in which we have sought them and I think that is generally the experience of others. The perception of responsibility has been sharpened greatly by certain happenings in the past, one of which, perhaps, is the move for universities to raise money from private sources. When governors, including staff and student governors, have to sign off on a statement of responsibility on a prospectus it does sharpen their appreciation no end of what is involved in being a governor.

266. LORD NOLAN: Yes. As Chairmen do you find any difficulty in determining the boundary between your own role and that of the Vice-Chancellor or the Chief Executive of the university?

LORD LIMERICK: I will speak very briefly and then ask Brian Heron to comment from his perspective. The answer is no, because we take quite straightforwardly a company model, that there is a board of directors, governors, who carry the defined and ultimate responsibility. A member of that board is the Vice-Chancellor, by whatever name, who is the Chief Executive and he is charged on the responsibility of the board for putting those policies into practice. So the board does not get involved in management at all. The Vice-Chancellor takes part in the discussions on policy and then has to implement them. We would expect that to be done in the way that a company chief executive relates to a governing body. This has not raised questions or problems in our experience or in what I know of other cognate institutions.

BRIAN HERON (Committee of University Chairmen): Yes, Chairman, I am chancellor of an old but not ancient university by definition and we take exactly the same view, that Council in the end is ultimately responsible for the policy and the execution of that policy in the university. Clearly the Vice-Chancellor is a member of Council. Lay members have to be in just a majority by one on our Council and we have no difficulty in recognising—as I say, I come from an industrial background over 37 years—and I have no problem at all in following a similar model under which our vice-chancellor is the senior executive responsible for executing the policy of Council.

Clearly the relationship between any chief executive and chairman is a fascinating one, as events over the last couple of days have perhaps revealed, but nevertheless it is recognised that any serious conflict—we have never had one—would have to be resolved by discussion and by agreement. That is the only way. In the older universities clearly the role of senate or academic board is a very important one because the academic responsibility initially rests with Senate, of which the Vice-Chancellor is normally chairman. They make recommendations and take prime responsibility for all academic issues, although ultimately the governing body has to accept over-arching responsibility. But clearly the harmony between the Senate, Council and the Vice-Chancellor is a crucial element in running any of the old universities as it is in the running of any successful organisation.

I think in relation to the organisation—and you asked a question slightly earlier—of course we are independent corporate institutions. The older universities are, by definition, usually established by charter and we are equally, by definition, organisations which bring with them implicitly the right to have a Visitor. Therefore, most old universities have an establishment under which Council is responsible to a court and court in itself consists very widely of representatives of the local authorities, the local councils, all the senior professional bodies, both nationally and locally. In turn, of course, the Visitor has over arching responsibility of inspection and authority in relation to resolving any disputes which arise internally from members of our institution.

267. LORD NOLAN: Thank you very much. I wonder if I could turn now to the code and as a preliminary to that ask you something I should have raised at the outset. You told us, Lord Limerick, that your Committee represents all the universities, old and new, now—all 72 of them, or whatever it is—how large is the committee?

LORD LIMERICK: One hundred. That is all the universities, other than Oxford and Cambridge, and the thing that is peculiar about them in this context is that they have no lay representation on their governing bodies.

268. LORD NOLAN: Yes, thank you very much. Two points in the submission to us: you refer to the events at Huddersfield—once as the stimulus that prompted the issue of the advice on guidance and, secondly, paragraph 3.3. for its relevance to a particular issue, namely the relationship between institutional governments and the community. I wonder if—this will revive the unhappy memories—you could just say again briefly what the trouble was at Huddersfield. There was a series of management difficulties, was there not, and a vote of no confidence, if I remember rightly in the Council. After it had excluded staff and student members the Council decided that as the vice-chancellor was, through no fault of his own, the focus of the discontent that prevailed, he should go and then there was a leaving package that had to be unscrambled. That was the broad outline of what went wrong, was it not?

MICHAEL SHATTOCK: Yes, that was the broad outline. Staff and students were excluded by the governing body, which the governing body was legally entitled to do, and this, of course, caused very sharp protests. There was a long-running political situation, I think, within the university and as one understands it from what has been published, the governors decided that the only way to solve that would be for the vice-chancellor to take early retirement and as you say, there was a substantial package created. A decision was taken to advertise a new vice-chancellor's post at a very high level salary and then this salary was reflected back to improve the position of the existing vice-chancellor, whose salary was then raised and a package was constructed around it which caused considerable unhappiness within the university and outside.

269. LORD NOLAN: Yes. What particular parts of the code were directed to the problems thus seen in so far as you have described them already?

MICHAEL SHATTOCK: Well, I think the first thing—as far as the CUC was concerned we took no part whatever in questions of the actual details of the severance pay.

LORD NOLAN: No.

MICHAEL SHATTOCK: However, our concern was in relation to the decision-making structure at

Huddersfield and in particular in the guide we suggested that if governing bodies were legally empowered—and, of course, it is not all governing bodies, it is only some of those in the post-1992 universities—but if a university governing body did decide to remove the staff representation and the student representation, then a very clear minute should be drafted explaining why this was being done and that minute should be published within the university.

The second point which we were concerned with was the position of the independent members of the governing body. This was raised publicly because the succession to them, the replacement of them, was entirely within their own hands: that is provided for in the 1992 legislation. And so the proposal that we advanced, which is in the guide, is for a nominations committee and for a process in which names are brought forward to the governing body. The nomination should be considered formally by the governing body, even though it is not able to intrude on the independent members' powers of making their own decisions. So what the guide proposes is a process which, if followed through, the independent members would have to take cognisance of.

270. LORD NOLAN: Yes. And so far as relations with the local committee were concerned, you have touched on that in what you have said. What was the particular problem?

MICHAEL SHATTOCK: Well, the Member of Parliament for Huddersfield, Mr Sheerman, argued, that the governing body at Huddersfield lacked what he would describe as public accountability. We have suggested in the guide that it is right and proper for governing bodies to take account, in so far as they are able to, of local opinion. Most of the old universities have bodies called "courts" which are very widely representative bodies and, therefore, give an opportunity once a year for local opinion and, indeed, other opinion to be directed to the university. But on the whole the new universities do not have that kind of machinery. What we have suggested in the guide is that universities should think their way through the process of taking account of local opinion. In particular the nominations committee should think actively of bringing people onto the governing body who have strong local connections.

LORD NOLAN: Yes, thank you very much.

BRIAN HERON: I think however, Chairman, there is a point here and that is, of course, that as polytechnics became universities and universities in general, of course, have much wider remit in terms of where they draw their students, their staff and their responsibilities as a whole compared with the past when polytechnics were perhaps drawing much more on local students. This is certainly not the case now and therefore the community of students, the community of staff, would be drawn much more widely than perhaps as previous organisations they were, certainly in comparison with older universities. It seems to work out that the chances of a local university having almost any students who live locally is extremely slim—part of the enthusiasm for attending university seems to be to get away as far from home as possible. And that is very relevant. That is why, I think, governing bodies have to comprehend the national scene as well as the local scene.

271. LORD NOLAN: Yes. Do you think the number of local students is likely to increase, as shortage of money makes it more difficult for them to get grants to live away from home?

BRIAN HERON: Yes, we keep on being told that. And the other aspect which is important in many universities is the involvement both of funds which are not from the public purse and the involvement of overseas students. In our university 25 per cent of our students come from overseas and that is a responsibility, obviously, which local organisations per se are interested in. Bringing overseas students in has a potential ultimately to involve local business and enterprise and to sell the community to many overseas countries. But it is in a different form and I think that is what was underlying the original question about local involvement.

LORD NOLAN: Yes.

LORD LIMERICK: Could I make a point? I think that the significance of Huddersfield was that it was a problem sufficiently serious and sufficiently well-recognised through all the publicity it attracted that up and down the country people in universities were saying "Is this something that could happen to us? What should we be thinking of doing about it?". Therefore it was immediately possible for Brian Heron's committee, when appointed, to get right into this subject and produce proposals that went much further and were adopted much more quickly than would have happened without that spark at the start, also almost certainly more quickly and effectively than it would have happened if somebody had attempted to impose procedures from outside, because I think there is something in the nature of universities that makes that unlikely.

That said—and we made this point in our written submission, of course—our power is the power of persuasion, no more. There is perhaps a model in what has happened in the company field with Cadbury and then Greenbury that codes emerge and they are kicked around until they are thought to be sufficiently suitable and then people are invited to conform to them. The next stage is that somebody—in that case the Stock Exchange—will say "we wish quoted companies to do these things or if they don't do them to explain what they don't do and why they are not doing it." And that is a model which might perhaps be applied in this case if it was thought important enough and attractive enough, that those who have sanctions which we do not have—and, of course, that starts with the Funding Council—should consider looking at the question of non-compliance with the code as one of their criteria.

272. LORD NOLAN: Yes, thank you very much. Michael Shattock, you carried out an enquiry into what had gone wrong with the Derby College at Wilmorton—not, of course, a university. Just looking a those two groups of incidents, what happened at Huddersfield and what happened at Wilmorton, there was a rather similar disturbance at Portsmouth at about the same time. Is your impression that there is something wrong, something to worry about, over general standards of conduct in further and higher education or were these, in your experience, isolated incidents?

MICHAEL SHATTOCK: Well, I think that if one takes the situation at Huddersfield and Portsmouth one does have to remember that you are dealing with two incidents which have affected, certainly the reputations, I suppose, of a hundred universities, but they have only taken place in two. As far as Huddersfield is concerned, Huddersfield was the only case which required some external intervention from the National Audit Office and ultimately from the Funding Council, whereas in the case of Portsmouth, Portsmouth did have difficulties but they appointed a QC to carry out an enquiry and he has written a report, which is the University's own Report, so in that sense I think one could say that the University has cleared up its own business. If you go back and you think about Cardiff, again, of course, that did become a matter of some national concern, but it was the university system and the University Grants Committee that sorted Cardiff out.

I think if you look at further education you are looking at a series of different problems. The new universities, as Lord Limerick said, became corporate bodies only in 1988 but they had had a period under the Polytechnics and Colleges Funding Council before they became universities in 1992. As far as the further education colleges are concerned 457 of them became, as it were, corporate bodies in 1993 and so were moving into a degree of independence a very large number of institutions that had been entirely under local authority control before, many of which were quite small institutions, who had to recruit governors and whose principals and senior staff were not experienced at running institutions completely independently. So I think the stresses on further education have been much greater than on the universities. I am now chairman of a governing body in the further education sector and this is a college which is again in great difficulty. I think there are some parallel features with Derby College, Wilmorton, in that the previous governors have resigned and it is clear that there was a degree of inexperience, as well as incompetence, in the way they took their responsibilities for the management of the college, which I think would not be the case if you looked at further education colleges maybe in five years time. So I think the further education sector is in a very particular situation, having been moved so quickly into independence.

LORD NOLAN: Yes, thank you.

BRIAN HERON: I am a governor of a further education college, as well as being a chairman of a NHS Trust and on a TEC board and the differences between those different establishments is fascinating, but it was amazing to me to join the board of a further education college which has turned out to be very successfully run but really their—naivety is a slightly unkind word—but the thrust of their new responsibilities and how they compared with how they had been run before, and I think obviously that depended to some extent on the local authority, but nevertheless I think most of them found themselves in a whole new world and therefore it is not surprising that, literally having been thrown in at the deep end, one or two have found it difficult to swim, at least in the very short time they have had to practice.

273. LORD NOLAN: Yes, thank you very much. That is very interesting and very reassuring. I have just one final question—it is of limited scope. Your guide deals with staff grievances. It does not, as I read it, provide for what have come to be known as "whistleblowers"—it is not really the exact term because whistleblowers are referees in my experience, but it is meant to connote the ability of staff with a grievance to make a confidential complaint. Do you see any scope for that as a general provision in the conduct of universities, or is it one that would vary from one case to another?

LORD LIMERICK: In my, admittedly restricted, experience there is no shortage of people prepared to make confidential submissions on most subjects, the problem is how they are dealt with. I think implicitly the invitation is always there and I suppose the main issue at Portsmouth—and it will be very interesting to see how the report deals with this—is how you get from the acknowledgement of fault and abuse or alleged abuse to the means of dealing with it. We looked at the procedures that were in here and came to the conclusion that the procedures in themselves were adequate. Now procedures can always be not applied or mis-applied and that is down to human failing, but we felt that there was little that we could add to the guidance that would provide a means that did not already exist of dealing with those situations.

LORD NOLAN: It is a most comprehensive guide. I am very grateful. I am going now to give some of the others a chance. Lord Thompson, I think you might have some questions.

BRIAN HERON: May I just pick up on that point?

LORD NOLAN: If you please, yes.

BRIAN HERON: As far as the older universities are concerned I think most of them do have complaints' procedures which are well-established. On the other hand, of course, they do have the role of Visitor, to whom any complaint by any member of the university—and that is all students, all academic staff and a number of non-academic staff—have recourse and, therefore, there is open access to that. And I think the philosophy is one certainly not of endeavouring to discourage anybody who has a genuine concern, genuine in their eyes as distinct from predetermining other people's views of being genuine. And the concept that there are somehow subjugated people sitting there who don't feel able to exercise their proper concerns is not quite one that I have come across in my experience.

274. LORD NOLAN: You do not find that in the academic world to the same extent as one sometimes hears of it, for example, in the Civil Service or even some commercial organisations?

BRIAN HERON: I have no experience of the Civil Service and, therefore, cannot speak for them, but I have 37 years of being in industry and responsible for operations throughout the world and I suppose it may be implicit in the sense that he who pays the piper ultimately there may be a feeling that he has the right to call the tune. But I have not seen this—I would have thought quite the reverse, I mean, the concept of academic freedom which may be sometimes smiled about but nevertheless is built into the establishment of universities, has always been an important tenet. I think if there is occasionally not academic freedom it is more likely to be imposed by other academics rather than by the governing body.

LORD NOLAN: Thank you very much. Lord Thomson?

275. LORD THOMSON: I would like to follow through the use to be made of your very good document of guidance. I think you mentioned in your paper that you intend to make a further survey in the spring of next year. Lord Limerick, you drew a very interesting analogy in

implementing the guidance with the Greenbury and Cadbury Committees. I was not quite clear—maybe I did not hear fully your answer—who would play the role of the Stock Exchange in applying the guidelines that you have in your paper? Do you see it as being the Higher Education Funding Council, do you see it as needing some legislation?

LORD LIMERICK: I think what I was reflecting was that we were able to produce something which so far at least seems to command general support—no doubt it will need amending in due course in the light of experience, we are not at all complacent about that—but at the moment it is the best document that we have to work on and it seems at least good enough. The point I was making is that we are not and cannot be policemen, we have no power and we are dealing with a lot of autonomous institutions, so the authority would have to be elsewhere and I did suggest the Funding Council, yes, as an obvious body which would have a role in this, merely to invite an explanation of any non-compliance. There may be perfectly valid reasons why particular universities feel that they would rather deal with an issue identified in this guide in a different way, or even not deal with it, but it is not a role that we can play ourselves. We shall, as you rightly picked up, be having a second round of monitoring on this next April, by which time there will have been a full season of meetings and procedures and we hope—and indeed we believe—that the level of voluntary compliance at that time will turn out to be really very high.

276. LORD THOMSON: Putting the matter more generally, your organisation now covers both the so-called old universities and the new universities and we keep coming up against the difference in structure that you have been mentioning amongst other witnesses. Do you think it would be a good idea for us to be thinking about recommending to government in due course that there should be an amendment or a change in the 1992 Act that would bring the new universities more into line with the old universities in terms of their practice of government?

LORD LIMERICK: Well, that is a red hot question. I think I can only answer it personally and invite my colleagues to disagree. I would say no. I think that one of the features, and one of the most valuable features of the university sector is diversity in the courses it teaches, and in the nature of its intake and its post-graduate population. I see no reason why that diversity should not be reflected in different models of constitution, provided they have sufficient built-in safeguards to ensure the essential things.

You did also ask whether we thought this might lead to legislation. I think my answer to that would be that it should be first given a real try, a good try, over quite a long period to see whether there are any reasons to suspect that is not succeeding. I will leave it there.

277. LORD THOMSON: Yes. Could I ask you one final questions that was linked a little and I ask it to you, Lord Limerick, particularly because of your very wide experience of business world-wide. Universities now are, of course, very important academic institutions but they are in an increasingly competitive world, both nationally and, indeed, internationally. They are going around the world trying to sell themselves in terms of attracting students and I just wondered whether you had any feel as to whether there is a danger in the balance, getting it

wrong, and the search for new students world-wide leading to a reduction in entrance qualifications at one end and perhaps a reduction in exit qualifications at the other end?

LORD LIMERICK: I will give you a quick answer and then again invite additions to it. There is a very strong financial incentive to attract overseas students because the unit of funding that remains with the university is higher. The proportion of overseas students varies colossally from, I suppose, at one end of the scale would be the LSE and Brian Heron mentioned 25 per cent at UMIST. In my case it would be very much lower than that. My experience of the overseas students is that they come extremely well-qualified certainly from Singapore —which is a pool in which everyone is seeking to fish—it is the students who are unable to get into Singapore University, which has extremely high standards, who are applying. They are expected by their families to come back with First Class degrees at least and the expectation of real added value — I have not seen that as a problem.

LORD THOMSON: Thank you.

BRIAN HERON: I have been concerned a little to read some of these later reports about people offering, shall we say, financial incentives to get students recently, which I think will hopefully wash away. But as far as the general question is concerned we only get our students in reality because of the quality of what we provide. We would not get an overseas student unless we were getting it on the basis of our reputation and that reputation certainly is something that we have to refresh regularly, in the Far East in particular. The Governments of all the Far Eastern countries regularly expect to be well-satisfied about the quality of what we are about and are providing for their students, whether they are privately or publicly funded and, of course, since many of those countries are in the throes of establishing universities of their own, with a mixture usually of private and public finance, then generally they are calling, I think, almost uniquely upon English universities to help them with the establishment of those universities and that is entirely because of our reputation, and I think that is absolutely crucial. If we allow our standards to drop—and I do not believe we will do—but if we were to do so then our position overseas would diminish very rapidly and, more importantly, even within the UK I mean, it is relatively well-known those establishments which have good reputations and those where they are not quite so good and, therefore, since generally students do have choice of which university they have, which is something which is very much cherished in the UK, then the voting with the feet is a very important incentive to make sure that we maintain our standards.

LORD THOMSON: Thank you.

LORD LIMERICK: It is very expensive for an overseas student to get an education at a British university, so on the whole it is only the brightest and the best who make that commitment.

LORD THOMSON: Yes, thank you.

LORD NOLAN: Clifford, you were going to ask something?

278. CLIFFORD BOULTON: I have just got one small question. Some witnesses have mentioned the fact

that work on the internal audit is done by the same firm of accountants as does the external audit. Is that something which you would normally not regard as good practice?

LORD LIMERICK: It is the subject of current debate. Some universities, as some companies, as a matter of principle say that the two functions should not be performed by the same firm. Others recognise the benefit, not least in cost, if you have a base knowledge of the institution before you start. I don't think there is anything peculiar to universities in this. I believe that gradually the practice will shift towards having separate firms engaged but so far, at least, we have not sought to be prescriptive on that point.

LORD THOMSON: Thank you.

BRIAN HERON: I am not aware that it is common practice at all. Many universities have their own internal audit consortia, just as many of the NHS Trusts do and I am not aware that it is any more common than it is in commercial practice.

MICHAEL SHATTOCK: I think that is absolutely right, Chairman. Most universities are of the size to have their own internal audit team and I would be surprised to hear of universities nowadays who have got internal and external audit from the same firm. I think the Funding Council would be concerned about that. It is slightly more common, I think, in the further education and, indeed, I have just stopped it in the college that I have become Chairman of the governors of because I do not think it is an appropriate practice.

LORD THOMSON: Thank you very much.

LORD NOLAN: Well, thank you all very much. I am sorry we have run out of time—I think we would have liked to keep you here a lot longer but you have been very helpful indeed in the evidence and advice you have given us. I am most grateful to you for coming.

Now we have Professor Peter Scott, Director of the Centre for Policy Studies in Education at Leeds University. Professor, thank you very much for the opening statement which you sent us. It was very helpful.

I am going to ask Diana Warwick to lead the questions to you.

279. DIANA WARWICK: Thank you very much, Lord Nolan. I wonder if we can begin by asking you to describe the scope of the research project on which you gave us some evidence and, in particular, the reports on changing patterns in governance, which you covered.

PROFESSOR PETER SCOTT

PROF PETER SCOTT (Director of the Centre for Policy Studies in Education, University of Leeds): It is based on two elements really. We carried out a questionnaire survey to all the council and governing body members in 25 universities, and we got a good response—64 per cent—and it was quite a long questionnaire. It asked them about personal details of their own lives and experience, their professional background and so on. It asked them about their views of their role as members of governing bodies, and it also, because this is an interesting group of people whose opinions are rarely asked on this matter, asked them their opinions on a range of higher education policy issues. So

that was the first element, and I think the Committee has a copy of that report.

The second was based on four detailed case studies of universities, two old universities and two new universities. Two happened to be in the north of England and two in the south of England, but I do not think that was essential. There we talked to the chairman of council or the governing body, the vice-chairman, the treasurer usually, also of course the vice-chancellor and the secretary or registrar in their role as the secretary of the governing body. We also talked to a range of other members of the council or governing body, both academic and lay members.

280. DIANA WARWICK: Did you find there was an increased awareness of the issues with which you were dealing?

PROF PETER SCOTT: We were pleasantly surprised by the level of response. It was a 12 or 13-page questionnaire. Given that many of these people have busy other lives, we suspected that we might get a rather poor response. In fact we got a good response: there seemed to be a lot of interest. When we visited universities, again I think people were very eager to talk about these issues and talk more generally about their role. Our impression was that there were very few occasions on which they had that opportunity—to talk in informal terms about their role—and obviously many members of councils and governing bodies are aware that their role has change quite significantly in the last 10 years or so.

281. DIANA WARWICK: You said that what you found in relation to the nature of governing bodies was unsurprising and you go on to say that most of them are male, middle-aged, well educated, think that higher education institutions should be run as businesses, are more likely to vote Conservative. You go on to say, I think, that the ones that are run on collegial lines are more likely to vote Labour or Liberal Democrat.

PROF PETER SCOTT: Yes.

282. DIANA WARWICK: In a way what you are reflecting there are the findings that we were given in relation to quangos—non-departmental public bodies—which we looked at in our last review. Because this is such an important area for all the institutions that we are looking at, do we think that universities should be concerned at the narrowness of background of their governing bodies?

PROF PETER SCOTT: I think they should. I am not saying that they are not. I think they often are. I suspect most universities would like to attract more younger people, certainly more women, people from a wider range of the community, but there are two difficulties. One is that those people are often very busy and have other commitments, and that may explain why you have a preponderance of older people on university councils and governing bodies. The other reason, which I refer to later in my opening statement, is the narrowness of the basis of selection. Because it is essentially an informal process, even when you have a nominations committee, people rack their brains for who they can have as new members of the council or the governing body, and not surprisingly they come up with people rather like themselves.

283. DIANA WARWICK: One of the things that you commented on in talking about the narrowness of the

range, I think in one of your suggested solutions, was opening up advertisement for these posts more broadly, but for many people that might not necessarily resolve the problem, because these posts, across a whole range of institutions but certainly in universities, are unremunerated. Is there an issue here about those people from unrepresented groups having permission, if you like, from employers to serve on such committees? Is there a problem that you have come across?

PROF PETER SCOTT: I do not think we have any direct evidence on that, only by the absence of people who perhaps are in that position, where they would require the permission of their employer, or else might be running small businesses in which it would be very difficult for them to give up the time to spend on governing bodies. I think that is a difficult problem. There is such a variety of practice right across the public sector, whether people get paid or not, that a particular role seems essentially arbitrary in many ways. But it is certainly an issue which university councils and governing bodies should bear in mind, to make sure that certainly their members are adequately compensated for any loss of earnings, expenses and so on. It should not be assumed that these are relatively well-off people who in a sense are doing this as a public service and that the cost is immaterial. If you are looking to attract new kinds of people on to these bodies, clearly cost might be a material consideration for some of them.

284. DIANA WARWICK: If I can move on to the differences between different types of governors, you seem to have found quite a considerable dividing line between the attitudes of lay members and the attitudes of academic members to the business of universities. Is this in reality a problem? Is there a problem also of conflict of interest?

PROF PETER SCOTT: I do not think there is a problem of conflict of interest. I do not think this arises in the case of universities, or would only arise in the most odd circumstances. I suppose it is some cause for concern that there appear to be two constituencies represented on governing bodies, and I think we have shown in our research that they have quite different attitudes to their roles. Some of that I think is inescapable. If you are a lay person and you come from outside, to some extent you are there to exercise your own personal judgment: that is what your role is. If you are elected by the senate or the academic board, even if you are expected to operate as an individual, there is a quasi-representative function, I think, so inevitably there will be differences.

I do not think necessarily that that creates great difficulty, certainly not in old university councils, where in a sense all members are treated equally, regardless of their origins. I think there is more of a problem in new university governing bodies, simply because the independent members are often seen as somehow more central to the decision-making process in the governing body than the other members, who may well be excluded from certain key decisions on the grounds that they are employees of the institution and therefore have a stake in the outcome of those decisions. Generally, I think we did detect, talking, particularly in the new universities, to members of new governing bodies, who in a sense represented academic staff or non-academic staff, that they had a sense of being the opposition really, not sharing in the collective decisions of the governing body, and I would regard that as a weakness. I think it is very

important that everyone in governing bodies should take collective responsibility, but, for that, everyone in a sense has to have a full share in influencing the decisions.

285. DIANA WARWICK: Was that so strong as to lead to actual conflict? Was it sometimes obvious that there were two sides, or is this simply a perception of those who from time to time are excluded?

PROF PETER SCOTT: There was a sense, I think, that the full governing body meeting often was operating to a rather formal agenda and the real decisions had been taken in other committees. Of course that happens in all complex organisations, but there was a sense that, although the meetings of the governing body themselves were transparent, the meetings of some of the committees and the papers that had gone to those committees—policy and resources committees, personnel committees and so on—were not necessarily as open in their procedures, and that created a difficulty, I think. These people felt that they had come along to a meeting where they were expected to take responsibility for decisions, although in practice those decisions had been taken elsewhere.

286. DIANA WARWICK: Taken elsewhere where?

PROF PETER SCOTT: In a committee of some kind of the governing body from which they might have been excluded on the grounds that they were employees of the institution or had an interest. It would often arise, I suppose, in employment issues, where it would be felt that an academic staff member who was a member of the governing body should not be involved in discussions about employment policy, conditions of service—these sort of issues—on the grounds that they had a personal stake in it. I understand that argument, but it leaves the person who is on the receiving end of that argument feeling excluded.

287. DIANA WARWICK: Do you think there continues to be an argument for reserved business or should all business be open and public, or alternatively do you think, if reserved business ought to continue, that there is a case for a better definition of what it should constitute?

PROF PETER SCOTT: I think inevitably there will be reserved business. I think there are two major instances where you have to reserve business. One is where personal cases are being discussed. Discipline might be an example. Promotion might be another example, although I am not so sure about that: I think promotion should perhaps be a more open process. But I can understand that there might be cases where individuals' lives and futures are being discussed when it would be inappropriate for it to be an open matter. Equally, I was listening to Lord Limerick at the end, when he was asked a question by Lord Thomson about the increase in competition between universities. That is a fact of life in universities nowadays, so there will be some matters which I suppose universities will regard as confidential in a commercial sense, that they will affect the university's competitive position. But the point I would make is that all members of the governing body should be trusted to respect those confidences, unless there are very strong contrary arguments or evidence.

288. DIANA WARWICK: You drew a quite interesting distinction, talking about openness and confidentiality, between the old universities and the new

universities. Can you say something about that? Are there general issues that we ought to be aware of which perhaps we should take into account when making recommendations?

PROF PETER SCOTT: There are two points. One, you have to take into account the different position of the old university council as opposed to the new university governing body in relation to other committees in the university. In an old university effectively the council, although the superior body constitutionally, in practice operates in a very co-equal way with the senate. In the case of the new universities, the academic board is clearly a subordinate body and it has quite restricted territory. Most academic boards of new universities will, as is right, have the first say on academic questions, but academic questions are quite tightly defined. Senates in old universities range pretty widely and see themselves as policy-making bodies. They would see almost any policy decision as having some impact on academic matters, and therefore they would have a right to be heard on it. So I think that is an important difference to bear in mind.

The other difference, which struck us very forcefully, is that the lay members on old university councils operate within a kind of environment of accountability. There are no strict ties of accountability, but they are very clear that they are to represent the community, the university has been there a long time, they have an understanding of the relationship between the university, the community and local business and so on. In the case of new universities, these are very fresh relationships, so there is no environment in which these informal ties of accountability, if I can put it like that, can develop. I think that anything that can be done to encourage the informal ties of accountability—I think those are the ones you have to rely on, rather than formal reporting back; I do not think that would be appropriate in these circumstances—should be done. That is why I think it would be sensible to advertise vacancies on governing bodies, not because I am naive and imagine that many people would necessarily come via that route. If I can give an analogy, when a university appoints a new vice-chancellor, it is probably not expecting to discover through public advertisement people it does not know about already. On the other hand, it is extremely important that a public institution should make a public declaration of such a vacancy, and I think the same might apply to governing bodies. It would also spread the word in the local community that there is a university, it has a governing body, it has people from the local community and the business community represented on it. I think that would encourage a better relationship with the governing body. A strong impression we had was that many of the independent members of new universities' governing bodies themselves felt they were operating in a bit of a vacuum: they were not quite clear who they were, in a sense, representing, and that can create difficulties at a personal level.

289. DIANA WARWICK: Do you think there is an argument for recommending a greater degree of uniformity between institutions? Perhaps I should ask you which way you would lean if you were to do that.

PROF PETER SCOTT: I think that is difficult. As I said in my opening statement, although there are important differences between the two types of university governing body, there is a degree of convergence, largely, I suspect, because the new universities are now universities and in a sense their governing bodies are now

perhaps behaving in a rather different way than when they were polytechnics. It is difficult to establish a national model, and I would be very against that. There is a high degree of diversity in the arrangements that old universities already make. Just to look at a simple matter, the number of people on the university council varies quite widely. There is a tendency to reduce the number of people on the university council to make it a more effective body. I think the kind of code that was being talked about in the previous session is very important, because that encourages people to ask the same kind of questions and think of themselves as operating in the same environment, but I would be against anything that went beyond that and in a formal way said what the constitution of a university council or governing body should be.

290. DIANA WARWICK: We have had various cases, not many of them, brought to our attention, notably Huddersfield, Portsmouth, Swansea, Cardiff, Derby; Derby is further education. Looking at the whole question of governance, from your knowledge of those situations, are there common themes which need to be addressed or do you think that, even though it is a small number of institutions, there are areas that should be cause for greater concern?

PROF PETER SCOTT: Not great concern. There are two points I would like to make. First of all, members, particularly lay members, of governing bodies are inevitably very dependent on the senior management of the institution for their information, so if the senior management are going wrong in some way, it may simply be that the governing body members are almost less well informed than other people in the institution, and that is a difficulty. So I think that anything that encourages greater transparency there is in a sense likely to discourage these kinds of incidents.

The second point I would like to make is that in the case of universities—it may be different in further education colleges, because of their lack of experience—one can rely very heavily on the integrity of the administrators who service these bodies to make sure that improper things do not happen, and I would regard that as a guarantee of high standards.

291. DIANA WARWICK: Perhaps I could ask one final question. With each of our witnesses we have raised the increased competitiveness and increased financial pressures on institutions which, certainly in some quite well-publicised cases, seem to have produced pressure or to influence universities perhaps to pack in numbers at the expense of quality. Is that something that came up in your investigations? Was that an area of concern that was raised?

PROF PETER SCOTT: We asked members of councils and governing bodies what their opinion was on the expansion of higher education, and the majority view was that they favoured a period of consolidation, which is in a sense what we now have in higher education. So I think there was concern that perhaps expansion had been too rapid. On the other hand, there was strong dissent from the view that standards had declined in any way. My sense is that that is not an issue that is discussed very often at the level of university councils or governing bodies. If there is a problem there, it is somewhere else in the institution; it is a matter that senates, academic boards or even departments should address rather than councils or governing bodies.

DIANA WARWICK: Thank you.

292. LORD THOMSON: I was, like others, fascinated by the research, particularly into the nature of the new governing bodies of the new universities. Can I begin with a very ignorant question? The new universities are very new. Where did the initial appointment of governors to them come from? How was it done?

PROF PETER SCOTT: That was formally made by the Secretary of State. I think that when the polytechnics were removed from local education authority control, formation committees were established, made up sometimes of members of the previous governing body, but also with new members added. In most cases the members of those formation committees actually became the new members of the governing body. But those appointments were technically made by the Secretary of State, which of course is a very important difference. There were no such appointments in the old universities.

293. LORD THOMSON: So they were made from the centre in effect?

PROF PETER SCOTT: That was the formal process. In practice, I suspect that the director of the polytechnic probably indicated which previous members of a governing body had turned up on time and been generally supportive and so on, and suggested that those people should be put on the formation committee. So the effective choices as opposed to the formal choices were in nearly every case made by the institutions themselves.

294. LORD THOMSON: We are of course as a committee a totally non-political body, although some of us are perhaps a little more non-political than others. We are not here to question decisions taken by government and by Parliament, but within these decisions we want to look at whether good governance requires any changes. It just occurred to me from your fascinating analysis of the declared political loyalties of people involved in these new governing bodies that there is a considerable dichotomy between the internal and the external members of the governing body. Would I be right in believing that the external members of the governing body are more Conservative in general character than would be true in the old universities?

PROF PETER SCOTT: Yes, there is more of a contrast in the case of new universities than there is in the case of old universities, and the contrast is at both ends. The lay members of new university governing bodies are more likely to be Conservative than the lay members of old university councils. Equally, the internal members of new university governing bodies are more likely to be Labour or Liberal Democrat, while there are still some Conservatives left among academics in old universities.

295. LORD THOMSON: You have experience of both old and new universities, because previously, as an editor, you had a wide-ranging experience of these things. Do you feel that inevitably in the new universities on the external side there is a degree of what one might call ideology? It was the transfer of an institution from having, very often with a strong element of local authority control, some kind of democratic legitimacy to an appointed body centrally funded. Is that so or is it all settling down in the rather pragmatic way that British people tend to in due course in these matters?

PROF PETER SCOTT: I think it is largely settling down, although what you say is true, that when the polytechnics were moved from local education authority control there was a sense that it was the job of the new governing body to change the culture of the institution. I do not think anyone on an old university council thinks it is their job to change the culture of the university, so there is that important difference. Another point is that it creates difficulties if there is a perception that the governing body has in a sense been packed with people from a particular side of the political spectrum, even if those individuals themselves operate in an entirely honourable way—I do not think there is any evidence that they do not—or if there are issues which in a sense are non political issues, where it would not really matter a great deal what your political views were. So I think the issue is more of public perception, as it might well be of magistrates. One would not expect the voting habits of magistrates exactly to mirror the voting patterns of the population as a whole, but if it was too much different, one might think that was a matter of public concern, particularly because it might undermine the authority of magistrates, and the same might happen in this case: it might undermine the legitimacy of the governing body if it was seen to have that biased nature.

296. LORD THOMSON: I was struck by your vivid and fascinating description of the mood inside some governing bodies, and that academic members have been marginalised, partly because the disputatious values of the academics are difficult to reconcile with the executive ethos of governing bodies. Is that a fairly wide description, do you think?

PROF PETER SCOTT: I think that is largely true. Some of the lay members of governing bodies, particularly those who come from business, are not used to the rather discursive ways of academics maybe, who want to debate things at length and exhaustively and in terms of principles rather than necessarily in terms of action, so I think there is a difference there, but in a sense these differences add to the variety of the discussion.

297. LORD THOMSON: Certainly. I wanted to ask you about that in my final question, but would that be different, if you were giving a comparable description of the older universities, even the more recent of the older universities? Is it different?

PROF PETER SCOTT: I think it would largely be true. It would be very difficult to generalise. There might well be a lay member who came from a background which valued that way of talking and thinking and arguing. Equally, there may well be academics who are extremely short and crisp and wish to get to the decisions quickly, so it is difficult to generalise, and I do not see that as a great problem.

298. LORD THOMSON: But I asked you the same question as you may have heard me ask Lord Limerick. Given the description that you have produced in this very interesting research study, would you feel that there was a case for trying positively to create a greater degree of uniformity in the governing bodies of universities, bringing the new universities more into line with the old universities, or is the better thing to say "First of all let there be a period of settling down, but in any case diversity and variety are better than seeking uniformity"? What is your view on that?

PROF PETER SCOTT: I think I would agree with what I understood Lord Limerick to say, which was that you should see it essentially as an organic process. I think there is evidence that there is convergence. I think that recent foundations as universities are already being substantially influenced by practice in the old universities. Equally, the reverse is taking place. I think there are many old universities who feel they should be a bit more business-like in their councils than perhaps they were in the past. As long as there are exchanges of views among not just the chairmen of governing bodies but also perhaps among individual members of governing bodies—that is a problem of course: it is very easy for the chairmen of governing bodies to get together; it is more difficult for the ordinary members of governing bodies to get together—so that they are operating much more on the same wavelength, that would be helpful, but I do not think that to have a fixed constitution, designed in Whitehall, would be a very desirable process.

LORD THOMSON: Thank you very much, very helpful.

299. LORD NOLAN: May I just ask one question. Do student members of governing bodies play an important part, in your experience, in their deliberations?

PROF PETER SCOTT: We talked to some students, although we did not concentrate on that. I have to say that our research concentrated much more on the external members of governing bodies. I personally was not involved in this, but one of my colleagues sat in on several governing body meetings—a fly on the wall, so to speak—and on those occasions the student representative made a very important contribution and was listened to with great attention, maybe because it is feared the student has more power or leverage to cause trouble if they are not listened to. But I think everyone we talked to felt that students made a very important contribution to governing body deliberations. In a sense the students did not feel excluded. I think it was the representatives of the academic staff, and the non-academic staff, who felt excluded more than the students. The students felt very much part of it, I think.

LORD NOLAN: I was thinking of the students particularly, because one imagines they produce rather greater variety in terms of age, gender and even ethnicity.

PROF PETER SCOTT: Certainly if you look at the age distribution, you can be sure that most of those in their 20's on governing bodies are the student members not the independent members from outside.

300. LORD NOLAN: My tutor always says that students nowadays are so much better behaved than we were, but they are not too well behaved, are they?

PROF PETER SCOTT: I think they are quite well behaved, yes.

301. LORD NOLAN: We are encroaching on Sir Peter Swinnerton-Dyer's time, but I wonder whether there are any questions that anyone else wishes to ask. No. Well, thank you very much indeed for the time you have given us. It has been very helpful and very interesting.

Sir Peter, good afternoon to you. You are presently the executive director of the Isaac Newton Institute for Mathematical Sciences at Cambridge.

SIR PETER SWINNERTON-DYER

SIR PETER SWINNERTON-DYER (Executive Director, Isaac Newton Institute for Mathematical Sciences, Cambridge): That is right.

LORD NOLAN: We are very grateful to you for coming along to us and bringing us the benefit of your very considerable and varied experience. In particular, you have been chief executive of the two funding bodies that were the precursors of the Higher Education Funding Council, I think.

PETER SWINNERTON-DYER: Yes.

LORD NOLAN: So you have seen some very substantial developments in that area. In a democratic way we take it in turns to take the lead in asking questions, and it is Sir William Utting's turn, so I shall ask him please to lead on.

302. WILLIAM UTTING: Sir Peter, thank you for your paper, which was a pleasure to read, if I may say so. The Chairman has referred to your previous experience with the predecessor funding councils, and in your paper you refer, I think, to a difference of ethos between them and the current Funding Council. I wonder if you would like to elaborate on that and perhaps suggest why this change has occurred.

PETER SWINNERTON-DYER: The University Grants Committee was in effect forced into becoming increasingly interventionist, partly because successive Secretaries of State under governments of both parties saw a real need to reform the university system and saw the University Grants Committee as the natural body to encourage such reforms and partly, I think, because the last few chairmen themselves saw that, unless the system reformed itself more rapidly than the natural pace of academic life would lead it to, it would be reformed from outside at the hectic pace of political life. So becoming interventionist and reformist could in some sense be seen as a defensive reaction on the part of the chairmen of the UGC.

When the UFC was set up, after a long and difficult search its first chairman was Lord Chilver. Lord Chilver sincerely believed in the abolition of all government and in particular passionately believed that the UFC should be a wholly non-interventionist body; and when you have a dispute between a tradition of non-interventionism and a tradition of interventionism, non-interventionism always wins, because it is far easier to stop things happening than to make things happen. Lord Chilver's ethos has in that respect, I think, continued into the Funding Council under my successor, both into the UFC and the HEFCE. Whether it will much longer continue, I am distinctly sceptical.

303. WILLIAM UTTING: Yes. I have heard the HEFCE define its role with considerable tact in relation to autonomous universities, while at the same time appearing to exercise considerable influence over the way they behave.

PETER SWINNERTON-DYER: That is true, and I think it will be more true with Brian Fender, because his instincts I believe to be interventionist, than it was true with Graeme Davies.

304. WILLIAM UTTING: Good. Could I move on to a more general point about the governing structures of

universities? I think you take the view that the governing structure for the older universities is to be preferred to that which has been devised for newer universities and that the size of governing bodies is not in itself an impediment to efficiency. If that is so, why was that system not devised for the new universities? Why was something completely new brought about?

PETER SWINNERTON-DYER: I think the only person from whom you could get a reliable answer would be Kenneth Baker, who was the Secretary of State and who to a large extent devised that system himself. I am not aware that he took much in the way of academic advice, though undoubtedly he took a little advice. It has to be remembered that he is among those Conservative Ministers who distrusted experts and who believed that anything run by businessmen would be wisely and efficiently run.

305. WILLIAM UTTING: That leads on to a point about the constitution of the new governing bodies that rather bothered me as a lay outsider, and that is the stipulation that a majority of the board must be independent members, namely "people who have experience in and have shown capacity in industrial, commercial or employment matters or a profession and are not members of staff or students, or elected members of local authorities". That seems to me to be a curious definition of "independent" in the first place, but that definition also seems to make it difficult for quite a wide range of people who might have something to contribute to university government actually to be involved in it.

PETER SWINNERTON-DYER: Yes. I think it is right that councils should have a majority of external as opposed to internal members, and I would count the local authority nominees as among the external members. How narrowly the external members of the council are chosen depends on how seriously the phrase you quoted is taken, and such phrases are only intermittently taken seriously. I doubt if it would be seen as a real constraint on appointing any outsider whom the council actually wished to co-opt.

306. WILLIAM UTTING: We have heard from other people that the majority of people on these governing bodies are chaps of my sort of age from a business or professional background, that there are not all that many women and that members of black and ethnic minorities or disabled people are not likely to figure on them either. Do you think there is a case for a broader representation of members of the community than this article appears to allow?

PETER SWINNERTON-DYER: I think there is a case and, as you will see from my written evidence, I think that the old universities are much better placed than the new universities in this respect. Because people of your age are by and large retired and therefore, with luck, have more time available, they are more likely to be willing to serve on council and to give to council the very considerable amount of time and effort which some members of council do have to give. So I think it will be difficult to get younger members of council to any significant extent. Nor do I think that what council does requires it necessarily to have a pro rata distribution of disabled people or to have a balanced age distribution. More women would be highly desirable, but the natural way to pick new council members is to find people who can be seen to have significant management experience. It

is worth saying that, with the older universities, where something like half the external members are by appointment by a diversity of bodies, there seems to be no higher a proportion of women than with the new universities—again, in both cases, too low.

307. WILLIAM UTTING: Yes. You seem to think that outside bodies make better appointments, frankly, than the Secretary of State does in this sector, although I think you exclude some Labour-dominated local authorities from that comment. Is this because you dislike the kind of keen, ideological edge that might appear as a result of those appointments?

PETER SWINNERTON-DYER: I do dislike the keen, ideological edge. As must be clear from an earlier response, I do not believe that businessmen have the monopoly of all wisdom, nor indeed that they can be relied on always to have wisdom at all. It is not so much that other bodies will do a better job than the Secretary of State but that a diversity of bodies will produce a more balanced collection of appointments than a single appointing person would.

308. WILLIAM UTTING: Some people have said to us that the idea of academic freedom has been imperilled by these recent changes, that the balance that existed between academic interests, the governing body and the executive of universities has really been shifted, so that the academic community is much less influential than it was. Do you think that academic freedom is seriously under threat now in universities?

PETER SWINNERTON-DYER: No, I do not think it is under threat at all. Academic freedom is one of those motherhood phrases which is imported into arguments where it actually has no relevant place whatever. The balance of decision making on keeping the university solvent, to put it bluntly, has shifted away from the average academic towards the Vice-Chancellor and his immediate colleagues and council. I think that was necessary, but I do not believe that that has anything to do with academic freedom properly so called. Academic freedom is not the right to be supplied with as much money as you think you need for your purposes.

WILLIAM UTTING: The new regulations leave the management of academic issues, it seems to me, firmly to academics.

PETER SWINNERTON-DYER: Yes.

309. WILLIAM UTTING: And you see that as operating in practice still?

PETER SWINNERTON-DYER: It operates in practice so far as purely academic issues are concerned, but suppose you are a university in serious financial trouble and the department of whatnotery turns out to have a remarkably high proportion of staff to students and a not very distinguished research record. Academics, being kindly persons, will say "Well, it's bound to get better in due course. We must leave it another 20 years and give it a fair chance." The more ruthless members of council will say "If we adopt that sort of policy, the university won't be here in 20 years. We must close it down as fast as is reasonably possible." That is a mixed academic and financial issue, and I think the evidence now is that councils with some academic advice do a better job on it than senates would.

310. WILLIAM UTTING: We are told that universities are now operating in a much more competitive market than they did and that this may be contributing to driving down university standards, in that they are more likely to admit people who will not do well and find it easier to give degrees to people who should not have them. Is that just propaganda or is there anything in that?

PETER SWINNERTON-DYER: I think that is just propaganda. Universities are being more competitive in some matters. There is a serious admissions problem in the not very popular subjects which government would like to encourage, which very roughly speaking means the mathematics-based subjects, notably engineering. Since there are not enough students to go round and you are financially penalised if you do not recruit enough, universities are advertising and competing fairly intensively to get students. But they are not very keen on getting students whom it will be totally unrewarding to teach. In contrast, in the popular subjects, universities may compete, but they are not going to spend money on competing. I do not think there is a serious problem of lowering standards at the undergraduate level. I am, as I said in my written evidence, somewhat concerned about some masters' courses, more in some institutions than others, because universities may stand to make a very tidy profit from recruiting overseas students to them.

311. WILLIAM UTTING: May I conclude with a point about what we are interested in. We have been very much directed towards accounting for the expenditure of public money and we have also spent time on the appointment of people to managing boards. Are there other non-financial areas in higher education that we should be looking at, and do you have any specific recommendations that you might put to us about how propriety generally might be improved in higher education?

PETER SWINNERTON-DYER: I do not think there are other issues you should necessarily look at, though you may wish to look at all the issues of assessment of standards, particularly in teaching, where the policy at the moment is more well-meaning than value for money. I do not think there is very much in the way of impropriety on a significant scale in universities. I have no illusions about the morals of the average academic, but the scope for significant impropriety is extremely small. That is also true of members of council, even if they have relevant outside interests, for example in building: it is almost impossible for them to misuse their position. All that sort of thing is looked at by the National Audit Office, which reviews the whole financial management of any university at regular intervals. There has been, apart from the embarrassment over golden handshakes, singularly little in the way of misconduct, even in universities that have been financially severely mismanaged. There was a period when universities got into real trouble through optimism, and I think it appears to be still true of some of the new universities, though probably no longer of the old ones, who have learnt from bitter experience. But with infinite respect to your Committee, curing optimism may be beyond your skills.

WILLIAM UTTING: Thank you, Sir Peter.

312. LORD NOLAN: Sir Peter, I only have one question to ask, and it arises out of what you have just been saying. It has been drawn to our attention that the membership of the Higher Education Funding Council can and indeed does include vice-chancellors of particular universities. Is that a matter that has caused any concern, anxiety or jealousy amongst other vice-chancellors, or is it regarded as a thoroughly good thing to inform the council better about what goes on?

PETER SWINNERTON-DYER: It has certainly caused concern. Most of the members of the University Grants Committee were academics and there was an absolute rule that no vice-chancellor or equivalent should ever be a member. Those academics rigorously did not favour their own institutions, though inevitably they sometimes exaggerated the importance of their own subjects. The problem when the new universities came under the Funding Council, was that they have a far more hierarchical structure, and if they were to be represented at all, it would have to be by their vice-chancellors. There are, in any case, far fewer academics on the HEFCE than there were on the UGC, so you cannot have a reasonable subject coverage. In those circumstances a small number of vice-chancellors seemed probably the only thing to do, though I regard the whole set-up as less satisfactory than the set-up was with the UGC.

313. LORD NOLAN: Thank you very much. Because of the fear, however ill-founded, of a conflict of interest?

PETER SWINNERTON-DYER: Because of the possibility of the conflict of interest, the suspicion that it happens, whether or not it actually has; and I think there is much more suspicion than reality there.

LORD NOLAN: The look of the thing?

PETER SWINNERTON-DYER: Yes, and incidentally the fact that the small academic representation has made the position of the chief executive actually very much more powerful than the position of the chairman of the UGC was, because to such an extent he is the only person who understands what is going on.

LORD NOLAN: Thank you very much, Sir Peter. I am now going to ask Sir Clifford Boulton if he would like to take up the questioning.

314. CLIFFORD BOULTON: Sir Peter, you said in your paper: "None of what follows applies to Oxford or Cambridge, whose systems of governance are so different from those other universities that they must either be put aside or made the subject of a separate inquiry." Which of those courses would you suggest to us that we take?

PETER SWINNERTON-DYER: I would suggest to you that they should be put aside. I do not think there is any reason to suppose weakness of standards or financial impropriety, and you have the ex-head of one Cambridge college who may be able to confirm that statement, not merely in respect of her own college but in respect of others as well. Though I believe that Oxford and Cambridge need significant constitutional reform and on a brisker time scale than they would themselves adopt, I do not believe that your Committee is the right body to tackle it and I think it would be an act of unreasonable courage for you to do so.

315. CLIFFORD BOULTON: Thank you very much for that encouragement. Obviously the other side of that particular coin is what you were talking about a moment

ago, which is the look of the thing. If we make pious recommendations about everybody except Oxford and Cambridge, and perhaps maybe London, there may be some who would say that we had run away from it.

PETER SWINNERTON-DYER: Yes. If you say explicitly that you have not tackled Oxford and Cambridge because their constitutional structure is so different and also so complicated, that I think makes it clear that the scope is still for other bodies to do so. Oxford and Cambridge in the past have only been reformed by means of Acts of Parliament, preceded by Royal Commissions specific to those two universities.

316. CLIFFORD BOULTON: Yes. Can I just return to the point of anxiety that you have about the possible devaluation of some further study courses—masters, you referred to—because they score so many points when it comes to university funding? You also say further on in your paper: "The danger is that examination results may be used by outside bodies as a performance indicator and that the grant to a university may be affected by the proportion of good degrees that it awards. This would be a clear incitement to debase the standard of degrees." If we feel that there is need to be concerned about this incentive to award more degrees or at higher level, would you see the oversight of any dangers that were beginning to build up as a matter for the Funding Council or a matter for the Committee of Chairmen, because there has been a little bit of pass the parcel, I think, between these two bodies so far as oversight is concerned?

PETER SWINNERTON-DYER: Yes. I do not have any fully satisfactory solution in respect of masters' degrees. I think it is too specialised a topic for the Funding Council to tackle and I do not see any other body well equipped to tackle it.

On the general question of undergraduate standards, examiners are kindly people and always have been, and that will prevent the standards being jacked up too high. In contrast, people like to keep the standards of firsts high, because most academics have themselves got firsts and wish that to be a notable achievement. What worries me is if universities are given a substantial financial incentive to debase their standards. Performance indicators have been used quite often as if academics were rats in an experimental psychology laboratory and did not know what judgments were being made of their performances, so that their performances were not affected by the judgments, but of course that is false: it is impossible to keep performance indicators secret, they are imperfect indicators of what you actually want to achieve and the temptation for anybody in any walk of life to improve his score on a performance indicator without necessarily having to do a better job must be nearly irresistible.

317. CLIFFORD BOULTON: So you think there may be room for almost a further body to reassure the Funding Council about these standards, because it is too specialised a task for the Funding Council itself.

PETER SWINNERTON-DYER: I think if the government adopted performance indicators which encouraged the university system to debase the standard of degrees, there is no machinery by which that event could be prevented, and I think what is needed is for those who determine what performance indicators are used, which is primarily civil servants in the relevant bodies, to

realise the situation and exercise more restraint and more common sense than they have been accustomed to.

CLIFFORD BOULTON: Thank you very much.

318. ANNE WARBURTON: I think Sir Peter made my declaration of interest for me, at least in part. I have just two questions. One of them I think is quite a short one. I was struck in your paper, Sir Peter, by your gloom, I would almost say, about the difficulty of having a systematic review of university management, but just now you spoke of the NAO as being active in that field. Does that mean that we as a Committee can rely on the NAO to check the accountability of management?

PETER SWINNERTON-DYER: I think you can rely on the NAO to catch most financial impropriety and a good deal of financial incompetence. You cannot, I think, necessarily rely on it to comment on constitutional structures of great clumsiness. There is a tendency in academic life to assume that the time spent on committees does not have to be costed and that it is right to set up machinery of unexampled thoroughness to consider any question, however long it may take.

ANNE WARBURTON: I think I will leave it there.

PETER SWINNERTON-DYER: You and Diana Warwick will I think be aware at first hand of that truth.

319. ANNE WARBURTON: Could I then ask my other question, which is one that we tend to put to witnesses, and that is summed up by saying: how can we help in the study of higher education and in improvement here and there, bearing in mind perhaps particularly the comment which we had last week from Sir Geoffrey Holland that we should beware of the search for uniformity?

PETER SWINNERTON-DYER: Yes, I would fully agree with that. Sir Geoffrey Holland is perhaps, of all the Vice-Chancellors, the one whose comments would be most useful to this Committee. I am sure you should beware of the search for uniformity. Increased uniformity is not, I think, a very grave risk. The natural inertia of the system and the natural eccentricity of individual governing bodies ought to be an adequate preventative of that.

320. ANNE WARBURTON: Then is there anything we can do to help the system, to help in accountability, in operation, in effectiveness?

PETER SWINNERTON-DYER: I think comments on the structure of council would be useful. I believe, as I have said, that courts, which only the older universities have, serve a valuable purpose, though it cannot be said to be as part of the government system. Beyond that, a statement that all the evidence available to you suggests that financial impropriety is not a serious issue, assuming you come to that conclusion, would be valuable, and particularly if you can tackle the rather peculiar and embarrassing problem of golden handshakes to vice-chancellors who have had to be got rid of.

If you felt you could assess the value of teaching assessment as against the cost of it, that would also be valuable to the university system. An enormous amount of wasted effort goes into preparing for the teaching assessments, not least because it is the sort of thing into which academics put far more effort than is actually sensible or productive. But I do not think the higher education system should really be high among the targets for a committee with your particular title and terms of reference.

321. DIANA WARWICK: I just had one question. It occurred to me that the problem with which you were particularly concerned was the problem at Swansea, and that was not a question of financial impropriety; it was a question about academic judgments and academic standards and the way in which limitations in them could be exposed. Would you say there were any general lessons for universities in that particular instance, or was it very much, in your view, from your knowledge of universities, a one-off?

PETER SWINNERTON-DYER: I think it was a one-off, as was the far more serious problem at Cardiff. If a university simultaneously has a wildly optimistic and charismatic vice-chancellor and a council whose senior members are senile and in some cases seriously ill, catastrophe is almost inevitable, but it is a very rare concatenation of circumstances.

322. LORD NOLAN: I would, for my part, describe your evidence as generally reassuring. Would that be putting it too high, Sir Peter?

PETER SWINNERTON-DYER: No, I think I intended it to be generally reassuring.

LORD NOLAN: One of the most difficult things we sometimes have to do is to try and reassure the public that some things are all right, but we are thought thereby to be white-washing, and we shall bear in mind with great gratitude what you have told us this morning.

PETER SWINNERTON-DYER: Well, I wish you luck. Thank you.

TUESDAY 22 NOVEMBER 1995

OPENING STATEMENTS

Opening statement from Higher Education Funding Council for England

I welcome this opportunity to give evidence to the Committee on standards in higher education. Since October I have been Chief Executive to the Higher Education Funding Council for England. Before that, I was Vice-Chancellor of Keele University. Altogether, I have been a member of governing bodies of three higher education institutions. I also have experience on the governing bodies of other private and public bodies.

As our written memorandum explains, the HEFCE's primary responsibility is to provide public funds to higher education institutions. Our concern is to promote high quality education and research, and to ensure that the funds we provide are used both effectively and with proper regard to the public interest.

We do not—and, I consider, should not—directly supervise in too detailed a way the conduct of business in universities and colleges. They are independent bodies, many of them with significant income from private sources. They are now subject to external scrutiny on a scale much greater than 10 or 15 years ago. I would need very good reason for imposing even more controls on them.

We are, however, prepared to intervene where we have reason to believe that failures of governance or of management are putting public funds at risk. We also promote good practice in standards of governance as in other areas. Our memorandum indicates ways in which we have been involved.

Overall my judgment is that the standards of governance and propriety in higher education are sound. The occasional failure, notably at Huddersfield last year, should not detract from this general conclusion. I do not consider we have grounds for greater formal intervention, and certainly not for imposing a uniform system of governance. The constitutions—and the practices—in institutions vary quite widely but they can and are working to secure high standards.

There is always room for improvement. We will continue to monitor the impact of the guide for members of governing bodies issued by the Committee of University Chairmen, and to encourage improvements on it in the light of experience.

Opening statement by Professor Peter Scott

In this statement I will cover three subjects: (i) the research evidence on which my observations are based, (ii) the main findings of that research and (iii) observations on two of the three issues identified by the committee, namely the appointment and accountability of board members and the role of boards in relation to the officers and staff. On the third issue, safeguards in respect of conflicts of interest, our research had little direct bearing.

1. Research evidence

In collaboration with two colleagues, Catherine Bargh and David Smith, I have recently completed research into the governance of higher education institutions. The field work was undertaken in 1994. Our first report has been made available to the committee and a second report is about to be published. We are also writing a book on the subject, which will appear next year. The research had two components:

(i)   A questionnaire sent to all the council/governing body members in 10 "old" and 14 "new" universities and four colleges of higher education. They were asked: (a) to provide biographical information (age, gender, occupation, experience of higher education, professional qualifications, voting intentions, membership of other public bodies, etc.); (b) to answer questions about their perceptions of the role of council/governing body members; and (c) to indicate their views on a range of current issues in higher education policy. Of the 745 questionnaires despatched, 494 usable replies were received, a response rate of 66 per cent.

(ii)   Four universities were chosen as detailed case-studies, two "old" and two "new" with one of each being in the north and the other the south of England. The chairman and other senior officers were interviewed, along with the Vice-Chancellor and secretary/registrar. In addition, interviews were conducted with a range of other council/governing body members. The following broad topics were covered: (a) appointment procedures and selection criteria; (b) the relationship between "core" and "peripheral" members; (c) roles of the council/ governing bodies; and (d) key relationships (for example, between chairmen and vice-chancellors).

2. The main findings

The main findings of the questionnaire survey have already been made available to the Committee in the form of the executive summary of our first report. These we found unsurprising. Most members are male, middle-aged and well educated. They are likely to be members also of other public bodies. Lay, or "independent", members prefer small councils/governing bodies, believe higher education institutions should be run as businesses and are more likely to vote Conservative, while internal members prefer somewhat larger bodies, believe institutions should be run on collegial lines and are more likely to vote Labour or Liberal Democrat. The differences are more marked in the "new" universities and colleges of higher education than the "old" universities.

The findings that have emerged from the case-studies are more difficult to summarise. On the one hand they highlight the persistence of difference cultures of governance. In the "old" universities council members tend to see themselves as trustees and their policy-making functions are shared with senates which, in practical although not constitutional terms, are co-equal bodies. As a result they operate in a comparatively open manner. In the "new" universities governing bodies are more likely to see it as their job to "change the culture" by encouraging their institutions to behave in a more entrepreneurial manner, and academic boards are subordinate bodies with restricted powers. Consequently they tend to place a greater emphasis on confidentiality.

On the other hand, our research found evidence that the two cultures of governance are converging. In "old" universities (lay) council members are less content to adopt an essentially passive role, particularly in external and financial affairs where they feel they have an important contribution to offer. There is renewed interest in involving the council more actively in strategic, and budgetary, planning. In the "new" universities, in contrast, there now appears to be less desire to emphasise the dichotomy between "business" and "academic" cultures, (particularly, perhaps, since the bestowal of university titles). To simplify, "old" university councils appear to be becoming more "efficient" and "new" university governing bodies more "dignified".

However, our provisional conclusion is that more weight should still be attached to the differences, rather than the degree of the convergence, between the two cultures of governance in higher education.

3. Issues raised by the Committee

(i) The appointment and accountability of board members

In two of the case-study universities (one "old" and one "new", both in the north) nominations committees had been established in order to identify potential new members on the pattern recommended by the Cadbury committee. In the other two more informal methods were employed—in practice, discussions between the Vice-Chancellor (and other senior academic colleagues) and the university's lay officers with the registrar/secretary acting as go-between. However, we found that the establishment of a nominations committee made less difference than might be supposed. Although the existence of a nominations committee is likely to encourage selection criteria to be made more explicit, in practice they appear to differ little from the rule-of-thumb criteria applied in the past. Also, although the proceedings of the nominations committee are formally noted, their proceedings remain confidential. Either way the processes of appointment are remarkably similar. Forthcoming vacancies are not advertised: instead reliance is placed on informal networks of contacts and acquaintances among existing members.

The closed, even incestuous, nature of the appointment process has important implications for accountability. Although all the council/governing body members we interviewed had a deep commitment to the well-being of their institutions, there were important differences between lay, or "independent", members on the one hand and internal members on the other. Our survey found that the former tended to define their right to be a council/governing body member in terms of heir own skills and experience, while the latter were more likely to see themselves as representatives or even delegates. There are arguments for both stances. Lay, or "independent", members are able both to exercise their individual judgment and to accept collective responsibility for the council's/governing body's decisions more easily than internal members who are beholden to their constituencies—but they inhabit an accountability vacuum which may deny them a proper context in which to exercise judgment and accept responsibility. Internal members, in contrast, may be inhibited from making up their own minds without undue reference to their constituents or accept collective responsibility for decisions of which those constituents disapprove; on the other hand, they are accountable for their actions.

The constitution of "old" university councils, perhaps serendipitously, embodies a balance between three principles of independence and accountability, ensuring that neither will predominate. In the "new" universities "independent" governors enjoy a substantial majority over other governors who, in addition, are generally excluded from key decision-making arenas. It can be argued therefore that the balance has been upset. It can also be argued that lay members of "old" university councils tend to be accountable to the constituencies from which they are drawn, directly so in the case of local authority nominees (although their calibre, and consequently effectiveness, have been questioned) and obliquely so in those who "represent" community, professional and commercial interests. In the "new" universities few of these informal ties of accountability appear to be felt, although this may simply reflect the absence of accumulated tradition.

(ii) The role of boards in relation to officers and staff

The questionnaire survey found that the majority of council/governing body members—in both "old" and "new" universities—felt their most important roles were strategic planning, followed by audit. The latter function is seen as a traditional responsibility; the former perhaps a more novel one. The case-studies throw an interesting light on the capacity of councils/governing bodies to become engaged in strategic planning. Our evidence suggests that, despite their desire to do so, the full council, or governing body, essentially reacts to proposals put to it by senior managers, the Vice-Chancellor and his/her colleagues. (In the "old" universities these proposals will first have been debated and approved by the senate.) Councils and governing bodies may (or may not) dispose, but they only rarely propose. They have only a limited capability to take their own strategic initiatives—generally only when the normal working of the institution has broken down.

There is a difference of emphasis between "old" and "new" universities in this respect. In the former lay members of council appear to be very reluctant to become involved in issues that are in any way academic; these are seen as the prerogative of the senate. In the latter "independent" members of governing bodies seem to be impatient with such constraints. They may emphasise the need to develop measures of institution performance that embrace academic as well as other indicators of "success".

Our research suggests that the key relationship is between the chairman of council or governing body and the Vice-Chancellor, occasionally mediated through the registrar/secretary. As a result two important issues are raised:

—First, all three principal actors must juggle ambiguous roles. The chairman's authority is not simply individual but derived from his/her ability to represent the collective voice of the council/governing body. The Vice-Chancellor is not only the chief executive officer of his/her university, and so subject ultimately to the authority of the council/governing body; he/she is also the accounting officer to the funding council and other providers of public funds, and so is directly accountable to them. The registrar/secretary is not only the head of the university administration and so a key member of the senior management team, but in most cases he/she is also the secretary of the council/clerk to the governing body and, as such, is their servant.

—Second, this relationship is essentially informal. Not only does it depend on personal trust (which, once undermined, can lead to damaging consequences); it also tends to exclude other council/governing body members from key decision-making. Our research found a clear demarcation between "core" and "peripheral" council/ governing body members. In some cases the inner circle is essentially informal: the chairmen and other senior lay officers meet the Vice-Chancellors and his/her senior academic and administrative colleagues to discuss, for example, the agenda of a forthcoming council meeting. In other cases it is embodied in policy and resources, or staff, sub-committees from which "peripheral" governors are excluded. Either way there is an erosion of collective responsibility. Instead of acting corporately the council/governing body is generally seen as a collection of more (and less) powerful individuals. This may strengthen the need to guard against conflicts of interest, although our research did not directly address this issue.

4. Conclusion

Our overall conclusion is that, in higher education, the present arrangements for institutional governance are unlikely to encourage a lowering of standards in public life. (The position in further education may well be different because the colleges are smaller with less-developed administrative infrastructures and less mature governance cultures.) However, we believe that these arrangements give some cause for concern. The main concerns, and possible solutions, include:

(i)   Lay, and "independent", members rely almost exclusively on senior managers for advice and, crucially, information. If, for any reasons, senior managers go awry, council/governing body members may pick up problems much too late. Best practice suggests that all council/governing body papers should be public documents—except in those very few instances where the privacy of individuals or commercial confidentiality would be threatened by disclosure;

(ii)   "Independent" members of "new" university governing bodies, in particular, operate in an accountability vacuum. There is no one to whom they need report (to the regret of more reflective "independent" members), and they effectively appoint their successors. Yet they are responsible for governing public institutions. One possible reform might be to require all councils/governing bodies to hold an open "Annual General Meeting", rather than simply making a formal report to the university court (in the case of the "old" universities; there is no such over-arching body in the "new" universities) or publishing a generally anodyne annual report. Another would be to require all vacancies to be publicly advertised.

(iii)   Council/governing body members are currently divided into first and second-class citizens. As a result their corporate responsibility is undermined, and full council/governing body meetings may be used merely to endorse decisions that have already been made. Good practice suggests that, where an inner circle of council/governing body members is required (as it generally will be), it should be formally constituted as a standing committee required to report its decisions in full to the council/governing body, and all members without exception should have access to its papers

THURSDAY 23 NOVEMBER 1995

Members Present:

The Rt Hon Lord Nolan (Chairman)

Professor Anthony King
The Rt Hon Peter Shore MP
The Rt Hon Lord Thomson of
  Monifieth KT DL

Dame Anne Warburton DCVO CMG
Diana Warwick

Witnesses:

David Edmonds, General Manager, Group and Property Central Services, National Westminster Bank

David Bebb, Chairman, Jim Coulter, Chief Executive and James Tickell, Assistant General Secretary, National Federation of Housing Associations

Sir Christopher Benson, Chairman, Michael Collier, Chief Executive, and Jane Markham, Board Secretary, Funding Agency for Schools

Dr Sheila Lawlor, Director, Politeia

323. LORD NOLAN: May I say welcome to our fourth day of oral evidence. Whereas yesterday we concentrated entirely on higher education, today we have a mixed bag, if our witnesses do not object to that expression. Our first two groups of witnesses will deal with housing associations, and the others with schools.

Our first witness today will also be the first witness we have questioned about housing associations. David Edmonds is the General Manager of the Group Property and Central Services at the National Westminster Bank. NatWest is a major private funder of housing associations, but Mr Edmonds is here primarily because he was Chief Executive of the Housing Corporation from 1984 to 1991, and I believe remains a Committee Member of a housing association. Mr Edmonds was also for a number of years Principal Private Secretary to Michael Heseltine when, as Environment Secretary, he was responsible for housing and, I understand, was then briefly Principal Private Secretary to our own Tom King.

Next, we shall hear from the National Federation of Housing Associations, represented by David Bebb, who chairs their National Council, and is Chief Executive of the Liverpool Housing Trust, and by Jim Coulter, NFHA Chief Executive. The NFHA celebrates its 50th anniversary this year, and we hope it will share its accumulated wisdom with us.

Third today we have the Funding Agency for Schools, represented by its Chairman, Sir Christopher Benson, its Chief Executive Michael Collier, and its Board Secretary Jane Markham. Sir Christopher has many business, public and charitable interests, but of particular interest today is that before taking up his post with the FAS he was Chairman of the Housing Corporation from 1990 to 1994.

Our final witness will be Dr Sheila Lawlor. Dr Lawlor was until recently Deputy Director of the Centre for Policy Studies, and now runs her own educational think-tank. She has written and worked extensively in the field of education.

That is our line-up, and Mr Edmonds thank you very much for coming along, we are grateful to you as to all our witnesses. I will ask Mr Peter Shore to take up the questioning with you.

324. PETER SHORE: First, welcome, Mr Edmonds, it is good to see you here before us.

We know that you have recently been connected, and still are, with the General Manager Property Services, National Westminster. Would you like to say a little bit more about your previous experience with housing associations, and if you wish to make an opening statement of any kind please do.

DAVID EDMONDS

DAVID EDMONDS (General Manager, Group Property and Central Services, National Westminster Bank): Thank you very much. My experience and involvement in housing associations dates back to the late 1960s when as a volunteer, together with six other people, I founded a housing association in the days of post Cathy Come Home. I remained with that association, which developed into a large and now very successful housing association operating in South London, until about 1979. In the mid-1980s I left the Department of the Environment, where I was then in charge of Inner City policy, to become Chief Executive of the Housing Corporation in which role I played a significant part in the 1988 Housing Act and the thinking that underpinned it, and the introduction of private finance into the Voluntary Housing movement. When I left the Housing Corporation some five years ago I joined the Board of a large housing association in South London which I left last year. My involvement with the Voluntary Housing movement is now as a Trustee of Crisis, more generally known as Crisis at Christmas.

PETER SHORE: So you are keeping your hand in as well as that very interesting past experience. You have actually been connected with the housing association movement really throughout the period of major expansion, which I think began in the 1974 period.

DAVID EDMONDS: Yes it did.

325. PETER SHORE: And then again was enormously increased following the election of the Conservative Government in 1979. What is your overall impression about housing associations, and whether they are properly run and accountable?

DAVID EDMONDS: I think that housing associations have a remarkable record of transmogrifying themselves through sets of legislation. They have been durable in the sense that the 1974 Housing Act produced for the first time very significant large sums of public money, the housing association grant, which associations used to expand very rapidly over a five-year period. They had previously often been a mixture of self-interest with people who had been involved in a professional capacity in the pre-1974 days, and the true voluntary sector. Post-1974 the true voluntary ethos, if you like, took over. Conflicts of interest were removed statutorily, and I think in the late 1970s, with very little risk because the public sector was creating the financial framework for them, they developed remarkably responsibly in terms of meeting housing need. I think in the late 1980s and the 1990s. There was a change to a much riskier environment with the advent of private finance. Local housing associations have now borrowed the best part of £6 billion I discovered last week from the private sector. Notwithstanding that impact of private finance taking away 100 per cent government funding and substituting private finance to the extent of 40 or 50 per cent, notwithstanding that shift, housing associations have a remarkable record in not wasting money, and few examples of corruption or malfeasance have been seen. I think it is a pretty good record in terms of effective delivery of a product to the people whom they exist to serve, those who are in acute housing need.

I think answering your question generally, it is a very good record in a rapidly changing external environment.

326. PETER SHORE: Just taking up that question of the record. What we have seen in recent years is a significant shift in the provision of social housing from the local authorities' democratically elected councils to the housing association movement. What would you say are the particular strengths of the housing association movement which might lead one, as it were, to think that that was a preferable or equally good way of providing social housing?

DAVID EDMONDS: I do not think it is necessarily the preferable way of providing social housing from the provision via local authorities. The switch into the housing association sector from it being the third arm, which was the policy of the Government in which you served as Secretary of State, was very much a political decision. Ministers in the early 1980s decided that social housing should be provided primarily and increasingly through housing associations rather than through local authorities. That fundamentally political decision was translated into action by effective actions through housing associations, and their ability to transform the way in which they worked during the 1980s. I would not argue, and I think few people involved in social housing would, that the housing association is a higher form of management, or a higher form of delivery mechanism, than a local authority. Some local authorities made some mistakes in their provision in the 1960s and 1970s of which we are all aware, but I do not think that was the real reason for changing their role.

327. PETER SHORE: On the face of it, of course, the switch from democratically accountable local authorities to housing associations—which are in some ways self-perpetuating oligarchies as I think they have been referred to—does raise the question rather acutely of how accountability is to be enforced on a large new non-elected sector. Has that put increasing strains on the Housing Corporation, and, if so, how has it been able to meet them?

DAVID EDMONDS: I think it has put strains on the Corporation. I think it has put strains on associations.

Accountability in the sense you were defining it in your question, and it is defined in the questions in the booklet, is manifested quite differently in housing associations. There is no doubt whatsoever that housing association committees and boards primarily are self-perpetuating oligarchies. The boards and committees I have sat on have always spent a fair amount of their time worrying over where they are going to get new recruits from, looking at the balance of the committee and thinking how can one fill a weakness there, how can one get in a special skill from that direction. I think housing association committees, in the way that they are now constituted, are in no sense formally accountable to the local community or the local electorate in the way in which a local housing committee or a local council is. That, I think, is an interesting philosophical question. Whether it has actually affected at all the way in which propriety has been maintained in housing associations, on the effectiveness of housing associations, is open to debate. I think from my long experience in the Housing Corporation, looking at housing association committees and boards and the way in which they operate, the standards of behaviour in terms of propriety, and in terms of adherence to legislation on the part of those Boards, was very high indeed, and the fact that they were not directly accountable to an electorate, although perhaps objectionable to some people because of the principle, I do not think in reality caused a problem in terms of conduct or propriety.

328. PETER SHORE: There are, of course, and it must add enormously to the problems of supervision, a very large number of housing associations of varying sizes—well over 2000 yesterday. Do you find in practice that your supervision tends naturally to concentrate on the smaller group of large housing associations rather than the very large number of small Associations that exist?

DAVID EDMONDS: Bearing in mind I am looking back five years, I think there is almost a paradox in my answer. Yes, the thrust of association monitoring and supervisory effort was directed towards the larger associations. The teams that went in spent longer, the accounts were more complex, there were more policies to look at, there were more quality standards to look at. I probably, as Chief Executive, spent more of my time concerned with problems that arose from small associations than I did from large associations, some of which related to the difficulties that small associations had in coping with the new financial world, some of which arose because of lack of professionalism in new or smaller associations. I do not know what the position is in 1995 and how much my successor's time bridges the two groups. Certainly my own clear recollection is I spent more time dealing with the problems of small associations in the regulatory arena than I did with the problems of large associations.

329. PETER SHORE: The powers given to the Housing Corporation I think were extended in 1984, and on the face of it they appear to be quite formidable, being able to get rid of Board members and suspend operations. These powers presumably have had a very strong deterrent affect against any potential wrong doing.

DAVID EDMONDS: I think the existence of the powers rather than the use of the powers, as you imply in your question, is very important in so far as the Housing Corporation's ability to regulate the housing association movement goes. Using the powers was often a difficult and cumbersome exercise. The need to abide by, for example, the rules of natural justice made what could look in legislation like a draconian and very easily usable power, quite often not as effective in reality. Again, going back to the experience of those six-and-a-half years, my colleagues and I spent far longer engaged in negotiations to persuade housing association Committees to behave in a particular kind of way than we did threatening them with the use of the powers. It was a much more, if you like, an iterative relationship where we suggested they might behave in a different way, a much more informal way perhaps of ensuring good behaviour and redressing bad behaviour when that was found.

330. PETER SHORE: One of the provisions of the 1974 Act which struck me as being a very strong one indeed, was Section 15 which, if I have got it right, says, "Individuals are not able to benefit personally from their involvement in an association".

That, presumably, thinking again particularly of small housing associations, would have a very strong deterrent affect on anyone hoping perhaps to rehouse themselves or their immediate relatives and friends through a housing association.

DAVID EDMONDS: I think that amendment which strengthened the duty on housing association committee members stemmed directly from the anxieties that related to the, if you like, old world of housing associations where quite often surveyors, solicitors, and others, for perfectly proper reasons were involved. Indeed, the housing association I was involved in in 1968 had a surveyor as a member of its committee to whom we gave work because we got the work done more cheaply, more effectively, he was a volunteer. Despite all those kinds of well-motivated reasons, the amendment to which you refer ruling that out of order was almost essential given the nature of the growth of housing associations, the huge amount of public resource that was going into them. Yes, it is a very strong deterrent. Whether in the context of the current need for highly professional management committees for associations, who after all these days are dealing with not only a very large chunk of public resource through housing association grant, but who may also be dealing with very sophisticated financial products being offered by the City of London, who may be having to carry through risk analyses of a quite complicated kind, it is still right is a different question. There is a bar that prevents, for example, paid board members with the responsibilities of board members of PLCs joining the housing association movement. Whether we are still using properly something that is very draconian in terms of propriety and preventing, perhaps, an improvement in the quality of management, I have some doubts on.

331. PETER SHORE: You have touched on a number of points in that last response. Let me just pick up one of them about paid board members. Of course, the origins of a housing association is very much a voluntarist and small scale local activity, but as you rightly remind us some of them are becoming a very big business indeed, and as they increasingly have to raise their own finances from the private sector a degree of professionalism and full-timeism must be involved. Did you come to any conclusion yourself during your time there about the desirability of actually rewarding members of perhaps the boards of the larger associations?

DAVID EDMONDS: I think my mind changed after I left the Corporation. While I was there the kind of

argument that you have just touched on, the voluntary nature, the way in which people came in as volunteers, I think weighed more heavily. Spending several years on the board of a large association in London, looking increasingly at the astonishingly complex issues with which that board and, indeed, of course, all others, had to deal. Looking at the responsibilities that were then vested in board members, because although board members or committee members are not paid, to all intents and purposes they have the same obligations as the director of any PLC. Looking at all of that, and, I have to say too, and this was something that I thought about hard over a ten-year period, looking perhaps at the lack of sustained quality. All this has changed my view. That is not a criticism of housing association committee members; I met thousands, many of whom were very good, but I also believe, and I think increasingly believe, that to get sustained quality I would remove the bar on payment and actually create now professional housing association Boards where they were big enough. I would equally bring on to those boards the key staff, the director and the heads of departments of associations, and I would move fairly quickly towards a much more PLC type housing association board than currently the law permits.

332. PETER SHORE: Thank you, that is a very interesting reply. Early on you had a quick mention about there being very few examples of corruption in the housing association movement, and I am sure that is generally correct. Do you think perhaps the Corporation has erred on the side of discretion and secrecy in its dealings with housing associations that have, in one way or another, performed badly in the past? Has there been a bit of a culture of secrecy?

DAVID EDMONDS: I think there has been, and still is, a culture which is to do with partnership and working together towards the same goals. The mission statement of the Housing Corporation used to, and I hope still does, talk about the Corporation working in partnership with the housing association movement. I think, therefore, when there were problems, whether of propriety or inefficiency or ineffectiveness, the first response of the Housing Corporation has been to find a way of sorting that out with the committee and/or staff of the association and putting it right rather than necessarily making a public example of the association. So, secrecy is perhaps a strong word, but, yes, it has not become public and therefore I suppose by definition if it is not public it is in a sense secret. Where the Corporation has had to use its statutory powers of course it then does become public knowledge.

333. PETER SHORE: You really illustrated the existence of a certain tension between your two roles of promoting housing associations and actually regulating them.

DAVID EDMONDS: There is both a tension and there is a reinforcement. The fact that as the chief executive of the Housing Corporation I had both an enforcement role and a funding role gave me enormous, if you like, extra statutory authority in dealing with a recalcitrant housing association, recalcitrant in the sense that it did not want to do what government policy said it should do, or what Housing Corporation policy said it should do, or did not want to put right something that we felt was wrong. Having the flow of information on the one hand from the regulatory supervisory monitoring side which had investigated, and then on the other hand being able to say to my colleagues who exercised the grant giving role, if this bunch does not get its act in order we will withdraw grant, gave the Housing Corporation a very powerful, and some people in the movement felt over powerful, and perhaps unaccountable authority. Again, I think, over the last ten years my mind on that has changed too. There is increasing complexity of housing association funding, and the way in which they are negotiating both with the private sector and with local authorities, and new changes in the laws that are proposed in the recent Government statement with grant going to purely private sector firms. I know that it is Government policy to retain the regulatory function in the Corporation. My own view has actually moved significantly away from that. I think that, in the new climate, I would have moved towards, would have been in favour of, am in favour of as an individual, a regulatory, supervisory authority which is independent, which confines itself to those issues. I think it would not necessarily weaken the authority because the funding would not be in the same agency because no funding agency is going to dole out cash to a group on whom the regulator has issued an adverse report. I think the focusing, the concentration, of the regulation and supervision is something that I would now like to see in an independent organisation, particularly as the Housing Corporation has become, if you like, more an agent of government in terms of its funding role. I think you can separate the two and there is a case for doing that, but Ministers who reflected on that have rejected that option, and that is very much a personal view.

334. PETER SHORE: Yes. From your experience now on the outside, as it were, as financing housing associations is it not the case that large investments from outside the housing association movement from commercial organisations in themselves require a rather greater degree of openness, accountability from the housing associations themselves if they are to inspire confidence in outside financing?

DAVID EDMONDS: Could I preface my answer by saying that my duties in the City do not involve lending to housing associations; I happen to work for a bank that is the biggest funder of housing associations. However, I spent last Friday chairing a seminar organised at the London School of Economics with a series of private funders talking about housing association finance and of the future. A very clear theme emerged from perhaps eight or nine funders in that room, and that was that the security offered to the funding agencies through having the housing association monitored and regulated by the Housing Corporation was a very significant factor in the faith of the funding agencies in the bodies to whom they were lending money. Therefore the existence of that regulatory framework, and this was certainly suggested by nearly all the private sector people present, is a very important factor indeed. It is an important factor in the initial decision about whether to lend to the housing association, and certainly it is an important factor in terms of the keenness of the terms that are offered, knowing that the association is regularly monitored, knowing that its performance and its outputs are looked at by the Housing Corporation and its team is a much more important factor than what you describe as openness and accountability. It is the effectiveness, efficiency, propriety of the association that really counts with the funders rather than accountability to the local electorate or to another external source.

335. PETER SHORE: Among the many changes in the housing association movement in recent years is, of course, the transfer by local councils of sometimes the whole of their stock to a particular housing association. This gives, in a sense, a kind of near monopoly of the provision of social housing in a substantial community area. Does this pose, do you think, particular problems for regulation? The business of priority and allocation of tenancies I would have thought was one of the things a Housing Corporation would have to satisfy itself about.

DAVID EDMONDS: I think that is right. Whole stock transfer, of course, came post the 1988 Housing Act. It is something that has taken off slowly. It is something that is subject, of course, to the will of the tenants, they have a chance to accept it or not. It is something on which the local elected councils can and often have influenced decisions, so there is quite a difficult process to go through in the first place. When it comes to allocation of tenancies to priority, I think increasingly good housing management practice has taken that out of the hands of boards, committees, whether housing association boards or local authority committees, and put it in the hands of the housing professionals both in terms of the setting of priorities on housing needs which perhaps is most important, and in terms of priority. So I suspect that the anxiety to which you point is probably not a real anxiety.

336. PETER SHORE: I hope that is correct. Are there any further points you want to add?

DAVID EDMONDS: I think not in response to your questions, sir, no.

337. LORD NOLAN: I wonder if I could pick up the point you were just talking about and that is the position where maybe the entire stock of the local authority's houses have been taken over by an association. I have been involved in many cases which showed how severe are the requirements placed on local authorities to house homeless persons, and this involves, as you know, not merely finding the accommodation but before that investigating the cases very carefully and making enquiries and so forth. How is that now being divided up between the local authorities and the housing associations? You think it would need a single hand on the tiller.

DAVID EDMONDS: I think that is a perfectly fair point. Post transfer housing associations have been almost the sole recipient of government funding since the early 1980s as the funding for local authorities was steadily diminished and that for housing associations was steadily increased. That placed upon housing associations even before transfer a key role in meeting homelessness needs. I have a personal view that the ability of local authorities and local associations to put together totally satisfactory liaison agreements is there. housing associations know what their statutory duties are; local authorities know what theirs are. I would not have thought that co-ordination and liaison should present a major problem.

338. LORD NOLAN: As between the housing association and the local authority it is not regulated by statute, is it? Isn't it regulated by contract?

DAVID EDMONDS: It is indeed.

339. LORD NOLAN: Contracts make adequate provision, do they, in your experience for this?

DAVID EDMONDS: They did in the experience I had way back, but the whole local authority stock transfer has moved on fairly significantly in the last couple of years and I suspect some of the later witnesses may be able to give you a more up to date answer than I.

340. LORD NOLAN: You told us that NatWest does not lend directly to housing associations but you have had a good deal of secondhand experience.

DAVID EDMONDS: No sorry, I referred to my role in the NatWest Group. The NatWest Group does lend very extensively to housing associations.

341. LORD NOLAN: I beg your pardon. May I ask one or two basic questions. What security does the bank have for its loan?

DAVID EDMONDS: Let us take the financial institutions generally, their security is the stock of the housing association, the houses, and it is the income flow that they can see generated by a stream of rents. It is a combination of looking at income and it is perhaps increasingly less to do with security.

342. LORD NOLAN: Yes, are there mortgages of the properties in the ordinary way?

DAVID EDMONDS: There can be; it depends on the nature of the private sector loan that is offered to the association.

LORD NOLAN: Personal covenants?

DAVID EDMONDS: No.

LORD NOLAN: Guarantees?

DAVID EDMONDS: Not in my experience sitting on a housing association board.

343. LORD   NOLAN: Have   many   financial institutions had difficulty in getting their interest or their principal back?

DAVID EDMONDS: As far as I am concerned, and I think other witnesses will be able to answer this, no housing association has reneged on a private sector loan since the 1988 Act.

344. LORD NOLAN: Do you attribute this to the care with which they are run and, for that matter, supervised by the Housing Corporation?

DAVID EDMONDS: I think it is a mixture. I spent a lot of time in the late 1980s in my Housing Corporation role persuading the private sector that this was a good investment, and my successor Anthony Mayer spends a lot of his time talking to financial institutions really explaining what the nature of the housing association movement is all about and that it does offer good security, it does offer a fair return on the investment.

I think the answer to your question is twofold. First it is the care of the institutional lenders. They look enormously carefully at the associations to whom they are lending. I was for a period a member of the board of the Housing Finance Corporation which was set up as a private sector institution in the late 1980s to lend to housing associations. In my role as a director of that

company with my co-directors we looked very carefully at the terms of the loans that we were offering, and we looked very carefully at the nature of the associations to whom we were lending. I think that is true of financial institutions generally. Secondly, the way in which the housing association grant links with private sector funding, the guarantee of income streams through rental income, the support given by the housing benefit system, at least since 1988, has made it a pretty safe bet, and all things being equal housing associations should not have had difficulty in paying the interest on their mortgages.

345. LORD NOLAN: Some witnesses have said, comparing the efficiency of the housing association movement with that of local authorities, that although you very often find the same people working in the housing associations who have been working in local authorities, and the individual expertise may be really no different, nevertheless the absence of political pressures has been a great advantage to the development of a commercial role. Is that your experience?

DAVID EDMONDS: It was my experience in the early days of stock transfer, yes. Talking to both the committee and staff of those early transfer associations one noticed a quite different approach, a quite different attitude. There was a freedom from what they may have previously seen as over control by their committees, from the hurly-burly of local political life. Certainly on a personal level, and this again is looking back five years, on a number of occasions people said exactly what you have said, that they were enjoying their new existence much more because they were able to operate with more independence and they were able to concentrate their efforts much more on housing provision and much less on satisfying their local political masters and mistresses.

346. LORD NOLAN: Thank you. Have you anything more you can tell us please about the proposed Housing Bill, the proposal, as I understand it, to put more money in the way of private developers in competition with housing associations?

DAVID EDMONDS: I think, again from a personal perspective and having now been out of the movement as a paid official for five years, I continue to be depressed by the extent of housing need that remains to be met. I continue to be depressed by the homelessness statistics. I continue to be depressed by what I see as a trustee of Crisis every night on the streets of London, and therefore I have a personal view that the maximum amount of housing that can be built and can be got into the social housing sector the better. I am increasingly less concerned about the way in which, using a not very elegant phrase, it can be got into the social housing sector. Therefore, if we are facing a run of years in which public sector investment is going to decrease, and the housing association movement has been on a roll for the last two or three years, but from all that one reads and hears about the next two, three, four years that investment level is going to be significantly reduced. I am strongly in favour of any device that can be utilised to get money to create social housing. If that means putting it direct to private developers, so be it. Actually I am fairly relaxed about that because I do believe that it is perfectly possible to create a system a bit like the Urban Development Grant where the money does go to a private developer, that you look at the return that he expects to get, and providing the accommodation is provided to an adequate standard, so be it. I think the management I would like to see in the association world, or in going into a regulated landlord, but in the actual provision of housing I think the private sector probably can take some more cost out of, it probably can produce more units for the taxpayer's pound—there was the case in the past—therefore I have to say I am strongly in favour of it there, yes.

347. LORD NOLAN: Can you tell me if it is envisaged that there should be a system of regulation of the private developers who get the money by the Housing Corporation?

DAVID EDMONDS: As I understand, reading the Government's documents, there will be a regulation by the Housing Corporation, but, again, I am not an expert on that and doubtless other witnesses will be able to tell you the detail. But, yes, there will be regulation.

348. LORD NOLAN: Just one final point as far as I am concerned coming back to the question of remuneration, and you said that on balance giving full weight to the value of the voluntary system you thought that the degree of expertise that is required, not to mention the time commitment, might justify at any rate consideration of a payment structure as, of course, has been found in the National Health Service Trusts. Had you thought how it might be regulated, whether there should be some central control of levels of remuneration, or would you leave that to the individual housing associations?

DAVID EDMONDS: No, certainly I would regulate it. I would do it in bands related to the size of the association either in terms of its asset base or in terms of its development programme. I do not think it is too difficult to work out what those bands should be. I think that in that way not only would you have regulation, but much more importantly you would attract, I believe, higher quality, more experienced people into the movement and perhaps redress some of the weaknesses that are now there. Equally, I think, you would reflect some of the real responsibilities that rest in housing association members of committees. I think many committee members are totally unaware of the true nature of their own responsibilities, and when pointed out to them often get rather nervous because they do have very major responsibilities under the law at the moment.

349. LORD NOLAN: Such as? What are the particular responsibilities you have in mind?

DAVID EDMONDS: It is a responsibility of a housing association committee to be satisfied that the accounts are right and proper and that the financial running of the association is to proper standards. I remember on one particular occasion a member of a board of a housing association being asked to agree this resolution at the end of a meeting and I had got 60-odd pages of figures in front of me, and I think for many committee members being faced with that mass of quite difficult financial data putting their hands up and saying "Yes I agree" is often an act of faith, it has to be.

350. LORD NOLAN: This is really something I ought to know, but what are the penalties for failure to carry out those responsibilities?

DAVID EDMONDS: I think my recollection is that the penalties for failure are those applying to directors under the Companies Act legislation, they are analogous

or identical to those, which of course has implications for those people who may be involved in other professions or in the financial sector. If something does go wrong I think the implications can be significant for them in the rest of their lives.

LORD NOLAN: So there could be a personal liability there, yes.

DAVID EDMONDS: If not a personal liability there could be a personal impact on their ability to carry out their professional life, yes.

351. LORD THOMSON: Could I just follow up Lord Nolan's question. Do members on the boards of housing associations take out personal liability and indemnity policies?

DAVID EDMONDS: I think all housing associations who are members of the National Federation of Housing Associations, and again Jim Coulter and David Bebb will be able to comment on this, have automatic insurance through their membership of the National Federation. My own association took out an additional indemnity policy for its board members, and I think that is absolutely essential.

352. LORD THOMSON. Could I just ask one further question. For the private sector funders is there any implied government guarantee of any kind? Do they feel that if a housing association gets into real difficulties that the government will stand behind them? Or putting it the other way round, if there is a problem with a housing association would the Housing Corporation do what the Building Societies Commission has tended to do, that is step in and ask some other housing association or other housing associations to come in with some kind of lifeboat?

DAVID EDMONDS: There are two separate questions there, sir. Can I take the second one first. I am again talking from personal experience. Yes, the Housing Corporation has on a number of occasions worked with perhaps a major housing association to get it to support, take over, work with a smaller association when it has got into trouble. I think that is well precedented, well documented, and I was personally involved in a number of cases where I talked to the chairmen and chief executives of housing associations to ask them to take on that role, and I think that is right and it is proper.

You first question, is there a government guarantee and do private sector lenders lend money on the back of that guarantee? The answer to that is an unequivocal no, there is no guarantee. Ministers and the Housing Corporation have made it transparently and abundantly clear that there is no guarantee, and if any private sector lender thought there was I do not think they would have been listening to all that both ministers, civil servants and corporation had said.

353. LORD NOLAN: Well, that has been very helpful indeed. It has also been a very helpful introduction to the evidence we are going to hear from our next group of witnesses. Thank you very much, David Edmonds.

Good morning, gentlemen. It is very good to see you here and I watched you listening closely to the previous witness. We shall be running over some of the same ground, but I wonder if I could begin by asking you to tell us a little more about the NFHA, its size, the extent of its membership amongst housing associations and its functions.

DAVID BEBB, JIM COULTER, AND JAMES TICKELL

DAVID BEBB (Chairman, National Federation of Housing Associations): Yes. The National Federation is celebrating its 60th year this year. It was established in 1935. Its history parallels the growth of housing associations this century, that is, its membership remained quite small, the level of achievement of its members was relatively small until the mid-sixties when a new range of housing associations—of which David Edmonds was talking about his involvement in one—was born, getting involved in rehabilitation in inner cities.

Those associations, acting on a small scale were supported very much by fundraising from Shelter. Their fundraising was of a voluntary nature and they were dependent upon charitable funds. Their example led to the passing of the 1974 Housing Act which was legislation drafted by the Tory Government in 1973 and enacted by a Labour Government in 1974. That characterised their cross-party support.

Since then, the role of housing associations has become increasingly central to the provision of rented housing and over the past 15 years, there has been a move from housing associations as supplementary or as a partner to local authorities—providing housing, as it were, as a diversity in the rented sector—to the point now where housing associations are virtually the sole providers of subsidised social housing.

There are something in the order of 2,000 members of the National Federation of Housing Associations. Many of those are very small associations with either no housing stock or a very small amount of housing. The number of housing associations which is funded each year by the Housing Corporation is about 400-450. Some of those receive funding occasionally, but there is core group of probably about 250 housing associations which takes the bulk of Housing Corporation investment.

In addition, local authorities still have the power to fund housing associations. That was a major feature throughout the seventies.

354. LORD NOLAN: May I interrupt. Is that mainly development funding?

DAVID BEBB: Yes.

355. LORD NOLAN: Is it still the case that outside funding is generally for development?

DAVID BEBB: Yes, with one exception. There was revenue funding in London. The Greater London Council provided revenue funding to keep rents down during its existence. Now, local authorities are very much a minor partner; because of reductions in the core funding for their own housing purposes, there is much less funding through local authorities. Our main source is the Housing Corporation.

356. LORD NOLAN: How many housing associations have you amongst your members?

DAVID BEBB: The majority of housing associations are members of the NFHA. We have an overlap with the Housing Corporation. Housing associations are registered with the Corporation, but many unregistered housing associations remain in membership of the NFHA and I think we have about 2,400.

JIM COULTER (Chief Executive, National Federation of Housing Associations): Slightly less than that. The main group of associations which are not members of the NFHA are almshouses, who are represented by the National Almshouses Association.

LORD NOLAN: I see.

JIM COULTER: But the primary providers are all in membership of the NFHA.

357. LORD NOLAN: Thank you very much. One of your functions, particularly in recent years, has been to give a lead in the establishment of Government's guidance and of course we have carefully studied the code you have sent out. It is, of course, a code and not a rule of law, but you tell us that although it is a recent document, it has been adopted enthusiastically by the majority of your members. Is that right?

JIM COULTER: That is right.

DAVID BEBB: Yes, there was much support for our setting up the inquiry panel. The inquiry panel was set up independent of the NFHA. We were very keen that its findings did not have the stamp of a trade body setting up rules and regulations for the benefit of its members. There has been intensive consultation with member housing associations—or housing associations which are not members—as well as individuals and its draft findings—the draft code—was also subject to consultation and has been very widely welcomed and accepted. It does allow a degree of freedom for associations to operate within it, but its broad principles have been very much welcomed.

I think there was a recognition that the nature of housing association work had changed radically from the days when their constitutions were set up. My own association was set up in 1965 by a committee who used to meet every fortnight and go out and do the work. They would go and collect the rents, buy the houses and so on. Now, the role of committees—they are now termed boards of housing associations—has changed so dramatically that there was a need for setting that new role in a different framework.

358. LORD NOLAN: In answer to the question, could more be done to encourage the widest pool of talent to come forward, you say the answer to this must be yes. You are "...currently setting up a data base for national recruitment of new board members and will be advertising widely to ensure that interested parties come forward. Housing associations will then approach our data base and identify particular board members.". Have you made further progress along those lines?

DAVID BEBB: If I can answer that.

LORD NOLAN: Yes, please.

DAVID BEBB: Yes, we have. We were very pleased to get the support of the Housing Corporation for this initiative and we are in the process at the moment of setting up the computer data base and will be advertising later this year and sending out information packs to interested candidates.

359. LORD NOLAN: Thank you very much. I wonder if I could come—having raised the question of board members—straight to the point about remuneration, which you have already heard discussed this morning. Am I right in thinking that you have adopted a relatively neutral attitude, though you recognise there are strong arguments in favour of payment? Is that your position.

DAVID BEBB: Yes. Can I allow James to answer this in a second?

LORD NOLAN: Please.

DAVID BEBB: Because he was our link with the governance inquiry and saw many of the representations of individual housing associations, but I would say that there are strong feelings, for and against, and I think our view is that there should not be any prescription, but there should be a degree of freedom.

JAMES TICKELL (Assistant General Secretary, National Federation of Housing Associations): Yes. The arguments in favour of payment are convincing, but against that needs to be set the fact that there is no crisis of governance amongst housing associations. We are hoping also that our initiatives to attract new volunteers will help to address any skill shortage that exists. The feeling of the NFHA and of the inquiry was that the case for payment was not yet strong enough and we felt that losing, if you like, the advantage of the voluntary ethos was too high a price to pay for the possibility of getting more people on at this stage.

We have also submitted evidence to the NCVO's inquiry on the Future of the Voluntary Sector and we shall be waiting to see what they have to say on this subject because we would want to move ahead with the rest of the voluntary sector, rather than in isolation.

360. LORD NOLAN: Yes. We have heard a number of witnesses about this. As you say, there are strong feelings in favour of retaining the voluntary system and the sense of pride that goes with the feeling that you are doing something without any sort of reward.

JIM COULTER: Could I just add a piece of information, which I think reinforces that.

LORD NOLAN: Yes, please.

JIM COULTER: As part of the governance inquiry's work, some research was commissioned among existing committee members of associations from Glasgow University and of the drawbacks which those polled described, loss of the voluntary ethic was the highest they saw. 80 per cent of those who objected identified loss of voluntary ethic and, linked with that, perhaps, 58 per cent identified that it was attract the wrong sort of person to become a member of a housing association board, so the feelings are very strong and the direction that we are pursuing is about compensation for loss of earnings, up to the jury level loss of earnings recommended by the inquiry, rather than some form of remuneration as recommended by your last witness.

361. LORD NOLAN: Yes, thank you. You say you are proposing to publish new model standards next year. What will they take account of?

JAMES TICKELL: This applies to the new Model Rules for housing associations—the constitutional document by which they operate. Currently, most associations use model rules which are based on a document 100 years old which was drawn up for a completely different type of organisation and our project is to produce new Model Rules in plain English which allow associations to put into practice the recommendations of our governance inquiry.

362. LORD NOLAN: The governance inquiry spent a lot of time on the accountability of boards. It does not seem to place great weight on the need for a shareholding membership to hold the board to account. What are your feelings about that?

JAMES TICKELL: I think the feeling of the inquiry was in some ways, when they were looking at the question, that we were starting in the wrong place and that the shareholding membership structure was not one that was going to produce balanced boards with the right range of skills to manage these very complex social businesses. There was also an acceptance that that is the constitution model that housing associations have and it was important to make it work as well as possible in the new environment.

In our new Model Rules we are hoping to produce a range of constituency options so that associations can develop the mechanisms of shareholding membership, without putting at risk their business efficiency and we are hoping to publish those early next year.

363. LORD NOLAN: I see. Is it right that membership is by permission of the board only as matters stand—that you have to clear it with the board before you become a member?

DAVID BEBB: It is standard provision within Rules that applications for membership have to be approved by the board of the organisation.

364. LORD NOLAN: Yes. The people you have to work with are obviously the tenants, the financiers from whom you get money, the Housing Corporation and, I suppose, the community generally. The latter may be the hardest to contact and to get to take an interest. Is that your experience?

DAVID BEBB: Yes. It is worth saying, about membership, just to clarify, that a range of associations have declared themselves open membership organisations so that anybody who applies is accepted, but when it comes to communicating or accounting to the variety of stakeholders in our work, then clearly it is relatively easier to account to tenants, because we can contact them straightforwardly. Indeed, many associations have actively involved tenants in their governance. I think you have had submissions from housing associations describing arrangements that they have.

LORD NOLAN: Yes.

DAVID BEBB: Many associations publish a wide range of publications which they circulate widely throughout the community. They hold open annual general meetings and there is a great commitment on the part of the housing association movement to make sure that information does flow about their activities. Frankly, many of us have grown up in the housing association movement recognising the political realities that the growth of our work depends upon political support. That, in turn, depends upon good reputations and we work very hard to make sure that those reputations are widely known about and are good.

If I can refer to an earlier discussion with the last witness about accountability: whilst we do not have the formal accountability in an electoral sense to local communities, I think we all feel that we are in fact much more answerable, certainly to our tenants and to local communities, because of the sensitivity of the organisation to decisions made by local politicians about our future by the Housing Corporation about the extent to which we do respond to local community needs.

365. LORD NOLAN: Yes. I was enormously impressed to hear Mr Edmonds talk about the reliability of housing associations generally as borrowers. From the little certainly that I have seen and that most of us have seen of the work of housing associations, it has been really remarkable to see what good quality housing can be produced at modest rents and yet without jeopardising the funding on which the work has been carried out.

It is particularly striking, is it not, because in so many other fields of the private sector, the opposite is the case. The banks are in danger of losing their money; the borrowers have almost a dominant position. If I can digress into a story which contained profound truth, concerning a female relative. I was helping her with her bills and she had a very rude letter from a big London store saying that unless she paid up promptly, they were going to have to consult their solicitors. And she said, "How dare they write to me like that? I owe them a great deal of money.". There is a lot of truth in that, but this is not so here, is it, and you confirm that the housing association movement generally has been a case in which money has been borrowed, not only responsibly, but also with the result that interest payments are kept up and principal repaid as required.

JIM COULTER: May I just give you a detailed answer on the performance of associations. David Edmonds referred to some £6 billion of private finance. The default record is not perfect, but something under £10 million only out of that £6 billion has been a default risk, and most of that in one particular association case, which the Corporation dealt with very effectively in the way that he described by securing amalgamation of the defaulting body, so the private sector's risk has been very well managed by housing associations and that has been endorsed by the Public Accounts Committee in its report last year and by the House of Commons Environment Committee in its report on the Corporation in 1993.

366. LORD NOLAN: One of the most sensitive and difficult parts of property management is, of course, collecting the rents and this, too, appears to have been conducted very successfully on the whole. Is that right?

JIM COULTER: The rent collection performance is very high and it is of course one of the performance indicators which the Housing Corporation collects in its annual data gathering.

367. LORD NOLAN: Yes. You mentioned the need for close co-operation with the local authorities. I wonder if you could give me your views on whether there have been any difficulties in the way of the local authorities fulfilling their statutory obligations, particularly towards those who are unintentionally homeless now that the local authorities have lost direct control of their housing stock. Has that been a difficult area as far as your experience goes?

DAVID BEBB: Can I ask Jim to answer this in a second and say that I think it is worth mentioning at the outset that housing associations all provide housing for local authority waiting lists.

LORD NOLAN: Yes.

DAVID BEBB: All associations provide at least half of their lettings to local authorities and there is a statutory duty on associations to support local authorities in housing homeless families, so it is not a loss of capacity and indeed in many areas associations make local arrangements with the local authorities to house substantially more than that 50 per cent.

In my view it would be wrong for them to completely cede their right of tenant selection to local authorities, because there is an important need for diversity and access to housing people who may be excluded for one reason or another from local authorities as not being, in their view, top priority, whereas the association may regard them as such.

JIM COULTER: If I may, I will just make three points. First, the statutory situation is that under Section 72 of the 1985 Housing Act, associations have a duty to help the local authority, where requested, with their homelessness duties and connected with that, most, in fact all, of the voluntary transfer arrangements which you referred to earlier have contractual additional agreements between the local authority and the receiving housing association.

Secondly, there is increasingly the growth of common housing registers, ie the local authority and the housing associations in a particular borough or district working together from a single, so-called waiting list, but with independently established criteria for establishing priorities.

Thirdly, we run a national monitoring system—a continuous recording of lettings—which our members send us returns about every letting and we are able to publish analyses which we do quarterly. The data is also available to the Housing Corporation, the Department and to local authorities so it is a very public set of statements about performance. In particular we concentrate on making sure that the performance data for local authority nominations, and especially for statutorily homeless households, are concentrated on in each of those publications.

368. LORD NOLAN: But the very difficult questions for which the local authority is answerable to the courts, which include, as you know, that of which a particular

individual has become unintentionally homeless and, if so, whether it was their fault or not, cannot be delegated to the Association?

JIM COULTER: No. We do not have those responsibilities. That is directly the responsibility of the local authority and in the chain of action, they take that decision and, so to speak, pass on the homeless household through the nomination system.

LORD NOLAN: Yes.

JIM COULTER: But there is a definite break between the responsibilities of the local authority and those of the housing associations.

369. LORD NOLAN: Yes. Thank you. There are three more questions I wanted to ask you. We have been asked by the Housing Corporation for our views on whether chief executives should be permitted to be members of the board or not. Is this an important issue in your view?

JAMES TICKELL: It is, yes. This was examined by the governance inquiry at some length. The first point to make is that chief executives and finance directors probably are, de facto, directors of housing associations under the Companies Acts, so that whether or not they are on the board, they would share the liability in the event of problems.

LORD NOLAN: Yes.

JAMES TICKELL: We became aware that most associations would not wish to have their chief executives formally on the board but that a certain number would think it useful in terms of governance. So the inquiry took the view, not that they should recommend chief executives joining boards, but that it should be a possibility for associations if they thought that was the best way of meeting their needs. Ultimately, the inquiry thought it probably was not a very significant point, in that the chief executive is, effectively, a director anyway and whether it was formalised or not, that would be the situation.

370. LORD NOLAN: Thank you very much. On the regime for avoiding conflicts of interest, you say in your evidence your views have changed since the Hancock Report. At the risk of over-condensing a number of paragraphs on page 9 of your submission, I understand that you are not pressing actively for any major structural changes in Section 15?

JAMES TICKELL: Firstly, we felt that given the interest of this Committee in housing associations, it would be appropriate to wait until you had considered it and made any views known. Secondly, we thought that although there was a case for reforming Section 15, in symbolic terms it could be misinterpreted and damage the reputation of associations.

We are hoping to discuss with the Corporation further ways of relaxing the regime in relatively minor ways to remove some of the irksome results, rather than wholesale reform at this stage. I think both we and the Corporation will be very much guided by any views put forward from this Committee.

371. LORD NOLAN: Is the major difficulty about Section 15, as you see it, that it adds to the difficulties in getting all the right people you want on the board?

JAMES TICKELL: I think that is right. Every once in a while, we come across cases where somebody entirely appropriate and able to serve is prevented by some extraordinary quirk of Section 15 because, perhaps, their brother is married to somebody who works for the association or whatever, in some very minor capacity. It does throw up these anomalies from time to time and we would like to try to sort those out.

LORD NOLAN: Yes.

DAVID BEBB: Can I just refer to one particular anomaly: as part of our drive to involve tenants in our governance, many associations have actually got arrangements for tenants to be formally members of their boards of governance and those tenants find their rights significantly diminished by being members under the Section 15 regime on the access of their families to housing and so on. That seems to me to be quite inappropriate. When we first sought the arrangements which were the precursor of Section 15 in the early seventies, it was specifically to distinguish the new housing association movement, with voluntary members, from some of the old housing associations which had been set up as fee-generating vehicles for professionals.

What has happened is that the net has been cast wider. There is no doubt that we recognise that it is the wideness of the net and its total exclusion of any personal benefit is a flagship for our own probity. I think that we have mixed feelings about its revision. There are many aspects on which we feel in practical terms we would benefit from its removal, but on the other hand, as James said, it is a flagship for us.

372. LORD NOLAN: Yes. If the statutory bar were replaced by a system of register of interests and declaration of interests when any possible conflict arose, would that work?

DAVID BEBB: That is the debate and that is where we would look for your guidance.

LORD NOLAN: What do you think?

DAVID BEBB: Can I speak as a chief officer? My board would want me to tell you that they want to move to a declaration of interests regime, because they find many of the requirements of Section 15 irksome. My view is that especially as we move into a wider range of providers being involved in developing social housing with grant, that it probably remains more important than it was before for us to actually be able to say with the absolute clarity we can at the moment that nobody involved in decision taking benefits in any way whatsoever from the decisions they take.

LORD NOLAN: Yes.

DAVID BEBB: So I have a personal view and a view as an employee.

373. LORD NOLAN: I suppose this to some extent conditions your attitude towards the new Housing Bill, the extent of regulation that will be imposed on private developers who are funded by central funds?

DAVID BEBB: Absolutely. In listening to the last witness who was suggesting the attraction of using private developers because of their possible savings in procurement costs, it occurred to us that the sort of regulation which applies to city grants and so on—the regime which he referred to—would be actually very attractive to associations. We end up with an obligation flowing from grants which were made in 1974 from the 1974 Housing Act.

LORD NOLAN: Yes.

DAVID BEBB: We remain obliged, as a result of those grants, and that has never been the case I think with grants paid to the private sector.

We watch very closely to see what sort of regulatory regime is going to be revised for private sector developers. I think it is fair to say that housing associations take a principled view about the involvement of the private sector and we would not object in principle to the access of private developers to grant. I think our general view is that we want to see more social housing provided and if they can provide more social housing and the arrangements for its long-term security within the sector are satisfactory, then there would be no objection in principle.

What we are concerned about is that the arrangements are not advantageous and give a false advantage to private sector developers, over and above those available to housing associations in terms of the simplicity of the regulation. There is no doubt that whilst there is a recognition that the regulatory function of the Corporation has been hugely successful in protecting our reputation and avoiding problems, housing associations generally, if they have a complaint, it would be about the heavy handedness of it. It is extremely time-consuming. There are personnel involved in many organisations whose job it is to service these regulatory functions and the idea that private sector agencies would come along that have much simpler regimes—which may just be subject, for example, to triennial review—would be very attractive to many associations.

374. LORD NOLAN: I follow that. Just leaving aside the Housing Bill for the moment and coming back to what you told me about the present regime as it affects recruitment and membership of boards, as I understand it, you have got along so far extremely well on the voluntary basis, but, as you say, times are changing. You wish to leave open the possibility of considering the payment of board members as something that might make it easier to get additional expertise when required?

DAVID BEBB: What we recognise is a diversity of view within our membership. Within individual associations, there tend to be very strong, single-minded views, but associations have different cultures and approaches. My own board is unanimously against the idea of payment. That includes people who are unemployed on very low incomes, for whom it would be very attractive. They think it would completely change the nature of their relationship, that they are volunteers giving their time freely and taking their decisions on the basis of wider interests, rather than exclusively for either their sectional interests or for the association's benefit.

375. LORD NOLAN: Yes. Is that the view of your colleagues as well on this count?

JIM COULTER: I think we see a very strong case for making sure that people are not deterred from membership, so, for example, the jury level loss of earnings proposals would, perhaps, compensate people on low incomes who find difficulty in getting time off. We would like to see eventually housing association board membership given the same status as serving on a jury itself—that it is an accepted public service which therefore Government, through legislation, encourages employers to give reasonable time off, as it does for trade union duties, for example. But I think on the whole we would, for the foreseeable future, want to avoid remuneration and reward for membership because in a sense there is much assertion, but little demonstration that the recruitment problem is producing a lack of talent. We are very open, however, to making sure that we avoid that problem emerging by the sort of initiatives we are taking on recruitment packages, training and development for board members, conferences, seminars and the rest of it.

LORD NOLAN: Thank you very much. And you?

JAMES TICKELL: I think the most important point made to the inquiry is that any costs of remuneration would be passed on to tenants and would result in higher rents, so ultimately I would agree with what Jim Coulter has said.

LORD NOLAN: Yes. I am very grateful to you. We naturally attach very great weight indeed to the view which you give us on behalf of your Association and I am now going to ask Mr Shore if he has further questions to put to you.

376. PETER SHORE: Yes, I have one or two. There is an aspect of your affairs which we have not really touched on and that is the accountability of housing associations to their own tenants. Are you satisfied with the present arrangements?

DAVID BEBB: I think it would always be wrong to say one is satisfied. Certainly we can see improvements and change. There has been a dramatic change over the years in the relationship between associations and their tenants. There is no doubt that most of the current generation of associations were set up as small scale philanthropic organisations. Their approach to their tenants was largely paternalistic and they regarded themselves as pretty much answerable only to themselves as a group.

As associations have grown and as the role of associations has become more mature, there is a recognition that we actually have to have a different relationship with tenants. Most associations of any size now have arrangements for involvement of tenants in their governance, either through local area committees, or through elections or appointments to boards.

My own association, for example, has a unit within the organisation which supports tenant associations. We have 15 tenant associations throughout the stock of the housing association. Each of those elects a representative onto one of two district committees. For those district committees, 90 per cent of their membership is tenants. They are responsible for taking decisions about estate management and evictions. They are not, in law, allowed to decide about rent levels because of Section 15 which deals with personal benefit, but they deal with all estate management issues within the framework of policy devised by the board.

In turn, the elect from those district committees, two members to the board, who are full members of the board. That gives tenants a democratic right of involvement. My view is that it has to go beyond that because democracy within tenancies, like democracy elsewhere, is the interest of a relatively small number and we have regular mechanisms for finding out what tenants feel about our services.

I do not think that we are untypical of major housing associations and that change has actually occurred mainly over the past 10 years. It was a growing movement in the early eighties. There is a very active involvement of tenants.

377. PETER SHORE: And the National Federation gives guidance to associations on this matter?

DAVID BEBB: Indeed it does.

JIM COULTER: One of our key tasks, as the trade body, is to promote good practice and that is certainly an area in which we have over the years regularly published good practice guidance.

378. PETER SHORE: There is also a sort of statutory provision, is there not—a tenants guarantee which I think is administered or supervised, again, by the Housing Corporation. Is that correct?

DAVID BEBB: Yes. The tenants' guarantee was established under the 1988 Housing Act as a document intended to suggest the service outcomes which tenants could expect and the Corporation, as part of its regulatory role, examines the performance of associations against the guarantee. It is almost certain that the guarantee will be reviewed and perhaps improved as part of the Housing Bill, which we are expecting shortly.

379. PETER SHORE: Good. Thank you. Can I just turn now to what you were saying earlier about relationship with local authorities. I got the point very clearly that with local authorities, who are obviously playing a smaller part in the provision of social housing, you frequently have agreements with them and furthermore there is a requirement of accepting 50 per cent of local authority nominations. Am I right?

DAVID BEBB: Yes.

380. PETER SHORE: Is that really satisfactory though in an area, for example, where there has been a holus-bolus transfer of local authority stock to a housing association?

DAVID BEBB: I think in those circumstances, as Jim mentioned in a previous answer, those large scale voluntary transfer housing associations in our jargon actually have contracts with the local authority which generally put a higher obligation on them than the 50 per cent.

I would say that the relationship between local authorities and housing associations—and again it depends on local circumstances—but the generality is that associations work very closely with and in partnership with local authorities. It is a relationship in which our access to new development funding is very important for local authorities. We can actually assist in the delivery of

their housing strategies and indeed in many areas there are social housing agreements which are formal agreements between local authorities and the housing associations operating in their area.

The governance inquiry report recommends that associations do enter into these social housing agreements with the local authorities in their area. It is very much an active partnership and I do not think you should regard the 50 per cent nominations agreement as actually being a limit on the extent to which we help local authorities with their rehousing. There is a great deal of overlap outside of that 50 per cent.

381. PETER SHORE: Yes. But one can envisage, perfectly legitimately, a local authority and a housing association having different priorities and a different assessment as to local needs.

DAVID BEBB: Can I exemplify that. Historically, in Liverpool in the early eighties, the local authority was absolutely committed to a programme of new building in contravention of central government policy. The then administration was knocking down large volumes of sub-standard local authority stock. The only people they wanted rehoused were people from that local authority stock. The housing associations, on the other hand, also had an obligation to housing special needs—people with either physical or support needs which we have done for some considerable time and we would not have got funding for that if the local authority had actually determined exclusively what the priorities within the area would be.

Since that time I think our priorities have become much closer, but it is important to recognise that there is a degree of diversity within the decision-making both from people rehoused and new housing which is built.

382. PETER SHORE: One rather large question. Is there increasing financial pressure on the housing association movement? As they have to borrow more and more money from the private sector and as the element of HAG decreases, does this put an increasing pressure on the housing associations in their efforts to provide social housing at affordable rents?

DAVID BEBB: Absolutely. With new developments there has been a terrific increase in the pressure that we have to reduce costs in order to make rents affordable. Certainly outside London there are parts of the country now which are receiving public funding which accounts for only 40 per cent of the capital cost of development and the result is that out-turn rents are forced up to levels which many of us thought would be inconceivable five or six years ago. Average rents across the country still remain relatively affordable, but on new developments, the level of rents—because the level of subsidy is so much lower—are forced much higher.

There is no doubt that as a result of that pressure, the associations have achieved great economies in the cost of building and we now have much more streamlined procedures for procuring housing and capital costs, with the benefit of what is a very beneficial tendering climate because the building sector is so depressed, have been kept very low.

It is also the case on revenue funding. There has been a total change in culture. Associations are now taking much more interest in trying to reduce costs, at the same time as maintaining service level. It puts us into a position which is much more analogous, I think, to private sector providers than public sector providers. There was I have to say very limited interest in economising and getting absolute best value for money prior to the 1988 Housing Act. There was a degree of underwriting of our costs which I think, on reflection, was unhealthy.

383. PETER SHORE: There is pressure on rents and costs. Does this almost inevitably lead to the increase in housing benefit as a way of squaring the circle?

DAVID BEBB: That is right.

JIM COULTER: The figures on housing benefit are very worrying. Two very quick figures illustrate how the change has come about. On average—because there was obviously a large pool of existing pre 1988 Act tenants—about 64 per cent of housing association tenants across the board depend upon housing benefit in full or in part. Of incoming tenants, the figure is 85 per cent and rising if grant levels continue to decline, although they have been held steady for next year by comparison with 1995/96.

DAVID BEBB: Can I just add to that: it is worth saying that the housing benefit bill for housing associations remains substantially below that of the private sector, partly because of the volume of the private landlords. The housing associations now provide one million dwellings and private landlords have something like twice that. Also the individual rent levels on which housing benefit is paid is much higher in the private sector. Compared to the private sector, we are relatively minor recipients of housing benefit.

384. LORD NOLAN: Very good value. Well thank you. We have I am afraid come to the end of our time. Was there anything else? We have got your extremely helpful submissions, which put down in black and white in summary form a great deal of what you have been telling us this morning. You have given us a very clear record and have expanded it most helpfully in what you have said.

Was there anything finally that occurred to you as we were talking that you wanted to leave with us?

JIM COULTER: Can I just offer one last sentence?

LORD NOLAN: Yes, please.

JIM COULTER: "Public confidence in the future of the housing association movement depends upon all associations maintaining the highest standards." That is a sentence from our code of conduct published in 1981, 14 years ago, and we still have that very strong commitment as a trade body.

LORD NOLAN: Thank you very much.

Good morning, Sir Christopher Benson, Mr Michael Collier and Jane Markham.

Welcome and thank you very much indeed for coming along to join us this morning. I am going to come straight to the point, if I may, because we never have enough

time, and lead into the questions, asking Professor King to go through your evidence with you.

385. PROF ANTHONY KING: Could I begin by making two, I think, important points? The first is that whatever else the Nolan Committee is in the business of doing it is not in the business of questioning the principle of grant-maintained schools. One of the things we do not want to spend time on is whether they are a good thing or not. For all I know members of the Committee may have different views but I think none of us regards that as relevant.

The second point I would want to make to start with is simply that there is no belief that I know of around this table that malpractice and impropriety of any kind widespread in grant-maintained schools. We are not studying grant-maintained schools amongst other things because we think there is something desperately wrong but simply because large sums of public money are being spent by new bodies in new ways. Against that background, can you clear up one mystery for me? In questioning of witnesses last week we found that people who were in favour of grant-maintained schools—and most of our witnesses were—confronted with any suggestion that certain aspects of the running of grant-maintained schools might be improved became very defensive. It was as though to suggest that one could tweak this arrangement here or perhaps develop some new safeguard there was to suggest that there was something wrong, either with the principle of grant-maintained schools or with the way in which they were being governed across the board. Can you explain this mystery?

SIR CHRISTOPHER BENSON, MICHAEL COLLIER, AND JANE MARKHAM

SIR CHRISTOPHER BENSON (Chairman, Funding Agency for Schools): I cannot think why anyone should be defensive about it at all. Quite simply, as far as we are concerned—you are aware of our function, it is to fund and to monitor the funding of grant-maintained schools and therefore to "follow the pound", as it were to see how that is spent and whether it is spent properly and giving value for money with the child's best interests at the end. I see no reason for anyone to be the slightest bit defensive about the handling or the categorisation for that matter of the grant-maintained school or its system. Can it be improved? I am sure it can. I am sure all the education authorities and local education authority schools, too, have room for improvement and that is what we are constantly looking for. And to that extent—and I am perhaps going a little beyond your question—to that extent it is why we have reconstituted what we have called the *Rainbow Pack* which is this rather large book which we carry around with us, which sets out what we consider to be the best financial guidelines for schools. Now, the fact that we have rearranged that just recently demonstrates that we are looking for improvement right down the line, so we are not the slightest bit defensive—we are not the slightest bit defensive—either of our own position or, indeed, of those of the schools, but look for improvement constantly.

386. PROF ANTHONY KING: Well, given that answer let me pull somebody's leg—I am not sure whose it is, I suspect it is Mr Collier's, because we asked him a whole series of questions, or rather he drew out rather cleverly, I thought, from our *Issues and Questions* paper a

whole series of questions which he then answered at twelve and a half pages length and there is no suggestion in any of the answers to the questions that there is anything wrong anywhere or that there is anything that might be done a little bit differently to bring about an improvement. I mean, it is I think—cricket is beyond my competence but it has a "straight bat" quality about it—is that the right analogy—that I found rather charming.

CHRISTOPHER BENSON: Let him answer for himself but let me preface that answer though. We take some comfort, but not huge satisfaction, from the reports of the National Audit Office recently into grant-maintained schools. Two major reports have taken place and they have shown in the first instance areas for improvement, both in our relationships with the grant-maintained schools and the grant-maintained schools themselves. We acknowledge that there are areas—there must be—there must be areas for improvement, there is no such thing as a perfect organisation anywhere. But we take comfort from the fact that in the second report it is very clear that many of the aspects have been responded to and responded to positively, not only by ourselves but also by the schools, and we think that is what we should be doing all the time, encouraging people to look for problems. In the rather generous reply which we made to you in our opening statement with the questions and answers before you had asked them, which we did not actually intend, I have to say—perhaps Mike could actually pick up that very point.

MICHAEL COLLIER (Chief Executive, Funding Agency for Schools): Yes, I will do that, Chairman.

387. PROF ANTHONY KING: Can I ask Mr Collier, before he answers, a very simple question. Are you technically a civil servant?

MICHAEL COLLIER: No, no I am not. I have been in the past in one of my several previous existences but I am not now.

PROF ANTHONY KING: No.

MICHAEL COLLIER: I apologise if our answers appear defensive. As the Chairman has said we have carried out quite a thorough review of a great deal of the regime that we inherited so in a sense the weaknesses that we perceived we think we have addressed. Now, I would be a fool to say therefore everything is a hundred per cent correct because I think behind your question is actually, I would suggest, quite a general point about administration in the public services, that probably one of the biggest besetting sins is to have self-satisfaction and complacency about whatever processes are in place. Processes and systems are important—of course they are—but it is the people who are working them and their approach to them that keep them fresh and keep them working. So if there is any sense, as I say, of complacency or self-satisfaction, I apologise for that. We would explain it by some of the changes that we have made.

Can I mention two, just to give you an example of things that we have taken head-on? One of the issues that we did encounter very early on was probably an ambiguity in the definition of the role of a Responsible Officer at school level. You probably will have seen from the background material that we have now had that redefined to separate away from that the responsibilities of the Principal Finance Officer from that of the Responsible Officer and I am sure you may want me to develop that.

The second one, again, is the making it now mandatory the setting up of registers of interests at school level. I have to say that seventy or eighty per cent of schools actually have them voluntarily but we found it was worth making them mandatory. Those are the two that immediately come to mind where we have made an improvement.

388. PROF ANTHONY KING: One of the issues we obviously have to deal with—and it was raised in the Issues and Questions paper—has to do with the tendency, I would argue, of anybody that selects its own members to perpetuate its own ethos, its own culture, and in your submissions, in response to the question "Is there a danger that boards will recruit in their own image and become closed to new people and new ideas?" you say in effect, "No, there is no such danger, but on the contrary governing bodies will have an incentive to ask round and attract new membership to reflect the composition of their local communities in that they need to be responsive to those communities."

Now, I am sure that many governing bodies feel that they have that incentive and do make those kinds of enquiries but I must say that it is false to my experience of corporate bodies that they always and necessarily do that. Several that I have been on, given a chance to perpetuate themselves do precisely that, unless stopped. Is there not a case to be made out for some kind of institutional mechanism simply for making it less likely that that will happen?

CHRISTOPHER BENSON: Well, if I can answer by our own example, because what we have done recently—that is the Funding Agency for Schools itself—with three board vacancies available, we could have reverted to the original pattern that the Secretary of State had at the very beginning and that was for the Secretary of State—for the Department—to identify people and then for us with them to interview them from a longish list. We have gone to advertisement, in fact, and we have had, surprisingly enough, 2,000 responses to that advertisement and 1,000 set of applications. So it is by the example that we have set that we would travel the path that you are suggesting and I think that we would be suggesting and recommending to governors that they should watch and follow our example.

389. PROF ANTHONY KING: In other words that advertisements should become a matter of course?

CHRISTOPHER BENSON: No, no, it is not a mandatory requirement for us either. Self-governing bodies are there to self-govern and what we are doing is setting an example which we think is a good example but we would not try and be too prescriptive unless we found real fault and we don't.

MICHAEL COLLIER: Could I perhaps add to this as well, that I think when you look at public sector organisations you have to look at them in the round and at what other mechanisms are in place when you look at a particular issue. Taken on its own, the dangers that I think you refer to are clearly there, where the majority of the governing body are nominated appointees rather than elected. But if you have got a framework, as we believe we have in the grant-maintained sector, where a significant proportion of the governing body are elected, albeit by different constituencies, where you have a set of external accountabilities that I believe that we have, where we have codes of conduct, best practice, auditing regimes and so on and so forth, as we have, taken in the round then it seems to me there are the checks and balances that would address what might be seen to be the long-term dis-benefits of self-perpetuation. I mean, self-perpetuation has benefits, of course, consistency and so on and so forth. It is whether all the other checks and balances operate, I would suggest, that need to be taken into account in making the judgment of that issue.

390. PROF ANTHONY KING: It is against that background, perhaps, worth reporting to you that in private conversations that some of us have had, but also in written submissions to the Committee, some worries have been expressed about this, it is not something we have just made up. For example, the Secondary Heads Association says, "A governing body is accountable only to itself for its composition. Schools in many areas are aware of the difficulties of finding suitable people willing to serve but there is also the danger of governing bodies and, indeed, heads, carrying out a "clone" search in order to avoid unwanted challengers to what might have developed into too cosy a relationship."

Is that concern expressed by the Secondary Heads Association not something that you playing your role and this Committee playing its should not be concerned about?

CHRISTOPHER BENSON: Oh, we should be aware—certainly aware of that concern—and, again, it is part of our function to respond, to use our eyes and ears and that also we do, not only in the various reporting systems that we have, but we have allocated board members to regions within the country to become acquainted with the schools in that area—not to represent them but to become acquainted with those schools in the area—and to be a sounding board for us, the board itself, to see and to hear if there are any apparent situations such as you may be describing. So far we have not had any reports back on that basis and we do have very very regular reporting from those regional board members.

391. PROF ANTHONY KING: Could I ask you a series of questions that arise partly out of the possibility of governing bodies becoming rather closed, cosy inward looking groups? Suppose that somebody, a governor say, discovers as he or she believes that there is some malpractice of a financial kind, or say the head teacher abusing his or her authority in a particular grant-maintained school, what should that governor do under present arrangements?

CHRISTOPHER BENSON: In the normal and proper sense of the situations in any organisation, whether it be a company or a school, that director/governor should immediately expose the situation to their colleagues. If no notice is taken then — we are the next line with auditors—they have their own internal audit, we insist upon external audit as well, there are regular and, in some cases—5 per cent of schools—monthly financial reporting to us, there are plenty of routes to us and if there is dissatisfaction in the total then there is the Parliamentary Commissioners to whom they can turn. But that is very much at the end of a long bumpy road.

392. PROF ANTHONY KING: This is jumping ahead to something I was going to ask later on. Are you at all concerned—you say there are a lot of lines to the Funding Agency for Schools—are you at all concerned that two things are true; first, there are two bodies to which somebody might have recourse, depending on the specific nature of the worry, one is yourselves the other is the Department, and that both of those bodies are very distant from the school? You have something like 1,100 grant-maintained schools under your tutelage, as it were, and a governor of a small primary school in Norfolk might feel that he or she really would not begin to know about how to raise an issue with these very distant bodies, especially when there are two of them.

CHRISTOPHER BENSON: Well, the management role, of course, is the one to which they would look to the Department for Education and Employment. With the financial side we would expect to keep our fingers very very tightly on the pulse of the schools. Not only do we have the regional board members walking the patch, as it were, but we also have our own department permanent officials who have a task and I think very successfully carry out the role of keeping close to schools, keeping evident and available. There is obviously a situation that could arise, as you indicate, but we are trying—and with the financial memoranda and the reporting systems that are in place and the encouragement to governors and to heads and teachers to identify with us, we spent again quite a lot of time doing that, too, when we produced our corporate plan; we travelled around the countryside and we invited heads and governors to come and talk to us about the corporate plan, how they should respond to us. So it is very much a reaching-out from us, making ourselves available and identifiable and friendly, in fact, so that we are approachable.

393. PROF ANTHONY KING: I am sure you are doing your best, but with the best will in the world, which I am sure you have, my experience of being at or near the top of organisations suggests that pretty consistently the way that organisation looks top down is rather different from the way in which it looks bottom up. If I could illustrate the point, I was talking to somebody involved with a grant-maintained school the other day who said that somebody else who was involved in the school, whom he knew and who he named, had found it totally baffling. This was a governor of the school who was worried about something that was going on in the school and simply not being somebody who was networked in British public life, or whatever, finding himself thwarted within the school simply did not know what kind of recourse he as an ordinary governor had and eventually simply leaked his problems to the local press, thereby damaging the school which was, in fact, the last thing he wanted to do.

CHRISTOPHER BENSON: And that was a grant-maintained school?

394. PROF ANTHONY KING: Yes. He simply did not know—he had no idea what the division of function was between the Department and the Funding Agency and even if he had been clear about that—in fact the problems that he was concerned with came under both of the two headings you referred to—but he just did not know, there was no sort of hotline, there was no name on a piece of paper or phone number that he could get in touch with and baffled, as I say, he turned to the Press.

MICHAEL COLLIER: If I might add on that, whilst taking the point—and I think that all the agencies have got to bend over backwards to ensure that people have adequate information to enable them to make those kind of judgments—and we do take note of the point you are making—but one or two things that we have been doing, and bear in mind that we have not been in the field that long and we started ourselves up from scratch, but some of the things we have been doing of late in addition to the new Rainbow Pack which we hope is totally more accessible, not just to the professionals in the school but the governors as well that will give them a better clue to what business we are in, but we have for instance instituted a monthly bulletin now from the Agency which goes to every school which should be making it increasingly clear what we are about. We have published a *Who's Who* in the Agency, which has gone to every school, split up geographically, names named, so there is plenty of information within a school as to who to contact, I would suggest definitely within the Agency and I would also suggest within the Department. I think that the issue of the division between ourselves and the Department is one that I would suggest at the moment operates okay, but it would be an issue, I would have thought—and it is recognised in the legislation—that we would all want to look at as and when the sector expands. I think that that division between the financial and the management surveillance would be something for further consideration.

CHRISTOPHER BENSON: Could I just add to that, please? The Who's Who that Michael just mentioned is not actually out yet—we have produced it but it has not got to schools yet. But that Who's Who was preceded by—before the bulletin came out too, which is a relatively new thing, too—but that goes out immediately after every board meeting and gives to schools, parents, governors and the public at large, if they wish, some indication of what went on at the board meeting the previous day. So we try to communicate quickly to all schools in that area. But also when we allocated each of the regional board members we not only sent out their own biographical details and how to get in touch with them, but we also sent a photograph, so we were actually trying to make sure that these people were identified—and easily identified—by absolutely everyone. I can understand the problem of the person, I am just somewhat bewildered that they were left, as it were, in the dark totally by their own colleagues as well by the sound of it.

395. PROF ANTHONY KING: Can I give you another example arising from a letter that was written to us? Suppose a teacher finds herself in the following situation, that she believes that the head teacher is engaged in malpractice of some kind, is aware that the head teacher and the governors are very happy with each other, what advice would you personally, or would Mr Collier, give to that teacher, about what that teacher should do?

CHRISTOPHER BENSON: Let's ask Mr Collier.

MICHAEL COLLIER: If what you are saying is that what might be regarded as the normal recourse within the school, i.e. the Responsible Officer or the Chairman of the Governors was not a very attractive route for the reasons you have said, then the first port of call would seem to me to be the External Auditors. If not there then us.

396. PROF ANTHONY KING: Can I just quote from the letter I was referring to—and I have come across instances of worries of this character. But the person writes, "I hope this information will be of interest to the Committee. I am not in a position to give the name of the school involved without assurances of confidentiality. Unfortunately a culture of secrecy and fear is common in grant-maintained schools..."—she alleges, I am not indicating that I agree with this, I am just reading what she said—".... and staff have clear instructions that talking otherwise than in a positive manner to anyone outside the school will be treated as a disciplinary offence." Do you find that worrying?

CHRISTOPHER BENSON: Astonishing, frankly. Again even I have trotted around quite a lot of grant-maintained schools merely to listen in, to watch and to hear what the people say and the openness of the school is one of the most remarkable things that I have found personally. So I do find that an astonishing statement and very worrying, of course.

397. PROF ANTHONY KING: Incidentally I am sure that what you have described is the "norm" but obviously one of the things we have to be concerned with is the "abnorms" and what might be done about them.

CHRISTOPHER BENSON: I have made it my business, in fact, to choose two levels of visit for myself. Those schools which are very small or those schools which are very large. You had the Housing Corporation people in earlier and when I was at the Housing Corporation I established there things that I call beacons of excellence and bad black areas and I looked to both and I found that as Chairman it was my job to identify, if I could, either of those. I have not found any bad black areas in the grant-maintained schools but I have been to the smaller ones and I don't find—I have not found personally—anything but complete openness. I can expect that, of course, as Chairman, because I am going to be shown what I am going to be shown, am I not? But I have been around and might be regarded as being a trifle streetwise.

398. PROF ANTHONY KING: Could I ask you about the position of a head who has worries about the behaviour of some of the governors? Again there are very few cases of this but they are known to exist. It has certainly been expressed to us that the head under these circumstances can be in a peculiarly difficult position and the Secondary Heads Association says, "One further aspect of the dangers of this situation that should be noted by the Committee is the frequent unwillingness of the head or deputy to come forward and expose a problem for fear of jeopardising his or her job or career should the exposure point the finger at the governors."

And later on in the same submission the SHA says, "In the grant-maintained school and the incorporated or designated college, if the head of establishment blows the whistle he is on his own while the governor in trouble may suffer slightly reduced local public esteem, the head or principal may lose career, livelihood and chosen way of life."

Now, the SHA sounds concerned, not that this is going on all the time but that this is a potential problem, given the present arrangements.

CHRISTOPHER BENSON: I suspect that is a potential problem in almost every company, in every school, in every organisation and in any corporate structure, that there must be potential danger for that and that is to do with management and governance. And when I say governors, these are things that we are trying to drive through in the *Rainbow Pack*, trying to ensure that people do understand their responsibilities, do understand the opportunities that are available for them confidentially to pursue their line, rather than to write letters to newspapers or elsewhere. Ultimately if the letter goes to the newspaper it is going to be public anyway, so why not take the approved route, as it were.

399. PROF ANTHONY KING: This is not meant to be a challenging question, it is a genuine enquiry. If I go to the Rainbow Pack which, as you have indicated, is thick, where in it do I find—can you give me the page reference for where I discover if I am a school governor or head or whatever what I should do if ——

CHRISTOPHER BENSON: I can't give you that ——

PROF ANTHONY KING: Not now ——

CHRISTOPHER BENSON: But certainly I could drop you a note of that, if that is satisfactory, and can indicate the line to take.

400. PROF ANTHONY KING: Sure. Can I put to you two positive suggestions that have been made in this kind of context? One of them is simply given the perceived remoteness of both the Department and the FAS, that there might be something to be said for encouraging or even requiring each grant-maintained school to appoint an office holder ex-officio to be their local point of contact, their local troubleshooter, their local scrutineer, their local Visitor, to have somebody to whom people with worries could have recourse and who would have a general oversight of the school. The sort of person who would read the local newspaper, perhaps, a little more carefully. Do you follow me? It does seem strange —-

CHRISTOPHER BENSON: Yes, the Visitor.

PROF ANTHONY KING: The Visitor, yes.

CHRISTOPHER BENSON: We are thinking—perhaps I should be more precise about it—we are thinking about that particular situation. What we have endeavoured to do at the present time is to identify two roles within the school, the Principal Financial Officer, of course, and the Responsible Officer. The Financial Officer will more often than not be the head, the Responsible Officer may be a member of the governing body or he may indeed not and that is a role that we have cast already, running down the mould that you are suggesting. To go outside altogether and to appoint a Visitor at the moment seems heavy-handed because it does not seem, as far as we are concerned, to be necessary. But if you are drawing our attention at the present time to areas that we should examine more closely because of evidence that you have received, then we must address that.

401. PROF ANTHONY KING: Incidentally I would have thought the appointment of an ex-officio Visitor need not be heavy-handed. I could imagine in your 1,100 schools all but three or four of them might want to make use of the services of such a person in any given year. For example, most of the older universities had Visitors and I am sure many of the Visitors are totally unaware that they are a Visitor until once every twenty years or so when they get called upon.

CHRISTOPHER BENSON: But they are self-governing schools, that is the essence of grant-maintained.

PROF ANTHONY KING: Universities are supposed to be self-governing as well, so were medieval monasteries.

CHRISTOPHER BENSON: But what you are suggesting is that they should be, in fact, forced by us to have this visitor. I would prefer the lighter touch for the time being, at least to follow the route that we are following, to make it evident that there is such an opportunity for them to appoint such a person if they felt that it was a wise and sensible thing to do and for us to monitor that situation. That seems to me to be a progression that makes a great deal of sense, but also makes use of what we have already put into place.

MICHAEL COLLIER: Might I just add and really return to a point I made earlier about seeing individual aspects in the wider context. I should like to remind the Committee that not only do the Funding Agency for Schools visit schools but so do their own external auditors, the National Audit Office, OFSTED and there are probably other regulators such as Health and Safety Inspectors, etc. etc.—there are all manner of external regulators actually visiting the school. In addition to that there is a regime of requirement for publicity about annual reports and so on and so forth and I think that, too, has borne in on the issue that we have just discussed.

402. PROF ANTHONY KING: I want to give you a suggestion of some of what we are getting that makes us a little concerned—I put it no higher than that. Somebody was telling me the other day of a meeting at a rather troubled grant-maintained school. There was, indeed, the annual parents' meeting and apparently it was very well attended because there were troubles in the school and some of the parents were very vociferous and when the temperature had got to a sufficient height the Chairman of the governors, in effect, told the parents present to "sod off" because the standing of this parents' meeting was zero. They could say what they liked, they could even pass a resolution condemning the governors, but nothing much would follow. I just mention this—I am sure it is not typical, please do not misunderstand me, I am sure it is extremely atypical, but these kinds of things can happen and it is for that sort of reason that some of us are wondering whether it might not be a good idea to have somebody from outside this hothouse who is yet pretty local in a position to help when schools get into that kind of trouble, as rarely they do.

MICHAEL COLLIER: Again, it is very difficult to talk of that particular case without knowing what is behind it and what the facts are and if it is a financial issue, an educational issue, a general management issue—what is the issue that they are referring to. The other thing that we have not mentioned so far which I think again starts to bear in on this, is where a school has, for instance, failed its OFSTED report, another external agency making a judgment as to the education output of the school. The Agency has now established a small School Improvement Unit which is a voice or a shoulder for the school to cry on or refer to, to introduce professional help, etc. etc. Yet another source, if you like, of information and openness between the school and an external body. But, again, it is quite difficult to deal with generalities on the back of a specific such as that. So the consequences of a troubled parents' meeting, the parents have a right to give a vote of no confidence in the governing body if that is appropriate in their circumstances and that clearly is not going to be kept quiet, is it?

CHRISTOPHER BENSON: If I may just add, because the word he used as "hothouse" in that parents' meeting. I cannot imagine for one moment that such a meeting would go unnoticed if it was a "hothouse".

403. PROF ANTHONY KING: It did not, you are quite right. One other practical suggestion I would like to raise with you—and I agree this is on the fringes of your specific remit but it does arise in connection with grant-maintained schools and again it has been drawn to our attention—and that is the business of a member of the teaching staff or the head who is going to be disciplined or, indeed, sacked and the relevant appeal mechanism, and the appeal mechanism as it stands at the moment is set out by the Department at page 41 is as follows, "The Appeal Committee must consist of an odd number of and at least five members of the governing body. The head and members of the staff committee cannot be members of the Appeal Committee."

Now on the face of it, if the suspension or dismissal or other disciplinary sanction has arisen in part as difficulties that involve the governors, it would seem on the face of it that governors and only governors should constitute the Appeal Committee and the National Association of Head Teachers, for example, has written in to us to say "Would it not be a good idea, on these Appeals Committees, to require at least one outside person who might be expected not to have the kind of stake in the outcome that even a governor who had not been involved in the original disciplinary procedure might have?" Does that seem to you a sensible idea?

CHRISTOPHER BENSON: We think at the moment that what we have put into place with the two officer roles, one not being a member of the staff anyway and the other being a member of the staff and probably the head, we probably accommodated to that and in the event we still would say, I think, that there is the recourse to the Parliamentary Commission for Administration if it became so serious a matter. At the moment we have not sufficient evidence that to impose another external body, person, onto these groups of people who are governors of schools is a necessary thing. I really don't believe it, too, at the moment, but if it became evidentially so then we would take the powers that were necessary.

MICHAEL COLLIER: You were also right, Chairman, that of course this particular issue is not one that is within the remit of the Agency and is one that was set up in the original arrangements. It is a classic question, is it not, about the appeal mechanisms on staffing matters? Clearly the system that operates here, that if an agreed member of staff has not found satisfaction at school level then it is to an industrial tribunal. I mean, I think there is law in place that addresses that and it is a question of judgment as to whether that is the appropriate law. I don't think I would like to comment any further on that. I have seen a number of models in a number of organisations, each of which have their strengths and their weaknesses. There are models in other parts of the sector where you have an interminable series of appeals and appeals and appeals.

404. PROF ANTHONY KING: I was not suggesting any additional layer, I was simply suggesting that a group

of at least five people might be required to contain one person who would, in the nature of the case, not have been caught up in whatever it was that was being suggested. Could I just ask one final question? Most of the bodies that we are looking at are unitary in the sense that, as with the Higher Education Funding Council for England broadly they are the body appointed by the Government to look after universities. Reading these papers and listening to you, you have actually emphasised several times the plethora of bodies to which grant-maintained schools are in some sense accountable or answerable. I found myself wondering whether there were not too many and that perhaps the system which has grown up a little bit like topsy might not be simplified to the advantage of the schools.

CHRISTOPHER BENSON: I think it is a debate that we have together, as you might imagine, that as the growth, if it is to be growth, of the grant-maintained sector takes its place we will, I think, with Government have to look at how the whole of that greater body is administered because it will get hugely bureaucratic in the very way that you are suggesting it might, or even be now. At the moment it works but I think we have to look beyond the horizons that if the grant-maintained sector does grow and grows to any major extent that there may well be a different role for this Agency, indeed itself, to play.

PROF ANTHONY KING: Yes, that is fine.

LORD NOLAN: Anne?

405. ANNE WARBURTON: I have been fascinated by this discussion. I approach it from a slightly different angle from Professor King because I know very little still about grant-maintained schools and I was very much impressed by the fullness of your submissions, the various forms they took. I think that there still may be space between words in one or two aspects. Particularly I would like to start on the auditing side. I have the impression that you and no doubt the schools think that they are subjected to a very thorough external financial audit regime. Should I pause there and see if you want to comment on that?

CHRISTOPHER BENSON: Well, the accountant is on my left and I will ask him to add to what I have to say, but we believe it is thorough, we believe actually that certain schools believe that they are over-audited because they do have the National Audit Office, they do have OFSTED, they do have their own internal auditors, because we insist up on it, they do have their own external auditors, because we insist upon it. We require them to provide us not only with the audit but also the management letter and their responses to that management letter. That to me is a very thorough audit trail and I would guess that a lot of the schools do believe they are a bit over-audited. But, Mike, you are the expert.

MICHAEL COLLIER: I think you have said it all, Chairman. That clearly is a danger. I think it has been quite interesting, though, to see that once you get past the slogan, the instinctive reaction and people start to talk about it then they recognise the strength of the NAO coming at it from a value for money perspective, their own external auditors very much focused on their particular school, their particular issue, and the more distant hopefully, strategic look, that we take.

406. ANNE WARBURTON: I was quite struck at the fact that you can insist that you get monthly returns, if not

weekly, I almost gathered, which seems to bring you much closer to the coalface than I think we found in one or two other of our enquiries. You do get early warning?

CHRISTOPHER BENSON: We attempt to get early warning, yes, and the moment we see any likelihood—and we do have quite a number of people on the ground identifying themselves with the school, so if there is the slightest hint that there is something amiss or that the financial regime is not being properly adhered to, then we will ask for more regular reports and, of course, we can put our own auditors in as well.

MICHAEL COLLIER: Can I add for the record—I don't think we have ever insisted on weekly returns.

CHRISTOPHER BENSON: No, monthly.

ANNE WARBURTON: Yes. And I take it that that is fairly rare itself, that you need monthly ——

CHRISTOPHER BENSON: Yes, it is very unusual.

MICHAEL COLLIER: But it wasn't. I mean, that is again going back to an earlier point. The regime we inherited—every school had to send in monthly returns in some detail. We have actually, we think, simplified it and improved it and now 95 per cent of schools report to us quarterly.

407. ANNE WARBURTON: Good. A small postscript, perhaps, on that side; we did, I think, in our first report when we were receiving evidence then, at one point have it suggested to us that it is a bad idea if external auditors go on being the same for any given institution year after year after year. Do you give any advice on that to schools?

CHRISTOPHER BENSON: I will say one thing, Mike may well say another. I agree with the principle. As a business man I do actually agree with the principle that there should be an opportunity to change one's auditor after a given period of time. Now, whether that is three—two or three years—I am not a judge, I think that is for the management to make its decision. But I am actually in favour as an individual of regular re-examination of one's own auditors, like the recommendations.

MICHAEL COLLIER: Yes. Well, actually we don't make any precise rule, as Dame Anne is suggesting. Certainly schools have to re-tender their audits after a number of years. I do think it is a live issue. In revising the Rainbow Pack this time we decided not to give the kind of advice that you are hinting at. One of the reasons behind that is that there are other ways in which we regulate the external audit. We, for instance, carry out our own quality checks, or are doing now, through our own internal audit section and, of course, the firms that are allowed to audit grant-maintained schools also have their own regulatory regimes, either through the professional bodies or through the Audit Commission. The Audit Commission is the auditor in some grant-maintained schools at the choice of the grant-maintained schools. So we did not feel, therefore, that we needed to insist that the auditors should be changed because, going back on an earlier question, there are advantages of continuity and again some schools in more distant situations might find it difficult to get alternative auditors.

408. ANNE WARBURTON: On the internal front we had one submission that I happen to have seen—we have stacks of papers still—which made quite a point of the importance of having an internal audit as well as an external audit. In the case of grant-maintained schools I take it that the Responsible Officer is the internal auditor but does the Responsible Officer have any committee to which he or she works.

CHRISTOPHER BENSON: We do not prescribe a committee for the Responsible Officer. We describe him elsewhere as being—quote—"the audit committee in the sense of Cadbury". My own personal view, once again, is that he would be well advised to have someone qualified to assist him or to report with him and that would actually help to iron out some of the earlier problems that were being alluded to.

409. ANNE WARBURTON: In your view, does the Responsible Officer need statutory protection for his functions or is it all right as it is?

MICHAEL COLLIER: We have not judged so far that he does. It opens up a series of other issues to do with Accounting Officer status, etcetera, etcetera. As things stand, our judgment was that we should not press for that. I know there is an analogy in the FE sector which you might want to draw but we have taken a different path for the moment.

ANNE WARBURTON: Thank you.

CHRISTOPHER BENSON: I am sorry, but, again, just once more to add to that. The Accounting Officer role, which is one that Mike holds within our organisation, is analogous to the one that we are describing so I think it is something that we need to keep a careful eye on for the future. They may need assistance.

410. ANNE WARBURTON: Thank you. I wanted to turn to the value for money audit as I found myself getting a bit confused as to who was doing a value for money audit on what and when. It seems to be not only a question of what is covered in a value for money audit but also the different layers, if I could have a little briefing on that.

CHRISTOPHER BENSON: We are carrying out the value for money audit and that is our function. Again, perhaps it is more for the accountant than it is for whatever I am.

411. ANNE WARBURTON: The NAO also carries out value for money audits?

MICHAEL COLLIER: Yes, again, I was going to pick up that point because, as the accountant, I have perhaps a slightly different view of the use of the word "audit". I understand the Chairman's use of it but in the strict sense of the word, it is the National Audit Office that carries out the audit of value for money. We carry out value for money studies which we are largely doing on the basis of not being too prescriptive, we are not setting up like the Audit Commission studies that we then go and see implemented and audited.

We are producing studies, research published for schools for them to take on board and to use as best practice so that the VFM audit side of it in a formal sense actually comes through the National Audit Office. They do not have the regularity audit function which, of course, is with the external auditor to the schools.

412. ANNE WARBURTON: So, when you do one of your studies you concentrate strictly on management issues, do you?

MICHAEL COLLIER: No, again, we are early in the field. We have not published anything yet but we are on the verge of. The first two or three studies were, I think, in the terminology you are using of, management studies but we are about to embark on a study into value for money for post-16 education in schools and we hope that will be a contribution to the wider debate that is currently taking place and I think will come to a head next year. So, we are widening that and, again, we are not doing it in a closed way behind closed doors in York but we are asking the other agencies to work with us and to make their contribution so we will have a broadly based educational segment to that.

413. ANNE WARBURTON: So that gets you into the area which is covered by OFSTED visits which otherwise come under the Department, do they not?

MICHAEL COLLIER: Yes, we are developing our relationship almost daily with OFSTED as we see common ground. Something again which will be obvious to the Committee, whilst the grant-maintained sector in total might be relatively small, in some ways it is quite significant, particularly in the secondary sector where nearly 20 per cent of secondary schools are grant-maintained. We are garnering now an enormous amount of financial information about grant-maintained schools and this, I think, as we draw it together will be complementary to the kind of information that OFSTED has about grant-maintained schools.

In the same way, OFSTED are one of a number of intangible less formal routes where we might have early warning of problems in a school. We do not use that in any formal sense but our relationships with OFSTED are such that we can get that kind of warning.

ANNE WARBURTON: It is a question of relationships. Obviously, it matters a lot across all this sector.

MICHAEL COLLIER: Absolutely.

414. ANNE WARBURTON: Is it worth my asking if you have anything more to say about the School Improvement Unit?

CHRISTOPHER BENSON: Yes, the School Improvement Unit is intended to be very much the light touch, once again, to try and identify problems as quickly as we possibly can, to put academics and administrators together—it is a very small unit, one administrator, two academics—to move in to help, to assist, to listen and to move out. We have described it rather more as cavalry rather than heavy artillery but that is really what it is intended to be. It is intended to be rapid response.

415. ANNE WARBURTON: Good. Thank you very much. My third general area was to have been how much had our first report affected the FAS itself. That has been touched upon but I wondered if there is anything more to add about that. It is gratifying to know that already vacancies are being advertised but is there anything more in that area?

LORD THOMSON: We are all rather flattered you paid so much attention to our first report and I think we want some further evidence on that.

CHRISTOPHER BENSON: The affect of your first report?

ANNE WARBURTON: On your agency.

CHRISTOPHER BENSON: I think our response is very positive actually. We believe that it is a very worthwhile thing that is being done. We think that we must respond as helpfully and as hopefully as we can. I think it has identified areas that we should address and have. We are very, very positive.

What we have been doing—we mentioned the bulletin earlier on that follows our board meetings and in that we have addressed the code of conduct within the whole of the grant-maintained sector. So, yes, you have spurred us into action a bit.

MICHAEL COLLIER: I think, Chairman, it is worth emphasising the point, and it may explain something that Professor King raised earlier, that I think the board wish to operate to the highest standards that the Committee drew up in any event, I have no doubts about that, but we are a controversial body. We are a body that attracts a lot of media attention and I think that that too has its effect, that we have to make sure that everything we do is absolutely right. One should not overlook that particular aspect.

CHRISTOPHER BENSON: And perhaps one should add that we do, hopefully by example within our own organisation, send the right messages down through to the schools themselves. The advertising is one thing, of course; the setting up of our own Register of Interests, that is one of the most comprehensive registers that I have seen anywhere. That has been something that by example we can only lead in that way. We have limited powers in other directions.

416. ANNE WARBURTON: If I may, following upon that, just ask one final question, a small one. Codes of conduct. I notice in your papers that you comment that grant-maintained schools are free to introduce codes of conduct. Would you consider, perhaps, encouraging them a little bit more than that?

CHRISTOPHER BENSON: Encourage is the right word, but yes.

ANNE WARBURTON: Thank you very much.

417. LORD THOMSON: Sir Christopher, you have already drawn our attention to the fortunate coincidence that in your long and varied voluntary public service you have both been chairman of the Housing Corporation and now chairman of this new organisation. We were hearing evidence from the Housing Corporation earlier this morning. I wondered if you would like to comment on your experience of the difference between the two organisations.

What I have in mind really is that the Housing Corporation have told us that they are both a regulator and a funder; they are, first of all, a funder and they are also a regulator. You have been really rather at pains to tell us that you are a funder and not a regulator and you say in the very useful paper you gave us, "management and governance issues are controlled by the Department for Education and Employment and not by ourselves." Would you like to give us your reflections on the difference between the two roles that you have experienced?

CHRISTOPHER BENSON: There are remarkable similarities. First of all, the atmosphere, if one is quite genuine about it, the atmosphere when I joined the Housing Corporation was somewhat hostile from local authorities. They did not want to see their housing stock taken away from them. They did not actually appreciate too much the advantages that were being given to housing associations on grant levels and by the amount of money that was being given. So, the atmosphere in the initial stages was not brilliant. I think the same comment could be made about the Funding Agency for Schools. When first we came into being there was the impression that there was going to be a hostile tension between local education authorities and ourselves, so the climate was very similar.

The objectives, clearly, were somewhat similar because both housing associations are voluntary, as are governing bodies of schools, so the end product was very similar. The disbursement of funds, again somewhat similar from the housing corporation to housing associations on, in their case, capital grant for proven projects. Similarly, with us again, we have the formula allocation but we also have the capital grant against shown needs so there are quite a lot of similarities.

The major, and very strong, difference is, of course, on the monitoring which we call monitoring. We monitor our pound. There is the heavy regulation in the housing corporations and, if I go back to the very beginning again, the first job that I did with the Housing Corporation was to insist that all housing associations within 18 months had PLC-type accounts. The accounting in those first days was archaic and absolutely meaningless and to follow a pound for value for money it was impossible to do it without having proper accounting systems. Here, we have them. They were here before we arrived and so we have not had to do the heavy-handed insistence upon accounting.

What we have done is to follow the accounting route but to recognise that ultimately the governance side is that of the Department for Education and Employment. There are those of us who, if the sector got larger coming back to an earlier question, there are those of us who might actually be seeking to persuade government to pass some of the more governmental roles on to us. I am not sure whether I have answered your question but I have talked a lot.

418. LORD THOMSON: You have indeed, you have answered my question and provoked a further question. Reading the Rainbow Pack one was not left in any doubt about the degree of supervision and responsibility you have on the audit front. It is the gap on the governance front that I think concerns me anyway in asking this question. We heard yesterday from the Higher Education Funding Council which has a fewer number of educational institutions to supervise than you have but they did indicate to us that through their funding responsibilities they regarded themselves as having some significant responsibility for the governance arrangements.

When you look at your arrangements I am much struck by the fact that you now have responsibility for more than

1,000 grant-maintained schools and there is a huge distance between your schools and you sitting in your headquarters and the Department of Education sitting in its headquarters and I just wonder whether there is not a governance gap to be more adequately filled.

We had some evidence the other day from I think it was the Association of Governors of Grant Maintained Schools which drew our attention to this very wide gap and said, I thought rather plaintively, it would be rather nice to have somebody filling that gap perhaps on the ground, a friendly outside source of information and encouragement and advice. Have you given thought to that?

CHRISTOPHER BENSON: I honestly think that the people sitting up in Darlington and York would be very disturbed and unhappy to hear what you have just said because they do actually spend an enormous amount of their time on the ground with the schools and the information that passes to and fro is very, very considerable—Mr Collier said earlier on, the "garnering" of data and information.

It is fundamentally to do with financial matters but it must inevitably cover other matters too. One cannot walk through a school when one is looking at a heavy audit without learning much more about it than that. Those people are encouraged to spend a lot of time on the ground. We also, both at officer and my own level, spend as much time as we can—more time than we would prefer on occasions—with ministers and with permanent officials at the Department in the hope that their regional arrangements which they have which coincide with our regional arrangements will provide some of the governance telltales, if you like. I am looking for a word that will signify something that might be going wrong at an early stage.

I do not know whether Michael would like to add to that, but I am of the feeling at the moment that the governance is working and that is the most important thing from our point of view. The thing that will worry us is if we get bellwethers that indicate that it might not be.

MICHAEL COLLIER: If I might, Chairman, just add a couple of quick points. I think also you have had evidence from other bodies who would take perhaps a different view and it illustrates the kind of balance that we have to strike, which is ensuring that things are not happening that are endangering childrens' education but we are not doing it in a heavy-handed, top down, bureaucratic way. The School Improvement Unit was, again, a case in point. Probably the governors you spoke to were unaware of that initiative. It is only just getting off the ground now. It seemed to me that that addressed some of the concerns that they had.

The other thing I would add is a thing that has come across on a number of occasions today about our accessibility and it is a good throwaway line that we are up in York. I have to tell you York is a very accessible place. As the Chairman said, our staff spend a lot of time on the road and visiting schools but also we live in a technological age now and we are finding things like mobile phones and fax machines and working from home and all different ways of arranging the way our staff work is contributing to our accessibility.

My punchline on this is that when we had our consultative conferences where all the grant-maintained schools were invited to attend, there was one unanimous thing that they said to us and that was their satisfaction with our accessibility.

PROF ANTHONY KING: So there!

LORD NOLAN: On behalf of the Committee, may I thank you all very much. You have supplied us with written information which was and is and will be extremely helpful, but it is most valuable to have had it supplemented by your answers to our questions. I am most grateful to you.

Dr Lawlor, thank you very much for coming to join us today. We are extremely glad to see you and grateful to you for your help. I am going to ask Diana Warwick to start off the questions to you.

419. DIANA WARWICK: Dr Lawlor, good morning. Can I say what we have said to other witnesses dealing with grant-maintained schools in particular and that is that our task is not to question the principle of grant-maintained schools or their existence, nor are we suggesting in any sense in this, or indeed in any of the other public bodies that we are looking at, that impropriety is widespread. We are simply looking at the way in which public money is spent and the propriety and standards associated with that.

Having said that, I wonder if we can just go back a little bit because you wrote a pamphlet I think in 1988 about how schools should opt out and I wonder perhaps if you could tell us about your interest in the whole principle of grant-maintained schools and perhaps something about your experience of them.

DR SHEILA LAWLOR

DR SHEILA LAWLOR (Director of Politeia): Right. Thank you very much and thank you very much for asking me to come along.

I suppose there are two things to be said of my interest. It really is in the wider principle of how we organise education in this country. I was particularly thinking of the wider principles on which education developed very successfully in this country, which was on a voluntary basis whereby once the 1870 Act came into force the aim was to fund voluntary bodies, to fund children, not to run a bureaucratic system. This principle lay behind schooling in this country.

If you look at the debates within the Liberal Party in 1870 about what exactly 1870 was going to do, Gladstone on the one hand was determined that what we should do was to supplement not supersede the voluntary basis of education and he, with the Conservatives, defeated those in his own party who wanted a much more collectivist approach—if you like, what they called the Prussian System. So, I think at the heart of the debate in this country, from the inception of maintained education, has been a debate between collectivists on the one hand who quite honestly feel—and it is a respectable view but I do not share it—that education can be best organised collectively through, in the case of this country, a local authority system.

Or, on the other hand, you have had, I think, a very successful voluntary basis for education where it was not a matter of public funding for education, as Salisbury said, "where education is compulsory it should be free", and there are all kinds of reasons why we should fund education publicly, but what is the best way to fund education so that we get maximum efficiency, so that we enshrine into the very system parental responsibility and choice and so that we can give the voluntary bodies who are doing a very good job the opportunity to continue to do it.

Those questions, in one way or another, have come back and I think that the 1980s were an attempt to redress the balance because from the 1960s and 1970s we had become a very collectivist and collectivised system where local authorities ran things, they appointed the teachers, they determined very often a curriculum. I have seen them, in fact, telling teachers how to teach and a system of preferment had grown up where if teachers and heads were not in sympathy with the ideology, educational philosophy which was in fashion, they were not necessarily promoted.

Grant-maintained was a very good way to try and circumvent this really rather top-heavy collectivist system in terms of finance, in terms of philosophy and in terms of being completely out of kilter with the great traditions of this country which had been deliberately set up that way. The idea was to devolve to those responsible the powers and the money to teach, not to set up an alien system, because in this country, unlike other countries, that kind of thing did not work.

420. DIANA WARWICK: That is very interesting that you are talking about not replacing a bureaucratic system or a costly administrative system. How do you react then to the introduction, to the setting up, for example, of the Funding Agency for Schools? How do you perceive its role?

SHEILA LAWLOR: You really are raising what is a question at the heart of what has happened since "88 and how things will go in the future. At its heart is really are we moving from a local collectivism or a local bureaucracy to a central one and the great danger is with all of Whitehall and all government reform you have, I think, a complete contradiction between the spirit of intended reform, certainly as I think intended by the government, and the implementation as implemented throughout Whitehall. There has always been this tension, certainly in education policy.

I think the Funding Agency for Schools in itself—the idea is a good idea. The idea that we should fund the child not the system because money gets lost in a system and any Chancellor of the Exchequer, going back again to Gladstone, will explain how you get better value for money when the funding follows the child. Also, I think, it is an inbuilt accountability mechanism if funding directly follows the child and it does not get lost.

The aim should be really to move to a clear and simple funding system where, I think, we have to move in over the decades to come to a common funding formula which is clear, which is transparent, into which will be built certain features—for instance, age weight, different ages require different amounts of money perhaps—other features such as small schools, local schools, inner cities and then one or two others. I think on the whole though it should be a simple formula, it should be clear so that every parent in the country knows that their child is having the same share of public money as another child, which does not happen now.

A simple formula would also have the advantage which the present byzantine formula does not, that it does not become then a basis for bureaucratic administration. I think the present way of doing things is very costly to administer. None of us know exactly how much money actually is spent on education. There are so many formulae to be got round and there are so many differences and weightings right around the country that it is a bureaucratic paradise but in the interests of efficiency and fairness I think it is a nightmare.

Let us move to a fair funding formula. Let the Funding Agency for Schools be the funding body but keep out of that the other decisions such as how teachers should teach, what system we should have for running schools, and so on. They should simply be a funding agency. I think that was the original intention.

421. DIANA WARWICK: Could I ask you then about accountability. How do you see accountability operating within this rather small still but new sector?

SHEILA LAWLOR: One of the best way for having accountability in schools is letting parents pick a school. One of the problems is that in, if you like, administration and in the exercise of policy much of the official advice is we must have more and more accountability mechanisms. They start off with league tables, say, for schools and they have value added this and that. It becomes expensive to administer and at the end of the time it really does not tell you very much more.

There is one very simple accountability mechanism and that is whether parents want a school or not. It is a very dramatic mechanism and in the old days, I think before you had much more direct parental permission to choose a school and to find what would suit the child, you had local authorities who allocated children to a school and you had no choice but to take what you were given. Now, we have only moved halfway away from that because until all schools are grant-maintained schools or Independent Charitable Trusts, whatever, you will not have proper responsibility and accountability between parent and school.

I would see accountability as a very straightforward matter. If a school did not manage to attract parents for whatever reason it would not have funding and it would simply wither. At the moment we still have artificial mechanisms in between the parent and the school, which says sometimes some schools must change, some schools must get rid of surplus places. There is still too much intervention between the parent and the school. It did not work in the old days. You saw before '88 that one of the reasons for the grant-maintained schools was local authorities artificially changed the character of schools, they lopped off sixth forms, they built schools on the wrong side of the tracks because that suited the philosophy of the day, they closed flourishing voluntary schools.

If you take authorities like Liverpool, look at what was happening then in ILEA, where very successful schools were being threatened with closure because they did not fit in with the bureaucratic plan.

I think we have moved a bit away from that but I still think there is too much interference and that is why we are trying to find other artificial accountability mechanisms. If you leave the parents to choose the school and if they do not choose the school the school would shut. I think that is the best accountability mechanism that exists.

DIANA WARWICK: Could I come back to the practical aspects of accountability. You have, I think, been presenting an ideological picture here.

SHEILA LAWLOR: No, this is not ideological, Miss Warwick. I think your position may be ideological but this is not an ideological position. I am saying that from time immemorial when State education was funded in this country we did not fund a system. It has become a matter of ideology for those who want a system to couch things in terms of other people being ideological. It is certainly not an ideological position to say that education developed on a voluntary basis in this country. We funded children. We did not fund a system. In 1988—and this was aspired to by both Liberals in the 19th century and Conservatives who inherited the mantle in the 20th—there was a period of collectivism which has been outlined in other ways in terms of the economic change by Robert Skidelsky in his *World After Communism* this year, into which, I would say, the education system fell in this country, along with all kinds of other things in terms of public policy.

A move was made in the 1980s to tilt the balance back to try and take that collectivism out. I do not think it is ideological to suggest ways where this might be further improved but I do think it is ideological for people who oppose this position and oppose grant-maintained schools to say you are talking from an ideological viewpoint. I am not. I am simply explaining, if you like, the background to voluntarism in this country and how some of the reforms aimed to tilt the balance back in that way and it is a different sort of way of thinking about things. But it is ideological and this has been one of the problems with the reforms that anybody who is not pro-collectivism has been dubbed an ideologue.

DIANA WARWICK: I hoped I had made it clear right at the start that we were not adopting either a pro or anti stance.

SHEILA LAWLOR: Sorry, in your last question—this is why I replied—just as you were opening your question, as far as I know, you were talking from an ideological standpoint.

DIANA WARWICK: I am sure I did ask you whether you were talking from an ideological standpoint.

SHEILA LAWLOR: Yes, that is a very curious question.

DIANA WARWICK: Only in the sense that—

SHEILA LAWLOR: Especially as I had explained my position. I had discussed it in terms of the historical evolution of the principle. That is not an ideology.

422. DIANA WARWICK: I was going to go on to make what I hoped was not a terribly contentious point actually. Quite a lot of our witnesses and the people who have given us evidence have felt it necessary to say that they eschewed any kind of political dimension in their support for grant-maintained schools and there seems to

have been in quite a lot of the evidence a defensiveness about it. I was only going to ask you, because you had been part of the political argument, whether you thought from the point of view of grant-maintained schools themselves that that political dimension was not an issue.

SHEILA LAWLOR: This is where I simply cannot accept the premise, the idea that in some way it is ideological or political. It happened to be part of a reform movement in the 1980s, a movement to liberalise what had become very hidebound. Opponents of that reform tend to dub it change made for political reasons because it is associated with the government which it opposed in every area of policy or changes made for ideological reasons. What I would like to contend, if I may, is that the opponents of such change, opponents who dubbed such change to be "ideological" or political, I would regard their position as extremely ideological because what they are saying, or what they are implying, is that they are defending a collectivist approach which grew up really in rather an alien manner in this country and they want to protect it.

It depends what you mean by political. The defenders of the status quo are not political and those who want to change are. So, if we get our terms clear then——

423. DIANA WARWICK: Let me ask you something that has been raised as a practical issue for the management of schools or the involvement of governors in schools because that has been an area where quite a lot of the comment that we have had has been focused.

The National Association of Governors and Managers characterised the new basis on which schools are governed as a great experiment, a great experiment in participatory public service by ordinary citizens. They then went on to say that there were inherent weaknesses in this particularly at local level, that the demands being made on governors were very, very challenging though lots of new powers, lots of new skills associated with exercising those powers. They were unpaid volunteers and there was always the danger that they might throw in their hands if the going got rough.

I wonder whether in looking at this huge number of governors whom we now want to see taking an interest in schools, are there ways which you can think of to strengthen that great experiment, of making it more surely based at local level?

SHEILA LAWLOR: There is no perfect solution to what makes the best governing body. You can look at the independent sector, you can look at the different sorts of schools, but I think an improvement has been made since '86 when, in the old days, you had really local authority dominated governing bodies. I think progress is being made.

There are two things that people who are making policy must remember. There is no perfect system and you cannot dot every "i" and cross every "t". What you can do is have a law of the land which will say that these are the duties and responsibilities of those appointed and it is up to you to ensure that those duties and responsibilities are fulfilled how you will. I do not think you can keep trying to perfect a system because every school is different, every budget is different, the challenges in every school are different. For instance, even two grant-maintained

schools which I know in London, grant-maintained voluntary aided schools, each of them is very good in its own way—the London Oratory and the Cardinal Vaughan school—yet they are so different. I would say different challenges meet the governors in both foundations.

I do not think that sitting in Whitehall or in a local authority you can keep perfecting a system of management for governing bodies. What I do think you can do is simplify and make absolutely clear what are the duties and responsibilities of the governing body vis-a-vis the head and vice versa and eliminate possible tension and friction there and then say you are responsible for your duties under the law. That is, I think, as far as you can go because otherwise you will develop management models, you will try to have a uniform system for all schools. It will be bureaucratic, it will be expensive and I do not think anybody will want to work with wodges of paper coming in. As Keynes said, what was it—"It is better to get something roughly right than precisely wrong."

424. DIANA WARWICK: There is one associated question with that that has come up in several of the representations to us and that is if we are to get governors from a wider range and perhaps also ensure that governors are prepared to take on these additional responsibilities we should introduce a system of payment for this, what is currently voluntary activity. Would you support that idea?

SHEILA LAWLOR: It is a very difficult question. I simply do not know. I do not know what the answer to it is. I think though if you want people to come forward as governors one must make absolutely clear what the duties and responsibilities are and they must be simplified. I think there are very good models in some schools for this, which might be a source of information. Some of the independent schools have managed it and if a school is good or if the head and staff are enthusiastic, if they are really doing something with their school, I think you do not have that much difficulty getting governors provided they are not given wodges and wodges of paper to read.

I would go along with some of the criticisms of the implementation of reform that what was intended to simplify accountability mechanisms to make for greater efficiency has ended up with much, much more administrative and bureaucratic work and this applies to governors too. I would say the best way is to simplify, to clarify the responsibilities, to simplify the relationship between the head and governors and to ensure that the school has the kind of autonomy and independence where it can flourish and I think it will attract good governors because that is what experience has shown. I am not sure that I would further complicate matters and as for payment, I do not know, I simply do not know.

425. DIANA WARWICK: Perhaps I can just ask you one final question before others have an opportunity. Where there are problems at local level some of the issues that have come up to us have been rows that have blown up often quite out of proportion and the only focus for those rows is the Secretary of State. We learned also from the funding body that they themselves can also take complaints and try to help resolve difficulties. Do you think there is an argument for what one of our contributors called a "critical friend" at local level acting as a mediator where it has not proved possible for conflict between governors and heads to be resolved.

SHEILA LAWLOR: Are you referring to rows which have occurred in grant-maintained schools specifically or LEA schools?

426. DIANA WARWICK: I think in other schools, in local authority schools in other words, the local authority probably exercises that dimension in some way. There is not a mechanism at local level for a disinterested observer but somebody who knows and understands the school to help.

SHEILA LAWLOR: I would be very reluctant to go down the route of having some sort of other tier. I do think if a system works well you do not have to legislate for the mistakes. The hard cases always make bad laws and one of the great problems with trying to decentralise here in this area and trying to devolve autonomy and responsibility to those concerned has been that we have given with one hand and then we have rather got worried about it and we have tried to legislate for the hard cases. I think that is a very bad basis for administrative change or regulatory change.

The best thing is to go for autonomy where you will. You will always have differences of opinion and perhaps differences of emphasis but a good head, supported by a good governing body, will deal with it and, if not, they will probably have to be dealt with elsewhere. I would be very reluctant to go down the route of setting up yet another tier of referral. I think that you really have to trust the schools and, on the whole, schools especially now as they are taking more responsibility and people who want to take responsibility are coming forward for the jobs and those who have grown up in the more dependency culture of the previous 20 years are retiring, I think we will see people well able to cope.

Remember, you are changing a system which for 30 years was dependent on the local authority for everything from the light bulb to the head teacher and a local authority whose schools were not anything to write home about in terms of standards, in terms of efficiency or whatever, and you are moving very rapidly to a new culture where people are coming forward having been trained in the old ways. If they wanted a window on their school they had to ring up the local authority, if they wanted a new teacher or a supply teacher. Of course, there will be teething problems but the best way is to allow them their heads subject to the law of the land. You must have faith in them. They will sort it out. I have seen schools do the most marvellous things over a five year change. It is terrific. But if you start thinking that you have to take it away or there has to be somebody else to whom they report or if we have a row—myself and my deputy head—there is somebody else, I think the governors can sort it out. I would not have extra mechanisms except where the law of the land applies. I would not down that route, no.

DIANA WARWICK: Thank you.

LORD NOLAN: Professor King?

427. PROF ANTHONY KING: You said something in response to one of Diana Warwick's questions that intrigued me and it had to do with this very difficult relationship, potentially very difficult relationship, between the head and the governors. You said that you would prefer not to establish some new mechanism or tier for dealing with problems that came up but rather that there should be a clearly stated definition of the role of the governors on the one hand and the head teacher on the other.

Let me put it to you deliberately slightly provocatively that these kinds of relationships between chairmen of boards of directors and chief executive officers, and so on, are very common in the world and that no one has ever succeeded, or ever will succeed, in defining the role sufficiently clearly that there will not be problems.

SHEILA LAWLOR: But there is a bottom line of clarity, that is all I was trying to imply, that there are certain things which are required. In company law there is company law and there are certain duties and responsibilities which are set out and different contracts will specify different things—I think that is right—but I would agree with the premise that we cannot have an absolute definition of every detail, so much depends on personality, the kind of challenge that is there and the kind of structure in the school.

I would err on the side of caution rather than trying to set it out and I think that possibly one of the problems with the '88 format was—and I remember thinking about it when it was being drafted even—it was this precise relationship between head and governors. I cannot say it because it is a public committee and I might get it wrong, but one of the people responsible, I think, was very keen to put in the head was responsible for the day-to-day running of the school and the governing body was responsible for the general strategy, or something else. I cannot think what happened in the end with that clause.

It was a minefield and it still is and I would say that the law of the land should be the bottom line rather than trying to work out the precise relationship. I would go more for giving heads their head. I think it is very difficult for a good head if governors think they are running the school, but then you need strong heads. In the independent sector the most successful heads whom I have met and known and talked to, they say governing bodies are a battlefield. It is like any company. You are the chief executive and the governors think they know it all, want to tell you what to do but you need all the talents which you need in dealing with people, shrewdness and charm and all kinds of things, but in the end you cannot resolve it. It is up to the head himself to resolve, provided the cards are not stacked in favour of potentially too interfering governors who actually want to go to every classroom and inspect every teacher when, I would say, that is on the whole a function for the head.

PROF ANTHONY KING: Yes, that is the only thing I wanted to ask.

LORD NOLAN: Any other questions? We have, in fact, more than exhausted our time. We are very grateful to you for answering our questions so fully, Dr Lawlor. It has been extremely helpful in helping us to clear our minds. Thank you so much.

428. SHEILA LAWLOR: Thank you very much indeed for asking me. The other thing is, if there is anything else you want to know I now am director of a new forum called Politeia and I am writing on some of these things and I can send over some of the stuff if you would like to see it.

LORD NOLAN: We would be very grateful if you would. Thank you very much.

THURSDAY 23 NOVEMBER 1995

OPENING STATEMENT

Opening statement from the Funding Agency for Schools

The Funding Agency for Schools is an executive NDPB of the Department for Education and Employment. Established under the Education Act 1993, we have statutory functions to fund grant-maintained schools and monitor their expenditure, and to plan school places in certain local authority areas. We are thus principally a funding and monitoring body; we do not have a quality inspection role, nor do we have a direct remit to control or regulate schools' governance and management arrangements.

When the Chairman of the Agency was appointed in October 1993, there were 6,592 schools in the sector. When the Agency was formally established on 1st April 1994, there were 926 schools operating within that grant-maintained sector. There are now some 1,084 schools in the sector.

The range of schools is diverse, divided approximately 60% secondary and 40% primary. There are special schools, including a hospital school; a range of comprehensive and selective schools; rural, urban and inner city schools; non-denominational and denominational schools including Church of England, Roman Catholic, and Jewish schools; single sex schools and mixed schools. The sector is also geographically widespread with grant-maintained schools in 83 of the 109 LEA areas in England.

The Agency was thus established to carry out its functions in relation to a considerable number of schools and has since continued its work during a period of sustained, if slowing, growth. (There are now signs that this trend is reversing and interest in grant-maintained status is increasing.) We were in the position of setting up many of our internal systems from scratch, although the framework for our relationship with the DFEE was laid down in the form of our Financial Memorandum with the Secretary of State and the framework for our relationship with schools was inherited from DFEE in the form of the individual financial memorandum executed with each school and the manual of advice and guidance on financial matters to schools, the *Rainbow Pack*.

In the 18 months of our life to date, we have reviewed and revised many of the components of the framework and regulatory regime of the grant-maintained sector (where such may be under our control and remit), in order to improve and to develop the sector's accountability and effectiveness. In particular, we have comprehensively revised the *Rainbow Pack*, we have agreed a revised financial memorandum with schools, and we have initiated a number of value for money studies in the sector, one of the most significant of which will be our work on unit cost comparisons to be published next year. The publication of our value for money studies will result in a dissemination of good practice within the grant-maintained sector. As far as our funding responsibilities are concerned, although funding policies are not ours to control, we have revised the capital bidding system and reviewed our system for paying special purpose grants to schools. We are also working closely with the Department to improve the revenue funding system by contributing to analysis work on the common funding formula and a national funding formula. Our work with schools on their proposals to plan new school places has also developed over the 18 month period; we currently have planning responsibilities on a shared basis with the relevant LEA in 47 areas for secondary education, and we have sole responsibility for secondary education in a further 3 areas. In 6 areas, we have shared responsibility for primary education. We are currently bringing forward our own proposals to establish new grant-maintained schools in two areas of the country. Although we have no direct accountability for quality in education, we have recently established a small School Improvement Unit to provide appropriate advice and assistance to grant-maintained schools who have "failed" their OFSTED inspections.

These developments and our ongoing work with grant-maintained schools at all levels give us a particular perspective on the questions you raise with us. This statement outlines our replies.

Financial monitoring by the Agency

We have statutory powers (S.84 of the Education Act) to impose requirements on schools, in accordance with grant regulations, in respect of any payment of grant. As a condition for receipt of grant, schools are required to enter into a contract with us, the Financial Memorandum, which governs their financial management. We issue further requirements, information and guidance in our *Rainbow Pack*.

We scrutinise schools' compliance with these requirements and conditions by means of our financial monitoring work. We require quarterly (or monthly for 5% of schools needing more frequent scrutiny by us) returns from schools which enable us to check schools' expenditure. Our teams visit schools to follow up on any issues and irregularities. We receive copies of schools' annual audited accounts and auditors' management letters. If there are any problems or a school has financial difficulties, we then work closely with a school to help it plan a way out of its difficulties. If the situation cannot be resolved in this way, we can advise the Secretary of State that further measures may need to be taken. We would, of course, need to involve the Secretary of State at an earlier stage if the difficulties extended to management and governance issues which are controlled by the Department.

We have found these powers sufficient in practice. In fact, the system seems to have worked well, in that, where in a small number of cases, problems have arisen, these have been picked up through our monitoring and scrutiny mechanisms and dealt with either by the school itself or in consultation with us or the Department.

Financial propriety and good governance

The required arrangements are set out in our *Rainbow Pack*. We had been working on substantial revisions to the manual and our proposals for new requirements to tighten up financial propriety arrangements were endorsed by last year's NAO review and subsequent PAC report. These revisions were also to make the manual more user-friendly and comprehensible. The main changes made were to clarify the separation of powers between the Responsible Officer and Finance Officer, an important way of preventing any concentration of power in the hands of any one individual. We have also introduced a requirement for schools to maintain a register of pecuniary interests for governors and staff with significant financial responsibilities.

These arrangements to ensure financial propriety are vital mechanisms in the governance of a school. A school that is well-run financially is usually a well-managed school. By requiring these mechanisms to be put in place, we are requiring schools to accept a good management discipline, within which, the respective roles of staff and governing body members are understood and each may carry out their separate roles and duties within a defined framework.

Role of Responsible Officer

In revising our *Rainbow Pack* of financial advice and guidance to schools, we found it necessary to clarify the role of the Responsible Officer so as to ensure a clear separation of function from the Principal Finance Officer. The RO has overall responsibility for control and supervision, like a Cadbury Audit Committee; the PFO, usually the Head or Bursar has day to day management responsibility for financial matters. This formal separation of powers is important so as to avoid the concentration of power in the hands of any one individual and to provide an objective health check on the school's operations.

External audit

Schools appoint their own external auditors who are required to submit copies of their annual accounts and their management letters to us. We provide advice to auditors on grant-maintained issues and also review the quality of external audit on a sample basis. We monitor the schools financially on a quarterly basis (monthly in the case of a small number of schools requiring more detailed oversight on our part), and, as a condition for giving grant to schools, we require them to comply with certain requirements set out in our "Rainbow Pack", which also includes advice and guidance to schools on financial matters. We may also initiate a specific audit of a particular school by our own internal Audit function. The National Audit Office also conducts value for money reviews.

This system provides for public oversight by means of our monitoring and inspection work, we being accountable for this to the Secretary of State and to Parliament, and because the grant-maintained schools' accounts are published and can be scrutinised by parents and the public.

Undoubtedly some schools may feel they are over-audited, especially those who have had a visit from us, from their auditors and from NAO in quick succession. However they do recognise that it is the system as a whole, comprising the different bodies to whom they are accountable and the various requirements with which they must comply, which provides the means to ensure that they operate properly and are publicly seen to do so. Grant-maintained schools are accountable nationally—they have to comply with national standards and are inspected by OFSTED (who requires them to draw up action plans to correct any deficiencies), they are subject to value for money review by NAO, they have to deliver the National Curriculum and they have to publish their results in a national performance league table. They are accountable both locally and nationally through the audit system, and through our financial monitoring work. We are ourselves nationally accountable for this work in that we are responsible to the Secretary of State and through her to Parliament. The Chief Executive of the Agency is Accounting Officer for the Agency and thus is accountable also through the Permanent Secretary of the Department of Education and Employment. In addition, grant-maintained schools are locally accountable to their communities and particularly their parents. They allow access to minutes and papers of their governor body meetings, they are required to publish an annual report and hold an annual open meeting for parents at which the report can be scrutinised. They have many other opportunities for formal and informal discussions with parents. They are required to send annual reports on each pupil to their parents. Grant-maintained schools' governing bodies are required to have a certain number of parent and teacher representatives; at least two of the first or foundation governors must be parents at the time of appointment. Where the school is an ex-VA or voluntary controlled school, the governors are also accountable to the trustees who have appointed them.

Within this system, grant-maintained schools are held tightly accountable. The schools recognise the reasons for the imposition of these requirements and inspection mechanisms and accept them.

Audit standards

The strength of the grant-maintained schools' audit regime is that it supports their self-governing status. grant-maintained schools appoint their own auditors, consistent with their status as self-governing business units. Consistency is then achieved across the sector as is compatible with requirements for public accountability, by means of the guidance we lay down for external auditors to ensure they work within common standards and quality requirements and our view of the quality of external audit on a sample basis.

TUESDAY 28 NOVEMBER 1995

Members Present:

Sir Martin Jacomb (Chairman)

The Rt Hon Tom King CH MP	Sir William Utting CB
The Rt Hon The Lord Thomson of Monifieth KT DL	Diana Warwick

Witnesses:

Geoff Mulgan, Director, John Plummer, Consultant, Norman Warner, Associate, DEMOS

Professor Robert Bennett, Professor of Geography, London School of Economics

Sir Garry Johnson, Chairman, Chris Humphries, Director of Policy and Strategy, the TEC National Council and John Troth, Member of the Council and Chairman of North East Wales Training and Enterprise

John Hedger, Felicity Everiss, and Andrew Tabor, Department for Education and Employment

429. MARTIN JACOMB: Good morning, everybody. I think it is about 10 o'clock, so may I start this morning by giving Lord Nolan's apologies. He is going to miss both the hearings this week—today and Thursday—because he is sitting in the House of Lords as a Judge, so I am taking the Chair today.

Our evidence today is mainly about Training and Enterprise Councils—TECs—and their Scottish equivalent, Local Enterprise Councils, which are sometimes called LECs.

First we hear from the think-tank, DEMOS, which is represented by its Director, Geoff Mulgan. He has with him Norman Warner and John Plummer. Demos has taken a particular interest in governance issues which have arisen during much of our work and, in particular, now arise in connection with TECs.

Our second witness will be Robert Bennett, the Leverhulme Research Professor at the London School of Economics, a leading academic commentator on TECs and LECs. And thirdly, we shall hear from Sir Garry Johnson, Chairman and Chris Humphries, Director of Policy and Strategy of the TEC National Council and John Troth, a Member of the Council and Chairman of the North East Wales Training and Enterprise.

Our final witnesses will be officials from the DFEE, John Hedger, Felicity Everiss and Andrew Tabor, who are concerned specifically with matters relating to TECs. We shall not be asking them about the other bodies with which the DFEE is concerned—simply about TECs.

Let us start off then with Demos. I shall ask Sir William Utting—who is on my extreme left—to ask some questions about your evidence, which has been put in, and your opening statement I think is taken as read.

430. WILLIAM UTTING: If I could just kick off with a clarifying question, my assumption is that the evidence that you have put in is based upon the whole range of your work across quangos or NDPBs and that you have not done specific research on the bodies that are the subject of our current review. Is that right?

GEOFF MULGAN, JOHN PLUMMER, AND NORMAN WARNER

GEOFF MULGAN (Director DEMOS): Our evidence covers all of the quangos and local public spending bodies, but in addition, John Plummer, on my right, has done specific research on TECs, which we have been involved in publishing.

431. WILLIAM UTTING: Perhaps I could hear from him about that at a slightly later stage. I noticed in your opening statement that you are arguing for a new institutional framework to oversee governance not subject to direct political control. I wondered how realistic this would be, given the amount of public money that goes into quangos and the most direct form of accountability perhaps being through the political system. Do you think it is really feasible to take all these bodies out of political control?

GEOFF MULGAN: The argument is not to take the bodies out of political control per se, but rather to shift the balance of control from the executive to Parliament and to introduce more arms length mechanisms both for appointments and for governance. Perhaps I could ask my colleague, Norman Warner, to further answer that point.

NORMAN WARNER (Associate, DEMOS): I think the question really is what legislative framework you place around any particular sets of regulatory bodies. In that sense, Parliament would have spoken on that legislative framework and would have been comfortable with it as a mechanism for supervising governance in a raft of local public spending bodies. In so far as any regulatory body was falling down on the job, there would be the parliamentary select committee system and the mechanisms of Parliament to actually supervise its activities.

432. WILLIAM UTTING: So it would remain firmly within our democratic system of government?

GEOFF MULGAN: Yes. In some respects, what we are recommending is perhaps not a million miles from a Northcote Trevelyan approach, but applied to quangos rather than to the Civil Service, to try and balance legitimate political direction with guarantees of effectiveness, transparency and accountability.

433. WILLIAM UTTING: Yes. So your argument would be that this would actually increase propriety in the conduct of public business. Would you like to specify any further ways in which it might increase propriety and the conduct of Government business?

GEOFF MULGAN: The thing that has overwhelmingly struck us in our research—and perhaps John can come in on this in a moment—is the extraordinary degree of both inconsistency and the governing arrangements of the different quangos—inconsistencies which do not appear to have any obvious rational explanation—and the extent to which the actual board members of most of them are remarkably unaware of what their obligations and responsibilities are. This is, one might say, a guarantee that there will be problems of propriety arising from their work. Perhaps, John, you would like to add something to that.

JOHN PLUMMER (Consultant, DEMOS): Yes, that is correct in terms of the lack of coherence and consistency across the bodies which you are looking at, but it also relates quite closely to the public perception of these bodies because it is actually quite difficult to find out how they are governed, how appointments are made and what regulations they operate under—which has a formal regulatory authority, which has a funding authority, but the funding department exercises regulatory functions and which do not. The contrast between the role of the Housing Corporation in its relationship with housing associations and the absence of any similar body with regard to the TECs is quite striking as an example of that lack of consistency that can cause confusion both internally and in the public mind.

434. WILLIAM UTTING: I can quite see that greater consistency is likely of itself to produce greater openness and awareness on the part of the people responsible for the system of what their responsibilities actually are. My problem is the actual diversity of the situation as one looks at it. Even within individual groups such as housing associations, there is an enormous disparity between the small ones and the big ones in the kind of business that they are running.

How does one produce consistency without a sort of bureaucratic uniformity? Norman Warner has been doing work on this has he not and he put in an opening statement a forecast of what his publication is going to be. I would be very interested to hear further from him on how this Governance Act and independent commission would actually work.

NORMAN WARNER: The starting point for it is that at the end of the day in democracies, the law sets out some sort of sense of society's values in a particular area and sets out conduct and behaviour which is acceptable and unacceptable. It usually has some mechanisms for enforcing that set of views.

The proposed Governance Act starts from that position. It also starts from an analysis of the present position where bodies, to some extent those who appoint them and, in particular, quite often the people who actually hold office, have a poor understanding of the expectations of them as a public body. They may well have a legal definition of the territory for which they are responsible, but they often have a rather inadequate set of expectations about how they should behave as a public body and that seems to be one of the shortcomings of the present system.

When you look across these different bodies, they all behave in different ways—in large part because they have

to make up their own rules about how to behave as there is no common framework which stretches across them. What I am arguing in the pamphlet that is coming out is that you need to step back from the present hotchpotch of arrangements that has grown up over time and try to reset the expectations of public bodies and office holders.

GEOFF MULGAN: Could I add to that: it is not the intention to try to recommend the imposition of a bureaucratic straitjacket which will try to fit very diverse institutions into a common frame. That would be inappropriate because their legitimate lines of accountability vary a lot, according to the type of institution.

What Norman has set out is a series of general principles of propriety, stewardship and so on which apply legitimately to all the institutions under discussion and give a degree of clarity and specification to things, which at the moment, tend to be assumed to be implicit and understood by people when in fact they may well not be.

Norman goes further and argues that some of those principles could, in addition, be extended to local councillors who, at the moment, have somewhat more stringent obligations on them than members of appointed boards but in our view, insufficient ones as many of the recent problems and scandals in local authorities under all political parties have demonstrated.

435. WILLIAM UTTING: One of the recommendations in our first report was that there should be a review of the whole of the public sector to establish a more consistent legal framework. In effect are you producing proposals that would enable that recommendation to be implemented? I gather that the review is underway at the moment and you may have had some contact with the people responsible for it.

NORMAN WARNER: We have tried to take up the challenge laid down in your first report really because we shared the view that there did need to be a more coherent framework. It is not just because of the work going on in Government, but also because of other exercises which are being carried out. I can think of one which is mentioned in a report in relation to the NHS where people have actually surveyed non-executives' perceptions of how they do and see their jobs. There is considerable confusion in their minds about what is expected of them as a non-executive member of a health authority. Some of the surveys that have been done, expose that some non-executives in the same authority have a very different picture of their roles and how they relate to the executive members of that body.

It is that kind of confusion in the minds of the people doing the job which I think is just as important a factor in trying to suggest that we need to sort out the legal framework.

436. WILLIAM UTTING: One of the confusions in their minds is often the nature of their accountability and to whom they are accountable. We have had a lot of opinion expressed to us on issues such as accountability to service users or to local communities. What do you think are the main elements of accountability? Is there an intellectual and moral justification for accountability to service users and the local community?

GEOFF MULGAN: In the survey work which has been done of board members, the overwhelming answer—and perhaps John can say something about this—is accountability upwards funding rather than downwards. Perhaps it is not surprising that there is felt to be a requirement for accountability upwards to funding departments and only fairly minimal requirements to be accountable downwards, either to local areas or to service users.

We do not try to specify precisely how accountability should be organised because, as I said earlier, the appropriate structure is different in each case, which is why instead we have argued as a first step that each body should be required to set out who it believes are its key stakeholders, which may include local authorities, other local public spending bodies, service users and non-service users who are indirectly funding it, and should in addition spell out precisely how they intend to be accountable to them over and above the basic requirements which a Governance Act would set in terms of transparency of information and reporting.

John would you like to add anything to that?

JOHN PLUMMER: Yes. I think what is significant from our inquiries is this domination of concern with accountability upline and quite properly because of the considerable amounts of public money involved, repeated complaints from bodies—including those that are the subject of this inquiry—about the onerous nature of their audits, multiple audits and so on and indeed your Committee has had evidence of that from other bodies in its second inquiry. That seems to be, to some degree, at the expense of accountability or at least openness to other stakeholders and therefore, as Geoff was saying, we are not proposing to tell them who their stakeholders are, but to require them to declare that publicly and how they report to them or how they attempt to involve them in their consultation processes and strategic planning.

It is significant, for example, that that need not fetter them in any way. The Housing Corporation, if I may use that example again, has responsibility for a very wide diversity of size, scale and focus of housing associations under its regulatory and funding control and yet you would find that housing associations are endlessly asserting their independence, autonomy and diversity, despite the regulatory framework under which they operate. Introducing the sort of requirements that we are suggesting here need not fetter independence and scope for imagination.

GEOFF MULGAN: May I add one point to that, particularly in relation to the TECs which, I think, have a very complex problem of accountability. This becomes clear whenever one speaks to any TEC board members. Not only do they primarily think of accountability upwards, but they are also unclear precisely how they should be accountable to their local area, their business community—the different elements of their business community, who may have rather different interests in terms of what the TEC actually prioritise—not least to, say, the unemployed who may depend on their services. What is required is to specify a process rather than to define and legislate who precisely they should be accountable to.

There is one other issue on accountability which concerns us and this comes both from talking to people who are members of boards and who might be members of

boards. If there are anything up to 70,000 appointed positions in this country—and there seems to be a wide variation in the estimates—clearly our system of government depends on a lot of people being prepared to give of their time and energy to making the system work. One of our fears is that the more there is lack of clarity on precisely what those jobs entail and who they are in turn accountable to, many people will be put off serving on those bodies and that will cause us enormous problems in the medium term.

Some of the media have tended to view the problem in terms of people using those positions for bad intentions. I suspect in a few years time we may see the problem precisely the other way round—us wanting to encourage people to give of their time to take part.

437. WILLIAM UTTING: Yes. In relation to those appointments, it seems to me that you are actually making a case now for payment of people who take up these positions in the voluntary sector. That is what I infer from your evidence. You do not make that explicit. Would you like to say why you think it may become necessary to pay almost everybody who is undertaking public work that is now often done on a voluntary basis?

GEOFF MULGAN: One of the reasons we think that some people serve now is that they do not properly understand their legal responsibilities. If we are to bring greater clarity to the responsibilities those roles entail, there may need to be a quid pro quo and that may be some payment—not payment equivalent to commercial rates, but something that signifies the importance of the job they are doing.

In addition, there is a lot of evidence that senior people in Britain, more generally, are working much longer hours than was the case 10 or 20 years ago and there is actually much greater pressure on time. So if the public sector is making claims on people's time, it is now doing so against greater competition from their workplace, family and so on. That may, in addition, justify some payment.

A very parallel argument is taking place in the charities world. It is not wholly dissimilar to the argument which took place around MPs a century ago. We would argue that there at least should not be a presumption against payment for membership on boards. I wonder if you would like to add anything to that?

NORMAN WARNER: It is in part reflected in the fact that there seems to us to have been a move in a number of appointed bodies towards getting younger people to participate as office holders. There is a certain symbolism also in the idea of giving public recognition through a payment for the time that they are giving up and the commitment they are giving to a body, especially if you are going to place them in an overt position of public stewardship in relation to particular bodies.

438. WILLIAM UTTING: You and other organisations have made the point about the individual liability that people may incur as a result of unpaid public service so that in a sense it may seem only right that they should receive some financial reward to compensate for that.

JOHN PLUMMER: I think that is right and I also think that there may well be a minimalist position which is very modest legislation to increase the range of people who can qualify for reasonable time off work, as for example, categories such as the Territorial Army and the Magistracy presently qualify for paid time off work when reasonable. To extend that to some other bodies might be a very reasonable way.

On the subject of consistency, we are of course aware that NHS trusts are not part of your present inquiry, but the analogy with some of the bodies that are within your inquiry would seem to be such that, again, it causes confusion in the public mind. We are aware that there are strong feelings on this subject and a member of a board of a substantial housing association said to me only yesterday that she would consider it like being paid for giving blood if she were to be offered payment for her service as a housing association board member, which she considered to be an honour and a duty. So there are wide ranges of opinion on this, but we feel that the present inconsistency is muddying the water and creating confusion in the public mind as to which jobs in this sector are valued and which are not.

439. WILLIAM UTTING: I share some of the strong feelings about it myself, but there are also practical problems. Where would the cut-off point come for example? We are told that there may be 300,000 school governors and being a governor of a school seems to me to be a responsible and perhaps quite difficult role. Do we include them as possible paid servants of the state?

GEOFF MULGAN: These roles would not be servants of the state. They would be engaged in public service. We would be saying that each institution should decide for itself what remuneration arrangements it has, but there should not be a presumption against them. If there is, in practice what already happens will continue: which is that there will often be payments made in disguised forms to people sitting on boards. In addition, there will be two other undesirable effects. One is a relative under-representation of people on lower incomes, simply because it will be harder for them to give up the time and, in addition, a degree of bias against younger people because they too will be putting more effort into earning incomes, paying off mortgages and so on.

We are not trying to say that every school governor in the land should be paid, but certainly for the larger local public spending bodies with responsibilities for millions or tens of millions of pounds, it is inappropriate and probably anachronistic to have people in positions of responsibility on those boards unpaid as at present.

440. WILLIAM UTTING: Could I end by inviting you to make any specific points about TECs that you might have in mind, in view of what you said earlier about John Plummer's work?

GEOFF MULGAN: One of the key things which we argue and which we have not mentioned yet, is that it seems anomalous that the TECs are the only major local public spending bodies which do not have a clear regulatory framework or body. This, in turn, seems to lead to quite a number of the problems of governance that we have identified and that some of the TECs themselves experience.

Obviously the TECs themselves would see any such regulator as an infringement in some respects on their independence of manoeuvre, but we would argue that this would probably in the medium term improve their effectiveness and certainly their legitimacy with the wider public. Do you want add anything to that, John?

JOHN PLUMMER: Just very briefly, it would be wrong to leave TECs without making some reference to the South Thames Training and Enterprise Council, an instance where the Department of Employment—as it then was—appointed a receiver in order to protect public money, but subsequently a substantial number of providers of training to that TEC have lost a lot of money.

It is significant that in the case of a housing association, the Housing Corporation has what are known in the jargon as "sub-nuclear weapons" that it can use when it has reason to believe that a housing association is getting into difficulty or going wrong. It can appoint additional board members; it can have a tighter regulatory grip; it can take a number of other measures before using the "nuclear weapon"—again, in their jargon—of actually closing the housing association down and ceasing to fund it. The comparison between that and what happened in South Thames is significant in terms of demonstrating the importance of a consistent approach to regulatory bodies without fettering independence or autonomy.

WILLIAM UTTING: Thank you.

MARTIN JACOMB: Thank you very much. Could I ask Mr Tom King if he would like to take up the questioning?

441. TOM KING: Can I just clear one point that is niggling at the back of my mind before we get into the other questions? I know your name well, but, in the current jargon, I do not quite know where you are coming from or who you are.

GEOFF MULGAN: Me?

TOM KING: No, Demos.

GEOFF MULGAN: We are an independent, non-party think-tank. We publish some of your colleagues and people from the other side as well and most of our work is fairly empirical research into issues ranging from public parks to taxation to companies employment practices.

Among the many topics we cover, we have been looking at questions of governance in local and other institutions. As part of that work, we published a report last year with research conducted by John, surveying large numbers of quango board members. More recently, we commissioned an executive search company to do a study of public appointments, on which we are drawing today. In two or three weeks we shall be publishing Norman Warner's paper setting out the elements of the Governance Act.

442. TOM KING: Where does your funding come from?

GEOFF MULGAN: From a mixture of private companies, foundations and bodies such as the Economic and Social Research Council. We are the only think-tank which publishes all of its funding sources.

443. TOM KING: Your papers are full of pleas for transparency, so that seems entirely proper. You talked

about the contrast between the structure of the Housing Corporation and the fact that there is no parallel in the case of the TECs. You call for consistency, so which do you think is the right model?

JOHN PLUMMER: I believe that the Housing Corporation has many attractive and important qualities. I argue that particularly because some of the other evidence that your Committee has heard has suggested that there can be, in the words of another witness, "governance gaps", where you have a funding authority—as in the case of grant-maintained schools—separate from and retaining still with the Departments the regulatory function.

It has also been argued that the Housing Corporation itself should be split into a separate funding body and regulatory body, but at the present time I think that model is easily replicable and has gained considerable support from both the bodies it regulates and funds and others. Your Committee has heard evidence that private sector funders of housing associations have been encouraged to invest money—we are now talking about something like 40 or 50 per cent of housing association funding coming from private sector sources—as a result of the rigorous, some say, draconian, standards of regulation applied by that body, which, nonetheless has not fettered housing association independence. We would certainly like to see a discussion about the replicability of that kind of body.

444. TOM KING: This seems to be the point that Sir William Utting was bringing out in his questioning. A phrase you used was that there is inconsistency for which there is no rational explanation. You could argue that the rational explanation is simply there by the extraordinary disparity of the bodies, that they have come from different origins and situations and have inevitably given rise, therefore rationally, to different structures.

The flavour of your paper seems to me to be harmonisation in the interests of greater public understanding—harmonisation above all, even if it means knocking some of these into shapes that would not be ideal for themselves. I do not know whether I make myself clear.

GEOFF MULGAN: If the divergence in governance arrangements followed reflected the very great divergence in functions of these bodies, one might expect the policy makers who had been responsible for framing them to be able to explain why the different frameworks had been built up and one might expect the members of boards on each different type of organisation to explain and understand why they had their particular governance arrangements. What is overwhelmingly striking to anyone researching this field is that neither group is able to explain rationally why their governance structure fits the peculiarities of their sector—housing, training, health or whatever it may be.

The explanation has much more to do with the fact that, understandably, ministers were setting up new structures in order to meet various policy goals and governance concerns were not uppermost in their minds. Their main concern was to get things done, to achieve tangible results and that is why the whole structure has this rather ad hoc feel. We are not proposing to standardise all arrangements, because that would be quite inappropriate to different fields. We are trying to argue for harmonising

the principles governing those arrangements so as to allow the appropriate diversity to genuinely fit the diverse realities, rather than to have simply happened accidentally.

445. TOM KING: You talk about a national council for public appointments. Who would appoint the members of the national council?

GEOFF MULGAN: Parliament.

446. TOM KING: Parliament or Government?

GEOFF MULGAN: We argue for a council which would be made up of a broad diversity of different interests, including the major parties and non-party interests. It would not be part of the executive crucially. It would be accountable to Parliament, creating this arms' length relationship between day to day party politics and appointments, which we see as essential.

TOM KING: But somebody has to appoint them.

GEOFF MULGAN: Yes.

447. TOM KING: And presumably the Government would have to move a motion through Parliament appointing the members of it?

GEOFF MULGAN: There would have to be a nominating process and there are issues in the British constitution of how one formulates and sets up arms' length institutions. Primary legislation would have to define it in such a way that it clearly was not directly under the patronage of the Prime Minister for it to be credible. Norman, do you want to add anything to that?

NORMAN WARNER: There are precedents for defining categories of members. There are also precedents for giving ranges of bodies nomination rights as well in some of these areas. There is quite a lot of other experience that one can draw upon in constructing bodies of that kind, or even the kind of public governance commission that is suggested in my own forthcoming pamphlet.

448. TOM KING: Your suggestion is that it should be protected from Prime Ministerial control? In other words, obviously there is a risk of this becoming super-patronage with total centralisation and then the actual body appointed by the Prime Minister of the day. That would be pretty devastating would it not?

NORMAN WARNER: The other point which perhaps should be emphasised is that over time, bodies come and go. They outlive their usefulness and new ones are appointed with new functions. Often, at the point of making change in an area of activity, there is such a rush to get something operational, that governance issues get lost sight of. If there was a stronger framework, it would make it easier and there would be a source, if you like, of guidance to ministers setting up new arrangements to which they would adhere and Parliament would be able to see that they actually had adhered to them.

449. TOM KING: Can I just ask one other question. You touched briefly on the problem of, in some areas, people queuing up and competition for posts and in others

a problem of actually getting people who would be willing to serve. Sir William Utting drew attention to the role of school governors. In recent times, some school governors have found the burdens pretty onerous and that may be an area where that might apply.

If we are allowed to go slightly wider, do you see areas where there are shortages now and difficulties in getting people to serve? In your research has this come up or is it generally the picture that people are queuing up for the opportunity?

JOHN PLUMMER: I do not think our research has revealed any area where there are shortages, but that is primarily because we have not looked particularly at that—it would have only come up coincidentally. I think, however, that our research and other research has indicated that there is very often an extremely narrow or small pond from which that recruitment comes, for some of the reasons that have been mentioned previously about the difficulty of attracting young people at an early stage in their career and those on relatively low-paid work. So there is a narrow pool; quite often there are waiting lists and we have heard of school governors, for example, regarding it as a position of considerable esteem within their local community, even within areas where one might have expected some difficulties. It is more, therefore, to do with the narrowness of the search area than the limited numbers.

NORMAN WARNER: I think it is worth just bearing in mind in the analogous field of the voluntary sector, who, over recent years, have taken on a much more service delivery role in many areas, that many voluntary organisations have struggled to find younger volunteer trustees who are not retired. In that field there some evidence of people sometimes struggling to get younger trustees.

GEOFF MULGAN: One additional point that is made is the research on business people and their experience of TECs. There has been some systematic research on this and there is an enormous amount of anecdotal experience from business people who have gone onto boards of TECs and found it a profoundly disillusioning experience and have told their peers not to follow in their footsteps, essentially because their room for manoeuvre was vastly less than they imagined because of the upwards accountability we have described. There may be therefore a medium term problem in winning over sufficiently high calibre business people to sit on some of these boards.

MARTIN JACOMB: Thank you very much. Diana Warwick would like to ask you a question.

450. DIANA WARWICK: I just have one question. In your recommendations about openness, you have made various specific recommendations on disclosure and so on, but you make a point that has come up in relation to several other of the groups that we are dealing with which seems to be quite problematic. In talking about the presumption of transparency you say that it should be overridden only on specified public interest grounds. "Commercial confidentiality should not be such a ground.". That seems to hinder a great deal of public comment and internal staff comment, particularly in relation to whistle-blowing and so on in various of the organisations we have dealt with.

Could you expand on that, because you are the only people who have actually said that commercial confidentiality should not be regarded as an argument for secrecy or confidentiality.

JOHN PLUMMER: Yes. We feel that commercial confidentiality is too often used as an explanation for concealing information which is not really of a commercially confidential nature and it is not in any way going to damage the business of the local public spending body to reveal this information. It does not necessarily mean that it would have to be revealed at the time of negotiations for purchase of property or land or price sensitive information of that sort. It need not necessarily be immediately available there.

We would draw particularly on the experiences of the local enterprise companies under the Highlands and Islands Enterprise—that is the north western part of Scotland, not Scottish Enterprise—where they have adopted a practice that they call "accountability through openness", which actually requires virtually every transaction that the local enterprise company makes to be revealed, effectively, to the local press and thereby through the local press, broadcast.

We are talking about grants to individuals to undertake training and to the local salmon fishing farm or local hotels to improve their competitiveness and performance —issues of that sort. It has been said by some that it is all very well doing that sort of thing within small rural communities, but you could not possibly do it within major conurbations. We are arguing that that is wrong and that in fact if you can do it in small rural communities where, almost inevitably, everybody knows each other, each other's business and interests and the board members of those local enterprise companies are very visible people, much more so than in England in the major conurbations, then you ought to be able to do it elsewhere.

They have found that the number of times they need to conceal or withhold information for limited periods is very small.

451. DIANA WARWICK: Could I just pursue that? Would you see that applying, for example, in the National Health Service or in higher and further education, two areas where exactly this argument has been made and where large sums of money are involved in a highly competitive situation?

JOHN PLUMMER: In principle, yes. Of course, we understand that there can be times when that information is price or competitive sensitive, as in research grants and things of that sort, but that does not necessarily mean that it needs to remain confidential. Indeed, we argue that it is actually contrary to good competition practice for it to remain confidential indefinitely.

GEOFF MULGAN: Just to add, there is in probably only a small minority of cases, an argument that over-transparency of price information can sometimes aid cartels of contractors to organise themselves against the public interest, but our analysis is that this is not likely to be a very significant problem in these cases. Overwhelmingly, the burden of change needs to be towards greater openness, not towards more flexible uses of commercial confidentiality to justify secrecy.

NORMAN WARNER: It is worth bearing in mind that over the past decade or so, contracting in local government has really advanced and the service specifications for contracts are to all intents and purposes public access documents which are available to people. It starts to become quite difficult to argue commercial in confidence, when the contract specifications are in the public arena for people to actually bid for contracts.

DIANA WARWICK: Thank you.

MARTIN JACOMB: Lord Thomson has one question he would like to ask.

452. LORD THOMSON: Could I ask a brief question, following up Tom King's remarks about harmonisation. A little later this morning, we are going to get evidence from the Department of Education and Employment, who are going to put rather a strong case against harmonisation, on the grounds that the institutions as such are a very diverse variety.

You have a good overview of these institutions that we are now examining. Which category would give you the most concerns in terms of internal governance?

JOHN PLUMMER: I think there is a great deal to be said in favour of all of them. They are all achieving remarkable performances and very often better than that before they existed. That said, the most difficult one is the Training and Enterprise Councils because of the absence of a regulatory authority and the fact that it has been up to them to invent their own governance rules, several years after Government created them. I find that an extraordinary state of affairs and although I think that they have done well in constructing internal governance arrangements, it is still not as good and the fact that 81 of them are accountable to one government department without a funding or regulatory authority in between, is I think a weakness for which we will be paying the price for some time.

453. TOM KING: Could I just come back on that. You said some of them were doing better than they were doing before. This is an evidence session on TECs: do you think that applies to TECs?

JOHN PLUMMER: I do. I think that vocational training, in many respects, is better than it was under the Manpower Services Commission. The fact that there are enormous funding difficulties, and so on, is obviously a separate question.

TOM KING: Thank you very much.

MARTIN JACOMB: Thank you very much for coming along. It has been a great help to us. Your evidence and your opening statement were a help and your oral evidence is a very great help.

Now we have Professor Robert Bennett from the London School of Economics.

Your initial statement is taken as read, as you know, but I daresay you would like to elaborate some of it but here I would like to ask, if I may, Mr Tom King to start with a few questions. Not necessarily a few, I may say, but to start with some questions.

454. TOM KING: Your book was called *Britain's Experiment* and the first question is you said in your paper that you wrote Part 1, Part 2, and you are going to stay with this now, I think you said, for the next five years, working on these issues. So it is still an experiment? Do you think that it should continue basically as it is because it is too early to really know to learn the lessons of the experiment and know what changes you make. Would you like to comment on that point?

PROFESSOR ROBERT BENNETT

PROF ROBERT BENNETT: Yes, I think from the Committee's point of view it would be useful to respond to specifics, but to take the general, I think, in many ways you can say that the TECs have been outstandingly successful in what they have done—you have heard previously about the increases in performance, and that can be quantified, doubtless the DFEE and the TEC National Council will tell you the dramatic increase in performance, on vocational programmes of training in particular.

The argument that I developed in the book—and I would still continue to develop—is that there are a number of fault lines, if you like, which remain as difficulties and many of these relate to issues of governance and accountability which are the central concerns of your Committee. The central dilemma, as I see it, is that the business community was to be empowered in the phrase of the prospectus launch and subsequent documents and, indeed, in terms of many of the pieces of vocabulary that the Department and its officers still use. The difficulty has been that the business community has not, on the whole, felt empowered by this initiative, it has felt that it has been too trammelled by very detailed lines of performance target setting, performance measurement, straight jackets on the way in which finance is allocated to these various targets and the way in which the accountability procedures in terms of financial accountability, rather than political accountability, straight jackets around those procedures.

The difficulty, I think, in the long term is that the business community will not feel committed to this as a long-term experiment unless there is some significant reform to the way in which they can operate the system. I have made the point in the introductory paper that TECs and LECs in Scotland are actually fundamentally different to the other local bodies you are dealing with because these bodies are intermediaries, they are not dealing directly with the client or the customer. They are dealing usually with a series of other contractors who provide the training or if they deal directly with businesses the businesses themselves, of course, are intermediaries dealing with the customers who purchase their goods and services ultimately.

The problem for the business community then is to work an arrangement with Government which allows them sufficient flexibility that they can deal with the customer appropriately and the planning framework which surrounds the TECs, in my view, is far too demanding in detail to allow that flexibility to be sufficiently client or customer responsive. That is the central argument that I put in the book. There have been a number of significant improvements in the procedures since that comment and evaluation but I think in fundamental terms the difficulties still remain to be addressed.

455. TOM KING: I mean, you were listening to the previous evidence and, of course, this argument cuts

—really it would appear to be in fairly direct conflict with the points they were making about harmonisation, that they are not the same and that your point that you make powerfully in your opening statement, that because TECs work through intermediaries whereas a hospital trust or whatever it might be deal very directly with the consumers. They are different in that respect. And so these ideas about harmonising and having national rules and national duties of non-executive directors and that you would think was actually not appropriate?

PROF ROBERT BENNETT: No, I think the issue can be unravelled in two directions here. It would seem to me that the Committee's concerns about public interest, audit and public accountability issues, for example the P.A.C. structures, interests of directors and seeing that probity and so on was maintained, these issues would be concerns that could be looked at as national questions rightly. But harmonising the detail of the way these operate for different forms of these executive agencies or local bodies seems to me to be inappropriate because you are dealing with entirely different animals here. The TECs, I have made the point, are very different from each other but equally further education, higher education, G.M. schools, all of the other things that you are interested or could potentially be interested in, are all dealing with very different areas of difficulty and problem, some having a very large social role, if there are disadvantaged communities, housing associations and unemployed trainees, others not necessarily having that strong focus to the disadvantaged at all there; for example, higher education and TECs clearly bridge some of these issues.

I think one of the benefits of the experiments of the eighties and nineties has been Government's attempts to try and find horses for courses that better fit specific design to the specific needs of those sectors. It has not always been successful and you would not expect it to be successful always, but in the process of development—and to take back the word of experiment again—you would expect these things to be refined and developed in the light of that experience. I do not see a strong case for harmonisation in the way that was being previously presented, but I think there are issues of probity which do run across all of these bodies.

456. TOM KING: Thank you very much. That aspect of harmonising was obviously much easier when it was all the Civil Service activity. Mr Plummer—just at the end I asked him—did he think it was basically an improvement over the previous system which was really entirely within the Department of the Manpower Services Commission. Do you hold the view that this is an improvement?

PROF ROBERT BENNETT: I think there is no doubt in general terms that in the vocational programme areas, for the Youth Training and Training for Work, as they are now called—they obviously had previous varieties of names—the outputs that have been achieved have remarkably increased. Now, it is actually very difficult to prove that in total detail. The TEC performance tables, which doubtless you will have presented to you, demonstrate the step by step improvement of the TECs themselves. There is no really reliable data of outputs under the previous regime. You might indeed ask the DFEE why there is not an appropriate national set of measures of what the previous programmes of YTS, YOPS and so on achieved. Some of the TECs themselves interestingly, in order to understand their own base lines, did indeed do some follow-up work with their

participants, the actual trainees in the programmes at the point at which that TEC started in 1989 or 1990. They found that the outputs being achieved on some of these programmes, in terms of NVQs, the vocational qualification achieved, were in the order of 3% or 4% of the participants, in fact almost no measurable output.

Now the TECs, when they started to measure the base line across the country, which was only one or two years later than that, 1992/93, found that they then were starting to achieve 20-30% levels and now they have pushed this up to 40-50% levels over the last one or two years. So clearly the output levels have radically increased and clearly the previous system did not focus on output measurement at all and, therefore, could not be claimed to have been achieving very much for the disadvantaged, youth trainees, in particular, in the system.

457. TOM KING: You have said that you thought that in vocational areas there had been improvements—in some vocational areas?

PROF ROBERT BENNETT: Vocational Training, qualifications achieved, yes.

TOM KING: Yes, right. But there were certain other areas where you thought there had not been an improvement.

PROF ROBERT BENNETT: I think the difficult dilemma that the TECs have suffered in their programme has been particularly focused on the business support enterprise services, what is now largely consumed within the Business Link initiative. This is a tricky problem because it is not entirely clear what the Government role should be in business support in any case, because there are ideological divides on this but there is also an exceedingly difficult number of technical problems, irrespective of whether you want to intervene a lot or a little and actually how to do it effectively. And the TECs in a sense have been thrown that job, initially without very much guidance. My evaluation in that "94 book demonstrated really they were floundering around, reinventing the wheel on a massive scale, not communicating with each other and not really learning from previous experience.

The Business Link initiative was very positive in the sense of focusing TEC minds on a particular agenda, defined from the President of the Board of Trade through the DTI. The difficulty, of course, was that the DTI were not necessarily perfectly equipped to define the programme as precisely as they wished to define it, so although Business Link, I think, can be said to be a very major step forward in TEC activities in actually focusing that programme and more or less directing them in what to do, there are still a lot of open questions about whether Business Link, which TECs are contract holders for are, in fact, the most effective way of intervening. That is another set of questions which goes rather beyond this Committee but I've looked at this in detail and I would say the key problem is the way in which the Personal Business Advisers, the PBAs, are defined, financed and what their terms of evaluation and performance are.

458. TOM KING: If you look at the operation of the TECs and the ideas of bringing in the private sector and trying to get that closer alignment between training and future employment, which is one of the concepts

envisaged, you have talked about the frustration of some of the people coming in from the private sector. One of the solutions to that, of course, is far greater autonomy which means almost by definition some diminution of central control and possible accountability. Is your view that actually so far for striving to get this greater central uniformity and autonomy you should actually be going for greater virement—I mean, the opportunity for, for instance, TECs themselves to be able to vire within their programmes, that it is too centrally controlled and that this would be the way in which to unlock greater local business interest and initiative.

PROF ROBERT BENNETT: There is no doubt in mind, if you want TECs to service business needs, which was the original objective and still remains the stated objective, that this cannot be done by detailed Civil Service guidelines and performance targets. I don't know whether the Committee has seen but it should look at the TEC licensing manual. Now, this defines performance targets in extreme detail and very numerous—a very large number of such targets. It sets up a so-called "Tariff System"—I use the vocabulary of the licensing arrangement—and an "Exchange Rate System between different performance targets. So each target has a price tariff and in order to be able to bring different targets together across different programmes there is an exchange rate so that one target can be traded against another. This reminds me of the way the Soviet system defined its GOS plan system, which was a whole series of artificial price structures, defined externally to the real market for sales. I have spent a lot of time in Central Europe is the last few years and one of the things that brought the problems home to me was a textile factory in former East Germany. A textile factory, it had a vast warehouse full of nails and they had nails because they knew nails would be in short supply, they did not need them but they would be able to use these as a barter good to get the textile raw materials they needed. So a system which mis-defines its targets is bound to accumulate both surpluses and, therefore, shortages because people who needed nails could not get them because they were being accumulated somewhere else.

In the TEC system, defining one set of NVQs, the vocational currency, in the way that is being done, incentivises the TECs to go for cheap NVQs, so it has amassed numbers of trainees in certain programmes which are cheap and quick to get. There is ring fencing to this, there are all sorts of constraints, but in practice that is how the system is incentivised to work. If you don't want it to work that way you have got to put more and more ring fences around it, you have got to change the tariff structures.

So if you want to centrally plan things, once you set targets you immediately have to set other targets, other constraints, other ring fences in order to achieve what you want to achieve. That is the dilemma of a central planning system. There is no limit to the planning once you decide to define it. So people sitting in the DTI or the DFEE are into a hopeless task which is ultimately bound to fail, is ultimately bound to lead to further stepping-stones of more and more detail.

The alterative is to say "These are the broad requirements we need, we need more vocational qualifications. We need the unemployed to get into jobs. We need businesses to get the support they require in terms of information, advice and whatever the businesses

locally feel that they need where there is a genuine market failure not supplied already by the very extensive market to business advice and information".

Having set that broad framework the TECs and LECs are then allowed to get on and set their own targets. Of course they should be scrutinised as to whether they are setting those targets properly and effectively, but they should be set free to do that. And this rule book of tariffs and exchange rates and terms of trade should be thrown away.

You will see also if you look at not just the TEC licensing but the detailed TEC contracts that follow from that, there is another 300 pages of rule books that follow, so this is really a system that is bound to break down and is one of the main reasons why business people become extremely frustrated with the whole system. It inevitably also produces a fracture between the officers who presumably know the rule books in great detail and are operating these terms of trade, and the board members who cannot possibly be expected to know them because they are non-executives, giving a day a week, a day a month, to this. So the design of the system is perfectly designed to achieve a fracture between the board and the officers, which is one of the key issues that the Committee should be concerned with, I imagine.

459. TOM KING: And that destroys the accountability that has been built into the system and by having too complex systems that are meant to ensure accountability in that way?

PROF ROBERT BENNETT: It is bound to undermine the local community accountability and the way in which the board is the intermediary between the community and the entity of the TEC, LEC, that is being dealt with.

460. TOM KING: Could I ask you a last question on quite a different subject, which is on the question of appointments to these boards is your image that in general TECs are self-perpetuating bodies, locally sort of recreating themselves in their own image?

PROF ROBERT BENNETT: That is the danger in the design. I think it is fair to say that in this stage in the development a lot of the potential abuses in the TEC, LEC systems are more potential than real. I think the media concerns have naturally got hold of a few particular cases, but the weight of evidence is that most boards and staff operate as well as they can within the system that they have been given. So impropriety and general questions of that nature are not a big part of the problem. But in the long term I think one of the ways that the Committee might like to think of this—I am sure is thinking of this already—is that there is an issue of justice being seen to be done rather than justice being done. I suspect that justice is being done in 95%, 99% of the system, but there is a problem of it being sufficiently open and understandable that justice can be seen to be done, that impropriety can be seen to be checked and to have checks and balances in it.

461. TOM KING: And a time limit on appointments as your predecessors suggested? They said, I think, five years?

PROF ROBERT BENNETT: I think there is an interesting debate here. This is an immensely technical area, TECs and LECs are dealing with a large series of programmes, many of which themselves are sub-sets of complicated technical programmes. There is an argument for turnover and refreshment, there is an argument that this may, in fact, undermine the quality of the board. I would have thought that a set term of reference, set term of office, may be the appropriate way to proceed but that that should be renewable if that is deemed to be appropriate. The question is who deems this to be appropriate and in the submitted evidence I made a comment on the nature of the membership and how this sort of accountability structure locally should be developed and that seems to me the only way that there is a proper check and balance on this.

TOM KING: Thank you very much.

MARTIN JACOMB: Thank you very much. Could I ask Lord Thomson to take up the questioning?

462. LORD THOMSON: Could I follow up immediately the line of questioning that Tom King has just been asking you about? In your paper you recommend really quite strongly the TEC/Chamber of Commerce merger solution. Would you like to develop that idea?

PROF ROBERT BENNETT: Yes. I come down very strongly in favour of it and recommend the Committee to think about it in detail, because it seems to me to get the TECs and LECs out of many of the traps of accountability that they got themselves into. They would have a membership, they are companies limited by guarantee but with no ——

LORD THOMSON: There is always the question about the selection of members of the board.

PROF ROBERT BENNETT: Well, the membership would then elect the board which can, of course, be subject to constraints if it is felt that the DFEE constraints on the seniority of the board members or appropriate balance between large businesses, small businesses and so on, should be maintained. All of those things can be built into the election process but this would provide an electorate, a true membership, to get around these problems. The difficulty is that the present Chamber system in Britain is a voluntary sector structure, it is entirely a private sector organisation, and it suffers as a consequence a number of classic areas of market failure. It is under-resourced, it is there to maintain a series of services to its members. You, I think, all the members of the Committee are, in different ways, yourselves part of voluntary sector organisations and bodies, you know the difficulties that many of these have. It is a classic situation in learned societies, voluntary sector bodies and, indeed, chambers and trade associations and so on.

So merger with the present system across the country is, I do not think, a total solution. It is a solution in areas where the Chamber is not a highly developed local entity and, therefore, is not sacrificing its assets or, indeed, its credibility. Indeed, it may well have previously depended a great deal on the TEC or previously the Manpower Services Commission for public sector contracts.

463. LORD THOMSON: Should it be an open membership, so that businesses in a particular TEC area could become members and be the body of electors for the board?

PROF ROBERT BENNETT: The idea would be that all businesses would be potential members.

LORD THOMSON: Yes, all businesses that wish to enrol as members, yes.

PROF ROBERT BENNETT: One can develop this thinking a lot further. In parts of continental Europe, of course, there is a de facto compulsory membership, that would be a French or a German model. In a Dutch or a Finnish model there is not a compulsory membership but the business register—what we would have, say, in Companies House, would be a de facto membership and your payment as a company for registration would be in effect becoming a quiescent member at least, not an active member.

There are other ways of doing it—the VAT register could be used in this way, the non-domestic rates register could be used. We have a variety of registers of business that could be used.

464. LORD THOMSON: One of the phrases I liked in your paper was that there was "too much scrutiny of the wrong type". I mean, would it be fair to say that one of the problems is that there is a sort of maximalist regulation on financial control and to some extent minimalist regulation on some of the governance aspects of conflicts of interest, all that kind of thing?

PROF ROBERT BENNETT: Yes. I think in practice the governance issue, as I said, is not really practically such a problem. Abuses are minor. Most people are in it for the good of their communities, there have only been a small number of proven instances, most of which have surfaced very publicly in the media and, indeed, the local media are a very good check and balance on this system, I think they have acted very effectively. So governance is not the problem. Clearly you do need financial accountability, there is just too much of it, too much checking of the same thing essentially. What I meant by my comment of the "wrong kind" was there was really very little client feedback. If an individual trainee, for example, feels that they are not getting a programme that really equips them for what they are supposed to be doing, that the NVQ trainer is not doing a good job, or, indeed, they have been put into the wrong programme altogether by the TEC or its advisers, there is virtually no comeback for that trainee to challenge the decisions.

Also if a business, to take another example, feels that it is not getting a proper quality of service and so on, there is very little potential comeback for them. Whereas in a real business the customer can walk away, in this sort of business the customer is, in effect, trapped.

465. LORD THOMSON: Finally, would you excuse the chauvinist remark that they order these things better in Scotland? Would it be better in England and Wales if there was the Scottish system of having an intermediary body like the Scottish Enterprise Council or the Highland and Islands Development Board?

PROF ROBERT BENNETT: I think it is certainly the case that many things are better in Scotland and I think the experience of Scottish Enterprise and Highlands and Islands Enterprise on the whole has been more positive. They have had other difficulties, of course, of a different kind and I gather the Committee is going to Scotland and will see some of the other tensions. But there is no doubt that the intermediary body of Scottish Enterprise and Highland and Islands Enterprise has helped greatly. What this has meant is that the Scottish office, is the Department in Scotland responsible for this, itself, of course, is one department, like a Government office for the regions but is more integrated than the GROs are at the moment. It has not attempted to give to SE and HIE, detailed contracts, it has given the rather general contracts, which I advocate, then SE and HIE has dealt with the LECs. They also (SE and HIE), have again been more arm's-length in the way they have defined those contracts, leaving more to the LECs to define for themselves. However, that has been tightened under some of the pressures that this Committee is part of, under NAO and parliamentary pressures, so there are difficulties in Scotland maintaining that arm's-length organisation.

But the biggest difference I see is the scale of the operation. The Scottish Office Industry Department, which mainly looks after this area, has thirty civil servants—three zero. The old TEED, Manpower Services Commission structure, had 1,000 civil servants in Sheffield and I think that really describes the essence of the different systems. One has a GOS plan methodology of defining immense rule books and has a thousand civil servants to do the designing and policing of it, the other has thirty civil servants who are on the whole much more pragmatic individuals who get on with the job and let the others do the work on the ground. So there is a lot to be said for the Scottish model, absolutely.

MARTIN JACOMB: Thank you very much indeed.

466. DIANA WARWICK: Can I just follow up the Scottish model because our previous witnesses referred us to the practice in the Highlands and Islands Enterprise Board on accountability—I think it was a process called Accountability through Openness, which appears to be almost a model of a series of efforts to communicate and to inform and to be accountable. Do you share that view and do you see it as a model, do you see it as something that we can look at as a series of processes that might be recommended for other LECs and TECs?

PROF ROBERT BENNETT: Yes, indeed. HIE, the Highlands and Islands Enterprise, piloted this process in Caithness and Sutherland, which is one of the most distant parts of the UK from London and if it can be made to work in that sort of area it can be made to work anywhere. HIE have adopted it as their recommended structure for all HIE LECs, Scottish Enterprise have more or less adopted it now for SE LECs, and the TECs code of accountability that went through approval by the TECs National Conference this July accepted more or less the same structure for the TECs. So it is now in place more or less for the whole system in England, Wales and Scotland.

You need to question, however, how far the TECs code of conduct, which has been implemented, fully meets all of the concerns this Committee would have. In the written submission to you I gave three or four areas where I thought there were some residual concerns and, indeed, where the TECs code of practice does not go as far as HIE, the Highlands and Islands Enterprise code of conduct. That particularly relates to demonstrated openness by ready access to lists of director interests and contracts assigned, which is available and, as was said in the previous evidence, given to the media and so on in a very easy way. It looks to me in TECs as if this is still quite an arcane area, that it is difficult for the average enquirer, member of the public, to ever penetrate. For the TECs, I think you can see this on your visits, you could investigate this to see how easy it would be. Perhaps the Committee would like to perform the activity of being a "blind" member of the public asking simple and naive questions about what was going on as if they were acting out the role of a trainee or an unhappy company that had got the wrong sort of advice and what the redress and grievance procedures might be. I think you would find them difficult to find out about in most TECs—not all—and to be an area which required an exceedingly high level of perseverance and, indeed, intellectual capacity to be able to see through to a successful conclusion. I think the TECs have yet to really implement the system in enough depth and detail.

MARTIN JACOMB: Thank you very much indeed. I think we may take up that suggestion—who knows. It may turn out to be a very useful question but what is certain is your evidence will have been very useful to us. So thank you very very much for coming along and giving it so very clearly. Thank you very much indeed.

PROF ROBERT BENNETT: Thank you.

467. MARTIN JACOMB: We now turn thirdly to Sir Garry Johnson, who is Chairman, and Chris Humphries who is Director of Policy and Strategy of the TEC National Council, with John Troth, who is a member of the Council and Chairman of what I think is called North East Wales Training and Enterprise. I hope I have got that right, so maybe I could ask you just to introduce yourselves to make sure that we have got no error between what I have said and the actual facts.

SIR GARRY JOHNSON, CHRIS HUMPHRIES, AND JOHN TROTH

GARRY JOHNSON (Chairman, TEC National Council): Certainly Chairman. Good morning, and I did not actually hear what you said—it is either the acoustics or myself—but let me do the introductions as you request. My name is Garry Johnson, I am Chairman of the TEC National Council and have been since September of last year. On my right is John Troth, who is a member of the TEC National Council and is the Chairman of the North East Wales TEC and on my left is Chris Humphries, the Director of Policy and Strategy at the National Council who, in a past existence, has been a Chief Executive of a TEC. So you have in front of you a trio of myself, who is busy asking many of the questions which you are about to ask us; someone with a direct connection, being the Chairman of their TEC and a long-standing member of the TEC National Council since it began: its present Director of Policy, who has hands-on experience of being the Chief Executive of a TEC. And we have two supporters from the TEC National Council with us, should you wish to get into more technical detail.

MARTIN JACOMB: Thank you very much. I did get it right. Could I ask Lord Thomson to open the questioning?

467. LORD THOMSON: Sir Garry, we are very grateful to you and your colleagues for bringing such an impressive team along. I expect you heard the last bit of advice we got from Professor Bennett that he recommended us to ask simple and naive questions. I have no difficulty in asking simple and naive questions. I think we have been hearing—first of all I think we are all agreed

that the purposes of the TECs, the training and enterprise, are two of the most top priorities for us as a country and what we are concerned about is to see how the system is working in order to achieve these objectives. I think it might be very helpful to us if you were to just start off by telling us something about the formation of your own National Council and what its nature and history and purpose is.

GARRY JOHNSON: I think perhaps I would reserve my comments and pass the direct question to my colleagues who have been in from the beginning. Perhaps John, you were a member of the original G10—you might like to take the thing to start?

JOHN TROTH (Member of the Council and Chairman of North East Wales Training and Enterprise): When the TECs were first formed, a representative body of regional chairmen was put together which was known as G10, which was intended to provide a representative, collective view to Ministers of the way in which TECs were operating on the ground and to act as a policy link for feeding back Government and Ministerial policies into the TEC movement—so it was a two-way communication channel, or intended to be as such.

I think in some of the evidence we have heard prior to our appearing here, the operation of the initial body left a lot to be desired; in fact it was very fragmented, had no support other than what we could produce from operational chief executives and so a secretariat was formed and eventually the TEC National Council came into being to assist with policy formation through a bottom-up process, if you like, feeding our own TEC movement views to Government and similarly acting as a central point for communication to the TEC movement from Government down to the TEC. So, in essence, the TEC National Council is a trade association for TECs, assisting with policy formation, assisting with representative activities.

468. LORD THOMSON: So was it created really from the bottom up or was it a creation of Government?

JOHN TROTH: The initial group was actually a group of four summoned to appear before Tim Eggar and there was such an outcry from the movement that only four people were called forward that in fact the group of ten rapidly appeared to represent the whole of the movement.

469. LORD THOMSON: And is it, if I may ask Sir Garry—you are an independent Chairman?

GARRY JOHNSON: Yes, I am a non-executive Chairman, appointed by the Council to carry out the functions of chairman on a two-day a week basis.

470. LORD THOMSON: But what are you independent of? Are you independent of the TECs or independent of Government or independent of both?

GARRY JOHNSON: I like to think I have a degree of independence of both. I certainly feel myself to be independent of Government as I am not a Government appointee. I believe that the TEC National Council informed Ministers and sought their view before offering me the appointment and Ministers expressed a view which was taken into account. I am, of course, remunerated by the Council but I do not feel myself necessarily to be the servant of the Council in all aspects. It is a curious evolving position.

471. LORD THOMSON: Yes. You will be aware that against the background of undoubted degree of achievement of the TEC movement, there is a feeling that the National Council came into being rather late in the day. The TECs were set up, what, in 1990, you started three years later, you have now produced a draft guidance for codes of conduct for the TECs which are going to take another two years really until you come to a judgment about how far they are being implemented. What is your answer to the fact that this is really rather late in the day for filling a gap which was there?

GARRY JOHNSON: Yes. Well you will understand, coming from the background that I do, that I have been accustomed to a more hierarchical structure and so many of the questions that I asked on starting was "how does this movement, as one might term it, function?" and I have been left in no doubt whatsoever that it is business-led, community-based, bottom up; and the last thing the movement was is any form of top down hierarchical command structure imposed on it. And I think that that lies behind, if you like, the slowness of development. I have also come to the view that this is an organisation which is still in evolution and as all organisations grow and gather structures to themselves they come to recognise that a greater degree of coherence and co-ordination, both at regional level and at national level, are required if they are to, in effect, be greater than the sum of their parts—as an organisation. I think that the trick that is necessary there is perhaps for myself and outsiders to understand the limits on any imposed development of that structural hierarchy, given the nature of the TECs' individual performances.

472. LORD THOMSON: Yes. Yet the fact remains that TECs are a very unusual, they are a very innovative but very unusual institution. They are really one hundred per cent funded by the rest of us as taxpayers and yet there is a fairly minimalist framework of regulation of their governance. I think there is perhaps an excess of maintenance—I would be interested in your comments of auditing and financial control—but in terms of your governance there does seem to be a rather—well, we just had very interesting evidence from Professor Bennett—I do not know whether you have had any chance to look at his papers as part of the documentation—but he is a supporter of the achievements of the TEC movement, it is a very sympathetic paper that he gave to us, but he does call your guidance the lowest common denominator kind of guidance.

GARRY JOHNSON: I think that what the movement has done is the Council has gradually developed a view of its own responsibilities and the weight that it should be given within the movement and, as your Committee has indeed exposed these areas of public life to greater view, the Council has approached the governance aspect of its duties in good faith and it has sought to put out guidance, rather than to act as a regulatory body. And the framework for local accountability and the code of conduct, which we have recommended to TECs, and which the TECs have accepted, would seem to us to set the pattern. We do not believe that it is in the remit of the National Council, nor would it be acceptable to TECs, to seek to impose measures as a regulatory body. We seek to work by persuasion rather than by regulation.

CHRIS HUMPHRIES (Director of Policy and Strategy, TEC National Council): If I may, Chairman, if I can pick up the specifics of Professor Bennett's statements on the framework, it is worth just highlighting three things. Firstly, the framework does ask TECs to have an established process for identifying their directors. What it does not do is seek to lay that down. I think that is right. One of the reasons for that is that there is a great difficulty for TECs in seeking, in ten private sector members on their board, to properly reflect size of company, sector of company, the geographical location of the company, the capacity they need in the individuals in choosing companies that actually practice the principles the TECs preach and ensuring that they have an adequacy of gender and ethnic representation on their board. Simple election is a very dubious mechanism for ensuring that a board does properly reflect that balance and, therefore, what you find both the merging TEC Chambers and other TECs doing is struggling to find an appropriate structure for choosing boards that actually ensures that the balance that results from that process does actually reflect the breadth of interest that a community needs. So I think there are some concerns about that issue there.

On the Register of Interests of Directors I think you should go and ask TECs whether that is available—I would agree with Professor Bennett's analysis. I think you will find it is available at the local level. And on the issue of the code of conduct for executive staff you will be aware that we have actually encouraged TECs to go down that route, but that is a matter for individual TECs in dealing with their own employees. What I would say is that I do not believe that it will take two years for that framework to be in place. We have actually developed that framework over eighteen months of consultation. TECs, when endorsing it and supporting it, all 81 last July were not endorsing something they would put into practice and start thinking about from then, they were actually acknowledging that most of them had started work on it during the consultation process and you will see results a lot sooner than two years from now.

473. LORD THOMSON: Do you feel satisfied, from what you have been able to find out about the way in which the conflicts of interest safeguards work, that boards of governors of TECs are fully apprised of the importance of that? TECs, after all, are bodies that are giving out contracts to various other enterprises in the area in which they serve and, inevitably, and quite properly, there are bound to be cases, if the board of a TEC is thoroughly representative, where the contracts will be associated with members of the board of the TEC. In these circumstances do you feel that the roles are very clear about dissociating themselves totally from discussion of a contract in which they have an interest?

GARRY JOHNSON: Yes, it is an area which I have enquired about as I have visited regions and TECs, and I find that directors are acutely sensitive to this and are being made increasingly sensitive over perhaps the recent couple of years and I believe that the safeguards are in place and are applied. But it might be helpful to ask John Troth if he would wish to describe to you how it works within his own TEC.

JOHN TROTH: I think you have to differentiate between the types of interest because certainly, particularly with the private sector members there is a possibility of one of the member companies wishing to contract for some commercial provision, not necessarily training provision. I have an example on my own board where the managing director of the local commercial radio station is also the majority shareholder. It is the only

commercial radio station in the area and if you wish to get a marketing message across to young people you have to use that. So, as a consequence, he is asked to stand down from the board every time there is discussion of that type of contract or dissociate himself from any commercial negotiation. All the members of the boards that I have come into contact with—not just on my own board—are acutely aware of that potential conflict of interest.

But there is another potential conflict of interest and that is in actual use of programmes and bearing in mind that we have chief executives of local authorities, directors of education of local authorities, college principals on our boards, they have a direct relationship in terms of education and training provision which may be funded by the TEC, as do the private sector companies on the board in use of youth training programmes and adult training programmes. It obviously would be wrong to disbar members of the board from making use of those standard Government programmes available for us in their company. So it is a question of differentiating between those two types of interest and in my experience the procedures are laid out in the framework for accountability and in the code of conduct, and certainly other people that I have talked to on boards are well aware of those provisions.

474. LORD THOMSON: What are the arrangements for monitoring this? Does your National Council take on a monitoring role or is that left to the central department?

GARRY JOHNSON: The National Council does not take on a monitoring role. In direct terms, when you asked me whether I was satisfied, one of the questions I asked was to what extent would I or the National Council be responsible for ensuring that this sort of thing happened, and the National Council is not staffed to carry out an inspection function. But, again, perhaps I may turn the detail of that to Chris Humphries.

CHRIS HUMPHRIES: Yes, the actual monitoring of that takes place in three ways. You suggested earlier that the framework for governments may be too light for TECs. It is worth remembering that the TEC operating agreement and TEC licensing process are only two of the government's management systems. TECs being private companies also, of course, have to have memorandum and articles of association which do govern their behaviour and, of course, these are laid down by government as a part of the formation of a TEC and cannot be changed without the permission of government, so there is another layer there that you need to be aware of. How that is monitored is by the government offices themselves as, in effect, the Secretary of State's representatives in signing the contract with the TECs, take on the responsibility in two ways for ensuring that these mechanisms are properly applied. The first is that they do it as a part of their normal monitoring of the work of the TEC—TECs are monitored and have monitoring visits and review meetings every month, and then much more detailed ones every three months with the government office. In most government offices cases they also review these directly with the board every six months, and it is during those meetings that those issues are actually investigated.

In addition, the licensing framework that Bob Bennett spoke of, lays down very clear requirements for the English TECs in relation to their capability as a board, as an organisation, and part of what is assessed by inspection during that process, both by the Government Office and by the TEC Assessors Committee, is the extent to which the board can demonstrate its effective management, its proper compliance with the rules and regulations that apply to it, and also the extent to which it has proper succession planning and director selection processes in place. That is necessary in order to gain a licence under the new three year licensing arrangements.

475. LORD THOMSON: I was sympathetic to the view that was expressed by our previous witness that there is an impression that TECs suffer from too much scrutiny of the wrong type. I think I am at the moment in the position of feeling that perhaps there is not quite enough scrutiny of the right type in certain areas. Would you like to comment on what your experience of scrutiny is, wrong and right?

GARRY JOHNSON: To go to the wrong type first, if I may take that, I was immediately struck when I took up my appointment with the similarities of feeling expressed by TEC directors and chief executives to those which I had been accustomed to hearing when I was in a previous Service as we struggled to make sense of the Government's intention to handle public expenditure in a different, fresh, innovative way, and the clash of cultures which occurs between a regulatory centralised civil service whose duty is to guard the public purse and, in so doing, their ministers' reputations and standing, and an organisation which suddenly thinks that it has been given licence to let loose energy, enterprise and initiative. The coming together of those two things is not an easy matter in my experience. I think what we here are talking about, is trust, that the TECs have to so conduct their affairs that they can demonstrate to those who would impose this regulatory system on them, that they are competent to handle public money in a way which delivers the objectives for which that public money is given to them. I think that that is building up over the period of time as the delivery of the programmes gives evidence that TECs are performing, are delivering. In a way this trust then has to be transmitted backwards by the civil service, by the Treasury, who must seek to encourage the initiative and not stifle it by the imposition of unnecessary monitoring.

I find that a totally familiar situation and we have been heartened, and I have been heartened, in the last month to receive the outcome of a Public Efficiency Scrutiny Report held jointly between the Cabinet Office Efficiency Unit and the Department for Employment and Education, of which in effect the recommendations go a very long way towards recognising the ability which has been demonstrated by TECs, and, if implemented in full, which we hope they will be, will ease the burden of administrative ennui upon the TECs while retaining in place sufficient controls to give that degree of trust and confidence which is required. That, I think, is a process that we have to go on pushing at from the TEC side. It is business-led, it is led by people who understand swift movement, swift decisions and initiative, and we have to go on demonstrating that we can do that within a framework of a whole new way of approaching public expenditure. We understand that responsibility.

476. LORD THOMSON: Would you have a view on the proposition that has been put to us that in Scotland there is an intermediary body between the government and the TECs (there are two intermediary bodies in different parts of Scotland) which can exercise a supervisory role of a lighter and perhaps less centralised nature than happens in England and Wales. How would your members react to that model?

GARRY JOHNSON: I have not had the opportunity to visit Scotland and experience that system at first hand yet, so perhaps I may turn this to Chris Humphries to answer.

CHRIS HUMPHRIES: Certainly TECs have considered the option and we do recognise that, under current and traditional public management and public accountability principles, an intermediary body, a funding council or a regulatory body, can actually lighten the burden that derives directly from ministers and the civil service. We also have recognised that there can be a difficulty in distancing businesses, and the businessmen who actually manage TECs, further from government and thus actually reduce the extent to which the government personal commitment to Training Enterprise Councils is demonstrated. That has led, I think, to a balance of views which is not overly favourable as yet to the idea of an intermediary body. They do as well note that the structure of Local Enterprise Companies in Scotland and TECs in England is quite different. Essentially all the employees of LECs are employees of Scottish Enterprise and it is essentially an agency with a company structure overlaid upon it. The TECs in England are truly independent businesses, and in that sense are subject in a different way to many of the requirements of law in the Companies Act. In other words, there is another layer of control over TECs.

Without going into too much detail, all of those have led to a certain nervousness on TECs about that proposition, but I think there would be an openness to studying what the implications might be of any specific proposal that came forward.

MARTIN JACOMB: Thank you very much. We are going to run out of time unless I turn over to Diana Warwick who is our other questioner this morning.

477. DIANA WARWICK: I have been much struck by the way in which our witnesses have identified the local business community as the main focus for the accountability for TECs. At the same time, of course, they are spending a very large amount of public money in helping to take decisions or initiatives which should be benefiting the local community. Are you satisfied that the arrangements for accountability, if you like to the public at large rather than to the business community, are adequate? You have described quite a lot of them as part of the code of practice on access and so on, but I wonder just how satisfactory those processes are, who knows what they are, and how does one get access given that our previous witness suggested it was really quite difficult to get information out of TECs.

GARRY JOHNSON: Perhaps I can give you a general feeling and then, again, turn to my colleagues for more detailed advice. It depends what you mean by accountability, and I think we are developing in the TEC world a new way of doing business and perhaps a different sense of accountability. It is accountability, not in the old hierarchical or local democratic control sense of accountability. The accountability seems to me to be demonstrated in a multi-faceted way. There are all these ways which have been laid down of showing what the TECs are about, but at the end of the day the accountability has to be somehow measured in the benefit which the TECs are bringing to the well-being, the wealth and the good standing of the community in which they operate. This, I think, can be essentially, subjective. There can be objective measures laid over it—how many people do you train? how many people stay in work?—all these measures are easy to get a grip on in the training and the provision side. Less easy, perhaps, to measure is the other side which also interests the businessmen who are driving the thing—which is what good are they doing for the community as a whole. If one can demonstrate in some way the success in that field, I believe you are looking to the true measure of accountability in the TEC business. That is a very broad view of it. I know what you are aiming at and there are strands and substrata of that, but, John, maybe I can ask you how you handle it in your TEC area?

JOHN TROTH: Again I think there are different levels in this particular point. I am not aware of any TEC boards that do not have high level local authority representation on their boards, so in the sense of having the local community presence in policy formation, strategy formation and so on, it is there built into the heart of the TEC itself. In terms of operating within the local community, certainly the majority of TECs that I know work closely with the other agencies involved in the community, and again, of course, there are other sectors represented on TEC boards—voluntary sectors, trade unions and so on—so you are starting to spread the principle applied to local authorities through to other sectors as well.

But then networking back into the community there is extensive consultation on local economic development strategies, because TECs are economic bodies at the end of the day, so working with the partners, local authorities and other agencies and bodies working in the economic development sector, and then throughout the education and training sector as well, working very closely on the ground with the communities in a two-way fashion, not just a one-way fashion from the TEC.

CHRIS HUMPHRIES: If I could give you some quite specific examples as well around this one. It is an important issue and one of the first things that any individual needs to be able to do to actually assert their rights is to actually know what those rights are. So TECs have developed over the last three years—my TEC was at the forefront of doing this—essentially statements of rights or charters for every participant in a training plan or a training activity. TECs, of course, do not deliver the training themselves, they commission a whole range of training providers to deliver it, and so an important part of the complaints process is for the individual trainee to be able to come to the TEC if the provider is not doing what is required of them. The common way of implementing it, therefore, is usually through some form of statement of rights or charter which is mandated to be given to every trainee. That will set out the procedures that can be followed in the event of training not meeting requirements. The TECs will normally provide a chain for complaints through which that can be taken which would culminate, as is expressed in our Framework of Accountability, with a mutually agreed independent arbitrator if such resolution needs it, but how they know they can do it is normally expressed by a statement of rights that are either included in the individual training plan or expressed as a separate charter for young people, and the same applies to adult trainees as well.

478. DIANA WARWICK: Just picking up the point about complaints, one of the issues that has been raised in relation to all these bodies is the whole question of

internal complaint, in other words of staff identifying impropriety or misconduct, wanting to identify it and finding a means to do that without personal threat. The whistle-blowing concept in other words. Is there a process by which that can happen within the TEC systems and, if not, do you see a need for it as a preventive rather than as a response to known problems?

CHRIS HUMPHRIES: In each TEC there will be a different approach to this. As much as anything else it often depends on the board structures that are established. In virtually all cases TECs will have an audit committee that is an internal audit committee: it is not just Finance, it is actually concerned with the whole issue of the behaviour of the organisation. In many TECs that organisation is identified to staff as the place to which they are entitled, encouraged, to bring concerns. That structure will normally report directly to the chairman or a group of directors designated for that purpose and enable the individual to bypass the executive. It is not designed for that purpose first and foremost, but is often used for that purpose by many organisations.

As well as that, of course, many TECs still have strong union structures, and in other places either through their trade union or their staff association structure they will have made provision for that opportunity and for the trade union or the staff association, often with external advice, to be able to take up an issue either by retaining the anonymity of the staff member or by protecting the staff member under existing trade union or staff association agreements. So it does vary from TEC to TEC, but certainly in most cases I am aware of such systems do exist.

479. DIANA WARWICK: Thank you. You talked about struggling to represent all interests at local level, and the problems of engaging the interests, for example, of women or of members of ethnic minorities and so on to get a broad spread. One of the solutions to that that has been posed to us is payment of members of governing boards. Do you see that as a sensible option from the TEC point of view, or, indeed, from any of the bodies that we are looking at, or do you feel that it is possible to retain the voluntary principle and still engage the interests of the range of people that you want to engage?

GARRY JOHNSON: The issue of payment has not come to me specifically. My instinct in response to your question on that is that it would be regrettable if payment were to be introduced into this. My sense as I go round looking at TEC Boards is that they in many ways operate in the same way as charities, charitable trusts, with which you or the committee will all have experience, as do I, in that there is a genuine sense of putting something into the community without getting remuneration back for it. It would be a tremendous pity to me if it were turned into a paid directorship. I do not see that that would necessarily be of benefit, but I would defer to John Troth in a moment on it.

I think it touches on another issue as to how you ensure that you get the right representatives on the board. You are well aware of the balance between the businessman member and the non businessman member, and I think it is important to keep that balance. The difficulty many TECs find is finding people of sufficient calibre to come forward to fill the vacancies. Local politics may come into it, local conditions, local requirements. There would be, perhaps, a temptation rather than saying pay for it, that you should have representative members on these boards to represent the interests of certain sections of the public. Again, I think this would be regrettable; we are talking about businesses. These are private companies, many limited by guarantee. They are run as businesses, they are not run as democratic fora to represent by statute every interest group in the community, and I have been struck by the number of those special interest groups that seek that sort of system in the hope that it will give them a place in the sun if you like. What I believe we ought to be doing is ensuring by encouragement and advice that the TECs do, in fact, represent those interests as best they may in their local community. If that sounds airy-fairy, it is airy-fairy because the different communities have different requirements. Where I think the thing would be proven not to be working is if, in general terms, there was a feeling expressed in a community that such and such a part of it was not getting a fair crack of the whip. I think that would come through many of the systems that we have.

I am sorry, that is a rather long-winded one to your first question about payment, and I wonder whether I could flick it to John Troth and ask what he thinks.

JOHN TROTH: Speaking as one of the few Englishmen on my TEC board I can speak as part of the ethnic minority I think. On the question of payment, it has been raised from time to time in my experience since TECs were first started, and I think the general almost unanimous reaction has been to reject that suggestion principally because the majority of private sector people, and certainly chairmen, involved in the TEC movement, feel that they have a direct relation with ministers as part of the operational process. While they value that relationship they do not want to be beholden in any way, and payment actually then removes the independent status and therefore part of the motivation in this process. So generally speaking, as Garry says, it is seen as making a contribution to the local economy, but one which is a voluntary contribution not a paid contribution.

480. DIANA WARWICK: Is part of the relationship with the local business community an understanding that if a member of a firm or a person you wish to have on a board is asked that they would get paid time off? I mean, is that a corollary?

JOHN TROTH: No.

481. DIANA WARWICK: It is not. Have you had any problems of that?

JOHN TROTH: Not that I know of. I know one member of the TEC National Council had to take holiday to attend National Council meetings, but that is the only instance that I have ever come across.

482. DIANA WARWICK: Can I just ask one final question because I raised it before. One of the criticisms that we have had about openness relates very specifically—it is not just in relation to TECs, it is in relation to almost all the organisation we have been dealing with—to the problem of effectively hiding information, or withholding information, using the excuse or the reason of commercial confidentiality. Is this something that could be done away with without any loss?

CHRIS HUMPHRIES: One of the very important differences between the committee structure of local

government and the structure of TEC boards is that TEC boards are doing two jobs at the same time. When they meet they are actually both seeking to shape, develop and monitor performance and policy, and they are also managing the financial concerns of a private company for which they have fiduciary responsibilities which are laid upon them by the Companies Act. Local authorities tend to separate their policy formulation structures which are open committees from the actual internal management of their finances which are done in closed rooms. There are always sound reasons for trying to actually deal with financial management issues which can impact upon staff and are highly confidential matters within and behind closed doors. TEC boards meet once a month; they are actually bringing volunteers from around their community in, usually within their working hours, and, as such, are seeking to fulfil a number of roles in a relatively short business meeting. To try and separate off those parts which are properly and appropriately conducted in commercial confidence from those parts which are properly and appropriately conducted, or could be well opened up, is actually not a simple matter.

What many TECs are doing now in order to address that is to find a whole variety of other ways whereby they can involve their community in consulting on what they do, how well they do it, and in monitoring the performance year on year and the way in which they implement and succeed in their plans. Not just a single public meeting, but going way beyond that in terms of drafting their corporate plans, setting their objectives, consulting with in many cases hundreds of organisations in their community to ensure that what they are proposing to do is valid, and actually then publishing and having public meetings to review their success in achieving that performance quite openly in a way that often even incorporates the local media to ensure that the public can be reached. By therefore taking their policy and their performance outside the board meetings to their community they are actually avoiding the problem that often lies behind keeping certain of the normal financial management activities where they belong in the board room, but actually ensuring that the public have a much greater access to policy and performance in a way that is totally consistent with local accountability. It is a difficult balance, as I said. Local authorities have a difference in structure which enables them to do it, and it is much harder to do that when you are actually gathering a board together for two to three hours only.

GARRY JOHNSON: I suspect also that TECs have a certain difficulty in actually encouraging public interest. I visited one TEC on the evening when they were going to hold one of their well-publicised in the local press annual meetings, for which they had hired Sir John Banham to speak and Trevor McDonald to introduce it, and I thought that would be a crowd puller. It got 230 people, which probably is a crowd, but it does not actually say to me that the whole of that community was thirsting for information which we withhold from them.

MARTIN JACOMB: Thank you very much. A moment or two ago when I switched the questioning from Lord Thomson to Diana Warwick I did so very abruptly, for which I apologise, but I think Lord Thomson probably has another question.

LORD THOMSON: I think Tom would like to.

483. TOM KING: I would just like to follow up exactly what Diana Warwick was talking about. I did not quite

understand the answer. TEC boards meet during normal working hours, do they?

JOHN TROTH: No, a lot of them meet outside working hours.

CHRIS HUMPHRIES: If you are looking for an average time I guess four until six, or four until seven, would be one of the most common meeting times of TEC boards which would, certainly for most businessmen, place that inside working hours.

484. TOM KING: And the majority of people serving on them do not actually lose any pay for the time that they may serve on the boards from their normal occupation?

CHRIS HUMPHRIES: Given that they are all chairmen or chief executives of their own organisation, I suspect the decision on whether to dock their pay is theirs.

485. TOM KING: And they do not, so that is one aspect of this point about should they be paid. How well have the objectives which you subscribe to been achieved about the majority of the private sector? Just to explain what I mean by that. I get the impression looking down some lists, chairmen of hospital trusts, chief executive of perhaps the county council, other public bodies of one sort or another, some of them seem to get classified because they are employers as the private sector, is that right?

CHRIS HUMPHRIES: No, the definition that is laid down in the TEC operating agreement makes it very clear that they must be private sector individuals, and it does actually define that. One third of the board can be the chief executives of the local authorities, the hospital trusts, the voluntary sector, trade unions, but two thirds are required to be the private sector employers who must be true private sector chairmen and chief executives. Every TEC is expected to have one third of its board drawn from the public and voluntary sectors, but, again, they must be of chairman or chief executive level in their respective organisations.

486. TOM KING: For instance, you are right about hospital trusts, are you?

CHRIS HUMPHRIES: Many TECs, but not all, would have the chairman of their hospital trust as one of their five public sector directors, but not as one of their ten private sector directors.

487. TOM KING: The impression that comes from some TECs is this sort of search for publicity and public understanding. You referred quite interestingly to Sir John Banham and I think Sir John Harvey-Jones does quite a bit of speaking at not inconsiderable expense to the TECs around the country. Is this the sort of image that you see necessary to build that public image as part of the accountability?

GARRY JOHNSON: One of the interesting things to me is the lack of visibility of TECs generally. Everybody knows various other sets of initials—TUCs, CBI, IOD. The TEC movement seems to me to have almost a deliberately low profile. Quite often you see it spelt with small t's, small c's, sometimes with big. I guess if you went out and spoke to the general public there is no ready understanding of what TECs are, what they do, and how

they set about it, and what place they play and where they are going in the business. I have asked within the movement whether people are content with that or whether they would seek greater publicity. The publicity seems to me to be sought at the local level in the ways that have been expressed in the press, local radio, to do the business, but publicity on a greater level as to what the TEC movement is delivering nationally, I do not yet think is particularly strong.

488. TOM KING: It interested me because the point has been made that you worked through intermediates, therefore you do not deal with the general public, you do not provide a service to the general public. Whether it is business-linked or whether it is individual training providers, or whether it is the college promoting its own courses, these sort of areas, is that not the areas that actually are more sensible and easier to promote?

GARRY JOHNSON: I think it is. TECs have essentially the role of facilitators, co-ordinators, generators, making it happen. Whether they should seek in any way by that to be visible in their own right I am not yet sure. I believe it is an open question in my mind. Whether that would be more effective in delivering what they are about, I think has to be the touchstone.

JOHN TROTH: Perhaps I could comment on that. I think as far as the public meeting aspect is concerned each TEC will have gone through a series of trial and error forms of presentation. On particularly large patches they will have several public meetings around maybe Devon and Cornwall spreading around so that they give access to the different geographical areas. We tried that in northeast Wales and eventually settled on one central meeting coupled with our AGM, so we have all gone through a different learning process from that point view.

In terms of general presentation there is substantial local marketing activity. For instance, the modern apprenticeships programme which is currently being promoted throughout England and Wales, and I think Scotland as well, there will be substantial marketing activities on the part of TECs making sure that young people and the employers are made aware of the availability of the programme and the availability within their own sectors of the frameworks and so on. Similarly with the adult training programmes, various branding issues and marketing issues revolve around that, some of which will highlight the TEC in its own right, and some of which will actually highlight the programme. So there is a substantial local marketing activity that goes on which brings the activities of the TEC to the notice of the local public.

489. TOM KING: Sir Garry and I lived through this inauguration of this process of trying to get greater local discretion and freedom in that area. Do you think that the report of the Efficiency Unit goes as far as you would wish, or is it a compromise between the attempts to see some relaxation of central control and intrusive control in that way and what the original system was?

GARRY JOHNSON: I cannot give you a direct answer because we have not consulted with TECs. I will ask Chris for his view. My own guess is that it goes about as far as the market will bear at this stage of development.

490. TOM KING: Who is the market?

GARRY JOHNSON: The Civil Service market.

TOM KING: They are not the market, are they?

GARRY JOHNSON: No, I am shorthanding the term.

TOM KING: They have a vested interest.

GARRY JOHNSON: Yes. It will go as far as we can persuade the civil service and the Treasury to allow us to go, given the constraints that they must necessarily still impose on us, which we accept. I think that their report, therefore, will go to the extent, and perhaps even beyond in some ways, in its recommendations that which we could reasonably expect at this stage of development.

TOM KING: Not far as you would ideally like?

GARRY JOHNSON: Not as far as many idealists would like in the movement, no, but perhaps we would never get to that extent. But I do not want to give you the impression that it does not go far enough, without taking a more technical view.

CHRIS HUMPHRIES: If I can just quickly respond to that one. The report has, in fact, surprised us with the breadth of the recommendations it makes, those surprises were pleasing ones. However, they certainly do not incorporate every proposal that we have made, and in particular I do not believe they would yet take TECs, for instance, to the comparable level of control that FE colleges experience. There is certainly scope for further negotiation, but I think it is actually, as someone who is normally a critic of bureaucracy on a large scale, worth saying that the report goes much further than we expected it would.

491. WILLIAM UTTING: I had a couple of questions about training. First, what methods TECs use to monitor the content of the training courses that they contract for with outside agencies? How do they determine whether they are getting value for money in this field?

GARRY JOHNSON: I would have to seek advice on that technicality.

CHRIS HUMPHRIES: There are two mechanisms that are primarily used. Every contract with a training provider is normally either reviewed or, more commonly, renewed each year. In order to assess performance of a training provider quite a number of different mechanisms are used. First, every training provider is monitored on the achievement of the contract it signs up for, that is in relation to the number of people who begin training who actually complete and are retained in training throughout and the number of qualifications they achieve. That is at the superficial performance level.

In addition, every TEC is required to implement a quality assurance system, and that system itself is audited, which involves them in visiting every provider, actually inspecting training on the ground, of interviewing trainees on a regular basis, of actually maintaining reports on those, of assessing the quality of management of the organisation and the financial management of the organisation, and retaining those reports for inspection by the government who assesses the extent to which we do this job properly. This system has one of the terrible acronyms which you may come across in other documents called TQASM, and the proper application of that system by the TEC is audited by the government office every year in order to ensure TECs do it properly.

492. WILLIAM UTTING: And these activities are carried out by officers of the TEC?

CHRIS HUMPHRIES: The inspection process and the contract management process are carried out by officers of the TEC, and then in turn their work is inspected regularly by officers of the government office of the region.

493. WILLIAM UTTING: Good, thank you. The second question also related to training because there are a number of groups of people in the population who might be considered to have special needs for training in the employment sector if one thinks of people with mental health problems or physical disabilities. Are there sufficient incentives in the system for TECs and the people they contract with to provide proper training for people with special needs?

CHRIS HUMPHRIES: No, we would say not always. I do not think it is merely a matter of incentives. Those with special needs do require quite close and continuous personal support, counselling, advice and guidance through the training process. It is not always feasible with the funding available to be able to both provide the quality and depth of support for special needs that we would think appropriate, and at the same time maintain the coverage for training for all of those without special needs. There is always a tension in managing budgets over the extent to which you either disenfranchise individuals who could benefit from training without special needs, or provide more support for those with special needs in order to help them through the process. That tension has been well recorded in public documents including the recent IES report. That report will highlight many of the mechanisms and techniques TECs use to try and minimise those difficulties, but the report itself does conclude that there is an overall resourcing level which is making that extremely difficult.

WILLIAM UTTING: Good, thank you.

494. LORD THOMSON: Going back to what I was asking about the arrangements for maintaining propriety generally. We inevitably have had some evidence from various quarters about individual cases with TECs. We are not an investigative body in any way and I think there is a general awareness that over the whole range of TECs that there is not serious impropriety, and when there is it has been mentioned a good deal over local publicity. What I would like to explore is when that occasionally happens, and it is very important that you should be seen to be dealing with matters adequately, who deals with them? Does your TEC National Council inquire into the matter and attempt to take steps to prevent the recurrence elsewhere? Is it entirely a matter for the department? What are the sanctions for dealing with the rare cases of impropriety by a TEC?

GARRY JOHNSON: I think I am prepared to tell you that in my time as Chairman we have had no personal experience of this problem.

LORD THOMSON: We are having some experience ourselves, so you must be hearing some of it.

GARRY JOHNSON: What I mean is that this matter has not arisen in a specific way during my time, but there have, as you say, been instances in the past. I believe I am right in saying that five cases of possible impropriety have been investigated and all found to be groundless. But each time something like that happens within a system, as you will well understand, the alarm bells ring and the lessons are learnt. The mechanisms which the Council have put in place in terms of the Code of Conduct are all designed to make sure that this sort of thing does not happen again. There is a rigour of supervision by government offices and this, again, is a tension in the degree to which you loosen the controls and the extent to which you maintain them, because there must be some rigour of supervision. There is the internal audit function that we have talked about, and John has talked about the conflict of interest problem. So gradually, my sense is that the scope for impropriety is being squeezed out of the system all the time.

You cannot in any system guarantee that there will not be some cases of impropriety which, in a round about way, brings me to the point of your question, as I understand it, of whether the TEC National Council has a sanction in that matter. I do not believe that it does, through the constitution of the TEC as a limited company in its own right. Again, I understand that the mechanisms for dealing with this are perhaps informal but nonetheless effective. In the end the Regional Government Office can exert an enormous amount of influence and pressure on any TEC and on its Board if it believes that it is going wrong through the mechanism of its contract. This, again, I am given to understand, has been done in the past to good effect where it has been felt necessary. Again, you will excuse me if I ask for more background from my colleagues to see whether it bears out my view.

CHRIS HUMPHRIES: Yes I think there are two things that could usefully be said just to set the scene. I do not believe the TEC National Council would actually be accepted as a body to investigate such allegations of impropriety anyway. I suspect it would be seen in the public eye as TECs investigating themselves, and I think appropriately wherever that has happened typically two bodies have actually stepped in to investigate. The first of these has been the government office itself which, as holder of the contract, is the appropriate body to investigate anything that breaches either the spirit or the letter of the contract. But in every case, certainly to my awareness, the National Audit Office has also been asked to take a specific look as a well recognised and totally independent body, and each case I believe the thing that made the difference was the statement that the National Audit Office was satisfied that propriety had been maintained. I believe it is essential to have a body like that to take a role where such a case is concerned, and I do not think that any intermediary body like the Council would have the level of public credibility that you would want to expect.

495. MARTIN JACOMB: Thank you very much indeed Sir Garry and also to your colleagues for coming along and giving us so much of your time. It is a great help to us to get the full picture from your point of view. Thank you very much.

I would like to welcome. Is that right?

JOHN HEDGER, FELICITY EVERISS, AND ANDREW TABOR

JOHN HEDGER (Director of Operations, Department for Education and Employment): That is absolutely correct, Chairman, yes.

MARTIN JACOMB: Would you like to start by describing the positions which you hold.

JOHN HEDGER: Surely. I have recently been appointed Director of Operations in the newly formed Department for Education and Employment. That means that I am responsible for the implementation of the government's programmes for training and for the careers service, in simple terms. Included in that responsibility is responsibility for the Department's, as it were, business relationship with the Training and Enterprise Councils. Felicity Everiss is currently the head of division with responsibility for our relationship with the Training and Enterprise Councils and indeed has been so involved almost from the ground floor up, and Andrew Tabor is part of her team in that division. His responsibility is also particularly for relationships with the Training and Enterprise Councils.

496. MARTIN JACOMB: Thanks very much. That is very helpful. Although your responsibilities are wider, we are going to try and confine ourselves to TECs. Could you tell us a little bit about the background to their formation and what the general idea was in relation to membership on the one hand and original board members on the other.

JOHN HEDGER: Sure. The guiding principle was that in relation both to the administration of programmes of training and for the wider objectives of economic regeneration in different parts of the country, it was likely to be more effective to engage the interests of, principally, employers than to operate as the former Department of Employment had done before, which was to rely on its own civil servants operating out of area offices in the region. That was what lay behind the White Paper and eventually the creation of Training and Enterprise Councils—a belief in the ability of employers to respond more flexibly and with a greater awareness of their own needs and the needs of the business community than civil servants could.

497. MARTIN JACOMB: Thank you very much. The point has been made to us this morning that, in relation to the membership, in order to achieve sensible accountability, it would be quite desirable to have a much more widespread membership, which is partially achieved through the combination which some TECs have done with chambers of commerce. Do you have any comment on that? I am talking about membership rather than board membership.

JOHN HEDGER: Yes. I think it is a difficult trick to take, for two reasons, though certainly it is a trick that we are constantly seeking to take. One is that we are here engaging the services of volunteers, and volunteers are not obtained easily, particularly when they have their own business to run. The second is that, in order to ensure that those who chair or act as directors on TECs have a breadth of experience and can, as it were, speak not only for themselves as employers but for the whole of the business community in their area, it is desirable that they have some, as it were, stature and breadth of experience. This is what lies behind the requirements for membership, in terms both of the directors and of the chairmen, but certainly the pilot schemes to combine the TECs with chambers of commerce have as part of their objective and their potential advantage the broadening of membership which the addition of a chamber gives. It may be that my colleague would want to add something to that answer.

FELICITY EVERISS (Department for Education and Employment): I expect you have heard already that there are some TECs who are operating with a model of that kind. I think some of those are formal company membership schemes; some of them are more what I would describe as a club membership, where they have a variety of benefits or services available to those who might otherwise be described as the "Friends of the TEC", or whatever. There are a variety of different models for achieving the main purpose, which is the breadth of contact and discussion and links with the wider community that the TEC board operates on behalf of and for.

Certainly in conversation with one of the new chamber TECs, and they have an electoral college system within the new chamber process, one of their concerns has been how to maintain the breadth of interests of different parts of the area, different parts of the industrial sectors, different interests of a personal kind that directors have from an electoral college system, so that they have a balance on the board. Secondly, they have some theoretical concerns, at least, about continuity of experience, because this is a very complex business and one of the issues for directors is getting a handle on the complex business that they are directors for. They think they will be able, as they put it, to manage that process through by the election system that they will operate, but it was of great concern to them in setting the arrangements up. Those are the issues that I think some TECs would have to think about in moving towards a broader membership or electoral system of that kind for directors.

498. MARTIN JACOMB: Thank you very much. We might come back to accountability in a moment or two, but while we are on the question of who runs TECs and the membership of them, on the other hand, could I ask you if you have a view on whether these qualifications for the private sector directorships are too strict? I am asking you that because in another sphere I have noticed that quite a lot of employers, big employers particularly, are willing to make more junior people available, both for the contribution to the public service and for the benefit they get through having those more junior people gain experience outside their employer's business. Do you think there is a case for modifying the qualification for board membership from the private sector boards to allow for something like that, or in any other respect?

JOHN HEDGER: I think the honest answer to that, Chairman, is that I have not had sufficient experience in detail of the way TECs work to give a personal view. What I can tell you is that both Ministers and the TEC assessors panel, which I imagine you are aware of, are actually rather chary of diluting the weight and stature of TECs. There is, I think, almost an inevitable trend, as organisations of this kind, particularly voluntary organisations, become more mature, for the initial sense of priority and importance somehow to get diluted and for the membership to be delegated progressively down the organisation. While that may have advantages in terms of the experience of more junior members of the organisation, I think there is a price to pay, and that is the reason for the caution.

FELICITY EVERISS: That view of Ministers I think is partly based on experience and observation of the private industry councils in the United States of America, where the controls on directorships of those bodies, or the equivalent thereof, are not the same as ours and were more relaxed. Over time, because those organisations are older, precisely that was observed, that the stature and status of those leading the councils deteriorated over time and that that led to a deterioration in their effectiveness, at least in some places, to engage at senior levels and in strategic and influential ways with the employer communities and others. I think that is partly the reason why Ministers are chary of this.

There is also of course an arrangement introduced relatively recently, partly in response to the issues, particularly for large multinational companies, where you may have a very senior individual in a location who does not quite meet the formal criteria about being head of operational activity. We call it the wild card arrangement, whereby a TEC may put forward the name of someone who does not meet the eligibility criteria in whole but who has a very good CV as an individual to be a TEC director. Those wild card cases are considered by the national assessors, who make recommendations to the Secretary of State. If my memory serves me right, there have been 11 such cases so far, all of which have been accepted by the Secretary of State on the advice of the assessors.

499. TOM KING: Can I just ask a question about that? Am I really hearing that right? One of the balances you have to strike here is between getting the group chief executive, or whoever it may be, which gives authority to a TEC board, and somebody who actually knows something about the people who are actually working in his company and the sort of calibre and training effectiveness of the people who he is recruiting—the production manager or somebody. Are you saying that that sort of person has to come through a wild card process, which actually has to come to the Secretary of State, and 11 such people have been appointed?

FELICITY EVERISS: More or less, yes. It will depend very much on the local circumstances. The criteria require the senior operational executive in an area, and that will vary according to company structures and the way companies are set up. It might be that a production manager is indeed the senior person in the company in the area, so it is difficult to be hard and fast about particular types of characters. Nevertheless, where there is a senior person in the organisation on site, such an individual would need to go through the wild card procedure, which Ministers have agreed is a way of addressing the problem of having people who have got relevant experience to offer being engaged as directors in the TEC. TECs also use a variety of other mechanisms to bring other people in board and bring expertise to them. They will have advisers attending the board, they have working groups, they have a range of other ways of drawing on expertise of different kinds throughout the community.

500. MARTIN JACOMB: Throughout the evidence we have heard this morning one of the general impressions I have got—maybe other members of the Committee have got different impressions—is that there are very tight regulations in some parts of the TEC activity but not at all tight in other part and, in particular in the latter category, not much accountability and control in the quality of the output. Do you have a general comment on whether you find the present system of measuring the output of TECs satisfactory?

JOHN HEDGER: I think it is true that, over time, we have moved from, as it were, volume to consideration of quality, and it is probably true that we are not as far down that road as we would ideally like to be. We certainly do have in place, I think, fairly complex arrangements for tracking expenditure, to make sure that the expenditure that we commit through TECs is incurred for the purposes intended. We have more recently begun to tighten up our expectations through contracts, so that they relate not simply to, if you will pardon the expression, bums on seats but also to qualifications achieved and to jobs secured—qualifications achieved particularly for the youth training programmes, both qualifications and jobs secured through training for work. That would be my first answer to that, that we have made considerable progress in quality assurance over the last five years, but that there is still probably a little way to go.

FELICITY EVERISS: There are some formal quality assurance requirements on TECs. We have, via the contract, a requirement that TECs operate a quality assurance system of all their products and supplies, which are very many—in any one TEC there will be upwards of 20 different services that they operate—and that is controlled and monitored by government office staff, both in terms of systems audits and a cycle of product audits, to make sure the systems work. That sort of quality assurance system borrows from the principles of the commercial sector in terms of quality control. We also have statistical analyses, nationally database analyses and a range of research and evaluation projects, across TECs and across the country, about what is happening to individuals who are going through the programmes and the range and quality of services run. So the Department has, both directly for each TEC and nationally for its programmes, a range of information available to it about quality. The outputs themselves are quality controlled by the system, in the sense that national vocational qualifications are what we pay for, and those are quality controlled by the organisations who set the standards and run the qualifications framework, and have their own quality assurance systems related to them, which gives us some assurance that an NVQ that is achieved is a quality product from the supply end of the qualification system—complex, but it works.

501. LORD THOMSON: Can I just ask on that very point: is it not a fact that the training provider is also the examiner for NVQs and is there not a real danger of providers needing to earn a living?

FELICITY EVERISS: There may be. They have to be accredited and assessed as assessment centres by the bodies that award. Not all training providers will be. Some employers may be.

JOHN HEDGER: I think the important point to make is that those who provide training have an important part to play in the assessment procedure, but they are not in control of it. The control over the total system and the part which providers play, whether they are private providers or colleges of further education, is exercised ultimately through the National Council for Vocational Qualifications and the awarding bodies, so there is a degree of partnership in the arrangements, but it is not, as it were, a provider-led, bottom-up system.

502. LORD THOMSON: But we are told that the provider is the examining body. It is true of course that the NVQ is there as a back-up, but the actual provider with the contract is also, we are told, the examining body when

the exams come on, not an independent exam of the kind that is taking place down the corridor.

FELICITY EVERISS: The awarding body, for example, the RSA—the Royal Society for Arts—which does a lot of these qualifications, will accredit around the country a number of places who are their agents, if you like, for assessment processes and for verifying the holders and the work. They will quality assure that those accredited centres do the job they are supposed to do properly, and the awarding body itself has an inspectorate to do that. The standards that they operate to are set by the National Council for Vocational Qualifications, so there is a chain of control of quality assurance through the system. At the bottom end some element of the assessment process may be done by a provider, though not necessarily, but always under that system of control of quality, and it will vary from place to place.

503. MARTIN JACOMB: I think Lord Thomson's question is a bit like a driving instructor changing his hat to driving tester. But could I just go on to the question of accountability? We were dealing there with output and the quality of output. The second theme I have got from this morning's evidence is that there is a great vagueness about to whom these bodies are really accountable. Are they accountable to you? Are they accountable to the private sector in the community in which they operate? What is your view about the people to whom these TECs are really accountable?

JOHN HEDGER: I hope it's not too glib to say that the short answer to that is "Both". They have important responsibilities for the use of pubic money, something like £1½ billion a year on the programmes that we contract to them, and for those programmes they are accountable to Parliament through the Secretary of State. It is for that reason that we have a fairly complex, certainly time-consuming, apparatus of contract management and performance monitoring, and of course information. Within those responsibilities, they have discretion as to how, in detail, they administer training programmes and how they respond to the wider objective of improving the skills base in a local community and thus contributing to economic regeneration, and not just the skills base but how they assist small businesses and growing businesses to meet the demands on them. In that sense it is important that they are sufficiently open to be held accountable, but not in a formal sense, to those whose views and needs they are expected to represent.

504. MARTIN JACOMB: Do you think you're open enough?

JOHN HEDGER: I do not think it is the case that all TECs yet fully comply with the framework for accountability which the TEC National Council has helpfully issued. I think that is something which we would expect all TECs to achieve, but I think it provides the basis for adequate openness to the local community, both in terms of membership and in terms of what their corporate plans are and how they intend to go about reflecting the business interests in their community.

MARTIN JACOMB: Thank you very much. I do not want to monopolise the questioning, so let me turn it over to Diana Warwick.

505. DIANA WARWICK: Could I pick up the theme of openness? It is something that I asked one of our other

witnesses, about the whole question of identifying problems that arise internally. It is an issue that has arisen within the Civil Service of course; it has arisen within most public service bodies. Is there anything in the contract that is negotiated with the TEC that provides for what is effectively whistle-blowing, to ensure that individuals can identify, without threat to themselves, problems that might arise?

JOHN HEDGER: Not in the contract, no.

506. DIANA WARWICK: Is there anything over which the Department has any control, where that might be operated?

ANDREW TABOR (Department of Education and Employment): This is a complex area, and I know some of the previous witnesses have covered this. One of the things that are available as far as the Department is concerned, is a regular monitoring process; there is regular contact between the Department, government office staff and TECs. There is a process of co-operation, we actually work very, very closely together and, through that process, there is a mechanism for persons who are concerned that they are not able to raise things through their own channels within the TEC to be able to open it up with government office contacts, if it is an issue relating to the delivery of the contract. We do require a TEC to have in place an audit committee, as required by the Cadbury code, and one of the functions that an audit committee has is the overall control and a watching brief of the operation of the company as a whole, not just from the financial audit. As I think Chris Humphries said earlier, that forms a channel within many private companies for people to take up issues and to blow the whistle where necessary.

507. DIANA WARWICK: One of the things that have come out in all the evidence, and I think Sir Martin alluded to this as well, is the enormous amount of financial control and the requirements that are exercised. It is almost suggested that it is overweening nit-picking from some of the evidence that we have had. Can I then ask you: having all these processes in place, why was the South Thames TEC picked up so late?

JOHN HEDGER: Since Felicity Everiss was there and I wasn't, as it were, I will ask her to answer this, if I may.

FELICITY EVERISS: The South Thames history is long and complicated, and I need to be careful, because the company is still in receivership and issues are still going through. I thought I should mention that. We knew there were financial control problems at South Thames TEC for quite some long time, which is about the risk to public funds as we perceive it. We have a scoring system for financial control, and South Thames had been high risk in our terms for a long time, and we were proactively working with them over a long period of time to try and sort that out. There were some difficulties of dialogue with that particular TEC, is probably all I had better say.

We were led, after a while, because we did this to all TECs, to issue a breach of contract notice to them to try and get them to remedy their financial control issues, and when that was still not coming to fruition in the way we expected and because we believed there to be a problem, from the company's own auditors and from information available to our auditors when they went in to look at the control procedures—there were some problems about the internal financial management of the company, which is a rather different issue—with the agreement of the TEC a firm of accountants were put in to look at the financial business, the financial operation, of the company. It was only when that report was received from that particular firm of accountants that it became obvious that the TEC was non-viable financially as an organisation. Until then it was not a case that that TEC, to put it crudely, was bust. We were worried about the way they were controlling the money, but until that report had been analysed, we did not have the information available to us to say that that company had to go into liquidation. So it did not take us a long time to know there were problems; it took quite a long time to get to the bottom of what was an incredibly varied and full-of-holes set of financial information.

508. DIANA WARWICK: It is interesting, isn't it, that we have all these controls and yet they did not show up something of crucial importance? Have lessons been learnt from that that have been translated into changes in the relationship?

FELICITY EVERISS: I think myself—it is a personal view—that lessons have been learnt by the Department, government offices and indeed Training and Enterprise Councils themselves, boards of directors in particular. One of the issues there was the amount of information—it is a company issue really—available to the directors and the management about their own financial affairs, and I think those lessons have been learnt. South Thames is pretty unique. It is the only TEC in the country that never ever got itself out of the high-risk control band. There has never been one like that before or since. Our analysis of annual statements of accounts and the returns that are given to us about the company's income and expenditure, for example, have been looked at in the light of those experiences. One can never be absolutely certain, but we do not believe that the chances of that happening again are very high, without being able to guarantee it, because you can't.

JOHN HEDGER: Could I add: the extent of audit controls over TECs is well documented. Every time I go to visit TECs I am assailed by a description which, on the face of it, does sound extremely burdensome. I think that this is one of the things we shall need to look at to make sure that, in the belt and braces approach to audit that we currently have, we are not, as it were, missing the wood for the trees.

509. DIANA WARWICK: In fact is that something you are looking at actively? Is it something we should take into account?

JOHN HEDGER: Yes, it is.

ANDREW TABOR: Can I perhaps add that in terms of the things that have actually progressed since South Thames TEC came along, particularly the work that was done by the Cadbury Committee, the publication of that code on corporate governance and the work that the TEC National Council has done now on standards for directors, had all that been in place before the South Thames saga started, and that is some time back, as Felicity has said, it might have meant that we would not have got as far down the road as we went with South Thames. One of the problems was—I have to be careful again with the words one says here—that some of the information that directors may have been working upon was not the information that would have been ideal for running a company. One of the things that setting up an audit committee does is that it actually gives the board a specific responsibility to ensure that the financial management and accounting systems are operating properly and are providing the board with the right sort of information. Had that right sort of information been before the board, it is possible that different decisions would have been taken by them, and therefore they might not have got into that difficulty.

510. DIANA WARWICK: Could I just ask one other question? It is something that came up out of very positive comments made by two of our previous witnesses this morning about the way in which the TECs have responded to the challenge of providing increased vocational education, vocational training. But we were then told that the measures that applied to previous schemes left a great deal to be desired, and therefore it was almost impossible to prove that there had been a very considerable increase in the provision. Can you say something about that and the way in which previous schemes were monitored, and the information that you have that enables a comparison to be made?

FELICITY EVERISS: Yes. I am not a statistician is my first qualification to what I say next, and some of this debate turns on the statistical interpretation of data. The programmes that were delivered by area offices under the previous arrangements did not work on a funding of output system for a start. They paid for the training process and they paid to providers directly. We monitored what was achieved by the young people. We have been monitoring what happens under youth training schemes for a very long time, but that is reliant on information provided by the young person in direct response to a questionnaire that they are sent some time after they leave the scheme. What we now have is a different system of measuring and paying for outcome and achievement of programmes. We have both financial information—how much we paid for—and management information, which comes from the company claiming the money—the TEC—which is not the same as the information provided from the individuals, and that is part of the problem of trying to demonstrate the effectiveness of one set of programmes against the other, as run under different organisations.

What is clear from the data is that over the lifetime of the TEC period the programmes have improved. They have done better over time, since they took on the work from area offices. If one assumes, and it is an assumption, that the level of activity in area office was roughly that when they started and they have had a progression since then, you can make not statistical assumptions, but you can draw some conclusions about the effectiveness of TECs as organisations. But it is quite difficult to prove statistically.

511. WILLIAM UTTING: We heard this morning that there has been an efficiency scrutiny of this sector. Did that cover whether or not there is a case for a new regulatory/funding body for TECs?

JOHN HEDGER: No, it didn't.

512. WILLIAM UTTING: It didn't? I find that rather surprising. Does it strike you as a surprising omission from an efficiency scrutiny?

JOHN HEDGER: No, because that was not within its terms of reference. It took the present relationship, if you

like, between the Department, the Secretary of State and the Training and Enterprise Councils as read and sought to come up with recommendations for improving the way in which that relationship was implemented. As to whether there should be, on top of a contractual relationship, a further regulatory body, which I think is what lies behind your question, is an interesting question on which we all may have personal views, but so far as I know, and I stand to be corrected, it is not one which Ministers have recently addressed.

WILLIAM UTTING: They may address it in the near future of course, depending upon what we have to say.

JOHN HEDGER: Yes, indeed.

513. WILLIAM UTTING: We heard from the TEC National Council earlier this morning that opinion in the field was ambivalent about this idea of a new regulatory body, but I thought the chief executive said one very significant thing, when he said he took the point that a body like this might actually be able to supervise TECs with a lighter touch than the Department itself. What would your view be about that?

JOHN HEDGER: I think my instant response to that would be "He would say that, wouldn"t he?" In a sense it's better the devil you don't know in this context. If we are to continue to operate, as Ministers currently wish, with a system in which our relationship with TECs is essentially contractual, I think that one has to ask a number of questions about the added value of a body which regulates that process. There are of course other ways in which the Department might establish a relationship with the TECs, and I think there it is not so much that the alternative would be a regulatory body, in the sense that there are regulatory bodies for the privatised utilities, so much as the relationship which the Department has, for example, with the further and higher education funding institutions through a funding council. That is an alternative model. It is not the one we operate, but it is an alternative. But I think that there are serious questions to be asked about yet more complexity, if on top of the contractual relationship one seeks to add a regulatory body, but perhaps that is not what is intended.

514. WILLIAM UTTING: You see, one of the points put to us is that this system, which was designed to empower business, is in fact not empowering business to get on with the job and that this is a problem which arises inevitably when there is a direct central government responsibility for what is going on, because both administratively and politically the central Department has to be over-involved in the detail. That seems to me to be quite a plausible point to make, that if it is taken away from a Department and another agency is created, the field may be freed as well as in some senses better controlled. One of my reservations about monitoring is that I doubt that individual TECs have the resource and skill base to carry out the monitoring satisfactorily, but one could see that an intermediary body with a quasi-inspectorate might do that rather well.

JOHN HEDGER: I think that where large sums of public money are involved, as they are in this case, there is inevitably going to be a tension between empowerment and accountability. I would not claim that we have got that balance absolutely right. Indeed, one of the reasons for setting up an efficiency scrutiny is to see whether it is possible to strike it in a rather different way. But it does not seem to me that the addition of a regulatory body as such is likely to produce more empowerment, nor necessarily would the removal of the Department's direct responsibility and its substitution by a funding council increase the freedom of individual TECs. They do have significant freedoms, in the use, for example, of their operating surpluses and in the choices they make in their locality for implementing the training programmes, but that is certainly circumscribed and would probably continue to be so under more or less any model you care to mention, while such large sums of public money are involved.

MARTIN JACOMB: I think the comparison with the arrangements with the LECs in Scotland was one of the things that came up, but just before we finish, could I turn to Mr Tom King, who would like to ask some questions.

515. TOM KING: Just a very quick question, if I may. Just let me get it quite clear. Each TEC is a private company.

JOHN HEDGER: Yes.

516. TOM KING: And they create themselves and the directors and the chairmen are their own appointments. Is that right?

JOHN HEDGER: Yes, that's right, within—

517. TOM KING: And they are without reference to the Secretary of State. I mean, they are approved as a company, but they make their own decisions as to who shall be on it and just the general balance is looked at and the company is then approved.

JOHN HEDGER: Yes, sir, provided they comply with the requirements as to composition, balance and so on.

518. TOM KING: Right. But the chief executive has to be notified to the Secretary of State, and an official from the Department sits in on the recruitment process—the interviews. Is that right?

FELICITY EVERISS: He has the right to do so.

JOHN HEDGER: He has the right to do so, yes.

519. TOM KING: I do not know whether you have got any record. Do you know what proportion of the chief executives are ex-Department of Employment people?

JOHN HEDGER: No, I certainly don't.

520. TOM KING: Well, you must have an idea. Could you give an off-the-cuff idea?

FELICITY EVERISS: Yes. Less than 20 per cent would be my instinctive feel for it now, but I can get the data very easily.

521. TOM KING: It wasn't originally, was it?

FELICITY EVERISS: No, originally, before they had an operating contract, most TECs spent three to six months setting themselves up. Almost all had chief executives who were civil servants and in many TECs that process continued for a time after their original contract.

For the first couple of years there were a great many ex-civil servants who were chief executives of TECs. That has changed considerably over the last six years, and I would say the numbers are now pretty low. Indeed, Mr Tabor is busy writing them for you.

522. TOM KING: Could you give us the figures for chief executives and could you give us an idea of the staff as well?

FELICITY EVERISS: Certainly, yes. The staff numbers are now very small indeed, and declining daily. All secondments will be finished by next year.

TOM KING: The what will?

FELICITY EVERISS: The secondment processes for civil servants end next year. There will be some—

TOM KING: I am sorry, I am not saying whether they are still civil servants with rights of return, or whatever.

FELICITY EVERISS: Right. How many were.

TOM KING: Who were.

FELICITY EVERISS: OK, fine. Yes, we can do that.

523. MARTIN JACOMB: Thank you very much. Just a final question: any comment on the comparison with Scotland?

FELICITY EVERISS: The only comment I think I would make is factual. The Scottish Office is a different organisation from the Department.

MARTIN JACOMB: I was really thinking of the intermediate—

FELICITY EVERISS: Well, Scottish Enterprise existed, but there is not an equivalent English Enterprise, and that I think is a real distinction between the way things operate in Scotland and in England, and Wales for that matter.

MARTIN JACOMB: I meant on whether it works better or worse.

FELICITY EVERISS: The performance data is slightly different, and I think it is inconclusive, is all that I can say.

524. DIANA WARWICK: But what about the reaction of the business community, since most of the criticism that we have heard seems to stem from the business community. Does the business community react differently in Scotland?

FELICITY EVERISS: I can't answer that. I don't know. I would have to ask colleagues in the Scottish Office.

JOHN HEDGER: I don't yet know, but I will make it my business to find out.

MARTIN JACOMB: No, I just wondered if you had a comment on it, but thank you very much indeed for coming. You've been a great help to us.

TUESDAY 28 NOVEMBER 1995

OPENING STATEMENTS

Opening statement from DEMOS

The Committee on Standards in Public Life has already begun a timely and important public debate about the governance of public bodies. In our evidence, we wish to suggest ways in which public trust in public bodies can be improved, by clarifying and harmonising the arrangements governing the various local public spending bodies.

We argue that there is a strong case for bringing coherence and clarity to arrangements which have tended to grow in an ad hoc manner, and for bringing governance arrangements under parliamentary rather than executive oversight. The aim is not to stifle good management or innovation, but rather to ensure common and adequate approaches to governance at one remove from the pressures of day to day political convenience.

In particular, we argue that:

- Common rules of openness should govern all local public spending bodies. Information on big contracts, appointees' interests and procedures should be open to inspection. A presumption of transparency could be overridden only on specified public interest grounds. "Commercial confidentiality" would not be such a ground.

- Appointed board members should be subject to five year term limits, other than in exceptional cases.

- Rules on the liability of board members should be harmonised across local public spending bodies.

- Failure by local public spending body board members to declare interests should be an offence and there should be a whistle-blowers' advice and hotline under the Council for Public Appointments (see below) which would also conduct investigations into alleged conflicts of interest.

- All local public spending bodies should provide and publicise systems of complaints and redress and codes of ethics and make information publicly available over computer-based networks.

We also argue for a new institutional framework to oversee governance, partly streamlining and clarifying existing arrangements. This should not be subject to direct political control.

- There should be a Council for Public Appointments—possibly only covering local appointments—to replace the existing machinery of ministerial patronage. Under cross-party control and with a range of expertise, it would register interests, maintain a database of candidates, establish codes of conduct, conduct ethics audit, provide advice, handle complaints, oversee recruitment and training and have long-stop powers to remove people not deemed "fit and proper" to serve.

- There should be a regulatory body for Training and Enterprise Councils and harmonisation of the powers of regulators for all local public spending bodies.

In a Demos report to be published next month, Norman Warner will be further arguing for bringing all governance arrangements for local public spending bodies under a Governance Act which would also cover local councillors. This would define the duties and obligations of public office holders, including appointments and compliance. It would establish an independent Commission on Public Governance to oversee the Act and serve as a tribunal to adjudicate on allegations of serious breaches of governance and misconduct.

All governments create appointed bodies. Inevitably, at the time of their introduction ministers are less concerned with accountability arrangements than with their purpose and effectiveness. The virtue of a clearer common framework for governance is that it would ensure that governance considerations are automatically given due weight as new appointed bodies are established.

Opening statement of evidence by Professor Robert J Bennett, Leverhulme Research Professor, London School of Economics

Local Public Spending Bodies—TECs and LECs

1. *Introduction*

This evidence is based on research on TECs and LECs gathered in two phases. *Phase 1* concerned the period from before inception, through start up, to the developments up to the end of 1993. This work involved interviews and analysis in the majority of TECs and LECs across the country. The report was published as an academic research text in 1994. It received considerable public attention and media coverage. This book is still a valid commentary on the TEC/LEC system, but does not cover the development of licensing, modern apprenticeships, merger of DFE and DE, or the recent developments concerning accountability with which the Committee is concerned. *Phase 2* has concerned the period since 1994 in which I have maintained closed contact with TECs and LECs, particularly with respect to government contractual changes and the emergence of Business Links Business Shops in Scotland) which are now the main TEC/LEC enterprise and small firms' programme. In that period I was privileged to act as adviser to the Scottish Affairs Select Committee on SE, HIE and LECs, and to give evidence to the Employment Select Committee on TECs.

My overall stance is as an independent researcher to persuade government and its agents of the form of changes required to improve its initiatives on economic development and its interface with business. This is a field to which I shall be devoted full time over the next five years with colleagues. I am pleased, therefore, to be called to present evidence to the Committee.

2. *TECs and LECs are different! They are predominantly arms' length bodies*

Before addressing the specifics of the Committee's questions it is first important to emphasise that the fields of TEC and LEC activities are fundamentally different from the other areas that the Committee is examining. Hence, the issue of accountability is also different. For FE, HE, grant-maintained schools, Housing Associations, or, indeed, for hospital trusts and most other government agencies at a local level, the agent has a *direct relation to the client* who receives the final service; e.g. as a student, or housing resident or patient. The government agent (as supplier) is, therefore, directly in contact with the source of final demand (the consumer).

TECs and LECs are different; their relations to clients is indirect.

They do not, in general, act as either the main source of supply nor are they in direct contact with client demands. In the field of training they overwhelmingly place contracts with suppliers who provide the service to trainees. In the field of enterprise services (such as small business advice and support) they place contracts, together with partners, through Business Links (England and Wales), or Business Shops (Scotland). In the case of Investors in People (IIP) and a few other areas (such as management seminars) there may be a direct contact between TECs and LECs and the business client, but even here inspectors, consultants, contractors, evaluators and organisers tend to be the main interface with the client. Only in the case of LEC activities in the fields of economic development (and in the case of HIE, additionally, some community support programmes) is there a direct funding and supply relation to the source of final demand. Even in those areas the directness of relations is diluted by the important role played by other partners, particularly local government.

In the case of services to business there is a further level of indirectness to clients. A business is not itself a client. A business services customers and it is these customers who are the final arbiters of choice and quality: if they do not like a business's services or products they go elsewhere. Hence, where TECs and LECs deal with business services they are at one further step removed from the final clients.

3. *Indirect relations to clients makes evaluation difficult*

The consequence of an indirect relation between the TEC/LEC as contract holder and the client is as follows:

(i) TECs/LECs make contracts with suppliers who are responsible for the majority of the outputs against which TECs/LECs are measured.

(ii) There is a low level of capacity for the development of technical or "tacit" knowledge of client needs at TEC/LEC level.

(iii) Technical knowledge at TEC/LEC level will not *rapidly increase* because there is unlikely to be sufficient direct feedback from clients i.e. there is little capacity for technical "learning by doing".

(iv) The client in turn tends to see, be aware of, and to evaluate the performance not of the TEC/LEC but of the provider (the training agent of Business Link/Shop).

Thus, in the words of the original TEC/LEC launch documents, they are *strategic bodies and enablers rather than doers.*

This means that when a TEC/LEC is evaluated its performance mainly derives from its contractors. This also applies to how accountability must be dealt with.

4. *The Government contract/licence to TECs fails to recognise the "arm"s length" relationship.*

Government is the ultimate contractor for TECs. In the case of LECs this contract (through the Scottish Office) is in the first instance with SE and HIE who then contract with the LECs. The Government contract has predominantly, and increasingly, focused on blocks of funding for the different main programmes, with low virement between. To the programmes have been attached government-defined performance targets. In the case of training these targets have been both output measures and cost measures. There are also "Capacity Indicators" which are evaluated as part of TEC licensing which seek to judge a number of management and effectiveness issues, including accountability. These are defined and assessed by DFEE staff. For all targets, points are awarded on the basis of which the budget of a TEC or LEC is allocated (though there are negotiations which are more complex in Scotland).

The problem that arises with this framework is that there is a very long "chain of command" flowing from government through TECs/LECs to providers to final clients. Moreover, each link in the chain is subject to a de facto fracture of knowledge and capacity since *feedback from the client cannot occur* in terms of quality and effectiveness measures. At government level, therefore, there will be an almost total incapacity to develop learning by doing and tacit knowledge. Without that learning, it is impossible to design performance targets (either qualitatively as to what is appropriate, or quantitatively of what constitutes a realistic level of achievement). Take two examples:

Example I. The difficulty can be illustrated in the case Investors in People (IIP) where the targets set in 1995/6 for many TECs have been so unrealistic that they cannot be achieved; the TEC must lose all its performance related finance for this programme, so that it might as well do nothing or act minimally (it is incentivised to be at most a satisficer!)

Example 2 In the case of business services the lack of ability to define targets is illustrated by the four chief TEC licence targets specified for 1995/6:

—expenditure

—counselling services

—diagnostic services

—management training events and numbers of participants.

These targets are being refined through Business Links, but they illustrate the key dilemma. None of these criteria involve any measure of client evaluation, they are purely volume measures. Indeed, it can be argued that TECs and LECs are encouraged solely to increase volumes, thus incentivising splitting or modularisation of sessions. Moreover, the whole process may be perverse to improving business performance: putting more business managers through more sessions may waste more of their time and thus reduce business performance. For government to be encouraging business to become involved in more sessions may be *incentivising a moral hazard by distorting the risk-taking behaviour of the manager or entrepreneur.*

The simple conclusion from this discussion is that since government and DFEE is at least two or three steps removed from the client it cannot define level of performance on targets with precision, nor can it ever expect to be effective in deciding what the detailed appropriate targets should be. Only agents directly in contact with clients can evaluate performance and only at one level of contract management above that level can it be realistically expected that targets can be drawn up effectively.

This can be looked at as a problem of contract between principal and agents. In the present arrangements, government is attempting to act, through DFEE, as principal in detailed contract design. But its agent (TECs or SE/HIE plus LECs) is itself a principal with the agents who deliver services; or in the case of businesses the TEC/LEC is dealing with agents who then deal with intermediaries (the businesses) which then serve clients. Considerable academic literature exists that demonstrates that this 3-level or 4-level principal-agent relationship cannot normally be expected to be effective, or if it is effective this is only one less probable outcome of many.

I believe the Committee should therefore be aware that the present TEC/LEC model of relations with government evidences all the worst aspects of a mis-designed principal-agent relationship. This has profound implication for any assessment of accountability.

5. *Financial and Management Accountability*

The consequence of the "arm"s length" relation of government through TECs/LECs to clients is that any hope of improving financial and managerial accountability to increase effectiveness has to involve a change in the contract relationship. The TEC licensing scheme recognises the problem but fails fully to solve it.

To be effective TECs and LECs have to be able to develop and define their own targets and to derive and use direct feedback from suppliers who are in contact with clients. Government, therefore, should do no more than set the broad framework for action e.g. on such issues as the relative weight to be placed on training unemployed people for jobs or to achieve a specified level of NVQs.

This means that the financial stream has to be a single block vote from which TECs and LECs develop their own targets without *detailed* DFEE/SO scrutiny. Much of this relationship already exists through SO and SE/HIE in Scotland. It is thus clearly possible for a much more flexible financial structure to be compatible with public accountability needs through the PAC and NAO.

In turn, the present system of auditing and scrutiny of TECs needs to be reformed. There are at least six different but overlapping audit procedures.

(i) normal professional accounting audit of accounts

(ii) Government Regional Offices annual audits plus quarterly and six monthly reviews

(iii) internal audit to a regime defined by DFEE (the FAM system)

(iv) internal management information and audit controls not covered adequately by FAM.

(v) Quality Assurance and Supplier management audit defined separately by each government department (chiefly DFEE and DTI).

(vi) scrutiny and audits for special enquiries by DFEE or DTI, NAO, European Commission and European Court of Auditors.

This is too much scrutiny of the wrong type. None centrally focuses on effectiveness from a client point of view of the individual business.

6. *Who are the "local community"?*

The Committee expresses concern in its *Issues and Questions paper* (para.15) with the weight given to the views of the local community. For TECs and LECs there are two communities—the population and business. Whilst the people are represented by local government, voluntary, community and other bodies, *TECs and LECs are fundamentally different from the other agents being examined by the Committee in having a large business community as well as a "people" community.*

The business community is relevant because such a significant part of the services are consumed by business: *directly* in the case of business advice, diagnostics, IiP, and management seminars; *indirectly* in the case of receiving trainees from government-sponsored training programmes.

Identifying and responding to that business community is a key aspect of TEC/LEC local accountability for which only a few have a fully developed approach. The "local business community" is clearly a diverse phenomenon and difficult to define. However, it does find an existence through a wide range of business organisations. The most important of these that is relevant to TECs and LECs is Chambers of Commerce. From my research it is clear that Chambers have memberships reaching thirty or forty per cent of the local business community in some areas, and an average of about 10% nationally. Although imperfect, this represents the best articulation of the "local business community" that at present exists.

Some TECs have developed close working arrangements with Chambers. Recently some TEC-Chamber mergers have taken place; perhaps 10 or 12 mergers will have taken place by the end of 1995. Merged TEC-Chambers offer a direct accountability of TECs/LECs to the local business community. They can have directly elected Boards (subject at present to eligibility criteria defined by DFEE) and this overcomes one of the key issues addressed by the Committee of producing a check to self-appointing quango boards. This represents a solution for some TECs and some Chambers. But for many of the main industrial areas of the country effective merger will not be on the agenda whilst the contract of government with TECs is so hands-on. An independent business body will never accept detailed line-by-line financial targets from government departments. The Committee might like to consider whether the TEC-Chamber merger model is so powerful in terms of accountability that it would wish to recommend its implementation throughout TECs and LECs. In so doing the Committee will have to recognise that this will be practically feasible only by modifying the Government-TEC contract model.

7. *Who are the members of TEC/LEC?*

TECs and LECs are (mostly) Companies Limited by Guarantee. They are controlled by a membership, but this membership is normally only their Board. They thus act as a form of "trust" on behalf of the local community (see above) who are the real "members" in the sense of being the clients for TEC/LEC services.

The TEC/LEC-Chamber merger solution would also help to clarify membership issues. The Committee's *Issues and Questions paper* (para.18) raises the question of members. The Committee could usefully clarify the field by recommending that the "members" of the TEC/LEC are the business community as a whole, who then elect the Board. This in turn would have the benefits of:

(i) Providing succession of the Board;

(ii) Removing lines of confusion as to whom the TECs and LECs are locally accountable;

(iii) Putting in the front line the "membership needs" of the business community. In turn this means freeing the TECs and LECs from governmental financial and regulatory straight-jackets.

(iv) Removing the highly ambiguous role of the TEC Assessors Committee set up by TEED to advise on eligibility criteria and calibre of TEC Directors.

Without TEC/LEC-Chamber mergers it is difficult to make effective use of the business community or to ensure an openness of Board recruitment. Most TECs/LECs have developed "task groups", "action teams", etc. which they use as means to develop knowledge of individuals and assess their appropriateness and commitment to the TEC/LEC. This is important and useful in itself, but it does not solve the problem of how people are recruited on to "groups" and "teams" in the first place. Only a membership and election process (subject to some form of pre-filtering and eligibility criteria) can be seen to be fully open.

TEC/LEC "membership" schemes (i.e. without Chamber merger) have been developed to cope with this issue in some areas. The Committee has seen the experience in South London TEC. This TEC has developed liaison with the local Chamber (Croydon and South London Chamber). Similar linked, as well as stand-alone, TEC membership schemes operate in other areas. Probably South London can be argued to be one of the best practice membership approaches of non-merged TECs although it is only one of a variety of models. The Committee should be aware that the Chamber in this area has only recently grown in size to approximately 29 staff, many of which are supported by contracts to the TEC. It is not therefore challenged by the TEC in the same way as a large and long-developed Chamber; in fact it is dependent on the TEC for over half of its income. South London is therefore a possible model for effective working in some parts of the country (probably about 30% of TEC areas) where the TEC de facto supports the Chamber to become a significant organisation. But it is not a model appropriate to areas with well-developed chambers.

8. *The TEC National Council "Framework for TEC Local Accountability and Corporate Governance".*

The Committee will be considering this document. It is a major step forwards, but its existence only in 1995, five years after the start of TECs seems to come late in the day. Despite this, the Committee will be aware that it was agreed by TECs only after some difficulty in some cases. As a result it is in some senses a "lowest common denominator". Whilst the majority of TECs have progressed rapidly in this area, some have been very reluctant. The committee's lead will thus be very important to encourage further and deeper acceptance of the code of conduct.

The present document suggests the following inadequacies:

(i) Principle 1(a) of having an established process for the identification and selection of new Directors and 1(c) of the selection process involving the wider community are inadequate in not specifying the details of how this is done. Local flexibility may produce variations in detail, but not sufficient to prevent a general procedure being laid down. As argued above, this begs the question of relations with local Chambers.

(ii) Openness. 3(g) a register of contracts funded by the TEC should be *easily* available for inspection. This is not yet normally the case.

(iii) Conflicts of interest e.g. 2(g). It does not seem clear why a Board member should not always withdraw from a meeting when decisions related to the interests of a specific director are being made. This would be normal, for example, in the Research Councils.

(iv) There is as yet no code of conduct for executive staff. Whilst TEC National Council have urged its development, the Committee should urge its urgent preparation and completion. A number of problems have arisen in this area; 2 resignations of Chief Executives have occurred in Scotland arising from impropriety.

(v) Complaints procedure. Principles 4(e) and 4(f) do not take account of the problems of the local context. Whilst a point of contact is helpful, there appear two gaps. The first is a clear approach to identifying the line of executive authority amongst TEC staff and that the Chief Executive will ultimately (internally) deal with complaints. Second, if as sometimes occurs, it is either difficult to complain to the local TEC or the complaint is dealt with unsatisfactorily by internal means, a clear procedure for going beyond the TEC should be laid down. The Scottish Affairs Committee considered the use of the Parliamentary Commissioner as an ultimate adjudication. This Committee might also consider this route. Whilst the number of complaints is very small, the existence of a known and certain independent means of resolving difficult complaints needs to be developed.

The Committee's overwhelming concern with the present code, in my view, should therefore not be just with its present form, but the quality and speed with which it is being implemented locally. In some cases local practice is unclear and difficult issues are being fudged. In main part this lack of clarity derives from the confusion of the government-TEC contract, which as I noted at the outset, is the key area where reforms are required. A properly designed organisation would respond without external pressure to the concerns this Committee has.

9. *Conclusion*

Organisations respond to incentives in their financial and management structure. If the principal who defines the contract (government in this case) does not and cannot know all of the technical requirements within each programme and locality, then it should not attempt to define them. Its agent (the TECs and LECs) must be free to determine their own targets and priorities within a much more flexible financial arrangement. The key concerns for the committee in terms of accountability, therefore, can be resolved by this redesign. This cannot be done unless there is a means (i) to ensure local control and local accountability, and (ii) to ensure effective client responses as a market-like body. TECs and LECs should behave like businesses as far as their clients are concerned, although subject to external parliamentary scrutiny. Many of the tensions between TECs and LECs and the local community and wider accountability would be resolved if their management was handed over to a fully *business-owned local structure* based on membership and election, rather than being *business-led* through de facto self-appointment subject to guidelines from government departments.

THURSDAY 30 NOVEMBER 1995

Members Present:

The Rt Hon Lord Nolan (Chairman)

Sir Clifford Boulton GCB
Sir Martin Jacomb
Professor Anthony King
The Rt Hon Tom King CH MP

The Rt Hon Peter Shore MP
The Rt Hon Lord Thomson of Monifieth KT DL
Sir William Utting CB

Witnesses:

Bill Garland, Assistant Director, Community Service Volunteers, Mike Stewart, Director of Services, NACRO, and Anne Weinstock, Chief Executive, Rathbone CI
Richard Best, Director, Joseph Rowntree Trust
Christine Laird, Chief Executive, John Perry, Director of Policy, and Sarah Edwards, Principal Policy Officer, Chartered Institute of Housing
Tim Brown, Chair, and Harry Perry, Director, Leicester Newarke Housing Association Ltd
Richard Clark, Chief Executive, Focus Housing Group
Professor Rudolf Klein, University of Bath

LORD NOLAN: Good morning. Our first group of witnesses today continue the theme of TECs which was our subject on Tuesday. They are Bill Garland, Assistant Director of CSV, the Community Service Volunteers, Mike Stewart, Director of Services at NACRO—the National Association for the Care and Resettlement of Offenders—and Anne Weinstock, Chief Executive of Rathbone Society and Community Industry. These bodies all provide training under contract to TECs. Some members of this Committee have a connection with CSV and I shall ask them to declare that—and, indeed, any other relevant interest—in a moment.

The remainder of today's witnesses will cover the subject of Housing Associations. The Joseph Rowntree Foundation is a major funder of research in the housing field and we shall be hearing from its Director, Richard Best, who was formerly Chief Executive of the National Federation of Housing Associations and has great knowledge of the subject.

The Chartered Institute of Housing has a membership of professional housing managers both in local authorities and housing associations. We shall hear from its Chief Executive, Christine Laird, formerly Director of Housing at Derby, and from John Perry, Director of Policy, and Sarah Edwards, Principal Policy Officer. We then hear from two Housing Associations which made written submissions. Tim Brown, Chairs, and Harry Perry is a Director of the Leicester Newarke Housing Association which is a small housing association providing mainly furnished accommodation for some 250 young people, especially students, in the city of Leicester.

By way of contrast, Focus Housing Group is one of the largest housing associations. It houses over 20,000 people and is based in Birmingham. Its Chief Executive, Richard Clark, was formerly North East Regional Director of the Housing Corporation. Our final witness today is Rudolf Klein, Professor of Social Policy at the University of Bath. Professor Klein has a specialist interest in issues of accountability and consumer representation and has done work—a very considerable amount of work—specifically on housing associations.

Can I now ask members of the Committee to declare any relevant interests, going round from the right. Sir William?

WILLIAM UTTING: I am a trustee of CSV and also of the Joseph Rowntree Foundation.

LORD THOMSON: I am a trustee of CSV.

LORD NOLAN: Thank you very much. Now we can get to work. I am going to ask Sir Clifford Boulton to open the questioning.

526. CLIFFORD BOULTON: Good morning. Thank you very much for the material you sent us. Perhaps I could start by making a point which, I think, you recognise yourself in the material that we are not a review of the general effectiveness of the TEC policy so you may be a little disappointed that we do not take up some of the issues that you quite properly mention in your general paper but you understand that our terms of reference are to do with standards of conduct and matters which could affect that.

Could I ask you just to set the scene for the record, to explain the range of work that you do for and with TECs.

BILL GARLAND, MIKE STEWART, AND ANNE WEINSTOCK

ANNE WEINSTOCK (Chief Executive, Rathbone CI): Yes, I will take that, if I may.

Between the three organisations we have something in the order of 20,000 training places, about 12,000 for young people a lot of whom are disaffected young people who have failed at school, and 8,000 places for long-term unemployed adults, many of whom have basic skills difficulties. I think I am right in saying between us we contract with something like 47 Training and Enterprise Councils and LECs, the Scottish equivalent. Is that sufficient?

527. CLIFFORD BOULTON: Yes, thank you very much. I think it concentrates our minds on the area that you are all concerned with. Now, could I ask who you worked with before the advent of TECs? How was this work done before they came along?

ANNE WEINSTOCK: Yes. The work we are now doing funded by TECs was previously funded by the Training Agency Area Officers, which was in fact an integral part of, I think it was then called, the Department of Employment but they change names so often I am not quite sure. In other words, it was run by civil servants and fully accountable within a government department in that sense.

528. CLIFFORD BOULTON: With a more focused purpose for the grants for that reason was there?

ANNE WEINSTOCK: I would not say necessarily it was more focused. I would have to say—and I am a TEC Director on the Manchester TEC—in some ways TECs are more focused than Training Agency Area Offices used to be but my view—I think our collective view—is that the focus is on economic regeneration rather than training the long-term unemployed or young people with special needs. I think for the majority of TEC Board members that would be their preference.

529. CLIFFORD BOULTON: But you did say somewhere in your material that you actually welcomed the inception of TECs so you must have anticipated that there was going to be some improvement in the delivery of services that you are concerned with by their creation. Did that happen and could you explain the areas in which you saw improvements and why?

ANNE WEINSTOCK: Yes. I think we are fairly clear about what the initial improvements were. I think that they did focus all of our collective minds on the challenge to raise standards for young people with special needs and for unemployed adults. In particular, it gave us a challenge of not undertaking training for training's sake but actually the links to the labour market and the links to employer networks through TECs gave us all the opportunity to move more people into the labour market than perhaps we had done before.

I think I would add that the initial element of output related funding—I do not want to get too technical—but some of the money being dependent on achieving qualifications and moving people into jobs challenged the mind enormously. I think our concern though is that that has gone too far and that it has been difficult within the TEC movement to make people truly accountable for that.

530. CLIFFORD BOULTON: We might want to follow that up. If I can just stick at the transition from one to another. Do your colleagues have anything to add?

BILL GARLAND (Assistant Director, Community Service Volunteers): Yes. I think one of the things that we certainly felt at CSV was that there were problems in the system of our offices with civil servants reporting to civil servants centrally from the area teams and we felt that people coming in from outside with different experiences would be more confident about dealing with government about some of the under-funding issues, some of the technical problems, that were faced and, sadly, I do not think that has actually occurred, but that was certainly our hope, that there would be a far more open exchange.

531. CLIFFORD BOULTON: What you saw could come out of this if it went as you hoped?

BILL GARLAND: That is right.

MIKE STEWART (Director of Services, NACRO): I think if I might just add another dimension to that. We are all national organisations. We are unusual, I think, in that as training providers in having an overview of the whole piece, as it were, working across the country. One of the dangers we felt of the implementation of the TEC system was a lack of a strategic overview and the potential for wide variations in practice, and so on, and I think, again, our experience would be that that has been borne out in practice. There are wide variations up and down the country—the same product being delivered in different parts of the country is administered in a different way, the outcomes are different, the prices are different, and so on. It is quite hard from where we sit sometimes to see why decisions are made differently in different places.

532. CLIFFORD BOULTON: You say that you have different employees involved in TEC Boards. Can you explain how they came to be appointed. Were they specially identified as having this form of knowledge and, therefore, ought to be on TEC Boards?

ANNE WEINSTOCK: As the one out of the three of us who sits on a TEC Board, perhaps I might take that. I wrote in and offered my services to Manchester TEC. I said that I thought I was probably the only female Chief Executive of a national organisation on the Manchester patch and I was wonderful and, therefore, they should have me. In point of fact, I think they wanted Joanna Foster from the Equal Opportunities Commission who turned them down so I was second choice. It is certainly the case that the expertise I hope I have brought to the Board has been to do with a very long and proven track record in the voluntary sector for disadvantaged people that spans 21 years.

BILL GARLAND: We have a South-West media manager who was invited by the local TEC because of their involvement in the voluntary sector and their involvement in women's issues.

533. CLIFFORD BOULTON: But the requirements that are listed for being a member of a Board might mean that it is almost a matter of chance whether there is anybody who has your kind of special knowledge who can get on. There is no special provision for making sure that somebody with an interest in the disadvantaged being on a Board, is there, none at all?

ANNE WEINSTOCK: No, none at all.

534. CLIFFORD BOULTON: Tell me about the staffs of TECs. We are always talking about the Boards. Do you find that the staffing policies and history of the TECs is satisfactory? Do you find that their staff stay long enough and can learn about, for instance, the special problems that your groups might have?

ANNE WEINSTOCK: I think, in all honesty, that varies enormously. I think we have said in the submission, I find it very frightening the number of Chief Executives who have moved on. In the North-West, I think, we have had three in the past two months. Amongst the generality of staff, certainly in the early days, a number of civil servants either chose to move back to the Department because they all came on secondment to start the TEC movement, or it was suggested that they went back. If I may say, both about the composition of the Board and the now composition of the staff, I think the bringing together strategically of private sector, voluntary sector and public sector has been in many areas a force for good. It has certainly been a tremendous learning curve for me. I do not feel so bad that I only spent a year in the private sector after university now and I would like to think some of the private sector people have learned from us.

I think the issue for staff at any level in the TEC who have this kind of interest is that it takes a very special kind of Board, probably through the Chair, and a very special kind of Chief Executive to fight for this given things like the funding structures and given things like, I believe, a tremendous confusion about what TECs are about. You will have seen recently should they merge with Chambers and Business Links and do that or should they be forces and catalysts for regenerating education systems in areas like Manchester.

I think there is a confusion and certainly I have heard a number of TEC staff say either directly to me or to my colleagues that they are not sure what they are about any more. They are not sure that they can take—you know, in private, off the record—that they can take all the people that we cater for and when we say whose responsibility is it everyone wants to buck pass.

535. CLIFFORD BOULTON: There is a weighted grant, is there not, to assist, or intended to assist, your particular problems?

ANNE WEINSTOCK: Yes, but there is no mandatory requirement for it to be passed on.

536. CLIFFORD BOULTON: I was going to say, can you tell me about what kind of openness there is about the way that is disbursed. Is that published in accounts or anything like that?

ANNE WEINSTOCK: No.

BILL GARLAND: Not as far as we know.

537. CLIFFORD BOULTON: Presumably, access is available to the National Audit Office, and that sort of thing. They could watch out for that?

BILL GARLAND: The contracts are private and in confidence. That is specified with each training provider.

CLIFFORD BOULTON: I am sorry?

BILL GARLAND: The contracts are private and in confidence and are seen, therefore, as between the TEC and an individual provider and, in some cases, providers were they to release details of their contract they may well be in breach of their TEC contract itself.

CLIFFORD BOULTON: I see.

MIKE STEWART: Can I add something to that? We were unaware, I think, until well into the financial year about the relationship of that weighting factor and the fact that it was there, as it were in theory, up for us to negotiate. There was a time when each of us was negotiating with each TEC annually and getting different prices for different people.

In recent years, that has been rationalised and because we talk between us we know that we are usually offered the same price now for the same product, which makes sense, and the negotiation is around the number of people that we work with, the type of people that we work with, and so on. But the price basically is not negotiable. Once we are offered it, that is it, by and large. I just thought I would make that clear because we were not party to the notion of the weighting and how it is passed on, until we were presented with it and it is only through actually talking with each other and doing some analysis of problems this year that we have discovered that some TECs do pass it on, some TECs do not pass it on and we are not quite sure why.

538. CLIFFORD BOULTON: Do you get the impression that the Government is not asking for enough information itself and collating it?

ANNE WEINSTOCK: Can I just make a plea on behalf of my own TEC and, I suspect, a lot of TECs. I think the system has gone awry since the collapse of South Thames TEC. I think there is so much paper required from TEC staffs, and indeed from providers, and we are so obsessed with getting the end output that we have all forgotten what the focus on quality training is actually about. I would certainly make a plea for no more paper trails.

539. CLIFFORD BOULTON: But you are worried—you cannot see what use is being made of the stuff that you are sending in, is that it? I mean, you are saying there is not enough transparency about?

ANNE WEINSTOCK: There is not enough transparency.

MIKE STEWART: We raised concerns with officials at the Employment Department earlier this year. We were informing the Employment Department what prices individual TECs were offering us. They had no means of assessing what price the TEC was actually offering the provider. The negotiation between the Employment Department and the TEC is about how much the Government office will give each particular TEC. From that point the officials do not know how the TEC operate that with individual providers and, from my perspective, that came as a surprise. They had no means of measuring what was happening in one TEC as compared to another TEC and it is only by us happening to be national providers, putting the prices down on paper that they could see how much they varied up and down the country.

540. CLIFFORD BOULTON: Can a provider sub-contract out to someone else?

ANNE WEINSTOCK: Yes.

541. CLIFFORD BOULTON: Who follows through the quality of that and the compliance with standards?

ANNE WEINSTOCK: If anything went wrong it would be the responsibility of the provider, the main contractor.

CLIFFORD BOULTON: So, it carries responsibilities?

ANNE WEINSTOCK: Yes.

542. CLIFFORD BOULTON: But it is an extra stage away from oversight?

BILL GARLAND: The provider would have to monitor that in the same way the TEC would monitor the lead contract.

543. CLIFFORD BOULTON: Does that go on quite a bit, sub-contracting work?

ANNE WEINSTOCK: I think it is happening more and more as TECs make decisions to deal with "preferred suppliers" to make it more manageable from their point of view. Quite whether it is a good thing in terms of choice or quality, I think is another matter.

BILL GARLAND: Some TECs rationalise their provider base by dealing with a dozen or so large providers who then, by necessity, would have to sub-contract to get the range of vocation provision.

CLIFFORD BOULTON: That is expected. When it actually happens everybody knows it is likely to occur.

ANNE WEINSTOCK: There is also an increasing number of TECs, of course, who are taking everything in-house. There may or may not be good reasons for that but I think there are certainly then questions of a monopoly position in terms of being the purchaser as well as the supplier.

544. CLIFFORD BOULTON: To return to the point I think you began to touch on earlier about the possible strains that are introduced by using the number of NVQs awarded as a basis for funding and rewards almost for achievement by measuring those kinds of achievements. NVQs, of course, are a kind of register of progress. They are not exams that you pass or fail—at least, you do not get something and then you get it; there is not a kind of ethos of competitive examination, is there? So, presumably, in your area NVQs themselves you presumably have nothing against, have you, as a concept?

ANNE WEINSTOCK: Not as a concept.

545. CLIFFORD BOULTON: Because they are rather more friendly things for the people you are concerned with to be involved in than in more orthodox examinations and certificates. But, you say that distortions can be produced by people wanting some creative returns, the risk of creative returns creeps in to get recognition. Is there much experience of that? Of course, we are now moving quite directly into standards of the sort that very much concerns us.

ANNE WEINSTOCK: If I can try and take that. In the very early days of TECs I was involved with others working with the National Council for Vocational Qualifications on its own equal opportunities, equal access framework. We were tremendously excited by the concept. You are quite right, it was not a pass or fail, pen and paper test, it was about proving one's competence, particularly in the workplace.

We were tremendously excited about it. We were more excited because that framework and the statement within the council itself talked of things like anyone, whatever their starting points, can achieve these competence-based

qualifications, however long it takes, irrespective of time, irrespective of place or mode of learning, irrespective of length of training. What has actually happened within the funding structure is that you have to get that many, you have to get it in that time and increasingly you have to do those qualifications because that is how quickly you can get them. Beyond it being a special needs issue I am not even sure whether it is good for the economy, but that is the basis on which the contracts work.

I think we did mention, and I will certainly leave a copy with the Committee, we led a piece of research which was commissioned and recently published from the Institute of Employment Studies that looked at the funding framework, TECs, output-related funding, and so on, and very certainly concluded that we are now into fast-tracking, creaming, selection into training of those who can reach the targets in the fastest possible time and for the lowest possible price. In fairness, I think the TEC Council would also agree with that.

Our problem, until we have had this research done, is that we, and particularly our local managers on the ground and staff, have been made to feel failures precisely because of the intake of clientele that constitutionally we are set up to take.

546. CLIFFORD BOULTON: But is there any evidence of abuse?

MIKE STEWART: I have an organisational concern. This is a personal view based on my experience within NACRO. I am putting severe financial pressure on my centre managers to achieve the outcomes that we are contracted to do. It is very tight financially. It is in the interests of the TEC, it is in the interests of my managers and it is in the interests of the awarding bodies to make sure these qualifications are achieved because the awarding bodies get paid on the number of qualifications that they are able to assess as being right. The TECs clearly are able to draw their output income from the Government office on the basis of the number of qualification and my staff clearly have an interest in making sure that these NVQs are achieved as quickly as possible.

I would not say that there is evidence of abuse. In fact, there are audit trails, there are checking procedures, there are checks and balances in. I am just concerned, from where I sit about the degree of pressure I am putting on my people to try and whiz these qualifications through as quickly as possible. I certainly have been concerned in one or two areas where rules have been bent, corners cut, in order to achieve the qualification. We have had that internally and I have dealt with that internally but I am just flagging up that there is strong pressure on all those involved in this system to make sure that people get as many NVQs as possible. I am not sure, in the context of the financial pressure, whether the people on the receiving end, or the ones that are wanting the qualifications, are wanting that to get a job, are actually getting the best deal from the system at the moment.

547. CLIFFORD BOULTON: Presumably, there is some kind of inspection of the maintenance of standards? Somebody comes along and says, "That girl manifestly cannot work a checkout till"?

MIKE STEWART: Yes, there are internal systems, there are external verifiers that come in and when they see a problem they do disallow. The systems there appear to be in place but I am saying it is in everybody's interest to get the NVQs. Clearly, it is in everybody's interest to make sure that the system is not abused. I am just flagging up that certainly from my point of view, in my organisation, there have been instances where people have cut corners in order to try and deliver a bottom line, break-even position. It is something that we have to watch constantly. There is strong pressure to deliver, is what I am saying.

ANNE WEINSTOCK: I think, on the question of standards, certainly in relation to quality standards, one of the fascinating things the research has thrown up is that TECs defined quality of standards of delivery when it was invited to respond to that question in relation to BS 5750 and ISO 9000, in relation to whether organisations who were delivering training had invested in people, in relation to how many qualifications they delivered and how many jobs they delivered. Of course, they are all the lines of income to the TEC whereas the training supply side, certainly the voluntary sector—specialist training suppliers—quite rightly defined quality and said it had deteriorated because we defined it in terms of equality of access, degree of learning support, length of time to take the qualification, to go at one's own pace, and so on. I think there are clear conflicts now between organisations like ourselves and TECs about what their true role is.

There is one point I would like to make and I would like to make it almost on behalf of the TEC movement as well because I think it is to do with the pressure that they are under—I think the system is grossly underfunded—which is that the research clearly shows the private and commercial sector are receiving more funding for training, higher ability trainees, than the voluntary sector for the same volume who are dealing with the most disadvantaged and less able trainees. It seems to me an issue of public accountability, bear in mind £1.7 billion-worth of public funds goes through the TEC movement, is a very live issue there.

548. CLIFFORD BOULTON: Just a final question from myself, and I was moved by your plea for less paperwork earlier, but the conclusion of all of you is that there really is room for and need for a new body, called OFTEC if you like, which will be a supervisory and information gathering body. That is the conclusion of you all, is it?

BILL GARLAND: It is indeed.

MIKE STEWART: I think it would help us about applying standards consistently, about balancing some of the extreme variations in practice that we are facing on a daily basis through our different TECs.

CLIFFORD BOULTON: I do not think anybody recommends that sort of thing lightly and unadvisedly but we are obviously very anxious to know that that is your firm conclusion. Thank you.

549. LORD NOLAN: I wonder if I could pick up a point on funding which you mentioned in your main response under the heading "Government and TECs". Computers nowadays do not number pages, do they, which makes life a bit more difficult. You say in one paragraph:

"Two years ago the embarrassment at the level of TEC reserves prompted the then Secretary of State to reduce

TEC funding to prompt them to spend their reserves. The consequence was widescale cuts in unit costs paid to those delivering the training for TECs. The logic of the system was that TECs could manage on less if they built up reserves. The reality was different for the training providers who were forced to close and for those voluntary organisations whose reserves were depleted in their attempts to train the most disadvantaged."

I was not quite clear about that. Was it the position then that the TECs refused to spend their reserves and having their grants cut?

ANNE WEINSTOCK: Some did and some did not and that will always be the problem if government does not mandate certain things to happen. I certainly recall that period in time. I think actually it was a bit further back the first time it happened because I remember Michael Howard was Secretary of State for Employment at the time and I was encouraged by one Sir Geoffrey Holland to encourage the North West TECs to come down and see him and say there was not enough money. He went around the table and said, "Now, you have £3 million in reserves and you have £4.5 million and don"t tell me you don't have enough money". Certainly a number of those TECs, rather than spend from reserves cut the funding to suppliers.

I think there is a very clear issue and there is certainly precedent in local authorities for actually capping very clearly how much TECs can take off the top of training budgets for all the other things they want to do—huge infrastructures, in some areas wonderful buildings, very nice cars and at the other end of the spectrum is, of course, the most disadvantaged people in dreadful buildings with insufficient staff and insufficient learning materials. So, I think there are issues there.

550. LORD NOLAN: Was the report that you were holding up just now, was that the Institute of Employment Studies report?

ANNE WEINSTOCK: Yes, we commissioned it from them.

551. LORD NOLAN: Yes, thank you, and you have quoted it quite extensively in your follow-up evidence, which I would like to come to actually. I think one of your main concerns is that the point of view of the disadvantaged is not adequately reflected in the policy of TECs. One question that raises is whether there should be greater representation on the boards of TECs of, for example, ethnic minorities or the unemployed.

If I could just put to you something that has been put to us. What is said is that the board should be the most competent businessmen. The answer to wider representation is good lines of communication from the board to ethnic minorities or representatives of the unemployed, or whatever. Is that enough or would it help to have somebody on the board from the disadvantaged areas concerned?

ANNE WEINSTOCK: I think there is a need for that, and we mentioned in the main submission that Manchester TEC has the concept of champions on the board and I am the champion, unsurprisingly, for special needs and equal opportunities. I am also, I suspect, in some areas regarded as the token woman and my colleague on those issues is Mohammed Amin who is probably regarded as the token ethnic. I think the issue is more about people being committed and they could be from the private sector, the public sector or the voluntary sector, to raising issues and not being afraid to raise issues that are clearly wrong with the funding structures and the accountability lines. On the board, yes, but I do not think it necessarily has to be a black man or a white woman.

552. LORD NOLAN: You need a champion, someone who knows what the concerns are?

ANNE WEINSTOCK: Yes. In Manchester we have gone beyond that. We have champions for education business partnerships and we have got champions for economic development so it is looking at very broad strategy. Certainly, in our area, I think I am right in saying this—I might now get a sackful of letters tomorrow—I do not believe there is anybody who wants to raise issues as far as Manchester TEC is concerned to the Board at the Board level about our strategy on special needs and equality of opportunity that would not know and would not feel comfortable about making contact with me.

553. LORD NOLAN: You were speaking also of the difficulty sometimes of keeping clearly in mind what the ethical functions of TECs are. We have been hearing something about the move towards amalgamating TECs and Chambers of Commerce. How has that worked out in your experience?

ANNE WEINSTOCK: Again, I am putting a Manchester TEC hat on. We have reached the stage in Manchester of having a joint membership scheme between the Chamber Business Link and the TEC and that is as far as it has gone at the moment simply because of cultures and a 200-history in the Chamber people are not yet ripe for any more merging than that but certainly it has brought some sensible cohesive frameworks to the business community. They have a single point of contact through the reception, telephone lines and so on, which I think is helpful.

I think I would want to add that given the balance of membership on TEC Boards—there is two-thirds private sector at a certain level and one-third the rest, if you euphemistically define people like me. It is unsurprising that people at that level from industry want to take an interest in the things that they have got an interest in and a clear expertise in and that is fine but I think there is an increasing issue of concern beyond the three of us and beyond the voluntary sector now about who represents the rights and who is accountable for the rights of the least articulate members of any TEC community.

BILL GARLAND: There may well be a mis-match because the TEC Boards with a minimum of two-thirds private sector representation receive 70 per cent of their income for training the unemployed and many TEC Directors say to us that their interest is about business regeneration, is about supporting small businesses within their community. I think to some degree that is where a lot of the tension and problems arise and that really needs to be addressed.

554. LORD NOLAN: One slightly related issue which we have raised with all our witnesses. What about the payment of some sort of remuneration to Board members? Would that get a better spread, a wider spread?

ANNE WEINSTOCK: Forgive me, Lord Nolan, I smile simply because I remember suggesting that in the very early days to Edward Roberts who ran the TEC Council or G10, or whatever the group of regional chairs was in those days, at a dinner. The point I was trying to make, actually, was to do with accountability. He said, "What would you pay?" and I said if needs be five thousand a year. There is something to do with accountability. I know in terms of my paid staff and volunteer staff there is always an issue in peoples' minds about accountability lines.

His response was given the salaries of the people who were on TEC Boards it would be small change so, in a sense I think, the point was missed. I think the point is a real one and I think it actually may help in terms of accountability.

555. LORD NOLAN: What, for example, to get payment for child care to a woman who would be a valued member of the Board but cannot come because you do not pay anything?

ANNE WEINSTOCK: Certainly, yes, certainly.

LORD NOLAN: I am putting words in your mouth—rather than substantial salaries to people, most of whom are well paid?

ANNE WEINSTOCK: Yes.

556. LORD NOLAN: What about your colleagues, do you have views on this?

MIKE STEWART: I was going to say there are mechanisms and structures for removing the obstacles for representation for the people that we might want on boards other than salaries which are about expenses for child care, about travel costs and so on, which I think most charitable organisations are into. Certainly, housing associations do that in order to encourage representation from people who might otherwise not be able to. I think the salary issue is one that is probably anathema to us. I do not know, it is difficult for us to say.

LORD NOLAN: Yes, there is a very, very strong feeling in many quarters that it would damage the voluntary ethos and remove a lot of the pride that people take in giving voluntary service.

MIKE STEWART: Yes.

LORD NOLAN: Thank you very much for that. I think Professor King would like to ask one or two questions.

557. PROF ANTHONY KING: Can I ask Mike Stewart to say a little bit more about one of his earlier answers. Clearly, in the world of education and training an awful lot of the financial pressure that exists is likely to result in a lowering of standards if it is allowed to. You alluded to that possibility, you referred to cutting corners, and so on. Could you give some indication of how serious you think that actually is?

MIKE STEWART: I will preface what I say. I am referring to my organisation now, I am not talking widespread, it is what I know about. If you will bear with me for a minute. In the past two years, which is what I have been responsible for, our training, I have needed to lay off 600 staff and close down about 10 different training centres. We are something like two-thirds of the size that we were two years ago.

The syndrome that occurs is that when we come under financial pressure at a local centre we do what we can organisationally to try and sort out if that is to do with poor performance, poor managers, or whatever. We have got to the stage in a number of training centres where it is simply that the money is not there to do the job that we want to do. The manager has a strong temptation to accept an offer of a contract to deliver more than he or she knows that they can deliver and it is at that point that from my point of view the dangers are in there. How can I gauge from my office in London what might be happening in Newcastle, or whatever?

At that point, there is a pressure on the local manager to deliver high outcomes and I know, from personal experience, that one of the signs, one of the signifying factors that things are not going right, is that suddenly the claims for NVQs start going up out of all proportion to what was happening previously, which is not justified in terms of any changes that we have made. When that starts happening obviously I then intervene but I think it is serious in the sense that the financial pressure is now so great that that sort of syndrome, that pressure, is there far more widespread than it was certainly two years ago. I am now extremely concerned about how I measure an understandable desire on the part of my manager to keep going for all the right reasons because we are working with the right people, and so on.

How on earth can they deliver the quality in order to achieve the outcomes that they say they can? I am concerned about that to a point where I am now making decisions to close rather than carry on because I think it is putting at risk, both in terms of our reputation and the service that we are providing for individuals, it is putting at risk the whole qualification ethos.

558. PROF ANTHONY KING: Absolutely rightly, but if what you say is true of NACRO it must be true of just about every other organisation in the country that is in a NACRO-like position, is it not?

MIKE STEWART: Perhaps my colleagues would like to comment. I am giving you a very personal view.

ANNE WEINSTOCK: Can I say a few words, if I may. I think you are absolutely right. I think any organisation who has as part of its brief the vocation, education and training of the most disadvantaged young people in society is facing pressure now in the sense in which amongst commissioning things like the research we were delighted to have the opportunity to come here today.

Clearly, we are national players. It seems to me that a lot of the smaller players who did not have national infrastructure, national resource, and so on, have already gone to the wall—and I am sure that the National Council for Voluntary Organisations would confirm that—but I think there is that clear pressure now in the system. There are 200,000 young people opting out of education, training and employment altogether in this country. That is research not yet released. I think the civil servants have at the Centre taken a view on it before it is released but it

was commissioned by the TEC Council sub group, of which I am a member, because we were concerned about what was happening firstly, in the education system, given the pressure on schools.

I think you will all have seen in last week's press, or the week before, that whilst there has been a commendable increase, although slight, in the number of pupils getting grades A to C, five of them and above, there has been another 8 per cent increase in the number of school pupils failing to achieve any qualifications whatsoever. That, of course, is only the percentage of those who sat for exams, not those who have not sat.

Then you come into youth training funded by TECs. I met a young lady in one of our projects recently, more articulate, I have to tell you, than any of my three teenage children. She had been sent to us from a Pupil Referral Unit, a kind of expulsion sin-bin, and I said to her, "Whatever are you doing here? Why are you not going to school?" and she said, very clearly and very perceptively, "If they decided not to sit you for the exams would you go to school?". They come into youth training. The payment is all on achieving the outcome, increasingly so even for providers like ourselves because that is the contract TECs have to deliver, and, frankly, as soon as they walk through the door somebody is checking, in a financial sense not in a quality of training sense, "Can I get them to that output with this amount of resource with the time I have to get them there in?".

559. PROF ANTHONY KING: Can I interrupt? My point was specifically on whether the standard of primarily the NVQs was actually tending to be pushed down by the existing funding system. You have raised another question I wanted to ask you about anyway. Is that your experience? Can I just ask Anne Weinstock and then come to Bill.

ANNE WEINSTOCK: I think it is very difficult to answer the question on the standards of the NVQs for those who achieve them because I think it is very comparable to saying to youngsters at school who have passed GCSEs, they must be easier to get. I am not in a position to make comment on that and, indeed, I think it would be unfair. Certainly, I think that pressure is there. The pressure must be there to cut corners and, of course, the response has been for the National Council for Vocational Qualifications to set up another regional layer of fraud officers so all the money is going out of the direct delivery end. I actually said to somebody running a TEC in the north-west very recently that I think in another year we will all only employ auditors, we will not employ any training staff.

BILL GARLAND: There are two particular pressures. We have dealt with it by losing £1.5 million over the past 18 months to support that infrastructure and to retain that provision for young people in most need. Other people have actually excluded them, they have taken those that are job-ready or who are already well on the way to a qualification and excluded those who have literacy and numeracy problems so that they do not have to spend quite as much and it does not take quite as long to achieve the qualifications. I think those have been the two options, quite honestly, in that situation. It is not just about watering down the value of the qualification, it is a bit about where you pick somebody up in terms of achieving it.

560. PROF ANTHONY KING: Could I ask one more question, which is Anne Weinstock referred to that very issue of the skewing of the resources in the system to, in a sense, those who need it least and you said that raised an issue of public accountability. Could you explain what you meant by that and what kind of forum might provide the kind of accountability you were talking about?

ANNE WEINSTOCK: If I just look comparably in my own family. I certainly look at many of the young people who pass through our centres. When we pick them up their individual starting point is such that for them to get an NVQ at Level 1, which of course is not in the national education and training targets so that is another issue, I do not know why when they were revised nobody thought to put that in because that is the baseline in a lot of areas of the country of where young people are at—that is a far greater achievement than my son who has just done two GCSEs a year early and got an A* and an A. It is a far greater achievement given the starting point.

561. PROF ANTHONY KING: If that is the issue. What I am concerned about is how is it not being addressed as an issue. You imply that the forums for discussion of these matters, for taking decisions about them, are somehow inadequate. This is happening but it is not a matter of policy.

ANNE WEINSTOCK: In fairness, the TEC Council sub group was set up to look at just these kind of issues and bring them to the TEC Council. I would have to say that we took this research outside of the sub group. I do not know what was happening at the top of the TEC Council, whether they were having a difficult time getting the points across, but certainly the research highlights, I think, in a very clear way that the public funding for training is going to commercial organisations who are dealing with more able people and, therefore, one can assume to organisations who are making profit for the same volume that the voluntary sector dealing with the least able is receiving and it is actually having to subsidise public funds.

We have all subsidised TECs, and indeed the Department, from our reserves and we are in a position now where we are reaching the stage where there is no more give in the reserves and, understandably, we feel cross.

MIKE STEWART: I mentioned earlier that we have been working with officials for some months now and one of the frustrations—and I am trying specifically to answer accountability because it is about where in the system it could be—there is no government policy that says that we want this programme to exclude people, in fact quite the contrary. We have actually met ministers and they are quite clear that what we want is for this "Training for Work" programme to be inclusive.

There is no TEC policy that says, OK, we know we are strapped for cash and the people that are going to have to suffer are the most disadvantaged. Nobody within the TEC movement is actually telling us that. Our problem is that we are the ones that are actually creating that policy because we are making the decisions at the point of entry as to who comes in and who does not. So, in a sense, it is us that needs to be accountable and that is why we are here because we are saying that we know we are doing this and we do not want to do this but nobody is holding us to

account and it is only by us flagging up at as high a level as we can that there is an issue here that we now have some recognition that there is an issue and we are working, I think, quite constructively.

I do not know, is the answer to your question, but somewhere somebody ought to have been saying what is the impact of this as it works its way through the system and who is looking after that group.

BILL GARLAND: We have been openly told in discussion with TECs, when we have raised the issue of value and access to training, that we should move up market and focus on those who are more job-ready to make the system work and that there is no more money in the system for those for whom we wish to cater.

ANNE WEINSTOCK: We have all been told that. I certainly have it on record filed away in a safe just about—from civil servants as well. But let us look at it from the TECs' point of view, because there is an issue about the accountability of the policies. The Department has not given—and has, to my knowledge—no target price per output point for delivery which it wishes to reach. If one thinks about that, it clearly means that even the TECs at the top of league table on this spurious value for money debate, can and have had their TEC budgets cut. Very recently we were all becoming concerned that the TECs were probably—whilst being private sector creatures when South Thames TEC collapsed, owing us all a not inconsiderable amount of money—suddenly going to take on the mantle of voluntary organisations in order to get money from the Lottery. There is therefore an issue about the accountability of the policy.

My strong view is that it is not that TECs do not want to have the responsibility or accountability, but that they feel that they cannot given the total amount of money and the funding structures. The issue for us as piggy in the middle is that the civil servants will say "We give them enough money, you know, but some of them just spend it all on posh cars," and the TECs will say there is not enough money in the system. Frankly, somebody has to decide whose responsibility it is to undertake vocational education and training for the least able members of society and somebody has to be accountable for that.

562. LORD NOLAN: We are very grateful to you. I am sorry that we cannot hear you for longer on this, but I think you have given us a clear view from a most important sector of the community—a sector in need. It has been particularly helpful that you have been able to present a combined view. Thank you all very much.

Mr Best, we know you were formerly Chief Executive of the National Federation of Housing Associations and therefore you know an enormous amount about this subject, on which I at least am in a position where I still have a lot to learn. Can you tell us a little about both your own and the Joseph Rowntree Foundation's involvement in housing matters?

RICHARD BEST

RICHARD BEST (Director, Joseph Rowntree Trust): Yes. Briefly, I started in the late 1960s setting up new housing associations. I was Director of the British Churches Housing Trust. We created new bodies at that time when we were still in the early, embryonic stages of the housing association world as it now is.

I became Director of the National Federation of Housing Associations in 1973 and was engaged in the run-up to the 1974 Act—a very busy time for us. I was Director for 15 years and I left in 1988 to run the Joseph Rowntree Foundation. The Joseph Rowntree Foundation is primarily now a source of funding and participation in research. We are most famous for our work on poverty—income and wealth we call it nowadays—but we also have a very big input on the housing research side.

Our origins, in fact, were as a housing association. Joseph Rowntree set up a housing trust in 1904 and started building homes, with the sort of special Rowntree thing of engaging the residents in civic society, as he thought of it—building communities not simply building houses. We have been a housing association for 90 years and seen all the changes before us over that time.

563. LORD NOLAN: Thank you very much. You mentioned the recent study commissioned by the Joseph Rowntree Foundation into the governance of voluntary bodies. How long will that take to report? Do you know?

RICHARD BEST: Yes. I had better be honest; we did in fact fund the Federation-initiated inquiry into the governance of housing associations. We also funded Rudolf Klein's study—you are speaking to him later. And as part of a body of work, we are funding that part of the NCVO's commission on the future of the voluntary sector: it is broader based and we are doing the governance part of that inquiry. That will report in the middle of next year and we are trying to get the governance bit in place by the spring.

564. LORD NOLAN: Thank you very much. In the paper you very helpfully sent us, it seems to me that you sound a warning against this Committee taking an inaccurate view of the nature and role of housing associations and tending to classify them as if they were something like NDPBs. If I can read your last paragraph,

"Classifying housing associations as public bodies, as quangos, brings the danger that this could diminish their sense of independence or their commitment to purely voluntary service. If so, reclassifying them in this manner could affect the motivation and willingness of trustees and board members to serve and that would undermine the ultimate strength."

I am sure that we note that, but if I could just try and clear our lines: if you have a body, whether it is voluntary in whole or in part, if it is providing public services—services to individual members of the public, if it is receiving substantial amounts of public funds and if it is involved in policy decisions, local or national, is that not an area where it is helpful to assist the bodies concerned—voluntary bodies as they may be—to interpret to the public the way they are carrying out their functions.

RICHARD BEST: Yes, of course, it is. I think I am the antidote to a long list of extra impositions, as I might describe them, on the voluntary members of housing associations. It has been always very difficult juggling the interests of public accountability and the proper desire of the voluntary organisations to be, and to feel, independent and to take their own decisions. It is only because of that sense of actually being in charge and responsible—not being local officers of the Housing Corporation—that we

get very high quality people who put in a tremendous amount of time, talent and energy. There are 25,000 of them out there and I am anxious to protect them from any encroachments, as they might see it, on their own operations, that go just an inch too far.

Getting this balance right is something I have been part of for something like 25 years. It is a tightrope and I do not think that the balance is wrong. Housing associations are not lacking in controls and equally they are not over-controlled. But the dangers exist all the time for the balance to tip and for people to get fed up and say, "We''ve spent our lives filling in forms for bureaucrats and we've had enough of this. We are not here to just carry out government policies and do what government thinks is right. We came in as independent people; we have something to contribute—a sense of service." And so on.

My special message is perhaps an antidote to many things; I could dream up a very long list of little changes that would add small burdens all the way round on committee members and their governance. But one must guard against the danger of losing the distinction between these and quangos and Governmental bodies. They are voluntary, they are entirely unpaid, as you know. They gain absolutely nothing from all the work that they put in and historically, legally and culturally they are voluntary bodies. So I think that I am saying they need to be treated with care.

565. LORD NOLAN: Of course. I do understand that. I hope, too, that I can assure you, on behalf of the Committee, that right from the start of our work we have made it clear that we derive enormous encouragement from the tradition of voluntary service in this country in its widest aspect and we see this part of our work as a means of helping the voluntary sector and certainly not of putting additional and unnecessary burdens upon it, but in helping to remove some uncertainties and suspicions that exist about where the money goes and what happens to it and who appoints the board members and so on.

May I pick up, without dwelling too much on the slightly negative aspect of the discussion, some points you raise. You say that it would be an enormous change in the relationship between the voluntary sector and government for any steps to be taken to apply to housing associations any measures currently reserved for public bodies—for example, for ministers to appoint or dismiss board members. I see that, but the Housing Corporation can, of course, appoint or dismiss board members. You would not want to change that would you?

RICHARD BEST: No. I would not. They use those powers with a relatively light touch. I think the last year for which they counted the numbers, there were nine appointments out of 25,000 volunteers out there; so it is something that is used and I certainly would not wish to change that.

The role of the Corporation—which is half way towards the housing associations and manages to retain their confidence and trust—as a body in reserve to appoint new members of the board is an important ingredient. But one would not wish there to be any sense in which Ministers were appointing or dismissing the boards of large housing associations as if they had become public sector agents.

566. LORD NOLAN: A sort of organ of central government? Yes, quite. One related matter: if the

Housing Corporation has investigated some case of unsatisfactory conduct or under-performance, do you think that its reports should be published?

RICHARD BEST: That is a difficult one because the housing associations, in a rather competitive market, depend on impressing the public sector investors, who are extremely easily frightened off. Any hint of inadequacy that is revealed in such a report, even if it has been rectified immediately and everything now is in place, tends to mean that that association is out of it in terms of borrowing more from the private sector.

It is probably wiser to be cautious in publishing such remarks. Or, if the Corporation is to publish reports, those reports—Rudolf Klein's work looked at this—need to embrace all the many good things as well as the three things on which the organisation is a bit feeble, and they do not. The reports that one gets from the Corporation have tended to be entirely on the negative points, just to save time—and as it is between them and us it does not matter too much. Often you have an extraordinarily good, competent, caring and helpful housing association and all one reads about is the feeble thing that they did not submit the HAR19, or whatever it was on the due date and this must not happen again. If one is going to have a report, one has to be sensitive to commercial factors—because of the rather odd world of private finance that associations are now in—and also it wants to be balanced with all the good stuff.

LORD NOLAN: There is a moral there for the press generally, is there not, in reporting individual mistakes and wrong doing. Those are what get the headlines and the good news is somehow overlooked.

RICHARD BEST: Yes.

567. LORD NOLAN: You mention also that you think it would be a pity if perhaps even the chief executive to have a duty to challenge where inappropriate decisions are made by the board. The chief executive in fact does have effectively the status of a director, does he not? He is a de facto director in most housing associations and one would perhaps expect him to, particularly if he also is the secretary—which I gather often happens.

RICHARD BEST: Yes, he often is. A signal would be sent out if you said that the chief executive should have a statutory duty to challenge the decisions of the board in certain circumstances. That sounds as if one is saying that the chief executive should be curbing the loony fringes of the movement, whereas in fact the whole thing has to work as a close partnership. Whether or not chief executives are on the governing boards—and they are not at the moment—they have to be like a board member and work with their colleagues, their trustees. It is much more like the model of a company, in which the managing director is round the table, than it is of a public body in which the civil servant is the officer implementing the desires and wishes of the elected members.

The chief executive is part of the process and it has to be a team in which everyone is as one and working together. The reality is of a very close-knit outfit. I think to distance the chief executive in a legal sense, making them have a responsibility to blow that particular whistle, might send a false signal about the kind of relationships that really work.

568. LORD NOLAN: You mentioned the membership. One of the aspects of housing associations which I find most hard to understand and come to terms with is what the membership generally consists of and what influence it has on the board. Is there a way of rationalising and simplifying that in a uniform manner, or is it better to let different housing associations tackle it in different ways?

RICHARD BEST: You are quite right. It is totally confusing. Membership, in terms of shareholding membership, nearly always means absolutely nothing. A handful of associations have huge memberships—several thousand members. I do not detect a great difference in the way that this ends up in terms of the governing board from those which have very few members and feel quite cautious about extending their shareholding membership. It is not, I think, a critical issue.

The charitable trusts, by definition, do not have a membership base at all—they have trustees. Some of them are among the biggest operators out there and they would always be different, whatever model one used. I do not think it is really the route through which one achieves accountability and finds the wider constituencies with which housing associations need to work. There are other much better and more important, mechanisms for ensuring that the residents in the accommodation that is provided, the local authority and the community around are all kept very much on board as part of the processes and the decision making. One is open and outward toward them but the shareholding membership is not really the method that has proved particularly helpful. We have tried it in all kinds of different guises and you can find good examples and bad examples of more or less all of the different illustrations. I would not depend upon it in any way.

569. LORD NOLAN: While realising that housing associations differ enormously in size and, for that matter, in origin, what are the better mechanisms that you would prefer, putting it as generally as you can, for keeping in touch with local authorities and tenants?

RICHARD BEST: Perhaps it will help you see it through the eyes of someone involved. I run the Joseph Rowntree Housing Trust, so there I am now, day to day, operating the housing association. Links with local authorities are much more extensive than perhaps I knew even when I was running the Federation and was more distant from the action. There is a constant interplay with the local authority. They may be providing funding; they are very often providing land; they are certainly providing planning consents; they nominate a large number of the tenants. My staff, down to the lettings level, are dealing, day to day, with local authority people, talking about exchanges of tenants working together. We have liaison arrangements with the Director of Housing for York; we see a lot of each other. He comes into the offices; we are around; councillors will open our projects on our behalf and commemorate them. There is an awful lot of to-ing and fro-ing and the thing is knitted together in a way that perhaps one would not imagine at a distance.

570. LORD NOLAN: But that is very crucial, is it not, because by and large the local authority still has the statutory responsibility for housing the homeless and maintaining a proper priority list. It is now done, in practice, more and more in consultation with housing associations is it not?

RICHARD BEST: Absolutely. The homelessness function of the council is obviously very high in its own priorities. We have been building quite a lot of houses recently, so we have been facing the question of what proportion of the incoming residents should be the homeless families at the top priority. At what point would it create a ghetto—to use a really ugly word—of poor people, exclusively on an estate. If all the residents in an estate of 130 houses, for example, that we have just finished in York came straight from short-term accommodation for homeless families, how bad would that be? We have had to work this through with the local authority and say that we think that if we put people all together in one place who are, by definition, likely to be poor and to have a number of problems, we may disadvantage them for life. The place will become stigmatised, residualised—all the words that get used. We would like to have a more balanced community there and we have talked to the local authority about having transfers, people who want to move from council stock, but have been there for many years,—more stable residents—people who are on their ordinary waiting list, vacating property from the existing stock. And then homeless families moving in behind, but not all in one place.

The kind of discussions that go on are very detailed and intense and we have to sort these things out. The local authority has 100 per cent nominations; they could choose all the residents ultimately for our estate, but one had to negotiate it through—in our case because we are particularly keen to ensure we have a strong community there and not just a bunch of people living in buildings, who then can feel abandoned.

One needs all those informal links and ways of working together. There is also a helpful role for proper liaison meetings that are regularly held between the local associations in an area and the local council.

571. LORD NOLAN: Do you have local authority representatives on your board?

RICHARD BEST: We do not. They have not actually asked to be there. We work very well; we have a long history—older than the housing department in York—and that has not been an issue for us. Many housing associations do. I have to say that I have been on a large number of committees and quite often the council members have not been the best attenders. They have a very heavy schedule with their own local authority and it has been something of a nominal relationship to have councillors on the list, but it can work very well and, of course, there are some people who have been councillors who continue their work with housing in a very intensive way in the voluntary sector and they are terrific people.

572. LORD NOLAN: The Joseph Rowntree Foundation has, of course, a long and distinguished history in York and no doubt has its own methods built up over the years in close association with the local authorities and with members. I wonder if I could just ask you this. One possibility we are asked to consider is the payment of board members. Putting it generally, would you be in favour of that, or oppose it?

RICHARD BEST: Personally I am very opposed to this. Again, this seems to me to send out entirely the wrong signals. It is a great strength of housing associations

to be able to claim, and properly so, that nobody gets anything out of serving on those boards. This really is voluntary service out of respect for others, a sense of duty and responsibility and, indeed, a good deal of satisfaction from being part of the voluntary sector.

Somebody said to me the other day that they thought it would be like being paid to give blood. They actually give blood, sweat and tears I think. But they would regard it as insulting and demeaning to be given money to do the things that they think are important and responsible.

I had to address the annual general meeting of one of the large scale voluntary transfer organisations the other day and somebody from the audience—and I did not blame them at all—got up and said "All the things that you are doing are all very well, but I want to know about those fat cats on the committee. How much are they getting out of all of this?". They did not have to defend themselves because I was able to say it for them: they are getting absolutely nothing. Indeed, our system would be unworkable in many circumstances because it is so stringent. But there is a very important distinction between the voluntary sector and other ways of doing things in society. It should be preserved and it will serve us well in the future.

LORD NOLAN: I am afraid I have been very selfish in taking up so much of your time. Lord Thomson, I know, wanted to ask you some questions.

573. LORD THOMSON: Just following up that particular point: I fully understand and sympathise with what you are saying about the importance of unpaid voluntary service, but would there be a case for paying some sort of expenses, loss of earnings and that sort of thing? Does the absolute unpaid character of voluntary service that you have in the housing associations limit the range of people who are able to serve? I am thinking about the mother with a child to look after and that sort of thing.

RICHARD BEST: Certainly payment of all expenses for starters. That goes without saying and that may well include the cost of the child in the creche.

574. LORD THOMSON: Does that happen in some instances?

RICHARD BEST: It certainly does, yes. We would also refund anybody any kind of expenses that they justifiably incurred—exact compensation for payment made. Equally, the idea of compensation for actual loss of earnings—I would say in brackets that I think it is a disgrace that employers deduct earnings when people give up their time voluntarily to participate in things like this—but only at the jury service level, sounds entirely right. I do not regard that as people gaining anything. In fact they may well be paid a good deal more than they would get as a member of a jury. But compensation, entirely understood. Payment of fees, regardless of loss to the individual, sends out the wrong signals.

575. LORD THOMSON: I am very ignorant about the kind of people broadly that give this very good voluntary service on housing associations. Is there any problem of conflicts of interest? You must want people on governing bodies of housing associations in many cases who have some professional experience of the housing market and that kind of thing. Do you have rules about conflicts of interest?

RICHARD BEST: Very fierce rules. You are right—they are a deterrent. Once you decide that you want to go on the committee of the housing association, you must give up any thought of your firm getting any contracts, sub-contracts or business associated in any way with the housing association. You are out of it. So you have to decide in an area—and in a small area like York you have to be careful, because we are big customers—because you are out of it indefinitely once you come onto the committee.

LORD THOMSON: That is quite a sacrifice then?

RICHARD BEST: It is. To give you a piece of history: it was the housing associations themselves that led to the stringent rules which finally came to pass that prohibit committee members from having any self interest, not the Housing Corporation—the regulator. I was involved in all these debates for years. The Housing Corporation believed in the principle—they had run from 1964-1974 an operation of cost-rent housing—of enlightened self-interest. They thought it would be necessary for architects, solicitors and estate agents to form the committee and have that self-interest to keep them there and involved. When we had the 1974 Act—first Anthony Crosland and then Peter Shore—those of us within the housing associations who did not feel that it was helpful to have the estate agents and others involved, pressed for a change in the position and that finally came to pass in law in 1980. But in practice really from 1976 onwards.

That was driven by the self-regulatory arrangements of the housing associations themselves—some of the old trusts, some of the new ones formed under the wing of Shelter and some of the middle-aged housing associations. There were strong feelings that that was an important point of voluntary principle and it was against the opposition of the regulator that we produced that change over a period of time.

576. LORD THOMSON: One final point: I was much interested in the distinction you draw between the voluntary sector and the public sector. I wondered, speaking more widely than housing associations, out of your very great experience, whether you have any thoughts on the new situation that has arisen over the past decade or so in which voluntary organisations are increasingly agents of public policy with public funds and how you get the balance right.

RICHARD BEST: Yes. You are quite right to identify it as a major issue for the sector. It will be debated long and hard in this commission that is now running on the voluntary sector. This is the delicate balance; when public money comes in in a big way, the danger is that the voluntary agency becomes absorbed into the public sector and becomes a creature of it. What we need is some variety and diversity, some independence of spirit, some innovation, some extra on top of what the public service is providing. We should not, as the voluntary sector, be bought. We must remain outside of that and this is where the delicate boundary lies.

LORD THOMSON: Thank you.

LORD NOLAN: I wish we had more time, but I am afraid we have run out. Thank you very much indeed for coming along and giving us the view of your Trust and your experience, which goes so much wider.

RICHARD BEST: Thank you.

577. LORD NOLAN: Now Christine Laird, John Perry and Sarah Edwards. Good morning. Thank you very much for coming along. We are running almost on time, which is nearly a record for us. May I ask Sir Martin Jacomb please to go straight into the questions we wanted to ask you?

578. MARTIN JACOMB: Good morning. Thank you very much for your opening statement. You describe your Institute as the professional organisation representing all those working in housing, with a view to promoting the provision and management of good quality housing at a reasonable cost for as many people as possible. Could you enlarge on that generalised statement and tell us how you see your role. In particular can you tell us how you distinguish between your role in so far as it affects housing associations on the one hand and privately provided housing on the other?

CHRISTINE LAIRD, JOHN PERRY, AND SARAH EDWARDS

CHRISTINE LAIRD (Chief Executive, Chartered Institute of Housing): The Chartered Institute of Housing is the professional body for people working in housing and access to the Institute is by qualification. It is a degree level qualification and we are in fact the national validating body for housing in the United Kingdom.

In addition to providing training and education for the housing profession, we also produce a professional practice series and run a good practice advice unit for people working in housing across sector and we provide policy advice and information to government and other agencies as well, so we have a fairly wide remit.

We have 13,000 members, 30 per cent of whom work in the housing association sector and 50 per cent in the public sector. The remaining 20 per cent work in the private sector for consultancy companies and in the education and training arena, so we cross the spectrum.

In terms of encouraging the profession to work towards the goal of decent, affordable housing for all, I would argue that one does not necessarily have to train one's values simply because one changes the sector in which one works. We have as a professional body specified common standards of housing management that cross tenure. The issue of affordability remains relevant whether or not one is providing housing for rent, shared ownership or low-cost home ownership. The principle is that the person living in the accommodation should be able to meet their housing costs.

579. MARTIN JACOMB: Thank you very much, but what I would like to ask you now is obviously directly to your role in relation to housing associations, leaving on one side the rest of your role for the moment.

First, a rather general question: do you think there is a problem of public perception about the nature of housing associations, their enormous variety and how they are financed and to whom they are accountable? Is their a public perception problem about that, do you think?

CHRISTINE LAIRD: If you were to ask the average man in the street "What is a housing association", you would get some rather peculiar answers. I do not think that the role of housing associations is as well known as perhaps it could or should be and if you were to ask to whom is the housing association accountable, again, I think you would get some rather odd answers.

Certainly when I was a director of housing in a local authority, I used to get letters from members of the community in connection with housing association activity taking place in an area, because they thought the association was accountable to the local authority, so I think there is some confusion in the public eye about what housing associations are and to whom they are accountable.

580. MARTIN JACOMB: Do you think you have a role there in trying to address that confusion?

CHRISTINE LAIRD: I think it would be quite difficult for a professional body to try to address that. We attempt to, but essentially I think that role would fall to the Associations' trade body in terms of promoting the role of associations.

581. MARTIN JACOMB: I would like to come back a little later to the question of accountability and the regulatory regime. Could I just go now to the boards of housing associations—how they are constituted and also their membership. You, I think, feel that chief executives should not be on the boards of housing associations. Have I got that right?

CHRISTINE LAIRD: That is correct.

582. MARTIN JACOMB: Why do you feel that? They are obviously, inevitably, going to be a dominant factor in the management of the housing association. Why do you make a special point of that?

CHRISTINE LAIRD: The chief executive has a unique role. He assists the board in formulating policy and is responsible for implementing the board's policies and is the manager of the organisation, but a chief executive should never lose sight of the fact that his ultimate responsibility is to implement the board's policy and not determine it, although he have an important advisory role.

It is also fair to say that in the National Federation of Housing Associations Inquiry into Governance, evidence was given that in some associations, particularly smaller ones, there was some confusion between the role of providing policy direction and actual management. It is important that the distinctions are drawn and that the boards are encouraged to focus on providing a strategic direction for the organisation, rather than getting involved in day to day issues, particularly as associations grow.

It is important that both boards and chief executives are clearly aware of their responsibilities, but that those responsibilities are kept separate. I do not think that, because a chief executive reports to and advises a board and because of the nature of the way in which boards are structured, it is necessary to make a chief executive a board member in order to expect the chief executive to be accountable and responsible for the implementation of the board's recommendations. Also, in the likelihood of a conflict of views between the board and the chief executive, it is important that the chief executive should

remember that his primary responsibility is to act at the direction of the board.

583. MARTIN JACOMB: I follow that, although, of course, it is quite different from the practice in the private business sector—that does not mean it is not correct. Could I just take that one stage further; I do not think you make such an issue of a case where the chief executive is also the secretary, which happens in quite a lot of housing associations, whereas I would have thought that board members who may well be unqualified in the legalities of their responsibilities, would have needed to turn to the secretary in case there was a difficulty, and in particular a difficulty as between them and the chief executive. I would have thought it was really quite important to have a secretary who was independent of the chief executive.

CHRISTINE LAIRD: The analogy I would draw is not with the private sector, but with the public sector. For example, a local authority housing committee will often comprise people who would not claim to be housing experts. Nevertheless, reporting to that committee is not only the director of housing, but a solicitor and, normally, a financial adviser. They have a responsibility to ensure that the committee are fully appraised of their legal responsibilities and receive the best possible advice that they can give, before the committee reaches a decision. I would argue that that situation is analogous with the arrangements in place in housing associations where the chief executive, the secretary and the director of finance have a responsibility to advise the board as to their legal and financial responsibilities and to ensure that the committee of management are in a position to be able to reach decisions, having had access to that advice.

I am not suggesting that chief executives and directors of finance and secretaries should be excluded from boards, but I am saying that I do not believe it is appropriate for them to be able to put up their hand when it comes to voting for example.

584. MARTIN JACOMB: Yes. Could I just go on then to the membership of the board. Do you have a view on whether local authorities, who obviously have a very close relationship with the activities of the housing associations, should be represented on the boards of housing associations or does it vary from case to case?

CHRISTINE LAIRD: It is inevitable that it will have to vary from case to case. For example, if you take the organisation for which I used to work, there were 22 housing associations operating in that local authority area. It would have been an impossibility for the housing committee to have actually nominated a representative to sit on each housing association board and expect that individual to perform their duties satisfactorily, simply because of the workload involved. It is possible to achieve accountability without necessarily expecting representation on boards. I think they are two separate issues.

JOHN PERRY (Director of Policy, Chartered Institute of Housing): Could I just add a point to that. We are doing some work at the moment in developing the concept of local housing companies, which I am sure you will be familiar with from earlier evidence. We are working quite hard with the Department of the Environment and the Housing Corporation on developing ideas for how local housing companies might work. We have looked at board membership by local authorities of housing companies, and that is something which I think will happen. Equally there are other ways in which links can be maintained between local authorities and housing companies and it may be that some of those ideas can be brought into relationships between local authorities and housing associations.

585. MARTIN JACOMB: Yes. Thank you very much. How about tenants? This is all leading on towards accountability, but so far I am still on the constitution of the board itself. How about tenants being represented?

CHRISTINE LAIRD: I would argue that it is quite important for customers to actually be represented on the boards of associations, not least because it is their rental payments that are contributing to the majority of the association's income. It is perfectly feasible, therefore, to suggest that tenants should be represented at board level. They may not be able to bring commercial or legal skills to bear in providing information to the board; what they can provide, however, is a unique perspective as a customer of the organisation. That is therefore a very valuable role which I would encourage.

If I may add to that, I would suggest that tenant representatives on boards should be elected rather than selected so that the tenants that they represent have confidence in their representatives.

586. MARTIN JACOMB: Yes. Of course, once they get into the board room, they have to be board members rather than representatives, have they not?

CHRISTINE LAIRD: Absolutely, but that, in my view, suggests that it is even more important that tenants, knowing that those individuals on the board are their representatives, have faith in their views and decision making, so that is more of a justification for election rather than selection.

587. MARTIN JACOMB: Right. And a strong view on payment of board members?

CHRISTINE LAIRD: given the voluntary ethos that has grown up with the housing association movement, it would be unfortunate if people were to regard becoming a board member of a housing association as something that one could do to generate income. It is perfectly appropriate, however, to compensate board members for loss of earnings, within previously agreed limits.

MARTIN JACOMB: Yes.

CHRISTINE LAIRD: Not least because it would enable associations to be able to have access to a more diverse range of potential board members. It is a pity that people on low incomes who nevertheless may be able to contribute a considerable amount to an organisation may perhaps be precluded from putting themselves forward, simply because they cannot afford to. We should not discourage the concept of good citizenship. I do think that we should ensure that simply because someone is on a low income they are not deprived of their ability to make a contribution to an organisation that is fulfilling a valuable role in their area.

588. MARTIN JACOMB: Thank you very much. So as not to monopolise the time entirely, I would just like to

come, rather briefly, to perhaps the most important question of all, which is the question of accountability and the regulatory regime.

As you may have heard from Lord Nolan's questioning of our previous witnesses, it is pretty clear that accountability to the membership of housing associations is not the right route to go down. That will not reveal effective accountability, so one has to find some other route for accountability to follow. I suppose the Housing Corporation has a role and the local authority has a role. There is not, as far as I can see, clarity about to whom the board members are really accountable. Who do you think they should be and feel accountable to?

CHRISTINE LAIRD: As a starting point, it would be helpful to define the stakeholders in associations because there are a lot of misconceptions surrounding the role of housing associations and to whom they are accountable. It is correct that they are accountable to their regulator. There are debates, certainly generated by the local authority associations, about whether or not the regulator is accountable—which I will not get into.

I would argue that if an organisation is in receipt of public money, it has to be seen to demonstrate that it is publicly accountable for the money they are responsible for spending. It is imperative in my view that they are able to demonstrate that. As we move into a situation where private sector bodies are going to be able to access public funds, it becomes even more imperative that we establish those accountability lines.

In my view, a lot of the issues surrounding debates about accountability are often not about the theory but the practice of accountability and often a lot of those problems could be resolved by better communication. Local authorities will argue in particular instances that an association is not accountable when really what they mean is that the local authority is not having access to that association's activities to the extent that they might like. In my view therefore, if we were to concentrate on the issue of how information in associations' activities in connection with the spending of public money distributed to the wider community, to Local Authorities, to stakeholders, then you would resolve a lot of those issues. I think the lending institutions would argue that the Housing Corporation performs a good role in ensuring the financial probity and viability of associations, but often in terms of issues of accountability it is not "Oh, well, the Association is not making the best use of public funds"—you will not hear that argument being put forward by a Local Authority or a Community Representative. You may hear, for example, that they say "Oh, well, they are not housing the right kind of people" and so forth, but that is often simply because the organisation does not have access to full and detailed information that demonstrates that, in fact, those perceptions are misplaced.

Because of that, we have suggested in relation to the development of local housing companies that there is perhaps a role for the Housing Corporation to contemplate entering into an arrangement with the Local Authority for the Local Authority to assume a role in monitoring and compiling information on the Corporation's behalf. We have suggested it may be appropriate for the Regulator to determine, within previously agreed parameters—mainly relating to the day to day activities of the company in the area in terms of its housing management performance—the information that it requires, but for the Local Authority to have the responsibility for compiling that information and then passing it on to the Corporation. And it could almost be like exceptions reporting, for example to the Corporation. Now that would mean that at all times the Local Authority was familiar with what the new company was actually carrying out, without impacting on either the financial viability or probity of the company, and it seems to me that in actually involving all the parties in that flow of information a lot of the debates and complaints about accountability would disappear because, in our view, a lot of the arguments or complaints about accountability are, in fact, complaints about a lack of communication.

589. MARTIN JACOMB: So that is your preferred answer to the question—and I completely understand it—because to make accountability work properly the person to whom the accountability is directed has to have some power to do something if the account is not very satisfactory, and that is why you have chosen to promote that route as a way of answering the difficulty?

CHRISTINE LAIRD: We have suggested that that route would be appropriate in the establishment of local housing companies where a critical factor will be in ensuring that the local housing company continues to meet local housing needs. We have suggested that it may be a solution round the difficulty in terms of the relationship that exists in some areas of the country between the Housing Corporation, Associations and Local Authorities. It may be a solution.

I think it is also important to ensure accountability to customers and that can be achieved by providing regular newsletters about the activities of the association and I think it is important to ensure that associations in receipt of public funds also publicise how it is possible to complain about the organisation in the same way that Local Authorities are obliged to.

MARTIN JACOMB: Yes, you deal with that in your statement, I think.

JOHN PERRY: Could I just add a point about the relationship between Associations and Local Authorities? There has been an idea that has been developed for the last two or three years, that has been developed between the National Federation and the Local Authority Associations about social housing agreements operating at local level between Local Authorities and associations. This actually stems from an idea of ours in 1991 in a report that we produced on working together between Local Authorities and associations. Now we put forward the notion of social housing contracts, as we call them, in which we suggested there should actually be a formal contractual relationship entered into freely by both sides between Local Authority and a local association in which what each would get from the other was spelled out in the nature of a formal agreement. We do think there is merit in revisiting that approach.

MARTIN JACOMB: Thank you very much. I am afraid I am monopolising you and I am going to ask Sir William Utting if he would like to take up the questioning at this point.

590. WILLIAM UTTING: Thank you. I had a couple of points about your evidence about the Housing Corporation, in fact—about the composition in the first place, because you say pretty plainly that the Housing Corporation ought to have in its membership people who represent housing authorities, Local Authorities, tenants, wider communities, and so on. Would you care to elaborate on the arguments in favour of that? I mean, this is a funding and regulatory body—what is the case for every stakeholder being represented on it?

CHRISTINE LAIRD: I think the argument is that, increasingly, funding for new provision is being channelled exclusively via the Housing Corporation, so in consequence, whilst a Local Authority has a statutory responsibility to identify the housing needs in its area, the responsibility for meeting those needs, the funding for meeting those needs, is being channelled via another body. That occasionally leads to disputes between perceptions of what does and does not constitute a housing need and I think as an aside it is unfortunate that we have no national mechanism for actually measuring needs because I think a lot of these disputes would disappear if it was possible to point to factual information as opposed to anecdotal.

But given that increasingly access to new housing provision is in the independent and will ultimately, perhaps, be in the private sector, and a group of people are reliant on having their housing needs met by looking to those sectors, I do think it is appropriate to say that future housing occupiers should have some say about the design of the homes that they will be living in, what they look like, where they are located, and so forth. And in terms of the wider issue of accountability, given that the social housing programme is funded by resources raised from taxes in addition to private finance, is it not reasonable to try and ensure that social housing provision in an area which is provided for the wider community reflects the wider community's requirements and views and could that not be achieved by actually having regional fora on which wider stake holders are represented?

591. WILLIAM UTTING: So that also depends then upon the creation of the regional structure that you refer to—that you would see the desirability of, if not actual representation, then people who come from these other interests being on both a regional level of the Housing Corporation and the Housing Corporation itself?

CHRISTINE LAIRD: Yes, I do. I think it is important to ensure that we make the best use of public resources that are available and to that end it is important to ensure, therefore, that the information against which spending decisions are being made is as extensive as possible. To that end, having regional advisory groups or fora committees, or whatever you choose to call them, can only be of benefit because the reality is that housing needs, for example in the North West, are not the same as London and the housing requirements in a rural area are going to be very different to the housing requirements of an inner city. We have no mechanism at present for reflecting them.

WILLIAM UTTING: The argument against that is that one does not necessarily establish the best funding and regulatory mechanism by requiring vested interests to sort out their problems within that body itself.

CHRISTINE LAIRD: I was not aware that I had suggested that.

592. WILLIAM UTTING: No, no, I was caricaturing your suggestion and just giving you the argument that is made against that. Could I move on to the role of the Housing Corporation because in talking about that you suggest ideally separating the roles of monitoring from regulation and strategy from funding. Again, the argument against that is that in reality questions of policy, resources and quality are in fact inseparable and are best dealt with by a unified body, even if that unified body gets in some external independent assistance. Would you care to comment on that?

CHRISTINE LAIRD: But the reality is that we do not have that system. I do think that it is important, particularly in the social housing sector, that we are working to one set of guidelines and one set of standards, not least so that we can actually ensure effective comparison across sectors to ensure value for money and that minimum standards are met. That mechanism does not exist at present. We actually have a situation where we have very similar types of housing being subject to two entirely different sets of housing management standards and it is not actually possible to undertake value for money comparisons between the sectors, simply because they are operating within different guidelines. It does seem to me that that is nonsensical—how does one measure value for money if you are not operating against clear guidelines?

I also think if we had one set of guidelines it would also assist to create healthy competition between professionals to ensure the very best standards are aspired to and value for money aspirations are met. And I do think there is the potential for a conflict of interest to take place. Of necessity the relationship between the Housing Corporation and associations is going to be a close one, but if one is to assess performance and value for money it is quite useful, in my view, to introduce a third party objective element into that review. Having been subject to external audit scrutiny in my capacity as a director of housing, it may from time to time have been unpleasant but it has certainly helped improve my performance as a professional and also to improve value for money of the organisation which I worked for.

So I do think it is possible to separate out the two roles because I would see the role of a housing standards agency or an arm's length agency providing detailed information to the founder on which they would be able to base their funding decisions and they would be able to make their funding decisions more analytically, perhaps, than is currently the case and that can only be to the good.

593. WILLIAM UTTING: May I slip in one last question, Chairman? We have had letters from people who are dissatisfied customers of housing associations—you will not be surprised to hear that. Are you actually satisfied that the system as it stands deals adequately with the legitimate complaints of individual tenants?

CHRISTINE LAIRD: The Housing Association Ombudsman in this year's report stated that in a review of the associations' complaint procedures, he found that 32% of associations did not advise tenants in their complaint procedures that they had a right of appeal to the Housing Association Ombudsman and that, in my view, is not acceptable. I do think all customers, irrespective of who they are the customer of, have the right to complain and to expect their complaint to be dealt with

appropriately. So I would hope that that improves. I do think there is merit in looking at complaint procedures generally for organisations in receipt of public funding and making certain that the complaint procedures are adequately publicised and that all members of the public actually know how to complain and who to.

WILLIAM UTTING: Okay, thank you very much.

594. LORD NOLAN: Thank you all very much. We would very much like to continue this but we have to ration our time. We are very grateful to you for coming along and for giving your answers so concisely and helpfully. Thank you very much indeed.

Now we have Mr Tim Brown and Mr Harry Perry. Good morning, gentlemen. Thank you very much for coming to join us. We are doing our best to cover a cross-section of Housing Associations and of the other bodies that we are looking at and we are particularly glad to see you because you are, in quantitative though not qualitative terms, a small housing association, is that right and you have a particular function which you have told us about?

I am going to ask Mr Peter Shore to lead off with the questions to you.

595. PETER SHORE: Thank you first of all for your paper and your opening statement, which we have all read with interest. As you have heard already, different views have been expressed about the Housing Corporation but in your submissions you have some really quite forceful things to say.

"The regulatory requirements of the Housing Corporation are backed up by powers of enforcement. In a number of areas the requirements leave far too little room for discretion."

You give an illustration of this, can you give an additional illustration?

TIM BROWN AND HARRY PERRY

TIM BROWN (Chair, Leicester Newarke Housing Association Ltd.): Another example apart from the right to repair example which we mentioned would be the detailed prescriptive requirements over development schemes. There are set standards that have to be followed and we find it quite difficult as an association that deals primarily with rehabilitation of older properties to meet all the requirements.

596. PETER SHORE: Would not their reply to that be quite simply "We have to enforce or maintain high standards, qualitative standards of workmanship in repair as well as in new development"?

TIM BROWN: I would say there are other organisations, such as planning departments of Local Authorities, environmental health departments of Local Authorities who also have regulations that we have to follow and there seems to me to be a case for at least some attempt to co-ordinate or to link together different requirements of different bodies.

PETER SHORE: Yes. Another criticism you make is the interest—perhaps over-intent interest—in financial regulation.

TIM BROWN: Yes. We as a relatively small association—250 tenancies—found over the last three or four years an increasing focus of the activities of the Housing Corporation on the financial side at the expense, we feel, of other areas such as, for example, equal opportunities. The Housing Corporation seems to put more emphasis on some aspects, particularly the financial aspects, than other areas and we think it ought to be a more level playing field of interest in practice.

597. PETER SHORE: Are you continuing to receive as a housing association funds for new development from the Housing Corporation?

TIM BROWN: We have received in recent years hardly any money from the mainstream approved development programme. We receive some money through special initiatives, such as City Challenge, which clearly includes some money via the Housing Corporation, but we do not receive at the moment mainstream approved development programme funding.

598. PETER SHORE: Thank you. My last question on the Housing Corporation arises really from paragraph 7 of your opening statement. You say that you

".... urge that a focused review of the Housing Corporation"s regulatory role .... with the objective of achieving a fairer balance between the interests of all stakeholders, while reducing the level of detailed prescription in all areas."

Can you expand a little bit on that?

TIM BROWN: Yes. We feel that some stakeholders, Local Authorities, local communities, and in particular tenants, have some difficulty in directly influencing housing associations of what they do. They have some influence through liaison, negotiation, but it seems to me that the Housing Corporation ought to take on board some of the requirements and views of these other stakeholders in their regulatory mechanism. We as a management committee discussed this in relation to the National Federation Enquiry into Governance and in relation to our submission to the Nolan Committee. We talked about the possibility of every stakeholder having some sort of regulatory powers but we felt that that would lead to quite a major problem of bureaucracy and I think myself, as a Committee Chairman—and certainly my director—would be aghast at having to fill in even more forms for even more organisations. So we feel that we need one regulatory body but they need to look and have a breadth of regulatory function covering the needs of a range of stakeholders, so all stakeholders feel that they are empowered in some way to influence through the regulatory mechanism.

599. PETER SHORE: Are you suggesting that the structure of the Housing Corporation itself should be changed to include representatives of these other stakeholders?

TIM BROWN: I am not necessarily sure that by having representatives on the board of the Housing Corporation from the Local Authority sector or from tenants, that that necessarily achieves what one wants to achieve. I think it is the regulatory mechanisms that are important, not the composition of the Housing Corporation Board.

600. PETER SHORE: The other stakeholders you mention—how important is private finance in your housing association and what relationships do you have to such providers?

TIM BROWN: Increasingly it is becoming more important, not just because of the 1988 Housing Act and the change in development funding situation, but increasingly we are looking to private finance to help us fund schemes entirely, so that we are not dependent on public finance. We therefore have developed quite good working relationships with a number of building societies and banks.

601. PETER SHORE: Do the building societies themselves, as it were, when they are providing the finance, themselves seek to regulate and to watch over your expenditure of money they have provided?

TIM BROWN: I feel they do not treat us in any different way to any other organisation they would lend money to. I think you may want to say something on that?

HARRY PERRY (Director, Leicester Newarke Housing Association Ltd.): Yes, that is right, they look at it as a business transaction and look at the strength of your balance sheet and your financial viability of projections and make decisions on that basis.

602. PETER SHORE: Could you say how that contrasts with the regulatory and supervisory role of the Housing Corporation?

HARRY PERRY: The Housing Corporation attempts to regulate us right across the board by setting down standards in almost every area of our activities and each year we have to complete a form called the R.14, which you may have seen, and if you have not I suggest you get hold of a copy, because it is very enlightening about the degree of supervision that the Housing Corporation gives and requiring statistics on every aspect of our activities and explanations about policies and procedures.

By contrast with that, dealing with a building society that is going to lend us money at risk is a much simpler business and you feel that you are being treated as mature and responsible managers of a business whereas with the Housing Corporation I think you feel that you are being treated as slightly dodgy customers who need a lot of supervision.

603. PETER SHORE: Thank you. I know that as an association you are concerned with your other stakeholders. I believe you have at least two tenant representatives on your own board of management, that is great. Is that an unusual practice in housing associations and anyway what sort of major advantages do you find, having representatives on your board?

TIM BROWN: I think many housing associations have tenants on their boards. I think obviously the practice varies enormously because of the diversity of housing associations. I think one point I need to make is that the two tenants on our committee are there as individuals, they are not there as elected representatives and one of the reasons for that, perhaps, is because of our rather unique role as a provider of housing accommodation for young people, especially students. We have a very high turnover of tenants each year—we have just been looking at our Tenant Satisfaction survey report that has just been carried out and roughly 50% of our tenants expect to move on within nine to twelve months. So it is quite difficult to have a tenants' association that is operating on a regular basis—we have tried all manner of means to get a tenants' association set up. So the two tenants are representing themselves but we think it is quite important to have tenants on our board because it makes sure that the rest of us as committee members appreciate the consumer's viewpoint. There would be a temptation for us to act in a very paternalistic way and think that we know what is best for our tenants and the tenants frequently say "Well, hang on a moment, that is not how I see it, or it is not how the people I talk to who are tenants see it" and I think it is a really useful function that they perform, to keep our feet firmly on the ground.

604. PETER SHORE: Yes. And, of course, tenants have, have they not, now this right to approach an ombudsman if they really have a serious grievance?

TIM BROWN: Yes, that is right. We think—I must say our management committee was rather surprised when we looked at the Housing Ombudsman's annual report to find that so few housing associations publicise their own internal complaints procedure. We have a newsletter and a tenants' handbook, which includes those, and we really think it is vital for any association to publicise their own internal procedures, as well as the Housing Association Ombudsman's system as well, which we fully support.

605. PETER SHORE: Yes. In your evidence—to move on to another but very important aspect of housing associations—you do have things to say about getting the right kind of people for your board of management and sometimes the difficulties of obtaining that. Your suggestion, I think I am correct in recalling, is that the Federation itself should keep a register?

TIM BROWN: Yes.

606. PETER SHORE: How have they responded to that proposal?

TIM BROWN: As I understand it, the National Federation of Housing Associations have been thinking about that and have made suggestions along those lines. We think that there are people in the community—and I think this point came out earlier in the discussions this morning—that we have got a lot of people in the community who do not really know what a housing association is and we think if more publicity was given to what housing associations are doing, particularly in terms of the management committee, the sort of voluntary ethos about wanting to be involved with organisations which are attempting to tackle housing issues and to meet housing needs, more people would be willing to come onto committees. And I think the National Federation of Housing Associations, as a trade body, could have quite an important role in this respect, to publicise what housing associations are and that there is a role for people in the community.

607. PETER SHORE: I am sure that would be very valuable. What about this rather fraught subject of payment of management members—or payment of expenses of such people—what do you have to say about that?

TIM BROWN: Our policy is that we will pay the expenses of our committee members—creche facilities,

etc. etc. In terms of payment—in income terms—our management committee is opposed to that. All of us on our committee got involved because of a commitment to do something about the appalling housing situation facing young people and students and I think that ethos is still very strong in our committee and we would, I think, see a payment leading to quite a change in the culture of the committee, if not the organisation as a whole.

608. PETER SHORE: There is one other point that I think you make very strongly in your evidence to us and that is the difference between the very large housing associations and smaller ones. I do not think you are a tiny one, I think you are a reasonable size housing association, but we know that some associations really are very large indeed, have a sort of national coverage and in some areas, of course, there have been the transfers from Local Authorities to housing associations. You make the point that it is sort of inherently more difficult to make large housing associations accountable. If accepted—that line of argument—what would you yourself be proposing in the way of additional, as it were, measures to ensure accountability where large housing associations are concerned?

TIM BROWN: I think for large associations, especially national or regional associations that operate across a wide range of Local Authorities and, indeed, a number of housing corporation regions, I think there is a real issue of accountability to local communities, Local Authorities and possibly tenants, but I think it is the first two that are of particular issue. I would have felt that the Housing Corporation is there for a much more important role in looking across the activities of that association and bringing in this point about making sure that stakeholders of Local Authorities have a role to play in this. I think that is where a review of the Housing Corporation regulatory procedures would be really important. I am aware of situations where Local Authorities have been rather unhappy with the way in which allegedly one or two associations play one Local Authority off against another.

609. PETER SHORE: You would actually like to see the very large associations broken up, would you not?

TIM BROWN: Yes. We seem to be in a situation where we are moving towards a much more diverse range of social housing providers. The representatives from the Chartered Institute of Housing talked about local housing companies. Now, if we are going down this direction of a more diversified range of social housing providers, certainly our management committee wonder whether there should not be an upper limit on the size of housing associations, so that we do not in a sense move to a situation, which has been talked about in the housing association movements where similar patterns emerge to building societies, where you move to fewer and fewer larger organisations.

610. PETER SHORE: You would argue, too, would you not, that the new, almost exclusive, social housing role had been given to housing associations until very recently and the great role of the Housing Corporation has tended to divert, as it were, public funds almost exclusively to the very large housing associations?

TIM BROWN: Yes, it's called the "Premier League".

PETER SHORE: Yes.

HARRY PERRY: I did start off some correspondence some years ago in the trade press under the heading of *The Hidden Agenda* which was hotly denied by the Housing Corporation at the time, that they had a hidden agenda to actually reduce the number of housing associations, at least that they would fund. But in practice that has come about and the engine behind that has been the concept of value for money in the use of housing association grant. The Housing Corporation has used this value for money formula in a purely monetary sense to get as many units of accommodation per pound of HAG as possible. That tends to favour large-scale organisations who can borrow money cheaply, who can do volume deals with building contractors and who can develop large sites provided by Local Authorities. Those things have their down side as the Page report showed and as can be seen now in various places around the country with dysfunctional housing estates and housing situations being produced. That process is continuing—the number of housing associations funded for new development is reducing each year and if you exclude the small housing associations which were funded under the ethnic minority initiative of the Housing Corporation, the number of mainstream or non-black small housing associations funded is very small indeed, compared to the pre-1988 Act situation. That process, as I say, is continuing and without a major change in legislation or the Housing Corporation's approach I do not think there is anything that will stop it.

LORD NOLAN: Peter, I am sorry to interrupt, I am afraid we have actually run out of time. Clifford, you probably have one or two questions to ask them?

611. CLIFFORD BOULTON: Well, I am very aware of the clock. May I just press this business about accountability a little bit further? You sent us a plan which looked rather like a dinner-table seating plan, which listed all the areas in which you feel accountable, but it is something we have been discussing on and off all morning and Sir Martin Jacomb made the point that accountability without sanctions is a bit hollow. Would it be helpful perhaps to distinguish, in the large numbers of way in which you feel accountable, between accountability and openness, or transparency, if you use the vogue word? You are saying you are very open and that there is quite enough of that and so far as sanctions for accountability are concerned you think the Housing Corporation should be regarded as the principal stick-wielder there, would you, and you say you feel misunderstood by the Housing Corporation. So the body that has got the principal power over you—you are not very happy with your relationship with them—but you think you are giving quite enough public information about your activities, thank you very much, we do not need any more?

TIM BROWN: I think it is vital that housing associations are open and transparent in their dealings and they provide information to as many bodies as they can. I think that is the basis. If housing associations are not doing that, or willing to do that, I think there is a real problem. So we attempt to put a lot of information out about what we are doing, so people can judge us by what we are doing.

But I think accountability is also about an organisation in the last instance having some enforcement power over us. Our view is that at the moment the Housing Corporation has enforcement powers over us—and quite rightly, we are not objecting to that, I think that is appropriate—our concern is that the Housing corporation

use their enforcement powers in a rather narrow way to look at particular activities, rather than taking a breadth look, that is our concern.

CLIFFORD BOULTON: Thank you very much.

LORD NOLAN: Thank you both very much. We would like to hear more from you but I am afraid we have got to try and cover more ground than is convenient. You have been most helpful and clear and it has been a great help to have you with us. Thank you.

Mr Clark, thank you very much for joining us today and also for the information with which you have supplied us. If I may get straight down to business I am going to ask Lord Thomson to begin the questions.

612. LORD THOMSON: Mr Clark, Focus is a housing association that is in what has just been called the Premier League, is that right—you are amongst the top twenty?

RICHARD CLARK

RICHARD CLARK (Chief Executive, Focus Housing Group): Yes, I would think so. Yes.

613. LORD THOMSON: Would you like to begin by just telling us something about Focus and its activity?

RICHARD CLARK: Yes. Focus is actually the product of a merger between a number of Midlands housing associations. There are four major associations who have been merged into one group in the last three or four years and so in a sense we are very much like Newcastle & Gosforth, in that we have got big by amalgamating from previous associations which were small and medium size. So it is actually one of the organisations which has responded to the post-1988 Act era, although the work that the founding associations has done goes back seventy years.

In terms of what we actually do, Focus has over 12,000 homes in management and one of the things we pride ourselves on is that we provide a very wide range of types of accommodation and so, for example, we not only do straightforward general purpose housing, we also provide low-cost home ownership accommodation for people who want to get on the bottom rungs of the housing ladder. And also we are amongst the top ten providers of supported housing in the country. So we provide a lot of special-needs accommodation and we consider that to be a very important part of our activity. And also we were a multi-regional association until last year—we now confine our activities to the West Midlands region and we have a very large staff of over 600, of which over half are in the supported housing area because of the very intensive staff levels. We currently have a structure which is broken down into three regions and we operate through a regionally-led structure so that although it is within the West Midlands within that there are three regions. I think that is in a nutshell the structure.

614. LORD THOMSON: That is very clear. Thank you very much. Leaving aside your special section of housing for sale what are the broad proportions of your funding between public funds and private funds?

RICHARD CLARK: Historically, of course, we used to receive 80-90% from public funds but since 1988 the percentage has fallen and in our current schemes—the new schemes which we provide—we have about 60% private investment and 40% public. So the majority is in the private sector and we are now moving on to a loan portfolio, I think at the last count, of £70 million. So it is a very substantial amount of private borrowing.

615. LORD THOMSON: You are a useful witness for us in the sense that you were previously employed within the Housing Corporation. I do not know whether that is the gamekeeper turned "poacher" or the other way around but you have the advantage of seeing it from both sides of the fence. Would you like to give us your comments on how you see the situation and whether there are changes in the relationship between the Housing Corporation and the Housing Association that you would like to see?

RICHARD CLARK: Would I like to comment on the changes I have seen, or that I would like to see?

LORD THOMSON: That you would like to see, yes.

RICHARD CLARK: Oh, right.

616. LORD NOLAN: You talk about, I think, in your paper the tightness of regulation?

RICHARD CLARK: Yes. I think there are two or three main things. The first is that I think the relationship between the various stakeholders in housing associations is very complicated and I think there probably is further work that can be done in relation to that area and I pick out in the original submission in my opening statement that the relationship with the Local Authorities is particularly complex, and that the Housing Corporation could well address that area in more depth, along with the National Federation, so that the actual way their relationships work is more articulated. There are a great many ways in which, on a day-to-day basis, on a month-to-month basis, those relationships exist, so I do not want to give the impression that there is no clear relationship either between the corporation and the local authorities or between associations and local authorities. I think the whole framework within which that works could be improved and it would benefit all parties if that was the case. That is the first thing.

The second thing is I think there is a problem with the type of competition which associations are currently asked to indulge in. There is a tension between providing structured social housing for the highest priority needs and having an open competition in the same sense as contractors compete for contracts, and you will not necessarily get the most effective social provision by associations competing on a scheme for scheme basis. At the moment the relationship between the Housing Corporation and the DoE and housing associations is that we are under immense pressure to provide value for money and the lowest cost per unit. I suppose I am a planner at heart, but I personally believe that if you want to solve long term social problems, a short term lowest price system is not the most effective. I do not mind being exposed to competition because I think we all should be, but I think that there is an excessive emphasis on it which is not necessarily in the interests of long term planning, and, in fact, the long term quality for housing products either.

The third thing is about regulation, and I do mention this in the statement. There is a tension between arms length regulation and close working, and the corporation over the years has gone from one to the other. One of the things I feel very strongly about is that I think effective regulation demands a close relationship between the person who is regulated and the regulator. For example, we have a very good relationship with our external auditor, but that does not stop our auditor, which is a national firm, from keeping a close surveillance on the activities of the company. We have a lot of respect for the person who carries it out, and when that person comments on the work we do there tends to be an immediate acceptance and interrogation of what the issue is, whereas if you have a very arms length relationship it tends to be very formal and the communications are very formal. I think in regulating associations the corporation needs to keep a close contact with associations, particularly large associations, and to see that there is both a relationship of respect but also there is an understanding and a grip on what is actually happening. One of the dangers of arms length relationships is you actually miss far more than you identify, and I think the Housing Corporation possibly strayed a little bit too far one way.

617. LORD THOMSON: That is very interesting. Now you very helpfully have given us as well as your paper a full note of your rules that you have been making various changes in, and I wondered if you could comment on these for us. You have been changing your method of governance, would you like to tell us something about that?

RICHARD CLARK: Yes, there are some minor changes, I will just focus on the main three or four. Obviously there are simple ones like changing titles of the committee to the Board of Management. The two or three main ones are that we have brought tenants into a constitutional position in relation to the association and have given them formal rights to representation on our regional committees, and that is now enshrined in the rules and a proportion of tenants have a right.

618. LORD THOMSON: Could I just ask on that particular point, are they appointed by the management committee or are they elected? How do they come on to it?

RICHARD CLARK: We have a bottom up system with tenants groups; we have about 40 tenants groups in the associations. The tenants groups elect a representative body called the Tenants Forum and the Tenants Forum elects the tenants onto the committee, so it fosters from the bottom those representatives. I would not like to say that that system works perfectly, it is still evolving, but the management committee do not pick their pet tenants and put them on the regional committees; it is all very much from the bottom up.

619. LORD THOMSON: Then do you have to have some special rules for the tenants representatives, when the matter of a rent policy comes up for example?

RICHARD CLARK: Yes, tenants are not allowed to vote on rent policy but they play an active part in all the rest of the business of the association. We have taken an interesting line, I think, on the relationship between tenants on the board and tenants on the regional committee which is that they have constitutional rights to be on the regional committees which are the service providers, and they are eligible for election to the Board of Management, but we are not giving tenants a position as of right on the Board of Management at the moment because we think that people who sit on the Board of Management are there for their skills and personal qualities. If tenants comes forward and offer themselves for membership of the Board of Management and for election they would obviously be considered, but they should stand in relation to the overall management of the association as people who can offer the Board of Management specific skills. Whereas at the regional level we believe that because of the emphasis is very strongly on the provision of the service that it is clearly essential that the customers, the tenants, are represented on that.

LORD THOMSON: I interrupted you.

RICHARD CLARK: I was just saying that apart from the rent policy issue, tenants have full voting and members rights to the committee.

620. LORD THOMSON: You have a shareholding membership, is that right?

RICHARD CLARK: Yes we do.

621. LORD THOMSON: How many shareholders do you have?

RICHARD CLARK: We have just short of 300.

622. LORD THOMSON: Is that a useful method of accountability? We have had various criticisms of it from various witnesses.

RICHARD CLARK: As you saw in both the original submission and the opening statement it is a concern to us. It is clearly a more complicated issue when you are an amalgam of previous organisations, and what happens when you merge housing associations is that the shareholders automatically are offered a share in the new organisation, so we actually have four or five groups of shareholders who have come together. Many of the shareholders have been shareholders for a very long time in the originating organisations, and, of course, some of the shareholding membership has become moribund. But more importantly the stake of the shareholders in the organisation is minimal. All the people have to have done is to have handed over a pound and received a certificate. They can live in Western Australia but they have a vote on our Board of Management. I think that that is unsound as a way of electing a Board of Management, and once people get on the Board of Management their responsibilities are extremely high and the expectations of them are extremely high, and the risks to them of negligence, as you know, are very large. To be elected by a group of people, many of whom we suspect have died and not notified us of the fact, is not healthy. We are trying to deal with that within our current rules and regulations, but once you start off you can only, for example, expel members for activities against the association, you cannot expel them for not turning up to meetings. So we do not really have any power other than to write to people and say, "As we have not seen you for 25 years would you like to hand your share in?", there are very few means for the association to actually rationalise this. We are attempting to do that within the rules and within sensible policies. For example, we are establishing semi-constituencies of shareholders and encouraging our stakeholders like local authorities to hold shares in the association, and we want 40 per cent of the shareholders to be tenants so that there

is a clear stakeholding from tenants, but it is very difficult to do it within the current guidance.

One of the things my association believes very strongly, this is my board's view as well as my own, is that there should be a much clearer basis for a shareholding constituency or an alternative way of electing a board. There is a huge gap between the responsibilities and powers of the shareholders and the board. I know you are aware that of course there is a huge variation between associations. There are associations with 12 members who happen to be the same people as the Board of Management, whereas in our position, as I say, there are many of our shareholders that nobody on the current Board of Management has a clue who they actually are, which seems rather unsound.

623. LORD THOMSON: I noticed one of the changes that you have made in the rules relates to retired employees joining the board. Would you like to comment on that?

RICHARD CLARK: I think Focus is very unusual in this. I do not think there are many associations who actually have employees in shareholding membership, it was an anomaly. We have had a situation with a recent ex employee standing to be on the Board of Management which was considered to be an unhealthy situation, and the shareholding membership have taken a decision to change the rules to exclude current employees from member of the association, and also ex employees from standing for the Board of Management. Of course, current employees cannot stand for the Board of Management because it is a breach of the Housing Associations Act, so even if you are a shareholding membership you cannot go on while you are an employee—I cannot go on as things stand—but ex employees who have just left six weeks ago, if they are a shareholder, are eligible for the Board of Management. We are proposing to the Housing Corporation and the Registrar of Friendly Societies that we exclude employees for five years after they have left. It is really an anomaly. I would be surprised if there were more than half a dozen associations in the country who have immediate ex employees as members.

624. LORD THOMSON: Just one other point on your rules, page 22 paragraph 60, you provide for the NFHA to appoint an arbitrator in the event of a dispute between the association and a member. I just wondered whether you thought this might also be used to resolve any dispute between, say, a chief executive and the board? Is it a formula that would have a wider application?

RICHARD CLARK: I would have doubted it. There are obviously powers as employers for disputes between a chief executive and the board to be resolved and the normal investigative methods if, in fact, there is a clear problem. It seems to me to be interfering with the contract between Focus Housing Board, for example, and myself to contract of employment to institute a separate procedure because obviously there are legal processes which need to be gone through, and legal ways of acting on them. I think to impose an artificial mechanism between the board and the employee I doubt very much whether it would work, and it would get so confused with legal rights I think it would be almost impossible.

625. LORD THOMSON: I understand. Just one final question, if you were a member of the Nolan Committee

what recommendations would you want us to make in the field of housing associations?

PROF ANTHONY KING: If any.

RICHARD CLARK: I would obviously like you to make a recommendation that large amounts of public money was put back into housing association funding, because I think our primary problem is insufficient resources to do the job.

LORD THOMSON: That is outside our terms of reference actually.

RICHARD CLARK: You did ask me what I would recommend and that would be one thing. I do believe that housing associations generally are well regulated and have responded very well to the 1988 Act which was a huge culture change for everybody and I think we have learnt very rapidly. The two areas I would suggest to you clearly need looking at is that the relationship between housing associations and the other stakeholders, in particular tenants and local authorities, could do with further elaboration. Secondly, in fact association committees are elected democratically in one sense because of the shareholders, but that is not a very stable way to be elected. That does need looking at and I think those would be the two areas I would pick out.

LORD THOMSON: That has been very helpful.

626. LORD NOLAN: I would like, if I may, to ask you about the policy for the allocation of development funds. We have a paper from Professor Klein which is very helpful saying funds are allocated to specific local authority areas by central government using the Housing Needs Index formula but local authorities effectively decide which schemes and which associations are going to be the investment vehicles for the money allocated to a specific area. We heard earlier this morning from witnesses who were saying they felt that there was insufficient unity and purpose in the way funds are distributed from central government and then applied by local housing associations. You yourself, I think, touch on this when you say one of the most difficult areas for housing associations is the lack of clarity about the relationship with local authorities, and the various assessments that are carried out for seeing how money should be spent.

First of all, can you tell me what is the Housing Needs Index formula?

RICHARD CLARK: The Housing Needs Index is related to the index which the Department of the Environment use to allocate funds to local authorities. It has slightly different factors in it but it is a combination of demographic data, housing needs data like homelessness indicators and the proportion of people who are homeless in a particular area. It is an amalgam of about eight factors which indicate the level of housing stress in a particular area, and the Department of the Environment use the Generalised Needs Index which has things like the local authority stock condition as a big factor, and the Housing Corporation use the Housing Needs Index which looks much more at shortage factors like the number of people on waiting lists, the number of people who are homeless, rather than the stock condition of the local authority. It is an amalgam of about eight factors and it is broken down by local authority.

627. LORD NOLAN: Is it a good criteria? Does it work well?

RICHARD CLARK: Not in my opinion, no.

628. LORD NOLAN: What would you substitute for it as a means for determining how funds should be allocated from central sources?

RICHARD CLARK: I would have an index. You have to have an objective measure to allocate funds, there is no other way of doing it, but I believe first of all that the indicator itself has tended to be very, very weak at local level. If you are dividing it by regions, given that certain decisions are political about what factors will be considered—are you going to put homelessness in or out—you need an objective index. At local level the Housing Needs indicator does not tend to work very well and therefore I think there is better data available which could indicate the level of housing stress which exists in particular areas and you could improve the index a lot. I am not saying you can do without it.

The other thing is, I am afraid I am talking as again as a planner, I do believe very strongly that housing should be provided strategically and that how money is being spent is fundamentally important to how you allocate it. At the moment the Housing Corporation allocates 80 per cent on the Housing Needs Indicator, which I think is in contrast to the Department of the Environment which I think is 50 per cent on the General Needs Indicator. I think there should be more stress in the Housing Corporation's allocations on the strategy of the local authority to deal with the housing problems it is tackling unless on an indicator where the data is flawed.

First of all I would try and improve the data within the index and then also I would change the waiting so that there is more money going to those local authorities who have a very effective housing strategy.

629. LORD NOLAN: The point was put particularly from the point of view of disadvantaged tenants which you have said are not sufficient protected by the existing set up for allocating money. That was something which would be better served by some central guidance for the allocation.

RICHARD CLARK: Was that referring to the conditions in which existing tenants live?

LORD NOLAN: The amount of resources allocated to their needs.

RICHARD CLARK: As my association has over 4000 houses which are pre 1919, and we are ourselves have launched into a £50 million home improvement programme almost exclusively out of our own resources over 10 years, I think that is absolutely right. We recognise we cannot provide a lot of new homes to a high standard and at the same time have run down properties for existing tenants, and I think many large inner city associations are coming into the same position as local authorities with the back log of repair and improvement to older stock competing with the need for new tenancies, and we are trying to balance it. Certainly there is a great need for investment in the existing stock as well as demand for new.

LORD NOLAN: We are very grateful to you, Mr Clark, I am afraid we have run out of time, but I am extremely grateful and glad that you were able to give us the amount of time you have. Thank you very much indeed.

Professor Klein, thank you very much for coming along to see us today. We have read with great gratitude and admiration the paper that you sent in for us, the one you did with Patricia Day, and we would like to ask you questions about that and other matters. The lead questioner will be Sir William Utting with Peter Shore following him, but I know Professor King who has to leave a little early has one particular question that he would like to ask you.

630. PROF ANTHONY KING: You have thought a lot more, Rudolf, about questions of accountability than I have, and I just wanted to raise one general question not connected specifically with housing associations at all. Partly from my own experience, but much more out of listening to people who have come before this committee, I am struck by the fact that there is often a marked difference between what one might call the declaratory policy in a particular area, that is to say what ministers and others had said their objectives were, and what might be called the operational policy, what is actually happening on the ground. So that for example a minister may say our objective is to deliver the highest possible quality of X; in practice the people on the ground feel that they are under pressure to deliver something less than the highest quality of X. There may be a hidden agenda there. The minister may not be saying in fact what his real objectives are, but equally it may simply be the result of muddle, of tension, of discrepancy between different objectives.

In the world that we are looking at there are constantly raised questions of accountability. Am I right in thinking, and if I am not tell me, that there is possibly in the world of next steps agencies at one extreme, and bodies like housing associations at another, a real problem of accountability arising out of precisely this tension between declared goals and operational performance? Do I make myself clear?

PROFESSOR RUDOLF KLEIN

PROFESSOR RUDOLF KLEIN (University of Bath): Absolutely, and I would totally agree that there is this tension. You can see it in the National Health Service where ministers say we have got these broad objectives but, of course, it is for people locally to decide how our objectives ought to be interpreted according to local need and so on. It is a sort of centralisation of credit and diffusion of blame. Ministers will always say, well, anything good, of course, that is our policies. Diffusion of blame, well, alas, we cannot be absolutely sure how people will locally interpret things. I think this is a tension, but I have no idea how it can actually be resolved. With a further tension, of course, I think one is talking primarily in the case of housing associations, as in the case of the health service, of bodies which have no independent source of finance. Which is where I have the problem when people turn round and say should there not be accountability to the local community etcetera, etcetera, when how can you in fact have these two streams possibly pulling against each other for accountability, one to the people who actually provide the money. Therefore Nye Bevan's phrase about health authorities, they are the "creatures of ministers", and how can creatures of ministers then at the same time also be accountable in the strict sense of their being sanctions to dismiss them if their

explanations fail to satisfy. So, I think your diagnosis of the tension is absolutely right; I wish I knew what the solution was.

631. WILLIAM UTTING: Rudolf, you make the ringing assertion that housing associations provide one of the outstanding success stories of the past 20 years. Bearing in mind that we are principally concerned with standards of conduct and propriety and regulation and accountability, have they been successful in those areas as well, and, if so, why is this?

RUDOLF KLEIN: I think I would like to take your questions in different aspects of it. Success in terms of producing the goods is what we had in mind when we wrote that particular sentence. They had just been successful in delivering lots of housing at reasonable standards though there are questions about their affordability.

They have been successful and have increasingly become tools of government, and I think that is one of the big changes over the last 10 to 20 years, while before that housing associations were sort of filling in their interstices of policy. They now are tools of government basically. The government is their source of finance and they have to jump through the hoops laid down by government. That is why I think we would argue that the system of accountability upwards to government through the Housing Corporation is pretty good.

One could argue endlessly about the precise nature of the regulatory system but it is pretty tough, and if you look, as you no doubt have, at the Committee of Public Accounts, which was published last year when they investigated the system of financial control, the Audit Office only managed to uncover one example of £300,000 being misappropriated in one particular one, which by the standards of National Audit Office reports is small change. So I think that upward accountability is pretty satisfactory. I think the real question is whether, and this goes back to Tony's initial question, there is sufficient "accountability" downwards, in other words for the sort of operational policies that are being pursued.

I wish one could devise a new vocabulary in keeping accountability for the flows of money and the sanctions, and another word, responsiveness possibly, responsibility, for the kind of operational issues of good management, sensitivity to tenant and other needs and so on. I think that that is the area of doubt.

There is an odd thing, when we went into housing, and it is not my main field of research which is much more than the NHS, there is an interesting phenomenon which is that bodies which are conscious of their lack of legitimacy in terms of democratic accountability sometimes, and I think it is true of the large housing associations which feel themselves very much in the public mind because they are conscious of their lack of legitimacy, actually do rather more than, for example, elected local authorities in terms of regional tenant committees sending out details of what they are doing and so on. It is almost the sense of insecurity which is the best guarantee of downward accountability. It is a tricky area.

632. WILLIAM UTTING: You throw a little cold water on some of the ready made answers that are provided to these problems of local accountability. You

are not too keen, it seems, on tenant members of boards, and you even have kind words to say about self-perpetuating oligarchies.

RUDOLF KLEIN: I would go back to the point I have just made that because they are conscious of being self-perpetuating oligarchies they are actually very sensitive to some of these needs. The study for our raw material really came from 10 of the biggest housing associations, and those 10 really very big ones are highly sophisticated operators in the political sense of being quite clear that they have got to win a sort of constituency of support in terms of downward responsiveness. I suspect there may be problems. We did not actually look at this in the next tier of housing associations which have not got quite the degree of professional and member expertise and sophistication.

I think we were sceptical about tenant participation on two counts really. If you actually look at the very large ones they operate all over the country. I think in one case we came across a housing association which had property in more than 100 local authority areas. They are also increasingly moving into new areas of activity—opening nursing homes and all sorts of things. I do not want to go into this, but it is an interesting case of entrepreneurship by largely the officers in a way driving organisations away from their original purpose. They are doing lots of good things in the process, lots of innovation buzzing away, but I think they are getting much more heterogeneous in their activities which, again, creates a problem of how you define the constituencies for any system of representation.

I think the main reason which made us sceptical was this. These are very big organisations. They are complex organisations, and it seemed to us the problem, as in all large organisations, is how does the board, nominally in charge and accountable for that organisation, actually control the officers who do the real business most of the time. That seemed to argue to us for really rather tough people with experience in the control of large organisations rather than any sort of participatory democracy.

633. WILLIAM UTTING: If one looks at the NHS, where you have done a great deal of work, some of these problems have been answered by making the officers executive directors of trusts. That does not seem to be a terribly popular suggestion with the housing association.

RUDOLF KLEIN: On the experience of the NHS so far I think one has to be agnostic about that as an experiment.

634. WILLIAM UTTING: What about the experience of the NHS in paying its authority and trust members then, because, again, there is some suggestion that you might need to pay people in order to get boards of housing associations of high quality, or have people with low incomes on them who can actually afford to do this work?

RUDOLF KLEIN: My hunch there is that because housing associations are a heterogeneous lot that argument probably does not apply to the 10 to 20 largest which are so prestigious that they can attract anybody they want. I think it may be a problem as you move down the size and the prestigiousness of the housing associations. As they get smaller and less prestigious they may have problems. One possibility which I have included in the short paper which I apologise, Chairman, for not having distributed it in advance, is attendance allowances rather

than salaries, because I think, and you would be in a much better position to judge than I am, there is a real danger if you go down the paying route that all the various bodies you are looking at will be competing against each other for the reservoir of the ablest people in terms of salaries. I think that is a risk which is why I would be rather cautious and urge possibly attendance allowances as a first step rather than salaries.

635. WILLIAM UTTING: Could I conclude on the question of the composition of the Housing Corporation because it has been put to us that there ought to be people on the Housing Corporation itself who may be tenants of housing associations, members of local authorities, other stakeholders and so on. The Housing Corporation was one of the quangos that we looked at in our last report, and we are now envisaging a situation in which there will be public appointments commissioners scrutinising the way in which appointments are made to these bodies, governance committed to principles of equity, appointment on merit, equal opportunities. Do you think that what the government is doing, plus our recommendations, will actually take care of the criticisms that are made about the composition of the Housing Corporation?

RUDOLF KLEIN: I do not think the government is specifically committed to the kind of change in the mix you outlined. It seems to me that public scrutiny of their appointments and so on will make sure that there are no odd appointments in terms of people's probity and so on. It does not actually address the question of what the composition ought to be in terms of experience or skills.

WILLIAM UTTING: Thank you.

636. PETER SHORE: We have this statement that you recently put round. In it you make reference to the Housing Corporation being required to publish the monitoring reports on individual housing associations. I gather from that that the present practice is not to publish such a report.

RUDOLF KLEIN: Precisely.

637. PETER SHORE: That is part of the secrecy of the Housing Corporation. Your recommendation there is, of course, confined to the category of the very large associations that you described at the beginning of your paper.

RUDOLF KLEIN: I am not sure. I think that is something I might be persuaded to apply across the board except, of course, if you look at the Housing Corporation's own activities. From their point of view, quite rightly of course, they concentrate their inspectorial activities on either the largest or the most vulnerable ones. I am not sure whether the quality of monitoring reports on the very small ones would be all that good. My hunch, and this is purely a hunch, is that the kind of patronage which you might be addressing the risk of that is highest amongst the very small ones.

PETER SHORE: Yes, I think that is correct. Thank you.

638. CLIFFORD BOULTON: I just want to follow up the point you make in some miscellaneous points at the end of your note where you say "there might be a mandatory requirement for large HAs to appoint a Secretary responsible for advising members on issues of propriety". Is it your experience that there are a lot of housing associations who do not have somebody with that

specific role? Is it a fact that the chief executive is taking on the job of secretary, or something like that?

RUDOLF KLEIN: I do not know of any systematic study of that, but my impression would certainly be that.

LORD NOLAN: Thank you very much indeed, Professor Rudolf, we are much indebted to you for the written material that you have given us, and in addition for putting, so speak, life on it in your personal appearance today. It has been very helpful and very interesting.

THURSDAY 30 NOVEMBER 1995

OPENING STATEMENTS

Opening statement of CSV, NACRO and Rathbone CI

1. Introduction

The organisations represented here today (CSV, Rathbone CI and Nacro) have already submitted a position paper to the Nolan Committee. This report now addresses the key points highlighted by the Committee in relation to our primary concern which is the:

> *"accountability of TECs for the training of the most disadvantaged in the community. We define the disadvantaged as including people with disabilities, moderate learning difficulties and mental health problems, as well as ex offenders and ethnic minority groups."*

It must be emphasised that this paper is not about criticising the entire TEC movement, many of which are doing an excellent job in regenerating local economies. Rather, it is about the relative willingness of some TECs to protect and indeed make a case for the rights of disadvantaged people to be trained in a way which takes account of their unique starting point. TECs willingness to do so is compounded, we believe, by the TEC funding structures and performance league tables which, in effect, value those TECs who deliver the greatest number of targets (qualifications and jobs) for the lowest possible price and in the fastest possible time.

Funding to TECs and therefore to those organisations with which they contract, is increasingly related only when "outcomes"(ie. jobs and qualifications) have been achieved. This is known as output related funding or ORF. 75 per cent of all funding in Training for Work, the government training programme for the long-term unemployed, now comes in this form, with up to 40 per cent in Youth Training. Increasing polarisation in Education and Training was exemplified in recent press coverage on the GCSE results, with another 8 per cent increase in the number of school children failing to pass any examinations.

The Institute for Employment Studies (IES) was recently commissioned by five voluntary organisations and seven TECs to look at the impact of recent changes in the publicly funded training market. The report focused on:

—recent changes in the TEC funding regime (including output related funding—ORF)

—the structure and use of TEC performance indicators and targets

—other changes in the policy environment affecting the overall approach to training provision

This report, "Winners and Losers"is highlighted in the following pages, and a full copy of the text will be left with the Nolan Committee.

Certainly, for those of us representing the voluntary sector here today there is a very real concern about the adequacy of monitoring systems, including through the TEC Contracts, if it has taken this research to expose problems which the voluntary sector have been raising for over three years.

The TEC Operating Agreement states that:

Suitable high quality and individually tailored Training shall be available to a Trainee who has a Disability or Special Training Needs"(paragraph B15.2)

On access to "suitable"training, however, it goes on to say that the TEC:

shall use its "best endeavours"to ensure that adequate support is available to residents" (paragraph B16.3)

The latter statement does much to dilute the commitment underlying the former. These two parts of the TEC Operating Agreement can serve to contradict each other and the second gives protection to those TECs who feel unable to deliver suitable training opportunities for all people with special training needs.

The Nolan Committee will form its own view on the ISE research findings. We wish however to add that:

a.   the Employment Department ignored a Coopers & Lybrand Report (reviewing 100 per cent outcome related funding pilots which it had itself Commissioned). It warned against the impact of too rigid a funding regime being imposed on TECs for the adult training programme, Training for Work (TFW). Instead, it forced upon TECs a system this year which penalises any organisation training the least able of the adult unemployed. Seventy-five per cent of total funding depends on outcomes being achieved.

We question why no TECs expressed concerns during the pilot phase or about the Coopers & Lybrand report before the new budget and output related procedures were introduced?

b.   Many TECs have been able to increase staffing levels and the remuneration package of their Chief Executives and other Directors, at a time when their reserves have been high and their turnover has reduced. These same TECs have been able to do this by offering prices to special needs training organisations which have to be refused unless they become more selective in their intake. Indeed, many TECs and senior civil servants have directly advised or strongly inferred that we should move "more up market". This is against our constitutional objectives.

We question why TECs and others feel the need to give such advice?

c.   Evidence has been given to the Employment Select Committee which is hugely unrepresentative and certainly misleading. For example, on 31st October the Director of the London TEC Council was interviewed. Angela Eagle MP asked the following question:

"On output related funding, we are very worried from some of the evidence we have taken that this is disadvantaging those who have specialist needs: ethnic minorities, women, people with disabilities. What is your view of the way that output related funding has been introduced?"

The Director said in reply:

"I would say immediately that there is no evidence at this time that this is the case. I think we all share a worry that any output related funding system can lead to "creaming"and that must be a worry with which we work.

Most of what we are getting at the moment is anecdotal and I have been working with a number of special needs interest groups to look at having proper research in this area".

The Directors' staff were fully aware of the IESresearch findings and the impact of the output related funding mechanism in the current funding climate. The TEC Council sub group on special needs had received scores of examples of this during the time the London Council TEC Director was a member of it. The research provided the factual evidence. The TEC Council sub group were fully aware of the Coopers report and its findings on output related funding and its increasing tendency to encourage selection and creaming. The proceedings of the Select Committee note that the cost of running the London TEC Council is £257,000. This funding will have been provided by London TECs from "top slicing"their Training and other budgets.

It is difficult to understand why the Director felt the need to be so economical with the truth when giving evidence to the Select Committee?

d.   The Opposition have begun to highlight the impact of continued reductions in funding to TECs; of training for the most disadvantaged. Such an article appeared in the Sunderland Echo recently. It prompted a reply from the local TEC Chief Executive that the story:

"painted a far worse scenario than has turned out to be the case".

Sunderland TEC was one of the joint sponsors of the IES research.

"Why is it the case that if facts emerge which may be uncomfortable for TECs people feel obliged to say so, at least for the public record, that the facts have always somehow been exaggerated or there is no evidence?

NB. It should be noted that in a questionnaire undertaken by the Financial Times earlier this year 61 per cent of TEC Directors said they were now unable and becomingincreasingly unable to train the most disadvantaged. The survey does not, of course, name individual TECs or TEC Directors.

2. Response to key issues

A.   *The arrangements TECs make through openness, membershipschemes or otherwise to be accountable to their local community.*

     Openness of TECs varies enormously, as does the willingnessto offer membership schemes. Our general view is that TECs perhaps because they are still relatively new organisations somehow feel the need to be on the defensive. Criticism of one part of the operation is sadly viewed as an attack on the entire TEC movement.

     Membership schemes, where they exist, tend to attract those who see clear and tangible benefits. For example, private sector companies looking for updated advice on export markets, regional supply networks, training/ expansion grants and so on.

     Manchester TEC, for example, has a unique joint membership scheme with the Chamber of Commerce and Business Link. It has several thousand members.

Our concern, however, is about those least able toarticulate their needs and/or to access training and employment opportunities. Young people on low incomes or on hardship allowance and the adult unemployed are likely to be part of a TECs membership scheme (for reasons which are self evident). However, Budgets to TECs to deliver Youth Training and Training for Work (for the adult unemployed) comprise up to ⅔ of the average TECs total Budget.

B.   *The advantages and disadvantages of the different approaches in making appointments to TEC boards.*

We are clearly not in a position to comment on the wide variations in making appointments to TEC Boards. In practice, it is probably more difficult to attract memberssince the collapse of South Thames TEC. There is an onerous time commitment to do justice to the work.

Few TECs are transparent in their procedure for nominations to the Board. Good practice TECs will seek to have a register of eligible members which reflect the economic position and needs of the area, as well as its wider composition.

It is frequently said that too few ethnic minorities or women are represented on Boards. The purported reason being that too few express an interest. It would be helpful if:

a.   A national framework for appointing Board members is developed.

b.   Boards adopt the practice of "Champions". Manchester TEC, for example, appoints members with an interest in a particular area, including for equal opportunities and special needs.

c.   A register is kept of people eligible from ethnic minorities and women. This could be compiled by relevant organisations being asked to propose names—IOD, CRE, EOC; Opportunity 2000.

d.   Where discrimination is shown at any time by the TEC Board members their position on the Board should be terminated forthwith.

C.   *The differing approaches within the contracts or licences to dealing with conflicts of interests of directors and staff.*

Again, we can take no broad overview of the different approaches of different TECs.

We would suggest that staff and Board members declare any interests they have with consultancy firms and others seeking work from the TEC. This should include direct and indirect relationships.

Further, that there should be transparency of staff appointments and random monitoring to ensure a robust recruitment procedure. It is certainly the case that some TECs have recruited to senior posts without recourse to advertisement.

D.   *Approach to handling complaints about the conduct of TEC staff and concerns about the board.*

Again, there will be different approaches. In practice, however, the relationship between the TEC is very often imbalanced by the nature of the contracts, the funding structure and the performance related award system for TEC employees.

The TEC Operating Agreement states that:

> *"The TEC shall be entitled to pay performance bonuses to staff. Such performance bonuses shall only be paid from the following sources:*
>
> *privately raised funds*
> *(which are unlikely to be given for such awards)*
>
> *operating surpluses*
> *(which means making profit out of the Training Budgets)*

TECs are commercial companies. As such they are encouragedto make a profit or operating surplus. Bonuses are well known to be regarded by staff in any company as an integral part of the salary and as such always payable.

Any sensible company when setting out its plan for the year looks to minimise its risks. Clearly, there are abundant risks to training many young people who cost more to train, take longer to achieve and "outcome"and who in fact may fail to do so. This puts the TECs own earning potential at risk.

Rathbone C.I. had a contract to deliver training forpeople with special needs in Durham TEC. The TEC decided to terminate the contract allegedly for "poor performance".The centre had a 15-year proven track record in training people with disabilities. It had won a Regional Training Award from the Employment Department the year before closure for "excellence in training".

It had overachieved on its contract with the TEC for the number of jobs, qualifications and literacy/numeracy packages delivered.

When local staff raised the question of this alleged poor "performance"the TECs response was "Other providers over achieved to a higher degree". This is, of course, going to happen if the training supply side takes more able people—those who can achieve qualifications and job "outcomes"in the shortest possible time and for the lowest possible price.

The TEC then suggested that Rathbone C.I. was being compared on a "like for like"basis. At this stage it was pointed out that on no less than 12 occasions in the previous year the local manager referred back cases of registered disabled people being sent through as having no additional support requirements!

The IES research has highlighted the wide variation in assessment procedures which is leading to inadequate provision in some areas. Further, which suggest that covert mechanisms are in place to reduce the numbers assessed as having special needs in order to reduce overall funding.

"Variation in endorsement rates (the funding mechanism of the assessment procedure) may also reflect in part variation in the extent to which TECs are effectively reaching groups of "disaffected youth".

"Whatever the precise case, however, the extent of variation recorded in the survey must at least raise questions about equity between TEC areas in terms of access to the programmes. It would seem that an individual with special training needs or other potential disadvantages may either face different likelihoods of being offered or of putting him/ herself forward for YT provision according to the TEC area in which he/she lives, or, if participating in YT, he/she is more likely to be endorsed as having a special training need (and therefore attract a higher unit rate of funding for his/her training) in some TEC areas than others".

REF P35 IES Research "Winners and Losers"

In the case of Rathbone C.I. the Durham TEC did eventually concede that there had been problems with its assessment procedures during the year in question, which had been raised by other providers too and which would now be rectified. Rathbone C.I. had closed its contract but ironically received a contract from the Employment Service because of its track record for people with disabilities!

During the year in question (1994/95) Durham TECs audited accounts showed the following:

a.   Turnover *decreased* from £27.4 million to £26.8 million.

b.   Staffing costs had *increased* from £1.64 million to £2.05 million.

c.   Staffing numbers had *increased* from 98 to 111.

d.   Reserves stood at £7 million.

During this same period Rathbone C.I. had cut staff and merged two centres under one manager in an attempt to remain in business.

a.   The consequence of making complaints about TEC staff is that it makes life difficult for voluntary sector staff on the ground.

b.   TEC staff themselves are under immense pressure to deliver sometimes unrealistic contracts. There have been a staggering number of Chief Executives who have had their contracts terminated. Some of these have been sacked for poor performance in the league table. We speak for those who have done their best to cater for people with special needs and have felt under pressure for doing so.

c.   It is very difficult for all Board members to absorb the complexity of the operation, in particular the adverse impact of funding structure on people with special needs.

All too often TECs and TEC Boards can be made to feel failures at strategic planning and direction, (by Government Regional Offices), whereas it may be the socio-economic area in which a TEC is operating.

Performance tables are constructed, inter alia, by the number of qualifications per 100 leavers and price per "output"point. There is no differential weightings given to different TEC areas which takes into account differing socio-economic conditions.

There is no known target price per output point which the DFEE wishes TECs to reach. This means that even those TECs at the top of the league table can and do have their budgets cut and have to improve their price per output point. The impact on those with special needs is obvious.

E.   *The procedures that are in place for non financial monitoring of compliance with contracts and licences.*

Sadly, we feel there are insufficient safeguards to protect the entitlement to suitable training for people with special needs and others at a disadvantage in the labour market. We have earlier highlighted many reasons which confirm this view. There is also a YT Guarantee which guarantees a suitable training place to every 16-18 year old. Yet, if enough suitable places were on offer, it is unlikely that up to 200,000 disaffected young people would be opting out of education, training and employment altogether. This figure is highlighted in research commissioned by the TEC Council sub group on special needs, and is due for imminent release.

The IES research states boldly that there is:

> *"clear and widespread evidence of creaming or trainee selection operating to the disadvantage of low achievers, as well as reductions in learning time, the additional support and guidance seen as necessary for clients with special training needs"*

The IES Research was jointly led by a group of voluntary organisations who were very pleased to be joined by seven TECs. The question must be:

If the Operating Agreement and YT Guarantee are working and being monitored effectively, surely it would not have taken this research to highlight issues of concern which the voluntary sector have been raising for many years?

We finish with the following extracts from the IES research, "Winners and Losers".

> *"some TECs at least are increasingly failing to pass on to providers the full changes in unit prices implicit in their current contracts with Government Regional Offices. This was a particular concern for many specialist providers who agreed that the weightings attached to endorsed (special needs) trainees in government TEC contracts was not being passed on to them". Page 49.*

> *"overall, TECs remain heavily dependent on the voluntary and charitable sector, in providing not only for trainees with disabilities and special training needs but also for trainees from the black and ethnic minorities". Page 11.*

> *"Thus, for example, comprising the two largest category of providers in the sample (voluntary and private) we can see that 35 per cent of voluntary providers (taking the least able trainees) had increased training weeks delivered (ie. volume) by more than 10 per cent, but only 8 per cent of them had an increase in YT funding of more than 10 per cent. The private sector, by contrast, (who were clearly for the most part with trainees of higher than average ability and lower cost to train) contained a smaller proportion of providers whose volumes had increased significantly (21 per cent) despite a larger proportion whose funding level had done so (15 per cent). Thus ... the date does not obviously support the claim (made by some TECs surveyed for example) of generally lower productivity and value for money among voluntary/specialist providers than amongst commercial providers". Pages 44/45.*

We leave the Committee to deliberate on a system which gives greater financial incentives (from public funds) Klein to commercial organisations dealing with higher ability groups, than is given to those voluntary organisations dealing with the most disadvantaged.

F.   *The ability to pick up improper behaviour—both financial and non financial on the part of either the TEC or those to whom it contracts.*

Our view is that financial impropriety in relation to those with whom the TEC contracts as well as the TEC itself, is well covered since the collapse of South Thames TEC.

In practice, however, this has meant an unheralded number of audit checks; the establishment of regional offices by the National Council for Vocational Qualification to monitor fraudulent claims; TECs still adding to and being cautious about their level of reserves.

All of this has detracted from the focus on delivering quality training to meet local economic needs, particularly for the most disadvantaged in the labour market.

"Quality" was defined by TECs in the IES research as being related to a training suppliers ability to deliver qualifications, jobs or the Investors in People standard. All these form the basis on which TECs receive their income. Clearly, the cheaper and faster they can be delivered, the "better" the performance of the TEC on the league tables.

We finish by concluding that the price being extracted is the continuing demise of the voluntary sector and the increasing marginalisation of those they seek to help—people who cost more to train and who take longer to produce a given "outcome".

The situation is intolerable and cannot continue. We hope the Committee will explore the reasons why so many TECs have failed to be accountable to all those within their local communities. We do not believe this was an intended consequence but can no longer maintain a situation where on the one hand the DFEE tells us adequate funds are given to TECs and on the other TECs saying the funding is inadequate.

Opening statement of the Chartered Institute of Housing

The Chartered Institute of Housing is the professional organisation representing all those working in housing. Our purpose is to take a leading and strategic role in promoting the provision and management of good quality, affordable housing for all.

The Chartered Institute has 12,800 individual members working for local authorities, housing associations and within the private sector.

Introduction

The Chartered Institute of Housing is delighted to accept your invitation to appear before the Committee on Standards in Public Life and we hope that you have found our earlier written evidence about housing associations useful.

We believe that your investigations could have a number of positive outcomes for housing associations in England, Scotland and Wales and it would be particularly helpful if the final report could:

- build on the recent work of the National Federation of Housing Associations into the governance of housing associations;

- raise public awareness about the important work that housing associations are currently doing in housing people in need, and the value of the service, that many dedicated and unpaid voluntary board members are currently giving to the public;

- objectively scrutinise the present systems of accountability in housing associations and identify any areas where there is potential for conflict or abuse;

- make recommendations, around principles of good practice, which associations could adapt to their precise circumstances.

In this opening statement we have concentrated on the issues raised in your letter of 30 October 1995 as we understand that you particularly want to hear the Institute's views on these areas.

1. Regulation of housing associations: nature and quality

The Corporation's regulatory role

The Housing Corporation, Tai Cymru and Scottish Homes regulate the activities of registered housing associations through powers set out largely in the Housing Act 1974 and amended by subsequent Acts (the principal powers in England and Wales being those contained in the Housing Associations Act 1985 and amended by the Housing Act 1988).

The regulatory powers of the Corporation are strong and wide and whilst they include responsibility for monitoring and assessing the management performance of housing associations, they have traditionally concentrated on:

- the registration of housing associations;

- the allocation of capital and revenue grants;

- housing association financial probity; and

- housing association financial viability.

It should be acknowledged that the financial probity and viability of associations is largely a confidential matter between associations and their regulators.

The recent Housing White Paper has raised the profile of the delivery of the social housing product which is a critical issue for the Government, the general public and all involved in the provision of social housing. The Institute is concerned to ensure that it is generally recognised that the delivery of the social housing product by housing associations and other potential social landlords must as a minimum include full and consistent consideration of the following issues:

- meeting local housing needs;

- development standards;

- management standards;

- rent levels and affordability;

- the appropriateness of development; and

- procurement costs.

We believe that the monitoring of housing management needs to receive more prominence in future, particularly as the Government encourages more diversity of social housing providers, including profit-making companies. It will be particularly important to ensure the delivery of effective management on a continuing basis, given the pressures on rents (for non-profit making bodies) and profit considerations for the "new"landlords. Whilst development standards are determined when a scheme is initiated, management standards can change considerably over the life of a project.

It is for this reason that we have said that it is worthwhile exploring new ideas for implementing the Corporation's regulatory role. At present, standards of social housing management are not set consistently. For example, the Audit Commission and the DOE set standards and assess performance in local authorities, whilst the Housing Corporation monitors housing associations. The Audit Commission is currently working with the Housing Corporation and housing associations in England to introduce a system of performance indicators for housing associations and is trying to develop an objective system to compare and monitor performance. However, they are having great difficulty in devising an acceptable method of comparing housing associations with other social housing providers such as local authorities.

For information, the Committee may wish to note that by comparison local authorities have been subject to a performance monitoring and an Audit Commission comparison regime for a number of years. However, we consider that objective comparisons will become even more difficult as the diversity of social landlords increases and we believe that it is logical that there is one agreed standard for all social landlords. To facilitate this process, the CIH has specified common standards in its Housing Management Standards Manual and has urged the DOE and the Housing Corporation to adopt these as a means of enabling cross service comparison.

It also makes sense to look at the scope for building on the new role which many local authorities have had to develop as clients in managing housing management contracts under the Government's Compulsory Competitive Tendering (CCT) regime. This does in some instances involve monitoring housing associations who are running such contracts. Furthermore, as Local Housing Companies develop, local authorities will have a contractual relationship with managers of social housing organisations to which they have transferred their housing stock.

Whatever happens to the Corporation's regulatory role, there is a need to consider how it relates to the similar and parallel role of local authorities. One way in which this could be resolved would be if the local authority was, in agreed cases, the first recipient of the housing associations monitoring information and compiled it on behalf of the Corporation as regulator. This is no more than they may increasingly be doing in relation to housing managers running CCT contracts in their area. Such a proposal would also address concerns expressed by local authorities that they are better placed than the Housing Corporation to monitor local delivery of service. The Institute is concerned that moves towards greater reliance on desk-top monitoring practices by the regulator may exacerbate this problem.

We believe that this proposal would have several benefits, including:

● assisting the regulator to implement its increasing responsibilities to monitor the delivery of the social housing product;

● enabling the regulator to have access to more detailed information at a local level;

● increasing local accountability by enhancing the local authorities' strategic and enabling role and improving the housing information database which local authorities currently compile in order to advise the Housing Corporation of its investment priorities; and

● improving relationships between the regulator, housing associations and local authorities by improving communication and the flow of information between them.

In suggesting this as a possible way forward to address perceived tensions between local authorities, housing associations and the Housing Corporation, we wish to emphasise that this proposal does not in any way indicate CIH support for local authority control of housing associations.

Location of the regulatory and monitoring roles
We recognise that the Committee is not directly investigating the role of the Housing Corporation, Tai Cymru or Scottish Homes, but we believe that it is important for the Committee to consider the debate about the appropriate location of the regulatory and monitoring role for housing associations.

The Institute has previously argued that there should be a national standards agency responsible for performance, monitoring and regulation of associations and local authorities. Ideally we consider that there should be a distinct separation or an arms' length relationship between the monitoring and regulatory and the strategic and funding roles to ensure that conflicts of interest do not arise.

Given that the Corporation's regulatory role is growing rapidly, we consider that it is appropriate to examine the scope for delegating some of these duties in relation to the delivery of the social housing product. We have already proposed in relation to Local Housing Companies that local authorities could perform some of the monitoring responsibilities on behalf of the Housing Corporation within previously agreed parameters. There may be merit in considering this suggestion in relation to housing associations. However, we do not consider that it would be appropriate for the Housing Corporation's role in regulating and monitoring financial probity and viability of housing associations to be delegated.

Need for regional committees for the Housing Corporation in England

We believe that it is not only imperative that housing associations, but also the Housing Corporation, Tai Cymru and Scottish Homes are actively able to demonstrate their accountability to the communities which they serve. We believe that they could respond to demands for more local accountability by local authorities by establishing regional fora on which local authorities and other interested parties could be represented.

2. Accountability of housing associations to stakeholders, including openness

Many of the issues of the openness and accountability of housing associations have been well covered by the recent NFHA Governance Inquiry. We believe that the NFHA's Code of Governance is an excellent code of good practice and we were very disappointed that the Housing Corporation has decided not to incorporate it within the regulatory framework in England. Whilst we acknowledge that some associations have already made rigorous efforts to embrace the recommendations contained within the code, we are concerned that it may not be fully implemented by all housing associations and social landlords unless it becomes statutory.

Given that the Housing Corporation in England has not required associations to embrace the code, we believe that it would be helpful for the NFHA to issue targets for compliance with the Code's recommendations by housing associations. We also believe that it would be helpful if the NFHA could define the stakeholders to whom it believes that associations should be accountable.

In our earlier written evidence, we emphasised the critical importance of an association's relationship with the local authorities. We believe that many of the criticisms of perceived accountability are not actually issues of accountability but are about communication. We believe it would be helpful if associations examined the extent to which information could be more openly shared within the wider community.

Finally, we also consider that greater accountability to stakeholders in the community can be achieved in a number of different ways, such as:

General
- the use of evidence of past performance such as housing association business plans or agreements between housing associations and local authorities;

- future proposals as expressed in consultation over revised business plans;

- performance indicators.

Tenant consultation
- regular meetings between housing associations and democratically elected tenant groups or customer panels;

- the democratic election of tenant representatives onto housing association boards.

Consultations with local authorities
- greater consultation with local authorities;

- the use of Social Housing Agreements;

- greater involvement of housing associations by local authorities in the Department of the Environment annual round of Housing Investment Programme meetings;

- continued consultation of local authorities by the regulator about housing associations' annual bids for allocations of the Annual Development Programme funds and revenue funding.

Wider consultation of other organisations
- Investigation of the potential greater involvement of other organisations such as health authorities, schools and voluntary organisations.

3. Recruitment of and responsibilities of management committees, including lines of responsibility between committee and staff

We believe that the NFHA Code of Governance deals adequately with many of the issues of recruitment and responsibilities of management committees. However, as we have previously reported, we do not accept the NFHA's view that individual housing associations should be able to determine whether or not it is appropriate for their chief executive to sit on their board of management. We consider that as there will inevitably be difficulties from time to time over strategic direction, it is essential that lines of accountability are not blurred and that the role of the chief executive as manager, policy interpreter and adviser to the board is not confused with the responsibility of the board to provide strategic direction.

We believe that there is also a need for a balance in the renewal and continuity of the appointment of new board members and think that it is important that tenant representatives are democratically elected rather than selected.

4. The conflict of interest regime for housing associations

The present framework for regulating the conduct and probity of associations is mainly derived from Sections 13-15 of the Housing Associations Act 1985. Section 15 prohibits staff, board members and relatives, together with any firms with which they have a defined connection, from deriving direct or indirect benefits from any aspect of the associations' work. It has undoubtedly served the housing association sector well, but it may now be partially out-dated and in need of minor reform. In addition, many housing organisations including the NFHA have argued that the existing framework acts as a disincentive to tenant involvement.

We agree with this view and consider that Section 15 should be reassessed and if necessary partially reformed, but do not believe that it should be removed in its entirety. We would also recommend that the regulation of housing associations moves towards a statutory declaration based framework similar to that operated in local government. It is essential that all associations should keep a publicly accessible register which records the interests of both board members and staff.

5. Procedures for responding to internal and external complaints

The Housing Corporation Tenants Guarantee in England requires associations to have and publicise policies and procedures for dealing with internal complaints about their service to tenants and applicants. These should be accessible and include an appeals procedure to the committee of management or a group of members not involved in the complaint.

Tenants should also be made aware of their right to make external complaints to the Housing Association Tenants Ombudsman Service (HATOS) and be provided with information about how to do so.

In June 1995, the HATOS published an analysis of 164 housing associations' complaints procedures. They found that although most associations had staged procedures culminating in appeal to the governing body or one of its sub-committees, most of the procedures failed to inform complainants about their right to take unresolved complaints to HATOS.

We are concerned about the extent and vigour with which some associations apply the Housing Corporation's regulations in practice. We do not believe that the system of annual desktop monitoring operated by the Housing Corporation always provides sufficient incentive for housing associations to rigorously implement its recommendations of good practice. For example, although the latest Housing Corporation performance monitoring form (HAR14) states that "housing associations must operate fair and accessible complaints procedures", it merely asks associations to tick a "yes/no"box to indicate whether or not they have notified all tenants, licensees and leaseholders about the HATOS service.

We do not consider that this approach to monitoring is rigorous enough especially when you consider that the information returned on the HAR14 actually forms the basis of the Housing Corporation's assessment of the performance of individual associations.

Furthermore, despite the Government's intention to put the HATOS on an independent footing from the Housing Corporation, we remain concerned that the Tenants' Guarantee only provides housing association tenants with contractual and statutory rights.

Opening statement of Leicester Newarke Housing Association Limited

1. Housing associations are a diverse group of organisations. They are also undergoing a period of rapid change partly as a result of the Housing Act 1988. Management committees and staff are having to respond to the changing environment in which they operate.

2. As a result, for housing associations, classification categories like "public", "private"or "voluntary sector"are of little value. Housing associations now have characteristics which fit all three and the situation is changing all the time. It is debatable to what extent the Committee on Standards in Public Life is relevant to their position but their "accountability"is now a key issue.

3. Housing associations already have to "account for their actions"to a large (and increasing) number of stakeholders. An important objective is to ensure that each stakeholder has an appropriate opportunity to influence the association's activities. In other words, accountability should reflect a fair balance between stakeholders.

4. Currently, the regulatory requirements of the Housing Corporation are backed up by powers of enforcement. In a number of areas the requirements leave far too little room for discretion. A recent case in point is the detailed prescription of repair time targets and compensation figures under the new "Right to Repair". In addition there is considerable bias toward financial regulatory mechanisms suggesting the Housing Corporation does not have faith in the ability of mature housing associations to manage their own financial affairs.

5. Some have argued for the separation of the funding and regulatory powers of the Housing Corporation though it is not always clear why. There is a degree of tension between the Corporation's regulatory function and its overriding performance objective of "committing the Approved Development Programme". In the past it is likely that this preoccupation has conspired with the development-led approach of some larger associations to result in poor

development decisions. We believe the Corporation should lessen its dependence on the development performance of a few large associations by allocating to a far broader range of associations in terms of size and client groups.

6. Associations should account for their actions to other stakeholders who do not have the "teeth"of the Housing Corporation, especially tenants, local communities and Local Authorities. The last of these has some regulation and enforcement powers in the form of planning and environmental health legislation, and can guide development also through its enabling role. But much of the influence of all three groups comes via moral pressure and the active willingness of associations to consult and listen. A fear of condemnation by the Housing Association Tenants' Ombudsman has recently added to the influence of tenants but the Housing Corporation's sponsorship of this service is perhaps less convincing than its concern to maintain the confidence of private lenders in the sector. The suggestion at the end of Para.5 above in itself would ensure greater accountability to tenants and communities because smaller associations are inherently more accountable. Consideration could perhaps be given to the suggestion that larger "trans-county"associations, beyond the influence of tenants and communities, ought to be subject to a tighter regulatory regime than small associations, or even broken up through a form of "anti-trust"legislation.

7. We urge that a focused review of the Housing Corporation's regulatory role is undertaken with the objective of achieving a fairer balance between the interests of all stakeholders, while reducing the level of detailed prescription in all areas.

8. In relation to the recruitment and responsibilities of management committee members, the key issue is to ensure an effective decision-making process. There have been well-publicised cases where decision-making and control has been flawed but these seem to be no more frequent than in other areas of private and public sector endeavour. Moreover, during a period of rapid transition it is surprising there have been so few cases of inadequate decision-making procedures.

9. Housing associations should not be complacent. There is a continuing need to ensure that management committees have an appropriate and broad range of knowledge and skills. Recruitment practices must help to achieve this aim. At present a range of methods are used, including advertisements, "word of mouth"and co-option of tenant representatives and nominees from partner agencies. We believe the National Federation of Housing Associations should actively recruit names to local registers of interested persons with appropriate skills from which housing associations could top-up their committees as and when necessary. "Federal"committees made up of delegated representatives of different interests would be a recipe for conflict and disaster. Payment of members is not necessary though modest compensation for time spent, on a flat rate basis, might assist broader recruitment.

10. In relation to the "conflict of interest regime" we would argue there are no significant problems with "Section 15".

11. On the topic of procedures for dealing with complaints we support the Housing Association Tenants' Ombudsman Service working as intended as a back-up to the operation of associations' own policies and procedures for dealing with complaints. These must be well-publicised among tenants.

Opening statement of the Focus Housing Group

1. Introduction

1.1. Housing Associations have altered totally in public profile, importance, and style of operation since 1988. Prior to the 1988 Housing Act, there had been relatively little attention paid in public to governance issues around Housing Associations. As Housing Associations received a major increase in the resources available to them between 1988 and today, there has been a major upswing in interest in the way Associations operate. The Housing Corporation has always maintained an interest in the management arrangements of Associations, but the number of new issues which have arisen since 1988 is legion, and both Associations and the Housing Corporation have had to adapt accordingly. It is against this background that the written submission from Focus was put forward, and the key points I wish to address are set out. I have tried to address both the points the Committee wishes to major on, and our own key areas of interest.

2. Regulation of Housing Associations

2.1 In my view, the regulatory framework of Associations is quite tight, and Associations operate under a fairly strict regulatory regime. I was a member of the Advisory Panel which oversaw the Joseph Rowntree report on Performance Monitoring carried out by Professor Klein and Patricia Day of the University of Bath. That report found that the effectiveness of regulation by the Housing Corporation was quite high compared to other regulatory frameworks studied by the University, and whilst there were weaknesses, the foundation was sound. Since that date there have been many changes in the regulatory framework. The most important of which is the changed relationship between desk-top monitoring and visits to Housing Associations. There is a very delicate balance to be maintained between arm's-length regulation and close regulation of bodies. In my view, it is essential that the Corporation retains a close relationship with the Associations in order to have a "feel" for the way Associations are operating.

2.2 One issue which is worth mentioning is the need for a degree of assessment of excellence in regulation. It seems to me if larger sums of public money are to be entrusted to Associations, then certain standards of excellence should be required and Capital Funding be linked to this. The tendency over the years has been to have a minimum line of acceptability with allocations, than solely linked to other factors. This does not seem to be the best way to encourage improvement in standards.

3. Accountability of Housing Associations to stakeholders

3.1 Housing Associations are very conscious of the fact that they are not accountable to others through the ballot box. Since the publication of the findings of the National Federation of Housing Associations Governance Enquiry, many Associations have accelerated their attempts to be seen to be accountable to Stakeholders. In particular, Associations have attempted to ensure that they are seen to be accountable to the Housing Corporation, Local Authorities, their Tenants and the public. Associations like Focus have adopted clear strategies to ensure that they are accountable to these Stakeholders and that their operation can be explained and communicated to others.

3.2 One of the most difficult areas for Housing Associations is the lack of clarity about the relationship with Local Authorities. Local Authorities are the strategic housing authority, and we are required to work closely with them in providing Social Housing schemes. Yet in relation to our performance, there is no clear method of doing this. This leads, of course, to many informal systems of assessment. Associations are required to publish large amounts of information about themselves, both through Annual Reports, regular reports to Tenants and information supplied to Local Authority. However, it would probably be better if there was more standardised information made public, and a standard code of openness of process. Associations are having more Performance Indicators published, and this is likely to help.

4. Recruitment and responsibilities of management committees

4.1 Management Committees are elected by Shareholders, and therefore the choice of Management Committee Membership is the result of this process. However, there are weaknesses in the Shareholding aspect of Housing Association Governance, which I will return to, which makes this a very flawed process. Traditionally, this has been one of the weak areas of Housing Association conduct, where local networks have often provided the basis for recruitment. Following the Governance Enquiry, many Associations have moved to remedy this. In Focus, the quality of Committee Members is high, and there is no difficulty in recruiting Committee Members for all our Committees, including the Board of Management. Following the Governance Report, Focus has decided to establish a pool of potential Committee Members who will be assessed against the skills and ethnic and gender balances of our Committees, and where recruitment will be targeted to meet identified deficiencies. We have also allowed for an increased number of co-options to allow this to happen. We are approaching Stakeholder organisations to help establish this, and through a selection process which is not dissimilar to the appointment of Staff, to ensure that we have Committee Members who are not members of a club, but who have the requisite skills to help run a major business. The line between the role of Management Boards and Staff, I think, is reasonably clear, and the need for Boards and Committees to set direction whilst Officers implement programmes is well understood. One of the key elements is the provision of accurate data to Committees to allow them to monitor the effectiveness of their decisions, and this is a constant source of monitoring within Focus. The idea of the Chief Executive being on the Board has been discussed with Focus; and was found to be an issue with very little support.

5. Conflict of interest

5.1 The Section 15 regime within Housing Associations is a very tight regime and restricts the benefits available to Staff and Committee Members very rigidly. It is probably one of the least understood aspects of Housing Association work and, in some ways, a great protection against misuse of power. However, the tightness of the regime does often make operating in a commercially sensible way difficult, and there is no doubt that aspects of Section 15 need reviewing.

5.2 Nevertheless, as Associations occupy this strange hybrid position between the public and the private sector, and are responsible both for large sums of public money and large amounts of public private loan, there can be no doubt that stringent controls over personal behaviour are needed.

6. Complaints

6.1. As the profile of Associations, and the size of their stockholdings has increased, the need for more effective Complaints Procedures is clear. Focus is one Housing Association that received an adverse report from the Housing Associations' Ombudsman Service, and understands the problem of an ineffective procedure. Much greater publicity has been given to the need for effective Complaints Procedures with Associations and we are required to publicise the existence of the Ombudsman Service. As the pressure from the Housing Corporation in this area, and with the continued development of the Ombudsman Service, it is likely that the accountability of Associations to their customers, and to the public at large, will be greatly enhanced. It is certainly Focus' experience that this has been the case.

7. Aspects of governance from Focus' point of view—a summary

7.1 It is essential that Housing Associations have a formal approach to governance, which can be communicated publicly, relating to all of the issues set out above. In order to persuade the public of the accountability and effectiveness of our operation, a simple and communicable structure is essential.

7.2 Associations must have an open operation, this means that the public, Tenants, the Housing Corporation and Local Authorities must have access to the information they need to assess whether or not the Association is performing well. Focus, like many Associations, is probably two-thirds of the way down the road where improvements can always be made. As I said in my submission, we are hampered by the lack of public understanding about Housing Associations in pursuing this.

7.3 Associations must have commitment to Stakeholders. This means that there must be a formal commitment to Tenants (which has been enshrined in Focus' Constitution). There must be a commitment to the Local Authority and other key partners, such as Health Authorities. Third, there must be a commitment to the community in which schemes are placed and no sense of "absentee landlordism". Lastly, there should be a commitment to the public in terms of information. This last commitment is more of a collective responsibility than the other three.

8. Shareholders

8.1. I mentioned earlier, Management Committees are elected by Shareholders. The problem Housing Associations face is that the Shareholder has such a minimal interest in the Association (a one pound share) that the level of commitment, responsibility and involvement can be close to nil. It is therefore possible for small groups of Shareholders to control the Association. In some cases, this can mean that the Association can be made a self-perpetuating oligarchy where the Shareholders and Committee Members are the same, or alternatively, those Associations can be placed at the mercy of a small number of Shareholders with a vested interest. Focus has had a particular problem in relation to ex-employees as Shareholders, which it is attempting to deal with through its Constitution. However, it is essential that as we put more and more responsibility on the shoulders of Board Members, who have to make a major commitment of time, energy, training, and legal responsibility, that more clarity is introduced into the Shareholding nature of Housing Associations. The Constitution of Shareholding groups should be made clearer, and their powers are both more circumvented and appropriate to the current situation.

TUESDAY 5 DECEMBER 1995

Members Present:

The Rt Hon Lord Nolan (Chairman)

Sir Clifford Boulton GCB
The Rt Hon Tom King CH MP
The Rt Hon Peter Shore MP

The Rt Hon Lord Thomson of
  Monifieth KT DL
Sir William Utting CB
Dame Anne Warburton DCVO CMG

Witnesses:

Sir John Bourn, Comptroller and Auditor General, Lew Hughes, Assistant Auditor General, and Caroline Mawhood, Director of Corporate Policy, National Audit Office

Robin Geldard, President, and Ron Taylor CBE, Director-General, Association of British Chambers of Commerce

Sir David Hancock KCB, Chairman of Inquiry into Housing Association Governance, and Executive Director of Hambros Bank Limited

Peter Cooke, Deputy Chairman, and Anthony Mayer, Chief Executive, Housing Corporation

639. LORD NOLAN: Good morning. Our evidence today covers both housing associations and TECs, but we begin with a wider view by welcoming an old friend, Sir John Bourn, the Comptroller and Auditor General. He is accompanied by Lew Hughes and Caroline Mawhood. Lew Hughes is the Assistant Auditor General and Caroline Mawhood is the Director of Corporate Policy at the National Audit Office. They are of course all specialists in the areas that we are covering in this part of our inquiry. Sir John and his team were very helpful to us in the preparation of our first report and it is a pleasure to hear from them again.

Our second group of witnesses come from the Association of British Chambers of Commerce. They are Robin Geldard, the president of the association, its director-general, Ron Taylor, and the chief executive of Glasgow Chamber of Commerce, Geoff Runcie. They will be concentrating on TECs.

We will then hear from Sir David Hancock, who chaired the recent review of governance of housing associations under the auspices of the National Federation of Housing Associations. He is of course well known to many of us as a distinguished public servant, having been the Permanent Secretary at the former Department of Education and Science between 1985 and 1989.

Finally, we shall be taking evidence from the Housing Corporation, the regulator and funder of the housing association movement. It is represented by Peter Cooke, the deputy chairman, and Anthony Mayer, the chief executive.

Now, Sir John and companions, thank you for coming in for your second innings. I believe that you have prepared a few remarks that you are going to make before we go into the questions. Is that right?

SIR JOHN BOURN, LEW HUGHES, AND CAROLINE MAWHOOD

SIR JOHN BOURN (Comptroller and Auditor General): That is right, Chairman, and thank you very much for your welcome to myself and my colleagues and your kind remarks about our contribution to your previous activities. Indeed, perhaps I could just start by

making reference to one of the recommendations that you made in your last report, because I think it is very germane to the local spending bodies that you are now reviewing. That is the recommendation that you made in paragraph 107 of your first report, where you said:

"We believe, in principle, that the propriety of all public expenditure should be capable of review by the appropriate public auditing body. We see much merit in the Comptroller and Auditor General being granted inspection rights over all pubic expenditure. Where such rights do not already exist, this could be achieved through contract terms or grant conditions attached to public funding. Care would be needed to ensure that no unnecessary bureaucracy would be introduced and, in particular, that duplication of effort by different auditors would be minimised."

I take that, Chairman, very much as a guiding principle in relation to my concern for the three sets of bodies we are talking about this morning, because I think that I could do good work for the public interest and for Parliament if I had the inspection rights that you set out in that paragraph and I was able to exercise them over those three sets of bodies. We would already have inspection rights over many of them, and I think that the extension over all three categories, arranged in the way that your committee recommended in your previous report, would very much meet the needs. This could be arranged, as you say it should be arranged, without extra bureaucracy, without creating extra sets of accounts, without employing extra sets of auditors, because our inspection work does not require bodies to maintain further records than they already retain. I think that the work that we have been able to do, for example in the health service and in the education service, where we have exercised inspection rights and brought before Parliament matters of public concern which have been acted on, has been useful. So, Chairman, my introductory remarks would be to suggest that the approach that you commended in your last report should be applied to this range of bodies, which, as I say, could be done straightforwardly, easily, without extra bureaucracy and without employing extra sets of auditors.

640. LORD NOLAN: Thank you very much. There does seem to be a curious imbalance in the present

situation. How did it occur? Was it accidental or was it the product of deep thought?

JOHN BOURN: Chairman, I think it was accidental. I think these bodies were set up at different times, different considerations were in the minds of those who set them up, and one can understand, by looking at the genesis of each body, how things came to be done as they were done. What your Committee is doing of course is looking at the matter in the round, on the basis of a number of years' experience, and saying "We have this range of bodies. How could financial matters and matters of public conduct be better attended to?" You are able to take stock of where we have got to now, so I think past history is the history of variation and now is the opportunity, as it were, to apply some principle, which, to repeat, should be the principle you have already enunciated.

641. LORD NOLAN: Can I safely assume, Sir John, that you have put these points to the Treasury Review Team, who are looking at the matter at the moment?

JOHN BOURN: We are putting these points to them, yes, Chairman.

642. LORD NOLAN: How are they getting on? Do we know when they are going to report?

JOHN BOURN: I do not know.

CAROLINE MAWHOOD (Director of Corporate Policy, National Audit Office): I think that they are likely to be reporting to Ministers in the first instance around Christmas time, but I am not entirely sure of that, and then I think the intention is to bring out a consultation document.

LORD NOLAN: I am told that they have promised to keep us in touch with the dates when they are likely to, so to speak, go public, but at any rate you are in communication with them and are putting your views to them.

JOHN BOURN: As you say, Chairman, we put evidence to them on a range of matters.

643. LORD NOLAN: Yes. One big area which you do not cover at the moment is individual housing associations.

JOHN BOURN: Yes.

644. LORD NOLAN: One view that has been expressed to us is that, many of them being small voluntary bodies, to bring them within the system of review of the National Audit Office would amount to an excessive degree of regulation. Do you share that view or would you confine yourself to the bigger associations, or do you think it should be across the board?

JOHN BOURN: I do not share that view, Chairman, because I think the point that has been made to you misunderstands the nature of our inspection activities. These are not great weights placed on organisations. As I say, it does not require them to maintain any further records; it does not require them to employ any more people. Of course in the nature of things, unless a particular reason has come to public attention which would require us to have a look, the approach to the

exercise of inspection rights is not to visit everybody over whom we have these rights every year, but to do it on a phased basis, so that we would, over a period of years, visit each body. I think that this would not weigh heavily upon them. There is sometimes a particular advantage in being able to visit a small body, because experience shows that sometimes it is the small bodies, out of inexperience sometimes, who have gone adrift in the handling of money, the appointment of people and the management of even quite simple contracts. So I think it would be a good idea for us to have these inspection rights over housing associations, which would be managed in ways which, as I say, did not impose a heavy burden at all. Other areas where our rights might be extended of course are the LECs in Scotland and there might perhaps be a rounding out of our rights as far as the TECs are concerned. In the education sector we do have inspection rights which are comprehensive and adequate.

645. TOM KING: Do you have it on all the grant-maintained schools?

JOHN BOURN: Yes, we do.

646. LORD NOLAN: I would like to come on to grant-maintained schools in a few moments, because you do express some reservations about the position there, but I wonder if, for the moment, I could keep to the general situation and ask you this. I think our present feeling on the basis of the evidence we have heard so far is that, while there have been isolated cases of maladministration and sometimes misconduct in each of the types of public spending body that we are looking at, there is no evidence of a failure across the board or a failure in the systems of widespread maladministration or under-performance. Would that be your view so far as you have been able to study the individual bodies?

JOHN BOURN: Yes, it would be my view, Chairman. I think that, if you take the system as a whole, the standards are high. People are working honestly and effectively to do their best. In the nature of things sometimes human affairs go adrift, sometimes out of carelessness, sometimes out of inexperience, sometimes, one has to say, out of deliberate intentions to deceive, but I think the overall standard is high and the case that I put before you is one, in a sense, of insurance and one that would assist in the preservation of generally high standards.

647. LORD NOLAN: Yes. We are aiming, would you say in general, to make what is basically a system founded on a generally satisfactory standard of honesty better, more open to the public knowledge and inspection, which in itself will help, one hopes, to improve public confidence in the way their money is being spent? That, I am putting to you, is what we might be seeing as our task at the moment. Is that how you would see it?

JOHN BOURN: Yes, I would, Chairman. I think that that is, if I may say so, how it should be looked at. The kind of extension, for example in my own sphere, that I have indicated to you I think would fit in very well with that. It would be a method of enhancing public confidence, where we have, as I have said, exercised inspection rights and drawn matters to public attention. Certainly Parliament has been pleased to see this, and people have, I think, taken some reassurance from the knowledge that we were there and were able to do that, and draw public attention to matters that needed looking at.

648. LORD NOLAN: And to the complaint that we have heard from some bodies about being over-audited you say that, if they are, this certainly would not add to their burdens as far as you are concerned?

JOHN BOURN: That is right, Chairman, because what we are talking about here is of course not auditing in the sense of requiring the annual examination of financial documents. One is talking about the right to inspect papers and records and to talk to the people concerned. So what we are proposing certainly does not add anything in the way of an audit burden.

649. LORD NOLAN: It would take time, and the question would be then whether the time was well spent. What you are saying, I think, is that, with the experience you can bring to bear on the problems of the organisations concerned, it would be time well spent.

JOHN BOURN: That is right, Chairman. Of course in most cases when we carry out inspections there is nothing to be brought to public attention. But what we are able to do when we visit a body is share a wider experience with them, draw attention to difficulties that may have arisen in their areas, not pointing the finger at other institutions but indicating general problems, shall we say, about the letting of contracts or the arrangements for appointing people. So we really share experience and draw people's attention to good practice, so that often the benefit of the inspection is the sharing of a wider range of knowledge.

650. LORD NOLAN: Do you think that the generally high standard of conduct and morale rests on the voluntary ethos in these bodies? Or, to put it another way, is there a case for paying board members, if only to compensate them for the loss of earning opportunities elsewhere?

JOHN BOURN: I think, Chairman, that standards of public morality do rest on the springs of action of each individual. I do not think that you will induce moral conduct by requirements. That has to spring from the individual, and springs from their education, their training, their experience of life. It can be reinforced by settled procedures, by such matters as codes of conduct, by training, by education, by, if you like, looking at where matters have gone adrift. All these things can reinforce the springs to moral conduct. On the question of whether, particularly, people should be paid when they take positions on the boards of institutions of this kind, I think there are cases where that is justified, because I think that sometimes people are making a contribution at the expense of their income and their families. It is good that they should come forward and do public work, and while people should not be able to make a fortune out of this voluntary commitment, it is worth looking at the extent to which some kind of compensation should be available for some of them, who would otherwise suffer hardship.

651. LORD NOLAN: Thank you very much. Now can we come to some of the more specific points? You mention the inability of the Secretary of State to intervene in the higher education sector and you make a number of references—I think it is five in all—to what went wrong at Huddersfield and the difficulty that arose over dealing with it in a prompt and expeditious manner. Is this right, that in the Huddersfield problem you were struck by the absence of a power to dismiss in the Secretary of State, as one of the factors?

JOHN BOURN: Yes, Chairman, we were struck by that and we drew it to the attention of the Public Accounts Committee, who made reference to it in their report, in the sense that you had a situation where the Secretary of State did not have the power in the higher education sector that he did in the further education sector and the grant-maintained schools, so there was a mismatch. The Public Accounts Committee, when this was drawn to their attention, made the recommendation in their report that it would be advantageous to introduce this power, so that there would be symmetry across the education sector. Our reason for pointing it out was essentially the difference of arrangements across the sector, but from our point of view the value and interest of that particular case was that it was an example of the exercise of inspection rights: we were not the auditor of the university, but we did have the inspection rights; we were able to exercise them. We were able to draw to the attention of Parliament, the funding body and the Department a state of affairs which was seen as worrying, and action was then taken. I think this was a good example of what we could do without, as I say, requiring the university to have a vast bureaucracy or keep extra accounts or papers, or anything of that kind.

652. LORD NOLAN: There is clearly a lack of symmetry in the Secretary of State not having the same power over universities as he does over colleges of further education and other bodies, but it would seen as very strong medicine by some of the larger universities, would it not, to put the Secretary of State in a position where he could dismiss board members? Is there, do you think, a sufficient body of evidence to justify that?

JOHN BOURN: Well, Chairman, you put me in the slight difficulty that it is a recommendation from the Committee of Public Accounts, and it would be difficult for me to comment on or question what they have put before the government, and they are the views and recommendations of the Members of Parliament on the Committee. For myself, I would say that it is a great prize of public life in this country that universities are seen as independent bodies and it is important that they should feel that they can conduct their affairs and carry out their academic and other work without constantly looking over their shoulder. But for us the point that emerged at Huddersfield was that too much was decided behind the scenes. It would have been advantageous for the university to have been able to show that these matters were in the open and that decisions were reached openly, and for everybody to see what had been decided. That seemed to me the most important thing that had come out of our inspection.

653. LORD NOLAN: The danger of the confidentiality clause?

JOHN BOURN: Yes.

654. LORD NOLAN: Do you link that with the case that has been put in many areas for having confidential lines of complaint from members of staff to someone suitable within an organisation, so that matters can be more easily brought to light without adverse reactions against the complainer?

JOHN BOURN: Yes, Chairman, I think there is advantage in having some procedure by which people who feel there is some matter which needs attention can draw attention to this and feel that their own position is safeguarded to some degree. In codes of conduct there is a great advantage in providing arrangements and making clear to people what these arrangements are, that there is somebody to whom they can go if they are seriously worried. At the same time I think it is important that, when people are seriously worried, while of course opportunities for confidentiality should be provided, they should, for the most part, be prepared to stand up and be counted. We have had many cases where people at low levels in organisations have been brave: they have been concerned about contracting procedures or whatever it is and they have spoken out. It is important that people should be able to do that and should be encouraged to do it. At the same time you need the reinforcement of confidentiality. One needs to have this in a well set out way, because you do not want to set up secret lines of complaint, through which people can, as it were, seek to inform on their immediate superiors or their colleagues. We do not want to re-erect in this country the world of the KGB, where it was always possible to inform on absolutely everybody and create great dossiers about people, which could then be used by the authorities to blackmail them. One has to be very careful and one has to know what the arrangements for confidential reporting are. I think they are, as I say, useful and helpful, but they should be clearly laid down and people should understand how they work.

655. LORD NOLAN: They need, do they not, very firm and sensitive handling, involving firmness over discouragement of malicious complaints?

JOHN BOURN: Yes.

656. LORD NOLAN: In paragraph 19 of your report you said:

"The office found that the quality of external audit at grant-maintained schools was variable and the Committee of Public Accounts recommended that external audit's role should be reviewed by the Funding Agency for Schools. The National Audit Office are assisting this review and new guidance to external auditors will be issued later this year."

I wonder if you could expand a bit on that. What was the chief concern over the quality of external audit?

JOHN BOURN: Chairman, could I ask Mr Hughes, who conducted this work for us, to deal with that point?

LEW HUGHES (Assistant Auditor General): Thank you. Chairman, there were a number of dimensions to that. The first was that a significant proportion of schools audited were audited by a firm who only audited one school, and therefore were not versed in matters scholastic. Secondly, there was a very large range in the fees charged for individual audits. On secondary schools, for example, they varied from under £1,000 to over £6,000, and the time allocated to those jobs varied from four days to 14 days, which rather led us to wonder what standard of audit was being achieved. Some schools, we found, in their tender evaluation process placed great emphasis on getting the lowest cost, which is not necessarily best value: quality is a very important dimension when evaluating tenders and reviewing what you are going to get in terms of an audit coverage. There were indeed some schools which had not formally had the audit process tendered but had just allocated the job. So those were some strands which we brought together in the C&AG's report, which led us to wonder whether this was going very well. Indeed

the Funding Agency for Schools has taken very positive action on that point. It has set up a review and that will report, I believe, in January or February 1996.

657. LORD NOLAN: I see. Did you mention that there was concern over tendering for contracts?

LEW HUGHES: I am not sure that we found any weaknesses in the contracting arrangements other than in the tendering before the contract was placed. That was the main focus of our concern.

658. LORD NOLAN: Can you be a little bit more specific? Was there a conflict of interests involved—or potential conflict?

LEW HUGHES: I am not sure there were potential conflicts of interest, no. We did find instances in grant-maintained schools of conflicts of interest or potential conflicts of interest in contracting, but not in the letting of contracts for audit.

659. LORD NOLAN: It has been put to us that the controls generally over finance and probity in the grant-maintained school area are much less strict than in the local authority area. Would you agree with that?

LEW HUGHES: Chairman, my own view of that would be that the grant-maintained schools are still learning their job. They are very young and they have taken on responsibilities from the early age which are new to them. One has to recognise as well that they are relatively small in size, so the normal weight of financial control and separation of duties that one looks to find in finance functions is just not workable at school level. Therefore, they are a different sort of challenge.

JOHN BOURN: If I could add to that, Chairman, as Mr Hughes says, here you have a range of institutions which have never had to have responsibility for their financial affairs before. It is a deliberate decision of the government that they should be responsible for this, and one can understand the reasons for doing that. You give these responsibilities to people who have not exercised them before, and it is not surprising that in the first year or couple of years some of them do not do it in a fully expert way. Again, I think it is very advantageous that when grant-maintained schools were set up we did have these inspection rights, because on the basis of being able to look at 70, 80 or more schools a year we are able to see the problem in the round and make these recommendations, which are being taken forward and will be a help to the grant-maintained schools in having a properly ordered way of running their finance. They are not usually very large institutions, the financial problems are not in themselves difficult, but sometimes inexperience can cause problems of the kind that we have highlighted. But I think that the sector will improve in its ability to handle its money over the next few years.

660. TOM KING: Can I make one point on that? Although we are talking about grant-maintained schools, there has been a major culture change right across with local management of schools. I think that the amount of expenditure now that is within the discretion of a school, whether it is grant-maintained or not, is 90 per cent. I think that is the national figure now for LMS. I have certainly seen one or two constituency problems where you could see conflicts of interest in that area. Does this general

problem about people learning and governors learning apply in the LMS as well as grant-maintained?

JOHN BOURN: Yes, that's right.

LEW HUGHES: As an LEA school governor, I can say, certainly.

661. LORD NOLAN: And the LMS has been generally very popular with schools?

LEW HUGHES: Oh, yes, absolutely.

662. LORD NOLAN: There are just two more specific matters that I wanted to raise with you before passing on the questioning to others. In the case of TECs there is no regulatory or financing agency corresponding to the Housing Corporation for housing associations or the Higher Education Funding Council for universities. Do you see any advantages or disadvantages in that arrangement or would there be something to be said for building in a responsible agency, so to speak above the TECs?

JOHN BOURN: Here you have the case of the direct relationship between the Department and the TECs. I think there can be problems about building in these intermediate bodies. On the whole our experience has been that if you administer something through several tiers of bodies and the money cascades down, you can get awkwardness, inefficiencies and difficulties. I think there is, as a general principle, something to be said for the direct relationship between the Department and the bodies that it appoints to conduct its schemes of implementation.

LEW HUGHES: Could I add to that, Chairman, that the TECs' contracts are actually overseen on a day-to-day basis by the 10 government offices in the region, which provides an extra assistance to the management of their affairs.

663. LORD NOLAN: Why were there such large losses when the South Thames TEC went down? Was there any explanation there that was of general interest and relevance?

JOHN BOURN: I think, Chairman, that here you had a body whose ability to handle its money was very weak. They quoted prices for their courses, for example, that did not cover their costs, there were deficiencies in their own management accounts, and they got themselves into a situation where they were not knowing exactly where the money was going, they were not knowing exactly how the money was coming in. It is a matter of common observation that one tends to find that, once you have a weak system, it gets totally out of control extremely quickly, and I think that this was the essence of the problem in that institution.

664. LORD NOLAN: The last question I wanted to ask you is really a continuation of something we were discussing earlier. What powers have you to inspect public expenditure by housing associations? Is there any direct method of inspection?

JOHN BOURN: No, we do not have the power to inspect housing associations, Chairman. It is one of the

extensions of inspection that, as I said before, we advocate. If we are to visit a housing association, it has to be set up as part of a special exercise, negotiated with the Department of the Environment and the Housing Corporation, and that, I feel, is not really a satisfactory basis on which to carry out this function. It is by their grace and favour, as you might say, rather than on the ability of the National Audit Office to discharge this function at our own discretion.

665. LORD NOLAN: And you say there is no independent examination of the regularity of grant expenditure at housing associations or whether publicly financed business is being conducted properly.

JOHN BOURN: That is right. Of course they are audited, but what one is interested to see in public expenditure is the concern, as you say, not only that the accounts should fairly represent the financial transactions of the body concerned, which is essentially what the basic financial audit will give you, but the contribution that we can make, by inspection, on matters of regularity, good practice and management and issues of propriety. That is why we think that, without supplanting or adding to an audit burden, we could make an useful contribution there by having those rights of inspection of housing associations.

LORD NOLAN: Thank you very much. I am going to ask Lord Thomson to continue the questions.

666. LORD THOMSON: Sir John, you are responsible for the TEC system. That comes under your authority, does it not?

JOHN BOURN: We are not the auditors of the TECs, but, as part of our audit of the Department, we have inspection rights over the expenditure of public money by the TECs. It is rather an unusual position. Our inspection rights for the TECs extend to being able to look at how they spend the money as a means, in a sense, of appraising the financial management of the Department. We have been able to do useful and extensive work in the TECs, but as I said before, the general right of inspection in the TECs would put matters on a clear, unequivocal basis and it would be valuable to have that.

667. LORD THOMSON: I ask, because we are going to have evidence a little later this morning which certainly summarised for me one of the issues relating to TECs for our Committee, and that is simply that TECs are private companies delivering a public service with public money. They are in a rather unique position from the point of view of the kind of concerns with which your duties lie. Could I follow that up then by asking you on a specific matter? Part of the evidence we have had so far from some of those who have been witnesses from TECs has been that the present auditing requirements in relation to their training obligations mean keeping a daily register of the number of students. I think the Cabinet Office Efficiency Unit has been investigating this and suggesting that it might all be a good deal more sensible if it was based on sampling techniques rather than a daily register of the kind that I remember when I was a schoolboy. Would you have any view as a professional controller on that view?

JOHN BOURN: Certainly the idea of taking samples of transactions is the only way in which effective audit can be done in a society. Since everything is to be checked, we should all be auditors. There is perhaps an area of care in this regard, in that we have investigated a number of cases where the claims have been put in to TECs by contractors saying that they have provided training for so many people, and it has not been entirely clear whether they have or they have not. While that is not to say that you necessarily need a system under which detailed records are kept of every person and every course, I think experience has suggested that you do need to have a system under which you have a fair degree of reliability to make sure that, when the TEC pays the contractor, the TEC is paying for the students who have actually been trained. If you have fuzziness there, you can find yourself paying money for things that have not actually been done. That is one of the things that we have been able to draw attention to.

Another one, which is a direct result of our being able to look at the TECs, was to see the way in which a number of them have built up substantial financial balances. Of course as companies you would expect them to have financial balances to take them from one year to another; it is not as if they had to draw stumps with their money on 31st March every year. But looking, and we have drawn attention to this, at the amount of money they have in their bank balances, sometimes you have to ask "Do you really need all that money doing nothing?" It is public money which has come down and it is sitting there, not actually being used. This again is an example of what we have been able to point out by looking at the system in the round, in the way that the individual auditor looking at particular TECs, doing his work, has not been able to see, because he does not see across the system as we do.

668. LORD THOMSON: One of the concerns that have been expressed to us in the regard to training responsibilities is that the need for the training provider, sometimes a commercial, private sector training provider, to maximise his profits means that there is pressure to reduce the standards of the non-vocational qualifications that are sought. Is that the kind of thing that the National Audit Office in its value for money responsibilities would look at?

JOHN BOURN: That is the kind of thing that we certainly could look at by the full range of inspection rights that I am talking about. One has to recognise that of course the training provider will in many cases be a company and has a perfect right to seek profit, but it would be interesting to look at a range of providers, to look at the quality control arrangements that the TECs exercised. I think we have on occasion felt, having a look at it, that it has been a question of giving the contract, taking a general look at what is done and then paying the money. Of course you do need to have the means of assessing the quality of what the contractor provides with training, as with all other purchases of goods and services.

669. LORD THOMSON: I think the concern that has been expressed to us has been, first of all, a recognition that there is some external control through the Royal Society of Arts or what used to be the City and Guilds, whatever these sort of bodies are, but the practice is also associated with the provider being the examiner, and I just wondered whether that is the kind of area that you look at.

JOHN BOURN: It is certainly the kind of area that we would be able to examine, which we have looked at in other areas. Certainly here the whole idea of the person who provides the training doing the examining themselves has to be part of an open system, so that everybody understands how it is done. We do have in the community experience of this kind of thing. For example, universities provide the tuition but also award their own degrees, so it can be done. But it does require a definite and considered system which is open to public inspection, where you have the activities of visitors and other matters of that kind. So it is possible to do, but you need to think it out carefully and for it to be transparent.

670. LORD THOMSON: Thank you. Just one final question. I was interested that you make the point that you could do a very useful job in terms of the concerns that we all share without increasing the audit burden. That was your proposition to us. I think it is fair to say that the evidence we have had on TECs from almost everybody associated with them is that, even under the present situation, they complain about being over-audited. I just wondered whether one of the things that a body of your particular role and standing would be able to look at is whether, in the formal auditing processes that take place in a sector like the TECs—though this could equally apply to other sectors—you could express a view as to whether there are too many auditors around and the auditing process itself might be simplified, while fully meeting the standards that you are seeking to sustain.

JOHN BOURN: Yes, that certainly is the kind of point that we can examine. It certainly has been the case that, if you take various aspects of British public life, especially where, in the last 10 to 15 years, you have had the phenomenon that I previously referred to of activities conducted by a tier of bodies, then each of them will have their own arrangements for external audit, but in many cases the immediately superior body, quite rightly, will have various ways of examining and checking up on things. I know that the people right at the bottom can sometimes feel they are examined by a large number of people. I think that, as we are now able to consolidate experience in some of these areas, there is a case for looking at the rationalisation and ordering of proper and sensible arrangements. Essentially what one needs is a proper system of external audit, you need internal audit arrangements, and as well you need a system of management accounting. Sometimes you may need an overall look at the area, which is something more than the annual audit. But to have too complex a system does get in the way of doing work and of course absorbs an enormous amount of money and resources in its own right.

LORD NOLAN: Thank you. Now we can go round the table. Were there any other questions you had?

671. TOM KING: I think you struck a chord with members of the Committee in talking about why TECs hold balances and what the case was for that. That seemed entirely compelling until I remembered that the way to avoid holding balances is to have a big end-year spend. This is obviously a wider issue and I wondered how you would advise proceeding on it and avoiding that alternative pitfall?

JOHN BOURN: I think the way to avoid it is to have a clear idea of what you need your balance for. One of the points that occurred to us is that when there was a large amount of money and you asked them "What is it for? What are you going to do with it?", the replies tended to be very vague. It is in some ways better that the money should be in the bank than spent stupidly in the last two or three weeks of March.

TOM KING: Absolutely.

JOHN BOURN: But it seems to us that you do not necessarily face the fact that you are going to have an end-year splurge.

672. TOM KING: Can I rephrase the question. The question I am really on about is a very fundamental one, right across government. As you know a lot of government departments see that if they have balances—underspends—coming up, the consequence will be a cut in their budget for the coming year. That has significant implications for government spending. Have you, the National Audit Office, addressed this as a specific subject in its own right which would apply to these bodies that we are looking at as well?

JOHN BOURN: You will remember from your own experience as Secretary of State for Defence, Mr King, that you presided over a department which negotiated some proper arrangements to avoid that splurge—the carry over of money in an orderly way between financial years. We have supported and encouraged the development of that and also the coming development of resource and accrual accounting and greater focus on these matters will be advantageous. It should work out in such a way that you have a properly articulated system of spending, that you are able to isolate those areas where in the last month or so you do not know when the bills are coming in, and therefore although you cannot be certain you will get down to the last penny by the end of the financial year, you can have an orderly system for moving between financial years. It certainly has been the case that in the past—and it still needs tackling in some areas—that people do fear this and they would rather spend it on matters of doubtful value in order to avoid that.

673. TOM KING: Thank you. Could I just then press you a bit further on a question Lord Thomson asked. You made the point very clearly that you thought your inspection rights should be significantly extended. There would be no extra bureaucracy, as I took it, for the clients you would be inspecting and no extra sets of auditors. But looked at from your end of the telescope, if we agreed that your criteria should be met and that you ought to have inspection rights under all the headings that you spell out in your paper where significant sums of money are spent, or even where they are not spent where it is a body that is involved in pursuing goals for which it is proper for government to take responsibility—which seems quite a widening to that extent—what would that represent in increased workload and staff cost for you?

JOHN BOURN: For example, we have been able to absorb the extra requirement to inspect the grant-maintained schools, which is an extensive programme for us—as I say, that is 80 to 100 schools to look at each year—by increased efficiency in the National Audit Office without employing any extra people or asking for any increase in the budget.

In the areas we are talking about now, if we were to be given these powers there would of course be some extra inspections. People would go out and visit places that they have not otherwise visited, so we would be making some extra output, but I would not see this as a sea change. I

should not be going to the Public Accounts Commission of the House of Commons and asking for 10 per cent increase in my budget, or anything of that kind. My way of approaching it in the first year would be to exercise those increased responsibilities within my present resources.

674. TOM KING: So that we can understand that, how many extra bodies do you think you are talking about?

LEW HUGHES: Perhaps I can help on the question of grant-maintained schools. As Sir John said, we have visited over the past two years, 150 schools. Each school has received a separate desktop published output from us.

TOM KING: Over the last two years?

LEW HUGHES: Over the last two years.

675. TOM KING: Two years. And there are how many now?

LEW HUGHES: There are just over 1,000. So we have visited 150 and each school has received a desktop published output pointing up things which they could do better—real value added to the local practitioner—and we have summarised that in reports each year to Parliament. They have been taken very seriously by the funding agency and without exception the points we have raised have been taken forward and improvements made. We have revisited a selection of the schools where we found problems and were able to confirm that they have put them right. We have achieved that with a programme of staff of about three people.

676. TOM KING: That is an inspection at the rate of every 20 years. Is that right?

LEW HUGHES: At that rate, that would be right—150 schools out of 1,000 over a two year cycle.

677. TOM KING: But where are the other areas? I am afraid I am ignorant on this. I am not quite clear; we call for this inspection and I am anxious to see how big the extension would be. Any other areas as well?

CAROLINE MAWHOOD: As far as the housing associations go, there are about 2,300 registered. Only about 275 of those receive 90 per cent of capital grants from central government so if the C&AG was to exercise inspection rights there, he would be taking a selection of the 275 and I am not sure of the precise figures, but I think a relatively small number of those receive the majority of the funds. Using the normal criteria as an auditor of risk materiality, he would judge on an annual basis how many he needed to do to fulfil his responsibility to Parliament. That certainly would not be anything like 275.

678. TOM KING: And otherwise? Is it just housing associations?

LEW HUGHES: There are 74 TECs and we visit about 12 a year currently under the present arrangements.

TOM KING: Could we have a note from the C&AG on this point so that we can see what is being covered by it and what it represents. That would be very helpful.

JOHN BOURN: Yes. I should be glad to do that.[1]

TOM KING: Thank you very much.

---

[1]*See* Evidence, pp. 465-468.

LORD NOLAN: Thank you. Now, Clifford.

679. CLIFFORD BOULTON: We came across cases where internal audit is being carried out by the same commercial firm as performs the external audit and to my inexpert ears that sounded a little bit like marking your own work. Are there in fact circumstances where it is acceptable and perhaps normal to have the same firm doing both?

JOHN BOURN: Sir Clifford, we share your view on that. We would expect the internal auditors to be different from the external auditor.

680. CLIFFORD BOULTON: Thank you. You will not be surprised to hear that I have been taking an interest in the potential role of the clerk or secretary of the boards of these bodies and I was encouraged to see in paragraph 4 of your memorandum that you say:

"The Clerk to a governing body can play an important role in providing independent advice on issues of governance and the proper conduct of public business. The National Audit Office found several examples of good practice during their inspection visits to further education institutions."

We have come across cases where it appeared that the role of clerk or secretary was rather that of the dormouse between an extrovert chairman and an extrovert chief executive and indeed the dormouse had been swallowed up in some cases by the chief executive, who was purporting to perform both roles.

Do you think that there is scope for encouraging a greater recognition of the advisory role and cautionary role that the secretary of a body can perform?

JOHN BOURN: Yes, I do. I think that very much. In the case where the secretary becomes, as it were, the dormouse caught in between the chairman and the chief executive, this from our experience very often happens because these two individuals have no experience of life in a large organisation—either a private or a public sector one—so that they do not see what a protection the role of company secretary, and the person who discharges that kind of role, is for themselves as well as for the public welfare. There is a great case for training and education and also, of course, for openness in recruitment procedures to seek to arrange that dormice do not get appointed. If you have the appointment made in secret—just fixed up between two or three people behind the scenes—they may very well select a dormouse because that is what they think they want. Openness in appointment procedure is an important safeguard there.

681. CLIFFORD BOULTON: Thank you. Just one other point because I am afraid we are short of time, is there anything you would like to say briefly about whether or not the funding agencies are the right bodies to be regulators as well. This is something which I know that the housing association area and the Housing Corporation has taken very seriously and there can be built-in problems of a fund granter trying to invent the rules and lay down all kinds of conditions which go much wider than the funding itself. Do you have any general comments on that?

JOHN BOURN: I certainly agree with the point that just as the funding council should have a care for the system for the proper handling of public money, they should not let that go to their heads and start regulating all kinds of other things that are not necessary. But perhaps I could ask Mr Hughes, whose sector this is in detail, to expand on that.

LEW HUGHES: I suppose that the one point I would make is that funding decisions have to be informed decisions on the basis of the quality of training provision and in the case of higher education on the basis of the quality of research. That implies to my mind that the funding body needs to have mechanisms for inspectorial arrangements for overseeing or at least monitoring the quality. Therefore I think they do sit together; an informed funding mechanism requires that they sit together I suspect.

682. CLIFFORD BOULTON: You think that it is probably not necessary to think in terms of always having a separate regulatory body and that the regulatory body can be the funding council in your view, so long as it is properly run?

LEW HUGHES: That is right, yes.

683. WILLIAM UTTING: Can I just pursue that as far as grant-maintained schools are concerned. It strikes me as odd that in a nation of this size, the Secretary of State might at any time become involved in the detailed administration of over 1,000 schools and in view of what you said earlier about the schools learning their job, that seems to me to be a situation that cries out for the kind of funding and regulatory body that has just been described.

LEW HUGHES: I think that is right. It is important to know that the Secretary of State has not become involved very often with the governance of grant-maintained schools. I think he or she has exercised powers in that respect on only two occasions so far.

684. WILLIAM UTTING: We do not know whether that was enough or too much, though, do we?

LEW HUGHES: I am not able to form a view on that.

WILLIAM UTTING: No.

LORD NOLAN: Or just right?

LEW HUGHES: Perhaps just right, yes.

685. ANNE WARBURTON: Chairman, in response to a question you put earlier, Sir John told us that TECs' contracts are under day by day supervision by regional government offices. I am sorry to say that I do not know what the composition of a regional government office is and I wondered how far it represents departments—how far, for example, perhaps the NAO itself is represented in it.

JOHN BOURN: It is a device of public administration introduced in the past few years, under which the government departments who operate on a regional basis, such as the Department of Trade and Industry, the Department of the Environment and the Department of Transport work from one office, the idea being that in the localities and regions, people should not feel that they have to go to a whole series of different offices but that central government should be represented by one office, one authority—the kind of one-stop shop idea translated into public administration. That is what the system is and what it encompasses.

686. ANNE WARBURTON: And it means that within the office there is a door saying "Department of Trade" and another saying "Department of Education" and contracts signed by the TEC would go to one or the other of those?

JOHN BOURN: Yes, that is right.

687. ANNE WARBURTON: And does the NAO have regional representation?

JOHN BOURN: Certainly we are the auditors of the bodies and our staff are distributed through the country, most of them are in London. Essentially, from the viewpoint of audit, with the development of a motorway system and internal airlines in this country, you can move around from an audit point of view more efficiently than by having relatively small groups of staff—half a dozen people—in a large number of towns. We are certainly very evident throughout the realm.

ANNE WARBURTON: Thank you.

LORD NOLAN: Thank you very much. We have slightly overrun our time, but it has been time well spent and it has been very helpful to have the clear and concise written material that you put before us expanded in this way by word of mouth. Thank you very much for coming.

JOHN BOURN: Thank you Chairman.

688. LORD NOLAN: Good morning, gentlemen. This is Mr Robin Geldard, President, and Mr Ron Taylor, Director-General of the Association of British Chambers of Commerce. We are lacking Geoff Runcie?

ROBIN GELDARD, AND RON TAYLOR CBE

ROBIN GELDARD (President, Association of British Chambers of Commerce): Yes. We thought that since the Scottish system is very different from that in England, for which we speak, it may be more sensible for evidence on that subject to be given elsewhere.

LORD NOLAN: We are proposing to visit Scotland in the new year, so possibly we can make up then for his absence now.

Thank you very much for coming to join us. I am going to go straight into the questions if I may and ask Sir William Utting to begin.

689. WILLIAM UTTING: I am sorry about Mr Runcie's absence, but it does mean that in talking to you I need say only TECs every time and not TECs and LECs.

Could I kick off with a pretty general sort of question to you that TECs were set up to look after the business development and the training needs of their local areas. In your view, how is this working out? Are they doing this job well and is there a reasonable balance between the enterprise and the training bits of their jobs?

ROBIN GELDARD: We would say that on balance they are doing the job reasonably well. That is not to say

that we do not have concerns that sometimes the programmes which they are asked to deliver are national programmes, not always suited to the particular needs of the region in which they are practising. On balance, though, their position has been entirely benign. Do you want to add to that one?

RON TAYLOR (Director-General, Association of British Chambers of Commerce): I would agree totally. When TECs were first established, we saw a degree of fear—TECs of Chambers, Chambers of TECs. That has now wholly disappeared. There is very close co-operation and importantly an understanding of some of the strategic directions and decisions at a local level which helps all those on the patch trying to do a job on behalf of British industry.

690. WILLIAM UTTING: Your suggesting that they have been directed towards national rather than local priorities, suggests that the parent department may in fact be too remote from TECs and is itself over concerned with the national view and not sufficiently knowledgeable about local need. Is that why this over emphasis on national needs occurs?

RON TAYLOR: Our hope when TECs were first established was that we would see a more local slant to a number of national programmes, particularly in areas of training and that is one of the reasons we argued strongly for TECs to be created. There has been a worry that that expectation has not always been carried through and the feeling is that it is because there has been a degree of national prescription about a great deal of TEC activity, which has left them little flexibility to deal with local issues and requirements. The worry is that the expectation has not been totally realised in many areas.

691. WILLIAM UTTING: Are there any bodies that can take national priorities and interpret them for application locally? Are there any useful intermediary bodies who can nag the department to get things right locally?

RON TAYLOR: This is, again, where the growing co-operation between chambers and TECs is proving helpful. One of the chamber roles is to articulate the views of its membership and if its membership actually believes that there needs to be more money and investment in a particular form of training or economic development, it can lobby with others to that end. That lobbying function is often with the local authority, with the TEC and the target is central government. That process is I think wholly healthy and welcome.

692. WILLIAM UTTING: Chambers of commerce have been involved in the setting up of a considerable number of merged Chamber/TECs and there is a programme actually to advance this. What are the advantages of this close relationship between TECs and chambers of commerce?

ROBIN GELDARD: One of the first advantages which becomes apparent is that up to now, TEC boards have been to a large extent self-appointing. The creation of the CCTE—the merged TEC and Chamber body—means that for the first time, this body, is actually answerable to a membership from which it draws its customers, which has a right to scrutinise its annual results and to scrutinise the way in which it uses its money, and to have an input into the thinking about training needs locally that perhaps was not as well articulated when TECs stood on their own.

RON TAYLOR: There is another feature in all this. We have seen during the eighties and early nineties the creation of a number of often competing bodies at a local level. If one looks at an area like Milton Keynes, the business community was asked to respond to chamber, TEC, Development Corporation, Enterprise Agency and so on and really that did not make a great deal of sense. Therefore there was a strategic value to be drawn by bringing these together under one roof with a common objective and direction. That has probably been the greatest motivation amongst the early CCTEs. We now have five—Oldham has joined the list since we submitted our evidence to you. There are two more whose applications have been agreed by TEC National Council and ABCC and are before the two Secretaries of State, three being processed and close to being submitted for approval, and we know there are another 10 in the pipeline.

That is quite a significant proportion—something like 20 out of the 80 TECs will in fact be merged Chambers and TECs within a year. That will start to change some of the ethos. It will not be a Chamber ethos or a TEC ethos; it will develop something of its own nature and being. But there is a ground swell out there, even beyond those 20, towards some form of unification, TEC plus Chamber plus business link.

693. WILLIAM UTTING: I can see the advantages of this closer relationship, both in enabling business to contribute across a broad front and also making TECs more responsive to business needs locally. One of the slight criticisms that has been made to us about TECs though is that they are perhaps less responsive to the needs of the rest of the clientele that they serve, that in fact they are weaker on the training side than on the business development side. What is your view of that?

RON TAYLOR: Again, we come back to almost your first question, that too much of their training related activity is driven by decisions taken at a national level, rather than at a local level. Therefore many of the businessmen who are sitting on either TEC boards or on the CCTE boards feel constrained as to the amount of direction they can give to training activity.

ROBIN GELDARD: It is arguable, of course, that that is almost impossible to avoid because TECs have had the duty of providing national programmes to help the unemployed and those seeking employment and that is very often not necessarily the training that is needed for those who are already in employment in an area and who require training of a different sort. So there is a diversity in the needs which a TEC is seeking to provide and it has sometimes been, I suppose, that the national need has overlooked the regional and local need.

694. WILLIAM UTTING: How do you think the membership of TECs can actually take sufficiently into account the needs of the diverse population of people who need training for employment?

ROBIN GELDARD: That has been the problem: TECs have not really had a membership. They have had a TEC board which is drawn from businessmen from a variety of backgrounds, but most have not actually had a

membership to whom they could go to find out what was needed locally. This is another of the advantages which flows from the CCTEs where they do have a strong and growing membership of the business community who are able to feed in their requirements in the local area. Before, perhaps, TEC boards were somewhat isolated. They relied on the experience of the boards themselves, which were very often in a fairly narrow compass.

RON TAYLOR: There is another fundamental issue here. TECs were established, very properly I think, as companies limited by guarantee. They therefore have a prior obligation to their membership and that is one of the key aspects of the CCTEs in that they are answerable to a membership which is 2,000 plus strong, rather than a very small tight group of individuals. That company limited by guarantee, however, has a number of objectives which relate to the greater good of Milton Keynes, Northamptonshire or wherever and that is what actually drives the company.

I think that I would want to argue that the accountability into the company law membership of the CCTE is as good as you are going to get. I would be very reluctant to see the TEC or the CCTE having to respond to wider issues because you get a very diffuse set of strategic directions and corporate strategies and we would be unhappy to see that widening of the membership.

695. WILLIAM UTTING: Yes. I think I am a long way from suggesting a kind of proportional representation on the board for every conceivable interest in the community, but I just wanted to test how far business membership of the board and of the membership actually extended. Does it go far enough? Do you take trades union interests into account for example in membership and on boards?

RON TAYLOR: If I were to be absolutely honest, the chamber of commerce view is that this is a business organisation. It looks very odd, therefore, to see trade unionists on the board. On the other hand, it is clearly a precondition of the Department of Education and Training that the characteristics of a TEC be carried into the new situation and that certainly allows representatives of trades unions to sit on the board and we do not object to that, even though we may not actually like it. We are happy to see, and in draft model articles which we drew up for the CCTEs it is confirmed, that there may be a trades union director, but we are unhappy about the thought of trades union membership. I think there is a distinction between the director and the owner of the company.

696. WILLIAM UTTING: And you might at a pinch take on rather broader equal opportunities issues, like seeing that there were rather more women perhaps?

RON TAYLOR: Yes. That is not a huge issue as far as we and the chambers are concerned.

697. WILLIAM UTTING: You have sat through some evidence already this morning I think and have heard that it has been suggested that TECs may be over-audited across the board, not only in strict financial terms, but also in relation to the amount of statistical information that they have to produce for the Department. Balancing that, though, a suggestion has been made to us that they tend to be under-audited on quality when it comes to the provision of training programmes—that the individual

TEC monitors what goes on for itself and that this monitoring is not as effective as the financial and statistical scrutiny of their work. What is your experience of this? Do TECs produce value for money on the training side?

ROBIN GELDARD: To start with my view is that it would be disastrous for TECs to have any more auditing requirements. They spend a great deal of money and very valuable time on producing statistics and other matters which are not necessarily of use to their main objects. As to the audit of their quality, there are times perhaps when their quality needs to be looked at a little more carefully and we have formed the view that, in a way, the best measure of quality is to make them answerable to the area of the business community that they serve. Concerns about quality will then surface very quickly. At the moment, there is not that ability. The business community does not have any way of articulating its desires or fears about the way a TEC behaves. It is entirely for the board members to decide how they are doing.

If I may pick up another point about the evidence which we heard, on this question about TECs having a certain amount of money stowed away in the bank, I think it is fair to say that if I were a director of a company, I would be very unhappy if I did not have a certain sum of money put away in the bank so that I knew I could at least meet my obligations over a three or six month period.

In addition to that, if I am answering local needs, it is perfectly clear that I may find, half way through a year, that there is a requirement for a special training project in the area, about which one knew nothing six months before. Therefore it is prudent to have a certain amount of money set aside.

On the other front, the question of the quality of the providers, it must be remembered that those who are providing training services for the TECs have gone through a bidding process and have therefore had to make their quality and their attractiveness in terms of price available to the TEC before they actually start work, so there are some checks and balances already there in terms of quality. That is not to say that it is perfect.

RON TAYLOR: There are many chambers who are training providers and therefore sub-contractors to their TECs and the feedback we have from them is that the auditing and regulatory procedures placed on the TEC are actually washing down to them and they feel themselves over-audited and over-monitored and spend too much of their time filling in forms when they could be training people. There is a very strong reaction from the training provider that the burden simply ought not to get any worse.

If there is a complaint about TECs from chambers as training providers, it is that the TECs in many cases have not managed the contractor-contractee relationship as well, as they might in some cases. They have not managed that process terribly well and the result has been that contracts have often only been signed after the work has started and there have been a number of issues around that. It is all about management—it is an operational issue, not one of major principle.

698. WILLIAM UTTING: You may on the training side, then, have quite a number of levels locally from the TEC

to a contractor to a subcontractor to the person who is actually getting trained. You then have a big leap from the TEC up to the Department for Education and Employment direct. Part of our conversation appears to suggest that that leap is actually too big—that you might actually be better off with some sort of intermediary body that stood between you and the Department that funded the process and also combined some sort of national quality check on what was being produced.

I take the point that was made earlier about the undesirability of having too many levels from top to bottom, but you can have too few and, again, it seems to me strange that the Secretary of State might become involved in the administration of an individual TEC somewhere in the country.

RON TAYLOR: I would have thought that it surely is not beyond the wit of man to have a sensible contractual relationship when all you are talking about is one government department and 80 TEC. I do not see the case for having any intermediate stages. To a degree, they already exist with the regional government offices, with the TECs bidding against single regeneration budgets; so it is there, but I have to tell you that our view, again, is that that actually has complicated things, not made them easier.

WILLIAM UTTING: You might be asking too much of a central government department. It is perfectly possible at high levels to combine great administrative and political skills with complete ignorance of the practicalities of delivering a service on the ground. Chairman, thank you.

RON TAYLOR: I am glad you said that and not me.

LORD NOLAN: Dame Anne?

699. ANNE WARBURTON: I wondered if I might explore with you a little bit more the match between the chambers and the TECs. I do not know whether it is a wild figure, but a chairman of a TEC told me yesterday that in his balance he has 60 per cent training and 40 per cent other—the business side as you might call it. How does that correspond with your own balance?

RON TAYLOR: It varies from place to place, but there are some chambers, such as Mid-Yorkshire, where the figure is much higher than that and can be of the order of 80 per cent being training related. That is not simply government training, but it is training of people in the workplace. I suppose the average is round about 40 per cent. Giving average figures, the chamber is funded by 15-20 per cent from membership subscriptions. There are another 40-50 per cent which relate to trading activity of one sort or another and then there are a range of government contracts from the issue of certificates of origin, through to contracts with the TEC to deliver various government schemes—that kind of proportion.

700. ANNE WARBURTON: So pre-TECs your interests were not so different from what TECs' interests are?

RON TAYLOR: Sorry?

701. ANNE WARBURTON: If one looks back to the time before TECs, what you were doing, what you were interested in, was already very much in the same field?

ROBIN GELDARD: Very much, but contracting with the Manpower Services Commission and its successor.

702. ANNE WARBURTON: Yes. You make quite a point in your paper about membership and the fact that if the chamber comes in then membership effectively becomes much wider. Some of the TECs seem to make it very easy for anybody and everybody, including individuals, to become members and certainly all businesses. Is it not the case that members of chambers could, if they were interested, become members of TECs as well?

ROBIN GELDARD: I think this is where the perception of TECs amongst the business community takes over. Generally speaking, it has been our experience that business people prefer to belong to an organisation which they are clearly seen to own and to control and which is therefore amenable to their wishes. The TECs have been seen as an arm of government because of their somewhat curious position between being a private company but with this enormous public funding, . That is another of the benefits that would flow from the unification of some of our organisations in that you would actually bring the TECs nearer to the business community which it is seeking to serve. It is seen by many business people as simply being another arm of government.

RON TAYLOR: Also this term "membership" needs to be defined. Chambers talk of membership as being company law membership. A member of a chamber is a guarantor and, therefore, part-owner of the company which is the chamber of commerce. TEC membership, all too often, is of a membership scheme. It is more akin to a subscription and is not a company law membership in the same way as ours. So there is a distinction. We are talking about control and ownership: the TEC usually—and it is a generalisation—talks about membership as being part of a scheme to encourage better communication. We are not knocking that, but we do not think that is the solution.

703. ANNE WARBURTON: Yes. Does your membership include a lot of small businesses?

RON TAYLOR: Yes.

704. ANNE WARBURTON: Or do you have a minimum size?

RON TAYLOR: Something like 90 per cent of businesses employing less than 200 employees—

ANNE WARBURTON: That is still quite large.

RON TAYLOR: Unfortunately these days it is, yes. Our targets are the businesses between 10 and 200, but increasingly we are seeing that proportion moving towards the smaller business. On the whole chamber membership is in that band of growing businesses between 10 employees and 200.

705. ANNE WARBURTON: Thank you. Could you say something more about what actually happens when a chamber and a TEC merge? What does it look like to me, the member of the public, who comes in wanting something from it?

ROBIN GELDARD: If you were to take Milton Keynes as an example, you go into one building and within that building, you find an organisation which is carrying out the role of a TEC. You also find other parts of the organisation which has to do with inward investment, lifetime training, the traditional chamber activities such as export advice, certificates of origin, and a development role, increasingly, with the local authority who now see this body as speaking for the business people of their area and therefore discusses the development of the area. It is much greater than the sum of the parts. It has become akin almost to a development corporation in its own right, something in which the business community are totally involved for the benefit of their area and providing all the services that a businessman might want, including business links.

I think it has the great advantage that Business Links, which is a development that we entirely support, does not become a third or yet another force and yet another problem for the business community trying to sort out where they get their help. It actually comes under the one roof and is directed by the business community.

706. ANNE WARBURTON: Thank you very much. In looking out for candidates, as it sounds as though you are, for mergers, is it a help or a distinct hindrance that the TECs themselves are so different?

ROBIN GELDARD: One of the main difficulties is the fact that the boundaries of TECs and chambers are not coterminous. Indeed, the whole boundary situation of local authorities, TECs, chambers and other organisations having these extraordinary boundaries which are not coterminous, can make for difficulty. If I may say so, we are not actually looking for candidates.

ANNE WARBURTON: No, I remember you said that.

ROBIN GELDARD: We at ABCC take a neutral stance until a TEC and a chamber come to us and say, "We want to get together", in which case we help them as much as we can, but we are certainly not driving people together, because we do not feel that that would be helpful.

707. ANNE WARBURTON: Geographically, do the two fit? Are there TECs were there are chambers and chambers where there are TECs, or are there gaps?

ROBIN GELDARD: I do not think there are gaps. The difficulty is, perhaps, the other way around—that you very often get a chamber area which has three TECs in it, or vice versa. That does cause problems because you get what might be called turf wars developing.

RON TAYLOR: Chambers are by tradition at their strongest in manufacturing areas and therefore there are areas, for example, mid-Wales, in the rural districts where you would find a less strong chamber and where there would be now a TEC which is clearly stronger, not least because it has public funding behind it. So there is an element of mismatch, but if you look at most of the major industrial conurbations, you will find a TEC and a chamber and roughly they match.

708. ANNE WARBURTON: If I may ask just one more question: your paper puts forward as an alternative suggestion a corporate director, sitting there representing in some way the chamber. It sounds to me rather a difficult

concept. I wondered whether you have tried it on the TECs for size and how they responded.

RON TAYLOR: I think the honest answer is they would prefer things as they are. They don't see the case, if you like, to have this stranger amongst their fold. There are some chambers, chief executives and, indeed, senior businessmen, who sit on TEC boards now. It is not a new concept. They can sit as one of the five, non-private directors, largely because they are economic development agencies. So you actually do find these examples already. We are saying that is a very valuable thing to have and you could actually formalise it for those TECs which are not ready or do not want to move down the convergent route.

709. ANNE WARBURTON: And generally speaking the corporate director you see as having much the same position as other directors, except that there is a link back?

RON TAYLOR: Yes, indeed. The director is a director and I would not want to change their fiduciary duties or responsibilities in any way, shape or form. If you take on a directorship you are a director and that is the end of the argument. Where it becomes valuable is where the TEC has a role, which we agree with, in setting economic development strategy for its area. There needs to be, if that is to be effective, a very strong communication between the business community and the TEC, an element of representational link. The chamber role is also that it acts as a lobbyist for local business, therefore to have a formal link via a director, a chamber director sitting on a TEC board, seems to us to be a useful and valuable thing, to make certain that the TEC is meshing in its strategic objective with the business community.

ANNE WARBURTON: Thank you, Chairman.

710. LORD NOLAN: I know we are running over time, but I wonder if I could ask you just one question. We have evidence from a number of bodies representing the disabled, or people under a disadvantage, such as NACRO, whose fear was that TECs run by very efficient businessmen very often tended to go for the cream of the working population and that the disadvantaged came some way down the list and we are considering ways in which that concern might be addressed. One suggestion was that there should be, if not a direct representation of unemployed or trade unions or prisoners who have served their sentence, a champion for the disabled on the TEC boards. Is that something that has been considered by you?

ROBIN GELDARD: We have not considered that. I think that that comes really within the purview of a board being run and having a proper concern for its statutory duties, or the duties that are laid upon it by the business community. If the business community had more input that position might well improve, and I can give an example of that. Down in Cardiff, in Wales, there is a special unit run by the chamber of commerce which looks after young offenders—the "last chancers", as we might call them—and seeks to put them into special training and they get training as motor mechanics, as cooks, and it has been remarkably successful but it has required funding by the local TEC. There came a time when the TEC budgets were being prescribed, particularly because of national training needs, and the help for that body was going to be withdrawn. The chamber was able to visit the TEC and to

persuade them that this was something which really should be done as a matter of social conscience and also as a benefit to the community, and the scheme was saved. I suspect that if the chamber had not had that input the TEC members would actually have been in ignorance perhaps of the gap in the armoury.

LORD NOLAN: Yes. Thank you. I think you have answered my question—in a well-run chamber it should not be necessary. We are very grateful to you both for coming along—you have helped us a lot.

ROBIN GELDARD: Thank you.

711. LORD NOLAN: Good morning, Sir David. Thank you very much for coming along to join us and since we can only look forward to having you for half an hour I am going to ask Lord Thomson to go straight into the questions, please. That is unless you wanted to make an opening statement.

SIR DAVID HANCOCK KCB

SIR DAVID HANCOCK (Chairman of Inquiry into Housing Association Governance and Executive Director of Hambros Bank Ltd.): Not really. But I wonder if I could just mention one or two points which I would like to register with the Committee, having had this opportunity. The first is I do hope the Committee will endorse the approach of guidance and encouragement rather than central regulation as the way to improve standards both in higher education, further education and in housing associations. I think there has been a tendency for too much top-down regulation and not enough encouragement of the people who are responsible for the management of institutions to take responsibility for their own decisions.

Secondly, I have seen evidence that housing associations should have their members appointed, either by the Secretary of State or by local authorities, and I am totally opposed to that. I think independence is a great virtue and should be encouraged.

Thirdly, I would like to say that I welcome the Housing Corporation's endorsement of our code of governance and their decision not to make it mandatory, which is consistent with the first point that I have made.

Fourthly, I welcome their support for our proposal that associations be free to reimburse the lost earnings of members of the boards of housing associations but I do rather regret that they did not see fit to endorse our recommendation on Section 15 of the Housing Association Act 1985 which, as I think the Committee knows, is the provision that aims to ensure proper conduct in housing associations. It is a very restrictive regime and we have recommended that it should be liberalised and made more consistent with regimes that are relied on by other organisations, including universities.

Finally, I did come under some pressure during my review to advocate that the boards of housing associations should meet in public. I would like to say that I am against that. I certainly think that boards should give an account of their decisions and our report includes numerous ways in which that might be done. But like other bodies that have to take difficult decisions I think they should be encouraged to deliberate in private. Thank you, sir.

LORD NOLAN: Thank you very much. Lord Thomson?

712. LORD THOMSON: Sir David, thank you very much for those opening remarks which lead into the questions, I think, that we want to ask you. You are, of course, as you will realise, a very valuable witness for us because you are, of course, a distinguished former Permanent Secretary of Education and I think Lord Nolan might want to ask you something on governance issues there. You are also now a merchant banker and I would quite like to ask you about some funding matters in relation to housing associations. But could I start with the main purpose of inviting you, which was your very important report on governance in housing associations. Could you just tell us what were the origins of it? One instinctively feels that nobody would ask somebody like you to chair a report on governance unless there had been some concerns that all was not as well as it might have been with governance.

DAVID HANCOCK: Well, it was not a crisis—there were not any really terrible things like Maxwell and so forth that led to the creation of the Cadbury Committee. There were one or two unfortunate incidents and I think you have had evidence from Circle 33, which was the one uppermost in people's minds. Governance was, I think, very much the fashion of the times. I mean, everybody is reviewing their governance—I understand that Her Majesty authorised a review of the governance of the royal household a few years ago. Cadbury in particular made everybody think about it, and quite right, too. But clearly housing associations are not like plc's and the National Federation decided that it would be a good idea to have an enquiry. The immediate cause was a debate at the Federation's annual conference. I think that one of the most encouraging things about the housing association movement is that this should have come from within and not from outside.

713. LORD THOMSON: Thank you. Perhaps you can help us on the question of accountability in relation to housing associations because it is, I think, a difficult area. You make remarks in your report about membership policies and we have had some evidence from other witnesses, I think it is fair to say, about the inadequacies of membership of housing associations as an adequate form of accountability. One witness gave us a very vivid description of the problems of tracing members of housing associations for purposes of the business of the housing association who had gone off to Australia and had forgotten to leave the forwarding address. I do not think that there is much agreement that membership, as such, is a very adequate forum. You, I think, in Chapter 5, certainly seem to say that boards are more accountable in reality in the strict sense only to the Housing Corporation. If I may say so, that seems—perhaps I have misunderstood—but that seems to fly a little in contradiction to your remark a moment ago that the independence of housing associations was their prime quality. We did have some very interesting evidence from Richard Best of the Rowntree Foundation the other day in which he made a passionate plea to us on the essential voluntary character of housing associations. What do you say to these rather conflicting elements in the problem of accountability for housing associations?

DAVID HANCOCK: I certainly think the shareholding members are a bit of a red herring. I think there has been a false analogy drawn with plc's which is simply misleading. After all, the shareholders of a company own it. In no sense do the shareholding members of a housing association own it. Some of the associations have open membership, ie, I could write in and send a pound and become a member of a housing association. I do not see that that gives me any particular right to have a say in the conduct of their business.

Perhaps the wording of the report rather gave an exaggerated impression to accountability about the Housing Corporation but you must remember I was an accounting officer for six years and the way these things get written do get influenced by one's experience. Associations have to be accountable through the proper procedures to Parliament for the use of the taxpayer's money. But we certainly did not wish to imply that that was the end of it—certainly not. We said a great deal about their relations with tenants. Whether you call that accountability or not I think is a semantic issue which is, perhaps, not very interesting; but associations certainly should seek the views of the tenants and explain what they are doing to the tenants and take close regard to what tenants have strong views about, which the evidence before our committee rather indicated was not about broad issues of governance, it was about mending the roof and I think that the well-run housing associations are well aware of that type of concern and give it special attention.

There is also the question of relating with the local authorities. In most areas housing the homeless is a joint responsibility of the local authority and of the associations. They must come to a civilised understanding with the local authority that is relevant about how they are going to do that. It is an important responsibility. Then there will be other representatives of the local community to whom they should clearly relate and explain their policies. I see it as a multi-dimensional type of accountability.

714. LORD THOMSON: Yes. I think what perhaps we want advice about is the fact that, as I understand it, although the housing association movement—I think one can properly call it that—is a very valuable movement with a very splendid history, its membership is very diverse and in practice, as so often happens in these situations, there are a few very big housing associations that, in effect, overshadow the rest. Given the vagueness about accountability, is there not some danger that in these big housing associations where you have a staff of perhaps a thousand, you have an unpaid, voluntary board of non-executives who are giving very creditable public service, but is there not a real risk there of the management team dominating the situation and not really being specifically accountable in any precise terms to anybody other than the Housing Corporation?

DAVID HANCOCK: That is precisely why our report and our code sets out in such detail the respective roles and responsibilities of the board on the one hand and the chief executive on the other. We have also stressed the importance of making sure that the board is capable of calling the chief executive to account by bringing in people with the right sort of background and from a wide variety of different professional and other interests.

I think this is one of the reasons why so many of the people from the associations who gave evidence to us stressed the importance of the voluntary principle, whereby the chief executive is not a member of the board but is clearly answerable to it. Although my committee was divided on this point, I myself have great sympathy with that point of view. If the decision-makers do not include the chief executive that symbolises a form of accountability so far as he and his staff are concerned, which I think is important. Of course, one does not want the board to interfere in his business, which does happen on occasions—I think that is equally bad.

715. LORD THOMSON: You have just answered very adequately the next question I was about to ask you about the chief executive. You made the interesting point in your opening remarks about Section 15—that you did not want excessive governance in this area—and, indeed, you made a plea for liberalisation. Could you expand on that a bit?

DAVID HANCOCK: Yes. I mentioned it particularly because it seems to me that both the National Federation and the Housing Corporation are being a bit coy on this issue. I think they are afraid of being accused of being "soft on sleaze", if you will forgive the rather crude vernacular that has become prevalent. Surely the more important thing is the merits of the case. It is not clear to me why housing associations should be subject to this very particularly restrictive top-down regime. It does not apply elsewhere. I was sent the other day, for example, a document which no doubt you have seen, which is the Guide for Members of Governing Bodies of Universities issued by the CUC and the way in which these matters are dealt with in universities is quite clear—it is a declaration of interest regime. In other words, if a matter comes up before the decision-making body where an individual member of that body has a pecuniary interest, he should declare it and if it is serious he should leave the room. This is generally regarded as a sufficient protection. I think the system in local government works in much the same way.

The disadvantages of Section 15 are important. It means that if you have a relative who has a very strong claim to a house owned by the association you may not give it to him, as I understand it, and that seems wrong in principle. Secondly, it means that business cannot be given to any company which is associated with a member of the board and the effect of that is most unfortunate—my bank will not allow any member of its staff to be a member of a board of a housing association, because we do a great deal of business with housing associations and if they were we couldn't do business with that one. I know of several young idealistic members of Hambros who would very much like to join the boards of housing associations and their contribution is, of course, extremely valuable. These are people who can say "Look, you are paying fifteen basis points too much for that" and say it with authority. I think it is wrong that there should be a system which prevents people like that from joining boards. The same may well apply, I don't know, to lawyers and accountants.

716. LORD THOMSON: You have spelled out in your draft code very clear rules about this and you think that these would be sufficient of themselves—the withdrawal when a matter comes up in which you have a direct interest, that kind of thing—rather than a blanket bar on people who actually have some professional knowledge or experience in this field, of giving that experience to a housing association?

DAVID HANCOCK: Yes, combined with our other recommendations about openness and the responsibility of the board as a whole and the responsibility of the chair to ensure that decisions which are of importance are taken by the board as a whole and not by any coterie within it.

717. LORD THOMSON: You do advise quite strongly, I think, in the code the benefits of advertising for

members of the board to get a wider range of recruits. Have you any sort of feel as to how far that advice is followed?

DAVID HANCOCK: Not universally and I think one of the reasons why some associations find difficulty recruiting is because they do it entirely in-house, so to speak, and do not go out to a wider public. I was very pleased to read that the National Federation have now established a data bank which will enable associations which are having difficulties in recruiting good members, members with the right sort of qualifications, to ask the data bank whether they have got any names on their list that they might look at. I think it will be found that the number of people who are willing to give service to worthwhile bodies like housing associations is much larger than you might expect.

718. LORD THOMSON: You have been very careful to emphasise how you want to get away from top-down and you don't wish the results of your report and your draft code to be prescriptive, but could you give us any sort of feel about how far it has been welcomed by the members of the housing association movement and how far the spirit and, to some extent, the letter of what you are advising, is going to be followed up?

DAVID HANCOCK: We went to very great trouble to make sure that our report was not top-down. In the first place, as I have said, the idea of having the review came from the movement, it came from their annual conference. Secondly, we asked for evidence and we received tons of it. I have never read so much paper about one subject in the whole of my life before.

LORD THOMSON: You have not yet had the good fortune to be a member of the Nolan Committee!

DAVID HANCOCK: Anyway, the report that we produced was intended to be an encapsulation of what the movement itself regarded as best practice and we made that very clear. The other thing we did, when we put forward our code, we put it forward to the Federation as a draft and we invited the Federation to consult about it, which they did. We and they received another ton of evidence of varying quality, with lots of comments on it. As a result of that exercise Mr Tickell of the Federation rewrote the code and it was then issued at the conference with a great deal of support behind it. The support has been so widespread that those who disagree with it are keeping very quiet.

719. LORD THOMSON: Thank you very much. Could I ask you just for a moment, finally, before I hand over to the Chairman, to don your merchant banking hat of Hambros and tell me how merchant banks view the funding of housing associations. Does Hambros, for instance, given your presence there when you are funding housing associations, do you worry about matters of governance or not?

DAVID HANCOCK: Well, I agreed to do it partly because Hambros recommends the credit of housing associations to other people and the better the governance, obviously, the more secure the credit. We do lend on our own book but chiefly we raise finance from other sources, from the investing institutions and the public capital markets and we syndicate bank loans. So we bring in other banks.

Yes, we take very close account of governance. Quite frankly asset security, the conventional recourse of a banker, is not a great deal of help with social housing. I mean, the tenants are already there, you cannot throw them out—the alternative use of the building is rather nebulous. Far more important is quality of the management and that is one of the first things we look at. Hambros, ourselves, we are rather choosy about the people we lend to. We take great comfort from the regulatory regime. Although it is complained about as being excessively onerous it does actually ensure that housing associations do not have great difficulty in raising funds for good projects.

LORD THOMSON: Thank you very much indeed.

720. LORD NOLAN: Thank you. Can I ask you one question about housing associations before turning right away from that and coming on to education briefly? In paragraph 3.22 of your report on page 25 you are in the middle of a passage advocating what I used to call, until people got rather bored with the expression, "government in the sunshine", that people can see what is happening and if it is good they can see that it is good and that is what we would all like to achieve and you list the sort of information that might be given, including information about decisions but not necessarily about the way decisions are made; you say board meetings should be in private and that, of course, one entirely follows. Amongst the specific items which you suggest might be covered in reports published to tenants and other interested parties was the gender and ethnic balance of the board. What significance did you attach to that?

DAVID HANCOCK: There is a lot of pressure for what is called equal opportunities. I think myself that the most important thing is that the person should be qualified to do the job. Equally I think that the tenants and others are entitled to know what the gender and ethnic balance of the board is. In the old days you could always tell a lady because it was Mrs or Miss, but you cannot these days—the way these things are printed it does not always make it obvious—and it is perfectly reasonable in an area with a lot of Bangladeshis to say that you do or do not have two Bangladeshi members on the board. It is important to the Bangladeshi community. I have quite lot to do with the Bangladeshi community in Tower Hamlets because I am chairman of a charity which was set up to help them—the St Katherine and Shadwell Trust—which I think Mr Shore is familiar with.

LORD NOLAN: And the purpose of this information would be just so that people could see if women and ethnic minorities were under——

DAVID HANCOCK: And if the Bangladeshi community thinks they have got a good candidate who ought to be they can write in and propose him or her.

LORD NOLAN: Yes, thank you very much.

DAVID HANCOCK: It is just another way of making it all open.

721. LORD NOLAN: Yes. Without necessarily laying down that there should be a particular number of women or a particular number of representatives of ethnic minorities?

DAVID HANCOCK: That was our approach throughout.

722. LORD NOLAN: Yes, thank you very much. Now, may I ask you to go back to the education system? Have you any comments on governance in the education system which you would put before us with a view to helping us decide what are the most important things in that area that we should concentrate on?

DAVID HANCOCK: In the case of universities and also, I think, further education colleges, the point I would most stress is respect for their independence. I think it is most important they should spend money well and they should be accountable for the way they spend it. But the trouble is that, if they are brought too much to heel, you will begin to raise questions about academic freedom. In my opinion academic freedom is just as important for the defence of our liberties as the freedom of the press, universal suffrage and the independence of the judiciary. This is a matter of prime importance. I make no apologies for the tightening up financial requirements in universities while I was at the Department of Education and Science—because their accounts were so difficult to read that some of them did not know whether they were in surplus or deficit. I also found in one or two cases that they did not have any independent scrutiny. I was very keen that they should all have audit committees which I believe they do now. Although this may have seemed very top-down at the time it was done, once it is done actually it is a reinforcement of local responsibility, which is what our intention was.

I am a bit worried about some of the quality control procedures that have been introduced. I am not intimately concerned with any university but they do seem to require an awful lot of paper and I think that might get in the way of the real business of teaching, scholarship and research, if one is not careful. So my general advice is hands off a bit—that is relax the pressure a bit rather than increase it.

723. LORD NOLAN: One possibility that was discussed earlier this morning was that the Secretary of State should have power to remove, to dismiss members of the boards of universities, so as to bring them in line with colleges of further education. Would you have any comment on that?

DAVID HANCOCK: I think it would be quite wrong. I think that the governing body as a whole should have the right to dismiss one or two of its members, on good grounds, but to put that in the power of Ministers I think would be a terrible mistake.

LORD NOLAN: Yes, thank you very much. I will ask any other members of the Committee if they have any questions to ask while we have got you here. (Pause) No, and I think it has been a very productive and interesting half-hour. Thank you very much indeed for coming to us.

DAVID HANCOCK: Thank you.

724. LORD NOLAN: Mr Cooke, Deputy Chairman, and Mr Mayer, Chief Executive of the Housing Corporation. Good afternoon, gentlemen, thank you very much for coming to join us.

PETER COOKE, AND ANTHONY MAYER

PETER COOKE (Deputy Chairman, Housing Corporation): Thank you, Mr Chairman. We have put in a short opening statement which we hoped would avoid the need for lengthy opening remarks, which we hope you have found helpful. I suspect that the echoes of the thoughts in that short note will perhaps come through in the answers to the questions which you may be putting to us, setting out the regulatory stance of the Housing Corporation. I should perhaps just say that I am here rather than the Chairman of the Corporation, perhaps most particularly because of my role as Chairman of the Registration and Supervision Committee of the Housing Corporation, which is the committee which has the principal regulatory responsibility within the organisation of the board, and that, indeed, we have just recently introduced some changes to the organisation of the board, which will give delegated responsibility to that committee for decisions on registration and de-registration of housing associations although, of course, fundamental issues and policy issues will remain with the board. So perhaps it is appropriate that I should be here, given the range of issues that you are likely to want to cover. These new arrangements, indeed, in terms of governance aspects more generally, will also make it possible for the Chairman and the board as a whole to act under this new arrangement to a degree as an appeal body in respect of individual decisions, should that be necessary.

I hope Mr Mayer and I may chip into each other's answers from time to time without causing undue disturbance to the process, as we go through the questions.

LORD NOLAN: We are quite sure you will not disturb us. Thank you very much. I will ask Sir Clifford Boulton to begin the questions, please.

725. CLIFFORD BOULTON: Good morning. Thank you very much indeed for the very full documentation you have provided us with. Speaking for myself it certainly reassures me that much thought has been given to these issues already and that we are not entering into some field of which you are not aware yourselves. Obviously there are some areas where we shall want to press you for a little more information but certainly we are aware that we are not starting on something which is not already taken very seriously.

I must apologise if sometimes the answers to my questions have already been provided in the material but I think it might help if I may do that because it not only gets on the record in a convenient way that particular point but it helps me and my colleagues asking you supplementary points if you have made an opening answer.

Also can I make it clear that I am well aware of the enormous variety and character of the housing associations—some 2,300 of them, I think—and that the very small ones present quite different problems and situations than the larger ones and, indeed, you are taking them as a separate subject, I understand, for appropriate forms of regulation. So my questioning will be primarily about the large housing associations.

We have been made well aware by individual housing associations of the value they attach to their own self-regulation and the responsibilities which they are very anxious and willing to carry themselves and, indeed, of what they claim to be their "private status" in a review of conduct in public life. So we are sensitive to the kind of situation you find yourselves in addressing them in a regulatory capacity.

I think we can agree, though, when we look at your code, for instance in the section on shareholding

membership, that you do not look at the shareholders as a central element of an association system of governance, that you do, in fact, have to fill what could otherwise be a vacuum in this world and, therefore, it is relevant for us to explore in these questions how far you go in that role. I think that you are proposing to do this by way of performance standards and I think that that is clearly a very sensible way of going about it, but I think you do rely very much on the boards of the individual associations to monitor themselves in that capacity. I see that you say in paragraph 32:

"However, our approach to regulation has moved away from the prescription of processes and now places emphasis on associations taking responsibility for, and being accountable to the Corporation for their own management and conduct."

I wonder if you could give us some examples of the way that this, in fact, works? In think in paras. 22 and 23 of your memorandum you do actually talk about the review performance that you undertake, annual returns, annual accounts, and so forth. Would you like to set the scene for us by describing the extent to which you do monitor performance standards and what you do about it when you have made that review?

PETER COOKE: Well, we have quite extensive procedures and sets of questions and areas of activity that we seek to cover in our regular discussions with housing associations and perhaps I could ask Anthony Mayer to iterate some of those.

ANTHONY MAYER (Chief Executive, Housing Corporation): All major developing associations that you are interested in, Sir Clifford, get a form they have got to fill in every year which includes a large number of questions ranging over the whole of the Housing Corporation's performance standards. On the narrow issue of the governance of housing associations we ask a number of detailed questions about committee composition, committee skills, whether or not they have arrangements for declarations of interest registers, whether or not they have rules of conduct, the composition of committees, the number of committees and the number of times they meet—the whole panoply of questions relating to governance.

The committee take responsibility for completing that form, return it to us and we look at the returns. So, for instance, if there were not rules relating to hospitality or a hospitality book we would immediately be concerned, go back to the association and say "Why haven"t you got a hospitality book, can you take remedial action?" If on the face of it we are satisfied, we then, on a sample basis, will go back to all the 300-odd associations filling in the returns—probably about a quarter every year—just to check on the accuracy of the returns. All associations know that they are expected, as with any self-certification arrangement, to provide accurate and reliable information. They all know that we will take a very dim view indeed, if we did this sample check and found that the committee was misleading us. Overall I am satisfied that this system of self-certification does work and does give us, in the particular item you are pursuing at the moment, an accurate over-view of the standard of governance of housing associations.

726. CLIFFORD BOULTON: But you do not just produce a synthesis/digest of everything that comes in and

issue it, you actually go back to the individual association if you do not like some of the answers that they give you, do you?

ANTHONY MAYER: If we don't like an answer we always go back. If we do like the answers we will go back on a sample basis to individual associations.

727. CLIFFORD BOULTON: Just to take an example, do you ask them how they recruit new board members—do you ask them about whether they advertise, which is one of the recommendations in the code, for new members?

ANTHONY MAYER: No, we do not. And it is an early exemplification of our opening statement. Our approach is to secure outcomes. We are therefore more concerned about the quality and range of skills of the committee rather than how they achieve it. If you are then to ask a supplementary question "Do you think associations should advertise, do we agree with Sir David Hancock"s report?", the answer would be yes. Our regulatory approach is we would prefer to leave it to the associations themselves to decide how best, if they need to strengthen their committees, they should do so.

CLIFFORD BOULTON: So that is an area where you will not be pushing them but encouraging them.

ANTHONY MAYER: Encouraging them, yes.

728. CLIFFORD BOULTON: You ask us very fairly for what our view is going to be about making any form of payment or monetary compensation. Do you have preliminary views yourself on either the possibility of remuneration or expenses actually incurred being reimbursed for members of housing associations?

ANTHONY MAYER: Two separate issues. One is that housing associations' committee members are allowed to claim expenses, within limits, for instance the cost of baby-sitting, petrol allowance——

729. CLIFFORD BOULTON: What about loss of earnings if there have been loss of earnings?

ANTHONY MAYER: In terms of remuneration our view is two-fold. One is that we do not see any sense of enthusiasm in housing associations themselves remunerating committee members. We do see a developing sense of concern that a voluntary committee member should not be worse off as a result of being a committee member and we are actively considering—and would welcome your views on the issue—the possibility, for instance, of allowing jury-level loss of earnings to committee members. That is the broad direction of our thinking. We are still developing our thoughts and any contribution you can make to this, I think, very sensitive debate, because it impinges so clearly on this crucial voluntary ethos, would be welcome.

730. CLIFFORD BOULTON: And some housing associations have got a very strong character of a charitable activity by their members, where we have had kind of shock horror reaction indicated that—"I would no more accept any money for serving on this than I would expect to be paid for giving blood"—I think was one example. In fact you would not be prescriptive, or feel the need to, because ——

ANTHONY MAYER: I find such a level of shock horror disturbing to the point of "methinks the lady doth protest too much". If there was, for instance, a jury-level of loss of earnings introduced—there would be no question of the Housing Corporation imposing such a system on an individual association. It would be entirely for the individual association committee to decide whether or not they wished to participate in such a scheme. So I do hope that those members of charitable associations that have given evidence can be suitably reassured.

CLIFFORD BOULTON: It would be hard to see that jury-level being an inducement, actually, to do all the things one has to do as a member perhaps.

PETER COOKE: Might I just slip in a comment, Sir Clifford, on this? I think the board as a whole—I am not quite sure how far you are personalising these questions—but the board as a whole certainly were very conscious of the need to be responsive to the variegated nature of the housing association movement and not to compromise the very deep-rooted voluntary principles that have enshrined its activities. We certainly did not, I think, regard payment as being something which was essential because without it the proper conduct of business by a management committee, or by a board, was otherwise being compromised because the right sort of people would not come and do the work that was necessary to achieve the appropriate degree of competence.

But we did also feel very sympathetic to the point of view that said that membership of a board of a housing association should be open to everybody who had an interest and who had a contribution to make. If there was something there in financial terms which was precluding a very proper contribution by, say, for example, a tenant who might be of limited financial means, then they should not be precluded because of the inability to pay from making a contribution.

731. CLIFFORD BOULTON: While I am just on boards, what would you like to say about chief executives on boards?

ANTHONY MAYER: Perhaps chief executives should not comment on that question!

PETER COOKE: Again, I think this is an issue which there will be differences of view about and I think the board of the Corporation feel that it is unnecessary to be prescriptive in this area. I think a lot will depend upon the nature of the existing governance regime in an organisation regarding the role of the chief executive, the degree of comfortableness of his role outside the board. My own personal view would be that there is a great deal to be said for associations to emulate the procedures in the Housing Corporation itself, whereby the chief executive is a member of the board. It does seem to make for a collegiate approach, if you like, to the running of the business, which provides this link between the professional executives and the management board of the organisation. But I do not think there is any wish to be prescriptive about this on the part of the Corporation.

732. CLIFFORD BOULTON: Is there not a counter-argument that the separate and proper roles and functions of the chief executive and the board are more clearly seen if he is not actually sitting round with them round the table?

PETER COOKE: One could certainly argue that. I think we have had a growing sense in the Corporation over recent years as the 1988 Act has come more and more into operation that, at any rate as far as the larger associations are concerned, one is looking at an organisation which is much more akin to that of a plc, and that in terms of the responsibilities and the scale of the business that is being undertaken it may well require an approach which is more akin to that of a public company where more often than not I think the chief executive will be a member of a board.

733. CLIFFORD BOULTON: If I can follow that analogy, you do not draw a very clear distinction between the chief executive and the secretary of the company. You talk about where the secretary of the association is a member of staff other than the chief executive, which rather suggests you think it is totally normal for him to be the secretary, and the chief executive will have ultimate responsibility for that member of staff.

We had evidence from Professor Rudolf Klein last week in which he said there might be a mandatory requirement for the large housing associations to appoint a secretary responsible for advising members on issues of propriety. He, in answer to my question on that point, said that he got the impression that much of the secretary's role was being swallowed up by the chief executive, and if the chief executive is then on the board isn't it rather a failure to provide proper checks and balances of somebody whose function it is actually to say "hold on a minute" and maybe interpose themselves between the chief executive and the board, or the chairman.

PETER COOKE: Yes, I understand that. I would rather assume that the cases where chief executives and secretaries exist in the same person applies substantially to small associations and not to large ones. I cannot think of any large association that I know anything of where these roles are combined. So I think the point falls away rather if you assume that they are not combined and, indeed, I would think it entirely appropriate for a larger association to have a secretary who has the kind of responsibilities and duties which you describe as well as advising on legal aspects and very often, the general responsibilities of the board. A very valuable role and certainly not one which should be provided by the chief executive.

734. CLIFFORD BOULTON: Thank you. I think to be fair to Professor Klein he did talk about this applying to the large housing associations, that it should do, but he also said that he did not have a systematic study to give figures. Anyway, thank you for pointing out the trap that we could fall into of equating the two in our minds and we know they are separate.

Can I talk to you a little bit about openness, because in an area which is not always hot in directly elected democratic features openness is a form of accountability, and you recognise in your own documentation that to be the case in your code. What I am concerned with here is your deep-seated reluctance to publish or press for the publication of the results of enquiries into where problems have arisen. I am reluctant to talk about particular cases but Circle 33 has been mentioned by others and so one can just use that as an example. There are areas where we find—in fact it has happened in higher education—where reports do get published. Perhaps you would like to say

what the inhibitions are which have led you so far not to publish reports of particular problems that have arisen.

PETER COOKE: I think there are some inhibitions. On the broad issue of openness we would take the view that openness is *per se* a good thing, and I think any regulator certainly regards transparency in the businesses that he is regulating, and all aspects of it, to be a valuable aid to the regulatory process because it enables those outside the regulatory process to make their own judgments and assessments and introduce elements of market discipline, if you like, into the process by which regulation is aided. So I think the concept of openness and of the provision of information is, on the whole, something which the Corporation would generally support, but I do think that approach needs to be qualified in the sense that it should be pursued only to the extent that it will not be compromising the proper objectives of regulation and the regulatory function. I think the particular case of the publication of our reports is one of those circumstances, most particularly because if it is known that that it is going to be published you can, in the course of the process of dealing with a problem situation, find that it can destabilise the way in which you actually handle that situation on an ongoing basis. There are also a number of issues which I think arise of a legal nature which Mr Mayer may like to comment on.

ANTHONY MAYER: If we could distinguish between Circle 33 and another association, Harambee, which was subject to a Section 28 Enquiry, there was some pressure for us to publish the report of that enquiry. The strong legal advice we got was that report effectively was the case for the prosecution. If we published it and the defendant decided to take the Housing Corporation for a judicial review, they would have been seriously disadvantaged by the pre-trial presentation of the case for the prosecution. On other areas I very much agree with Peter Cooke that we favour openness except to the point that it makes our regulatory process more difficult. So for instance with Circle 33, shortly after the particular crisis had been resolved, there was a new chief executive, and a new chairwoman who I believe you are meeting with next week, who were trying very very hard to implement the necessary changes. I think if there had been a publication of our regulatory report on Circle 33 all that would have happened would have been a further destabilising and uncertainty in their efforts to basically make sure that the affairs of Circle 33 were being run in an acceptable manner. I think very much openness, yes, unless there are legal constraints, or unless our view, and this is a judgment, is that the regulatory process would be damaged as a result of publication.

PETER COOKE: I think there is one other thought in this and that is we are dealing particularly with large associations in organisations which are providing a very substantial public service on a continuing basis, and that there is no particular point, as it were, in publicly rapping somebody over the knuckles just for the sake of doing that if in doing so you somehow compromise or constrain the degree to which the association, the organisation, can then continue to perform its duties, as it were, in this case in meeting housing need.

735. CLIFFORD BOULTON: I am certainly not going to, not least in present company, argue the legal problems of the first case you mentioned. I think in the education sphere where reports that have been prepared with a view to publication they have been very valuable in

drawing general lessons for other people. Two things occur to me. One is that is it right to leave it to the individual association to have to publish this unfortunate information about itself? Is that not a little bit hard and one can understand their reluctance, but would it not be possible perhaps to have a policy whereby the reports were prepared with a view to chopping off at the end particular details and particularly embarrassing or awkward matters of the kind that sometimes quite properly can be left out of premature retirement agreements or something like that without falling for a total gagging clause. The sequence of events and the lessons could perhaps be prepared in the report consciously in advance with a view to publication.

PETER COOKE: I guess that might be possible. I certainly regard it as a very important part of a regulator's role to, as it were, learn the lessons from events that have come about which have led to problems. My own approach to this would be very much one which seeks to address, identify, describe and learn lessons from the issues rather than the cases. You know, I think, that we have a stewardship report which we produce for the Department of the Environment and which in future years we are intending to publish, and I would see as a very important part of that report an account, if you like, of the areas where problems have arisen in the area of regulation, in particular where there are specific lessons to be learnt where people can learn from others mistakes. That that is a very important part of the regulator's role to bring such lessons to the attention of the sector that is being regulated to ensure that the same mistakes are not made elsewhere. I think that can be done very effectively without getting into the tangle of taking apart the confidential and sensitive issues from the less sensitive issues. It is particularly so in the case of the Section 28 inquiry, for example, where there is an outside person, usually a legal person, who will be appointed to write this. They could certainly make these distinctions, but I think the freedom and the flow perhaps of the analysis and recommendations of the investigation and inquiry would come more naturally and more easily without that distinction being made. The same positive results can be achieved by, as I say, addressing the issues involved rather than the particular circumstances of the case.

736. CLIFFORD BOULTON: Thank you for the constructive suggestion about the stewardship report which I take on board.

Just one final question before other members ask a few questions. I wonder if you could say a word for the record on the combined funding and regulatory role because this is something which I know a thought has been given to and there are potential tensions which have been identified. Is there something you would like to say about that?

ANTHONY MAYER: A point of principle by me, and then if I may some practical points by Peter Cooke who has much experience in this area. The point of principle: I am the accounting officer responsible not only to the Department of the Environment but also to Parliament and the Public Accounts Committee for what stands at the moment as £19 billion worth of taxpayers' money which is going to organisations to provide social housing in this country. In being able to act as a responsible steward for that £19 billion worth of money, I have got to be in charge of an organisation who can satisfy itself that that money is resting in suitably conducted organisations. If I cannot have the direct line control on what is happening in housing associations, their suitability for remaining social landlords and be able to improve performance if one has doubts about that performance, if I cannot have that satisfaction I do not think it possible for me to act responsibly as an accounting officer. Against that rather sombre point of principle, it was with some relief that on the record the government in their Prior Options Review of the Housing Corporation have supported the line that regulation is an integral part of the funding process. It was also with relief that I heard the Shadow Minister of Housing, Nick Raynsford, also make the point that funding and regulation as a matter of principle should be under the same roof.

PETER COOKE: I am not sure that I am able to address the practicalities as such, but I certainly would accept the statement that regulation in some circumstances can appropriately be separated from other functions which an organisation carries on because there is tension and it exists in a number of regulatory bodies, not just the Housing Corporation. I am certainly convinced, and the board of the Corporation are convinced, that it is essential, in our case, for the board and for the Corporation to fulfil its function effectively that those responsibilities should be combined. At the regional level in the Housing Corporation, in the regional offices where the grass roots work is done on allocations of funding resources and on the regulatory activities of the Corporation, they are separately conducted but they have a relationship, as it were, and an opportunity for dialogue which is critical, and in my view, quite invaluable for the fulfilment of both the functions. I think it is extremely important in the particular circumstances of the Housing Corporation to have them within the same organisation. Indeed, I would go further and say that in the event that it were decided to make the regulatory function a separate body independently responsible for that function alone, I think, given the circumstances of the funding of the social housing sector and the way it is structured at the moment, you would probably have to recreate a regulatory function within the funding organisation in order to satisfy the kinds of issues to which Anthony Mayer has referred.

I think that it is an issue which is properly one which should be addressed, and in some cases you can make a case for separation. In this particular case, in my judgment, and I think this seems to be shared by those who have looked at it over the last year or two, specifically it is best to leave it where it is.

737. CLIFFORD BOULTON: Do you use funding to steer policy? Do you tell them that they have to make a provider, spend a proportion of the money on housing for the disabled or something like that, or hypothecate the funding for particular purposes which might not have been the preferred policy of the association?

ANTHONY MAYER: A potentially huge answer; I will be brief. Every year the Minister will allocate a certain sum of money and will basically make some divisions between national sub-programmes, for instance housing for rent, housing for sale, and also make a sum of money available for special needs projects nationally. Our first port of call is very much to the local authority to discuss with the local authority, the director of housing, the chairman or woman of housing, what the local authority's priorities are for the year within the basic programmes that we have money to allocate. We then invariably get a joint plan that there should be this or that special needs project, this or that new housing scheme, and then on the back of that invite housing associations to make competitive bids to us to have the particular programme achieved. I do not think it is therefore so much a question of us influencing particular patterns of provision. I think it is working very, very closely with local authorities to ensure that there is a marrying up, if you like, of the national programme with local housing strategies.

CLIFFORD BOULTON: Thank you, that answer convinces me that we are right to be looking at housing associations.

738. LORD NOLAN: I wonder if I could pick up a legal point arising out of what Sir Clifford was saying before we go on. This is about the publication of Section 28 reports and I noticed in paragraph 19 of your supplementary memorandum you say:

"The Corporation has taken legal advice on whether it should publish a Section 28 inquiry report. That advice was strongly against publication, not on grounds of secrecy but essentially on grounds of natural justice. To publish in advance of any appeal to the High Court what is in effect the case for the prosecution could seriously prejudice any challenge of the Corporation's decision. Furthermore, without the protection of absolute privilege, a commitment to publication of an inquirer's report would seriously restrict what could be said in the final report given the law of libel."

I am certainly not questioning the advice you were given, but I am a little puzzled by the description of the report as the case for the prosecution. Was this not a conclusion based on hearing the evidence from both sides?

ANTHONY MAYER: We can provide you with the supplementary memorandum on the particular point. The Section 28 report was an examination commissioned by the board of the Housing Corporation into whether or not there was mismanagement and/or misconduct by the committee of Harambee. To the extent that misconduct and mismanagement was found, then that particular case was more nearly akin to the case for the prosecution where the defendant has a right and natural justice to say "Well, look, I disagree, I do not think there was mismanagement and/or misconduct". That was my understanding of the spirit in which that legal advice was given. If you want further information, because I can appreciate the sensitivity of this particular case, we will gladly give it to the committee.

739. LORD NOLAN: Was the advice given in general terms or in relation to a particular report? In other words, was the advice you should never publish a Section 28 report, or you should not publish this one?

ANTHONY MAYER: The advice was given in respect of this particular report. One would have to revisit as to whether or not that advice is invariably of general application. I do not know the answer to that question. It is potentially a very important point in the context of any further inquiry we have.

740. LORD NOLAN: I appreciate it is a very difficult issue, but supposing the report is not ultimately found to be 100 per cent accurate, I think it was Harold Wilson who said that "the falsehood is halfway round the world before the truth has got its boots on", and you never quite catch

up an adverse report once it has been published. But other bodies, as you know, in many fields do publish the reports, and the possibility of an application to the High Court does not disqualify that, nor the law of libel if it is properly written. Would you have these reports written by a Queen's Counsel or somebody like that?

ANTHONY MAYER: I do not know what the context of reports are in other bodies. All I can tell you is that in this particular sort of report it is specifically focusing on misconduct and/or mismanagement which I fancy, but I do not know, puts it in a slightly different category. To answer who did the report, it was Patricia Scotland QC on our behalf.

741. LORD NOLAN: The last thing we want to do is to cause further trouble or expense, but this is a point that has been put to us by a number of people. I do not know whether it would be possible for you to put in a short supplementary memorandum about your general approach to the publication of these reports on the lines you have indicated?[2]

ANTHONY MAYER: Delighted.

742. PETER SHORE: Further to the use of your powers, first of all the powers themselves are very extensive indeed, and looking at the memorandum you gave us, under paragraph 18 the Corporation has a great range of powers with regard to lapses in management or conduct of an association. Then again with regard to action to safeguard public investment and the security of tenants following an inquiry. You can get rid of people, you can appoint people, you can establish inquiries and so on. Do you ever in your annual report give information as to the number of occasions on which you have used these powers?

ANTHONY MAYER: The answer is, yes, in our annual report in summary form. I think you are entitled to say, Mr Mayer, why only in summary form? To which I then say, yes, I think arguably we should have published fuller reports before. I think it would be helpful given the very wide range of our powers if we could also publish our stewardship reports to give more detail about the use of our powers. For the committee's information, I have been chief executive of the House Corporation now for four and three quarter years, we have only had one Section 28 report. Since 1974, let us say a handful. In terms of Section 17 appointees, that is us making appointments to committees, at any one time there would be between five and ten Section 17 appointees on committees. This is a range figure. We can give the precise numbers. The impression I want to give you, is that these albeit extensive powers are used sparingly and only with the specific approval of the board of the Housing Corporation and the chairman of the Housing Corporation.

743. CLIFFORD BOULTON: Could I ask are those big or small associations?

ANTHONY MAYER: The Section 17s can be to any association. In practice, and relying just on memory for four and three quarter years, the appointments have been overwhelmingly to small associations, and within the family of small associations to newer associations where, for instance, the initial enthusiasm of the committee when the association was set up might have been slightly dissipated. What we try to do is get the Section 17s in, turn

---

[2]*See* Evidence, pp. 468-470.

the situation around, get new committee members and then leave. It is not a permanent appointment.

PETER COOKE: Perhaps I might just add that my hesitation in responding to your question was because of the catalogue of powers that you read out. I was not sure quite how many of those was actually specifically referred to in our annual reports, but certainly my own view as far as the Stewardship Report on regulatory activities is concerned is that it is entirely proper and, indeed, probably necessary that there should be an accounting of the use of those powers, and that those should be specified in whatever degree of detail seems appropriate and helpful.

744. PETER SHORE: I think that would be helpful, frankly, and no doubt when you are responding to Lord Nolan's request for a note on Section 28 you could add further points arising from our exchange a few moments ago.

PETER COOKE: Sure.

745. PETER SHORE: Just going back now to what you were saying about the fact that the two functions of regulation and funding are married together. My impression from reading your very interesting memorandum was that really your whole performance review system depends upon, in a way, the integration of the two functions, because here you arrive at these performance assessment and investment summaries for each association and, as you say, the Corporation's decisions on allocation of funds for new investment is based upon a satisfactory PAIS report. That is so, isn't it?

PETER COOKE: Yes it is.

746. PETER SHORE: So you really do have this very strong leverage that if they are not up to it they will not get any further funds, which is an obvious incentive on their behaviour.

PETER COOKE: Certainly. It is, of course, only a leverage in so far as associations wish to avail themselves of the money which is available from the Housing Corporation. It does not impede or impair any of the rest of their business that they may as independent organisations choose to carry on.

747. PETER SHORE: That naturally leads me to turn to the very large number of, I suspect, smaller housing associations who are not seeking further funds established, but who still you have to look at and look at their behaviour and make sure that they are behaving properly. You refer in your paragraph 27 to what you call "Regulation Arrangements for Smaller Associations" —RASA. I gather that you are actually thinking further about what this should be, but could you indicate to us perhaps generally in what ways the regulatory functions that you now perform, and you will continue to perform, in relation to larger associations, how they will be different in future when you are applying them to the smaller associations.

PETER COOKE: This, again, is a subject on which one could speak extensively, and we are still in the process of developing our thoughts on this. I think the Corporation starts from the proposition that although there are a very large number of associations who have been at some time in receipt of public money and therefore it is sitting there, as it were, within the balance sheet of these organisations, it is very unlikely in our experience that many of them will want to come forward for more public funding. They are running along perfectly satisfactorily—a four unit almshouse somewhere—and the full panoply of the regulatory framework being applied to them has the appearance of beginning to look slightly ridiculous. So we are taking steps to devise a regime whereby probably I think at least half, or something of that order, of the housing association membership would fall within a category which allowed a rather less extensive system of regulation to apply to them. It will actually consist of still a lot of the same basic information which will be required on a continuing basis for all associations, particularly in relation to the board and the governance of the housing association, but will contain much less information on the ongoing activities and the detailed financial arrangements although, of course, the fundamental assessment of their financial wellbeing will be an essential part of the arrangements, but perhaps Mr Mayer wants to add a bit.

ANTHONY MAYER: Fine.

748. PETER SHORE: I am reasonably content with that. I assume that the Section 15 would still apply to the smaller housing association. I do not know whether you were here when Sir David Hancock was asked about Section 15. His reply, if I remember it correctly, was that it was really too strong a power of control, and he cited as an example of this the close relative of a board member who had a genuine case for being rehoused on grounds of need but he would be disqualified, as it were, from consideration because of his relative who was a member of the board. I am interested in your comments on that, but could not one say in reply to that, it is precisely the danger of the relatives of a member of the board being given preference in the very needy short area of social housing that would discredit a housing association?

PETER COOKE: This is a difficult area and the board has given quite a lot of thought to Section 15 and to the recommendations that were in the Hancock Report. We concluded that we should remain with Section 15, but we also, I think, concluded that there was scope for further examination of the possibilities of particular sorts of exemptions from the full rigours of Section 15 which might be appropriate to alleviate the regime to some degree. More generally I think perhaps I should convey to the committee that the board generally were instinctively sympathetic to the idea of moving from a more prescriptive regime to a conflicts of interest regime in the sense that this was an area in which integrity could still be relied upon in the delivery of public or semi-public office. We concluded that, not just as Sir David was mentioning if I heard him correctly, because of fears of sleaze, if you like, but because of the whole aura, the whole environment within which the housing association had become used to operating over a period of years, it seemed inappropriate, particularly at the present time, to contemplate a serious moving back from a position which had served the movement very well over a number of years. I think the conclusion that we reached was that we should remain with the Section 15 regime but that for precisely the reasons that you put forward in relation to this particular example one must be very careful about the nature of the exclusions that one actually agrees to. That there may be scope for some alleviation of the full rigours of this particular regime as it is drafted in the Act.

PETER SHORE: Thank you.

749. WILLIAM UTTING: If I could just follow up a couple of points. I saw that the White Paper *"Our Future Home"* proposes that profit making bodies should come into this market. Will this cause any change in your regulatory functions, or will the same principles and practices apply to the new boys as to the old boys?

PETER COOKE: I think that is quite a difficult question to answer at the moment. Clearly there are two main areas where changes will be proposed in the Housing Bill arising from the White Paper. The first of these relates to housing companies, and the second relates to private landlords—profit making bodies. As far as housing companies are concerned, I do not think we have any particular problems with it in terms of the existing regulatory regime in that it seems to us that that regime can be well applied to these new housing companies which may be set up.

With respect to private landlords, I think we are still, to some extent, thinking through our approach to their regulation, and I am not quite so clear that it can be simply the full and comprehensive adoption of the existing regime. There may be some special features which we have to take account.

ANTHONY MAYER: There are two particular difficulties and this is a very current question, it is still being thought about. First of all the propriety of our being able to appoint Section 17 appointees to subsidiaries of publicly quoted companies with shareholders is a difficult one. The second difficulty, coming back to Mr Shore's area of interest, is that almost intrinsically the board member of a subsidiary of a private landlord is receiving a benefit. This brings into question the appropriateness of Section 15 in this area and the difficulty of drawing up Section 15 in a way that can apply properly to a private sector company. Two very difficult issues where the only reassurance I can give you at the moment is that we are very seriously considering both with a view to reaching a satisfactory conclusion.

750. WILLIAM UTTING: And the Nolan Committee ought to keep an eye on how this develops presumably.

Secondly, you will not be surprised to know that we have had a number of letters from dissatisfied tenants of housing associations. What is your view about the adequacy of complaints procedures now?

PETER COOKE: I will ask Anthony Mayer to comment on that in relation to the organisational detail in the Housing Corporation, but I think that we were certainly very happy as a board to see the introduction of HATOS, the ombudsman service, and that degree of removal, if you like, from day to day routine complaints. I think that is working well and we were also very gratified to see that in the White Paper it is proposed that this service should be established totally independently from the Housing Corporation which I think we felt was an appropriate step. On the whole I think the complaints procedures in associations is something which we pay considerable attention to in the course of our regulatory investigations and enquiries and conversations, but perhaps Anthony Mayer would like to comment further.

ANTHONY MAYER: As a result of the Environment Select Committee Inquiry into us three years ago we did make a step change to improve complaints procedures. All developing associations have to have written complaints procedures. As part of the Tenants Guarantee every tenant is entitled to have their complaint dealt with within the association, and is then entitled to the extent that the association has not given him or her satisfaction to refer the complaint to the Housing Association Ombudsman. The ombudsman will then do one of two things. One is, first of all, and I think it is in the spirit in which it is operating, try to arrange for a conciliation between the tenant and the housing association. Most often the particular difficulty is with service delivery. Only if that fails will the Housing Association Ombudsman, Roger Jefferies, then do a full inquiry which will then be published very much following the model of the national ombudsman. I am satisfied that a serious improvement in this area has been made in the last two years. As always, one does not sit on ones laurels; one looks for any further improvements that one can make.

WILLIAM UTTING: Thank you.

LORD NOLAN: We have finished on time which is a record for us. We are extremely grateful to you. We have covered a great deal of ground with you this morning, and we have been enormously helped by the written material you have sent us, and are grateful also for your promise to supplement it yet further. Thank you very much indeed.

TUESDAY 5 DECEMBER 1995

OPENING STATEMENT

Opening statement of the Housing Corporation

The Housing Corporation's approach to the regulation of housing associations

1.   We welcome the opportunity to appear before the Committee. In the light of questions put to us ahead of the hearing, we believe the Committee might find it helpful if we submitted a brief opening statement to set out the Corporation's approach to the regulation of Housing Associations and how that role has changed since the 1988 Housing Act.

2.   Our starting point is that, along with universities, housing associations are not creatures of government or public authorities. They are independent bodies, many of very long standing, set up by volunteers and philanthropists who wished to improve the housing conditions of their fellow citizens. For example, 606 of the 2,300 housing associations are almshouses, many of whose origins go back to the sixteenth century or earlier. Housing associations now act as agents of government in the provision of social housing. They need not do so if they do not wish to do so. There are therefore implicit, necessary and justifiable limits to the right of government to interfere in their constitutional arrangements.

3.   The focus of the Corporation's regulatory function is to ensure that the social housing product, substantially funded by the tax-payer, is and can be seen to be delivered. Only to the extent that we need to secure this objective or to ensure that it will not be frustrated do we interest ourselves in the constitution, finances, management and performance of associations. In meeting this objective, our particular concerns are to sustain confidence in this system which delivers the product and to protect the interests of the tax-payer and the tenant.

4.   The Housing Corporation thus has no specific constitutional model for housing associations and their governance. We believe this would compromise the crucially important voluntary ethos of the housing association sector. It would also be impracticable given the diversity of registered housing associations which range from small co-operatives and almshouses to multi-thousand home associations like Peabody and the William Sutton Trust with their own order of parliament governing their constitution.

5.   Since 1988, the Corporations' regulatory focus has changed significantly. Associations are now major private sector risk-taking businesses, with un-guaranteed market borrowing amounting to over £8.5 billion. The change in housing associations' funding pattern from one of 100% public funding has resulted in a parallel shift in the Corporation's regulatory approach. Before 1988, we focused on processes. Now we have a less prescriptive approach which focuses on outputs and the achievement of set performance standards.

6.   Within this general approach to our regulatory role, we continue to work to improve our performance and procedures. We are receptive to constructive suggestions and welcome the Committee's views on some current issues. In making improvements, however, we believe we have constantly to bear in mind the need to avoid compromising the voluntary ethos of associations and to avoid regulating committees (or boards) out of their basic responsibility to run their own affairs in an orderly manner, which the vast majority do, year after year.

WEDNESDAY 6 DECEMBER 1995

Members Present:

The Rt Hon Lord Nolan (Chairman)

Sir Clifford Boulton GCB
Professor Anthony King
The Rt Hon Lord Thomsonof
Monifieth KT DL

Sir William Utting CB
Dame Anne Warburton DCVO CMG
Diana Warwick

Witnesses:

Brian Sherratt OBE, Headteacher, and Hon Alderman Mrs Judy Watts-James, Chair of Governors, Great Barr Grant Maintained School, Birmingham

Tom Johnson, Headteacher, and Lawrence Upton, Chair of Governors, Katherine's Grant Maintained Primary School, Harlow

Rodney Skidmore, Chief Executive, Central England Training and Enterprise Council

David Rossington, Chief Executive, and Mary Lord, Deputy Chief Executive, Lincolnshire Training and Enterprise Council

Sir Jeremy Beecham, Chairman, Association of Metropolitan Authorities, Elgar Jenkins OBE, Leader, Conservative Group, Association of District Councils, David Heath CBE, Leader, Liberal Democrat Group, Association of County Councils

David Hart, General Secretary, and Sue Nicholson, Assistant Secretary, National Association of Head Teachers

951. LORD NOLAN: Good morning, today we will be focusing primarily on grant-maintained schools and training and enterprise councils.

We will hear first from the head teachers and chairs of governors of two grant-maintained schools. Our first witness are Brian Sherratt and the Hon Alderman Mrs Judy Watts James, respectively head and chair of governors at Great Barr School, Birmingham. They will be followed by representatives of a grant-maintained school in the primary sector, Katherine's: the head, Tom Johnson, and the chair of governors, Lawrence Upton.

Next we will hear from the TECs. Rodney Skidmore is chief executive of Central England TEC, and he will be followed by David Rossington, chief executive of Lincolnshire TEC. Mr Rossington was, I understand, suffering from heavy 'flu and may not yet have recovered, but his deputy chief executive, Mary Lord, will be here in any case.

Our penultimate witnesses today are making their second appearance before the Committee as the spokespeople for local government. They are Sir Jeremy Beecham, Chairman of he Association of Metropolitan Authorities; Elgar Jenkins of the Association of District Councils and David Heath, of the Association of County Councils. Robin Wendt, secretary of the ACC, will be with them.

Our last witnesses today have had a busy last 24 hours in the media; they are David Hart, the general secretary of the National Association of Head Teachers, and the assistant secretary, Sue Nicholson.

Now, Mrs Watts James and Mr Sherratt. With many thanks to you for coming and for the very early, extremely cold start you must have had a bit of a day. As we are always in these hearings short of time may I go straight into the questions, thanking you first for all the material

you have sent us and asking Professor King to take up the questioning?

752. PROF ANTHONY KING: Could I first repeat the Chairman's thanks for this extremely useful document. I would like to begin with a couple of points that are raised in the opening statement that have not played a very prominent part in our discussion so far. In one of your paragraphs, 2.9, you say "With some governing bodies there is the possibility that a group of governors may take control and seek to perpetuate their power. However, it is the duty of other governors to ensure that this does not happen. "Chairman's Action" under emergency powers should always be justified at a full governors' meeting and the action with its justification minuted. This is an area [you say] of weakness requiring attention." Could you just say a little bit more about that and perhaps say something about the kind of attention you think it should get?

BRIAN SHERRATT OBE, AND HON ALDERMAN MRS JUDY WATTS-JAMES

BRIAN SHERRATT (Headteacher, Great Barr Grant Maintained School, Birmingham): I took the prompt from the wording of one of the questions which did in fact suggest that it would be possible for a small number of governors to exercise a particular influence in a governing body. It seems to me that this might happen where perhaps the chairman is a member of that small number and that by taking chairman's action it would be possible to impose a view or a will upon the larger number of governors. This would be a cause for concern.

753. PROF ANTHONY KING: Have you heard on the grapevine that it does in fact cause problems?

BRIAN SHERRATT: No, I have not. I took my cue there from the wording of one of the questions. But it does seem to me that it is essential that chairman's action should always be justified and justified at the next statutory governing body meeting and properly minuted, so that the nature of the action and the thinking behind it is always in the public domain.

754. PROF ANTHONY KING: One issue that we have thought about quite a lot but we have come to no conclusion about it, is the problems that seem to arise, or may arise, when there are difficulties in a grant-maintained school given that there are two bodies that deal with grant-maintained schools at the national level—two rather than one—and both at a considerable distance, the Funding Agency for Schools and the Department itself. You raise this in your opening statement and you say "Rather than introduce mechanisms of external scrutiny it would help if the powers of the clerk to the governing body were strengthened by making that role advisory with direct channels of communication with the FAS and the DFEE." Do you think that the clerk is the right person to do that particular job?

BRIAN SHERRATT: At the moment the status of the clerk to the governing body, either in a LEA or a grant-maintained school, is an inappropriate status. What I am suggesting is that we should be looking at the status of the clerk so that in addition to furnishing the governing body with the necessary information they require, both legal and otherwise, and furnishing them with documentation regarding their meetings and so on, that the role should be expanded to encompass the possibility of individuals, both on the staff and, indeed, governors themselves, and members of the wider community having access to the clerk having established for the clerk proper channels of communication with the FAS and with the DFEE. In other words, a different concept of the role of the clerk, a kind of internal ombudsman, I suppose.

755. PROF ANTHONY KING: There are already something like 1,100 grant-maintained schools. Do you think a person with that degree of competence could be found one by one for every one of them?

BRIAN SHERRATT: I think clerks would require additional training. The majority of clerks, it seems to me, are perhaps the head's secretary or somebody on the administrative or secretarial staff of the school, and in order to do the clerking duties they are currently required to undertake they need and receive appropriate training. I think it is the level of training that is of significance here.

PROF ANTHONY KING: There is an alternative possibility, which is that the person who performed that kind of ombudsman role could be somebody appointed by the school but from outside the school.

BRIAN SHERRATT: Yes, indeed. A possibility that springs to mind is someone from another grant-maintained school, not that grant-maintained schools consider themselves as a kind of exclusive club but certainly if the external person was associated with another grant-maintained school then they would understand the workings of most grant-maintained schools.

756. PROF ANTHONY KING: If you had to choose between an exalted clerk on the one hand or some such person from the world of grant-maintained schools on the other, which would you be inclined to go for?

BRIAN SHERRATT: Well, perhaps having heard what you said I might take the via media and have the exalted clerk, but perhaps supported by a clerk or some other person from another grant-maintained school to

bring an objectivity which perhaps might not be there were the matter solely left to the clerk of the school in question.

757. PROF ANTHONY KING: Now in the case of people who have grievances or, more precisely, feel that something is seriously going wrong in the school, which you refer to in paragraph 6.1 of your opening statement, might the same kind of ombudsman person play the role of the external appeal under that heading as well?

BRIAN SHERRATT: Yes, I would not take exception to that, I think that that would be sensible, given that it may not always appear appropriate to a person with a grievance to go to the chairman of governors, or any governor, or other clerk because the governors are the employers and, therefore, it would be helpful for them to feel that they were discussing the matter in confidence with a person who was not going to report the matter back to the governing body. But at the same time had channels open to the FAS and the DFEE.

758. PROF ANTHONY KING: In that same general connection one problem that may not have arisen frequently but I think has arisen and it does seem a little difficult and perplexing on the face of it, arises out of the fact that when teachers, including head teachers, are disciplined or even dismissed, their appeals against whatever has been inflicted upon them are heard by committees that consist entirely of governors within that school.

HON ALDERMAN JUDY WATTS-JAMES (Chair of Governors, Great Barr Grant Maintained School, Birmingham): I am sorry, I would have to disagree with you there because we do have outsiders who sit on the disciplinary panel and it is actually in the governors' legal manual. So if somebody is dismissed—a member of staff is appealing against dismissal there are so many governors and so many independent people sitting on that panel.

759. PROF ANTHONY KING: The manual must have changed jolly recently. I looked at what I took to be the latest edition this morning before I left. It did not give that impression. But at any rate the point of principle is the point that matters and you would actually approve of that kind of arrangement?

BRIAN SHERRATT: Yes.

760. PROF ANTHONY KING: You would, right. Can I ask you a little bit about this vexed question of the recruitment of governors and against the background that everybody understands that there are not large queues of people waiting to be governors and that one does have to go out and recruit them. Is there a case, however, for making it a matter of routine that when a governorship at a grant-maintained school falls vacant that the school should make it known through the press, ideally, in a formal advertisement that the post is vacant, perhaps indicate what qualities they are looking for in the next holder of the office and invite people either to nominate themselves or to nominate others. Should that, in your view, be a matter of routine?

JUDY WATTS-JAMES: I think one must bear in mind that governors are voluntary and give up their time and expertise and obviously in a school of our size we will want certain expertise. If the governor, shall we say, who has retired is the chartered accountant that we have and deals with finances then obviously we would be looking for expertise in that field. And we would look around, we do have people who approach us asking if they can come on the governing body. I think we need a CV and I think that the governors need to look at it very carefully indeed. We are in the happy position—and I appreciate that all schools are not in that position—in that we do have people who come and apply, if you like, ask if ever there is a vacancy would we consider them. If that situation altered then I would not object to an advertisement but I think one has to draw a very fine dividing line as it is a voluntary organisation and we want the best people, with the right expertise for the vacancy that is occurring.

761. PROF ANTHONY KING: Suppose for some reason a meeting of a board of governors has to or it would be desirable if it did take place in the early afternoon. Do you have any provisions at your school for reimbursing people for travel, for perhaps creche facilities for a child? Is that something that you ——

JUDY WATTS-JAMES: We have always offered to reimburse travelling expenses and the governors know that that is available. But at the moment no one has ever taken up the offer, have they?

BRIAN SHERRATT: This raises an important issue. If one is a JP and is required at the Magistrates' Court, my understanding is that there is an obligation on the employer, all things being reasonable, that the JP should be given leave of absence with pay and it may be worth looking at the possibility of governors not being out of pocket—if the role of governor is important and clearly it is, then it may be important enough for governors to be able to attend meetings, for example in the afternoon, and be reimbursed, not from the school, but by their employer.

762. PROF ANTHONY KING: You ask the question in your opening statement "Should there be a system whereby governors qualified for paid leave of absence as with JPs?" Is your answer to the question "yes"?

BRIAN SHERRATT: Yes, I think it is something which should perhaps be looked at because good governors are going to be busy people and governors with the expertise that grant-maintained schools perhaps will be looking for are going to be very busy people. I think there are two points; first, they are going to think twice about coming forward. If they see an advertisement they are not going to be rushing forward. If they are approached, if they are head-hunted, they might be more amenable to taking on these additional responsibilities. But it would help if they did not have to go out of their way to ask for time off with pay from their employers.

763. PROF ANTHONY KING: Is any governor of your school also a local councillor?

JUDY WATTS-JAMES: Yes.

PROF ANTHONY KING: One, two, three?

JUDY WATTS-JAMES: Well, I was until May and in May the other LEA governor became a City of Birmingham District Councillor.

764. PROF ANTHONY KING: And do you have at your school, as part of your thought process about the

board of governors, that ideally at least one governor would be a local councillor? Is that something that you would look for if you did not happen to have one?

JUDY WATTS-JAMES: Not ideally no. The other governor and myself were originally LEA representatives.

BRIAN SHERRATT: I think nevertheless it is important, particularly from the head's point of view, to have balance within the governing body and that there should not be, as it were, one particular political point of view being expressed, but a breadth of political perspective within the governing body.

765. PROF ANTHONY KING: I was thinking of the local councillor not so much as the expresser of a political point of view but as potentially a rather useful link with the thought of the local authority. Might just be useful there as a liaison person. Do you happen to know from your experience of other grant-maintained schools whether or not they either have local councillors on their boards or think about having them?

BRIAN SHERRATT: Well, I think that many of them do, because when grant-maintained schools came into existence a number of the governing bodies had to appoint first governors and I think you will find that many first governors have political affiliations on local or borough councils in that way.

766. PROF ANTHONY KING: Just one final point, you say again, in this very useful opening statement, in paragraph 3.11. "A better balance between the defined responsibilities of the head, supported by professional staff, and those of governors would be useful in clarifying both policy-making and managerial functions..."—and you go on to say a little bit more about that. Are you saying in effect that you think that the division of responsibility between the head and the governors could be defined clearly and is not now defined clearly?

BRIAN SHERRATT: I would suggest that in the majority of schools which operate well the understanding of the role of the head and the role of the chairman or the governing body is well defined by that group of people. I think it would be helpful, however, for all schools if the role of the head and the role of the governors were more clearly delineated.

767. PROF ANTHONY KING: Could that in practice be done? We all know that in almost every part of the world where there is this kind of division of function, whether it is the chief executive officer at the Corporation and the Chairman of the board of that Corporation, difficulties can arise. Is it really possible to define ——

BRIAN SHERRATT: I would say so. I mean, the danger lies in—and I am not speaking from experience here, I hasten to add—but one knows that the danger can lie where governing bodies become intrusive into the managerial responsibilities of the head. For example, if they took a view that they wished to exert pressure on the head to suspend a particular pupil, that is clearly a statutory obligation of the head and the head's duty alone. I think that that is where the danger lies and it would be helpful to heads if the demarcation of responsibilities could be more clearly stipulated.

JUDY WATTS-JAMES: I must say that when we became incorporated as a grant-maintained school, as you will see in my submission, we did pass a resolution so that the head clearly knew the way forward. You know, giving the day to day running of the school, the well-being and the learning environment, the responsibility to the head, which meant that his role was very clearly defined, I think you would agree, you knew what you were doing—otherwise you could have had the chairman of the governors coming in every time there was a naughty pupil in school, which is not our role—we are there to be supportive.

PROF ANTHONY KING: Though it has been known to happen! Thank you.

LORD NOLAN: Diana?

768. DIANA WARWICK: Good morning. Can I also say how much I appreciated both the comprehensiveness and the thoughtfulness of your evidence. I wondered in general terms, because you covered each of the aspects in our document, how representative you thought those views were. We have had views from, for example, the NAHT and other bodies. Do you think that you felt that you were speaking for other heads in your evidence?

BRIAN SHERRATT: I would like to think that my views were not too dissimilar from those of other heads in terms of the governance of schools, the management of schools and leadership of schools, yes and I would be very surprised if David Hart's views, for example, were dramatically different from my own in terms of school management. So I think the answer to your question, with some hesitation, is "yes".

769. DIANA WARWICK: Fine. I mean, is it something that has exercised heads in a way that irrespective of our investigation these issues have been pretty generally discussed amongst heads of—I presume not only grant-maintained schools but other schools as well?

BRIAN SHERRATT: I think only because some time ago there was some publicity given to a grant-maintained school, or grant-maintained schools, where there was more than a healthy tension between the role of the head and the role of the chairman of governors. I think only that.

770. DIANA WARWICK: Right. In your answer to Professor King on that very topic you said both of you, I think, felt that it was a good idea to have those roles defined. In fact the NAHT goes even further than that and says that there ought to be provision by the Articles of Government—statutory provision by the Articles of Government. Would you concur with that, would you think that is a sensible way forward or is that pretty much a sledgehammer to crack a nut?

BRIAN SHERRATT: I think it is a very sensible way forward and, in particular, in that the 1988 Act appears to have given very, very great powers to governors. The circulars which then followed after 1988—many of them—seemed to not exactly back-track on that but seemed to interpret the law in terms of heads carrying out, in fact, these responsibilities which had been given to governors. And it seems to me—and I am not trying to be cynical—that the system works as well as it does because in the majority of cases the governors do not use the very significant powers which, in fact, have been given to them and they delegate those responsibilities and powers to the

head. It would be very helpful indeed if that could be made explicit, laid down in the Instruments and Articles of Government, so that there could be no confusion and if, indeed, there were confusion that those documents could be referred to in the formal context of a governors' meeting.

771. DIANA WARWICK: Could I just ask you about your response on the role of the LEA? You were talking about LEA governors but you sent us a copy of a trenchant article that you had written about the—I think you called it "the dependency culture".

BRIAN SHERRATT: No, I didn't send you that actually—somebody else must have done. It was published in *Times Educational Supplement*.

772. DIANA WARWICK: Well, it was fascinating and I do not particularly want to comment on that but to ask you, just in this general area of accountability, whether the point about the accountability to the local community is something which exercises either you or the governors and whether it is possible to define it. You do comment on it in your evidence and I wondered if you could say something about that—and quite what it meant to you.

BRIAN SHERRATT: Yes. It is a very very interesting area. As head I am accountable to my governors, they are my employers and I am responsible to them as head. I think I am answerable to all parents of children in my school. The accountability to governors is formal—I am accountable to them in terms of running the school, reporting to them in a formal context. I am accountable in terms of the way I manage the budget, in the way I provide value for money for pupils in their learning and for maintaining the standards of the school at all times in the community.

I am answerable to parents in the way that my staff and I deal with their children because pupils have a right to a good education, free from disruption. I am answerable in terms of the ethos of the school, the discipline. I am answerable in terms of the appropriateness of the curriculum, whether pupil achievement is commensurate with pupil ability, and I am answerable in the sense of providing them with the kind of school which they would wish to send their children to.

Now, I am responsible to the wider community—I am differentiating between accountability, answerability and responsibility, I suppose. I find it very difficult to see how a school can be accountable to the wider community which subsists of various communities, some of which I may not even know about or which may come into existence without my knowing, but I am responsible to the wider community for maintaining the status and good discipline of the school so that it is a school which they think well of in the local community. I am responsible for the behaviour of my children to and from school, so that they are not making a nuisance of themselves to members of those communities. I am responsible for links with local industry, with commerce—in our school they are very extensive and work well. I am responsible in the sense that I have many points of contact with the community, I am invited to speak at various events, attend certain functions and so on, and I am high profile there and that promotes the school.

In particular I glean a huge amount of information about what the community thinks about us and its expectations of us as a school from my links with the primary schools. We have about forty or fifty contributory primary schools and I have links with every single head and go into every single school and my staff go into those schools and so we plug in, as it were, to a school information network in terms of parental expectation—that is parents who are not currently parents of pupils at the school. And I suppose also in the way I manage the press, the kind of information I give to the press to publish about the school.

So I would make a distinction between the formal kind of accountability I have to governors, my answerability to the primary client community, the parent community, and a different kind of responsibility that I have towards the wider community, which is made up of many communities, ethnic, cultural and otherwise.

773. DIANA WARWICK: An extraordinarily comprehensive answer, thank you very much. Could I just ask you one final question because it is exercising us in relation to all the bodies we are looking at. You emphasised the voluntary principle, the fact that all governors of grant-maintained schools are not paid. Do you think that there is any problem about recruiting governors to schools, just simply in terms of the people you think you need and want, whether they are coming forward, whether you can find them, and if there is a problem could it be solved by making more people accessible, simply because they are either paid or there is a guarantee that they can get paid time off work?

BRIAN SHERRATT: I know that there are many schools where it is difficult to recruit governors. I know that there are many schools where it is difficult to recruit governors of the right quality. In our particular case we have recruited governors of good quality. However when, for example, our Responsible Officer who is 70 now, does eventually decide that he no longer wants to fulfil that role, I think we will have some difficulty, given the kind of area we serve, to find someone of equal status and ability.

I am wholly against the idea of paying governors because governorship is not a job, I see it as an unpaid responsibility to the community and to the school. It requires commitment to the school and it seems to me that it would be a retrograde step to employ governors, but as I have already suggested I think that it would be helpful if local employers could recognise the responsibility of governors and, indeed, perhaps it would be helpful if they saw the fact that some of their employees were governors that this was, in fact, useful to them in having, as it were, influence in the wider community. So I would be in favour of governors being remunerated—given time off with pay to fulfil governor duties where that is appropriate. I do not think that all the governors would wish to take advantage of it but in some cases it would be helpful.

774. DIANA WARWICK: So you are really thinking of them not losing money rather than having money?

BRIAN SHERRATT: That is right, yes. I do not like to think of them being paid for being a governor but I do not like to think of them losing money because they are a governor.

775. DIANA WARWICK: That was going to be my final question, but you made very interesting comments

about your contacts with the local business and industrial community. Have you found in those contacts that there is resistance to that idea or has it just not come up?

BRIAN SHERRATT: Within the school or within the——

776. DIANA WARWICK: No, within the business community, amongst employers. Has this been an issue which has been raised, i.e. paid time off, and has it been resisted?

BRIAN SHERRATT: No, I haven't raised it with them.

JUDY WATTS-JAMES: It has not been raised, I think. If we have required a working party to meet in the afternoon they seem to have either done it by going in earlier, you know—they have managed to work it through but they have not lost money and they have been able to come in. But it could prove difficult. I mean, we have been very fortunate, as I have said, and we do have people applying to be governors, but I have seen other governing bodies where they are not as lucky as we are.

BRIAN SHERRATT: There have been one or two occasions when we have invited representatives of the commercial world and industry at a very high level to come into school to discuss certain issues and they have been more than willing. In fact we were staggered on one occasion at the number and we had to revamp our arrangements and have a very large hall because they were very willing to come. So we find that there is considerable support from the world of industry for what we are doing in schools.

DIANA WARWICK: Thank you.

LORD NOLAN: Thank you very much. I wish we could keep you a lot longer because you are, in many ways, a unique institution and the largest school, I think, in the country.

BRIAN SHERRATT: Yes.

LORD NOLAN: Could I just make it clear that the evidence which we shall retain as part of the evidence before us will include not only your full submission but also the much briefer opening statement which contains much compact information of a more personal kind, including quotations from the very complimentary OFSTED report and some indication of the progress made at Great Barr since 1991. So, although I am afraid we have not had nearly as long as we would like to ask you questions we have been greatly helped by your additions to the written material and we shall study them both. Thank you.

BRIAN SHERRATT: Thank you.

777. LORD NOLAN: Good morning, gentleman. Mr Tom Johnson and Mr Lawrence Upton? Thank you for striding through the wet weather to get to us in such good time this morning. If I may, as with the previous witnesses, go straight into the questioning, unless you would prefer to make a short opening statement?

TOM JOHNSON, AND LAWRENCE UPTON

TOM JOHNSON (Headteacher, Katherine's Grant

Maintained Primary School, Harlow): No, we haven't——

LORD NOLAN: In that case that will enable Lord Thomson, please, to open the batting from this end.

778. LORD THOMSON: Thank you very much for coming and for me it is particularly nice to welcome people from a school in Harlow where my children had a very happy primary education and my wife was once a school governor, although that is many years ago and in very different circumstances. Mr Johnson, you have an advantage, which will be a great advantage to us, of having, I think, an overview of problems of governance in grant-maintained schools. I think you sit, do you not, on the National Advisory Committee for Grant Maintained Schools?

TOM JOHNSON: Yes.

779. LORD THOMSON: I just wondered if you would like to begin by giving us as frank an appraisal as you feel you wish to about the nature of any problems that lie in the relations between governors and heads?

TOM JOHNSON: Yes. Generally speaking, where it comes up, it is usually addressing a problem—and there have been one or two problems nationally and they have been concerned with a head teacher being disciplined in one way or another such that there was a consideration on whether or not that head would continue in employment in the school. Remember the SAC is both governors and head teachers, it is a body representing both. I think the feeling there is that where this sort of occurrence happens it would be very difficult to repair it with an outside intervention in order that it should resume again in perfect harmony, that by then it has come to such a pretty pass that it would be very difficult to go on and therefore one is relying more on good practice and good relationships occurring which is the majority. I mean, there are very very few where these have broken down.

780. LORD THOMSON: Are you saying that you would be opposed to somebody from outside acting as a mediator in matters like that?

TOM JOHNSON: I think the view is—and it is certainly my view—that it would be by then rather difficult, whatever judgment any independent person came to, it would be rather difficult for the management and the governance to continue in harmony for the good of the school thereafter. I mean, one or the other might have to go and usually it is the head teacher that is on the line. It is an issue that we have found the governor members of the SAC and the head teacher members have a different perspective about and we are looking at devising some kind of code of conduct where it would be possible perhaps not to get that far down this road where it seems, by the time you get outside intervention, it is too late.

781. LORD THOMSON: You have, I think, been listening to the previous evidence we have had from Birmingham. Does what you are saying mean that you think there is a need for a clearer definition of the respective responsibilities of the governors and the head teacher?

TOM JOHNSON: In detail, probably, yes. I mean, there are some overall guidelines which determine governance as being strategy and policy-making and so on and management as managing the school on a day to day basis and so on. But probably yes, in more detail. Though I have to say that I think it is quite healthy for there to be some tensions and that where we've experienced this it has actually been to the advantage of the school. It draws the governors in to a full understanding of what actually is happening in the school and it makes the management realise that there are other views and that there is a lay view that is an important thing to be aware of. So where we have had occasional tensions it has actually been healthy in my view.

782. LORD THOMSON: Yes. I understand the advantages of constructive tension—you get it very usefully in all sorts of fields of life—but turning a little more widely and leaving aside problems of disciplining staff and that kind of thing, to the wider arrangements of grant-maintained schools. Grant-maintained schools seem to have the positive advantage that they excite a great deal of voluntary public service from the people in the community that they serve. But they are very far away from the ultimate funding authority and the ultimate administrating authority which finally is the Secretary of State and we have had evidence from other people associated with grant-maintained schools that they might feel helped if they had some kind of provision of what I think one of them called a "friend critic" in the area that they could have dialogue with and get advice at certain times. I am not thinking about bringing back the local education authority into that role, I think that would be unacceptable to many people, but I wondered if you had given any thought to whether there is a vacuum between the FAS and the Department—one in York, is it not, and one in London—and yourselves, that might be usefully filled in some way.

TOM JOHNSON: I don't feel the need for this, speaking personally, and from my own experience ——

783. LORD THOMSON: You have a regional Association of Grant Maintained Schools you are very active with, are you not?

TOM JOHNSON: Yes, but on a wider basis. I do not think that generally speaking it finds favour in the SAC, I think the view is that the very nature of grant-maintained schools is their independence and that there is adequate appeal to the Secretary of State or the FAS and physical distance is not a problem. In a school like mine, for example, where we have always been some distance from the centre of the LEA and, indeed, that centre being very different in its cultural background to the area that we work in, it has not been a problem in the past and it isn't any more a problem now. But I don't have any strong views about the possibility of this being of assistance but I haven't felt the need.

LAWRENCE UPTON (Chair of Governors, Katherine's Grant Maintained Primary School, Harlow): I would have to say, if I can, that I think that that would tend to muddy the waters a bit and, in fact, as grant-maintained schools we are clearly accountable for providing the appropriate standard of education for the children in the area and that, in fact, once you do have someone else who is in fact going to come along and say "Well, maybe you should do this, maybe you should do that"—someone else other than, maybe, OFSTED, who have got a statutory responsibility to do that. Then, in fact, you start to get away from part of the ethos of, in fact, grant-maintained schools and as Tom was saying, I think that one of the things that we have found at Katherine's is that in fact the fact that there is now no other person who is sort of behind us sharpens us up, makes us become much more aware of the local community, of our accountability, of our responsibilities than previously, when someone from the LEA could be there as a backstop to pick up the pieces, to sort things out and maybe to tell us what to do. We have to decide ourselves what to do, we can get advice, we can buy advice from appropriate people on appropriate issues, but it is for us to decide and I think we actually start to lose some of the benefits of grant-maintained status if in fact other people have come along who are there to sort of tell us how we should be doing things, however well intentioned that particular approach might be.

784. LORD THOMSON: Thank you. Do you have any ideas about how best to ensure that those who are governors of a grant-maintained school are reasonable representative of the community that they serve?

LAWRENCE UPTON: I think that in fact one of the great dangers is that you may be trying to get "the butcher, the baker the candlestick maker" on the governing body and just say a "Well, as long as we have got all of them we are okay". The key point, I think, about membership of the governing body is that, in fact, they are people who are personally committed to the school and personally committed to the advancement of that particular school and are prepared to put their time and their efforts behind that. Then obviously one would hope and one would aspire to have on the governing body expertise which may give us intelligent advice and intelligent guidance in terms of what we should be doing, but my experience is that, in fact, if one goes out and tries to recruit all the various professionals and all the various people who could represent whatever the local community could be, you might end up finding those people but they may not be personally committed, in fact, to the school and so they don't necessarily turn up for meetings and when they do they are not able to contribute because, in fact, they haven't come in with the kind of burning desire and purpose to support the school which is, I think, essential for a governing body.

785. LORD THOMSON: What do you do in practice about finding replacement governors when terms of being a governor come to an end. What is your maximum term—seven years?

LAWRENCE UPTON: Yes, 5 to 7 years is for a first governor. For parent governors it is shorter than that because they are elected but for first governors it is a 5-7 year period. We have experience recently. Tom, do you want to explain?

TOM JOHNSON: I've written to a number of local organisations, not just businesses but also social organisations, churches and so on, and said that we had a vacancy for a first governor and would they be interested to nominate somebody and in that way we have recruited recently the vicar of the local church, although we are not a church school, and we have a representative from another local business. We've only ever had two vacancies to fill and so it hasn't been an issue. But when we have it has not been difficult to fill them.

LAWRENCE UPTON: And this work has been done following discussion with the governing body as to who should be approached.

786. LORD THOMSON: You have perhaps heard the evidence we have just been listening to with great interest from Birmingham—a very clear answer as to who the head was responsible—accountable to. The head was accountable to the governors. I wondered what the Chairman of governors would like to tell us about who he thinks the governors are accountable to.

LAWRENCE UPTON: The governors are quite clearly, I think, accountable to the local parents and their children because they are responsible for providing the children who come to the school, and those who may come to the school, with the standard of education which those parents can reasonably expect and it is their job, in fact, to do as much as they can by whatever means to ensure that that is in fact done. And I see that as a very clear accountability.

787. LORD THOMSON: How many grant-maintained schools are there in Harlow these days?

LAWRENCE UPTON: Only three. We were the first and we have been followed by two of the Roman Catholic schools, but none other. Which is unusual because Essex is known as the centre of the grant-maintained movement and we are rather an unusual outpost.

788. LORD THOMSON: How do you deal with your admissions policy? Do you have a queue of applicants for your school?

TOM JOHNSON: We published our proposals at the time of going grant-maintained and it just happens that we have a very large capacity because it is a new part of Harlow—a bolted on estate—and the actuarial advice was that over 12 years we would go from nothing up to 470 down to 280. That was precisely correct and we have got capacity for 350 or more and we have a role of about 280, so it has not been an issue.

LAWRENCE UPTON: It is also a fact, of course, that it is less of an issue for primary schools. It is secondaries which tend to have the problem about admissions because there is much more choice exercised. In most cases, parents send their children to the nearest primary school because it is convenient.

TOM JOHNSON: And we concur with that; it is not our job to go recruiting children from areas where they ought to be in their own school.

789. LORD THOMSON: Yes, thank you. What is your annual budget in broad terms?

TOM JOHNSON: £400,000.

790. LORD THOMSON: So you, as headteacher, not only have to perform all the traditional roles of a headteacher, but you are the chief executive of a quite considerable financial business in one sense—a financial service?

TOM JOHNSON: Yes.

791. LORD THOMSON: To what degree do you feel the arrangements for that, the control of it from the FAS and so on, are excessively onerous or adequate? Have you any comments from your experience about how the financial arrangements go, whether the safeguards are adequate and that sort of thing?

TOM JOHNSON: First, it is not very different from local authority schools in the sense that one still has the responsibility for managing that kind of budget. It is true that in some areas cheque books are in the school and in others they are not—they shadow the spending, so to speak. But because we are grant-maintained and have independence, we have our own money.

We are audited every year, as you know, and those audits are rather more thorough than in LEA schools. We make regular returns to the FAS and so there is a monitoring of our spending over a month or two at a time, both in our cash flow and in our budgeting and we have a Responsible Officer who is able to make periodic checks on what we are doing. It is my responsibility to report to the governing body so that they have regular information about our income, expenditure, how much money we have in the bank, whether that matches our budget and so on.

792. LORD THOMSON: Do you feel you are over-audited and over-regulated or are you reasonably content with the arrangements?

TOM JOHNSON: It is not a bad thing. It is quite a responsibility and it is important that a very thorough audit is made of that kind of money. No, I do not have any problem about that. It is right that we should be thoroughly audited.

LORD THOMSON: Thank you, Mr Johnson. That has been very helpful.

LORD NOLAN: Would any other members of the Committee like to ask questions?

793. WILLIAM UTTING: If I could ask one quick question, Chairman. There are comparatively few grant-maintained primary schools; the great majority are secondary schools. I wondered what the head does for his own professional context here. Do you rely on the National Association of Headteachers, or are there other bodies which will provide you with, say, a professional reference point?

TOM JOHNSON: Yes, indeed. The National Association of Headteachers is one, but then so is the Standing Advisory Committee, where I meet both secondary and primary headteachers. We cluster too into primary headteacher groups, both grant-maintained clusters and also mixed clusters of LEA and grant-maintained.

On the professional level, on educational matters, I have access to colleagues in exactly the same way I had before. There has been no change there whatever—neither from their point of view nor mine. I do not go to meetings with the LEA officers though—I did to begin with, but I found it was not relevant. I can meet my colleagues and we draw from each other just as we did before. It is as if there were no differences at all.

WILLIAM UTTING: Good. Thank you.

794. LORD NOLAN: Any others? Well, thank you both very much indeed. This has been an extremely helpful clarification of the position from the point of view of your school and those like yours. We are most grateful to you for coming along.

Good morning Mr Skidmore. We thank all our witnesses for coming to see us, but particularly on a morning like this. I hope you have not had too bad a journey. Did you wish to make any opening statement, or would you like to go straight into questions.

RODNEY SKIDMORE

RODNEY SKIDMORE (Chief Executive, Central England Training and Enterprise Council): I submitted a short opening statement, which I hope was helpful by way of background. I should welcome your questions.

LORD NOLAN: Thank you. We have your opening statement in front of us and we have of course all read it. It is Dame Anne's turn to lead off with the questions.

795. ANNE WARBURTON: Mr Skidmore, good morning. You will think I am asking some fairly naive and simple questions, to start with anyway. This is partly because I, and I think some of my colleagues, are finding a certain amount of difficulty in getting a "three-dimensional" feel for TECs. They are strange animals in the realm of government and public life and I wonder if perhaps I could begin by asking you to give us a little more depth on exactly what you do. I have seen your annual report, but I doubt that others have. Could you indicate something of your activities—a little more than just the headlines.

RODNEY SKIDMORE: Yes, of course. Our main focus, as you probably appreciate, is upon the things which government contracts for us to do. Of that, some 50 per cent of our budget, and therefore our activity, is devoted to the vocational training of young people, primarily 16-18, but maybe up to the age of 24 or 25. The way we add value to that is firstly in the TEC understanding its local economy—the needs of its local businesses, the aspirations and the abilities of its local people. We are a dating agency if you like: we have to know our market. That is the main piece of added value on which any Training and Enterprise Council builds.

We therefore tailor, within the regulations that we are set by government, the type, level, nature and target groups of the training and the linkages through from the world of education into the world of work. That is probably the largest portion of our work, to which we devote both our budget and our energies.

We have, of course, a considerable responsibility towards our local businesses. We are concerned not with land, premises or investment in machinery. We are concerned with investment in the local people—the employees, the skills and the managers. We are concerned therefore with the competitiveness of businesses and to assist them. That, again, takes something like a further 30 per cent of our energies.

I guess it is probably the remainder where people—including myself sometimes—find it quite difficult to see what our boundaries and responsibilities are. It is encompassed under something which we head, helping to develop the local economy. That is a fairly broad church, because clearly TECs as the new boys on the block in the past four years are not coming into something which is cold. Local authorities and other bodies have long had responsibilities and carried out an excellent amount of work in what we would class as economic development, so infrastructure, transport, in terms of land and premises availability, are all the bedrock of developing the local economy. What we add as a TEC is developing the skills, capability, professionalism and some of the personal attributes of local people and when you match all those things together with the business and infrastructure, we really start to see some clear drive in the local economy.

That in a nutshell may not include as much detail as you would like, but I am happy to amplify it.

796. ANNE WARBURTON: It may be all we have time for. Can I ask you a little more on that. Does each TEC decide for itself what is appropriate in its local environment and context? How much help do you get centrally to decide your priorities?

RODNEY SKIDMORE: There are certain things that we recognise and accept are national priorities, in terms, for example of the targets set for us through the national targets for education and training, which we frankly welcome. But if I can use those as an example, what we see is a rate of increase and improvement which is required, but all areas are starting from a different baseline, so the line we are taking is that provided we can make that continued step change in the skills and qualifications of our people and managers at all levels over the next four or five years, we shall certainly have contributed the best we can. If we can do better than the national rate of improvement in those skills and qualifications, then of course we shall be extremely pleased with that.

797. ANNE WARBURTON: You spend how much a year roughly?

RODNEY SKIDMORE: About £12 million turnover. An increasing proportion of that comes not through the government mainstream contract, and I am thinking particularly of levering out contributions from employers, but especially increasing reliance on European funding.

798. ANNE WARBURTON: Yes. I saw that figure had gone up quite substantially. Is that in a particular area for training?

RODNEY SKIDMORE: Yes, primarily with regard to the European Social Fund targeted on groups who might otherwise be disadvantaged and that includes everything from concentrating on people with disabilities, ex-offender projects, helping women to get back into work and working with our ethnic minorities—which represent less than 5 per cent of our population. That has gone up from our first year of something like £7,000 to this current year of over £700,000. We have worked very hard to diversify our income stream and particularly help those who perhaps are not the main focus of government funded mainstream activities.

799. ANNE WARBURTON: One of the things I find difficult to grasp is that one sees figures for the number of people who go into training. Does that get compared clearly with the numbers who exit from training having achieved what they were being trained for? Do you ever do things such as "What did it cost to train that person?".

RODNEY SKIDMORE: We have a clear handle on our costs, certainly. I can sympathise with where you are trying to get, which is that there are a plethora of agencies, of which the Training and Enterprise Councils are only

one, in this country who are charged, in some cases, with overlapping responsibilities and the development of the individual. The lifetime learning ethos we are all striving for is still very much fragmented between different organisations.

Again, one of the pieces of added value that the Training and Enterprise Councils can bring—given that we do have such a large remit—is to play a major part in bringing together all those organisations in the local area so that there are no overlaps and—more importantly—no gaps.

If I could give you one example, we were very pleased yesterday that the consortium of which we are part as a TEC have just won the bid to run the new careers service in the County of Hereford and Worcester. We were delighted with that and it typifies the strategic influence which a TEC can bring to bear, as well as what will then flow from that, which is some day to day operational level impact through the achievement of various programmes.

Going back to your original point I think, Dame Anne, at the moment, TECs, by and large, only have the capability of tracking what they do. What we must have in this country is a far more coherent system if we are truly to achieve lifetime learning, which does not drop a young person from the records when he or she leaves school at 16, then find them when a TEC picks them up and drops them again at age 21, for them to come back into the system and back onto someone else's register, say, with the Job Centre if they happen unfortunately to be unemployed at the age of 31. We need a coherent system and some incentives not to, what I would consider, lose customers. They are our customers and if we allow them to drop out, it is our fault. I get very annoyed if I lose customers.

800. ANNE WARBURTON: That seems to bring us into the area of relationship with the local community—again very hard to define. Can I perhaps start on your contact with advisory sub-groups. I would like to know what subjects they cover, how they come about and how you use them.

RODNEY SKIDMORE: I came into the post in the development phase of the TEC, so I was able to bring some help to bear on this. It came about because our Board identified very early that with the maximum laid down of only 15 people, that really could not be seen to be totally reflecting the broader community and the input which we felt was necessary for the TEC, so we did two major things.

First, we set up a number of advisory groups, invited and proactively sought people to come onto those, the majority of whom would never qualify to be a main Board TEC director because of the rules laid down by government on that—i.e. being a chief executive or a chairman of a company etc. We identified early on those people who would otherwise feel excluded from having an input and from shaping their local Training and Enterprise Council. So we set them up and we have refined it over the past four years, but they cover the whole spectrum. We have a sub-group which advises on economic development policy to the Board and a sub-group which focuses on equal opportunities for those who have special training needs, to make sure that the Board receive advice from the grass roots on those aspects.

801. ANNE WARBURTON: Do you put these groups together? Do you invite people to join them?

RODNEY SKIDMORE: We put them together, advertise for them and welcome people to come onto them. If the response is still perhaps not as great as we would like, we take some positive action and in some cases positively discriminate if we feel that our advice is under-represented by a certain group.

We have a group which deals with the whole spectrum of individual learning, training, education, career development and advice. We have one which deals with communications and marketing which is charged with trying to increase community involvement in their local Training and Enterprise Council and we have another which looks at the activities we are currently running—the established programmes—constantly seeking feedback from the ultimate customers as to how we can either improve those programmes or how we can bring on new activities better to serve the local community. Of course we also have statutory sub-groups such as the financial and management committee and the audit committee of the Board and so forth.

802. ANNE WARBURTON: Could I ask about a particular group which might be relevant. What sort of relationship do you have with your local chamber of commerce?

RODNEY SKIDMORE: We have to recognise that it was primarily people prominent in the local chambers of commerce movement who were responsible for helping the TEC to be set up in the first place so we owe them a great debt of gratitude. We are an interesting area actually, as a Training and Enterprise Council. If you can imagine Birmingham there, we have it surrounded on three sides—south, east and west of Birmingham. We have a number of the advantages of being on the periphery of England's second city without, perhaps, some of the disadvantages. The point is that we have three chambers of commerce within our boundaries. They are members of different core chambers so that there is no unity even within the chambers with which we work in the sense of unity of chain of command, although they network very well together.

Certainly we have worked hard trying to work in true partnership with them. I think that is probably an over used word and we have to be careful to unpick it. In some cases, partnership of course is a legal joint venture, as in *Business Link* where we are equal stakeholders legally in the establishment of these new companies. Similarly in the two new companies called the Career Services. There is a joint venture partnership in there.

In some cases, what we call partnership is actually a buyer-supplier relationship. We are a purchaser of services both for individuals and for business support services.

803. ANNE WARBURTON: From the chambers of commerce or from members of chambers of commerce?

RODNEY SKIDMORE: From both. We contract with some of our chambers to provide business services and youth training, for example. There is a different sort of relationship there and then, of course, there is a third relationship which is a true partnership, which is coming together truly to identify our mutual objectives and, where we can, in a more informal partnership, help to develop strategy rather than the direct delivery, purchaser-supplier relationship. We work fairly closely with them in all those three ways.

804. ANNE WARBURTON: We heard yesterday from the chamber of commerce side that mergers are happening. Is that something that you have considered?

RODNEY SKIDMORE: It is something which we are considering. I think if we were a single TEC, single chamber area, it would be easier to pick our way through that. With three chambers—and two different cores of chambers—we are actually having to think quite deeply and it is not quite as straight-forward in our area, but it is something we are looking at—not driven from a structural point of view. Part of the ongoing debate is how we can better serve the local businesses and people and make how they can be helped more clear to them. I still think there is a lack of clarity amongst local businesses and people and I mean TECs, chambers and *Business Link*. Whilst they may be right, and they all came about for very good reasons, sometimes it is still confusing to the customers.

805. ANNE WARBURTON: I have one more question on the chambers of commerce side. There was a mention also of the possibility of a corporate member—a chamber of commerce representative really—on the Board, which would surely run a bit counter to the rule that people are there as individuals.

RODNEY SKIDMORE: We have a particular membership scheme in Central England TEC which we established from the outset and it was done for a number of reasons. It is a free and open membership scheme, open both to businesses and to individuals—going back to the issue of enabling individuals to contribute and feel that they are part of the ownership of the local TEC. Because that is a free and open membership scheme, we particularly did not charge because for one thing that would have brought us into conflict with the local chamber of commerce who do charge and we did not want to undermine their paying membership scheme.

The second reason we set that up separately from the chamber scheme is because the chambers are membership organisations and their services are therefore exclusive or at preferential rates to their members. Again, it was our TEC Board decision, rightly or wrongly, that we did not want to be an exclusive organisation, that TEC services should be freely available and accessible for all—either individuals or businesses—and therefore we did not go down the route nor go into competition with or into a merging a scheme with our local chambers. That may come with *Business Link* and as we get closer together, but we have to be very careful that as a TEC we are not an exclusive organisation. That is the main concern of my Board.

806. ANNE WARBURTON: I was very struck by your term "free and open to all local companies and individuals". How many actually take you up on it?

RODNEY SKIDMORE: At the moment we have something like 160 individuals who are members.

807. ANNE WARBURTON: Are they people who have benefited in some way or helped you?

RODNEY SKIDMORE: No, not necessarily. I have 48 staff and about 40 of those are members. They do not have to be, but it is a way, again, of empowering our staff so that they can come to the AGM as well as the other individuals and legally vote—vote directors off or not vote them on, or refuse to accept the annual report, all the normal things that shareholders do. We do not have shareholders, we are limited by guarantee, but we have tried to ensure that not just the perception, but the reality, is that the local community, the individuals and the businesses, own the local Training and Enterprise Council. We are not as far down that road as we would like to be. People have still to be totally convinced, there is still cynicism, but with something approaching 400 corporate/individual members we are getting there and we believe it is working.

808. ANNE WARBURTON: Can I come onto the question of membership having a say in who becomes directors. That is an area I find puzzling, because your papers tell us that the membership can put up nominations and vote, but somehow the result has to come out in conformity with a plan of balance and so forth. Presumably you have some kind of Board committee which vets applications? How does that work.

LORD NOLAN: May I just butt in while you are thinking of the answer and say to Dame Anne, will this be the last part of your questioning?

ANNE WARBURTON: It was not going to be Chairman. I have to point out that we started very late.

LORD NOLAN: We did.

ANNE WARBURTON: Can we have another five or 10 minutes because I think there are one or two more points.

RODNEY SKIDMORE: I will talk more quickly, Chairman.

LORD NOLAN: Very well.

809. ANNE WARBURTON: Perhaps you could give us some help on how the balance inside the Board is arrived at if you have membership voting for it?

RODNEY SKIDMORE: It is in the hands of members. We feel we have to walk the talk on this one, having had the membership scheme. We are constrained by the restrictions placed on us by the Secretary of State's regulations, so it still has to be a chairman or chief executive and we publicise that in the local media. You are right that there is an issue there of managing people's expectations.

However, the members themselves are responsible within the confines laid down by the Secretary of State, for nominating potential directors to the main TEC Board and that they do. Those nominations come forward: they have to be nominated and seconded by members, either corporate or individual, and then go forward to the Annual General Meeting at which all the legal members are present and they vote for those non-Executive Directors whom they believe should be on the TEC Board.

We have not yet had a conflict, but it may come. For example, as you know, up to one third of the Board may come from the public sector. We have not yet had a conflict whereby more public sector people than there are places have been nominated, but it may happen. We shall simply have to fall back on the operating agreement if that does happen, to say that there are only a maximum of five places allowed for public sector. That is a conflict which could arise.

810. ANNE WARBURTON: On possible conflicts of interest of Board members, you keep a register and it is a full one. I stop on it really because in your annual report, the interests listed seem to be just their present appointments, but you have a fuller list than that?

RODNEY SKIDMORE: We have a full list, not only of financial, but non-financial interests, and not only of the directors but also of their close family too. That is available for public scrutiny.

811. ANNE WARBURTON: It may not be quite the same area, but I was also struck by the arrangements for delegation—that the Board can delegate to any one member, anything. That sounds very sweeping. Is it really like that?

RODNEY SKIDMORE: That was, I think, a phrase that was taken from the model memorandum and articles which I think most TECs adopted in their ignorance in the early years. The Board does not delegate to any one person; however, it does delegate to some of the sub-groups and sub-committees. They believe of course that it would not be perceived to be good practice to actually put complete delegation in the hands of any one person.

812. ANNE WARBURTON: Does the composition of your financial management committee include non-executive members?

RODNEY SKIDMORE: Yes. It is chaired by one of the non-Executive Directors. There are two other non-executive Board members who sit on it and then, as and when necessary, there are three members of the Executive, including myself and my Director of Finance, but we withdraw of course when that committee becomes, for example, the audit or remuneration committee. That is entirely composed of non-Executive Directors.

813. ANNE WARBURTON: Some of us were struck by the fact that your internal and external audit is run by the same firm.

RODNEY SKIDMORE: There are two simple reasons for that. One is that they know us and the second is that it is cheaper and we are burdened down with ever rising administrative costs. We feel it is totally defensible that it should be done by the same organisation and those are the reasons. I should actually say that those auditors also audit the TEC National Council, so there is an interesting third leg to that stool.

814. ANNE WARBURTON: That brings us perhaps into the area of auditing. You say that you are audited by three different bodies at least. Is that what you need by way of auditing?

RODNEY SKIDMORE: The public needs the confidence that someone is scrutinising very carefully the money which we expend, whether that is the European

Commission auditors, the National Audit Office or the audit for our local government office in the West Midlands. I do not think it is necessarily the audit itself in principle; what I should have added to my previous remark is that there are actually too many rules and regulations and too much bureaucracy which then has to be audited. I believe that we can get equally good public accountability, particularly for the expenditure of the funds, the openness and the way in which the TEC conducts its business, without so many of the rules and regulations which actually lie below the surface.

815. ANNE WARBURTON: Is there a need for a body which more specifically compares with the funding organisations that exist elsewhere in the general sector of local public spending bodies? I am not suggesting it would be an additional layer, but that possibly it would replace.

RODNEY SKIDMORE: That is an interesting question. I would be fascinated to look at the options, particularly if you say it would have to replace something else, because that something else at the moment is the West Midlands Regional Government Office in our case, with whom we contract.

816. ANNE WARBURTON: Do you keep in very close contact with them?

RODNEY SKIDMORE: Ever closer contact with government office, particularly now that we are a licensed TEC. We are moving into a closer relationship with government office, which itself is just reorganising better to enable them to focus on the TEC in a more holistic way. Rather than having three or four different contacts in government office, we are now told we are only going to have one person who is responsible for the contract with the Central England TEC. We can only applaud that: it is good practice.

ANNE WARBURTON: I think I shall be fired, Mr Skidmore, if I do not yield, but I would just like, if I may, to ask whether there is anything you want to talk about that has not been covered.

817. LORD NOLAN: Anything that you would like to see coming out of our report?

RODNEY SKIDMORE: I would just welcome the recognition that, although the TECs do work to national priorities and within a national framework, they are 81 independent, local bodies, who are charged in addition with being accountable to Parliament through the Secretary of State, with being accountable to their local community—the individuals and the local businesses. I believe that is the strength, for example, which locally elected people onto TEC Boards bring. They know their area and if we do not respond—and in some cases help shape and understand local needs—then I would suggest to you that we are not adding the true value which local bodies such as Training and Enterprise Councils should be adding.

818. LORD NOLAN: We are very grateful to you indeed. Thank you very much for answering the questions so comprehensively and clearly.

Moving on to Lincolnshire: good morning. Thank you very much for joining us. Mr Rossington, I hear you have not been well. Have you got over the "flu now?

DAVID ROSSINGTON, AND MARY LORD

DAVID ROSSINGTON (Chief Executive, Lincolnshire Training and Enterprise Council): I think you are far enough away, Chairman, not to catch it from me.

LORD NOLAN: That is the least of my worries! Thank you very much also for the material you sent us about the Lincolnshire TEC. This we have before us and have all studied. So as to make the best use of the time, I should like to go straight into the questions we wanted to raise, if that suits you.

DAVID ROSSINGTON: Certainly.

LORD NOLAN: I shall ask Sir William Utting to start please.

819. WILLIAM UTTING: Thank you, Chairman. You sent us your paper on local accountability and corporate governance, which is based on the TEC framework. Does your production actually depart from that framework, or perhaps even improve on it?

DAVID ROSSINGTON: We think it meets the needs of that framework and in some cases perhaps goes beyond what is required. It is interesting that the development was to a large extent in parallel. The development was not prompted directly by the production of the TEC National Council framework. It was more prompted by the fact that we needed to move in this direction to ensure that we become more accountable at local level. We recognised that in many instances we were not sufficiently accountable and we wanted to address some measures, particularly those of getting a wider group of people involved in the TEC Board as directors for example.

820. WILLIAM UTTING: Can you recall any particular areas in which you, so to speak, improved on the framework?

DAVID ROSSINGTON: If we look at that area of recruitment of directors, then we went down the road at a fairly early stage in these developments of saying that we wished to advertise for our board directors. Lincolnshire is a very large county—2,300 square miles. We have to ensure that we bring people from a range of different sectors and from the total geography of the county. If we think back to when the TEC was first formed, then by necessity, government set out an invitation, local employers responded and the initial board was perhaps three or four people who knew each other. There was a danger therefore that as directors left, others were replaced by people who the current directors knew. We wanted to broaden that and we thought that advertising in the local press was the best way of ensuring that a range of people both had the opportunity to apply and that we broadened those things out, so I think we go beyond there.

In seeking to communicate, we do a great deal by way of surveys. This year we surveyed 1,000 employers, we do a household survey—a telephone survey to several hundred households asking them a range of questions about what they know of our organisation, what they think we do and what we ought to do, we have a radio programme which is intended for the same approach. We fund the cost and radio journalist; the editorial control is with the radio station itself and nothing whatsoever to do with us and in fact that gives a platform for a range of different organisations to have their views and that is aimed primarily at small business. Finally, we place our minutes and papers in the reference library so that people can actually see the minutes of meetings and the supporting papers. Perhaps all of those things go beyond what is required by the framework itself.

821. WILLIAM UTTING: Yes. The framework is described as a voluntary framework. Are there any measures to encourage people to get this in place? Should adherence and implementation of this framework become a condition of contracts with DFEE, for example?

DAVID ROSSINGTON: An interesting question. It is voluntary to a large extent because you have 81 autonomous TECs and this is produced by the TEC National Council, which is something to which we all belong, but do not have to belong and does not control those TECs.

You could argue that it would be rather pointless having a TEC National Council working on our behalf if in fact we were to ignore anything and everything that came out of it if a particular TEC did not like certain aspects of the framework. The framework itself has been carefully thought out and makes a lot of sense. I would not want to encourage government office to see this as part of the future licensing agreement for example. I do not think it is necessary—I think we can deal with that ourselves—but it would not worry me either if adherence to that framework was something that was required because that would be yet another way of helping to demonstrate accountability.

MARY LORD (Deputy Chief Executive, Lincolnshire TEC): If I could add to that: the licence currently has capability aspects which implicitly talk about the capacity of the TEC board to deliver. It is not quite as specific as the kind of accountability framework we are talking about, but there is potential within that to interpret it in a future licensing round in a more focused way.

822. WILLIAM UTTING: Could I ask you about membership because I was interested in what the last witness was saying about the membership of his particular TEC. I did not gather from the documentation that you have that sort of wider membership, but I did see that you have a system of regional advisory committees. If that is so, could you say something about your thinking behind that.

DAVID ROSSINGTON: Can I deal with that in general terms and ask Mary to talk about the regional advisory committee side of things, with which she is particularly involved?

WILLIAM UTTING: Of course.

DAVID ROSSINGTON: No, we do not have a broader membership scheme as such. We considered that in the very early days, but like the previous witness we were concerned about conflicts with the chamber of commerce. Even if this was seen to be a free membership, that may also be seen as a conflict with the chamber of commerce because they may be asking for funds to join their club and we would be saying "You can join ours for free.". We therefore agreed with the chambers of commerce that we would not operate a membership scheme in that way.

We are currently developing a joint membership scheme with *Business Link* and the chambers, which is a slightly different option because the chamber is part and parcel of our *Business Link* operation.

The regional advisory committees have been there from day one. They are there partly because of our large geographical area. The needs of Lincolnshire vary from the north to the south. If you look at unemployment rates, they vary widely from the coast across. We needed to make sure that anything that was run from or devised in the centre was also relevant to the whole of the county and we wanted to get the feedback the other way so that initiatives were developed on the coast to meet the needs of the coast. One also finds in sheer operational terms that if you operate in a rural county of this nature, if you think you can sit in the city of Lincoln and do things on a central basis, the people in Skegness will soon put you right, so we needed to ensure that we got that sort of support. Mary can talk about the membership of regional advisory committees.

MARY LORD: Yes. On the point about the RACs being in place from the outset of the TEC, they were very helpful in steering the TEC from day one and they have fulfilled that function ever since. They were set up basically in the first instance on the model of the TEC board that was designed to keep private sector leadership in those committees, but to have the opportunity to be more inclusive than maybe TEC board membership would allow us to be. While we wanted to keep the private sector leadership, we wanted to get a broader cross-section of the community interest at the RAC level than we might be able to with the main TEC board.

That has enabled us to have the flexibility to involve particular interest groups in an area within Lincolnshire, so if there is a particular voluntary sector group or trades union interest in one area and not in another, we can reflect that in the membership of the RAC.

There are five committees. The actual committees are chaired by a TEC director and there is a vice-chair who is also a TEC director so every committee has two TEC directors and that provides a two-way communication link between the RACs, directly into the TEC board. The RAC chairs produce a report to the TEC board on a quarterly basis and that is commented on and feedback given to the RAC so issues can be raised directly through that committee.

In terms of recruiting people for those committees, in theory, anybody can ask to join the RAC. Decisions about participation in the RAC are taken by that RAC and the chair of is a member of the TEC board in consultation with executive staff and so on. The main criteria for that is the contribution that they are likely to be able to make to that committee—what are they bringing to the table to help the committee and group meet the interests of the community in the area. That is not as formal a process as it might be and it is questionable whether making it more formal would actually inhibit it, but there is a process where the committee discusses potential nominations or interests from people within the locality to join the group.

823. WILLIAM UTTING: You have already said something about the ways in which you publicise the activities of the TEC to local communities, but this system of regional advisory committees is really the principal

means you have of enabling local communities to contribute to your programme of work?

DAVID ROSSINGTON: It is one of the ways and it is an important one. The committees themselves will set up ad hoc groups to look at particular issues and involve a broader range of people. The TEC board has functional sub-committees—for example, we have an economic development subgroup, which involves all the local authorities. It involves the Chief Executive of the County Council and the economic development professionals from the district councils so there are other ways of involving the local community and if we look at our rural areas in particular, we have a programme which we call Rural Challenge. That starts with a public meeting which we organise with the local community and then it is based on a computer generated and analysed questionnaire that goes out to everybody in the community from the age of 12 and above. The intention of that is to produce a bottom-up business plan for the community. We then work with that community to try to find ways and means of implementing that plan. If it means they need to get money to do things, we try to find ways of helping them to do that, but that is a way of involving a very wide range of people. In one location, 75 per cent of those eligible to complete the questionnaire actually did so and therefore had an input into that process.

824. WILLIAM UTTING: Have you had much turnover of board members since you were established?

DAVID ROSSINGTON: Yes, we have actually had a total turnover of board members within the past 18 months or so.

WILLIAM UTTING: My goodness.

DAVID ROSSINGTON: To some extent that was to be expected. Many of the original people had been with us through the original development phase and then for a three year period, so they had done a four year stint.

WILLIAM UTTING: Yes.

DAVID ROSSINGTON: We make quite high demands on people and they do this in the best traditions of public service, but they recognised as well that it was important for us to move on and not to have the same group of people. We want to bring fresh ideas to the board, as well as demonstrating to the outside world that this is not a closed club and that others can get involved.

825. WILLIAM UTTING: You have then had the experience of inducting and training a substantial number of directors in recent months. What is your basic programme for this?

DAVID ROSSINGTON: In many ways we involve the board directors. The process is controlled by our personnel training department in the same way as it would be for staff, so we have an induction process and programme for our staff and we have the same people, because they are professionals, controlling the process.

We produce an individual induction plan for a particular director. That would normally start off with a discussion with myself and possibly Mary and others who are involved, to identify what they already know and

where their particular areas of interest lie. In many instances they may have been involved with a regional advisory committee for a couple of years or so. There is no need to go over the detail of what the TEC is and how it works. Other people may be fresh to that, and we need to explain some of the mechanics of that and their understanding of the company itself. We then produce an individual plan for them. That would normally involve them coming into the company and spending time with individual members of staff who are experts in that particular area. That programme is driven by the individual, to a very great extent. The more our directors understand what we are doing and understand the detail of that programme, although their job is not the day-to-day operation, the more value they can add, so it is in the board's interests in general terms to ensure that it has a group of people who understand the business and can make a major contribution to the business.

MARY LORD: Could I just add something to that? After the induction process, there is an ongoing process for continuing updating and training, and that involves things such as twice a year holding workshops for the whole of the board outside of the main board meetings; they are very much about taking an overview of developments that the board need to consider. Then there are ongoing presentations to board meetings about areas of interest that all the board members need to be updated on, and the board is particularly active in terms of its involvement in our day-to-day activities, so they get involved in development activities with us as an organisation, which is part of their ongoing personal development.

826. PROF ANTHONY KING: I will end on just one question. One of the occasional criticisms that have been made of TECs is that they are rather better at the business development side of their activity than on the training side, but I see from your papers that you have the right to include in your logo the slogan "Positive about disabled people". I wondered what you had done to deserve that and what it actually means. I assume that it is connected with training, for example.

DAVID ROSSINGTON: The "Positive about disabled people" is an initiative—a programme—run by the Employment Department, and you have to satisfy particular criteria as a company. It is primarily aimed at private sector companies and it is aimed at their recruitment and training processes. So you have to demonstrate, for example, that your buildings are totally accessible to people with disabilities and you have to demonstrate a range of other issues about recruitment processes and training processes. If any registered disabled person applies and they meet the basic criteria for a job, they are guaranteed an interview—things of that nature. Once you satisfy those criteria, the Employment Department decide whether you may use that symbol. So it is an external programme operated by the employment service which provides that symbol. We decided that, as an employer ourselves and as someone who, within the local community, wished to set an example to others—we do quite a lot of work in the field of special needs and disability in particular—we wanted to set that example, so it was right that we should lead by example by going through the process ourselves, so that we could have that badge. We then have to maintain those criteria. We can lose the symbol if we do not stick to the rules of the club, as it were.

PROF ANTHONY KING: And those values are reflected in your training programme as well.

DAVID ROSSINGTON: Those values are reflected in our training programmes. All our training suppliers do not have that symbol, though we would encourage them to do so, but they do have to have equal opportunity policies in place and proper action plans to implement those policies.

PROF ANTHONY KING: Good. Thank you.

828. CLIFFORD BOULTON: Can I just follow that up? Do you get a weighted element in the grant you receive for training of disadvantaged groups—they might be disabled or they might have learning disabilities—which you are expected to make use of in that particular area?

DAVID ROSSINGTON: Yes, we do. It depends on the particular programme. If we look at the training for work programme, for example for long-term unemployed adults, we are paid purely by results. We are paid for the number of jobs we get, the number of qualifications we get, but we will get an increased payment for someone who is disabled or who has been out of work for a very long time. In total, it brings no additional funds into the TEC, because we have a contract value that we negotiate with the department and we pull that down as we deliver the training.

828. CLIFFORD BOULTON: Would it be possible to show from your accounts how much money was being spent on disadvantaged groups or in another way in your report? The reason I am asking you that is that we are to do with standards, not policies and that sort of thing, and we have had a suggestion that money is not going to these groups because TECs get so preoccupied with economically directly useful training. Could you make more transparent how money for that purpose is actually being expended?

DAVID ROSSINGTON: It is possible in two ways to identify that with any TEC. One is in its business plan itself, setting out the range of things it is doing, and in its annual report. We have what we call a training support unit, which is a specialist organisation. It has some direct staff; it has others who are seconded. For example, we have a seconded probation officer, so we have a full-time secondee from the local probation service working with us to try and ensure that we meet the needs of ex-offenders. We are doing some work at the moment with the probation service, social services and the employment service to look at the very long-term unemployed among 18 to 25-year-olds, people who have been out of work several years, to see if there are additional things we can do. What we decide to do will be set out quite clearly in our business plan and will be costed in that plan, and that will also be reflected in the annual report itself.

829. CLIFFORD BOULTON: I have one quick question on the structure. Do you serve on the board? Are you a director yourself?

DAVID ROSSINGTON: Yes.

CLIFFORD BOULTON: Is that normal in the TEC world?

DAVID ROSSINGTON: Yes, it is. Yes.

830. CLIFFORD BOULTON: Do you ever feel that the respective functions of a chief executive and the directors could be more clearly seen if you were not sitting round the table with them as a colleague? Do you see any direct advantages in separating them out more clearly? For instance, we have taken evidence from the education world. A teacher does not sit as a governor, and they probably prefer it that way. But you prefer to be a member, do you, and you are comfortable with that?

DAVID ROSSINGTON: I have not found any problems with that at all. We have tried not to get into what I might term the officer and member relationship that perhaps a local authority might have. The TEC is a private company and we try to run it in a businesslike fashion. We believe that my position on the board enables me to do that. The day-to-day operation is quite clearly delegated to me, so I am, by necessity, involved in all the activities of the board itself. I think this enables me to do a better job for the organisation than if I was excluded from some of that process.

831. CLIFFORD BOULTON: So it can place quite a lot of responsibility on the company secretary, who might have functions which might involve pointing out where interests conflict. I am a little bit surprised to see that you regard it as a duty of the chief executive to draw attention to conflicts of interest. I would have thought that might have been the secretary's job, but that is how you do it, is it?

DAVID ROSSINGTON: That is how we do it and how the board has decided to operate that. Our company secretary is external to the organisation, he is a lawyer who works for us for those sort of purposes, and again that does seem to work effectively on a day-to-day basis for us.

CLIFFORD BOULTON: Thank you very much.

832. LORD NOLAN: Thank you both very much. I am afraid that the clock requires us to stop there. You have certainly improved our education and training this morning and we are very grateful to you for coming.

Good morning, Sir Jeremy, and, if I may say so, welcome back. It is nice to see you again. I am sorry we are running a little late this morning, but we have covered a lot of ground, both mentally and physically.

May I begin by asking this? Did you wish to make any opening statement to supplement the very carefully prepared written material you have given us?

SIR JEREMY BEECHAM, ELGAR JENKINS OBE, AND DAVID HEATH CBE

SIR JEREMY BEECHAM (Chairman, Association of Metropolitan Authorities): Very briefly, and it is just to say this. We do not come here, any of us, saying that local government is perfect. We do think that local government offers good examples of accountability and probity in practice and, importantly, with an appropriate framework so far as possible to ensure that accountability and probity are observed. We in our evidence are suggesting ways in which those criteria can be met in local public spending bodies. We identify some shortcomings that we see at the moment in the way those bodies function, both in relation to their appointments and, potentially, in relation to their practices. If public confidence is to be secured and maintained, we think that some improvements need to be made to facilitate greater accountability and to ensure that probity is observed at all times. That is the thrust of your evidence.

833. LORD NOLAN: Thank you very much. I have just seen the news release that was issued this morning, which of course reflects what you have been saying. It concentrates our attention on your proposed *"Framework of Democratic Good Practice"*. I wonder if we might start with that. We find it on page 3 of the first part of the written evidence that you have given to us, in paragraph (1). It confers of course a substantial role on local authorities:

"the members of boards providing public services should be elected ... and removable by the people."

Pausing there, with many of the bodies that we are looking at, especially the smaller ones, this would be an ideal, but it could not, could it, practically be obtained?

JEREMY BEECHAM: We are not saying that all members of all boards should be appointed: that is neither appropriate nor, as you say, practical. We do think that, in most cases, there should be an element of representation by those who are directly elected to local authorities.

ELGAR JENKINS OBE (Leader, Conservative Group, Association of District Councils): I think (1) and (2) in fact hang together, Lord Nolan. We say "as far as possible" in the first one and in (2):

"If this is not possible, then local authorities should have a power of appointment",

and it is fairly critical to notice those words—"as far as possible" and "a power". We are not trying to be unreasonable in what we are saying.

LORD NOLAN: Because failing the possibility of direct elections, you say that you and the local authorities are the nearest thing to a locally elected body who can exert an influence on the membership of these boards.

JEREMY BEECHAM: Locally elected and therefore locally accountable.

834. LORD NOLAN: Yes. On page 17 of the same document—paragraph 3.37—you have your conclusions, which are that

".. standards of appointment and accountability ... could most easily be improved if the following principles were adopted:

(a) Rights of appointment and nomination for local authorities should be used more extensively. Other interested user or community groups could also be granted rights of appointment to allow for more representative boards."

No doubt you have in mind, for example, trade union membership or community organisation.

JEREMY BEECHAM: Chambers of Commerce.

ELGAR JENKINS: User groups

JEREMY BEECHAM: A regional body, perhaps the CBI?

DAVID HEATH CBE (Liberal Democrat Group, Association of County Councils): I think we have been very careful not to be over-prescriptive in our suggestions to the Committee, because quite clearly they are only suggestions, but we are very conscious of the point that your Committee itself made in its first report in terms of its seven principles, and particularly that of accountability to the public—the public in the instance of local public bodies is clearly the local public—and trying to explore some means by which we can ensure that accountability, and at the same time ensuring as far as possible, which is the underlying theme of what we said last time and what we are saying today, that the same underlying principles apply whatever public body and whatever public service you are talking about, with different mechanisms obviously. I think that is the essential point of what we are trying to get over.

JEREMY BEECHAM: Self-selection and self-perpetuation, as we refer to it in that paragraph, are dangers to be avoided where possible, but equally important is transparency in operation. That we also touch on in sub-paragraph (c). The system must be seen to be working effectively.

835. LORD NOLAN: Yes. What makes the bodies that we are looking at at the moment so unusual, distinctive and important is the extent to which they exist and are chosen, not normally by election, not by appointment by Ministers, but largely on a self-selecting basis. I have been trying to clear my mind—I am sure we all have—as to how best one can compare them with local authorities with a view to seeing how the common standards which the public expect from all those who voluntarily engage in public service and voluntarily undertake responsibility for large sums of public money can be observed. Some of them are, so to speak, deliberately not associated directly with the local authorities now, are they? This is not a matter for us to say is right or wrong, but, for example, grant-maintained schools and housing associations are independent bodies and they tend to be served by people who attach great importance to independence. I was thinking of what one headmaster called, rightly or wrongly, the dependency culture, which he felt had affected at any rate some headmasters when they were in the local education authority sphere. So one has to look at the nature of these bodies to see how best to regulate them, without infringing on the willingness of people who, almost by definition, are not wanting to become involved in the political process to come and serve on them.

JEREMY BEECHAM: Yes, that's right. There is a balance to be struck between independence and accountability, both to the users of a particular institutional service and to the wider community, which of course is paying for that service, and the components of that balance will differ, no doubt according to different circumstances. Housing associations are in a sense at a further remove, for example, than, one might argue, an FE college which at one time was, if not local authority-controlled, at any rate closely engaged with the local authority and from which local authority membership is now specifically excluded. Many housing associations seek nominations from local housing authorities for a member to serve, because they wish to foster that link. FE colleges are effectively pretty much restricted from doing that.

DAVID HEATH: I think, my Lord, if I might add, there is an unhappy equation between perceived independence and non-accountability, or indeed the view that, as soon as you are elected by a local community in whatever capacity, you cease to exercise independent judgment. I think that that frankly is not a logical position, but it is nevertheless the way that a lot of these bodies have evolved, by a rather spatchcock mechanism up to date.

836. LORD NOLAN: Yes, I follow that. I think that we have heard from many of them, as one would hope and expect, and I am thinking in particular of evidence we have heard today from training and enterprise councils and from grant-maintained schools, that the relationship with the local authority is an important one, as with other local communities. Putting it broadly, is it your experience that many of the larger local public spending bodies in your areas have a representative of the local authority on their boards or do they keep in contact by other means, or is the relationship too distant for comfort?

ELGAR JENKINS: It is very variable, I would have thought. Quite honestly it is almost impossible for us to answer it.

JEREMY BEECHAM: Many TECs have local authority representation. Originally this had to be an officer. Now I think there is more flexibility and I think some elected members have been admitted to the ranks of TEC membership. It is the our experience from the metropolitan authorities that TECs generally have a reasonable working relationship with their local authorities, but it must be said that that is not universally the case, although there is some cross-membership of the kind I have indicated. With other institutions it is less the case and, as I have indicated, in FE it is virtually impossible, although, interestingly, I heard evidence given by an FE college head in respect of another inquiry recently, and she was strongly urging that FE colleges should have a capacity to have local authority membership of their board. She felt it would actually strengthen the further education sector if that were the case.

ELGAR JENKINS: I think there are two things, my Lord. One is the idea that some local authority representation on these bodies would be useful to the body and an important link with the community, which, after all, they seek to serve. But there is also the other side of the coin. We want these bodies to be open, as you say in your seven principles. Some of them are very good about being open and seeking to go out and communicate, and some are less good. What we really want is a governance approach, of which an important element would be that you have a duty to be as open as you can, in having your meetings open where possible, in having an annual meeting at least, in publishing an annual report which is open, in going out and being prepared to talk to your local councillors and to important groups in your local community. This is part of the idea that each of the organisations we are talking about should have a proper approach to governance, both in the probity of the way in which they manage their financial affairs and declare their interests and in the way in which they endeavour to communicate, as they are public bodies, to the people in their area and the interests which they seek to serve on behalf of all of us.

837. LORD NOLAN: I think I can say for the Committee that one of the main objects of this part of our inquiry is not to expose wrong-doing: on the contrary, it is to help to reassure the public, as we hope we can, that what is going on at present, sometimes behind closed doors, is going on properly. This is a very important factor, is it not, in the restoration of public confidence and in the ability of the bodies themselves to demonstrate that they are doing a good job and doing it honestly?

JEREMY BEECHAM: That is why you need a clear and common framework.

LORD NOLAN: Yes, I follow that.

DAVID HEATH: There is that aspect of good governance which I think is very important. There are also purely practical considerations and advantages from a close working relationship in the case of the TECs between TECs and the education authority and the authority acting in its economic development role, for instance in the case of FE colleges. There is the really quite absurd position that a sixth form within a school context is within the local authority educational planning framework, but, should that be a sixth-form college, which is established on precisely the same basis, or indeed an FE college, it falls without, and we do not have the same sort of contact, which I think is actually to the advantage of both parties.

838. LORD NOLAN: When you consider housing associations, which you mentioned a few moments ago, there are so many of them and some of the larger ones cover so many different local authority areas that one cannot, can one, have a simple rule saying there must be a local authority representative on each housing association board? The best we can do, is it not, is to try and get to the principles that we are aiming at, and you have identified one of the main ones, of establishing openness about what is happening, and then see what the best means of achieving that are in the different contexts? We have heard from a number of further education bodies, for example, that they have well-organised and well-advertised public meetings, and about 10 people turn up who are already parents. Then they have to look for other ways of getting the word round.

I wonder if I could pick up one or two other points which appear in your framework. Other members of the Committee will no doubt have others. You say at your point (11):

"Appointed bodies should also be subject to investigation by an ombudsman on the same terms as local authorities."

Had you in mind enlarging the powers of local government ombudsmen or different kinds of ombudsmen for different kinds of bodies?

JEREMY BEECHAM: I think our feeling would be that it may not be appropriate generally to extend the role of the local government ombudsman, save that in relation to grant-maintained schools he should have a similar role to that which he enjoys in relation to LEA schools. But for organisations like TECs and so on, it may be that a different person—a different organisation—is necessary. But the principle that there should be some recourse is one that we would advocate.

839. LORD NOLAN: Yes, as we already have it in the housing association context, and it seems, if not to be

universally admired, to command a good deal of respect. There was one word in point (12) which surprised me and I think some others on the committee. You refer to "a national code of practice ... covering ethical conduct by members", "declarations of interest", yes, certainly, and "surcharge". You are defenders of the surcharge, are you?

JEREMY BEECHAM: We feel that, as long as it applies to local government, it should apply to others. We would be happy to see it abolished for everybody.

840. LORD NOLAN: Speaking as a judge who is not liable to surcharge if I get a decision wrong, I have very great sympathy for JPs, whose position is still, to put it mildly, difficult in this respect, and for that matter for what amount to very heavy, sometimes impossibly heavy, fines on local councillors, which do not seem to be related either to their means or to their fault. But I have your point. You are just saying if you have them, why shouldn't others?

JEREMY BEECHAM: Yes. We are not pressing it.

LORD NOLAN: No.

DAVID HEATH: I should explain that my county council at the moment is subject to an, in my view, unjustified accusation, which may result in surcharge of members, but we do not expect that it will.

841. LORD NOLAN: If I could turn to some of the specific bodies which you deal with in part 2 of your evidence, you express considerable concern about grant-maintained schools and the role of the first governors and you note that parent governors will always be in a minority, although they are elected. Would you feel, though, that the parents of children at present in the school for a few years should be a majority?

JEREMY BEECHAM: I do not think we necessarily say that. Clearly they must be adequately represented. I take the point that it is implicit in what you are saying that there is a longer-term interest which needs to be reflected in those governing bodies—parents of future generations of children going to the school and indeed the wider community which, as I said before, is in fact paying for the body. So again it is a question of balance. I think our principal concern was that the first governors assume a rather critical role in subsequent appointments, and that is a major difficulty. But, given that there is a significant presence of parent governors, then that, from that standpoint, would be acceptable. It is the other appointments that one would need to look at, to ensure that the wider interest is represented.

842. LORD NOLAN: Yes. The view is sometimes expressed that the Funding Agency for Schools has an incompatible combination of roles, as something which is there to support and encourage the system and at the same time to act as a regulatory body. Is that your feeling?

JEREMY BEECHAM: Yes, we do feel that there is a potential conflict between the advocacy role and the regulatory role, and they ought to be kept apart. There is a publicly-funded body which advocates grant-maintained status. There is a trust established to provide finance for that purpose. The advocacy role, in our view, should be left to that body or anybody else who wishes to play it, but not the body that regulates it.

843. LORD NOLAN: The same situation, I suppose, obtains in the case of the Higher Education Funding Council and the Further Education Funding Council. Is there, there too, something that needs to be watched to make sure that there is no conflict between the two roles?

DAVID HEATH: There is not really an expansionist interest there, is there? The entire sector is within their province, rather than the rather odd position that we have that of a declared government policy of expansion of a particular form of governance and a body which is responsible not only for the furtherance of that policy in terms of advocacy and also the discharge of its regulatory duties. I do not think the same analogue applies in the other funding councils.

844. LORD NOLAN: Thank you. If I may turn to TECs, you advocate a more restrictive framework for the operation of TECs. In paragraph 4.18 of your second volume you say:

"Some in local government believe that local authorities should appoint the whole of the TEC board in consultation with local interested parties. Failing this, local authorities could be regarded as the prime source of proposed nominations. In either case, local authorities should have a duty to ensure that sectors operate a fair system of selection of their representatives."

That is pretty strong medicine, is it not? I was wondering how this would be greeted by the TEC representative organisations. Have you discussed this with them?

JEREMY BEECHAM: No. We have actually got quite a civilised dialogue with the TEC national body at the moment, and I dare say we will be revisiting this issue. We are not seeking a restrictive framework; we are seeking a broader-based representation. The paragraph is rather carefully worded. "Some in local government", it says, believe that they should be entirely appointed. I think the majority would not necessarily take that view. We do feel that local authority presence on TEC boards should be increased and that we should be consulted on the wider representation, but I think we would be content if we felt that other members were appointed in a way which allows the people who serve on that genuinely to be representative of particular interests that they are supposed to reflect, so that the local chamber of commerce or the CBI or trade unions or whatever should be asked to nominate to these bodies, rather than have the existing board again select those who would serve and with whom they would no doubt feel comfortable. It is that principle of having external appointment of a representative character that needs to be reflected in the system.

DAVID HEATH: There is a huge variance in practice in TECs across the country. Some are very good and some are less good, shall we say. We are not trying to encourage a restrictive model; we are simply trying to suggest to you that the Committee's seven principles should hold firm when it comes to TECs. They are public bodies. In saying that, I would take slight issue with evidence that you received earlier this morning. I notice that it was suggested that

"money leaves the public domain via the Government-TEC Contract".

I think we would challenge that. We would see TECs very much still as public bodies, despite their form of governance and their contractual arrangement with government. I think the National Audit Office would probably challenge that statement as well, in following public money through to its end destination.

LORD NOLAN: I'm sorry, which statement is that from?

DAVID HEATH: I am referring to what I have written here from, I think, Lincolnshire TEC in their statement to you earlier. I am assuming that that was the evidence that was actually presented. But, as I say, I think we in local government would challenge that view. We would feel quite clearly that the TECs were in the body of public life. If that is the case, it follows by our logic that there should be a regime of accountability and openness and a method of appointment which is consistent with what we have said earlier in other forms of authority and public body.

JEREMY BEECHAM: Can I just come back on one point? The most restrictive thing about TEC membership is that which is imposed by government at the moment: members are supposed to be chief executives of, in effect, fairly substantial organisations. That is a restriction which in our view is unnecessary. I can quote directly from the experience of the Tyneside TEC, whose first chairman, in shadow form, was very acceptable to everybody in the business and local government community, but because he had retired by the time the TEC formally came into being, he could no longer continue to serve, he was no longer a serving chief executive of a private sector company, and his experience and talents were lost in that capacity. So there are restrictions now which in our view are unnecessary and should be removed to allow wider access, from the business community itself.

LORD NOLAN: Yes, I follow.

ELGAR JENKINS: There is one point I was going to add. We have very good evidence that the most effective TECs are those with the best developed consultation and partnership arrangements. We think that, therefore, by having a link in the way we are suggesting with local authorities, we are building on that good practice. That really is the thrust. We are not seeking to be restrictive. We want these organisations to succeed, to flourish, to be effective in their communities.

845. LORD NOLAN: One of the questions that has to be resolved, on which we must do our best, is how far you would achieve that by prescriptive rules and how far by encouragement and perhaps codes, certainly guidance, rather than law.

DAVID HEATH: That is something, I think, for your side of the house, I would suggest, my Lord. We will come and write the final paper, if you like.

846. LORD NOLAN: Did I understand you to say earlier that you would favour an ombudsman or some similar regulatory body for TECs in particular?

JEREMY BEECHAM: Yes.

LORD NOLAN: For the reasons you have given.

JEREMY BEECHAM: Yes.

847. LORD NOLAN: There is just one topic I wanted to cover with you before handing over to colleagues, and that is to go back to housing associations. Here of course the trend has been very largely to take the housing of disadvantaged people away from local authorities and put it in the hands of housing associations. This is an area which plainly calls, does it not, for the closest co-operation between housing associations and the local authorities? The local authorities still retain most, if not all, of the legal obligation for housing the homeless. Somehow they have to equate that in their relationships with the housing associations. What is your view of the present situation there? Would you favour, again, some rule or firm guidance for the representation of local authorities of the larger housing associations to whom the local authority housing stock is gradually being transferred?

JEREMY BEECHAM: Yes, I think we would. Notwithstanding the fact to which you have already referred that some are national organisations now, I think there is scope for facilitating local authority representation. Indeed, speaking from an area which has the headquarters of North Housing, which I think has now changed its name, it is, if not the largest, one of the largest national organisations and it does have local authority members on its board. I think that is important. It is right to say that housing associations increasingly take a responsibility for housing disadvantaged people. One might almost delete the adjective, because they have perhaps more potential, and have had, than local authorities in terms of new build for some time.

Interestingly, there is an article in in the "Environment" supplement of today's Guardian about the increasing role of housing associations now in social care. Social services departments are, perforce, contracting out residential care, and indeed domiciliary care, to other organisations, and housing associations are beginning to assume a role in that field, which makes it all the more important, given the vulnerability of the people we are talking about and the importance of the service, that there should be very effective links with local government and, again, with users of the service in terms of the management of those organisations.

ELGAR JENKINS: I think it is true generally to say that relationships are good between housing associations and local authorities. One thing the housing associations recognise is that they are doing the work which was formerly that of local authorities and they need to have access to infill sites, forward planning and in all sorts of other ways, and also I think local authorities recognise that, as the thrust now of providing social housing rests with housing associations, clearly they want, in the interests of the people they seek to house, to work closely with them. So in making the comment that Sir Jeremy has made about membership, although we cannot be prescriptive as to which council, if it is a regional or national organisation, we also ought to record that good working practices do exist at the moment and we want to build on those in fostering the ideas that we are putting forward.

LORD NOLAN: Thank you very much. I am going to ask Sir Clifford Boulton to take over.

848. CLIFFORD BOULTON: May I stay with housing associations for a moment? I notice that you said:

"A Code of Governance for Housing Associations ... should be given mandatory force."

Then you go on:

"Although the Code should not be rigidly applied",

leaving it to us perhaps to fill in the gaps. But you do then say:

"... variations from it should have to be formally authorised by the Housing Corporation.

Have you got some actual variations in mind? Are there things that you felt would be appropriate for relief from the otherwise mandatory code?

JEREMY BEECHAM: It is difficult to be prescriptive in advance about that, because of the very diverse nature of the organisations we are talking about. At one level you have, as we have heard, national organisations with many thousands of homes; at the other you have a small, locally based housing association catering maybe for a very small number of people in a particular area, and you would not want to over-burden such an organisation with too heavy a regulatory framework, because it simply would not be able to cope. So a light rein will be needed in some respects, not so much in terms of probity as of some of the other aspects that one might cover. It is a field that would require careful elucidation before you defined things too closely.

849. CLIFFORD BOULTON: So you would have to trust the judgment of the Housing Corporation, and that is not so terribly different from what is actually happening at the moment, I do not think, is it?

JEREMY BEECHAM: No, except that one might wish for a more active role. I think the Housing Corporation at the moment is, perhaps naturally, very bound up with the financial aspect. The housing association movement has suffered considerable financial pressure. It has been increasingly driven to the market for finance, its rental structures have changed in response to all of that, and the Housing Corporation's concern, I think, has primarily been to do with resources and perhaps less with management and outputs of a social kind than one would like, and I think that is a balance that needs to be redressed. So it is perhaps the Housing Corporation's brief that might need to be rewritten, or perhaps some of those functions might be administered at a lower level, perhaps at a regional level, than at the national level.

850. CLIFFORD BOULTON: Can I be clear in my own mind what you are actually asking for by way of representation on TECs? Are you actually asking that local authorities should have the right to nominate someone as a representative?

JEREMY BEECHAM: Yes.

CLIFFORD BOULTON: You would like there to be a place for the various local authorities perhaps that some TECs might cover.

JEREMY BEECHAM: Yes.

CLIFFORD BOULTON: You say about the involvement of senior executives that:

"These individuals may "have little time or inclination to play a meaningful role in such boards"."

I have to tell you that we have had some evidence about people's experience of having local councillors on their boards, that those are very busy people too, though they may have lots of inclination. Are you asking for the right to nominate either a councillor or somebody else who would be your representative?

JEREMY BEECHAM: Yes.

DAVID HEATH: If I may intervene, wherever we have said "local authority nominations", we are importantly not saying that that should necessarily be a local councillor. He may not be the appropriate person.

CLIFFORD BOULTON: No, I had gathered that from somewhere else in the paper. It does apply across to all these.

JEREMY BEECHAM: Yes.

851. CLIFFORD BOULTON: So you would claim that putting somebody from the council, either a councillor or somebody the council had in mind, would give some kind of reassurance that the thing was more open and accountable, because they had nominated somebody?

ELGAR JENKINS: Provided that the council has arrangements to report back to the council. All of us have seen cases where people were put on bodies and there is no communication then between the individual who is representing the council and the council itself, so it is very important that there is a proper reporting back process to the council.

CLIFFORD BOULTON: You see, some of the bodies who come before us say they attach enormous importance to the fact that people on these boards are there as individuals and not as representatives of some group, but your person would kind of be a representative of the local authority and a two-way channel of communication.

ELGAR JENKINS: I think they are a bit of both. Any of us who are put onto bodies, and all of us sitting here sit on a variety of bodies, recognise that we have an individual contribution to make, but we also recognise that we have a duty to report back to the body who puts us there and it is a way of making sure that both those roles are correctly applied.

JEREMY BEECHAM: I think the distinction is the old distinction between the delegate and the representative, and I think bodies should have representatives rather than merely individuals, but on the other hand they should not be delegates.

DAVID HEATH: I think there is also a danger, again coming back to the concept which is a very prevalent one, that local authorities are just another interest group amongst others rather than the least bad means of providing democratic accountability to the local community.

CLIFFORD BOULTON: I am aware that is what your objective is and I was testing it against the kind of reception you might get from the people who were having this cuckoo.

I only have one further supplementary on that and that is that I was not very clear as I read your paper that you were distinguishing very much between higher education and further education institutions. Wouldn't they distinguish themselves rather clearly, and higher education institutions would sometimes feel that it was not appropriate particularly for them to be associated with the local authority in which they operated and that their whole purpose really was to have a more national standing and HE was not the same as FE. Would you agree that we might have to notice the difference between the two if we were making recommendations in this area?

JEREMY BEECHAM: Yes I think there is some truth in that. On the other hand I think increasingly the civic universities, and the new universities which have acquired that status having previously been polytechnics, generally speaking value and are developing communications with local government in their areas. That is not to say necessarily that they look to have representation on the Senate or whatever the appropriate body might be, nor are we specifically saying that they should at this stage. Personally I believe that they should be but I do not think that is an agreed position of local government as a whole. But the relationship is one in which there is a degree of mutual interest transcending merely the presence in the community of a large institution. In areas like planning, student housing, the contribution of the university may make to the economic and cultural life of the area there are, in fact, strong links which people on both sides wish to foster.

ELGAR JENKINS: I certainly have served for over 25 years on a university so I can speak from experience. It is usually appointments to council and they are important. Senate is, after all, the academic body of the university and nobody would think of putting a counsellor on there unless they got there because they were an academic, but they are part of a range of advice and opinion to council. I must say, I echo what Jeremy said, I think universities generally value as part of a contribution from society in issues that arise.

CLIFFORD BOULTON: Thank you very much.

ANNE WARBURTON: I have none, Chairman, other than the ones that Sir Clifford just raised.

852. WILLIAM UTTING: I had one point and it really arises from the comment that Clifford Boulton was making about the defensive reaction one encounters when one raises the question of restoring local authority members to bodies that they have been turfed out of, and one gets the answer that Clifford came up with. One also gets the comment that they are awkward because they introduce party politics into a non-political situation that they are not committed to the individual institution, and that there is a kind of revolving door in that they are re-appointed annually and you do not have the same person, it seems, for longer than six months at a time. I wonder if you could offer a few observations on that kind of defensiveness?

JEREMY BEECHAM: It is impossible to say that individual members may not occasionally indulge in political rhetoric and neglect their duties or disappear quickly, but then it is equally impossible to say that people who have been appointed by other methods may not do similar or different things which may not fit the ethos of

the organisation. I think what would be fair to say, and this touches on what Elgar was saying earlier, is that local authorities have an obligation to ensure that the system works in the interests of the institutions upon which representation is sought that there ought to be, if you will, almost a code of conduct for members serving on public bodies outside the local authority as there is for the local authority itself. It may be that that is something we should look at, but I am doubtful from my experience of bodies on which I have served, and on which I know colleagues have served, whether it could be said that, for example, in the FE college in which we had something like 50 per cent representation that it was a sort of battleground of party politics and matters of that kind in Newcastle. I am sure that is not the case. Inevitably individuals will behave in a less than wholly desirable way, but that is true of all members I think.

ELGAR JENKINS: I think it is a bit like I remember one of my priests once saying, the problem is you will get the odd priest who goes wrong in the Catholic Church, but the trouble is we have to choose them from the laity, and the truth of the matter is we are all capable, whether you come from business backgrounds or council backgrounds, of having somebody who does not perform in the way that one would hope they would as a representative of the public. That is no argument, I think, for saying that we should not, in fact, have people from local government, the locally elected community, as members on these bodies, and that we should ensure ourselves that, in fact, we choose people with care, that we do ask a lot about how they are doing their work and we do have some continuity. I think there is some case, particularly with large organisations, for trying to maintain continuity over time even if political control may vary over time, but it is in the interests of the local authority to have people who actually know that institution well, whether it is a university or a major body like a TEC, and whether that person is on the council or not on the council. Yes, we have our part to play in it and I think that is the answer really to your question, but I do not think that negates the fact of the point we are fundamentally making.

DAVID HEATH: Can I say with some deference it is not self-evidently true that having a political position that is known to the public is necessarily a debarring interest from taking part in public life, and there is some argument that suggests that if that is in accord with the views of the general public as tested by election there might actually be a supporting factor in contributing to that particular body's activities.

JEREMY BEECHAM: Nor is it self-evident to the governing purpose businessman, and it usually is a businessman, he is necessarily fully equipped to take on all manner of public responsibilities in a way that is apparently denied to other people.

853. WILLIAM UTTING: I am afraid the bowling is now getting knocked over the field. If I could just make one further observation, if one puts the representative role on one side it also seems that local authority members have the kind of experience and ability in managing large public service bodies that is likely to be of use to most kinds of other institutions, and it seems strange that they should actually be excluded from the membership of some of them.

JEREMY BEECHAM: Well, that is exactly true. They also have to deal in their daily and weekly lives with the users of these services, and so they have another perception.

DAVID HEATH: That was a very friendly ball!

854. PROF ANTHONY KING: I was going to ask Bill Utting's question perhaps in a slightly less tendentious form, but since you have answered it so effectively I will ask another question of a much more restricted character. Could you say a little bit about what the local government ombudsman does in connection with local authority schools? What is that person's role because you want it extended to grant-maintained schools?

JEREMY BEECHAM: It is, I think, primarily to do with admissions policy. There is usually an appeal mechanism within the local authority. Of course in theory parental choice governs the allocation of school places. In practice, almost by definition, popular schools are full schools and it is very difficult obviously to accommodate those preferences and so local authorities have appeal systems but not infrequently dissatisfied parents want to test the procedures that have been followed, so the ombudsman has a clear role there. In other respects regulation, of course, is within the province of the auditor and the Audit Commission in terms of the probity aspect, and that is something that would need to be considered separately for grant-maintained schools.

855. LORD THOMSON: When local authorities enter into contracts with outside bodies of one kind or another, am I right in believing that always has to be fully recorded in your public accounts so that everybody knows to whom you have made what sums of money?

JEREMY BEECHAM: Yes.

856. LORD THOMSON: Against that background do you feel it would be reasonable to ask that TECs do the same thing in terms of the funding that they make available under contract to training bodies or to businesses of one kind or another? Do you see any argument against doing that which would also, of course, bring out into the open any question of a contract with a company with which one of the board of the TEC has an interest?

JEREMY BEECHAM: There should be exactly the same regulatory framework that local authorities are obliged to follow under financial regulations and, indeed, legislation. I cannot see any difficulty.

857. LORD THOMSON: Is there any feel as to how far any TECs do this?

JEREMY BEECHAM: I think a parliamentary question has elicited some failures, but one would not want to generalise too much on one or two unhappy experiences with TECs that may have transgressed. After all it is not unknown for local authorities to occasionally transgress too.

LORD THOMSON: I apologise for asking you a question that I would have asked the TEC witnesses this morning but time got a little short.

858. DIANA WARWICK: I just wanted to ask something that was brought to our attention this morning because I want to raise it with the next witnesses as well,

and in a way it is a kind of follow-on to Sir William's question about control. It is an article about the role of local authorities vis a vis grant-maintained schools. It was an article about dependency but this is not really about dependency, it is about the way in which local education authorities can place heads in a difficult position in making the choice about grant-maintained status and the control they exercise. It is written by a head teacher of a grant-maintained school and says——

"Ambitious heads wishing to move to a larger school are dependent on the authority for their promotion. Those seeking early retirement are dependent on the authority for their retirement enhancement."

Has there been any indication to your knowledge that that sort of subtle control is being exercised?

JEREMY BEECHAM: No I do not quite understand it because schools now appoint their own head teachers, and the local management of schools, schools appoint staff, they appoint heads. In fact there is an argument that the role of the LEA in the appointment of head teachers has, if anything, been diminished too much. In my authority we have some concerns about the manner in which a head teacher appointment was made by a particular governing body. I do not follow the logic of that, I think it is a misconceived statement, and nor do I think that prospects of early retirement and so on will enter into that picture. I think it is bizarre.

ELGAR JENKINS: The difficulty is in pinning it down because there seems to be some evidence now after a big story today in the press of statements by a headmaster in Mr Blair's constituency.

JEREMY BEECHAM: It was the *Daily Telegraph*, Elgar.

ELGAR JENKINS: Well, it is in the press today, I do not think the *Telegraph* is any less saintly than *The Guardian* or vice versa. I mention that because from time to time this has been repeated that overt or covert pressures are put upon people when votes are being carried out. That may not be in the way quite in answer to the question of the future of appointments, but I think it is worth recording that time and time again this is said that when votes take place local people are saying things. It may not be the official council but certainly local people who are against the proposal for a grant-maintained school are making all sorts of statements in order to endeavour to stop it. Now I think there are enough of these, but you really ought to put these questions back to people who deal in this field rather than to us to come up with some precise examples.

JEREMY BEECHAM: But the decision to ballot is a decision taken by the governing body not just by the head teacher, and presumably it is not going to be suggested that governors are being bought or deterred in some way.

ELGAR JENKINS: It is while the ballot process——

JEREMY BEECHAM: The question as raised was specifically about the role of head teachers who might be dissuaded from taking a particular course.

DIANA WARWICK: Improper control is really what I was getting at.

JEREMY BEECHAM: I was widening it.

DAVID HEATH: I cannot see a mechanism by which that improper control could be applied because, as I said, local management of schools has meant that head teacher appointments particularly are well within the province of the governors and not of the LEA. I think any attempt to manipulate by means of references given or whatever would be rather easily spotted by any half competent governing body. It is not directly apposite to your question, but I think it is an appropriate point at which to say that I think some of the problems that we perceive with grant-maintained schools and their governance apply to an extent also with locally managed schools within LEA control which is a point that has been made by the Audit Commission OFSTED report and others, and if that is part of your concerns within this section of your investigation, which I suspect it is not, it is something we would draw your attention to.

LORD NOLAN: Maybe why grant-maintained schools do well.

DAVID HEATH: The head teacher of Stratford School might have a different view given experiences there where the governing body was not exactly supportive of the head.

LORD NOLAN: We are very grateful to you, it has been most interesting, as before. If we are asked to write a report on local government no doubt we shall be seeking help.

JEREMY BEECHAM: It might be three strikes and we are out.

859. LORD NOLAN: Good afternoon Mr David Hart and Miss Sue Nicholson. Thank you very much for coming to join us and for the help you have already given us in what you have written. Do you want to add to it by way of opening?

DAVID HART, AND SUE NICHOLSON

DAVID HART, General Secretary, National Association of Head Teachers: No we do not, we are happy to rely on our written evidence.

LORD NOLAN: Thank you very much. I will ask Diana Warwick to open the questions.

860. DIANA WARWICK: First of all perhaps I should say from the start that we are not looking at the principle of grant-maintained schools, nor are we suggesting that there is any evidence of great impropriety. I say that because in your opening statement you say that you regard it as unfortunate if the impression was to be given that somehow the grant-maintained sector is in need of particular attention. That is not why we are looking at them; we are looking at them because they are new bodies being asked to be accountable in new ways.

Having said that, the National Association of Governors and Managers characterised the new basis on which these schools are governed as a "great experiment in participatory public service by ordinary citizens". Do you share that view? Do you think the great experiment has worked, or are governing bodies in your view too narrow to reflect legitimate community interest?

DAVID HART: I think it has certainly worked, yes. I would make the same comment in respect of local educational authority schools as well. An enormous increase, of course, in governor responsibility across the board, but dealing specifically with grant-maintained schools, yes, I think it certainly has worked. I think that in the vast majority of cases the governors are governing grant-maintained schools well. They have to undertake a range of responsibilities which are way beyond those which were expected of governors, certainly pre-1988. I think that in some cases one could argue that the governing body's composition is perhaps too narrow. Clearly the governing body is composed of various categories of governor. One could, I think, make a case for extending that to a reasonable degree. You certainly cannot under the current system guarantee by any stretch of imagination that you have a full spread of skill, knowledge and expertise because you obviously have to rely upon the people who come up through the elected process or through the appointed process, but I doubt very much if you could ever guarantee you have everything you particularly want on a governing body in terms of skill and knowledge and expertise. So I think there is a case to be made for perhaps widening the categories of people who come on the governing body, and perhaps we do not have enough governing bodies who do truly reflect the community that they serve, if, indeed, you can define accurately what community a school serves with the catchment areas gone and with parents exercising their right of preference, and pupils coming from a much wider geographical area than they did in the past.

861. DIANA WARWICK: Again in your evidence, which is really comprehensive and very, very helpful, you say that there ought to be a form of process for appointing governors, and you go on to say that selection criteria might be used. I wonder if you could say something about that and also perhaps add why you think job descriptions would not be appropriate, because some of the evidence that we have had has suggested that job descriptions, not just for grant-maintained schools but elsewhere, might be a very useful way of signalling the kind of people that are required or might be useful.

DAVID HART: Maybe I am guilty of engaging in semantics. I just do not think it matters really what you call the document you are talking about. I think there has to be a document, whether you call it a job description or selection criteria I do not think matters too much. What I certainly think you do need is a document which sets out exactly what the responsibilities are of a governor of a grant-maintained school, what can be expected of somebody who is seeking election to or appointment to a governing body. Attached to that, of course, or incorporated in that should be a list of the sort of skills and knowledge and expertise that you are looking for to fill that particular vacancy. My own view, from quite a lot of experience of grant-maintained schools, and Sue Nicholson actually looks after the grant-maintained sector within the NAHT headquarters structure, is that governors are selected too often on the basis of "Well I know Fred Bloggs, he is a good person, let us have him" or her as the case may be, and that person comes on the governing body because that person is known to one governor or maybe a group of governors and it is thought that that person will fill the need that the governing body has. I think more comprehensive processes should be gone through.

862. DIANA WARWICK: You are thinking of a sort of a search process or an advertising process, something like that?

DAVID HART: We are talking about reasonably small enterprises, and very small enterprises in some cases, and one has to watch the costs and the bureaucracy involved in this process. Certainly I think a method by which one can make it clear to people who are being sought or people who are volunteering exactly what is expected of them, and certainly the sort of skills and knowledge that they ought to be bringing to the governing body would be very helpful.

863. DIANA WARWICK: How would you ensure that and avoid the sort of self-perpetuating committee problem, like replacing like with like in other words.

DAVID HART: For all grant-maintained schools who went grant-maintained since 1993 you have to have a Code of Standing Orders. I think we ought to move on beyond that. I think we ought to have a compulsory Code of Standing Orders for all governing bodies in the grant-maintained sector. That ought to be a requirement by law, and I think you can incorporate within that Code of Standing Orders issues such as the method by which governing bodies fill vacancies on the governing body, and the issues which you have been raising such as job descriptions or selection criteria or a document of information.

864. DIANA WARWICK: Could I move on to the main area of your representation which, of course, is on behalf of head teachers. In paragraph 12 of your document you say you are extremely concerned—I think it is one of the areas where you do express extreme concern about an aspect of grant-maintained schools—at the failure to clearly set out a division of responsibilities between the governing body and the head of the school. You go on to say that "Only statutory provision, via Articles of Government, will ensure that every governing body observes such a division".

There are always sensitivities in these areas between governing bodies and chief executives or heads and so on. Are you confident that you would be able to define the distinctions between the two roles sufficiently for it to be embodied in statutory form?

DAVID HART: Yes, I have had frequent discussions with the current Secretary of State and, indeed, her predecessors, about this very issue, and she takes the view that you cannot legislate for relationships, as she calls it, and I keep telling her I am not asking her to legislate for relationships, I am asking her to do for grant-maintained schools, and I would also say the same for delegated budget schools, what she did for the FEFC sector. I can see no difference between a grant-maintained school and FEFC college in legal terms where both employ the staff and are the actual de facto employers, and *de jure* employers for that matter. But the issue is this, why is it that a college principal, or chief executive as they are now called, has these powers by statute through the articles of government for the college, and the grant-maintained head does not have them? I do not see any logical distinction between the two, and it is possible, and has been done in the FEFC sector, to lay down by law what is the appropriate balance, particularly in this very difficult area of personnel management. The NAHT takes the view that if you are talking about taking responsibility for the management of an institution, unless you have the personnel management powers to underpin that management role you are, in effect, being asked to walk with at least one stick and maybe two.

865. DIANA WARWICK: That leads me on to another question and that is really about what happens when rows occur? They can blow up very quickly and maybe no means of diffusing them other than, as far as one can see within the grant-maintained structure, the Secretary of State which seems a vast great leap. We have been looking at the possibility of what one witness has called "a critical friend" who understands how the schools work and would look and see how performance could be assessed, how to diffuse that issue. How would you react to that?

DAVID HART: Let me start by saying that I share the view that the problems in the grant-maintained sector, whether they be small or great, are very difficult to resolve in terms of an appeal mechanism. We have at the moment two bodies, the FAS and the Secretary of State. The FAS really has a role which is devoted to financial overseeing of the sector, and a role in connection with obviously places, admissions and new schools and so on and so forth. It does not have any role that permits it to take action where you are, in effect, complaining about the conduct of a governing body, say financial irregularities, so everything gets channelled to the Secretary of State. It does not matter how minor it is. If you are talking about a minor complaint which the governing body does not wish to resolve, or says it is incapable of resolving, it goes to the Secretary of State. I do take the point that without an FEFC type structure where these things are more susceptible of being dealt with, and I will come back to that in a minute, we will have to have some method by which these low grade complaints can be resolved.

Just very quickly on the FEFC, we had two colleges there who had to be the subject of immediate action, one in Derby and one in Birmingham, and the FEFC did put in an enquiry in both cases which led to some pretty drastic recommendations. These were high grade disputes, if you like, but that method of dealing with what was a very difficult situation in both those colleges is not open to the Secretary of State according to my understanding under the current situation. So the Secretary of State really has this very difficult position where she either says "yes, you have hit the button under Section 68 or Section 99" or "you have not hit the button", and if you do not hit either of those buttons really she has to say "I have got no locus in this, I cannot intervene".

I am not sure whether we are talking about a critical friend. I am quite interested in pursuing the idea of a role for an ombudsman where maybe an extension of the local government ombudsman, because they operate on a regional basis, who can perhaps take on board complaints which are not susceptible to being dealt with by the Secretary of State. That may be a way forward.

866. DIANA WARWICK: Do you think there is a greater role for OFSTED or even for a regional structure that might engage?

DAVID HART: I would not like to give any more powers to OFSTED than they have at the moment. They have quite enough powers in terms of what they are supposed to be doing which is inspecting the quality of the teaching and learning that is going on in the school, and, of course, the leadership of the school. I do not honestly think you can give OFSTED that role.

867. DIANA WARWICK: But do you think there is some sort of intermediary structure that it would be wise

to have in place in order to ensure that the number of instances does not increase?

DAVID HART: Yes I do. I think it is ridiculous that if we have a case, and Sue Nicholson and I have had a number of cases, and so have our internal legal department and external lawyers, where we scratched our heads and said where the hell do we go now, and the only place we can go is the Secretary of State, and we know we are taking to her what is a relatively low grade complaint.

SUE NICHOLSON, Assistant Secretary, National Association of Head Teachers: But many of the cases arise because these functions are not clearly defined. So by clearly defining the functions between the head and the governing body one would immediately, in my view, limit the number of disputes that arose. Because the area is so great, it is open to debate who does what, inevitably disputes will occur.

868. DIANA WARWICK: Fine. Could I ask you about another aspect of your paper? That is paragraph 16 where you say, "Greater openness is not in practice a great "spur". We would be concerned if "gagging" clauses were outlawed because it might prevent governing bodies entering into settlements which were in the interests of Heads and Deputy Heads". I take the point, but you say "there has to be another way of subjecting severance payments to external scrutiny", that is the corollary of your comment and this is obviously an area where there has been some considerable cause for concern in these bodies. What do you have in mind? Is there something that you think could be done that does not relate to gagging clauses but relates to the openness of severance payments?

DAVID HART: Again taking a line from the FEFC because we have quite a big involvement there through our links with the Association of Principals of Colleges, and we provide them with services in this area. Whether this is an informal operation or a formal operation, I am not sure, but I do know for a fact that the FEFC have intervened and have given advice to college or corporation governors where they have been negotiating a deal with the principal which involves a severance payment. I know for a fact they have in some instances said, "you cannot do that, it is too much money", or they have said "No, this is inappropriate". I do not quite know the basis upon which the FEFC operates there, but clearly within the FEFC structure there appears to be some mechanism by which severance payments can be subject to reasonable scrutiny.

Within the grant-maintained sector the decision as to whether a severance payment would be made is obviously the governing body. The decision as to whether the head's or deputy head's pension and lump sum will be enhanced is a matter for the governing body. The funding for that will come through the special grant provided by the Funding Agency for Schools. There is no public scrutiny that I know of of the actual payments except any scrutiny that the FAS may undertake, or any scrutiny that the National Audit people may undertake of the sector as a whole.

The point I was making was this, that although I can understand some people thinking that gagging clauses are bad, and I do not like to see gagging clauses, wearing a negotiators hat I would not like my staff responsible for

negotiating these things with governing bodies to find that, because everything has to be out in the open in the sense that you cannot have a clause in it saying you will not speak to the press or the public about the circumstances surrounding your departure, the access to reasonable settlements which might ease problems in schools is cut off. I do not say it will be, but it might be.

869. DIANA WARWICK: I am very conscious of not wanting to take up all the time and my colleagues to be able to ask you questions, are there two or three main features that you feel in relation to grant-maintained schools we should address, and, if so, what would you suggest?

DAVID HART: I think firstly there is the question of whistle blowing. I do feel very strongly that there is a possibility of increasingly difficult situations arising because members of staff, and in particular the head of the school or possibly the bursar, are aware of situations which clearly are either improper or illegal or a combination of the two which clearly should be brought to the notice of external authorities, but they are unable so to do because they feel that their employment status may be at risk if they were to undertake action which would be clearly frowned upon by the governing body. I think that is a potential real issue. We have certainly come across it in two or three cases of some importance, and I do believe that some method by which a senior employee of the institution were able to record, not just have it noted in the minutes, but record more formally or more directly their concern about malpractice ought to be seriously considered. I do not say it is frequent, far from it, it is very infrequent, but when it happens it causes quite catastrophic consequences for relationships within the school or the college. So that is one issue.

I think the other issue which is of fundamental importance as well is referred to on the first page of our evidence, and that really is the accountability of governors, not just as a corporate governing body as a whole but individual members of the governing body. We have governors in place for lengthy periods of time and yet, within that lengthy period of time, short of disqualification for the reasons set out in the Articles of Government, they can be acting quite clearly contrary to the interests of the governing body, maybe quite clearly contrary to the interests of the parents and the community, and yet there is no mechanism by which a governing body can remove one of their number. They are stuck with that individual whether they like it or not, and that individual, despite all the rhetoric about corporate responsibility, can cause mayhem within that governing body and within the community, and I find that rather a strange omission, with safeguards of course.

870. WILLIAM UTTING: If I could return to the arguments you put forward about a statutory statement governing the respective functions of the head and governors. You are proposing this presumably for the grant-maintained sector only, and you do not think it necessary in the local management of schools context?

DAVID HART: No, I proposed it for both categories of schools.

871. WILLIAM UTTING: So it would go right across the educational sector. I thought that there were sort of long established systems within local authorities for

dealing with the kind of issues that are worrying you in separating functions between a chief executive and a board of management, but no?

DAVID HART: No, there are no long established systems. Even before the 1988 Act there was a grey area, less of a grey area in one sense because obviously the local authority have much more control pre 1988 than it has now. What happened was that the 1988 Act and subsequent legislation rewrote the map, or redrew the map, and vested in the governing bodies, either as real employers like the grant-maintained sector or as quasi employers like the delegated budget sector, very substantial responsibilities not least in what I call personnel management areas, but failed to resolve this inherent conflict which exists between giving to the governing body all these responsibilities and then hoping that the governing body will, because it is good practice, undertake necessary delegation.

872. WILLIAM UTTING: Thank you for that, that is extremely helpful. Could I also go back to what you said earlier about the role of the Secretary of State in relation to grant-maintained schools. You say in your evidence that the Secretary of State ought to act quickly when action is necessary, but you speak about this being governed, so to speak, by other circumstances than the actual merits of the case. I could, having worked in central government, see quite a lot of reasons why the Secretary of State might be advised not to intervene quickly in the affairs of a single small institution, especially if she is responsible for a thousand of them. This sort of leads in the direction, with your earlier remarks about the FEFC, actually about some sort of intermediary body between the Secretary of State and the individual school that soaks up or co-ordinates the activities of the wide range of different organisations that a single school has to relate to.

DAVID HART: I see no reason why the Secretary of State cannot establish, albeit for 1000 or 1100 schools or whatever it is, a body along the lines of the FEFC, because although the FEFC controls an entire sector it does not seem to me to mean that an FEFC type body cannot also take responsibilities given to that body by the Secretary of State so it would be an FAS merged with some of the Secretary of State's powers to create a body of that nature. I cannot see any way round that unless you are going to create a sort of ombudsman situation on a regional basis where the ombudsman would have a role to play in non Section 68 and Section 99 situations. The Secretary of State quite clearly has to be advised by her civil servants and by the legal department at the DFEE that a case is susceptible to being dealt with under those sections or it is not, and then of course she will then be advised as to

whether, as I said, the Section 68 button should be pressed, or the Section 99 button should be pressed, and if not she will so rule. I understand that process can take time and should not be rushed because she has to watch her back in case somebody want to challenge her by judicial review or something. I can understand all of that. That is a good reason, therefore, for trying to take what I call the lower grade stuff out of the Secretary of State's domain and vest it in some other body, or some other group, that can deal with that perhaps more expeditiously and certainly less formally, otherwise everything goes to the Secretary of State.

873. WILLIAM UTTING: One last question if I may Chairman. The DFEE evidence to us says, "grant-maintained schools intended to be self-governing, accounting to their local communities for their performance". Are you satisfied that they can and do actually account to their local communities for their performance?

DAVID HART: Yes they certainly do account. Whether, in fact, the local community is sufficiently active or interested to place that level of accountability on the governing body is another issue, but we have the school prospectus, we have the annual report, we have the annual meeting, badly attended or not as the case may be, we have other more informal links between schools, and obviously not just their parents who are frequently in the school on all sorts of bases, but also with the local community, if you can define who the local community is. I think there is quite a lot of accountability there. After all, if the governing body, as advised by the head, get it wrong and the school is perceived to be failing to deliver in various areas, the parents or prospective parents will vote with their feet. As soon as the pupil numbers start going down all sorts of things start to happen. The budget starts to reduce, redundancies start to come on stream, and the governing body soon has to direct its attention to what action should be taken to make sure it is more in tune with the needs of the community as expressed particularly through the parents.

WILLIAM UTTING: I am grateful, Chairman.

LORD NOLAN: I suppose, as the Headmaster of Great Barr School was saying this morning, you can feel very responsible indeed to the local community for the behaviour of your school children when they are out of school and on the streets. Thank you very much indeed, I think your pupils this morning have learnt a lot. Thank you.

WEDNESDAY 6 DECEMBER 1995

OPENING STATEMENTS

Opening Statement from Brian Sherratt OBE, Headmaster and Hon Alderman Mrs Judy Watts-James, Chair of Governors, Great Barr Grant Maintained School, Birmingham.

Great Barr is a non-selective, co-educational comprehensive school in North Birmingham. It is the largest school in the country with more than 2,300 pupils on roll and one of the largest employers in the area.

I have been head of the school for twelve years and was previously head of a comprehensive school in Derbyshire.

Great Barr became a grant-maintained school in April 1991 and since then improvements to all aspects of the school have been very considerable. Grant-maintained status has brought to the school a new vitality and corporate sense of purpose as we work together to provide the best possible learning environment for our pupils.

The school received a very positive OFSTED report in April 1995 a synopsis of which is attached. I would wish to draw attention to the sections on Value for Money and Efficiency because I believe that they reinforce the point that grant-maintained status is a means of ensuring that all the money available to the school directly supports pupil learning.

Preamble

It is perhaps unfortunate that the section of the Paper concerned with schools concentrates only on grant-maintained schools in that there are key issues which are of equal importance to both grant-maintained and LM schools. The Paper's concentration on grant-maintained schools may suggest to members of the public that grant-maintained schools are a particular focus of the Committee's attention. OFSTED evidence would suggest that generally grant-maintained schools are efficiently and effectively managed and that the quality of governance is of a high order. There are obviously some exceptions but it would be unhelpful should the majority of grant-maintained schools, which would fare well in examination on Standards in Public Life, be perceived as being in particular need of the Committee's attention.

It is also important to ensure that full account is taken of the self-governing, autonomous nature of grant-maintained schools (schools differ from other public bodies) and to avoid generalised solutions to problems of propriety which may not work in the interest of grant-maintained schools.

1.   How are governing bodies accountable to parents and the local community and could this be improved?

1.1   Governing bodies of grant-maintained schools are demonstrably accountable to parents in that generally there are more elected parent governors on grant-maintained governing bodies than on those of LEA schools. This accountability is strengthened by the fact that following incorporation as a grant-maintained school at least two First Governors (of a former County school) must also be parents. First governors represent business (a legal requirement) and other interests (e.g. the police, the church) in the area served by the school. Thus parent governors and first governors of a grant-maintained school are by definition local people in that they live or work (or both) in the area served by the school. They are thus more accessible to parents than locally elected members serving on an LEA school governing body and their interests are specific to the grant-maintained school.

1.2   Accountability to the community is perhaps a more difficult concept to define because governing bodies are more tangibly accountable to parents through the Annual Report and Annual Parents' Meeting. In this context how can a school give due emphasis to the view of local community/communities? The inclusion of governors representing local business interests adds an important local dimension but in what sense is the school accountable to the local business community? It may be more helpful to think in terms of accountability to the parent community and answerability to other local communities.

1.3   The point to be stressed, however, is that in a grant-maintained school governor accountability is local and clearly focused on the school. Elected members or LEA-nominated governors serving on LEA-school governing bodies are less likely to focus their efforts on a particular school and may well see themselves as having a party political role to play on an LEA governing body. With the best will in the world, elected members, who usually also pursue their own career outside politics, are busy people and, if remote from the school, will find it difficult to give it appropriate attention. With grant-maintained governing bodies the reverse is the case. Governors are locally accessible and accountability (or answerability) is to the local community.

1.4   The proceedings of all meetings of the Governing Body are recorded as minutes. Minutes include the names of governors present at the meeting. Copies of the agenda, minutes and supporting documentation for each meeting must be made available at the school for any parent or member of the public to read. As with LEA governing bodies, the minutes of any part of a meeting that are confidential are kept separate and are not available for public inspection.

1.5   Governor accountability is formalised by law in that the governing body of a grant-maintained school, in accordance with the school's Articles of Government, must publish and make available to each parent of a registered pupil at the school an annual report on their governance of the school and which addresses the areas of the school's activities for which governors are responsible (ie, how the governing body has implemented its plans for the school since the last annual report). The annual report must also contain the names and status (parent, teacher, first governor or otherwise) of each member of the governing body, together with their term of office and information concerning the next election of parent governors. Publication of these details further ensures the accessibility of governors to parents.

1.6   Governors are obliged to hold an annual parents' meeting at which the annual reports can be discussed. This meeting provides parents with the opportunity of taking part in the running of the school and, provided there is a quorum (the number of parents at the meeting must be equal to at least 20% of the pupils on roll) parents may pass resolutions which must be considered by the governing body or referred to the head. The next annual report must include a comment on any resolution so passed. Resolutions may refer to the work of governors or to the duties of the head. Effectively, therefore, parents may pass a vote of no confidence in the governing body which governors would then be required by law to address. The fact that the number of parents at the meeting must be equal to at least 20% of the pupils on role means, in most schools, that such a vote of no confidence would have to involve a large number of parents. This obviates the possibility of the stability of the governing body being undermined by a minority of parents who are not representative of the wider parental perspective.

1.7   Unlike the somewhat superficial audit procedures applied by many LEAs, those applied to grant-maintained schools are rigorous. The accounts of a grant-maintained school must be audited annually by external auditors in accordance with FAS requirements. The school's accounts are then made public and published as part of the Governors' Annual Report to Parents. Governors are quite literally accountable for the way in which they have used grant made available to them by the FAS and may have to answer questions on value for money at the Annual Meeting.

1.8   The FAS monitors schools financially through its own procedures. Further scrutiny of a school's public and non-public accounts may be undertaken by The National Audit Office and by the OFSTED. In both cases the reports produced are in the public domain.

1.9   In the case of an OFSTED report the governors must produce an action plan which is sent to parents and made available to any member of the public. The action plan must be included as an agenda item in the Governors' Annual Report to Parents and governors must explain to parents at the Annual Parents' Meeting how they are implementing their action plan and what progress has been achieved.

1.10   In a grant-maintained school the accountability and responsibility of the governing body is far more precisely delineated than in an LEA school. Governors cannot pass on a problem to the LEA nor can they absolve themselves from blame by suggesting that the fault lies with LEA bureaucracy. Parents, staff, pupils, the local community and the media are all aware that governors of a grant-maintained school carry very considerable public responsibilities. This is likely to lead to recruitment of governors of a high calibre who will take their responsibilities very seriously. Indeed, governing bodies of grant-maintained schools often enjoy an enhanced status within the community served by the school by virtue of the increased responsibilities which self-governing status brings. The status of the governing body and the standing of the school in the community will be reflected in parental satisfaction and application for places at the school. School performance is a form of accountability to the local community.

2.   Do governing bodies rely on informal networking for recruitment rather than a formal nominations system? Could published job descriptions and selection criteria be more widely used?

2.1   Each grant-maintained governing body includes a significant number (between 4 and 7) of governors formally appointed through an election process (every four years). The remaining first or foundation governors are appointed, or re-appointed, formally by the governing body. Elected governors ensure the introduction of new ideas whereas first or foundation governors (who serve from 5 to 7 years) ensure continuity and consistency. First governors are important in that they bring to the governance of the school a local perspective beyond that of the elected parent governors.

2.2   The selection process may include networking but this will depend on the local circumstances of the school. Given that governorship of a grant-maintained school requires considerable commitment in terms of time and work, schools will want to search for potential governors with the appropriate kind of expertise to meet current needs so flexibility is important. Networking may well draw a governing body more effectively from the local community than one with LEA-appointed governors where, particularly in the Shire counties, the local government administrative centre may be thirty miles away.

2.3   It would be unhelpful to legislate for the involvement of local interest groups since schools vary considerably in terms of the communities they serve.

2.4   Many grant-maintained schools have devised formal procedures for the recruitment of new governors and this approach is to be encouraged. Where first governors are concerned it is less likely that schools will have as yet devised formal procedures since only a few schools will have been self-governing for more than five years but similar procedures based on good practice should be developed throughout the grant-maintained sector.

2.5   Since the roles and responsibilities of grant-maintained school governors are more precisely defined than is the case with LEA school governors it is not surprising to find that recruitment of governors to a grant-maintained school is relatively less problematic than in the LEA-maintained sector. Grant-maintained governors are the employers of the school's staff. In LEA schools the governors are responsible for appointment and dismissal but the staff are the employees of the LEA. This kind of complication does not help recruitment. In addition, many governors of grant-maintained schools wish to do their job as governors without the intrusion of the political perspective inevitably associated with LEA governing bodies. The LEA bureaucratic culture is not conducive to persuading volunteers to come forward to serve on governing bodies.

2.6　This is not to suggest that recruitment of first governors is necessarily straightforward. For example, it is particularly useful to have first governors with financial, legal or personnel expertise and successful recruitment is more likely to result from head-hunting than from members of the local community volunteering their services. The governing body needs to define its needs and appoint accordingly.

2.7　Individually, schools need to develop their formal procedures for the appointment of first governors and all grant-maintained schools should be encouraged to have these in place. Advertising may be appropriate but the real problem is not so much how governors are recruited but the fact that they are expected to conduct virtually all their governor business after business hours. Should there be a system whereby governors qualified for paid leave of absence as with Justices of the Peace?

2.8　Selection criteria might be useful but job descriptions for governors would over-complicate the role confusion that apparently exists between heads and governors. To describe the governor's role as a job is to misunderstand the nature of governorship.

2.9　With some governing bodies there is the possibility that a group of governors may take control and seek to perpetuate their power. However, it is the duty of the other governors to ensure that this does not happen. "Chairman"'s action' under emergency powers should always be justified at a full governors' meeting and the action with its justification minuted. This is an area of weakness requiring attention.

2.10　The regular need for re-appointment of first governors and re-election of others helps to obviate the problem of self-perpetuation. However, the introduction of regulation prescribing a maximum term of office makes no sense at all. Given that it is now difficult to recruit governors, that they give their services voluntarily and that they are essential in terms of accountability to parents and answerability to other local communities, such a regulation could only lead to the loss to the education service of a significant number of experienced governors. This could only be harmful to schools in the long term and serves to reinforce the point that grant-maintained schools need in place effective formal procedures for the re-appointment of first governors.

3.　How do you draw the line of responsibility between governing bodies and head teachers?

3.1　It is helpful for the Head to be recognised by the Governors as acting in the role of a chief executive of a company, of which the Governing Body, under its chairman, is the board of directors. However, whereas this analogy is useful it should not be pressed too far, since a state school is manifestly not a commercial company, nor are its "directors" paid. The Head is also the leading professional, a concept that also helps to differentiate the role of the Head from that of governors and, indeed, from all other members of the school's staff.

3.2　A Governing Body needs to bear in mind that it:

- has important statutory responsibilities;

- makes policies and gives the Head scope to implement them;

- has an essential function to perform in setting the strategic framework for the school;

- oversees the work of the school, but does not oversee the work of individual teachers;

- does not perform an inspectorial role, but considers the advice of those who do;

- performs a voluntary service, not a full-time function;

- is not involved in close day-to-day supervision; and

- has a corporate role and that no individual governor has the right to act independently of the governing body.

3.3　The Governing Body should determine both the educational character and mission of the school. The Head's responsibilities include making proposals for these. However, the process of forward planning is continuous and the Head has a responsibility to ensure that issues related to the school's future development are brought before the Governing Body at the appropriate time and with relevant advice. In particular, the Head will play a major role in updating and developing the school's strategic plan.

3.4　Once the Governing Body has decided on a course of action, then it is for the Head in the role of chief executive and leading professional, responsible for the running of the school, to carry out its decisions personally, or to ensure that they are implemented through the school's management structure. It is the responsibility of the Governing Body to ensure that the Head has the delegated powers necessary to achieve this.

3.5   In respect of the Head's responsibilities which are not delegated functions of the Governing Body but which are laid down in the Instrument and Articles of Government and the current Pay and Conditions document it is essential for governors to appreciate that there are important statutory requirements that only the Head can undertake, such as the exclusion of a pupil and the temporary suspension of the National Curriculum for a particular pupil.

3.6   More frequently the responsibilities that are given to the Head have to be carried out within the framework of the policies determined by the Governing Body. This should not be seen as interfering with the Head's management role, but as giving the Head a framework of accountability to the Governing Body.

3.7   However, for governors to play an effective role they will have to acquire a working knowledge of the school and this will involve visits to the school. These need a clear purpose and careful planning, if such visits are not going to undermine the Head's authority in relation to managing the school. Guidelines should be established by the Governing Body in consultation with the Head for such visits.

3.8   Getting the balance of power right between Head and governors in a school depends on two central factors: the character of those concerned, and the framework of law under which they operate. The question facing grant-maintained schools is whether the school has established the right framework.

3.9   In terms of routine organisation and administration, schools generally function perfectly well without the direct assistance of governing bodies. The system as we experience it works largely because most governing bodies do not actually exercise in detail the powers potentially available to them. This is not to suggest that there should be no accountability or that the existing accountability of heads to governing bodies should be transferred to DfEE or FAS officials, a notion that certainly would not sit easily with that of the self-governing school. Accountability within a decentralised education system, however, needs to be made explicit. In any event, if a school cannot win the support and approval from parents and its local community—from which its governors are drawn—it will go out of business.

3.10   In broad terms, heads are responsible for implementing the statutory requirements and governing bodies are responsible for ensuring that they fulfil their statutory duties. The governors determine the character of the school: the head runs the school. They are each responsible for supplying the other with any necessary information. Nonetheless the balance in favour of governors appears, perhaps, excessive to the extent that it may not always helpfully complement the operational responsibilities of heads.

3.11   A more equitable balance between the defined responsibilities of the head, supported by professional staff, and those of governors would be useful in clarifying both policy-making and managerial functions. A certain creative tension between head and governors might well be a healthy one. Given, however, that self-governing schools will wish to retain the autonomy to decide for themselves the procedures for policy making and implementation, there is nevertheless a strong case for making the respective roles clearer. Clarification of respective functions would make for greater efficiency and avoid confusion and misunderstanding.

4.   Should mechanisms of independent scrutiny be introduced to resolve staff grievances? How might these work?

4.1   All grant-maintained schools have formal systems in place for grievances to be raised. The present system of checks and balances should enable schools to deal with such grievances at the appropriate level. In this respect the distinctive roles, with reference to powers and duties, of the head, governing body, bursar and clerk to the governors are important. Staff concerns can be made known through the appropriate channel of communication. Staff concerns about propriety are also brought to light through the established procedures of audit and inspection.

4.2   Rather than introduce mechanisms of external scrutiny it would help if the powers of the clerk to the governing body were strengthened by making that role advisory with direct channels of communication with the FAS and the DFEE. Concerned staff could discuss their concerns in confidence with the clerk who would then be obliged to pass on those concerns through the established channels to either the FAS or the DFEE—in other words, a mechanism to accelerate procedures that already exist.

5.   Do you think the proposed code of conduct will improve propriety? Should adoption of a code be mandatory and compliance be a condition of appointment?

5.1   There is a requirement for all grant-maintained schools to adopt Standing Orders and there are examples of guidance on good practice. The Further Education Funding Council's Code of Conduct on Governance provides a useful model.

5.2   It is of vital importance that all grant-maintained schools should operate procedures to safeguard against governors using their position for any form of personal gain. The same applies to LEA schools where there are fewer checks and where LEA appointees, particularly elected members, can exercise considerable influence in a variety of contexts.

5.3   Governing bodies should:

adhere to a code of conduct for the full governing body and for individual members

adhere to Standing Orders for the full governing body and its committees

produce Terms of Reference for each committee

keep a register of interests to include details of
> paid employment
> self-employment
> directorships of commercial companies
> significant shareholdings
> elected office
> trusteeships or participation in the management of charities and voluntary bodies
> public appointments (paid or unpaid)
> membership of professional bodies and trade or other associations

invite members to provide the same information, if known to him or her, in respect of his or her spouse or partner, children or other close relatives (e.g. living in the same household or a dependent). A member should ask him/herself whether members of the public, knowing such information, would reasonably conclude that the relevant interest might influence his or her judgment.

produce Agreed Terms of Employment for senior staff

circulate all minutes of all committees to all governors promptly

5.4   The new Rainbow Pack produced by the FAS requires all grant-maintained schools to keep a Register of Interests. The National Audit Office also considers this to be good practice and many grant-maintained schools already have such a register in place.

6.   Is there a role for whistleblowing in the grant-maintained sector?

6.1   With the proviso that the school's internal procedures have been properly followed there may well be a case for a formal, independent means of considering staff concerns with regard to impropriety. There is obviously a risk that staff who would wish to complain about standards of probity in school governance may feel unable to do so by virtue of the employer/ employee relationship. Staff may feel that there is no body of people of an independent nature between the school and the FAS. There is, of course, no reason why a member of staff should not register a complaint with the FAS, with the school's external auditors, with the Responsible Officer or with the Clerk to the governing body (see 4.2 above). To ensure independence and confidentiality, however, an independent panel, not dissimilar to an appeals panel may provide a possible solution avoiding the setting up of some new bureaucracy. It is for the DFEE and the FAS to encourage the establishment of non-statutory principles in all grant-maintained schools.

6.2   However, the influence of the FAS, the NAO and OFSTED is very considerable. Good governance is the norm, not the exception, in grant-maintained schools. The machinery to ensure propriety is already very effective. All governing body minutes are in the public domain, governing body have a statutory duty to report to parents on all aspects of their governance and to discuss their performance openly at the Annual Parents' Meeting; there are checks by auditors, the FAS, the NAO and OFSTED on governors' conduct of school affairs; the Secretary of State may intervene if she is of the opinion that a governing body's activities are ultra vires. Already the procedures employed in the grant-maintained sector are at least as effective (and in most cases more effective) than those in LEA schools.

**Opening statement from Hon Alderman Mrs Judy Watts-James, Chair of Governors,
Great Barr Grant Maintained School, Birmingham.**

Great Barr Grant Maintained School serves an area of high deprivation and high crime rate. Housing in the area consists mainly of a large pre-war council estate and pre and post-war semi-detached properties.

Because of the nature of the area the school consists of children with a wide range of abilities. Approximately 15% of the school population is from ethnic minorities.

1. Quote from OFSTED

The School is highly valued by the Community and the atmosphere of the school is generally very positive and welcoming

A strongly led PTA with many events open to the public.

Through the House System parents have easy access to voice concerns.

Pupils take an active part in the community—Christmas parties for Senior Citizens—Concerts in sheltered accommodation—Working with activities in primary schools.

Any suggestions or comments to improve our already good relations would be discussed and welcomed.

2. Parent governors and teachers by the appropriate elections. First governors were appointed on incorporation. LEA governors became first governors. Co-opted governors who had been appointed previously by the Governing Body also became first governors. All had given valuable service to the school and had expertise and the specialism necessary for grant-maintained status.

Mainly by recommendation. Friendly interview to explain the workings of governors and time needed. Governing body then to make decision.

It should be remembered that governors are voluntary and give of their time and experience without any thought of payment. The Governors booklet and guide to the Law clearly set out responsibilities. If appointments and interviews are mandatory this may prevent many people becoming governors.

It should be borne in mind that governors prime purpose is to support and improve the quality of education.

3. The Head Teacher was appointed for his professional expertise and knowledge to provide strong leadership in the school. This is recognised by the Governors who are very supportive in their dealings and discussions.

There are regular and frank discussions between the Head and Chairman.

A resolution was passed by the Governors stating that the Head was responsible for the running of the school and for the well being and learning environment in the school.

This gives the head a very clear directive and he in turn keeps the Chairman fully informed.

4. A Staff Consultative Committee is composed of Staff Union Representatives, 6 governors, Deputy Head responsible for staffing and Headmaster.

Minutes of this committee are reported to Statutory Governors Meeting.

The Disciplinary panel for appeals and grievances has independent members as well as governors. This has proved to work well.

All documents on policy are sent to National Union Representatives well in advance of meetings for their comments.

5. It was a monument of neglect in previous years. We have improved the building for the learning and teaching environment. We are the envy of other schools in the area. The success is in the number of applicants for entry.

I do recognise, however, that there are cases where money is not spent for the benefit of the learning environment and would welcome a mechanism to define the lines to the bodies which already exist.

Opening statement from Mr Roddy Skidmore, Chief Executive, Central England Training and Enterprise Council

I am pleased to have this opportunity to give evidence to the Committee with regard to Central England TEC. From the outset in 1990, the Board has sought to ensure that the TEC is fully accountable to the local community which it serves in Solihull, Redditch, Bromsgrove and the Wyre Forest. We serve an extremely diverse area and it is extremely important to us that the TEC should be open in its dealings and seen to be acting in the very best interests of the local economy.

From its inception, Central England TEC instituted an open membership scheme, which was free and available to all individuals and all businesses based in the TEC's area. This has encouraged businesses and local people to take ownership of their local Training and Enterprise Council, to nominate and vote for its non-Executive Directors and help shape the direction of the company. We advertise openly for potential non-Executive Directors and all candidates must stand for election by the membership at the Annual General Meeting. Our non-Executive Directors are not remunerated and give freely of their time and energy because they truly believe that the local Training and Enterprise Council can make a positive contribution towards the development of the local economy, enhancing the competitiveness of our local businesses and to raising the standards of living for local people.

The TEC, including its non-Executive Directors, recognises that it has a responsibility for the wise application of public funds and continuously seeks to demonstrate the highest standards of integrity and leadership. A register is maintained of the financial and non-financial interests of Directors and employees, which includes close family. Where a conflict of interest does arise at a Board meeting, this is fully minuted, together with a decision whether the Director should be present, participate in the discussion or have access to relevant papers. Central England TEC publishes in its Annual Report and Accounts details of the contracts which it places, including any placed with an organisation in which a non-Executive Director has an interest.

We have a robust procedure for dealing with complaints and for the monitoring of compliance with Central England TEC's Code of Practice.

Central England TEC is proud of the quality of the services which it provides and of its steadily increasing success in developing the local economy. In this, the TEC works very closely with its local partners, such as the local authorities and chambers of commerce. We recognise that the quality of our Board has been a major contributory factor to success.

Opening statement by the Lincolnshire Training and Enterprise Council

In our evidence, we wish to build upon the information contained in our submission of 24 October. In relation to the particular issues raised in your invitation of 21 November, we will make the following additional comments:

Openness/Accountability

We have established five Regional Advisory Committees (RACs) based broadly on District Council areas within the county. Membership is open to any local organisation including employers and we make a particular effort to ensure a representative cross-section of community interests in that locality. RACs are chaired by Board Directors and provide an effective two-way communication link directly with the TEC Board. Board Directors often have previous involvement with RACs prior to appointment.

Other methods for ensuring community involvement and accountability include:

- Network News—a quarterly newspaper, circulation 8,000 (open to whole network).

- In Business—a weekly half hour radio programme focused on small business.

- Board minutes and supporting papers—placed in the public domain by library service including quarterly performance reports.

- Rural Challenge—a community based economic development initiative involving everyone from age 12 in the development of sustainable community regeneration activities.

- Business Plan Executive Summary
  Annual Report
  Corporate Plan*   } all widely circulated
  Annual Public Meeting
  Close relationship with local media

* Developed via comprehensive countywide consultation.

TEC Board Appointments

Policy of advertising has two key benefits—opens up TEC Board to wider community than otherwise possible and for those not appointed, provides an opportunity of involvement with the TEC in other ways. Our succession planning process helps ensure that we appoint people with a genuine interest in the local community.

Conflicts of interests

Our ISO 9001 quality procedure sets out clearly how we deal with conflicts of interest. A register of interests for Board Directors and staff is available to the general public on request. Staff are required by terms and conditions to declare activities which may have a potential for conflict of interest.

Complaints

We have an established complaints procedure as part of ISO 9001 quality system. The Board Audit Sub-Committee deals with any appeals from complainants.

Contract compliance

We have monthly performance reviews—a two-way process which is mutually beneficial. ISO 9001 accreditation has proved extremely valuable in maintaining compliance. GOEM licensing and contracting conditions are not, in practice, unduly onerous.

Improper Behaviour

A number of points made earlier impact on this issue, in particular, the complaints procedures, contractual requirements, quality/financial monitoring, openness and availability to local media.

In conclusion, we believe that TECs have now matured to a position where it could be accepted that money leaves the public domain via the Government/TEC Contract. We, at the same time, recognise that there is legitimate public interest in the use to which that money is put. We believe the systems described above and in our submission of 24 October meet that interest and there is no need for more onerous demands to be placed on the TEC organisations.

TUESDAY 12 DECEMBER 1995

Members Present:

The Rt Hon Lord Nolan (Chairman)

Sir Clifford Boulton GCB
The Rt Hon Lord Thomson of
Monifieth KT DL

Sir William Utting CB
Dame Anne Warburton DCVO CMG
Diana Warwick

Witnesses:

Auriol Stevens, Editor, *Times Higher Education Supplement*
Roger Brook, Chairman, and Andrew Foster, Controller, Audit Commission
Donald Hoodless, Chief Executive, and Margaret Hodge MP, Chair, Circle 33 Housing
Association
Baroness Perry, President, Lucy Cavendish College, Cambridge
Professor Gareth Roberts and Professor David Melville, Committee of Vice-
Chancellors and Principals

874. LORD NOLAN: Welcome to our fifth and last week of oral evidence in London.

We have five sets of witnesses today, from a number of different sectors.

First we welcome Auriol Stevens, Editor of the *Times Higher Education Supplement.* Ms Stevens has over 20 years' experience as an educational journalist and has done voluntary work in the fields of higher and school age education, including a period as chair of governors of a secondary school. Her journal has been covering our hearings and now we look forward to her own insights on the subject.

Next, Roger Brook, the new Chairman of the Audit Commission, will be accompanied by the Controller, Andrew Foster, whom we met during our first set of hearings. The Audit Commission audits local government and also the health service at local level. We found its evidence particularly helpful during our first study, and its experience in studying the organisation of service delivery at local level will again be useful today.

Our third set of witnesses are Margaret Hodge MP and Donald Hoodless, the Chair and Chief Executive respectively of Circle 33 Housing Trust. Ms Hodge and Mr Hoodless took over the management of Circle 33, which is one of the larger housing associations, after it experienced a major fraud some years ago, and among other matters we hope to hear some of the lessons which Circle 33 learnt from that.

Fourth, we shall welcome Baroness Perry, President of Lucy Cavendish College, Cambridge. Lady Perry has had a distinguished career in education. In addition to being Chief Inspector of Higher Education and Director of South Bank Polytechnic, as it was, and later Vice-Chancellor of South Bank University, as it now is, Lady Perry has undertaken voluntary activities too numerous to mention. One of our Committee has a connection with Lucy Cavendish College and indeed was Lady Perry's immediate predecessor, and I shall ask Dame Anne Warburton to declare that formally on the record in due course.

Finally today we hear from Professor Gareth Roberts, the Chairman, and Professor David Melville, representing the Committee of Vice-Chancellors and Principals. Professor Roberts is Vice-Chancellor of the University of Sheffield and Professor Melville is Vice-Chancellor of Middlesex University.

Can I now ask members of the Committee to declare interests relevant to today's witnesses?

DIANA WARWICK: I have to declare my interest as Chief Executive of the Committee of Vice-Chancellors and Principals, who are one of our witnesses today.

LORD NOLAN: Dame Anne, did I describe you correctly?

ANNE WARBURTON: Chairman, I was President of Lucy Cavendish College until about 18 months ago. I am still a member of the Council of the University of East Anglia.

LORD NOLAN: Ms Stevens, it is very nice to have you with us. Thank you very much indeed for coming along. It is very good of you. We take turns in a democratic way to ask questions of the witnesses. I am going to ask Lord Thomson to begin questions this morning to you.

875. LORD THOMSON: Ms Stevens, thank you very much for coming to give evidence to us and for providing us with an opening statement, which was very useful and which I have read with great interest.

We have heard from a number of witnesses in the higher education field. Basically the message we get is that the standards of conduct in higher education are pretty high. You mention in your statement to us that broadly you agree with that, but you have some reservations. Would you like to start off by spelling out some of your reservations?

AURIOL STEVENS

AURIOL STEVENS (Editor, *Times Higher Education Supplement*): I think the standards are indeed pretty high. I think they have got a lot higher very recently as a result of the investigations of your Committee, and I am not sure how well entrenched all those high standards yet are. I don't think that the low standards, if that is what I am referring to, are wickedness, but I think that they are quite complacent.

876. LORD THOMSON: I used to be a chancellor of what I always regarded as a new university, but one of the bits of education I have received during these hearings is that I realise I was chancellor of what is now called an old university and that there is a new breed of new universities, and there is a broad distinction in the governance between the two. Would you like to tell us from your great experience of these matters what are the advantages and disadvantages of the two systems of governance in terms of standards and propriety?

AURIOL STEVENS: Yes, it varies a lot, does it not? I think that the advantage of arrangements in what are now the old universities is that they have a very open and democratic system. Everybody knows what is going on, vast numbers of people are involved; and the disadvantage of that is that it is extremely difficult to get any decisions made. In the new universities, by contrast, and probably as a result of observing that, the management structures are much leaner and it is much easier to make decisions, but, by contrast, it is much more difficult for people to know what is going on and to feel that they are participating. Whether anything needs to be done about that or whether that is just something that maybe time will change I do not know. I notice that the new universities are putting in place large bodies equivalent to what would be the court of an old university—the great and the good, the local MPs, people from the neighbourhood who are interested—who have no real power but are there to advise the university. All that paraphernalia is coming into place in the new universities, I think, so they are moving in that direction. The old universities have been trying ever since the Jarrett report to streamline their decision-taking. I do not think they have been altogether successful. I think they are somewhat hog-tied by procedures which prevent serious mistakes of commission being made but encourage mistakes of omission. It is very difficult for the university to react sometimes.

877. LORD THOMSON: The occasional scandals that have been drawn to our attention during the course of our inquiry—we are not investigating particular situations, and in any case bad cases make bad law, do they not?—have tended to arise in the new universities, and yet you draw attention in your paper to the fact that one of the scandals was Cardiff University and how long it took to deal with that. Is that inherent in the governance of an old university?

AURIOL STEVENS: I think it was. For instance, the document produced by the Chairmen of University Councils is newly come and suggests all kinds of rigorous things which were probably not in place in University College Cardiff, though I do not know. I just think there has been a lot of tightening up, partly as a result of Cardiff and of subsequent moves that were made by government forcing upon the old universities changes in the ways in which they are publicly accountable, which they did not like at all. It would be foolish to suppose that all this had been done purely out of the kindness of their hearts: they have done it under pressure.

878. LORD THOMSON: You make what I suppose is a kind of compliment, that perhaps the fact that we have been conducting these inquiries has helped to create a situation of fear of something worse, but I notice that you make the rather menacing recommendation to us that we ought to become a permanent feature of public life. You are proposing to give the Nolan Committee a life sentence, are you?

AURIOL STEVENS: This is a rather peripheral and not-thought-out thought, I am afraid, but I am interested in questions of regulation in this new world we live in and I wonder if regulation behind closed doors always works and whether there are not things we should learn from the American system about structures which allow more frequent open hearings. We have a case this morning, do we not, of Richard Branson and the regulator for the Lottery, where what did or did not happen happened behind closed doors and who will ever know? So the regulatory mechanisms might perhaps be more open themselves.

879. LORD THOMSON: Yes. You speak from your wide experience not only as an educational journalist but also as a television presenter.

AURIOL STEVENS: I am afraid I speak from absolutely zero experience over regulation.

880. LORD THOMSON: I was very grateful to you for drawing my attention at least to the definition of academic freedom in the 1988 Act, which seems an admirable definition. I did not realise Acts of Parliament were as wise in their definitions as that. Would you like to comment on getting the balance right between academic freedom and managerial efficiency in universities?

AURIOL STEVENS: What a nasty question. First, let me say that I think academic freedom is one of the most precious things that the universities exist to protect—the universities particularly, but education in general. It applies also to schoolteachers discussing with classes: people must be free to discuss. But I think that it is much more easily defensible if it is somewhat narrowly drawn. There has been a tendency among threatened groups to cry academic freedom in cases which were not cases of academic freedom but cases of academic sloth or misbehaviour or whatever, what my newspaper would refer to as the Dr Piercemuller phenomenon, when much time is spent in Tuscany and little time with the students. I think that the concept has been abused. So I would look for standing absolutely solid for a narrow definition of academic freedom and then being quite tough on abuses which purported to be academic freedom but were not. President Mary Robinson gave a very interesting lecture the other day on the "academic space", and she said that that to her was vital but that it did not include the freedom for academics to write their own cheques.

881. LORD THOMSON: Thank you very much. That is a very interesting, useful comment. Could I follow that immediately on the same subject area? In your submission to us you mention that there have been a number of examples of gagging clauses recently as part of severance packages and that there is a growing use of confidentiality clauses and contracts which have a gagging effect, and you suggest that one of our recommendations might be that we should outlaw gagging clauses in contracts and agreements. I should be interested in your views about whistle-blowing generally, which is obviously a very important part of our inquiry. The education sector in a sense is fortunate, if I may say so without being flattering, in having its own journal, which you edit. Not all aspects of public life have a specialist journal covering their activities and, quite clearly, one of the best methods of dealing with the problem of effective whistle-blowing without destroying somebody's career prospects is to go to a journal like the *Times Higher Education Supplement*,

where you would of course protect to the death your sources. I am not a regular reader of the journal, I confess. I just wondered how often you find instances of this kind. How often do you find yourself in this role?

AURIOL STEVENS: I suppose the mischievous answer would be not as often as we would like. It is not very frequently. It is a very risky thing for people to do. It requires a great deal of courage and, whatever protection may be offered, there is always a risk that people will guess who it was. So I think people are very cautious about doing it. I should add that there are always a number of cases which come to us which never get any further. There will always be discontented, malcontented, slightly nutty people who will come to us hoping that we will make a cause célèbre out of their case. Most of the cases that come to newspapers are not followed up, but some of them, if we reckon that they are well-founded, are, but they are quite few and, by definition, those that we regard as well-founded you would know about, because we publicise them. I suppose that Portsmouth—it did not start with us; it started with the local paper—was a whistle-blowing case. The Swansea case was another. I think that in both those instances gagging clauses were used by the management of the institution to try to prevent things coming to public attention.

If I may add, it was not only in that kind of respect that I was referring to gagging clauses. There is a very difficult area, which I think is under-investigated, of, for example, research contracts which now restrict the right to publish the results—these are often government department contracts—and that has been forced on the academic community against their wishes. They were powerless to do anything very much about it and in the current funding situation, when you need the money and you are in competition with others, it is very difficult to resist.

882. LORD THOMSON: Yes. Just on that point, is there a developing tendency for almost everything that an academic produces to be the subject of a rather restrictive copyright approach by the institution itself?

AURIOL STEVENS: No, not by the institutions, but sometimes by the funders, and the funders are not necessarily the institutions. There is a very strong case, which I would wish to make, and it is part of my evidence in a way, that the institutions need to be strong enough financially to support a number of people who, if they were supported by outside funders, could find that they could not publish their results or that the outside funders would withdraw when the results were something that they did not like. It is very important that their home institution be able to sustain them if that happens.

883. LORD THOMSON: I attended a conference at the weekend, as it happens, on the future of broadcasting, one of these endless conferences, but this one had a difference to it at the end, when it became clear that a number of those taking part might very well want their contribution to be the subject of copyright rights and therefore royalties, and any publication that emerged from the conference. In all my years of attending these kinds of conferences that was the first time I had ever heard this raised. Is that happening more generally?

AURIOL STEVENS: Yes, it is, and I think it is a very important issue, which I am very interested in, because we in the newspapers are now beginning to deliver what we produce electronically, and after the first use of their material in the newspaper the copyright reverts to the writers. The question is arising: what is first use? Is it in the newspaper and its electronic derivatives or should we be paying again for electronic reproduction? You can imagine that, as part of News International, the *Times Higher Education Supplement* might not be a significant player, but News International is, in this market. It is also very important in the United States. The writers are saying, "We should be paid twice". I think this is very important for the academic world too, because what we produce in this country is knowledge and information, not training shoes or widgets, and how are we as a country to be paid for that, if all knowledge is freely usable, repeatable and copyable?

884. LORD THOMSON: So intellectual property is a very interesting, difficult and important area, is it not?

AURIOL STEVENS: Intellectual property is becoming a very important issue in a way that it was not.

885. LORD THOMSON: Could I just go back for one moment to the narrow question of whistle-blowing? You quite rightly draw attention to the limitations even of press security in this matter. I wondered whether, in trying to make the kind of recommendation you are suggesting to us, we would need to draw a balance between proper confidentiality for commercial matters and the fact that, in general, gagging clauses should be wrong. If we make such a recommendation, how is it monitored in the university world? Is the visitor system a good system for dealing with problems like that that might arise? Is there a case for a higher education ombudsman?

AURIOL STEVENS: I am not sure, and I am not sure that I am not back to my question of open hearings of some sort. First, may I say that I think that academic institutions should put up with a higher degree of whistle-blowing than commercial companies. That is partly what academic freedom is like and that is one of the crosses that the management of higher education institutions have to bear: all kinds of things will be said and they must cope with that. The trouble with all these things like a visitor or an ombudsman, where things are heard in private, is that you never really know whether this was not just an establishment stitch-up. That is why I wonder whether there is some open mechanism for hearing things.

886. LORD THOMSON: So you go for openness more than anything else?

AURIOL STEVENS: I go always for openness.

887. LORD THOMSON: What is called the sunshine approach. Is that right?

LORD NOLAN: Government in the sunshine. The Americans, as I am sure you know, have a Government in the Sunshine Act, although it is not directed so much to open hearings as to freedom of information. It is a phrase I have always liked.

AURIOL STEVENS: It is very nice, yes.

888. LORD THOMSON: I just have one final, very general question. Higher education institutions are now in a much more competitive and market-orientated world.

Do you have any fear that this may be putting downward pressure on entrance standards at the one end, when university principals scour the world for students, or on exit qualification standards at the other end?

AURIOL STEVENS: Let me say that I thought the entry standard thing that erupted in the summer was one of the most disgraceful episodes by my professional colleagues in the media that I have ever witnessed. In saying this, please understand that journalists know nothing really, we only suspect, but I understand that it arose from Whitehall briefing that the entry standards were falling, that universities were scouring the bushes for ill-qualified entrants. Our assumption certainly—it may easily be wrong—was that this was in order to justify a continuation of the restriction on numbers in higher education. It was a Whitehall spin-doctor exercise to cut off at the pass pressure for renewed expansion. My personal view would be that the more people who come into higher education, the better. If the entry standards go down in the pursuit of that, so what? As long as the courses provided are appropriate and people come in and learn useful things which will help them and help the society, so much the better. I think that this notion that we have got too many people learning things is bizarre.

As to the output standards, I think the output should be clearly what it purports to be. I think that, increasingly, the classified degree—first, 2.1, 2.2—is absurd, and it would be better to have a degree with a document which said "These are the courses this person has done and these are the grades they scored on them", so that an employer could see what that person knew and could do.

LORD THOMSON: Thank you very much. I am glad I asked you my last question.

889. CLIFFORD BOULTON: Can I follow up that area a little, because one of the things that we are set up to do is to address public concern, so we have to have regard to what people are saying about things and find out for ourselves to what extent they are justified and, even if they are not, set up some reassuring mechanism, if possible, so that people can see what is happening.

It is said that there is a tremendous scramble to offer further degree opportunities in universities and it is said that there are some masters' degrees which perhaps would not bear too much sunlight. It is even said that the external examiners who go around to keep an eye on the standards in universities are not really detached from the subject, because the universities as a whole consider themselves as looking after their own interests and nobody is going to go around seriously criticising standards of further degrees. Are you aware of much anecdotal evidence about all this and of any substantive evidence about strains that commercial pressures have put on the quality of further degrees?

AURIOL STEVENS: I think there are areas in which some, particularly, of the overseas recruiting is difficult and I would worry about that. I think there need to be mechanisms for scrutinising some of the methods—it is almost trade descriptions kind of peddling—of looking desperately for overseas students. This is a function of the under-funding: overseas students pay fees, home students do not. There is not enough money and that, I think, is corrupting the system to some degree, yes. I think the rushing after overseas students is causing an element of

corruption: people will create courses, take in students. I would rather see the effort expended on training up our own people, but there is no money in it and you have to survive. So, yes, I do think that the commercial pressure is producing an element of corruption there.

890. CLIFFORD BOULTON: You talked about the preservation of academic freedom. It is in two sections really, is it not? One is that the institution itself does not bully or pressurise its own members of staff, but also that the funding councils does not pressurise the colleges or universities and reduce their academic freedom in that way. You are saying that both of those areas are matters for concern at the moment, are you, that the funding policy produces strains on standards as well as the possibility of internal bullying, if you like?

AURIOL STEVENS: No, I was not really referring to either of those. I was referring to the desperate need for money, which might be compromising the standards of some of what was offered in the overseas market. The funding mechanism is a way of rationing money. I do not know that that has much to do with standards.

LORD THOMSON: I was just concerned that you might be saying that it was a policy only to fund the economically useful subjects and that economically useless subjects, in which I must declare my own interest, having read one, might be under pressure, which then would cause strains on academic judgment.

AURIOL STEVENS: Yes. There is a great push to vocationalism. I suppose my view would be a slightly robust one, that the Government is entitled to ask for whatever it wants for its money, and people either deliver that or they do not. My worry is that when a government has that particular thrust, as it does, and perhaps rightly so, that should not be the sole source of funding for the activity of higher education, which I think should be broader than that. That is why other sources of money become very important, so that you are not victim to a particular political spin on the funding, which, you are right, I am sure is at the moment very vocationally orientated and likely to remain so.

891. CLIFFORD BOULTON: Just a question about whistle-blowing, because you will agree, will you not, that we can make a distinction between an internal system of the examination of complaints about the working of an institution, which in some way protects the person who feels they have a duty to get some investigation started, and that is really a responsibility of the institution to have in place, and legitimising leakers to the press about matters which they feel they would like to get covered, because so often these are subjective judgments and public interest is confused about what the public would find interesting? We know the Press Council has that problem. So they are two separate matters really, are they not? I just wanted you to accept that there can be areas of legitimate confidentiality within any organisation like this where the institution can be justified in asking for confidentiality.

AURIOL STEVENS: Yes, I think it certainly can. What I am saying with whistle-blowing is that it puts a tremendous load on the conscience of the individual who is going to do that. Some of it is done frivolously, some of it is done maliciously, sometimes the complaints are not taken up, as I said, but sometimes an individual who has gone through the normal procedures of complaint within the institution and still feels there is something wrong may, out of deep, conscientious commitment, go to the press, knowing the likely downside of that, and I think that in the end we are dependent on those people to keep the system good.

CLIFFORD BOULTON: Thank you.

892. LORD NOLAN: I wonder if I could ask just one question. You spoke about the desperate need for money, and of course no one is more conscious of that than the less well-to-do students, which we have all been in our time. We have heard from more than one source that a substantial number of students would qualify for university places but are not taking them up because they are not prepared to saddle themselves with borrowings at that stage of their lives, and they are therefore going straight to the jobs market if they can find a job. Have you had much evidence of that?

AURIOL STEVENS: No. I notice that the participation rates continue upwards, that the social class participation continues to broaden. I know people do not like to be in debt. I think that the debt arrangements currently are very unhelpful and that a proper loan system with a proper repayment mechanism would greatly help, but I think that there is a lot of equating of hardship with debt, and they are not quite the same thing. People do not want to take out loans, but they are going to earn a lot more later, and I am not sure that I am totally sympathetic to people who are in hardship because they will not incur a debt, provided that debt is properly handled and the repayment mechanism is equitable and spread over a long time, and unlike the present arrangement.

LORD NOLAN: That is interesting and, if time permitted, I would like to hear you more on that. You do not think the present arrangements are entirely satisfactory.

AURIOL STEVENS: I think they are ridiculous. There is a very rapid mortgage cliff over which you go for repayment. I am unable to understand why it was done so badly and why it continues to be proposed to go on doing it so badly. The mechanisms for doing it better seem to have been proposed, and I am not sure I understand why they are not being implemented—which is to collect the debt through national insurance or the tax system.

LORD NOLAN: Yes, fine. We have really overrun time, but was there anything that anyone particularly wanted to ask?

893. ANNE WARBURTON: I would like to follow up an earlier question if I might. I think it is very difficult to find the exact line between the sort of audit which we are mostly interested in and quality audit. I happened this morning, on the train coming down, to have been reading the passage in the CUC guide about the auditing of teaching quality by the funding organisations. I hoped to hear you reassure me that we can assume, whatever the niceties and whatever the detail, and the details might be improved, that the quality audit and the quality assessment deal with the quality of education in higher education.

AURIOL STEVENS: I think the quality assessment has been a useful exercise in a sense, in that it has, rather

like your own Committee, forced the institutions into doing things better, but as a mechanism I think it is not good and should not continue, because it produces a compliance culture. We have a lot of evidence coming into the paper about how academics cheat; they are very clever at it. The right lecturer is put on to lecture when the assessors are there, the students are coached in what to say. There are all kinds of carry-on in order to pull the wool over the assessors' eyes and to get an excellent rating, because an excellent rating is good for marketing. I do not think that is helpful for the genuine assessment of teaching quality. The mechanism which I have been persuaded, from looking at this, works best is departmental review with outside people. That is an internal mechanism in which the academics are free to shred each other, as they are perfectly capable of doing, within that group and to produce working reports for improvement within the institution. If the result of all of this going on is that the auditing arrangements require that there shall be departmental reviews in every institution, then in the end it could all come out right, but to have government inspectors going into higher education I frankly think is absurd—and damaging.

894. ANNE WARBURTON: Do you feel that about the quality audit as well as the quality assessment?

AURIOL STEVENS: No, I think the audit is much better, because that is an arrangement to see that the mechanisms are there, but not to purport to be inspecting the quality of teaching in the classroom. In higher education the quality of teaching is not the important thing; the important thing is what goes on inside the student's head, and one teacher is good for one student and another for another. Even the most incompetent lecturer may be brilliant with certain groups of students.

LORD NOLAN: Diana, do you have a question?

895. DIANA WARWICK: I just have one, if I may, very briefly. To come back to the gagging clauses issue, you say that there have been a number of examples of gagging clauses, usually as part of the severance package. The first part of my question is: if there are examples that you could let us have, could we have them? The second part is that another witness suggested that it was often a useful ploy in negotiations for severance to be able to comply with this clause because there was a quid pro quo in financial terms, and we were urged not to legislate in a way that you are suggesting we should. Can you comment on that?

AURIOL STEVENS: I think the cases are well known. Professor Pickering in Portsmouth was subject to a gagging clause, and so were the people in Swansea, which I think they broke in the end, but they were. We have another case of a gagging clause which we shall be reporting on Friday, I hope, which we are currently investigating, which is a government agency gagging people. Should you legislate? I have referred to a climate of corruption. If the sort of deals that are being done mean "You can have even tens of thousands of pounds more, if you do not reveal the disgraceful things we have been up to", they should not be given house-room. It is not a good way to carry on—is it? Even if what were once your members benefit individually from that, it makes poor law.

896. LORD NOLAN: Thank you so much. You have packed an enormous number of very useful and

interesting answers into your half an hour. You have made quite sure also that we shall all be studying Friday's edition of the *Times Higher Education Supplement.*

Now we greet Mr Roger Brook and Mr Andrew Foster. Good morning, gentlemen. It is nice to have you here. Did you wish to make anything by way of brief opening statement before we get into the questions or would you be happy to go straight into them? We have of course read your very helpful written evidence.

ROGER BROOK, AND ANDREW FOSTER

ROGER BROOK (Chairman, Audit Comm-ission): Maybe I will just say one or two brief things, Chairman. As you know, I am a very recently appointed chairman. I have been conducting a very intensive learn-in over the last few weeks, but I just thought I would pass on one or two impressions to you from somebody coming principally from the private sector, although I used to work in the public sector. In fact I was a councillor when Sir William was a very distinguished director of social services at Kensington and Chelsea.

The Audit Commission, as you know, works primarily in local government, in appointing auditors and doing studies of value for money, local government and the health service, and also covers the police and fire services. It therefore does not strictly work in the areas which you are studying at the moment, but it does have a lot of knowledge of those, because, by definition, its work is in the local communities all over the country: it has its regional offices and people, district auditors, and the auditors work all over the country, so there is a good deal of understanding and knowledge about these bodies that you are currently reviewing.

Coming from the private sector, what has impressed and interested me most is the ability of the Audit Commission to do what they call value-for-money work. They do not just appoint auditors, which is a crucial part of their job, ensuring that they are independent and accountable and that public bodies are accountable, and they do all sorts of things to try and prevent bad practice in local government, but they have this policy, which they have built up since they were founded in 1982—13 years ago—of taking particular aspects of local government and the health service and studying them. They have a staff in London, helped by staffs around the country, they bring in experts from the bodies they are studying and they go into a particular aspect of the work of local government or the health service to try and highlight two things. Two things always come out of it.

First of all, you find that one local authority does things quite differently from another local authority, similarly with health service bodies, and also that certain practices are much more effective in one authority than in other health authorities or local authorities. The effect of this is to produce a document which is the result of this work, which if I had had anything like that in the private sector I know would have been enormously useful to me, because it shows how to do it right, basically. In any regime which you decide to recommend or the Government decides to implement for these other bodies a similar kind of opportunity exists to do this kind of work. After all they are, in their different categories, groups of bodies which have similarities. You cannot do it in the private sector, because no company is like another and anyway you come into hopeless areas of confidentiality. But in these other bodies there are similarities between further education

bodies, grant-maintained schools, housing associations, and I would certainly urge you to consider very carefully whether in any recommendations you make you want to suggest this kind of aspect. It is not just auditing; it is looking ahead and trying to improve the effectiveness of these bodies. But, as I say, coming new to it, this is what has impressed me most about the Audit Commission.

Just as interest, I asked for this. This is a list of all the studies the Audit Commission has done since it was set up. You will see that it is like the Forth Bridge. They gradually cover all aspects of local government and the health service. They have not completed it yet, there is still a long way to go, particularly in the health service, because they have only been doing that quite recently. But I think it is quite impressive and it shows how a corpus of knowledge can then be used by the auditors in all these bodies to try and help the bodies that they are auditing to improve their practice.

I am going to ask Andrew Foster to deal with most of your questions. He is very much more deeply involved in and knowledgeable about this than I am, but I thought it was worth making that point, coming to it new.

LORD NOLAN: And I am going to ask Sir William Utting to ask the questions.

897. WILLIAM UTTING: I did not think, Chairman, that I was going to have to declare as an interest that I had been the director of social services for the Royal Borough of Kensington and Chelsea, but I am afraid I now have to do that in view of what Mr Brook said. But it is good to see him again and also to see Andrew Foster here again giving evidence to us.

You set out in the first four sections of your evidence a number of extremely important principles, with most of which, if not all, I am sure this Committee would agree. I wanted to ask you if you regarded these as being of equal weight or whether there were some principles there that you considered to be outstanding and of particular import.

ANDREW FOSTER (Controller, Audit Comm-ission): The general approach that the commission has taken to producing this is wanting to elucidate principles and a framework and, as such, I think that all the principles are part of that framework, against which we try and work and we think are relevant for public sector audit. But to answer your question and say which is the most important I would probably choose three, and this is in fact in our evidence on page 5. Perhaps I could briefly speak to the three I think are most important.

Frankly, point 1 there about "principled leadership of able people" is absolutely at the heartland of this: so much else would follow and flow from that. The second that I choose is in fact the second there—2—to make sure that there are some good checks and balances. I think that, frankly, good people very often want to see that that happens, but that would again seem to me to be important, as we spell out there. Some of the things that go wrong are sometimes when people somehow, be they a chairman or a leading official, get in an unduly dominant position. So that would be a second point of importance to me. For my third I would go to the last point in our evidence, which goes to an environment of culture which creates openness and trust. It is about having systems in place that promote good practice, but would also mean that there is some deterrent around if bad practice were in place. Frankly, I think that some of the other things we spell out there would follow and flow from those three. In putting this together, I think the commission also finally thought we were very much against some response to any public concern that was unduly bureaucratic or stifling, and I hope that the ones I have chosen are ones that emphasise principled leadership by good people, well chosen, in a system that has sensible, solid checks and balances and an open culture.

898. WILLIAM UTTING: It is particularly interesting that you select those three items as being of particular importance. You also say in the paper that there is a need to understand that public money is special and that there is a distinctive legal framework which governs its use and that it imposes unique duties and responsibilities, and yet you are able to say that and yet to put that in the context of these other values.

ANDREW FOSTER: That is absolutely how we choose to do it.

899. WILLIAM UTTING: One of the criticisms that has been made to us by some of the bodies we have examined is that they are, in fact, over-audited on the financial side and yet, at the same time, appearing to lack the kind of evaluation of quality that you are joining with the financial audit. Do you have any observations about how this balance is best achieved and what kind of intermediary body is, perhaps, best equipped to undertake those combined operations?

ANDREW FOSTER: Can I just start with a statement of principle about management and audit. I am a public service manager by background rather than an auditor so I, perhaps, would start there but, for me, responsibility actually rests in managing public bodies with management itself, be it the board of governance and the top managers, that is where prime responsibility rests for me.

Second responsibility might rest on an internal auditing regime which would be set up by the management itself and a third level of responsibility is external audit and, for me, external audit is principally about financial probity but certainly in the way that we approach things we have a substantial chunk that is about effectiveness in comparative information. I think it is important to spell out those levels of responsibility.

I am absolutely opposed to too much auditing or confusion about it, which is why in our evidence we seek to start from a statement of principles and of main approaches. In terms of the nature of intermediary bodies the Commission feels, I suppose not surprisingly, that there are elements of our own regime which work well and just to remind members of the Committee, the national role of the Audit Commission is to have a code of practice, a best practice for auditors, against which they then carry out their job. It is not to do detailed auditing at all, that is done at a local level.

The role of the Audit Commission is to push on quality and make sure that the quality of local auditing is being done well. In our case, it is about some value for money work too and, if you look in the Commission's case when we took responsibility for the Health Service at the time of those reforms some five years ago, we actually left in place existing auditors and then expected them to work to the regime we had.

In answer to your question, I think I am saying two things. One is that you need to be clear of what the responsibility is between different auditors, internal and external, and management and then, frankly, I think you should have the simplest regime you possibly can which demands and requires auditors, if they are in interface positions, to collaborate and co-operate together Certainly, that is a requirement we make of auditors who work within our framework.

ROGER BROOK: In the Butler Report which the Commission organised last year, which was a report on its own operations, one of the criticisms made was that the Commission had not yet got it right—the method by which the auditors get the value for money work done at the local level; in other words, the transfer of the information from the studies down to the local level. Of course, all the auditors have to do is to try and persuade the local body itself to make changes to reflect these studies and a lot of work is now being done by the Commission to help auditors do that better. It is interesting that this is something that the local government associations are very keen on.

900. WILLIAM UTTING: In the area that we are currently studying it actually seems quite difficult in certain parts of this area to bring these different matters together into one place or one agency. I notice that the Further Education Funding Council does combine financial support and scrutiny with resources for evaluating the quality of the product—it has its own inspectorate—yet, if one looks at grant- maintained schools there is the Funding Agency and then a variety of external bodies which may provide advice or, in the case of Ofsted, turn up every four years or so to carry out a quality examination.

What is your view of the kind of body that one would actually look for to combine these activities?

ANDREW FOSTER: Can I just make an answer of principle before giving a little bit of detail. The Commission's own approach both to the Treasury Review of audit and to submitting evidence to you is not actually necessarily saying that we are an appropriate body to do this work but to try and do an analysis of what does require to be put in place to do things well. Seventy per cent of our work is about the probity of the expenditure of public funds. We find it is tremendously valuable to have a cross-fertilisation from that into value for money work and back the other way. That argues to me possibly for the same organisation doing it or very close collaboration between. I make the point there about we are not particularly propagating ourselves but we are propagating the notion of integration of the work because they genuinely feed each other and, frankly, serve the principles which we think are important.

ROGER BROOK: I mean, an auditor who understands intimately the operations of a school or a TEC is well placed to work with the management of that organisation in improving its value for money. That is the point, I think, we are making. You can help the auditors, reinforce them, but it is the process of audit that fits in naturally with changes to improve effectiveness and efficiency of the organisation. The Audit Commission does it through your body of auditors principally reinforced by Commission staff.

ANDREW FOSTER: If I were just to give you an example. Later on this week we are going to publish something on the level of fraud and corruption in local government over the past 12 months. What we have done there is to bring together evidence and information from our auditors across the country. We give some examples of bad things that have happened that others could learn from. We give some examples of good practices that others have put in place and we are only able to do that because we have (a) set a frame for it nationally and (b) then required our auditors to do it. So, we take a backwards look but very much try and say, "So, what are the lessons for the future?" and you get that by bringing together an approach to value for money along with an approach to probity and regularity.

901. WILLIAM UTTING: The Audit Commission, of course, is not a funding body. Do you think that it is reasonable and proper to combine regulatory with funding responsibilities or is there an issue of principle here that says they ought to be separated?

ANDREW FOSTER: I am not sure that the Commission itself has spent a lot of time debating that particular issue. My own view is that it may well be easier and clearer if those functions are separated but I would believe that if you were clear about the principles it could be made to work within the same body, but I give a personal view there rather than one that the Commission has debated extensively.

902. WILLIAM UTTING: There was an interesting comment in your evidence raising a point about whether the regulators should audit their own work. I wondered what suggestions you might have for auditing the work of regulators.

ANDREW FOSTER: The Commission has always been in favour of independent external scrutiny by bodies that have good knowledge about the work in hand. Roger Brook has already mentioned it in our own case. It depends on what sort of auditing you are meaning—whether you are meaning the financial audit or an effectiveness audit.

Frankly, because in our own case our role varies between some regulation and some purchasing of auditing services, the Commission was always being asked the question, "Who audits ourselves?" that the Commission agreed—as we are a quango ourselves—to set up an external scrutiny of ourselves which, as Roger Brook has said, was published last summer.

I think my principal answer would be an independent body that puts the information into the public domain with people working for it who have good working knowledge of the matters in hand.

903. WILLIAM UTTING: Could I ask you one question of detail? You say in your reports when you speak about schools that there ought to be written agreement between heads and boards of governors. It has been put to us that, in fact, there ought to be a statutory framework governing this relationship. I wondered if you thought it necessary to go quite that far?

ANDREW FOSTER: I expect members of the Committee have had the chance of looking at the joint work that we did with Ofsted recently on the roles of governors. We visited 50-odd schools, people from Ofsted and ourselves, and I think the general view of the Commission when we discussed it was to have clarity of role well discussed between governors and head teachers and other support staff. I do not think that we felt there was a need for statutory framework. In fact, I do not think we discussed it very much. We felt, however, that the issue of clarity of role was absolutely critical and that that could come about from sensible and proper discussion at the senior level in the institution.

ROGER BROOK: It is interesting that, as Mr Foster told you, that publication has been selling like hot cakes. If you read that, if you are a member of a school board and you read that, I would have thought that it is so obviously sensible, blindingly clear, that if somebody then tried to ride roughshod over you alarm bells would start ringing immediately. I would have thought that was better than legislation.

WILLIAM UTTING: Good. Thank you. Thank you, chairman.

LORD NOLAN: Dame Anne.

904. ANNE WARBURTON: I wonder if I might start with one or two questions about over-auditing and various aspects of it. One of them is the one about how many audits are appropriate. I think the CVCP have added up that their clients can be exposed to four different levels of auditing. Does that sound excessive to you or does that sound reasonable?

ANDREW FOSTER: No, it sounds excessive to me. As I have said, I very much favour the idea of an integrated audit, of bringing your probity audit and your effectiveness audit together. I would have thought that fours sets of auditing is clearly far too much and it has the potential of being wasteful. It may be that there is a lot to be looked at but the more it can be managed and targeted in a sensible way and reported in an integrated way it seems to me that the board of governance is going to get a much better view of what is going on.

905. ANNE WARBURTON: Then I look for what can be taken out, squeezed out. Are you familiar with HEFCE and its arrangements?

ANDREW FOSTER: I know about it in passing but in truth this is not the Commission's central area of work. I know about it as an informed lay person rather than somebody who works with it.

906. ANNE WARBURTON: I ask that really because just looking at it it looked to me as though perhaps what is needed is the particular, the institutional level and then the top level and there must be something in the middle that has to go not out of the top or the bottom. Does that sound sensible?

ANDREW FOSTER: There is certainly a need to look at auditing of what happens at an operational level. That is where financial regularity is important. It seems to me it is quite important as well that you look at a strategic level in the institution, both in terms of its management of its financial affairs and the sense of its longer term direction. At an institutional level I see two levels that need looking at.

907. ANNE WARBURTON: Thank you. Then there is also the complaint about being over bureaucratised, too

much unnecessary detail. As you have done a rather useful comparative look at these things, have you a view on that, if that is a valid complaint and, if so, what should be done about it?

ANDREW FOSTER: To make a broad comment, a number of these concerns seem to have developed since we have had a market place or a purchaser-provider arrangement put into the public service, which has clearly had some major benefits and some difficulties by way of the fragmentation of services. You then have had public concern and many peoples' response to public concern has been to put masses of new processes in and, frankly, as a Commission we are fundamentally opposed to that. I mean, that would be to take the system back 30 years where you had the public pound being very important but so much so that people were frightened to do very much with it and it was stifled and bureaucratic.

Some of my first answers to Sir William were the important things about clarity of principle, good leadership but then being prepared to give freedom to those boards at a local level to make sensible delegated decisions as long as they could justify them by reasonable sets of reasonableness. Such things do exist and you should be able to explain to people but some people's response has become very pedantic and nit-picking and that is not at all the answer.

908. ANNE WARBURTON: I find it a little hard to know how one can impose or bring about the streamlining—organisation by organisation, I take it from what you say?

ANDREW FOSTER: The Commission has taken the stance that you do it from some principles, in a sense not dissimilar to the principles you yourselves, as a Committee, have spelled out, that you should have those for auditing and then have an over-arching approach to audit in the public sector, which does not mean to say you have to then have a uniform organisation that does it, but you require them to behave against it in a sensible way.

Frankly, it does feel very fragmented and different at the moment. If you look at how central government carries out its affairs, how local government carries out its affairs and how the bodies you are currently looking at have been allowed to behave since they were taken in the main away from local government control. You actually have a very piecemeal and ad hoc situation.

909. ANNE WARBURTON: "To which in part a common code of conduct and common principles for dealing with conflicts of interest"—I quote from your paper—may be the answer.

Can I ask what ideas you have about how this common code of conduct might actually be arrived at? How do the principles—your principles and others—become properly disseminated and at what level? Are we talking about some institution which could do this or are we talking about a kind of gathering of representatives of all sorts of institutions? How can dissemination best take place?

ROGER BROOK: I suspect that if the Audit Commission was asked to do it what would happen is that they would consult widely with people in these bodies first in drawing up a code of practice so that the code was relevant to the particular nature of the bodies that they

were looking at. You would not necessarily have exactly the same code of practice for TECs as you would for further education establishments, for example.

Once one had done that one would set up the code of practice and then the auditors would be briefed on it and would become steeped in it and in dealing on a regular basis with those bodies they would be able to deploy it, so to speak. That is how it would work.

ANDREW FOSTER: I can give an exact example from one of the sectors we are involved in and that is in local government. In the document I will leave behind for you the Local Government Management Board has developed a code of conduct in just the way that Roger Brook has said. That has been promulgated widely and in our audit of last year we are now showing that 72 per cent of local authorities are using their own interpretation of it. What actually happens it that our auditors then comment back to the body on how they are doing against it.

Just to bring that forcefully home, that covers things like hospitality, it covers things like gifts, it covers things like members and the definition of their own pecuniary interests and so it is codified and the majority of authorities are on their way to using it. I do not see any reason at all why similar, sensible, voluntary, professional codes could not be developed and then policed by the appropriate auditors.

910. ANNE WARBURTON: You speak of policing and you see that as being better than setting up best practice and leaving it to people to choose?

ANDREW FOSTER: No, I would definitely come at it from the profession developing it themselves and best practice. I probably use the word "police" inappropriately there but I think that for the auditor to be commenting back about how they had done against their own code is not far from policing actually.

ANNE WARBURTON: Thank you very much.

911. DIANA WARWICK: Could I just ask you one question and it is a rather general one. It applies to all the bodies that we are looking at. Under accountability you place enormous emphasis on local bodies being truly accountable and responsive to their communities. One of the things that we have been concerned about is this problem of self-perpetuating oligarchies, effectively, people choosing themselves and their successors.

Have you, in the work that you have done, developed any view about just how representative the various governing bodies are? Do you have any views about how to make them more representative and do you have any views about whether or not local governors should be paid?

ANDREW FOSTER: If I could just say, in terms of the effectiveness of local boards, the example I know best is the Health Service which, I know, you looked at last time. Some of the issues are the same. Frankly, NHS boards were introduced amongst a lot of political contention with the different parties all saying different things, which was not helpful to their operation, but I do not think in the beginning it was very clear what their role was.

If you just take an example of the health authorities. They are meant to be looking at the health needs of their community and the trusts are meant to be running the hospital business. I do not think, for instance, enough was done in their case to look at having people who genuinely represented the community. Similar sorts of people were selected on both sides and, clearly, the charge was made that they were unduly politically biased and I think a lot of people believed that that was the case.

If you look at the paper we have done on the role of non-executive directors, the issue of community responsiveness, it seems to us, is a very important one and if you are going to have people on your boards who are genuinely responsive it starts to tell you something about the personnel specification of that sort of person. Frankly, in the earliest years of the Health Service reforms the charge definitely was laid that it was self-perpetuating and, frankly, you need to have people who have sets of experience which reflect what is happening in the community.

I would come at it from some of the principles that we have spelled out about what you need to be on a board of governance and some of the other things that we said to you last time and which I understand from all that, as a Committee, you have said—the issues of openness and it being clear that the person fulfils the job specification. On the issue of whether school governors should be paid, the Commission has not taken a stance on that at all.

DIANA WARWICK: I was thinking in terms of the ability of people to serve, the physical ability of people to serve, if they were not, for example, given paid time off.

ROGER BROOK: There is an argument. If people are making big sacrifices and are not well off I think there is an argument for some pay. There are arguments on either side, are there not—they should be doing in the interests of the public good—but I think it slightly depends on the degree of sacrifice the person incurs. As long as the payments are not excessive I would have thought they might be justified but I have not given enough thought to this to give you a serious answer.

DIANA WARWICK: Probably a bit unfair.

912. CLIFFORD BOULTON: We have had some examples where internal audit is carried out by the same commercial auditors that perform the external audit. Is that something you have a general view about, that it should be avoided, or can it be justified?

ANDREW FOSTER: In the Commission's code we run a very rigorous quality control which I will happily explain to you but, we generally would not favour that as an approach. External audit is about bringing a separate level of scrutiny to affairs and the notion of conflict of interests between any of the contractors—we use eight of the big firms, we use our own agency and others and unless a compelling argument could be taken we seek to avoid conflict of interest in external scrutiny.

CLIFFORD BOULTON: Thank you.

913. LORD NOLAN: You mentioned in one part of your evidence that you produce an annual report on local government audits which shows how the results of individual audits are brought together to produce a national picture of the total probity, regulatory and VFM audit work. You say you also produce such a report for the

National Health Service as well as for local government bodies. You suggest that it would be helpful if a similar exercise could be carried out for local public spending bodies. I thought that was a very interesting idea. Have you given any thought to who would do it?

ANDREW FOSTER: I think the Commission's general stance would be that that would be a matter for the Treasury review and for the government. Clearly, a variety of bodies could do it but the Commission has not taken a stance on that other than to say that it would be valuable.

If I could just give you a couple of examples to bring it to life. In the past month we published something on hip fracture in the Health Service, a tremendously growing issue. If you talk to any group almost everybody has a granny or an aunt or an uncle who this has happened to. We looked at 10 hospitals and we took all the Royal College's different standards. For instance, one of them—and I will only tell you one—is that a senior doctor should carry out this particular procedure. In the 10 hospitals we looked at, in 10 per cent of them not only was the operation being done by a junior doctor but it was being overseen by a junior anaesthetist as well. Frankly, that is not something I would wish on my granny, my uncle, my aunt or any other citizen. In the ten there were two or three where that was happening and there were others where it was always being done by an experienced doctor. I could give you that story again and again.

Why I make the point of saying it is that responsible boards of governance, when they have that sort of information fed back to them, do not like it at all and it is a tremendous spur for change. We have done exactly the same in the police service. If you look at work we did with the CID in terms of how effective they are around burglary. We have done exactly the same in relationship to how many policemen are actually on the beat at any one time.

I labour the point because actually good professionals do not like that to be said against them and informed boards of management say, "Gosh, why is this happening to us?". We do that at a local level and a national report would draw out those examples and that then is very valuable for the government departments concerned. I strongly believe that there would be very great power and influence to be had by doing the same for local spending bodies but, as we have a vested interest in this matter, we do not seek to make a case for ourselves.

913. LORD NOLAN: Well, you have declared it. One final question. The second appendix to the evidence you have sent us contains a checklist for action, questions for board members in the NHS to ask themselves. That was entirely your own compilation, was it?

ANDREW FOSTER: Yes. We visited a massive number of hospitals. We consulted with the National Association of Health Authorities and Trusts. We consulted with the Trust Federation. Frankly, we are arch-plagiarists. If there is a good idea to be had we will steal it but we will also happily give credit for it. The thing that matters is does it make any different at a local level. We put it together but from discussions with hospitals and other bodies.

914. LORD NOLAN: Is this in regular use as far as you are aware?

ANDREW FOSTER: Yes, it is. We have recently run six or eight road shows around the country based on that particular document and it was very interesting to us. Lots and lots of non-executive directors came—we did them through a lunchtime—and chairmen and chief executives and directors of finance. So, clearly, there was a perceived feeling out there that people should be discussing this more. We were actually inundated. We did them all round the country. It was meant to be a 15 or 20-minute read for a non-exec. Then we encouraged people to discuss it at their board meetings as well.

LORD NOLAN: Mr Brook will have noticed, as I have, that it includes a question about the behaviour of the chairman. I think Sir William Utting wanted to ask you a final question.

915. WILLIAM UTTING: It really follows from that. I take it from what you say that you believe that people's performance should be appraised or assessed against codes of conduct so that assessing performance against a code of conduct is as central to performance in other ways of achieving targeted objectives and so on so that competence includes really this idea of conforming to a code of conduct.

ANDREW FOSTER: That is absolutely what we say and no more so than for non-executive directors or people on boards. Some of the worst performing boards that our places visited, what was happening was that there was a cabal or there was a chairman and chief executive who were running things by themselves. The more there can be open discussion about what the expectation is and what is actually happening in this board and some proper discussion we felt there was some chance that might diffuse.

WILLIAM UTTING: Good, thank you. Thank you, chairman.

916. LORD NOLAN: Thank you both very much indeed. That has been an extremely valuable and helpful three-quarters of an hour. We are most grateful to you for coming.

Now we welcome Margaret Hodge, Member of Parliament, the Chair of Circle 33 Housing Association, and Mr Donald Hoodless, the Chief Executive. Good morning and thank you very much for coming. Thank you also for the evidence you have sent us and for the opening statement which we have all read.

917. LORD NOLAN: I wonder if I could begin by picking up something you say in paragraph 6 of the opening statement about the Housing Corporation. You say that it:

"needs to be very clear in whose interests it acts as regulator, and tailor its regulatory activity accordingly. Regulation is not the same as accountability. It has limited goals, namely the safeguarding of public money, in relation to those goals, and considering the complex nature and scale of some housing associations who receive most of the public money, a reliance on a bureaucratic form filling process is unlikely to be successful in the longer term."

Would you accept that regulation should go further than just seeing that the money is honestly handled but

also see that it is effectively used because I think you are in favour, are you not, of the housing executive taking an interest in performance indicators and in the quality of the houses?

DONALD HOODLESS, AND MARGARET HODGE MP

MARGARET HODGE MP (Chair, Circle 33 Housing Association): Yes. It is a difficult area. Of course, we want to see value for money and them looking at the effectiveness of public expenditure as well as the probity issues. That is fair enough. There are a number of issues that we think need to be examined in relation to how they currently operate. We would say that, firstly, a lot of their regulation is process driven and not outcome driven and I have pulled out some examples because I thought you might deal with this.

When they did the special performance audit report on the fraud that we had in Circle in 1994, among the recommendations——

DOUGLAS HOODLESS (Chief Executive, Circle 33 Housing Association): That was the follow-up report.

MARGARET HODGE: Yes—among the recommendations were things like numbered shared certificates should be issued to trust members or the trust should reconstitute the finance subcommittee pending the outcome of the review of committee structure. These are all slightly process-driven recommendations which we felt did not really get to the point of the matter, which was to ensure the probity and then moving on to effectiveness.

There is another problem, we would say, with the Housing Corporation and I do not know the answer to it—all these things are quite difficult—but as they are both the funder and the regulator they have a dual purpose interest. In one sense they see us as their agent delivering a certain number of units of housing to meet government policy and sometimes that role interferes—I do not know if "interferes" is the right word—but sometimes that role does not fit properly with the role of being the regulator. I think there is a muddle in intent and whether those two should be separated is an issue which perhaps you should address.

918. LORD NOLAN: It is a basic central issue. The present position is that they pay the piper and they call the tune which is a principle which has been quite widely applied in life in the past. Do you think they should be separated, those two functions?

MARGARET HODGE: My own personal view is I think that would be better, yes, and there are various models that could emerge. You could do the funding via the Department of the Environment regional offices and that way work in with local authorities. The structures are partly there anyway because local authorities have to be consulted on what happens and that might make a more logical division of responsibility.

The other way of looking at it—you have just had the Audit Commission—is whether you take that bit of it out to the Audit Commission. The difficulty with doing that is that the Audit Commission could become over-burdened with the number of bodies that it is overseeing.

DONALD HOODLESS: If I could add that I think it is important to remember that the word "regulation" to the

Housing Corporation is a relatively new one. It came in about a year ago. Up till then they saw their role as one of supervising and the supervision was really in a sense to order and protect the investment in housing associations through Housing Association Grant. They have used the term "regulation" but I do not think they have sorted out how regulation is different from supervision.

There is a clear difference in the way regulation—OF-this and OF-that—has developed in this country if you use that as a framework. I do not think the Corporation has reached that stage yet although perhaps that is what it is driving towards. Currently, and certainly our experience back in January 1994, it was much more of supervisory process-driven rather than setting a framework in which housing associations should operated and be accountable to them for performance in general.

919. LORD NOLAN: It is absolutely essential since they are one of the main bodies to whom you are accountable that there should be clear understanding on both sides of what your respective roles are. Do you think there is more work to be done on that?

DONALD HOODLESS: I do. I think they have talked about regulation but I do not think they have set out sufficiently clearly how that varies from what they were talking about a year ago, which was the supervision of associations. My experience is that the supervision is much more driven towards the investment decision about which housing associations get what money to provide new housing and an order to inform that decision than it is to look at overall performance of housing associations in terms, for example, of the quality of their housing management or what value for money they are offering in terms of rent levels or standards for that housing.

MARGARET HODGE: Can I also say that one of the problems, because they are both the funder and the regulator—and, clearly, you are anxious to keep the momentum of providing more homes so you are anxious to please—I think that is the wrong approach for a relationship between us as housing associations and the Corporation. You will tend to always want to please the Corporation because you want the money, which is a different relationship from wanting to meet objective criteria of regulation or even having an argument about what is appropriate in terms of structure or ways in which you work. It is a muddled relationship.

920. LORD NOLAN: I am not sure that I really followed that. What would please the Housing Corporation?

MARGARET HODGE: Let me go back to our examples in the post-fraud era when we both came in. We were new after the fraud and we had to pick up and sort out an enormous range of problems and some of the obsession with process that was coming to us after the fraud from the Housing Corporation really was irrelevant almost to what we saw as the immediate problems that confronted us in the situation of the association as we entered into the arena. We were there trying to sort out our systems to make sure that no such fraud would recur. They were pushing us to simply set up a finance committee without us having thought through how we could best control all the expenditure and business of the association, whether that was appropriate, so we thought we might as well set up a finance committee, that will get them off our backs on that.

921. LORD NOLAN: I would like to come back in a moment to the precise faults which you identified in the failure of your predecessors in this matter and the most important steps you have taken to remedy them. May I just pick up one reference you made and that is to the Building Societies Commission. You applauded the principle adopted by the Building Societies Commission in its activities. What particularly had you in mind?

DONALD HOODLESS: I think that one of the issues about the Corporation becoming a regulator is understanding the business which housing associations are in and what they are doing and what their plans are and having a greater understanding of how they are setting their decisions on rents and why they are developing. I think the building societies are not necessarily a perfect model of regulation but it points to more senior people talking to more senior people about plans and the future and understanding the business better and I suspect that the Corporation do not always quite understand exactly the direction some associations are going in and what their plans are, many of which can, of course, fall outside simply developing with Housing Association Grant.

They can be involved in CCT with local authorities; they can be involved in developing community care projects with health authorities; so they can be in a range of business which is relevant to their objectives but which does not directly impact on the funding through housing association grant which is administered by the Corporation.

922. LORD NOLAN: Can you tell us what you regarded as the most important steps needed to avoid a repetition of what happened before 1993?

MARGARET HODGE: I think quite simply setting up systems and reporting mechanisms so that we were aware. It is always easy to be wise after the event but I was pretty astounded that nobody uncovered it sooner and I think the systems for monitoring were simply not in place. You will never be able to ensure that somebody who wants to steal money does not do so but I hope we get sufficient monitoring data to enable us to spot any fraud that is taking place and I think we have to set those systems up now.

923. LORD NOLAN: You think you have got it now?

MARGARET HODGE: Yes, systems and they are open. I mean, they are now reported to the full committee and we have taken ownership of that very clearly.

DONALD HOODLESS: Could I add that that is absolutely right but there are other factors. I am aware, as a Chief Executive, that Circle 33 grew very rapidly and as it grew it ignored its core business of managing its stock. That neglect led many of the staff to be—how can I put it—they were quite defensive, they were task-orientated, they would follow procedures but would not accept responsibility for the whole task. In some senses, that culture where there was not an acceptance of responsibility, there was not a willingness to develop an outward-looking service to tenants did, in fact, enable the fraud and those issues to fester in a way that, hopefully, we have overcome because now we are much more directed towards providing a service to tenants; that people accept responsibility; that we are seeing tenants as customers in the sense not that they have choice but we have to see the service we give from the perception they have of what we are doing.

That cultural change is also important to ensuring that the service is delivered and that it goes alongside the reporting and systems and procedures that support good service delivery.

MARGARET HODGE: And, going back, if the Housing Corporation is to regulate us, I think they have improved their system since the fraud, but it was interesting that they had been in and done a detailed review of Circle 33 a few months prior to the fraud being uncovered. So, if we go back, if they are too process driven and do not monitor the outcomes properly they could miss it.

924. LORD NOLAN: You wrote a letter to the Housing Association's Weekly complaining that the magazine had published extracts from the Housing Corporation's Special Audit Report and had quoted it selectively. We noted that some other regulators not in this field do publish their reports when something has gone wrong. The Housing Corporation does not routinely do so, but does ask the association concerned if they would like it reported. Did you consider asking for a full report to be published?

MARGARET HODGE: We did not because it was part of a negotiated settlement at that time with the previous chief executive. I have read the Housing Corporation's evidence to you. I tend to be of the view that we should be more open in publishing these reports, but if we are going to do that there has to be, which there is not at the moment, probably more negotiation between the individual association and the Corporation on the content of the report so that, in a sense, how the Audit Commission do it with local authorities so that factual inaccuracies, for example, can be identified before it comes into the public domain, which are those sort of issues which are sometimes in conflict in local authorities and the Audit Commission. If you can have some form of negotiation with everybody preserving their rights, for the Corporation to publish for the Housing Association to argue against it, at the end of that I think it would probably be preferable to publish, but there was a specific reason for Circle 33.

DONALD HOODLESS: There does need to be a process if reports are to be published. Looking back on it, and it is before I arrived, if that report had been published as it was, which was very narrowly focused on certain events, I think it would have undermined confidence in lenders and others in the association at the time which would have threatened its independence. I think that is an important point to remember. In principle, yes, but there is not at the moment a procedure where there is the dialogue between the Corporation and the housing association about the content and the accuracy and the impact of reports, so I think that would have to be take into account. It is part of this business of actually determining what the Corporation is to do as a regulator and how it presents that information.

925. LORD NOLAN: As you know, this committee is very much in the business of openness and, of course, I quite understand the essential need for a report once published to be one that is fair, and if the facts are not

agreed for the person about whom it is published to have advance warning and an immediate right of reply. Would you be in favour of a system on that basis where the association criticised has a chance, as in the Scott Inquiry but one would hope rather more quickly, to put its points to the investigator and for the report then to be published as a routine matter?

MARGARET HODGE: Yes.

926. LORD NOLAN: And it would avoid what is really the worst of both worlds which is selective votes and underlying suspicion as to what has not been revealed.

MARGARET HODGE: Yes.

LORD NOLAN: Thank you very much. I mentioned the Scott Report. We have always been very clear that it is not our job to examine individual cases. We do not have the resources, we do not have the time, but we do, of course, take note of them as an indication of things that have been looked into or may need to be looked into again. We have had very full submissions from the Circle 33 area committee steering group and, although I do not want to go into any issues between them and you today for the reasons I have given, they said one or two things which I would like to take up with you. One is they say that housing associations are about people and not about numbers of houses; you would accept that, I am sure. They argue that there is a risk that the larger developing housing associations, especially when they lose their local base, may lose touch with their true objectives. You are a large housing association, are you not, over 9.500 houses and growing? Do you operate in the areas of 22 councils? You have a very large staff, your revenue budget is £30 million. What is the future? Do you see yourself getting bigger and bigger?

MARGARET HODGE: In the wake of the fraud we have reviewed entirely our strategy, and I think there was a huge thrust, and there still is among some of the larger housing associations, just to grow bigger. We as an individual housing association have taken a very clear decision that that is not our prime objective. Our prime objective is to provide a quality service to our tenants.

Equally, on the other hand, we are the main vehicle for providing new social housing, and that is in our charitable objectives so we will continue to expand but in a way which gives priority to tenants. We have a responsibility to existing tenants but we do also recognise our responsibility to future tenants. The way that that is converted into practice, for example, is every year when we look at our policy for expansion and our programme for expansion. We ensure that the overall cost of that programme will not fall on existing tenants, so there will not be a burden on existing tenants from what we provide for future tenants. We have been able to hold that so far by a mixture of our various funding sources, some reserves, some housing association grant, and private sector finance. If the housing association grant were to diminish enormously clearly we could not sustain that.

Housing associations originally were very complementary to local authorities and were very local. I was chair of a housing committee in the '70s and I remember them emerging. Now, since local authorities are not providing any new social housing and the whole burden has been shifted onto housing associations, there is this complete drive all the time to get bigger. The other problem is, since there has been a shift from public finance to bringing in private finance, the bigger associations have the bigger asset base and therefore are more likely to be able to attract the necessary private finance to expand. So that whole system is throttling the small local housing associations, and I think that is a real big public policy problem. The advantage of a housing association is that it is a single purpose organisation which is completely committed to providing housing. That is its strength and one hopes that on the whole it gives a better service therefore to its tenants than a local authority which has a whole range. The disadvantage is as it gets bigger it loses that link back to its tenants.

DONALD HOODLESS: In a practical sense we decided that we will only develop where we can successfully manage the properties and provide a good service, and therefore one of the first decisions of the committee was to determine where we operated, which we have told you about, and where we hold stock in other areas we are divesting ourselves of it. For example we have got rid of stock in South London, we will pass ownership to other associations. The same in Oxfordshire, we had a few units there, and in Hounslow we have some as well. What we are saying is we will develop where we have a management base in order to provide a good quality service for the tenants in those new homes. That is our decision and that is how we are approaching it.

927. LORD NOLAN: You have moved from the former area associations, or area committees, to the new sub-committees. Are the new sub-committees up and running now?

MARGARET HODGE: It has been a very successful exercise. The problem is the old area committees had no executive power at all, we established them 18-20 years ago, but they had fallen into disrepute and if you were to examine their proceedings there were more officials from the housing association than there were tenants. There were just very few people who participated in it, so we wanted (a) to bring more of our tenants into that decision making process, and (b) we wanted to bring it in as a formal part of the decision making processes of the housing associations so we are going to devolve power to them. We advertised and we have had 100 people respond to show a willingness to serve on those area committees, which I think is not bad for a first stab at it.

LORD NOLAN: Sorry to interrupt you, are those 100 all tenants?

DONALD HOODLESS: 48 are tenants.

MARGARET HODGE: And others community representatives.

928. LORD NOLAN: Would they include local authority representatives?

DONALD HOODLESS: Yes, we ask local authorities to nominate and we will get local authority nominations, we have a number. In practice they can be set up by the committee. Their first meetings are at the end of January, and we are holding a training day in January to bring people as a sort of day's induction into the work of the Trust. What we have to say is that we will have 75 voluntary committee members involved in the work of the Trust of which 30 are tenants, and from those 30 tenants five serve on the main board which is about a third.

929. LORD NOLAN: With these sub-committees I am not quite clear about the relationship between them and the board. Is there a board member on each sub-committee?

MARGARET HODGE: Yes.

DONALD HOODLESS: Two.

MARGARET HODGE: The tenant and a non-tenant. The tenant representative who will come from the sub-committee to the main board, and a member from the main board who is a non-tenant who will also attend the sub-committee.

930. LORD NOLAN: You are, like all housing associations, charged really with taking the burden of social housing off the local authorities. Is the structure suitable for doing that at the moment, or is there a good deal of overlap?

MARGARET HODGE: Overlap?

LORD NOLAN: Yes between different housing associations and different local authorities, different housing associations and the same local authority.

MARGARET HODGE: Again, government policy has deliberately introduced competition between housing associations and this has its good and bad parts. There is one bit that personally I find does not work which is where you have three or four housing associations operating on the same estate. If they do not have similar rent policies or similar management policies, tenants living under a different landlord on the same estate will have a different service, and I do not think that is a particularly good way of serving your tenants. I think you could introduce a healthy form of competition between housing associations which is not quite as absurd as we are currently ending up with too many landlords on one estate.

DONALD HOODLESS: In a practical way we seek to work very closely with local authorities. We do not run our own waiting list. Our main referrer for all our tenancies is the local authorities, and therefore we see our role as fitting their local housing strategies and meeting their particular needs because the responsibility to the homeless rests with them but we would expect them to nominate homeless families through the referrals we have.

LORD NOLAN: I am afraid I have been rather greedy with the time. Sir Clifford Boulton was due to ask you some questions as well.

931. CLIFFORD BOULTON: Most of the ground, Lord Nolan, that I had in mind has been covered. Could I just ask you about your internal complaints and grievances procedures because you very commendably explain to your tenants how to set about it. Are you satisfied yourselves with the way it is working out at the moment in the handling of these problems?

MARGARET HODGE: We are never satisfied, no, so we are constantly trying to improve. We see complaints simply as one of several mechanisms for us to raise quality.

If you know what your tenants are complaining about, and if you handle it effectively and you take the general from the particular you may do something to enhance the quality of the service you provide to all tenants. So we are trying to improve. For example, we have just brought in a new computer system which is far more effective. It tells you how long you are waiting to have your phone call answered and things like that, so all that is better, but it should also enable us to do some spot checks back to tenants on repairs. So rather than waiting for them to complain, we will go pro-actively to them and say did the contractor arrive on time, was the job done efficiently, is there anything you want to say to us? We are also supplementing that, which I think is quite important because somebody has got to want to complain, with regular annual surveys, basically a MORI tenant survey once a year, which will again give us a handle on what are the main issues of concern to our tenants. Then hopefully we will have these area committees functioning effectively in the next calendar year, so our mixture of area committees, tenant representatives on the main committee, complaints mechanisms, MORI surveys.

We have various other participation mechanisms. If we are doing an estate improvement we will encourage some sort of tenant participation in that business, or we encourage the formation of tenants associations. We employ development officers to encourage tenants associations on particular estates to emerge as well. So all those bits together ought to help us be better listeners to what our tenants are saying about the service we provide.

932. CLIFFORD BOULTON: Good, because a lot of the complaints must be really about the standard of management, of not coming to mend a broken window, or something like that, others are rather more deep seated and might be really concerned with worrying aspects of maladministration or something. Those kind of things can eventually work their way up through the system and then go to the ombudsman. Have you actually had many cases go to the ombudsman?

MARGARET HODGE: We have, too many. We have been pretty radical in reviewing our housing management services just this year, and I think it was part of the legacy that we inherited. We have completely restructured and everybody had to re-apply for their job. At the moment we are in a flux, so if you ask us in the next six months or a year it will not be good, but hopefully in 18 months time there will be a substantial improvement in the quality of the housing management service.

933. CLIFFORD BOULTON: Have you any complaint you would want to make, or comment you would want to make perhaps, about the actual standard of the ombudsman service itself? It is going to be moved out from the Housing Corporation, isn't it?

DONALD HOODLESS: We think it was quite fair. I think one of our concerns was some of the cost of arbitration. We have had two cases and in one of those the cost of arbitration was quite high which is an issue I took up with Roger Jeffreys which he was grateful for because he is looking at how he can set up procedures and have feedback and obviously control the costs of going through the arbitration process.

I come back to something I said about the fraud and what staff attitudes were like, they were very defensive.

What we are saying is that we should welcome complaints because they will help us put the service right, and we are changing attitudes so that people should first apologise then put it right if we have got it wrong. That is a very significant cultural shift that we are making in order to get ourselves out of the position that allow the events of the fraud to happen.

934. CLIFFORD BOULTON: You did refer to the staff in some areas not being well directed or well focused or co-ordinated in the way that the work was being carried out. Could I just ask you a question about the salaries structure of the senior staff? Do you they have performance-related pay, or are they on fixed pay?

MARGARET HODGE: We have just reviewed that. It is not performance related, but there is now a mechanism whereby a staffing sub-committee will review the performance of the senior management team. We review Donald's performance, he reviews the rest of the management team but we take the final decision thereon, and it is quite a complicated performance review process that we have just completed our first year of doing.

935. CLIFFORD BOULTON: The reason I raised it really was we had someone saying that in one area senior staff pay was linked to what one might describe as the profit emanating from the trading activities, so you do not pay according to that kind of return?

MARGARET HODGE: No, but we do set criteria at the beginning of the year on which we tell the senior members of the staff we will be judging their performance.

DONALD HOODLESS: In essence we have a planning process where we set an annual plan, and clearly if we are to be measured on performance is how far we have met the objectives in that plan. They are not about profit on services, they are about have you let the properties, how have we dealt with complaints.

CLIFFORD BOULTON: That was just the reassurance I was looking for. Thank you very much.

936. WILLIAM UTTING: I saw reference in the papers to members of the trust, I assume that these are shareholding members and I wondered how many of them there are?

DONALD HOODLESS: About 30 I think. The membership of the trust?

937. WILLIAM UTTING: Yes, and it is these shareholders who formally appoint the board but you have adopted a policy that leads to, as it were, a completely different and open method of appointing the board?

DONALD HOODLESS: Yes.

938. WILLIAM UTTING: What is your view about the importance of shareholder members of housing associations?

DONALD HOODLESS: Given the complexity of housing associations in trying to find committee members, all members, who have skills across a range of functions—finance, property, housing management—and equally to represent across the geographical area we operate, open membership policies are not going to work and achieve that balance, and therefore we have not seen open membership as a method of ensuring that we have an effective board membership.

WILLIAM UTTING: Thank you.

939. LORD NOLAN: So what recommendation would you make about membership generally?

MARGARET HODGE: Membership of the board or membership of the trust?

LORD NOLAN: Membership of the trust.

DONALD HOODLESS: We have a membership policy which, in some sense, could be described as circular which says that we will take into membership people with the skills that are required to serve on the board. In a sense it works that way round, but it is a circular argument.

940. LORD NOLAN: It is one of the more puzzling features of the housing association with their diverse backgrounds. I am afraid we have run out of time, there is a lot more we would like to ask you in view of your unusual and interesting history and the steps that you are still taking to make sure things go right for the future. We will follow them with great interest and we are very grateful to you for telling us all about them.

Lady Perry, we are very glad to see you, thank you very much indeed for coming along. We have followed your career with great interest and admiration, and we are looking forward to hearing you this morning. Did you want to say anything by way of a brief opening statement?

BARONESS PERRY

BARONESS PERRY (President, Lucy Cavendish College, Cambridge): Not really thank you very much, except to say that, as you kindly indicated, I really am speaking from personal experience of having gone through a lot of changes. Obviously I was involved in the inspection of higher education and, indeed, it was my team, in Her Majesty's Inspectorate who first negotiated any inspection in universities, (of education departments), as well as having inspected in polytechnics, for a total of 17 years in my case: then moving to a polytechnic which went through the rather heady period of coming out of local authority control and then into university status. I am now very happy to be in Cambridge, so I have seen a lot of different things in my time.

941. LORD NOLAN: You saw South Bank through its change of life, didn't you?

BARONESS PERRY: That is right, yes.

942. CLIFFORD BOULTON: Lady Perry, I wonder if I can take advantage of your very wide experience by starting with a very general question. You have experience at several levels of teaching work, both educational work at schools and then the new universities, and you are actually in charge of one as it turned itself into a university, and also trans-Atlantic experience. I will not ask you how Manitoba winters compare with Cambridge, I should imagine both of them are fairly severe.

Before we talk about specific areas, would you like to say anything in general about standards of conduct in academic life? Has there been a change? Has there been a shift in the last decade? Is there public concern which is justified in any way? What is your general feel about it?

BARONESS PERRY: I am not aware of any great public concern about standards of behaviour in the public aspects of higher education. I think there are other quite vocal concerns about standards of academic performance and so on, and we might touch on those. It is my own view that the standards of governance and of management in higher education have immeasurably improved in the last 20 years, particularly I think from the mid-'80s onwards. First in respect of increased accountability, and I would date that as starting from the days of the first selectivity exercise in research assessment. Secondly the greater clarification of the roles of governance which came first of all with the 1988 Act and then with the 1992 Act. I think thirdly with a much clearer distinction (and I feel very strongly about this), between the role of governance and the role of management within higher education. These I think have immeasurably improved matters rather than, as you suggest, raised any cause for concern.

943. CLIFFORD BOULTON: Good, that is very good news for us because we are in an area where a great deal of thought has been given to these matters already, and we are almost looking at the quality of that rather than working in a completely new field ourselves.

Could we take it then, talking about management, that the new universities really did emerge with a strong managerial test to their constitutions, a stronger managerial role. Would you like to make a comment on the transformation that came over the South Bank institution and, using that as an example, whether you thought areas that you think are of interest to us were an improvement.

BARONESS PERRY: I would not suggest that it was so much an improvement in managerialism. I have always thought of that as rather a deleterious word. The outstanding thing about the change was that it removed from South Bank, and from other polytechnics up and down the country, the control that was exercised by local government. That control was exercised across every aspect of life. Academic freedom was a meaningless phrase within a polytechnic because the local authority could interfere in any academic matter it wished. The local authority determined a great deal of the decision making which properly, I think, in a well run institution would be done internally within the institution. For example, in the polytechnics outside inner London the employment of staff and all matters concerned with personnel were done in shire hall or county hall or whatever: they were not done within the polytechnic, so any attempt to develop a proper staffing policy or a staffing plan was impossible. We were more fortunate in inner London because the five inner London polytechnics were set up as companies limited by guarantee from 1970 when they were first designated, so we did have the right to appoint staff. However, that was entirely within the ILEA guidelines. The ILEA gave us a precise budget for each individual appointment and precise numbers. There was no way that you could say, well, we will do without two secretaries and have one extra academic, or we will do without one academic and have two extra secretaries so to speak. The establishment for each category was laid down and every single appointment had to be approved by county hall. That made it extremely difficult to develop any strategic policy for what you wanted to do with the staff and, indeed, the budget of the polytechnic.

944. CLIFFORD BOULTON: I can understand a university feeling that a local authority does not know anything about how to run a university. Of course the local authorities that have regretted losing their influence over local universities have said to us that there is a loss of accountability and control of a kind of democratic kind as this openness because of the loss of that link. Is there an anxiety about any loss of accountability and openness that you see continuing, or are there systems in place that are adequate?

BARONESS PERRY: I think the system of accountability came into play with the '88 Act. I do not think there was any real accountability before in any sense of the word. Again speaking from personal experience only, the governing body was predominantly the ILEA, they had the largest single voting block on the governing body, so in the sense that they both made the decisions and then applied them at governance level, there was no accountability within the polytechnic at all. None of us really had any room for manoeuvre or freedom because the ILEA gave us the money, told us how to spend it, and then came as governors to make sure it was spent in the way that it should be done. So if you call that accountability I suppose, yes, though it was not accountability, it was control.

I think it was President Mitterand who said once that the exact counter balance to autonomy is accountability, and I think what I experienced as one running such an institution after the '88 Act came into effect in '89 was a much better balance of autonomy with accountability. The accountability is very fierce; we are audited four times over, as I think you have been told. The quality of our research is assessed. The quality of our teaching is assessed, there is no way you can dodge that. Our customers bring us our income; if we do not do well and perform well for the students, and if the students themselves do not believe that we will give them something which has coinage in society outside, we shall go broke. There is plenty of tight control of accountability. What is welcome, and I think is right, is that the degree of academic freedom and the degree of freedom for management to make decisions within the policy framework set by the governors has vastly increased. It has not just increased, it has appeared having not been in the new universities before.

945. CLIFFORD BOULTON: So the accountability and necessary responsiveness that now exist are much more relevant and appropriate you think to a university. I suppose it has been drawn to our attention that the most conspicuous examples of poor practice has cropped up in the new universities, but I do not know whether there is any general lesson to be learnt from that or they were perhaps just isolated cases which at least have to come to light.

BARONESS PERRY: Indeed, that is the point I was going to make, that at least the system works, that the bad practice now comes to light whereas before, of course, it could be totally concealed within the local authority structure. Yes, I am sorry that there have been one or two bad examples: I think that one or two bad examples out of a large number of institutions is still too many. Nevertheless I think these are the early teething troubles of a very different and new system, and perhaps for individuals within the system the headiness of autonomy was a little intoxicating and led to behaviour which perhaps was not as desirable as it should have been. I do

think the important thing is that these were instantly picked up. You cannot do these things secretly or privately any longer, they are open deals and there is transparency in what happens.

946. CLIFFORD BOULTON: So some lessons were learnt pretty sharply and quite quickly.

Can I move on now to Cambridge because we are always trying, of course, to frame recommendations and findings which have general application, and then we look at Oxford and Cambridge and perhaps London Universities and perhaps roll our eyes a little because these are such complex bodies which just grew in some many ways, but they do have some characteristics which are not necessarily found throughout the higher educational world. For instance, the concept of a Visitor and an external person who can be held in reserve and, in fact, made use of from time to time. Are there any Cambridge things that you would like to tell us about which you think are good, or worrying examples of university administration which could be extended anywhere?

BARONESS PERRY: I do not know that I can speak for the University of Cambridge, I can only speak for one small college within the university, but my experience of Cambridge at university level is that it has very, one might almost say, rigid structures which are a protection. They may be frustrating at times in that they are rather tortuous procedures, but they are there and have been there for a very long time for the protection of individuals and for ensuring that the way that the university conducts its business is a way which allows all voices to be represented and heard. Of course that does make for very long drawn out processes, but nevertheless I believe that within an academic community that kind of total involvement of the community in decision making is wholly beneficial. I think it is right.

I think the problems come, not just for Cambridge but for any university, when they need to make decisions which are more commercially edged where those academic timescales, consultation and discussion and committees and so on, are no longer appropriate, or at least no longer efficient. Perhaps there are problems there, not specifically for Cambridge but for every university as it faces a more commercial world, of how to cope with that.

Speaking from the college level, of course the Cambridge and Oxford systems have a quality, which I think is almost unique, of involving the whole of the academic community in the governance of the institution. That is the concept of what is a college, it is the community of all the scholars, so to speak. That, I believe, carries within it some of the same tensions, but it is absolutely right for academic decision making that the decisions should be made by all the scholars concerned, all the fellows of the college concerned in modern terms.

There is, I think, a tension related to the need for day-to-day management decisions, and I think, as I said earlier, one of the most important aspects of university governance, or of higher education governance, is clarity between management and governance. I think we still have not perhaps anywhere in the system yet got that quite as clear and as right as it ought to be. I am not sure that the 1992 Act helped, although it moved a long way along that path. The 1992 Act was meant to move the distinction and make it clearer; I am not sure that it has yet gone far enough.

947. CLIFFORD BOULTON: There is ultimately a very large governing body at Cambridge and Oxford. Have you had any experience, or is it said that that is really a drag on desirable change, that in fact it is very difficult to get changes through if they are at all controversial, and that there might be something to be said for a more expedited procedure of getting to the Privy Council for some issues which really need attention? Is that something that is said?

BARONESS PERRY: I have to say my lifetime of experience in consultative committees, which involves those I have experienced as a civil servant as well as in higher education, leads me to believe that if you cannot get it through a large committee then you should not get it through at all. That large committee is representative of all the constituencies which will be affected by the changes, and if there is genuine resistance within that large committee then they are speaking quite properly for the constituencies who will be affected. I do not think that there is a case for making change without the consent of the people who will be affected by the change. It may be very frustrating, and of course it is frustrating for all of us who wanted to put changes through which we can see absolutely clearly are right, but the fact that others tell us that they are wrong, that they will affect them in ways which will not be to their benefit, I think is very healthy for us to hear.

948. CLIFFORD BOULTON: You find it a safeguard?

BARONESS PERRY: Absolutely a safeguard, yes, but I still come back to this business of the separate function of management and governance. Just as in Parliament, for example, we are very careful that the executive does not take powers away from Parliament.

CLIFFORD BOULTON: Or should be.

BARONESS PERRY: Well we have special scrutiny committees, of one of which I am a member, which scrutinise legislation to make sure that the executive is not taking powers away from Parliament. So I believe it is quite right that management does not take away from governance, from governing bodies, the powers that they quite properly have to make policy. There is a quid pro quo for that, and that is that the governing bodies, the parliament if I may put it that way, the committee structure, does not try to pre-empt the day-to-day management decisions which have to be made within the policy framework they have set. I think the thing goes wrong if it tilts in either direction. If you get managers making decisions which are policy decisions which ought to be part of governance, and if you get governing bodies of whatever kind, or senates or whatever, or councils, trying to make decisions about the day-to-day running of an institution, either of those is an imbalance and is wrong.

949. CLIFFORD BOULTON: I think that is something that cuts across a great many of the areas we are looking at in addition to education.

Finally, may I just ask a question about strains that are introduced by financial needs and demands that are made nowadays both for getting private finance for academic activity and research, and by the shortage of funds which perhaps could be a temptation to universities to introduce rather thin further degrees in order to get foreign students. The whole of the area that money can, in fact, distort the ideal academic programme of a university. Is there anything you would like to say about either of those things?

BARONESS PERRY: Yes, there is always a tension between quality and access in higher education, as in many other areas of education, and I think there always will be and it is one of those tensions which it is the job of governing bodies and managers to resolve all the time. Almost every decision involves some aspect of that. The implication of a shortage of money leading to bad practice I think is one which assumes that you have bad management and bad governance en route. There is no inexorable relationship between a squeeze on finance and people behaving in irrational and less than honourable ways about the measures they take to make good their financial difficulties.

Perhaps I could take it back one stage. I am not entirely convinced that we have in this country reached a resolution yet of how we want to finance our higher education system. Certainly as access has increased, and the numbers of people coming into higher education have more than doubled, there has undoubtedly been a cutting back of the amount of money per student that we have to spend. Overall, the higher education budget goes on increasing but, of course, not in proportion to the increase in student numbers. There are many, of course, in other countries who still believe we are over-funded. I spoke to a group in the World Bank a few months ago about British higher education and their comment at the end was "all very interesting stuff, but you still have not gone far enough in cost recovery in the UK, you ought to be spending more on basic education and less on higher education"—not a message that was very welcome to hear! But I think it is important to see it in that international perspective—that we still do in this country have a sizeable budget available to higher education.

So that leaves us with the question over how we spend it. Now, we have had this dreaded awful phrase of "level playing-field" in higher education—not a pretty phrase at the best of times, but also one which I think has bedeviled our thinking about funding in higher education. After all the richness and the value of our higher education system, as it now is in the UK and as it was not twenty years ago, is its diversity; it's a very rich diversity and it's a proper diversity which produces graduates particularly, and post-graduates, who fit the very diverse needs of a modern economy. There is everything from the Oxford PPE who has gone on to do a PhD in philosophy who is just as much needed by modern economy as somebody who has done a degree in hotel management, let us say, who is a skilled hotel manager and will run an effective, and efficient and pleasant hotel.

All of that diversity is important but there is nothing it seems to me written in heaven which says we ought to fund all of those activities as if they were equal and as if they needed the same amount of money. And I think that is where we have gone wrong. I do not, for example, accept the argument that the new universities needed access to basic research money—they were doing very well with applied research and that seemed to me to be a very good and healthy thing that they were doing—it was proper to their mission that they should do so. But it has meant that the butter of research funding is now spread very thinly across the whole system instead of being concentrated in places where it can be best used. And I think you could make exactly that argument with costs for teaching and so on. I think we ought to be more honest and more open about the fact that if you are doing very different jobs you should expect different kinds of funding for those jobs.

950. CLIFFORD BOULTON: You are not alarmed about the actual quality and standard of some of the further degree courses that are being offered at the moment? You think that a respectable standard of academic requirement is being maintained?

BARONESS PERRY: In this country, yes.

LORD NOLAN: Thank you. Now Lord Thomson would like to ask you a question or two.

951. LORD THOMSON: Could I ask you two questions? The first one really relates to the new universities and the old universities. You are in a special unique position to give us advice about this. They are very different systems of governance, are they not? You have just mentioned what you thought was the value of the large committee in relation to experience of Cambridge, even though it might be frustrating to the actual academic management. Would the new universities benefit from having more large committees to supplement their governors?

BARONESS PERRY: Well, my Lord, they have them. They do have very large academic boards, for example, I think one of the strengths of the system that was put in with the 1988 Act was—again I seem to be hung-up on clear distinctions—that there was a clear distinction within the '88 Act between decisions which were made about the finances and the property and the overall ethos of the new universities, and the structures which were needed for academic decision-making. In the Articles of Governance of the former polytechnics, the new universities, there is, by the law, absolute freedom for academic board to make decisions about academic matters within the university. The board of governors has no remit in academic matters at all.

Now, obviously to us in the new universities that was a terribly important thing because we had lived through the local authority business where there was no distinction between those. The '88 Act, I think, was a very wise act in that it made those things quite clear. Academic board is the supreme decision-making body over all academic matters. It can be very big and it can, indeed, just as in the oldest of universities, sometimes be extremely long drawn-out in its decision-making and very frustrating to those who are trying to manage the institution. I would still defend that—I mean, against the frustration of decision-making I would still defend that. Where I think it's important to be swift and fast is in the decisions which I would call more commercial decisions. I mean, if you are trying, for example, to respond to requests for a consultancy or applied research from industry, you cannot say to them "Well, we have got four more committees to go before we can give you an answer"—they need an answer very quickly and I think you have to find ways to create different structures where that kind of decision can be made.

952. LORD THOMSON: You mentioned the inelegant phrase the "level playing-field". Another very inelegant phrase that we had to deal with, but an important one, is "whistle-blowing". Could you just say a word about how you feel, in terms of universities, about dealing with problems of personal behaviour? We have had some evidence that, in fact, universities tend sometimes to deal with them not by the sort of normal legal or public channels that are available but by what has been called "a bribe to take early retirement", gagging clauses in terms of people retiring. Would you like to comment on that—should we be making recommendations to try to deal with that area?

BARONESS PERRY: I find that a very difficult question to answer. It is undoubtedly common practice in industry to give people golden handshakes if you want to get rid of them. Our universities—certainly the new universities—are now run by people who are used to that climate, they are business and industry men and women. If they see a major personnel problem with a senior member of staff or even in the Vice-Chancellor herself or himself, then they are liable to think in those terms. Who am I to say that their wisdom is misplaced when it comes to carrying over industrial practice into academic life? I do not feel comfortable with it myself. On the other hand I recognise that it is sometimes a way of avoiding very public and very painful procedures of trying to get rid of somebody whose fault, if I may put it that way—whose sin—is something which is often very nebulous and very difficult to prove in an industrial tribunal, for example. When a senior academic is under-performing it is extremely difficult to produce the hard evidence that would be needed. I am not suggesting that people are doing anything which is criminal or fraudulent, I simply mean if they are a block to where the institution wants to go—if they have ceased to be effective or ceased to perform, it is very difficult to go through the open procedures of firing them and then facing an industrial tribunal and defending the firing. It is much easier—and perhaps that is cowardly, but it is much easier—to persuade them to go with something which makes it more attractive for them to go than to stay.

953. LORD THOMSON: Is there not the difference between universities and private, commercial, industrial businesses, that universities are public institutions, that very often the financial arrangements that have been made have been made with public money and that in any case, even in the business and commercial world, there are annual reports and company law to be followed and generally speaking these arrangements sometimes come out more in the open in the business world than they have in one or two recent cases in the academic world?

BARONESS PERRY: I would not for a moment defend their being done secretly, my Lord—that is not the point I was making, no. I think that the institution itself, through its annual report and through its books, needs to show exactly what has been done. What I was suggesting was that it was much more painful and difficult to have a public firing and then an industrial tribunal. There is an enormous difference between the governing body and, indeed, the staff of the institution, knowing that somebody has gone with a golden handshake and being able to make a very shrewd guess that that was because they were under-performing, and the kind of massive publicity that would happen if the thing was done through a dismissal and a tribunal and so on.

LORD THOMSON: Thank you.

954. LORD NOLAN: May I just ask one question, please, Lady Perry? You mentioned earlier in your

evidence that you did not think the 1992 Act got the balance right between management and academic affairs. You perhaps covered some of that in your answers to Lord Thomson a few moments ago. Was there anything you wish to add on that point?

BARONESS PERRY: I think what I said, Lord Chairman, was that it had gone further than the "88 Act did—I think there was some recognition that the "88 Act had left a rather untidy position—and I think you may wish to pursue this about grant-maintained schools as well—where the governing body was really given the total executive authority for the institution and that clearly is ridiculous. I mean, I used to enjoy telling my governing body at South Bank that they gave about as many hours in a year as I gave in a day to the institution. Clearly they could not run it in quite the same way that I could. But I think the "92 Act did push that forward—I mean, it did try to make it clear, for example, that the Chief Executive, the Vice-Chancellor, was a chief executive and was the chief accounting officer, so that the buck stopped there, so to speak. And I think most vice-chancellors found that extremely helpful. That was a universal change.

I am not sure that the clarity between the two has gone quite far enough yet. If you read the "92 Act carefully with the "88 Act, there is still a sense in which the governing body could be held responsible for every detail of what happens within the institution, details which they could not possibly inform themselves about, and I think there is still a difficulty there to be resolved.

955. LORD NOLAN: Is there one single recommendation—assuming that we take into account what you have just said—that you would like this Committee to make, one above all?

BARONESS PERRY: I think certainly it would be enormously helpful to have greater clarity, yes.

LORD NOLAN: Thank you very much indeed. You have been most helpful. Thank you so much for coming along.

BARONESS PERRY: Thank you.

956. LORD NOLAN: Now we have Professor Gareth Roberts and Professor David Melville, please. Thank you very much, gentlemen, for coming to help us. We are most grateful for the information you have already supplied and for what we are now about to receive, if I may say so in advance. Had you anything further you wish to say by way of opening statement before we go to questions?

PROFESSOR GARETH ROBERTS AND PROFESSOR DAVID MELVILLE

PROFESSOR GARETH ROBERTS (Chairman, Committee of Vice-Chancellors and Principals): Well, thank you very much indeed, Lord Chairman. I am Gareth Roberts and David Melville, my colleague, is with you this morning. It is a pleasure to be here. Perhaps as Chairman of the CVCP I ought to declare an interest at the outset because my Chief Executive is actually on your Committee.

I have read most of the evidence that has been put to your Committee concerning universities and at some point, not necessarily now, there are a couple of points I

would like to make to really, I think, correct a couple of misapprehensions that may have crept into sort of the information you received.

957. LORD NOLAN: Would you like to deal with those now?

GARETH ROBERTS: Certainly, if you wish. I think the first point I would like to make is that successful universities have very very influential executive teams. Normally they comprise the Vice-Chancellor, three or four pro vice-chancellors, the Registrar or Secretary, Director of Estates, Director of Finance, with the three main lay-officers coming in as and when required. And it is in that forum—and it is called within the University of Sheffield the Strategic Planning Committee—that the strategic thinking is carried out. But even more than that, because the rate of change in the environment now is so rapid, one has to make very rapid decisions and it is very often that group that makes decisions and very often the Vice-Chancellor is trusted as the accounting officer to make some very quick decisions on important issues and these are then reported to Senate and Council—because universities really are very large businesses. In my own institution the annual turnover is about £180 million, more than five thousand staff, but it is important to point out that less than 50 per cent of the income in the University of Sheffield comes directly from undergraduate student fees and from the Funding Council.

The size of the councils and senates in the old universities—and David Melville will comment on the new universities—are such that you just cannot have executive decisions made in these bodies. The council at the University of Sheffield has seventy-one individuals on it. The senate is close to 200 in number. And so, although there may be variations from one institution to another, I think it is important to point out that decisions very often are made in another forum and then approved, I think, by senate and council and, in particular, lay-officers do not normally provide the strategic direction perhaps that has been conveyed in the documentation that you have received up to now. It is the Vice-Chancellor who is seen, not just as the academic leader but the administrative leader as well.

Now, that is background to saying something which I think has been missing in the evidence that you have had up to now. I have had three industrial jobs and three academic jobs and therefore I have been in a position to compare governance on both sides of the fence. I think it was true—and maybe still is true in industry—that the motto is "if at first you don"t succeed, then your successor will". That seems to perhaps be the driving force in industry and commerce. Many years ago in universities the motto was "if at first you don"t succeed then you've got ten, twenty, thirty years to try again and put it right". Now that situation has changed profoundly in the last five or ten years and as I see it one of the key roles of the Chairman of council and the lay-officers which, perhaps, has not come through in the documentation I've seen, is to monitor the performance of this important individual that I have mentioned, the Vice-Chancellor, because the Vice-Chancellor, being the accounting officer, being the leader of the institution, that institution's success will depend enormously on the energy and on the vision of that individual.

This is where I think the new universities possibly have the edge over the old in terms of instructions to the lay officers, the board of governors, to monitor very carefully the work and the performance of the Vice-Chancellor.

If one looks at a lower level than the Vice-Chancellor, if you look at heads of departments and Deans, I think the reverse is true, that all old universities have the edge on the new, because in the old universities deans, heads of departments are only appointed for a limited time whereas in the new universities the norm is to have permanent people in these positions. So I have tried to indicate, perhaps, this very very important role of chairman of council together with his or her colleagues to really monitor the performance and to take effective action, not because the Vice-Chancellor has filled the books, or anything like that, but purely because he has lost the zest or lost an interest in that particular job or institution.

The other point I wanted to make, Lord Nolan, was to do with the fact that standards of conduct have improved enormously in the university sector. We do now have pressure from the Funding Councils, our auditors, of course, to conform, but I thought it might be valuable to the Committee if I brought along the Financial Directors and Financial Procedures Manual of the University of Sheffield, just as an indicator to you of just how carefully we do try and govern the institution. This covers not just financial issues but conflicts of interests and so on. So that is the Bible that those at the University of Sheffield are supposed to conform to.

958. LORD NOLAN: Would you be prepared to add that to your written evidence?

GARETH ROBERTS: I would indeed, yes.

959. LORD NOLAN: Thank you very much, it will be a very useful matter for us to study and for the record. I do not know whether, Professor Melville, you wish to add anything by way of opening?

PROFESSOR DAVID MELVILLE (Committee of Vice-Chancellors and Principals): No, not at this stage, my Lord.

LORD NOLAN: Thank you very much. I am sure it will come out in the form of questions. I am going to ask Dame Anne Warburton to begin the questions.

960. ANNE WARBURTON: May I begin by saying thank you for your very succinct and very to-the-point submission to us and thank you, too, for the comment in your covering letter, Professor Roberts, in which you tell us that you see the governance of the UK universities as increasingly capable of measuring up to external scrutiny. You have just told us other points relating to that—you have just spoken of the enormous improvement that you have seen recently. I think in some of the questions I would like to put to you may find that they come back on ground you have just covered. Do not feel you have to say it again but if there are other angles which you would like to bring out then perhaps it will give you the opportunity. We start, I suspect, on the common ground in assuming that the standards in higher education are already high, even if still improving. If I can take it that that is so, then I think I would just say has the change in size of the higher education sector, particularly in the last three years or so—the doubling of that sector—has that in your view changed the standards applied?

GARETH ROBERTS: I think the answer has to be yes on one count and no on another. If you look at the funds that the higher education institutions now receive, they are about 25 per cent less than three or four years ago. There is a three per cent efficiency gain built into the system for the next three years and, therefore, there will have been an enormous drop in the unit of resources that institutions receive. Therefore, inevitably, the quality of provision will have decreased; staff/student ratios are now very much different from where they were ten years ago, the level of capital for laboratories, the sizes of tutorial groups, and so if one is making the distinction between quality and standards, the quality of education you feel must have decreased because there is a strong correlation between the resources that an institution receives and I think the quality that they can provide of education to their students.

In terms of the size, it is not just the size that has changed, of course, it is the diversity of institutions that is probably the more significant factor. If you look at a degree course these days in some of the new universities, they will be very different to degree courses in the old. That is not to say the one is better than the other, but they are different. When you look at a degree course, I normally look at three components, the skills base, the knowledge base and the level of understanding, and you will find that certain engineering courses, although they might be labelled the same will have a much higher skills content than another. And, therefore, a degree in a certain subject is possible rather confusing to employers because one needs to look rather more clearly at what the content is and that balance between skills, knowledge and the level of understanding. So if people do claim that there is a variation in standards I think it is because possibly they are not always comparing like with like.

961. ANNE WARBURTON: Thank you very much. You probably heard a question put to Lady Perry a little while ago about standards of degrees and—academic standards—I think I will not pursue that angle now. You have emphasised the importance of the Vice-Chancellor, and quite rightly so; I would like to turn, though, to the balancing question of the recruiting of members of the governing body. In your experience—in the CVCP experience—is there these days difficulty in recruiting appropriate members of governing bodies?

GARETH ROBERTS: I have been involved now on three governing bodies of three different universities and in the experience I have had there has been no difficulty recruiting staff at all. In fact there has been quite a great deal of competition, especially for some of the very key positions of chairman of council and treasurer. I think one of the reasons for this is that in the last five to ten years it has been quite common policy for people to retire earlier, perhaps at the age of fifty or fifty-five, and I think now we do have an abundance of people, certainly in large cities like Sheffield, that are just wishing to become involved and therefore, if I could just relate my own experience—I am not sure how David would like to respond—I just feel that there really has been no difficulty whatever, we recruit national figures as well as local figures and we do try and make sure that there is a good balance. And, as I say, there is a competition for places rather than there being a dearth of people. But perhaps my colleague, David, would like to add something.

DAVID MELVILLE: Yes, I think the situation in the new universities, as you are aware, is slightly different in terms of the size of the body but my experience in two new universities, or a polytechnic as it was and a new university now, is that there is similarly quite a strong desire for people who are approached to actually join the governing body. I think it is still seen as something where senior members of communities, or experienced members of communities, can make a real contribution.

The most important thing, of course, is the process and the process that we use is one where we advertise in our internal newspaper, so get suggestions from staff and students and anyone else and then we have what we call a governance committee, one of whose prime tasks is to, besides overseeing the work of the board of governors, actually to provide nominations to the board. This way we have, in fact, introduced governors who have been suggested from all of those categories and it has also been possible to create a waiting list of governors with particular skills so that we could also ensure that we had expertise in areas like finance, the law, buildings, estates and so on.

962. ANNE WARBURTON: Thank you very much. Would you describe that now as best practice?

DAVID MELVILLE: We shall, in fact, be discussing this at an "away-day" that we have for our governors in January, just to see what further we can do and I was hoping that I might feed back some of your deliberations into that process. The extension that we might consider is advertising in the local community and we have just introduced, I think we are one of the first new universities to introduce the idea of a court and we are also going to use the court as a means of suggesting further names for the governing body.

GARETH ROBERTS: Perhaps I could add something here? The code which has been introduced by the CUC, the Committee of University Councils of Universities, I think you will find that in most of the old universities that code of practice has been in existence for some time. In Sheffield the only action we were not taking consistent with that code was to advertise for positions on the council. And so I do think that that good practice code that the CUC has produced is a very very good document. It is so vital for universities to have people who have got the time to contribute, people with real experience. Not so much for their time on the main board of governors or the council but for the excellent sub-committee work that they carry out. This is where our lay-officers really come into their own, where they chair the estates committee, the finance committee, the staffing committee, and they also participate there. And we have once a term a meeting of all the council people at the university for about four hours, bringing them up to date on various activities. And so it really is important that people who agree to serve on councils and boards of governors are able to set aside two or three days a month, I would think, on average, to become involved and most of them do very very willingly.

963. ANNE WARBURTON: Thank you. A closely related question, I think, has already arisen in what Professor Melville said particularly. Is the size laid down for governing bodies of new universities seen as being rather too small?

DAVID MELVILLE: I wouldn't say so in my experience and I think that the thing to remember is that the model is slightly different and I think a word of caution is that because there is a different structure in new universities—and I spent seventeen years of my career in an old university at an earlier point—as the structure internally is different it is very difficult to draft different parts of the system. One of the real benefits, I think, is that we have diversity—we are different kinds of institutions—we have diversity of governance and I think the possibility of spreading good practice.

But to answer your question more specifically there are some members of my board who believe that at 24 it is too large, it is their experience is that you really cannot have a company board which is as many as 24. There are some who have come from a different direction who say it is too small because the tradition in academic life is to have boards of 60 or more. So I would suggest probably we have it about right and the key is actually being able to operate within and to do the right kind of business and the earlier discussion that I had of defining the roles of the executive and ensuring, as Gareth indicated earlier, that the board of governors had the specific role of overseeing the operation of the executives which, in particular, is the Vice-Chancellor and a few of the senior members of staff, is very important and is of course laid down in Articles for the new universities.

964. ANNE WARBURTON: But you are finding the idea of a court something which helps to extend your contacts?

DAVID MELVILLE: Yes, it does not ape precisely the old universities, it is a new university style of court. We will have our first meeting in January and its aim is to provide greater accountability, a group of people who are more aware of what is going on in the university in the local community—community in its widest sense, business, local authorities and community groups—and who will take an interest and hopefully make comments throughout the year on the way the university is operating.

965. ANNE WARBURTON: Thank you very much. If we were to ask for a comparison of the new and the old university's system of governance, would you be prepared to say which you thought more efficient and where drawbacks might lie?

DAVID MELVILLE: I don't think I would, in actual fact, because I think it refers back to my earlier comment that institutions operate differently right from the centre. New and old universities actually are driven from rather different points in the way they operate. In fact, they are in diverse bits of business, if we can use that kind of description. Therefore I think that there have been benefits, if you like, in the new funding climate for the new university system of governance, that is it is one which is lighter on its feet, it is more able to respond, it is more used in the kind of lay members that we generally have and who dominate the governing bodies, they are more used to the idea of responding quickly, restructuring the services, restructuring the university. And, therefore, I think there have been advantages in that way. I think some of the old university governing structures have benefits in terms of what is generally called greater collegiality—we have to work rather harder at the collegial process of involving staff in a broad way in debates and discussion in the institution.

GARETH ROBERTS: Could I——

966. ANNE WARBURTON: What about accountability?

258

ANNE WARBURTON: I am sorry.

GARETH ROBERTS: I was simply going to add that a board of governors in a new university should not be equated to a modern board of directors. A modern board of directors would only have six or seven people on, so I suppose as soon as you get into double figures you really can't equate the two. Another comparison I would like to make is with the old universities—in my own case in Sheffield about one-third of the members are people from Borough and City Councils—you know, maybe 80 or 100 miles away—they do not have the same impact and the same contribution, of course, as those who live much more and have been nominated for very special reasons. And so, even if you have maybe seventy people, as you do in Sheffield, only perhaps a third of them actually contribute in a meaningful way to the work of the university. The other two-thirds are there, obviously helping with governance, but not contribution in anywhere near to the same measure.

DAVID MELVILLE: Let me respond to the question on accountability. I think that the way in which boards of governors generally in new universities have responded to the freedom that they have in their membership has been generally in the direction of accountability and there have been one or two exceptions to that. But I think, if you like, the fact that we are discussing so few exceptions is a good indicator that accountability generally has been taken—generally very high store has been put on this. If I can take the example of my own board of governors at Middlesex, it chose to maximise the number of staff on the board of governors, that is to take nominations both from the general staff but also from the academic board. It chose to include the maximum number of non-academic staff, it chose to increase the student representation from one to two within this 24. We have the fortune of sitting within three local authorities, three London boroughs, and it chose to maintain its links after it was no longer required to do so and it did it in a very interesting way. It had an elected member from one authority, it had a chief-executive from another authority, now replaced by a chief education officer, and it had a member of the local community, a local community group, in the third authority. And that is built into the way the governance committee—this committee responsible for staffing the board, providing membership of the board—it is built into their terms of reference, to ensure that as vacancies come up those targets are met continually.

So it effectively is something that comes out of mission, it comes out of what the university and the board of governors decides it wants to do and I don't think that there is a need to build in any further requirements for accountability. They do seem to have been responded to.

967. ANNE WARBURTON: Thank you very much. The few conspicuous examples of poor practice do seem to have come from the newest universities. Is that in itself significant, do you think? Have lessons been learned in consequence, has action been taken?

DAVID MELVILLE: I think all bad cases are good learning exercises and I think that it has led all boards of governors, certainly mine, to very rapidly review itself and say "Could this happen to us?" and I think that has been very good and I think the greatest strength of all that process has been openness and if we can argue for anything in your principles in our education then it must

be openness. The more openness there is on a whole set of issues then the more likely we are to pick up inevitable bad practice that will result from a whole range of issues. You can't legislate for occasionally having the wrong person in the wrong place.

I think it is also—and maybe Gareth can back me up on this, but I will stick my neck out on it—it is perhaps unfair to describe this only to the new universities. Cardiff was a very good case in point, which in fact was not dealt with as satisfactorily or as rapidly as these cases in the new universities have been. And I think maybe there have been others that have not even risen above the parapet in the past. I think it is simply that we have now greater accountability and greater openness and so these cases (a) came to the fore very rapidly and (b) were dealt with very rapidly.

GARETH ROBERTS: I think given the complexity and size of our education system, the instances of bad practice have been rather few. Clearly in Huddersfield the mechanisms of institutional governance were not adequate and I would like to think that what has happened in the last year or two will have changed that situation. Certainly when I read the newspaper, like everybody else does, and hears about cases of mis-management and bad practice in the commercial or business sector, we are really talking about something which is on a smaller scale—it is still not forgivable, of course—but was it not Henry Kissenger who said that the reason politics is so important in academe is because the stakes are so low. I think this was his comment, that we are really not talking about the opportunity to deviate from proper practice and having huge repercussions, I think.

968. ANNE WARBURTON: Perhaps two or three little quick questions, as time is getting very close, which run a little bit together. We have spoken of the business influence now, particularly in the new form of governing bodies, has there been discerned yet a tendency to over-emphasise confidentiality, to use commercial or individual confidentiality as a way of cutting off debate or restricting participation in debate, or is that not something we need worry about?

GARETH ROBERTS: If I could maybe kick off on that. Universities now are in a very very competitive situation. We are pitched into that position deliberately by various agencies in this country and abroad. So whether it is bidding for a new medical college in Malaysia, which I have been involved in recently, or bidding to take over the local nursing college, universities have been forced into a very competitive situation. Therefore, it is hardly surprising that strategic planning committees, in particular, play their cards fairly close to their chests until they are about, I think, to make some important decision where, of course, senate and council then is asked to become involved. And so there is a great deal more asked of colleagues now in terms of confidentiality. I think that is to be expected as we are in this very competitive environment. The way we try and cope with it in my own institution is on a "need to know" basis. If people really want information—and it is clearly confidential information—then we do not make it available to all senators or all council people until, as I say, that very last stage.

I should perhaps add that our senate papers, our council papers, are regarded as public documents. When you have

200 people on senate and 70 people on council it would be foolish to regard the information in any other way, I think.

DAVID MELVILLE: Yes, I think I generally reflect that. I think there has been no desire that I have been aware of to have what might be described as unnecessary secrecy. But my own board adopted what they explicitly called an openness policy, which implies openness of absolutely everything unless declared otherwise; and we also have a reporter from our internal newspaper present at all board meetings and he operates entirely independently—those stories are not vetted—and there have only been in the last three years three or four occasions where he has been asked to withdraw while something was discussed. So I think generally there seems to be the opposite desire—in fact one member of my board suggested recently that we should perhaps consider having the press in general present. I sense a feeling for greater openness and accountability, rather than the other way around, within the confines that Gareth describes, which of course do refer to what might be described as commercial secrecy and also matters that might affect an individual member of staff.

969. ANNE WARBURTON: And your assessment is that that is general, it is not just your two institutions?

DAVID MELVILLE: Yes. And my assessment would be that that is a general process and I think that the recent examples have actually helped in that because I think that there is a feeling that the problems that were reached did result from too great a level of secrecy, that in fact it is possible to get into a mode of thinking which is not very helpful when you are restricting your discussion to a very small group.

GARETH ROBERTS: And I am not sure how relevant it is but at the Committee of Vice-Chancellors and Principals we have always had an annual conference in September which has been a closed conference, but Diana Warwick and myself have decided that in future that conference will itself be open to outsiders, too.

DAVID MELVILLE: If I could just perhaps add one more example. The Education Reform Act did have some rather restrictive requirements in the involvement of staff in staffing affairs' committees and also financial matters. This can be somewhat restrictive in terms of involvement of staff and so my board about eighteen months ago introduced a speaking observer, which is a way of working within these restrictions, which actually means you have people present. It effectively makes it an open meeting and the Chairman will welcome comments from anyone who is present. We hardly ever come to a vote and so it is possible to actually involve people and for people to see the decisions that have taken place.

970. ANNE WARBURTON: I have several questions I would like to ask but I must not. May I just end with this short one—I think it is a short one: is the sector over-audited and if it is, what is the remedy? A short one to put, anyway.

GARETH ROBERTS: I think the answer is we do not want any more, is the best answer to that. I do believe that in certain areas like quality we are now moving to a single agency which will embrace both quality assessment and audit and that will increase, I think, efficiency in the system. The auditing that we have seems to be entirely

proper in terms of internal financial audit and external, the information that we need to provide to the Funding Councils, I think, keeps us on our toes. It is very important to have an information centre that does prepare interesting statistical analyses. It is a good way of helping you plan strategically if you have that information. So my own personal view—David might differ—is that we have just about enough now, we certainly do not want any more.

ANNE WARBURTON: Thank you.

LORD NOLAN: Lord Thomson?

971. LORD THOMSON: I was interested in what Professor Melville said about the importance of extending openness as far as is practicable. I wanted to ask on another aspect of confidentiality. When you are dealing with personal problems, somebody taking early retirement or somebody whose performance demands that really in the interests of the university he should leave, that there have been cases where the processes involved were commonly known as "gagging clauses". What is your feeling on the principle of that and how should it be dealt with?

DAVID MELVILLE: I believe that gagging clauses are inherently the wrong approach and I can perhaps answer by an example because as it happens I have had such an incident since Huddersfield—if I can put it that way, post Huddersfield and Portsmouth—where it was determined that largely on the basis of someone not having a future in higher education one of my deputies came to precisely this point. This is an individual who is within the concept of senior staff in the new universities, that is within the hire and fire of the board of governors, very broadly, as described in the Articles. There was a discussion which I primarily had with the individual, I involved the senior staff service committee, which is the senior staff remuneration committee of the board, in the discussion of what the appropriate guidelines might be. We came to an agreement which did involve a financial settlement but that was reached, if you like, considering the possible costs the university might engage in should it go to an industrial tribunal, I kept in touch with the Higher Education Funding Council chief auditor to consider what kind of limits they would regard as not appropriate. When the arrangement was reached, and it was one that was amicable on all sides, it enabled him to progress on with his career and thus the university to progress, it was reported with the actual sum involved to the board of governors in open session and this sum, of course, is reported in our annual accounts this year. There were no gagging clauses. There was, of course, an agreement reached between the individual and the university but I believe this kind of practice is one that can be reached and having just listened to what Baroness Perry was saying earlier I think within the requirements of institutions to operate efficiently, within the requirements of individuals to progress with their careers, that it is possible to, as it were, reach a settlement that stands up to public scrutiny in the use of public funds. And, of course, the level of that is an appropriate issue.

GARETH ROBERTS: If I could perhaps add to that, the only difference, I think, in an old university would be that that equivalent information would have gone, let us say, to the finance committee which, again, has a majority of lay people on it and they would then have signed it off and then it would have gone to the main council and the finance committee chairman would have reported without mentioning the name of the individual, without mentioning the size of the settlement, but the fact that the finance committee had unanimously approved that particular action.

972. LORD THOMSON: Would it be regarded as one of the roles of the CVCP to offer guidance on what ought to be good practice in this area?

GARETH ROBERTS: It would be very helpful, I think, for the CVCP jointly with the CUC to perhaps add to their existing terms of guidance. Obviously most universities now have remuneration committees and it seems to me very straightforward to add to their duties a clause that includes that with a recommendation to finance committee, or whatever.

LORD THOMSON: Thank you very much.

LORD NOLAN: May I just mention one remark of Professor Melville's? I think you said that some of the new universities were creating courts now. We would be very interested to know what the procedure is. I will not ask you now, unless you can do it in a couple of sentences, but it would not be able and be kind enough to let us know about that we would be most interested.

DAVID MELVILLE: Yes, I would be very glad to, my Lord.

LORD NOLAN: Thank you very much. And thank you both very much indeed, you have been most helpful and it has been very kind of you to come.

TUESDAY 12 DECEMBER 1995

OPENING STATEMENTS

Opening Statement by Ms Auriol Stevens

Thank you for giving me the opportunity to give evidence to this inquiry. My evidence will be confined to further and higher education. I have no useful experience of the other areas of the Committee's current inquiry. In giving evidence I will be speaking in a personal capacity, but I would also like to recommend to the Committee a set of articles which will appear in this week's (December 15, 1995) *Times Higher Education Supplement* on the subject.

The Committee has already received a great deal of evidence that codes of practice are already in existence for further and higher education, that scandals are quickly spotted and dealt with and that additional rules and regulations would be more damaging than is the risk of misdoing. I would like on the whole to endorse this view with some amplification and some reservations.

1.   Detailed external requirements specifying how people must behave and decisions must be taken can produce a compliance culture which is the enemy of creativity and innovation. In order to avoid doing something which may attract blame, there is a tendency to do nothing. At a time when economic and social demands are changing fast, further and higher education institutions need to be able to move rapidly if they are to flourish and serve society well. This is already difficult in what are rightly relatively open and democratically run institutions because such institutions are liable to capture by those within them who oppose change. This inertia is more apparent in old universities than new. I hope the Committee will not recommend the imposition of codes and practices which would make it easier to impede adaptation.

2.   Sanctions against improper personal behaviour already exist. Some are contained in the law of the land. In addition if institutions have—as they should—their own rules for the conduct of staff or governors (disclosure of interests, for example) they are in a position to discipline persons who infringe the rules as well as those who break the law. Fear of using these remedies (dismissal, or calling the police, for example) arises from the hassle, bad publicity and expense involved. This tempts institutions to try to preclude bad behaviour by regulation, to hush it up if it occurs or to bribe offenders to retire. This is conducive to a climate of corruption. Perhaps the Committee would like to inquire into the way institutions handle such cases when they occur and make suggestions.

3.   These first two points will look to many in further and higher education like endorsement of what is seen as the worst kind of macho managerialism—managerialism being one of the dirty words of the education world. The point I would like to make to the Committee is that the protection of academic freedom as defined in the 1988 Education Act is one of the most important duties of institutions of education especially, but not exclusively, higher education. [The 1988 Education Reform Act defined academic freedom as "Freedom within the law to question and test received wisdom and to put forward new ideas and controversial and unpopular opinions without placing themselves in jeopardy of losing their jobs or privileges that they may have at their institutions".] This freedom, essential to the resilience and creativity of our society, cannot flourish if the employing institution is subject to constant interference from outside, if it is at the mercy of factions, nor if it is in such financial difficulties that it cannot afford to employ people who offend powerful pay masters. The best defence of genuine academic freedom lies in the strength and independence of the employing institution. The Committee might like to consider the implications for the health of further and higher education institutions of staff dislike of effective management.

4.   The Committee has been given much evidence to the effect that adequate codes of conduct and guidance already exist. The Committee's present investigation, along with the publicity which has surrounded some recent cases, has done a great deal to accelerate the compilation, promulgation and adoption of these codes. The action already taken or being taken may indeed be sufficient. However, such desirable arrangements as open recruitment procedures, registers of governors' interests, remuneration committees, etc. are not yet universal and where they exist are sometimes very new. Fairly recent history does not justify too much complacency. It took a long time, for example, before anyone acted to curb overspending at University College Cardiff in the 1980s. Demands for accountability were resisted for a number of years by what are now the "old" universities. If the Committee is minded to accept that houses have now been put in order, as it is being urged to do, it might like to consider how the salutary fear of something worse can be built in so that self-regulation does not mean reversion to earlier complacency. Perhaps the Committee itself—or some other body which holds open hearings in this way—should become a permanent feature of public life.

5.   There is however a less cumbersome remedy to hand. The press, though often disliked and excoriated, has been one of the main agents in uncovering unacceptable behaviour and producing rapid remedy. The press is only able to report that of which it is aware. We depend on whistle-blowers. The definition of academic freedom to which I have referred accommodates whistle-blowers and critics of institutions to a degree which would seldom be tolerated in an ordinary commercial organisation. Provided this is protected there is a reasonable chance that codes of conduct will be observed and infringements will become known. Institutions greatly dislike whistle-blowers who can be said to bring the institution into disrepute. There have been a number of examples of "gagging clauses" recently, usually as part of a severance package. There is also growing use of confidentiality clauses in contracts which have a gagging effect. This applies to government agencies as well as institutions. The

Committee might like to make recommendations on outlawing gagging clauses in contracts and agreements. It would also be helpful to discuss where the line might be drawn between gagging clauses and the kind of confidentiality clauses which may be proper for commercial contracts.

Opening statement of Circle 33 Housing Association

Introduction

0. The Committee has indicated five issues on which it wishes to hear our views and we address each of these in turn. This note supplements our written evidence.

Regulation of Housing Associations by the Housing Corporation

1. The principal regulatory objective of the Housing Corporation is the safeguarding of public money invested in housing associations. It has been generally successful. No housing association has defaulted on its loans, and, as our written evidence demonstrates in our own case at Circle 33, there has been no loss of public funds.

2. We have some doubt, however, as to whether the methods it uses to achieve the objective are the best available. Housing associations vary enormously in size and complexity. Circle 33 is a large and complex business with a range of activities. As a result our Board members include people with a range of skills and experience necessary to direct that business and our senior staff are recruited for their ability to manage it. In this context, it often appears that the regulator is more concerned with the way in which things are done than with the outcomes which are achieved.

3. In our own experience, this was demonstrated by a concern with matters such as the length of our agendas and a prescriptive view of committee structures rather than a focus on service outcomes for tenants.

4. The Housing Corporation has itself been considering and developing its regulatory role, and is now paying more attention to indicators of performance. This is a move that we welcome. In doing this, it has been assisted by the Audit Commission, which has been working in a similar way with local government for some years.

5. The Housing Corporation needs to be very clear in whose interests it acts as regulator, and tailor its regulatory activity accordingly. Regulation is not the same as accountability. It has limited goals, namely the safeguarding of public money. In relation to those goals, and considering the complex nature and scale of some housing associations who receive most of the public money, a reliance on a bureaucratic form filling process is unlikely to be successful in the longer term. There has to be a dialogue between regulator and housing association at a senior level, so that regulators are able to understand the nature and development being undertaken by the Association and the direction in which it is going. For example, this is the philosophy of the Building Societies Commission in relation to their regulatory activity.

Accountability to stakeholders

6. Our principal stakeholders are our tenants, and in our written evidence we set out in some detail the ways in which accountability to tenants is addressed by Circle 33.

7. Other stakeholders include local authorities, people and organisations in the communities in which we work, the Housing Corporation as the agent of our government funding, our lenders and our staff.

8. Accountability to the various stakeholders takes different forms. Our Area Subcommittees are part of the management structure of the Trust. They include tenants, nominees of local authorities and other representatives of local communities, recruited through advertisement and invitation. Applications to join the Area Subcommittees have been invited through advertisements in local papers, and by contacting relevant local organisations. We have regular liaison meetings with local authorities, at all levels in the organisation. We publish a regular newsletter for our tenants, and another newsletter which goes to councillors and officers in local authorities, lenders and other organisations with whom we work.

9. Our accountability to the Housing Corporation as funder is through the Corporation's Scheme Audit procedures. This concentrates on cost control and value in the sense of quantity of output for the cost incurred. More recently, in particular in the light of the Government's proposal to make Housing Association Grant available to the private sector, there has been an increased emphasis on the need to account for the quality of homes produced. In its Schemework Procedure Guides, the Housing Corporation has set down very clear standards which associations are expected to achieve. We would like to see these standards strengthened and would suggest that the Corporation should do more to check that the required standards are achieved in practice.

10. Accountability requires that we are open and transparent about the work we do and the results we achieve. We publish an annual report, and our full accounts are available on request. An effective Board must be able to have full, frank and open discussions, and this requires that our meetings are private. A report on decisions taken is available publicly within 72 hours of each meeting.

Recruitment of and responsibilities of management committees

11. We have adopted a formal policy on the Appointment of Board Members. This sets out the range of skills that we require on the Board, the obligations of Board members, and a process of annual review of the Board's performance and composition. We have set a target of recruiting at least one new Board member each year. Appropriate recruitment

methods will vary according to circumstances. We intend to use open advertisement in many cases. We have set out a formal appointments process, supervised by a sub-committee of the Board, requiring Board members to sign letters of appointment in which their responsibilities are set out. We have set a maximum term of office for officers of the Board, and we have limited the numbers of those who work for other housing associations who may serve on the Board.

12. We have a clear statement of the responsibilities of Board members, the Chair, and the Chief Executive. The Chief Executive's responsibility is to manage the organisation and to deliver the objectives, policies and strategies determined by the Board. This division is needed for effective direction and management in an organisation that is as large and as complex as Circle 33, where overall responsibility is with a voluntary committee. We believe also that this division of responsibilities should be recognised in the legal and regulatory framework within which Associations operate.

The conflict of interest regime for housing associations

13. The existing regime is a tough one, in our view rightly so. We do not advocate a change, and have introduced a further control at Circle 33 by limiting to 20 per cent the proportion of our Board who may be staff members of other housing associations. The Committee may consider that the housing association regime provides a model that could be adopted by other local public spending bodies, many of whom derive a greater proportion of their income from government.

Complaints

14. Circle 33 is committed to improving the service it gives to its tenants and leaseholders. The way in which we deal with complaints is an important tool in improving service quality and ensuring accountability to tenants. In this context, we see complaints as an opportunity to put right any service failure which has affected a particular customer, and also an opportunity to see where more general service improvements are needed.

WEDNESDAY 13 DECEMBER 1995

Members Present:

The Rt Hon Lord Nolan (Chairman)

Sir Clifford Boulton GCB DL	The Rt Hon Lord Thomson of Monifieth KT DL
Sir Martin Jacomb	Sir William Utting CB
Professor Anthony King	Dame Anne Warburton DCVO CMG

Witnesses:

Tony Clark, Director, Higher Education, David Forrester, Director, Further Education and Youth Training and Peter Shaw, Director, School Places, Buildings and Governance, Department for Education and Employment

Sir Geoffrey Chandler CBE, Chair, and Stuart Etherington, Chief Executive, National Council for Voluntary Organisations

Professor John Tarrant, Vice-Chancellor, University of Huddersfield

Dr John Strickson, Principal, Ray Morgan, Chairman of Governors, and Barry Wastnidge, Clerk to the Corporation, North East Surrey College of Technology Further Education Corporation

973. LORD NOLAN: May I welcome you all to our last day of oral evidence in London for our current study. We are starting a full three minutes late, which may be put down to this being the last day of our London term. In fact it resulted from there being an unusual amount to prepare today, but I am so sorry to have kept you waiting.

We have four sets of witnesses today. First, we welcome again officials from the Department of Education and Employment. We have already discussed training and enterprise councils with the Department. Today's team will, I hope, share with us some of their expertise on education matters. They are Tony Clark, Director of Higher Education, David Forrester, Director of Further Education, and Peter Shaw, Director of School Places, Buildings and Governance. Together they cover a very wide field, to which I hope we shall be able to do justice in the short time available.

Second, we welcome Sir Geoffrey Chandler, Chair, and Stuart Etherington, Chief Executive, of the National Council for Voluntary Organisations. The NCVO, as we have heard before, is doing work on the governance of voluntary organisations, which is of interest to us, and I believe they may also have comments about the relationship between the voluntary organisations and the TECs.

Third, we shall hear from Professor John Tarrant, newly appointed Vice-Chancellor of the University of Huddersfield. While a past incident at Huddersfield has attracted a great deal of interest, I know Professor Tarrant is keen to look forward rather than back. Professor Tarrant has moved from the University of East Anglia, where Dame Anne Warburton and he were colleagues.

Our final witnesses are Ray Morgan, Chairman of the Governors, Dr John Strickson, the Principal, and Barry Wastnidge, Clerk to the Governors, from the North East Surrey College of Technology Further Education Corporation, a title which happily is normally abbreviated as NESCOT.

Gentlemen, thank you very much for coming along to join us this morning and thank you also for the very helpful and clear written evidence you have already given

us. Was there anything you wished to say by way of opening statement before we ask you questions?

TONY CLARK, DAVID FORRESTER, AND PETER SHAW

TONY CLARK (Director, Higher Education, Department of Education and Employment): Thank you, Chairman, no. We thought we would stand by the memorandum that we submitted at this stage.

974. LORD NOLAN: The first question is, I am afraid, fairly wide-ranging, indeed fundamental. We would find it helpful if you were to outline as succinctly as you can the working and legal relationships between the Department and the various NDPBs—the Higher Education Funding Council, the Further Education Funding Council and the Funding Agency for Schools.

TONY CLARK: Yes, Chairman. I will start by saying something generally and then something briefly about higher education, and then my colleagues will come in.

Each of these bodies is set down in statute, so the relationship between the Department and the bodies concerned is clearly specified in statute, and we have to develop working relationships that reflect that statutory position. In practice, in each case we have a financial memorandum between the Department and the body concerned; we are able to monitor the performance of these bodies through management statements and corporate plans. In the case of governance, which I know is one of the Committee's main interests, it is fair to say that the Department is concerned with the broad framework and structure of governing bodies, whereas the funding bodies are concerned primarily with governance in so far as it affects financial relationships. So the Department's interest is slightly broader.

Very briefly on the higher education side, we have the Higher Education Funding Council for England, with which the Department has closing working relationships. The Funding Council is responsible, as an independent body, for distributing the aggregate money which the Government makes available each year, and is solely responsible for that. The Secretary of State is entitled to offer general guidance, but that guidance is subject to certain restrictions set out in the law, in particular restrictions concerned with academic autonomy. And, as a working relationship, we have an assessor on the council, which meets about 10 times a year, and we have regular informal contacts.

LORD NOLAN: And now the Further Education Funding Council.

DAVID FORRESTER (Director, Further Education, Department of Education and Employment): Chairman, thank you. I do not wish to add very much to what Mr Clark has said, because everything he says applies pari passu to the Further Education Funding Council and further education colleges.

The only general point I would make at this stage to distinguish between the two sectors is that, reflecting their different origins—further education coming essentially out of local government background and it being a new sector—when the sector was set up there were some tighter controls that the Secretary of State retained. For example, she determines the general instrument and articles of government, which is a model which is applied, unless an institution wishes to seek an amendment, to all institutions in the further education sector. There are variations which we allude to in our written evidence as between different categories, but essentially there is a common framework of governance. But as regards the overall framework and the principle that the Secretary of State deals with the funding body and the funding body deals, in turn, with the individual institutions, that principle, I think you find, applies across all the bodies that we are talking about.

975. LORD NOLAN: Thank you very much, and what about the Funding Agency?

PETER SHAW (Director, School Places, Buildings and Governance, Department of Education and Employment): The same general principles that Mr Forrester just referred to apply, the same sort of control arrangements—financial memorandum, annual grant letter, management statement and corporate plan. This body was set up fairly recently, in 1993. There are some differences. The Department annually issues grant regulations, which control the way the agency calculates and pays grants to schools. The FAS has a wider discretion on the use of funding on elements of expenditure which are not recouped from local education authorities than on expenditure which is directly recouped from LEAs.

976. LORD NOLAN: It is an agency. What is an agency?

PETER SHAW: It has "agency" in the title, but it is an NDPB in the same way as the FEFCE and the HEFCE. It is not a Next Steps agency. The title may give that impression, but that is not the case.

977. LORD NOLAN: One of the things we must try to examine for our own minds, if for nobody else's, in the reports is again these widely used and, to the outsider, rather confusing uses of the word "agency". A Next Steps agency is not an NDPB, is it?

PETER SHAW: No. The relationship between the Secretary of State and the Next Steps agency is much closer than in respect of an NDPB.

978. LORD NOLAN: How did the funding agency become called an agency? Has that anything to do with its

rather wider discretion that you describe, or is it simply an accident of history?

PETER SHAW: I was not involved at the time. I have in fact only been in my job for a couple of months, although I was working on grant-maintained schools when there were a very small number, when all these matters were done within the Department, so I cannot throw any light on the particular title. But, as to discretion, they have a similar level of discretion to FEFCE and HEFCE on capital expenditure matters. On recurrent expenditure matters their work is guided by regulations made by the Secretary of State, so in terms of recurrent expenditure there are more controls in relation to the funding of grant-maintained schools than in relation to the funding of FE and HE institutions.

979. LORD NOLAN: Yes. Gentlemen, I deliberately have not asked you about TECs, which we have covered previously, but are you able to compare the legal and working relationship for the educational side of the Department's work with that for TECs?

DAVID FORRESTER: Chairman, perhaps I should take that, though I am not principally responsible in the Department for relationships with TECs. My directorate has a great deal of interest in the relationships with TECs, as they are the delivery mechanism through which the Government seeks to develop the work-based route, for which I am responsible in relation to young people.

You will have heard that a key difference is that the TECs are private sector bodies, and all the bodies that we are talking about here are, though incorporated, incorporated either in statute or by some sort of charitable deed. That is a fairly key difference. There is also the key difference that, going with that, there is a contract relationship (a) between the Secretary of State and the TECs and (b) between the TEC and the individual provider, whereas formally, and I use the word advisedly, the relationship is not a contract relationship between the Secretary of State and the statutory body, the Funding Council, and, in turn, between the Funding Council and the independent further education college, in the case that I am talking about, which receives a grant from the Funding Council.

However, in practice one of the things I have been interested in is that there is a convergence of behaviour—best practice convergence of behaviour—so that the relationship in a competitive environment but where all are substantially dependent on public funding becomes quite similar. I know that the Further Education Funding Council when they gave evidence mentioned this to you. They in effect are contracted with individual institutions to secure the achievement of their objectives, the meeting of their duties, because at the end of the day the duty is on the Funding Council not on the individual institutions. The individual institutions are simply a means by which to achieve that. That is not very different, it has to be said, from the relationship between an individual TEC and an individual provider, which of course can include a further education college for those functions that the TEC is discharging.

That will not be a very helpful comment, I am afraid, for the Committee, Chairman, because I am simply indicating that there is quite a blurring here, but we are achieving—I think it is fair that the new Department has a mission to achieve this—common, best practice standards of behaviour, including very much an endorsement of the principles that the Committee has been promoting.

980. LORD NOLAN: On the contrary, Mr Forrester, I think it is very helpful, because in our selection of these five groups of bodies that we are at present looking at, we were hopeful that there would be enough common threads, in spite of their diverse origins and their different aims, for us to be able to deal with them together, and I think what you said is very useful in that connection.

I wonder whether, arising out of what you said, we could spend perhaps a little more time on the powers which the Secretary of State has to intervene in education bodies in the event of maladministration or misconduct. They are of course, as you set out in your memorandum, quite different. For example, in the case of the further education bodies, you note in paragraph 2.15 on page 4:

"The Secretary of State may intervene on the recommendation of the FEFCE where there is evidence of mismanagement and may remove some or all of the governors, and may also modify the instrument of government."

How often does that happen in practice?

DAVID FORRESTER: Chairman, the way you have put the question is in relation to further education initially, so I shall answer if I may. We have had two inquiries, as that paragraph says, in relation to colleges—very different circumstances, I may say, one in Birmingham and one in the Derby area, only two. In both cases they were inquiries where complaints were made and the Secretary of State invited the Further Education Funding Council to commission the inquiry, and I believe you have had evidence from one of those who conducted one of the inquiries, Mr Shattock. In each case the Funding Council then made recommendations to the Secretary of State on which, substantially, she acted.

There has been another case which is a little similar but did not actually require an inquiry, because what happened was that there was a damning report by the FEFCE's inspectorate on governance and management of one of the colleges, and the Secretary of State might well have been minded to intervene directly, had a recommendation been made to her. In fact the governors chose to resign on receipt of the report and a new governing body was instituted in place of them, and indeed Mr Shattock is now the chairman of governors in that case.

But that is only three cases out of approaching 500 colleges, and there is indeed only one case where there has been cause for concern over the governance to the extent that there was in the case of that inspection report. We are not complacent about it, but we regard that as quite reasonable, given how new the sector is and the extent of their responsibilities and challenges.

981. LORD NOLAN: Were you reasonably satisfied with the way the procedure worked—that is to say, being able to find out what was happening and report within a reasonable time to the Secretary of State, and get an effective remedy put into operation promptly?

DAVID FORRESTER: Yes, I think so, Chairman. As I have indicated, the circumstances were different in each case. We had to proceed by way of formal inquiries in two

cases, which were triggered by complaints, and then by invitation to the Secretary of State. In one case we had, as it were, accidentally a report coming through on the cycle of inspection reports. I suspect that if that report had not been coming through within a matter of weeks, concerns would have been voiced informally and then more formally, which would have triggered some sort of inquiry. In brief, the procedures are there, and we are satisfied that they are adequate for the purpose.

982. LORD NOLAN: And that the complaints are made responsibly and without fear of consequences? Have you any fear that people may be restrained from making complaints because of the adverse reaction that may result for the complainant?

DAVID FORRESTER: It is very difficult for us here to be complacent about that, because in local areas, which may be dominated by local interest groups, there may be very high pressures on individuals. I believe that in the case that Mr Shattock reported on in Derby he alluded to the great pressures that were put on a number of individuals in the college and he gave credit to one who, in effect, acted as a whistle-blower. But the fact is that that person was able to act as a whistle-blower, had the support of locally-elected Members of Parliament and was able to make representations in various ways that triggered the inquiry and triggered what we regard as adequate action.

983. LORD NOLAN: As you know, what is called whistle-blowing—it almost seems to be not quite the right phrase: it is the referee who blows the whistle, isn't it, whereas this is actually talking about a complainant who appeals to the referee?—is something that we felt should have a place in the other departments of public life which we have looked at. It is clearly a highly sensitive and not always very attractive method of making a complaint, but there are occasions when it is the only way of getting at the truth. This is one of the areas that we are looking at, so I am interested in what you have told us on that score.

DAVID FORRESTER: We would accept that, Chairman. Is there anything my colleagues want to add? There are formal arrangements in place—for example, the principal, as chief executive of an institution, has a responsibility to inform the chief executive of the Further Education Funding Council if the governing body is likely to be engaged in anything that would make it ultra vires in terms of its financial management. I know you have been informed that the Further Education Funding Council is considering the role of the clerk of the governing body similarly and indeed will be taking a paper on that later this week.

984. LORD NOLAN: Thank you very much. I wonder if I could turn to Mr Shaw and ask about grant-maintained schools. On page 13 of your paper you tell us:

"If the governing body of a grant-maintained school are believed to be failing to discharge their duties or to be acting unreasonably, a complaint may be submitted to the Secretary of State. If she finds the complaint justified, she may issue a direction to the governing body.

The Secretary of State also has powers, where serious problems have arisen, to appoint up to two additional governors or to replace any or all of the existing first governors."

PETER SHAW: Can I speak to both those subjects in turn?

985. LORD NOLAN: If you would be so kind. What would be the nature of the direction that the Secretary of State
might issue to the governing body in the first case? Can you give us an example?

PETER SHAW: I can give you an example under sections 68 and 99, when there has been a complaint to the Secretary of State and the complaint has been investigated. A formal direction is a last resort. What often happens is that the process of investigation itself leads to the solving of the problem. But an example I can give from last year was when the governing body of one grant-maintained school, a primary school—Hawkedale Primary—was directed to reinstate a head teacher whom they had dismissed, so it was not properly going through the procedures. So there was a direction to reinstate the head teacher. So that was the remedy on the first leg.

On the second leg, which is the appointment of up to two additional governors, the Secretary of State has the power to do this when she considers the governing body are not carrying out their functions satisfactorily. She is also able to replace any or all of the first governors where the governing body failed to carry out the duties they have by law, or an inspection report says special measures are needed at the school, or the Secretary of State considers that the governing body has acted in a way prejudicial to the provision of good education at the school.

If I can give you a couple of examples of those, in October 1995 an additional governor was appointed to a grant-maintained school in Lincolnshire to bring additional expertise to the governing body in the light of comments in the inspection report, in the light of an Ofsted report, that the governors were not playing an appropriate role in planning and policy-making at the school. So the trigger was part of Ofsted's regular cycle of inspection: they expressed these concerns. There was clearly correspondence with the school, and the Secretary of State decided that an additional governor should be appointed, who was an ex-head teacher and who would bring new expertise to the governing body.

In another case, in Essex in November—last month—two additional governors were appointed as a result of advice from FAS, which expressed concern at the financial management at the school. So the trigger there was FAS who, because of their regular monitoring of expenditure of the grant-maintained schools, raised concerns with the Secretary of State; hence the appointment of the two additional governors. So in both those cases Ofsted and FAS were the triggers, and the Secretary of State used the powers available to her under the legislation.

986. LORD NOLAN: Yes, thank you very much. Has the Secretary of State power to remove governors other than the first governors?

PETER SHAW: I do not know off-hand. The provision that I was referring to was the removal of first governors. The others are elected, and parent governors having been elected, I think the presumption there is that it would be unusual for the Government to want to replace those who had been elected. Mr Forrester, who dealt with this subject in a previous incarnation, may be able to answer your precise question.

DAVID FORRESTER: Chairman, I was going to comment partly on the particular case of grant-

maintained schools, but there is also a general point, that where the power exercised by a Secretary of State enables her in effect to influence the composition of the governing body to the extent that she determines the majority, then that majority in turn can substantially influence the overall composition, because there is provision for co-options. So even though she may not directly be removing co-opted governors, she would, by determining the majority of the governors, be determining substantially the overall composition.

987. LORD NOLAN: Yes. What are the powers of the governing body to remove one of their number? Can that be done by a majority vote, or how? This is a worst case test, but supposing one had a really difficult and irresponsible member of the board who was being a complete pain in the neck and holding up business, is there a machinery there for getting rid of him or her?

DAVID FORRESTER: It is a very valid question. I can think of cases that I have heard of where governing bodies have in effect called upon a member to resign, which comes to the same thing, provided that the member takes the hint. But I cannot give you chapter and verse, and perhaps we ought to give you further evidence on that.

988. LORD NOLAN: Would you be so kind, thank you very much, just to tidy up that point. Staying for a moment with the grant-maintained schools, who have explained how the machinery worked and, I gather, worked satisfactorily in the cases that you have mentioned, is it not rather a cumbersome machinery to involve the Secretary of State in the affairs of so many grant-maintained schools? Is it rather a lot to saddle a busy Minister with?

PETER SHAW: The reason behind the approach that Ministers took was part of the background when grant-maintained schools were set up. Originally they were maintained by local education authorities and, when the relevant legislation was going through Parliament, Ministers were very keen to set up these schools as self-governing schools, very much with the philosophy that they should solve their own problems and work out locally any issues that arose. This has been very much the experience in the great majority of cases. Recently one head teacher in a grant-maintained school said to me that one of the great advantages of being grant-maintained was that they did have to solve their own problems. They could not use the excuse that they could always go to the LEA: it was the LEA's fault. That ethos has in most cases meant that problems are solved locally. The difficulty of having any intermediary in terms of grant-maintained schools is that it might reduce that focus on self-government. Hence the provisions in the legislation that the Secretary of State is there as a power of last resort, but the very point you make about the distance was part of the design, in order to try and ensure that schools solve their own problems.

989. LORD NOLAN: I follow. Thank you. Perhaps this ties in with a point I was going to put to Mr Clark, because there is no power, is there, in the Secretary of State to remove members of the governing boards of universities?

TONY CLARK: No, Chairman. This is on the basis that universities have been managing themselves for rather longer than some of the other institutions which we have been discussing. That applies even in the case of former polytechnics, because many of those were essentially self-governing in the "80s before they were given their statutory independence.

990. LORD NOLAN: But there is here too, I suppose, the question of academic freedom to be borne in mind. It is defined in the 1988 Act as

"Freedom within the law to question and test received wisdom, and to put forward new ideas and controversial and unpopular opinions, without placing themselves in jeopardy of losing their jobs or the privileges they may have at their institutions."

That is of course statutory language. Does that play a part in the Department's policy towards these various institutions?

TONY CLARK: It plays a part in the sense that we have model articles of government for the post-1992 universities. These are models, they are not requirements, but the models do incorporate this particular phrase about academic freedom. So this requirement is enshrined within the articles of government of all the post-1992 universities. I would expect a similar article to be in many of the pre-1992 chartered universities and, even if it is not there, I would expect them to follow it.

991. LORD NOLAN: Thank you very much. You mention in paragraph 4 of your evidence, starting on page 13, the principle of voluntary service and the fact that

"The government believes this remains fundamental to school governance in both the grant-maintained and the local authority sectors",

and of course it goes across the board, does it not? Do you see a case for limited exceptions to the prevalence of purely voluntary service for some small allowance being given for loss of earnings, rather on the lines of those given to members of juries, to special payments for exceptional out-of-pocket expenses which might be incurred by a mother with young children? Would you regard that as representing a possibility of a dangerous inroad on the principle?

TONY CLARK: Chairman, I think that the present legislation, and I think this applies across all the sectors we are talking about, enables out-of-pocket expenses to be paid to governing body members. That is at least possible within the Act. I am advised that this does not, however, allow for loss of earnings, which would be regarded as a payment. As far as your question is concerned, we are not aware that there have been significant difficulties over recruiting governors under the present financial arrangements, and since we certainly endorse the principle of the voluntary approach, we do not see a need at this stage to change the law in the way I think you were indicating.

992. LORD NOLAN: Thank you very much. If we were to recommend that some general alteration be made in the systems of governance of either the pre or the post-1992 universities—suppose, for example, the post-1992 universities were to introduce consultative councils or courts on the lines of those that we tend to find in the older universities—would that be likely to create difficulties for the Department?

TONY CLARK: If the universities themselves wish to change their articles of government to allow for the

creation of a formal consultative council, there would be no problem. They would submit that to the Privy Council, and the Department in advising the Privy Council, depending on the individual circumstances, would be likely to support that approach. But we do not have the power to require that approach to be taken amongst all the universities. If we were to go down that road, it would require primary legislation.

Perhaps I could add, Chairman, that when the Committee of University Chairmen were consulting universities about the question of openness, consultation and so on, the view was expressed then by the universities concerned, including the post-1992 universities, that it would be best to leave open the way in which these consultations were carried out, although the principle that there should be consultation with the local communities was accepted and indeed is part of the advice which the CUC offered at the time.

993. LORD NOLAN: Thank you very much. One feature which has caused some concern in a number of quarters is the possible personal liability of governing board members for decisions made by them. Is there an authoritative legal view within the Department as to the possible danger of board members being defendants in actions for negligence?

TONY CLARK: Chairman, I have a piece of legal advice, which I am happy to read out. It is consistent, incidentally, with the advice which has been given, certainly by the Funding Councils to governors in the past from time to time, although I have to say as well that it is a point that does come up from time to time and questions are received about it. The advice that we have is as follows:

"Liability is likely to rest principally with the corporate body, which is a separate legal person from the individual members of the corporation or governors. It is only in wholly exceptional circumstances that an individual member or governor would be personally liable. There first has to be established a breach of fiduciary duty. Secondly, for the individual to be held to be personally liable, there has to be a valid claim by someone with a sufficient interest to bring a claim. In practice, the courts are very unlikely to hold that there is any personal liability in cases where individual governors or members act within the scope of their functions and procedures, act honestly and reasonably, with care and common sense and without ulterior motive, and seek to persuade their colleagues against acting other than in this way."

That is the sense of the legal advice that we have and indeed, as I say, it is the advice that we have offered in the past.

LORD NOLAN: Very little likelihood?

TONY CLARK: Very little likelihood, yes, assuming that governors act in the way outlined in this note.

994. LORD NOLAN: Yes. I know it is a most difficult question and I do not expect an immediate answer, but I take my personal lead from the fact that judges are immune from this. I think it is assumed they act in good faith. It does seem a little surprising that others in responsible positions acting in good faith are either not given some immunity or are covered by an assurance that

if legal liability were found, then, excluding, for example, criminal action or fraud, their position would be covered.

TONY CLARK: Chairman, we have looked at that in the different Acts since about 1988 and the view that we have taken has been that we do not want to offer indemnity in respect of the kind of actions that I have just set out as leading to personal liability. In so far as there is a grey area in this, it is open to governing bodies to insure against that grey area, but they cannot insure themselves against the kinds of things that are set out in this legal advice. So far as we are aware, governors accept that position.

LORD NOLAN: Thank you very much. I think I have taken all and more than my share of the available time. I am going to ask Sir William Utting to carry on the questioning.

995. WILLIAM UTTING: Thank you, Chairman. Perhaps I could address the point of the constitution of governing boards of further education institutions and post-1992 universities. I can quite see that these criteria were set to give effect to a strong policy thrust at the time, but, as we look at them now, they do seem to bias the constitution of these governing bodies in favour of white males from a business or professional background. I wondered if there was any likelihood of these criteria being reviewed in the light of the government's new guidance about public appointments, with its strong emphasis on merit being the criterion for appointment and its strong equal opportunities thrust.

TONY CLARK: Perhaps I can comment first on the post-1992 universities. One of our objectives in establishing the constitution for these universities was to put them on at least a similar basis to that for the older universities. That is why their instrument and articles are handled, if you like, by the Privy Council rather than by the Department. Another factor was that the former polytechnics concerned in all cases had a strong vocational bias. So we considered that the governing body should reflect that, and that is the reason for the reference to professional persons, employers and so on. There are of course co-opted governors as well, and it is open to any governing body to open up membership to other persons. Not only that, I think the definition is open to a fairly wide interpretation. So although in practice what you have suggested is probably borne out by the facts, in principle, even with the present requirements in the Act, it would be open to it to widen membership in the way that you have suggested. I think the answer to your suggestion is that, at this stage at any rate, we have not seen a case to review the schedule as far as the post-1992 universities are concerned. I will ask Mr Forrester to speak on FE.

DAVID FORRESTER: Chairman, if I may, again I have very little to add, in the sense that the picture is really quite similar. It is of course in no way the intention that the requirement of accountability to the local business community that is essential for further education colleges, which are essentially serving a local employer market, a local labour market, should lead to the composition of the governing body being essentially white, middle-aged male——

WILLIAM UTTING: Elderly males in my case!

DAVID FORRESTER:—as I have seen previous witnesses suggest to the Committee, but it is indeed a fact

of life across public life, as many of us are aware, that one has to work quite hard to seek to address that balance. I think it is fair to say that many colleges are conscious themselves of that need, that they have in place search committees or other formal procedures to try to widen their composition. I think it was Sir Robert Gunn who said to you at an earlier point, and reminded ourselves, that these institutions and their governing bodies are on the whole in their first round of membership. I am sure that for their second round, as they come up to renewal and changes, with the natural turn-over of governors, they will be looking to widen the coverage in the way that the Government has been seeking to do in relation to those bodies that it appoints.

WILLIAM UTTING: I think you say in your evidence that no specific guidance has been issued on these points. It may be that guidance might be a more appropriate and easier vehicle to produce change than altering statute, if change is needed.

DAVID FORRESTER: We certainly would not rule out guidance. There is nothing in the various codes of practice and the various guidance at present. There has been guidance both from the Further Education Funding Council and from the representative bodies of the colleges, which I think included something about equal opportunities and extending the membership, but, if it did not, that is certainly something that we would be very happy to look at with them.

TONY CLARK: It is certainly the case, if I may just add to that, that in the post-1992 universities there is guidance about opening up the nominations process, not specifically on the point that you have raised. So that at least gives, as I say, opportunities to a wider section of the community to have their names put forward.

996. WILLIAM UTTING: Thank you. Could I move on to some of these intermediary bodies that exist between the institutions that we are concerned with and the Department? They seemed to be described in various ways, as funding bodies or supervisory bodies or regulatory bodies, and I am interested that a body like the FEFCE combines not only funding but also a quality assurance element, in that it has its own inspectorate, and that the HEFCE, in addition to funding, carries out assessments, both of research and of teaching. How would you describe bodies that exercise those sorts of functions? They are rather more than funding. Are they supervisory or do they go as far as being regulatory?

TONY CLARK: Perhaps I could start and then Mr Forrester will come in. There is a distinction between the Higher Education Funding Council and the Further Education Funding Council, which I am sure Mr Forrester will come on to, in the sense that the Further Education Funding Council has wider responsibilities in terms of planning. The Higher Education Funding Council is essentially a funding body, but, as one might expect with a funding body, it has responsibilities for accountability as well. I would see its quality assessment role as relating to that accountability interest. That is to say, it needs to satisfy itself that the money which it is allocating is not only used for the purpose for which it is intended but that it is being well used for that purpose. So I have seen the assessment process as being part of that. It may also influence, and indeed it does in a limited way, the distribution of funds, because quite clearly if you have a limited amount of money and you want to expand, you might want to expand in areas where there is high quality rather than low quality. So there is a case also for the assessment regime to relate to the distribution. But I see the role primarily as one of accountability.

DAVID FORRESTER: Chairman, through you, if I may, that applies very much also to the Further Education Funding Council, but I would make two additional points about that. First, as regards its remit, it does have statutory responsibility for securing adequate and sufficient provision for further education, particularly for 16 to 19-year-olds but also for all ages. That is a very major responsibility and, exercising that, it has to have regard to issues not only of quality in order to underpin its funding, but also obviously to securing an adequate range of provision across the country.

The second point I would make is that the quality assurance responsibility which it has, which to some extent parallels that of the Higher Education Funding Council, is deliberately set at one remove from the Funding Council. Although it is a responsibility of the Funding Council, what the Council has chosen to do is establish a committee which does not include any members of the Council to which the inspectorate of the FEFCE is answerable. That is seen as giving a measure of independence so that it is somewhere between the Funding Council and the client bodies, the colleges that are funded.

As to whether that is a regulatory model, I do not think it is particularly helpful to describe it as that because that carries overtones of the sort of Oftel or Ofgas regulator, and it is not quite like that, but there is obviously a power of regulation to do with the attachment of conditions of grant and that is the key function of the body. It is essentially a funding body and it would be irresponsible of it not to have powers and not to exercise powers to attach conditions and to put itself in a position to attach conditions on the basis of good evidence.

WILLIAM UTTING: Both bodies were tactful in describing their role to us in that respect. I was actually going to come on to grant-maintained schools. Perhaps you would like to offer an answer before I ask the question.

PETER SHAW: All I was going to say there was that the FAS role is different again to FEFCE and HEFCE because of the particular circumstances. The quality control is the principal responsibility of Ofsted because it is looking across not only grant-maintained schools but also LEA maintained schools. So, it is important that the inspection body, in terms of educational content, is looking across both sectors and that is a structural difference to the circumstances in FE or HE. So, the educational quality inspection responsibilities are with Ofsted.

FAS, as well as having strictly funding responsibilities in terms of the payment of grant and the financial monitoring of schools expenditure, also has a responsibility to ensure that sufficient school places are available in certain parts of the country and certain authorities where the proportion of grant-maintained schools is above a certain level. Again, that is because of the particular circumstances of grant-maintained schools which are different to HE and FE.

WILLIAM UTTING: Yes. My concern was that the value for money elements might not be quite so well integrated as far as grant-maintained schools are concerned as they are in the further and higher education sector. That was really my point.

PETER SHAW: I think both FAS and Ofsted are very concerned about value for money through their different ways. The key role though of Ofsted has got to be both LEA maintained and grant-maintained and because of that reason there is a separation.

WILLIAM UTTING: Yes, I appreciate that, boundary problems wherever you draw the line. Chairman, thank you.

997. MARTIN JACOMB: I would just like to follow up what Sir William was asking you. I think it was Mr Shaw who drew a distinction between financial management on the one hand and management on the other but what I would like to ask you is this. Most of these bodies are the subject of a financial memorandum which is quite a long and detailed basis on which you extract accountability. Is that right?

PETER SHAW: Yes. There is a financial memorandum both between us and FAS and then FAS have a financial memorandum in relation to each institution.

998. MARTIN JACOMB: Right, and this applies to nearly all the bodies, does it not? It is a very detailed thing and it gives rise to the paradox that the more accountability you extract in that way, the more your responsibility is for ensuring that the institutions are managed correctly. That is a paradox of extracting detailed accountability, is it not?

DAVID FORRESTER: Chairman, could I attempt a comment, not necessarily a direct answer. The principle is that all these institutions should, to the greatest extent possible, be independent and self-governing and stand on their own two feet. The framework within which they operate is a competitive one, one where they are responsible for large sums of public money and, therefore, it is right and proper there should be quite a detailed financial memorandum that specifies that.

The onus for securing an adequate response rests essentially with the individual institutions and, as I was hinting before when we were contrasting the position of further education colleges with that of the private training providers, the TECs fund, these institutions do not have, and do not see themselves as having, a God-given statutory right to permanent existence. They have to fend for themselves now. They are in a competitive market. Of course, they are in receipt of public funds but there is not an automatic responsibility on someone else to support them in perpetuity. The real responsibility rests in the individual institution.

Now, in order to have a system and a network that copes with that there is a measure of responsibility also to provide benchmarking, indications of good practice, support mechanisms and in each sector, I think it is fair to say, these have been developed and are being developed all the time. I come back to say again the responsibility rests principally in the individual institution.

999. MARTIN JACOMB: So, insofar as it arrives at your end it is like a longstop, is it?

DAVID FORRESTER: Yes.

1000. MARTIN JACOMB: Could I just ask you this. One of the things you principally look at is the financial management, as it has been described, and how the money is actually spent and how the buildings are looked after and whether people are paid too much, and all that kind of stuff. That being the case, how do you begin to judge value for money without directly relating all that to the quality of the output?

DAVID FORRESTER: I do not want to hog all the questions but perhaps I will say something initially and then my colleagues doubtless will come in.

First, of course, the principal responsibility for that monitoring rests in each case with the intermediary body, the funding body, and if you are thinking of the Secretary of State and her officials, we would be looking to that body to be discharging those responsibilities. We, in turn, in order to be satisfied that the body knew what was going on, would expect it to have mechanisms, obviously, of audit, inspection, monitoring, information and some way of digesting that information.

The Further Education Funding Council, for example, from next year will be including in its annual report performance indicators and measuring the achievement of its institutions against those indicators and those will be giving an indication of quality but the quality ultimately is judged principally, obviously, by reference to whether people attain the qualification they were seeking, notably in further education where, I think it is fair to say, all students are there essentially to gain a qualification, but also through the inspection system which gives quite detailed advice and information on the quality institution by institution.

PETER SHAW: Could I say something in relation to grant-maintained schools. The Department regards itself as having a role in promoting good management within grant-maintained schools as well as issuing detailed guides to the law and what the formal responsibilities are. We worked up with Ofsted some brief documents trying to set out very clearly annotated agendas for governing bodies to consider about what their priorities are, what their management priorities are, deliberately doing it quite shortly so that governing bodies can use that in discussion. These were *"Governing Bodies in Effective Schools"*, also *"Lessons in Teamwork"* which is an Audit Commission and Ofsted document again designed to put forward examples of good practice to be pressing governing bodies to be looking at the value for money issues across the whole patch for which they are responsible.

There is also work in progress at the moment about the preparation of a code of practice within grant-maintained schools. The lead on that has been with the NAHT and the "Action for Governors Information and Training" working with the Department and other bodies. This would address things like the relationship between the head and the governing body but also standards and the work of the governing body more generally. So, that is one approach by the government not being absolutely prescriptive but working with the relevant bodies to produce clear publications to assist and also working now to assist NAHT and HEIT and other bodies like the Grant Maintained Schools Advisory Committee to put together a standard code of practice.

1001. MARTIN JACOMB: Yes, thank you very much. Could I just ask one final and very general question. I am coupling you, I think,—the Department—with the intermediate agencies, NDPBs if I can call it that. Do you think the level of accountability and the types of accountability being extracted from the institutions has gone about as far as it can go? If you take, for example, a restaurant the requirements of its kitchen being clean are treated as more important than the quality of the cooking?

TONY CLARK: I will be bold enough to make one comment as far as higher education is concerned. One of the problems there, in terms of accountability, is that the standard of the qualification, which in other sectors is standardised externally, is solely a matter for individual institutions and so it is difficult to measure output because the standards of qualifications may vary. In that area, I think there is scope for doing even more than we are doing at the moment in terms of accountability and, indeed, the Secretary of State is pressing the academic community to seek to draw together common threshold standards. That is an area where there is perhaps even more to do.

Generally speaking, I would say that the accountability that is required of universities by the Funding Council is recognised by the universities to be a reasonable requirement in relation to the very substantial sums of public money that the Funding Council is distributing—a substantial sum of money and, what is more, a significant proportion still of the income which universities receive.

PETER SHAW: As far as grant-maintained schools are concerned, the memorandum which we have put in listed about ten types of accountability, some of which are relatively new in terms of the regular Ofsted cycle and the action plan requirement in certain cases. Also, the publication of pupils' examination results is another form of accountability to parents and the local community. So, it is quite wide ranging.

I know the FAS has reviewed this year the Rainbow Pack to see whether that has the right balance between freedom and discretion on the one hand and financial clarity and accountability on the other. I think they have made some changes, including the requirement for setting up a register of interests at school level. I posed your very question to a group of grant-maintained heads last week and said, "Is the burden too much?" and their general response was that they welcomed the financial security which came from fulfilling the requirements of the Rainbow Pack which the FAS issue and they were glad that there were clear procedures that they had to follow, so I did not get from them any strong reaction against the auditing requirements.

What they did draw to my attention was general relief and pleasure that in the words of the NAO report recently, the schools they visited were generally well managed to secure propriety and financial control. Clearly, I think it is right that FAS and the Department keep an eye on the accountability requirements for the reason you suggested, that they just do not get more and more without periodically looking to see whether the balance is right.

MARTIN JACOMB: Thank you very much.

LORD NOLAN: Our hour is up but your evidence is of such interest that I know at least one or two members of the Committee would like to ask a short further question. I know Professor King is one of them.

1002. PROF ANTHONY KING: It will be very short and very general. Whether the answers will be, I am not sure.

The question is this. In a situation in the world of education and training when money is perpetually short and when the way in which the money is distributed depends to a very considerable extent on throughput and output, there obviously is inevitably downward pressure on academic standards. That pressure may be resisted or it may not be resisted. We have had some evidence before this Committee of problems in this connection and as a university teacher and administrator I am very conscious of these pressures. What kind of thought is being given in the Department to this endemic problem, given the funding situation?

TONY CLARK: Well, I guess that is a matter that relates to higher education as much as to any of the sectors we are talking about this morning. The simple answer to your question is that in the universities at least they are responsible for academic standards, they have to take the action that is required to ensure that the pressures to which you have referred do not lead to a reduction in academic standards. We have from time to time received assurances from the academic community that despite the pressures to which you have referred those academic standards have been maintained.

1003. PROF ANTHONY KING: But they would say that, would they not?

TONY CLARK: Not a unanimous view, I have to say, but that is the view that we receive. Your question, I think, is what can the Department or the Funding Council do to assist in this and all I can say there is that the Funding Council do fund a number of initiatives that are indeed designed to provide even more value for money within universities. These are initiatives concerned with such things as new technologies in teaching designed to assist universities in improving the efficiency of their operations. There are initiatives of that kind from the Funding Council to assist what I think is primarily a task for the institutions.

LORD NOLAN: Dame Anne, do you have a question to ask?

1004. ANNE WARBURTON: Chairman, yes, I would like to ask two quick questions, please, on which I think it would be useful to have the Department's views. Your memorandum specifically omits from consideration the structures of Oxford and Cambridge. I think this has been true, in fact, of all the general studies we have had of the sector. I just wondered what your advice to us was on that point.

TONY CLARK: I am inclined to say leave well alone.

ANNE WARBURTON: Shall I go on to the next question then?

TONY CLARK: They are the only universities—and I think this point has already been made to you in evidence—that do not have external independent people on their main governing bodies. On the other hand, their constitution is really quite different from any other university in the sense that they comprise a group of individual colleges and their parent university and so, in a sense, there is a degree of externality provided by the independence of the different colleges.

My advice is this. If one is willing to accept that as an argument then the present system is suitable for its purpose. To a large extent I think one would have to say that the two universities concerned in terms of reputation, output and everything else, have performed extremely well. In all the measures that one can think of they perform extremely well. I come to the conclusion that the universities concerned could be encouraged to review their arrangements. Indeed, Cambridge reviewed theirs a few years back and Oxford are in the process of reviewing their arrangements. I would be inclined to leave it on that basis.

1005. ANNE WARBURTON: Thank you very much. The second question arises from one of the answers which I think you, Mr Clark, gave to the chairman. You made it clear that you did not think that compensation was appropriate for the voluntary members of governing bodies, and so forth, but I do not think you mentioned the question of time off, perhaps on the lines of jury duty. Would there be any possibility that perhaps there might be official encouragement to employers to give time off for a certain amount of public service in the educational sector.

TONY CLARK: I think if this was seen to be a significant problem we could raise this with the employer representatives, yes. Yes.

DAVID FORRESTER: Chairman, I think it would be fair to say that the Department would see it as part of its new mission as an integrated Department for Education and Employment to seek to promote best practice in that regard and certainly to encourage that. We have a newly established integrated division responsible for all links between education and business at large to bring together an improved, coherent view on that and that is something that I would think would be on their agenda.

Whether one would go further—and I think you are implying one might although you did not directly ask us to consider that—and give it as some sort of statutory entitlement I think is another question but I think encouragement would be what responsible bodies would expect to receive anyway.

ANNE WARBURTON: Thank you.

LORD NOLAN: Thank you all very much indeed. You leave us much better educated than we were an hour ago.

1006. LORD NOLAN: Sir Geoffrey Chandler and Mr Etherington, good morning. Thank you very much for coming along and for the written material which you have already supplied to us. It included an opening statement which is very helpful. I wonder, Sir Geoffrey, if I am right in thinking that you were minded not so much to read it out as to pick out the points made in it by way of introduction.

SIR GEOFFREY CHANDLER CBE
AND STUART ETHERINGTON

SIR GEOFFREY CHANDLER CBE (Chair, National Council for Voluntary Organisations): Chairman, thank you very much indeed. Certainly, not to read it out and only some very brief words; really to say we much appreciate this opportunity for two reasons. Partly because public sector bodies impact on voluntary organisations at many points and, secondly, because the aspects of governance you are looking at have a very strong resonance in the voluntary sector.

If I say that the voluntary sector is ahead of the game, that is not meant to be complacency or that we think we have got it right but that we have been tackling this subject in principle for a good many years. We regard the voluntary sector as value-led and, therefore, governance has to reflect those values and that purpose and, therefore, issues such as openness, representativeness, accessibility, equal opportunities, have to be reflected in governance and those are not incompatible with effectiveness. It is for that reason that the Commission on the Voluntary Sector, which we set up but it is independent of us, has governance as one of its main tranches of examination. Within NCVO we set up three years ago the Trustee Services Unit which is to advise our membership and the sector at large about governance issues and trusteeship issues and in that we work very closely with the Charity Commission.

That is really all I would like to say to emphasise some of the values within the sector which we think are particularly relevant to our chief problem area, which we see as TECs, and if I anticipate the first part of the first question on the exam paper, my answer would be "No".

LORD NOLAN: We shall have to see if you have anticipated rightly. Of course, the voluntary sector is absolutely central to this stage of our inquiry and so we are particularly glad to have you here for that reason alone.

In this Committee we try to practice, amongst other things, equality of opportunity regardless of gender and, on that basis, it is Professor King's turn to ask the questions. He will be supported by Dame Anne Warburton.

1007. PROF ANTHONY KING: I am not sure I know the question to that answer. I think I can guess and perhaps we will come back to it. Since we are running a bit late, can I just pick out a few points from your very extensive submission which I read with enormous interest. I think if I had read it without knowing anything at all about the sector we are looking at I would have come to the conclusion from what you have said that it must be in truly terrible shape, that there must be all kinds of dreadful problems besetting it. You use language like——

"the suspicion of (these bodies) being shadowy creatures operating in a semi-secret world"

and there is a good deal of language of that character, references to suspicion and mistrust.

Can you say, in very general terms, how serious you think the problems really are?

GEOFFREY CHANDLER: We are now talking about the TECs?

PROF ANTHONY KING: You more or less invited us to focus on the TECs.

GEOFFREY CHANDLER: Indeed, those adjectives or epithets did not apply to the voluntary sector but the TECs. Yes, I think it starts with the fact that these are very curious animals. They are, in a sense, an unknown species. They are limited companies. They are monopolies. They are supplied by public money. I think our main concern is because they are animals which interact with the community their governance is of a kind that prevents that interaction. Some of the attributes I described in our own examination of governance—openness, communication, involvement and particularly, as we see it in the voluntary sector, involvement of the consumers, those who actually use the money and the services—we think is totally inadequate.

1008. PROF ANTHONY KING: Could you spell that out a little bit more because the people who have given evidence to us from the world of the TECs, if I may say so, paint a totally different picture and lay enormous stress on their openness, their accountability. They claim they have all the characteristics that you claim they do not have. Can you just say a little bit more about why, in your judgment, they are wrong?

GEOFFREY CHANDLER: Openness is in the eye of the beholder. If you look at the governing boards of TECs we would say that there is inadequate representation—of course, this is not the case in all TECs—the ability of the voluntary sector to know who the governing boards are. There are no job descriptions or person descriptions which one might expect for this sort of body. There is inadequate advertising of the openings on governing bodies and, on the whole, they operate, if I may say so as someone who was an industrial manager, with the closed spirit of an industrial company rather than something which should be rooted in the community. In many ways they ought to be nearer a voluntary body in the spirit in which they operate rather than an industrial company which, as an aside I would say, is one of our reasons for fearing that the Association of Chambers of Commerce would compound the problem.

1009. PROF ANTHONY KING: Could you say a little bit more about that specific point. What do you think would be the adverse consequences of a tendency for TECs which is developing to merge with Chambers of Commerce?

GEOFFREY CHANDLER: As an aside, I would say in most cases Chambers of Commerce are extremely weak entities and that in itself is a problem. It would increase the dominance of the business side of TECs and, as I was implying earlier, I think that needs to be diluted or enriched with people who are the consumers. I think Chambers of Commerce have a totally different objective from TECs and, therefore, you are marrying like with unlike.

1010. PROF ANTHONY KING: Going back to the more general point, you say at one point in your submission:

It is a widely held view that the members of TEC boards abuse their position of trust to benefit their private sector companies, or the companies of other members of the same beneficiary group".

You say that it is a widely held view. When my students use that kind of formulation I always say, "Do you hold that view?"

STUART ETHERINGTON (Chief Executive, National Council for Voluntary Organisations): As we indicated in our submission, it is mainly based on the fact that we actually run a network of voluntary sector providers and certainly it is the view of those people who most intimately understand and know the TECs and have direct experience of trying to provide services to them that there is a sense in which they are becoming self-perpetuating. There is a sense in which they are closing off elements of the community in the voluntary sector and not really giving a clear indication of why that is happening. Certainly, that is their view and they would have the most intimate knowledge of TECs as far as the voluntary sector was concerned.

PROF ANTHONY KING: The suggestion here being that they are doing it partly in order to line the pockets of themselves and their friends.

STUART ETHERINGTON: I would not say necessarily that there could be a direct conclusion that they are actually involved in corrupt practices but the suspicion has arisen because of a growing lack of openness by TECs in the way that they actually undertake their business.

1011. PROF ANTHONY KING: A growing lack of openness?

STUART ETHERINGTON: That is certainly true. Amongst voluntary organisations that we have contact with there is, I think, a growing suspicion that they are being closed out of decision making when they actually represent quite an important local constituency. There is also fear, I think, that TECs are expanding their role into areas in which the voluntary sector itself has been traditionally more involved. So, there is a growing fear at a local level that relatively unaccountable bodies are beginning to take on wider roles that were traditionally the roles of the voluntary sector but also that even in the roles that they are actually being required to play the voluntary sector should have an important say in their governing bodies and that is not actually happening.

GEOFFREY CHANDLER: Might I just add to that. Given Richard Branson this morning, we would not dream of libelling individual members of TECs by suggesting they are lining their pockets, but the sufferers when things go wrong have often been the voluntary bodies, and the network to which Stuart referred has suffered considerable pain when the policies—and they may be Government policies—interpreted through TECs have changed and voluntary bodies have lost many millions of pounds when they have geared up for particular programmes which have then been changed.

When the South Thames TEC went into bankruptcy, the voluntary bodies were insufficiently aware of what lay behind it and had insufficient knowledge that this could happen which, again, comes back to the secretiveness. Had they had greater knowledge they could have made some preparation because they could perhaps have anticipated what was happening. So, if the wording was coloured it is because these organisations are suffering.

1012. PROF ANTHONY KING: Looking at the general problem and looking at TECs in what is already their traditional role, leaving aside the question of whether they are expanding their role, what would you like to see us recommend in connection with the governance and operation of TECs that would mitigate the kind of problems you have been referring to?

GEOFFREY CHANDLER: The setting of standards, I think, in the first instance is essential so TECs operate to standards which would relate to communication, which would relate to openness. We have mooted a regulatory body. One can say pejoratively that is another layer of bureaucracy but I actually think the regulation is more important than if it is interposing something different. There are a whole number of things and I think this is where the voluntary sector has attributes it could offer in shaping a TEC to its purpose.

If you are going into the deeper question that do TECs do their job in their community, that is a much deeper and more political question. I think they take on far too wide a scope but I think that is outside the ambit of your consideration probably.

1013. PROF ANTHONY KING: Just one very specific final question, although I have lots of others and if provoked I will ask those too. You mention the possibility of setting up what you call a new King's Fund Library. Could you say a little bit more about what you have in mind and, more particularly, what good you think this would do?

STUART ETHERINGTON: I think it is about reassurance and it is also about the way in which information is made available and the general thrust of our evidence to you is about openness, about demonstrable standards, about regulation where regulation does not exist. The issue about the availability of information is quite critical. I think it is important not to blanket the whole thing and some TECs are actually quite good at making available information locally about what they are doing but the problem is that not all are, some appear extremely secretive.

If there was a requirement to have a depository of information about TECs which was accessible then I think that would be reassuring. The sorts of things that I think we would like to see in there are what their annual plans are, what their overall corporate objectives are, listings of their board members, publishing of the audit, of training needs locally. That would be extremely useful not only in reassuring people that actually this was open, that the work was being done, but also in actually providing a comprehensive view of what TECs were doing and that would not only make them more transparent in their operation, it would enable information to be available for policy analysis of what they are doing as well and that would, I think, be quite useful. Some centre of information about what TECs are doing, I think, would be reassuring to the voluntary sector.

1014. PROF ANTHONY KING: What are the principal problems the solution to which might be aided by having such a depository?

STUART ETHERINGTON: I think there are two. One is that not all TECs make information available easily and that means that you have to work extremely hard to find out what is actually going on and voluntary sector organisations are often not equipped to do that.

The second reason is that I think it will allow an easier way of actually analysing what they are doing over all, which is actually quite difficult for voluntary organisations to do.

PROF ANTHONY KING: Thank you.

LORD NOLAN: Dame Anne?

1015. ANNE WARBURTON: Thank you, chairman. Could I ask you another question about TECs. We seem to have focused on that in some way. We heard last week from a representative of a TEC of concern that in the process of lifelong education there was some duplication but he was even more worried about gaps, that, as he put it, customers could disappear and that was a bad thing. He was indicating that perhaps TECs were rather well placed to make sure, to co-ordinate a bit better between different bodies concerned with persons from the age of 16 onwards. I wonder whether this is a point which has engaged your attention and what you think about it.

GEOFFREY CHANDLER: I think if one were to interpret this into special needs training where the voluntary sector has a particular strength, yes indeed we would expect TECs to support voluntary sector bodies to fill what could otherwise be a gap. If I might just turn that into a concern, it is a particular concern where there are TECs which do not give sufficient attention to special needs. Would you add to that, Stuart?

STUART ETHERINGTON: Yes, I would just reinforce that point. The special needs issue is absolutely critical for the voluntary sector's relationship with TECs. It is there where they actually are major stakeholders. It is mainly voluntary organisations that are providing that particular training.

Our concern would be if it was lifelong learning, and some of it may well be now, if TECs are moving away from just training for work and beginning to see training, lifelong learning, as a much more comprehensive intervention within local communities then the role of voluntary organisations would become much more critical in terms of actually providing that because they would be in a better position to do that than what one might call formal training providers for work.

Our experience has been—and it is not an issue of probity, it is an issue of the way in which special needs training is structured—that, in fact, many voluntary organisations are finding it increasingly difficult to provide special needs training because the outcome conditions that are being placed on TECs are such that it actually dissuades them from engaging in that.

I would welcome the thought that TECs may be involved in a wider area of lifelong learning but the *quid pro quo* for that seems to me is (a) that the outcome-related funding issues need to be revisited to ensure that they are in a position to provide that and (b) because of the absolute centrality of voluntary organisations to that area of work then it seems to me they would have to engage the voluntary sector more both in discussions about their policies but also in serving on their boards.

1016. ANNE WARBURTON: I was thinking of asking you whether you have adequate opportunities to discuss these things with TECs and perhaps more widely in communities either at national level or locally.

STUART ETHERINGTON: Certainly, at national level we have not engaged in a lot of those arguments. I think we have found TECs reluctant to engage in discussions with the voluntary sector at a national level. At a local level, our experience varies. Some TECs are quite keen to engage the voluntary sector, and we have several examples of them. Some TECs are members of the Training and Enterprise Network which NCVO runs and, therefore, they are showing their willingness to engage in the debate. Some TECs do not and our worry is that, if anything, we detect a move away because of a whole range of issues—an increasing business focus, changes in funding patterns, all of those things—a move away from engaging the voluntary sector so it will make it slightly more difficult in the future unless there are requirements on TECs to involve the community, to involve voluntary organisations.

1017. ANNE WARBURTON: Thank you very much. Could I ask just one more question. You recommend the introduction of Ombudsmen. I say it in the plural. I think you intended a different one for each of the local public spending bodies. Would you care to say anything more about that because not everyone we have talked to has agreed that an Ombudsman is needed or would be helpful.

STUART ETHERINGTON: Our argument would be that there should be a different one but they should be operating to general principles which apply to all Local Public Spending Bodies. The reason I think there should be, or some relationship with the regulatory structure is that there are options there, whether it is an Ombudsman or some appeal mechanism to a regulatory structure, which currently does not exist for TECs.

Let me give you an example of that which might illustrate the case. A voluntary organisation could be engaged in a clear contractual relationship with a TEC to provide a service for people with special needs and that contract is removed. That does happen, there are examples of that and on occasion no clear explanation is given as to why that contract has been removed or how the voluntary organisation has failed to meet the standards being set by the TEC. In those circumstances, it seems to me to be quite important that voluntary agencies have a right of appeal about that particular contract. It may be critically important in terms of the voluntary organisation's programme of work. That has to be independent from the TEC's governing body itself. There has to be some form of open appeal mechanism when contracts are cancelled.

Some of that appears to be happening in a fairly arbitrary way with very little explanation being given as to why it is happening, which is why I think we need some form of open appeal structure. Whether that is an Ombudsman or whether that is some relationship with a regulatory framework we do not have particularly strong views on.

ANNE WARBURTON: Thank you very much.

LORD NOLAN: I know Lord Thomson would like to ask you a question.

1018. LORD THOMSON: I have two questions, one very specific and brief. Would it be helpful if there was a mandatory requirement on TECs in their annual reports, as I think there is a legal requirement on local authorities, to provide a list of the organisations with which they have entered into contracts during the particular year of the annual report and the value of these contracts?

GEOFFREY CHANDLER: My direct answer would be yes, certainly. We believe there is very little justification for commercial secrecy in TECs. The question is raised at some point, should minutes be available to which my response would be, "Why not?". Commercial secrecy on the whole is simply not justified and the terms of contracts and the terms of the relationship of government funding to those contracts, which is often obscure, is most important and, yes indeed, we would support that.

1019. LORD THOMSON: That would then be an open record of any TEC board member whose companies were in contractual relationship with the TEC itself?

GEOFFREY CHANDLER: That is correct.

1020. LORD THOMSON: Thank you. I would also quite like to hear your view on the problem of liability these days for trustees and members of voluntary organisations. I do not know whether you heard the departmental evidence which was very interesting in answer to the chairman's question, but there is obviously a grey area here in the case of TECs as you have mentioned. There was one case where voluntary organisations found themselves liable for the losses because the Government did not stand behind the TEC. Is it your view that the Government stands behind grant-maintained schools or further education colleges if they get into trouble or would voluntary organisations who were providers in these cases simply find themselves liable, as they did in the TEC case?

GEOFFREY CHANDLER: Of course we have fewer members on that front. Can you respond on that, Stuart?

STUART ETHERINGTON: No not really. I can just reflect not on the question of the government standing behind organisations, but our experience in terms of the liability of trustees from our own field, if that would be helpful. In relation to our own field trustees of voluntary organisations actually have unlimited liability, and one of the reasons why it is actually quite difficult to attract people to serve on bodies of this kind, and increasingly difficult to attract charity trustees, is that since the passage of the recent Charities Act it has become much clearer that you have unlimited liability. For a whole range of community organisations who are registered charities, and some who are associations, they have unlimited liability and people are not coming forward for the very reason that they face unlimited liability. I think it is a deterrent in actually people coming forward to serve on trustee boards, and the same would apply to some other local organisations, so that is one particular problem. We have been pushing in other spheres to create legal entities which combine elements of limited liability and trusteeship, because at the moment there is an extremely complex situation where you are trustees of a charity and also directors of the limited company which constitutes the same entity. There are very few test cases as to what happens when that comes collapsing down. We think that the legal structure needs clarifying. If it were, and this is

just speculative, there is no reason that some of these bodies could not actually be constituted with that sort of legal form.

GEOFFREY CHANDLER: If I could, Lord Thomson, just pursue that a little further, perhaps you do not want to go down that route. When we surveyed trustees we found there were half a million in the country of whom 75 per cent did not know they were trustees, therefore in law with unlimited obligation. Again, the majority are white middle class and middle aged, and one of the things we have been looking at is how you attract other parts of society into it, and the whole question of payment or time off comes into it. We have a great problem of pluralism, a lot of people who have a lot of trusteeships, but at the end of the day we are trying to spread it which is a related problem.

LORD THOMSON: Thank you very much, you interest me greatly. Thank you.

1021. LORD NOLAN: I know that there is at least one other question to come. I wonder if I could take a turn on the way and ask you about housing associations which, unlike the other local public spending bodies, are considered to be an important part of the voluntary sector. I am concerned really to hear your views on the larger and growing housing associations which one finds often spanning a number of counties, and depending to a substantial extent on public money but also to a very considerable extent on privately raised funds, and assuming in some respects the appearance of large property investment companies. The difficulties they encounter in maintaining local contacts with tenants and with councils are therefore greater because of their diverse locations. Have you given any thought or had any worries about the need for special arrangements for the larger housing associations, particular in matters of openness?

STUART ETHERINGTON: Yes, I think the tradition of housing associations is different from some of the other public spending bodies that you are examining in that their history is within the voluntary sector. I think the difference that has happened to them is that there has been a massive injection of public funds and they have become an instrument of housing policy in a slightly different way. I think what they have demonstrated though, particularly the NFHA's work on governance, is that they actually have tried to address these issues head on. Where they do meet problems is when they are no longer local, as you say. They actually have pockets of housing development across the country. I think that they have to find ways of having more localised management structures in those circumstances where tenants can actually relate more closely to local housing management, because if they do not do that they are likely to become extremely remote from the people for whom they are actually there to provide services. This is true also, I think, because they are increasingly developing in areas like community care services in order to expand their area of operation.

So my answer to your question is that they have actually got to develop more localised forms of housing management and control in order to offset the fact that they are now quite large and national organisations with often pockets of localised housing across the country.

1022. LORD NOLAN: Will you be playing a part in this? Is it within your sphere to offer advice?

STUART ETHERINGTON: We certainly have contacts with the National Federation of Housing Associations and our member organisations would.

1023. WILLIAM UTTING: I wonder if you had any feedback from your constituency about the makeup of the governing bodies of further education colleges? The rules say that at least half the members must be business people, but there is provision for representatives of community organisations. I wonder whether people told you whether this worked and whether the community was sufficiently represented on these governing bodies?

STUART ETHERINGTON: We do not have any information on that because it is the least well developed part of our own constituency, but certainly, if it would be helpful to the committee, we could find out.[3]

WILLIAM UTTING: That would be very helpful, thank you.

1024. LORD NOLAN: Thank you very much indeed, gentlemen. It has been a very useful and interesting half hour you have given us, thank you very much for coming.

Good morning, Professor, and thank you very much for coming along to talk to us today. You are here representing an institution which has had a troubled past but, of course, we do not so much want to go into that unless you have things to say about it in so far as it has provided lessons for the future. Is there any opening statement you would like to make before we go straight into the questions?

PROFESSOR JOHN TARRANT

Opening Statement (see page 290)

PROF JOHN TARRANT: Thank you, I should make one or two preliminary statements. Firstly, although I am here as the Vice-Chancellor of the University of Huddersfield, I am not really representing the institution here today. I regard myself as being here in a personal capacity, and the submission I made to you was also made in a personal capacity. I think that is important both because my views are not necessarily shared by the entire Council of the university, nor, indeed, by the entire staff of the university. Nor, I believe, are my views necessarily shared by my fellow vice-chancellors of the new universities.

Finally, I come at this session today with very limited experience indeed of the new university sector. I have been in office about eight weeks, and all the management guidebooks tell you not to make a decision in the first six weeks. Well, we are only just past the first six weeks, so I come very much as a new boy. That is all I need to say I think.

LORD NOLAN: Thank you very much. We take it in turns to ask questions of our witnesses and I will ask Lord Thomson to begin in your case.

1025. LORD THOMSON: On the other hand, Professor, first impressions are often particularly vivid and valuable and perhaps to us who are not an investigatory body, but we look for lessons out of troubled situations that may be helpful more generally in terms of good governance. I just wondered what your first impressions were of the lessons that might be learnt out of the troubles of the past at Huddersfield?

PROF JOHN TARRANT: Again, I have to stress I was not at Huddersfield during the troubles, and the public understanding of what the troubles were all about is only one dimension. I think there were many other dimensions to the stresses and strains inside the organisation during that 18 months to two-year period. I think what we saw, the removal of staff and students from the governing bodies and the remuneration package for the previous incumbent, were just the surface of a breakdown of trust and confidence within the organisation, both upwards and downwards. There was a substantial loss of trust by the academic community in the governors and by the governors in the academic community.

The lesson I think I come away with in so far as I know the details of what happened is that universities have three characteristics which make them rather different from some other public bodies, and therefore perhaps make the style of governance which the Education Act imposed upon the new universities not entirely appropriate. Those three, I think, are: first of all in universities we guard jealously academic freedom and the right to dissent, and to dissent publicly. You could say we almost encourage dissent, and the management of an organisation, and the governance of an organisation that positively encourages dissent is, as I say in my submission, slightly more challenging than it is in some other types of organisation, and requires a different sort of hand on the tiller than might be true in some other bodies.

The second characteristic is the diversity contained within universities. Again I make reference to the fact that the culture and traditions and ways of behaving in a physics department are light years away from the way in which faculty in a music department might interact with each other and wish to be managed and manage themselves. There is a great deal of internal diversity which we need to maintain and hang on to.

Thirdly, because of the nature of universities and the emphasis on individual work, the outcome of a university is the summation of individuals and teams all working away to some degree independently of each other. The governance and the governance structures of universities require a high degree of common ownership, and that responsibility implies on the one hand and trust on the other.

Those three dimensions, I think, make for the need for a style of governance which is more broadly based than that which is enabled by the Act. A rather rambling answer, forgive me.

1026. LORD THOMSON: Not at all, it is a very helpful answer. Would you conclude from that that we ought to be thinking about recommending that the 1992 Act requires some changes in terms of the new universities?

PROF JOHN TARRANT: I am cautious on three grounds in recommending changes in legislation. One it takes a long time. Two the legislation has been seen to work in the great majority of the new universities, and I do not in any way wish to appear to be denigrating what has gone on in other new universities. I come with a particular perspective which is different from some of my fellow vice-chancellors in the new universities in coming from an institution where it has not entirely worked. The third reason why I am cautious about change in the legislation is

---

[3]*See* Evidence, pp. 470.

that I am not sure we can legislate against the sort of incidents which happened in some of the new universities. I think incidents like that may well arise regardless of what the legislation says.

However, I would like a bit more flexibility than is provided for me in the legislation about the makeup, the constitution and size of the governing council. I would like the constitution more flexible, I would like the size rather larger.

1027. LORD THOMSON: Do I take it from that that you would feel it an advantage to have a wider consultative body? Do you have the impression one could have that without changes in the Act? Can you do that within the present provisions? It would be rather like a University Court in an older university.

PROF JOHN TARRANT: I can certainly set up something like a University Court without a change in the legislation. It would not be a Court, it would not have the powers that a Court has, but it would have many of the functions that a Court has. I could do that and in fact I am working towards persuading my council to do that now. No, I think it is in the governing council itself where the legislation comes to bear most critically. I am confident we can make it work within the legislation. I would be just slightly more comfortable if the legislation allowed me to increase the size of the council and to increase the diversity of membership of the council.

1028. LORD THOMSON: Does the council now have staff and student members of the governing body? What has happened?

PROF JOHN TARRANT: Yes it does. Very soon after the events that are so well known staff and students were brought back onto the governing council, with the full support of the governing council. I think it is fair to say that they recognised that the exclusion was an error.

Just a word about staff members of council if I can take advantage of that question. It goes back to my point about diversity of new universities. I think it very difficult for there to be two staff governors of an institution as diverse and as large certainly as the University of Huddersfield is. If one is looking for the staff to elect, or to approve of, two staff governors across a whole institution that ranges from engineering to music, it is quite difficult to find people who will be acceptable to that whole constituency and will speak with confidence for different elements of that constituency, will speak with confidence about what happens, about what the attitudes of mind and the behaviour in humanities schools, in social science schools, in engineering schools, in physics and education etc. really are. That is one reason why I would like to have more staff members on the governing body as full members of the governing body, more in line with what the old university sector has, which is, of course, the background I come from.

1029. LORD THOMSON: That is very interesting and you have the advantage of coming from a different background into this new environment. I just wondered whether you find in terms of the new universities and their particular structure that there is a greater degree of emphasis on commercial confidentiality than in the older universities, and is this something that some attention should be given to?

PROF JOHN TARRANT: I certainly think all universities should write down quite clearly what their rules on confidentiality are. I think there was a tendency, from what I have heard anyway in the University of Huddersfield, to regard too many things as being confidential. What we have tried to do over the last few months is to narrow down and make quite explicit both the areas of confidentiality and the reasons for them. They are coming down to issues about individuals on the one hand and issues that are I suppose commercially confidential but in rather a special way. If, for example, we are interested in expanding our estate, or selling off elements of the estate, the decision to expand or sell would be in the public domain but the prices around which negotiations would take place would be kept confidential until after the deal had been struck. At that point, and immediately at that point, that information would then go back into the public domain. So we are trying to write those guidelines down—they go before the Council on Friday, as it happens.

1030. LORD THOMSON: Putting the matter more generally, quite apart from the particular circumstances in Huddersfield, what is the present position now about the requirements of the Higher Education Funding Council with regard to openness regarding the salary and other arrangements in respect of the Vice-Chancellor, for example, and what are the arrangements now for bringing out totally into the open any arrangements for severance payments for senior staff, that sort of thing?

PROF JOHN TARRANT: Both of those items now have to be declared in full. The Vice-Chancellor's salary has to be stated in the annual statement of accounts and, indeed, the salaries of senior staff in salary bands, but the Vice-Chancellor's is explicitly one which is identifiable immediately.

LORD THOMSON: Rather like company reports.

PROF JOHN TARRANT: Yes indeed, directors' emoluments and so on. The Vice-Chancellor's is the only one which is immediately identifiable with an individual; there are other ones, x number of people in various salary bands and, of course, a lot of detective work goes on to identify who the people are.

With regard to severance payments, those also have to be declared to the Funding Council now.

LORD THOMSON: Thank you very much.

1031. WILLIAM UTTING: Perhaps I could begin by soliciting a little further comment on some points you have already made. I was particularly interested in what you said about seeking greater flexibility in the constitution of your council and making it bigger. I wonder if you could say what sort of flexibility, why this was and what sort of size you thought might be optimum for a governing body.

PROF JOHN TARRANT: I am not sure there is a single size which would be optimum for what is quite an extensive range of institutions. For my own institution I think we could usefully have a governing body of about 35. That sounds rather high but I think that one of the corollaries of that is that you have an effective executive committee, if you like, which in my submission I refer to as a Planning and Resources Committee. This is something which the Jarratt Report recommended to us many years ago now and, indeed, reflects very closely what the HEFCE requires of us to integrate academic, financial and estate planning together and that, I believe, can only effectively be done by a very small group, a group of about half a dozen to eight perhaps, reporting through for full discussion with the council. I do not think a council of 13, which is what Huddersfield had during the troubles, is any better able to cope with the writing and drafting of major strategic planning issues than a group of 35 would be. So I think it is important to separate the function of approval of the major strategic direction of the institution (and that can be done comfortably with a larger number of people) from the drafting and preparation of that direction which has to be done by a smaller group of people, even smaller than the legislation requires.

In order to conduct the council's role of approving and steering the major strategic direction, it does have to be larger and to be more representative of what I identify as the three separate communities which need to be involved. I think it needs external people, very important, and these should be in a majority. It needs the internal executive directors. I do not believe there is a company in the land that would expect to have its major strategic direction provided for it by a board which was almost exclusively made up of non-executive directors, and that in a way is what we are asked to do. So the internal executive directors and a broad cross-section of the institution's staff. That is necessary, I think, for confidence and ownership of the strategic direction which that governing council can lay down.

1032. WILLIAM UTTING: What do you think were the principles behind the thinking that made staff and student representation optional? Was it felt that staff interests were taken up completely by a separate academic board and that they could get on with the academic business there while people managed the affairs here?

PROF JOHN TARRANT: I think you would be better to ask the drafters of the legislation and the advisers at the time.

WILLIAM UTTING: Yes, but I am asking you.

PROF JOHN TARRANT: I honestly do not know the answer to that question.

WILLIAM UTTING: You do not think it is a very good idea, obviously.

PROF JOHN TARRANT: I certainly do not, no. Because of the nature of universities I do not believe they could be governed by a body which is so divorced and separate from the staff of the institution who are themselves the institution.

1033. WILLIAM UTTING: What about the student representation on the council?

PROF JOHN TARRANT: I would be a strong supporter of student representation on council as well, and I am delighted to say the students are back on our council and will remain there.

1034. WILLIAM UTTING: As far as the external members are concerned I notice you had a section in your

evidence about interaction with the local community. Are you seeking specifically a more representative group of people from the local community than those that are allowed by statute at the moment?

PROF JOHN TARRANT: No, I think the statute allows us to have a broad representation of the local community. I am just cautious that we do not go too far in this direction and remember that universities have a national and an international constituency. They are not local bodies exclusively. They have a local role but it is not by any means all of their role. Some universities are more strongly locally based than others. My own is very strongly locally based, but even in that circumstance I would not want the board of governors to be dominated by local representatives.

1035. WILLIAM UTTING: Would you be looking for more adequate representation then of the community at national level?

PROF JOHN TARRANT: Yes I would, and I do make a suggestion right at the end of my submission that it is very difficult to find members of council with the time and the experience necessary to deliver a good job. It is particularly difficult to get people from a national constituency to serve any one particular university. I think there is a case to be made for some way of easing the bringing together of potential candidates with the vacancies that might occur, and I drew a parallel with the PRONED organisation that does that in the private sector for non-executive directors. I do not want to set up a parallel organisation, but some body which achieves that sort of objective for the quasi public sector organisations like universities would, I think, be quite helpful.

1036. WILLIAM UTTING: Could I end just by inviting your views about the role and functions of the Funding Council for England here in relation to universities. The body has been described in various ways as a funding body or a supervisory body or a regulatory body, and obviously does combine some quality assessment functions as well as funding. How do you view this? Is this right or should those functions be separated?

PROF JOHN TARRANT: Should the functions of quality assessment from funding be separate?

WILLIAM UTTING: Yes.

PROF JOHN TARRANT: No I do not believe they should be. I do not believe they can be, actually, because to some degree at least funding has to be influenced by the quality assessment process. I do not believe that the Funding Council should be exclusively responsible for quality, but it should share in the process and I think the initiatives which the CVCP and the HEFCE are now working on in terms of a joint body with joint responsibility for quality assessment and quality audit is the right path to be taking. I do not think the exercise should be dominated by either the HEFCE or the universities themselves.

In more general terms that question points to the conflict which exists between universities as autonomous bodies with academic freedom and central control. That is an issue which we need to keep coming back to, the need to protect the ability to dissent and the dangers if one goes to a central national body which controls the universities.

So there is a tension between the funding which clearly has to be done centrally and the autonomy of the institutions which has to be protected, and we have to settle for a reasonable compromise between central steering and local autonomy. It is quite difficult and the boundary moves a bit over time, but it is important to recognise that universities do need a strong measure of local autonomy.

WILLIAM UTTING: Thank you.

1037. LORD NOLAN: I wonder if I could ask you one question before inviting other members of the committee if they have any questions to raise. It is one you may find difficult to answer because, as we all know so well, you were not at Huddersfield at the time the difficulties arose, and you have only been there a short time now. There was a Public Accounts Committee Report on Huddersfield and also on Portsmouth, and one of the questions we have been asked to consider and have been looking at is whether there should as a general rule be reports where something has gone wrong in a local public spending body. The danger, of course, is that it will be unfair or be thought to be unfair and give a lot of adverse publicity which may not be fully justified. That is the danger on one side. The danger on the other side is that if there is no public report the suspicions that remain are worse than the realities. Can you tell us whether the report on Huddersfield has left any lasting effect good or bad, or is it something that people are now putting out of their minds?

PROF JOHN TARRANT: I do not think the report had any serious impact at all inside the institution. I think it added to a large and growing pile of adverse publicity which certainly damaged the institution in terms of admissions, for example, because with a large group of the population the only thing which they knew about Huddersfield was, if you like, the accumulation of bad news, so that certainly damaged the institution. I do not think the Public Accounts Committee Report itself cleared up that bad news or significantly added to it. The damage outside the institution was done by the adverse publicity, and the damage inside the institution was already there. So I am comfortable with a large degree of public accountability for organisations like universities. I think it was quite right and proper for the Public Accounts Committee to have had that enquiry. I do not think my immediate predecessor, Sir William Taylor, enjoyed the experience very much, but I think it was a valuable thing to have done. In a way it put the seal on the whole occasion. I could then close the door when I came in, fortunately. I could regard the door as shut and move forward in the other direction.

1038. LORD NOLAN: I say this very tentatively and personally, and not in any sense a committee view, but part of our job has been to set out what we have heard and come across that has been unfavourable, but to try and balance it with what has been favourable so as to cover nothing up but not to leave an unduly depressing result because much depends on the success of the report in achieving that. I am grateful for your answer, you think that the Public Accounts Committee Report was not in itself harmful to the university?

PROF JOHN TARRANT: Not seriously so and it did allow me, and others to, close the door and say, right, it has been fully investigated, there is nothing left to uncover, the HEFCE audit was carried out, the Public Accounts Committee have scrutinised everything, that is the end of

that chapter, let us move on. In that sense it is quite a valuable thing to have passed.

LORD NOLAN: Thank you.

1039. ANNE WARBURTON: I have one slightly maverick question perhaps. Attention was noted earlier that the fact that Professor Tarrant had experience in what are now called old universities had perhaps been a useful background for going to the new universities. I wondered whether after eight weeks he has yet noticed anything in the new universities which might usefully be put back into the arrangements obtaining in old universities.

PROF JOHN TARRANT: It is indeed a maverick question which I was not expecting. I was expecting the reverse of that question.

ANNE WARBURTON: I think we have had your answer, so I do not press the question.

PROF JOHN TARRANT: I think it is too early yet. It is said that the speed of decision making is better in the new universities than the old universities. I am not at all confident that that is true. Seeing a little bit of one side and quite a lot of the other I know that the old universities can make decisions very fast if the need is pressing. I equally know, judging from limited experience, that the new universities can take an age over things that should be done very fast. So there is a tendency for people on either side of the fence to think either that their way of doing things is the best, or that the grass is greener over there, isn't it. In fact, I suspect that both have advantages and disadvantages. I cannot see a clear winner.

LORD NOLAN: I think Sir Clifford had a question he wanted to ask.

1040. CLIFFORD BOULTON: In some ways it has got an echo from the previous one. I think I recall from your paper that you are not minded to have a Chancellor at the university.

PROF JOHN TARRANT: No, certainly I am minded.

CLIFFORD BOULTON: You are minded, I beg your pardon, I misread that. Is that in any way, apart from the decorative business of degree ceremonies and so forth, any way connected with having a sort of arm's length figure who could also be someone to whom problems or even complaints could be referred, is a kind of Visitor role which is something found in the old universities, or would you have some other idea for the handling of complaints by an arm's length person?

PROF JOHN TARRANT: I do not think the Chancellor should have that role. Of course, if you have a Chancellor he or she will have that role because people will write to the Chancellor and hope that that person will become a sort of court of last resort, but I do not believe that that is appropriate. I think the Chancellor has three roles. One is the ceremonial one which is the least important. The other is to be a friend and advocate of the university in one of the corridors of power, and it does not actually matter what corridor of power that is, whether it is government or business or the commercial sector generally, or the arts or the media, wherever. Some important spokesperson for the university on a national, or preferably even an international stage. Thirdly as an adviser, almost a sort of counsellor for the university vice-chancellor. I think it is very useful for a vice-chancellor to be able to turn to somebody who is outside the institution and the day-to-day affairs of things for advice and guidance, and I know that the three vice-chancellors under whom I served in East Anglia certainly used their Chancellors in that role to good effect.

Those are the three roles of what I would hope a Chancellor would do, and I think it is very important that they are all three fulfilled and I am moving as fast as I can to persuade the University to appoint a Chancellor. They do not take any persuading, but just finding the right person is not easy.

That goes on to the question of the Visitor and whether there should be such a sort of court of last resort. I am not convinced myself, I have to say. Two reasons; one that you have to stop this process somewhere, and I am not confident that just putting yet another court of appeal, if you like, beyond the institution will actually achieve very much. In my own experience in academic life I have no examples of where cases have gone to a Visitor and been resolved. There are some in the higher education sector, but I certainly have no direct experience of any such cases. I am not sure that in practice it would actually solve anything to have a Visitor, but I do recognise that there are many people who think that it might have prevented what had happened in Huddersfield if there had been a Visitor to whom people could appeal. My view is that I do not think it would have stopped it happening, and it would be better to put the checks and balances inside the organisation rather than outside the organisation. I think that if at the time the Council of the University of Huddersfield had been more broadly representative than it was, I suspect that some at least of those incidents would not have happened.

CLIFFORD BOULTON: Thank you very much.

1041. LORD NOLAN: Thank you very much indeed, Professor. It has been very interesting and helpful. We are most grateful to you for coming.

Now we welcome Dr John Strickson, Mr Ray Morgan and Mr Barry Wastnidge. Gentlemen, I do not know whether you had it in mind to make any introductory remarks. We have, of course, read your submission, for which we are most grateful. Was there anything you wished to say before we start the questions, or would you like to get straight on with those?

DR JOHN STRICKSON, RAY MORGAN, AND BARRY WASTNIDGE

JOHN STRICKSON (Principal, North East Surrey College of Technology Further Education Corporation): We will go straight on.

LORD NOLAN: Very well, then I shall ask Sir Clifford Boulton to begin.

1042. CLIFFORD BOULTON: Thank you very much for your paper and for the opening statement, which I found very succinct and you very clearly dealt with the points that you have got in mind.

I notice from a report I saw of the Annual Meeting of the Further Education Funding Council that many of the points you raised were also raised at that meeting. Were you present at the recent annual meeting? No? One or two of the points I have seen covered there will come up in your own evidence.

You draw attention to the formal requirements of accountability which involve the funding and other authorities being able, to a large extent, to indicate policy and what you should do as part of their funding role and then you contrast that with the responsibility you feel to the community and clients you serve and say that the two can get into conflict. Would you like to mention some of the things that you do to your clients to have the relationship with them which you feel you must have—for instance, the local community, the local authorities and so forth?

JOHN STRICKSON: Can I open by saying that, first of all, the college is slightly unusual in the sense that it has some 40 per cent or so HE work as well as 60 per cent FE work and in relation to the work that it does, it has one or two specialist customers, particularly regional health authorities and it has a very substantial contribution to make to the training of nurses.

The local community therefore is difficult to define. There is the immediate environment of the college, perhaps the Borough of Epsom and Ewell and going a little wider into the County of Surrey, but many of our students travel quite long distances because we offer specialist programmes, some in nursing and some in other specialist areas. The community therefore is the local community, the employers that have used the college for the past 30 years and there is in some sense a community which is overseas—we have some students who come from France and Germany on linked programmes.

To what extent all of these bodies have a contribution to make to the governing body to the Corporation of the institution is not clear. An added problem in terms of responsibility is that with a mix of levels of courses, we are funded substantially by the Higher Education Funding Council, which has one set of rules and regulations, and by the Further Education Funding Council, which tends to have a different set of rules and regulations. The health authority being a major funder also has its own rules and regulations. To whom do we turn for advice, other than to split the institution into several different groupings, and from whom do the Corporation get their advice and instruction? To whom are the Corporation accountable—to the funding bodies? To the local community? This is the general area of uncertainty as to whom the Corporation is responsible. To whom do they report? Who feeds advice into them so that they can advise the executives in the colleges what actions to take? We find the whole process very unclear.

Back in the days of local authority control, at least there was a body. The chief education officer was the boss and everything you did had to conform with county policies, but we now have a diversity of people who have a legitimate interest in what we do based on our service to the various communities, not all of them, as I say, local. There are one or two programmes in which we have a national catchment. How we would select people who would help us to meet those requirements we know not. That underlies one of our problems in respect of accountability and relationship with the local community.

1043. CLIFFORD BOULTON: Are you typical in having that split between FE and HE or untypical?

JOHN STRICKSON: There must be of the order of between a dozen and 20 college which are in this particular situation. We are not typical and that does lead to difficulties that perhaps many other institutions do not have, but we are not unique. There are a group of colleges which have similar problems.

1044. CLIFFORD BOULTON: Have you not rather made the point? There is no one local authority that could solve all these problems by being your godfather or something is there?

JOHN STRICKSON: No.

1045. CLIFFORD BOULTON: Is not the idea of this form of establishment that you will take responsibility for having a policy and will be answerable for being sensitive to all these? You are not saying, are you, that the rules and requirements of the Funding Councils are making it impossible for you to perform that role—or are you? Are you saying that they are not flexible enough in their understanding of what you have got to do?

JOHN STRICKSON: They are not clear enough and there are differences in the approach made by the different bodies. The FE Funding Council has very different policies from those of the Higher Education Funding Council and there are often occasions where the College is torn between moving in one direction or another because both are significant contributors to the overall funding of the institution.

The Further Education Funding Council are by far the largest contributors, but the others are significant. Of our funding something between 51 and 55 per cent comes from the Further Education Funding Council, with the rest coming from other bodies. We do have academic responsibilities to the validating bodies, particularly for our degree and postgraduate work, and there is a conflict between what the Further Education Funding Council would have us do and what we see that we must do in order to meet the needs of our external educational validating bodies. There are conflicts which we as managers have to resolve and this we think we do quite well, but the conflict is there. We are very well aware of the fact that when the Corporation members come to make their decisions, they have to assimilate the problems that arise from each of the large funding bodies and that does produce conflict. We go in one direction to meet the needs of the higher body, even though it is in direct conflict with another one and that is a problem.

1046. CLIFFORD BOULTON: Can I just concentrate on the technical accountability side of this equation. In your paper you said—

"In the capacity of Accounting Officer the Principal may be required to appear before the House of Commons Public Accounts Committee, alongside the chief officer of the Funding Council on matters relating to funds paid by the Council to the College. This may conflict with his/her position as an employee of the Corporation and appropriate safeguards need to be given."

What risk were you envisaging there?

JOHN STRICKSON: I think it is the problem of being accountable to the Corporation for general policies, but being accountable to the Funding Council for the day to day operation and in part also to some of the longer term programmes within the institution. There are two masters and at any one time the conflict between the needs of the two masters can lead to a difficult choice and whichever choice is made could be seen as inappropriate by one of the two bodies. There is a potential for conflict there. Sometimes it is fairly low key, but in other cases it could be quite significant. In the appointment of certain types of staff, one body could want you to follow one pattern—particularly the Funding Council—because such a policy would fit in with their general philosophy of the way things should go and the Corporation members might well determine that you should go another way to meet the needs of either local industry, the professional bodies or indeed of one of the other major funding bodies. There is a potential for conflict.

1047. CLIFFORD BOULTON: When I saw you felt in need of safeguard, I thought I would perhaps give you a little Christmas present by pointing out the existence of the Witnesses' Public Inquiries Protection Act, under which it is a criminal offence to punish, damnify or injure a witness before a select committee and you can be fined, imprisoned and ordered to pay compensation if you offend. I hope that is some comfort to you.

JOHN STRICKSON: Yes.

1048. CLIFFORD BOULTON: Going back to the actual work on the ground, how are you affected by the need to keep in with the local TEC, because you refer to that situation?

JOHN STRICKSON: At this time our relationship with the local TEC is very good and that has been the situation since the TEC was created. Indeed, certainly in its early days college principals within the County of Surrey were consulted about the structure of the TEC and about the boundaries within which the TEC works, so there has been an extremely good working relationship.

There are times when the college responds to particular TEC initiatives and there is the potential that for financial reasons it would not wish to respond, whereas the TEC clearly has the need to protect its client groups. We at the moment find it very difficult to work within the financial constraints imposed by the TECs. They, like many government bodies, are trying to reduce their expenditure.

We feel under an obligation to the community to offer certain programmes, but when we analyse the viability of those programmes in financial terms, we conclude that we cannot possibly bid for them. There is therefore a conflict between what might be feasible if money were unlimited—which we know it never can be—which would be good for the community and for the TEC and what would be good for the College in the eyes of its responsibilities to the Funding Council. There are some very serious difficulties there because of the never ending stream of edicts which say "You should become more efficient." Sometimes that efficiency leads to lack of quality and there is a demand for quality by the customer, which in this case might well be the TEC, which cannot be met by the College in terms of the financial constraints it works under. There is a possibility that we will not be able to fulfil the requirements of the TEC because we are required to fulfil the financial requirements of the funding body.

1049. CLIFFORD BOULTON: On the question of getting nominating bodies you rather liked the idea that somebody else would look round for members of the council for you on their own behalf, as nominating bodies. Presumably you could consult them already informally for suggestions of people to be on your governing body? Perhaps you do.

JOHN STRICKSON: Yes.

BARRY WASTNIDGE (Clerk to the Corporation, North East Surrey College of Technology Further Education Corporation): I think this goes back to when we had delegated responsibility under local authorities. To be truthful, we actually identified the people we wanted and then searched for a body to nominate them.

CLIFFORD BOULTON: Yes.

BARRY WASTNIDGE: But even with that process there was a feeling that outside bodies were contributing to the governing body. With the current arrangements—all the comments, for instance, with regard to self-perpetuation—governing bodies seem to be set up in a way which seems to imply that there is a requirement that they are run by businessmen. They have powers of veto over various types of appointment and they are in the majority. It says in the statement that you can end up with a governing body within the governing body which, because it is in the majority, will always have power. It seemed to me that if you had these external nominating bodies, it would at least give you a safety valve to prevent that from happening.

The other issue that is not covered in the legislation, and again it is mentioned in various documents, is that at present there is no limit to the time that a member can serve on a Corporation.

1050. CLIFFORD BOULTON: Would you like to see that built in?

BARRY WASTNIDGE: Yes.

1051. CLIFFORD BOULTON: Are you having fairly severe difficulty in finding members of the range that you would like to see?

BARRY WASTNIDGE: Yes. We have one longstanding vacancy where we are trying to find a person with financial expertise, but a large number of the governing body are still those people who were members of the governing body under the local authority. One or two of them now feel that they have been doing it long enough so over the next couple of years I suspect that we shall have severe problems as those longstanding members decide that they would like to step down.

1052. CLIFFORD BOULTON: You would quite like to see more than just an expense allowance for out of pocket expenses? You would like to see some remuneration—is that right?

BARRY WASTNIDGE: In terms of where we are in Surrey, the majority of businesses are small—a recent survey said the businesses had five employees or less—and if we are asking those people to give up time, they are in some difficulty in giving that time free. We

have a large number of accountancy practices—one man professional organisations—where if they are at a Corporation meeting, they are actually losing professional fees.

1053. CLIFFORD BOULTON: Are meetings during working hours or in the evenings?

BARRY WASTNIDGE: We hold them at 8.30 in the morning.

1054. CLIFFORD BOULTON: How often would you be expected to attend both a full meeting and, perhaps, a committee that you find yourself on? How many days a month would be required?

BARRY WASTNIDGE: It probably works out about a day or a day and a half a month, unless you were the chairman and he will comment on that later I am sure. But for a normal member of the Corporation, if they were on a committee——

CLIFFORD BOULTON: One or two days a month?

BARRY WASTNIDGE: Yes.

1055. CLIFFORD BOULTON: And so on this £155 a day, which you seem to suggest as about right, you would not be making a lot of money, but it would be some consideration. This is not, I may say, the very general kind of evidence we get about the service in these kind of things.

BARRY WASTNIDGE: It may be a symptom of our area.

CLIFFORD BOULTON: Yes.

BARRY WASTNIDGE: As I say, in the type of businesses around us, it is difficult for people to give up the time. The other issue on that is the position of female members. We have three, but, without wishing to insult them, if we wanted younger professional women, it would help if we could give some contribution towards childcare costs.

1056. CLIFFORD BOULTON: We got rather an encouraging answer from the Department this morning which seemed to suggest that childcare could be considered to be an out of pocket expense, so it might be worth following up to see whether that is the case or not. I rather gathered that from the tone of an answer we got.

BARRY WASTNIDGE: This is an ongoing problem we have. It is not until something is raised as a problem that something is done about it. In terms of the FCECE guide to governors it was retrospectively decided that expenses were really only for travel and subsistence, but that was 18 months after incorporation.

1057. CLIFFORD BOULTON: Yes. Can I ask about the role of clerks because we have a clerk in front of us. We understand that there is some advice expected to come out quite soon about the constitutional role of the clerk in guarding the constitution of the body. We will look at that with interest because I can understand that it can rub up against the role of an accounting officer who has been given the duty of reporting back irregularities or problems in that capacity. I can see there might be difficulty there, but can I ask about the profession of clerk or secretary in the further education world. Are they people who get together and communicate with each other? Is there any exchange of information or procedural information?

BARRY WASTNIDGE: There is a professional organisation, the Association of College Registrars and Administrators. At the time of incorporation, the membership dwindled a bit, but it is becoming a more powerful force again. My membership lapsed at incorporation because I did not think it was fulfilling the role it should and nothing has come up that is better at the moment. There is no formal contact at the moment between clerks of corporations on that basis.

1058. CLIFFORD BOULTON: No. Thank you. Dr Strickson, I understand you are a member of the Higher Education Funding Council; is that right?

JOHN STRICKSON: Yes.

1059. CLIFFORD BOULTON: Do you think we are dealing with much the same sort of issues in FE and HE or are the universities really different animals about which it is not easy to make sideways comparisons and comments?

JOHN STRICKSON: Within the higher education sector and the further education sector there are very wide differences between institutions and there is an element of overlap between the two. The dozen or so colleges that I mentioned probably have as much in common with higher education colleges as they do with other further education colleges. It is a spectrum, with colleges like NESCOT in the middle.

Each area has rather different overall problems, but at the moment perhaps there are a large number of commonalities. The financial constraints within which we are all working at the moment are causing major stress within both groups of institutions, whether in the HE or the FE sector. Those of us who sit on the dividing line find it particularly difficult because, as I think your previous witness said, the grass can always appear to be slightly greener on the other side of the fence. I do not think it is. I think we all suffer in rather different ways, but if you are near to the fence itself, you are perhaps more aware of the pluses on the other side and perhaps the HE colleges which are not universities (and there are many of those) are aware of some of the pluses on our side of the fence. But there is a spectrum: it is not that there are two types of institutions. There are many types of institutions and there will be overlaps between the two.

Some of the biggest problems that are developing relate to the provision of capital. Your brief is probably not to look at the detailed problems of institutions, but there are very different ways in which colleges can have access to capital and to funding for different types of activity and because there are differences, there is often conflict that if you are one side of the fence your students are entitled to one set of services and if you are on the other, they are not. So while saying that there is overlap and a continuum, there are some differences that are significant because FE colleges do not have access to certain types of facilities and I am sure there are corresponding circumstances on the HE side, particularly in terms of ability to expand student population and there are conflicts there.

I am sure that in terms of the accountability on both sides of the fence there is much similarity. I would guess

that the chief executives of the two funding bodies have very similar ways of dealing with the colleges responsible to them.

CLIFFORD BOULTON: Thank you very much.

LORD NOLAN: Dame Anne?

1060. ANNE WARBURTON: Thank you. I find myself very perturbed to hear what trouble you have in recruiting good people for your board. I was glad that Sir Clifford gave you the reassurance we had this morning from the Department, so perhaps that will influence what the funding council finally says about childcare.

In your paper you raised one or two other particular points on which you would like some action. The last is the one that it is perhaps asking too much of voluntary board members to fill out a complete register of interests and you ask whether that is not really the last straw. From the point of view of accountability, the answer I think has to be, no, it should not be the last straw. Are you really unhappy about that one? Would you like to speak to it.

RAY MORGAN (Chairman of Governors, North East Surrey College of Technology Further Education Corporation): One has to take that particular point in the context of the whole really. No member is unhappy about declaring personal interests. I think what happened was that that recommendation came at the end of a long line of increasingly apparently restrictive recommendations on governors and sooner or later one felt one should draw a line as to what was going on.

There is no objection to declaring interests. We are all perfectly happy to do that. I think there was some interpretation that the declaration of interests should go beyond the individual and be transferred to members of families and so on and I think one would not wish to follow that in detail. The whole question of accountability is one of definition or lack of it. I started to write a job description for a governor and you start with, "name, title, responsible to whom" and the scene becomes a little cloudy and "responsible for what" requires a great deal more definition than we have at the moment. One of our major problems in recruiting suitable people onto boards is lack of finite definition of the responsibilities. So as a simple point of declaration of interests, I do not think there is a problem. What I think is a problem is ever-increasing responsibility being imposed or recommended as good practice, none of which individually one would necessarily object to.

It is the build up of an atmosphere of apparent increased responsibility without proper definition. It is the definition we are trying to get to I think.

1061. ANNE WARBURTON: I noticed from your submission that you are obviously feeling that the unclarity may be almost intentional in order to get at members of the governing body. Chairman, you were questioning the Department about whether they would go so far as to give a legal statement about liability.

LORD NOLAN: Yes.

ANNE WARBURTON: I would hesitate to summarise it for the present purposes, but it seemed to me that possibly it might help our present witnesses if they knew what the Department had said in synopsis.

LORD NOLAN: I would prefer to abide by their exact words because it was a very carefully phrased description of the position.

ANNE WARBURTON: Yes, it was.

LORD NOLAN: "Little likelihood of liability" was the key phrase that stuck in my mind.

ANNE WARBURTON: It was a way of saying what perhaps you will feel you have heard before, that it is very unlikely, but they would not go as far as to say it could not happen. They did make the point that it would be the corporate body rather than the individuals who would normally be held liable.

LORD NOLAN: Again, yes, that was their view, but as you say, I think it was again qualified by the word "normally".

RAY MORGAN: The point has already been made, and I understand that we must not get into detail, but one does automatically. We have an Audit Committee and we are not a very big body of governors—we are 14 strong. A decision was made to invite two elected members of the staff onto the governing body, in accordance with the rules. Those members of staff cannot, by the regulations, be members of any other committee than the Audit Committee. We appointed the two members of staff to the Audit Committee. We have been severely criticised as a board for making that appointment because it is not "in the spirit of the legislation". I cannot deal in spirits. Again, I must have definition as to what we are about, otherwise I think we are lost.

1062. ANNE WARBURTON: I think I have read somewhere that it is quite usual to have the Audit Committee comprised of non-executive members, as it were, but I am not an authority on that.

Can I ask just one other question. It struck me as strange, and I wondered if there was more to be said about the statement that after extensive debate, the board decided that all decisions must be taken at board level—that they could not use the committees to get on with business. Is there more we should hear on that?

RAY MORGAN: I think it is fairly simple: the legislation appeared to us to preclude us from delegating responsibility and therefore authority to sub-committees. As each member of the board felt that he was being held personally responsible for what was going on, then the ultimate decisions had to be made by members of the board in totem in committee.

1063. ANNE WARBURTON: I am bound to ask if you feel you have sufficiently good relations with your funding or regulatory agency to be able to discuss such things with them?

RAY MORGAN: We have had some internal debate on the subject and if I might return to my job description point, I do not feel that there is a good relationship between the board, the Chairman and whoever, because the whoever is not defined. Who is the Chairman or the

board responsible to? The Secretary of State? I am unlikely to have discussions with the Secretary of State. Once one moves out of that finite definition as to the line responsibility, who am I responsible to? Who can I have discussions with in the terms that you put the question?

ANNE WARBURTON: That is what you would like cleared up?

RAY MORGAN: I find great difficulty. I need—and I think we all need—more definition, not more restriction.

ANNE WARBURTON: Thank you, Chairman.

1064. MARTIN JACOMB: Two quick questions. Your answer on the Audit Committee interested me because in the private sector it is axiomatic that the audit committee should consist of non-executive people, simply in order to provide a forum for a detailed conversation between the auditor and the people they are auditing.

RAY MORGAN: I do not say they are the only people on the committee. Perhaps I have missed the point.

MARTIN JACOMB: I was just interested by your answer which seemed to imply that you found it difficult to deal with the spirit of an audit committee consisting of non-executive people.

BARRY WASTNIDGE: The point was that it was clearly within the regulatory framework that we could appoint two independent members of the corporation and two staff members of the corporation. There is nothing anywhere that lays down that you cannot do that. The FCECE came along afterwards and said "Although it does not say anywhere that you can"t do that, we think it is against the spirit of the legislation.".

Quite often it is the retrospective interpretation of something where we thought we were working within the rules. Some of the retrospective decisions seem to be based on opinion rather than on what is actually laid down in the statutory framework.

1065. MARTIN JACOMB: They were saying that it was a mistake rather than just advice for the future?

BARRY WASTNIDGE: They have actually written to us and advised us to remove the staff members from the Audit Committee.

1066. MARTIN JACOMB: Yes. Could I ask one other thing. When you referred to the difficulty of recruiting outside people, you mentioned the fact that a lot of the businesses in your area are small businesses, professional partnerships and so forth. Do you exclude businessmen who do not work in your area, but live in your area, because there must be hundreds of those?

BARRY WASTNIDGE: We tend to deal with that through advertisement in the local press because obviously we are aware that we are a large commuter residential area and there will be a lot of suitable people who live in the area, but do not necessarily work there.

1067. MARTIN JACOMB: When I say businessmen, I include business women. I ought to make that clear.

It surprises me that you find that there is a difficulty in getting businessmen and women, but that really is your experience is it?

BARRY WASTNIDGE: Yes.

RAY MORGAN: I think part of the problem may be that if those people are travelling up to London, or wherever, on a regular basis, they simply are not prepared to put the time in to the local college for the local need. If they live there, work somewhere else and their main interests are somewhere else, a large group of the people will therefore by indifference preclude themselves from interest in college activities. The thing works both ways. A dormitory area has those sort of problems. We advertise widely.

MARTIN JACOMB: You might try posters on the station because they will have plenty of time to read those!

JOHN STRICKSON: One of the elements of this has already been touched upon and it is that people are reluctant to take on a post where the responsibilities are not defined. One of the questions asked by people with small businesses is "What is the financial liability to me if I join your board?" and at the moment that is not totally clear. Many small businesses are on the margin of viability even in the relatively affluent areas of Surrey. There is a great reluctance to become involved in things where the quality of life can be affected by decisions made by a body that you are not totally familiar with.

There are some problems there that need to be resolved and it is true that when we have discussed the possibility of people joining the Corporation, a question has been "What is the financial liability if the Corporation as a whole gets something wrong?" and I do not think there is a clear answer. I know that Barry has tried on a number of occasions to get clear definition from government departments and at the moment we can make no statement that says "The liability is zero, unless you break the law.", or "unless you are fraudulent". Obviously there are circumstances there where everybody has to accept liability, but it is the murky ground that we are not able to clarify and we would appreciate it if there were a clear statement of the limits of liability. If it said "There is no liability unless you break the law" at least it would be a clear statement. I think our relationship with our funding body makes it very difficult to get any definition from them.

The funding bodies are remarkably reluctant to clarify the rules of the game, for good reason. I can understand it totally. Having been the member of one, I can understand the reluctance to be so specific that you could be held accountable for your statements at a later date, but it is very difficult. Well educated people understand the nature of the law and are very worried about the legal implications for their families and their own businesses and it is difficult to go to them and say "Please accept this job with the institution. We cannot actually tell you what the liability could be." They withdraw at that stage.

One of the other things we have found increasingly to be a problem is the fact that with the multiplicity of rules and regulations that are emerging, particularly from the funding council, more and more time is being taken up with Corporation business. I can recollect—and I am sure my Chairman can—the days when the average Corporation meeting was no longer than two hours and when most of the business of the main board could be conducted within between an hour and a half and two hours. There have been many occasions of late when it has

taken a whole morning, starting at 8.30, through to one o'clock, with an extension sometimes into the middle of the afternoon. The nature of the business and the need to discuss issues that have emerged from the funding body have taken a great deal of time and those people who are very active within their company and their own business increasingly object to spending these very long periods discussing college business. Given the difficult path that most of the education system is treading at the moment, the time element will increase rather than diminish. We are confronted with an increasing number of problems to solve. We have problems because of the schools, because of the universities and competition therewith, pressure on students and so on. There are many issues that our Corporation should look at in detail, but such an investigation takes a lot of time and those who have an active business career find it increasingly difficult to devote that time.

1068. LORD NOLAN: We are very grateful to you. You have given us an extremely clear and vivid picture of the experience you have had in North East Surrey. We have tried to combine the evidence of national institutions and departments with those of individual organisations in different parts of the country and the experience of the latter has always been most interesting and helpful, as yours has been, so thank you very much for coming. Have a good journey home.

JOHN STRICKSON: Thank you.

1069. LORD NOLAN: I am going to make a closing statement to mark the end of this session of our hearings. Today we have come to the end of our public hearings in London, although we still have to take evidence in Scotland and Wales. We have heard from and about a diverse range of bodies. Our witnesses this week have covered most of them.

Housing associations are "not for profit" organisations, many of which are registered charities. Although there are over 2,000 registered housing associations in England and Wales, the 30 largest account for the lion's share of this year's public sector capital funds of £1.2 billion.

There are nearly 500 colleges in the further education sector in England alone. Since April 1993 these have been independent corporations, with their governing bodies responsible for £3 billion of public funds—around two-thirds of their income.

Including the individual schools of the University of London, there are now nearly 150 universities and colleges of higher education in England, accounting for over £6 billion of public funds through various sources such as direct funding and research funding. We have heard of the fundamentally different approaches to governance of the so-called "old" universities established by charter and the "new" ones set up by legislation.

Over 1,000 grant-maintained schools in England and Wales spend over £1.6 billion of public money each year. Their boards have taken on functions which previously rested with local authorities. Their funding is provided through the funding agency for schools, but ultimately problems and disputes must be settled directly by the Secretary of State.

Finally, the Training and Enterprise Councils are entrepreneurial "not for profit" private sector companies, working under contract with the Secretary of State, but despite their private sector status, they receive over 90 per cent of their income from public funds—some £1.4 billion a year in England and Wales—and the Secretary of State has a major say in how they work, including approval of their Memorandum and Articles of Association and setting the criteria for board membership.

All this adds up to major changes over the last few years in the ways in which public money has been channelled through to the final user. Undoubtedly in the early days there were a few incidents where things went wrong or were not done properly. Equally, we have heard over the past five weeks of new control mechanisms that have been or are being put in place. A key part of our deliberations will therefore be to take a view on whether these systems are sufficiently robust and transparent.

But before getting to that stage, we move to Wales and Scotland to hear about their institutions. On 24 and 25 January we shall be in Cardiff and on 30 and 31 January in Edinburgh. While the institutions in Wales are similar to those in England, Scotland has very few grant-maintained schools and their equivalent of the TECs—Local Enterprise Companies—have a wider remit and work to Government through intermediate "Enterprise" bodies.

The view of those in Wales and Scotland who have a close knowledge of the bodies covered by our present study are essential to our work. We want to make sure our conclusions are relevant to their institutions and there may well be lessons from Scotland and Wales that we can apply more widely.

Thank you very much.

WEDNESDAY 13 DECEMBER 1995

OPENING STATEMENTS

Opening statement from the National Council for Voluntary Organisations

Background

NCVO was established in 1919 as the representative voice of the voluntary sector in England. Its membership comprises 650 national voluntary organisations. NCVO also co-ordinates the Training and Employment Network (TEN) which brings together members and local organisations concerned with vocational training. NCVO provides services to members on such matters as management and governance including trusteeship.

NCVO's submission to the Committee is based upon consultation with voluntary organisations. It is influenced by the fact that voluntary organisations have most contact with TECs in comparison with the other local public spending bodies under review. As distinct from other local public spending bodies under review Has are regarded as part of the voluntary sector and NFHA is a member of NCVO.

NCVO has established the Commission on the Future of the Voluntary Sector. The Commission, which is independent of NCVO, has three areas of study-relationships between voluntary organisations and other sectors; governance and management; and the legal and fiscal framework. Issues of probity, accountability and governance will therefore be considered in detail by the Commission.

In NCVO's submission to the Commission, a number of recommendations were made concerning boards, including that larger charities should be allowed to appoint staff members to trustee boards and, if they wish, to remunerate trustees, on a scale equivalent to magistrates.

Key recommendations

Regular authority

NCVO believes that all local public spending bodies should be subject to the supervision of a regulatory authority; to ensure that minimum standards are observed and that the responsibilities of boards are strengthened.

Board appointments

The process for selection of Board members should be widely broadcast; candidates should be sought from a wide range of community interests; the names and particulars of those chosen should be published; and the period of office should not exceed 6 years.

In particular, after appointment TEC Boards become self selecting which creates an inbuilt bias towards perpetuating current make-up of boards.

Accountability of Board members

There should be better access to information about decisions made; the process for appeals against decisions should be widely broadcast; and appeals should ultimately be able to be heard by an independent agent.

Role of Boards in relation to officers and staff

There should be a clear statement of the role of the board, chairman and chief executive and the duties and responsibilities devolved to staff.

Safeguards re Conflicts of Interest

Registers of interests of directors and staff and their immediate families should be held by local public spending bodies and their regulatory authorities and be publicised; a mechanism for "whistle-blowing" by staff and members of the public should also be publicised.

Standards of openness

There should be greater openness in local public spending bodies about their activities and decisions. Only in rare circumstances should personal or price sensitive information be withheld on the grounds of commercial sensitivity. In such cases the reasons for refusing openness should be made known.

The need for access to data

There is a paucity of information about local public spending bodies and limited access to data at local offices and public libraries which is unacceptable and which puts a constraint on legitimate interest and inquiry.

A new national centre or regional centres based on the Government Offices for the Regions should be established with information on local public spending bodies including annual reports; corporate plans; lists of board members; registers of interest and other materials.

Opening statement by Professor John Tarrant, Vice-Chancellor and Principal, University of Huddersfield

Introduction

The University of Huddersfield is a former Polytechnic which became independent from Kirklees Metropolitan Council on 1 April 1989 under the terms of the Education Reform Act 1988. In common with other former polytechnics it is a statutory corporation, called a Higher Education Corporation and the members of the corporation are the members of the University Council. They are legally responsible for the University. The Polytechnic became a University as a result of the Further and Higher Education Act of 1992 and the constitution and appointment of its Council is governed by an Instrument of Government made by the Privy Council pursuant to that Act. Internal bylaws of the University are contained in Articles of Government which also require the approval of the Privy Council. There is an Academic Board or Senate which is responsible to the University Council for academic affairs. Whereas the majority of the University Council members are external to the University, all the members of the Academic Board are internal and the majority are teaching staff. The University has about 13,400 students, 1,235 employees and an annual budget of approximately £55m.

The Issues

During 1994 two issues at The University of Huddersfield came to public notice:

(a)   the removal of student and staff members from the University Council; and

(b)   the severance arrangements of the former vice-chancellor.

I did not join the University of Huddersfield until 15 October 1995, have no direct knowledge of the issues and do not intend to comment on them. I do know, however, that both issues were resolved with the full co-operation of the Council of the University of Huddersfield well before the hearing of the Public Accounts Committee on 20 February 1995 where the University was so ably represented by my predecessor, Sir William Taylor. He joined the university as vice-chancellor and principal for a year from October 1994. During his period of office there were significant changes in the governance arrangements at the University of Huddersfield. The changes are fully in line with the CUC Guide for Members of Governing Bodies of Universities and Colleges in England and Wales issued in June 1995 although most of the changes were implemented before that, and many of them were conceived even before the CUC issued its two page "Advice on University Governance" in December 1994. The University was given the opportunity of commenting on the draft of the CUC Guide and its input into the final version was not insignificant.

The Changes

The changes instituted at Huddersfield are directly relevant to the three broad themes of the Committee's work as set out in the "Issues and Questions" document, issued earlier this year, namely:

(a)   the appointment and accountability of board members;

(b)   the role of boards in relation to the officers and staff;

(c)   the safeguards in respect of conflicts of interest.

The first tranche of changes, and the most significant, were decided upon at the Council's meeting in December 1994. They are as follows:

(1)   the size of the University Council was increased from 13 to 20. Nominations have since been sought in order to increase it to the permitted maximum of 25;

(2)   a Nominations Committee was established to advise the Council on the appointment of independent and co-opted members and on the appointment of a Chancellor. The Nominations Committee consists of the President, three members of the Council, a member of the Academic Staff and the Vice-Chancellor;

(3)   nominations for vacancies on the Council and its Committees are sought from staff and students on a confidential basis. Vacancies have been widely advertised within the University.

(4)   a Dean, a member of academic staff and a member of non-academic staff were appointed to the Council on the nomination of the Academic Board. The latter elected the Dean from among its number and organised elections to choose the two other members of staff;

(5)   the President of the Students' Union was also appointed to the Council;

(6)   a three year, once renewable term was introduced to all members of the Council. This maybe extended in the case of members of Council who are subsequently appointed Chairman of the Council or of one of its Committees;

(7)   the Committee structure beneath the Council was reorganised. A General Purposes Committee was discontinued and its functions divided between three new Committees namely the Finance Committee, the Estates Committee and the Personnel Committee. An Audit Committee and a Remuneration Committee were already in existence and are continued;

(8)   three Joint Committees of the Council and the Academic Board were established namely a Planning and Resources Committee, a Student Affairs Committee and an Honorary Degrees Committee;

(9)   a review of the constitution and operation of the Academic Board was initiated. The results of this were incorporated into new draft Articles of Government which were required by the Further and Higher Education Act 1992. These are at present with the Privy Council for their approval. The main effect of the changes in relation to the Academic Board (or Senate as it will be called) is to increase its size to enable it to be more broadly representative of the teaching and other staff of the University;

(10)   following the Annual General Meeting in 1994 members of the Council attended an open meeting to which all staff and students were invited. The meeting took the form of a question and answer session, ran for about one and a half hours and was attended by approximately 200 people.

In addition to the above changes, I put forward the following points which are relevant to some of the matters raised in the Committee's Issues and Questions document. Many of these points go beyond openness and transparency to address issues of effectiveness.

(a) Interaction with the local community

The University Council is discussing methods by which it can more effectively interact with the local community outside the University. Many of the external members of the Council bring, among other things, a wide range of local experience. Although the constitution of the University Council does not include a member who is nominated by the local authority, the Council has appointed, in her personal capacity, a member who is the Chair of Education Committee of the Local Authority. In my view further representation of the Local Authority would be inappropriate to an independent Corporation which has a national and indeed an international constituency.

The University Council and the Local Authority have a Liaison Forum which meets approximately every six months where matters of mutual interest are discussed. In addition senior officers meet regularly for the same purpose.

I am working on proposals for an annual public presentation of the work of the University along the lines of the meeting of Court in many chartered Universities, but without the formal power to appoint a Chancellor of the University. There have been some preliminary discussions with members of the Council and I will put a recommendation to the Council shortly.

Of small, but symbolic importance, was the involvement of the Mayors of our three Local Authorities in the award ceremonies last month.

The most important links with the local community will always be at the "grassroots" level—as they remained at Huddersfield even when formal relationships with the Local Authority were at their worst. Examples are the involvement of the University in the Huddersfield Contemporary Music Festival, the Festival of Contemporary Women Writers and bids to the Single Regeneration Budget, including proposals to develop an integrated Manufacturing Centre of international standard in partnership with local industrial and educational interests.

(b) Paragraph 8 membership of Council

Advantage has been taken of a paragraph in the University's Instrument of Government permitting non-Council members to be appointed to Council Committees. There are currently six such individuals from varied walks of life outside the University who have been appointed to Council committees because of particular experience which is relevant to the Committees on which they serve.

(c) A code of practice for Council members

The Council has a Code of Practice which was adopted in mid 1994 before much of the adverse publicity arose. (attached as Annex A)

(d) Familiarity of members of Council with the University and with Higher Education

A university is populated by people who are charged with challenging accepted views, and we rightly protect the academic freedom which allows this. The management and governance of an organisation in which dissent is expected is especially challenging. It requires a partnership between the Council, the senior management team and the staff of the University with respect, trust and confidence between the partners. To help develop this trust and partnership it is essential that the members of the Council develop an understanding of the work of the University, notwithstanding the time commitment which this involves. It is also important for staff to understand and accept the role of the Council.

With an enlarged Council and many new members of the University of Huddersfield it was desirable to hold an "Induction weekend" this autumn involving all Council members and the senior management team of the University. There were discussions and presentations on the national higher education scene, the workings of the University, and effective governance. The event was judged a success and will be repeated in the spring of 1996, when discussions will focus on strategic planning issues. I have no doubt that these occasions will continue, probably annually.

One of the independent members of Council (a retired vice-chancellor) and a co-opted member have been chosen for their experience in higher education and their experience complements that of three members who are full-time members of staff (one of whom is a co-opted member).

I am discussing other ways in which the external members of Council can be more involved and known throughout the University, for example by associating members with the different parts of the University on a rotating basis. It is not intended that the members should be involved in the management of these areas, nor that they should act as spokespersons for these areas on the Council, but the informal links are intended to improve the members' knowledge of the institution they are charged with governing.

The establishment of the joint committees also helps the Council to be more familiar with the working of the University.

Finally, in my view the effectiveness of the Council could be improved by changing the balance between internal and external members—a matter discussed below.

(e) Internal and external membership of Council

I believe that the experience of University affairs, and the Institution's confidence in its Council would be improved by increasing the internal membership of the Council. Although it is possible for all the co-opted members of the Council to be members of staff of the University (in addition to 2 of the ordinary members), under the legislation the co-opted members have to be nominated by the independent members and such an increase in staff membership may not be acceptable. (There are, however, other needs to be addressed through co-opted membership—including, for example, local authority membership.) I realise that the great majority of the new Universities have made a success of their governance and management arrangements under the terms of the legislation, but, for the improved effectiveness of the governance of the University of Huddersfield I believe there is a need for a better balance of membership, and, in common with the commercial sector, I would wish the executive of the University (the senior management team and perhaps three Deans) to be members of the Council alongside the external "non-executive directors".

Universities are very diverse organisations, and different cultures and styles of management tend to characterise, for example, science and arts based departments. If staff membership of the Council is confined to two members there will be a limited set of people who are acceptable to the whole electorate. It would be helpful to increase the number of staff members—perhaps to three or four who can more appropriately represent this diversity.

The model articles make reference to the exclusion of staff members from discussion of the framework for staff terms and conditions of service and of matters referring to individual members of staff. We have to be careful not to give the impression of two classes of Council member. This does not help to engender a sense of trust. As far as possible these matters should be delegated to a smaller sub group of the independent members who report the results of their deliberations to the full Council, from which the staff members need not be excluded.

To retain a majority of external members (co-opted and independent) which I support, it would be necessary to allow for a somewhat larger Council than the maximum of 25 laid down in the legislation—see **g**) below.

(f) The Senate (Academic Board)

The draft Articles presently before the Privy Council propose a Senate of up to 40 members with a broad representation across Schools and staff grades with the University. For a University of 13,400 students organised into nine large Schools of Study, I believe that this is effectively the minimum number rather than a maximum.

(g) The size of the Council

Many of the clauses of the Education Reform Act of 1988 and the Model Articles were apparently based on the belief that the bodies which plan and oversee the management of Universities had to be small to be effective. I believe this is open to question. The Council of the University of Huddersfield recognised that for decisions to be well-informed, and to be "owned" by the University as a whole while retaining that delicate balance of effective management with the encouragement academic freedom, both the Senate and the Council needed to be enlarged. Any disadvantages of a larger Senate and Council can be overcome through an effective Planning and Resource Committee—as was recommended by the Jarratt Report (Report of the Steering Committee for Efficiency Studies in Universities [March 1985]). Such a Committee can act as an executive committee of the Senate and the Council, bringing together (as the HEFCE requires) the planning of academic, financial and estate matters. In my view the Council could usefully be larger (30 to 35 members) than is provided for in the Act to be more able to achieve the balance discussed in paragraph **(e).**

(h) Finding Council members

The Committee should not underestimate the difficulty which the Nominations Committee has in finding people with suitable experience, combined with the time to devote to the governance of such a complex organisation as a university. We canvass nominations for Council members widely within the University and would consider local advertising. The Council should not, however, be dominated by external members with only local interests. Given the difficulty which the Nominations Committee has in finding suitable people (a difficulty shared with other such bodies outside Higher Education) there might be a case for a parallel national organisation to PRONED which finds non-executive directors for the private sector.

(i) Openness and transparency

The agendas and minutes of meetings of the University Council and all its Committees are made available to students and staff in the University Library, although it is necessary from time to time to exclude sensitive commercial or personal information from what is published in this way.

(j) A register of interests

The University Council has decided to establish a register of interests of members and is at present discussing the form which it should take. This is in addition to the obligation placed on all Council and Committee members by the Articles of Government to declare interests at the time the relevant matter is discussed.

(k) The role of the HEFCE

Under the terms of the financial memorandum which each University has with the Higher Education Funding Council in England, I as Chief Executive have responsibility for advising the University Council if at any time any action or policy under consideration by it appears to me to be incompatible with the terms of the financial memorandum. If the Council decide nevertheless to proceed with the action or policy, I am under a duty to inform the HEFCE in writing.

Conclusion

The changes at the University of Huddersfield are relatively recent and, alongside the ideas outlined above, will be kept under review. As a result of all that has been done, I believe that the University is now an example of good governance, with the necessary checks and balances coming into place. Throughout all its difficulties the University has maintained its academic and financial soundness. It is coping well with the demanding environment of higher education and in the last two or three years has carried out some exciting developments. There are more to come.

The views expressed in this report are those of the Vice-Chancellor and Principal of the University of Huddersfield. They are expressed in a personal capacity and should not be taken to represent the views of the University Council, nor the University as a whole. They have been discussed with senior colleagues who endorse them.

Postscript

I greatly value the time and effort which external members of Council devote to University affairs. They bring an essential external perspective to the workings of the university. The advantages of such connections could be increased if the links were reciprocal. There are very few companies which use senior people from universities as non-executive directors. They would help to bring just that external dimension to company governance that Sir Adrian Cadbury suggested and would add to the breadth of experience of senior university managers.

Opening Statement by North East Surrey College of Technology Further Education Corporation

Thank you for the invitation to give evidence on behalf of NESCOT to the Committee on Standards in Public Life. The major concerns set out in NESCOT's submission to the Committee relate to

> Accountability
> Personal Liability
> Responsibilities

Accountability

The College's major concern is how to resolve the conflict between national and local accountability. Statute and funding council regulations deal exclusively with national accountability. National financial pressures, to conform to national norms, are likely to lead to the decline in traditionally expensive vocational provision in areas such as construction and engineering irrespective of the needs of the local community. Colleges have a funding mechanism for further education under which they have to continually increase student numbers to maintain a constant level of funding. Whilst accepting that Colleges have a responsibility to be cost effective, we believe that such a mechanism will eventually lead to concentration on courses which can be provided at the lowest cost. Under such circumstances accountability to the local community, which colleges are intended to serve, can only be secondary.

The College is not convinced that the establishment of search committees will necessarily increase accountability. It is possible, in fact, that they may do little more than formalise the closed nature of some corporations.

The College believes there is some merit in the use of nominating bodies being identified by Corporations, similar to the process used under LEA delegated responsibility to Colleges. As indicated in the College's original submission there is a potential danger that the independent members may become a self perpetuating "corporation within a corporation".

In general terms Colleges in the further education sector provide highly vocational courses and the structure of Corporations should reflect the mix of provision. However in areas where small businesses and self employment are the norm the lack of ability to properly recompense members for loss of earnings is regarded as a particular problem. The inability to assist with child care costs for female members is also seen as a deterrent at a time when women are under represented on Corporations.

Where Corporations cannot recruit members with the necessary mix of expertise they are encouraged to co-opt additional persons onto their committees. The attached summary of a recent CEF survey indicates severe difficulties in recruiting and retaining Corporation members so it seems extremely unlikely that these additional co-optees will be forthcoming unless they can be engaged on a consultancy type basis.

Personal Liability

As set out in the College's submission our major concern is that the current arrangements for College Governance rely on asking people to be responsible for running multi-million pound businesses on a voluntary basis without being able to tell them what their liabilities are. The fear then is that they may be subject to retrospective action by the funding agency who may, with the benefit of hindsight, choose to interpret the current ambiguous situation in a manner which is critical of decisions taken by Members in good faith and on the basis of information they had at the time.

Responsibilities

The term "member of a further education corporation" should be properly defined in law in order that their powers and responsibilities are properly clarified. It is not particularly helpful to define them as trustees or akin to trustees for the purposes of not paying them remuneration when clearly they could not act as Charity Trustees under the terms of the Charities Act 1993.

What members require is a clear definition of their powers and responsibilities set within a statutory framework not a vague interpretation of the situation which may or may not prove to be correct until it is tested in the courts.

WEDNESDAY 24 JANUARY 1996

MORNING SESSION

Members Present:

The Rt Hon Lord Nolan (Chairman)

Sir Clifford Boulton GCB   Dame Anne Warburton DCVO CMG
Sir William Utting CB   Diana Warwick

Witnesses:

Professor Robin Williams, Vice-Chancellor, Dr Emrys Evans CBE, LLd, FCIB, Chairman of Council, and Victor Carney, former Registrar, University of Wales, Swansea

Professor Adrian Webb, Vice-Chancellor, Rudi Plaut OBE, Chairman of Governors, and Leigh Bracegirdle, Secretary, University of Glamorgan

Dr Wyn Williams, Dr Geoff Simmons, and Brian Lloyd, University of Glamorgan, Trade Union Alliance

Professor John Andrews, Chief Executive, Richard Hirst, Director of Finance, and Linda Gainsbury, Head of FE Division, Welsh Funding Councils

1070. LORD NOLAN: It gives me great pleasure to open our first session of oral evidence in Wales. The very tight time constraints on our first study compelled us to have all our hearings in London, and although that did not prevent us from drawing on evidence from Wales and Scotland, we were anxious to travel beyond London on this study, especially since it is very much concerned with bodies whose activities are of interest to local communities and which are subject to separate governance arrangements in Wales.

Our hearings are in many ways more in the nature of informed discussions in public rather than inquisitions. Inevitably we have to take our oral evidence from active participants in the institutions we are studying so that we can test on them their reactions to issues that have been raised and propositions which we are considering. But we attach great importance in this Committee to proceeding as openly as possible, to making the public aware of what we are doing and to trying to draw in the widest possible range of views and opinions. So I very much hope that any members of the public who are prompted to offer views as a result of these hearings will not hesitate to write to me as soon as possible.

Of our ten Committee members, as you see at the moment we are at our lowest ebb, numbering only four. Another two will be with us for the afternoon session and we will be the strength of six for the rest of the hearings. Our two Members of Parliament are unable to be present because the House is sitting, and Sir Martin Jacomb has had to make his apologies because of business commitments. Lord Thomson has particularly asked me to make his apologies because until the weekend he had firmly planned to be here, but his doctor has now confined him to bed with flu.

We have four sets of witnesses this morning, mainly concerned with higher education. We welcome first Professor Robin Williams, the Vice-Chancellor, Dr Emrys Evans, the Chairman of Council, and Mr Victor Carney, former Registrar of the University of Wales, Swansea. In the context of this study, and perhaps more widely, the University of Wales counts as an old university. It was established before 1992 and it is a good deal older than that.

Our second group of witnesses come from a new, 1992, university, the University of Glamorgan. We shall hear from Professor Adrian Webb, the Vice-Chancellor, Mr Rudi Plaut, the Chairman of Governors, and Mr Leigh Bracegirdle, the University Secretary.

Then, for a view from another angle, we have Dr Wyn Williams, Dr Geoff Simmons and Mr Brian Lloyd of the University of Glamorgan Trade Union Alliance.

Finally this morning, from a third stratospheric viewpoint, we have the Welsh Funding Councils, represented by Professor John Andrews, the Chief Executive, Mr Richard Hirst, the Director of Finance, and Ms Linda Gainsbury, the head of the further education division.

With that introduction we now come, first, to our opening witnesses, Professor Robin Williams, Dr Evans and Mr Carney. Thank you very much for coming to us, gentlemen. Like all our witnesses, you have come forward totally voluntarily and you have already given us great help with your written submissions. I am well aware of the demands that this kind of occasion makes upon those taking part in it.

I believe—am I right?—that you have a short opening statement that you would like to make to fill in some of the background to the questions we are asking.

PROFESSOR ROBIN WILLIAMS, DR EMRYS EVANS CBE, AND VICTOR CARNEY

DR EMRYS EVANS (Chairman of Council, University of Wales, Swansea): Very briefly, my Lord Nolan, I think—I underline "I think"—we welcome the opportunity of giving evidence to your committee. I do not think I need introduce my colleagues, Professor Robin Williams, the Vice-Chancellor, on my left and Mr Victor Carney, the immediate past registrar, on my right.

Perhaps it would be helpful if I were to remind the Committee that the University of Wales, Swansea, is an autonomous university institution incorporated a long time ago, as you said—we are in fact celebrating our 75th anniversary this year—and is governed by its own royal charter and statute. It awards degrees, though, of the federal University of Wales, of which Swansea is a full member.

We have received the correspondence and guidance from your committee, sir, and are prepared to the best of our ability to answer any questions that are listed thereon or any further inquiries that you may have.

1071. LORD NOLAN: Thank you very much. The University of Wales, Swansea, you say, is autonomous. I wonder if you could clear my mind on this. What then is the specific function of the University of Wales as distinct from the component parts? Is it the academic function, concerning itself purely with the contents of the academic courses and examinations?

EMRYS EVANS: Perhaps it would be proper for me to report right at the outset that, apart from being Chairman of the Council at the University in Swansea, I am an independent appointee of the Lord President of the Privy Council on the Court and Council of the University of Wales.

You should be informed that the federal system of governance was the subject of a major review in 1992-93, as a result of which a revised system was approved by the Privy Council and it came into effect in January of last year. Two of the primary concerns of this review were the relationship between the member institutions of the federation and indeed the role of the federal authority.

Major changes in the structure of higher education under the 1992 Act, the setting up of the Higher Education Funding Council for Wales in 1993 and increasing evidence of internal resistance to the perceived shift of planning authority away from the constituent institutions towards the federal centre all combined to make an early review of the system a matter of urgency. A working party was set up and, being sensitive to the autonomy of the constituent colleges and of the university as a chartered body, it was faced with the task of producing meaningful recommendations that could be seen to command the willing support of all bodies concerned.

The report's advocacy of partnership, based on the utmost good faith, was the only foundation on which all parties could work effectively together. The key features of the new system of governance which came into effect last year were a mission statement of the university as distinct from the individual constituent members; a new and influential body, the Vice-Chancellor's Board, was formed; the size of the university council was reduced, but with the proportion of lay members still maintained; and other features were also radically changed, including the machinery to facilitate the development of relationships with universities, and associated institutions of higher education.

The mission statement identified, and I am coming to your question, my Lord, four primary functions within the distinctive role of the federal university—core responsibility for awarding degrees and maintenance of academic standards, the provision of those services, both functional and financial, that it is agreed are more effectively based at the centre, the creation of a forum for the discussion of long-term academic strategy and a

facilitating role in the development and promotion of inter-college collaboration, both in teaching and in research. At the same time the mission statement confirms the university's commitment in all its activity to the educational, cultural and economic needs of Wales and to the enhancement of the university's international standing.

The federal system of governance consists of four main bodies—the University Court, Council, the Academic Board and the Vice-Chancellor's Board. Details of these four bodies can be given if required, but in order to save time, my Lord, I conclude by saying that I am anxious to assure the Committee that the University of Wales Council welcomes the Council of University Chairmen's guide for members of governing bodies, has accepted the general thrust of the recommendations and has set up a working party to see how those recommendations can best be put into effect in the particular circumstances of a federal system.

I think possibly the Vice-Chancellor would like to add to that statement.

LORD NOLAN: Thank you.

PROFESSOR ROBIN WILLIAMS (Vice-Chancellor, University of Wales, Swansea): Could I add a brief note? Essentially the degrees and related matters are dealt with by the University of Wales. They approve the courses and the syllabi, they appoint the external examiners and they receive the examiners' reports, etc. The federal university is the guardian of the degrees, essentially. The constituent institutions, of which we are one, are responsible for the delivery of teaching and research. The division of responsibilities is reasonably clear and the system works reasonably well.

1072. LORD NOLAN: Thank you very much. That is most helpful. I wonder if I could ask you about one specific aspect of the arrangements. The question arises out of the problems that were referred to the Visitor in 1972–73. We have no interest whatever in reopening that matter in any detail, but it does raise for us the interesting and important question of the structure by which conflicts and disputes—perhaps covering both academic and disciplinary matters, because they cannot always be neatly separated, can they?—are best resolved. Both the university itself and Swansea, have the Visitor machinery to invoke, and the college invoked it on that occasion. We wonder how far that system, which is peculiar to what are called the old universities, might usefully be more generally extended or whether there are better ways of doing things. Looking back on the matter, would you say that Swansea felt that the Visitor system had done what was expected of it on that occasion, that it had worked as it should?

EMRYS EVANS: I think we will invite Mr Carney to answer that.

LORD NOLAN: If you please.

EMRYS EVANS: Then I might have an observation to make.

VICTOR CARNEY (Former Registrar, University of Wales, Swansea): Yes, sir, I am sure that using the Visitor system in the specific case mentioned was the way in which that case could be resolved, and we decided as council and university to go forward with that. However, it was protracted; it took a very long time. The Queen is our Visitor and, for reasons that will be obvious, Privy Council had to find somebody who would make judgment for the Queen. That proved a very, very difficult task because of the complexity of the problem that we had, so it was very, very protracted. However, whether one agrees or disagrees with the outcome, it was helpful in resolving the dispute in this case, yes.

1073. LORD NOLAN: The principle, I suppose, of common interest is whether it is important to have, if only as a fall-back, an independent source of authority to deal with disputes that it is felt have not been or cannot be satisfactorily resolved within the university and, if so, what form that outside, independent genie should take. One other candidate which has been put forward, as you know, by a number of people, is that there should be, rather than a Visitor for each university, an ombudsman figure. One associates ombudsmen, I suppose, particularly with maladministration, but their general function, as you know, is investigatory and reporting from an independent angle. Have you considered whether there were alternatives to the Visitor system that might be of interest to Swansea or are you going to carry on with it as it is?

EMRYS EVANS: Our experience of the Visitor system, my Lord, as Mr Carney has mentioned, was time-consuming; getting to the Privy Council was very protracted; the Lord President's committee had to make several approaches to people of standing before they could find anyone to take on the mission. So maybe, on reflection, we believe that a good case could be made, possibly, for establishing a regular channel, and that perhaps would point us to the ombudsman's office. Our feeling is, and we have not been able to give a great deal of thought to this, that with an ombudsman's office that was already in operation there would be case law to refer to and there would be experience at hand to deal with such disputes and no need to start from scratch.

The Visitor system has without doubt a debilitating effect on all, so I suppose our immediate reaction, at least speaking personally, is that we would have no objection to setting up an ombudsman system. If such a course was considered, some would possibly argue that there would be a loss of status, but the Queen is not directly involved, although the Lord President of the Council is. He has to give active, detailed consideration to all submissions, and perhaps a case could be made for not involving Ministers. Ministers are exceptionally busy people, and their direct involvement inevitably delays the procedure. In fact, my Lord, I discussed this particular issue with our immediate past President, the Lord Callaghan, and I think he would agree with that point of view.

LORD NOLAN: That there might be advantage in having an independent body or person, independent both of Ministers and of the university itself.

EMRYS EVANS: Yes.

LORD NOLAN: And able to deal quickly, because he would have the expertise and the staff, with problems as they arose.

EMRYS EVANS: Indeed, I think that is the case. The long delay, dragging it out, directs officers' attention from

other important issues and it inevitably has an effect on morale as well.

LORD NOLAN: Speed is very important, isn't it?

EMRYS EVANS: It is important.

LORD NOLAN: If I may digress for a moment, it was one of the factors that the Committee took into account in recommending to the House of Commons that they should consider the appointment of a parliamentary commissioner, and one is pleased to see that a dispute has been resolved speedily, in a matter of weeks, by that method, but I appreciate that that is a very different setting. Your experience of the Visitor is of course unique: it is not a situation that is going to arise, one hopes, very often.

EMRYS EVANS: We sincerely hope not.

1074. LORD NOLAN: Even so it is an important matter to bear in mind with universities generally, and I am very grateful to you. I wonder if I could turn now, please, to what you told us about your Council. How big is the Council?

ROBIN WILLIAMS: Fifty two.

1075. LORD NOLAN: Fifty two, and you have, I notice, local authority representatives amongst the lay members. Are they delegated by the local authority or do you ask for people?

VICTOR CARNEY: They are delegated normally, sir.

1076. LORD NOLAN: The note you sent us says that the register of members' interests of the Council has recently been instituted, but it is not published. Is there a particular reason for that? Would there be objection, do you think, to publishing it?

VICTOR CARNEY: No, sir. Our fear and worry was that each individual might have a reason or a case for not wishing the world in general to know what some of his or her interests were. Apart from that, there is no reason at all why the interests of members of Council, or indeed members of the whole staff of the university, could not be made public.

1077. LORD NOLAN: No, quite. It is a very natural feeling, which I think we all share. I think the immediate instinct is "This is my business. What does it matter to anybody else?" On the other side of the coin, if an institution is entrusted with a large amount of public money—this is really why we are here—are the public adequately informed about those who are spending it?

EMRYS EVANS: We have this form of disclosure in mind, my Lord, but we feel that we would have to have the authority of the person concerned to disclose publicly such involvements.

LORD NOLAN: Yes. That would certainly be so unless there were legislation.

VICTOR CARNEY: I was thinking, sir, we would want the authority of the Council to ask its members to let this be published, and then if a member dissented from that, he would have to consider his position in terms of the Council's decision.

1078. LORD NOLAN: Yes. Thank you. Do you have members of the staff on the Council?

VICTOR CARNEY: Yes, sir.

1079. LORD NOLAN: How are they chosen?

VICTOR CARNEY: They are elected from among the senate of the institution primarily or, secondly, from the lecturers' association, which is that group of staff which is non-professorial.

ROBIN WILLLIAMS: I should perhaps add, Lord Nolan, that we are also reviewing the membership of the Council at the moment and its operation, with a possibility of trade union representation, and of course also there is student representation.

1080. LORD NOLAN: There are students, are there?

ROBIN WILLIAMS: There are students, yes.

1081. LORD NOLAN: I see. Are they again put forward by the student council?

VICTOR CARNEY: Yes, sir. The students' union elect a president chairman treasurer and a welfare officer, and a number of sabbatical officers, who then serve on the college council. Four of them in fact serve on the college council.

1082. LORD NOLAN: The last question I wanted to raise with you before I ask Dame Anne to join in the questioning is this. You refer in your letter to us to the imposition of a model statute on the position of the staff by the University Commissioners. The University Commissioners, I think I am right in saying, are five individuals appointed by the Secretary of State under the 1988 Act, but we haven't come across them before. Who are they?

VICTOR CARNEY: Maybe we used the phrase slightly wrongly. I think it was formerly Lord Justice May who actually looked at charter and statutes and worried particularly about the arrangements for disciplining of the tenure in universities and the powers of the chief executive in terms of managing that area of dispute within a university that is becoming all too common. It was this group under Lord May who first of all sent us a draft. We worked on the draft and sent it back. But ultimately they sent us a document, which became, through the Privy Council charter, a statute of the university.

1083. LORD NOLAN: I see. And although the word "imposition" rather caught our eyes, it was accepted quite freely and happily by you.

VICTOR CARNEY: Oh yes, sir. Our Court and our Council accepted it, with a little grunting, I must say, in fairness to the chairman, and indeed had to accept it, because it had come from the Privy Council as an amendment to our charter and statute.

ROBIN WILLIAMS: I should add perhaps that in my first year as vice-chancellor we did have to make use of it,

and it was very useful having the statute in place, although, operating it, we will need to gain experience.

VICTOR CARNEY: Yes, it is a difficult one to operate, you are quite right, vice-chancellor, as we found.

1084. LORD NOLAN: One of the things we constantly find in this part of our inquiry is the amount of new development and progress that is being made in each of the types of body we are looking at in conscientious efforts to improve the transparency and efficiency with which their affairs are conducted, and of course we are all feeling our way.

I said that was my last question. May I just ask shortly about the Court of Governors. You say you have 350 members and they cover a wide range of professional bodies, both locally and nationally. You say that in practice busy industrialists and professional persons are often reluctant to commit too much time to university business. That one can understand, but who is in practice mainly responsible for the commercial decisions? Is it the Court or the Council?

VICTOR CARNEY: It is the Council normally, sir, yes. The Court has specific functions—I will outline them if you wish—but it is the Council which in a sense is the executive commercial arm of the university.

LORD NOLAN: Yes, and of course great financial expertise is always at a premium and is in practice provided voluntarily for yours and all these bodies.

EMRYS EVANS: We are very fortunate in that respect, my Lord. We have a finance committee and a planning and resources committee before going to Council, and the treasurer, a layman, is a qualified chartered accountant. We have two senior, albeit retired, bankers as well on the finance committee and another chartered accountant, who is in business, so we are well advised in that respect on commercial decisions.

1085. LORD NOLAN: Thank you very much. I wonder if I could just say this. We have a phrase in our laws "liberty to apply". May we have liberty to apply, having studied your answers this morning, to ask for further written information of the kind which has recently come into existence which we have not seen yet? If we are going to ask for it, we will do so soon, because our time is drawing near to a close.

EMRYS EVANS: We will be only too pleased to help in every way.

LORD NOLAN: Thank you very much indeed. Dame Anne.

1086. ANNE WARBURTON: I wonder if I might first say that, having been a bit involved in model statutes myself in the past, I was not shocked by the word "imposed". Could I pick up some points which have already been covered in general? I should like to start with the question of grievances, but move to a different angle. I do not speak about grievances, I speak about concerns and these are points which arise very much in the administration and management of the university. Is there a system in the university for people to signal to elsewhere that there are problems—there might be problems of propriety, for example—in such a way that it does not risk their job?

VICTOR CARNEY: There is no formal way, apart from normal departmental structure—the Vice-Chancellor was a head of department before he came to Swansea; he could tell you more about that—in which concerns about academic work are taken through the system into the faculties and up to the Senate. As to other sorts of difficulties and concerns, I think there is no formal way for that to happen. Swansea is not unique, I am sure. We are a smallish university in terms of the system generally, and concerns do come through the system by staff talking to staff.

1087. ANNE WARBURTON: But, for example, does the Registrar serve as the Jiminy Cricket for the university or do certain members of the Council perhaps have a role in having these concerns referred to them? I am talking about concerns which do not necessarily directly involve the person concerned.

VICTOR CARNEY: I think it is true to say that the Vice-Chancellor and the Registrar have open doors, and people come regularly to talk about obscure as well as very detailed problems.

ROBIN WILLIAMS: The way it works is that certainly staff can communicate, and they often do, by letter, and matters are investigated, and if there is found to be cause, then it would be taken further. We would immediately look at the charters and statutes as well to see how to handle a situation that arose.

EMRYS EVANS: As Chairman of Council I have been approached a few times over the years as well, so we are able to progress those grievances in the correct manner.

1088. ANNE WARBURTON: Yes. Good. Thank you very much. Talking about the composition of the Council, you have put some weight on the financial expertise. Could you tell us a little bit more about what other criteria you apply in setting up the Council and indeed how the Council is made into a well-balanced whole?

VICTOR CARNEY: I think one has to look first of all at what the structure of the Council is. Where does the membership come from? First of all, there is the academic staff. They would be represented, as we have said. Then there are the students.

1089. ANNE WARBURTON: But the students elect their own representatives.

VICTOR CARNEY: They elect their own. Then there are six each year—total 18—members of the Court elected to the Council, so they come from the whole diaspora, if you like, of the 350, if they want to, and then there are people that we co-opt, and it is in that key area, the co-option area, that we can draw on specific expertise. There, for example, we would be looking to draw on specific expertise in finance or in commerce or in business, and then the local authorities appoint their own, and they bring presumably, and they do indeed, a sort of "political" interest to our affairs, so broadly we get everybody, I think.

1090. ANNE WARBURTON: Can I ask you two questions on that? First of all, are the local authority appointees mandated appointees? Do they come with a brief from their local authority or are they there as persons who are chosen by their local authorities but bring their own views?

VICTOR CARNEY: Judging by the work they put in, they come on their own. They are not mandated by anyone. They have views, opinions, which they share with us at great length.

ANNE WARBURTON: It has been suggested to us in some of the evidence that, if they are mandated, it is quite often difficult for them to change their position in the light of discussion.

VICTOR CARNEY: We have never had that sort of problem in Swansea.

1091. ANNE WARBURTON: No. And then secondly the co-options—are they additional to the 52?

VICTOR CARNEY: No, they are included in the 52.

1092. ANNE WARBURTON: Yes, I see, and how large a section are they?

VICTOR CARNEY: Twelve.

ROBIN WILLIAMS: Could I add that we have a nominations committee, so we are able to look at the balance of the Council and bring in the expertise, so having the co-opted members is very, very important to get that balance. We need a balance covering the region, we need a balance covering the academic side of things; we need expertise on the finance, on the buildings side, so it does work quite well.

1093. ANNE WARBURTON: And the nominations committee are who?

VICTOR CARNEY: The Chairman is in the chair, and shall be in the future at any rate. The Vice-Chancellor—it is a pro-Vice-Chancellor—one of the vice-presidents and the treasurer.

EMRYS EVANS: As we are in a highly competitive business nowadays, Dame Warburton, we cast the net very widely in order to get as much expertise as we possibly can on to Council. We are responsible for a large amount of public money and we think we really must seek the best possible people to serve on our Council, and we try to do that to the best of our ability, and we did welcome the suggestion of a nominations committee as is recommended in this guideline.

VICTOR CARNEY: Sorry, I might have misled you. There are nine members co-opted and not 12. I am sorry. I just checked my own charter.

1094. ANNE WARBURTON: And the movement of members? Are they co-opted for the same length of time as other members?

VICTOR CARNEY: Three years.

ANNE WARBURTON: So your new blood comes in all sectors.

VICTOR CARNEY: Yes.

EMRYS EVANS: There are some of us who do not take very kindly to the recommendation in this book, and I was party to it, that they should retire gracefully having reached the ripe old age of three score years and ten, but there is a slight escape clause there, so we manage to operate that quite effectively.

1095. ANNE WARBURTON: It is a very difficult balancing thing, isn't it?

EMRYS EVANS: It is.

VICTOR CARNEY: The point you made about new blood of course is important: two sets of three years should be enough and then the co-opted member should move, and we are very aware of that problem, Vice-Chancellor, aren't we?

ROBIN WILLIAMS: Oh yes.

1096. ANNE WARBURTON: I have been struck by the evidence we have had from the new universities that they are very pleased that they have got smaller councils. Would you expect business to be transacted more efficiently, more effectively, if the Council were smaller?

EMRYS EVANS: There is no lack of participation in our council. We normally have an attendance of 40-plus. They are very good at attendance and they are certainly very active. They make the chairman's life pretty uncomfortable at times.

ROBIN WILLIAMS: For the operation we have then to divide things into committees, so there is a finance committee, which is small and very active, there is a buildings and estate committee, which looks after the estate, so those committees are very important. I do not think we could run these with a large council if we did not have that structure.

1097. ANNE WARBURTON: On committees, I notice that you refer to your internal and external audit committee, as opposed to the internal and external audit. Can you tell me a bit more about the committee and what its role in the internal and external audit is?

VICTOR CARNEY: Yes. It is a committee of the Council. It has an independent role and reports directly to the Council actually. We have an internal audit system linked into the University of Cardiff and the College of Medicine. These internal auditors that we all have report to this audit committee, and that audit committee actually makes the chairman's life even more miserable on the Council, frankly.

ROBIN WILLIAMS: A very important thing is that it be totally independent, so the members of the audit committee are not members of any other major committee of the college. They are on the Council.

1098. ANNE WARBURTON: Who does the internal and the external audit?

VICTOR CARNEY: The external audit is done by a firm that the Court have to authorise every year. Is it Touche Ross or Coopers & Lybrand?

EMRYS EVANS: Coopers & Lybrand.

VICTOR CARNEY: The internal audit is done by a group of staff that we have that commonly audit Cardiff, the College of Medicine and ourselves.

ROBIN WILLIAMS: Essentially our own employees, together with the other colleges.

ANNE WARBURTON: And do you then have a series of further audits going up into the——

EMRYS EVANS: Indeed we do—to the National Audit Office ultimately.

1099. ANNE WARBURTON: What is your view? Do you think that the auditing is all right and effective?

ROBIN WILLIAMS: Could I say that we also of course get audited on the teaching side—quality assessment—and also on the research side for the research assessment. My belief is there was a need for tightening up, and I think that has been done. There is a danger of us being over-audited. It is again getting this balance right. Our staff have to put a great deal of work into preparing for the audit visits and so on, but by and large I think the present system works quite well.

ANNE WARBURTON: They are two different sorts of function of course.

ROBIN WILLIAMS: Yes, they are.

1100. ANNE WARBURTON: If you were asked which of the financial audits might be dispensed with, would you be able to answer that? I do not want to put you into difficulties.

ROBIN WILLIAMS: I do not think we could reduce any of them.

EMRYS EVANS: I subscribe to the view that we look as if we had been over-audited, but I would not like to make any decision regarding doing away with any of them.

ROBIN WILLIAMS: On the financial side I think all of them are needed.

EMRYS EVANS: All of them are needed. We are dealing with vast sums of money and we cannot, I think, be over-audited in that respect.

1101. ANNE WARBURTON: Then one last question because of the time: on the teaching assessment side, how would you make the assessment process fit the needs more closely?

ROBIN WILLIAMS: At the moment the institution is assessed for its structure. In addition to that, the departments themselves are assessed, and it should be possible to combine those so at least only one of these would be needed. So one could reduce the load quite a bit that way.

ANNE WARBURTON: Thank you very much.

1102. LORD NOLAN: You are all well aware that although you receive and handle large amounts of public money, there is not a penny to spare at any level—the staff, students or the college itself—so we wish you all possible success in continuing to meet the very difficult financial as well as auditing problems that you face. We have heard evidence of the tensions that can arise between universities by way of competition because of the financial pressures that they are under, but it is not one of the subjects that we have time to talk to you about this morning, I am afraid. We would like to keep you here all day, but this is true of all our witnesses, so we can only thank you very much for coming along.

EMRYS EVANS: I would like to add that, even with a lot of public money, the shoe is hurting and we could do with a lot more, sadly. Can I, on behalf of us, thank you, my Lord, and all of you.

1103. LORD NOLAN: Thank you very much.

We now have Professor Adrian Webb, Vice-Chancellor, Rudi Plaut OBE, Chairman of Governors, and Leigh Bracegirdle, Secretary, of the University of Glamorgan. Good morning, gentlemen. Thank you very much for coming along.

I am going, if I may, to move straight on to the questioning. In a democratic way on this Committee we take it in turns to lead off, and it is Sir William's turn now, so, Sir William, would you like to start, please?

1104. WILLIAM UTTING: Thank you, Chairman. I would like to pick up straight away, if I may, on Professor Webb's experience at senior levels in an older university and now as vice-chancellor of a new university. I think it would be very helpful if we could have the benefit of his experience of both those systems. I am obviously not seeking for the particular institutions to be compared, but you have worked in both systems and it would help us, I think, to know what you think the advantages and disadvantages of each of those systems might be.

PROFESSOR ADRIAN WEBB, RUDI PLAUT OBE, AND LEIGH BRACEGIRDLE

PROFESSOR ADRIAN WEBB (Vice-Chancellor, University of Glamorgan): Thank you very much. Chairman, may I briefly make a historical comment as background to that. I think it is important to remember that the old universities themselves have diverse traditions and governing structures, the ancient universities starting very much as self-governing groups of academics—collegial government—the civic universities beginning with a very strong involvement of local communities, regional communities, which was usually represented through courts and councils, as you were hearing just now of the University of Wales, and this was quite typical. In the mid-1980s it was very clear that many people in government felt that the balance of power in the old universities was too clearly with senates and that courts and councils particularly were not as able effectively to ensure and control the management of the university at a time when resources were beginning to become very much tighter, and I think that was what really precipitated discussion of the governing structure of the old universities, and there were requirements at that time on the old universities to ensure a more effective control by councils and the creation of joint committees on resources, academic planning, etc.

The importance of that is that when the new universities came into being under the terms of the 1988 Education Act that thinking was reflected directly into the constitutional structure of the new universities, so the new universities operate under a legislative structure which puts in place small governing bodies. It involves student membership, it permits up to two members of the staff to be elected from the academic board, which is the equivalent of senate in the new universities, but it requires a clear majority of independent lay members.

Of course I do not know what has happened at the old universities in the last three or four years, but my experience is that the dynamic of the governing body is quite different, that the terms of trade—the terms of debate, if you like—are clearly influenced by the fact that the independent members are in a strong majority on the governing body, they are relatively few in number, they are deeply involved in the life of the university, and the terms of debate in the governing body and in the committees of the governing body are very much set by the independent members, and I think that is a significant difference. Their expertise in the university is, I would argue, very well honed, and that compares, in my personal experience anyway, with the independent members in an older university and a large court being less expert about the detail of the university, with the exception of that smaller group of independent members who are on the resources and planning committee. So I think the whole dynamic of the governing body is different because of the constitutional arrangements.

1105. WILLIAM UTTING: Good. Thank you very much. Could I broaden the questioning then, but still staying on constitutional points? General criticisms have been made to us about the means of constituting the governing bodies of new universities on the ground that the criteria for appointment actually bias appointments towards white males who come from professional and business backgrounds, so that a very narrow range and not necessarily a genuinely independent range of people is represented, and also on the ground that the proper interests in running a university cannot be accommodated on a governing body as small as that. What is your reaction to those sorts of general criticisms?

ADRIAN WEBB: I would not argue that the method of appointment necessarily biases towards white professional males. I have no doubt at all that the membership probably is biased in that direction nationally, but new universities are not the only institutions with that problem. We have certainly actively sought in the university to avoid such a dominance, but it is not always easy. It is important to note that constitutionally it is the independent members who make the formal decision or recommendation about new members to the board. There is a membership or nominations committee, which makes recommendations to the board, but the whole of the board does discuss new membership, but constitutionally it is the independent members who have the decision-making power in terms of the selection of new members. As we have indicated in evidence to the Funding Council, we trawl widely within the university and outside for names, but there is no doubt at all that with a small board what the independent members typically are looking for is expertise of particular kinds. They are looking to ensure that the board contains a high level of financial expertise, a high level of legal expertise, expertise in estates, in audit, etc., so that necessarily tends to bias choice to a significant degree towards people from professional backgrounds.

1106. WILLIAM UTTING: You find it necessary still, with a small governing body, to have a number of committees.

ADRIAN WEBB: Certainly. Yes.

1107. WILLIAM UTTING: Would you care to say something about them and how they are appointed and how they report to Council—how they are made accountable?

ADRIAN WEBB: The governing body has established a series of committees—finance committee obviously, audit committee obviously, employment committee, which sets policy for the employment of staff throughout the university, broad policy framework, etc. We have just established a new health and safety committee, because we think that is now of such significance, not least in terms of governors' liability, that there must be a committee of the governing body. The committees and the governing body operate on a cycle which brings committee business to the governing body and, as I indicated, the terms of that business are very substantially influenced at committee level as well as governing body level by the independent members, because they are in a majority in committees as well as in the governing body itself. But membership of those committees is itself determined by the nominations committee of the governing body. I am sorry, they make recommendations to the whole of the governing body, which then accepts or otherwise.

WILLIAM UTTING: But they are the engines for policy development in specific areas within the university.

ADRIAN WEBB: Very much so.

WILLIAM UTTING: But all their decisions are, so to speak, recommendations to the council

ADRIAN WEBB: Of course.

WILLIAM UTTING: So that every member of the governing body is involved in approving major decisions affecting the universities.

ADRIAN WEBB: Committees and the chairs of committees do have areas of delegated responsibility, and chairs will take chairs' action, and indeed the involvement of chairs of committees with the senior officers of the university may be weekly or even daily on particular issues, such as major building programmes, and chair's action is essential to expedite business, but the chair obviously is working within a framework established by the committee, which framework in itself is established by the governing body, and all matters are reported of course to the governing body and open to debate at the governing body.

1108. WILLIAM UTTING: I should be interested if you could say something about what difference incorporation actually made to the running of the university. You have spoken, I think, about life since incorporation. What was life like before that? How much better and in what areas is it now?

ADRIAN WEBB: Can I pass on that point, because I was not an employee of the university before incorporation?

RUDI PLAUT OBE (Chairman of Governors, University of Glamorgan): I was not a governor until incorporation. The only one of the three of us is the clerk.

LEIGH BRACEGIRDLE (Secretary, University of Glamorgan): It is very clearly over to me. We made some comment about this in the submission we made. As a new university we came much later to incorporation—1992 as opposed to 1989 in England—so we have had a much shorter period of development after becoming an incorporation. From my own experience, the key thing that I see is the very clear accountability of the board of governors, the responsibility of the governors without reference to the county council, which we had before then. It makes a very key difference—a much greater involvement of governors. The expertise, which has been mentioned earlier, that was brought to bear on the governance of the institution has made a tremendous difference in terms of the involvement of governors in the university. That is one of the strengths, as I see it, of the new system.

ADRIAN WEBB: Can I add one footnote to that, which I think may be helpful? It is important to remember that as a polytechnic managed by a local authority the polytechnic was effectively acting as a high-level clerical function on a number of activities to the relevant expert departments in the local authority—for example, estates and finance—so that what we have had to do since incorporation is to establish that level of expertise at officer level, but what was fundamental to that was having that level of expertise at governor level in the first instance to ensure that it was established at officer level, and it is important to remember that a polytechnic becoming incorporated lacked the expertise of managing those functions as opposed to administering them to a managing local authority. It is a very sharp difference.

RUDI PLAUT: It may just help if I add that, being chairman of a single board, you know where the responsibility lies. There is some personal liability, but you know where the buck stops, you cannot shift from it, and that helps greatly in having clear thinking, because you know you are responsible full stop.

1109. WILLIAM UTTING: Could I follow up the point about the local authority and what you see desirable relationships with a local authority and local authorities now consisting of and how, if you think this relationship is valuable, it is established and maintained?

ADRIAN WEBB: Can I at least begin to respond on that one by distinguishing between formal and informal? We are at this very moment in the process—indeed, yesterday I was in discussions with the new Association of Local Authorities in Wales—of establishing the mechanism by which the local authority member of the board will be chosen in future. We have an interim mechanism. So there is a formal representation of the local authorities. It is important to remember that, while we are highly local in one sense to the valleys communities of mid-Glamorgan, we deliver education throughout Wales to 23 partner colleges, so we are quite clearly saying that we wish that local representation to move around Wales in due course. In addition, we have the ex-director of education of the ex-county as a member of the board and we have the chair of the education committee of the new authority as a co-opted member of one of our committees, and indeed there is a bilateral relationship between us. I have an involvement in the local education authority as well.

In addition to that, we have a formally structured liaison committee with local residents. What I am now going to suggest is that it is very difficult to define community for a university, because we live within a local community, we operate regionally, we operate nationally in a Welsh sense, we operate nationally in a UK sense and we operate very much internationally with something like 20 partner institutions throughout the world in addition to 23 partner institutions in Wales and the UK. So for the immediate local community we have a residents' liaison committee, and that is very much about the university in the local community, the inevitable friction in having 11,000 students walking through local streets and parking in local streets, etc. We have a local authority liaison committee with both the town council in the old structure and the borough council. So that is a formal liaison committee with the local authority's committee structure, and it covers all matters of interaction between the university and the community, including things like advanced discussions of the university's plans with the local authority members, indications of what we might be looking for in planning permission terms, traffic control problems, etc., and then we have these formal methods of representation—I prefer not to say "representation'; it can be interpreted as delegation. We have the formal method of incorporating a local authority member or members on the governing body and on committees by co-option.

1110. WILLIAM UTTING: There are inevitably tensions —you have referred to them—in this kind of operation, but from what you say it sounds as though, even with a comparatively small governing body, you believe that all the major stakeholders, to borrow a phrase, in the university are actually in membership of Council.

ADRIAN WEBB: I am not sure how large a governing body you would need to involve everybody who thought they were stakeholders. Clearly, as I said just now, we operate with a very wide range of communities. Even within the region we operate very clearly with local authorities themselves, with other kinds of public bodies—the WDA, the Welsh Office. We operate through businesses—companies. We have nearly 10,000 UK and international companies on our active business list and many hundreds of public bodies. So I think the definition of community for a university, because it is local, national and international, is actually extremely difficult, so what we attempt to do is to ensure we have mechanisms in place for each of these functionally different styles of interaction with different communities.

To give an instance, all the relevant departments in the university have formal or well developed informal committees to engage with local business, and that operates on a departmental level. We also have a university business club, so we interact with the business community in that way. I have membership of the CBI. So we seek to structure interaction with a variety of different communities, functional and geographical, and I do not think you could achieve that by direct representation only, however big your body was.

1111. WILLIAM UTTING: I perhaps conclude with a couple of specific points. There is a section on openness in your written submission and you say that minutes of the

board are circulated to heads of department and included on the agendas of academic board, so they get through the academic bit of the works all right. "Minutes of meetings with the board and its main committees are available to staff and students in the library."

That does not strike me as being a very proactive form of informing people of what is going on. What does it mean in practice?

ADRIAN WEBB: I do not think it is proactive. That is to ensure that the minutes are publicly available, and that includes, by the way, the declaration of members' interests, which is something you raised earlier on. We have a formal structure for declaration of members' interests annually, and those interests are publicly available in the library as well. But we publicise the decisions of the directorate weekly to all the heads of departments, we publicise the decisions of the directorate and the governing body through the university's internal newsletter and we also have an agreement with the editor of the newsletter which says that he has complete editorial freedom within the law to report whatever he believes is right and proper in the university newspaper, and he regularly interviews myself or others about policy decisions. So we would see the internal newsletter as the active means of communicating to staff.

In addition to that, annually I make an oral and a written report about the university's past year to all members of staff. We follow that report session, which is an open public occasion, usually organised on two or three different occasions to allow different types of staff access to it within their timetables, with an informal "meet the directorate", where we simply sit down over tea and biscuits at tables and the members of the directorate move around the tables. That is immediately following my policy statement of the year, so that staff can pick up policy issues directly with the directorate, or indeed they can pick up grievance issues of an informal kind if they wanted to, and they do. We also similarly have a "meet the governors" occasion, exactly similarly structured: a general introduction from the chairman and myself and then informal groups of governors moving around the tables over tea and biscuits. The chairman and I annually visit every department and seek in that visit to meet every member of the department, so that every member of the department not only knows who the chairman is but has the opportunity to say quite bluntly, as they do sometimes, "We don''t agree with this particular policy", or whatever. So I think our formal publication of minutes is very much the tip of the iceberg.

1112. WILLIAM UTTING: What about the circulation of board papers? You say that restricting these to the board leads to more open debate. I think that is an arguable proposition.

ADRIAN WEBB: As one of the members of your previous team of witnesses mentioned, universities have become very much more commercially sensitive. We discuss an awful lot of matters which, if they became public knowledge before we had negotiated or made decisions, would affect, for example, the price of land or would affect, for example, the way we organise transport, etc., so we are actually much more conscious, I think, nowadays, of the commercial sensitivity of a large amount of what we do, and of course many of the decisions we make are about, I am afraid, competing with our local universities, so we do not want to make those public until we are actually at a stage where we do want to make them public.

WILLIAM UTTING: And the code of confidentiality is directed to the same end.

ADRIAN WEBB: Yes, in broad terms.

1113. WILLIAM UTTING: Could I finish by inviting the chairman to expand on the comment he made about the individual liability of members of council. You had said something in writing and it is something that has cropped up throughout our deliberations on local public spending bodies. You obviously see this as a problem and something that inhibits people.

RUDI PLAUT: Yes, Sir William. The problem that we experience is that there is a fear that with much new legislation, particularly concerned with the environment, there is personal liability on governors for which they cannot insure. Going to government is a standard reply, which is "Nothing has happened in 100 years, so it won"t happen now". When one then points out that new legislation is coming almost daily, which therefore makes that first statement a little unreal, one is told "Go and insure yourselves". So we have done that very carefully, but we find that of course the most important thing that we are concerned about—environmental pollution—is excluded from all commercial policies, on top of which we as governors naturally have to go to the lowest cost, or very nearly the lowest cost, insurer. The very first insurance company we used, Municipal Mutual, went out of business. There is then a major gap in getting new insurance, and they actually refused to pay out for several days until they were rescued. I believe that universities are in a better position than schools, because we do have experts on the board and we do have very good professional advice, but school governors are in the same sort of position. One of these days one of them will get things wrong, something will happen and once governors have to pay out major sums for something which may legally have been their fault under new legislation but was not something that the ordinary man on the Clapham omnibus would have realised was an error, the whole system of governance by outside experts, people who give their time voluntarily, will collapse, and that means that the whole system on which really our modern education system is based will very quickly disappear. Already there is undoubtedly a lot of discussion on this point, and I do not know how many people may already not have become governors: we never do know; it is a negative thing. I think it is something that could be taken out of the way quite easily. We say that if you do something wrong that is of benefit to you, then you are liable, quite rightly, but if you do something innocently, you are working for the public good, then the public will protect you.

WILLIAM UTTING: Right. So you obviously believe that people who provide unpaid public service ought to have a higher degree of protection than they currently do.

RUDI PLAUT: Indeed, sir.

WILLIAM UTTING: Yes. Good. Thank you. Thank you, Chairman.

1114. DIANA WARWICK: I wonder if I might ask just three questions. Could I pursue with you the question of reserved business, because it is something that has been raised with us by virtually every one of the institutional representatives that we have had evidence from. Can you tell me whether those who are excluded are certain categories from within your council or certain individuals and, secondly, do you have a laid-down list of what is excludable, what you regard as reserved business, because again that also has varied enormously between institutions?

RUDI PLAUT: We do have a list—two things. The first one is anything to do with staff, and all staff are then excluded. If it is to do with the Vice-Chancellor's pay, for instance, then there would be no staff present at all; if it is something further down the hierarchy, the Vice-Chancellor would be there. So it depends on who is involved. The other category was on finance. However, we have found that in fact the members of the board are able at all levels to keep financial information to themselves, and it is now an open matter that the whole of the board is there for financial matters, but that used to be a reserved item.

1115. DIANA WARWICK: And those are just the two?

RUDI PLAUT: They are the two.

LEIGH BRACEGIRDLE: That is right, yes. It is where individual staff are concerned.

1116. DIANA WARWICK: So it is actually quite a limited category of issues. Could I move on to an issue which again constantly comes up with us and was raised with our previous witnesses here as well, and that is the general problem of whistle-blowing. Both Swansea University, who gave us evidence previously, and you in your own evidence indicate that there are no formal procedures whereby a complaint can be progressed. There are probably procedures, but no formal structures. I wonder if you can say something about that and how, if somebody wanted to make a complaint, they would go about it in your institution and whether you think the processes are adequate.

ADRIAN WEBB: Can I correct slightly a misimpression perhaps? There is a clear formal process. I should say there are separate formal processes, in the sense that students and staff issues will be handled slightly differently. It is indicated that staff are very free to make complaints to their line manager or, if they believe it is not appropriate through their line manager, to the next level of management or, if they believe it necessary, directly to myself, or if they believe it is inappropriate to bring it to me, directly to the Chairman of Council via the university secretary, who of course is a servant of the governing body of the university and not of the directorate for these purposes. We are in fact discussing at the moment, and have progressed some way in that discussion, the possibility of a Visitor in the old university style—i.e. an independent person standing outside the university—who would be available either to the Vice-Chancellor or to the chairman of governors in appropriate cases.

We do of course in particular instances also seek the advice of our chancellor, Lord Merlyn Rees, though it is important to recognise that in the constitutional position of new universities there is no constitutional role for a chancellor. It is slightly strange that there is a constitutional role for a vice-chancellor but not for a chancellor, so we have a chancellor who has no constitutional role but who has a very real engagement and involvement in the university, including advising us on these matters. Indeed, he has been deeply involved in some whistle-blowing problems in another major university and has been advising and talking to us about this. There are clear mechanisms, but they are through the managerial process, but it is quite clear that the staff can bypass that managerial process and go to the top, if they believe that the managerial process is inappropriate.

1117. DIANA WARWICK: Could I just follow that up then? I do not know if you heard the questioning earlier about whether it would be appropriate to have an ombudsman who would be available, given what has been said to us about, apart from anything else, the slowness of the visitorial procedure. Do you think a person of that kind would be of help in the university context?

RUDI PLAUT: What we were looking for was somebody outside ourselves, so that it could be clearly seen that justice could be not only done but seen to be done. I can see nothing wrong with having that outside person provided by an ombudsman. If there is not an ombudsman, what we are talking about is creating our own, which is a local visitor, but an experienced outside organisation should be able to do it much faster, because they do not have to lay down new rules each time, and—this is purely a personal view, because we have not discussed it as a board—I would have thought it was a good idea.

ADRIAN WEBB: Can I just add that it is not necessarily obvious that an ombudsman system would be quicker than a Visitor. It depends who your Visitor is, and I think the more prestigious and purely formal your Visitor is, the slower the process might become in practice.

1118. DIANA WARWICK: Could I ask one final question? Both you and other witnesses have referred to the increasing competitiveness of the university world. That obviously has an impact in all sorts of areas, but one area which it has been represented to us is under threat is the whole question of academic freedom, that there is a conflict between the new managerialism, if you like, and the protection of academic freedom. Do you perceive that in any sense to be at issue or a problem?

RUDI PLAUT: Speaking from the governors' point of view, I very much hope not. The academic board is independent of the board of governors, although they are represented on the board of governors. There is always a difficulty in any organisation between the executive and the non-executive and exactly where borderlines are drawn, and obviously it always depends on personalities, but we certainly see the maintenance of academic standards as being absolutely central to the future of the university. Reputation depends on quality, and we have a large number of overseas interests which are totally dependent on our having a good name, and therefore the board is absolutely behind the Vice-Chancellor in saying that standards must come first. If we let our standards drop, we believe we are really finished.

ADRIAN WEBB: May I add, I think the issue of academic freedom is far more complicated than we can discuss in a brief time now. There is a sense in which academic freedom always has been, but is more, curtailed by the availability of resources, in the sense that if you mean by academic freedom the right of any individual academic to undertake whatever research he or she might wish to undertake, clearly in some disciplines that requires resources of a very substantial kind. If somebody wishes to undertake expensive areas of research in physics, for example, it is dependent upon the availability of those resources. The direction of the resources in the university has had to become increasingly managerial, and that is within of course a very, very strict allocation of those resources in a national context. So we ourselves, as universities, could argue that we have lost a lot of academic freedom as an institution by the allocation of resources nationally on a very much tighter rein. But if you leave aside the resource issue, we make no attempt whatever as a university to control in any sense what academics research or what they say about issues that they research. Of course any member of the institution could be accused of bringing the institution into disrepute by virtue of their behaviour, but we do not argue, and have certainly not sought to argue, that the expression of opinion is itself a means by which you can bring the university into disrepute.

I just give a slight example. We had a very interesting art exhibition about a year ago which many members of the university felt was offensive. We went out of our way to ensure that that exhibition, which was chosen by members of staff in creative art and design, could continue, while limiting the possibility of causing offence, and, if you like, that is the kind of balance you have to strike in maintaining academic freedom, in this case through the creative medium on the one hand and the good governance of the university on the other, and it is about common sense and maintaining a balance.

DIANA WARWICK: Thank you.

1119. LORD NOLAN: Thank you very much. I am afraid we have come up against the clock. You finish on a reassuring note, an invocation of common sense, which we as a committee will, I assure you, always try and bear in mind in all our difficult problems. We are very grateful to you, gentlemen. Thank you very much indeed. You have been most helpful and clear.

Now we welcome Dr Williams, Dr Simmons and Mr Brian Lloyd, the secretary, of the University of Glamorgan Trade Union Alliance. Dr Willliams, I do not know whether you wish to make any kind of short opening statement or introductory remarks before we proceed to the questions, or whether you are happy to go straight to the questions.

DR WYN WILLIAMS, DR GEOFF SIMMONS, AND BRIAN LLOYD

DR WYN WILLIAMS (University of Glamorgan Trade Union Alliance): First of all, we would just like to welcome the inquiry you are setting up.

LORD NOLAN: Thank you very much.

WYN WILLIAMS: We believe there are problems, especially with the new universities, in the way they govern. Apart from that, we will take the questions as you pick them up.

LORD NOLAN: I am much obliged. We are extremely grateful for the information which you have already given us, which we have all carefully studied, and I am going to ask Diana Warwick to open the questions for us.

1120. DIANA WARWICK: Good morning. Can I pick up instantly then on that point, because it is one that you explore in some detail in the evidence that you gave us. I do not know whether you had an opportunity to listen to the other witnesses before coming in, did you?

WYN WILLIAMS: Shortly.

DR GEOFF SIMMONS (University of Glamorgan Trade Union Alliance): We would have been able to listen to a lot more of it if we had been able to park here.

1121. DIANA WARWICK: Oh! I am afraid we can't answer for the parking problems of Cardiff. I wonder if you can say something to us about the differences in perspective on governance and accountability that you perceive. You have linked it in particularly to the new universities. We are obviously interested in the sector as a whole, but it would be very helpful if you could explore some of those for us.

WYN WILLIAMS: I suppose this comes from a historical perspective, when the new universities first appeared. When these new universities were formed it was thought that they would have a mode of governance which was similar to the old universities. However, what has arisen is more of a quango-type governing body, and in our particular instance there is a large group of people with business and commercial aptitudes on the board. There are also co-opted members from the academic board and other interested parties, but they are relatively few in number as compared to the core of the board. There is some concern at our institution and generally that the university, when compared with the old university, is being run more on commercial lines as opposed to what were thought to be academic lines or educational lines. So there appear to be some differences in attitude, as we perceive them, between new universities and old universities.

As far as accountability is concerned, there is a group of members of the board who seem to predominate on many of the sub-committees which work with the board. The dealings of the sub-committees and the boards themselves are sometimes restricted for various reasons, and we would welcome more openness in what is being dealt with by governors, more communications and decisions of governors. It would help staff understand better what is going on at the institution.

Also we feel that when the new universities were formed we lost a lot of local community involvement in the institution. We feel that a great deal can be done for the university by the local community to help it to blend in with the local environment at Pontypridd, and as far as I know this is generally the case across the new universities.

1122. DIANA WARWICK: Could I come back to the first point that you made—I obviously do not want to explore the differences between you and Glamorgan—that the university is being run on commercial lines. That is a very common feature of much of the evidence that we have received. Indeed, it is clearly now the case that all universities are being run as competitive businesses. Inevitably that will produce a change in attitude than if you were operating in a non-

competitive environment, so I wonder if you could say a little bit more about that difference in attitude and how it is perceived to be damaging or harmful to the university or undermining perhaps its main function.

WYN WILLIAMS: What some staff have seen is that the board of governors, obviously for reasons of confidentiality, does not publish its paperwork as widely as in previous times, so there is some suspicion as to what is going on in governors: the openness may not be as it was, and also the means by which the university operates. Our heads of department and schools and senior staff operate on different contracts from the general academic and other staff at the institution, so we are not aware, basically, of the terms and conditions of senior staff, how they are appointed and so on, which causes some suspicion again among staff in general.

1123. DIANA WARWICK: So how do you think that could be improved?

WYN WILLIAMS: Recently, very recently, the university has adopted a communications policy, which is just about starting. It would be very useful if staff were able to receive information from governors and the senior executives of the institution as to how it operates and where it is going in greater detail.

1124. DIANA WARWICK: Would this go beyond publishing minutes and so on in the library? Are there practical ways in which decisions can be communicated without damaging the institution's commercial interests?

WYN WILLIAMS: I am sure there must be ways. We are not really privy to all the information of governors, so we cannot really say what goes on there—that is another difficulty we have—but surely there must be a reasonable amount of paperwork which is not confidential, either financially or otherwise, which could be communicated, especially the workings of sub-committees perhaps.

1125. DIANA WARWICK: I wonder if you could explore that a little bit. You place quite a lot of emphasis on the workings of sub-committees in your evidence and that obviously underlines the points that you are making about the difficulties in tracing accountability. Could you say how it operates and how it might be improved?

WYN WILLIAMS: The academic board obviously has sub-committees, which report to the academic board. It is not clear to us, as we look in on governors, whether all the machinations and paperwork of sub-committees are presented before governors or whether a synopsis is provided. Also, various names which have a business interest seem to be appearing on sub-committees and the odd few co-opted or other members, so there is a suspicion that there seems to be an inner group of governors who hold the reins of power perhaps. This is just a suspicion. I would not like to say it was something which is fact as such.

DIANA WARWICK: But you do go on to say that you would prefer a clearer regulatory framework.

WYN WILLIAMS: Yes.

1126. DIANA WARWICK: I wonder if you could say precisely what you have in mind, because that seems quite a heavy way to approach things.

WYN WILLIAMS: The way we see the new universities or indeed higher education in Wales operating is through the Higher Education Funding Council for Wales. This, as we understand it, discharges money to institutions for their use, but we are not clear about the lines of accountability from the institutions to the Funding Council, to the Welsh Office and to government. We feel that the Funding Council could play a more prominent role in scrutinising the dealings of governors, perhaps financially, or monitoring the suitability of governors or whatever for the institutions as a whole in Wales.

1127. DIANA WARWICK: I was going to ask you about the relationship between the Funding Council and the university and the autonomy of the institution, which I think many universities would call in aid on that point.

WYN WILLIAMS: We feel that if public money is being spent on education, there should be some accountability for it, and from our perspective it is not clear who the University of Glamorgan, or any university, is fully accountable to. If there is a big financial problem at an institution, the Welsh Office or the Funding Council may be tempted to step in and help out, but it is not clear if the Funding Council is particularly interested in the individual allocation of money within institutions perhaps or the directions in which institutions go in spending money. We would welcome a mechanism by which the Funding Council would at least ask for some account of how the universities are operating.

1128. DIANA WARWICK: How do you respond to the point that has been made to us by vice-chancellors and governors of institutions that, going back to the point I made earlier, everybody is now operating in a more competitive environment and therefore certain elements of decision-making have to be kept reasonably confidential until they can be made generally public?

WYN WILLIAMS: That is probably the case in terms of procuring more space for universities, hiring staff and so on, but there might be other matters regarding, for instance, planning of the institution—the corporate plan, strategic planning—which would have a wider audience in its setting up, including local people, because the university obviously impacts locally, and within the institution itself, so we believe that that is one thing that could be done in this area.

GEOFF SIMMONS: As regards the work of one of the sub-committees—the employment policy sub-committee, for example—we as trade unionists would be very interested to learn what they talk about, but I understand—I am not sure, because of the atmosphere of secrecy surrounding the governors—that their deliberations and so on are reserved items, that it is only the inner clique of business governors who ever learn about what goes on there.

1129. DIANA WARWICK: I wonder if I could move on to another question that I have raised before, and that is the general point about whistle-blowing and the way in which a member of the staff can make a complaint within an institution. Do you see the need for a formal process by which that can be followed through and, perhaps more particularly, do you see the need for an external and independent body or person to which somebody who has a complaint can eventually refer it?

GEOFF SIMMONS: Well, here you are. We would welcome your arrival every year.

DIANA WARWICK: Our task is not to take individual complaints.

WYN WILLIAMS: Perhaps I should just say that there is a grievance procedure in place within the institution which goes through the line manager system and ends up with the Vice-Chancellor or possibly a group of the board of governors. However, if there is a matter within the institution which could embarrass the institution, it is not clear whether that could be adequately dealt with within the institution. I am thinking of various events that have taken place at other new universities, where information has leaked out through the back door, as it were. I think we would welcome a procedure—ombudsman, Visitor, whatever it may be—an independent scrutineer for the new universities, as a whole or in part, whereby complaints could be addressed outside the institution. I would not know which mechanisms would be best for that.

1130. DIANA WARWICK: Can I ask you one final point? We have talked about the role of individuals as members of the governing body. There are various categories of membership of the governing body. In certain institutions members of staff, students, members of local authorities and so on are represented, but it has been put to us that there are problems about members of governing bodies who have, if you like, delegated powers, who come as delegates, and who therefore do not bring a free mind or an open mind to a discussion. Do you have any views about that?

BRIAN LLOYD (University of Glamorgan Trade Union Alliance): It is our view that the governing bodies should be as wide as possible in their composition, representing wide-ranging interests. Prior to the institutions becoming independent, it would appear that the Government saw the predominance then of local authority representation as not being conducive to the new form of institutions that were to emerge. However, the new boards that did emerge had another prominent group, not appointed by local authorities but appointed by the Secretary of State. It is our view that there should be no prominent group and there should be a wide, broad range of interests, with a particular interest obviously, in a competitive market, in higher education. This wide-ranging group could include the business and commercial interests but should also include the community, the staff and other suitable interests, and, equally, each of those represented on the new boards should have equal status, equal representation, in terms of their responsibilities, duties and powers, which we believe does not currently exist where some boards have individuals who are executive governors as opposed to the other governors.

DIANA WARWICK: You do not see that there might be a conflict of interest where somebody who is representing a group of others comes mandated to a discussion.

BRIAN LLOYD: If you are referring possibly to what used to be the local authority that could have been mandated or to a staff representative who could have been mandated by a trade union, then my personal experience is no: they are there for the betterment of the institution and the higher education that is being provided.

1131. DIANA WARWICK: May I pursue one final point? It is something I should have picked up on in terms of appeals. In your evidence you indicate that your appeals procedure is an internal procedure and ceases with the Vice-Chancellor, and you then contrast that with the position of the students who have recourse to an external arbitrator. Could you explain that process?

WYN WILLIAMS: For the students?

DIANA WARWICK: Yes.

WYN WILLIAMS: I can't say I am too familiar with that.

DIANA WARWICK: If you do not know the process, it would be quite useful to know how that system within the university operates, if we may come back to you later and ask you about that.

GEOFF SIMMONS: It is a relatively recent introduction—the students' charter. I do not know quite what the intermediate steps are, but if all else fails the student can appeal to this external arbitrator. The staff have no such right of appeal. The Vice-Chancellor's word is final.

DIANA WARWICK: Yes. Thank you very much.

LORD NOLAN: Thank you, Diana. Sir William.

1132. WILLIAM UTTING: Thank you, Chairman. The problems you perceive seem to originate in two areas. One of them is with the way in which the university conducts its business, but the other seems to originate from the legislation itself, because the legislation does not appear to permit the kind of governing body that you would recommend. Would you like to elaborate on any other issues about the legislation, which restricts the size of the council in the first place and says that it has to be composed in a certain way?

BRIAN LLOYD: Since the institutions became independent there have been number of changes in the composition of governing bodies governed by legislation and the categories of those that are allowed in that composition. We would like to see the instruments and articles that dictate that composition changed to allow for a wider-ranging interest and particularly not to have any predominant group. If it was good enough to change the composition from what was perceived as a local authority dominant group towards a more commercial group, we should possibly be looking at a composition which has the interests of the institution at heart. I am not saying that all our governors on governing bodies across higher education do not have the interests of the institution at heart, but it is perceived by many that, because there is a predominant group, influences can be one particular way, and we would rather see a broader-ranging composition, with no predominant group. Particularly we would like to see the composition include representatives of the community, local authorities, other educational interests and business and commercial interests as well.

1133. WILLIAM UTTING: So you would like to see a fairly radical revision of the statutory composition of the governing body then. At the moment there is a maximum of 25 and there has to be a majority of people who are called independent members, who appear to be qualified by coming from a business or professional background,

and that group of people has to approve the co-opted members, of whom there may be a maximum of two staff and two students.

BRIAN LLOYD: Yes.

1134. WILLIAM UTTING: What sort of size do you think is the optimum one for an effective governing body of a university then? You are obviously going above 25 to brigade in all the interests you think should be represented.

BRIAN LLOYD: I do not think personally it needs to go a lot higher than the 25 to 30. It becomes unmanageable if it becomes too big.

1135. WILLIAM UTTING: So it is really this so-called independent element that you would wish to diminish in favour of, say, increased staff, increased student, increased local community representation and a local authority representation in its own right instead of just being co-opted.

BRIAN LLOYD: Yes.

GEOFF SIMMONS: We would be happier if on a committee of 25 there were 25 different interests represented rather than just one.

WILLIAM UTTING: Only one of them for the staff then, in that case, if there were 25.

GEOFF SIMMONS: Well, that is an improvement.

1136. WILLIAM UTTING: That is helpful. If I could turn to some of the points which you raised about the way business is conducted at the moment, it seems that, even with a relatively small council of 20, it is necessary or desirable to have some additional committees which in fact develop policy in different areas, and you have an academic board which is independent of Council, which presumably develops policy on the academic side, and a policy and resources committee and a finance committee. Your sense is that too much business is carried out in these sub-committees that does not actually see the light of day. Does that apply to the academic board as well as to the other two, by the way?

GEOFF SIMMONS: No. The business of the academic board is relatively open. We have in fact seven elected staff representatives on the academic board, so we know what is going on there.

1137. WILLIAM UTTING: Yes, but you think there ought to be more access to the actual deliberations of various sub-committees?

GEOFF SIMMONS: Absolutely, yes.

WYN WILLIAMS: There are staff representatives on academic board and the circulation of information from academic board and to academic board is much better structured than it is with governors.

1138. WILLIAM UTTING: Yes. Are any of the academic members of the governing body on the policy and resources committee or the finance committee?

WYN WILLIAMS: No.

1139. WILLIAM UTTING: It would seem that constitutionally the position is OK, in that those bodies are making recommendations to Council which then have to be approved by the governing body, so that staff and student representatives at least get a sight of them at that sort of level.

GEOFF SIMMONS: There are some reserved items that they do not get, I understand.

WILLIAM UTTING: Yes. I am not seeking to reassure you but really to try to establish what the position actually is.

GEOFF SIMMONS: We have a problem here of trying to establish a lack of openness. If we had the evidence, then we would prove that it is open.

1140. WILLIAM UTTING: I asked the Vice-Chancellor a question about communication and I got quite a long answer about the attempts that what is called the directorate, which is presumably the caucus of senior officers of the university, make to disseminate information about what is going on. But you still do not find that system wholly satisfactory.

WYN WILLIAMS: We see that as a one-way communication system, where information is disseminated down from directorate, vice-chancellor, down through heads of department to individual staff. There can be much selectivity in what information is transmitted, and it does not allow for information to be passed back up through the system. There has been put in place recently a communications strategy with a newsletter, but these are early days. I think communication through a newsletter or some other means is a most vital part in getting the new universities to work much better. It helps staff understand what is going on, it keeps the governors and the senior management in touch and it provides a means of disseminating information which is relevant to what is happening at the institution, which is sometimes not clear, such as building work for instance. You may turn up one day and find that building work is going on in your part of the university, but no information has been forthcoming on that. It sounds a simple matter, but it does affect the work of staff.

1141. WILLIAM UTTING: Good. If I could end on another matter, it concerns the potential role of the Funding Council as a regulator. In practice a body such as a Funding Council, which audits the expenditure and the management of an institution and is perhaps getting into the evaluation of academic work too, exercises, or can exercise, a great deal of power. It does not necessarily need, so to speak, to be established by statute as a regulatory body. Do you think that if your Funding Council flexed its muscles and made, say, adoption of the CUC guide a condition of financing, that would help to meet the kind of points that you have in mind about the need for tighter regulation?

WYN WILLIAMS: We certainly welcome the CUC guide. Indeed, our university is now adopting some of the advice given in that—fairly recently. Whether the funding of the university should rest solely on that I think is a difficult issue, because the university may not be able to fulfil all the requirements in a quick enough time. However, I would like to see some mechanism put forward by the Funding Councils by which the institution

is called to account for its spending and its development plans over future years. We are not privy to what goes on between the institution at governing level and the Funding Council, so we hear I won't say gossip but information from other sources as to what goes on. So we are not really in a position to formulate a mechanism by which our concerns in this area can be addressed.

WILLIAM UTTING: I am much obliged.

1142. LORD NOLAN: I wonder if I could just clear my mind, with your help, on one point. You spoke, Dr Williams, of suspicion, and I think it covered, for example, the award of contracts about which you had had no knowledge before and you suddenly found them being carried out. We were told that there is a procedure whereby all governors are asked to complete a proforma annually, declaring relevant interests, and this is available for scrutiny. Do you have any difficulty in having access to the relevant interests of governors? I know this would not tell you perhaps all you would like to know, but it is a starting point, isn't it?

WYN WILLIAMS: I do not think this information has been communicated to us. We are not aware of that procedure.

1143. LORD NOLAN: We were told it was certainly in the library, but I was not clear where they were available. Is that the kind of thing you feel you would like to know more about and, for example, who gets the contracts? Well, that is apparent when they are being carried out, isn't it?

WYN WILLIAMS: That information should be available, yes.

LORD NOLAN: You know who has got it, you do not know why he gets it, and that may be a difficulty there.

WYN WILLIAMS: Yes. We would like to see, basically, that there is openness and that there are no conflicts of interest for governors in these matters.

1144. LORD NOLAN: Are these matters that have been discussed between you and the university fairly regularly—your wish to have fuller information about certain aspects?

GEOFF SIMMONS: It is a permanent item on our JNCC agenda.

LORD NOLAN: Thank you very much. Thank you for coming along. That has been, again, very instructive and we take careful note of what you say. I am much obliged to you all.

WYN WILLIAMS: Thank you for your inquiry.

1145. LORD NOLAN: Not at all.

Now we welcome Professor John Andrews, Chief Executive, Richard Hirst, the Director of Finance, and Linda Gainsbury, the Head of the Further Education Division of the Welsh Funding Councils. We have been saving the most important till the last this morning, as you see. Have you any opening statement or brief introductory remarks you would like to make?

PROFESSOR JOHN ANDREWS, RICHARD HIRST, AND LINDA GAINSBURY

PROFESSOR JOHN ANDREWS (Chief Executive, Welsh Funding Councils): We have provided you with a statement, my Lord, which we are happy for other people to have copies of.

LORD NOLAN: You have. Thank you very much.

JOHN ANDREWS: There is nothing I would wish to add to that.

LORD NOLAN: We are very grateful for all the information that you have provided us with. We know that these things do not just come straight off the word processor: a lot of work and thought have gone into them. We know how busy you are, and it has been of great benefit to us. May I please go straight ahead with the aspects of the information that we would like to follow up and ask Dame Anne Warburton to begin the questions.

1146. ANNE WARBURTON: Good morning. Could I first ask a question about your introductory passage in the very full paper you have given us. I am not quite clear who decides how much money goes to each of the institutions concerned. Is that in your responsibility or is that a given, so far as you are concerned?

JOHN ANDREWS: No, that is decided by the Council, but almost the whole of the funding is in fact determined by formulae. The formulae were arrived at after consultation with all the institutions and representative bodies.

ANNE WARBURTON: Particularly for Wales in this case?

JOHN ANDREWS: Oh, yes. These are the formulae for recurrent and capital funding respectively of FEFCW and HEFCW.

1147. ANNE WARBURTON: Perhaps as a slight diversion I might just ask: are you closely in touch with your English equivalent?

JOHN ANDREWS: Yes.

1148. ANNE WARBURTON: Do you find it is useful to exchange experiences?

JOHN ANDREWS: We exchange papers and we have cross-observer status on the English and the Scottish Funding Councils.

1149. ANNE WARBURTON: Yes, good. How much actually are you dispensing annually roughly these days?

JOHN ANDREWS: Across the two Funding Councils?

ANNE WARBURTON: Yes.

JOHN ANDREWS: That will be something over £400 million.

ANNE WARBURTON: Of which—?

JOHN ANDREWS: Of which something over £250 million on HE and something over £160 million on FE.

1150. ANNE WARBURTON: Good. Thank you very much. We are very conscious of course that you are a funding body; you are not in the regulatory business. I kept on being impressed when going through your paper, though, at the number of sometimes perhaps marginal, at other times more important, changes which you think would be advisable and I wondered to what extent you find yourselves wanting to use, or actually using, your influence to promote these changes. Is it within your remit to say "Unless you do so-and-so, we have a whip hand"?

JOHN ANDREWS: I think there are very real dangers in that. We were fortunate that we heard the last few minutes colleagues from Glamorgan talking. If a funding council was to assume a regulatory role over universities, I think that really would mark a significant change in the constitutional position and the responsibilities of that council, which basically is to fund institutions. If we are to be a regulator as well, that is to give us a very different role. The problem is that if the funding body is also the regulator, if you couple being a regulator with the sheer clout which you might be seen to hold by virtue of being a funding agent, there is a very real danger of a sort of big brother relationship. Essentially we have seen ourselves as a funding agency to achieve the best possible systems of further and higher education in a sort of partnership role with institutions, recognising that it is an uneven partnership, that at the end of the day the Funding Council has to take the funding decisions, but it essentially recognises the other side of the coin, which is their autonomy, their constitutional position and their governors' position, which essentially relates back to the instruments and articles of governance agreed by the Secretary of State and not by ourselves.

ANNE WARBURTON: It is also this tension between academic freedom and the accountability for funds.

JOHN ANDREWS: I am not sure that the tension is not perhaps exaggerated on occasions.

ANNE WARBURTON: Creative tension.

JOHN ANDREWS: Yes, but here you are reliant on public funding for a very substantial part of your income, I think it is understandable that Government would seek a return on this and would expect the Funding Council to seek a return on this. So the money we give to institutions is tied in terms of student numbers and balance between subject areas and is dependent on the outcome of the research assessment exercise. But all of that is concerned with academic affairs. If it was tied also to the way in which they govern themselves, that is to make a very sharp change.

ANNE WARBURTON: You have already answered a question which I might have put to you—whether you would like a greater regulatory function—and you tell me no.

JOHN ANDREWS: No, I did not say that. Or, do you mean as a Funding Council?

ANNE WARBURTON: Yes.

JOHN ANDREWS: Not as a Funding Council, although if it were put on us, then we would do it.

1151. ANNE WARBURTON: But what about your inference? Do you discuss the sort of points which were made in your paper with your beneficiaries as you go along, questions like the process of appointment being more formalised or guidelines on nominations committee or declarations of interests and how they should be handled, that sort of thing? Do you discuss them or do you circulate papers which set out your view of how they should be done, or what?

JOHN ANDREWS: We have provided a guide for HE institutions jointly with the English HE Funding Council. The Welsh Office itself is producing a guide for FE institutions. In the course of our relationships with the institutions we do, on occasion, seek information from them and we make recommendations to them. Significantly, a number of these were prompted by the reviews that the Public Accounts Committee has conducted of HE and FE institutions.

1152. ANNE WARBURTON: Thank you very much. Can I move on to the systems of government which the pre- and post-92 universities have? From where you sit as a Funding Council what advantages and disadvantages do you see in those two different systems?

JOHN ANDREWS: I think it fair to say that our view on the whole is that the new higher and further education corporations have advantage in terms of their smaller size. They are more nimble, I think, in consequence and, because of the smaller size, the impression that we have is that the governors feel much more personally involved and much more personally responsible for the decisions which are being taken, compared with those who are members of college councils of the University of Wales, which could be 50-plus membership—80-plus in one case—and of courts of governors of several hundred people, only a small proportion of whom would turn up.

If I could add a little, I think the one disadvantage perhaps of the smaller governing body is in the case particularly of larger institutions, where it might be desirable to have more sub-committees and working groups and there is a relatively small number of people to choose from. I do not know whether my director of finance would like to come in on this. I should perhaps make a declaration of interest for him: he is a governor of Filton College in Bristol.

RICHARD HIRST (Director of Finance, Welsh Funding Councils): Yes, Filton FE College in Bristol. I think I would echo what Professor Andrews has said, in the sense that sometimes we have an impression that, because of the size of the pre-92 universities' councils, substantial proportions of their business are done not in front of those full councils but in front of finance committees and whatever, which may be an appropriate way of doing business, but could perhaps to be seen to be taking away something of the accountability of the full council, and I think that is a flavour that comes through to us on particularly, for example, financial matters.

JOHN ANDREWS: Linda Gainsbury is closer to the FE sector in Wales and you might like her view.

ANNE WARBURTON: Thank you.

LINDA GAINSBURY (Head of FE Division, Welsh Funding Councils): I had some contact with governing bodies pre-incorporation and, although they were semi-independent in the wake of the 1988 Act, there was not a

sense of real ownership, because the LEA was still there and ultimately accountable. The change over the last three years, while gradual, is now becoming really noticeable in terms of the extent to which governors are taking their responsibilities more seriously and growing into their roles in a way that one just did not see between 1988 and 1992.

1153. ANNE WARBURTON: Thank you very much. Perhaps that leads me into another area of questions, a little bit by the side entrance. I wanted to ask more about the difficulties in recruiting governors. You refer to the importance of clear and open policies in recruitment, and I would like to explore that a little bit more with you, but the reason I picked up what Linda Gainsbury has just said was that one of the things that I was interested to know was whether, when the LA link was altered, LA representatives have always stayed on the councils and, if so, in what form they are there, what sort of remit they have. But perhaps I should open with the general question: what are the real problems of recruitment? You have mentioned particularly financial expertise, but what other problems do you perceive?

JOHN ANDREWS: I think the difficulty in part is that the institutions need on their governing body financial expertise, ideally estates expertise and legal expertise, and here they tend to be looking for busy people of a particular type, who are sought after quite frequently for other committees as well, and it may be that in a sense there is an over-demand for those sorts of people in the voluntary sector. It is there that some institutions do have some difficulty. As we have mentioned, it is often more difficult in rural areas, small towns, than in large towns.

I think it could be said that the difficulty may be in the lines of communication, the lines of search, and that there may be other people who would be only too pleased to serve on these bodies but links are not there. For that reason particularly, I am attracted by the idea of an extended search system and possibly advertising for people. There are other reasons as well. But if I move away from there, elsewhere I do not think there is the same difficulty of getting people to serve on these governing bodies, albeit there has been a tendency since the 1992 Act, and it is echoed in the 1988 Act, to move away from some of the traditional types of person you might see on governing bodies, who one might describe as people with an interest, with a concern, in public affairs, and that would include elected representatives. In a sense, while I feel it is important, and it has been a very valuable exercise, to get on to these bodies people with the professional experience which helps them with the management function and with their efficiency functions, I do not think we should lose sight of the other sort of person, who can be very valuable on these bodies.

Linda Gainsbury may be able to add some experience if it would be helpful for you, on the local authority representation and the way it has gone.

ANNE WARBURTON: Thank you very much.

LINDA GAINSBURY: I think post-incorporation quite a lot of the LEA representatives disappeared automatically. They came to the end of their period of office within LEAs, or the governing bodies sought not to retain their services; so the picture is mixed. Some ex-LEA representatives remain in the chairs of governing bodies, although one I met last week was very quick to say that he was now acting in a personal capacity rather than in relation to his LEA link. Talking with principals, I find they appear to see this retaining of the link as valuable, because after all they are looking at relationships with schools in order to ensure progression within the curriculum, and I do not think they want to sever that link.

ANNE WARBURTON: So they are now better able to listen to the debate and amend their own views in the light of it, and that sort of thing.

LINDA GAINSBURY: Yes.

JOHN ANDREWS: It is perhaps worth bearing in mind that under the legislation local authority elected representatives can only be co-opted on to governors; they cannot be elected. I am not sure that that is a wise distinction.

1154. ANNE WARBURTON: Is that true both of higher and further education?

JOHN ANDREWS: I think it is, isn't it? It is certainly true of further education. I believe it is of higher education.

1155. ANNE WARBURTON: I have one other question on the finding of candidates. Do you see as in any way a problem of finance—that is to say, personal finance—either meeting their expenses or even paying them a per diem allowance or perhaps, and this is a point that has been made this morning quite cogently, the question of what they are letting themselves in for and how far they are covered by insurance provisions?

JOHN ANDREWS: I think overwhelmingly the people who serve on the governing bodies do so out of a genuine interest in the institution and a genuine interest in public service. I would regret very much if it became a paid position. I think it would have a considerable impact on the nature of the bodies and particularly on the regard, the attitudes which would be struck between staff and students and a governing body, if they were seen to be being paid rather than to be performing a public service. So I would not personally wish to advocate payment of members of governing bodies—expenses certainly, payment for loss of earnings I would have thought no, not least because of the disproportion in the loss of earnings of some people and the impact that might have on colleges. In most cases they meet in early evening anyway, but to have a governing body where some people were on high earnings and were therefore paid very high sums and others not does not seem to me to be the sort of thing that would promote teamwork and the sense of commonality that one would look for.

1156. ANNE WARBURTON: Thank you very much. I wanted to ask you where you see the initiative lying for some of the improvements that you think should be introduced, questions like the training of new members. I noticed particularly your point at paragraph 14 about declarations of interests and the practice which is followed there. I have the impression that it is now fairly common for members of boards to declare their interests. What happens then seems to be rather more vague, as to whether the register is available publicly, or how publicly, and, in particular, whether, when an interest does arise, the interested party stays in the discussion and so forth. Is

that something which you would want to pursue further or is it something which should be done somewhere else?

JOHN ANDREWS: I do feel that the *Guide for Governors* is very helpful on a number of these things and has prompted such things as the setting up of registers of interests. Practice, I suspect, is very varied between institutions and in most cases I think the register of interests is probably regarded as a confidential matter. There are arguments for and against the confidentiality of it. I can myself see, however, advantages of both a code of practice for governing bodies and a code of conduct for individual members of governing bodies being agreed and coming out with the authority not simply of the Funding Councils, which is largely the position of the *Guide for Governors,* but of the sponsoring Departments—the Department of Education, the Welsh Office, the Scottish Office, as the case may be—and having greater authority in dealing with things like registers of interests, nominations committees, the whole range of things of that sort, in terms of the code of practice, and then, on the conduct side, the sort of things that are covered in codes of conduct for members of NDPBs.

1157. ANNE WARBURTON: Good. Then one particular category of members—how widespread now is the practice of having staff and student representation? Perhaps I am not even right in saying "staff and student". Perhaps I should separate the two.

JOHN ANDREWS: I would have thought very common indeed—not universal, but very common, by which I mean more than 90 per cent, I would have thought.

ANNE WARBURTON: Presumably there is still some differentiation in how widely they participate in the work of the Council.

JOHN ANDREWS: I think that for all governing bodies, certainly in the case of university councils, the Privy Council in the past has insisted that certain items should be reserved areas of business. Primarily they are items concerning staffing, and particularly individual members of staff.

1158. ANNE WARBURTON: Thank you very much. I have one other question I would like to put at this point, a question about the competitive position of the universities in the world around them. Does it concern you at all that the fact of competition might be disadvantageous in some of its consequences? Some people talk about the poaching of students, perhaps a lowering of standards, or perhaps about the poaching of academics as well as students, or of secrecy being injurious to academic debate. We were hearing a little earlier also that the business side of universities is such now that perhaps this is one reason for not circulating minutes of discussion very widely.

JOHN ANDREWS: I am not aware that it has deterred institutions from, for example, circulating their council minutes or their senate minutes. You are raising a number of issues under that one umbrella. I think it is inevitable that there will be competition between institutions, because they will naturally aim to be working at the highest levels, and in a sense it is just a short step from that to being the best. Both the Funding Councils in Wales have sought to encourage collaboration between institutions and partnership between institutions, and we have seen the growth of that. Partly, I think, because of having a Welsh funding environment which is relatively small—a smaller number of institutions—we have seen much more working together, but there is still competition and it is not necessarily competition between neighbouring institutions; it may be competition with institutions in Wales and England or even European institutions in terms, for example, of links with industry, which can be very valuable to institutions not just in cash terms but in terms of research platforms, placing of students, a whole range of that sort of thing. If we are to encourage our institutions to become more and more involved in industry, to develop their research from basic and strategic through to work which has a relevancy in the economic world, it is inevitable that some of the tensions of that world—the need for confidentiality—will come in.

ANNE WARBURTON: Thank you very much. May I leave it there, Chairman?

1159. LORD NOLAN: Thank you very much. I wonder if I could pick up one or two small but I think important points which we have already covered in general terms. We hear much disquiet about the danger of legal liability attaching to board members rendering their services voluntarily, and the position appears to be that no government department is prepared to say firmly as matter of law "This won"t happen". The advice appears to be "It probably will not happen, there is no real danger of it, but you should insure", and we are told it is not easy to insure satisfactorily. Is this a matter which, so far as you are aware, is causing grave disquiet in Wales and is it one that the councils are addressing?

JOHN ANDREWS: It has caused considerable disquiet among the governors of one institution in Wales and it has been raised in the meetings of Chairmen of governing bodies and councils in the HE institutions. I do not get the impression that it is a major worry for FE colleges or for most of the HE institutions. It is possible to insure against the personal liability of governors. There are exclusionary clauses which it is not possible to shake off. For example, they will not insure against potential liabilities arising from pollution—a specific issue.

1160. LORD NOLAN: Thank you. Could I turn back again to something that you covered, but I just wanted to be a little more specific about it? In your submission you express the view that registers of interests should be mandatory. I notice that in the very helpful note that we had from the tertiary college Mr Smith mentioned two of his governing body's members who declined to complete a register of interests because they felt it was an intrusion on their privacy and then there is a sentence in quotes: "I believe it should be made compulsory". I think that is probably what Mr Smith is saying. In effect you are saying that, aren't you? You are saying it should be mandatory.

JOHN ANDREWS: I think if it was mandatory, particularly if it was in a code of practice which was seen to come from the Department, those two governors would probably have recognised the writing on the wall and would have been content to fill in the register of interests.

1161. LORD NOLAN: One understands the reluctance: it has been evident and not surprising in almost every organisation which has had to consider it, I suppose, from the House of Commons downwards, but one must simply present people with the argument that the responsibility for public money imposes demands in terms of transparency which one would not otherwise seek to impose on people.

JOHN ANDREWS: On this one, my Lord, we had no difficulty in either of the Funding Councils in obtaining declarations of interest from the members, and they are available publicly if anyone wishes to see them, and I would expect that to be the position with most of the members of Councils. One of the things which might be considered is the possibility of allowing a registration of interests with the clerk of the Council but under a confidential cover, so that it is not necessarily available to everybody without some good reason for it to be seen. I cannot imagine that many governors would ever want to make use of it, but I think one has to accept that there might be certain reasons why they should be held confidentially, the more so perhaps if the register of interests were to be extended to the interests of a spouse as well.

1162. LORD NOLAN: Yes, thank you very much. If I may say so, I think that is very helpful. The submission also refers to guidance about appointment procedures and advertising, and the need for widening the selection for membership. Have the Funding Councils issued any guidance statements on these matters?

JOHN ANDREWS: No. We have been parties to recommendations that institutions should establish nomination committees, but we have not done anything beyond what is contained within the 1992 Act in terms of composition and the instruments and statutes established under them.

LORD NOLAN: Thank you very much.

RICHARD HIRST: We have endorsed the guidance given by the Council of University Chairmen. Clearly that pertains to those issues, and we would support the kind of suggestions made in that.

LORD NOLAN: Yes. Possibly with all these things too one does not necessarily get the best results by great speed. A number of these things are happening, we find, all over the country spontaneously, which is really the best way, but I note what you say.

LINDA GAINSBURY: We are finding that in FE governors are taking considerable heed of the model nominations committee sheet which the Colleges Employers Forum has issued and of the code of conduct. So although there has not been anything from the Council, they are getting it from their own association, as it were.

1163. LORD NOLAN: Thank you. May I ask you about what we call whistle-blowers, confidential lines of complaint? These, too, you encourage. Can you give us any impression of how widely they are being adopted?

JOHN ANDREWS: The position is very uneven. Under the FE charter there is an appeal to the Funding Council. There is not a similar appeal on the HE side. So whilst I can give you some details of appeals that we have had on the FE side, what comes to me on the HE side is very fortuitous. It really is only where people have complained to their MPs and the letter has then been sent on to the Secretary of State and comes to myself. The impression I have is that most institutions do have a complaints procedure and that works effectively in respect of individual members of staff. In respect of students normally this works well, but the FE charter does have the bolt-hole, as it were, of the appeal to ourselves. In HE there is nothing quite so clear.

There are, I think, broader issues in the colleges, which would not be concerned with the individual position of a member of staff or the individual position of a student, but where there may be concern about issues of governance, senior management or what you will, where at the present time there is no set procedure, but in most cases good practice, common sense, resolves these issues. But what one does find is that, because of that, occasionally there are clashes or occasionally there are rippling undertones of "How can we get hold of this issue?"

I come back to where we began, whether the Funding Council is the right body to get hold of this, and I still have misgivings as to whether the funding body is the right body, but it is probably fair to say—this is not the view of the Funding Councils; we have not discussed it—that the view of ourselves here is that we do see a potential advantage in having some system, whether ombudsman is the right title or not, whereby—and I am not thinking so much of the whistle-blower with a particular issue but of the broader issue of where there are concerns—they can be teased out without putting funding at risk or wondering what effect it will have on your relationships with the Funding Council, but in a situation where somebody is above and beyond a college and therefore would be seen to be detached. In many cases I think that would be in the best interests of the institutions as well as of those who are concerned for some of the things that are going on.

1164. LORD NOLAN: Certainly what I had in mind were two different things—one, a confidential line of inquiry, which would normally exist, assuming the organisation was big enough, within the organisation—you need, obviously, an organisation big enough for confidentiality to be preserved—and that, one would hope, would bring to light things that would otherwise lie hidden in the junior levels, or at any rate behind closed doors, and would enable the proper authorities to be alerted and to do whatever was necessary. One knows, too, that it might be a way of encouraging a lot of frivolous complaints which whoever was responsible for dealing with would have to be very firm at disposing of, so that unnecessary trouble was not caused. That would be one thing.

The other point you mention is really for dealing with complaints that cannot be resolved within the university, or not satisfactorily or not quickly. That is an area where earlier this morning we were discussing the comparative attractions of the old style of Visitor system or, as you say, the ombudsman, or conceivably both. It may be that the universities who have Visitors thank heavens rarely have to call in the Visitors, but do on occasions find them extremely useful and would be happy to go on with that. But the alternative argument was for a regularly appointed ombudsman with a fairly wide territorial or national jurisdiction, who would be there and available with staff and with experience and who could provide the necessary independent element in considering internal disputes and, one would hope, perhaps deal with them more quickly than others who are instructed ad hoc. I appreciate that you, not being a regulatory body, are not directly concerned with these matters, but you have such a wide overview of the whole field that we were interested, and are interested, to hear your comments about it. Have you any particular views on, let us say, the argument for

not merely preserving but advancing and extending the Visitor system to other universities? Do you think the Visitor system is in itself a useful thing for a university to have?

JOHN ANDREWS: I would not wish the burdens of visitorial law on anybody. I think the Visitor system is archaic. For most of my time in the higher education world I think the vast majority of people within the university system were not aware that such a person existed, and if they were they thought he was somebody who came down every couple of years in a ceremonial fashion. I frankly do not think that the Visitor system really meets the bill. It does work where a major issue has arisen and requires ultimate resolution, but then it can be very expensive and time-consuming. It does not really work for getting hold of the issue before it has gone too far and getting hold of the issue in a way which can resolve it by conciliation and discussion and reaching a common-sense view. It pushes everything up into this cocoon of rather archaic law, which is why I would prefer, if one was to have any procedure of that sort, something less formal, such as an ombudsman system.

One problem one would have to recognise is that, if one were simply to set up an ombudsman system for further and higher education, you would need a degree of staffing and one would have to ask whether this would be justified for the number of complaints that would arise. I think one of the possible advantages that you have is that you are able to look at this issue and see whether it can be cascaded down from the recommendations that you have already made for a broader range of local bodies than just further and higher education.

LORD NOLAN: Yes.

JOHN ANDREWS: Would you like me to comment on the other point you raised, which is the internal issue—

LORD NOLAN: Yes, please.

JOHN ANDREWS: There it does seem to me that there are advantages in procedures being available and being widely known to people, and I think you probably need two sorts of people. You need somebody within the institution on the staff who can deal with issues, and normally one would expect to find that in a personnel section of a university, and somebody outwith the line management running down from the principal. We have suggested that the chairman of an audit committee is the sort of person, but it does seem to me that what one is looking for there is an agreement by the governing body that one of their number, who has the time and willingness to take this on, should be available. I would not go for one person, either within or without, because if you have a governor picking up everything, that could lead to a desperate overload of a lay member which would not be right, and an internal member of staff picking up everything does not allow that slight outwithness that you would get by going to a governor.

1165. LORD NOLAN: Quite so. Yes. I have little direct experience of this, but I believe that in the commercial organisations which have adopted them it is just that sort of procedure normally, a two-stage process, if you like, so that it is not just one person with all the responsibility for dealing with the matter, but does provide a mechanism which is probably as effective as any could be to enable matters to be brought to light without unfair prejudice to the individual who is raising them, which is, as we have heard from many areas of public life, something that it is widely felt needs to be addressed.

I have a note from Dame Anne saying "I overlooked asking about layers of audit. How necessary is it to have them all?"

ANNE WARBURTON: You will have been surprised not to be asked that.

RICHARD HIRST: If I can answer that, Chairman. Clearly institutions have to be externally audited under their own statutory provisions, and I do not think anyone would query that. They are also required under our audit code of practice to have internal audit, and I think again any organisation of the kind of size that we are talking about would expect to have an internal audit system to ensure that it is running efficiently and, more particularly, that expenditure is properly committed and so forth.

We are conscious of the danger of over-auditing, and therefore the council's own audit service tries very much to avoid duplicating what is already there and going in for hands-on audit, so in order to satisfy the accounting officer that public funds are being properly accounted for we tend to operate, if you like, at arm's length by assessing institutions' own procedures through the reliance we can place on external audit, the reliance we can place on internal audit and the reliance we can place on institutions' audit committees. If we are content that those are working as they should, covering the areas that they should, that the reports are thorough and so forth, then we would regard that as providing us with the kind of assurance that the accounting officer obviously needs to have for public funds. So we are conscious of the issue and we try to minimise the degree of duplication by standing back and looking at those systems themselves rather than looking directly into the institution. So I think the issue is there and we attempt to minimise it in practice, and although there are some mutterings within governing bodies, as perhaps one would expect, I do not think there is a great ground-swell of opinion against that. I think there is a recognition that in publicly-funded organisations that is an inevitable trend.

LORD NOLAN: Were there any other questions, Anne, that you had, or anybody else?

1166. DIANA WARWICK: I wonder if I could just ask a question of clarification. It reverts back to the point

you were making about whether the Funding Councils would make, for example, compliance with the chairman's advice on governance a condition of grant. You said you did not think it would be at all advisable. In fact are you able to do that?

JOHN ANDREWS: We can impose conditions on grant only after consultation with institutions, and whilst we could ignore what they said, it would be a very cavalier thing to do, and normally when we consult it is a very genuine consultation. I think one of the things, though, that has to be borne in mind with the chairmen's guide is that it is quite a long document and much of it is setting out good practice, not necessarily best practice, and it is not necessarily ideal in all its content for all the institutions; there is a tremendous diversity.

The potential advantage of a code of best practice is that it could be slimmed down to the core of what is needed, and if that came forward as a result of your proposals or came forward from Departments, it would carry an imprimatur rather than as if a Funding Council was being fussy and intruding. It would then be possible for us to make it a condition of grant, and indeed some of the conditions which we impose are as a result of requests from the Secretary of State, and the same would apply in England, in the PES letter. We already are asked to do that, for example, in respect of observance of government pay policies. We would be very loath as a Funding Council to take the initiative on that, but quite clearly since the money is coming from government, if we are told to do it by government, then we will do it.

1167. LORD NOLAN: One point of detail. Could we establish whether you have the principals or vice-chancellors of the Welsh institutions on your councils?

JOHN ANDREWS: No. We have on the FE Council two principals from Welsh institutions. On the HE Council we do not. We do have two vice-chancellors from English institutions with Welsh links.

LORD NOLAN: Thank you very much. We are very grateful to you all. We leave you much better educated than we met you. We do appreciate the time you have taken and the amount of work you put into the evidence you have given us. Thank you all very much indeed.

WEDNESDAY 24 JANUARY 1996

MORNING SESSION

OPENING STATEMENT

Opening statement from the University of Glamorgan

1.   The institution, as Polytechnic of Wales, was the last polytechnic to be incorporated in 1992 and therefore has relatively recent experience of the transition from local authority control to fully independent university status.

2.   The current Vice-Chancellor, Professor Adrian Webb, who was appointed in 1993, was the first vice-chancellor to cross over from an "old" to a "new" university and therefore has recent experience of both systems of governance. His evidence may therefore be particularly useful to the Committee.

3.   The size and composition of the governing body has occasioned debate at several meetings since the university came into being. There is an inevitable tension between such desiderata as the effective and efficient management of business, the full involvement of all members, the recruitment of individuals with specialist relevant skills, the effective guidance and control of the executive officers and the representation of a diversity of community interests. The overwhelming view of the board members is that a comparatively small board can facilitate most of these desiderata, and Professor Webb's experience of both systems would tend to confirm this, but not, arguably, the representation of a diverse local/regional community. Glamorgan, however, is a highly "local", community-oriented university and the diversity of its community is represented by direct involvement of different interests and groups in specific steering/liaison committees (e.g. many departments have a "business club", the Community University of the Valleys programme, etc.) Taken together, we believe such mechanisms enable close community liaison to be maintained and good governance to be prosecuted.

4.   Professor Webb's initial experience, since 1993, suggests that a comparatively small governing body (20 in the case of the University of Glamorgan) is able to exercise a clear and direct authority in a way that a much larger, more diffuse governing body such as exist in most old universities may not be able to do.

5.   We believe that the university secretary's letter of 30 October 1995 addresses the key issues which are of concern to the Committee.

WEDNESDAY 24 JANUARY 1996

AFTERNOON SESSION

Members Present:

The Rt Hon Lord Nolan (Chairman)

Sir Clifford Boulton GCB   Sir William Utting CB
Professor Anthony King   Dame Anne Warburton DCVO CMG

Witnesses:

Tim Blanch, Chairman, and Gareth Hughes, Director, Welsh Federation of Housing Associations

Chris Jones, Chief Executive, Carl Hadley, Board Member, and Ian Raybould, Company Secretary, West Wales TEC

Molly Owen, Chief Executive, Wales Chambers of Commerce and Industry, and Helen Conway, Chief Executive, Cardiff Chamber of Commerce

John Stone, Headmaster, Bishop Vaughan Catholic Comprehensive School, Morriston, Swansea

1168. LORD NOLAN: Good afternoon. This morning we were mainly concerned with higher education. This afternoon we range more widely across housing associations, TECs and grant-maintained schools.

First we welcome Tim Blanch, Chairman, and Gareth Hughes, Director, of the Welsh Federation of Housing Associations. We are sometimes told that housing associations in Wales are different from those in England and we shall be interested to know if that is indeed the case.

We then hear from West Wales Training and Enterprise Council, represented by Chris Jones, who is the Chief Executive, and Ian Raybould, the Company Secretary.

This will be followed by a business perspective on TECs from Mrs Helen Conway, the Chief Executive of Cardiff Chamber of Commerce, who is accompanied by Ms. Molly Owen of the Welsh Chambers of Commerce.

Finally this afternoon we shall have our first witness from a grant-maintained church school, when we hear from Mr John Stone, Headmaster of Bishop Vaughan Catholic Comprehensive School at Swansea.

So we come back, please, to our opening witnesses this afternoon. Welcome, gentleman, and thank you very much for coming to join us. Thank you very much for the help you have already given us with your written presentations. I am going to ask Professor Anthony King now to open the questions but before he does so was there anything you wanted to say by way of opening remarks or statement or would you be happy to straight into the questions?

TIM BLANCH AND GARETH HUGHES

GARETH HUGHES (Director, Welsh Federation of Housing Associations): Well, happy to go into the questions. I just would like to make the one point I think we feel quite strongly about in the Welsh Federation of Housing Associations, that we are very worried about being categorised as local public spending bodies in terms of those that you have been looking at because we come from the voluntary sector. Indeed, gradually, because of

Government policy, we are getting less and less public money, so we see ourselves very much as part of the voluntary sector and we have tried over the years to educate the public in Wales to the fact that we are voluntary bodies, even though we receive money from a quango, but we are in ourselves not a quango and trying to get that message across I think is quite important to us and in a sense the Committee enquiring into housing associations has done us a bit of a disservice in that respect. So I would like to get that off my chest before I start.

LORD NOLAN: Of course we note your remarks. They are not the first remarks of this kind to be made. But there it is—we feel that this is a proper subject for us to look at with full understanding of the background of the housing associations as distinct from the other bodies. Professor King?

1169. PROF ANTHONY KING: You have got that off your chest. Can I just ask you whether the following description is accurate; that housing associations in Wales as well as in the rest of the country are local voluntary bodies spending public money. Is that a fair description?

GARETH HUGHES: Yes, I think we spend a mixture of public money and private money and also in some instances raise charitable money as well. So, yes, in part it is true that we do spend public money.

1170. PROF ANTHONY KING: I am just making the obvious point that one of the reasons why we thought it worth enquiring into housing associations, even if they have been rather clumsily lumped with genuine local quangos, is simply that there is quite a lot of public money involved. Could I ask you—I do not hold you personally responsible for what appears in the *South Wales Echo* but it is a newspaper——

GARETH HUGHES: I don't take any responsibility!

1171. PROF ANTHONY KING: —— one is told in England to take seriously and is often quoted in England. You are quoted as saying—and obviously it would be disconcerting if you were right—that "the enquiry by the Committee on standards in public life might do more harm than good". Now, clearly we would not want to do that, better we should not have come at all than we should have that effect. How do you think we might achieve that effect?

GARETH HUGHES: Well, I think, one, it is slightly an abbreviation of perhaps what I might have said, but I think the way it can do some harm is that certainly with many of the people we deal with, especially local authorities, in the last few years we have been trying desperately hard to point out that housing associations are not quangos, that we are voluntary organisations, we are independent. We are controlled by a quango, because we take money out of them, but we also take money from the building societies and the banks and they, too, exercise control. Bracketing us together with all the bodies that in Wales come under the general category "quango" does do us a disservice and creates in the mind of the population of Wales that matter to us this feeling "Ah, the housing associations are the same" and I can assure you that quangos are not the favourite animal of most people in Wales.

1172. PROF ANTHONY KING: Not just in Wales, is our impression! And you go on to say—I just want to be clear what you mean by this—you go on to say, or to have been quoted as saying "we depend heavily on volunteers sitting on our committees and there is a possibility that potential volunteers might be turned off if they hear the Nolan Committee has questioned us". Again, could you spell that out a bit?

GARETH HUGHES: Yes. As far as the general public are concerned—and we rely on the general public for volunteers to become members of housing associations and, in turn, be elected to the committees of housing associations—your Committee is associated, whether it is true or not, with sleaze. Let us make no bones about it, I think in the *Western Mail* today you, sir, are described as "the witch-hunter general", I think, or something along those lines—"the sleazehunter general". So as you can see that is the public perception of your work and therefore I was pointing out, we might suffer from guilt by association and we would not want people to be deterred from, real public duty in a voluntary sector that is contributing a great deal to Wales by any guilt by association.

1173. PROF ANTHONY KING: Could I say rather emphatically that obviously that would be very unfortunate and that the reason we are looking at housing associations is not because we think there is something desperately wrong with the governance, or whatever, of housing associations but simply because housing associations do, over the country as a whole, spend very large sums of public money and do raise the kinds of questions of audit and accountability and so on that are raised by bodies that really are quangos, even though, clearly, you are not.

One of the things that has been said to us more than once is that if you look at the housing association movements in England, Scotland and Wales separately they do turn out to have rather different features. Could you tell us a bit about how, if at all, you think the Welsh housing association movement differs from that in, say, England?

GARETH HUGHES: I think the one thing we can say that is very different, we tend to be very very much smaller bodies. The largest association in Wales has about 6,000 houses. The average association would probably be in the range of between 500-1000 properties and I think they are much more accountable to their communities. In the main most of them either cover one local authority area—at the most, apart from the one national one—at the most they would cover three local authority areas. I think that is very different from English associations. Scottish associations would probably be on a par with Welsh associations. The only difference is, I think they have slightly more tenant controlled associations in Scotland than we do in Wales.

1174. PROF ANTHONY KING: You have described the smallness of Welsh housing associations as a fact. Do you think it is also a virtue?

GARETH HUGHES: It does allow those associations, to be more sensitive to the communities that they are operating in—and, I think, also sensitive to the people that they are serving, those people that we have the privilege of actually providing our houses as their homes. And I think that is the kind of approach that the housing association in Wales has tried to develop. That is partly because of its size—it can be more sensitive and can be more influenced, by the community around it.

1175. PROF ANTHONY KING: How do you set about institutionalising the sensitivity? How do you set about making sure that your associations are actually sensitive?

GARETH HUGHES: Perhaps if I could duck that one and pass it to my Chair who actually runs a community-based housing association. Although Tim is Chair of the Welsh Federation he is also Chief Executive of the Rhondha Housing Association and I think he can actually demonstrate in practical terms how they do it there.

TIM BLANCH (Chairman, Welsh Federation of Housing Associations): I think it is difficult to institutionalise things. Obviously one of the problems—your first comment that I was going to pick up but I did not was that not all housing associations are actual local spending bodies, some may be specialist and if, for example, your specialism is housing people with learning disability for example, you know, you may have a very different approach to local sensitivity than, say, my organisation which is very heavily concentrated in one particular geographical area. And I think there is, therefore, going to be a pretty wide diversity between the approaches. I mean, openness and accountability to members and to the local authority is very very important, obviously, for a locally based organisation like mine, but it would not necessarily apply to all.

1176. PROF ANTHONY KING: But still speaking of your own association how do you actually set about—I will resile from the word "institutionalising" but creating and maintaining sensitivity to your clientele?

TIM BLANCH: Well, partly it's because your committee —I mean, my association has a large membership, mainly composed of tenants, we have tenants on the committee of the association, the association committee is made up of local people, you have clearly direct links with the elected local authority members and with officers. It is those sort of connections which actually create that sensitivity—and obviously the local authority has a direct input into the work that we are doing.

1177. PROF ANTHONY KING: Could I just ask you about your document *Standards of Conduct and Good Practice?* You say at one point in paragraph 3, I think, that "it is the member"s duty [that is the member of committees of housing associations] to ensure both that the committee represents the interests of those it seeks to serve"—that is your sensitivity point—"and that the committee contains sufficient expertise to handle its duties in controlling the affairs of the Association". Now obviously there could be a tension built in there between, as it were, the experts, the specialists running the thing, perhaps wanting to increase its size, wanting to increase its staff or whatever, and the sensitivity to the tenants that you talked about. How conscious are you of that as a problem and how do you set about dealing with it?

GARETH HUGHES: Well, first of all we do advertise quite considerably for committee members. The purpose of that is that we can actually, or the committees concerned, can interview people to try to get a balance within that committee. I think a substantial number of our associations are charities on charitable rules and we have a rule of thumb, because I don't think there is a law there that says that you can't have tenants on a charitable committee. There is a lack of clarity there and perhaps that is something that you might care to comment on in your report. But we have used the rule of thumb that there should not be more than a third of tenants on the committee of the charitable associations because you can't be a beneficiary of a charity that you are running. So there is that problem when you are trying to involve tenants on a charitable committee. We are trying to encourage most of our associations to move on to charitable rules for reasons that really basically I can't see—and I don't think the public can see—the difference between the types of housing associations that are on charitable rules and those that are not.

TIM BLANCH: Coming in there, though, I think this has often been floated—this question of this tension between different groups represented on association committees. In my experience it is more a problem that people think about than in reality. I have not actually come across this problem in reality at all and I have worked for a number of associations where there have been substantial or majority tenant participation and in my experience the tenants are more interested in an efficient and well-run organisation and there isn't that tension in practice, though in theory one could postulate it.

1178. PROF ANTHONY KING: Picking up something Mr Hughes said a moment ago and moving on from there, Section 15—we have heard a fair number of horror stories of people who have felt that a particular housing association has been less than well-served because of these very tight Section 15 rules. Would you want to see Section 15 loosened up in some way and if so how?

GARETH HUGHES: Yes. I think that one of the difficulties we have with Section 15 is that it is so tight that we actually have had to get determination orders passed to actually loosen it up. Let me quote some examples: if you were on a community-based housing association and you are living in a fairly tight geographic area you find that some of the committee members of housing associations are disadvantaged in members of their families being housed in that association, even though they have a genuine housing need and they can be demonstrated to have a housing need.

Again the same thing—and this is an actual example—a committee member of a housing association in a rural part whose daughter would have been entitled to and did require a home in that association and he had to resign and the daughter couldn't have been helped for another year because of his involvement. And there are real difficulties with Section 15, especially in areas where there is, I think, a very tightness of a community, rural areas particularly, I think, and I would certainly like to see us move more to the system adopted by local authorities of declaration of interests, so that you can actually make it absolutely clear when there is a problem of duality, rather than this blanket prevention that the law at the moment insists on.

PROF ANTHONY KING: I thought I saw Mr Blanch looking a little quizzical as you said that.

TIM BLANCH: No, I agree, it applies as well in valley communities, like the one I work in, where you have very very tight communities with large numbers of members of the same family living in a small area and where you have large tenant participation it is a problem, yes.

1179. PROF ANTHONY KING: Do you think—and this is addressed to both of you, I am not trying to divide you in any way—do you think that mere declarations of interest would be enough, because Section 15 was clearly drafted in the tight way it was to prevent some pretty obvious abuses that could otherwise arise? Do you have specific notions as to how you might loosen it up without the worries coming to the surface?

GARETH HUGHES: I think if you were to loosen it up and simply have a declaration of interests and leave it at that then I think it could be abused. But it is not leaving things just like that because we have a whole programme of committee education, we have a whole programme of developing good practice. In Wales we provide every new committee member and every committee member with a pack which we update and we hold training events on them, so that it is not just about saying "Well, you"ve got to declare an interest", to explain why the circumstances ——I think it is an ongoing education process and a reminder all the time that these things are important and we do hold it important that we are seen to be acting with fairness in all our dealings and I think it is important, you know, that we underline that. But we do genuinely want to overcome some of the difficulties that Section 15 does cause.

1180. PROF ANTHONY KING: The question about members of the housing association: going round the country we get the impression, not only that different housing associations have a very different attitude towards their members, but that they take them with varying degrees of seriousness. Some associations try to build up their membership, some of them seem to regard members as largely irrelevant. Could you tell us what you think the role of members should be and whether you actively want to recruit them and have more of them?

GARETH HUGHES: I think we, certainly in Wales, have I think a large number of associations that have actively gone to encourage a substantial number of members of an association. But I don't go down the route of saying that that should be the answer for all housing associations, because I think there are some housing associations—I am particularly concerned and interested in those that have a speciality—that perhaps are doing, if I can describe it as the most difficult type of housing, housing people that in the community at large people would not be welcoming with open arms in that particular type of housing. Now to have those associations perhaps with large membership may well act as a brake on them actually pursuing a particular housing need.

PROF ANTHONY KING: Can you be a bit more specific?

GARETH HUGHES: Yes. We are at the moment experiencing, just with ordinary housing, because we are housing people in the main that are quite under-privileged. Now we are having difficulties with planning authorities, especially with new building, because the "nimby" syndrome is "We don"t want these people living near us". You know, we have got to be frank about it, it is happening more and more often with social housing. If you are actually dealing with a particularly difficult group, for instance an association that might be specialising in people that have been offenders and are now back into the community. Now, to get those kind of housing schemes off the ground is particularly difficult. I would not want to see the use of the membership—and membership of housing associations has to be particularly open, so if anybody applies to be a member then there has to be good reason why the association should refuse membership. Now, my worry with those types of associations is that you could have people applying for membership that really want to frustrate the ambitions of that association. So that is why I wouldn't give a blanket, say "yes, let"s have full membership". I do think that the association would have to justify why they limit membership. I think normally there should be open membership. Unless an association comes out and says "We want to limit membership and we want to limit membership because of these reasons".

1181. PROF ANTHONY KING: Could I finally just ask you a couple of questions about housing for Wales which does not, as you say, fund all of the associations in your membership but funds a fair proportion of them at least in part. It is obviously both a funding body and a regulatory body. We are told rightly or wrongly that housing for Wales is a pretty interventionist organisation. How would you describe the relationship between your member organisations and housing for Wales? Do you think it is a satisfactory relationship, if not how would you change it?

GARETH HUGHES: I think there are always tensions between a body that acts as a police person and those people that are actually being policed. We actually feel that as public funds have declined intervention has increased. I think associations are genuinely worried about the amount of information that is required in this instance from our quango, Tai Cymru Housing for Wales. For instance, associations have to submit quarterly accounts to the quango. Obviously the organisation has to have rules as to which way they give the public funds but I often feel that instead of actually looking at the broad principles of what we should be doing there is a direct and almost an intimate wish on their part to run the business. I think our members feel quite often that they are now not independent bodies but are simply local agents of a national housing body and I don't think that is particularly healthy.

1182. PROF ANTHONY KING: Finally, can I just pick you up on what you say in your evidence at one point, and it is consistent with what you have just been saying,

that we are in danger of being over monitored and I am sure you think that we are another bad example of that process. Leaving us out of it how could you, consistent with the public good, be less monitored? What sort of monitoring would you like seeing rained back?

GARETH HUGHES: I think the broad thrust of what we say is—let's agree the general principles of what an association ought to be doing, in receipt of public money. But at the moment we are monitored by Tai Cymru. We also have the building society world and the banks making their demands. Also, because we have to work with local authorities, we have to satisfy them in terms of the work we are doing in their areas. We also have, because of our rules, either to respond to the demands of the Registrar of Friendly Societies because in the main they are Industrial and Provident societies or those that are on charitable rules or are charities have to answer to the charity commissions. So there are plenty of people that seem to have an interest in our affairs and I can assure you also from the kind of correspondence that I receive that individual members of parliament and other people take a great interest in our affairs because housing, whether we like it or not, is one of those areas where there are real difficulties of society and certainly generate a fair amount of correspondence backwards and forwards because a lot of people are frustrated in their housing, there is not enough to go around and when you have a scarcity you also have problems. So everybody has an interest in the work of housing associations.

1183. PROF ANTHONY KING: That is the complaint which we have heard before and almost certainly has some foundation, but what is the remedy?

TIM BLANCH: I think from our point of view we are worried not so much about the general overview monitoring but intervention in much more detail. One of our concerns, I think, is that where associations are aiming to be sensitive to local need that is very difficult if there is very detailed regulation coming down from a national body and the evidence from the past is that centrally-determined housing policies have not been a great success.

PROF ANTHONY KING: Thank you.

LORD NOLAN: Thank you very much. Anne?

1184. ANNE WARBURTON: Could I just at the beginning stick my neck out a little bit on this question of whether we are doing you a disservice by talking to you—I hope we are not. I don't altogether see the distinction between you and, for example, universities, whose board members are also unpaid voluntary people and which are also charities and, of course, on the point about the private sector TECs are also in the private sector. I just want to say that we are not really looking at quangos this time round, is what I am really saying. I hope that helps to put your mind at rest, Mr Hughes.

GARETH HUGHES: Yes. I think it is unfortunate perhaps that the organisations that you are looking at in terms of the Welsh——they are always controlled by government on all those other bodies in the way that they are established. Whereas we come from another area completely, the voluntary sector. If I can just give you an example why it is particularly sensitive. As you know there has been a Welsh Language Act and there is a Welsh

Language Board. Now, the Secretary of State is in the process of determining whether we are a public body from the point of view of the Act or whether we should be part of the voluntary sector. There are different kinds of demands for a voluntary body to that of a public body. All the time we seem to be moved into that kind of quasi public sector whereas we want to be seen as that quasi voluntary sector. Now I know the voluntary sector is very wide and very broad and there are very different types of organisations and I think it is very difficult to——perhaps that is the beauty of the sector, that it is very difficult to pin anyone into it being quite like any other. But that is the sector we see ourselves in and that is why we are making that particular point.

1185. ANNE WARBURTON: I knew I might be refuelling the discussion! Could I just limit myself, in view of the time, to one question and that is following on the audit, the question of whether it might help to reduce the hierarchy of auditing, make that easier to wear, if some of your own auditors also looked at performance, whether perhaps reassured on that score that some other detailed financial auditing might not be so important. Have you thought about that?

GARETH HUGHES: Actually at the moment we are paying an outside consultant to look at and make recommendations to us as a federation and to housing associations as to how we can actually get real performance indicators into housing associations. Not the performance indicators, the kind of number crunching indicators that are used to compare housing associations to local authorities but, real quality indicators, so that we can actually say "Look, this organisation, this business, if you like, this housing business is actually meeting its targets well and these are the indications of how it is meeting its targets and how it actually is providing a good service to its client group." I think it is not easy and we are developing it because we are centring that development on the housing association's business. Too many other performance indicators are, if you like, to measure dissimilar organisations and they are not true comparators and, you know, in other fields—you may have asked questions this morning, in terms of education performance indicators and how they can be misused and misinterpreted and this is what we are trying to move away from in housing, although Government and Tai Cymru do require us to produce indicators that compare us to local authorities, which I find particularly frustrating because again they are misleading because they are too simple.

1186. ANNE WARBURTON: There is one just general question which perhaps can be answered almost with a "yes" or "no". We are not able to talk too widely to housing associations in Wales—can we take you as being representative, the points you have been making are representative of what others would think, or do you have particular angles which are special for you?

GARETH HUGHES: No, I think we have in our membership all the housing associations in Wales that receive public funds and we have quite a number that don't receive funds at all. We've discussed the kind of issues that you are asking questions on today; (a) in the context of, as you know, the National Federation had an enquiry into this whole area of governance of housing associations. We, too, have had our own look at our roles in view of updating them and seeing whether they are relevant today. So the issues are well aired. For instance, we took a vote in a general meeting six months ago as to

whether committee members of housing associations in Wales should be paid or not and I can tell you that it was almost unanimous that none of the committee members in that room and, therefore, none of the associations in Wales, wanted to go down that route.

TIM BLANCH: I think it is broadly true to say that associations in Wales are more similar to each other perhaps—you have a much wider range of housing associations in England than in Wales, we are a fairly united movement in Wales, small and fairly common in our approach, I think.

ANNE WARBURTON: So it is not so difficult for you to represent.

TIM BLANCH: No.

1187. PROF ANTHONY KING: Can I just cut in to ask, do you think that some of the English housing associations are too big?

TIM BLANCH: Yes.

1188. PROF ANTHONY KING: Could you make that "Yes, colon", rather than "yes, full stop"?

GARETH HUGHES: Yes. I think actually that there is a great deal —I am convinced that the Schumacher arguments are right, smaller in this instance is particularly beautiful. I think if you actually have housing associations that are 27,000 or 28,000 units, they have the problems of a large local authority and I know that they have problems. I am not saying that you cannot overcome those problems but if you were to ask me as to my preference for an association it would be a small association, but as all my members are small I would say that anyway, wouldn't I?

TIM BLANCH: There is also an additional point, I think, about the extent to which an association is a monopoly provider in an area. I mean, I think it may be very different if you are talking about, say, Anchor, or something, which is a large organisation but providing a specialist service right across the country, from say any organisation which is the main provider of housing in that area and obviously the question of accountability is more central if you are a monopoly provider.

1189. LORD NOLAN: And as you know in England we have been looking at some very large housing associations including some that have become virtually the sole providers of social housing which do, of course, raise different problems. So let me thank you very much for improving our education over the situation in Wales. We are still on our learning curve and we have learned a lot this afternoon. Thank you very much for coming.

GARETH HUGHES: Thank you.

PROF ANTHONY KING: And we will try to do as little harm as possible!

1190. LORD NOLAN: Good afternoon, gentlemen. Now we welcome the West Wales Training and Enterprise Council in the person of Mr Chris Jones, Chief Executive, and Ian Raybould, Company Secretary. I have only got the two names, I am afraid.

**CHRIS JONES, CARL HADLEY,
AND IAN RAYBOULD**

CARL HADLEY (Board Member, West Wales TEC): My name is Carl Hadley—I am a Director.

LORD NOLAN: Thank you very much, Mr Hadley. Did you wish to say anything by way of opening remarks or would you like to go straight into the questions?

CHRIS JONES (Chief Executive, West Wales TEC): We have submitted a public statement, but only basically to say that we appreciate the validity of the constitution of the Nolan Committee and its remit and its applicability to TECs, not necessarily because we think that TECs need to be probed or investigated so much but because we are happy to have the chance to respond to some of the perceptions that exist that sometimes give rise to concern about the way that we are structured and constituted. So it is nice to be able to have the opportunity to give some insight into how we are structured, what is in place to satisfy some of the concerns that I know you are investigating and the flexibilities that exist within that system to develop that further. So thank you for inviting us.

LORD NOLAN: Not at all, and thank you. It is certainly an important part of our task to reassure as well as to criticise and we hope we shall do that much better with your help. Now I am going, if I may, to ask Dame Anne Warburton to open the questions in your case. Anne?

1191. ANNE WARBURTON: Thank you, Chairman. Could I first ask a sort of office question: have you yet seen a summary of the report of the Parliamentary Committee which is making its views on TECs public today?

CHRIS JONES: I saw it in the witness room just before we came in.

1192. ANNE WARBURTON: You did, good. Because there was one point there I thought we might come to and if you had not I would ask that you be·shown that. But to begin with I would really like to ask you if you could just give us rather more background on the West Wales TEC, like how long has it been working and how did the first Board get constituted. I will leave those as the first two questions.

CHRIS JONES: I can certainly tell you how long it has been in existence, because it has just had its fifth anniversary—it was the first TEC in Wales to be constituted. It covers the two counties of Dyfed and West Glamorgan, it has a turnover of about £28 million a year, it covers a population of 750,000, which is about a quarter of the Welsh population. I wasn't around at the time that the first Board was constituted by Mr Hadley was and so he could probably give you more insight as to how that came about than I could.

CARL HADLEY: We started really because Peter Walker was encouraging us at great speed to form a group of people to start a TEC and we pulled together people that we knew from organisations that we felt represented what was wanted in business—local government and health and other related organisations—and we started off, I think, with about seventy people forming sub-

boards, forums, groups, to form a plan and out of that we did not elect but, we ended up with fifteen people who became directors and then after that we looked to make it more representative and we have been developing it ever since.

1193. ANNE WARBURTON: Have you had a rapid turnover?

CARL HADLEY: We have had a turnover. I am not sure what a rapid turnover would be, really. We have had a turnover and some of us have been there since the beginning and some have only been there two or three months, in fact.

1194. ANNE WARBURTON: And what does this large population largely do—is it mostly industrial, or rural or what?

CHRIS JONES: It varies. I mean, the patch itself is diverse. Of the two counties I have mentioned, West Glamorgan is a more urbanised, industrialised population. Dyfed, with certain exceptions, like Llanelli and perhaps to an extent Carmarthen is a far more rural area, so the spread of sectors with which the TEC has to deal is along quite a large spectrum from heavy manufacturing, constructing industries, to largely rurally based agricultural industry.

1195. ANNE WARBURTON: That fits in rather well with the question I wanted to ask about relationship with the two development bodies, the Welsh Development Agency and the Development Board for Rural Wales. Does the work of these bodies overlap with the enterprise work of the TEC and if so, more on the urban than on the rural side, or how closely do you work with them?

CHRIS JONES: We work closely with them. The WDA has an office which covers West Wales which, in fact, coincides in boundary terms with our own West Wales patch and our own officers and those of that division meet on a regular basis to share our own strategies and operational intentions for ensuing months, so there is a working relationship that exists with the WDA in that context. There is a potential perception—and it does exist—of conflict or overlap between the work of the WDA and the work of TECs which has often sort of bottomed out in a mis-understanding of the word "enterprise" which exists within the TEC acronym. It doesn't actually operate like that in practice because I think that enterprise from a TEC's perspective is about the creation of enterprising people, they are not just people who are not in business but people also in business and people who are in business in order to make those businesses more enterprising, but our focus is clearly about an approach, a style—it is a conceptual philosophy, a willingness to explore, to experiment, to risk-take, if that is what business needs to develop, but it is about people's understanding of how best to contribute to business.

The WDA is a far more infrastructurally focused organisation in terms of enterprise where it is clearly more about inward investment, it is clearly more about the making available of premises for lease, for rent, or for acquisition. There is a distinction—you could look at it in a sort of micro-soft/macro-hard distinction—there is no inherent competition between the two because one is infrastructurally focused and one is clearly people focused and West Wales TEC is undoubtedly a people focused organisation, not an infrastructure focused organisation.

1196. ANNE WARBURTON: That is interesting. I think I am right in saying that the Welsh TECs share with English TECs having no intermediate sort of regulatory authority, whereas in Scotland I understand that the two development bodies there, north and south, actually not only make contract with their LECs but actually are both funders and regulators. What would you see as the advantages and disadvantages of having something similar to that in Wales?

CHRIS JONES: So that the TECs remit was, in effect, enmeshed with that of the WDA?

ANNE WARBURTON: Yes, and does not have to go straight back to the Department.

CHRIS JONES: Well, the straight back to the Department issue is largely one of logistics because Wales in many contexts of England and Wales-wide TEC administration—and we belong to the TEC National Council for the UK, which covers all TECs in England and Wales—is a region because its demography and the logistics of the number of organisations that are represented within that region are consistent with other regions as part of England. For us in Wales to have a line between us in Government would make a little bit of a nonsense of the logistics of it, in so far as there are not enough of us—there are only seven TECs in Wales. You would find as many TECs, if not more, in certain regions within England. So we are for those administrative purposes a region of the UK. I don't think that logistically it would be sensible to impose another layer of bureaucracy in between the two.

CARL HADLEY: Could I add a comment to that as well? We also feel that if you brought all these organisations together, the TECs and the WDA and the DBRW, you would lose the focus that we have, and our focus as TECs is to train people, train people for existing businesses as well as any new businesses coming in. Whereas the WDA, they concentrate more upon inward investment and they also encourage development of existing businesses but then emphasis is more on inward investment and if you brought them together you would lose something.

1197. ANNE WARBURTON: Thank you for that. Rather like the housing association we have been talking to you put a lot of emphasis—and I quite understand it—on the private sector nature of your work. But as ninety per cent of the funding comes from Government and I gather the Welsh Office does lay down quite detailed criteria for the board membership, perhaps one must not push that too far on the private side. But are there specific advantages for TECs to be clearly in the private sector status and are their any disadvantages from it?

CHRIS JONES: I think that the advantages are probably borne out by the acknowledged change—progressive increase in performance that TECs have delivered since becoming constituted as TECs and populated in the main by individuals from the private sector. So what TECs inherited from the Manpower Services Commission and have taken on board in terms of the delivery of Government programmes has been seen to be an improvement, an increase in the value for money

obtained from it and I think that is largely occasioned by the fact that you have got individuals used to dealing with and working within the private sector, who can bring to bear that individualism, that flexibility, that flair, that enables TECs to look in a more visionary way to their remit and to their responsibilities. I think it would be a loss to lose that particular focus. Having said that, one appreciates that we are wholly dependent, to all intents and purposes, on the public purse for the money that we contract with Government to receive in return for what we deliver and it would be folly of any TEC not to openly acknowledge and to work within the realisation that that framework exists—without public money TECs would not exist, there is no other way that we could draw money for what we do. So we must regard ourselves as a half-way house between the public and the private sector and give due deference to both sectors for that reason.

The disadvantage, as I see it, of private sector emphasis on a Board is more one of perception than practical manifestation. There is no issue that manifests itself in terms of an inability to discharge a publicly funded role but I can understand why a perception might exist that said "if you are focused upon private sector individuals that automatically excludes representation from the community at large". I can understand that to be a perception. I don't think it's a problem in practical terms—as the previous witness himself was trying to emphasise—it is more perception than it is application. However, in giving due deference, as I think is required, we have, as our public submission has already stated, recognised the need to be open and flexible in endorsing the principle of advertisement for appointments to TEC boards. I am not saying that applies across every TEC and we are not here to talk about every TEC, but we have recognised that there is a need to secure that comfort, that acceptance, because it will generate positive outcomes for us in terms of representation across the community. I think there is a role, in other words, for the amalgamation of both philosophies and both concepts in the way that a TEC structures itself. I think that there should be an element of co-option to the board because one needs to be able to focus upon and to pick out those with flair and individuality that can add impetus to what the TEC does, but there also is a role for openly advertising, even if it is focused upon sectors, of making it an electoral college system, by which some of the TEC directors are appointed. I think that that would be a sensible thing and a valid thing for a TEC to do.

1198. ANNE WARBURTON: I think you are just getting into my next question, that last bit, which has to do with membership—we are coming back to the membership. Really the question is who are the members—can anyone play?

CHRIS JONES: Yes, the membership of the TEC——it has been a thorny issue since the start, to be honest with you, the membership scheme of TECs because, at the end of the day, when we first constituted the membership scheme it carried with it a financial tag whereby people had to pay £25 to become a member of West Wales TEC. Different TECs organised membership schemes in different ways but that was the way ours was originally constituted. One has to ask what does the TEC actually give in return for its £25 that *the* individuals or businesses or entities within the community don't receive, and the truth of the matter is there is very little that a TEC can give that is special in return for a fee of that nature. That explains why membership schemes are often very low in TECs and I would be the first to acknowledge—and it's open information anyway that up until recently our membership scheme stood at the sum total of thirty-five, which is a very small number of members for an organisation of that size.

Now we have looked at the reason for that and discovered that in essence TECs are actually working on a membership basis most of the time without necessarily realising it, because we all—and we are one of them—maintain a series of forums and sector groups that derive commitment and involvement from a whole host of people throughout the community, throughout different sectors, who meet regularly and help us define and draft and implement strategic plans across the patch. We have a number of these forums, as we call them, in West Wales, construction forums, engineering, manufacturing, women and one parents' forum—a whole host of them—and they are extremely highly populated. Now we have taken a decision as a board to recognise those members of those forums as members of the TEC, as constituted within the term of the Memorandum and Articles of Association of the company. That immediately boosts the membership to close on 200 at a stroke which is a hugely different scenario. That is not simply a question of seeking to find a body of people that we an use to call members, it is recognising that as TECs have evolved they have built up this mechanism to consult with, to liaise with and to act with active members of the community but have never necessarily called them or considered them eligible to be called members. So I think membership is manifest, if not necessarily termed as membership. Membership is a problem but not an insurmountable one in so far as I think it is a question of recognising what actually happens on the ground and formalising its recognition better than perhaps some TECs have done in the past. I think membership schemes are important because we must be seen and must be able to act on an annual basis at the AGM on a vote of opinion as to who should or should not sit on a board and that must come from more than thirty-five people. So membership schemes are important and I don't think that they should ever be relinquished. But recognising what we have got on the patch our new membership is, in fact, already there.

1199. ANNE WARBURTON: Who is eligible to nominate directors, your thirty-five or your two hundred?

CHRIS JONES: Anyone is eligible to nominate a director but they would have to be a member of the TEC in order to become a director.

1200. ANNE WARBURTON: Yes. And is it at the AGM that the directors are formally appointed?

CHRIS JONES: Yes.

1201. ANNE WARBURTON: We have had a lot of discussion in England—back there—about TEC and Chamber of Commerce mergers as being a way to help to get the membership the right sort of size. How does that look from your point of view?

CHRIS JONES: As a concept, TEC and Chamber mergers which we have only really sort of broadly debated—we are quite open and flexible about the idea of TECs and Chambers coming together. As a mechanism by which one secures an enhancement or an increase in membership it's a different story in Wales. Chamber of Commerce membership is not as expansive in Wales as it is in England—I think the total Chamber of Commerce membership in Wales is in the small thousands for the whole of Wales, it is not large. In West Wales TEC/Chamber mergers would not secure an increase in membership that would be anything like we would secure by recognising forums such a I have just outlined.

CARL HADLEY: And also we feel that if the Chambers want to merge to give themselves more strength and to use their services, which would be training services and give priority to that, and also to keep their eyes on our surpluses that we have got allocated for other purposes, we would be a little reticent in bringing them along, I think. They have to come along for the right reasons, I say.

1202. ANNE WARBURTON: Yes. I think I shall probably only put one more question myself and yield the questioning. The question I would like to stop on is that of conflicts of interest, to hear what your procedure is for dealing with potential conflicts of interest.

CHRIS JONES: We have, again as you will have read from the submission, endorsed, embraced, implemented both the National Council advocated framework for local accountability and the code of conduct for TEC directors. We also have included within our own Memorandum and Articles of Association, as do other TECs, but also expanded upon in our own standing orders, which I have also made available to the Committee, a series of rules and systematic requirements whereby declarations of conflict of interest have to result in either the removal of that individual, having so expressed such a conflict, from any further participation in discussion and certainly removes eligibility for voting on any issue in respect of which a conflict has been declared or if it is felt that the degree of the conflict of interest is insufficient to warrant that exclusion, then it must be formally and detailedly minuted as to why it has been determined by the rest of the board that that extent is sufficient to allow continuance within the debate.

1203. ANNE WARBURTON: And in your experience does that meet, though, the problem—we have had some evidence suggesting that those not in the TECs see the TEC as a way of getting business to one own's advantage. Does the procedure that you have outlined make sure that in your case that does not follow?

CHRIS JONES: I am 100 per cent confident that in our case it certainly has done and there never has been, and certainly isn't any evidence to substantiate any claim to the effect that a board director of the TEC has been advantaged in any way as a result of his or her being a board director of the TEC. I am 100 per cent confident about that.

CARL HADLEY: I endorse that as well, but also to say that we have never encouraged people to be directors who have had a strong link with the TEC business itself. So we use the TEC but only in the same way as a business, as a company, in the same way that anyone else can. But any training provider, we have always kept them as far as we can at arm's length.

ANNE WARBURTON: Good. Thank you very much.

LORD NOLAN: Sir Clifford?

1204. CLIFFORD BOULTON: Do you get a certain amount of your grant specifically for the purpose of training disadvantaged groups, disabled or such groups?

CHRIS JONES: We certainly will do in the ensuing year.

1206. CLIFFORD BOULTON: So at the moment you have no experience of administering those special cases?

CHRIS JONES: There is always contained within the contracts which we negotiate with Government through the Welsh office a targeted commitment to deliver a certain level of programme delivery for defined groups, defined disadvantaged groups, yes.

1206. CLIFFORD BOULTON: And you have arrangements for getting access to the right kind of specialist advice, you do not have trainers on a board, do you, trainers are people that you deal with? Do you have access to expertise for knowing how to grant contracts for this particular type of work?

CHRIS JONES: Yes, I think that presence on a board is very different—a different issue—from the one which would impinge upon how we actually go about setting contracts——

1207. CLIFFORD BOULTON: It is just that some of the evidence we have received is suggesting—you are not and we are not suggesting anything, we are only asking—but there have been some suggestions that the composition of boards is too specialised from one point of view and that it would help to enrich it with, let us say, some trainers and some other sorts of people on the board and I was just asking how you would acquire the expertise you would need for looking after special needs of that sort which are not directly market orientated in the way that you pride yourself in being in the main part.

CHRIS JONES: Yes, we do have a forum—one of the forums I have already mentioned, which does actually assist us in looking at the issues that impinge upon that facet of the social infrastructure and we use it, as we do others, not just to feed into in terms of what our particular intentions or current draft plans are, but also to receive back from it what the potential pitfalls might be in implementing those plans. That is not the only way in which one does it, of course, because contract negotiation as far as a TEC is concerned, or so far as West Wales TEC is concerned, exists largely at a senior staff level and not at a board level. The board themselves do not get involved in negotiating contracts with training providers, or businesses for that matter, they specify a broad policy framework within which contract negotiations with providers should take place, in terms of what areas we should focus upon—that is sector areas as well as geographical areas—but the actual contract negotiation mechanism itself does not rest at the level of the board, it rests at the level of the senior staff who themselves will draw up on contacts for the seeking of advice from outside of the organisation.

1208. CLIFFORD BOULTON: Yes. But, of course, the board has to be able to pass judgment on how successful these things will be. I suppose once in a while you might have some disappointed clients, individual trainees who feel that the thing has been a failure for them, or hasn't helped them. Do you have an inbuilt system of looking into complaints that are received?

CHRIS JONES: If I may I would pass that question to our Company Secretary who does deal with the complaints' procedure.

IAN RAYBOULD (Company Secretary, West Wales TEC): Yes. Since we have been established as a TEC we have set up a complaints procedure which is mainly dealt with internally within the TEC organisation and that is dealt with at a senior management level and we respond to the complainant within ten days of receiving any complaint from them. They then have the right of appeal to the Chief Executive, if necessary, and then on to the Board if that person feels that their complaint has not been dealt with justly or correctly and then we have now in-built a means of external arbiter, should that be necessary. However, it perhaps should be stated that in the five years of our operation we have had complaints—not necessarily directly about the TEC itself but possibly about the training providers and the service that the provider has given—but we have, as yet, not even had to refer any of those complaints to the Board itself, we have been able to answer and sort out those complaints satisfactorily for the complainant without them going to the Board even.

1209. CLIFFORD BOULTON: Good. But some information is reasonably readily available to people who might wish to complain—how do they find out about the system?

IAN RAYBOULD: Well we have a published TEC charter which is available and is distributed widely which outlines that there is a complaints procedure available and encourages them to complain, because that is obviously one way of learning perhaps where we are going wrong.

CLIFFORD BOULTON: I imagine you want to know about these things.

IAN RAYBOULD: Indeed, yes.

1210. CLIFFORD BOULTON: What is the general ethos—do you reckon you get a reasonably favourable press about the work of the TEC? Is it a controversial business here or is the TEC reasonably comfortably accepted in the work it is doing locally?

CHRIS JONES: I would say that times change and things move on and if you were to have asked me that question a year and a half ago then I might have answered it differently from the way I would today, because a year and a half ago in the aftermath of the just concern that existed about the PAC reports on TEC risk status levels, when that applied equally in Wales as it did in England, it did lead to a flurry of interest and activity in what TECs did and perceptions which are often exaggerated and, indeed, were exaggerated, resulted in a heavy focus of criticism and questioning of whether TECs should actually exist in the format and in the style in which they did. That is not news to anyone because we have all seen the reports consequent upon PAC across the country. We dealt with that appropriately to the extent that we were able to ensure those external commentators that we had in place the wherewithal and the means to satisfy the low risk status that was demanded. We have never incidentally been anything other than low risk status as an organisation. But today the press coverage that I would summarise the TEC as receiving is extremely positive and, of course, again as the previous witness said, I would say that, wouldn't I and why should I declare it to be otherwise, but I am an honest man and that is the truth!

CLIFFORD BOULTON: You are in a public forum and we should soon hear if you were trying to pull the wool over our eyes! But public concern is in our terms of reference that we have to address—the level of existence of it—so thank you very much.

1211. LORD NOLAN: May I just conclude with one point—it is really a follow-on from what Dame Anne was putting earlier. What you have just been saying and what, indeed, appears from your submission is that you set an example in a way of openness of your activities—in public meetings you have an open register of interests which anybody can come and look at, you have a published complaints procedure and you have an extensive and positive programme of communications in the 25,000 businesses in West Wales. You also, as you say, are heavily audited. You list on page IV of the submission eight separate audits. I daresay you have got them all in your head, but shall I read them out quickly for the benefit of the public?

"1.   There is the internal audit, which despite the implication of the term is conducted by an external professional firm of auditors.

2.   Company external audit conducted by a different firm of professional auditors.

3.   Welsh Office Audit.

4.   Welsh Office Audit of our Internal Audit.

5.   Audit consequent upon extensive involvement in European funding programmes.

6.   Audit by the National Audit Office.

7.   Welsh Office FAM Team of Audit contract arrangements between the TEC and its providers.

8.   Formal TEC Audit of Providers' Contracts."

Are you over audited?

CHRIS JONES: Yes, most definitely.

1212. LORD NOLAN: Which of those eight do you think could be dispensed of without damage?

CHRIS JONES: Well, it's probably not so much a question of which of the eight should be dispensed with because I can understand the validity probably of each one of them. It is just that each one of them is implemented to a very full extent, so that there tends to be the obvious potential for cross-over and questioning that has already taken place. I think incidentally that since a large part of our audit is Government orchestrated audit that it is fair to say that the Government itself—the Welsh Office itself—is cognisant and recognises the fact that there needs to be an opening up of the flexibility within which TECs operate because the extent to which we are audited can be stifling and counter-productive in terms of our ability to deliver with flexibility the programmes that we have over the last five years been successful in delivering. So it is not so much a question of which one shouldn't be but a rationalisation of how they relate and interact with one another which I think as a concept is one which Government has already embraced.

1213. LORD NOLAN: They should talk to each other more and less to you, is that it?

CHRIS JONES: It is not necessarily an issue of not talking to each other more because there is not necessarily any mechanism or system in place that demands it at present. It is just more a question of talking to each other.

CARL HADLEY: Can I comment on that point? I think with too many auditors going in—I mean auditors have been proven to be quite fallible and if you feel that seven other people have been in and audited the organisation that you are going in to do today you may not be quite as sharp as if you knew that it was you who was responsible and I think if a single team went in with a brief drawn up from all of those things there and actually did the job properly once a year, it would be a much sharper focus for the TEC itself and also it would be better for the auditors as well.

LORD NOLAN: Thank you all very much indeed. Well, on that constructive note we finish your evidence and thank you for all your help, both in writing and in what you have told us this afternoon.

CHRIS JONES: Thank you very much.

1214. LORD NOLAN: Now we welcome Molly Owen, the Chief Executive of Wales Chambers of Commerce and Industry and Helen Conway, the Chief Executive of the Cardiff Chamber of Commerce. We are very grateful to you for your help and for making time to come along and talk to us as well as providing us with the written material which we have all looked at. Was there anything, in addition to what you have written, that you wanted to say by way of opening remarks or would you like to go straight into the questions?

MOLLY OWEN AND HELEN CONWAY

HELEN CONWAY (Chief Executive, Cardiff Chamber of Commerce): I'd like to go straight to the questions.

LORD NOLAN: Very well. Then I will ask Sir William Utting to begin them, please.

1215. WILLIAM UTTING: Could you offer me a couple of pieces of factual information first, please? We were told by the last witnesses that there was a Chamber of Commerce membership of about a thousand in Wales. Is that right or do you have a more specific figure than that?

HELEN CONWAY: We have a membership of over 2,000 in Wales. Cardiff consists of 1,400 members and the balance is made up of a Chamber in Swansea and a Chamber in Newport, having roughly equal members.

1216. WILLIAM UTTING: Right. Could I ask how many members there are in the Cardiff Chamber?

HELEN CONWAY: 1,400.

1217. WILLIAM UTTING: 1,400, good. Thank you very much. And I take it that Chambers of Commerce were involved in the setting up of TECs when these were established. That is correct, is it?

HELEN CONWAY: It is correct. Perhaps I could call on my colleague, Mrs Owen, who was actually instrumental in the evolution of the TEC in South Glamorgan.

MOLLY OWEN (Chief Executive, Wales Chambers of Commerce and Industry): My memory serves me as going back to, I think it was, 1989 when I first became involved. The Secretary of State, Peter Walker, at that time wrote to the Chamber and asked for us to be actively involved in helping to set up the first TEC in South Glamorgan and I certainly attended meetings by invitation and also my colleague at that time—he was very heavily involved—unfortunately he died very suddenly so I took over the role. We were asked in actual fact to assist in putting forward the sort of people who we could see would form the board and giving names and addresses. All the meetings took place in our Council room in the—I was Cardiff Chamber of Commerce, I am actually Wales now—in the Cardiff Chamber of Commerce and I would say that was the inception of the South Glamorgan TEC. It was built on from there. I think at the time it must have been the Manpower Services Commission that we were dealing with—as my memory serves me.

WILLIAM UTTING: That sounds as though it ought to have been the beginning of a very fruitful partnership between the Chambers and TECs.

MOLLY OWEN: Certainly that was the impression that we were given, that Chambers of Commerce in particular would be heavily involved in helping to develop the training programme through the TECs and the Chambers themselves we hoped—the impression we had at the time—would certainly benefit from that. In any case at that time we already did have a training scheme in place and the TEC came on board and then that was further developed with the TEC.

1218. WILLIAM UTTING: And that partnership has developed satisfactorily to the present day?

MOLLY OWEN: To the best of my knowledge. I have to explain that I moved on into the Wales Chamber of Commerce some three years ago and the Cardiff Chamber of Commerce is closer to that now and, in fact, it is Mrs Conway who has been so closely associated with TECs, much more so than I have. I was more affected in those first few formative years than I am today, so this is why—unfortunately our senior officers could not be present today—and so Mrs Conway has been nominated because of her close association to speak on behalf of the Chambers as far as that is concerned. But where I can chime in and assist I certainly will.

WILLIAM UTTING: Yes, thank you. Did you want to add something to that?

HELEN CONWAY: Just to pick up on your point about the fruitful relationship and what currently is the activity between the TEC and the Chamber. The Cardiff Chamber is involved in two very separate areas of TEC activity; one in the training of young people through Youth Training Schemes and in particular dealing with a scheme which the Cardiff Chamber took over from NACRO and has traditionally dealt with young people from deprived backgrounds and who have been in trouble with various authorities. And we are also involved in their Enterprise Training through the delivery of certain programmes to the business community.

1219. WILLIAM UTTING: Yes. And has a satisfactory geographical coverage of Wales been achieved now since 1989—is the whole of Wales covered by TECs?

HELEN CONWAY: Yes, it is. You are obviously aware of the merger between the two TECs in North Wales and then we have a TEC in Powys, the South Glamorgan TEC, Gwent, Mid-Glamorgan West Wales TEC. There is some debate, I believe, about the exact number of TECs which is the optimum for Wales and whether there are some advantages to combining certain geographical areas as they currently exist.

1220. WILLIAM UTTING: Do you think that they have achieved the right sort of balance between developing enterprise and providing training for people? Are you satisfied with the way they are actually conducting their remit?

MOLLY OWEN: Should I just come in on that? I think it tends to differ around Wales. I think they are all operating slightly differently, probably relating to the demands. One would hope and one would think they are relating to the demands in their particular area.

1221. WILLIAM UTTING: You do comment in your written evidence about a lack of focus for spending public money and I was really wanting to approach that really from my earlier question. I mean, it seems to be outside but that if an organisation has got the responsibility of developing enterprise on the one hand and providing training on the other that looks like a fairly simple brief. I mean, how does the loss of focus arise?

HELEN CONWAY: My hesitation really stemmed from the fact that one questions the flexibility that the TECs have in developing programmes for their local community, given the targets that are set for them by central Government. That also obviously impinges on accountability but I am sure we will come to that later on. Yes, the experience is different across Wales. As far as training is concerned—training in either the unemployed context or in a social context rather than an enterprise context—yes, they are responsive to the needs of their community and the different TECs have different social needs. South Glamorgan is a different economic base from that found in Mid Glamorgan, from that found in Powys—you go from industrial to service sector to rural economy—and as such they tailor the programmes to fit.

As far as the enterprise side is concerned I think the TECs have been constrained perhaps by targets imposed on them by Central Government to deliver Central Government programmes—perhaps Investors in People is one to name—and then the flexibility which is available to the TECs to deliver training which is appropriate to company needs as opposed to the need to achieve a certain target set for a number of companies subscribing to IIP, or committed to IIP. So one can say that there is an element of flexibility where surpluses perhaps have been generated and those surpluses are then put into specific local schemes and projects whereas pure enterprise training tends to be geared towards Central Government objectives.

1222. WILLIAM UTTING: So one of the difficulties in the situation is actually outside the TECs' control and appears to stem, as far as you see it, from an over-prescriptive approach on the part of the central department, but not just an over-prescriptive approach, an approach that is designed to delivering, so to speak, national policies rather than meeting the particular needs of different parts of the country?

HELEN CONWAY: Yes. That is not to deny the validity of Central Government programmes such as Investors in People.

WILLIAM UTTING: Especially if it is paying for them.

HELEN CONWAY: Indeed. It's a question of assisting local enterprise development by identifying company needs and perhaps then fitting them into a framework, if that is applicable, but not using IIP or a similar national Government target or framework to——I have to be careful how I phrase this——encourage companies strongly to adopt a particular programme because that, in fact, reflects well on the TEC in its league status with Central Government.

1223. WILLIAM UTTING: Yes. So in a sense you are looking for a little more freedom for TECs to apply resources to the needs that they perceive locally?

HELEN CONWAY: Yes, absolutely.

1224. WILLIAM UTTING: We heard from our earlier witnesses in West Wales TEC that they regarded the enterprise part of the brief as really being to help enterprising people, so that in a sense it seems to me that they tended to regard themselves as an overall training organisation, to help develop enterprising people at one end and then right at the other end to help disadvantaged people acquire employment skills. Would you regard that as a common sort of recipe for issues confronting TECs in Wales or are there other ways of meeting the enterprise requirement than this training approach?

HELEN CONWAY: Without getting into specifics certain TECs around Wales that have generated perhaps a surplus over which they have more control have taken an approach which allows them to look at company infrastructure, or the capital equipment, the capital needs, of small companies, developing companies. They are committed to training—obviously that is one of their central functions—but they are committed in other ways to encourage companies in the development of their own resources other than human. To take one example, there is a programme which one of the Wales TECs is just putting into place, which encourages companies who are renewing their computer infrastructure, their IT infrastructure, to donate equipment which is then given to small companies who have a need who perhaps don't have the capital to invest but they will then receive both the hardware and the training to enable them to use their time and their resources more effectively. So there are creative ways of applying enterprise to both TEC activity, as being a business and being enterprising in themselves, and also in looking at enterprise in addition to training. So it does exist.

In terms of focus—to go back to your question—the focus on developing enterprise, developing companies, developing individuals needs to be adequately provided for, but in taking individuals I think you do develop the companies on the back of those individuals, in that you once again have to come back to the different economy or economic bases which the various TECs in Wales actually have to operate within.

1225. WILLIAM UTTING: That is very helpful. Could I ask you about one of your other comments—your belief that the eligibility criteria are too restricted for TEC directors? Why is this and in what ways could they or should they be relaxed?

HELEN CONWAY: There are some concerns that TEC boards consist of Chief Executives and Managing Directors of either public or private companies that are larger perhaps than the economic base that the area would suggest it ought to be. If you were taking a cross-section of the business community and saying the TEC, to be responsive to local business needs ought to be representative therefore of the area in which they operate, it would be helpful to relax the criteria in the sense that you encourage small businesses who may well not have a Chief Executive or Managing Director in the context which is applied by the TEC but had something to bring to the development of the TEC, its programmes overall.

1226. WILLIAM UTTING: Again that is very helpful because people have said to us that if you relax the criteria and get second and third level people in there is an almost automatic loss of clout and status locally because of that, but you are saying that you will actually gain because you are getting people who really understand the local situation and can actually react to it more appropriately?

HELEN CONWAY: Yes.

1227. WILLIAM UTTING: One of the other things that has been said to us about mergers with Chambers of Commerce is that as well as reinforcing the business base to these organisations it actually turns them virtually into business monopolies and reduces still further the prospects of building in acknowledgment of other interests in the community. What have you got to say to that sort of comment? I mean, do you think that it is valid to try to build other interests in the community into the management of TECs?

HELEN CONWAY: In the context of mergers between Chambers and TECs?

WILLIAM UTTING: Yes. Or generally.

HELEN CONWAY: We currently don't have a merger between a Welsh Chamber of Commerce and a Welsh TEC. The concept has been explored but we acknowledge the difficulties that exist in terms of perhaps compromising the accountability or restricting the representative base. You have to acknowledge the breadth of interest. The TEC fulfils a certain function with regard to the development of the local economy; the Chamber can be a provider to the TEC in terms of training but fulfils a separate and independent function. Our main concern in regard to mergers between Chambers of Commerce and TECs lies in the control which Central Government necessarily has over a TEC because it is its prime funder and identifies training programmes for it to deliver and how that might compromise the independent business voice which can be represented on a TEC board in trying to influence its policies and strategies. But once the organisations become merged you have to enshrine an element of independent accountability to the local business community within that set-up. I am not sure that I have completely answered your question but——

1228. WILLIAM UTTING: Well, I think the only other piece is whether you see in any case the argument for some sort of wider representation of community interests on the boards of TECs. I mean, people have said to us that there ought to be representatives of the local community or trade union representatives. Do you think that TECs are actually taking those interests on board anyway from the way they are constituting themselves?

HELEN CONWAY: Across Wales there are various mechanisms which TECs use to be accountable to the local community. They may have fora, such as West Wales TEC do, they may have Sector Advisory Groups which meet on a regular basis and in terms of influencing policy and to take a representative view back to the board there are other mechanisms which can take the community view into account. The TEC is a business and the board has to run the business but in terms of directing its policy the board should be as representative of the local community as possible and where it isn't possible to —- We have experienced it in the Chamber movement, where you are as representative as possible and end up with a board of 45 which does not make for the best business practice in the world and the TEC can use other mechanisms to feed local community needs into that. Whether it is a board issue is another matter. But, yes, they should be accountable to and find mechanisms, therefore, to glean local community needs and wants within their system.

WILLIAM UTTING: Good, I am most grateful. Thank you.

LORD NOLAN: Sir Clifford?

1229. CLIFFORD BOULTON: Can I go back to the eligibility point for a moment? There is this restriction about the members being very senior people indeed. I just wondered—has it been a particular problem in Wales where someone who might be extremely senior here and very familiar with the Wales scene happens to belong to such a large organisation whose headquarters are elsewhere, probably in London or somewhere, that the person has failed to meet the technical criteria, while nevertheless being a very senior person in Wales? Has that arisen at all in your awareness, or not particularly?

HELEN CONWAY: I am not aware of any specific instance where that has been the case.

1230. CLIFFORD BOULTON: You said you supported the paper which we got from the Association of British Chambers of Commerce in general terms and particularly the point about "We believe the eligibility criteria too restricted". In their paper they then said "However, this is not the view held among the Chambers of Commerce Training and Enterprise who hold that the present rule governing eligible persons works well and does not need change". Now, you did not write that—they wrote that. Do you happen to know what the issue there is, why they felt like that?

HELEN CONWAY: It comes back to Sir William's point about clout, one would imagine. The role of a Chamber of Commerce Training and Enterprise varies from that of Chambers of Commerce as an individual group and TECs as an individual group and in terms of the economic development remit and the level to which one can approach local Government, Central Government, perhaps that is the context. But other than that, no, I am afraid not having any direct experience of a Chamber of Commerce/TEC merger I couldn't comment.

1231. CLIFFORD BOULTON: Fair enough. I just thought it might have been something you might have followed up with them, having seen it. Can I just turn to a point that was made in their paper under "Officers and Staff", where they said in paragraph 13: "As in any company and under Company Law there is a requirement placed upon the Company Secretary to challenge decisions he believes to be ultra vires against the true interest of the company and the shareholders. We accept that this could put his job at risk but if there were a corporate director appointed by and responsible to the Chamber of Commerce, the Company Secretary or other staff member could have an impartial director to approach." Is that anything you have given any thought to, the question of almost a compliance officer or someone who had a role slightly outside the immediate working of the board to guard propriety and its general good name?

HELEN CONWAY: Not to a compliance officer, although my understanding in setting up a South Glamorgan TEC was that the Chamber did have a director on the board to fulfil that type of function, to be the voice that was accountable to the local business community. But perhaps Mrs Owen could expand on that.

MOLLY OWEN: I think that was at the very outset. On closer investigation most recently there isn't a Chamber of Commerce representative on the board, of certainly South Glamorgan TEC—I really couldn't speak for the other TECs in Wales. But at the moment we haven't got any input there. After that initial year or so, in the first year, I can recall once or twice that we were trying once more to get somebody on that board but for some reason that didn't materialise. I really don't know the answer to that—of why that was.

1232. CLIFFORD BOULTON: I was more thinking about giving perhaps more recognised weight in the job description of the Company Secretary who might have a reason——Company Secretaries can sometimes feel very much under the authority of the Chairman or the Chief Executive or both but there is scope perhaps—and we touched on it in our *Issues and Questions* paper for perhaps giving a recognised role for such a person in these circumstances.

HELEN CONWAY: Just to make a general point about the directorships; given the size of the business communities within which we operate—and it was one of the points made about Chamber/TEC mergers and boards and the rationale behind not expecting business people to commit their time to various organisations and that to obtain this focus you have one board of local business people who can actually achieve more by sitting on one board than sitting on several. The Chambers of Commerce across Wales have actually at various times had most of the TEC board directors as members of either their Council or certainly as members of the Chambers of Commerce, so one would imagine that compliance and challenging decisions is done at board level within TECs by more than the Company Secretary in terms of questioning the validity of certain programmes within the local economic base. So I would imagine that it's actually covered and a compliance officer as such may be over-statement of a case which is currently being fulfilled.

1233. CLIFFORD BOULTON: I asked the last witnesses a very general question about the degree of satisfaction there is about their work. Have you got any specific points that you want to leave with us that you yourself feel call for change in the way that the TECs are operating in Wales or are you broadly satisfied but within the context of the particular points that you have made?

HELEN CONWAY: There is one final point which I would like to make, particularly on behalf of training members of the Chamber of Commerce, and that is that they have found that procedures for becoming recognised providers to TECs are restrictive. There are myriad schemes by which one can become quality assured by TECs; there is not one common scheme throughout the UK and there are perhaps up to five or six different fees to be paid by trainers to be quality assured by one body or the other or, indeed, directly by the TECs. And, again, we have evidence from training members of the Chamber that in certain areas training needs are identified by a trainer and a company. A proposal is then put to a TEC and that training is either subsequently not carried out or, because the individual trainer might be assured by one TEC but not particularly by the TEC in that area, that they are then excluded for delivering that training and that the contract is passed to another training provider. So in terms of the accountability of the TECs to their deliverers there are certain issues which we would like to see addressed in terms of a common quality assurance programme for training providers to the TECs.

CLIFFORD BOULTON: Thank you very much.

1234. LORD NOLAN: There is just one point of fact that I would like to clear up with you if you can help me and which I really should have clarified with our last witnesses, and it is about the question of membership of TECs. You say in paragraph C of your letter of 1st November last: "TECs in Wales have to a varying degree sought to involve the local business community through membership schemes etc. In each instance the membership is either free of charge or has a nominal charge attached to it and confers no rights in terms of Company Law membership to its members". So what rights does it confer? What is meant by being a member who is not a member for Company Law purposes? Is it just a kind of club of supporters?

HELEN CONWAY: Yes, indeed.

LORD NOLAN: As simple as that, yes.

ANNE WARBURTON: They can nominate board members.

1235. LORD NOLAN: They are not members of the company? Dame Anne says——I would have thought, with respect, that you would need to be a member of the company——

ANNE WARBURTON: Representatives said that they could nominate.

HELEN CONWAY: It may well be that in certain instances but generally, no, they do not nominate.

1236. LORD NOLAN: It would surprise me. Well, I am grateful to you because it has clarified that point for our own minds, but the general point you were making was that this leaves accountability with the TEC board itself, not with the "members" who are just a club?

HELEN CONWAY: Yes.

LORD NOLAN: Or a sort of club.

HELEN CONWAY: Indeed.

LORD NOLAN: A very interested club. Well, thank you both very much indeed, you have been very helpful.

HELEN CONWAY: Thank you.

1237. LORD NOLAN: Good afternoon, Mr Stone, and welcome to our meeting. It is very good of you to come along and give us your time. I am sure that at this time of day your minutes are as precious to you as any others and like all your witnesses you are a volunteer and all the more to be thanked on our behalf for coming. We have got a number of questions that we would like to put to you. Was there anything you wished to say by way of introductory remarks or are you happy to go straight into questioning?

JOHN STONE

JOHN STONE (Headmaster, Bishop Vaughan Catholic Comprehensive School, Morriston, Swansea): Happy to go straight to questions, thank you.

LORD NOLAN: Very well, I'll ask Professor King to start, please.

1238. PROF ANTHONY KING: Could I start with a few straightforward nuts and bolts questions? The foundation governors in a school like yours are in the majority on the school governing body. How are they appointed?

JOHN STONE: They are appointed by the Trustees, Church Authorities.

1239. PROF ANTHONY KING: What does that mean in practice?

JOHN STONE: In practice it means the Bishop and three or four others and one would guess that the Bishop has a fair amount of influence in such matters.

1240. PROF ANTHONY KING: You say "one would guess". Does the school itself—do you have any direct input into the choice of these governors?

JOHN STONE: None whatsoever.

PROF ANTHONY KING: None at all?

JOHN STONE: None at all.

1241. PROF ANTHONY KING: So that the people who show up to form your governing body might be people with whom you had had no previous association, of whom you knew nothing?

JOHN STONE: Yes, and sometimes that is the case. Not in most cases, however.

1242. PROF ANTHONY KING: Now, on the face of it there could be a question in your mind or in the mind of your teachers or parents as to whether those school governors were there to do their level best by your school or whether they were there, as it were, as the instruments of the Bishop and the other people who had appointed them. Do issues or questions of that kind ever arise?

JOHN STONE: I am sure they do and there might be that confusion in the minds of some of the parents who might not know the workings of individual governors, but I do know that each of these governors as an individual is well aware that he or she represents his or her own views and their prime duty is to serve the school, although they are foundation governors. So they will always be balancing the needs of the future and the trustees' correct interest in the school at the moment and in the long term—they will balance that with the needs of this school of which they are governors.

1243. PROF ANTHONY KING: But do I take you to be saying you have no complaints either about the way in which foundation governors are appointed or by the behaviour of foundation governors you have known in terms of their willingness to serve the school?

JOHN STONE: None at all. I have found them to be very co-operative and they mesh in well with the rest of the group—the elected members.

1244. PROF ANTHONY KING: Has the relationship changed at all since you went grant-maintained?

JOHN STONE: The relationship hasn't changed very much but what I have noticed is that there is a greater commitment. This can be seen in many ways but the plainest evidence for that will be their attendance at meetings. Now there is almost 100 per cent attendance at all meetings and there are about three times as many meetings now as there used to be.

1245. PROF ANTHONY KING: One of the ways in which a school like yours differs from a former LEA school is that there are fewer prescriptive rules saying what kinds of people the governors should be. There is no requirement that they should represent the local business community or whatever. Do you think there should be a clearer indication in the rules as to the kinds of people that should be, or perhaps shouldn't be, school governors?

JOHN STONE: I think in practice there usually is a cross-section of interests. However, this could be by chance but I am sure that the trustees are looking at a balance. They would like to see people with experience of finance etc. represented on the board of governors. However, I think the prime pre-requisite in a governor is commitment to the school and a willingness to serve and I think that would come above and beyond any individual expertise which they could bring. After all if the governors wished to have expert financial advice they can buy it in.

1246. PROF ANTHONY KING: Since you opted out how has the character of your relationship with the local authority changed, or rather since it has changed in some pretty obvious ways I will rephrase that—what is now the character of your relations with your local authority?

JOHN STONE: We buy in many services, particularly in-service training, from the local authority. In our early days as an opted out school we bought in other services but we tend to buy more in the private sector now. That is not a conscious decision but it is a matter of looking for the best value. Our relationship with West Glamorgan authority is not harmonious but it certainly is not acrimonious.

1247. PROF ANTHONY KING: That is the most tantalising thing anybody has said in this room for quite some time! Perhaps you can spell that out in a little more detail.

JOHN STONE: Well, all my staff meet the staff in other schools regularly at in-service training sessions. As a matter of fact more of my staff attend these sessions than staff in other schools. Often we send two members of staff whereas other schools send one or none. So that we are well represented locally in that way and, more importantly, our staff do have professional contact with staff in other schools.

PROF ANTHONY KING: That is the harmonious bit, I take it.

JOHN STONE: There isn't too much which is non-harmonious, discordant. The area in which there is discord is in the area of finance and in agreeing what the figure *in lieu* of central services is. So sometimes there is some conflict over what the correct figure is. But it is a professional one and, you know, there is no personal animosity about it. It's a professional argument, usually conducted firstly by telephone and then by letter.

1248. PROF ANTHONY KING: Could I ask you a few questions about your relationship, in so far as it exists, with the Welsh Office? Obviously as you know in England there is a completely different kind of set-up with the Funding Agency for Schools on the one hand and the Department for Education and Employment on the other. From where you sit does the fact that the Welsh Office is both the regulator and the funder pose any problems or, alternatively, do you think that is the way it ought to be?

JOHN STONE: I haven't a view on the second—I probably would have to think about it. But I have experienced no problems with the former relationship and I don't think any of my colleague heads has.

1249. PROF ANTHONY KING: What happens if problems arise? One of the things which is clear about any school and grant-maintained schools not least, is that there can be all kinds of tensions and difficulties that come to the surface, clashes between the Chairman of the Board of Governors and the Head, whatever. In England the situation is on the face of it a slightly strange one in that if problems of that kind arise, if they become at all serious—and probably in practice at rather a late stage—they go all the way to London to the Secretary of State. Now presumably in Wales they go all the way—although in this case it is not very far—to the Secretary of State for Wales. I mean, on the face of it that seems rather odd. Do you think it is sensible to have the Secretary of State playing this kind of visitor role?

JOHN STONE: I suppose it does seem rather odd. I am at an advantage in one sense and at a disadvantage in answering your question in that I have never experienced any serious conflict with my Board of Governors. So I am probably not the best person to answer your question. If I could imagine myself in that position I feel that my main recourse professionally would be to my professional association, the Association of Head Teachers, who would come and represent me and advise me in the first instance. But where there is conflict I would have thought that one seek to solve it by reasoned argument and then one would look outside to the Welsh Office for a ruling as to where the decision should lie.

1250. PROF ANTHONY KING: But one suggestion that has been put to us and one with which I have a good deal of sympathy, is that especially in a part of the country where there are a lot of grant-maintained schools it might be a good idea for each grant-maintained school to appoint some local person, possibly *ex officio* to be the person who would try to sort these things out without their having to go all the way to a Cabinet Minister and senior civil servants. Does that idea commend itself to you at all?

JOHN STONE: Yes, on the face of it it would appear to be a very sensible and sound suggestion. I wonder where, you know, we can get a person of the right calibre but if such a person could be found it could only be helpful. I couldn't see how it could have the opposite effect. In the case of an ex-voluntary-aided school and a grant-maintained school which is still a church school, like ours, we do, of course, have the diocese and there would be a diocesan director. We also have the Catholic Education Service in London to whom we could appeal as a sort of an independent arbiter. So we are fortunate in that sense. But I think the suggestion has a lot of merit; I just wonder whether there are enough people of the right calibre and the right experience to assist.

1251. PROF ANTHONY KING: You said a moment ago that if you got into trouble with, in some sense of the term, your board of governors you would have recourse to your Head Teachers Association, or might have. There seems on the face of it to be something rather strange about the required structure of the staff appeal committees, such that one lot of governors decide that, for example, a Head should be disciplined in some way, or another teacher in the school. If the teacher or Head does not like the outcome he or she then appeals to another lot of governors. Does that strike you satisfactory? You can infer from my tone of voice that it seems rather strange to me.

JOHN STONE: Yes, but that is only stage number 2. If the teacher or head teacher was not satisfied or felt that there was an injustice in the second group, that is the appeal. Then there is an appeal to an independent committee, is there not?

PROF ANTHONY KING: To an industrial tribunal in practice.

JOHN STONE: Well, I think firstly—perhaps I am mistaken here—but——

PROF ANTHONY KING: It is a measure of your situation that you are not sure what the answers to these questions are.

JOHN STONE: I am only not sure because you are questioning me and putting doubt into my mind. I think that the next stage is that there would be an independent panel which would have a lay person, an independent chairman and one governor who had not been involved with the case. But I stand to be corrected.

1252. PROF ANTHONY KING: We can go back to the book of words and find out about that. There is a general requirement of grant-maintained schools allowing for the specific church-related element in your situation that they should be accountable to, sensitive to, various other phrases of that kind, the local community—to, I think we are now supposed to call them, the "stakeholders" in the school. How does your school set about doing that?

JOHN STONE: Well, we are accountable, obviously, to the local community. The local community can be identified chiefly but not solely as the children—they are the chief stakeholders if we call them that—we can hardly be accountable to the children except through others for the most part anyway, but their parents—we would consider that the parents are the people to whom we should be chiefly accountable. We are also accountable to, in our case, trustees; we are accountable to the Welsh Office; we are answerable to all sorts of people who have all sorts of expectations. In day to day terms how do we discharge this accountability to parents, for instance? The law requires that governors present an annual report to parents. In our case it is a document about half an inch thick—of course distance narrows the size—but it will be about forty or fifty pages which more or less describes everything that the school has been engaged in over the whole year. So parents are able to peruse this and ask any pertinent questions. So we go beyond the minimum requirements of the law in that. Then we are required by law, aren't we, to have an annual parents' meeting when parents, although there has to be a certain number of parents in order to pass a motion. Our governors always freely take any questions and will try to answer any questions which are put to them. So that is a sort of statutory discharge in that way.

Further than that, we have a very strong parent-teacher association in our school. The school itself communicates very regularly with parents; on the last Thursday of every school month there is a newsletter which is sent to parents so they are kept fully informed and I think that is half the battle. If the staff keep the governors informed, if governors and staff keep the parents informed, then I think people are generally happy and they can ask appropriate questions.

So that is one way. The school also for the last six months has been surveying parents on a host of questions, for instance homework policy, anti-bullying policy, school meals, and so that is a new direction that we have taken. We at random choose fifty parents and fifty children and we give them questionnaires and then we analyse the results and then feed back to parents. And that way the school is informed as to what parents want and where there is a discrepancy between what we are providing and what parents would like to see provided then that forms a basis for discussion in the school and then later at a governing body level

1253. PROF ANTHONY KING: Just out of curiosity, how many pupils are there at your school?

JOHN STONE: 975.

1254. PROF ANTHONY KING: And how many parents show up to the annual meeting?

JOHN STONE: About thirty, which is above the going rate, I know.

1255. PROF ANTHONY KING: And suggests a pretty satisfied clientele, you think?

JOHN STONE: Yes. I think those who turn up turn up out of support and duty rather than because they have any serious questions to ask. You see, at our parent/teacher association meetings, parents will just come along to those because although there is a committee there is open membership—all parents are encouraged to attend—so whenever they have something to ask they come along and ask the question under "any other business". We are very open about it; we allow them just to bring up their concerns.

1256. PROF ANTHONY KING: Finally another question that you may find it hard to answer because you probably will not have thought about it for reasons that you have given already: it has been put to us that the division of labour between the head of the school and the school governors should be much more clearly spelt out, that in cases where there has been trouble between heads and school governors part of the trouble has arisen out of the fact that the lines of demarcation are not clear enough. The view has also, however, been put to us that there is no way in which you can clearly define the division of labour in this kind of situation, that so much depends on personality. Do you have any views about which of these views is more nearly correct?

JOHN STONE: I think if there are these conflicts and these disagreements between head teachers and their governors or staff and their governors then something has to be done about it because it cannot be good for the school for such conflicts to remain. I have not experienced them myself. However, my own view is that in that case then clearer guidelines or a code of conduct has to be helpful. However, if this is spelt out in too much detail it might encourage governors and head teachers to say "this is my territory and that is yours", whereas I feel that staff and governors ought to be working together.

I think I have a reasonably clear idea of where I stand in the day to day running of the school, that sort of thing, where governors stand, policy etc. and certainly the Chair and Vice-Chair of governors are well aware of this and on the rare occasions where, after an open discussion, there might be one or two governors who are continuing with their point of view (because there is often quite vigorous debate at our governing body meetings), the Chair will come in and will in a gentle way guide people back and say "I think here we ought to leave this with the head teacher as he is in charge of this and we hold him accountable and we will review it in future"—and in my opinion that is a very wise way of dealing with potential conflict.

So in a sense one has the strength of knowing where one stands without insisting upon saying "this is my right". So if governors want to discuss the day to day running of the school I see they have every right to do so and it is in my interests to explain in great detail everything.

1257. PROF ANTHONY KING: But you did say a moment ago that it could not be a bad thing if the demarcation were more clearly spelt out. Suppose I were to give you a week and ask you to go away and draft a set of demarcation rules, do you think you could pretty comfortably do that? I am not about to.

JOHN STONE: Well, I could do them but they would probably be very deficient. But I believe that there are some groups, certainly in the grant-maintained sector, there are groups already working on a code of conduct and I believe that David Hart from the NAHT is also involved in this. I am confident that there'll be at least a discussion document that would lead to a finally agreed code of conduct.

PROF ANTHONY KING: Yes, fine, thank you.

1258. LORD NOLAN: I have just a few questions to add: one again as part of the background. How many are on your governing body?

JOHN STONE: 15.

1259. LORD NOLAN: You have told us—and it is very impressive to hear it—how conscientious they are and how lively the meetings are. Do you have difficulty in replacing them when that is necessary?

JOHN STONE: We haven't, no. We have a vacancy now for a foundation governor and we are waiting for that to be filled. Our Bishop at the moment is seriously ill—he has leukaemia—and so there is a slight delay. That would be the Bishop's responsibility anyway. We have just replaced three parent governors and on this occasion we only had three nominations for the three places. That was disappointing really. We were careful to point out how many meetings they would be expected to attend and what their duties were; and I think this might have frightened people off because they might have seen the bad side of it and, of course, they wouldn't know in advance, you know, how invigorating and how satisfying it could be to be involved in a school in that way. So, perhaps, next time the governors thought they might give less information in advance and let people find out for themselves.

1260. LORD NOLAN: But talking about the terms on which governors serve—of course they get no remuneration, but what about expenses? Have you got a scheme for paying expenses?

JOHN STONE: Yes, there is a Welsh Office approved scheme for the paying of expenses but this is my twentieth year of headship and I have never known any governor ever claim a single penny in expenses. So that is how "amateur" they are, if you know what I mean. Amateur perhaps in a bad sense, if they have got families!

1261. LORD NOLAN: And on the other side of the scale there is the question which has been raised with us from many different quarters and different organisations and that is the possible legal liability of governors. Is that something that worries your governors?

JOHN STONE: Sorry, the possible?

LORD NOLAN: Legal liability of governors for negligence, for example, if there were some catastrophe in the school.

JOHN STONE: Yes. Well, we have insurance which does indemnify them. But it is a source of concern and quite often individual governors say "Are we responsible for health and safety?" You know, "we are responsible for this, we are responsible for that" and the advice they are given by the Chairman—and I tend to support it and I hope I am right in this—is to say that no governor is responsible as an individual but it is a corporate responsibility. That usually assuages it somewhat. But, yes, they are concerned and worried about it. Quite honestly I would like to see the State indemnify them and insure them against such claims. After all, they are working unpaid, they are giving up an awful lot of time and they ought not have that worry upon them.

LORD NOLAN: And going back to your number 50—it seems to me to be a very large number. I have never been on a governing body with——

JOHN STONE: Sorry, fifteen.

LORD NOLAN: Oh, fifteen, yes. That explains it. And how many of those are parents?

JOHN STONE: There are four elected parents and two of the foundation governors have to be parents but in effect we have seven parents at the moment and three former parents—that is three governors whose children have recently left school. So the parent representation on the governing body is a high one, a significant one.

1262. LORD NOLAN: I think my final question is this: is there anything that you would like to put to us from your experience of the way in which the grant-maintained scheme is operating in your case that would improve matters?

JOHN STONE: In Wales, in common with all my colleagues, we would like to see a national funding formula so that we did not have to waste so much time negotiating, you know, for the correct central services figure—the figure for central services formerly provided by the authority. So the Welsh Office is aware of this and they are taking it into consideration. They are taking it very seriously, we know. We are not talking of a common funding formula but something which is a common formula across the whole of Wales and it might be more possible because there are only sixteen of us. So, all of us are committed to that.

1263. LORD NOLAN: Would that ease your relationships with the local authorities?

JOHN STONE: It probably would because there would be no area of conflict—I hope! Well, I would not guarantee that but——

1264. LORD NOLAN: No, no. But that and the point you mentioned about legal liability you would like to see looked after by the State for the benefit of these voluntary workers?

JOHN STONE: Yes, indeed.

LORD NOLAN: Thank you very much indeed. Was there anything else anybody wanted to ask Mr Stone? No?

Well, that has been a helpful and encouraging piece of evidence and we are very grateful to you for coming along and giving it to us. Thank you.

JOHN STONE: I think one thing I would want to leave you with is the fact that I am in my twentieth year of headship and I have been head of a grant-maintained school for the last four and I am so thankful that I had this experience because it has been so invigorating. I was beginning to become quite depressed, you know, with my lot when I got to my fifteenth and sixteenth year and it has just made me—I won't say a young man—but young in activity for a 58 year old.

ANNE WARBURTON: Why?

1265. LORD NOLAN: Dame Anne is asking why.

JOHN STONE: Well, the reason is that the whole of the community, but especially the parents, teachers and governors—and head teacher, of course—we feel now that we are responsible for this school; it is "our" school (it is on loan to us, I know) but this is our school, we are totally responsible for it, but we now have the power to act in its interests, we don't have to deal through a third party. So we are able to deliver at the point of need—that is the phrase which is usually used—but it really is so in action. All the staff feel the same; it is just a release of energy, and our school has never been involved in so many educational initiatives as we now are because there is just a whole new way of thinking. We are always looking to raise standards and looking for new ideas which will take the school forward. And there is really a tremendous difference between the school now and what it was previously.

LORD NOLAN: Thank you very much.

JOHN STONE: Thank you.

LORD NOLAN: Well, that concludes our first day's hearing. Thank you all very much.

WEDNESDAY 24 JANUARY 1996

AFTERNOON SESSION

OPENING STATEMENT

Opening statement from West Wales TEC

The Board of West Wales TEC has considered the Consultative Document which constitutes the Committee's second report, on this occasion looking at local public spending bodies in the light of the work of the first report.

This response is evidently submitted from the perspective of this organisation only and is based upon the practice and procedures adopted by West Wales TEC Ltd. It cannot be taken as necessarily indicative of the general procedures followed by all TECs in England and Wales, but we believe that our procedures, codes, method of audit and scrutiny, and role definition, provide good examples of that which satisfies the many valid considerations outlined in the Consultative Document.

We feel it necessary firstly to note that in accepting the report's conclusion that the seven principles of public life should apply without modification to TECs, to emphasise that TECs are, of course, not public bodies but private limited companies and much of their success in the past, and that upon which we rely for continued success in the future, is fundamentally dependent on the maintenance and development of the private sector nature of TECs. We believe this because its main strength is derived from the voluntary commitment of key private sector businessmen and women, drawn from a wide representation of sectors including manufacturing, engineering, tourism, agriculture, leisure, services, big and small business without whose personal commitment the TEC would be an entirely different entity.

Having said this, the standards sought are enforced by the Board in terms of the openness of recruitment, the establishment of appropriate codes of conduct, the necessity for a framework for ensuring propriety and accountability, and investing in an individual officer a responsibility for such.

The Board have considered the Consultative Document by reference to the three threads identified of:

1. The existence of Codes of Conduct.

2. The independence of scrutiny.

3. The provision of appropriate guidance and training to Directors.

In the context of this consideration we have concentrated upon the three areas detailed, namely:

  (i) the appointment and accountability of Board Members;

  (ii) the role of Board/staff;

  (iii) conflicts of interest.

Taking each in turn:

Appointment and Accountability

A key question in the Consultative Document focuses on whether the expectations outlined might be too great for voluntary Boards, and a related question asks if more could be demanded of a paid member than an unpaid one. We do not necessarily believe that the latter sentiment holds true, and in many cases voluntary commitment will enable the provision of greater input than if payment were made. However, we are able to relate to the former sentiment, in that we believe that the definition of job descriptions for Directors, for example, would place a disincentive on the interest and willingness of those currently serving and who might potentially serve, and we believe this would be a serious problem for most TECs. We appreciate of course that the interpretation of the term "job description" could rest along a spectrum from that which is very general to that which is very specific. The nearer to the latter, the greater would be the problem from the TEC perspective. In any event it is imperative that TECs remain flexible in their requirements of senior executive who sit on Boards. Demands on their time are large and increasing, often involving extensive duties occasioned by Government imperatives of short notice. Too rigid a statement of role would hinder this vital necessity.

The appointment of Board members within this TEC has to all intents and purposes been conducted on an informal basis, albeit that due consideration is openly given to ensure that as many interests in business sectors and geographical areas are represented. The appointment is, of course, subject to the scrutiny of the full Board, but it has to be emphasised is in due course subject to the approval by the full membership of the TEC at the next Annual General Meeting of the Company. This has to be held annually in line with the Articles and Memorandum of Association. The TEC has, however, recently established a more formal process and have in accordance with this principle established a nominations committee and adopted the principle of openly advertising for the vacant Board seats where such seats are not directly targeted at specific or key sectors. Even here, however, we have in certain key sectors (Further Education, for example) sought a nomination from that particular sector rather than approaching an individual specifically. In the same context following Unitary Authority reorganisation, we will be approaching the Unitary Authorities as a group to nominate two of their Chief Executives to take a seat on the Board, as opposed to approaching individuals directly. To this extent we would argue that we have (and it is therefore possible to) achieve a working balance that provides representation by nomination but without the need for prescription. Prescription would, in fact, be counter-productive.

It should also be noted, as part of the regulations governing us under Company Law, that we are required to ensure that a proportion of the Board must resign at each AGM and formally stand for re-election by the Membership and that membership of the TEC is open to all and is publicised as such.

Role of Board/Staff

The Board of West Wales TEC has a very clearly defined strategic role and an open delineation of responsibility between the Board and the staff, the latter being charged with the implementation of policy. We would keenly maintain that the Board do not assume too much operational control, and that the Chief Executive of the Company is demonstrably able to exert influence on Board decisions. This is most evidenced by the fact that, although the Operating Agreement under which all TECs work does not prescribe that the Chief Executive should be a Director of the Board, it is nevertheless open to Boards themselves to determine that he or she should be offered such a position. In the case of West Wales TEC the Chief Executive does sit as an equal voting member of the full Board.

We have defined the documented formal Codes of Conduct, remits of various Groups and Sub-Committees which include the very important and vital Sub-Committee functions of Staffing and Remuneration and Audit and Finance. We have reviewed and updated the remit and responsibilities of the respective sub-groups since their inception last year. Details of our Standing Financing Instructions, Standing Orders, Sub-Group remits etc. have been provided to the Nolan Committee in the form of the TEC's "Director"s Handbook" which contains all such documented procedures and protocols.

As regards openness of meetings, we would emphasise that Directors of TECs have, of course, to answer for their actions to the Welsh Office with whom we are in contact, and to the Membership of the Company via the AGM. We also operate a published and robust Complaints Procedure which has recently been extended to incorporate the right to third party arbitration on Board decisions. We publicise and organise an Annual Public Meeting (separate from the AGM). Moreover we operate an extensive and positive programme of communications to our staff, clients, partners and the 25,000 businesses in West Wales.

As regards independence of scrutiny, TECs are heavily audited. Indeed, the following listing of such audit intervention may serve to highlight the validity of this point:

1. Internal Audit—conducted by an external firm of auditors.

2. External Audit—conducted by different external auditors.

3. Welsh Office Audit.

4. Welsh Office Audit of our Internal Audit.

5. European funding programmes audit.

6. Audit by the National Audit Office.

7. Welsh Office FAM Team Audit.

8. Formal TEC Audit of Providers' Contracts.

Conflicts of Interest

As the Consultative Document acknowledges TECs are required, under the terms of their Operating Agreement, to maintain a register of Directors' Interests, which we do. The register also includes any recorded Expressions of Interest. The register is, moreover, openly and freely available for inspection (by visit to the office) by whosoever would care to avail themselves of this opportunity.

Summary

In summary, the Board of Directors of West Wales TEC Limited welcome the opportunity to comment on the issues and questions raised in the Nolan Committee's recent publication, and fully endorse the principles identified. We hope to have demonstrated that a significant number of the standards and procedures exhorted by the Consultative Document are, in fact, already in place within this organisation. The robustness of our activities, policies and procedures is, we believe, such as to warrant the maintenance of current methods and styles of operation of TECs (including most importantly the avoidance of job description definitions for Directors, a mandatory recognition of interest groups with powers of nomination, and the specification of open monthly, or bi-monthly public meetings). Our argument is in essence for the status quo, albeit that this argument is not based on a belief that everything is currently embedded perfectly and, indeed, we will continue to review our Codes of Conduct and the formalisation of the methods by which we implement our appointment procedures, but such formalisation would occur within the context of the concepts outlined above. An example of progress in this regard is our recent adoption of the nationally promoted Local Accountability Framework.

THURSDAY 25 JANUARY 1996

Members Present:

The Rt Hon Lord Nolan (Chairman)

Sir Clifford Boulton GCB   Dame Anne Warburton DCVO CMG
Professor Anthony King

Witnesses:
Professor John Williams, Principal, Gwyn Bartley, Board Member, Dr Lynn Griffiths, Clerk to the Board of Governors, and Alwyn Roberts, Board Member, North East Wales Institute of Higher Education
Dr Colin Williams, Principal, and Gillian Burns, Assistant Principal for Human Resources, Coleg Glan Hafren
Michael Cohen, Secretary, and Dr Gill Evans, Council for Academic Freedom and Academic Standards
Sir John Allen, Chairman, and Adam Peat, Chief Executive, Housing for Wales

1266. LORD NOLAN: I am told it is one minute to ten but there is no harm that I can see in starting a minute early, if this breach of regularity will be accepted, as we have our first witnesses here. May I say welcome to everyone here to our second and, I am sorry to say, last day of taking oral evidence in Cardiff. Today we have witnesses who will talk about higher education, further education and housing associations. Our first witnesses will be from the North-East Wales Institute of Higher Education and they are led by Professor John Williams, the Principal, together with Mr Gwyn Bartley who is an independent governor from the private sector, Dr Lynn Griffiths who is the Clerk to the Board of Governors and Mr Alwyn Roberts, Pro-Vice Chancellor of the University of Wales, Bangor, and another independent governor. All four, whom I will ask Professor Williams in a moment to introduce individually, have distinguished records of public service both in the academic and in other fields of public life.

We then move on to further education and we will welcome Dr Colin Williams, the Principal of Coleg Glan Hafren, which is a further education college here in Cardiff. He will be accompanied by Gillian Burns, the Assistant Principal for Human Resources, and they will be followed by Michael Cohen, the Secretary of the Council for Academic Freedom and Academic Standards, who will have with him Dr Gill Evans and Professor John Griffiths.

Last, but not least of course, we shall hear from Sir John Allen, the Chairman, and Adam Peat, the Chief Executive of Housing for Wales, Tai Cymru, who will close our session by discussing with us the governance of housing associations in Wales.

Now, Professor Williams, we meet happily again. Would you be kind enough, please, to introduce your team.

PROFESSOR JOHN WILLIAMS, GWYN BARTLEY, DR LYNN GRIFFITHS, AND ALWYN ROBERTS

PROFESSOR JOHN WILLIAMS (Principal, North East Wales Institute of Higher Education): Thank you very much, Lord Nolan. I could give the evidence in Welsh, of course, but we did not think that we would lumber you with translation services at this early time in the morning.

It is a pleasure to introduce on my left Mr Alwyn Roberts, as you rightly pointed out, an independent governor, Pro-Chancellor of the University of Wales in Bangor. Mr Roberts' particular interest is in the interests of members, the comparison of governance systems really, between the old universities and, possibly, the new higher education corporations and the relationship between the governing body and permanent staff which issues were highlighted.

On my immediate right is Mr Gwyn Bartley, also an independent governor, as you rightly pointed out, a solicitor by profession. He is very much interested in the Nominations Committee proceedings, revelation of members' interests and particularly the notion of an independent involvement in a Nomination Committee, for example.

On my far right Dr Lynn Griffiths who has been Clerk to the present governing body for three years, was previously Clerk to the old Council when we operated under the Local Education Authority and Clwyd County Council, which was only three years ago. Those are the members of my team and witnesses and, if you would permit me, Lord Nolan, I would just like for a few minutes very briefly to paint a general picture.

LORD NOLAN: That would be very helpful.

JOHN WILLIAMS: The North East Wales Institute is a relatively small higher education institution. It is exclusively dealing presently with higher education. We have about 3,500 enrolments, a mixture of full and part-time students. We do not have degree awarding powers but we are validated to deliver the courses of the University of Wales and we have that arrangement of an associated college with the University of Wales. That, I think, is important.

We retain our own quality systems but, of course, we also have an involvement with the university and their own quality procedures as well. In previous times, we have had associations with the University of Salford, who also validated some of our courses in our early years.

As I said, we were incorporated, possibly the last of the higher education institutions, in 1993 and, therefore, we are a relatively new corporation. This present governing body has been in operation for the three years. Their terms of office now come up for renewal and we are now going through that procedure, that process involving Nominations Committee of renewing that particular body. We have natural retirements and resignations and we are filling these positions by as open a process as we can get our hands on but I must say that in these three years the governing body has behaved extremely responsibly, as you would expect of the professional people that are involved.

We have our difficulties. As a small institution we also have a relatively small governing body. It is a governing body of eight independent members and a total of 14 members in all, involving three staff members and a student member. It is not, as you would expect, a representative body and those people are there in their own right and that principle now is well accepted by the staff and by the students and it has been operating relatively efficiently over the past three years.

As I said, it is sometimes extremely difficult because of availability and time constraints to actually get membership of all the sub-committees that we have. With 14 people and in some instances we have to exclude the staff and student memberships, we are running an Estate Committee, an Audit Committee, a Remuneration Committee, a Nominations Committee, an Employment Committee and a Finance and General Purposes Committee. Therefore, you can imagine that juggling and looking for expertise across the board has not been easy for us with but the 14 members.

Those, Lord Nolan, are my introductory comments, just to paint a general picture and to put what we are saying this morning into some sort of context.

1267. LORD NOLAN: Thank you very much. As you would expect, you have anticipated some of our questions by what you have already told us, which is a great help.

Still on the background to this morning's talk, I wonder if I could ask you to tell us briefly about something which you mention in your submissions but do not spell out in detail and that is about some difficulties which you experienced in the past and how you have had a recovery plan to get rid of them. We do not want in the least to go into the detail of whatever individual problems may have arisen but we are, of course, very interested in case problems have arisen—in particular, organisation—to see how they have been dealt with and whether the machinery for coping with problems has worked properly. Are you able to help us on that one?

JOHN WILLIAMS: Yes, indeed. Prior to incorporation and in the very last days of local education authority control we undertook to the Clwyd strategy for the disaggregation of further and higher education in the county. That strategy involved itself in the formulation of a higher education institution, which we now have in being as our institute, and also the disaggregation of further education into two separate colleges that are also now in existence, one as a separate further education college on Deeside of about 1,500 students and also the further education in Wrexham went to the Yale sixth-form college, as it was then, to form a truly tertiary college.

All the expenditure of that disaggregation predominantly fell on the Institute. In a period of

considerable change—and I will not bore you with the details, you can have them if you want them—we went into some financial difficulties. We were running a deficit last year and in order actually to recover a report was commissioned by Touche Ross which our governing body and the funding council agreed to. That led to a recovery plan which was formulated. That took effect in January a year ago and we have been involved in a monthly monitoring process since that time.

There has been a steering group of governors involved with me in the monitoring and control of that recovery plan and I am delighted to say that at every stage we have been ahead of targets set by the Funding Council. That paints a general background. Therefore, this governing body has very much been involved not quite in crisis management but they have been preoccupied in establishing a firm, financial base for what is a relatively new institution in order to move forward to the future. I think we now have that firm base on which to grow and on which to build.

It is a difficult period because consolidation has not allowed us to expand as we would have wished to but the student numbers are buoyant and our finances are sound and are being monitored effectively and efficiently in collaboration and in association and, indeed, in partnership with the Funding Council and some very, very tough decisions have had to be taken over the past 18 months. The institute basically has been turned round and that is, if I might say, a tribute to this very small governing body and I must emphasise that the smallness and fleetfootedness and general consensus and agreement of this governing body has assisted us considerably in this process.

1268. LORD NOLAN: Thank you very much. I wonder if we could come in just a little bit more detail to some of the aspects of the way the governing body is appointed and how it operates. You have told us about its composition and about the staff and student representatives and the very small number of extremely busy people, in particular the independent governors who have their own outside responsibilities, in managing so many committees which is very impressive.

You mentioned also in your written submissions that amongst those whom you consult about possible future members are suitable local public bodies. What sort of bodies have you in mind there?

JOHN WILLIAMS: Yes. Can I ask Dr Griffiths first who has been involved as the constitutionalist in contacting these people to provide some of that information and then Mr Bartley will add some of his own perceptions of the work essentially of the Nominations Committee which we put into existence some six months ago.

LORD NOLAN: Good. Thank you, good. Yes, please, Dr Griffiths.

DR LYNN N GRIFFITHS (Clerk to the Board of Governors, North East Wales Institute of Higher Education): In the renewal process that we are going through at the moment the Board are very concerned to be as transparent and open as possible in finding new members to replace those who did not wish to continue beyond 31 March, so two strategies were invoked. One was to advertise in the local press, and it was specifically local to Wrexham, North Wales and the Borders, Cheshire in particular. That was placed, but in addition the Board felt that there were certain organisations with whom we have worked over the years, have a professional affinity with—such as, the health authorities in particular because of our course portfolio, a number of professional bodies, such as the CBI, the Institute of Directors, from where some of our members originally came. I think they were selected through those organisations in 1993.

We also, as a Nominations Committee, discussed areas which we would like to approach because one thing that we are concerned about is to have a balance of specialisms and professional interests within what has been described as a very small body so that we are not replicating, if we can possibly avoid it, people with employment interests, human resource interests. We have as wide a breadth as possible. That has proved very successful, in my opinion. As the evidence has indicated to you, we have had 14 applications of stature and I do not think the Board will have any difficulty whatsoever in coming to a conclusion in renewing that membership.

The other observation I would make is that we are also concerned to have or be cognisant of gender interests, gender balance on the Board. That is difficult. In defining the selection criteria to be people who are holding executive positions by definition, it is going to be very difficult to find women, although we have a number of applications.

LORD NOLAN: Thank you very much.

GWYN BARTLEY (Board Member, North East Wales Institute of Higher Education): Mr Chairman, there are two matters that I would like to address to the Committee but the first one follows exactly on from what Dr Griffiths has said, and that is the replacement and the nomination of members to the Committee and, in particular, the view submitted to you, I believe, by the Higher Education Funding Council for Wales that the Nomination Committees ought to have represented upon them an outside member who has no connection whatsoever with the Institute. In my view, that is not a way forward.

I cannot see why there is a need for outside members to be appointed purely to a Nominations Committee for the purpose of appointing or nominating members of the board of directors of NEWI. I am not sure that they can add anything to what NEWI already has amongst its board members. I do not believe that they would know sufficient about NEWI, or any particular institute or college for that matter not particularly related to NEWI, I do not think the principle is a sound one to have outsiders on the Nominations Committee. The board of a small institute like NEWI will have very many professions and skills represented and we will know what we need to replace. It might be personnel expertise, it might be estate management, and so on, and I do not think that outside members can add to that. We advertise sufficiently, and significantly in my view, for members and, as you have heard from Dr Griffiths, we have had 14 people express an interest.

The danger is that if outsiders are nominated to a Nominations Committee there will be some political influence, perhaps, brought to bear by the local council

wanting to be represented and if they are represented the local trade union organisations would like to be represented, the CBI and so on. You will never please everybody in having people nominated to that committee. I think you can end up with the silly scenario of having a Nominations Committee to nominate people to sit on a Nominations Committee.

We have a system of bringing co-opted members on to the Board from time to time where we need particular skills that are not represented on the Board and the system of co-option is the one that ought to be relied upon rather than having enforced upon us from above the idea of having to have by rule some outside members on the Nominations Committee. This is a small Board of directors with a significant responsibility and it is never far from the minds of the independent members that they have significant and substantial duties and responsibilities and I do not think their effectiveness can be added to in any way by putting outside members on the Nominations Committee.

The other matter that I wanted to address, but perhaps I can come back to this when the topic arises, is the HEFCW proposal that there be a register of members' interests.

1269. LORD NOLAN: I wonder if, before we come to that and it is a matter on which I would be grateful to hear what you have to say, I could just follow up the trend of your remarks which reflects what has been said in your written submissions. Indeed, I think it is Professor Williams who says, talking of the new corporations:

"the new corporations appointed by the Secretary of State may not have the political balance essential to operate effectively a geographical area where political opinion is largely at the other extreme."

As against that, of course, as he says, decision-making is a much sharper process with a smaller body.

GWYN BARTLEY: Yes, it is.

1270. LORD NOLAN: Now, are there any ways in which you can, so to speak, bridge the gap? For example, what are your links, informal or otherwise, with the local authority? Is there any criterion or guidelines for that or is it done very much on a case-to-case basis as and when they are, you think, properly involved?

GWYN BARTLEY: I think Professor Williams would be better placed to answer that, my Lord.

JOHN WILLIAMS: I just detected that Mr Roberts was taking a deep breath. Did you want to respond to that before I do? There was quite a significant change of breathing pattern here.

ALWYN ROBERTS (Board Member, North East Wales Institute of Higher Education): I think it touches upon the matter in which I am most interested, Lord Nolan, namely the comparison between the more traditional university council type governance of universities and the rather more corporationist type represented by NEWI. I do not think there are perfect ways of running institutes of higher education. Both models have their advantages and their corresponding disadvantages and it seems to me that the concern ought to be to compensate in each case for the weaknesses which they have compared to the other.

I would have to say that the NEWI Board is lacking in terms of a community representation. I would be happier not if there were local government representation but if there were members of communities other than the business community in North East Wales more fully represented. Obviously, university councils derive their membership from separate interest groups including local authorities and that certainly can create problems but there are opposite problems, in perception in particular, when governing bodies cease to be perceptibly representative of various kinds of interest in the community and seem to concentrate on one particular aspect.

JOHN WILLIAMS: This was partly the reason why you had two responses, which I am sure you detected, from our institution. The response from our Chairman of Governors who, unfortunately, is in Australia today and cannot be with us, agreed by the Board, and my response, also agreed by the Board, because I could say things that our Chairman, for example, could not say. This is a particular point to which I would like to refer and this is the balance, and the perception of the balance, and the work and the bridges that we have to build with the local community despite the fact that we would be accused of being undemocratic, unrepresentative and unelected. That is a particular problem, clearly, that the so-called quangos which we are identified with have at this particular point in time.

We, as executives, as managers, have to counteract that by involving ourselves on a regular basis with people in the local community, with the local members and also with the officers.

1271. LORD NOLAN: The point made by Mr Bartley very strongly is that with at least half your members as independent members from a wide variety of outside interests and organisations you are going a long way, if I understood Mr Bartley correctly, to meet the need for an independent approach, at any rate not only to the selection of the board of governors, as he said, but to its operations and, of course, the two interests are to some extent in conflict and, of course, a high priority must be to pay the bills, which is very much a matter of good business.

JOHN WILLIAMS: Absolutely, absolutely.

1272. LORD NOLAN: This is really where we are coming closer to this Committee's specific concern—the fact that public money is involved and the need to combine ordinary business prudence and, to an extent, confidentiality about what you are doing, certainly in advance of making a particular deal, with the requisite degree of openness towards the public about actually how things are conducted.

I wonder if, perhaps at this point, we could come back to Mr Bartley's mention of registers of interests. What would you like to say about that, Mr Bartley?

GWYN BARTLEY: I am hesitant to be again against the HEFCW submission but I am not sure that a register of members' interests on a board of this sort, not limited to NEWI but to the Higher Education Corporation boards of management as a whole generally involves, I do not think the register of members' interests is a step that we ought to be taking.

The board members are appointed now by a Nominations Committee. They were appointed in the past—certainly I was—by a representative of the Welsh Office. We now have a Nominations Committee which will scrutinise the applications, the CVs will come before us, and then the full Board will make an appointment from the Nominations Committee recommendations. So, you have a scrutiny by the Nominations Committee and by the full Board before anyone is nominated to the Board. It ill becomes us to say to any new nominee thereafter, "By the way, although we have scrutinised you twice, we don"t really trust you to declare an interest, we must have a register of members' interests".

This is unlike an elected body where a Member of Parliament or a member of a local authority would not be subject to public scrunity—public, perhaps, with a small "p" as far as we are concerned—not to be subject to scrutiny by a public accountable body in the same way as a nominee for the board of governors. I can put that better.

If you stand for Parliament or if you stand for election to a local government body you are not scrutinised in the same way as you are scrutinised if you have to become appointed to a board of this sort. Therefore, you cannot transplant the register of members' interests that perhaps some governmental bodies readily sit with to a board like NEWI.

LORD NOLAN: Is that—I am sorry, I interrupted you.

GWYN BARTLEY: I was going to say, my Lord, that if it is insisted upon from those above then you are going to have all sorts of problems about how extensive it should be. For example, is it only limited to business interests? Should it be limited to family ties because my daughter is a student at NEWI, by coincidence, and has been for the past six months. Would organisations of particular bodies have to be disclosed—such as, in the police service, the Masonic movement? Where would it end?

Having decided where it ended, to whom would it be open? Is it open to all members of the public or is it only open to certain members, staff representatives, or certain executive members in NEWI—the Chairman, for example? It would be a disincentive to sometimes onerous unpaid public service if peoples' private lives had to be made the subject of scrutiny by the man in the street, as it were. If people are nominated to the board after the scrutiny that is sufficient and you put them on their honour to declare an interest where appropriate.

1273. LORD NOLAN: Is that a Board view, Professor Williams?

JOHN WILLIAMS: No, it is not. Can I say that this is a matter that we have not yet discussed and, clearly, it is Mr Bartley's view and it will be heard in the governing body as we move forward. On the other hand, I have to say that in terms of the scrutiny systems, etcetera, we very well respect the need for audit and one recommendation of the HEFCW audit report is that our Audit Committee should now take responsibility for putting out a register of members' interests. We are at that point at the current state of play in that the debate has not occurred within the governing body. We have a view, strongly expressed by Mr Bartley. We have a recommendation from the HEFCW audit report, something that our Audit Committee must consider at this point in time before the Board considers it and that is the situation at the moment.

Another deep breath from my left, Lord Nolan.

ALWYN ROBERTS: Mr Bartley and I would be totally agreed that in the discussion of any matter and in the making of any decision all those involved should be aware of the interests of everybody else involved. The difference lies in the mode of arriving at that state of knowledge. I, personally, would have no difficulties about a register of interests but we would all be agreed that the interests involved in decision-making should be known to everybody within the process.

JOHN WILLIAMS: Yes, and can I say that up to now any matter that has involved potentially members' interests then those members have been asked clearly and explicitly to reveal those particular interests. Of course, if the answer is positive they will then take no part in those discussions in the usual way, but we are talking about something slightly different.

LORD NOLAN: I think so.

ALWYN ROBERTS: There are so many grey areas, if I might take my own position, for example. To an extent, NEWI and my own university are co-operators. To an extent, also, we are almost necessarily competitors. The fact that I am associated with another body is perfectly well known. Anything I say in the Board might conceivably be seen to be interested but, given that the position is well known, I suppose one manages to live with it.

1274. LORD NOLAN: Quite, yes. I see that. It is a common problem to all registers of interests and the need is, of course, as you say, to make sure that the information is available to those who need to know it, which may or may not include the public in the particular case.

There is much I would like to ask you but there is one closing matter I would like to cover with you. It is still on the need for reasonable commercial competitiveness which is assisted by the smaller board that you describe in comparison with the old and perhaps more widely representative board for the protection, of course, of academic freedom and of ordinary standards of employee regulation. Do you have confidential clauses in your service agreements and do you have provisions about the use of intellectual property? Is there a standard form of agreement for your employees over this?

JOHN WILLIAMS: Yes, yes, we do and also we have clauses in the contract which effectively prevents an individual from using or divulging information that could be of use to the institution at the termination of his or her employment with us. That is as far as we go.

1275. LORD NOLAN: Is that a standard form of agreement?

JOHN WILLIAMS: That is within the contract of employment. That is within the professional contract certainly for academic staff.

1276. LORD NOLAN: Yes, yes, but is that one that has been drawn up in your own institute or is it one that is in common form throughout the sector?

JOHN WILLIAMS: It is generally a part of the professional contract drawn out by the negotiators but I think it is acceptable. We have gone through the professional contract with the local branch of NATFE, for example. We have quite an understanding with them at this point in time and it is acceptable to them.

1277. LORD NOLAN: I see. You have discussed it with their representatives?

JOHN WILLIAMS: Absolutely, absolutely.

ALWYN ROBERTS: In clarification, Lord Nolan, it probably is a contract which applies totally within the old public sector colleges in Wales where there was a common negotiation on the revised professional contract. Practices amongst the older universities would vary.

1278. LORD NOLAN: Yes, I follow. Thank you very much. Would it be possible for us to see a copy of that contract?

JOHN WILLIAMS: Yes, indeed.

LORD NOLAN: Thank you very much indeed. I have taken up a lot of time. I know Dame Anne Warburton wanted to ask some questions. Anne?

1279. ANNE WARBURTON: If I may, in view of the time, concentrate first of all on a hopefully brief question or two about the governing body and then come on to the more general question of audit.

On the governing body, am I right in thinking from the way it has been put that you had a rather surprising number of governors standing down?

JOHN WILLIAMS: No, we did not. In the three years we have had one with personnel experience stand down, retire, and we have replaced him with another person with personnel experience. We are now——

1280. ANNE WARBURTON: But governors not wanting to be re-appointed?

JOHN WILLIAMS: Sorry?

ANNE WARBURTON: Governors not wanting now to be re-appointed?

JOHN WILLIAMS: Yes, we do have now two or three resignations that will take effect this April and, therefore, we are in the process of filling those positions.

ANNE WARBURTON: I ask the question because you make rather a point about the view taken locally of the Board and I just wondered if that had an influence on these decisions.

ALWYN ROBERTS: If I might speak personally. I am retiring at the end of March. It has nothing to do with any kind of dissatisfaction with NEWI; it is the sheer burden of work and the feeling that it is time to get some movement at least within the system. Nothing to do with dissatisfaction.

JOHN WILLIAMS: Could I say that another Board member has been appointed on the board of the Funding Council, of HEFCW, and naturally we have been advised that that individual, a she, cannot serve on those two boards. These are natural, if I might say, retirements or resignations for personal reasons.

1281. ANNE WARBURTON: Fine. Do you give induction training to new governors or will you be?

JOHN WILLIAMS: We did in the early days and in changing over from local authority control to become a corporation we really trained quite extensively. Therefore, we have a training programme in place and it is likely that we will be implementing that for the new members.

ANNE WARBURTON: A lot of institutions seem to find that very helpful.

JOHN WILLIAMS: Extremely useful.

1282. ANNE WARBURTON: I am puzzled by one phrase which was used in your papers:

"ensuring that the vice-chair assumes the chair"

Does that mean on a meeting basis or a three-year basis?

JOHN WILLIAMS: No, no, on an annual basis or a two-year basis but that is currently under review.

1283. ANNE WARBURTON: So, the idea is that you do your apprenticeship as vice-chairman and go on?

JOHN WILLIAMS: The idea there is that we appoint a vice-chair with a view to him or her assuming the chair at a certain point in the future. That is a position we took about two months ago. We need to review that again and one possibility, for example, is to view one of our meetings at the end of the year when, for example, we consider the statutory accounts, as an AGM.

ANNE WARBURTON: Yes, that is an unusual idea.

JOHN WILLIAMS: And we are considering, or likely to be considering, that in the near future and balancing the merits and disadvantages of those two systems to see which better fits the aspirations and the needs of the governing body.

1284. ANNE WARBURTON: Thank you very much. I am sorry to be rushing but you can understand why. The question of funding and of auditing, and so forth, I was struck by the passage at the end of your paper, Professor Williams, on what you saw as the coming problem of the decreasing public share of your funding. I think you were suggesting that perhaps auditing by public bodies was not going to go on being as suitable as it may have been in the past.

JOHN WILLIAMS: I do not think—I am sorry if I gave you that impression.

ANNE WARBURTON: I have misunderstood you, have I?

JOHN WILLIAMS: I think it is natural for any institution, any HE institution, in the light of government funding to look for outside sources of funds and those are likely to come from the private sector. Therefore, there is

a balance between the need to audit. We are, after all, a public body so it is right that we should be audited but there needs to be a balance of audit for the public funds and also the ability for a board of governors, if you like, to use the funds that are generated from the private sector perhaps in a slightly different way.

1285. ANNE WARBURTON: What do you mean when you say that the audit has to be both ways, the responsibility has to be both ways? It is in your comment on paragraph 10:

"accountability to funding bodies, be they public sector or private, must work both ways"

LYNN GRIFFITHS: If I may, that reinforces what Professor Williams says. We are looking to derive a lot more of our income from private sources and we need to be cognisant and have an empathy with the systems and the structures that govern that particular market. There is sometimes a conflict in terms of the private sector seeing institutions such as ours as being less than responsive, sluggish. It is the feeling that we are a quasi-local authority body which carries that baggage still around with it.

There is a contradiction or a tension between the needs of being a singularly public accountable body which overtime will have, I suspect, a diminishing level of resource coming from that with a greater orientation towards the private sector for more income which gives us greater freedoms in terms of what we can do. It is managing both systems equitably to the satisfaction of a variety of public and professional perceptions and we need to have an empathy-strike relationship with different kinds of people who have very different expectations of us.

1286. ANNE WARBURTON: Just on the pedestrian straight audit point, would the Welsh Funding Agency, for example, and other official audits cover also the private part of your funding?

JOHN WILLIAMS: Yes, they would, undoubtedly.

ALWYN ROBERTS: Yes, they would.

1287. ANNE WARBURTON: And you are content with broadly the present structure of the auditing process?

JOHN WILLIAMS: Yes, we have, as you know, quite an extensive audit process. The Funding Council itself comes in and it has been with us—indeed, the second time in 18 months. We have an internal audit committee and we have external auditors. Two important documents come out of that. It is the HEFCW auditors' report. It is also the external auditors' management letter which can carry important recommendations and it is how an institution like ours responds to those two reports and then adopts systems, say of project management, to make sure that those actions are actually delivered in the timeframe which is expected of us.

ALWYN ROBERTS: I have to say that there is within the sector a feeling that this is a field where deregulation has not been applied and that we are exceedingly heavily audited, almost to the point of distracting some of us at least from other equally pressing duties.

LORD NOLAN: It is a lesson that we try to bear in mind ourselves in these inquiries.

ANNE WARBURTON: Thank you, chairman.

1288. LORD NOLAN: We are very grateful to you. We have slightly exceeded your busy time as well as ours but it is because it has been an extremely interesting and helpful talk to us. Professor Williams and your colleagues, thank you very much indeed for the trouble you have taken and the time you have spent both in writing to us and in coming to talk to us. We are very grateful.

Now we have Dr Colin Williams and Gillian Burns. Good morning to you and thank you very much for coming to talk to us. Was there anything you wished to say by way of opening statement in addition to the written material you have let us have.

DR COLIN WILLIAMS AND GILLIAN BURNS

DR COLIN WILLIAMS (Principal, Coleg Glan Hafren): Yes, I think it might be useful if I give you a brief pen portrait of the college.

LORD NOLAN: I am sure it would.

COLIN WILLIAMS: We are the primary provider of further education and general education in the City of Cardiff. We are a tertiary college, established in 1989. We enrol approximately 10,000 students of whom 2,600 are full-time. On the staff we have 580 on the payroll, although not all are necessarily active in the college. We have two major sites, one in the centre of the City, one at the edge of the City. We have operated since 1989 with a governing body of approximately 15 and moved into incorporation with more or less the same governing body, all bar one elected to transfer. So, to some extent, in the early year of incorporation the issue of recruitment of new governors was not really at the forefront of development.

We have been on a steep learning curve in the past 2½ years, having to set up a whole range of systems in the college that previously would have been provided, or services provided, by the LEA and perhaps I could sum up that experience by saying that the primary lesson the college has had to learn—and I think we have learned it—is that you need professionals to do a professional job. Using perhaps bright and well-meaning academics to discharge certain key functions is not necessarily a prescription for dealing with those functions effectively.

The governing body currently, with the two resignations I have just received in fact, is now down to the minimum of ten. We have been functioning with 12. The board saw advantages in that but at times found the pressure on themselves, particularly in terms of committee work, quite onerous so I am not sure that they are totally sure on the issue of numbers. My own recommendation would be—and has been—that they move back to 14 or 15 members.

The range of skills and people we have on the board reflects the requirements over the past two years, which is really that the college establishes itself in terms of its systems and concentrates on that rather than perhaps other issues. We have legal representation, financial representation, personnel expertise; we have a link with the local authority; we have estates expertise available as well.

Mrs Burns is our Assistant Principal for Human Resources but I should also perhaps point out she was formerly in effect Chief Executive of the Mid and South-Glamorgan Trading Agency so herself has significant experience as a Chief Executive and, indeed, has a particular perspective on the effectiveness of governance of the college as Clerk to the college Audit Committee and has perhaps an interesting view of governors in committee.

LORD NOLAN: Thank you very much. We take turns on the Committee to start off the questions and it is Dame Anne's turn now so I am going to ask her, please, to begin.

1289. ANNE WARBURTON: I can foresee it is going to be difficult to fit everything into this discussion too, Dr Williams. Can I start right away with the point you have just been making about the size of the governing body. I was quite surprised to see that you were down to 10 because that sounded a terribly small number, especially if you have an Audit Committee as the membership is not allowed to overlap with other committees, and so forth. How does it actually work in terms of particularly the lay members, independent members?

COLIN WILLIAMS: We find that is a problem in that they are all committed to the three key committees we have, which is Audit, Finance and General Purposes, Personnel and, of course, Remuneration, so that is a problem and the view that is developing on the Board is that they can solve that problem by co-opting members who are not necessarily members of the Board of the college but provided they have the right professional expertise.

1290. ANNE WARBURTON: They can be supernumerary?

COLIN WILLIAMS: Yes, yes. That is probably the direction in which we will go.

1291. ANNE WARBURTON: Good. Thank you very much. You talked also about the change, your coming away from local authority control. Could you summarise for us the differences from the management point of view both then and now and advantages and disadvantages. Is there a balance sheet or is it clearly one or the other?

COLIN WILLIAMS: I would not mind admitting that I was not one of the greatest supporters of the concept of incorporation but would say now that I would be reluctant perhaps to go back to the old system. The management team at the college has changed quite significantly and that in itself brings certain tensions perhaps between people I would describe as professionals in finance and estates and people who are professional academics. Since incorporation, we now have a Personnel Manager and a Finance Director. We have built a finance team up to ten members from scratch, for example. We have an estates team of five, with an extremely professional Estates Manager. We buy in all our legal expertise. Expensive though it is, we do not feel we can afford to have our own legal team in the college.

The management team of the college has changed, certainly in the balance. Previously it was entirely composed of people with a sound academic background. It is now approximately 50-50 people with an academic background and people with what I would describe as this professional background and there are tensions in that.

1292. ANNE WARBURTON: So, on the skills side you have done well. Were you helped with extra resources where you needed it for setting up the new arrangements, financial resources?

COLIN WILLIAMS: Perhaps, as a college, we were in a rather more fortunate position than many in that we had consistently turned over significant financial surpluses and was one of the perhaps few Welsh colleges that moved into incorporation with substantial balances in our favour. So, the recruitment of these extra staff was never really a problem for us, as I imagine it may well have been for smaller colleges and as I imagine it may still be. We did not receive very much support, I have to say, although we did receive some pump-priming funding but that was quickly used up.

ANNE WARBURTON: That is behind you now?

COLIN WILLIAMS: It is indeed, yes, well behind us.

1293. ANNE WARBURTON: There was one small point which we noticed in your report and that is that you tell us that a member of your staff is on the Audit Committee. That is rather unusual, I think, and may be even disallowed in some cases.

COLIN WILLIAMS: Yes. I think it is an interesting point. We were not aware that it was unusual and believe there are other colleges where this is the case. As far as we are aware, this was not disqualified. That person brings a very interesting perspective to the functioning of the Audit Committee, as I think Mrs Burns would confirm. It does actually, quite interestingly though, cause—how can I say—the members of the Board who are members of the Audit Committee see themselves as slightly different from the member of staff and they do not always recognise the presence of that individual, as it were. That person is almost invisible to them at times.

1294. ANNE WARBURTON: It sounds then as though they are treating it as would be more normal, that the member of staff is there to help the Committee rather than being a member of it?

GILLIAN BURNS (Assistant Principal for Human Resources, Coleg Glan Hafren): Yes, that is certainly true. One of our members is a very irregular attender and, consequently, there have been issues of quorum. There have been at least two occasions when I have had to point out that we are, in fact, quorate because of the presence of this member of the Committee who is a member of staff. Perhaps I should add here that she is the only member of the Committee currently who has financial expertise and that is why she was appointed.

One of the difficulties that you pinpointed earlier of the small number of governors meant that the person with financial expertise is on the Finance and General Purposes Committee which, of course, disqualifies him from being a member of the Audit Committee and it was for this reason that this individual was co-opted. We also saw a benefit, and the Board initially acknowledged the benefit, of having somebody on the Audit Committee who understood the sometimes rather arcane workings of certain of the college systems. For instance, internal audit reports on things like the enrolment procedures could be interpreted from within by somebody who was a part of those procedures, so there is a useful purpose.

1295. ANNE WARBURTON: You are not worried about conflict of interests?

GILLIAN BURNS: The member of staff who has been appointed would not raise that particular worry although it would be a consideration. One has to look at the individual and there are individuals who are capable of handling that kind of issue.

1296. ANNE WARBURTON: Thank you very much. Shall we turn to the governing body? I am bound to say in answer to the first paragraph of your recent letter, Dr Williams, to Martin Le Jeune—you rather wonder how members of the two councils are appointed. I have to say that the Nolan Committee in its first report suggested to government how this might come about. I do not know how it is done but our views are on record anyway. Could I ask you, how does the college go about choosing and getting its governing body?

COLIN WILLIAMS: It is an issue, perhaps part of the wide issue of governance, that I find a matter of increasing concern to myself. We follow the pattern that many colleges have followed which is that we seek nominations from various bodies. We seek it by recommendation from individuals and what we have done to date is that the chair of the board and myself normally meet with the individual concerned and spend several hours with them—we usually have lunch with them as well—in order to get to know each other and also for them perhaps to decide whether they really wish to get involved with us.

Having met them in this way, and we occasionally bring in senior staff as well to meet the individuals, we then attempt to form an opinion of the person concerned and then request a CV from the individual if we think we are going to go forward with it, making it clear to them that we would be making a recommendation to the board. That CV, together with our recommendations and our rationale for appointment, is then advanced to the board of the college who, of course, make the actual decision.

In some ways that has worked quite well but I, personally, have felt increasingly uncomfortable with it as the Chief Executive of the organisation because it is possible to criticise it in the same way as one can criticise boards as being self-perpetuating. It could be argued that the Principal is always going to support someone he or she is going to feel very comfortable with. It is occasionally—your own papers quote this, I think—of use to have a member of the awkward squad present as well. Therefore, I feel it is better that we move away from that model to a nomination committee composed of members of the board and that they should deal with the matter, against a strict specification of what is required. In the past, perhaps, recruitment has been somewhat ad hoc and not against a structured consideration of the skills required on the board. That is essential and if the board itself defines what it is looking for in terms of the skills and experience then it would make it easier for a nomination committee, and easier to rationalise an appointment.

1297. ANNE WARBURTON: If I may say so, I found the way you set that out in your paper as very comprehensive. You go on in that same section to suggest that the view that the appointment of governors should be as open as possible being an advantage is questionable. You say it might perhaps be an example of the liberal sentiment that openness of itself is a good thing. Do you want to develop that thought?

COLIN WILLIAMS: Yes. I must stop writing letters to people. We considered the advice given generally on ways of recruiting members to boards and one of the pieces of advice offered is, for example, advertise. I believe the previous speakers, as far as I can recall, seemed to support that concept. The problem I have with that sort of approach is you may well attract very capable candidates, you will also attract a large number of people, perhaps, who represent single interest groups, who have an axe to grind, etcetera, and who may merely be very happy to sit on a committee. I would not wish to move in that direction myself and that is what I was touching on in terms of that sort of openness.

ANNE WARBURTON: In general, we have found people thinking that openness has the advantage that people are less suspicious that things are being done behind the scenes.

COLIN WILLIAMS: Yes, I would agree, but if the governing body itself is very upfront and open about the way it goes about selecting, about its criteria and the process and is then prepared to justify its appointments, that would give a sufficient degree of openness. It should always be prepared to explain what it has done.

1298. ANNE WARBURTON: There was another of your remarks which caught my attention. I enjoyed reading your papers, as you will gather. You said:

"It might be argued that the designation of the chairperson and the appointment of the principal are too important to be left simply to the board."

I wrote—if not, then who?

COLIN WILLIAMS: Yes, I asked myself that question having written it. Again, I am aware of not exactly a trap a board can fall into but there is a temptation, is there not, always to go for what you are comfortable with and not necessarily for what you need. It may be that having established a particular pattern of governance and functioning of the executive, the board would seek to perpetuate that. That might not be what the board would require.

Also, with the resignation of the principal you have to ask the question, who exactly is going to advise the board and guide them on the selection of an incoming chief executive, for example? What I had in mind with that remark was that the board should, at the very least, seek advice from professional organisations on issues to do with person specifications, job specifications and, indeed, take advice from those who understand the local context in order to build up a picture of the sort of person that they should be looking for.

For example, I would recommend the board to go to the College Employers' Forum or the Association for Colleges—hopefully, they will be merged in the not too distant future—and that organisation could provide what I would call the professional support and advice the board would need and it would be independent advice as well. Again, the board would be seen to be squeaky clean in the way it sought to deal with the matter. What I did not mean in making that remark—I was not suggesting that an organisation like a funding council should necessarily have a major say in that, although I would not rule out the board, should a vacancy arise, going to the funding council and discussing with the funding council their view of the college, the main issues and problems associated with that college, because it would certainly help them, the board,

to put together a picture of what exactly was required at this stage in the development of the college.

1299. ANNE WARBURTON: Thank you very much. Because of time, I shall not mention the word "audit" unless you particularly want to but I would just like to ask you, as my last question, accountability—accountability to different sectors, those interested. What would you like to say to us about that?

COLIN WILLIAMS: I will say something as a Chief Executive on the processes of auditing because they are linked to accountability. I would share the concerns that many chief executives and boards express that currently we are being almost driven to distraction by the weight of audit being brought to bear on colleges. I have rationalised it in my mind as a necessary stage in the development of colleges. It is better perhaps to be sure and come in hard early in the development of a college than try to put it together later. We have tried to bear with the pressure and I accept it as part of the process of accountability, which was never particularly clear when we were part of the LEA, I would add.

The problem, however, that I find personally is that there is a real danger that you could develop into a very effective bureaucratic organisation that totally lacked any dynamism or any exciting view of the curriculum and the student. You could function extremely effectively in terms of audit and, quite frankly, be going down the drain on your curriculum. I find the pressure on myself and on senior staff is to concentrate on systems at times perhaps leading you into a situation where you become too dependent on others to deal with what the core business is, the student. All chief executives are feeling that sort of very real tension but I am rationalising it on the basis that the colleges are at a very early stage in their development as corporate establishments and audit is a probe that is useful not only, obviously, to organisations like the funding council but is also an extremely useful tool for the management of the college as well.

You will note in my submission the comments I made on management were that there were insufficient levels of management expertise, of which financial expertise was just one component. That is certainly my view. In the current year, for example, we have set aside £50,000 to provide middle management training in the college.

1300. ANNE WARBURTON: Accountability outside the college?

COLIN WILLIAMS: Yes. I accept that at the very least the college has to justify what it is doing with, what appears to me anyway, to be the large sums of money made available to it—they are not necessarily adequate but they are certainly large sums of money—and also that you are accountable to your community, I feel, the public and the people of Cardiff, to reassure them that you are providing quality education and training.

You will notice in the submissions I made I did not actually respond to the question on the importance of quality in education. The reason was that it is such a vast topic I realised that I would have great difficulty containing myself to a reasonable response. Yes, the accountability, as I see it, is to the community, that is my personal view, and that is why I have striven extremely hard to maintain close and effective working relationships with the local authority. It could be demonstrated that in this area we have been significantly more successful than many other colleges and many other authorities.

1301. ANNE WARBURTON: How long have you particularly done that, it would be interesting to know?

COLIN WILLIAMS: I have a very good working relationship with the Director of Education and meet him quite frequently; indeed, we were meeting yesterday on a very major development project relating to the provision for 16 education and training in a particular part of Cardiff where we are working on a very exciting development that involves the college and the authority and a school in making particular provision. I see that as essential because the authority is, after all, still the major player in the provision of education up to the age of 19 in this area.

That really was the basis of my doubts about incorporation. At the time I felt what was needed was a reform of the relationship between establishments and the authority rather than a sundering of the links and so I have done my very best to maintain those links with the authority and it certainly works to the benefit of the college.

1302. ANNE WARBURTON: But you do not have anybody who is either elected to the authority or works for it on your governing body?

COLIN WILLIAMS: Yes.

ANNE WARBURTON: You do?

COLIN WILLIAMS: We currently have county councillor. He was retained on my advice expressly to maintain that link with the authority and particularly with the LEA. I am currently actually exploring the recruitment of another individual who also has similar links to the local authority.

ANNE WARBURTON: Thank you very much, Dr Williams.

LORD NOLAN: Professor King?

1303. PROFESSOR ANTHONY KING: I only have a few questions. Dr Williams, you described yourself several times as the college's Chief Executive and you used phrases like "management team" and "middle management" and "core business" and that is the way people in further and higher education tend to talk at the moment. Do you see the Coleg Glan Hafren as a business?

COLIN WILLIAMS: Yes, I do. Again, perhaps I am becoming schizophrenic about these things. I have always felt very strongly that the funding provided to us is funding that is earned by people out there in industry and commerce and in employment and in the community and, therefore, I have always felt we had a major responsibility to be seen to be using that funding effectively and efficiently. That does not, therefore, excuse an educational establishment from operating, certainly in terms of its financial management, as a business. There are tensions but the bottom line is your budget. You cannot, at least over a prolonged period, go into deficit. I do see us as a business in that respect.

1304. PROF ANTHONY KING: You are certainly saying that the college should be run in a business-like way?

COLIN WILLIAMS: Yes, yes.

1305. PROF ANTHONY KING: Suppose I asked you a slightly different question. In what ways does a college like yours differ from a normal business?

COLIN WILLIAMS: We differ perhaps—I am not sure whether people would agree with me—I mentioned we have approximately 10,000 enrolments. I have always maintained we have, therefore, 10,000 products. It is very difficult to apply assessments of quality, BS 5750 etcetera, to an establishment like ours. I am not suggesting it is easy outside in an industrial concern but if you are producing a limited range of products then it is easier to apply those sort of quality measures. The difference is in that domain.

1306. PROF ANTHONY KING: Is there not one crucial difference that on the whole if I am selling widgets the customer is judging the quality of my widgets, I am not judging the quality of the customers? Is not one of the differences in an institution of education that the customers are being judged by the sales staff, as it were, the whole time as well as the other way round? Is that not a crucial difference?

COLIN WILLIAMS: Yes, it is, indeed. In the enrolment and recruitment of students the staff of the college are constantly going through that sort of process obviously with the idea, however, of determining the most suitable provision for their particular needs and aspirations at the time. In fact, one of the major problems we face is organising ourselves to do that effectively. The time that it takes, as you would appreciate, Professor King, is enormous. I would agree with you, yes.

1307. PROF ANTHONY KING: What about their qualifications at the other end of the process because, to the extent that an institution like yours, or mine for that matter, operates like a business with the students regarded as customers, is there not going to be a considerable emphasis possibly on achieving customer satisfaction at the expense of demanding of the customer—as we normally call students—the kinds of performance that either ourselves or outside validating agencies would require?

COLIN WILLIAMS: Yes. That is an extremely interesting question that we could go on for a very long time about. What I would say is that there may be some evidence to suggest that in education we have been somewhat self-indulgent in that respect in the past in not, in fact, making it clear to students what exactly was expected of them so that they knew what they were expected to achieve at the end of the course. They appreciate this sort of guidance. I think that is what you are suggesting.

On the other hand, I have always believed very firmly—and this is the thing that attracted me from HE, to some extent, to further education in particular—I always believed that people, as I put it—and I hope you will not misunderstand me—had the right to fail. In other words, we are there to provide them with opportunities and provided their aspirations are not wildly at variance with what they are asking us to provide for them, they should be given that opportunity. I have a problem, for example, with league tables which I accept in a way but it does not always measure, does it, exactly how much has been achieved. Indeed, the achievement can be considerable but will not show up in a league table.

I am wedded to the notion of the college giving people opportunities. If, at the end, it leads to a National Training and Education Target, or whatever, I am very pleased. That is good. It is good for them, it is good for us, it is good for the country. But I am wedded to the notion of FE as that second opportunity for many people.

1308. PROF ANTHONY KING: Suppose that a large number of your students exercised their right to fail, that has an effect, does it not, on the competitive position of the institution, even though the institution may be doing its academic duty by examining them in a sufficiently tough way that they do fail?

COLIN WILLIAMS: Yes. Fortunately my experience is the majority of them do not exercise that right to fail. On the whole, provided the induction and initial counselling is right and you match them with their consent to the right provision then the success rates, certainly in our college, are well up to national standards. It would be a nightmare situation, I suggest, that you are pointing out to me but, no, it is not one I have any experience of.

1309. PROF ANTHONY KING: The background to these questions, by the way, is in part the fact that we have had some evidence that people whose income as an institution is measured by output are under considerable pressure to produce what the funding people regard as output even though they have qualms about the quality of what they are doing.

COLIN WILLIAMS: Yes. I would share those qualms and I do not necessarily feel particularly comfortable with that aspect of the current funding system that is represented as payment by results.

Again, I am not absolutely sure what the answer to that is. Part of our accountability is, in fact, to ensure that there is an acceptable level of success among our students and that success is measured primarily by most people by examination results, by the achievement of NTETs. We have to accept the reality of that.

1310. PROF ANTHONY KING: Just one other question. I will make it deliberately not ad hominem. It is inconceivable that your board of governors would want to sack you, but suppose they made a mistake in choosing your successor and after two or three years decided that this was a person without whom they could do. What, in fact, in your college is the formal procedure for sacking the head or, presumably, a teacher? Maybe you do not know. That would be a sign of great confidence.

COLIN WILLIAMS: So far the occasion has not actually arisen.

PROF ANTHONY KING: I am sure it has not.

COLIN WILLIAMS: Thankfully. Can I look at the question in a slightly different way perhaps. At the level of the Chief Executive then perhaps the safeguard should be present in the form of the contract used so that you have the principle and if you wish to be the chief executive of a college then you should be prepared to accept the sort of contract that puts you on a three or four-year rolling appointment. If you have that in place then there are ways of dealing with that sort of situation, which will become more frequent, that would be acceptable to both sides. There are, of course, the usual disciplinary processes for dealing with, perhaps, behaviour that is not acceptable.

1311. PROF ANTHONY KING: What are, in your college, the usual disciplinary processes, what form do they take?

COLIN WILLIAMS: We have a set of procedures which we negotiated—in fact, I negotiated—for the whole of South Glamorgan with the main teaching union which divided the process into disciplinary matters, into health and competency procedures—three procedures. The previous one, in fact, rolled them all together in a very muddled form and I felt they had to be separated, which we did.

We had—and I would not want to go into detail here—an almost unique experience 18 months ago in the college relating to disciplinary matters affecting senior staff when it was very apparent to me that, in a sense, the instruments and articles were perhaps not defective but certainly not helpful in that there was a tension between what the instruments and articles advise you to do and natural justice. We had quite a problem with that. In the end we came down on the side of natural justice.

1312. PROF ANTHONY KING: Could I just ask you finally in that connection—indeed, in any connection—whether there is any kind of outside involvement at all, short of an industrial tribunal; in other words, if you have a disciplinary problem, however you want to define that term, with, say, a senior member of your academic staff, does it end entirely, apart from the possibility of an appeal to an industrial tribunal, entirely within the college?

COLIN WILLIAMS: It does end entirely within the college although I am very aware that the main teaching union probably has a view that recourse to outside arbitration, or whatever, would be appropriate. On the whole, the governing body would tend to resist that.

PROF ANTHONY KING: Would you?

COLIN WILLIAMS: Yes, it can be dealt with adequately within the college and there are, of course, the usual processes outside the college, industrial tribunals.

1313. PROF ANTHONY KING: So, you do not think there is anything to be said for having somebody like a visitor or an ombudsman, or something, either for the FE sector as a whole in Wales or for your individual institution?

COLIN WILLIAMS: I would not rule that out, no. That, properly examined, could be an extremely useful device and could be used quite widely even outside the immediate domain of disciplinary matters.

PROF ANTHONY KING: Thank you. We are out of time, are we not?

1314. LORD NOLAN: I am afraid so, just about. On that last point, Professor King asked you in terms of a visitor for the individual institution or an ombudsman covering the sector and you were in favour. I was not sure whether you were in favour of one or the other or both.

COLIN WILLIAMS: I think perhaps an ombudsman. There are issues that arise between colleges and the funding council, for example.

LORD NOLAN: It may depend on the type of issue, of course.

COLIN WILLIAMS: It would, of course, but I am more concerned, particularly at the moment, with certain issues of principle relating to growth in colleges, in terms of what is allowable and what is not allowable. There is sometimes a contradiction arising between the funding mechanism and policies on growth, for example. On the one hand, they say, "We want you to do this but we are going to make sure that the instruments are in place to prevent you doing it in effect" and in that case someone who could sit between us would perform a very useful function.

1315. LORD NOLAN: Thank you very much. You clearly have treated us as somewhat superannuated pupils and we are very grateful for the care you have taken in this extremely full and clear memorandum and in the frank and helpful answers you have given us this morning. Thank you both very much.

Good morning. This is Dr Gill Evans and Mr Michael Cohen. We were hoping to see Professor Griffith but I gather he is unable to be here.

MICHAEL COHEN AND DR GILL EVANS

DR GILL EVANS (Council for Academic Freedom and Academic Standards): Yes, I am afraid he was hoping to be able to come but he could not in the end.

1316. LORD NOLAN: No, I see. Thank you for coming. Was there anything you would like to say by way of opening remarks before we go to questions?

GILL EVANS: Mainly that we speak not as an institution but as a body of concerned academics. Our membership is about 200 individuals with some institutional affiliations and it extends right across the sector from further education to the oldest of the old universities. It includes a number of academic lawyers and academic accountants so that we are able to bring a good deal of professional expertise to bear on the cases that we deal with.

What we mainly do is to seek to act as mediators in cases where individuals in institutions have raised concerns or, in some cases, not raised concerns at all but found themselves in difficulties and where they have not been able to utilise the internal procedures to help. Therefore, we are in a unique position both in the experience we have in a non-adversarial way in trying to bring two sides together and in the extent to which our case material covers, as is not true for either the AUT or for NATFE, the whole sector. We are able to see patterns which it is not so easy for some of the other bodies doing variants of this kind of work to see.

LORD NOLAN: Yes. Thank you very much. Now, if I may, I will ask Sir Clifford Boulton to start the questions.

1317. CLIFFORD BOULTON: Thank you very much for the material that you sent us. You will understand that we do not follow up individual cases in any detail but, on the other hand, it was extremely useful for you to have produced examples to illustrate the problems as you saw them. Nor can we really address ourselves to cases of rank bad management. We are not able to solve the inadequacies of managers if that is the cause of problems. We are more interested in structural changes or methods of solving organisational problems or injustices through systems. That is what I want to explore; any positive

suggestions that you have been making that could improve institutions. Of course, we are talking about this issue of apparent conflicts very frequently between academic freedom and organisational necessity or whatever it might be.

The 1988 Act, as you are aware, defines the academic freedom that people in this sector should feel entitled to—freedom within the law to question and test received wisdom and to put forward new ideas and controversial and unpopular opinions without placing themselves in jeopardy of losing their jobs or privileges that they may have at their institutions.

You are really saying to us that on the ground this is not working entirely satisfactorily. On the other hand, it has been put to us, perhaps cynically, that one definition of academic freedom in some people's minds is the right to be supplied with as much money as they think necessary for their purposes. What we are asking you to do is to give us your own vision of this tension between academic judgments and managerial decisions and some specific ideas of where you see the boundary lying or how it could be operated.

GILL EVANS: The hardest area to protect, either legislatively or in terms of the framework of good principles which you are trying to lay down, is the very subtle ways in which a person can be disadvantaged who has become known to be a questioner or, at least, an asker of awkward questions. What the Act provides for is fine as far as it goes but we all know how very subtly a person can be disadvantaged.

I do not know what the answers are about that but there is a lot more scope for the setting out of much more detailed ground rules which it ought to be possible to make those in senior positions require to know and to operate on. The natural justice issue has already been raised by previous speakers. Again and again we find someone in a senior position doing damage to someone else's life and career out of what is clearly ignorance of the rules of natural justice and then it is impossible to call that person to account because the structures do not allow it. It would seem a fairly simple thing to do a spot of required education for people in senior positions. There is a bit of scope for tidying up in that area. That is one thing I would say.

1318. CLIFFORD BOULTON: We are looking for specific ways of dealing with these things. Could this be tackled by greater induction training, to use that rather horrible expression, for people who are in these positions of boards of governors with clearer rules. You actually call at one point for clarification of the differences between these academic judgments and managerial decisions. How do you see them being clarified? Standing orders or rules which are operated by the officers of the council?

MICHAEL COHEN (Secretary, Council for Academic Freedom and Academic Standards): It is very difficult. There are two slightly different issues here. One is an issue of what one might call day to day problems that arise. Very often academics feel that very large decisions are being made about how things are to be done in their institution without proper consultation.

It was very instructive listening to some of the evidence given earlier this morning and I noticed that when one of the speakers was asked about accountability he spoke in terms of audit. It seems to me that part, at least, of what accountability ought to mean is that those taking decisions ought to listen to those on the ground who are actually having to implement them. I am thinking, for example, and I do not want to comment on the rights or wrongs of the specific issue, but the introduction of modularisation in my own institution which many people on the ground are not at all happy about and feel it is something which has been imposed from above.

One of the things that is needed in universities is an approach in which more people are involved in decision-making than at present. At the moment there are a great many people who feel that they simply do not have any serious part to play in important decisions like that.

There was the other issue where things actually get to the point where people are dissatisfied about something that is being done and this is becoming all too common a pattern, where somebody makes a complaint and institutions simply are not capable of dealing with it. They will not deal with it. They will not take it seriously and the person involved finds themselves on the wrong end of disciplinary charges.

GILL EVANS: I wonder if we have quite answered your question because you wanted, clearly, to focus on the difference between a managerial and an academic judgment decision. I would say that where there is a conflict there it is likely to be in terms of the tension between such constraints as the financial and being seen to have a healthy output of firsts, if possible, and those considerations which people in a culture of scholarship might wish to put forward as being productive of rather intangible benefits, at least in the short term, but importantly protective of, if you like, the future of Western civilisation.

That has much less edge—it has much less cutting edge—if you want to put that forward against a person in a professional, especially a professional, managerial position who will say that is all very well but we have to pay the bills.

1319. CLIFFORD BOULTON: We have annual estimates, and all the rest of it?

GILL EVANS: Yes, quite so.

1320. CLIFFORD BOULTON: I am afraid we are rather now on two fronts but can I just follow up what Mr Cohen was saying and then we can come back to this business. Again, without talking about lack of consultation in your own institution, managers are free to consult now as much as they like, or people in authority can consult and if they do not it might just be what I was talking about earlier. Are you saying the situation is so bad and the extent to which junior members, or junior teaching staff and so forth, are being kept out of formulation of decisions is so general that something institutional ought to happen. There ought to be some rules which require formally much more consultation to happen. Is that what you would like to see?

MICHAEL COHEN: Consultation would prevent at least some of the problems that are coming into our ken on a regular basis which is what I said was the second aspect of this, that people were dissatisfied. I can give you

examples of the kind of case. Our own case was such a case where people make complaints about the standards and practices on a course and the institution simply fails to deal with it and tries to discipline them.

I could give several similar examples of that kind of thing, where people are, for example, put under such pressure that they take early retirement or are made redundant but have to sign gagging clauses in order to get their redundancy money. That has happened too often now for it to be purely accidental. It grows out of a general atmosphere in which those lower down the hierarchy are simply ignored so if they say something they are going to be stamped on.

1321. CLIFFORD BOULTON: Yes, marked as awkward squad. Talking now about the strains that can grow up between the people providing the finance and the academic perspective. You say that the present assessment system for deciding how much money universities will get has been running long enough for its deficiencies to be apparent. What is wrong with it?

GILL EVANS: A great many things in terms of its distorting effect. The degree to which people whom it surprises one to learn it of will now ask themselves first the question—"Can I get this out by 31st March 1996?"—and only secondly the question—"Have I finished this book?".

The old traditional driving force which, after all, has to keep someone going from the age of 21 when he or she first graduates and begins research to, in most cases, well beyond retirement. Most academics go on writing books indefinitely. That driving force of passionate interest has to come from within and if an attempt is made to judge it from outside by criteria which are unavoidably crude and have these short-term effects, that in some cases actually prevented people embarking on very long-term pieces of work. Even people who have that internal drive are being affected visibly by this.

1322. CLIFFORD BOULTON: You have a few problems about the British Academy being a source of funding for research. What is your answer to that?

GILL EVANS: That, of course, is part of a much larger question to do with the apportionment of funds for various subject areas of which that is only one.

1323. CLIFFORD BOULTON: What would you replace them with as a system?

GILL EVANS: We need what one could loosely call core funding, something which is much less up for grabs every few years, so that there can be commitments to very long-term projects. In other words, part of the answer has to do with the placing of sums of money in a context where they can be relied upon for a while.

The other area has to do with the selection of the persons who disburse it and, for various complex reasons, that has been slightly cobbled together, particularly in the humanities. It is very much a trial run at the moment and I would like to see it looked at after running for a year or two to see what the drawbacks are.

To take an example: the present state of play is that persons who are not in full-time employment in a UK university and who are beyond the age of 35 will find it very difficult to get funding from the Leverhulme people or from the British Academy because, amongst the options, they fall between stools. In that category of people is a huge number of very able academics, scholars with serious and important pieces of work on hand, who have not been able to get jobs because there have not been any in the sector very much. We are wasting intellectual and human resources here by not rethinking the grounding of that kind of funding.

1324. CLIFFORD BOULTON: At the end of the last witnesses we raised the question of a visitor system and ombudsmen. You back both those horses. Would you like to say why you think it is necessary to have both and what respective fields you consider them to have?

MICHAEL COHEN: My own view, and perhaps I should say this is my own view, I am very much in favour of a visitorial system. The advantages of it seem to me—and this is partly because of my own personal experience with it in two cases—its informality is one thing and it does seem to me that, with respect to lawyers on the committee, it is sometimes possible to establish what has happened, it is sometimes easier to do that in an informal way than in a court of law and, given that one has established what has happened, easier to work out what you are going to do to resolve it.

What the visitor pronounces is binding. There is no appeal against what the visitor says. One can, of course, seek judicial review in certain circumstances but one cannot appeal it and these seem to me to be good reasons for supporting a visitorial system but whatever system we have it seems to me that there is need for something. Institutions themselves are all too often quite ignorant of very fundamental principles governing the way in which disciplinary matters should be handled and if they cannot be brought to see how to do it themselves, and as long as that situation continues, then there must be a long-stop, there must be some external body which is capable of righting the wrongs which are all too common.

GILL EVANS: I think we would both feel that whatever is provided ought to be provided evenly across the system because at the moment we have an untidy provision of visitors here and no visitors there. Whether it takes the form of a revised visitorial system or an ombudsman is not very important except that if it remains a visitorial system it is important to have another look at the law because of the recent restriction on the powers of a visitor.

The positive proposal we would both want to put in here is that it would be useful to begin to build up a body of expertise in the handling of these cases because visitors are, in fact, very rarely called on and we have run into difficulties in even getting to them, that is on the part of the junior person who needs to appeal to them, because a university which has a visitor can, in practice, put a blockage in the way. Since the visitor is often the Queen or the Archbishop of Canterbury, or somebody of great seniority who clearly is not going to come himself and talk, there is a need to delegate the task anyway and we would like to see some positive effort to create a pool of people with a real knowledge of the sector and the relevant legal expertise who can build up a bit of relevant practical expertise in this area.

1325. CLIFFORD BOULTON: I think there might well be room for some sort of co-ordination and wider

understanding because a witness yesterday rather implied that to him a visitor was someone who was far away of whom he knew little, who just turned up occasionally to give out some honorary degrees, or something like that. Clearly, the attitude to visitors is not uniform but you are not making a separate job for the visitor and an ombudsman really, you just want the matter to be co-ordinated.

GILL EVANS: I think we are at the beginning of our researches—when I say "we" I mean the whole sector—in terms of sitting down and thinking hard about what is needed here and out of such an investigation the answer to the question—"Do we need more visitors or do we need an ombudsman?"—might very naturally emerge.

LORD NOLAN: Or something of the same sort?

GILL EVANS: Some equivalent, yes.

1326. LORD NOLAN: For example, a panel of senior lawyers and academics any one of whom might have the relevant expertise and resources?

GILL EVANS: Yes, that would do the job. What we need is two things, a pool of relevant expertise and the power to enforce a solution in the end.

1327. CLIFFORD BOULTON: You want the ability to discipline senior academic staff to the point where they can be dismissed. You are going to have problems there over academic freedom, are you not, I suppose, in introducing a system of senior figures being accountable, from the Vice-Chancellor downwards, to some sort of a body?

GILL EVANS: You mean because it is a reality of life, and especially of public life, that the more senior you are the harder it is to shift you unless you have actually embezzled a great deal of money?

1328. CLIFFORD BOULTON: No. The disciplinary force would be being exercised for something from outside the body. I think you quite like the system of Oxford and Cambridge where you say that the safety valves are much more real and that relatively junior people can, in fact, get a decent amount of support and can get something taken right up to the top. It just happens that those are self-governing institutions without any lay members, close to this academic ideal of academics governing themselves. This is not going to be a practical affair if you are talking about disciplining Vice-Chancellors in provincial universities is it? You are going to have to bring some people from outside into the process there of disciplining, are you not?

GILL EVANS: Yes, and that actually touches importantly on the question that arose with your last witnesses of the degree to which it would be helpful or proper for the internal disciplinary procedures to overflow into the public arena. One would run at once into the question of enforceability of statute against internal procedures, would one not?

CLIFFORD BOULTON: Yes.

GILL EVANS: That, in fact, has interestingly been showing up problems in relation to the implementation of the 1988 Act because, of course, the regulations the commissioners drew up are binding on the old universities but not on the new. Even in the old ones they have not always been honoured to the letter when it comes to it and we find again and again that going to the public courts, even where a statute has clearly been broken, is not easy. Again, I would not presume to speak to the lawyers on the Committee about this, but there are clearly technical issues of great interest and importance here, are there not, about the boundary between those two arenas?

1329. CLIFFORD BOULTON: You also talked about the diffidence that judges would have in pitting their opinion against an academic judgment on someone's own subject and the enormous freedom that the courts would be inclined to give them in that respect.

GILL EVANS: I think our feeling about the matters on which it would be proper for a vice-chancellor or a chief executive to be brought to task in this way, and this perhaps reflects our direct experience, is that the damaging of human lives which is going on in some institutions and which, of course, carries with it all these questions about academic freedom, where we would like people to be, in practice, accountable is where they are distorting careers and damaging lives and it is impossible to do anything about it.

1330. CLIFFORD BOULTON: So, you are going for the lesser of two evils in conflicts?

GILL EVANS: Yes.

CLIFFORD BOULTON: This is a fascinating area because it is so close to what we have been talking about all the time in higher education but perhaps I could be fair and offer some opportunities to colleagues.

1331. PROF ANTHONY KING: I am tempted to entertain my colleagues with horror stories about the oddities of university funding. One of them they may not be familiar with is the now existence of a transfer market so that if I am bought off by another university just before the closing date for research assessment the entire volume of my research output over the previous period goes with me to the new university, as though a football player transferred to another team took all his goals with him from the previous five years. That is only the most obvious of a number of examples of dottiness that I could entertain you with.

Having failed to resist the temptation myself, can I invite you to resist the temptation to run together, which to some extent you were, questions of management, of funding, of good sense in these areas, with what we have to focus on much more tightly which is standards in public life, malfeasance, malpractice, misconduct, and so on. Partly because your written submissions were so extensive, one of the things I found I could not quite focus on was what you think, under that heading, the principal problems are that a body like ours ought to address itself to. Where are the worries? I mean, could you codify them for us?

GILL EVANS: Are you focusing here primarily on the upper echelons of governance questions?

1332. PROF ANTHONY KING: No, I want to know what you want to focus on, what you think we ought to focus on?

GILL EVANS: One of things we wanted to say is that we would like very much to encourage you to look as seriously at the issues of improper use of human and intellectual resources as you have been doing, and were doing, in your previous report—at those areas of finance and very much senior management because the talk about boards of governors over against chief executives takes us to a level of the stratosphere above that at which the problems we are seeing in the lives of ordinary people working in those situations.

1333. PROF ANTHONY KING: I may not have expressed myself clearly enough. I am not clear what these problems are, what are the difficulties that you think might fall under the heading of raising questions about standards in public life. In other words, could you illustrate the kind of things when ideally one would like to hear you say, well, there are three kinds of problems that we run up against in our work frequently, one, two, three. I find I am dealing—if I can put it this way—with a kind of porridge of different issues and I cannot quite separate them out.

MICHAEL COHEN: A pattern has emerged and probably the sort of person who has contacted us most often is the person who has made a complaint about the academic standards or the academic practices on a course which they either know about or are directly involved with and they have found it impossible to get their institution to take seriously. There are various different outcomes to that sort of thing.

We were contacted once by a man who told us that he was in a science department and that a post-graduate student was getting some results using some apparatus which were unbelievable. They were just not plausible and to test his hypothesis that the results were faked he disconnected the apparatus and the results kept on coming in as good as before. When he went to his head of department and pointed this out he was told to keep quiet about it, that the issue was one of "bums on seats", as they say in the theatre, and that he was not to rock the boat. This man contacted us but he asked us not to do anything about it. He said it was more than his job was worth. We cannot do anything in circumstances like that.

1334. PROF ANTHONY KING: So, one of your categories, number one, is the frustrated whistle-blower?

MICHAEL COHEN: Yes, yes.

1335. PROF ANTHONY KING: OK. Can you give us two or three others?

MICHAEL COHEN: Not to go into our own case again, that was such a case, but again I was contacted by someone who was complaining about certain practices involved in a course that she was involved in which she felt were unethical. She told her employer about them. She was made redundant and since she had been employed for less than two years at the institution she had no statutory protection. She was made redundant but, in order to pick up her redundancy money, she had to sign a gagging clause, a clause which said she would never discuss the issue anywhere ever again, in public or in private.

1336. PROF ANTHONY KING: So, in your view, the illegitimate use of gagging clauses is another issue?

MICHAEL COHEN: That is a common feature. I noticed one of the witnesses spoke in terms of severance agreements which protect the information which is of value to the institution. That is rather a slippery sounding phrase. What concerns us is the suppression—I think I had better use that word—the suppression of information which is of disvalue to the institution, that is which they would sooner nobody know about.

1337. PROF ANTHONY KING: Do you want to add a third or fourth? You see what I am trying to get in my mind is a map of the kind of things.

GILL EVANS: Yes. One of the reasons why it has been difficult for us to give you a map, especially in this very short span of time, is that these issues are so intimately inter-connected and they, in fact, form a mesh but, as you say, we must pick out things.

I would add the climate of fear question which is affecting not only those relatively junior academics who wish to raise questions and, as Mr Cohen has said, come to us, tell us all about it, often ask if we will act and then cannot quite bring themselves to have the courage in the end to let us do so. Also, the climate of fear which is causing their seniors not to investigate and this is a fear both of consequences to the institution in terms of loss of funding, loss of reputation; in many cases fear of damage to their own personal reputations, which is a slightly separate question from their being bringable to account in terms of possible dismissal in the future.

My feeling about the spirit of your Committee is that you very much want a loosening up, an opening up, in public life so that a lot more healthy debate is possible, where the shutters come down much later on in the process of airing things, than they routinely do at the moment.

PROF ANTHONY KING: Have I time for another couple of questions?

LORD NOLAN: Yes, indeed.

1338. PROF ANTHONY KING: You will shut me up when I have outstayed my welcome. Could I ask you rather specifically about a sentence in one of the documents you submitted that, in fact, Gill Evans touched on earlier on. You say that the visitor system is inadequate and you then give two reasons for its inadequacy. The first is because of new legal restrictions on the powers of a visitor. Could you explain to a confirmed non-lawyer what that refers to?

GILL EVANS: That is the new formulation in the 1988 Act which means that it is employment issues, is it not, that the visitor cannot touch. Of course, it is precisely in areas which in some sense are employment issues that most of our people end up having problems, though that may not be how it begins. This is a legal point. There is a great deal in the 1988 Act it would be a good thing to look at again and that is one of the points.

1339. PROF ANTHONY KING: The second reason you say the visitor system—I think I heard you say "visitorial" a moment ago; I have never heard that word before—is inadequate is as a result of restrictions placed by certain institutions on access to their visitors. Could you again explain?

GILL EVANS: Let me give you an example case there. One lecturer in an old university found himself in danger

of dismissal at the end of a process where what he had done, in fact, was to refuse to obey the orders of his head of department. The discipline issue as presented to him was simply that he had failed to obey orders. That is a very dangerous thing in its own right in the academic arena. In due course, he wished to appeal to the visitor and the university told him that he could not do so until certain preliminary stages had been gone through by the university and, in the meantime, while this was hanging fire, it proceeded with further stages of the process against him.

In that case, we intervened with the visitor directly, with his consent, and, first, got a reply in terms of the visitor—of course, this was through his lawyers—his concern about the jurisdiction he had in that situation. It was a genuine concern. It was quite unclear what his jurisdiction was, not as a visitor but in the context of that particular situation. Because one of us happened to know that visitor personally it was possible to ring him up and say, "Look, just lift the phone and have a word with the Vice-Chancellor. Tell him just to let this go for the moment while we sort out the tangle further down the line" and, as far as we know, that is exactly what happened.

A situation in which, to get the creaking joints to operate you have to be able to lift the phone, you have to know the man, is not satisfactory.

1340. PROF ANTHONY KING: Could I finally just ask you a favour. I do not think it is misdescribing the material you have sent us to say that it is long on instances of real or imagined abuse but rather short on what you would actually like us to do about it. If you think there should be a revamped visitor system or an ombudsman, or whatever, my colleagues and I would find it useful if you would tell us in very specific terms what is it that you would see as the ideal rather than inviting a group of ten people, only one of whom is a somewhat bemused academic who has not had much experience of these matters, to figure out what it is that we ought to do.

GILL EVANS: Clearly, one has to give a rather brief answer.

PROF ANTHONY KING: Not here and now, no.

GILL EVANS: I was going to say we can do this on paper for you and, certainly, we would be very glad to do that. If I might just say one thing here and now it is this. In our experience, only a proportion of those senior people who have caused this damage to individual lives or got into a muddle have been at the outset persons of illwill. It has much more often been a matter of muddle and muddle after which, for the sake of saving face, it becomes very difficult for the man to reconstruct things.

There is an educational task to do, as I think has already been said, and one which has both to be done person to person in actually training the chaps and also could be done partly by the publication of really very detailed guidelines which could constitute a handbook to which people could refer when they are trying to implement a grievance or a disciplinary procedure which, in the nature of things, they will very rarely have to do.

I was talking to one vice-chancellor yesterday describing to him some of our cases in an outline form and his immediate response was that it would take so long in the internal processes of his institution before he even heard about what was going on here that by the time it got to him it would be very difficult for him to salvage it. Now, were there to exist such a handbook there would be helpful and preventative remedies there.

1341. LORD NOLAN: Thank you very much indeed for that. Following up very briefly Professor King's request, which you are going to consider, I wonder if I could mention one of your comments which struck me in which you said, "No individual officer with a clear, formal responsibility for ensuring propriety seems to exist in universities with which CAFAS has had dealings unless one counts the Vice-Chancellor."

Of course, one counts the Vice-Chancellor but in many organisations one finds a specific compliance officer. Now, in the House of Commons we have a Commissioner for Standards. Was that the sort of thing you had in mind?

GILL EVANS: I think that would be rather useful.

LORD NOLAN: Possibly you would like to consider that a little further?

GILL EVANS: Yes, yes.

1342. LORD NOLAN: Thank you very much indeed both of you. It has been most helpful.

Now we meet Sir John Allen and I have down both Mr Adam Peat and Mr Peter Lawler.

SIR JOHN ALLEN AND ADAM PEAT

SIR JOHN ALLEN (Chairman, Housing for Wales): Chairman, Mr Adam Peat and I will deal with any questions.

1343. LORD NOLAN: Fine. May I begin, please, by thanking you for coming and asking you were there any introductory remarks you thought you would like to make before we come to the questions?

JOHN ALLEN: We have put in an introductory statement which we hope will be helpful and other than to say that we are very pleased to have the opportunity to be here to answer any questions, it will be better to deal with any matters in discussion.

1344. LORD NOLAN: I am much obliged. Your introductory statement, I assure you, will form part of the records and so we can take that as read although naturally we shall be referring to matters raised in it in the course of our questions. I would like though, if I may, to begin by quoting from something that you tell us about in the introduction to your submission, paragraph 1.2: "The Committee may wish to know that Housing for Wales was the subject of a National Audit Office study in 1994. The National Audit Office concluded that Housing for Wales had generally performed well since their inception in April 1989. They have met or exceeded most of the medium and short-term development programme targets set for them by the Welsh Office, adopted a comprehensive approach to monitoring associations, exercised tight control of associations' development programmes and taken initiatives aimed at achieve better value for money in procurement."

That makes good reading. Some people rather tend to treat this Committee as almost synonymous with the pursuit of sleaze and, in fact, as you know, we are looking at all sides of the picture and are very happy to find, and report to the public—which is part of our job—on the good things that happen in this country and why they happen and how they can be extended and made to happen always and in all places, if that is not too much of an idealistic aim.

Now, having started on that basis, you are an organisation, quite plainly, that we can look to for experience from a high level of the administration of housing associations in Wales. You may be able to tell us this. A number of people have said that the movement in Wales, and for that matter in Scotland, is different in many ways from housing association movements in England. Would you agree and tell us why that is so?

JOHN ALLEN: Certainly, in the question of scale to start off with, we are a very much smaller movement in Wales. We have in total some 100 housing associations and only 30 of them participate in the development programme. Geographically, it is a smaller area to cover and it means that Mr Peat and I can visit, and do regularly visit, all of the principal players in the movement and they are known to us so that there is a dialogue that goes on which is very helpful.

The housing associations themselves are smaller than the housing associations in England and we have deliberately encouraged this. They tend to be close to the communities that they serve and this has worked to the benefit of them. A lot of the individual problems that face a housing association in England are obviously the same as in Wales but it is the scale that is the principal difference between us.

1345. LORD NOLAN: Would I be right in saying that in Wales you have conformed much more closely to the traditional pattern according to which housing associations were first formed and have grown up?

JOHN ALLEN: I think so. One of the questions that was posed to us when we were first formed was how we faced up to the movement now that we had Housing for Wales responsible for Wales as an entity. One of the things we first decided was that we wanted all the housing associations that were going to be funded through us within the development programmes to be registered in Wales and that they should have their registered offices in Wales and that their management committees should have 75% of their members domiciled in the areas. We have also taken care to zone the housing associations in Wales into the areas they serve so that there is choice available in the different local authority areas, but, at the same time, the associations generally can concentrate on areas where they have local knowledge as well as skill.

1346. LORD NOLAN: Yes. This interests us very much because, as you and I know from personal conversations, the Committee has found in England in many areas very large and growing housing associations, associations of a size comparable with those of a large property investment company, with their houses scattered over different counties, sometimes widely different areas; in some areas taking over completely the housing stock of local authorities and thus becoming effectively, though not as a matter of strict statute law, responsible for enabling the local authority to discharge its statutory responsibilities.

Of course, all these things have not just happened by accident. There are principles and planning behind them. Do I take it from what you are saying that you see no advantage in pressing for larger and growing housing associations?

JOHN ALLEN: No. We find actually that the efficiency or the performance of housing associations is nothing to do with size. We have some very effective smaller associations and we have some very effective and efficient larger associations with good management. It has nothing to do with size and we tend to really look at them in the amount of programme they need to spend in the areas they serve.

Some of our areas are the urban areas of the big cities, like Cardiff, Swansea and Newport, others are in the rural areas of Wales, some of which are very sparsely populated, and then you have the valley communities which, again, are very high levels of population and present special problems in their own right. Would you like to add anything?

ADAM PEAT (Chief Executive, Housing for Wales): Yes, if I could just add to that, Chairman. When you said that in our experience efficiency and performance has nothing to do with size, that is true once an association has got beyond having about 500 units in management. You have some associations that are very small indeed, perhaps only having one scheme, one property in management. They can function very well on a purely voluntary basis with perhaps staff at the front end actually managing as warden or caretaker. Once you get to the point of needing paid administrative staff then you need to get some sort of minimum take-off point which probably is about 500 units in management before it is cost effective to have full-time staff.

Beyond that, it has certainly been our experience that a good "little 'un" at 500 units can be just as cost effective and deliver just as good a service to its customers as a very much bigger association.

1348. LORD NOLAN: Yes. It is clear from what you are saying that you know your associations very well. You visit them all. I think I saw somewhere that the maximum period between visits would be something like four years but much more frequent visits would occur in the case of associations which were developing.

JOHN ALLEN: They would have an audit visit every two and a half years but Adam and I would visit them all at least once a year and sit in——

LORD NOLAN: The developing associations?

JOHN ALLEN: The developing associations—on one of their management committees. Various members of staff have an ongoing interface with them in the various aspects of performance audit and, of course, we receive quarterly management accounts from them which enables us to keep fairly well informed on what is happening.

1349. LORD NOLAN: I was interested to note that you get the management accounts. Can you tell us, are there any signs of possible trouble that you can tell from those accounts? Are there typical signs that make you raise an eyebrow and say, "We'd better have a look at this"?

JOHN ALLEN: Yes. They are an absolutely wonderful way of getting an early warning system.

1350. LORD NOLAN: Is it simply a question of the amount of debt being taken on in comparison with the assets, the terms on which the debt is taken on? Is that the kind of thing in which you would take a close interest?

ADAM PEAT: That is one of the things, Chairman, but generally my performance audit staff are analysing, and they always analyse, the management accounts very promptly after we receive them to see if there is any worsening of trends. If, for example, you had seen that an association had been projecting a surplus and, indeed, making a surplus in previous accounts and suddenly the projected trend is moving sharply downwards then you would say, "What is happening? What is going wrong?". It is often just a question of picking up a telephone and having a discussion and reassuring oneself that there is a rational explanation. Of course, if there is not a rational explanation, or a satisfactory explanation, we would probe further.

1351. LORD NOLAN: Yes. I wonder if I could come on now to the guidance you give to associations about the manner in which they should recruit committee members and over their relations with those to whom they are responsible. I see in the introduction to the paper which you very helpfully sent us, paragraph 4 says: "Performance standards are aimed not only at housing associations' committee members and staff but are also intended to inform tenants, local authorities, funding institutions and the public at large of the conditions under which associations are required to operate."

If I may say so, this is all precisely in line with what you understand to be one of our main concerns, which is to inform the public who, to a large extent, are relatively uninformed about the way public money is spent by the bodies we are looking at, including housing associations. Then you go on, rather in the same vein when it comes to composition of the committee, with the heading: "The association should have a suitably skilled and broadly based committee of management which is free from undue influence by any other body and specifically should ensure its composition contains an appropriate balance of skills and is committed to the communities it serves. It should make use of co-optees where appropriate; ensure that sub-committees contain appropriate skills; ensure that all committee members devote sufficient time to the association's business and make an efficient contribution; ensure that committee members receive adequate preparation for and support in their roles; review regularly its composition to ensure the current membership reflects the needs of the association and be aware of the need to bring in new members from time to time; determine the maximum consecutive terms in office for chairmen."

This guidance is, in its present collected form, fairly new, I take it? When did it come out?

ADAM PEAT: It is, indeed, fairly new but it follows on from earlier performance standards and is not new in substance. We have been saying things along these lines to associations from very early on in our existence but, after a process of feedback, this is a substantial redrafting to clarify and to extend certain of the points that we found in practice were a little bit unclear. One major extension in this from our previous guidance was to give guidance to committees about the kind of relationship they should have with their chief executive and what they should be expecting of their chief executive because we found that in practice that was a fairly common source of difficulty.

LORD NOLAN: Yes. So, as you explain, it is in the nature of what in legal terms would be a consolidating or a codifying act, bringing together what might have been, up until then, the sort of common law, the actual practice, the best practice observed.

ADAM PEAT: We did actually have a document called, *"Performance Standards"* before. This is now the third edition of *"Performance Standards"*. We have always, from the outset, seen it as important to try and say very clearly to associations within the compass of a single document what it was that we thought they should be aiming to do and the standards they should be trying to achieve.

1352. LORD NOLAN: Yes. Can you tell us a bit more about how links with bodies in the community, and in particular with the local authorities, exist?

JOHN ALLEN: We view as very important what we term as a tripartite arrangement to really produce social housing in Wales. The local authorities are undoubtedly the largest landlord of social housing. They would have probably something like 80% of the total social housing stock and the housing associations about 20%. We are in a position at the moment where we are, through our funding, the providers of new housing but it is very necessary in the usage of social housing that the interests of both parties, in particular, be taken into account and the housing associations' views be taken into account as a deliverer of that programme.

We endeavour to visit, and have done for a number of years, each of the local authorities in Wales. With the unitary authorities there are slightly less than the 37 that we used to go round, and we endeavour to have strategic agreements with a number of them and did enter into formal agreements with about a third of them. We have set out the strategy and objectives that we would try to meet in the developing programmes. These have been very successful and we are now endeavouring, as the new local authorities come into being, to set up a whole series of consultations. We listen very carefully to the views of the local authorities in the preparation of our strategic plan, as we do to the housing associations.

We meet the housing associations in a number of ways. We have a Chairmen's Conference once a year when all the chairmen of the developing associations come and we have a full and frank exchange of views. Then, at various other levels, Adam and his executive team meet the various executive members of the associations. There is a dialogue going on pretty well the whole of the time.

1353. LORD NOLAN: The problem, as we have heard from many associations—I think it would be fair to say more often the larger ones—is how to communicate with local people outside their own tenants' organisations. Do you find the local press helpful on these occasions? Do you have regular links with the local newspapers and getting articles into them?

JOHN ALLEN: Yes. Would you like to deal with that one?

ADAM PEAT: One of the things that we ask of housing associations is that at least once a year they should

hold a public meeting and try and get as wide a cross section of people along as possible. They often will combine that with a formal annual general meeting. A number of our larger associations that actually operate in more than one local authority area have recently started trying to ensure that they hold a series of meetings so that they will have at least one meeting in each centre of population that they serve. That is one way of getting the message across. They try to ensure that they invite their tenants and lay on the necessary facilities, buses and so on, to enable people to get there but also a wider cross section of people from the local authority and others who are interested in their work.

JOHN ALLEN: We have also published a number of pamphlets actually, starting with *"What is a Housing Association"* and *"What is Housing for Wales"*. These are distributed through various sources, through Citizens Advice Bureaux, through housing offices, through building societies and we have a series of these which help to tell people a little bit more about the movement. Of course, quite a number of housing associations themselves now advertise for voluntary committee members when they are looking for members, for people who would like to be considered for membership. All of this helps to widen the knowledge of the movement.

1354. LORD NOLAN: One of the things we found right across our inquiry can fairly be generalised by saying the better the job you are doing, the less public interest it attracts. You can take a lot of trouble to organise a public meeting and if everything has gone well in the past year you get five people turning up. Conversely, if something has gone wrong then there is considerable interest in it.

I was interested to see in the one case where you have had a Section 28 report you published it, though in somewhat bowdlerised form on legal advice?

JOHN ALLEN: Yes.

1355. LORD NOLAN: Was that a difficult decision to make?

JOHN ALLEN: No. The Board always wishes to have openness and to publish as much information about what we are doing and what we are trying to achieve as possible. In this particular case, it was fair to say that whilst we had to take legal advice on what we could or could not say, we felt that the matter was of such importance that it should be brought as far into the public arena as was possible.

ADAM PEAT: If I might add to that, chairman. Firstly, it was clearly a matter of wide public concern that a respected association had got into difficulties and the general public was owed an explanation as to how this could have come about. Secondly, we felt specifically that there were various useful lessons and dire warnings that were directly relevant to other housing associations and they could best take those lessons on board by having access to an authoritative account by an independent inquiry team as to what exactly had gone wrong.

1356. LORD NOLAN: While, of course, we reach no conclusions about this or any other aspect of the matter, we have received strong evidence supporting the line you took as a matter of general policy unless there is some specific reason for non-disclosure. Although, as we all know, housing associations to a large extent are now being encouraged to finance themselves other than from public money, there is, of course still, a very large public interest, both financial and in the service that housing associations provide for the community. You took the view in this instance that openness was the criterion to follow.

You have, I think, favoured a strict line on a number of matters, one of which is the Section 15 requirements. You are supporters of Section 15 as it stands, I take it?

JOHN ALLEN: No, actually. Like all these things, we reviewed them and towards the middle end of last year the Board looked at the Section 15 requirements to see if there was any need for any amendment to be made. We came to certain conclusions which we put out for consultation with the Federation and subsequently submitted certain amendments for approval to the Secretary to State. Adam, would you like to report on the latest position?

ADAM PEAT: The Board made a determination, as it can do under the Housing Act 1988, to bring about certain relaxations of the Section 15 requirements. That determination had to go to the Welsh Office for confirmation but we have very recently had that confirmation and will be issuing the determination. It will, for example, cover a specific matter which the Welsh Federation of Housing Associations mentioned to you—namely, the ability of an association to offer housing to a relative of a committee member which can, of course, be of particular importance in the life of that association and that community if a large number of tenants are in membership and a number of them are actually members of the committee. It would be unfortunate if people felt that they could not go on to the committee because they were thereby debarring themselves, or their relatives, from any chance of being offered improved housing.

1357. LORD NOLAN: I am very interested. I said what I did because in your letter of 12 January you say: "It has been suggested from time to time that the Section 15 regime is unduly restrictive. We disagree".

ADAM PEAT: Yes, that very much is broadly our line. We would not want to see Section 15 done away with. Over the years it has been a very valuable safeguard for the probity of the movement and its reputation but there is no question about it, in particular circumstances its unmitigated application straight out of the Act can be rather harsh or unreasonable and that is why it was welcomed that the 1988 Act gave us a facility to make some relaxations in its applications. What we are saying is that given we have that ability, then we very much support the continuance of Section 15 and would not want to see Section 15 abolished.

JOHN ALLEN: At the root of what we are agreeing, it is not that we just relax the whole of Section 15 in certain areas, on certain aspects—as the case that has been mentioned—they could make an application to us for approval to relax them in that case so there is still a procedure where a watching brief is kept very much on any relaxation to it.

1358. LORD NOLAN: I was actually going to put to you the very point you have anticipated yourself in what you have told us today. We have felt that although there appears to be very wide support for the principle of a strict rule, like the Section 15 rule, there are cases in which it appears to operate with quite unjustifiable hardship and in a way which could reasonably discourage good people from wanting to serve on committees. Would you be kind enough to let us know what your latest written material is on that?

ADAM PEAT: Yes, we will let your secretary have a copy of the determination as we issue it.

1359. LORD NOLAN: The last thing I wanted to mention to you is—I will not call it a chestnut but it is a matter with which, of course, we have become very familiar in our inquiry. It is the question of payment for committee members. You would be against having fully salaried members on the lines of National Health Service Boards?

JOHN ALLEN: I think so. I have the greatest admiration for the voluntary members of the movement in Wales. Their commitment is a vital part of the housing association movement. It creates the whole ethos in which they operate. It is a matter that has occasionally been discussed. To my knowledge, it has been raised as a peripheral item twice at a chairmens' meeting and on each occasion it was very, very heavily voted down—not voted but dismissed. People came out saying that they felt themselves that it was something that they would not wish to happen in Wales and it would affect the movement as a whole. As far as we can see, that is still the prevailing position.

1360. LORD NOLAN: As far as I could summarise, I would have thought the evidence we have received on the whole has said—expenses, yes, reasonable expenses; in some cases, an allowance for loss of earnings, a flat rate allowance on the lines of jury members' allowances not an actual recompense for the highly disparate earnings that are, in fact, given up by people—not even that, no actual pay, you just get your expenses at the most or salaried members.

The final matter, I suppose, which one should bear in mind is this: ought boards to have the right autonomously to decide, within the reason of finances that can be made available, which of these lines they wish to pursue, or do you think it is better to have an uniform rule across the organisation?

JOHN ALLEN: I would have thought it would be better to have a uniform rule across the organisation. I am talking right off the top of my head at the moment but I would feel instinctively that if you are not careful you would introduce a competition between people on various boards and that would be regrettable. At the moment people go on to the management committees for entirely other reasons and they are not competing between one committee and another.

The structure of the management committee of an association has had to change very much over the past six or seven years, particularly as private funding has come in. The responsibilities of a committee member have increased and the sort of areas of financial management that they need to take to them have increased so, therefore, the mix of the management committee has changed and we have been delighted with the fact that so many people who have the necessary professional expertise have come into the management committees of the associations to support those who have this great social awareness and social drive to make a contribution to the work of the community.

1361. LORD NOLAN: It has been made clear to us by a number of people that it is a source of great pride to members of the boards of associations, and indeed to this country, that this is still a voluntary activity. You would rather see no breakdown of the corporate unity over that matter, such as giving discretion to individual boards? You would rather have the same rule for everyone?

ADAM PEAT: We would certainly not want to see discretion given to individual boards to pay committee members. We would be quite happy to see discretion given to committees to pay a very modest level of expenses so that one did not deter perhaps, in particular, tenants of associations from being able to take part in the deliberations of the committee because the cost to them of so doing was one that they could not bear. Certainly, the present voluntary nature of committees in Wales has, in our experience, not disabled them from finding the skills and the expertise that they need and while that commitment is available on a voluntary basis it would be a great shame to lose it.

In many ways, as a personal view, to make it possible for associations to pay salaries to committee members might be something of a signal that the voluntary commitment was not valued.

LORD NOLAN: Thank you very much. That was very clear. I am going to ask Sir Clifford Boulton to take over now.

1362. CLIFFORD BOULTON: We received stacks of letters from the tenants of English housing associations and from board members for that matter. We received hardly any from Wales and, following Lord Nolan's hint, you are perhaps entitled to draw comfort from that fact.

There was one particular point that was put to us in a letter from a board member and I am sure you will be familiar with the point. He says his concern arises from the practice used in one or two housing associations in Wales of remunerating senior staff in part on a profit-related basis. "Since senior officers must, as part of their responsibilities, recommend policies in relation to rent levels, methods of filling voids in levels of service to tenants, there is the possibility of a conflict of interest between the derivation of profit and the obligation within the social housing framework to tenants."

He thinks the pay-for-profit link is not only an unhealthy arrangement but also, in the public sector, unethical. Do you have any comment on that point of view?

ADAM PEAT: Yes, we have. This is a point that the board member concerned has raised with us before and we have looked at it. We are satisfied, in the circumstances of the particular case, that the scheme is one that is approved by the Inland Revenue; it is a perfectly proper scheme from that point of view and it is done for that reason. It is actually enabling extra remuneration to go to the pockets of the staff of the association concerned at no cost to the association. It is essentially a scheme that is designed to take advantage of the rules that the Inland Revenue has offered.

We were satisfied on the detail that there was no improper incentive to staff to counsel rent increases that would not otherwise be justifiable. If the Committee would be interested we could certainly let you have a more detailed note on that case.

1363. CLIFFORD BOULTON: There is some credibility to the suggestion that performance related pay is all very well but there can be some areas where you should not be seeking to generate performance. I bounce that on you. If you would like to send me a written answer, I would be grateful.

ADAM PEAT: Certainly.

1364. CLIFFORD BOULTON: Thank you very much. Can I just ask you a little bit about how the complaints procedure works. As a lead-in, you have a policy that there should be informative tenants' handbooks available to all tenants. Are those handbooks universally available, does every tenant have a handbook?

ADAM PEAT: Yes, that is certainly the intention and, as far as I am aware, it is indeed the case. It is certainly something that when our performance audit team visits an association looking at their housing management practice they would certainly look to see that there was not only a tenant's handbook in existence but the thing was reasonably comprehensive, up-to-date and written in language that people can understand.

1365. CLIFFORD BOULTON: Would that include how to complain?

ADAM PEAT: Yes, it would. We have very specifically sought to ensure that all associations have recently made their tenants aware of a complaints procedure that exists. We have asked, as a standard feature, that the complaints procedure shall include a right for the tenant to appeal if not satisfied with the handling of his complaint in the first instance to the committee of management of the association and also, to make it absolutely clear to tenants, that if they are still not satisfied that their complaint has been fairly treated they can ultimately come to us and ask us, as the regulatory body, to investigate. Indeed, a number of complaints do reach us and we do investigate them.

1366. CLIFFORD BOULTON: Yes. I see that you welcome the proposal that there should be an ombudsman in Wales, as there is in England. Could you just give me a little more detail about the use that is made of the complaints procedure? Is it an anxiety, the volume of complaints, or is it exactly the sort of thing that one would expect, a tolerable level?

ADAM PEAT: No, I do not think that we deal with an overwhelming flood of complaints and in all probability the fact that the number of complaints reaching us has increased as it has over the past couple of years is more a function of the fact that we have ensured that wider publicity is given to people of their ability to complain, rather than tenants of associations have suddenly become more dissatisfied.

Nonetheless, we would welcome now the setting up of an ombudsman service in Wales. An ombudsman is a concept that is very well understood and perhaps would be yet more clearly understood by tenants as being a separate figure who would investigate absolutely impartially. Tenants may perhaps not always feel that we are, as it were, equidistant between them and the association in investigating a complaint.

1367. CLIFFORD BOULTON: Yes. What are most of the complaints about, the quality of management, the fact that repairs are not done, or something like that, or are they very wide ranging?

ADAM PEAT: They are fairly wide-ranging but most of them relate to issues of housing management, either a complaint about repairs or a complaint about a failure to give sufficient weight to the tenant's views in some matter which might either be a neighbour dispute or a desire to transfer properties. Nothing has come up to us out of the complaints that we see and that we analyse as being something that overwhelmingly needs to be addressed and put right.

Where we have investigated an individual complaint and found that it was justified, we always ask the association concerned to consider whether this was a one-off incident or whether there are wider lessons that need to be learned.

1368. CLIFFORD BOULTON: Can I just ask you lastly about how well the registers of interests are being maintained. Do you keep an eye on that? You have a policy of registers of interests for board members, do you not?

ADAM PEAT: Yes, we do. Again, one of the audit visits that an association will receive focuses specifically on what we call committee control and, as part of that, we look at the proceedings of the committee to see whether they are regularly and properly documented and,

certainly, one of the things that we always look to see is that the register of interests is being properly maintained and kept up to date and not just gathering dust in a corner.

1369. CLIFFORD BOULTON: Do you get a lot of complaints from people who have to register their interests, new members; do they find it oppressive that they have to do that?

ADAM PEAT: I cannot recall that we have ever had a complaint on that score, no. People who serve on committees fully understand the need for this and it has never been a source of complaint to us.

CLIFFORD BOULTON: Good, because we do come across areas where people say, "I"m not going to do this voluntary service and be required to reveal my private life to all and sundry", but you have it working in a way that is accepted and recognised as sensible. Thank you very much.

LORD NOLAN: Thank you very much, gentlemen. That brings to an end these sessions of oral evidence in Wales for our study of local public spending bodies. It has been a short but concentrated visit. We have gained a great deal of valuable information, both in our formal and in our less formal discussions. Welsh witnesses have all been frank, very thoughtful, very helpful and we have covered some extremely important issues. We also much appreciate the warm welcome we have received in Wales. I hope in turn that we shall be able to make recommendations which will be regarded as helpful to the institutions and to the people of Wales and not simply as another bureaucratic burden. We shall do our best. Thank you.

THURSDAY 25 JANUARY 1996

OPENING STATEMENTS

Opening statement: North East Wales Institute of Higher Education

This statement addresses the previous written responses submitted by the Principal/Chief Executive of the Institute and the Chairman of the Board of Governors. It identifies a number of developments which have taken place since the responses were drafted. The statement also seeks, as outlined in Martin Le Jeune's letter of 19th December 1995, to address some of the issues which may be explored in the meeting with the Committee. For ease of cross reference with the previous written responses, the same paragraphing numbers are used in this statement.

Paragraph 4: As a consequence of the process for renewing the Board of Governors and filling vacancies from 1 April 1996, the Institute has received 14 applications arising from the placement of advertisements and writing to selected organisations. The majority of these applicants have stature within the local community and possess the necessary levels of professional experience. The fact that the position of governor carries no remuneration does not seem to have been a problem in attracting suitable persons. It is probably fair to assume, however, that questions relating to governor liability are more likely to be raised in informal discussions with applicants prior to selection and given the ambiguity surrounding legal interpretation, the Institute will be floundering to give a coherent response.

The implementation of a "process for ensuring the vice-chair assumes the chair" regulated by a maximum period of tenure is now likely to be revisited. New members, joining the Board in April, would be unable to effectively participate in the selection of these positions. They would not necessarily know their colleagues already on the Board, yet in terms of their own credentials they could be worthy candidates for the post of chair or vice-chair. Therefore, it is likely that the Board may move to identify one of its meetings within an academic session as an AGM where statutory and procedural business is taken, eg. acceptance of the end of year accounts; the appointment of auditors; appointment/re-appointment of chair and vice-chair, and sub-committee chairs. Occupancy of the chair would be given a ceiling, say of three years.

Paragraph 5: The Audit Committee have agreed to develop a proforma for recording the interests of members of the Board. The principle of declaring interests, together with proposals on process and implementation will be discussed at a meeting of the Board in the near future.

In addition, the Board of Governors has adopted the recommendation of the Audit Committee to co-opt an independent financial expert to support the work of the sub-committee.The role of internal and external auditors including the Welsh Funding Council Audit Service is vital in giving the Board advice and assurance that both the Institute's financial systems and management structure are effective.

Paragraphs 6 and 7: Underlying reasons for conflict between governing bodies and the permanent staff emanate from the tendency for staff to view the role of staff governors as representational. Where disputes arise, staff will attempt to avoid procedural routes via line management and instead will communicate directly with the chair or lobby members of the governing body. This appears to reflect what used to happen under the old regime where staff were employees of the County Council and would approach members directly in relation to any disputes. Staff are also uncomfortable with the dominance of independent governors on governing bodies who, in their view, seem not to understand academe. This may also relate to a reluctance on the part of academic staff to accept the need for "business practice".

Paragraph 10: There is potential contradiction between public accountability and the apparent increasing drive for higher education institutions to operate more commercially to compensate for reductions in core funding. The PFI initiative, for example, encourages governing bodies to borrow money and enter into significant long term debt without quite knowing the financial implications and certainly without being able to anticipate the implications of swings in future government policy. There are tensions attendant in straddling two worlds; that of the public sector where there is some degree (albeit diminishing) of safety netting in terms of guaranteed income, and the world of business where entrepreneurship and even financial risk management can reap rewards and retribution. Business imperatives do not sit comfortably with open governance, particularly in a market which is becoming increasingly competitive. Accountability to funding bodies (be they public sector or private) must work both ways. The central regulation of higher education institutions, which is becoming ever more onerous, could be construed to be interference and as the percentage of income derived from the public purse declines, that regulation may become increasingly out of step with the aspirations of managers and governors for the development of their institution.

Introduction statement by Housing for Wales

Could I first of all thank you for giving us the opportunity to appear before the Committee. We are submitting this opening statement to amplify and elaborate our evidence submitted last October.

Housing for Wales in a non departmental public body (NDPB) set up under the Housing Act 1988 to fund and regulate the activities of registered housing associations in Wales, with functions and powers equivalent to those of the Housing Corporation. The Board of Housing for Wales has between six and eight members appointed by the Secretary of State. The Chief Executive is also a member ex officio.

The defining characteristics of the Welsh housing association movement are that associations are relatively small (by English standards) and have a defined local area of operation.

100 housing associations are registered with Housing for Wales of which around 30 are regularly in receipt of public money and have professional staff. These are usually referred to as the "developing associations". The other 70 would typically be very small with perhaps one scheme or house. Many of them are almshouses or Abbeyfield associations. Only five developing associations own in excess of 3,000 houses; the majority own between 500 and 2,000 homes. The scale of the housing association movement in Wales makes it possible for the Chairman and the Board of Housing for Wales, as well as senior officers, to be familiar with many of the voluntary Committee members, as well as senior personnel in the movement. The Chairman, accompanied by the Chief Executive or other senior officers, seeks to visit the Committee of Management of each developing association every year. Further, Housing for Wales hosts a conference for Chairmen of associations each year.

Housing for Wales has established a regulatory regime that consists of formal audit visits and submission of financial and statistical information. This naturally focuses more heavily on the developing associations, since they are continually in receipt of substantial sums of public money. Every two years, each developing housing association will receive three audit visits, one from a housing services team (which would cover issues of access to housing, housing management and maintenance); one from a financial and management control team (which would cover issues of governance and financial management); and one from a technical team (which would look at compliance with Housing for Wales' Technical Standards and Capital Grant Procedures).

The extent of the audit visit would vary depending upon the associations' assessed performance. Associations who are good performers would receive correspondingly shorter visits of a narrower scope, whereas associations performing less well would receive more extensive visits. The visits would assess the associations performance against Housing for Wales' published Performance Standards for developing associations. These Performance Standards were developed after a very wide consultation and have been approved by the Secretary of State for Wales as statutory guidance under Section 49 of The Housing Act 1988. Less onerous Performance Standards apply to non developing associations; typically a non developing association would receive a single visit, covering all aspects of its operation, every three or four years.

In addition to the formal audit visit, associations are also required to submit the following documentation to Housing for Wales as part of the regulatory process:

a) statutory audited accounts;

b) quarterly management accounts (developing associations only);

c) annual performance indicators covering a range of housing management and maintenance issues (developing associations only at present);

d) an annual return giving details of their governing body.

The purpose of the regulatory system is to provide as early as possible warning of potential problems in order that these can be tackled before they become serious.

The Committee specifically sought our views on the following matters:

1. **Appointment and accountability of Board members of housing associations**

    Our Performance Standards require associations to have a "suitably skilled and broadly based Committee of Management which is free from undue influence by any other body". Housing for Wales has not been prescriptive about how Welsh housing associations should achieve this. However, a number of associations have advertised for Committee members and have recruited numbers of competent and committed Committee members from this route. Housing for Wales has on occasion encouraged individual associations to recruit particular specialist skills and has from time to time assisted associations in the identification of particular individuals.

    Housing for Wales strongly supports the ethos of the voluntary Committee member and opposes the idea of remunerating Committee members beyond re-imbursement of expenses and perhaps modest allowances for loss of earnings. It has been suggested that this introduction of an allowance for loss of earnings equivalent to that applicable to jury service might be appropriate, and we would not be opposed to this. It has not been our experience that the voluntary nature of Committees has inhibited them from recruiting competent members.

2. **Tenant Participation**

    Housing for Wales is committed to the principles of tenant participation, namely ensuring that associations are accessible to their tenants, that they provide tenants with good information; take account of tenants views and encourage tenants involvement in the association's affairs. Through our Performance Standards we have ensured that associations have a public open meeting annually (this is usually the annual general meeting), that they have produced informative tenants handbooks and have actively sought tenants' views on the quality of the service provided.

3. **The Role of the Chief Executive in relation to the Committee**

    Housing for Wales believes there is a need for associationsto specify clearly the role and responsibilities of the Chief Executive, and we have given guidance on this in Performance Standards. We have no strong views as to whether the constitution of associations should permit the Chief Executive to be a member of the Committee of Management. The Chief Executive has a duty to serve the Committee of Management whether or not he is a member, and if he loses the confidence of the Committee of Management he has to go.

4. **Safeguards in respect of conflicts of interest**

Stringent statutory safeguards with regard to conflicts of interest and benefits are set out in The Housing Association Act 1985, Section 15. It has been suggested from time to time that this regime is unduly restrictive. We disagree. The operation of the Section 15 regime does much to preserve the high reputation of housing associations for probity and disinterested service. Difficult cases do of course occasionally arise, but the Housing Act 1988 allows Housing for Wales to make a determination permitting such class or classes of payments or benefits as are deemed appropriate. Housing for Wales has done this from time to time with appropriate safeguards.

5. **Section 28 Inquiries**

The Housing Association Act 1985, Section 28, enablesHousing for Wales to institute an inquiry into the affairs of a housing association to establish if there has been misconduct or mismanagement. Since its formation Housing for Wales has only commissioned one such Section 28 Inquiry, when Corlan Housing Association got into financial difficulties in 1990. Notwithstanding the lack of precedent for doing so, the Board of Housing for Wales firmly believedthat publication of the substance of the report was in the public interest.

However, the version published was a modified version from that received by the Board. This was based on legal advice that if the original report were published in full, Housing for Wales was at risk of defamation proceedings.

Should a Section 28 inquiry be necessary in future, Housing for Wales would again wish to publish the report of its findings, unless there were compelling legal reasons not to do so.

6. **Complaints about Registered Housing Associations**

Housing for Wales has ensured that all of the housing associations have complaints procedures and in the case of developing associations we have audited the operation of this procedure, and where appropriate made recommendationsas to how these could be enhanced.

The current situation is that there is not a housing association ombudsman in Wales. When complaints have exhausted the associations' own complaints procedures, complaints are dealt with by Housing for Wales, with the right ultimately of appeal to the Board of Housing for Wales. The governments' White Paper, "Our Future Homes" now proposes the introduction of a housing association ombudsman for Wales and Housing for Wales welcomes this development.

7. **Funding and Regulatory Matters in One Body**

Housing for Wales is of the view that there is a definite added value in having both funding and regulation in one body. This is because we are able to use the granting of further funding as leverage to ensure that recommendations that come from audit are effectively implemented. Our statutory power of inquiry is clearly cumbersome and is only appropriate for use in extreme situations. Nor is our ability to use statutory power to appoint additional committee members one which we should use over frequently. By making our recommendations the condition of future funding, we are very clearly able to get associations to raise their standards to meet our Performance Standards. Conversely, were the funding and regulatory functions to be separated, it is likely that associations would be exposed to increased bureaucracy, since the funding body or bodies would be unlikely to be content to fund associations without themselves seeking to be assured that associations were performing satisfactorily and were fit recipients of public funding. This would inevitably duplicate to some extent the work of a regulatory body.

TUESDAY 30 JANUARY 1996

MORNING SESSION

Members Present:

The Rt Hon Lord Nolan (Chairman)

Sir Clifford Boulton GCB

The Rt Hon Lord Thomson
of Monifieth KT DL

Dame Anne Warburton DCVO CMG

Diana Warwick

Witnesses:

Ray Baker, Chairman, Michael Webster, Vice-Chairman, and John Sellars, Secretary, Association of Scottish Colleges

Donald MacPhail, Vice-Chairman, Dr David Kennedy, Principal and Vice-Chancellor, and Gavin Ross, Vice-Principal, Robert Gordon University

Professor Sir Stewart Sutherland, Principal, Dr Martin Lowe, Secretary, and David Smith, Convenor of Finance and General Purposes Committee and Member of the Court, University of Edinburgh

Anthony Schmitz, Chairman, Rae Angus, Principal and Chief Executive, and Roderick Scott, Secretary, Aberdeen College

Councillor Rosemary McKenna, President, and Douglas Sinclair, Secretary-General, Convention of Scottish Local Authorities

1370. LORD NOLAN: It gives me great pleasure to open our first session of oral evidence in Scotland. The very tight time constraints on our first study compelled us to have all our hearings in London, and although that did not prevent us from drawing on evidence from Scotland and Wales, we were anxious to travel beyond London on this study, especially since it is very much concerned with bodies whose activities are of interest to local communities and which are subject to separate governance arrangements in Scotland.

Our hearings are in many ways more in the nature of informed discussions in public rather than inquisitions. Inevitably we have to take our oral evidence from active participants in the institutions which we are studying, so that we can test on them their reactions to issues that have been raised and propositions which we are considering. But we attach great importance in this Committee to proceeding as openly as possible, to making the public aware of what we are doing and to trying to draw in the widest possible range of views and opinions. So I very much hope that any members of the public who are prompted to offer views as a result of these hearings will not hesitate to write to me as soon as possible.

Of our ten Committee members, seven will be with us at various times during the hearings today and tomorrow. Our two Members of Parliament are unable to be present because the House is sitting, and Sir Martin Jacomb has had to make his apologies because of business commitments.

We have five sets of witnesses this morning, mainly, but not exclusively, concerned with higher and further education. We welcome first Mr Ray Baker, the Chairman, Mr Michael Webster, the Vice-Chairman, and Mr John Sellars, the Secretary, of the Association of Scottish Colleges.

They will be followed by Mr Ian Souter, the Chairman, Dr David Kennedy, the Principal and Vice-Chancellor, and Gavin Ross, the Vice-Principal, of Robert Gordon

University at Aberdeen. In the context of the study Robert Gordon constitutes a new university, because it was established in 1992. All universities established before 1992 count as old universities.

Our third set of witnesses come, therefore, from a very old university. We shall be hearing from Professor Sir Stewart Sutherland, the Principal, and Mr Martin Lowe, the Secretary, of the University of Edinburgh. One of the more minor differences between the system in Scotland and those in force in England and Wales is that the term "Principal" is in common use in Scotland for what would normally be called a Vice-Chancellor in England.

Our fourth set of witnesses is Mr Anthony Schmitz, the Chairman, Mr Rae Angus, the Principal and Chief Executive, and Mr Roderick Scott, the Secretary, of Aberdeen College, which is a college of further education.

Finally this morning, we shall be hearing from Councillor Rosemary McKenna, the President, Mr Peter Peacock, the Vice-President, and Mr Douglas Sinclair, the Secretary General, of the Convention of Scottish Local Authorities. We trust that they will range fairly widely over the relationship between local authorities and the various bodies which we are looking at.

With that introduction may I again extend a warm welcome to our first witnesses in Edinburgh and our thanks to you for the time you are giving this morning and the time and trouble you have taken in presenting us, with great care, with written advice about your activities.

You were formed, I think, as an association in July 1995, which makes you about eight months younger than this Committee and an equally lively infant to judge from all the work you have been doing since then. I wonder if you could please tell us, Chairman, a little more about how you came together, how you are organised as an association and what your role is in further education in Scotland.

RAY BAKER, MICHAEL WEBSTER, AND JOHN SELLARS

RAY BAKER (Chairman, Association of Scottish Colleges): Thank you, Lord Nolan, for the opportunity. We will be very much, we hope, the voice of FE in Scotland. Prior to last July a number of disparate bodies spoke for the FE sector in Scotland, and we got together and decided, through a steering group, that it would be a good idea if we could form one association of all the colleges in Scotland, and we did that. As you know, there are 43 incorporated and three which are still with local authority, but they are all members. We have not yet actually had a meeting with all the colleges—that is due next month—so our answers to some of your questions may be a bit difficult and we will give you a personal view of the way we think things will go. As I say, the raison d'être for the organisation is to be, we hope, the voice for FE in Scotland, which was rather fragmented in the past.

1371. LORD NOLAN: Unlike the English position, and indeed unlike the position in Scottish higher education, the further education colleges are funded and regulated directly from the Foreign Office—sorry, the Scottish Office.

RAY BAKER: Yes, devolution and all that.

1372. LORD NOLAN: Do you know why this model was adopted?

RAY BAKER: I think it is the interim, as we move forward from the association that all the colleges have had with the Scottish Office. That has worked extremely well and they have participated fully with the Scottish Office in the funding formula, but perhaps John Sellars, our company secretary, could give a little more background to where we are at the moment.

JOHN SELLARS (Secretary, Association of Scottish Colleges): Thank you. Clearly, Lord Nolan, legislation was coming quickly on board in 1992–93 or 1991–92. The legislation does include the ability for Scotland to have a Funding Council—it is already in the legislation—but there was considerable debate at that time about whether it should be set up immediately or not, and I recall, as we look in *Hansard*, that one or two of the key players at that stage put forward the view that possibly it was a bit early, because of the all the other changes, the fact that they were inheriting colleges with different funding backgrounds and so on, and that there should perhaps be a cautious approach in Scotland. During the parliamentary debate they considered in particular a letter from the Association of Principals in Scotland at that time—the APC Scotland—which is now part of our organisation, which at that time supported the view that there should not be an immediate move towards a Funding Council. So it was all speed for the Higher Education Funding Council and I think the debate is now open on where we go to for the next stage.

We have, over the last two or three years, moved very quickly through change into incorporation, with the full support and collaboration of our colleagues in the Scottish Office. The funding formula is there. We now have to take stock and review how the money is distributed to the colleges, whether we have the right model, whether there should be changes, and from now on I think the debate is now open.

The other aspect of setting up a funding council is that, as we all know, the public sector is very tight on resources and one would have to look not only at the philosophical arguments but also at the cost grounds of where the money would come from. The Scottish Office are perhaps rather lean in their staffing.

1373. LORD NOLAN: As I understand their evidence, they look to your association to a considerable extent for help in offering guidance to colleges—would this be right?—as to some extent acting as a link between them and individual colleges.

JOHN SELLARS: Yes. As the chairman said, Lord Nolan, it is early days yet, but as we move through to the philosophy of relationships with the colleges on the one hand and the various agencies—the Scottish Office and so on—on the other, I think the Scottish Office Industry and Education department will be looking for some help in that.

1374. LORD NOLAN: Yes, and it is the Scottish Office that has the ultimate power to remove governors in the event of mismanagement. I think that power has not been exercised, has it? There has been no case in which there has ever been any consideration of the removal of a governor, but they have to that extent a regulatory power.

RAY BAKER: They have the power, but it certainly has not been necessary.

1375. LORD NOLAN: No. The main effect of the Higher and Further Education (Scotland) Act 1992 was, was it not, to move the colleges from local authority control to independence? What effect do you think this has had, if any, on standards of conduct, accountability, conflicts of interest?

RAY BAKER: I think it has worked extremely well in those areas and it has brought the responsibility that they had into sharper focus. Also I would like to think that we did not throw the baby out with the bath water, and we have maintained excellent relations with the local authorities, so that in fact has worked extremely well. In terms of conflicts of interest, different boards use different methods, but it is certainly widely accepted that papers go out in time, so that people can and do declare conflicts of interest, at particular board meetings. There are also registers now in all the colleges covering the individuals' interests, so that they know when certain items come up at boards that they do declare a conflict. To the best of my knowledge, that is working extremely well. It works well in my own college, and I think I am fortunate in that I am also involved, in public life in other ways, with health board, enterprise company, industry and so on, and it is good to see that there is now a standard that we can apply across these boards. That is working extremely well in my view, and the conflict of interest issue is one that I think we have rationalised, mainly.

1376. LORD NOLAN: I would like to explore that a little further with you. Before we leave the links with local authorities, is there a common system for ensuring that the link is maintained? Do you have guidelines for local authority representatives on boards?

RAY BAKER: As an organisation we do not at the moment, but certainly in the case of my own college we have local councillors on our board, so we have maintained those links. The Depute Chairman is in fact a councillor and former chairman of the education committee.

MICHAEL WEBSTER (Vice-Chairman, Association of Scottish Colleges): I was going to say that there is pressure on colleges to make sure that their communities are well represented in whatever form, because they will not survive if they do not. The colleges exist to serve their local communities and to provide further and, in some cases, higher education for their local communities. If they get that wrong, if they get the offering wrong or the quality wrong, they will suffer, and there is quite a pressure coming, if you like, from the market, whereas previously it came through elected members, to do that, and most boards will take cognisance of the need to make sure that local elected representatives have a place on the board and that the relationships with the new education authorities as they emerge, because local government is being reorganised, are maintained. My own college is certainly engaged in discussion with the new education authority to make sure those links are maintained, and strengthened in fact.

LORD NOLAN: I am sure that all the members of the Committee will find that a very encouraging answer. We have not found that in all areas of the three countries we have been looking at there is quite the same closeness of association and community of purpose.

RAY BAKER: I think that is one of the strengths in Scotland. We have not had the sort of problems that they had down south with incorporation, and the relationships are very much better.

JOHN SELLARS: I have two points, Lord Nolan. In terms of the legislation, in its college development planning process a college has a requirement to consult both with the local education authority—the local authority in which the college resides—and also with the local enterprise company. So there we have, hopefully, the ability to discuss educational links and industrial and commercial links on a regular basis. Many colleges are doing well on that; perhaps there could be some improvement in other areas.

1377. LORD NOLAN: Thank you. Now I turn back, if I may, to possible conflicts of interest and how you guard against them causing difficulties. Throughout this inquiry into each aspect of the various departments of public life that we have been looking at we have been very conscious, as you are, of the need to avoid over-regulation, particularly of bodies that are doing an extremely good job, and discouraging people who take a pride in their honesty as well as their efficiency, and of the danger of getting to a model which functions perfectly in terms of accountability, openness and all the rest of it, but is not actually very good at its job. There is always that balance to maintain, remembering that you are dealing with public money and that there must be safeguards over the way it is handled, and at the same time not over-regulating it so that people feel frustrated and rather humiliated by the regulations put on them. I was interested to see in your documents that you had a model register of members' interests—a guidance note—and of course all these are, aren't they, guidance rather than prescription? That is very full. It calls upon members, "to disclose relevant business interests in a manner which is open and transparent and demonstrates to the public that such interests have not influenced the Board's decision making process. The Register is open to public inspection. Board members are also invited to provide the same information, if known, in respect of close family members."

I was a little puzzled, because in the paper marked IV there was a rather more guarded reference in paragraph 5.5: "The Secretary will maintain a Register of Members" Interests which will be open for inspection by any member of the Board."

The public are not mentioned there. Similarly, under the heading of "Confidentiality": "agendas, minutes and other papers——are normally available for public inspection when they have been approved for publication by the Chairman."

If I may say so, one can understand both approaches, but which is the recommended approach—complete openness of the member's interests and his spouse's?

RAY BAKER: Certainly that is the approach that we as a board are taking, yes—complete openness. I think there is nervousness in some areas, because they have not perhaps been used to that sort of thing, but it is certainly, as I say, very helpful in a number of boards that I am involved in, where we now have a standard that we can work to. But openness is the key.

1378. LORD NOLAN: Yes, and you do not find—am I right?—serious objection to the disclosure of family interests, where relevant, as well.

RAY BAKER: We have not encountered that, no. No one has complained, to the best of my knowledge.

JOHN SELLARS: In terms of the ambiguity, Paper IV actually went out before paper III in chronological order, and Paper III is the one which goes towards complete openness. You did stress, Lord Nolan, the guidelines, and those have only been issued over the last three or four weeks, it is the timescale. Again, as you said, we do not want to go through regulated prescription, so these are guidance notes, so at this stage we are looking to colleges to respond positively in ways that suit their local circumstances, but, as the chairman says, one would want to see complete openness.

MICHAEL WEBSTER: Colleges will still be under the same pressures as local government used to be to protect individuals from publicity. There will be some information which is personally sensitive, where disciplinary cases, student appeals and all the rest of it are concerned, and those sorts of things would remain confidential. There can now, in the new position in which colleges are no longer within local government control, be situations in which colleges are considering investment decisions which are commercially sensitive in some way, and that too, for a period of time, would not be published, but eventually everything is open.

RAY BAKER: But, as I said earlier, our first meeting with all the colleges is next month, so we will be able to feed back views that we are getting this morning.

1379. LORD NOLAN: Yes. One point, I noticed with interest, was that the setting up of a remuneration committee was made a condition of grant in, I think, November of last year. Was there any particular impetus behind the singling out of remuneration committees? Had there been problems in that area or was it just thought a natural area for an especially cautious approach?

RAY BAKER: I think that at an earlier stage there were one or two comments in various areas that it was not sufficiently open, and we saw no problem with what was being suggested by the Scottish Office, so that is part of our recommendation.

JOHN SELLARS: Yes, indeed in this evolutionary approach, Lord Nolan, the annual report now has to identify clearly the total remuneration of the Chief Executive and Principal, so again we would move into that openness. Before it was not necessarily obligatory, but now it is there. Our former association did issue guidelines, and by and large those have worked very well in Scotland in terms of how they should set about assessing the top executives in the colleges. But this is just formalising, hopefully, a process which has been developing.

MICHAEL WEBSTER: This is actually more open than it used to be under local authority control. Such things were not public.

1380. LORD NOLAN: Yes. All over Scotland, England and Wales, as you will appreciate, the process is evolving, and evolving very rapidly. It has been doing so for some years, but the process is by no means over. We hope that, if the Committee can help at all, it will be to guide and offer information about how these matters are being tackled in different institutions in different parts of the country, and with what ideas and what success rates so far. I do not think our report will be the last word on this, but we hope it will be helpful, as we are being helped by hearing of your experience.

Do your members have the impression that they are being over-audited on the financial side? Do you hear that as a complaint?

RAY BAKER: I have not heard it as a complaint, but there is a nervousness that we may go that way.

MICHAEL WEBSTER: I have heard it as a complaint.

JOHN SELLARS: I think again, Lord Nolan, as you develop new systems, our colleagues in the Scottish Office in their regulation guidelines have perhaps been very zealous, naturally, and I think in time there will be perhaps more local autonomy, more flexibility, but you have to have the auditing and accounting systems in place. There is no question about that.

1381. LORD NOLAN: It, I suppose, also marches step by step with the development of a very money-conscious and commercial attitude on the part of the colleges, which is necessary, to the need to pay the bills and to take care over the commercial aspect of their activities, so one expects a high degree of auditing. The question that has been raised with us by some institutions is that there are some areas in which the auditing could be simplified and consolidated, with a smaller burden on the bodies being audited. But you say you have had some evidence to the same effect from your members.

MICHAEL WEBSTER: Yes. Anecdotally, in the year in which the college was incorporated we had internal audit, external audit, an accountant's visit sponsored by the Scottish Office as part of a pre-incorporation check and a visit from the National Audit Office. I do not know whether my college is regarded as particularly shady, but that was our experience. On the educational side we had

an HMI inspection and what is known in the trade as a blitz by Scotvec, where they check through the quality of the college curriculum offerings. We had a clean bill of health on all these counts, but that was quite a volume of audit and inspection for one college to bear in the space of a few months.

1382. LORD NOLAN: There is just one topic that I would like to put to you before handing over to Dame Anne Warburton, who also had some questions. As I understand your letter of 30 October in particular, a number of your members would at any rate wish you to consider and perhaps take up with the Scottish Office the question of some form of remuneration for loss of earnings. Is that right?

RAY BAKER: Yes. A number of boards have written to me on this issue. It is not one that we to date have pursued very vigorously, but there is a problem where people may be in partnership—self-employed and so on—where it is very unfair on that business, on their partners, if there is no remuneration. Also there does not appear to be any commonality between the quangos: some are paid and some are not. Health boards are.

1383. LORD NOLAN: It is very striking, isn't it, that the health boards are so different from the majority of the other bodies in that respect?

RAY BAKER: Yes.

LORD NOLAN: And some see it as a trend towards recognising the very great skills that are required and the very great responsibility that is undertaken.

RAY BAKER: Yes.

LORD NOLAN: I think we are probably going to hear from Robert Gordon University strong opposition, but we shall see.

RAY BAKER: I think there are My vice-chairman, I think, would challenge that.

MICHAEL WEBSTER: My own college would be opposed to paying board members in any way, except for major travel expenses. Boards vary in their approach to their style of governance, and my board takes the view that it should have a light touch and should be exercising strategic direction and not day-to-day management. There will be colleges in which chairs and other elected officers of boards take more of a hands-on approach. There is that variety within the sector, and I think there is probably a link between that and the demand for some form of recompense.

1384. LORD NOLAN: There is payment of proper expenses, which I think no one objects to. Otherwise, it is most unfair for people who have to come a long distance. There is the question whether, particularly with, as you mention, the self-employed, perhaps small businesses, there should be some allowance for loss of earnings, possibly on a limited scale, of the kind that is paid to jurors. Thank you for your views. You are still fairly open-minded about it, but you are looking further into it.

RAY BAKER: Yes. It would be the exception rather than the rule. If there is a clear distinction between executive and non-executive, then I do not think the problem arises, except in the instance we have mentioned. John, I believe you wanted to say something.

JOHN SELLARS: I was just going to confirm that I think it is important that in the early days of further education incorporation we have to try to ensure that the board of management and its office bearers look to the strategic aspects and allow the office bearers—the principal and the executive of the college—to enact those strategic decisions. Payment possibly could result in the chairman saying "I must spend more time with the college", and therefore you get the confusion, as the chairman said, between the executive and the non-executive role.

LORD NOLAN: Yes, quite.

JOHN SELLARS: The other aspect is that in Scotland we can only pay loss of earnings up to a maximum of £40 per day, because those are regulations from the Secretary of State, and that is not very much in this day and age.

LORD NOLAN: Thank you very much. I am now going to hand over to Dame Anne Warburton. I hardly dare mention, in the context of my previous slip of the tongue, that she has had a distinguished career with the Foreign Office, but we are under no instructions, any of us, from that quarter and her experience in education, particularly in higher education, is very considerable. Anne, would you like to carry on?

1385. ANNE WARBURTON: There is not much time left, but could I ask one short question and then come to a broader one? In Wales we found some apprehension, not very widespread, about liability of members of boards and whether they were properly covered if anything did go wrong. Is that a concern here?

RAY BAKER: In the early days of incorporation it was a great concern. That has all been resolved, and I am not aware of any problem from any college on that score.

MICHAEL WEBSTER: The general view seems to be that if a board acts in accordance with what is recognised as good financial practice, accords with the Financial Memorandum that the Scottish Office has signed with boards and does not go against advice from either the accounting officer or the Scottish Office, it would be very difficult for them to get into difficulty.

JOHN SELLARS: Most college boards have taken out insurance—governors' liability and officers' liability. I do not know whether that has ever had to be used.

1386. ANNE WARBURTON: So it is done by the college. There is no sort of government cover. Good. Thank you very much. I read the paper of 30 October and found a number of remarks to the effect that work is in progress or is about to start and then I read the later ones and found that a lot of work had been done. Do you still have other projects on the stocks which will be relevant in the next short period, in the way of guidance papers?

JOHN SELLARS: No, Dame Anne. The guidance that went out two or three weeks ago, which I think is the first stage, will perhaps be as far as we go, but depending upon the outcome of your report and the way we proceed

forwards, we will possibly have to take further steps, but we are working within the concept of guidelines and guidance, and that was the way we wanted to see it.

1387. ANNE WARBURTON: Something I am not quite clear about, as you have not yet had a meeting, is how well assured you are that what you have written down is acceptable. Do people write back and tell you "This is fine", or what?

RAY BAKER: Yes, there are regular bulletins to colleges and we get feedback from them.

MICHAEL WEBSTER: While we have not had a full and formal meeting, we have had meetings with most of the colleges on different bases, so I think we are reasonably well in touch with what people are thinking.

ANNE WARBURTON: And the feeling is very general that you go for best practice rather than for prescription.

RAY BAKER: Yes, absolutely.

1388. ANNE WARBURTON: One suggestion I saw somewhere was that perhaps the Scottish Office might monitor performance, particularly with our famous principles. I like to call them "famous principles", and you have very encouragingly accepted them. Do you see a monitoring role at all from the Scottish Office and, if so, would it be linked with the provision of grants?

RAY BAKER: I would not have thought so, but I would not see any problem with it, frankly.

MICHAEL WEBSTER: The Scottish college system is fairly small and problems, whether our problems or others', are fairly apparent fairly quickly, so I would not have thought a heavy-handed approach would be appropriate.

ANNE WARBURTON: I am wondering whether to go on, but my eye has fallen on my watch and perhaps I had better stop there, because it is difficult not to carry on too far. Thank you very much.

LORD NOLAN: We are almost up to the hour. I do not know whether there was anything particular which other members of the Committee wished to put to you. No. The time constraints being what they are, we must resist the temptation. We have, as I hope you appreciate, carefully studied your written material and we shall be watching your progress, as you will ours, with close interest. Thank you all very much for your time and trouble. It has been very helpful to us.

RAY BAKER: Thank you very much, Lord Nolan, for the opportunity.

1389. LORD NOLAN: Good morning, gentlemen, and welcome. Thank you very much for coming to see us. It is Mr Ian Souter, the Chairman, is it, and Dr David Kennedy, the Vice-Chancellor and Principal?

DONALD MACPHAIL, DR DAVID KENNEDY, AND GAVIN ROSS

DONALD MacPHAIL (Vice-Chairman, Robert Gordon University): May I make a correction, Lord Nolan?

LORD NOLAN: If you please.

DONALD MacPHAIL: I have come in place of Ian Souter. Ian Souter, unfortunately, due to business commitments had to go away and try and salvage 300 jobs as a liquidator. I do not think you would hold it against him if he decided that 300 jobs were more important than coming here at the present moment.

LORD NOLAN: Thank you very much. So we have the Vice-Chairman, and Gavin Ross, the Vice-Principal. We are very grateful for the material you have given us, which we have studied with close interest. We take it in turns on this Committee to ask the lead questions, and it is Sir Clifford Boulton's turn to start us off, so I shall ask him to begin.

1390. CLIFFORD BOULTON: Good morning, and thank you for the care you took in addressing the questions that we had raised and in giving us your response, which is very useful in asking you some questions when you come to see us. Could you first put on the record briefly the history and status of your university?

DR DAVID KENNEDY (Principal, Robert Gordon University): Yes. The university started 110 years ago as a private institution that grew out of the Aberdeen Mechanics Institute. Its funding was then taken over by the Scottish Office in 1903, and in 1992 it became a university. So that is very briefly something about the background.

1391. CLIFFORD BOULTON: Thank you very much. You gave us your views on the need for a balanced membership of a governing body. Could you indicate the composition of your own governing body In the categories that you like to see on such a body?

GAVIN ROSS (Vice-Principal, Robert Gordon University): The composition has changed of course. Up until 1989 there were a number of nominating bodies and they were generally able to provide a range of governors that reflected the purpose of the institution. Subsequent to 1989 we have a different composition, with core governors, who initially were nominated by the Secretary of State and then can nominate replacements, and a number of ex officio governors or governors who are specified, so there is now a different mix. We have 12, I think it is, core governors and a total membership of about 24, I think.

1392. CLIFFORD BOULTON: And is there, for instance, staff representation on the governing body?

GAVIN ROSS: Yes, there are three members of staff, two of whom are nominated and one elected.

1393. CLIFFORD BOULTON: I see. They choose one from amongst their own body to be on. They have a right to nominate.

GAVIN ROSS: Sorry, could I just correct that? There is one nominated by the Academic Council and there are two members of staff who are elected. One is elected by and from among the academic staff of the university and the second is elected by and from among the non-academic staff of the university.

CLIFFORD BOULTON: I see. That is an interesting example for us.

GAVIN ROSS: And of course the president of the Student Union is also a member, ex officio.

1394. CLIFFORD BOULTON: Indeed. Do you have any formalised way of what one might call an induction for new governors, explaining the role or in any way showing them the ropes, or is it a question of turning up and seeing how things are run?

DAVID KENNEDY: What has happened since 1989 is that there is an informal process whereby lay governors have been more or less given some background information about Scottish higher education, about the awards system and about the institution itself, but that has all been done in an informal way. It has been very difficult, because enormous changes have been made, and therefore no sooner have you prepared material than it is out of date. We have conferences of the governing body annually, and this is an opportunity for new governors to acquaint themselves both with one another at a personal level and also with the senior staff of the university, and usually the agenda covers issues that are very material to the well-being and the future of the university. What with the informal process and with the formal conferences, I think it would be true to say that new members very quickly learnt about the situation that the university is in.

1395. CLIFFORD BOULTON: And you have a Nominations Committee, which looks for candidates, so to speak.

DONALD MacPHAIL: The Nominations Committee has recently been set up. It basically is a chairman's committee which meets under a different head. We are in the process of formulating its remit in greater detail and the methodology that it should use, but it has been utilised. It comes from the ad hoc arrangements that we had before and it has now been used once or twice to find out new members for the board of governors, taking particular care to ascertain from other members of the board which areas we feel we would like to have representation on the board—for instance, the oil industry, which is such a great aspect of the commercial life of Aberdeen and Aberdeenshire.

1396. CLIFFORD BOULTON: Do you have any difficulty in attracting people to serve?

DONALD MacPHAIL: Not really, but there is always a difficulty of people and their priorities and trying to establish if they can give the time. There has been the odd occasion when we have found that people have given the commitment and have then found that they have been unable to meet the commitment. While for most governors board meetings take place three or four times a year, we also have a sub-committee structure which sometimes takes up a considerable period of time.

1397. CLIFFORD BOULTON: You have a very severe view about governors not doing, so to speak, any business in areas where they have an interest. You avoid conflicts of interest of your governors by effectively saying, as far as I could see, that their businesses are to be excluded from consideration, whereas I notice that another university which is going to come before us said: "Because of the need to attract people with commercial and business experience to the Boards, there is always the opportunity of contracts being awarded to companies with which Board Members are connected. If too many strictures were imposed on such members, Boards may well be deprived of their services which would be detrimental to the operation of such Boards."

You have not experienced any difficulty in that?

GAVIN ROSS: I think it is experience that leads us to this view. In the past there have been instances perhaps where governors have been involved, to a certain extent, with the business of the university, and this was a view that was articulated by the committee that was responding to your "Issues" paper, so it really brought it into focus, and this was the view the governors felt they should now articulate. It is not that there has been any difficulty, but it does seem, when you sit down and think about it, almost impossible to draw a half-way house line. I think it was the view of the governors who were considering in detail the "Issues" paper that it would be far better if this line was articulated rather more clearly. That is why we have put that in the response to you.

1398. CLIFFORD BOULTON: It is perhaps a little bit odd—perhaps it does not matter very much—that there should be different practices in such an important matter amongst higher education institutions. I gather that in fact the Funding Council is contemplating issuing some general guidance on such things. Do you think that might be a healthy thing, to have at least some general thoughts brought together from across the board on that subject?

GAVIN ROSS: It is always helpful to have considered views from authoritative bodies. I think it is an area where there should be simply no doubt. If you are not clear, then you down to ad hoc interpretation. I think the feeling was that this was unlikely to discourage people coming forward as members of the university and it would be much clearer for all concerned if this view was adopted.

1399. CLIFFORD BOULTON: And you also have, I think, a clear view about the payment of governing body members: you do not feel that is appropriate.

DONALD MacPHAIL: No, we do not feel it is appropriate. How much could you pay them? Particularly if you have somebody from the top of a very large oil company coming in, what do you pay them, and payment might not wish to be paid for that. But what we were trying to get at is that there is this line between the day-to-day management under the Principal and the broader view taken by the board of governors. I think the governors did not wish to get into running the college on a day-to-day basis and they felt that being salaried might impose some pressure on them to go and poke their nose in where at times it would be better if they stayed out.

DAVID KENNEDY: There is another argument that one can put forward. My institution serves industry and the community. If industrialists give their services free, they are getting something back in return anyway, so it is a mutual benefit. I think we have been very fortunate that up to now the people from the local industry and the local community have been very happy to come forward and serve. We have not found any difficulty in getting people from the various industries to come forward and serve on the board of governors.

1400. CLIFFORD BOULTON: They see it as a service rather than as a job, but there might be a temptation to slip into thinking of it as a job if it were remunerated.

DAVID KENNEDY: I think that, without exception, sir, they have taken it as a service.

1401. CLIFFORD BOULTON: You define the university as a self-governing, academic community. One Scottish academic has told us that universities today are more readily described as "managed institutions than as self-governing communities of scholars". This is a very general question, but how well do you think the balance is being maintained between the economic targets that are pressed upon you and academic ideals? Is there a tension there?

DONALD MacPHAIL: Yes. I think the universities find it very difficult at the present moment to do this balancing act between becoming figure manipulators in some ways and their core business, if you like, of teaching and learning. I think that we have to look at a wider overview of what is happening in the universities and, if targets are being set, the targets should be discussed before they are set. Quite often targets are coming down in which we have had no input whatsoever. It is extremely difficult for us then to understand how they have arrived at them. If they have arrived at them by a process of auditing, for instance, the utilisation of staff and how they are allocated to certain areas of work, fine, we could go along with that, but if it simply comes down to a sum of money—that is what is underlined there—and then it is reduced by a percentage year after year, it makes it extremely difficult for the university to understand what is happening and to take the necessary action. It causes tremendous tension between staff and the management side, and the Principal is at all times back on his heels defending something into which he has had probably no input whatsoever.

1402. CLIFFORD BOULTON: Is it producing strains on the standards that you are required to produce? Do you find the formulae that are used for deciding what your financing grants should be helpful? Are there strains there on the quality of the work that you are prepared to give further degrees to, or anything like that?

GAVIN ROSS: I think there are strains. I would like to draw the distinction between quality and standards. I think standards are maintained and I do not think that any responsible university would allow standards to be threatened: the line would be held. The quality of the experience of either being a student at an institution or indeed working at an institution is undoubtedly affected every time resources are not available to do what, in professional terms, you would deem to be the right or proper way to do something. So clearly, when the unit of resource has dropped to the extent that it has over the last 15 years—it is not a recent phenomenon—one has to do things differently and sometimes, not always, that affects quality. So, yes, there is that tension.

Getting back to your earlier point about being a self-governing, academic community, what we were trying to say there was that that is the ethos, and I think an appropriate ethos, of a university. It does not, however, contradict the notion of efficient management. We take a pride In our own university of managing with financial accomplishment, and our records show that.

1403. CLIFFORD BOULTON: Are you satisfied with the reassurance that is given by external examiners and external supervision of the quality of academic work? Could you tell us how that operates in Scotland?

GAVIN ROSS: Yes, external examiners have their part to play in the general quality system, if I could call it that, of the university. The Principal outlined a little bit of the history of the institution, and of course prior to 1992 we were a member of the CNAA, a much lamented body, I think, who spent 20-odd years developing quality control systems for their member institutions. That is the culture that we have come from recently and we have continued to abide by the fundamental principles that the CNAA adopted, namely that one's quality assurance systems would have a high degree of external involvement. All our courses are scrutinised and examined by external peers, both from academe and from the appropriate receiving industry or profession that the course is leading to, and they come at the invitation of the university now to scrutinise our course proposals. These panels we require to be chaired externally and they therefore advise Academic Council as to the appropriateness and standard of the proposal. We also have a system—again it is a voluntary university system, but it derives from the old CNAA practice—of quinquennial reviews of all our schools and departments, and the people undertaking that again are externals. That system has been in place and operating effectively in the university ever since we were accredited by the CNAA in 1988, so it is a quality system that we are used to and one that we happily invest in.

To that extent we feel that some of the more recent initiatives that have been brought into the higher education sector, namely and in particular, I think, quality assessment, are rather redundant and not as effective or credible as the processes that we already use. I think we would subscribe to the HEQC process of quality audit, because, after all, that is there to come and appraise how effective our systems are, and we see that as being an extremely useful exercise. We have just gone through it and I think we will learn a lot from it. It is a professional dialogue and it is very helpful. Quality assessment I think is rather naively founded and not altogether helpful, and indeed can be misleading.

1404. CLIFFORD BOULTON: Is there a specific example you could give of how it does mislead?

GAVIN ROSS: There are a number, and I would be in danger of giving you a lecture on quality assessment and its failings, but we have had one particularly upsetting example recently, which has led the governing body of the university to inform the Funding Council that we simply do not accept the outcome. The reason for that is the adoption of a rather mechanistic and thoughtless approach to the way that a conclusion was arrived at.

CLIFFORD BOULTON: They get stuck on their own method and the result just has to come out in a mechanical way.

GAVIN ROSS: Yes. I have a lot of sympathy with the people trying to make it operate. The problem is that the scheme is badly conceived.

1405. CLIFFORD BOULTON: Can I ask one more question before Lord Nolan invites colleagues to join in, and that is on the system of a Visitor who comes from outside with a remit to look into internal difficulties that have arisen and as the alternative or even something that could perhaps be run in tandem, having a kind of external ombudsman who would provide a general service for listening to complaints throughout the higher education

service. Do you have views about the usefulness of someone who can intervene in problems like that and sometimes provide a solution?

GAVIN ROSS: It is not something that we have adopted, but it is something that we might want to weigh up. Like everything else, there will be pros and cons, but obviously tensions rise and viewpoints are formed, and sometimes these can appear to be irreconcilable, especially when it is over a rather hurtful or emotional issue. Clearly, as a sector, we must be heading, sadly, into this, as the financial environment gets ever harsher. So issues can arise and, if it is an academic community, as we have said, stances can be taken and people can get too close to one point of view or another. It may be that a little bit of external wisdom and detached objectivity would help the institution. So it is something that I would certainly like to give further thought to within the context of our own university.

1406. CLIFFORD BOULTON: But you have not at the moment thought as far as a choice between a common ombudsman for the whole university sector and individual Visitors for each institution?

GAVIN ROSS: No, we have not given that any formal consideration.

CLIFFORD BOULTON: Thank you very much.

1407. DIANA WARWICK: I wonder if I could pursue that, but from the other end, if you like, and look at the question of internal whistle-blowing. It has been an issue that we have raised with most institutions, and I wondered whether there were any formal processes or systems within the university which people could take advantage of if they wished to be critical of what was going on.

DONALD MacPHAIL: Other than through the representation on the board of management and the board of governors, no.

DAVID KENNEDY: Obviously there are systems in place such as grievance procedures, so that if any individual member of staff has a grievance, there is a clear procedure that the person can follow and, failing satisfaction within the employed staff of the university, they can then appeal to the governing body, to lay governors. So formal systems of that kind are available and, as Mr MacPhail says, obviously through the representation on the governing body matters can and are raised at the level of the governing body.

1408. DIANA WARWICK: There have been very few real criticisms of the processes in universities, but in those where they have been criticised—I think particularly of Swansea—there was no real internal procedure, and it has been asserted to us that this is a fairly common omission in university processes. Is it something that has ever come to your attention as a problem or have there ever been problems within the university?

DAVID KENNEDY: I think some staff will perceive a problem. At the end of the day everything comes down, I suppose, to personalities and people and so on, so on occasions you do find that staff feel worried about using the formal procedures in case they are victimised. It is like saying that everybody has the freedom of speech, but not everybody wants to use that freedom of speech: they are afraid they will be intimidated. So although it is all right to say it is there, people may still be afraid to use it, and sadly that is true in the case of grievance procedures. But we are a relatively small institution, relationships are usually very good and, when there are people who feel aggrieved about something, it usually permeates out sideways anyway and, probably because of that, we have not had any major incident of the sort that perhaps you have in mind.

1409. DIANA WARWICK: Could I turn to another element that we have been exploring, and that is the whole question of openness of process? Could you say something about the way in which the decisions of your governing body are communicated and whether there are elements of business, for example, that are regarded as closed business?

DAVID KENNEDY: Yes, there are areas, clearly, that may need to be closed, when they are dealing with personal aspects of individuals. Clearly in any business there are bound to be things which must be confidential, because there are personal details about individuals' lives that they do not want to have made public and nor does anyone else, quite properly and not improperly. Clearly there are times also when the affairs of the governing body must be conducted in private. I can think of quite a number of incidents in my own rather lengthy experience in the public sector.

If I can take one particular example, there was a case where a senior member of staff was going to be disciplined, and it led to an industrial tribunal. The governors had to conduct their case in the industrial tribunal. At the governing body as a whole the representatives of the staff were anxious to know what the governors' case was, which clearly would have prejudiced it in the industrial tribunal. So a smaller body had to be empowered to deal with the case and see it through to its finality before the thing could be made public. So clearly there are areas where litigation may be involved, where one has to be very circumspect in what one makes public before the hearing. There are other issues which also can arise where it would be imprudent to make the things open and public.

For example, there are certain conflicts in which education is placed. On the one hand, we are told to go out, to earn money from full-cost commercial activities. If we are going out into the market place, which we are quite happy to do and we have done with some success, we cannot divulge everything that we know which has a commercial sensitivity, so the very fact of having to act with due commercial sensitivity in itself may preclude total openness of the sort which Lord Nolan's Committee recommends. I do not know of any firm that is willing to divulge all its secrets to rival firms.

1410. DIANA WARWICK: Do you think it is possible to define these, because one of the criticisms we have had, and it has varied between large numbers of institutions, is that in some institutions a very large degree of business is limited and in other institutions they are much more open. Is there a general understanding in your institution about the nature of the business that might be regarded as closed?

DAVID KENNEDY: I think most of the activities that are paid for from the public purse are totally and utterly open. There is no secrecy, as far as I am aware, in that

regard. I think that where the secrecy comes is where there is a possibility of litigation, where there are personal details of individuals that it would be improper to make public and, thirdly, where it does not involve the public purse but may have something to do with commercial sensitivity.

1411. DIANA WARWICK: And does the same general rule apply to any sub-committees that you set up within the institution?

DONALD MacPHAIL: Yes, they follow the same standing orders and they follow the same general rules and regulations.

1412. DIANA WARWICK: Fine. I realise that we are running out of time. I have an awful lot of questions here. Perhaps I can just ask you one question, because I think it is an interesting difference between new universities and old universities, and that is the very well established link with the local authority. Has that link been maintained through incorporation and could you say how you feel accountable to your local area, your local community?

DAVID KENNEDY: Unlike the English polytechnics, we were a Scottish Centre institution and as such since 1903 have been funded by the Scottish Office and not from the local authority, so there was not that funding link, or that controlling link, with the local authority that would apply to the polytechnics. As it happens, because of the strong sense of purpose of the university with both the community and local industry, we have involved ourselves very closely with all the local authorities—the regional authority, district councils and so on—and there are numerous ways in which we interact with them. I would have said the relationship was extremely good, to the point that in 1991, when we were not going to be made a university, the title was going to be denied us, quite unjustly in my view, it was because of the pressure of the local authorities and the local community that the Scottish Office was persuaded to change its mind.

1413. DIANA WARWICK: But do you see a line of accountability with the local community?

DAVID KENNEDY: Very strong indeed, and I think it is bound up with previous questions asked about whether governors were paid and about standards. We try to involve industry and people from the local community in everything we do, from the design of courses to the validation of courses to the operation of courses to the evaluation of courses to the assessment of students—the whole lot. We belong to the locality and we try to involve them in everything we do, and if we fail to do that, we are not fulfilling our purpose.

1414. DIANA WARWICK: Thank you. I know I have gone over my time. Can I just ask one last question very quickly? Sir Clifford raised the point about your quite hard and fast rules about conflicts of interest and people becoming associated with business and university. Did you lose any members of your governing body as a result of taking that strict rule?

DAVID KENNEDY: No.

DIANA WARWICK: You didn't? Fine.

1415. LORD THOMSON: Does it any way, do you feel, restrict your choice of future members of the board?

ALL: No.

1416. LORD NOLAN: Thank you very much indeed. You have added further weight to the views already pretty clearly expressed to us by our member Lord Thomson and, I may say, our Secretary Alan Riddell about how much England has to learn from education in Scotland, and we have learnt a lot in the last half-hour. Thank you.

Good morning, Sir Stewart and Dr Martin Lowe.

PROFESSOR SIR STEWART SUTHERLAND, DR MARTIN LOWE, AND DAVID SMITH

DR MARTIN LOWE (Secretary, University of Edinburgh): Good morning. We also have Mr David Smith, who is Convenor of our Finance and General Purposes Committee.

1417. LORD NOLAN: Good. Thank you very much, all of you, for joining us.

Thank you for the information you have already given us and the very substantial amount of detail which we have studied and which will of course form part of the record. I wonder, Sir Stewart, if it would be acceptable to you if we go straight into questions, unless there is anything else you wish to say by way of opening remarks.

PROFESSOR SIR STEWART SUTHERLAND (Principal, University of Edinburgh): No, our statement was effectively as we sent to you.

LORD NOLAN: Indeed, yes. Thank you very much. It has been very helpful to us in preparing our questions. I will ask Dame Anne Warburton to lead off, if I may.

1418. ANNE WARBURTON: Good morning. Your statement begins with our seven principles and you tell us that you are initiating a process of review to ensure that they are given full effect in the manner appropriate. Have you anything more to say about that at this point or is it too early?

STEWART SUTHERLAND: It is a little early. In fact at our next Court meeting we will be looking at some of the specific implications raised in your report, but we have had a review group looking at this, and one or two of the suggestions that you independently are making have been put into place over the last two years—for example, the creation of a Nominations Committee and of a body to review salaries of senior staff and so on. The next stage is the full discussion by the University Court of some of the matters that you have raised.

1419. ANNE WARBURTON: Coming from the south, I am particularly interested in the Court, because it has very distinctive features. Could I begin with the position of the Rector? The Rector, I know from your paper and otherwise, is elected by students and staff. Does that mean that the Rector is a person who already has a university experience, because I see that he or she chairs the Court?

STEWART SUTHERLAND: Not necessarily so. The field of potential applicants is as wide as the nominations the student body wishes to make.

1420. ANNE WARBURTON: So it could be a pop star?

STEWART SUTHERLAND: Yes, has been.

1421. ANNE WARBURTON: And does then still take that leading role?

STEWART SUTHERLAND: Yes.

ANNE WARBURTON: That is interesting. Another very unusual feature of your Court, for me, was the General Council of graduates.

STEWART SUTHERLAND: Yes, assessors.

ANNE WARBURTON: And this is not just graduates in residence, as it would be at, say, Oxford or Cambridge.

STEWART SUTHERLAND: No. I think now there are some 70,000 members of the General Council, all of whom have the responsibility of helping appoint assessors to the Court. There are various ways in which they can do this, and inevitably it tends to be assessors who have a local base, otherwise it might not be very practicable, but it does not have to be.

1422. ANNE WARBURTON: How does such a large body get together a list to choose from?

MARTIN LOWE: We have a statutory responsibility to maintain a register of our graduates. it is called the General Council Register. I think that responsibility goes back to the 1858 Act, and that is one of my duties. We now have it computerised of course. I think we have about 56,000 names and addresses that we are reasonably confident of. Of course it is difficult to keep in touch with everybody and we rely on them telling us where they are, but there is this massive circulation, and that is how it is done. They meet twice a year. Probably around about 100 to 110 people turn up, and of course they are largely from the Edinburgh area, and I think they recognise that it is difficult for them to represent the entire constituency, but they do it to the best of their ability, and then they have a Business Committee, which is quite a large committee, which meets regularly between their twice-yearly meetings.

1423. ANNE WARBURTON: And do you find that, once on the Court, there is a distinctive voice, a graduate voice?

MARTIN LOWE: No. I think our Court tries to operate as a group, and people do not speak from their particular constituencies; they speak as individuals and make their own individual judgments. If you were to hear a Court debate, you would probably find it quite difficult to identify who were the General Council assessors just by virtue of being General Council assessors.

STEWART SUTHERLAND: And of course other Court members may in fact be graduates of the university who have come to that position through another route.

DAVID SMITH (Convenor of the Finance and General Purposes Committee, University of Edinburgh): Yes, I come into that category.

STEWART SUTHERLAND: Precisely, yes.

1424. ANNE WARBURTON: You have really answered another of my questions, which was: do you have a problem, if you have, as you have, persons appointed by local authorities—for example in Edinburgh itself—of them having a mandate? They do not, I take it from what you have just said.

STEWART SUTHERLAND: They do not act as if they have a mandate. They take part in discussions as other members of the Court do.

1425. ANNE WARBURTON: Fine. Then there are the nominations by the Court itself, in which all members of the Court take their part, I take it—the co-opted people. You say that, on reflection, you might work to widen it a little bit. Do you do anything in the way of public announcement of vacancies?

STEWART SUTHERLAND: We have not done that so far, but one of the possibilities we are considering, for example, is indicating at the beginning of each academic year which Court vacancies will arise, whether through an elected constituency or through the nominations process, indicating whether the possibility of re-nomination or re-election exists, so that the community whom we serve—I mean largely the university community, but the material goes out more widely than that—would be aware which vacancies were coming up and what the remaining balance of the Court was, and would be able to make nominations through the appropriate route.

1426. ANNE WARBURTON: And the Nominations Committee receives suggestions as a result of that as well as from looking around on its own?

STEWART SUTHERLAND: "As a result of that" is perhaps slightly premature. This is a route down which I propose that we should go. The Nominations Committee at the moment can receive nominations from any member of the Court, and the Court of course very much represents the wider community.

ANNE WARBURTON: It is quite a large Court.

STEWART SUTHERLAND: Yes.

ANNE WARBURTON: It functions well, does it?

STEWART SUTHERLAND: Yes. I have come recently to the University of Edinburgh, so I speak with a slightly dispassionate voice in this, and my colleagues, who have been there longer, will make their own comment, but I think the number is about right. Inevitably there are times when one or two members are not able to come and, taking account of that, I think the group who sit round the table can conduct a serious and intelligent discussion. But I pause for my colleagues here.

DAVID SMITH: It certainly was larger and it has been reduced in recent years. Coming from commerce, I must say that when I first attended a Court meeting I thought "My goodness, this is a very large body indeed", but, notwithstanding, I am impressed, continually, by the focus that is always apparent and the way the debate runs and the decisions are made. It may look slightly ponderous to the outside, uninformed eye, but I am quite satisfied that, as far as can be, it is a well-balanced, properly structured Court.

1427. ANNE WARBURTON: You have no difficulties in finding people who will take it on?

DAVID SMITH: That is a difficult one, I think, isn't it? The process that we go through at the moment seems to find the right people. It would depend on the extent to which these processes might change or the extent to which business life or outside public life might change as well. At the moment we seem to be able to get people of sufficient calibre to fill the Court vacancies, and I am speaking particularly as a lay member. The other members of Court find their own way through, as it were, either by nomination, as you have heard, from the General Council as assessors or otherwise.

1428. ANNE WARBURTON: How does the balance between the executive and the Council define itself?

DAVID SMITH: In practice.

STEWART SUTHERLAND: I think it would be very useful if you answered, David.

DAVID SMITH: This is always a difficulty, because a keen governing body will be tempted at times to stray into executive areas. I think we have been quite careful as a Court, particularly the lay members, who have perhaps some experience in commerce and some experience of working with non-executive boards, not to interfere in what I would regard as the proper management and day-to-day running of the university. When a university sets its policy, that is where the Court should properly have a role to play, and then I think it has a role to play in monitoring how that management process is carrying out those policy matters. The Court has a number of mechanisms, which are described in the paper which you have, which will tell you how that happens. I would not want to elaborate at this stage.

1429. ANNE WARBURTON: Good. Thank you very much. Can I come on to a point where you have made your view clear that a code of conduct is not something which you think is needed in the circumstances of the university. Some people see the code of conduct as being as important for the perception outside of what happens as it is for guiding the people inside. Is that an angle which has been thought about?

STEWART SUTHERLAND: I think there are a variety of ways in which it can be made plain to the wider community that the business of the university is properly conducted. One of them clearly is the possibility of a formal written code of conduct. By and large the business that we have is governed by the statutes that have been laid down, and are published and are available. I think, and I take the point you are making, that there may be sense in looking to cull from those quite complex documents the list of points that refer specifically to the University Court as the governing body, but clearly the statutes, and indeed the regulations and ordinances that we have, refer to a much wider range of activities, and I understand what you are saying on that.

1430. ANNE WARBURTON: Good. Thank you very much. On a comparable thing, the register of interests that you are thinking about, you raise a couple of questions which I think do puzzle people about it, about families and how far non-financial interests should come in. Do you see yourselves moving towards answers to these questions or are there any points about them you want to make?

STEWART SUTHERLAND: It is certainly the case that we will have a stated practice with regard to declaration of interests, and I do think that is very important. In practice this has happened, and if there is a need to declare an interest, which has not happened very often in my experience, members of Court have clearly done so, and appropriately their words have been understood in that context. I do think it important that the Court make it plain, particularly to new members but equally to all existing members, when such occasions would be understood to arise. How far does one go beyond that and say "You've got to have a list of interests that is published"? How far that would be helpful I think depends on the detail in which the devil usually lies: how much goes into this?

MARTIN LOWE: I think it is true to say that there is probably an inclination to rely on the common sense of members of Court and I think that is probably quite a sensible way to approach it, rather than to have a very didactic list of things that they have to comply with.

1431. ANNE WARBURTON: Do you already have a procedure for what happens if a declaration has been made—that the person with the interest withdraws or does not take part in the discussion?

STEWART SUTHERLAND: Certainly such an individual would be expected to withdraw, depending on the nature of the interest. But it may well be that simply not taking part in the discussion is appropriate, or possibly that, having declared an interest, the view is then heard. I think that circumstances will dictate in the individual case. But I would certainly regard it as part of my responsibilities, if I thought there were to be a clash, to ensure that a member of Court knew in advance that this was an issue that ought to be addressed before the discussion of a particular item began.

1432. ANNE WARBURTON: I know that Lord Thomson has questions that he wants to put and I want to leave him time to do so, but there is one combination of questions I would like to raise. Am I right in taking it that, when you speak of academic autonomy, you are talking essentially about individual academic freedoms?

STEWART SUTHERLAND: The academic autonomy would include freedoms to define what a syllabus is, to award degrees for appropriate subject matters at appropriate levels, setting standards. That all is part of what I regard as academic autonomy. In more detailed cases I would regard academic appointments as a matter in which the question of academic autonomy arises, that appointments should be made on academic merit and quality in line with the objectives of the institution, for example. These are the broad principles that then define the detail, and the responsibility for academic judgment lies of course with the Senate of the university rather than with the Court.

ANNE WARBURTON: The Senate being the academic body.

STEWART SUTHERLAND: That is right. That is a wholly academic body in fact.

1433. ANNE WARBURTON: Yes. There is a lot to be said there of course, but I wanted to come down to the question you put in your last paragraph, which you obviously are concerned about. In case others do not have your last paragraph in their mind, it is the question about

suppression of reports by government sometimes and failure to publish by sponsors of research. This is not something which has arisen elsewhere, so I wondered whether you would like to tell us a bit more about what the problem is, as you see it.

STEWART SUTHERLAND: I think there are three different contexts. One is where a department or research group in the university is carrying out research for a government body, on what may be socially sensitive issues. I think it is fairly clear that there is a natural reluctance on the part of politicians to publish at inappropriate moments and there is sometimes a tension, therefore, between the wish of those who have carried out the research to put their research, as academics do, into the public arena and, on the other hand, perhaps the wish of the executive to ensure that it goes out at a time that is suitable to the formation of public policy. I do not make a universal judgment on that and I can wholly understand what the tensions are, but these are real tensions.

I would mention two other areas. One, if we have contracts with companies to carry out research on matters that could have significant commercial import, it is not unreasonable for those companies to have clauses in the contract which indicate when this information might become publicly available, and then we make a judgment as to whether that is the sort of research we want to do and carry on, and it will vary according to the particular contract. I think the more difficult area is that in a context in which, increasingly, the funding of research in universities is expected to draw on industrial and business money, there is a risk that the degree of compliance expected of the institutions will increase with regard to publishing. It is a situation we have to watch, because a shift is taking place in the way in which research is funded. We attract a lot of research money—it was over £50 million last year—so we are quite sensitive to currents beginning to flow.

1434. ANNE WARBURTON: So it is not altogether just an issue of academic freedom—I am seeing it under that heading—but I suppose the university and the individual academics are not always in a very strong negotiating position with the contracts.

STEWART SUTHERLAND: That is sometimes the case, but I think academic institutions have to make a judgment as to whether that is the sort of work that they are there to carry out. My colleagues are actually very good at drawing quite fine lines in this area.

1435. ANNE WARBURTON: Where else other than in the Nolan Committee would this sort of issue be addressed?

STEWART SUTHERLAND: I think it is being addressed by the universities in their responses now to, for example, the DTI, which includes the Office of Science and Technology. It is addressed in our discussions with Funding Council and indeed, in our case, with, significantly, the Scottish Office. We would raise questions with them if there were a particular problem on a particular piece of research.

ANNE WARBURTON: I think I should pass the word. Thank you very much.

1436. LORD THOMSON: I do not have very much more to ask, because Dame Anne has covered most of the issues, but could I probe a little further on one or two of her points and then ask one very general question that I do not think has been raised? It is on the conflicts of interest. I think you probably heard the evidence that we were receiving from Robert Gordon University in Aberdeen.

STEWART SUTHERLAND: Yes.

1437. LORD THOMSON: I just wondered what your view was about their proposition that their governing body believes it is not appropriate that contracts should be awarded to companies with which their board members are connected. What would Edinburgh University do in a case like that?

STEWART SUTHERLAND: I think we would examine the nature of the connection. If it were a very close connection, it would be very difficult indeed, but on the other hand, if there is a way in which that particular item of business can be isolated from the involvement of an individual member of Court, then one might regard it as unfortunate that membership of a public body which is unpaid actually prevents the possibility of fair and open tendering in an open tender process for a particular contract.

MARTIN LOWE: I might just add that the Court did have a careful discussion on this very point quite recently in connection with the co-option of a particular individual whose firm does significant business with the university. It was stated that it would be expected that, if that were to continue, a different partner in the firm would be involved and that any interest would be clearly explained to the Court. So this is very open. We would not have invited this individual to join the Court if his firm would thereby have suffered. Indeed, he would not have been able to accept the invitation.

LORD THOMSON: So it is an issue you have been facing and making judgments about.

MARTIN LOWE: Indeed, yes.

DAVID SMITH: It could almost be put the other way, that the Court and the university would perhaps be the poorer for not having his expertise, if we were to have such rigid rules.

1438. LORD THOMSON: Yes. Thank you. Can I just ask about the position of the Rector? I have to confess that I cannot remember who is the present Rector of Edinburgh University.

MARTIN LOWE: Our present Rector is Dr Malcolm Macleod, who was president of the Students' Association in, I think, 1988–89. At the time of his election he was a junior hospital doctor. He is now, rather interestingly, a member of the university staff. Had he been a member of staff at the time of his election, he would have been ineligible to stand for election.

DIANA WARWICK: A conflict of interest!

1439. LORD THOMSON: It is a peculiar Scottish institution with the ancient Scottish universities, and I did think that perhaps, for my English colleagues, you were a little bland in your description of the role of the Rector in your statement, because there must have been times when the Rector of Edinburgh was not in a position to chair the Court. What happens then?

MARTIN LOWE: In those days the constitution was different and the Principal took the chair. That has now been changed. We now have a Vice-Convenor of the Court, elected from among the lay members, who will take the chair in the absence of the Rector. You go back to the Gordon Brown days in the early 70s when the students did not feel they had proper representation and they elected a student as Rector. The second such election of course produced Gordon Brown, and I think that led to a number of changes in behaviour. And of course that was also the time when all four ancient universities were looking for what they called working Rectors, and I think the tendency since the mid-70s has been on the whole—apart from Winnie Mandela at Glasgow, who never of course came—to elect people who would come, and those who could not come have generally—there have been examples—been asked to resign, in other universities. But there is also a fifth university which has a Rector, which is Dundee, and Dundee of course inherited that from St Andrew's. But the interesting thing at Dundee is that the Rector there is not the chair of the Court.

LORD THOMSON: He appoints an assessor in Dundee, I think.

MARTIN LOWE: I do not know whether he has an assessor or not. He probably does, but I would need to look at their constitution. But he does act in an ombudsman's role, I think, in the same way as our Rector does.

1440. LORD THOMSON: At the moment in Glasgow there is a possibility that there might be a very interesting appointment as Rector, of Dr Muhammad al Mass'ari. He might find things difficult from the Dominican Republic, mightn't he?

STEWART SUTHERLAND: It is an interesting nomination, yes. It is open to the student body to nominate whom they wish.

LORD THOMSON: I am not a wholly unprejudiced asker of questions of course, but I rather think the newer Scottish universities, without their Rectors, have a more relevant, more modern procedure.

STEWART SUTHERLAND: I think the advantage of the Rector's post is that there is clearly someone who has the confidence of the student body, who can act as an ombudsman, and I do think that is important, but on the other hand, whether it is the wisest way to appoint someone to chair a body of this sort, as the nature of the business of the body has changed dramatically over the last 20 years, is a much more open question, and it seems to me that Dundee have got a very good solution to that.

LORD THOMSON: You have clearly been fortunate in Edinburgh, I think.

STEWART SUTHERLAND: Yes, indeed. All that we say is without prejudice to the fact that actually we have had a string of very good Rectors, who have done the job well.

DAVID SMITH: And very hard-working Rectors.

STEWART SUTHERLAND: Yes. They have rarely been absent.

DAVID SMITH: The present Rector's predecessor, who I suppose was a pop star—still is a pop star—was extremely hard-working and in my view, having served through his whole term, was very able. I was constantly amazed at his grasp of some fairly complex issues, which he was coming to fairly new, as it were.

1441. LORD NOLAN: Who was that, if I may ask?

MARTIN LOWE: Donnie Munro, the lead singer of Runrig.

1442. LORD THOMSON: Could I just ask about one other point? You mention a reluctance, I think, to publish minutes. Again it is a matter of degree, isn't it, but there are many publicly funded institutions who do not find the same difficulty about publishing minutes that you appear to find, from the evidence you have given us? Would you like to comment on that?

STEWART SUTHERLAND: I suspect that what one would find is that the character of the minutes varies very dramatically between institutions that do publish and those that do not publish. The value of a full minute, which we do have, is that Court members and new Court members have access to these and can have a fairly full picture of what went on at any meeting, not least if they have not been able to be there. If you publish minutes, almost inevitably they will be possibly more bland and certainly less detailed.

LORD THOMSON: Yes. I have noticed that occasionally about Cabinet minutes.

STEWART SUTHERLAND: There is no specifically right answer on this, but you alter the way in which you carry out your business.

1443. LORD THOMSON: Could I ask one very general question? The newspapers are full today of the financial problems of the universities and the fact that, unless the Government behaves a little differently, you may have to impose a poll tax on students coming into universities. In the face of these financial pressures, is there a problem about maintaining standards? You mention the difficulty—you mention it very well and put the balance very well, if I may say so—about research projects that are commercially funded as against the very important tradition of academic independence and freedom to publish. In your search for other sources of revenue, your search for students outside of the United Kingdom who bring very welcome revenue, does this put pressure on your entrance standards at the one end and possibly on your exit standards at the other? We have had suggestions that there is concern about this and I wondered if you would like to comment on it from the Edinburgh University point of view.

STEWART SUTHERLAND: I am confident that our exit standards have not altered. If I thought that they were altering, I would be very concerned indeed and would take a whole string of actions. That is point one. Point two, in terms of entry standards, this is a much more complex matter, because we have very good access courses, where people, within usually the Edinburgh and Lothian community, who have not had an opportunity at earlier stages of their lives to come to university, through an access process come into university with less than the normal formal qualifications. Our experience there has been that, once they are in the institution, they are indistinguishable in terms of performance from those who come in through the normal route, but it is a well structured access programme. I make that point just to say that entry standards are a slightly different question.

The danger you are pointing to is the risk that we might take students who are able to pay full fees, coming from overseas, of a lower quality. We have not been doing this, and I think that the numbers of overseas students that we have would bear this out. We could probably recruit many, many more and we may be looking in that direction. How far these are students who might currently be going elsewhere and how far they are new to the market remains to be seen.

But we are very concerned about standards. Can I make this point very firmly? I do believe that the cuts in funding are having a very severe impact on the quality of what we can provide. The way in which this is showing in the university, and in specific changes we have made, is that the profile of subjects we can offer will reduce. This is our initial response to the problems of reducing funds and maintaining quality of experience and standards. We do not think we will be able to do it over the very wide range of subjects we currently teach. This has begun to show through and it is in the public arena, and it will continue. So there are changes, and I reject any suggestion that we cry "wolf" and do nothing about it. We are doing something about it and changing the profile of the university.

LORD THOMSON: That is a very useful note, for me to end up on anyway, Chairman.

1444. LORD NOLAN: Thank you very much. There were several points in your submissions and in what you have said to us where you reminded us gently that some of the questions in our paper about non-elected bodies and about the lack of a straight line of accountability back to Parliament were not applicable to your university, and I think in other respects you have been warning against the dangers of over-prescription and the advantages of leaving well alone. If I may use the familiar Americanism in the Hilton Hotel, "If it ain't broke, don't fix it". We take note of that. Are there any particular recommendations that you would like to see coming from us in our report, any particular areas in which you would like to see strengthening or improvement, leaving aside for the moment the specific danger which concerned you and which you were talking to Dame Anne about?

STEWART SUTHERLAND: I hope this does not sound presumptuous—it is a personal view rather than a university view—but I would add an eighth to your seven principles. The eighth would be acceptance of responsibility, because I do believe that in governing bodies of the sort that we have that is absolutely fundamental to the business of the governing body. I take my hat off to my colleagues, who come from a wide variety of areas of public life and serve the university, that they are not simply spectators but accept the responsibilities that go with the post which they have accepted. On reflection I would add that to the seven principles, all of which I think are admirable, appropriate and pointed. But that is not a specific recommendation that I would be looking for. It is simply an awareness of what is involved in membership of such governing bodies.

LORD NOLAN: I do not know whether your colleagues had anything they would wish to add to that. Are they content?

MARTIN LOWE: No.

DAVID SMITH: Very content.

1445. LORD NOLAN: Well, thank you very much indeed for your improvement of our education. We have learnt a lot in a short time. We are very grateful to you.

We now have Anthony Schmitz, the Chairman of the Board of Management, Rae Angus, the Principal and Chief Executive, and Roderick Scott, the Director of Finance and Administration, of Aberdeen College. Gentlemen, thank you for your submission to us, which we have all read with great interest. I do not know whether there was anything you wished to add to it by way of a brief opening statement or whether you would be happy to go straight into questions.

ANTHONY SCHMITZ, RAE ANGUS, AND RODERICK SCOTT

ANTHONY SCHMITZ (Chairman, Board of Management, Aberdeen College): Happy to address questions, I think.

LORD NOLAN: Very well. Thank you very much. I will ask Diana Warwick to begin.

1446. DIANA WARWICK: Thank you. Good morning. You sent us a most impressive list of the standing orders and the rules on appointment of members and so on. I wonder if you can tell us something about the evolution of that, where it came from, what prompted you to produce these sorts of codes—the code of ethics and so on—which seemed to me to be very interesting. I wondered whether this was something that had resulted from your own experience or that you had drawn from elsewhere.

RAE ANGUS (Principal, Aberdeen College): A number of our policies and procedures were established at incorporation, but clearly the movement from the local education authority to incorporate status required us to take on board a number of procedures, policies and approaches which were not, if you will, part of a normal non-incorporated college's business. Others have evolved over time, and the code of ethics is one where essentially we thought we wanted to place as a matter of record how our Board Members should conduct themselves. It says "code of ethics", but, of course, it is concerned with conduct: the ethics, hopefully, informing the conduct of Board members; so a mixture, if you will, of imperative and the evolution of our approach as a Board.

1447. DIANA WARWICK: And have you found it satisfactory? Have you found it a good part of the learning and induction process for new members of the board?

RAE ANGUS: I have to say that we have not appointed any new Members of the Board. We are in the process of doing so. Initially, Board Members were appointed by the Secretary of State under the 1992 Act. A number of Board Members have since left, and we are in the process of advertising for, and appointing, new Board Members. We require to do a little more in that respect, because we have to ensure that there is a proper induction process for Board Members, given the very different nature of college Boards as compared with, for example, those of universities.

1448. DIANA WARWICK: Yes. I just wondered whether you thought it might have wider application. It is a very interesting combination from the very basic, that members should not use their membership for their own personal benefit, to being willing to take up opportunities to meet staff informally and formally. It seems a happy blend of restriction and of assistance in knowing what their role is. Do you think that sort of thing has wider application, because codes of conduct and so on are something that the Nolan Committee has been quite keen on?

RAE ANGUS: I think the code of conduct has a general application. We hopefully have adopted best practice. Our college is a very large one and is multi-site. If, for example, you look at the requirement on lay Board members to visit sites, and to meet with staff, outwith the normal board meetings and liaison committees, our practice reflects our own particular circumstances. We operate on something like eight sites, and it is very difficult with a Board membership of 10 to 16—because that is the legal range for us—to get a proper appreciation of the feeling of staff, and, indeed of students. So that particular aspect of our approach reflects the nature of our institution, but in general terms we would hope that other colleges would also have something along these lines. I am afraid I do not have personal knowledge of whether they do or not, but I certainly would hope so.

ANTHONY SCHMITZ: May I just add that that code was formulated at an away-day of the board, when a number of things were being discussed and we were looking at our conduct of the past year, and the question of visiting other sites was one that arose quite naturally for the reasons the Principal has just stated. A lot of the board of managers came into the principal meeting on a regular basis but did not naturally go to some of the other sites, so that was just an opportunity we took to include that in the code.

1449. DIANA WARWICK: Could I move on to something rather more general? In contrast to the English system, you are funded directly, as I understand it, through the Scottish Office. How does that work? Is it satisfactory from your point of view? Is it rather overbearing having a government department that has a direct role in an academic institution? Could you say something about that?

RAE ANGUS: Yes. It has worked very well indeed. Obviously we learned something about the system south of the border—about the FEFC. Our system has worked effectively. The Scottish Office has not been overbearing, but in the initial two years following incorporation, it kept a very close watch—quite correctly in my judgment—over the financial aspects of college activities. Some of our colleges are very small, and they were moving quite quickly from what I would suspect was an over-reliance on the Regional and Island Councils to one of almost complete independence, so the participation of the Scottish Office in our activities, in the early years, was very welcome indeed.

1450. DIANA WARWICK: Could you say something about the transformation? What would you say were the key differences in governance and in demands on you as an institution, which it would be interesting for our Committee to know about, between your previous existence and your new existence?

RAE ANGUS: I think it is fair to say that, across Scotland, there is quite a wide range of relationships between individual colleges and their Regional and Island Councils: from Strathclyde—a very large region—to the Islands, which are obviously quite small. Governance, I would argue, has been strengthened in relation to colleges as institutions. Prior to incorporation, a layer of Education Officers was interposed between the members of staff of colleges (and Principals) and Elected Members, so that distance has been shortened. In terms of governance, the previous College Councils—and I refer to the ones before the 1989 Act, which brought in a "half-way house" of college councils—were very much advisory, and played very much honorary rather than onerous roles. So, in many ways, it has strengthened the governance of institutions.

1451. DIANA   WARWICK: Robert   Gordon University talked about its relationship with the local community. Does your college have a similar link and have there been any instances where those links have caused problems in terms of conflicts of interest, for example?

RAE ANGUS: We have on our Board the Convenor of the Education Committee of the outgoing Regional Council. Obviously we do not know who the new Members will be, but we have tried to maintain links with the local authorities. The practicalities of our business, are quite different, I think, from those of Robert Gordon University. They are such that we could not perform our functions properly without very close links with the local education authorities, not only because there is an overlap in their provision and ours in certain areas, but also because our history as independent institutions is very short, and the relationships between the Regional Council and ourselves, and between the schools and ourselves particularly, have been maintained. We have worked quite hard to do that, particularly with the forthcoming unitary authorities. We have gone one step further, from simply maintaining relationships which were in place, to positively cultivating relationships in the unitary authorities. It also makes sense for us in curriculum terms. The introduction of a new curriculum arrangement for the upper years of secondary school is such that it would be, quite frankly, wasteful and counter-productive to meeting the needs of local people if we did not co-operate on the curriculum. The same is true also in finance. As the unitary authorities find it more and more difficult to finance their activities, it makes sense for colleges and the local schools (and the local education authorities) to co-operate more closely. It is a mutual benefit. It is a "win-win" rather than a "win-lose" situation.

1452. DIANA WARWICK: I wonder if you could say something in relation to that about accountability to the local community. Do you see it in terms of meeting the needs of the local community or do you see it in a broader sense?

RAE ANGUS: I think it is appropriate to distinguish our courses from other services that we, as a college, may provide. Most of our courses are vocational. For those

which are not, the curriculum is determined by examining bodies—for example, the Scottish Examination Board, and the Scottish Vocational Education Council. The content of most of our vocational courses is determined by Industry Lead Bodies, so that in terms of a client-supplier relationship, we are very close to our clients. That, of course, is not the local community at large. What we have done in Aberdeen is try and ensure that the local community has access to user-friendly information on the college. We also have liaison groups—now have about 40 of them—which involve local industry representatives and other organisations we serve. We have to try and use an indirect form of accountability to the community at large, but a much more direct form of accountability to our specific clients.

1453. DIANA WARWICK: Could I ask you now about internal processes, particularly linked with the concept of openness? Can you tell us how you ensure that the business of the college is widely known? Do you distribute minutes of your main meeting and of your sub-committees? How do you ensure openness?

RAE ANGUS: We ensure that all papers, save those that are reserved items of business (relating mainly to individuals perhaps, or to commercially sensitive information), minutes, records of meeting, are open to the public in each of the College's libraries and we also have them posted on notice- boards, so that there is very wide access to the day-to-day working papers of our Board and its standing committees. Of course, access does not mean to say that people automatically take it up. We are not deluged with demands for the records of meeting of our standing committees. So what we have tried to do is present what I have to admit is rather glossy information in terms of the facts and figures relating to our performance; how long students remain with us; success rates; post-course success rates; and a whole range of performance indicators (in hopefully a palatable form) so that people can come along and pick them up as they will. We also take a lot of time and attention in putting together our Development Plans and also our Reports and Accounts, and these are transformed, again, into a glossy form and the language and approach changed, so that they are fairly easy to read—hopefully easy to read. We make sure that main client bodies, including local authorities, are sent these documents. We were fortunate enough to win some prizes for their quality and readability. So we do take positive steps.

DIANA WARWICK: I was just going to make a comment about whether there was a Plain Scottish campaign as there is a Plain English Campaign.

RAE ANGUS: The problem with the Plain English Campaign is that you have to pay. And, of course, in Aberdeen we are very, very careful not to pay. Careful with public money—let's put it that way.

1454. DIANA WARWICK: You mentioned reserved business and you have in fact, in your standing orders, attempted to define areas of reserved business. Have you had difficulties in that, because it has been one of those issues that has come up from many of our witnesses? Their views have varied enormously on what should constitute reserved business, and it has clearly been an area of criticism internally in institutions that there is often too much reserved business. Have you a) had that criticism and b) found any difficulty with your definition?

RAE ANGUS: We have had some criticism from teaching union representatives—for example, if we are about to enter salary negotiations—that we, at that time, do not publish, in great detail, our financial update. That is because we have established separate negotiating fora and arrangements. So, we have had some criticism on that account. In fact the necessary information for the unions is there, but they would have to collate it from different papers.

DIANA WARWICK: So work a bit harder at it?

RAE ANGUS: Yes, but the information is there—with a little effort, yes.

ANTHONY SCHMITZ: In my experience as Chair, if I may just supplement that, the reserved items of business have virtually in all cases been reserved precisely to this question at the time of negotiations with a teaching union.

1455. DIANA WARWICK: You have mentioned the staff representatives and so on. Thinking in terms of the other area of openness, the question of whistle-blowing, do you have a process within your institution whereby an individual can exercise the right to criticise in the knowledge that they will not fear for their jobs or fear any reprisal?

RAE ANGUS: I can give this Committee an absolute assurance that the staff in Aberdeen College feel in no way intimidated. When we were, for example, in the process of recognising trade unions, the staff representatives—individuals, indeed—felt quite free to go to press, even to make assertions which were untrue. We also have the normal grievance procedures that are open to members of staff. We have very full and complete recognition of trade unions and participation of trade unions, including full-time officials. We also have the practice that was mentioned earlier of Board Members visiting the different centres, and I make a point of not being there, and of encouraging my colleagues in management not to lean over the Members' shoulders. I think that individuals have taken the opportunity, where they have felt room for criticism, to speak to the Members. The Chairman perhaps is better placed to talk on that than I am.

ANTHONY SCHMITZ: Yes, there have not been any particular instances that I would describe as whistle-blowing, but things have been brought to our attention in the course of the site visits that would not have come about if we had not done that, but I feel comfortable with the arrangements that we have. There have been a number of exchanges which have been very frank, in the course of board meetings, between the Principal and staff representatives on the board, which would indicate that there is no fear at all about bringing things to the attention of the board at board meetings.

RAE ANGUS: Could I just say, without wishing to bring levity to the Committee's proceedings——

LORD NOLAN: Please do. We could do with it.

RAE ANGUS:—that staff representatives on our Board have felt free to ask who pays for my dinner when we take guests from other colleges out. I think that is an indication of how searching the questions can be.

1456. DIANA WARWICK: Could I just ask one final question? I am conscious again that we are running out of time. Each of the institutions that we have talked to today, and I think you have heard them, have talked about the problems that reductions in funding have placed on institutions and others have argued with us that funding which is based on results creates tensions within any academic institution and, in particular, that there is a possibility of it having an impact on the quality of the work done in the institution. Do you have any views about that?

RAE ANGUS: Yes. Like most principals, I am in favour of more resources being allocated to further education. It is, of its nature, a good thing, but there are also opportunity costs involved in that allocation. My own feeling is that the leaders of our institutions are there to manage within the resources which are allocated to them, and of course it is quite proper that they argue for, negotiate for, and seek more resources. I can say that fairly freely in Aberdeen's case, because we have been a beneficiary of a new funding formula in which the funding follows the student. Last year, and indeed this year, we had a real gain in our funding, so perhaps I speak from a position of comfort, whereas some of my colleagues might not. That funding mechanism is doing much to ensure that the resources go to where the student demand is. Obviously, I would argue for more resources for further education, but I do think there is a balance to be struck, and that balance is in the management of those resources, because it is a fact that a pound needlessly spent on further education is a pound not spent on a hospice or not spent on some other useful purpose, and I think that managers of educational institutions should be aware of, and practise, the fact that their organisations are economic entities, and that the public money they spend has alternative uses.

DIANA WARWICK: But you would not then argue, and I think this is really the issue that has been put to us, that the quality of the institution and what it delivers have suffered as a result.

RAE ANGUS: In the case of further education, our quality is very well monitored by the Scottish Vocational Education Council, by the local enterprise companies, because they manage the Scottish Quality Management System audits, which is a single quality management system for vocational education. We are also audited in terms of our quality by Her Majesty's Inspectorate, which, of course, in Scotland remains part of the Scottish Office and has not been privatised. We are also audited in terms of quality by a number of other external agencies, and the College itself maintains an internal quality assurance and audit team, which is independent of the management of our curriculum and our services. I am assured, in our own college's case, that quality has not suffered. It is sometimes too easy to say that changes in funding automatically lead to the deterioration of quality. I think, for example, that there is more requirement for the measurement of quality and objective measures of it, rather than simple assertions that it goes up or it goes down.

DIANA WARWICK: Thank you very much.

1457. LORD NOLAN: Just a few questions. What is the size of the college roughly?

RAE ANGUS: The college, if I could give a few words of background, was formed in 1991 from the merger of three colleges, a technical college, a business college and an agricultural college. We have about 20,000 enrolments per year and are Scotland's largest college by about 20%, in terms of student numbers.

1458. LORD NOLAN: How many sites did you tell us earlier?

RAE ANGUS: We have eight sites at the moment.

1459. LORD NOLAN: And you were saying that that is not very easy for your board members to get round. Have you got a full complement on the board?

RAE ANGUS: No, we do not, which is why we are seeking to appoint new Members. We are at the lower end of the permitted range.

1460. LORD NOLAN: Mr Scott mentioned in his letter to us that a study had been undertaken by Leishman Associates in the early part of 1995, which said: "The conduct and operational effectiveness of the Board of Aberdeen features favourably in the resulting report. The Board is cited frequently as an example of good practice".

So we must congratulate you. Would it be possible for us to see a copy of the report of Leishman Associates? I don't think we have that.

RAE ANGUS: I have to say that, as is the manner of these reports, the references are shaded references, but we understand and have been assured, that that is the case. We have a copy of the report.

RODERICK SCOTT (Director of Finance and Administration, Aberdeen College): Yes. I have a copy here, if you want it.

1461. LORD NOLAN: I am told that there is no need for us to trouble you individually over it. We can get it from the Scottish Office, but I am sure that it will be helpful to us. So far as openness is concerned, do you have associations of your former students, of your graduate members?

RAE ANGUS: No. Unlike the universities where someone may be there for two, three or four years, some of our students are there only for months. Two years is perhaps the upper end of attendance. It is very difficult to maintain student participation where large numbers of students are coming perhaps in the evenings, or perhaps on block-release or day-release. It is difficult to do that.

1462. LORD NOLAN: Yes, it is very understandable. The last question is this: you have not, as I understand it, had serious staff problems. You do not see the need for an independent adjudicator in the college. Is that right?

RAE ANGUS: Within the college itself? I think that the representation on our board of management and representation on other bodies gives both the students and the staff a fairly direct route to the governors of the college. We have tried—it is for others to judge whether we have been successful—to maintain a good balance between governance and management, so the governors of the college are not seen as too close to the management. So we have not really seen the need for it and perhaps have not given it as much consideration as we might. It is something we will certainly look at.

1463. LORD NOLAN: Yes. We have had much evidence about confidentiality clauses, both in standard service agreements and in termination agreements. Have you any particular policy or standard form of agreement in that respect?

RAE ANGUS: Through negotiation with the teaching trade unions we have introduced new contracts, which do not have gagging clauses whatsoever. The senior management of the College, at least Mr Scott and myself, have normal clauses of confidentiality, but they are concerned with ensuring that we do not leave, go somewhere else and take some of the College's business. It is not a gagging issue as such.

LORD NOLAN: No. Restrictive clauses in service agreements are a common feature of employment law generally, but gagging clauses are something different, and those you turn your faces against.

RAE ANGUS: Yes. We do not have in any of our contracts what might be called gagging clauses. As I said, Mr Scott and myself do have confidentiality clauses. In fact, we have avoided that, quite frankly, like the plague, because it is not fitting in an educational setting to seek to do that.

LORD NOLAN: Yes. This has been very helpful and encouraging evidence. Thank you all very much indeed for coming along and giving us your assistance.

RAE ANGUS: Thank you, Chairman. We appreciate the opportunity.

1464. LORD NOLAN: I can now say good afternoon. We now have Councillor Rosemary McKenna, the President of the Convention of Scottish Local Authorities, and we were hoping to see Mr Peter Peacock and Mr Douglas Sinclair.

COUNCILLOR ROSEMARY MCKENNA AND DOUGLAS SINCLAIR

ROSEMARY McKENNA (President, Convention of Scottish Local Authorities): Can I apologise on behalf of Councillor Peter Peacock, who is the convenor of one of the new unitary authorities—Highland—and unfortunately has had to stay in Inverness? He is extremely busy, as I am sure you will understand. So I do apologise on behalf of Councillor Peacock, but Mr Sinclair and I are here.

1465. LORD NOLAN: Good. We are very glad to see you. You have kindly provided us with an opening statement, which we have all read and which will form part of the record.

Was there anything you wished to add by way of preliminary statement before we go to questions?

ROSEMARY McKENNA: No, not at all, just to welcome the opportunity to speak to you and appreciate very much the fact that you have come to Edinburgh.

LORD NOLAN: We are delighted to be here. I will ask Lord Thomson, if I may, to open the questions.

1466. LORD THOMSON: We appreciate the opportunity to pick your brains a bit about these matters, because anybody who is active in Scottish public affairs knows how much experience and the resources that lie behind COSLA and what authority they have on these matters.

Your starting point, I was happy to see from the paper you gave us, recognises that our remit excludes the political decision to exchange local government control for quango control. That is not something that we are concerned about, but we are concerned about the consequences of that political decision and to try to deal with some of the problems that have been raised. I wanted, therefore, to start off by asking you where you think things are in Scotland at the moment in relation to the bodies that are either directly appointed by Ministers or, in the cases that we are examining in detail today, are not appointed by Ministers nor of course are they the result of election, where they command substantial quantities of public funds. You refer in your paper at paragraph 5 to bodies continuing in their present form "on the basis of ministerial appointment". I thought I might just remind you that in our first report this was the area that we addressed ourselves to. We made a series of quite substantial recommendations, including the appointment of a public appointments commissioner and the recommendation that appointments to quangos should be done on the basis of advisory bodies that contained an independent element and so on. I just wondered, before we went any further, if you have any impression about how far these recommendations, which are recent recommendations, recently accepted by government, might be beginning to apply in Scotland.

ROSEMARY McKENNA: We are assured by the Scottish Office that they are taking on board all the recommendations and are going ahead. I am not quite sure yet that we are at the stage where we can assess where that is at the moment, being as it is very recent. We welcome the advisory body on the health boards, which was set up to look at the appointments last year. That was very welcome. I do not think that there is yet a recognition that there has been any change in that situation. We welcome the recommendations. I think it is very important that we get away from that, and certainly the noises coming from Scottish Office are very positive, but we are not yet able to assess, and this is no evidence at all to say that this is yet in place.

1467. LORD THOMSON: No, I understand that. That is very helpful. Now can I turn to our immediate concern, and that is the question of nomination rights to bodies like further education colleges, local enterprise companies and that kind of thing? Would you like to develop your ideas about what might be done to improve matters there?

ROSEMARY McKENNA: Yes, I do think it is very important. I think that the one area that we would want to improve considerably is the partnership role that local authorities play with the bodies within their area. We believe that local authorities have a democratic legitimacy to speak on behalf of their communities, and it is therefore very important that, whatever body is working within their area, a very good relationship is developed between them, and we do think there has to be a partnership there. What concerns us is that the self-appointed nature of many of the bodies means that local government does not have an automatic right to place their people on to the boards of, for example, the LECs and the colleges. I feel that it is important that local authorities decide who their representative will be, because people are elected to speak for the community, and it is important that the local authority should have the right to say who their representative would be and not the board of the LEC, the education college or the housing association. It is the local authority who should be able to decide on that representation.

LORD THOMSON: I suppose that there is varying experience throughout Scotland, and Scotland has the advantage over England of having a single local authority association, so you have an overview.

ROSEMARY McKENNA: Yes.

1468. LORD THOMSON: Would you like to give us any information about how things vary? Are there places where there is good practice and co-operation between the local authority and these newly-funded bodies and cases where there is much less good practice?

ROSEMARY McKENNA: Yes, there are. Without being specific, there are areas where there is a very good relationship and where the local enterprise company has worked extremely hard to make sure that the local authority has been involved right from the very beginning in deciding the shape of the enterprise company and the agenda for the enterprise company. That is very important, and it is important to state that that has happened. There are other areas where that has not, unfortunately, been the case, where there is a tension between the organisation and the council. With the unitary authority status that we have now, there ought to be an opportunity for that to be much more effective, for the relationship between the bodies to become much better, because there will not be the tension among the councils to decide who the representative should be, but it should be an opportunity to make that much better.

LORD THOMSON: An opportunity really in a sense for a fresh start, I suppose, with the new pattern of unitary authorities.

ROSEMARY McKENNA: Yes.

1469. LORD THOMSON: And that would involve what—arrangements for the local authority perhaps to have an opportunity to scrutinise the operations of the particular body, whether it was a further education college, a housing association or a local enterprise company?

ROSEMARY McKENNA: I actually think that is very important, and I do not think the bodies should have anything to fear from that. After all local government has quite rightly been subject to all the scrutinies for many years, and the bodies should not be afraid of that being applied to them. I think it would be appropriate for the local authority to be able to do that.

1470. LORD THOMSON: Would you in general be ready to accept a situation in which there were local authority people on these bodies, but they were not there in a sense as mandated representatives but were there as people bringing their experience of the local authority to the work of the new body?

ROSEMARY McKENNA: In actual fact that is where some of the tension arises. I am currently, and have been for some time, a member of the board of a development corporation, which is appointed by the Secretary of State, in my town, which was a new town. I was appointed by the Secretary of State on the recommendation of the authority, but appointed on the basis of my expertise and my local knowledge and very clearly told that it was not on the basis that I represented the authority. That always creates problems for the authority and for the member, because I was always very clear, and the board accepted, that I was there to represent the views of the town and the people of the town. That was very clear. That actually causes some tensions on the board, and it causes tension for the individual concerned. I always had to make it very clear that I felt I was speaking apart from my role as local councillor, that I was speaking on behalf of all the people of the town, because I was the only one who actually lived in the town, which again was a problem with a nine-member board. The role there I would like to see clarified. I think that if you are a member of a local authority, they should be able to appoint by right to be there to represent the local authority.

1471. LORD THOMSON: Is it not sometimes the experience—to be fair, I think it would be my experience, looking back at my time as a Scottish MP—that local authority people are very busy, with many demands on their time and that, where there is a statutory right of representation that is taken up, they are not the most regular attenders?

ROSEMARY McKENNA: Yes, that is an issue. I quite agree with you, there is an issue there, and I think it is appropriate to make sure that standards are laid down for involvement and attendance. I recognise that that could be a problem.

1472. LORD THOMSON: Turning to your local authority experience and applying it now to the procedures inside these new bodies which, as you have perhaps heard from some of the evidence we have been getting, are feeling their way in many ways—one of the big issues is conflicts of interest and all that side of things—I just wondered what you would like to see happen in that field. Do you think there is a need for a more effective code of operation within these new bodies in terms of conflicts of interest? In local authorities you have some very rigid statutory rules. I just wondered whether you feel that some of the rules in local authorities, on surcharging and so on, can lead to criminal charges, whether they are excessively draconian, whether there is a middle way to recommend to government between what is imposed on councillors and local authorities on the one side and at the moment seems to be rather an open question in regard to the procedures for these new funded bodies.

ROSEMARY McKENNA: I do think that they should be subject to exactly the same code of conduct as local government and I think that it would be appropriate if that were the case. Openness and access to these bodies are also important. Openness and access very often allay the fears. A lot of it is suspicion, and openness is something that local authorities are very well used to and do not have a problem with, and I think it is very important. So I would be very happy about that. I think the issue of surcharge is so draconian when you consider that local authorities are spending in Scotland less than 50% of the public purse and are subject to the kind of surcharge that they are if they behave improperly and spend over the government's capping levels, for example, and that does not apply to any of the other bodies. So it does seem to me that that is an area that should be looked at.

But I think it is important that anyone who is responsible for spending public money should be accountable, and there obviously have to be different ways of looking at accountability, whether it is elected accountability at the ballot box or appointed accountability to the Scottish Office. I think that the standards that apply in local government should apply to the bodies. I know a lot of them are feeling their way. They are new and they are feeling their way towards achieving that. The others are imposed by law on local government, and yet we are elected at the ballot box. The electorate have the right to say, and we have to be open and available to the electorate. There is also another issue there: they know who we are, they know their local councillors, they do not know the members of the boards of the LECs or the colleges. All local councillors have surgeries where people can go along and give them their problems. That does not apply to the bodies which are, again, spending public money. So there is a whole host of issues that ought to be looked at in terms of accountability, access and openness, and codes of conduct. I think that is very important.

LORD THOMSON: Thank you very much. That is fine.

1473. CLIFFORD BOULTON: I enjoyed reading the report on the conduct of the local government of Scotland, which seemed to be, if I may say so, a very useful piece of work, a joint effort, which also appeared to have attracted the Secretary of State's interest in his response. Interestingly, in that paper it was pointed out that with current methods of conducting the business of local government, if you like, it is likely to be more common for local authorities to pursue their objectives through organisations which fall to be audited under the Companies Acts, so that in starting to set up, almost, businesses in conjunction with contractors and so forth, in many ways some aspects of local government are getting a little closer to some of these bodies that we are talking about. Do you think there is scope for almost a co-ordinated view right across the board, to get the same standards of conduct introduced across the board, which would span all those activities?

ROSEMARY McKENNA: Yes, I agree. I think we have to realise that today people have much more information in the media and the press. People want to see what is happening in companies, and I do not think there is a problem about that. I think we should approach it in that way. One of the things that surprised me, just after the first two years of the local enterprise companies, when people began to probe where the spending was going and there were suggestions that it was not open and fair, was the reaction of the members of the board—that they should be surprised that this was happening, because it was something that had been happening to local government for years and something that we thought was perfectly appropriate. So I do think there is a case for saying yes, let's look at the whole aspect of behaviour and standards, and agree standards that would be appropriate in every area.

1474. CLIFFORD BOULTON: On the apparent anomaly about the risk of surcharge, which applies in local government, of course there is a difference, isn't there, in that local government is a taxing authority which can take money directly out of people's pockets, and the bodies that we are talking about are not so: they are grant-aided. So there is some extra element in local government which is not common to these bodies.

ROSEMARY McKENNA: A very small element, I have to say, currently. It is 15%.

CLIFFORD BOULTON: It is the classic explanation.

ROSEMARY McKENNA: It is the classic explanation, but very draconian for the very small amount that local government actually raises by itself.

1475. CLIFFORD BOULTON: Many university statutes have the opportunity to appoint, amongst others, persons having experience of local government as independent members of their court. Do you know whether many take advantage of that?

DOUGLAS SINCLAIR (Secretary, Convention of Scottish Local Authorities): There have been occasions in Scotland where that has been done. I know of former colleagues in local government who have been appointed to the boards of universities, and indeed the case is not unknown of the Permanent Secretary of the Scottish Office who became the Principal of Glasgow University, so there is some link there between local and central government.

1476. CLIFFORD BOULTON: So it happens, but of course people with experience of local government are amongst other people who have been identified as desirable people to keep in contact with. Do you think that if one went down the road of the local authority actually choosing their representative and feeling entitled to expect their representative to advance their policies, all these other groups would start coming along, also in some way under instruction? We get evidence, as you can imagine, from the other side of the coin, from people who say "We want these people to sit round as free agents to form a joint policy on matters. We don't want people coming in from all over the place with their marching orders."

DOUGLAS SINCLAIR: The distinction with the other bodies that you refer to is surely that local government is based on democratic election, which gives it a unique legitimacy. It is not unreasonable, it seems to me, that, say, the new City of Edinburgh Council should have the right of nomination to bodies like that, because it will be a key player in the development of the city in partnership with bodies like the university. That would seem to me to be in the selfish interests of the university as well: there is a mutual benefit there.

1477. CLIFFORD BOULTON: You say there are examples of, for instance, universities having this kind of representation. You are not aware that it has caused particular problems by some kind of rigidity or a lack of flexibility by the representative. You think it works.

DOUGLAS SINCLAIR: I think universities are probably at the other end of the scale. I think it is the bodies the President has referred to where there is a closer relationship in terms of the impact on local communities with local enterprise companies, health trusts, housing associations. The key partner for many of those bodies will in fact be the local authority. The problems of unemployment in Scotland will not be solved by agencies acting in isolation from one another. They can only be solved by the agencies working in partnership with one another.

1478. CLIFFORD BOULTON: And are you telling us that at the moment the relationship between the LECs and local government is not happy?

DOUGLAS SINCLAIR: I am saying that, as the President has indicated, it is not even across Scotland. There is no consensus as to the right of representation of elected members on local enterprise companies; the practice varies across Scotland.

CLIFFORD BOULTON: But there are some good examples.

DOUGLAS SINCLAIR: There are some good examples, yes.

1479. CLIFFORD BOULTON: In England TECs are still seen as relatively closed, secret organisations. In Scotland both the Scottish Enterprise Network and Highlands and Islands Enterprise claim that there has been some work done on this. Would you agree with that?

ROSEMARY McKENNA: I am a member of the board of Scottish Enterprise, so I do know that work has been done on that. I do not know yet that it is perceived as being as open as they would want to be, as we would want them to be. There is still the self-appointed nature of the LECs, the self-perpetuating board, where people invite their colleagues on to the board, and it is not clear why they are being invited, who is on the board. There is a lack of knowledge about that. So I think there is work to be done in opening that up to let people see why they are there. And it is not only the local government community who are saying it. The business community have been saying for some time that they want to know how the boards are set up. They are fairly new and they are working towards it, and there are recommendations coming out from the parent bodies to say "We want more openness". But I believe that it is the self-perpetuating nature of the boards that is causing concern to everybody in Scotland and, yes, work is being done, but I think more needs to be done.

CLIFFORD BOULTON: But you are on Scottish Enterprise personally.

ROSEMARY McKENNA: Yes, I am.

CLIFFORD BOULTON: This is an example of what Lord Thomson was pointing out, that COSLA is in on the action in Scotland——

ROSEMARY McKENNA: Yes, we are, very much.

CLIFFORD BOULTON:—in a way we do not normally find in England.

ROSEMARY McKENNA: But not in all.

DOUGLAS SINCLAIR: Not in all national quangos—Scottish Homes, for example. There has been a tradition of the COSLA President being a member of the Scottish Enterprise board. That does not apply, for example, to Scottish Homes, and yet again there is a very close relationship between local authority housing and the housing-enabling role of Scottish Homes.

1480. CLIFFORD BOULTON: Do you have any attitude to this suggestion that every organisation should have an external adjudicator for complaints? Is that something you have given any thought to?

DOUGLAS SINCLAIR: Yes.

ROSEMARY McKENNA: Yes, we do.

CLIFFORD BOULTON: That is your policy.

ROSEMARY McKENNA: I do not have a problem with that at all. I do not think you would find anyone in local government making any objection to that, because they are subject to so many scrutinies, and we think it is appropriate.

DOUGLAS SINCLAIR: I think it is interesting that the local authority ombudsman did not exist in Scotland before the last reorganisation. It has now been accepted by local government as a perfectly reasonable, and indeed appropriate, mechanism to have in place. If it is good enough for local government, surely it is good enough for other non-elected bodies.

1481. CLIFFORD BOULTON: We are not examining individual cases, and I suppose, if we are not going to look at individual complaints, that individual praise is also probably inappropriate or invidious, but could you give us an example, not necessarily naming somewhere, of the kind of good practice of co-operation and partnership between councils and some of these bodies, where it has been organised to a point where there is exchange of papers or information?

ROSEMARY McKENNA: Lanarkshire Development Agency has probably done most to encourage the partnership approach with their local authorities, perhaps because they had the biggest problem, in that they were created at the same time as Ravenscraig was closing and therefore there was a very serious problem to be addressed there. They certainly did that and they worked extremely well with the local authorities. I would hope that in the unitary authorities that would continue and that the other bodies could look to that kind of relationship to develop best practice. It is patchy across Scotland. I think that one of the areas where it is particularly bad is in Highland. I have to say that the islands authorities do not appreciate the relationship with Highlands and Islands Enterprise. There is an area there where they have to get together a bit. That is one area where I would say some work probably needs to be done.

CLIFFORD BOULTON: Thank you very much. I do not think I have any more questions, but could I just end on a personal note? I began my association with the Scottish Grand Committee and Scottish parliamentary affairs in 1953 and it has been a great pleasure for me to come up here and continue that relationship. Thank you very much.

1482. LORD NOLAN: I wonder if I could just ask something. I may have overlooked it. We have heard a lot of conflicting evidence on the question of whether board members should receive remuneration, or at any rate some allowance for loss of earnings, or whether, as many of them feel is important, they should remain on a voluntary basis. Have you as an organisation expressed a view on this?

ROSEMARY McKENNA: I do believe that people ought to be paid appropriate to the time, the effort and the expertise that they bring to a task. I think it is inappropriate to ask people to give up a lot of their time, and for a lot of people it means giving up some earned income, to take part on bodies. It is one of the most difficult areas, I think. Certainly that has been our experience. For the first time local government has worked out a proper scheme of remuneration. There was no problem when the scheme was worked out, interestingly enough. When the scheme was proposed, it was accepted across party and non-party bounds: everyone agreed and signed up to the scheme. But the minute names were put beside appropriate levels of remuneration, the press and the public began to take an interest. I believe, yes, that people ought to be paid, but I appreciate how very, very difficult it would be to come to an agreement on that.

1483. LORD NOLAN: Yes. You would not, would you, suggest that there should be full compensation for, say, a very wealthy director of a public company for the time he gives up?

ROSEMARY McKENNA: I think that is something that should be part of the discussion. I do think many people do it out of public interest and the public good, and that is appropriate, but we want to encourage everyone to take part in public life and there are people who would be barred from that, because financially they would not be able to take part, and I think you have to try and find a balance between the two, which is what we have been trying to do in local government for some time.

LORD NOLAN: That is very helpful. Thank you very much. Just looking again at what Lord Thomson pointed out to me, the Secretary of State, looking at the proposals of your convention, has revealed that he is inclined to reject only nine of the proposals, that he was favourably disposed to more than half of the total. It is not a bad score.

ROSEMARY McKENNA: Yes, except that it was about deregulation, and some things were off the agenda before the consultation began.

LORD NOLAN: I see.

DOUGLAS SINCLAIR: The weight of the nine was much heavier than the 43 others.

LORD NOLAN: So you are not letting it go yet. Councillor McKenna and Mr Sinclair, thank you very much indeed for your help. We have been interested and it has been a most enjoyable meeting. Thank you.

ROSEMARY McKENNA: Thank you very much.

TUESDAY 30 JANUARY 1996
MORNING SESSION

OPENING STATEMENTS

Opening Statement from the University of Edinburgh

Introductory contextual comments

1. The Court is the University's governing body. It welcomes the opportunity to comment on the issues raised in this paper. It fully recognises the importance of exercising the highest standards in its governance of the University. It is more than willing to learn from experience and good practice elsewhere and to contribute to development of best practice. The Court fully endorses the "Seven Principles of Public Life" identified by the Nolan Committee and has initiated a process of review of its operation in order to ensure that they are given full effect in a manner appropriate to a university environment.

2. The comments set out below need to be seen against the framework within which the Court and the University operate. The University is an autonomous body with a history extending over 400 years and with its roots firmly in its local community, having originally been established by the Edinburgh city authority. Its present constitution derives from Acts of Parliament (the Universities [Scotland] Acts) dating from 1858 to 1966. It is presumably not necessary here to set out the strong reasons why higher education institutions should retain autonomy: these were recognised by Government as recently as 1992 in its enactments which *inter alia* brought about the end of the binary line in higher education. In Edinburgh's case, it is the further and Higher Education (Scotland) Act 1992 which regulates the relationship between Government and it, via the Scottish Higher Education Funding Council. The Court fully accepts that the corollary of autonomy is a very high degree of responsibility for the continued well-being and future development of one of Scotland's, and the UK's, leading universities. That responsibility extends to over 17,000 students and over 5,000 staff, as well as to the local, national and international community.

3. The University receives approximately 34% of its operating income direct from the SHEFC, and a further 13% comes from the public purse via the student fee mechanism (1993/94 data). Whilst the University is therefore by no means wholly dependent on state funding for its activities, such funding does form the core of its income, especially in regard to teaching and fundamental research. The University's relationship with SHEFC is governed statutorily by the Further and Higher Education (Scotland) Act 1992 and by the Financial Memorandum between the Funding Council and the University, which sets out the terms and conditions on which funding is provided: these include compliance with SHEFC's Code of Audit Practice governing internal and external audit arrangements and value-for-money studies.

4. The Universities (Scotland) Act 1966 is the most recent statute which governs composition of the Court. It provides for members who are internal and external to the University, with some appointed on a representational basis and others in a personal capacity. The Act also makes provision for the Court to initiate changes to its composition by an Ordinance procedure, subject to comment by the University Senate and by the General Council, the statutory body which comprises all the graduates of the University. Final approval for any such changes rests with Her Majesty in Council. The current composition of the Court is set out in Annex 1.

5. For reasons which are explained more fully in the following sections, the Court strongly believes that the framework summarised above, and in particular its own composition, provides checks and balances which form a strong safeguard against many of the areas of potential concern set out in the Nolan Committee's paper.

6. The University Court's specific comments on the issues raised by the Nolan Committee, and some associated matters, are set out below, using the same sub-headings as in the Committee's paper.

The Appointment and Accountability of Board Members

7. As explained above and shown in Annex 1, the University Court is *not* "largely responsible" (paragraph 15) for appointing its own members. Only eight out of 23 members can be appointed by the Court itself. Its mechanisms are not "self-perpetuating" (paragraph 17), and its broad composition offers strong safeguards against a "relatively small group" assuming and perpetuating "their control of it" and against the other potential problems referred to in paragraph 17. Periods of membership of elected and co-opted members are staggered, such that a balance between continuity and change can be achieved.

8. The Court has a Nominations Committee comprising internal and external members, whose composition and terms of reference are set out in Annex 2. The Court recognises the crucial importance of co-opting able and active members from a wide range of backgrounds. The Nominations Committee considers suggestions for co-option against published criteria (Annex 2) with this objective very much to the fore. A particular feature of this process is the practice of including one co-opted member nominated by the Senate Assessors. The existence of vacancies amongst the co-opted places is made known within the University. The Nominations Committee is able to take into account the performance of co-opted members when considering renewal of their appointment (paragraph 20). Generally, co-opted members are restricted to two three-year periods of service.

9. The Nominations Committee has been active for two years: on reflection, the Court accepts that more could probably be done to widen the range of individuals considered for co-option, perhaps by more actively encouraging

suggestions from within the University and from the wider community (paragraph 20). It will consider further how to enhance current performance in that respect and how to ensure that the process is as open as can reasonably be achieved. However, the Court sees no additional benefit being derived from external involvement in this process: the balance of internal and external members provides sufficient checks and balances.

10. The Court views the issue of accountability (paragraph 21) as falling into two parts. The first is financial accountability. This is very adequately covered by the statutory framework within which the University operates, notably the Further and Higher Education (Scotland) Act 1992 and the Funding Council's Financial Memorandum and Code of Audit Practice. The University's accounts are open to the Comptroller and Auditor General. The chain of accountability to Parliament is not "lengthy" (paragraph 15): as the "designated officer" in the terms of the Financial Memorandum, the Principal can be summoned to appear before the Public Accounts Committee together with the Chief Executive of the SHEFC. In addition, again arising from the terms of the Financial Memorandum, it is already the case that the Principal has the duty formally to advise the Court if it is considering any action or policy contrary to the Memorandum and, if the Court decides to proceed, to notifying the Funding Council (paragraph 23). In broader terms, the University is also accountable to the Funding Council for the utilisation of its grants for the intended purposes. This is reflected in the need to recruit at least the number of students for which it receives funding for teaching and to account for the allocation of funding received for research and for the use of any funding provided for specific purposes at the initiative of the Funding Council.

11. The second and broader area of accountability relates to performance in the non-financial sense. In many regards this is a more complex matter. At one level it relates to the performance of individuals as members of the Court; at another—albeit linked—level it relates to the performance of the University as a whole in relation to its academic and wider objectives. The Court, as a body corporate, is collectively responsible for the effectiveness of its work. It is accountable to the General Council, the statutory body comprising all graduates, in the sense that it submits an Annual Report to a meeting of that body which, through the terms of the Universities (Scotland) Act 1858, is empowered to exercise a broad oversight of "all questions affecting the well-being and prosperity of the University" and to make "representations to the Court" on issues which must be considered and responded to.

12. In the context of being an autonomous academic institution, the University regards itself as accountable to the wider community in a variety of ways. Members of Parliament, local councillors and members of the public raise matters with the Principal, the Rector, members of the Court and senior officers: they expect and receive proper responses. The University actively seeks to communicate its activities and achievements to the local community and beyond, and recognises that such communication should be a two-way process. It is accountable to the Funding Council for complying with broad higher education policy which can be underpinned by the Funding Council attaching conditions to its funding. Moreover, in a very real sense it is accountable to the market in terms of student recruitment and ability to attract external income for research and other activities. Ultimately, however, the Court recognises and accepts that the corollary of academic autonomy is a collective responsibility for the University's welfare and development which cannot be transferred to any other body. It strongly believes that what some might regard as a consequent curtailment of its formal comprehensive accountability to any external body is wholly appropriate and acceptable because of the fundamental importance to a democratic society of its institutions of higher education retaining the autonomy to teach and to pursue research without fear or favour.

13. Individual members of the Court nominated by other bodies, whether internal or external, are to some degree accountable to those bodies. This is not in the sense of them being mandated delegates, required to pursue whatever line their nominated body requires and to report back to them. Rather, it is in the sense that whilst they can and do consult with their nominating bodies, they act to the best of their abilities and in good faith as individual members. If, for example, the University were to run into an area of difficulty, they would be able to explain to their nominating bodies how this had arisen and why, and what the Court intended doing about it, and to bring back to the Court the results of this consultative process. The chair of the Court (the Rector) is elected by staff and students for a three-year period of office.

14. The University Court very much doubts that any benefit in terms of improved performance or greater accountability would be derived from paying members (paragraph 20). Whilst it might sound trite, there is a very real sense in which the service and the wider involvement in the University's affairs is its own reward. For most members the time which requires to be devoted to the work is fairly limited and any financial reward would be relatively small, not least because the University would be anxious to avoid individuals seeking appointment to the Court for financial reasons. Such payments, or the danger of their loss, would not be likely to provide any additional incentive to performance.

15. The University is also very concerned that undue pressure of accountability or detailed scrutiny should not be placed on individual members of the Court. It would be all too easy to deter able but usually very busy people, active in other walks of life, from joining the Court by imposing an intrusive or bureaucratic performance-monitoring regime, which at its worst could carry a flavour of "guilty until proved innocent". That would be to the benefit of no one. It is the Court's firm view that there has been no trace amongst its membership of the inappropriate behaviour which the Nolan Committee's paper postulates as being possible, or indeed which is reported to have occurred elsewhere in, it is understood, differently constituted governing bodies. Whilst appropriate measures can be put in place which should prove acceptable and effective, it would be very unfortunate indeed if individuals of the highest calibre were to be deterred from serving the University, and through it the wider community, as members of Court by wholly disproportionate measures.

The Role of Boards in relation to officers and staff

16. The University Court believes that it does maintain an appropriate division of responsibilities between itself and senior officers of the University (paragraph 22). The Court's role is one of setting policy and broad strategy for the University: the executive manages the University on a day-to-day basis in the light of the Court's policy and strategy decisions. There is inevitably a grey area at the boundary between implementation of policy and strategy and its formulation: the Court and the executive are able to explore these together and to learn from the experience of so doing. Moreover, there are some areas where the executive find it helpful to seek the Court's guidance on the implementation of policy and strategy, and there are areas where the Court rightly expects to have a more detailed insight than a simple delineation of responsibilities might suggest.

17. It is certainly the case that all major policy decisions and all major financial decisions are taken by the Court or by a body formally delegated to do so by it (paragraph 24). In the latter case papers are available to all Court members on request. The Court's agenda is divided primarily into items for information, which largely constitute the executive reporting back on actions taken or reports from Sub-Committees on decisions reached, and items for discussion and decision by the Court itself. Whilst the Court would certainly recognise that there is some scope for improvement in the efficiency of its decision making and the delineation of responsibility between itself and the executive, it is firmly convinced that the procedures it employs offer a secure safeguard against the dangers set out in the final three sentences of paragraph 22 of the paper.

18. As indicated above, the Principal, as chief executive, already has the duty set out in the opening sentence of paragraph 23. The Secretary to the University also has a clear duty to advise the Court if it is about to take a decision which is beyond its powers or in some other way *ultra vires* (paragraph 23).

19. Sub-committees of the Court have clear terms of reference approved by it, and report to the Court as indicated above (paragraph 24). In a large organisation such as the University there is an important role to be played by sub-committees, not only for greater efficiency in the processing of business but also to permit wider involvement of the University community in the decision-making process. The Court's powers to delegate to sub-committees are governed, in generalised terms, by the Universities (Scotland) Act 1889.

20. The University's Audit Committee oversees both internal and external audit, which are conducted within the framework laid down by the Funding Council's Code of Audit Practice (paragraph 25). The Funding Council itself is empowered to initiate efficiency studies of the University's activities. The University's financial health is monitored closely by the Funding Council through bi-annual returns. The University does not believe that there is need for further layers of audit. A Remuneration Committee (paragraph 24) has recently been formed. Its role is formally advisory to the Principal and relates to senior members of staff of the University (Court members are not paid for their service).

21. Court meetings are conducted in accord with its Standing Orders. It is not clear to the Court that formulation of a "code of conduct" would result in any practical improvement to its operation over and above adoption of best practice in a number of specific ways arising from the Nolan Committee's suggestions and otherwise (paragraph 24). Such a code of practice would presumably be no more than a statement bringing together a set of separate decisions by the Court on the way in which it conducts its business and the standards members are expected to observe. The concept of making public funding conditional upon adherence to such codes raises the obvious and very real question of how this would be monitored in practice. The Court strongly believes that if able and eminent people are to continue to be attracted to membership, and whilst appropriate checks and balances can and do exist, ultimately the members themselves must carry responsibility for their integrity and compliance with best practice in the conduct of business. Moreover, they must also carry responsibility for dealing with circumstances, which experience hitherto suggests would be very rare, where an individual member departs from these standards.

22. Like other Scottish universities, Edinburgh does not have the equivalent of the Visitor found in older English institutions (paragraph 25). Viewed from the outside, it is not entirely evident that this function is wholly effective. The Court feels no need for such a post to be created. The University does have a well-defined internal complaints procedure, which needs to be seen in the context that, along with the other "ancient" Scottish universities, it has the unique post of Rector. The Rector is an external person elected by all the staff and students of the University for a three-year period. He or she chairs the Court and in addition has traditionally played the role of "ombudsperson" in the sense that they can be directly approached by any student or member of staff who has an unresolved complaint or dispute. The Rector is uniquely placed to take such matters up with the appropriate officers of the University. The University finds that in practice this is a very effective mechanism for dealing with such difficulties, and the need has never been expressed for a wholly external person to play such a role.

23. The question of greater openness in the Court's proceedings requires careful consideration (paragraph 26). The Court attaches great importance to communication between itself and the University community, and with the wider outside community. In particular, the Court believes it to be very important that the processes leading up to consideration of matters are open, that it has mechanisms for ensuring that account is take of all relevant views and that the outcome of Court decisions is effectively communicated to the University community. It seeks to achieve these objectives by encouraging its members to consult within the University with regard to matters coming up for discussion by using the existing sub-committee structure, and through an internal newsletter in which its decisions are made known as quickly as possible after meetings. Agendas and minutes are, however, not routinely made available within the University. Whilst the majority of papers could probably be made available, it is far from clear that this would be the best practical way of giving members of the University greater opportunity to influence the Court's work. Court

meetings are not open to members of the University, and the Court is very doubtful that there would be any real benefit to be gained from this. It concurs with the view that public bodies must be allowed to have private thoughts. Holding meetings in "public" would be likely to change the character of the Court and quite possibly could be counter-productive. There is a real danger that this could result in the tendency for decisions to be taken in practice outwith meetings or in smaller groups, which would be wholly contrary to the Nolan Committee's intentions.

24. It is also important to recognise that not all discussions within the Court result in decisions. Consideration of some matters can spread over a number of meetings. It would be counter-productive to release half-formed views to the University community, and indeed the whole process of governance of the University could become very inefficient in such circumstances, although there are occasions when the Court will wish to interrupt its consideration of a matter in order to seek wider views within the University. The Court must also bear in mind its responsibility to third parties: some of its discussions must remain confidential until external bodies affected by its decisions have been notified of them. Account also need to be taken of the fact that the University is in a competitive position vis-à-vis other higher education institutions and that it operates a number of income-generating activities, some of them within the framework of commercial companies. The details of some decisions taken by the Court will need to remain confidential for competitive or commercial reasons.

25. The Court accepts that some further thought is needed on these issues, particularly in regard to effective communication between it and the University community and beyond. It will pursue these matters over the coming months.

Safeguards in respect of conflicts of interest

26. Hitherto the University has not maintained a register of members' interests (paragraph 29), but its consideration of this enquiry from the Nolan Committee has led it to conclude that it should do so. However, it must be emphasised that the Court is very firmly of the view that none of the potential difficulties raised in paragraphs 28-32 have been experienced: there is no doubt whatsoever that members of the Court have always acted with total integrity.

27. The Court accepts that there should be a register of interests open to public inspection, and that this should include senior officers as well as members of the Court. The definition of what should be included in the register raises some difficulties (paragraph 30). It clearly should include individuals' financial and business interests, but how far, if at all, it should extend to Court members' families requires further consideration. Moreover, given the nature of the University's activities, an element of judgment will be needed as to where the boundary should be drawn with regard to inclusion of non-financial items on the register, including involvement with other public bodies. The current view is that the register of such interests should be limited rather than extensive, with a clear expectation that members would raise particular potential conflicts of interest as and when relevant matters came up for discussion at Court meetings. It is emphasised that this is not a way of dodging the issue, but rather a practical approach to resolving the difficulty of knowing what non-financial interests should be included in a register.

28. The University would expect the register to be updated at least annually, with members notifying major changes as soon as they are known. Whether a potential conflict should bar a member from participating in the meeting or voting would depend on the circumstances and on the scale of the issue. If members were in any doubt, they would be expected to consult the Convenor or the Vice-Convenor, or the Secretary of the Court.

Conclusion

29. The University Court strongly believes that ultimately, as an autonomous body, it should take responsibility for identifying and observing best practice in the conduct of its business and in its governance of the University (paragraph 34). As indicated at the outset of this response, the Nolan Committee's seven principles are very helpful in this context. It is very important that these should be interpreted in the context of the particular institution or organisation under consideration. Very real harm could be done to the character of organisations and to good governance of them if a simplistic approach were taken requiring a high degree of consistency in the detailed way in which the principles were implemented. The Court therefore strongly believes that it should carry the formal responsibility for ensuring that the principles are put into practice at the University within the existing statutory and regulatory framework for higher education in Scotland.

Other issues

30. Although not raised in the Nolan Committee's enquiry, one other area of concern has been identified during the Court's consideration of these matters. This is the apparently increasing tendency of Government to suppress research reports which it has commissioned from academic institutions. Not only is this potentially seriously disadvantageous to the academic concerned, it is contrary to the principles of open government. The Court is similarly concerned that there is an increasing tendency for the results of research projects funded by industry not to be published, even after an appropriate delay for commercial reasons. It is hoped that the Committee might be able to give these matters some consideration.

Opening Statement from the Convention of Scottish Local Authorities

1. COSLA welcomes the opportunity to give evidence on local public spending bodies to the Committee on Standards in Public Life. In Scotland since 1978/79 expenditure by Scottish quangos (including national and local public spending bodies) has doubled in real terms, increasing from £3.5 billion to £6.9 billion (but excluding water) and involving some 4,000 appointments.

2. While it is not part of the remit of the Committee, the removal of responsibilities from local government to appointed bodies has been, in the Convention's view, an important factor in weakening local government. Whilst the Convention accepts no Government will abandon government by appointed body, there is a need for a review of local appointed bodies to determine whether there is a continuing need for each of them or whether (a) their functions might be more effectively undertaken by local government or (b) there is a need for them to be subject to some form of strategic monitoring by local government, given their close relationship to local government—for example, giving rights to councils to require explanation from such bodies or to require representatives of them to appear before scrutiny committees of the council.

3. Having regard to the areas of interest of the Committee and the questions posed by it in relation to local public spending bodies—namely, appointments, accountability, membership and performance, the role of Boards in relation to officers and staff, and safeguards in respect of conflicts of interest—COSLA would make the following submission.

Appointments

4. Informal and networking methods of recruitment smack of "jobs for the boys" and are inconsistent with best employment practice of equal opportunities. Open recruitment would secure transparency.

5. If most bodies are to continue in their present form, on the basis of ministerial appointment, it is essential that the process of appointment is made as transparent as possible, as well as being strengthened to increase its accountability. Accountability would be strengthened if local authorities individually and through COSLA had rights of nomination to a number of places on such bodies. This will enhance the legitimacy of these bodies and at the same time would strengthen the relationship between each body and its council.

6. Consideration should also be given to the possibility of direct election to increase accountability, although this carries potential pitfalls, for example of confusion for the public and of worsening the already fragmented nature of the way local services are governed.

7. In terms of financial accountability, the Government has accepted the Committee's recommendation that there should be a review of the arrangements for external audit. COSLA believes that all appointed bodies should be subject to the same standards of external auditing and performance measurement as councils. Given their use of public funds, there is a strong argument in favour of extending the remit of the Accounts Commission to include all such bodies.

8. In terms of strengthening local accountability, COSLA offers the following suggestions:

(1) *Improved public access to meetings.* Meetings of such bodies should be publicised, and some or all meetings, and most of the agendas, should be open to the public and agendas and meetings should be easily accessible. Access to information legislation should be extended to them. There should be an effective complaints procedure and COSLA supports the principle of extending the remit of the Parliamentary Commission for Administration.

(2) *Securing an effective partnership with councils.* Local authorities are, in most cases, a key partner for such bodies. There is a need to secure a climate of positive co-operation, mutual openness and positive joint working. The fundamental basis of a positive and productive partnership must be equality and a willingness to discuss issues openly in an environment of trust and co-operation. Clearly issues of sensitive commercial information on both sides cannot be ignored but, as a general principle, there should be a culture of openness in which both sides agree that the overall objective of delivering real benefits to local communities justifies working together in a spirit of genuine partnership..

Membership and Performance Issues

9. Whilst the Government has accepted the Committee's proposals in relation to appointments, eg. a presumption in favour of advertised paid appointments, the appointment of Advisory Panels and the appointment of a Public Appointments Commissioner to oversee and approve the appointments procedures of Government departments, the position remains that, ultimately, appointments to public bodies will be the responsibility of Ministers. In order to avoid any perception of "self-perpetuation", COSLA supports the concept of maximum period of office of two terms.

The Role of Boards in Relation to Officers and Staff

10. In local government maintaining a clear distinction and understanding of the separate roles of elected members and officers is a well established principle; members have responsibility for the development of strategic policy and a review of its implementation; responsibility for operational management and the implementation of policy rests with officers. A similar principle should apply to local public spending bodies. There should be a statutory code of conduct equivalent to the statutory local government code setting out respective responsibilities. Similarly the concept of the monitoring officer, which is a useful addition to the safeguards that exist to prevent unlawful decision-making or expenditure, should be extended to local public spending bodies for the protection of both members and staff.

Safeguards in regard of conflicts of interest

11. The provisions applied to local government should be extended to local public spending bodies. All members (and their spouses or cohabitees) of such bodies should declare their interest generally and at meetings. The current local government legislation provides for three separate thresholds as to how interest should be treated. COSLA supports the concept of a single threshold of £1,000, above which interest must be registered and the member may not participate in discussion or vote.

TUESDAY 30 JANUARY 1996

AFTERNOON SESSION

Members Present:

The Rt Hon Lord Nolan (Chairman)

Sir Clifford Boulton GCB	Sir William Utting CB
The Rt Hon Lord Thomson	Dame Anne Warburton DCVO CMG
of Monifieth KT DL	Diana Warwick

Witnesses:

Professor John Sizer, Chief Executive, Dugald Mackie, Secretary, and Professor Robert Jack, Council Member, Scottish Higher Education Funding Council

A H Bridge, Former Chairman of the Court, A Lindsay Stewart, Chairman of Court, and Ian Miller, Secretary and Registrar, Napier University

Lex Gold, Director, Scottish Chamber of Commerce, Geoff Runcie, Chief Executive, Glasgow Chamber of Commerce, and Derek Marnoch, Chief Executive, Aberdeen Chamber of Commerce

Eileen Mochar, Chair, and Alistair M Tyre, Principal, Langside College, Glasgow, and Walter MacLellan, Member, Strathclyde Regional Council

1484. LORD NOLAN: This afternoon, on what is perhaps our most intensive day of evidence, we shall be hearing from a further four sets of witnesses. Once again they will be mainly, but not exclusively, concerned with the fields of Further and Higher Education.

First, we welcome Professor John Sizer, Chief Executive, Mr Dugald Mackie, Secretary and Professor Robert Jack, Council Member of the Scottish Higher Education Funding Council.

We shall then be hearing from Mr A H Bridge, Former Chairman of the Court, Mr A Lindsay Stewart, the present Chairman of the Court, and Mr Ian Miller, the Secretary and Registrar of Napier University here in Edinburgh.

Our third set of witnesses this afternoon will mainly be covering a different field. Lex Gold, Director of Scottish Chamber of Commerce, Geoff Runcie, Chief Executive of the Glasgow Chamber of Commerce and Derek Marnoch, Chief Executive of the Aberdeen Chamber of Commerce will mainly be talking to us about the business perception of the Local Enterprise Companies.

Finally today we shall be pleased to welcome Eileen Mochar, the Chair, and Alistair Tyre, the Principal, and Mr Graeme Hyslop the Deputy Principal of Langside College, Glasgow, which is a Further Education College.

We begin, please, with our witnesses from the Higher Education Funding Council. I wonder, Professor Sizer, if, for the benefit of the record, you would be kind enough to introduce your colleagues so that we are clear about who is who.

PROFESSOR JOHN SIZER, DUGALD MACKIE, AND PROFESSOR ROBERT JACK

PROF JOHN SIZER (Chief Executive, Scottish Higher Education Funding Council): Thank you, Chairman. First, may I offer Sir John Shaw's apologies. Sir John is the Chairman of the Council and unable to be with us today. On my left is Professor Robert Jack who is a

member of the Council and Chairman of the Audit Committee of the Council, and on my right is Mr Dugald Mackie who is Secretary of the Council.

1485. LORD NOLAN: Thank you very much. We are very grateful for the written material with which you have already supplied us. I wonder if I could start by asking you a quite general question about your approach to the area. You are essentially a funding body rather than a regulator, and you make it clear in what you have written that you are very careful to respect the autonomy of the institutions with which you are dealing. What is the right balance between independence and accountability in this sector, and if I may follow that up a little by reference to what you have written. On page 3 of the response of the Funding Councils to this report in paragraph 14 you urge this Committee to—"recognise that every increase in the burden of expectation placed on governors either by funding councils or by government must be tested and weighed before it is introduced. Responsibility brings with it accountability for actions taken. It is essential for the public interest that governors continue to feel that sense of responsibility. The imposition of rules, conditions and its own standards by a third party has been shown in the past to lead to a diminished feeling of responsibility as control is taken out of the hands of those in whom it should rest."

You return, Professor Sizer, you and Mr Mackie, at the conclusion of your separate paper to speak of the key factors which need to be observed if institutions are to account more rigorously for what they spend, and demonstrate that they are using funds economically, efficiently and effectively. You, in effect, as I read it, say that so far the shift is towards more autonomy, leaving it with them, but it may be necessary to impose stricter checks if you have any disasters. Is that how you see it?

PROF JOHN SIZER: I think we feel in Scotland we have very high quality governing bodies, and we believe that they are the first line of public accountability. We make funds available to the governing bodies on condition that those funds are used for the purposes intended. So we have to satisfy ourselves that not only are the funds being used for the purposes intended but are achieving the purposes intended, and that the governing body operates within a framework that ensures that the executive of the institution does, in fact, account to the governing body in the same way as we require the governing body to satisfy us that the funds are being used for the purposes intended.

Our concern is that if we assume the roles of the governing bodies, these very high quality people, who work closely with the executive managements at universities in very difficult times, will feel that their role is being taken over by ourselves and we do not feel we can fulfil that role. If they do have that feeling, then we will not be able to attract the high quality of people that we currently have. All our experience since the Council was established in 1992 is not only that the governing bodies in Scotland do contain very high quality people, but they take their responsibilities very seriously and are fully aware of the expectations of the Council and do set out to deliver them.

I will ask Professor Jack to add to that because he has had experience both as a member of a governing body and as a member of the Council.

PROF ROBERT JACK (Council Member, Scottish Higher Education Funding Council): Chairman, this balance between accountability and autonomy is, of course, at the crux of our problem. It is perhaps accentuated in our case by the fact that universities, certainly the ancient universities, were there before we were there (if you take the comparable case of LECs they came in the wake of the network). So the institutions were there with an established history and an established ethos, and, in the case of the ancient universities, with very ancient privileges and constitutional arrangements which have served them well for quite a long time. As Chairman of the Audit Committee I have a special responsibility to look at the problems of the financial health of the sector, and to see that they are being (this begs a lot of questions) properly run.

The thing to be said about Scotland, and I think you will hear this *ad nauseam* while you are here, is that we are a very small constituency. We know one another. I used to say when I was involved with the Financial Services Regulation, we did not have big frauds in Scotland because everybody knew one another. If you did not know the chap you, to use the Scottish expression which Lord Thomson will appreciate, "you kent his faither". He can translate that for the rest of you. Or certainly you went to school with them, or somebody you knew went to school with them. So you know them, you know who the rogues are.

I think it is perhaps part of the sort of presbyterian ethos that we have very strong views about honesty, and these permeate our institutions. I, I may say, am a part-time academic. I am really a lawyer. I do not know how that ingratiates me or otherwise—a bit of a fraudulent academic—but in my experience, people who come into the service of the university with which I have a connection are motivated by the highest of motives. They are not there for any thought of reward, certainly not any thought of financial reward; it is just a service to this institution which they regard as an important element of their community. Therefore to impose on them rules suggesting that we question their integrity, their honesty,

is very counter-productive and, in fact, may drive them away. But, on the other hand, we (at SHEFC) have accountability to the Scottish Office for the money which we get, and we have, by the same token, to impose accountability on our customers from whom we buy services. Therefore we have an interest to ensure that governing bodies run their universities properly (that there are no scandals, there are no frauds, there are no irregularities). We, to some extent, have to rely on the checks and balances which they themselves have and which we, to some extent, monitor; that they produce a climate which, while it does not prevent innovative action, in fact also ensures that irregularities are detected and properly exposed. It is a balance which is never totally adequate at any given time. When a scandal erupts people say it was inadequate; but on the other hand when monitoring is over-intrusive there are problems the other way.

1486. LORD NOLAN: But you have been short on scandals, to put it mildly, haven't you, in this area of Scottish public life? There have not been any scandals in recent years that have crossed our path that we know about.

PROF JOHN SIZER: I think that is true, Chairman.

1487. LORD NOLAN: And this is a reflection of the very high standards which you say prevail, and long may it last. One respects the feeling of almost indignation which you have spoken about when, with no evidence to suggest that there is any malpractice, people find that effectively outside bodies are saying, but we do not trust you.

If I can go back to an earlier experience of mine which the other Committee members have heard me mention before. I suppose it must be at least 20 years ago at the English Bar, we had a complaints system, we had disciplinary tribunals, it was all internal, we thought we sorted out the rotten apples in the barrel quite satisfactorily, but it became borne in on us that people outside thought we ought to have an independent element in the tribunal and it was quite a shock. We had to say to ourselves, don't they trust us? It became clear that not only didn't they trust us because they were suspicious, but we would have to do something about it. I think this is something that has happened in many areas of life, isn't it, including, as we now see following our first Report, the House of Commons itself has accepted the presence of an independent element. One hopes that, in so far as we are proposing greater openness, those to whom we propose it will not take it in any sense or reflection on them, but an opportunity for them to show the public what a good job they are doing, which is, I hope, one of our tasks.

Coming back to the big demands made on those volunteers who serve higher education in Scotland, one of the views you express is that remuneration should be introduced or at least considered for governing body members. Why do you propose that?

DUGALD MACKIE (Secretary, Scottish Higher Education Funding Council): The response which we sent in fell between two meetings of our Council, and I interpreted one meeting in putting these views forward. Subsequent to the response being sent in I think members of the Council considered this very point again, and I think by and large, although we have said it is a point that should be considered, and I do not think it can be ruled out, the majority view among Council members is that if institutions can get members of the governing bodies to serve without remuneration that is preferable to there being remuneration to them. I think the point we were trying to make is that this has always been the expectation in the past, and it is possible that it may no longer be the expectation.

PROF ROBERT JACK: Can I elaborate a little on that. I came from a professional practice where if I took on a job like this then my partners expected there would be some compensation to the firm for the loss of my time. In most cases they would accept that the university is a public service which they ought to take account of, but in my professional lifetime the profession has moved from a recognition of this obligation to a much more cost-driven, cost-recovery basis. All I say is, it perhaps helps to make a better case in such a situation which I have envisaged if, in fact, there is at least an element of compensation. The obverse of that is, if it is so minuscule that it does not matter perhaps we should not do it.

I am intruding into another area, but I am a member of a LEC as well and I think this issue is actually stronger in LECs, partly because the Scottish Enterprise Network Board are themselves paid.

1488. LORD NOLAN: Thank you. It is one of the most difficult and perplexing bodies of evidence that we have had to consider, and even today we have from the Association of Scottish Colleges the evidence that they are going to consider it at the request of some of their members. Robert Gordon University of Aberdeen, on the other hand feels very strongly that it would be damaging to the morale of those members who give voluntary service if any sort of remuneration were to be introduced. But we have, as you have just mentioned, in the highest degree reputable public bodies whose members are paid, including, of course, many of those in the National Health Service. So it is a difficult balance and you have not formed a concluded view, is that right, certainly not a view that should be applied universally?

PROF JOHN SIZER: No, I think there are differences of view within the Council, with people not feeling they want to come to a firm view. I think what we are conscious of is that as the financial environment in which institutions operate becomes increasingly difficult, as they are faced with increasingly difficult strategic choices about the future direction of the university, and as the governing body's role in monitoring the relationship between the academic strategy and the financial health and the physical environment of the university increases, this is placing increasing demands upon lay members and therefore requires throughout very high quality lay members. Certainly for those institutions facing difficult financial circumstances, the lay members have to have more interaction with me and my officers in terms of discussing how the institution will address the circumstances they face. Therefore there is always the risk that some people may say, "well, I have enjoyed making my voluntary contribution but I am not sure that I necessarily want to be continuing to do this in this sort of climate". I think it is that balance between the desire for public service—it is a strong tradition in Scotland—on the one hand, and the increasing demands that we are placing on them and the difficult environment in which they operate, that Council members recognise.

So far I have not seen any evidence that the institutions we fund (some of which one has to recognise are very

prestigious, distinguished institutions) have said that they are having difficulty attracting members of their governing bodies. One of the reasons is partly, as Professor Jack says, that it is a small country and it is very well networked and therefore people know the sort of people who can fulfil these roles. But also we have very able chairs of governing bodies and those chairs are clearly influential in attracting able people to join them. I think at the moment the view of the Council is that they do not want to take a firm position but it needs to be kept under review.

1489. LORD NOLAN: Thank you very much. Although not specifically a regulatory body, you have, have you not, attached conditions of reporting and the like on particular types of expenditure? I am thinking of the research grants and the study you made of that, and your view that the expenditure must be carefully accounted for. Would you welcome a wider regulatory role or do you feel that, having effectively control of the purse strings, without exerting too much leverage and without being too prescriptive, you can do effectively what you feel you need to do in safeguarding the expenditure of funds under your control?

PROF JOHN SIZER: I am content with the position we have at the moment. Unless the Secretary of State placed extra demands on the Council I think we can operate effectively. We have considerable experience both within the Executive and the Council in these areas, and if you looked at the history of how we have addressed research accountability perhaps, because we are a smaller sector, we probably have been just a little bit ahead of our counterparts in England because the problems they face are much larger and more complex, as you have probably found from your discussions with them.

1490. LORD NOLAN: As we all know, the systems of governance in what we call the old universities and the new universities are different. At the risk of over simplifying, one might think that the new universities have generally smaller boards and boards perhaps more easily adaptable to the more commercial role which universities now seem to play. Have you a view on whether the new universities are better able to face up to the financial challenges that they meet today than the older ones?

PROF JOHN SIZER: I do not think I can express a view, Chairman. It is not my responsibility to monitor in detail the effectiveness of the boards, and therefore anything I say I think would be hearsay rather than based on a careful examination. But I repeat what I said at the beginning, and in a sense you reiterated by saying there were no scandals in Scotland, we believe that the governing bodies of all the institutions we deal with are competent and have high quality people who we can deal with in their different circumstances. I do not think it would be appropriate for me to make comparisons and draw conclusions about the relative effectiveness of three different types of situation in Scotland. There are those appointed in the ancient universities under the Universities of Scotland Acts; there are the new universities who were previously funded by the University Grants Committee and have different charters, like Heriot-Watt for example, of which Lord Thomson was Chancellor; there are the new universities and colleges of higher education formerly funded by the Scottish Office. They each have different arrangements and it is not our responsibility to draw conclusions other than to say that we have had effective relationships with all of these, though they all have particular problems. I think it best to discuss with them individually rather than for us to draw a conclusion.

LORD NOLAN: But I suppose you are very closely concerned with their financial viability and how much money they need, and how they can supplement it in other ways.

PROF JOHN SIZER: We have very rigorous financial controls and monitoring procedures. It just happens that my chairman is an accountant and I am an accountant in our first professional lives, so we do have very rigorous forward-looking control systems that are designed to anticipate problems and to enter into discussions, if necessary, as to how the Principal and, if necessary, the governing body as a whole is addressing those problems. But we have not had any institution in serious financial difficulties. Our procedures are designed to ensure that institutions do not get into serious difficulties because we anticipate them and have discussions with them. So I have no evidence that when governing bodies are faced with the consequences of undertaking their financial forecasts that they are not addressing the issues. As you know, we make our financial memorandum available to every member of the governing body. We require the institution's plans and financial forecasts to be approved by the governing body before we receive them, and there is certainly no evidence that this is simply a rubber stamping operation by the governing body. But again, I rely on Professor Jack and his committee to ensure that the Executive is delivering that.

PROF ROBERT JACK: It is true that we do impose obligations of accountability, and to that extent we rely and we have sought to improve upon the quality of accounting. There is now a statement of recommended accounting practice which applies to the sector and we are hopeful that we will see where problems are and that accountability will be improved. Of course, we do rely to a considerable extent on external auditors. One can never be totally sure that the obligation to ensure that money given to the university or other institution for a specific purpose is used for that purpose without an excessive degree of monitoring. One has to rely on certification, internal and external, and hope that one gets that one. You cannot be sure, but, as auditors will tell you, they cannot be sure that any audit discloses everything. But I think, so far as one can reasonably expect, we have put in place a system of accounting between ourselves and the institutions which should disclose problems before they become crises, or whatever the advertisement says. So far it is working but there is a reasonably easy dialogue, I think it is true to say, between ourselves and the institutions who will tell us of problems even before we get to know about them, and there is hopefully a bit of trust between the two of us that there would no kind of attempt to deceive one another. We have responsible people on these bodies, both on the non-executive side and the executive side, and so far, and touching all sorts of wood, it has worked.

1491. LORD NOLAN: That certainly answers my question in so far as we are concerned with the proper monitoring of the public money which comes through you to the universities. I was wondering whether the universities feel they have enough, and whether, by supplementing funds or practising more competitive approaches to their task, they were causing any problems as far as you were concerned. For example, I do not say in Scotland but there has been some fear in England about the risk of academic standards being lowered to attract more students, of poaching between one body and another. Has that been a problem that has come your way?

PROF JOHN SIZER: No, but again we are not the body responsible for monitoring standards; that is undertaken by the Higher Education Quality Council which is a body owned by the institutions themselves. Our quality assessment procedures complement those, but clearly as institutions have to reduce their dependence on government funding and develop other sources of funding, and they are actually having to compete for students in priority areas, the risk and uncertainty attached to their operations increases. So in terms of financial monitoring we have to recognise that, and therefore we do ask institutions to undertake sensitivity analysis, we do discuss with them whether they have contingency plans. They are reluctant to make those contingency plans available to us, which you can understand, but they have to satisfy us that they have those plans in place.

Clearly part of my role is to look at the overall financial health of the institution because it may well be that public funds are put at risk because of the other activities they undertake. For example, institutions are increasingly making use of loan finance and are encouraged to participate in the private finance initiative. That, again, has an impact on the financial health of the institution, it increases the risks they undertake, they need to have income streams to service the debt and so on. So our monitoring procedures have to make sure that the institution fully understands these things and that, if we are not satisfied that their assumptions hold water, or that their governing body does not fully appreciate the overall health of the institution, then we will bring it to their attention. There are various ways of doing this. They range from me writing a letter, to me asking if I might go and talk to the principal, to me asking if I might go and talk to the principal and the chairman of the governors, to inviting the principal to come and see me, to inviting the chairman of the governing body and the chairman of the finance committee and the principal to come and see me. Those are all different levels of dialogue that address the extent to which that institution is facing a difficult financial scenario. I have to be satisfied that they can address it effectively, and they are addressing it effectively so that public funds are not being put at risk, and also that they are able to deliver their contract with the Council in terms of providing teaching and undertaking research.

1492. LORD NOLAN: Yes, and if the universities reach the point of saying that "We are so short of funds we are going to have to take an entrance fee off the students of £300 a go", is that something in which you have a part to play? Does that come back to you to advise Government?

PROF JOHN SIZER: The Secretary of State has not sought my advice or the Council's advice on that, and I would rather not comment.

1493. LORD NOLAN: No, well it is clearly at very early stages of discussion.

I think the only other question I wanted to put to you was this. It has not so far been necessary in this country as it seems, but in the English universities and to some extent elsewhere there have been occasional disputes which have called for the intervention of an outside regulator. In the case of the old universities we are told that the Rector can effectively play the part of Visitor in the English universities and could act as a kind of ombudsman or trouble-shooter or a medium for insuring an independent investigation. Would you favour a regular outside body for settling disputes about the use or improper use of money in the universities? Would an ombudsman for the university sector help do you think, or is it something you have not considered?

PROF JOHN SIZER: It is not something we have considered and, I think as far as the proper use of public funds is concerned, that is my responsibility as Accounting Officer, and I really do not think I can delegate that responsibility to some outside body. I wonder how the Public Accounts Committee would react, if I was called before them to explain why proper use had not been made of public funds, if I said "well, I had assumed this outside body was doing my job for me". That is a personal reaction but I do feel very strongly that as Accounting Officer it is my responsibility to satisfy myself that funds are being used for the purposes intended and achieve the purpose intended. I do not really feel I can delegate that to other people, and the Council's role is to ensure that I am doing my job effectively and also to satisfy itself that the procedures laid down in the financial memorandum between ourselves and the institutions has been properly carried forward. But we have not discussed it, and Professor Jack has an interest in these issues and reflects upon this from various perspectives, so I would ask his view as well.

PROF ROBERT JACK: I am not sure. Certainly I would second what Professor Sizer has said that, in the terms of financial control and accountability, I do not think an outside party really has any part to play. Normally, as you know, when there is a sort of financial scandal an independent firm of accountants normally produces a report and says why it has happened. I do not suppose it is impossible that we would have to resort to that device, we have never had to thankfully. The sort of issues which one envisages a Rector being involved with are not the sort of issues that would impinge very directly.

LORD NOLAN: Not normally money issues.

PROF ROBERT JACK: They are not normally. The other side, as you all know, is that in the ancient Scottish universities there is a body called the General Council which, in fact, comprises the graduates of the university. They actually do meet—they meet twice a year in the case of my own university—and I know within my experience when there was a problem about a student who was expelled from the university, his own council did act, albeit rather slowly and perhaps not very effectively, but it did act. As someone said to me, the General Council is there as a sort of court of last resort if things get out of hand in the relations between university and the public, or the university in any element to its constituency. It is an institution which has not been brought into play very much, but it is there.

DUGALD MACKIE: There are times when we have grievances which are referred to us, I suspect sometimes as a last resort, because we are a Funding Council and people may see us, perhaps slightly wrongly, as in some way a regulatory body. Certainly, in responding to such grievances I am careful to point out that we have a certain statutory authority which we cannot exceed. By and large

I will try to deal with them on an ad hoc basis either by referring them to the Rector where possible, possibly even to the Chairman of the University Court because that may be appropriate, or to the Principal. But I have to say, and this is my personal view, that I think there is a slight problem here. I personally consider that if I am an aggrieved person and I wish to deal with a higher education institution, at the end of the day I may not be able to have that grievance properly solved, and I think that there is a difficulty.

PROF JOHN SIZER: Whether we are the organisation to deal with that, or whether the equivalent to a Visitor system as exists in the English universities is the way forward, I think we look forward to hearing what you conclude. I do not think it is our role.

1494. LORD NOLAN: Quite so. If I may say so, to my mind at least, your report is very reassuring on what you see as your fundamental role which is preserving proper accountability for the public money that goes through your hands.

Is there any recommendation which you have in mind that this Committee might make which would improve the situation from your angle?

PROF JOHN SIZER: I do not think so, Chairman. Is this overall or in relation to this particular issue?

LORD NOLAN: In relation to your functions.

PROF JOHN SIZER: I think we feel that we have a very good set of relationships with the institutions we fund, that they understand clearly where we are coming from, and they understand what our view is on the role of governing bodies and our view on clear lines of accountability, so I do not think so. There clearly have been problems elsewhere which you have no doubt addressed elsewhere, but these problems have not arisen here, as you said, and I think if there are to be changes made I would rather they evolved through the process of consultation that we have pursued right from the start. We believe in securing ownership for everything we do through extensive consultation. Therefore I think I would much rather, in a sense, read the evidence and read your report and bring this to Council, and then say to the Council, "do we feel that something should be done?" Rather than making a recommendation off the top of my head.

LORD NOLAN: These are early days and you are still evolving, as you say, and it is not a time to rock the boat unless there is some good reason for doing so. Thank you very much. I will ask Diana Warwick if she would like to carry on.

1495. DIANA WARWICK: I feel I ought to declare an interest every time a university or a higher education institution comes to give us evidence.

First of all, thank you for what I think is very clearly set out in your paper, the nature and level of your responsibilities. You have explored almost all the questions that I wanted to ask, but if I can press you just a little bit on one of them. When you are dealing with private funds you said that you needed to reassure yourselves, as a body which has responsibility to ensure financial probity, that there were structures in place which ensured that public money was not going to be affected by the way private money was dealt with. Does that mean that if an institution received, let us say, 75 per cent of its money from the private sector and only 25 per cent of its money from the public purse, might you find yourself in conflict with that institution if you chose to investigate the 75 per cent to make sure that the procedures were appropriate?

PROF JOHN SIZER: I think one exercises judgment clearly.

DIANA WARWICK: I was thinking of powers rather than judgment.

PROF JOHN SIZER: I think the important thing is that it is very easy, as you know from your declared interest, for institutions to take on research contracts without fully reflecting the costs of taking on those contracts, particularly in terms of not fully covering the overheads. Therefore an institution, even if it raised 75 per cent of its money from outside, if it was actually taking on a series of marginal contracts that just covered their out of pocket costs there is the possibility that public funds are being used to subsidise that. Now if I was providing my 25 per cent specifically for teaching, it is quite possible that students are actually getting a bad deal because funds that have been provided to ensure that they are taught satisfactorily are actually being used to subsidise research for commercial organisations. That is not only a concern of myself, it is a major concern of the National Audit Office and the Public Accounts Committee, and therefore I have to satisfy myself that these situations do not exist. It is not easy because anybody who is familiar with costing joint product situations knows that it is difficult, and therefore we want to be satisfied that there are procedures. Of course, the CVCP is currently undertaking a review of the procedures and will be recommending proper practices to all institutions very shortly, and I shall be monitoring it to ensure that institutions do implement those procedures. Whether it raises its money from 75 per cent or 25 per cent, either way the fact is money can be misused. But clearly I have to exercise judgment and I do not rush in with both feet and start on the assumption funds are being misused, but rather monitor very carefully. If the evidence I am receiving on the macro level suggests that there is some problem, I think I should be able to send in my audit team to check the facts on the ground because that is what the public expects.

1496. DIANA WARWICK: What would you say as a consequence of that? I know I was putting a very exaggerated position, but what does that say about the relationship between the Funding Council and the governing bodies of institutions? What is the difference in the responsibility of the governing body and the Funding Council in such situations?

PROF JOHN SIZER: If I was not satisfied that funds were not being used to subsidise research contracts, clearly I would bring this to the attention of the accounting officer and the chairman of the governing body and ask them how they intended to address it. If I did not get a satisfactory response I would bring it to the attention of the Council and then the Council would have to decide whether it wished to take any action in terms of the funding of that institution. But in the end the governing body designates, usually the Principal, the Accounting Officer, and they have to ensure that he does his job

effectively and I have to ensure that he operates within guidance that we provided to his governing body, and therefore if it is not being followed then I need to take it up both with him and with the chairman of his governing body, which I do.

1497. DIANA WARWICK: I am reflecting on the situation that arose at Cardiff University, and I am not entirely sure how the role of the Scottish Department for Education would relate to the English Department, but one of the problems there was precisely whose responsibility it was to take up the issue, whether it was the Department or whether it was the then UGC, and what the role of the governing body of the institution was. I think I am trying to push a case here which, since it has not arisen, is not likely to be readily accessible. But trying to work out who is the prime mover or the last resort, or who has the prime responsibility seems to me rather a grey area. I was struck very much by a comment in your report where you were quoting the Carnegie Foundation for the Advancement of Teaching, where you say that that—"concluded that how universities govern themselves remains one of the most confusing and tension-ridden issues in higher education."

That is an interesting comment because what we have been told from many witnesses is that things are reasonably well sorted out and that there are not too many problems.

PROF JOHN SIZER: I think there are clearly problems about the interface between senior management and academic departments, resulting from moves to executive styles of management and away from the traditional collegial way that universities were managed. That is a separate issue from the relationship between governing bodies and executive management. As you may or may not know, I was heavily involved in sorting out the mess at Cardiff and was part of the three-man team advising the then Permanent Secretary of the Department on the question of whether funding should be provided, and I was the sort of hard-nosed accountant in this. I distinctly remember having a meeting with the governing body and pointing out their responsibilities, and clearly they were not aware of their responsibilities. But there was no financial memorandum between the University Grants Committee and the governing body of the institution, so we have learnt a lot from the Cardiff situation. Cardiff was a situation where you had a very weak governing body that was not fulfilling its role to supervise the executive. You can read the report produced to the Public Accounts Committee and the detail, but that was a very exceptional situation and much of what has happened since, as we referred to in our article, was partly as a result of Cardiff and partly the Jarrett Report, which could also be linked in some ways to the situation that arose at Cardiff. But I cannot see any way a Cardiff situation would arise in Scotland.

DIANA WARWICK: It is quite interesting, the point you have made about a weak governing body and effectively a chief executive who has considerable power and exercises it is one that has come up in relation to lots of other institutions with which we have been dealing.

PROF JOHN SIZER: I can think of the examples you may be thinking of but hopefully they are not examples in Scotland.

DIANA WARWICK: No, I am not referring to any examples, at least I do not think I am.

LORD THOMSON: Not examples in Scottish universities.

PROF JOHN SIZER: Scottish universities, I apologise. There may be other examples in Scotland, yes, but not within my patch.

1498. DIANA WARWICK: Am I right in thinking that even were you to apply a condition of grant, which you have powers to do, it would not be appropriate for you to apply such a condition in relation to any element of governance?

DUGALD MACKIE: Our general view is that conditions of grant are conditions of last resort. Our view is that we tend to trust in the good faith and common sense and responsibility of members of governing bodies. It is an easy option for a funding council to making something a condition of grant, but our general view is that it is slightly paternalistic, it is heavy handed and it rather does take away the responsibility from the members of the governing body in whom the responsibility should really lie.

1499. DIANA WARWICK: Can I just make one point because I think it may come up when Napier gives us evidence, and they say here—"It is understood that there is a delay in SHEFC publishing any guidance for Members of Governing Bodies similar to that issued by the Committee of University Chairmen in England and Wales"—and in the absence of guidance Napier has established its own code. From what you have said, is that a misunderstanding about what SHEFC is likely to be doing?

PROF JOHN SIZER: We have been in consultation with the two organisations that represent governors in Scotland, and as a result of those consultations we made a final draft of our Notes of Guidance available to them. They asked if they could have an extension of the consultation time so that they could fit it in with the timing of the meetings of their governing bodies, but I think it is fair to say that we are expecting no negative response to this document. Mr Bridge, who I think you are meeting later, was chairman of one of the groups and it was at his request that I extended my consultation period, but I did work closely with Mr Bridge and Mr James Miller who is the Chairman of the Court at Heriot-Watt University who represents the Chairman of Courts in another grouping, and they both were involved in developing this and we had help from Secretaries of two universities. So, we have gone through an extensive process of consultation and ownership; we are content that the guide reflects all of the points that we wish to raise, and they are content it raises all the points they wish to raise, but they need to carry it through their own individual governing bodies. So we have now given an extension till the end of February at their request, but I assure you that it is fully in hand.

1500. DIANA WARWICK: What I meant was, is it going to be published by SHEFC?

DUGALD MACKIE: No. The difference in our approach to that in England and Wales is that this is a blueprint. There is a level of information and guidance on a number of different issues relative to governance which, in a sense, we are saying to each institution—following consultation we think that it has been proved that having such things in the guidance that you give to members of your governing bodies is useful. But what we have said is

(rather than publish a single document which, although it might cover everything, can be fairly generalised in its scope) that each institution should take the blueprint and then tailor it and add to it things which are particular to its local circumstances. Which is why the process has taken slightly longer in Scotland. But at the end of the day I think will be no less effective than what exists in England and Wales, and they own it and that is the important thing.

PROF JOHN SIZER: It is an insert that they will each fit in in their circumstances because there are three different types of governing bodies in Scotland, and therefore each one wants to consider it in their own context. What we have agreed, subject to dotting the i's and crossing the t's, is the section that we feel should be incorporated in appropriate ways in each of the guides.

DIANA WARWICK: Thank you. Sorry, Chairman, I went over my time a bit.

1501. LORD NOLAN: We are very grateful to you all. You have supplemented your written evidence in an extremely helpful way and answered all of our questions very clearly. Thank you.

Now we have Napier University and Mr Bridge, former Chairman of the Court, Mr Lindsay Stewart, the Chairman, Mr Ian Miller, Secretary and Registrar. I wonder, gentlemen, if for the record you would be kind enough to identify yourselves.

A H BRIDGE, A LINDSAY STEWART, AND IAN MILLER

LINDSAY STEWART (Chairman of Court, Napier University): I am Lindsay Stewart and I have just taken over as Chairman of Court. I have been a governor and a member of Court for ten years so I have a two-year term left as Chairman.

TONY BRIDGE (Former Chairman of Court, Napier University): I am Tony Bridge, I am past Chairman and my 12 years of duty finished in December of last year.

IAN MILLER (Secretary and Registrar, Napier University): I am Ian Miller, Secretary and Registrar for the past eight years.

LORD NOLAN: Thank you very much indeed. Gentlemen, would it be convenient to you if we go straight into the questions? We have read your written submissions with great interest and we would be happy to start straight off if that suits you, unless you would like to make an opening statement as well.

IAN MILLER: We did not submit an opening statement. If it is useful to the Committee we have some documents which we could leave with members of the Committee; our Constitution and Standing Orders, the Code of Conduct which we devised for the Members of Court, their Annual Report and the current membership of the Court and its committees. I have these here which I can leave with the Secretary if it would be helpful.

LORD NOLAN: That would be very helpful. Thank you, we would like those. I will ask Sir Clifford Boulton please to start off on the questions.

1502. CLIFFORD BOULTON: Good afternoon, and thank you very much for the thought you gave to our issues paper and for having gone through it so carefully. Can you please, just to put our questions into context, briefly describe the history and status of your university for us?

IAN MILLER: Napier University originated as Napier College in 1964 as really a technical college. It developed very quickly over the years and became a central institution in 1985 having previously been administered by the regional council. In 1989 it became a polytechnic, and in 1992/93 one of the new universities.

1503. CLIFFORD BOULTON: Thank you very much. Can I talk a little bit about the composition of the governing body. You use as a Nominations Committee a Chairman's Committee, I understand. I know you are going to give us these details later, but could you just describe who is on the Chairman's Committee?

LINDSAY STEWART: The Chairman's Committee is made up of the Chairman and the chairmen of all the sub-committees, and the sub-committees are the Audit Committee, Student Affairs, Staff Affairs, Health and Safety, and the Buildings Strategy Group. I as the Chairman am also the Chairman of the Finance and General Purposes and the Development Sub-Committee.

1504. CLIFFORD BOULTON: Many institutions have a separate Nominations Committee distinct from the Chairman's Committee, but you feel that that is the sort of body you would have in any case, is it?

LINDSAY STEWART: The Chairman's Committee accept nominations from right throughout the whole university, and then start and look at these nominations and then recommend nominations to the Court who make the final decision on the nomination.

1505. CLIFFORD BOULTON: But because they consist entirely really of chairmen, perhaps it is not the cause of that, but at least you do not have any independent members on your Nominations Committee, do you?

ALL: No.

1506. CLIFFORD BOULTON: Do you happen to know whether that is normal in Scottish universities who have Nomination Committees?

TONY BRIDGE: I do not think it is normal to have a Nominations Committee.

CLIFFORD BOULTON: So there are no conclusions drawn from that.

LINDSAY STEWART: The other important point is that all the chairmen of the sub-committees are external members of the Court.

1507. CLIFFORD BOULTON: I see, yes. Do you have any difficulty in attracting people to serve on the Court?

TONY BRIDGE: I do not think so. In my experience, for every one vacancy we had in the order of about seven nominations.

CLIFFORD BOULTON: So you say you do not think advertising is appropriate; you just have not felt any need for it from your own purposes.

TONY BRIDGE: No that is the case.

1508. CLIFFORD BOULTON: You do not feel that simply almost as an exercise in openness that it would be a good idea to let it be known that there were vacancies?

TONY BRIDGE: Edinburgh is a very small community and I do not think lack of openness is one of our problems.

1509. CLIFFORD BOULTON: We have just been told that by an earlier witness. You say in your paper that although you do not have the obligation to have people, so to speak, wished on you from various representative organisations, nevertheless you do still have those sort of people on your Court who come from various areas like Headmasters' Conference or local government and so forth, but do I take it that now they do not send you somebody, you choose who shall be, is that right?

IAN MILLER: That is correct.

1510. CLIFFORD BOULTON: Is that different from what it used to be?

IAN MILLER: Yes, when we were a central institution there were nominees by various organisations, Scottish Trade Union Congress, CBI, Edinburgh Merchant Company, but that ceased in 1989 when we became a polytechnic and no longer exists. But I think the principle has continued in that we have chosen Members of Court from still a wide range of bodies within the community.

LINDSAY STEWART: We try and create a blend so that if we need a judge or we need a lawyer then we are looking for a judge or a lawyer or an accountant and so on to get a nice blend right through the external members.

1511. CLIFFORD BOULTON: Not thinking in terms of judges so much as perhaps people with local government experience, you do not find that they come to you mandated with some kind of policy which they feel bound by? You find the individuals who come with that background act as fully participating members in their own right?

TONY BRIDGE: I think so.

1512. CLIFFORD BOULTON: You do not get a sense that they have come with a mission or their instructions?

TONY BRIDGE: Some of our trade union colleagues perhaps have a mission, but that is understandable.

CLIFFORD BOULTON: They do feel very much in a representative capacity I suppose.

TONY BRIDGE: Yes.

1513. CLIFFORD BOULTON: I suppose you sometimes get issues where they would like to be on certain restricted business and cannot be for that very reason. Do you find that?

TONY BRIDGE: That is correct. There has been conflict of interest on one or two occasions and that has been declared and we have dealt with it very amicably.

1514. CLIFFORD BOULTON: I am not going to ask you about interests myself because I think those questions will come later. Do you feel that you have a comfortable relationship between the respective roles of the Court and the Principal? Is that fully understood and worked out in your case?

TONY BRIDGE: I am not sure it is a comfortable relationship. It is a very professional relationship where both interests are identified, and it is a very good working relationship.

1515. CLIFFORD BOULTON: When new Members of Court come on is there some kind of explanation or induction or guidance issued?

IAN MILLER: Every new member receives a fairly large package of documents from myself. I am sometimes concerned about the amount of information I give them in the early stages. I then meet with them individually and spend some time going through the history and background of the university and its rules, regulations and procedures. Then we normally meet with the Chairman of Court, Principal and the new Members and have a general discussion. Beyond that we have continuing visits by new members to individual departments of the university so that they can get a feel for what it is all about, get to meet the staff, and I think we develop a good rapport between the Members of the Court and the university staff.

LINDSAY STEWART: Having taken on the Chairmanship, I have regular meetings now once a month, maybe possibly twice a month, with the Principal and we deal with all the various aspects, so there is a very, very good role of communication between the Court and the Principal.

1516. CLIFFORD BOULTON: But the new Members of Court are made aware of what their responsibilities are and they are heavy enough without straying into the executive responsibilities of the Principal. What about the role of the Secretary himself? Is there a role there of almost someone whose responsibility it is to see that these matters are appropriately handled and to blow a whistle on some occasions if matters might be going adrift? I saw one of our witnesses at university said "the function of the Secretary in regard to decisions of the governing body is to ensure that the debate is properly informed and recorded". I suspect, from reading your paper you might have a slightly stronger view of your role than that.

IAN MILLER: I think it goes beyond that and I would certainly regard it as my role to advise Members of the Court if they were straying into any decision that looked illegal. It happens that I am a lawyer and that probably helps, but beyond that I do regard my role as being there, being available for discussion, for informal comment, and I think my colleagues here would agree that I have an open door and am always available for the giving of advice.

TONY BRIDGE: I think you use the term, Sir Clifford, "blowing the whistle", and I think our Secretary is a very good referee and his whistle blowing skills have to be called upon from time to time. I see his role as an ombudsman and he keeps the Court right. Certainly in my period of office he kept me aware of any tensions which he felt I ought to address, and I found his proactive role very, very helpful.

1517. CLIFFORD BOULTON: Thank you very much. You told us how you keep accountable to your local community by making sure that various interests are represented in the governing body. Is there a wider advisory body or meeting of graduates with a role in the governance of the university itself?

IAN MILLER: There is a Graduates' Association which has a representative on the University Court, but being a young institution and a new university it is not yet a very strong body, that will build as the years go on. We are building steadily a body of alumni with whom we keep in close contact. That will grow as the years develop.

CLIFFORD BOULTON: That will help give a personality and ethos to it.

IAN MILLER: That is correct, yes.

1518. CLIFFORD BOULTON: In England many universities have a Visitor or someone like that. Do you have any independent method of resolving disputes and complaints?

IAN MILLER: No.

1519. CLIFFORD BOULTON: We got a little whiff from a previous witness of some possible scope for the redress of deeply held grievances which do not seem to be settled within a university by someone who has some deep feeling of unfairness that has happened. Not linked to Napier itself but to the wider university scene, would there be any scope at all for some system of almost a safety valve from outside the heated atmosphere of a university for someone to go elsewhere for a view on a grievance, or do you think that the importance of the university being a self-regulating body is supreme?

LINDSAY STEWART: I think to date, because I was Chairman of the Staff Affairs Committee prior to taking on the Chairmanship, we do not really seem to have had that problem. We have two joint consultative staff committees who report to the Staff Affairs Committee, and one of our great difficulties has been finding an agenda to have a meeting of the Staff Affairs Committee. So that shows you there is a fairly good link there. As far as grievances are concerned there obviously are grievances, yes, and we have a proper grievance procedure, and the Chairman of the Staff Affairs Committee chairs any grievances and they have always been, to date anyway, quite satisfactorily completed without any problems.

TONY BRIDGE: In addition to that, on the informal side there are many functions which the Court attend and staff attend, and there is plenty of opportunity for discussion and the raising informally of grievances. I would say that as far as Napier is concerned, without seeming arrogant, there is no evidence that we would benefit from having a Visitor. I cannot speak for other institutions in Scotland.

CLIFFORD BOULTON: No, fair enough. We are certainly not in the business of inventing cures for which there is no apparent disease. I think that covers very well the issues that I had in my mind, having also, of course, got your paper in mind.

1520. LORD THOMSON: I want to follow up one or two of the matters that Sir Clifford has already raised, and

I just wondered in terms of the membership of the Governing Body. I was interested and encouraged by what you say in your paper to us about the fact that various interest groups that you used to have by statute or by edict, I am not quite sure which, from the Scottish Office when you were a central institution, these interest groups are still represented on your new Governing Body. May I just follow that up a little further; I hope it is not an embarrassing or invidious question, but it would help us to clarify our mind about this area. Although the interest groups are still there, has a change of method meant a change of personnel, the kind of person that you now invite to serve on the Governing Body, rather than the kind of person that was sent by the interest group before? Associated with that, do you have a feeling that you have better quality now than you had under the old method?

TONY BRIDGE: I think the answer is yes, but I think it is the self-selection process. As Lindsay said, our Members of Court are proactive and the chairmen of our committees are external Members of Court. It therefore follows that if the quality that we select in the first instance does not meet the need and meet the demands of being a Court Member, then they choose not to continue after their four-year term of office has been completed. So it is a self-selection process, and I think the quality is very very high and it has happened, if you like, not through desire or wish on our part, but through the ethos of the university and the work that has to be done.

1521. LORD THOMSON: That is very interesting, but perhaps to be a little more precise about my question. We have had evidence earlier today from COSLA about their general concern about local authority representation on these various bodies where previously they were either under the local authority or had some statutory rights and that has vanished under the new regime. Do you have local authority people on your Governing Body from inside the Edinburgh local authority system, the area you serve?

LINDSAY STEWART: We have one representative who was a chief executive in local government on the Court.

LORD THOMSON: So he is a senior official.

LINDSAY STEWART: He is no longer in local government, but the experience is there.

1522. LORD THOMSON: Does that mean that you prefer not to have people coming from elected councils in the area that you serve?

TONY BRIDGE: I do not think it is a question of preference; the names were not put forward to the appointments committee.

1523. LORD THOMSON: I see. Well that then leads me to the other question I wanted to ask. I personally agree with your strong reservations about the necessity to advertise and then have to cope with a large number of applications in a conscientious way, and I take the point that you have a pretty wide governing body and you ask for suggestions from them. Even at that it could be said, certainly in terms of outside perception, perhaps unjustly, that if your nominating body are the existing governors, however widely based you argue they are, it is a rather self-perpetuating formula. Have you considered whether

there is not some middle course short of advertising, the kind of thing that Sir Clifford did mention about a wider awareness? You gave me the answer, Edinburgh is a wee village, well, even in wee villages in my experience there are even wee villages within them and there are all sorts of walls between different groups and so on. Have you thought about trying to widen the catchment of nominations?

TONY BRIDGE: I do not think we have seriously considered doing that because the number of nominations far exceeded the demand for Court members.

1524. LORD THOMSON: I was interested in that, but without getting too many nominations you might have a wider range of suggestions. I think one of the things we have to consider in terms of the kind of evidence we heard from COSLA, for example, is whether there is not something that we can recommend in a constructive way that would improve the atmosphere between the local authorities, who feel that they have been rather deprived and downgraded a bit, and the new bodies without going back to the old regime. That is why I was asking you whether you did not consider the advantage in terms of your community relations of having, on your own selection, individuals whom you chose from the local authorities and invited them if they might come and give public service on your governing body. Have you thought about it?

LINDSAY STEWART: We have had local authority representatives on the Court, but at this moment in time there are not any.

IAN MILLER: We would certainly not rule that out as a possibility, and, indeed, on our staff we have at least two local authority councillors, so we feel we have an input nevertheless and we do consult widely within the university both from staff and students. It is not just the external members of the Court who are considering nominations, it is totally university-wide.

1525. LORD THOMSON: Can I ask you about a matter that I found quite fascinating out of today. We are having evidence from many people and we finally have to make up our mind about what kind of recommendations we put forward. We have had two almost directly contradictory bits of evidence, from you on the one hand and from Robert Gordon College in Aberdeen on the other, both splendid Scottish education institutions with somewhat similar histories, both former central institutions and now both good universities. On the difficult business of conflicts of interest in the governing body, and, as the Chairman said, this is not a belief that there is something wrong at the moment, but this is the problem of external perception and the public mood about these matters. Robert Gordon said, very forthrightly—"The governing body believes that it is not appropriate that contracts should be awarded to companies with which their board members are connected."

They felt it was wiser to adopt the absolute stance there, they said. You said I think almost exactly the opposite—"Because of the need to attract people with commercial and business experience to the Boards, there is always the opportunity of contracts being awarded to companies with which Board Members are connected. If too many strictures were imposed on such members, Boards may well be deprived of their services which would be detrimental to the operation of such Boards. It is generally believed that this situation is adequately dealt with by the need to declare an interest when any such contract is being considered." You cannot have two more opposite points of view. Would you like to comment?

IAN MILLER: I would disagree with Robert Gordon on this, as you would expect. I do believe that any Member of Court who happens to be involved in a company who may be wishing to tender for a contract should obviously not be deprived of being a Member of the Court. Equally I think it would be wrong, because he was a Member of the Court, that his company should be deprived from submitting a tender, provided the safeguards are there, provided he declares the interest, provided that interest is known, and provided he is not involved in voting in the event of a vote being required in placing any tender.

TONY BRIDGE: I think it also fair to say that if a Member of Court does not declare an interest our Secretary has CVs of all Court Members and he will winkle out an interest, even if it is not declared.

1526. LORD THOMSON: I see, but would it not perhaps be better from your own point of view to have a register of interests? You set your face against the register of interests I think on the paper. There are two kinds of register, there is one that would be internal for your own use, and then there is a separate question as to whether it should be available either on request or more generally available.

IAN MILLER: I have no problems with an internal register and, indeed, I hold such a register, perhaps on an informal basis, but I have a list of all the Members of Courts directorships, members of other public bodies and the like. I have more reservations about that becoming a public document because, again, I think it may preclude people wanting to get involved and becoming a member of the university Court if they felt they had to disclose interests and make them public.

LORD THOMSON: You feel it might limit your choice of good people.

IAN MILLER: I think it might limit the choice, yes.

TONY BRIDGE: I think the other aspect is that all the appointments are on a voluntary basis and, as such, that just adds to what Mr Miller has just said.

1527. LORD THOMSON: As a last question could I just ask a very general one that I do not think has arisen before today. We found in the evidence we have been getting in England, and I find it with interest as a Scot listening to it, that the changes that have taken place in higher education in England have led to two very distinct categories of what are crudely called the old universities and the new universities, and this definition of new universities are the former polytechnics generally previously under local government control that have been converted into universities but it has been under statute, whereas the older universities in England are under charter, Privy Council arrangements. This is a very sharp difference between the two, and one of the issues that has been raised with us is whether it might be better to abolish that distinction in one way or another and create a greater degree of uniformity. As I understand it in Scotland, we

have done it differently. The Napiers and the Robert Gordons and so on that were central institutions, you are not in a separate category of university, you are universities with the same privy council, background as Heriot-Watt or the University of Edinburgh, is that right?

IAN MILLER: That is basically correct, yes.

1528. LORD THOMSON: Would you like to express to all these innocent Sassenachs who are beside me whether you think the Scottish system has advantages over the divisive English system? Not a leading question, of course.

IAN MILLER: I am happy to take that one. When we were looking at the constitution of Napier before we became a university, we looked at the constitutions of ancient universities, of the 1960s tranche of universities, and we actually sat down and devised what we thought was the ideal constitution. I am glad to say that the Privy Council agreed with us, and I think Napier actually devised a model constitution which was effectively taken on board by the five new Scottish universities, and that went through the Privy Council. We had the benefit at that time of Lord Clyde's advice who was a member of the governing body at that time, and we really sat down with a clean sheet of paper. I think we have a very clean constitution that is very straight forward, it is very short, and it enables us to make decisions quickly and it clearly defines the roles of the different Members of Court, officials of the university, and I will be leaving you a copy of the constitution for perusal at your leisure.

LORD THOMSON: Thank you, I am glad I asked that question.

LORD NOLAN: Was that Lord Clyde, Lord James Clyde?

IAN MILLER: Yes, indeed.

1529. LORD NOLAN: A great man. Well, thank you very much indeed. This has been very helpful and a very lively piece of evidence which we have all enjoyed and gained from. We are most grateful to you.

Now we have from the Scottish Chamber of Commerce Mr Lex Gold, Director, from the Glasgow Chamber of Commerce Mr Geoff Runcie, and from the Aberdeen Chamber of Commerce Mr Derek Marnoch. I have been asked not only for the benefit of our members but also for the benefit of the record to make sure that we know who is talking when you are all talking. Is that quite clear? Thank you very much indeed.

Many thanks to you for the information that you have already given us which we have studied. I do not know whether there was anything else that you jointly wish to say before we start, or whether you would like to go into questions because we have a number of questions we would like to ask you.

**LEX GOLD, GEOFF RUNCIE,
AND DEREK MARNOCH**

LEX GOLD (Director of Scottish Chamber of Commerce): It might be helpful, Lord Nolan, if we gave a short clearing the ground statement. Since our written evidence was put forward there have been some developments which impact upon it. As the Committee will know, the Scottish Affairs Committee looked at the working of the Local Enterprise Companies and reported, and the Secretary of State for Scotland responded to that on 11 January. His response actually covered a lot of the areas that the Chambers of Commerce in Scotland had concerns about, and if I may define those for you.

Leaving to one side the question of accountability up the official line to Government for the spend of public money, which is not a matter directly for the Chambers but may be of interest to you as a committee in a different context but on which we did not comment, other than if I could perhaps by way of a parenthetical thought point out that there do seem to be a great many auditors in that process. First of all, each of the companies have the private auditors, then you have the National Audit Office. You have the European Commissions auditors, particularly in relation to training money. But that form of accountability and the propriety linked to it has not been the issue for the Chamber Movement directly.

In relation to the Chamber Movement's concerns it is about accountability to the business community and the wider community more generally, which is a looser form of accountability I suspect. There the concerns have been about the openness of approach and about how inclusive or exclusive that has been, whether it includes or excludes the wider community and the business community, and in that would be the Chambers. So, in that territory there was a question of rotation of membership of the Local Enterprise Company Boards, and we are pleased to see that the Secretary of State has been encouraging Scottish Enterprise in particular, and the Highlands and Islands Enterprise to adopt a code of best practice in terms of corporate governance, and that there will be a financial management review of that whole process in the course of this year. That was an area of concern which was reflected in the paper that went forward from Peter Dunn who was standing in in the period before my appointment.

The other area was membership schemes. They are one way of involving the local community, and the business community in particular. Where those operate well they do involve the business community, but they are certainly not a panacea in terms of accountability in the wider sense because, if you look at some of them, you will find that two-thirds of membership consists of those who may perhaps be wishing to sell something to the Local Enterprise Company. So they may not necessarily resolve all the issues of that broader accountability. We are delighted to see that there is now going to be openness in terms of the publishing of the grants, equity funds and loans emerging from the Secretary of State's response, and above that that there will now be a system of adjudication when an individual or a company has some cause for complaint against the Local Enterprise Company. That has been accepted by the Secretary of State and has moved on some of the points about which my predecessor wrote to you.

By way of a general comment before taking any questions you have, we believe that in this territory there can be no absolute. We welcome the structure of the Local Enterprise Companies. There is a general belief that they are an improvement upon the moribund approaches that you found in the likes of Area Manpower Boards under the old Manpower Services Commission which were consensual bodies but largely, by the very nature of their operation, turned off the business community and caused business people not to attend. They are an improvement but in this whole territory we believe that there is a need for constant vigilance. It is quite clear to us that there are areas of Scotland today where the Local Enterprise Companies are not drawing in the business and other community in the way that they might, whereas in general we believe they are doing a reasonable job.

LORD NOLAN: Thank you very much. That has been, as you say, a positive development since you wrote to us and it is useful to have your summary of it. We have, of course, seen the report you speak about.

I am going to ask Sir William Utting to ask the first lot of questions.

1530. WILLIAM UTTING: Thank you, Chairman. I think you said in your written evidence that you do represent 8,000 member companies and they account for more than half of the workforce in Scotland, so a very large and important and influential body. You repeated what you said in your written evidence about being overall impressed with the performance of LECs, but, of course, in the written evidence you did go on to make quite a number of suggestions about how that performance might be improved. Although there may be the promise of a new dawn coming along, we could, I think, today perhaps go further into your thinking about what that promise might consist of in reality. So I would really like to draw out from you some more detail about the improvements that ought to take place.

One of the things that interested me was the contrast you drew, or comparison, between the constitution of TECs in England and LECs in Scotland. I do not know how conversant you are with the TEC structure in England; I found it quite difficult to become conversant myself. Do you have a patriotic preference for the Scottish setup, or do you see things in England that ought to be translated north of the border?

LEX GOLD: Sir William, let me declare an interest to begin with. I was formerly in the Manpower Services Commission and I was also involved in setting up the Scottish Enterprise and Highlands and Islands Enterprise structure in a former existence, so I have some knowledge. I would claim better knowledge of what happens north of the border, but I certainly have some knowledge of what happens in England and Wales.

Dealing with your questions in reverse order, I believe that the arrangements for economic development and training being in the one enterprise network is to be preferred, so I declare a personal bias in that regard. I actually think it brings together both the skills and ability of the individual with all the other commercial developments that are required to help an economy to develop and grow. Given this personal view, and I stress this is not necessarily Chambers of Commerce view, that people lie at the core of economic development, I think it is right that those two interests are brigaded together. A slightly Panglossian view because the ideal construct is not always the one that delivers the ideal result, but I have seen nothing since its inception to dissuade me from the bias with which I started, that north of the border the arrangements are better and might, with advantage, be adopted elsewhere.

I am bound to say to you we tried to encourage our colleagues in Wales in the Manpower Services

Commission days that they might also go the route that the Scots took. They, for a variety of reasons, and I will not attempt to describe those reasons to you now, chose to stick with the system that was being developed for England. I actually believe the nature of economic development and skill development are closely related and are best taken together. That is a personal view; my colleagues may have a different one. Before I move on to the first question, I will check with either Geoff or Derek.

DEREK MARNOCH (Chief Executive, Aberdeen Chamber of Commerce): I would not disagree with that at all. I think it is essential that business development, economic development and training are closely allied, and certainly in the LEC in the Aberdeen area, and we are perhaps fortunate in that we have a very low level of unemployment, they have concentrated on training people in employment rather than people who are unemployed looking for employment. In that context it is perfectly right and proper that they run side by side.

GEOFF RUNCIE (Chief Executive, Glasgow Chamber of Commerce): I think to some extent from the Glasgow point of view, which has the very opposite set of circumstances from Aberdeen with high unemployment, the international competitiveness, and even the domestic competitiveness of the businesses, is directly related to the ability to train and upskill the people in the businesses. Therefore there is a serious benefit to having the Government publicly funded training and enterprise companies together, particularly as they share boundaries and therefore their focus is the same. We believe that the structure in Scotland is reviewed by other parts of the United Kingdom, mainly because of the skill and integrity which it can bring to the challenge. There are downsides to that as well, but I think on balance the two activities, enterprise development and training development, are best managed as one corporate structure within one simple and singular programme per area.

LEX GOLD: I am sure this is a point which has been made to you elsewhere, but I think both sets of arrangements would benefit if the Government were to provide a little more freedom of national training programmes, in terms of how they are constructed and delivered to reflect more the conditions locally. I am not certain that we as a nation gain the bang from the buck that we might were greater freedom given in terms of how that training money was spent, but I am sure that is not the first time you have heard that.

1531. WILLIAM UTTING: No, and it has also been put to us that in the kind of integrated model of combining enterprise with training, it is training for employed people that tends to get preference, and training for unemployed people gets put down the list, and disadvantaged people tend to do worst of all. Do you think that the needs of those people can be met adequately in the kind of model you prefer?

LEX GOLD: I would be sad were what you describe to be the case. But there is clearly a debate that goes on about training for opportunity, or training to deal with need, and that is a constant debate. I do not think there is any line that you can actually draw in the sand and say that is the right place. What I believe would be helpful there is if it was clearly determined what money was for what purpose; what was going towards need and what was going towards opportunity. However, that is kind of glib

because I actually believe a great many of those who are disadvantaged, those who are unemployed, actually can benefit from the opportunity spend as well. But there does need to be some system to ensure that the disadvantaged in society do not get left behind if you go completely for a model which appears to be based on opportunity.

GEOFF RUNCIE: Can I just comment that my experience of the Glasgow Development Agency who have some of the biggest problems, particularly as far as the disadvantaged are concerned. In their strategic plan and their operational plans I see considerable focus on people who are not necessarily in the business environment. I see focus on a number of significant programmes which are about addressing the social and educational needs of people past school age which, of course, fits on top of local authority responsibilities with regard to education. So to some extent I would defend the experience we have, certainly with one of the biggest LEC in Scotland, and say that a substantial part of their programme is clearly targeting groups that you might have suggested that were going to be further down the priority list than they were.

1532. WILLIAM UTTING: Thank you. You say that, even though you are impressed with performance so far, there have been some concerns about the failure to resolve conflicts of interest. Although we should not talk about individual cases here, I wonder if you could give examples of that kind of problem and how you think that it is best avoided in future, bearing in mind that you gave some pointers in your opening statement.

LEX GOLD: This is your "new dawn" which was the point which I was reversing. In relation to that issue we went round all our Chambers asking for their views and their experience, and you are getting only one side of a debate when you do that, but there is clearly certain parts of Scotland where still those people representing the business community do not feel they are being drawn in to the process of (a) developing the strategy adopted by the Local Enterprise Company, or (b) being consulted in some of the projects and the way ahead. If that is true for the business community, it may well be true for the wider community. You asked whether there was any splendid ideas that we could share with you. It sounds terribly wet that we really do not other than trying very hard to draw in and consult as many as possible in the process. There are areas of Scotland where the LECs actually have shown very good practice in producing draft strategy documents and drawing in comment from the business and wider community. That best practice is what we would recommend be adopted across Scotland in the other areas, so the adoption of best practice would be the main approach.

The second point would be recognition that people are human and they are going to err and there will be occasions where they fail, because you cannot provide a structure that will actually do it for you. One of the biggest areas of failure is likely to come where you rely on the structure to do it for you.

1533. WILLIAM UTTING: If I can just end on a constitutional point. You set out a kind of master plan combining the role of Chambers, LECs and Local Enterprise Trusts which you say would clearly require Government legislation, and it is not for us to propose that. If that does not come off, why do you see advantages to Chambers having a statutory right to appoint to LECs rather than go down the combination between Chambers and LEC route?

LEX GOLD: The first point I should make, Sir William, is that our evidence may give the wrong impression and, indeed, it appears to have done so in the sense that there is not a common view. There is no unanimity view in the Scottish Chamber movement about the question of whether the Local Enterprise Companies and Chambers should come together in much the same way that, for example, there is pressure down south for the TEC/Chamber movement to come together, so there is not the unanimity of view of that kind. The evidence that was put forward by Peter Dunn, who was the stand-in director, is actually reflecting what I think many people say about the very vague nature, not only of business representation but of the business support activities, that you find not only in Scotland but throughout the United Kingdom. Indeed, were you to come from Mars you would be surprised at what you found, and I think you would take a bit of convincing that it was the product of a logical mind.

The standpoint of the Scottish Chambers on this is pragmatic. We do not believe that you will change that world, certainly not overnight. What the Chamber Movement in Scotland is looking to do is form pragmatic relationships to carry forward the work of business in the best way possible, and to form those relationship and partnerships with those in the wider community where it will add value. I hope that clarifies the point. You may have been misled by the evidence put.

WILLIAM UTTING: Or I may have misunderstood it.

LEX GOLD: I think you may have been misled.

1534. ANNE WARBURTON: I think I was misled as well without having been in cahoots with Sir William, because my first remark I wanted to have made was that the Scottish Chamber seemed to be rather more pro merger than the English Chambers gave me the impression that they were. May I take it that you do stand by your support expressed in the paper for single local business support organisations?

LEX GOLD: Yes.

1535. ANNE WARBURTON: I was struck in reading this very succinct paper by some positions which were taken in it which were a little more forward than those we have met elsewhere. For example, the point that is made in the paper that the Chambers should have a mandatory right to nominate to the Boards of LECs, and, if I am not mistaken, to other comparable organisations, local public spending bodies.

LEX GOLD: Yes, I am in some difficulty here because the Chamber Movement actually supports the approach adopted to the appointment to the Local Enterprise Company Boards, namely that it should be on the basis of ability, not on the basis of representation. Going back to the point I was making about the moribund area Manpower Boards, which is fairly strong words but as a former member of the Executive it served my purpose perhaps better than it may have served the purpose of good governance that they did not have the attention that they might have done given their advisory nature.

Therefore there is broad based support for appointing on the basis of ability.

I think what you find reflected in that paper, written by the chap who was standing in ,is the feeling of frustration that is felt in the Chamber Movement that a great many very good people who are in Chambers of Commerce have not yet had an opportunity to serve on LEC boards. I mentioned in my clearing the throat opening statement that the rotation of LEC board membership, which has been addressed by the Scottish Affairs Committee and by the Secretary of State's acceptance of their findings, goes in large measure to tackle the concerns that we in the Chamber Movement have. But I stand to be corrected by either of my colleagues. I mean, I speak with the advantage of all of five weeks in the job.

GEOFF RUNCIE: Dame Anne, if I could possibly comment with some two years in the job and not a great deal more experience. One of the benefits that some representation from the Chambers Boards, for example, would bring is that the Chambers are engaged daily in interfacing with the activities of the Local Enterprise Companies. As a consequence of that we are just across the fence on the side of the consumer of many of the services and products and programmes of the Local Enterprise Companies. Collectively, as a result of that, we have a reasonably good feel for the focus and the directed approach that the Local Enterprise Companies take. I think the proposition that we might make a nomination or nominations to the Board was really on the basis of the fact that we bring through the Boards of the Chambers of Commerce a good feel for the general views of the consumers of the service, and the constitutional elements about the nomination being representative or being skills related is another part of the issue. But I would contend, and I am sure Derek would agree, that the Chambers of Commerce Movement as businesses ourselves are pretty close to the views and the needs and aspirations of the business community. But, again, as representative organisations we tend to aggregate a lot of views together. The Chambers do have their finger on the pulse and I think the proposition that was put forward was the basis of taking that expertise up through into the Boards of the Local Enterprise Companies.

1536. ANNE WARBURTON: But as individuals a lot of the members of the LEC Boards presumably are also members of Chambers?

GEOFF RUNCIE: Indeed that is the case, although there is no requirement on them to report down through the Chamber Movement to disperse information coming back. To some extent that was one of the aspects of accountability, possibly even reportability rather than financial or fiscal accountability. It was the requirement or the desire to report back to the collective group, whereas the individuals who are on the Boards in their own right have no requirement on them to report to the Chamber as possibly a nominee would have.

1537. ANNE WARBURTON: You would not envisage giving those who were nominated the task of representing your Chamber views in a mandated way?

LEX GOLD: That is the difficulty that the Chamber movement finds itself in against what was in that paper, because if on the one hand you accept that it is best that people are there because of the individual contribution they make, be they from trade unions, be they from local authority, wherever they come from, the mandated route runs counter to that principle and we recognise that. Indeed, in terms of this conflict that you have picked up, Dame Anne, the Chamber Movement would err on the side of the freedom of the individual.

DEREK MARNOCH: I would agree with that. I think it is dangerous to have a mandatory appointment. In Aberdeen our President of the Chamber is actually on the LEC Board and he is not mandated to report back to us on what the LEC decides to do. That is an issue at executive level. But there is an argument that, for the benefit of corporate governance, there ought to be more interchangeability between organisations so that a view point can be expressed rather than finding that something has been decided that we might have disagreed with, when we could actually have an input as it is happening. Certainly, from our point of view, I think it is right to get the proper people on these boards, and if we have the right to perhaps nominate somebody who may or may not be selected, that at least would be a step in the right direction.

1538. ANNE WARBURTON: I think given the time probably I must only ask one more question and it has to do with conflict of interest, again going back to the paper it may also perhaps have a nuance to be put on it. The paper suggests that there really is a problem about conflict of interest, personal business interest, and suggests that—

"This Committee might look at every LEC annual report published to date with a view to interrogating conflict situations."

I somehow doubt whether we will get around to that, but I wondered if it is a point which you feel strongly about, whether possibly the Chambers or some other body might do it. Is it something which you still would stand by?

LEX GOLD: I think the force of that point is covered in the response from the Secretary of State about the greater openness in terms of the publication of the details of grants, equity, funds and loans. I was intrigued listening to your interview with our colleagues from Napier moments ago and the question about how far members of the boards should be debarred because of other interests. Life does not, in my view, break itself down into neat compartments in that way, and given that Local Enterprise Companies, particularly the Highlands and the more rural parts of Scotland, operate in areas of fairly sparse population and where there is not a great many businesses, you would be debarring from membership of the Local Enterprise Companies some very talented people were you to say that they could not in any sense benefit from grants etc. that were there and agreed could be used officially. Indeed, it would be thoroughly unfair if public spiritedly they came forward and became members of boards, and their companies could not benefit from that from which they would normally have benefited. The view that we have here is the question is about the openness of the process, and since the submission was put in we have seen that whole process opened up in a way which we find most satisfactory and covers our concerns. We would not now wish you therefore, Dame Anne, to bother reading all the reports. But the public interest is now served by the response I think we see from the Secretary of State.

1539. ANNE WARBURTON: May I slip in just one more question. It shows great ignorance on my part, I was

not all together sure what an LET as opposed to an LEC is, and I observe in the last paragraph the forecast that LECs have a future but there is a growing feeling that LETs' days may be numbered.

LEX GOLD: LETs, and I take some distance from the view that they may not have a future, we are talking here about Enterprise Trusts, and the L before it is Local Enterprise Trusts. I am not sure whose feelings those are that they do not have a future. The distinction that is being made there is that I think there was a feeling in the Chamber Movement that the Enterprise Trusts were being used by the Local Enterprise Companies as a means of delivery in a way which led the Local Enterprise Company to believe that they had passed on a responsibility for accountability for what was being delivered in that territory. So that is the context in which it was put. But I am pretty certain the Enterprise Trust Movement will continue in Scotland. How far it flourishes is for others to judge.

ANNE WARBURTON: Thank you very much.

1540. LORD NOLAN: Thank you all very much. It is precisely the kind of evidence that you have given us that we came to Scotland to hear. It has shown us a slightly different perspective on a number of problems from what we have heard before in England and in Wales, and, if I may speak for myself, we are all very impressed with the constructive approach you are making to solving those problems, and we wish you luck. Thank you for coming.

Good afternoon to Langside College, Glasgow, to Eileen Mochar, Alistair Tyre and Graeme Hyslop. I wonder if, for the benefit of the Committee and for the record, the two gentlemen would identify would identify themselves so that we know which is talking to us.

EILEEN MOCHAR, ALISTAIR M TYRE, AND WALTER MACLELLAN

ALISTAIR TYRE (Principal, Langside College, Glasgow): Thank you very much, Lord Nolan. Alistair Tyre, Principal.

WALTER MacLELLAN (Member, Strathclyde Regional Council): I am, in fact, Walter MacLellan, just to confuse the issue.

1541. LORD NOLAN: Well you did not confuse us for long. Thank you for putting us straight.

Thank you also very much for your written material which we have all read and studied with interest. As you know, we proceed by way of question and discussion, and we would all be glad, I am sure, to get on to that straight away. Was there anything you wished to say by way of introduction before we get into the questions?

EILEEN MOCHAR (Chair, Langside College, Glasgow): Only that we are delighted to be here; thank you very much for asking us to come along this afternoon. I am very proud of Langside. I have been on the Board one way or another since 1986 and have seen great changes since incorporation on 1 April 1993. Great challenges have been put to FE colleges, and I think Langside are rising to the occasion very well indeed. My board and the principalship and staff are, to my mind, one of the best.

I am delighted that Walter MacLellan can be with me. Walter, again, has been on the board and a previous college councillor quite a while. He is one of my fellow board members and is a member of the present regional council and the new Unitary Authority in Glasgow.

We had a brainstorming session last week trying to guess what you might be asking us this afternoon. A typical solicitor, I like to be prepared beforehand, hence all the papers, but we have prepared some bullet points that we have written down for you and if we could leave those with you at the end, matters that might not be able to be covered in that half hour which we thought important to get across to you.

LORD NOLAN: That is very kind. Thank you very much indeed.

EILEEN MOCHAR: That is really all I wish to say at the moment.

LORD NOLAN: I am going to ask Dame Anne Warburton to start off the questions.

1542. ANNE WARBURTON: Might I begin by asking you just to give us a little precis of the size and the particular interests of the college? How does it fit in to the national picture in Scotland?

ALISTAIR TYRE (Principal, Langside College, Glasgow): The college and staff size is approximately 333 members of staff from various grades, and I include all members of staff within that. We have approximately 7,900 students as a head count, 2,600 in further education speak which is known as a further FTE full-time equivalent, so you will forgive me if I break into jargon. It sits in size within the further education community in Scotland of 43 colleges and a further three incorporated colleges, two in Islands and one is Skye. Within that we are probably tenth in size as an approximation I think it would be easy for the Committee to follow.

It sits within the south side of Glasgow, a catchment area of approximately 300,000 of population, although we do draw from students further afield from that, and, indeed, we have a fairly strong connection with students from overseas. That is a link with the universities. We take students on to our Higher Scottish Certificate of Education programme, and they then move from us to the university of their choice after going through a foundation programme which is centred at Glasgow University, but all universities in Scotland are involved as members of it.

So that gives you a rough thumbnail sketch of the college. It is also a multi-ethnic college; I think that is quite important for the Committee to know. We have at the present time 66 different nationalities studying at the college, some of which come from abroad and others who are resident or second generation within the Scottish community.

1543. ANNE WARBURTON: Thank you very much. Do you regard yourselves as in some way likely to have very different opinions to the other 40 however many colleges it was?

EILEEN MOCHAR: We are one of some 20 in the Strathclyde region at the moment, and I am not sure how many in the Glasgow area but there is quite a lot. Our strength we feel is in our community college title, very much serving the local community and the wider community as Alistair has indicated. We joined some two years ago with four other colleges ringing the Glasgow centre to form the five community colleges who very much have the same ethos of serving the community in their hinterland.

It is quite a large square mileage that we actually do cover; we were just talking about that earlier. It is quite wide triangle or a pair of triangles on the south side of Glasgow that we do cover.

1544. ANNE WARBURTON: Thank you very much, and perhaps that takes us into one of our main questions which is the appointment of members of the board. What could you tell us about the composition, and really what formal methods are used for identifying members?

EILEEN MOCHAR: Most of the present board members have been there for some time prior to incorporation on 1 April 1993 and come from a wide area of expertise and knowledge. Some are employees of Scottish Power, big organisations that have their staff in our area and who send students to us. Small companies, individuals who live in the area who are involved at our councillor. I am a solicitor but I am also a lecturer in higher education so I can bring those two areas of knowledge in. As a former member of Glasgow Junior Chamber of Commerce, not the Chamber of Commerce, that is how I got on to the College Council in the first place.

1545. ANNE WARBURTON: Is it laid down for you in some way what the composition should be?

EILEEN MOCHAR: Yes, Schedule 2 of the Act of 1992 sets out what our membership should be and the Secretary of State did confirm a lot of us still in those positions when incorporation and independence came. Since then we have had three vacancies and we have managed to fill those vacancies and co-opted another member, so we have four newish members who have come to us since 1st April 1993.

We do not have any formal procedure other than discussion among the board members that we are looking for a replacement. For example, we were able to get a replacement member from the Transport and General Workers Union in place of the lady who had been a member and resigned from our board, so we network amongst ourselves and our composition is quite wide. At one point in your actual paper you were concerned in case we became too narrow. We are very keen to ensure that we remain reflecting all possible interests in the area.

WALTER MacLELLAN: As I recall the discussion when places have been filled, we have really looked at ourselves and looked for the gaps and then thought how can these gaps in our skills be filled. There has been a very strong feeling of identifying with the communities in which the college is situated, and through that of relating to the issues that arise within the communities. These come up both in the forms of the needs of the companies that are within the area and also in terms of the social needs, because there is a campus in Castlemilk which has been closely related to the development of urban renewal partnership which the Scottish Office and the local authorities have been involved in, and the college has played a crucial role, I would say, in terms of bringing the opportunity for education and widening the horizons of people within that community. So in that sense I think the college board in terms of looking at its membership, looks at a very wide spectrum for a way in which it can create the strongest board possible.

1546. ANNE WARBURTON: The board is how large?

EILEEN MOCHAR: Sixteen and that is including our academic staff member, our support staff member and the student nominee.

1547. ANNE WARBURTON: Do you have any nominees from other bodies or from the local authority?

EILEEN MOCHAR: The Glasgow Development Agency have a nominee who has been with us for several years now and has actually chaired one of our standing committees. We have a very strong standing committee structure which reports back to the board of management at our quarterly meetings and, again, I am delighted to say that we have a very good representation at standing and board meetings all the time. There are not many apologies tendered throughout the year.

In our bullet points that we will be leaving with you we always have at the front of our mind the college operating values of transparency, flexibility and empowerment and performance review. So far, as Walter highlighted, we reckon that we needed more support on the accounting side of life, and two of the four members who have been appointed bring those skills with them as qualified chartered accountants with a wide experience in private practice and public bodies already.

1548. ANNE WARBURTON: I think the Association of Colleges is suggesting that there should be more formality in proceedings of this kind, will that influence your thinking? Perhaps you have not got that far.

EILEEN MOCHAR: It might be needed in some colleges. So far we have not felt that we needed that because of the way that we did all work well together.

1549. ANNE WARBURTON: From what you say I take it that you concentrate quite precisely on your relationship with your local community. Your accountability to the local community, do they know what you are doing and why do they take part in it?

EILEEN MOCHAR: Yes.

ALISTAIR TYRE: I think it would be useful just to very briefly dwell on the fact that the college is a community college and we set ourselves out in that particular fashion because of the location and the multi-ethnic groupings that we have to serve. We work very closely both with the present regional council and its community education arm which takes us into the area of community councils per se and the locality in which we serve. They are actually not on the boards. I did attempt to suborn one of their members to come on but she decided it was not really what she wanted to do. Despite that, she has very close links, and we have close links, with her through an open door policy to the college of the Community Council. In fact there is now two of them within the

college itself which brings people in. They then can see what is happening within the college; they do meet not only board members but my own staff and myself, so there is an accountability and a transparency which I think comes first, I daresay, before the accountability. People have to know what you are about before they can pose the questions on whether you are doing it properly and with probity.

I think the membership that we have on the board, and if we can just reinforce the Chair's words there and perhaps emphasise it again, the decisions in the selection procedure were taken at full board meetings, at which I have to say there was a full board representation there and everyone was involved in that. I think I was least involved as the Principal within that, and that is only appropriate that I should not try to influence in any shape or form other than looking at the competencies and skills that we should have a representative of the board. The background is sometimes difficult to always get people from the areas that you would like to get them from. Our ethnic communities are not always easy to attract onto the full board. We have had two and unfortunately in both cases they became so heavily involved in their own businesses that they had to withdraw; I have to say that was prior to incorporation.

ANNE WARBURTON: But you are up to strength, you do not have real impossible difficulties.

EILEEN MOCHAR: Yes. As far as the formal procedures, I indicated we feel we do not need one because we have been very well served by the interpretation of the 1992 Act by Strathclyde Region's solicitors in the preparation of our constitution and standing orders. The Scottish Further Education Unit were very helpful initially with some seminars etc., as the Association of Colleges are continuing to do. Also I found tremendously helpful the Secretary of State's *Guidance to Public Body Board Members* issued in September 1994 which we adopted as a board at Langside right away, we adopted it in the November meeting of the Financial Control Committee. I do not think that guidance is known to all the colleges. It has been filtered back via John Sellers to the Association of Scottish Colleges in the correspondence of the autumn when everybody was responding to yourselves. We found that tremendously helpful as part of our ethics, integrity responsibility involvement etc. at all our committees, so we have had that in place since September 1994 already.

In our written response in October I did indicate the list of items that we had in place formally, and the bullet points will give the actual dates of those. The object of the exercise is continual improvement, and that is something we have always been doing at Langside as a board and formalising procedures etc.

1550. ANNE WARBURTON: One of the points you made there was open reporting of board decisions. How is that done?

EILEEN MOCHAR: We have very full minutes of the board meetings. We have, of course, at the board meeting itself the academic, non-academic staff members, and the student association nominee. The minutes are then placed in the library of the college. Alistair Tyre had tried to get the minutes exhibited at the local public library in Langside, but they were going through renovations at the time and have not yet been able to put them on a relevant board, but that was offered quite a while ago. As I say, all the minutes etc. are available for the general staff, not just through their representatives.

1551. ANNE WARBURTON: Thank you very much. If I may just switch the subject a bit, you say that the college does not presently favour an additional layer of scrutiny or accountability in the form, for example, of a Funding Council. I wonder, have you thought at all about pluses and minuses on an extra layer in there? What is your thinking?

EILEEN MOCHAR: We seem to have been very well served so far by the unit within the Scottish Office. I know, even before I went on to the Financial Control committee, that through the board I was getting lots and lots of instructions and "Dear Accounting Officer" letters to let us know what we should be doing. My initial feeling, which could be wrong, is that if we had a separate council it would be a cost which would just come out of the cake that we are all trying to work with already, and we are well served by the Scottish Office at the moment. I could be wrong.

WALTER MacLELLAN: I think one of the greatest strengths of a good FE college, and I think Langside is a good FE college, is that it is an incredibly flexible machine, it can respond to the social issues that arise from industrial closures and the need for helping, being part of picking up a community and reorientating it. It has to respond to the day-to-day changes and the needs of industry, and these are getting more and more common as industry becomes more involved in new technology etc. I do not need to make a meal of that, but I would be very worried at another layer of scrutiny. There is, as has been mentioned, the control through the Scottish Office. There is also, in a sense, through consultative mechanisms with the LECs, with the education authorities, and obviously having that link through the board as works in Langside, I think there is a lot of scrutiny of what the college does. I feel adding another layer to that could really mean that more of the college's resources are put in to form filling on the one hand, and on the other it could also really threaten the flexibility of the college to respond quickly to changing needs in the community and in the business world, which is the greatest strength that the further education system has I think.

1552. ANNE WARBURTON: I just want to put one more question because of time and that is to do with the Register of Interests which is one of the things you have had for a long time. My papers did not include a copy so I have not actually read it, but does it include family? I saw that you went as far as to include staff which is going further than a lot of people do. What sort of procedures do you have to make sure that conflicts of interest may exist but are not put into reality?

EILEEN MOCHAR: We have had a code of ethical behaviour since March 1993 for staff, although it is something put on by the board so they adopt it by asking their staff to take it on board by requiring the staff to take it on board. Really the conflict of interest was a natural follow on as part of the overall picture that we wanted to formalise our procedures. We took advice from the Glasgow Development Agency and our external auditors so far as what we should be putting in it is concerned, and, yes, we do have partners/spouses involved in the conflict

of interest information as well. That has been in place since August. It was June 1995 that the policy was proposed by the board, and the letters came out in August 1995 to all of us for filling in the bits and pieces that we require. The board's membership details are available for information of staff and board members, and it is open to the public generally although from the staff point of view we cannot let outsiders see what their interests are, that is confidential to the board really.

ANNE WARBURTON: Thank you very much.

1553. WILLIAM UTTING: I think it is very important that we note your satisfaction with the present relationship with the Scottish Office. I think the question we all need to put to the Scottish Office is whether it is happy looking after the interests of how many is it, 43 further education colleges. I am especially gladdened to hear of your satisfaction, so presumably the Scottish Office also finances you so it determines how much money you get as well.

EILEEN MOCHAR: We are never satisfied with that allocation! But that is probably limited by the Scottish Office purse.

1554. WILLIAM UTTING: If I could persist with constitutional matters, as I read the arrangements your board of 16 members is just about in the middle of what the legislation permits. I read it as permitting a minimum of 13 and a maximum of 19, and as in England it says that the majority have to be persons experienced and with capacity in industrial, commercial or employment matters, or professional practice. In England, local authority members are apparently not permitted to be full members of boards, they may be co-opted. Is that the position in Scotland also?

EILEEN MOCHAR: No.

1555. WILLIAM UTTING: They can be full members of the board. Is it your experience that this prescription about the majority being drawn from this sector actually does limit your choice? It reads to me like a prescription for boards that are filled by middle-aged white men from business and professional backgrounds, and that you are going to have difficulty finding enough women, certainly difficulty finding enough people from black and ethnic minorities, to become board members.

EILEEN MOCHAR: I am laughing because we have quite a few lady members on the board.

ALISTAIR TYRE: If I could just answer one or two of the issues that you have raised there. First of all, legislation in the 1992 Act for Scotland has 16 for the maximum members of the board of management, of which there are specified areas. For example, a representative from a local enterprise company has to be on, the student representative and the two staff representatives who are nominated and are voted on according to each of their stations. I think we find it fairly easy to look at a fairly wide gender balance within the board. There has not been the difficulty, dare I say it since I am wearing one, of the grey-suited white bearded people appearing on the board. We have not had that experience at all and I think that has been useful. In the first instance, in answer to Dame Anne's question earlier on, in selecting board members there has been a full and open discussion at the board, and I have to say that the ladies on the board, I am sure, can hold their own just as well as anyone else. I think the gender balance has been important to us. The ethnic balance we do not have right and that is partly our fault and I think also the problems facing our local ethnic business community as well. I think it is vital, though, that we actually have democratically elected members on the board, and that is a decision that Langside board. thank goodness, took my recommendation back in 1992 when we were talking about forming the board. I actually ensured we had elected members there, so it is not a problem with us under our legislation in Scotland.

1556. WILLIAM UTTING: Good, thank you very much. I thought you knocked aside the question of a code of conduct for board members perhaps rather too easily. If one has codes of ethical behaviour for staff, isn't a code of ethical behaviour or conduct for board members quite a good idea too on the basis of what is sauce for the goose ought to be sauce for the gander?

EILEEN MOCHAR: That is where I feel that the Code of Best Practice which the Secretary of State issued in September 1994 which we have adopted has made us toe the line as well as the staff toeing the line.

1557. WILLIAM UTTING: You implied that other colleges might actually not have heard of this guidance, did I hear you aright?

EILEEN MOCHAR: I have no evidence on that. I know that one college did not have a note of it, but I am sure they have something else in place that is equally as good. I do not know, I can only speak for Langside. We liked what we saw there, we thought it was very appropriate for us to take that on board to balance up, as you say, the code of ethical behaviour.

1558. WILLIAM UTTING: The Code of Guidance from the department that allocates your money controlled by the Secretary of State who can sack you all, that is pretty strong, isn't it? That is perhaps, in reality, a bit more than guidance, is it not? It is the sort of advice that people would disregard at peril, isn't it?

EILEEN MOCHAR: I do not see why we would want to disregard it.

WILLIAM UTTING: No, but if people did?

EILEEN MOCHAR: Well, if they decided to do that then they should be sacked.

WILLIAM UTTING: It could be backed up pretty strongly by the responsible department.

EILEEN MOCHAR: Yes.

WALTER MacLELLAN: If I could possibly add to that. I do not know what it actually says in the minutes, but I think that when the board approved the Code of Conduct relative to staff it presumed itself to be bound by the appropriate parts of that code, and that certainly was my presumption. I do not know what the minutes said, mind you.

ALISTAIR TYRE: The Code of Ethical Behaviour actually covers members and staff and their actions were

quite clearly stated which was in August 1993 when I wrote it.

1559. WILLIAM UTTING: Delighted to hear it. There was, I think, one point of detail; you attached the Code the papers so I actually read it. I was a bit surprised by something in it that said that members of staff should not issue any unauthorised statement to the press or other media of mass communication unless delegated to do so. You are not actually wanting to prevent members of staff writing to the press on academic matters presumably? Do they have to get permission from you if they want to write something on an academic issue?

ALISTAIR TYRE: *Mea culpa*—I think I have to answer to that one. It really related to a slightly different issue. We were looking at the press relationships and we felt it was better focused into probably myself and the Deputy Principal and one Assistant Principal rather than public statements coming from the institution by any member of staff which could run contrary, for example, to the policy of the board. No, there was never the intention of stopping anyone from writing on academic matters. I have to say it does not happen and we have two of our staff members who contribute regularly to national newspapers.

WILLIAM UTTING: I did not really think for a moment that it did, but I felt we ought to make that clear.

ALISTAIR TYRE: It was badly phrased.

WILLIAM UTTING: Thank you, Chairman.

1560. ANNE WARBURTON: Chairman, might I add one point. I was gratified, I think, really to see that you have gone further than I think anybody else has about the seven principles, that you wish to make it a condition of grant that they be accepted. I was not quite so clear just quite how there could be departmental scrutiny and regular audit in relation to the seven principles.

EILEEN MOCHAR: We have internal and external auditors, and it could quite easily be done that part of the audit in the financial years state these seven principles could be brought into that particular box by our auditors.

ANNE WARBURTON: So it is more questions of the background that illuminate the discussion.

ALISTAIR TYRE: If I could add to that that we also, as all colleges do in Scotland, publish an annual report and I would see that as being part of the annual report as much as the objectivity and transparency and accountability. Selflessness etc, I think might be more difficult to audit. I think so long as we can demonstrate as transparently as we possibly can to as a wide a church within Scotland I would feel that we were going some way towards the initiative to make it a condition of grant. I think that it is up to the Committee to decide whether that would be appropriate within the Scottish context or not, but it is an issue we felt we should raise with you otherwise it is liable to slide away to a Code of Best Practice or a possible recommendation. We felt, perhaps, a strengthening within the grant-in-aid on the conditions attached to it, and we have several already. I do not think it is particular onerous that others, particularly in standards in public life, should be attached to it.

ANNE WARBURTON: Thank you.

LORD NOLAN: Thank you very much indeed. My only regret about your evidence is that our Secretary, Alan Riddell, who is a Glaswegian, was not here to bask in your reflected glory which he would have enjoyed—he is seeing other bodies this afternoon. We are also very grateful to you not only for coming along and for the written evidence you have already put in, but for providing us with your bullet points because we do rely very much on our volunteer witnesses to let us know what points they want to make, what they think we can usefully do in this report, and I am very glad you have. If we have any questions on the points you are leaving with us I hope you will not mind if we trouble you yet further.

EILEEN MOCHAR: We will be delighted.

LORD NOLAN: That is very good of you, and thank you so much again for coming. Goodbye.

WEDNESDAY 31 JANUARY 1996

MORNING SESSION

Members Present:

The Rt Hon Lord Nolan (Chairman)

Sir Clifford Boulton GCB

Professor Anthony King

The Rt Hon Lord Thomson
of Monifieth KT DL

Sir William Utting CB

Dame Anne Warburton DCVO CMG

Diana Warwick

Witnesses:

John Ashworth OBE, Chairman, Vernon Murphy, Vice-Chairman, and Bob Beaty, Director, Renfrewshire Enterprise

Iain Robertson CBE, Chief Executive, and Sandy Brady, Director of Executive Office, Highlands and Islands Enterprise, and Sandy Cumming, Chief Executive, Ross and Cromarty Enterprise

Stephen Maxwell, Assistant Director, Lucy Pratt, Head of Research, and Ian Brown, Enterprise and Training Officer, Scottish Council for Voluntary Organisations

Sir Donald MacKay, Chairman, Crawford Beveridge, Chief Executive, and Ray MacFarlane, Director Network Services, Scottish Enterprise

Peter McKinlay, Chief Executive, Frances McCall MBE, Board Member, and Carole Oatway, Head of Registration and Monitoring, Scottish Homes

---

1561. LORD NOLAN: Welcome to our second day of oral evidence in Edinburgh. This morning we welcome five groups of witnesses. Whereas yesterday we dealt mainly with further and higher education, this morning we are dealing mainly with Local Enterprise Companies and then with housing associations.

We welcome first Mr John Ashworth, OBE, the Chairman, Vernon Murphy, the Vice Chairman, and Bob Beaty, Director of Renfrewshire Enterprise, which is a Local Enterprise Company which operates within the geographical area of Scottish Enterprise, the sponsoring, non-departmental public body.

Our second group of witnesses comprises Iain Robertson, the Chief Executive, and Sandy Brady, the Director of the Executive Office of Highlands and Islands Enterprise. They will be accompanied by Sandy Cumming, who is Chief Executive of Ross and Cromarty Enterprise. I think it important to make clear that, like Scottish Enterprise, Highland and Islands Enterprise, as will be well known, is the non-departmental public body which sponsors Local Enterprise Companies in its area. However, Ross and Cromarty Enterprise is, itself, a Local Enterprise Company. I might just add that the sponsoring arrangements between Scottish Enterprise and its Local Enterprise Companies on the one hand, and Highland and Islands Enterprise and its Local Enterprise Companies on the other, are slightly different. No doubt, we will be hearing something of that this morning.

Thirdly, this morning we welcome Stephen Maxwell, the Assistant Director of the Scottish Council for Voluntary Organisations, who will give us their perspective on the Local Enterprise Companies from the point of view of training providers. Fourth, we complete that chain by hearing from Sir Donald MacKay, Chairman, and Crawford Beveridge, the Chief Executive, and Ray MacFarlane of Scottish Enterprise,

Our final witness this morning will change the subject completely. We shall be hearing Peter MacKinlay, the

Chief Executive, France McCall, a board member, and Carole Oatway, the Head of Registration and Monitoring of Scottish Homes.

Now then, if I may turn to our first witnesses, Mr Ashworth, Mr Murphy and Mr Beaty. Thank you very much for coming and I know that for one of you at least this has meant a very hectic early morning and late night. Diana Warwick, whom I am going ask to open the questions, will sympathise with that because she has had much the same time this week.

1562. DIANA WARWICK: I wonder if I can ask you, first of all, to say just a few words about the range of areas and organisations that you cover because it really is vast. Could you tell us something about that?

JOHN ASHWORTH OBE, VERNON MURPHY, AND BOB BEATY

JOHN ASHWORTH, OBE (Chairman, Renfrewshire Enterprise): Yes, certainly. Good morning, thank you for having us along. Just as a background, Vernon Murphy runs Scotland's airports; I am in the whisky business, Bob Beaty latterly was running IBM's operations in Scotland.

Renfrewshire ranges from pretty well the airport—for the Glasgow boundary, the airport—and all the opportunities that that lifts, down into the Inverclyde area, Greenock, Gourock, where there have been substantial shipbuilding job losses over the years. So, there is a whole range of opportunities and problems. The key thing about the area is that it has a number of big, multi-national companies, the Compaqs, the IBMs, the airport is a big organisation, National Semi-Conductors, so a substantial modern business infrastructure that we are trying to build around. The area produces 40% of Scotland's manufactured exports so, on the one hand, old skills, big problems and, on the other hand, modern opportunities. That is a sort of flavour of the area.

1563. DIANA WARWICK: Thank you. I wonder if you can help me a little bit further. Tell me what you see as the differences between you and the TECs in England?

JOHN ASHWORTH: I am no expert on the TECs but I understand that our brief is much more business development, economic development orientated, as distinct from just purely the skills. We have found in our work that the skills issues, the training issues, are so vitally integrated with business development issues. You go in and you are working on business development with a company, you find that part of it is the normal business development, economic opportunities, and part is the skill base that is required. That is how I perceive the fundamental difference.

1564. DIANA WARWICK: Could I ask you to say something about the relationship between you, Scottish Enterprise, and the Scottish Office. Can you describe those links and how they work?

JOHN ASHWORTH: Yes. We are accountable to Scottish Enterprise who, obviously, are accountable to the Scottish Office. It is that line of communication. The way that it works is that Scottish Enterprise is allocated an annual block of money with some guidance as to what activities it is to be spent upon. Individual LECs go forward, meet with the board of Scottish Enterprise, argue our case for next year's budget allocation and then wait with baited breath to see what we get. That is how the process works.

1565. DIANA WARWICK: I wonder if you could just say something about the introduction, turning now to our main area of interest, the introduction of the Scottish Enterprise code of best practice on corporate governance. How has that had an impact on you and on your organisation?

JOHN ASHWORTH: It has sharpened up the focus but it has not had a dramatic impact in the sense that virtually all the board are from big organisations with their own codes of practice so standards of propriety and behaviour is just integral in board members. It has focused us into double checking our practices.

VERNON MURPHY (Vice Chairman, Renfrewshire Enterprise): Can I say something there? I had a couple of discussions with Scottish Enterprise over this before it came out. One of the real issues which I felt, being a LEC member, is that the system has evolved. It was such a different approach than the SDA approach previously that some of the problems which we had in the initial years were only identified in the light of experience and then resolved in terms of the code of practice. That came out in 1994, I think, John, did it not. the code of practice?

JOHN ASHWORTH: That is right, yes.

VERNON MURPHY: It would have been helpful to have had it a bit earlier but no doubt if we had had it a bit earlier it would not have tackled the problems which actually we experienced on the hoof.

1566. DIANA WARWICK: How do the people of your area, Renfrewshire, know about the code of practice and what their rights are and how to get access to information?

JOHN ASHWORTH: When we have our public meeting we dwell on this. It is available and we issue it at every opportunity. So, through the public meetings we make people aware of it and also the partner bodies that we are with. Most of our activities are in partnership with local authorities, chambers of commerce, individual companies and we make them aware of it as well. Our client base is made aware at first hand of the existence of our code.

1567. DIANA WARWICK: Could you say something about the way in which you seek to make your work and your decisions accessible to the public? How open are the decisions? What are the processes that you adopt to try and ensure that people are aware?

JOHN ASHWORTH: Obviously, the annual report which goes out is a comprehensive document of what we have been doing. When we produce a business plan for the ensuing year we publish an abridged version so that the programmes and our areas of activity are clearly publicised in that way. If we have specific things we use the media, perhaps periodically put a full insert into the local papers just to bring people up to date.

You have to be careful to target information so that it is fresh and relevant rather than blanketing people with a miscellany of information. Through this process, and briefing local authority Economic Development Groups, which we do on a quarterly basis, and meeting with the chambers of commerce and passing on to them our programmes, we are putting it down the channels of communication as well as publicly publicising the bigger things through the media.

VERNON MURPHY: The basic approach we take is networking, is it not, John?

JOHN ASHWORTH: Yes.

VERNON MURPHY: The way we see putting information out and getting information back is through networking with people face to face.

1568. DIANA WARWICK: Is there a role for the more formal method of communication. For example, some TECs in England publish their minutes, they make copies of board papers and the agendas are available publicly, either through the public library service or in other ways. Would you see a programme with that? Do you do that?

JOHN ASHWORTH: No, we do not. Quite a lot of what happens at the board is, if you like, steering the executive on various programmes and saying, "Yes, that is something we should explore", so it is development work. Certainly, there are a number of decisions which are taken at those board meetings, not all that many you might be surprised to learn. If you have projects then approval will be given for that expenditure and that would be publicised, that we are going to do this in this area and that in that area. The board also works up our business plan submission and that is developed and approved by the board and then that is publicised once we have had the allocation communicated.

A lot of what the minutes are doing are more administrative things, some of which are slightly sensitive, not in a political sense but involving companies or people. It is sensitive information and not relevant to the general public. The general public quite clearly sees what areas of activity we are involved in. We list all the companies we work with, so that is public knowledge.

1569. DIANA WARWICK: In essence, what you are doing is producing a summary of board decisions and communicating those?

JOHN ASHWORTH: Yes, yes.

1570. DIANA WARWICK: I wonder if I could turn to board membership. The Scottish chambers of commerce in their evidence to us say: "Although prominent business people are appointed to the Boards of LECs, these are generally regarded as political appointments. For this reason and because there is no formal communication link between these appointees and the business community, LECs cannot be regarded as Business lead organisations."

What is your answer to that?

JOHN ASHWORTH: I am at variance with that line of thinking. First of all, there are four public body people on there, not representing per se the organisations that they are within but, as we are in partnership with the local authorities—we have three in our area—a significantly senior elected member of each of those organisations is on our board, bringing local knowledge and cementing the partnership with the local authority. That is all the more important now that the new local unitary authorities have enhanced economic development responsibilities. Those four provide that sort of role.

You are then looking at eight private sector people whose prime role, although it goes without saying that they have to be accountable and responsible and declare interest, their prime role is to contribute to the process, steering the executive, bringing their knowledge and experience to bear, passing this on, making sure that what best practice these eight people who have a lot of experience in the industry perceive as being the way forward and getting the best bang for the buck. That is the prime role of these people.

As for the election of them, I would like to think it is open. I am a little surprised at some of the comments that are made. What we do when we have our two annual public meetings is stand up, go over our work and invite nominations. We are always on the lookout for people who can contribute. Please write to us, either nominating somebody or volunteering in confidence, because we want to build up a list of people who would like to partake.

We talk along the same lines to the chambers of commerce—we are not asking you to nominate somebody representing the chamber of commerce but if you are aware of an individual who is out there who you believe could contribute. The same with the local authorities who we meet with quarterly. Also, between our board members or another will know all these people. It is a relatively small community and comprehensive feedback comes from that. For example so and so is a very bright chap; he seems to be very interested in joining us. Also sometimes we have to go out and tempt people to join us where particular knowledge is required.

Bear in mind it is a group of eight; the other four public sector have a different role. These eight people have to have a balance of skills, knowledge, industry knowledge, and so on. The world is not exactly full of volunteers for these jobs which, as you well know, are unpaid.

BOB BEATY (Director, Renfrewshire Enterprise): May I just expand on that a little bit. Good morning. You will remember me if for no other reason that I am the one with the Scottish accent.

DIANA WARWICK: Exactly. We had noticed.

BOB BEATY: I have to say something just so you realise Scotland was represented.

I am one of the newer members of the Board, two years has been my stint so far. I have to say that I am probably typical of the other Board members, particularly those from industry on Renfrew Enterprise, in that we are all extremely busy people where time is absolutely critical to us. So, we are giving of our time not for any reason because of a political appointment for any political reason; we are doing it because we believe it is the right thing to do for the area. As businessmen who work and employ people in that area, we want to do whatever we can to assist the generation and the development of those areas from an economic point of view. We are there for very honourable reasons and I certainly did not feel any kind of political pressure at all on my appointment to the Board when John approached me.

1571. DIANE WARWICK: Given the amount of public information you seek to make available, and given that both you and the chambers of commerce aim to represent the business community in promoting enterprise, how, having rejected their claim, would you go about trying to ensure that they recognised that it was not valid?

JOHN ASHWORTH: The simple answer to it is to try harder to build up the communications. Obviously, if they feel that there is a communications gap that we have to address. I cannot think of any simpler answer than that.

1572. DIANA WARWICK: Some LECs have introduced membership schemes, or similar mechanisms, to try to broaden the scope of identifying directors, and so on. Have you thought about that?

JOHN ASHWORTH: We have thought about it and we have looked at and listened to the experience of the three LECs who have done it. As I say, the directors and the executive know everybody in the area. We can get to people one to one and, indeed, visit 30 or 40 companies a year because there is some issue that is worth talking over with them and to brief them and we get groups of them in for informal lunching briefings. We find that that networking and direct face-to-face is a more dynamic way of doing it.

Then we look at what the chambers of commerce are trying to achieve. They have membership schemes and they have their own agenda that is filtered up the way. By feeding off them and feeding back to them, we would like to think that, in effect, we are feeding a membership scheme rather than trying to replicate one outside that network.

VERNON MURPHY: Probably a couple of minor things which might help with this: firstly, if you look at the period since we have been set up, we have probably lost about eight private sector directors.

JOHN ASHWORTH: All the private sector people have rotated.

VERNON MURPHY: Not only have we rotated but we have replaced about eight private sector directors, so there has been no suggestion that new blood has not been coming in or that it is a self-perpetuating clique.

The second thing we have done, which may be interesting to you, is that we have a supplementary group of members called Management Committee. They do not actually vote on the Board but they are there to give help and assistance. In many ways, it is also a sounding board to see whether they are the sort of people who would help as board members in future times. We have found that quite useful, have we not?

JOHN ASHWORTH: Yes, absolutely.

1573. DIANA WARWICK: Perhaps I can just finish—I am conscious of the time and others will want to ask questions. Thinking in terms of local accountability, which has been one of the areas where both TECs and LECs have been criticised, are there ways that you have perceived where this might be improved? Things that you think it would be useful for our committee perhaps to recommend for a wider takeup?

JOHN ASHWORTH: I will be quite honest, nothing specific comes to mind. We believe passionately in our networking, trying to talk to the actual people on the ground and I cannot think that a global thing that you will issue minutes, or something like that, would necessarily help us in our area. We have to work harder and harder and harder at communicating with our population and we are all seeking to do that but there is no simple answer how best to do it.

VERNON MURPHY: What John has done, which is interesting to me, is that we did not start off by having meetings with the local councils on a quarterly basis. These have developed. We have found that the contacts we had through the executive of the council, the executive of the Local Enterprise Company, and then the meetings you had one-to-one with them, really needed to be developed into a wider form so we have about four of our directors go quarterly down to, for example, Inverclyde council, and we will have an afternoon meeting with them. They can raise whatever are their concerns and we can raise our concerns.

The idea of communication may be a simple answer but it is a simple answer I would recommend to you. Where these things have blown up it is probably because the communication channels have not been right.

DIANA WARWICK: Thank you. Thank you, chairman.

1574. LORD NOLAN: It may be that our report will shed light on matters such as the manner in which your operations are conducted, yours and similar bodies, which the public is lacking possibly through lack of deep public concern. You hold public meetings, do you not?

JOHN ASHWORTH: Yes.

LORD NOLAN: Are they well attended?

JOHN ASHWORTH: Regrettably not, no.

LORD NOLAN: It may be a sign that people are not too worried. Dame Anne I know has some questions to ask you.

1575. ANNE WARBURTON: I am sure Diana will not mind if I say that on the quotation that she gave you from papers we had received previously, a good deal of gloss was put on that yesterday and I am not sure that you should charge off and accuse the Scottish chambers of commerce of having said this in their entirety.

JOHN ASHWORTH: Point taken.

1576. ANNE WARBURTON: Can I ask you—are you happy with your relations with the media locally?

JOHN ASHWORTH: We are currently. We have had problems along the way with one of the local papers who seemed to have an aggressive agenda but we have worked hard at that and we are now getting a very fair and constructive press. Yes, we are quite happy with them.

1577. ANNE WARBURTON: Do they come to your meetings?

JOHN ASHWORTH: Yes, they do.

1578. ANNE WARBURTON: Can I ask you a bit about the financial auditing side, one of the things we always have to look into. How audited are you?

JOHN ASHWORTH: To death! There is a very rigid process. We have internal auditors who work, in main part, within a framework of audit work that Scottish Enterprise require, which, I have to presume, satisfies the Scottish Office as well. So, our internal auditing is within a Scottish Enterprise framework. We can add on bits that we want for ourselves, external auditors, and there is a lot of monitoring within the network. It truly is Scottish Enterprise network. In many of the areas, be it training, there are monitoring processes going on and I feel very comfortable about the propriety of the financial control, I am very relaxed about that, but there is an awful lot of attention paid to it in the system and we spend a significant amount of our staff budget on areas of monitoring like this. We are investing in it.

BOB BEATY: If I could just amplify that a little bit with a little bit of industrial experience. My background is with a company which, in many cases, is one of the most internally measured and internally audited companies you could ever imagine, so I have been brought up in an ethos of audit and measurement. I have to say I have been both pleasantly and unpleasantly surprised since I joined the Board. Pleasantly surprised in the sense that I am on the Audit Committee and the discipline that both Scottish Enterprise and the company put into the management of their business and the control of their business is really exemplary. The slight bad news is that, if anything, it is overdone, it is too much, and that is just from an industrial perspective.

1579. ANNE WARBURTON: Can you point to where the surplus lies?

BOB BEATY: I could but I would have to go into detail.

1580. ANNE WARBURTON: There were a couple of detailed points which I noticed in your papers, which are relevant. One was that, under code of conduct, board members do not receive papers where there may be a potential conflict of interest. I heard this from someone last evening too. It seems to me it almost requires a sort of sixth sense actually to carry that out. Does it work?

JOHN ASHWORTH: I believe it does. You can identify when something is potentially a conflict of interest. Perhaps you are negotiating commercially with one of your partners who is represented on the board or somebody who is on our board. The whole board is not quite paranoid but bordering on this conflict of interest issue. There are certain categories of employment which would inevitably bring conflict of interest and we do not invite people from those areas to come on the board. We are very careful in that concept who can come on the board and contribute without potentially being in conflict.

We have a culture of watchdogs. It is up to each of us to say, "Please, I have a conflict of interest", but any member of the board can, if you like, blow the whistle. So, if I had not declared an interest and Bob Beaty here said, "I know about that", he would be expected to tell the company that this should be looked at. It has happened on a couple of occasions.

1581. ANNE WARBURTON: Do you have trouble getting across to your public the extent to which the watchdogs are vigilant?

JOHN ASHWORTH: I think we do have difficulty in getting it across. You can say it but it does not necessarily register in mind. Over the learning process of the Enterprise Network there have been a few alarms and excursions in the paper and that has potentially stuck in peoples' minds rather than listening to the good news.

VERNON MURPHY: Could I add something, if I may? One of the strengths we have in Renfrewshire is that we do have, as John said right at the outset, a number of major international companies who we can call on for board members. I know from talking to them that there is no way they are going to compromise their own positions in their companies by getting involved in any way in public criticism over decisions that have been taken. I just could not and I know, Bob, that you feel that same.

BOB BEATY: Absolutely.

VERNON MURPHY: One of the points John made in passing was that we have looked at the constituency of the board and we have felt that in one or two particular areas of recruitment it is just not fair on the individual to ask him to be an Enterprise Company member because too many of the issues coming up could be potential conflicts of interest. In those circumstances, the operation of the company would actually cease to work properly.

That was one of the learning curves we went through when we realised we had to be responsible in who we asked to go on the board so they were not faced with a continual succession of potential conflicts of interest.

1582. ANNE WARBURTON: It is the board itself really which is the kind of organising committee for the slate of elections, is it?

JOHN ASHWORTH: Yes, it is, yes, but, as I say, we will receive any nomination or volunteer. The board looks and maintains a list of potential people and maps it out so

that in future we know that so-and-so is going in a year's time and to replace him or her we need this sort of person. It is not just a question of picking down the list.

It has to be clearly understood that particularly the private sector people are there for delivering their skills, contributing their skills, and that really is why they are in it but there are plenty of other responsibilities that go with it and, therefore, you have to make sure you have the right skills, the right experience being brought to bear on the issues of the day. The profile of the board changes overtime.

I have to say that when we think about the comment of "jobs for the boys", a number of people coming on to the board did not know many people on the board. It is a very democratic process and anybody can get on to the board.

1583. ANNE WARBURTON: Your management committee is a sort of nursery for potential talent, is it?

JOHN ASHWORTH: It is. We have one, very knowledgeable private sector person who, for his own good reasons, does not want to be a board member, he has some business reasons that legitimately do not want him on there, and we have three local authorities, and up to now Strathclyde region. We could not accommodate all the representatives, people with knowledge of all those organisations, within the board constitution so we facilitate doing it that way.

1584. ANNE WARBURTON: As a last two minuter, as it were, do you have any proposals, any suggestions for us to take away of things which we could do either to help you or to help the way you are seen locally in your work?

JOHN ASHWORTH: The main thing is to find ways, which is probably your prime role, of making sure that the public and interested parties understand the openness and the detailed role of what the LECs do. I think publicising those angles would do us a great service. I am not so sure that you could decree who will issue your board minutes. I think you would be putting too much information out.

LORD NOLAN: We try to avoid over prescription. We are very conscious of the dangers of that.

VERNON MURPHY: One thing I would add, because I have been in both the public sector and the private sector, is that this is still a fairly young group of companies and the sort of experience which you can get from other groups you are talking to would be of assistance to us because we are very much on a learning curve and we do not have a unique answer to any of the questions you have raised. We are doing what we think is best practice but you may well have some better practice you can add to our best practice.

JOHN ASHWORTH: One closing thing I would like to add. We have developed a very strong network of inter-relationship between the chairmen of the various LECs. We meet very regularly. We address issues. We try and follow best practice, as do the chief executives across the LECs. It is a very close networking arrangement and I do not think there would be any one of the LECs doing something that we would not be aware of but we say that that is not for us, membership is not for us, we would rather do it this way. That is not to say membership is not right in those areas. It is very strong networking.

1585. ANNE WARBURTON: It sounds an efficient way to sift out what best practice is?

JOHN ASHWORTH: Yes, that is right.

ANNE WARBURTON: Thank you.

1586. LORD NOLAN: Thank you very much. Just one final standard question, please. You do not remunerate your board members. Is there a case for remunerating board members?

JOHN ASHWORTH: There is irrefutably not, not even the chairmen. People would be in for a different reasons. Bob Beaty articulated why we are in it. We want to help our community. We are big employers in the area with a dependence of, in my own case, probably 6,000 people in the community are dependent on the company that I run and you want to put something back for the youngsters, and so on. To remunerate people would be getting people involved potentially for the wrong reason and I think it is safe to say none of us would serve or none of us would accept the pay.

VERNON MURPHY: No, we would not. I would not accept the pay.

LORD NOLAN: Yes. Thank you very much indeed. It has been extremely helpful and clear.

JOHN ASHWORTH: Thank you.

1587. LORD NOLAN: Now we welcome the representatives of Highlands and Islands Enterprise and also Mr Cumming, the Chief Executive or Ross and Cromarty Enterprise. I wonder, gentlemen, if I could ask you, please, to identify yourselves both for the benefit of members of the Committee and for the record.

IAIN ROBERTSON CBE, SANDY BRADY, AND SANDY CUMMING

IAIN ROBERTSON, CBE (Chief Executive, Highlands and Islands Enterprise): Certainly, Lord Nolan. My name is Iain Robertson. I am Chief Executive and a board member of Highlands and Islands Enterprise and, like my two colleagues, I am a Scot, indeed a Highlander. On my right is Sandy Cumming, who is the Chief Executive of Ross and Cromarty Enterprise, one of our 10 Local Enterprise Companies, and on my left is Sandy Brady who is Director of our Executive Office, which is personnel, media relations, European Affairs and a number of other departments in our organisation.

1588. LORD NOLAN: We have studied with care and gratitude the written information which we have been given by Highlands and Islands Enterprise. I do not know if there is anything you wish to add by way of a brief opening or whether you would prefer to go straight to questions.

IAIN ROBERTSON: I am perfectly happy to go straight to questions, except to say that we are very much the little brother or little sister in development terms in Scotland. We are the development agency for 51% of Scotland, the northern half of Scotland, with only 7% of the population, over 90 inhabited islands so we are a very diverse community and, in fact, we are a classic rural development agency.

1589. LORD NOLAN: Yes. You refer to yourselves as the small brother. Of the 22 Scottish Local Enterprise Companies, you are responsible for nine and half a tenth, are you not?

IAIN ROBERTSON: Nine and a half exactly. We share Moray Badenoch and Strathspey with Scottish Enterprise.

1590. LORD NOLAN: I see. So, you have nearly half of the responsibility for Scottish LECs?

IAIN ROBERTSON: Yes, our LECs are very small, however. They are very close to the community. For example, the catchment area for Skye and Lochalsh Enterprise contains only 12,500 people so we are very close to communities which we have found to be a tremendous advantage in our work.

LORD NOLAN: I am afraid I am poaching because we take it in turns on this Committee to ask the questions and it is Sir Clifford Boulton's turn.

1591. CLIFFORD BOULTON: Thank you for coming half way to meet us by coming down to Edinburgh like this. You are an executive NDPB, in terms of the jargon. Could you explain briefly, first of all, the nature of the contract you have with the Scottish Office and then the nature of the contract you have with the individual LECs?

IAIN ROBERTSON: Yes. We work under what is called our management statement to the Scottish Office and once a year we prepare an operating plan under our strategy which we present to them in a bid for funds for the succeeding year. It is done in a three or a five-year rolling horizon and, depending on how good our bid is and how much resources are available at the time, the Scottish Office then awards us a contract with a set of targets and we operate that contract.

In turn, we contract with the 10 Local Enterprise Companies for a delivery of the contract terms in the local areas. So, we have a similar contractual relationship with the Local Enterprise Companies based on their bidding to us once a year in an operating or business plan and setting targets for themselves which we monitor and follow up. We also work with them in a three-year rolling horizon as well. We find this quite an efficient system. We are heavily into management and measurement and value for money, which we might mention later on.

1592. CLIFFORD BOULTON: And do those negotiations throw up typical problems which then tend to get learned from in order to negotiated further contracts? What sort of things have emerged from the renegotiation of these contracts?

IAIN ROBERTSON: Everything really because we have targets in each of our four sectors, if you like. We operate economic, environmental training and a unique set of social development powers which, again, we might talk about later, and within each of these sectors we set the Local Enterprise Companies targets and they will tell us what they plan to do in their area. It literally throws up issues twice a year, in fact, because we do a six-monthly review with them, we work together quite continuously to make sure the targets are being achieved.

It is a very good discipline on all of us to make sure that we are actually in each of our programmes, delivering what that programme intended and not just satisfying numbers with them.

CLIFFORD BOULTON: It is ongoing really. If you have a six-monthly review they feel they are always under surveillance.

IAIN ROBERTSON: Yes, but they are doing it themselves—that is the beauty. We do not actually do the review on them; they review themselves and report back to us. They prepare their own business plans. Sandy Cumming is on the receiving end.

CLIFFORD BOULTON: Yes, he is, yes.

SANDY CUMMING (Chief Executive, Ross and Cromarty Enterprise): Yes, and we do so willingly, the way we operate. We are in the process at the moment of hoping to finalise our budget for next year and the rigour is very much looking at the "what if" situation: what if we were able to secure an extra 5% funding, what if we actually have to take a 5% cut, what would be the impact in terms of business growth, in terms of people development and the impact on communities in our area?

We are a small business with a turnover of £8 million, that is the value of our contract each year. We, clearly, have a management reporting system for our own board. We have a very rigorous quarterly review of the company's performance, very much against the contract that we have negotiated with Highlands and Islands Enterprise.

1593. CLIFFORD BOULTON: As you know, with Scottish Enterprise, LEC staff are on their payroll. Did you consider adopting a similar model and why is it not the situation with you?

IAIN ROBERTSON: We did consider it, but when we were formed we had 25 years experience of the very excellent HIDB behind us and we were able to evolve from the HIDB so we left it up to the individual LECs how they constituted their staffing arrangements, with the result now that a number of people are directly recruited into the LECs and some are still recruited into LECs and parented to HIE if the LEC board or if HIE wishes that to happen. So, we have a mix of people coming and going.

The one advantage in having staff parented to HIE is it offers them the opportunity to transfer around the network and a number of people have taken advantage of that. We actually like the idea of the LECs recruiting locally as well because that encourages them to take local people and, in turn, turn them through their organisation and back into the local community.

SANDY BRADY (Director of Executive Office, Highlands and Islands Enterprise): The current proportion of those working for LECs is approximately 50% directly employed and 50% on secondment from HIE.

1594. CLIFFORD BOULTON: I see. So, you think that is better really, that gives you a flexibility and the possibility for movement?

SANDY BRADY: It does give us a flexibility, yes.

1595. CLIFFORD BOULTON: I can imagine it is quite important for people who feel almost trapped in a very, very small area to expand their own personal experience?

IAIN ROBERTSON: Yes, and we are trying to encourage staff movement and to encourage people to sort of come out of a LEC into HIE for a while and then go back into the LEC because some of the functions we do at the centre capture economies of scale for the whole network. So a staff member coming from a Local Enterprise Company into the centre will see a bigger picture, the whole Highland picture, and a bit more of the Scottish picture. It is good, career-broadening stuff.

1596. CLIFFORD BOULTON: It makes the application have more sense when he is back in a LEC. We talked a little bit earlier, when you were talking about renewal of contracts, of the ongoing exchange of information that you have. We get complaints in England that the burden of information requirements put on them is pretty heavy. Can I ask you, Mr Cumming, if you feel sometimes that it is too much that you are being required to supply HIE with?

SANDY CUMMING: No, I do not think so at all. Taking one step back, if I may, without avoiding the question in any way, I myself have been someone who has worked at the centre to begin with and now I am out at the coalface, actually running a Local Enterprise Company. That has been a very helpful experience.

We are determined that we see ourselves as running a business and a business should be managed very effectively and I believe the information that is required under the contract that we have to supply HIE is, in any case, the sort of business information we should know ourselves. I do not see a duplication. I do not see it unnecessary in terms of the volumes, or anything else. I think it is right. It is the correct level that we report back.

1597. CLIFFORD BOULTON: Do you join the chorus of LECs and TECs who say they are over-audited?

SANDY CUMMING: Occasionally, yes, but there are areas of our work where we are examining the level of monitoring work that goes on. One area, perhaps, is the degree of auditing that we have in our training programmes. It seems to be out of kilter with, say, the degree of auditing we have in our business growth programmes. What we are seeking at the moment in discussions with HIE is to get a balanced approach to this if we can.

We believe very much in the role of internal auditing. We are also very fortunate that we have a very good relationship with HIE in calling in their internal audit team whenever the opportunity arises and they move very quickly and help us in any situation.

1598. CLIFFORD BOULTON: I should imagine that if you get your internal auditing right in the first place, subsequent audits are less painful, are they not? You have your material ready to show off.

SANDY BRADY: That internal audit function that we run is a very pro-active one in the sense that one of the duties that they fulfil is benchmarking. So they are not only in the process of auditing individual LECs but where they come across examples of good practice they prepare benchmark reports which are then circulated around the other LECs to say, "Ross and Cromarty Enterprise has developed a particularly good way of doing this. Here is how they do it. You might want to think about this for your own LEC".

IAIN ROBERTSON: If I may just add, some of the criticism on the audit front comes from the number of audits because we are, of course, subject to the National Audit Office and to the Scottish Office and, whilst we are able to combine our internal audit function with our compliance function, which is like a bank's compliance function and we operate this somewhat uniquely in the Highlands, we can combine audits and do them altogether at the local level. We are not always able to do that with a National Audit Office, for example, value-for-money study as we are going through just now, or the Scottish Office quinquennial review, which is going on just now. Also, there is the annual NAO review of our books and accounts, which is also going on at the moment.

So, in a sense HIE shelters the LECs from a bit of the burden of audit in that we co-ordinate with the National Audit Office how they will do their detailed audit but, in turn, we have to have our own internal audit and so do the LECs. That is where it comes from but we try to get the maximum benefit out of the process. Indeed, we have asked the NAO in doing their current value-for-money audit, if, instead of just being critical, as sometimes the NAO are, they could actually look at our measurement functions and see if there is any aspect of our measurement functions that they would suggest we make changes to that can add value to that measurement, to try to turn their audit into a pro-active exercise as opposed to just a critical one.

1599. CLIFFORD BOULTON: Is it not the case that the NAO has less access to the individual LEC accounts than they have to TEC accounts in England?

IAIN ROBERTSON: That certainly was the case to start with but now the accounts of the Local Enterprise Companies are consolidated with the accounts of Highlands and Islands Enterprise and the same is happening in central Scotland in Scottish Enterprise and their LECs. So, really now the NAO has pretty good access to the LECs.

In fact, we started off on the premise that there was no point in trying to draw up a barrier between the NAO and our LECs and we actually worked with the NAO in going into the LECs right from the start and I think they actually appreciated that. We found it quite helpful.

1600. CLIFFORD BOULTON: Individual LECs get visits from the NAO?

IAIN ROBERTSON: From the NAO, yes, certainly.

1601. CLIFFORD BOULTON: Can we talk a bit about board membership? Obviously, we are sensitive to the fact that you have special geographical considerations, and so forth. Can you talk a little bit about the relevance and help of membership schemes as a way of building up a body of support which might help in the recruitment of board members? Somewhere we have been told that it is very hard to see a function for membership schemes; they tend to be just a bit of a supporters' club with a role that has to be virtually invented for them and made to feel welcome and given something to do. Would you like just to tell us your thoughts about membership schemes and their relevance to the healthy working of a board?

IAIN ROBERTSON: The fact is membership schemes can be helpful in certain circumstances but a lot depends on the individual area. In our area, several of our LECs have membership schemes and draw their future directors from that pool of resource. The numbers in these membership schemes vary from the largest of about 45 down to 16. In other areas, instead of having membership schemes, our LECs have drawn up—the Argyll LEC, for example, Argyll and the Islands Enterprise—has some 13 consultative committees around their area because Argyll is a very diverse area with a lot of very inconvenient pieces of water in between so it is difficult to get from Point A to Point B. They take meetings in local areas using these consultative groups and they have drawn their board membership from these groups.

In other areas our LECs do not have membership schemes or consultative committees but rely on direct contact with the local community in their annual community groups, much as Renfrewshire Enterprise mentioned they do in their local area. So, we have a range of approaches.

Most of our LECs do not see a huge advantage in membership schemes because they do not have a lot to offer. We are not in the business of offering discounts with credit cards. What we can offer members is the potential for a lot of evening work, a lot of travel and a lot of very difficult decisions and the opportunity to give up a considerable amount of their own time only to be criticised often in the press for so doing.

CLIFFORD BOULTON: There seems to be an endless supply of masochists offering themselves for public service throughout the United Kingdom.

IAIN ROBERTSON: Yes, that is right. We are actually very lucky, particularly in the Highlands, that people are willing to put in the effort to spend two days, one day going to a meeting and the other day coming from it, to attend a board meeting once every month or once every couple of months because it is quite an imposition. There is a story of one of our LEC chairmen who set off on a Monday for one meeting and did not get back to his business until the following Saturday because of ferries and weather. He was from Barra.

CLIFFORD BOULTON: One has been familiar with the problems of Members of Parliament in your area of Scotland in attending both to their constituencies and their duties in Westminster.

IAIN ROBERTSON: Yes, it is the same problem.

1602. CLIFFORD BOULTON: This kind of serious difficulty must inhibit the willingness of people to come forward. Does that have any bearing in your case on the question of whether remuneration would be appropriate? Do you have any views about remuneration?

IAIN ROBERTSON: We do, actually, and it is a little different to Renfrewshire Enterprise. We consulted all the LECs about remuneration. Bear in mind, we largely are comprised of small businessmen who, in giving up time to come to LEC business or HIE business—and we have meetings of LEC chairmen on a regular cycle—are giving up time to their business and we felt that it would be appropriate if they had the option of being remunerated, something like the attendance allowance that local councillors get. Indeed, we made that suggestion to the Scottish Office and I do not think I am speaking out of turn in saying that in the Scottish Office the suggestion found some favour but they could not get it any further through the Treasury because, obviously, at the national level it would be a considerable cost.

Sometimes, with purely volunteers—Lord Thomson will understand this—there is an element of the kirk session about things so perhaps a little remuneration might add a little more order to events from time to time.

LORD NOLAN: We will have to ask Lord Thomson about that because it raises an intriguing question in my mind as to what goes on at kirk sessions.

IAIN ROBERTSON: I am a son of the manse so I know.

1603. CLIFFORD BOULTON: Obviously, if we enter into this area we shall have to think about the form in which remuneration could take place but you are talking about having a set rate or fee which could be claimed, rather than actually demonstrating a precise amount that has been lost and reclaiming the damage to your business or your partnership, and asking for something like that. Clearly, there would be extreme variations.

IAIN ROBERTSON: Absolutely.

CLIFFORD BOULTON: A flat rate.

IAIN ROBERTSON: Yes, but it does take small businessmen away from, as Sandy put it, the coalface to go to meetings.

1604. CLIFFORD BOULTON: How much local attention —press and so forth—does the work of the LECs generate?

IAIN ROBERTSON: A huge amount. We are blessed with a number of very excellent local papers in the Highlands, just in case there are any of them here, and they pay very close attention to what we do. In fact, when we announced our "Accountability through Openness" policy a couple of years ago now that was actually welcomed, even by the West Highland Free Press, which tends to be one of our fiercest critics in that it is owned by a Labour MP, Brian Wilson. Brian actually published "Hooray for Highlands and Islands Enterprise" which was an unheard of accolade from the paper. Of course, it has gone back to the normal situation now.

That has meant that in any edition of the West Highland Free Press once a month you will see a report from each of our LECs whose area they touch, giving a list of the grants and loans that have been awarded to businesses and to people in that area. It has given them unrivalled access to exactly what is the product of the Local Enterprise Companies. The benefit for us, as I was mentioning to Dame Anne Warburton last night, is that that has actually been a form of quite good advertising for us in that other people see, "Oh, that business got assistance to expand, there is no reason why I shouldn't step in and try and get that", or "So-and-so did that training course. That is very interesting. Maybe I should be going after that or trying to get this kind of support or that kind of advice".

The press attention, on the whole, is to our advantage. You cannot listen to the radio in the Highlands in the

morning without something being mentioned about one or two of our LECs and what they are doing.

1605. CLIFFORD BOULTON: Our terms of reference require us to address public concern. Is there some common theme that either the press or other commentators pick up and go on about which relates to concern about standards?

IAIN ROBERTSON: At the moment there is a general quango-bashing theme in the press which does not always distinguish between those quangos that are trying to evolve and trying to improve all the time in their openness and, perhaps, those that are not. That is the particular theme.

There was a strong concern before the Scottish Affairs Committee looked into Scottish Enterprise and into HIE about potential sleaze and conflict of interest but, as the Scottish Affairs Committee reported, they were largely quite content that there was none of that sleazy type of activity going on and that, in fact, the LECs in Lowland and Highland Scotland were trying their absolute best to have good conflict of interest procedures in place that would prevent that.

In the Highlands, our LEC chairmen are really local businessmen so, if they or their board members, were involved in anything questionable not only would their reputation suffer but they would be likely to find one of their customers in their shop or in their hotel or in their garage remonstrating with them or not buying their products, as was the case with one of our LEC chairmen who lost a customer because he had been turned down for finance. So, it can work greatly to the disadvantage of the LEC chairmen as well.

1606. CLIFFORD BOULTON: But there is, as you say, a lively interest taken in the work which perhaps has the effect of keeping people on their toes or, at least, feeling vulnerable?

IAIN ROBERTSON: Yes.

1607. CLIFFORD BOULTON: I notice that there is a practice of making an announcement every time a contract is awarded in a case where a director has a relevant interest. The alternative to that, and probably the more normal thing to do, is to make that publicly available in an annual report. Is it not possibly a little unsettling? People always say it is very unsettling if your airline pilot suddenly announces there is no cause for alarm. Is it not a bit unsettling constantly to be reminded that contracts are being given where a director has an interest, or is it best to get in first?

IAIN ROBERTSON: Frankly, it is much better to get in first and to show that you have nothing to hide and there is this benefit that it draws other people in. We have found that to be very productive. If you do it in your annual report—your annual report is often coming out a year afterwards and there is not always much room in annual reports for any detail but if you put out a press release about it you can actually explain the whole case so the facts are getting into the public domain, whereas in an annual report it is only a byline at best or, perhaps, even just a statistic.

SANDY CUMMING: Yes. In fact, picking up the point you make, the practice that we operate is that we were concerned that we were over-emphasising the situations when they arose, so we have introduced, as have all other LECs in the Highlands, a monthly set of approvals so the ones in which our directors may have an interest are very much put into the public domain as part of the overall package. There is very much more a sense of perspective and balance so people get a feeling in terms of the percentage of the value of the total approvals in that month; how much has gone to any LEC director who has a particular interest.

CLIFFORD BOULTON: That very much meets the point that I was making in my question.

IAIN ROBERTSON: We announce them individually as well. I was thinking particularly of the Milton Hotels announcement recently where one of the directors of Lochaber Limited got assistance with his hotel. It was a big development for the town so we put out a specific press release on that.

SANDY BRADY: It is also fair to say that a number of the examples of interest are non-financial interests. For example, we have a number of the college principals on LEC boards throughout the HIE network and a number of those, when we are involved in assisting a training course at the local college, certainly may have an interest but it is not a personal or financial interest within that, but we cover that by the same policy.

1608. CLIFFORD BOULTON: I have just one final question and then I will ask colleagues to take part. The Secretary of State said that he has asked the enterprise bodies to appoint external complaints adjudicators. Is there any news about how that is going in your area?

IAIN ROBERTSON: We are talking to the Scottish Office about how to do that just now. We welcome the opportunity. Again, there is an advantage to us in doing that because, as you will understand, we get a number of what the lawyers would call "vexatious complainants" in that there are people who continuously complain, perhaps because they are not well or perhaps because they feel very strongly about a point. Often you just cannot satisfy them and the correspondence goes on year after year after year. So, having an external adjudicator can be a device for dealing with that, so we welcome that opportunity and we are about to start talking to the Scottish Office about who should be selected, what sort of remuneration they would be offered and what terms of reference they would be given.

CLIFFORD BOULTON: Good, because it is an area which is, obviously, very relevant. Perhaps we will be getting some more news in the course of our inquiry about this.

IAIN ROBERTSON: The Highlands Islands Development Board, which was our predecessor body, actually was part of the Parliamentary Ombudsman system, was it not?

SANDY BRADY: Yes, that is correct, but it was not transferred to Highlands and Islands Enterprise on our establishment.

CLIFFORD BOULTON: No, I can understand that. Thank you very much.

LORD NOLAN: Sir William?

1609. WILLIAM UTTING: Thank you, Chairman. I would like to go back to your overall role because there is not in England an intermediary body between TECs and the relevant department doing the job that you are doing here. Your job in, so to speak, superintending LECs was added on to what you described as a classic rural development agency?

IAIN ROBERTSON: The LECs were actually added on to what the Highlands and Islands Development Board had done. The Highlands and Islands Development Board was started by the Labour Government in approximately 1965 and examined by the House of Lords in 1988. The House of Lords came to the conclusion that it really was a unique rural development agency but there were two or three things missing. (1) was that it did not have enough businessmen on the board; (2) it did not have training powers; (3) it did not have environmental powers, but they thought it was an excellent example of a rural development agency, especially because it had social powers.

When the Highlands and Islands Enterprise Network was announced five years ago these missing pieces in the jigsaw were added so we got the local motivation through the LECs, we got the businessmen through the LECs and on the HIE board and we got the powers of the training agency and we inherited the environmental renewal powers that the Scottish Development Agency had held for the whole of Scotland.

We have been able to evolve what the HIDB did on a central basis from Inverness by passing it out, devolving it to the local enterprise companies, and keeping in the centre processes that display economies of scale. For example, the Skye LEC only has 12 people on the staff so we run their finance for them; we give them legal advice; we do their personnel work for them, so the LEC is very much staffed with calling officers, people who are actually dealing in the product.

We are aiming and working with the LECs just now on the training side to try and be more product orientated and less administration orientated as the old Training Agency was. That is, perhaps, one of the areas that all the LECs throughout Scotland are going to have to try and tackle, to simplify the process—and Sandy mentioned it—for dealing with the administration of training which just now requires more attention to individual employees, or young people involved in training, than perhaps is required for dealing with a major grant and loan. You can spend more time on a £2,000 training programme for an individual in terms of checking than you can on a larger grant and loan application that is going to a business.

Somehow, throughout the whole network, throughout Scotland, we have to try and simplify that and reduce that and, perhaps, go on to a more random sampling, random testing basis, as is done in the accounting in most corporations now, as was not the case through the Department of Employment, through Sheffield, under the Training Agency.

1610. WILLIAM UTTING: I think you must have added mind reading to your other qualifications for your post since you have answered four of my questions in one go.

If I could summarise something about the role: if you are successful in working with LECs, this is partly due to the fact that this responsibility forms part of a coherent responsibility that extends well beyond the comparatively narrow remit of TECs in England?

IAIN ROBERTSON: Yes, absolutely. We are very much dealing with improving the economy of the Highlands and Islands but doing it through the people of the Highlands and Islands. Our job, to a large extent, is to prevent depopulation in villages on the west coast and the Western Isles.

The community aspect is very strong in everything we do; indeed, our strategy is about developing prosperity for the people of the Highlands through business growth, through community growth and through developing people. These three strategic thrusts overlap because each one benefits the other and capable people will mean strong communities; work for people will mean strong communities. The medical analogy is quite good. You cannot address one symptom without treating the whole person as well.

1611. WILLIAM UTTING: How does your social development role relate to any local authority responsibilities in that sector? How are these responsibilities apportioned between you and the local authority?

IAIN ROBERTSON: Our role is not on the social work side of things. It is really concerned with local facilities and starting groups and getting community entrepreneurship and community initiatives going. For example, encouraging a group to get together to raise a third of the cost of a swimming pool for Islay, encouraging a business to donate the premises and then getting either European funds or our own funds to come in and complete the picture so that between you and the community—obviously led by the LEC—you can produce something that is of community benefit.

SANDY BRADY: We have a small budget of just over £1 million each year for what we call community action grants and those go typically to things like village halls, swimming pools, assisting the local bowling club or the local Brownie pack, or whatever. More important than that in some ways is the fact that because of our community powers it suffuses a great deal of what we do on the economic side.

For example, if we are assisting fish farms on the remote west coast the community impact of that in the creation of four or five jobs in a small community is equally important because that often means putting half a dozen kids into the local school and enabling the local school to stay open with a very small roll which, in turn, creates a community facility for the people living locally. So, particularly in small communities, economic and social development are inextricably bound together and we find that time and again at the local level.

SANDY CUMMING: Just to add a point quite uniquely in the Highlands, there is also the whole question of cultural development. For instance, the distinctive Gaelic language which is very much central to many parts of the Highlands and Islands. We are able to assist with the development of that particular key part of our environment. It is very important that we progress on that front.

1612. WILLIAM UTTING: Presumably, your area covers a large number of local authorities so that it would

be the local LECs who linked most closely with the individual authorities. I do not know if Mr Cumming wants to say something about relationships with individual local authorities?

SANDY CUMMING: Yes, we have an excellent relationship in Ross and Cromarty. I would like to use this opportunity, if I may, to highlight a situation. On our board we have a member who has served on both the district council and on the regional council. In our register of members' interests it is quite interesting to note that there are 38 items against that individual, in none of which he has a pecuniary interest but, for instance, if we helped the local authority, because in the Highlands a local authority, as you may know, plays a very leading role in training delivery, so if we awarded a grant as part of our training programme delivery that would be noted against that member's interest although he would have no financial interest.

That is the sort of situation we deal with. Other listed of interests that we notify in our annual report and our register of interests will range from things like he is part of the Gaelic movement, he is on things like the hydrotherapy pool, he serves on the board of management there. It is a very unique, close working relationship we have.

Another clear example of good working relationships with the local authority was where we had a major rundown in oil fabrication at Nigg about three years ago. We formed a very strong alliance with the local authority at that stage, to the extent that we had on secondment on our staff their deputy Director of Development and it was very much working together to try and find a lasting solution to the problems which emerged at the time.

IAIN ROBERTSON: If I could just add on the relationships with local authorities, we actually changed the conceptual approach to the relationship with local authorities when we were formed. It was not universally popular. We moved away from what was known as the Montgomery system of the past which was regular, formal meetings every six months or every year which were, in some instances, fairly aggressive meetings. We moved on to a much more working relationship where we said to the local authorities, "Our doors are open. We expect your doors to be open. We will work together on a huge range of activities at the local level throughout the Highlands and Islands, working day to day, and we will drop the set pieces".

That has been unpopular with some of the local authorities but the facts speak for themselves. The last time the Highlands tried to win something like Objective 1 they did not get through. This time the local authorities and the Highlands and Islands Enterprise Network worked so closely together with all the local authorities that a successful case was made. There are hundreds of examples now of on-the-ground working relationships with the local authorities, but there are still a number of people who like these big set piece meetings.

What we do now is take our board round the area. The HIE board and the LEC boards meet the local authorities in their area, not on a regular basis but we meet every local authority probably once every 13 months, or thereabouts, in their local area, talking about local problems with the LEC board present. The aggregate level of contact has hugely gone up but the formal level has actually gone down.

1613. WILLIAM UTTING: But at strategic level, would you have regular contact with COSLA, for example?

IAIN ROBERTSON: We do not have a huge amount of contact with COSLA, although we do exchange correspondence with them and I have gone and talked to them, for example, and explained our strategy in the past. I have not been to see them in the past year.

1614. WILLIAM UTTING: Very briefly, if I could conclude; what about your relationship with the relevant Government department?

IAIN ROBERTSON: We have had a very good team in the Scottish Office looking after us, our sponsoring division, for the past five years and in our annual report we actually complimented them because we found them helpful. I came from the private sector and I probably expected the Scottish Office to be quite bureaucratic and quite difficult to deal with and I found the first team that we had to deal with very interested in the Highlands and I hope that will continue in the future.

We are now looked after by the same team as looks after Scottish Enterprise. There is a danger that we might be dwarfed. I rather liked having a person who was wholly interested in the Highlands to the exclusion of everything else to deal with, but that is a luxury that the Scottish Office cannot afford any more. We still regard them as very much on the team in terms of, as we are doing just now, fighting cases through for assistance from Europe to get some investment in our fabrication yards and helping us with the major projects that are going on all the time in the Highlands. We need that Scottish Office backup.

WILLIAM UTTING: Thank you. Thank you, Chairman.

1615. LORD NOLAN: Thank you very much. I wonder if I could just raise one point you touched on earlier and that is the three-year contracts of which, I think, Mr Cumming spoke. I think you said that you found those very helpful?

SANDY CUMMING: I do, personally. I find the rigour that is attached to that in terms of strategic planning, moving the business on, fundamentally important. Having worked in the HIDB since 1973, one of the real differences that we have made is that now, for instance, back working in my native patch of Ross and Cromarty, we have a very localised focus. We have now an Invergordon office which is our HQ with 19 staff, dedicated to the task of taking Ross and Cromarty forward. We also have a sub-office on the west coast.

These access points really were not available in the past. On top of that we have the board working, helping us to take forward issues in Ross and Cromarty. It is a unique extra dimension to economic development in our area and it is good value for money.

1616. LORD NOLAN: Yes. It has been more broadly considered, as you know, in England and, indeed, Scottish Enterprise but there was a fear that it helped build up excessive reserves. What do you say about that?

SANDY CUMMING: No, I do not think so.

1617. LORD NOLAN: You have not had any difficulty over that?

SANDY CUMMING: No, none whatsoever. If I may, there was one point that I really wanted to bring out and that is our closeness to communities. Iain mentioned this previously. If I may, I would just like 10 seconds on that.

For instance, several of our board members are active community councillors as well, which is a tremendous demonstration of their commitment to the community but we also, at the staff level in the company, place strong emphasis on working very closely at that level, the community council level. We attend as many of their meetings as we physically can and we find that very helpful to get feedback from the local community.

LORD NOLAN: Yes. You have been very clear and very helpful. We have covered a lot of ground with you. Our thanks to you all for coming and for your help.

IAIN ROBERTSON: Thank you very much for the opportunity.

1618. LORD NOLAN: Now we welcome the Scottish Council for Voluntary Organisations, represented by Mr Stephen Maxwell, the Assistant Director, Mr Ian Brown, the Enterprise and Training Officer, and Lucy Pratt, the Head of Research.

May I just make it quite clear, if you do not mind Mr Maxwell, for the benefit not only of the members of the Committee but also for the record, that you are Mr Stephen Maxwell sitting in the middle?

STEPHEN MAXWELL, LUCY PRATT, AND IAN BROWN

STEPHEN MAXWELL (Assistant Director, Scottish Council for Voluntary Organisations): That is right.

1619. LORD NOLAN: So we are all now identified. We are very grateful for the information you have already given us and that includes, of course, a short opening statement, which we have already accepted as part of the record. It is a statement which, if I may say so in summary, is somewhat critical of the LEC system as it at present stands in a number of respects. This is one of the aspects of the matter that we would like to explore with you.

Would you be happy to go straight into questions or would you like to add anything else?

STEPHEN MAXWELL: Could I say something very briefly first?

LORD NOLAN: Yes, indeed.

STEPHEN MAXWELL: First of all, I would like to apologise for the absence of our Director, Martin Sime, who actually led on the written evidence. He has been called away to jury duty, I am afraid. Secondly, to say that SCVO's interest in the LEC network is, in some ways, a quite specific interest and our comments reflect our particular experience and the experience of many of our member organisations in dealing with the LEC network. It would also be true to say that our comments probably apply more strongly to the Scottish Enterprise Network than they do to the Highlands and Islands Network, although insofar as they relate to the broader regulatory framework, they of course apply to both. We are aware that the Highlands and Islands Network, through accountability through openness and the close community contacts, is perhaps less open to some of the strictures we make than perhaps the Scottish Enterprise Network is.

LORD NOLAN: Thank you very much indeed. We take it in turns to take the lead in asking questions and it is Sir William Utting's turn, so I will ask him to begin.

1620. WILLIAM UTTING: Thank you, Chairman. You spoke in your written evidence about the important role that voluntary organisations play in life in Scotland right across the board and you said that in this context they provide 25% of training for work places in Scotland. What would that mean in volume terms? It is fine as a percentage, but can that be converted roughly into cash or number of people helped?

IAN BROWN (Enterprise and Training Officer, Scottish Council for Voluntary Organisations): It roughly means round about 3,000 to 4,000 places in the training for work scheme. It is rather difficult to give a set figure for places because Government schemes like "Training for Work" are organised on trainee weeks. The LECs, Local Enterprise Companies, pay for trainee weeks delivered so it is not always the case that someone will stay on a scheme for 52 weeks or six months. The rough equivalent would be round about 3,000 to 4,000 places.

1621. WILLIAM UTTING: Good, that is very helpful. What kind of organisations are providing this training?

IAN BROWN: Quite a mixed bag. Voluntary organisations tend to specialise in special needs training for particular client groups and these could range from people with mental health problems, physical disabilities, mental handicap, ex-offenders, single parents, and that type of thing. There are also many other what we call more generalist voluntary organisations who are training providers, who compete openly in the training market and are recognised as leading providers in Scotland.

1622. WILLIAM UTTING: Yes. So, you have a mix of what might be called "not for profit" training organisations and other organisations that have special concerns for socially disadvantaged people?

IAN BROWN: Yes.

WILLIAM UTTING: I ought to say that I am a trustee of CSV, which provides a good deal of training in England and I know that NACRO does as well.

IAN BROWN: CSV is a prime example.

1623. WILLIAM UTTING: This area of social disadvantage was one that I actually wanted to pick up because you speak, in your opening statement about—'continual downward pressure on trainee unit costs and numbers" and "a hostile payment regime having a serious impact on the quality of training"

It was represented to us in London that this sort of regime was producing a peculiarly adverse set of

circumstances for socially disadvantaged people. Would you like to say something, first of all, about what you mean by this downward pressure on unit costs and the hostile payment regime and its effect on training?

IAN BROWN: Certainly. SCVO's research showed that round about four or five years ago when the LECs first came on stream that the average unit price offered for a "Training for Work" place was round about, we estimated, £40 per week. We now think it is almost definitely below £30 a week and we find it hard to accept, even with numerous efficiency savings, that there is any more fat to cut. We really are down to the bone now and every year more and more training providers drop out of the LEC training market because they simply cannot make the economics of it work.

The problem has been compounded by the fact that under pressure from the Treasury the LECs and the TECs have been forced to introduce a system known as "output related funding" whereby a proportion of the money they offer to training providers is withheld and is dependent on trainees getting specified outcomes which tend to be either vocational qualifications, jobs or moves into further education or self employment.

That proportion has increased gradually. It started at 10%, I think, a few years ago. It is now up to round about 40%. In England it is even worse. It is something like 75% and it is causing massive problems. I think the Department for Education and Employment recognises now that it is causing massive problems, particularly for special needs trainee people because these are the kind of people who will be least likely to get jobs and will be least likely to attain vocational qualifications and, of course, they will need longer on schemes so providers will have to keep them longer on schemes, which means they can have less people coming through which means they have less chance to maximise their income.

Output related funding has been introduced on LECs and TECs which are forced to pass it downline to the training providers. We know that just two months ago the Department for Education and Employment pretty much conceded the point that output related funding was not helping providers of special needs training and the Department is talking about piloting a separate adult training programme simply called, "The Basic Skills Programme" for certain client groups.

I would just mention too that a Coopers and Lybrand report commissioned by the Department also found that increasing the output related funding element was causing severe problems for all training providers but particularly special needs training providers.

WILLIAM UTTING: But that is a requirement from the central department that the LECs have to conform to so, in a sense, their behaviour is being heavily influenced by the central government requirement.

IAN BROWN: Yes, though it is up to LECs whether they do pass output related funding downline but I think they are pretty much obliged to. They can vary it a little bit.

1624. WILLIAM UTTING: The problem quite simply for disadvantaged people is that it is going to take longer to train somebody with learning disabilities up to a level of achievement than it does the average, so to speak, employed worker?

IAN BROWN: Yes, and encouraging providers, of course, to be increasingly selective about who they take on when we know even the most conscientious of voluntary sector training providers, simply to remain economically viable, really have to think twice now about the kind of people they take on. You know, "If we take this person on our scheme for 12 months will they get an output at the end?" because, if they do not, they will, frankly, be an economic liability to the organisation.

1625. WILLIAM UTTING: On the constitutional point, you say very clearly that you believe that the status of LECs should be reviewed. What have you in mind here? Are you looking for a radical review that changes the nature of these organisations altogether or are you saying that there is something here that can actually be improved upon and worked with?

STEPHEN MAXWELL: I certainly think we are suggesting that their status as private companies, although of course dependent on public monies, makes them less accountable to the interests they serve and to the wider community than is desirable. We certainly believe that their status as private companies should be looked at more closely and questions should be asked as to just how consistent that status is with the principles of accountability.

1626. WILLIAM UTTING: It is one thing to say that these ought to be made public sector bodies but another to say that their working might be improved if the community were, in a sense, more widely represented on the management boards. For example, one of your points is that they actually ought to include a representative from the voluntary sector. Which way would you really want to go, the comprehensive review or improving the present situation?

STEPHEN MAXWELL: We would favour a comprehensive review of the status they have. We are very keen that the voluntary sector as a major provider of training places and, if you like, as a champion of some of the most disadvantaged groups in the community, should be properly represented. One of the contrasts between the TEC network and the LEC network is that the LEC boards, as far as we are able to identify, have fewer members with a voluntary sector background proportionately than the TEC network has. We are really only able to identify in the total board membership in Scotland two members, both in the Highlands and Islands, both in Highland LECs, who have voluntary sector backgrounds.

That may be partly because the LECs have a smaller number of board members than the TECs and that limits the scope for representing the whole community of interests on the LEC boards. That is perhaps one of the elements which should be reviewed. We think it is a serious disadvantage in the LECs that the voluntary sector is so poorly represented.

1627. WILLIAM UTTING: Yes, I can quite see the case for its representation as a kind of advocate for groups in the community whose interests might not otherwise be represented. There are problems if it is itself a major training provider. There would then be an obvious conflict of interest. Somehow, those issues would have to be satisfactorily resolved, would they not, if voluntary organisations were to participate in the management?

STEPHEN MAXWELL: Yes, although the number of voluntary organisations which are training providers is a tiny, tiny fraction of the total voluntary sector constituency in Scotland. We are talking of, perhaps, 30 organisations which are significant training providers and the voluntary sector has well established representative structures which are not training providers themselves and which represent the wider voluntary sector interest to public bodies and those might well be the base for representation on the boards of the LECs.

1628. WILLIAM UTTING: Yes, I accept that. That is good. But if that is accepted, does it open the door to requests for representation from other groups in the community with legitimate interests that it would be difficult to resist or that actually you would advocate? There is the position of local authorities, for example, and perhaps other bodies in the community?

STEPHEN MAXWELL: I think we would welcome the representation of local authorities on LEC boards and local authorities are represented on the great majority, if not all, of the LEC boards in Scotland.

IAN BROWN: All of them.

STEPHEN MAXWELL: The problem is that the small size of the board membership in Scotland means that once you have satisfied the requirement for private sector membership there are relatively few places left and once local authorities have their representation then there is usually just one or two places left over and the voluntary sector does not always, we feel, get proper recognition for the variety of roles it plays with the client groups and the wider economic and community interests which LECs are meant to progress.

1629. WILLIAM UTTING: I would like to conclude my questioning by moving into an area that you mentioned in your evidence but which has not formed any part of its substance. That is the reference you made to the voluntary sectors' contribution to social housing in Scotland. We are also concerned with housing associations and these are described to us in the United Kingdom as being quintessentially voluntary organisations.

We have had some difficulty on the accountability side over the question of the membership of housing associations, the idea that their being a membership provided a body to whom the organisation could be accountable was, I think, rather dismissed by the Hancock Review of the governance of housing associations. There is, perhaps, something rather odd about the idea of anybody coming along and putting up a pound and becoming a member and being able to vote in people who are commanding quite large public and private resources.

Do you have any thoughts really about how voluntary bodies of this nature ought to be constituted and whether the membership idea is a good and useful one at all?

STEPHEN MAXWELL: Presumably your question is about the division of accountability for expenditure of public monies between elected committees of voluntary organisations and their stewardship of the public money that becomes available to them?

WILLIAM UTTING: Or whether the concept of membership actually provides a reliable basis for exacting accountability at all.

STEPHEN MAXWELL: The membership basis of voluntary organisations is a pretty complex and diverse matter and I do not think that the voluntary sector would argue that just because a voluntary organisation is representative of its membership that that justifies a claim to a wider role as representative of the public in any grand sense. The claims the voluntary sector makes for representation on bodies like the boards of LECs is a more specific claim which depends on the actual role it plays in supporting client groups or that the contribution it makes to progressing the interests which that body, the LEC or other public body, is officially committed to advancing.

I am afraid I could not venture an opinion on the housing associations. There is a Scottish Federation of Housing Associations and I am sure——

WILLIAM UTTING: Whom we shall hear from later on.

STEPHEN MAXWELL: And I am sure I would get into trouble if I ventured too many opinions on housing associations.

WILLIAM UTTING: Thank you. Thank you, Chairman.

LORD NOLAN: Dame Anne?

1630. ANNE WARBURTON: Chairman, I have been sitting here being very conscious that it would be lovely to have a dialogue because we still have with us the HIE representatives. It would be very interesting but perhaps time does not allow even if they wanted that.

Could I ask you particularly, given your wish to be more involved in the LEC decision-making, and so forth, do you have a strategy for, as it were, getting in there amongst them? We have been being told that meetings are open. Do you take the initiatives?

STEPHEN MAXWELL: Certainly. The voluntary sector is a very active contributor to dialogues about training provision and the needs of different groups in the community for training and other forms of support from LECs and at central level in relation to Scottish Enterprise and, indeed, to Highlands and Islands Enterprise. The Scottish Council for Voluntary Organisations and other representative voluntary sector bodies have argued their case both for a continued high level of provision for the vulnerable groups they represent and for a greater representation for the voluntary sector on the boards.

We do what we can to present the voluntary sector's interests and the interests of its clients. Whether we do it vigorously enough and mix it persistently enough, I am not sure, but we certainly put a good deal of effort into promoting the case.

1631. ANNE WARBURTON: We heard earlier from the Renfrew Enterprise that they have a management committee which sounded as though it was a fairly elastic body which might perhaps be used. Are you aware ever of representatives of the voluntary sector coming into that?

IAN BROWN: I deal probably most with Local Enterprise Companies within SCVO. I have not come across that, I must admit, and I do not know any of our members who feel they have any sort of significant input into any of the LECs decision making processes, certainly in the Scottish Enterprise Network, but I had not heard of the Renfrewshire example.

1632. ANNE WARBURTON: There was one other question that struck me. Your paper covers both LECs and TECs and I wondered if you would like to pinpoint—we have mentioned one or two of them in the talk now—pinpoint practice which perhaps might well be looked at by TECs which already exists in LECs and vice versa?

IAN BROWN: Our key thing is, as my colleague said, the size of the boards, the number of directors on the TEC boards in England. The Training and Enterprise Councils actually have a narrower remit than the Scottish Local Enterprise Companies because they do not have quite the same powers over economic development. Despite that, the TECs in England and Wales have boards of up to 15 members. They must satisfy the same requirement that two thirds of the seats must be given over to senior figures from industry and commerce but that leaves more seats on the non-private sector side for a wider range of interests to be represented from the community.

We know in England in many of the TECs, or at least some of the TECs, there is quite strong voluntary sector representation. In Scotland the Scottish Enterprise Boards only have up to 12 directors on the boards which means fewer on the non-private sector side. For Highlands and Islands LECs I think it can be as few as seven, which means it is very squeezed once you have the business people on board. We have always campaigned heavily for Scottish LECs to have a wider board structure.

I think perhaps it is an advantage when I liaise with our English colleagues, how they work with Training and Enterprise Councils, voluntary sector organisations find it an advantage in England that the TECs are more focused simply on training. They do have an enterprise remit but they are more focused on training whereas the Scottish LECs, and particularly the Scottish Enterprise LECs, also have this very strong economic development remit and, to some extent, that might take precedence at board level and at director level.

ANNE WARBURTON: Good. I do not think I have any burning questions still.

PROF ANTHONY KING: Could I ask a question?

1633. LORD NOLAN: Yes, please. I wonder, Tony, may I ask one that is in my mind and then I will hand over to you. Mine is a short one. Both the Highlands and Islands Enterprise and the Scottish Enterprise enjoin their LEC members to have registers of interest which are open to the public. Is that a requirement observed generally in your experience?

STEPHEN MAXWELL: I am not sure that we would feel qualified to comment on how widely registers of interests are kept or publicised. I think we would probably duck that question.

1634. LORD NOLAN: That is quite an important venture into the open, is it not?

STEPHEN MAXWELL: Yes, indeed. I do not know if Ian has an impression of how easily accessible the register of interests is.

IAN BROWN: I do not, I am afraid, no. It has not come up as an issue, I do not think, in the voluntary sector so far.

1635. LORD NOLAN: You say it has not become an issue?

IAN BROWN: I have not heard of it as an issue, one of the key issues with the voluntary sector.

1636. LORD NOLAN: Thank you. In other words, you have no reason to doubt that that requirement is generally complied with? It is certainly down in black and white.

IAN BROWN: Sure.

LORD NOLAN: Thank you very much. That is all I wanted to clear up. Tony?

1637. PROF ANTHONY KING: I just wanted to look back to something that Sir William Utting was asking you about. Clearly, if an organisation providing training is paid in part in terms of results there may be a lot of pressures on it to do a variety of things, including cutting corners, and claiming it has achieved results when it does not actually have them, provided any validating body is half asleep at the time. When we talked to the equivalent organisation in London they said that the pressure to cut corners was there and that to their dismay corners were on occasion being cut. What is the Scottish experience on that?

IAN BROWN: There have been some scandals in England actually of commercial training organisations claiming people have been submitted for exam courses which they have not. The pressure is there. Yes, the pressure is there to cut corners. We find the problem more simply at the front end is training organisations just will not take on people now if they are not very competent.

PROF ANTHONY KING: So, instead of cutting corners in the normal sense you cut that corner instead?

IAN BROWN: We cut that corner, yes. But the system does lean towards that, does tempt you to cram as many people through as possible.

1638. PROF ANTHONY KING: You said there had been scandals in England. Have there been scandals in Scotland?

STEPHEN MAXWELL: No, I am not aware of any.

1639. PROF ANTHONY KING: Should there have been? Have things been happening that the public does not know about?

STEPHEN MAXWELL: No, we do not have evidence that there are uncovered scandals. I hope we would have helped to uncover them if we had such evidence but we do not have such evidence.

1640. LORD NOLAN: Just one other question that occurred to me when I was reflecting on what you have

been saying. Do not community minded people and councillors who are on the boards of LECs also sometimes become involved with voluntary organisations? We heard of a councillor on the Ross and Cromarty LEC who belonged to at least two voluntary organisations. Is there a substantial number of people in that capacity who are able to bridge any gaps that exist between the approaches of the two types of organisation?

STEPHEN MAXWELL: I have no doubt that there are people on the boards of LECS who have connections with voluntary organisations but the issue is not just whether they have an incidental connection, the issue is whether they feel that they have an obligation to account to a voluntary sector constituency for the policy of the LEC and to take up and be in active dialogue with the voluntary sector on some of the issues which are of most interest. I am afraid there are very few LEC board members who are so rooted in voluntary sector networks that they are able to conduct that sort of dialogue with the voluntary sector.

LORD NOLAN: Thank you very much. We are very grateful to you. Our prime concern, as a Committee, is to address concerns, as you know and as has been said this morning, and you have raised, very clearly and very objectively, the concerns which you feel which will certainly help us in pursuing our further inquiries and concentrating our thoughts. We are most grateful to you all. Thank you for coming.

STEPHEN MAXWELL: Thank you.

1641. LORD NOLAN: Now we are going to hear from Scottish Enterprise itself—Sir Donald MacKay, Mrs MacFarlane and Crawford Beveridge, Chief Executive. That has at once identified each of you, which is one thing we always have to do at the outset, both for the benefit of the Committee and for the record.

You, or course, have in your jurisdiction, if I can call it that, 12 of the Local Enterprise Companies and half of a thirteenth, is that right?

SIR DONALD MACKAY, CRAWFORD BEVERIDGE, AND RAY MACFARLANE

SIR DONALD MACKAY (Chairman, Scottish Enterprise): That is correct.

LORD NOLAN: Sir Donald, we take it in turns on this Committee to lead off with the questions and, if it is convenient to you, we will go straight in. We have, of course, read with great care what you have sent us and then I will ask Lord Thomson to start. Will that be convenient to you?

DONALD MACKAY: Yes, certainly, Sir.

1642. LORD THOMSON: Sir Donald, thank you very much for coming with your colleagues. Maybe I could start whilst it is fresh in our minds with what has just been said by the Scottish voluntary sector. I am sorry they have now gone from the room. You heard the tail end of their evidence to us and, basically, they were saying to us that there was a lack of effective voluntary organisation representation on LEC boards. They attributed this partly to the fact that in Scotland the number of people on LEC boards is set at a smaller number than in England where there is, therefore, more room for manoeuvre. They were also arguing that, in the English TECs the emphasis is more on training than on enterprise, whereas in Scotland the emphasis is more on enterprise than on training.

Whilst it is all fresh in our minds, would you like to comment on their concerns?

DONALD MACKAY: There are a lot of concerns expressed there, Lord Thomson.

LORD THOMSON: They are linked concerns.

DONALD MACKAY: Of course, the size of a board is given to us in guidance from the Scottish Office. It would be our view that the size of board is appropriate. It is not necessarily true that larger boards are more effective and we certainly feel a board of a dozen can encompass a wide range of interests. It is also true that many of the persons, particularly those from the private sector, are actually chosen to become board members because, in addition to their business experience, they have direct experience of working with voluntary organisations.

We take very seriously our responsibilities as a network towards special needs groups. The percentage of persons who are trained in the special needs category has not fallen since Scottish Enterprise was established. The amount we spend per trainee on special needs groups is roughly twice as high as on other groups and we fund them quite separately from other people to make absolutely certain that we do not overlook their interests. There is a social responsibility as well as the economic development responsibility and that is shared by the whole network.

1643. LORD THOMSON: Thank you very much. That is a very interesting reply. Can I move on to wider matters and could I just start by asking you this. We have been hearing evidence from the TEC sector in England and Wales and what is of great interest to us now is to compare what happens in Scotland with what happens in England and Wales in this field and perhaps see whether there are lessons to be learned both ways.

I just wondered whether you wanted to make any comments, you or your colleagues, on what you see as the relative advantages and disadvantages of the two rather different systems that operate on either side of the border.

DONALD MACKAY: The major differences, I would suggest, are that the powers which are vested in Scottish Enterprise are far wider than the powers vested in TECs. In addition to our training responsibilities, we have responsibilities for the development of enterprise; we have responsibilities for environmental improvement and, going alongside that, then we have substantial powers for property and site development, and so on and so forth.

The Act, of course, creates only Scottish Enterprise. It does not create the LECs. The Act of Parliament only refers to Scottish Enterprise so we operate through the LECs with guidance but our powers, if you like, are devolved down to LECs. They have no less powers and no more powers than we have and, by their operating contract, they have to operate within the Act, as we have to operate within the Act.

It would be a mistake to believe Scottish Enterprise is a regulatory body. It is not actually; it is a doing body.

National programmes and projects are our responsibility and, together with the Scottish Office, we are responsible for "Locate in Scotland" and we are responsible for Scottish Trade International. We have the overall responsibility for creating the policy framework within which the LECs will operate and we have the responsibility for the allocation of resources and generally for the oversight of the LEC programme. But we regard ourselves as a network—that is, we are a deliberately de-centralised network. Most of our expenditure is actually at the hands of the LECs but they work within the system set for Scottish Enterprise as a whole.

1644. LORD THOMSON: One of the interesting things from our point of view about the Scottish pattern here is that we have in Scotland Scottish Enterprise which is a quango in the classic sense of the term. In England there is nothing between central Government and the TECs. We have already been looking at quangos in our first report, quangos being defined in this sense as bodies publicly funded but with ministerial appointment. In this area now, in our second report, we are looking at bodies that are publicly funded but are not subject to ministerial appointment and that is where the LEC layer in Scotland comes within our present review. Could you just say a word about the nature of your contract with the Scottish Office, with the Government?

DONALD MACKAY: I will defer to our Director of Network Services in a minute because she has legal training and she is better than I am at these things.

We are required to ensure not only that we carry through our own services but also that the LEC network works within the powers given to us by Parliament and the operating contract requires the LECs to operate within that Act. The operating contract goes on to specify some other things but, basically, it is a situation of devolved power. I think it was once said that power devolved is power retained and so by devolving it we do not lose the overall responsibility for ensuring accountability and, on my left, Crawford Beveridge, is the accounting officer for the whole of the network and for all expenditure within the network and it is a requirement on us to ensure that they operate within the Act. I am sure Ray will put it much more elegantly than I have.

RAY MACFARLANE (Director Network Services, Scottish Enterprise): You asked us specifically about the relationship between us and the Government. We are a statutory body so we have an Act and we can only act within the Act and the powers that that devolves to us. We are managed by Scottish Office and the relationship between us and them is governed by a management statement and so we are given full guidelines from Scottish Office on exactly how we are expected to behave and the management statement incorporates in particular Treasury guidelines on financial issues and programme rules on the way that we should go about appraising projects and the way we wish to approach our business. So there is a set framework for our relationship with Scottish Office.

1645. LORD THOMSON: Thank you very much. Another interesting difference in Scotland is that you have both Scottish Enterprise and you have the Highlands and Islands Enterprise. We have just heard some very interesting evidence earlier this morning from HIE. Could you just say a word about the relationship between

Scottish Enterprise and HIE? As the Chairman mentioned, you have 13½ LECs under Scottish Enterprise. That half must be shared with HIE, I suppose?

DONALD MACKAY: That is correct. We have 12½ and half is shared with HIE. I would say our relationships with Highlands and Islands Enterprise are extremely good. I put that down to the fact that the chairs of both organisations are from the Highlands. Both at that level and at Chief Executive level we have a very good working relationship.

We have fundamentally the same interests. We both wish to see a stronger Scottish economy and we both fundamentally believe that if we are going to achieve that then that should apply, as far as is possible, to all parts of Scotland.

1646. LORD THOMSON: We were told earlier this morning there is now one single bit of the Scottish Office that is responsible for the relations both with Scottish Enterprise and with HIE, whereas previously HIE had a separate bit of the Scottish Office looking after it. I detected a certain concern, no more, from HIE that perhaps because you are the big brother and they are the smaller organisation that this might mean that their interests might not get the same equal treatment from the Scottish Office under these new arrangements. Would you like to reassure HIE, who are sitting at the back and their ears are flapping?

DONALD MACKAY: I would be very pleased to get the same budget per capita as HIE have.

1647. LORD THOMSON: That is an adequate reply for the moment anyway. Could you then also tell us about another very interesting feature of the way you do things in Scotland. The actual staff of the LECs, I think I am right in saying, are employed by the Scottish Enterprise Network. Could you tell us how this works in practice? Is there any danger of a feeling of conflict of loyalties with the staff as between the LEC that they serve and the network that employs them?

DONALD MACKAY: Can I ask my Chief Executive who has to deal with this on a daily basis if he would like to answer that?

CRAWFORD BEVERIDGE (Chief Executive, Scottish Enterprise): I do not think there are any particularly observable conflicts with this. We have discussed several times in the past five years whether we would want to change this with chairs of the Local Enterprise Companies and the conclusion we have come to in each case has been that the system actually works rather well. It allowed us, since many of our LECs are in fairly close proximity in the central belt, to allow for some quite good career movement for staffs between the Local Enterprise Companies and ourselves without having to worry about whether there were significant conditional changes between the organisations.

It seems to work well for us at the moment. We have not seen any concerns of conflict amongst the staff involved. They feel very much part of the Local Enterprise Companies they are working for.

1648. LORD THOMSON: Could I then turn to the questions that relate to the composition of boards and the

way that their interests are recorded and any conflicts are dealt with.

Just on the boards themselves, I noticed that Mr Beveridge in his evidence to the Scottish Affairs Committee is quoted in their report—I do not know how far it is a quotation taken out of a wider context, Mr Beveridge will tell us—he said: "Board members do indeed select themselves" and the Committee itself went on to say that, of course, this is a very important matter of perception; whatever the actual reality, there is a perception problem and—"At worst safeguards are felt to be required to protect LEC boards degenerating into self-appointing and self-perpetuating cliques".

What do you say about that?

CRAWFORD BEVERIDGE: The context of that was in trying to make sure the Committee understood that these LEC boards were not appointed in the way that the boards of quangos are appointed and that the boards were indeed responsible for making their own selections of board members. It was not meant to imply to them that this was done in some secretive form and, in fact, part of the guidance which all of the Local Enterprise Companies adhere to is that there be a system in place by which board members are put forward from various different kinds of organisations for the selection of the board itself.

It has been very important, as it is in other private companies, to make sure that boards are able to work on a unitary basis with a wide ranging set of skills there, with a group of people who can work well together. It is important that the boards themselves, as a private board would do, are able to select the best possible people to go on and continue the board work.

1649. LORD THOMSON: Do you feel you have a duty to monitor this and to seek to influence particular situations if you feel that they need influence?

DONALD MACKAY: We do monitor. We are required to monitor because the intention was to create boards of a particular structure and to operate in a particular way. Therefore, obviously, we look to see whether they meet those guidelines. We do not seek to influence individual appointments. We would if we felt it was an inappropriate person but, effectively, if LECs wish to consult us they can do so and they often do.

You must remember here, Lord Thomson, that it was the intention to create boards where two thirds of the members were drawn from the business community because it was felt that was particularly important to the process of economic development. I do not think I can stress that enough. It is absolutely critical to us.

It was also the intention that the boards should operate as business boards. Their company is limited by guarantee. They operate on the unitary principle. People are on the boards because of their individual merit. They are not there, and should not be there, to represent particular views. That is very important too. Therefore, it is essential that the board should decide how to consult with its community, how to represent those interests and should seek our guidance when it feels it needs it.

It is necessary for our system to work well for there to be a certain element of creative tension in the system. The job of a Local Enterprise board is to make absolutely certain that Scottish Enterprise National understands the needs and opportunities of its local community and can accommodate those within a national strategy. Therefore, it requires that the boards have a certain standing which is independent of us. If we appointed them they would not have that independent standing. I think it is very important for effective operation.

1650. LORD THOMSON: I think we understand that and, of course, we understand their unitary nature and the fact that they have legal obligations as companies. Perhaps I might just say that it has been put to us by the previous witnesses from the voluntary sector that there ought to be a reappraisal of this structure and the question ought to be raised as to whether the private company structure is the appropriate one in the light of experience or whether it should be more a public institution, a publicly funded, public service institution. Would you like to give us your reaction and what your experience is of the pros and cons of the present structure?

DONALD MACKAY: The first thing I should say is that it is our duty to ensure that we try and represent the nature of the delivery mechanism which is intended by our guidelines. If our guidelines change then we would have to operate those different guidelines. You asked me a different question.

1651. LORD THOMSON: I asked you a wider question. You have to operate the law as it stands. We have to consider whether we want to make any recommendations that the law might be changed in this respect. We have an open mind on it. It is not a leading question in any way.

DONALD MACKAY: If you think of the nature of our powers: firstly, we have training powers like the TECs have. We have operated our training powers not actually to cut corners, as was suggested, but quite deliberately to drive up standards of vocational qualifications which we have done, I would suggest. The number of persons achieving vocational qualifications when we came in was 2,000; this year it will be 12,000 and most of those are at NVQ level 2 and 3 and we will introduce this year modern apprenticeships.

It is also the purpose of our training programmes to place people in work wherever possible, not just to train them and put them back on the dole queue. For that, through the Skillseeker schemes, we need very close relationships with employers because we find, if the training is done in the workplace, there is a far better chance of getting work.

Then, if you take our enterprise powers, they mean what they say. It is our intention, through our enterprise powers, to build a wider and a deeper business base. Therefore, necessarily, we must have skills which are appropriate to that task. The same goes for many of our environmental powers which are used not just to improve the environment but enhance the quality of the environments within which businesses operate. They have economic development functions as well. Therefore, for all those activities we need people who have experience of industry and that is what our LEC boards give us. They also give us the local knowledge.

I would say to you that if you judge us by results your motto should be—"If it ain't broke, don't fix it". It ain't broke.

1652. LORD THOMSON: Just to finish the questions relating to membership of the boards, the composition of the boards. Two propositions that have been canvassed—some of them in our evidence taken south of the border and some in evidence we have had here—is the possibility of membership schemes on the one side and the other separate proposition is a closer relationship with local chambers of commerce. I just wondered whether you had any comments to make about the pros and cons of these propositions?

DONALD MACKAY: Four of our enterprise companies have membership schemes. Three of them are very happy with it but the fourth is actually ruing it because they feel it is not working as well as they would like. The other LECs have certainly considered them—we have asked all our LECs to consider them—but they do not feel it would best meet their needs. What we do emphasise, and I am very serious about this, is that we believe that if a LEC is to operate effectively in its area it needs a good working relationship with its chambers, with other business organisations, with the voluntary organisations and with the local authorities and we very much believe in the principle that they should try to effect working partnerships on the ground with these various bodies.

We do understand also that circumstances vary a great deal from one part of Scotland to another and what is appropriate in one part is not appropriate in another. We feel that the local boards are best able to decide what working arrangements suit them in their particular circumstances but if any LEC wishes to develop a membership scheme we would encourage it.

I may just say also that at the time we were giving evidence to the Select Committee we discussed membership schemes with the Scottish chambers of commerce and we found a certain reluctance on their part to their extension because there was a feeling that it might lead to competition for membership, which we did not want, and the chambers, like ourselves, believe that there is a very big distinction between what a chamber does and what a Local Enterprise Company does.

I understand south of the border there has been some talk of mergers between these organisations. North of the border we think that is quite inappropriate.

LORD THOMSON: That is very interesting.

DONALD MACKAY: Both sides of the house feel that. Therefore, we had regard to one of the persons with whom we seek a working partnership, but if a LEC thinks it is appropriate we will certainly encourage them to develop it.

1653. LORD THOMSON: Could I ask you about your code of good practice, particularly in relation to a register of interests of members of the board and publication of conflicts of interest.

When the Scottish Affairs Committee was meeting there was a difference of practice, I think, between HIE on the one side and Scottish Enterprise on the other. HIE had gone in for the interesting innovation really of regular publication of contracts that were made with members of the local boards. You have moved on this since the Scottish Affairs Committee report was originally published but you have not yet gone quite as far as HIE do. Would you like to comment on what your present practice is?

DONALD MACKAY: We may be mixing up two different things, Lord Thomson.

LORD THOMSON: I am talking about members of the board who have contracts with the LEC of which they are on the board.

DONALD MACKAY: Scottish Enterprise has always had a system where all members of boards must register their interests. These registers are open to the public. All members must declare their interest and must not take part in any decision in which they might have an interest. Our guidance to LECs, apart from the legal guidance which, again, Ray will put to you elegantly, is that if you feel there may be a conflict of interest, there is; in other words, you have to declare it.

LORD THOMSON: I understand all that but I am going one step further about contracts.

DONALD MACKAY: All contracts with LEC board members are published in their annual reports. I think you are thinking about something quite different. You are thinking about the publication of information to do with grants and loans where HIE was earlier than us.

LORD THOMSON: Yes.

DONALD MACKAY: Indeed, they were earlier than us but from Spring of last year Scottish Enterprise itself, and from October this year the LECs, will be publishing on a six-monthly basis all details of loans and grants above £5,000.

LORD THOMSON: I see.

RAY MACFARLANE: The difference is between contracts with board members and all contracts. We have always published contracts with board members. We are now moving forward on publishing all contracts awarded.

1654. LORD THOMSON: I see, on a six-monthly basis, is it?

DONALD MACKAY: All contracts. As to contracts with members of boards, they are published and always have been, in the annual reports of the Local Enterprise Companies.

LORD NOLAN: But not separately, not as they are made?

DONALD MACKAY: Not as made, on an annual basis.

1655. LORD THOMSON: The annual report is certainly a very important element in this. We have been pressing this point on TECs in England and Wales where the practice is by no means universal. Annual reports, as we all know, come out sometimes 18 months after the events that they report. Is it not better to do it more quickly than that?

RAY MACFARLANE: In future they will be brought into the six-month rule as well. That will be the change there.

DONALD MACKAY: But they will still also be published in the annual reports.

1656. LORD THOMSON: Thank you very much. The other thing I wanted to ask and then I will pass this on to my colleagues is the new complaints procedure which is just being developed at the moment. I wondered if you could give us any information about what is happening on that front—an independent complaints procedure?

CRAWFORD BEVERIDGE: Yes. One of the recommendations from the Scottish Affairs Committee was indeed that there should be an independent adjudicator appointed both for the Highlands and Islands and ourselves so that somebody who had gone through the complaints procedure and felt they had not been satisfied could go further. We were clear with the committee at the time that we would welcome such a move, as we do now, and we are in active discussion with the Scottish Office at the moment to try and figure out how we can get this set up as quickly as possible.

LORD THOMSON: I see. Thank you very much.

LORD NOLAN: Thank you very much. Sir Clifford.

1657. CLIFFORD BOULTON: I do not have a large number of questions, you will be pleased to hear, because a lot of the ground has been covered by Lord Thomson. Can I just pursue a little further the point that was made to us by the voluntary organisations. I understand that in general terms, as a sanction really to ensure that contractors are producing productive results, you have a way of withholding the final grant to be awarded on the basis of certain success rate tests as to the amount of qualifications that have been gained and the number of jobs that have been obtained. That is the case, is it?

CRAWFORD BEVERIDGE: We partly fund the Local Enterprise Companies on their outputs so we would expect that from their training programmes people actually end up with a qualification and that, as far as possible, they end up with a job.

1658. CLIFFORD BOULTON: When it comes to the disadvantaged groups, you told us that you have special financing for them directed at their needs and the impression that was left with me this morning was that that same performance test is applied across the board to the disadvantaged groups in precisely the same way as to everybody else. Is that the case?

CRAWFORD BEVERIDGE: That is not correct.

CLIFFORD BOULTON: That is very important, to me anyway.

CRAWFORD BEVERIDGE: There are two differences that it is very important that you understand. The amount of money that we allocate to the Local Enterprise Companies for the disadvantaged groups is between two and three times the amount that we allocate for the non-disadvantaged groups and we also have a flexibility on their output to allow much lower levels of vocational qualification to be achieved before they can actually get that trigger.

We felt it was very important that we try to push for the same treatment to the disadvantaged group so that they could end up with jobs, that we were not just doing this to make a statistic and leave them completely outwith the economic system that we were trying to run here. It has been very important to us to make sure that we put pressures on to make sure that these people try to end up with qualifications and in employment, in the same way as other people do.

1659. CLIFFORD BOULTON: That is very helpful because, as you know, we are not actually supposed to be concerned, and we are not concerned, with giving you marks out of ten for performance. We are concerned with standards of conduct and the public perceptions of things that might be adrift and worrying. Obviously, if disadvantaged groups were somehow being left out in the cold because of some heartless formula or other that would come within our terms of reference. I am very glad to have had a chance to pursue that point.

DONALD MACKAY: May I say that most of our training expenditure, whether it is for special needs groups or elsewhere with young trainees or in adult training, is with groups who are disadvantaged in some sense in the labour market. Our approach to it is that we have a particular responsibility to look after these groups, to try and create a framework where they can get qualifications and where they can get back into employment for all of them. We run our training programmes very much with that in mind and, if I may say so, through the Local Enterprise Companies we try to take account of the differing circumstances in differing labour market areas. Some are more disadvantaged than others.

1660. CLIFFORD BOULTON: Yes, I understand. Can I ask a question, again it is only a supplementary one, about the code of best practice. Do you actually give specific guidance? I know you do not impose anything and you prefer LECs to make their own specific rules but do you give any detailed help on the form in which a register of interests should take place?

I can remember from my own experience in the House of Commons that you cannot really get these things off the ground unless everybody knows what the rules are and what they are expected to do. I just wondered if you do actually provide a standard form of help so that there is some similarity between the degree of declaration of interest which is taking place across the board?

RAY MACFARLANE: Yes, there is a set list of things which ought to be registered and the LECs all have that although, in the network, many go beyond the basic requirement.

1661. CLIFFORD BOULTON: Have you given any guidance on the extent to which this ought to apply to families and what we are told are called "partners" these days?

RAY MACFARLANE: That is included. They are asked to include that, yes.

1662. CLIFFORD BOULTON: This business about public perception. What do you normally read about LECs in the press?

DONALD MACKAY: It varies, according to the press. Some days it is good news and some days it is bad news.

1663. CLIFFORD BOULTON: It is not a sort of one string fiddle? There is not a sort of bleat about the problem which they have with overall performance?

DONALD MACKAY: There is certainly not much question about performance because in terms of performance I think the network has delivered. There has been a certain uncertainty and concern over the nature of the delivery mechanism and particular questions you are addressing but I would have to say that we do not have a single case in which we have had a serious conflict of interest in any of our Local Enterprise Companies and, just possibly, that is sinking in. I hope it is.

1664. CLIFFORD BOULTON: Good. Can I just ask a rather detailed question about auditing? I imagine you, in common with everybody else in this area, feel that you are quite adequately audited, if not excessively so. Is that your feeling, that there is rather too much of it?

DONALD MACKAY: I have to say that, listening to the question on training, I hoped you would not conclude we needed more auditing in the training field because I can assure you we do not. Maybe I should ask my Chief Executive who bears the brunt of this.

CRAWFORD BEVERIDGE: There is, particularly for the Local Enterprise Companies, a significant amount of auditing going on. Because they are private sector companies they all have external auditors appointed, they have their own internal auditors and internal audit committees. We have our internal auditors who would also, in turn, work with them on an audit plan. The National Audit Office agrees with us a programme of audit for ourselves and now for the Local Enterprise Companies as well and, as well as this, we from time to time have visitations from people like the Scottish Affairs Committee, the National Audit Office to do value-for-money audits, the Treasury quinquennial review that we are going through at the moment. I would certainly say it is adequate.

DONALD MACKAY: It might be worth saying that we are actually at the present time introducing a system where we will create a system of networking the auditing services so that we will have like a seamless roll so that the people responsible for it will do both ourselves in Scottish Enterprise and the Local Enterprise Companies which will provide an even better flow of information. Auditing is very strict, as it should be in any public sector agency.

1665. CLIFFORD BOULTON: HIE told me that they had now resolved the question of access by the National Audit Office to individual LECs. Is that also the situation with you?

CRAWFORD BEVERIDGE: That is correct.

1666. CLIFFORD BOULTON: They do pay visits to the individual LECs?

CRAWFORD BEVERIDGE: They will as of this year. The nature of the way we had the system set up made that difficult for them in the past. We agreed with them last year that legally the LECs would be viewed as subsidiary undertakings and that we would consolidate the accounts in our own accounts and, as of that happening, we would work out with them a programme that would give them adequate access and they are very happy with that.

1667. CLIFFORD BOULTON: Lord Nolan just touched on the question of the external complaints adjudicators. Have you been part of the consideration of the form in which that is going to take place?

CRAWFORD BEVERIDGE: We are a part of it. We are in discussion with the Scottish Office on that now. There are, obviously, a fairly wide range of choices. We had some concerns, as you may know, that we were being asked actually to appoint this person because it did not come within the terms of reference of the Ombudsman and, apparently, would have taken some primary legislation for such a thing to take place.

We were somewhat uncomfortable about that and so we have been working now to see if there is some way we can have a very hands-off approach to that appointment so there will be no suggestion that this is somebody that is essentially being looked at and monitored by ourselves. We will be doing that over the next 60 days or so with the Scottish Office.

1668. CLIFFORD BOULTON: Good. So, we may see something in the fairly near future out of that. What about internal complaints? Do you have mechanisms and safety valves for dealing with internal staff complaints about the handling of staff, and that sort of thing?

CRAWFORD BEVERIDGE: We have both an internal complaints procedure for managerial style complaints but we also have a cross-network committee that we have recently set up on fraudulent issues particularly so that an employee who felt there was something going on that was inappropriate in the network and was uncomfortable about going through their own management chain to ask about that will have the ability to call this body and, quite anonymously if they want to, press a complaint with them.

1669. CLIFFORD BOULTON: Does much of that happen? Is it used?

CRAWFORD BEVERIDGE: The internal one happens from time to time, like you would expect in any company where an employee feels they have been unfairly treated in some way but certainly no more so in my experience than I have seen in companies I have worked for in other lives. We do not have enough experience yet of the fraud committee, if you will, to find out whether that will happen but I would be surprised, based on the work that we do in audit anyway, if we had not caught anything along the way as it was happening.

1670. CLIFFORD BOULTON: But internal staff complaints about unfair treatment or bad behaviour of some kind or another, they are dealt with internally within the LEC?

CRAWFORD BEVERIDGE: They are dealt with internally within the LEC. If there is no satisfaction there then, because we are a single employer and we are the final employer of choice, they can come up through the personnel organisation. We are also represented by three different unions and so the employees have the opportunity to go, as they would in other companies, through the route of using their union representative to come and press a complaint with us if they felt they wanted to go that way.

1671. CLIFFORD BOULTON: Is there any demand at the moment from the unions for a different system or are they content as far as you know? They may not be content with all the results but are they content with the system as far as you know?

CRAWFORD BEVERIDGE: As far as I know, they are broadly content. We have a joint negotiating committee which deals with the unions on behalf of the network. The union, to be fair, has asked from time to time if they might negotiate separately in each of the Local Enterprise Companies. We have not felt that that would be particularly productive, nor have the Local Enterprise Companies at the moment, so we have agreed to a joint committee on which the Local Enterprise Companies are represented when they speak to them and that seems to be working all right for the time being.

1672. CLIFFORD BOULTON: I think I have really exhausted the questions that I had in the front of my mind, but I would ask you if there are any points that you were hoping to have a chance to make to us when you came here today which have not come up? Is there anything that you would like to put in our minds? You have already encouraged us not to take any unnecessary steps, and I think we are already of that mind anyway.

1673. LORD THOMSON: Are there any ideas where you might like us, with some reforming zeal, to see if we could apply to the English?

DONALD MACKAY: I would hesitate to recommend any such course of action, Lord Thomson, they are just a source of trouble either way.

What I would like to say to you is not so much a recommendation but I believe that we have a rather unique organisation here in which private persons undertake public duties for which they receive and seek no remuneration. It may be important for you to know that I asked the LEC chairs whether they would want me to recommend to you that they, or their members, should be paid and the view was that no, they did not wish to be paid. They saw this as a voluntary task that they undertook willingly.

I would have to say that the level of accountability, integrity and commitment shown by people on the LEC boards is something which I doubt you will find equalled in many other countries around the world.

1674. LORD NOLAN: I am very interested in that. I was going to ask you what is really one of our standard questions and that is to say what view you and your member LECs took of the question of remuneration. We have already heard this morning from the Renfrewshire Local Enterprise Company strong opposition to the idea and a firm statement by their representatives that they would refuse it if offered.

On the other hand, the view from HIE was not so specific. The HIE representatives, joined I think by Mr Cumming from the Ross and Cromarty Enterprise, spoke of the hardship that could be felt particularly by a one-man business, or possibly a small partnership, if considerable time was taken, as it is, on the affairs of the LEC and of the possibility, it was put no higher, that there might be an option for a member to put forward a case for an allowance on the lines of the loss of earnings allowance given to councillors or, perhaps, to jurymen, a flat rate allowance that is not something that reflected the actual value of his time or the loss of his earnings.

DONALD MACKAY: I cannot speak for HIE and I would not dream of doing so. There is quite possibly, even amongst the members of the board of Scottish Enterprise, probably including myself, a view that there would be a strong case for paying chairmen of LECs but it is not our job to impose on them what they do not wish. I report to you what the chairs quite unequivocally said to me; they do not wish to be in a situation where they, or their members, are paid. They do this out of a sense of public duty and that is how they wish it to remain.

1675. LORD NOLAN: And they do not even wish to be offered the option?

DONALD MACKAY: And they do not wish to be offered the option.

1676. LORD NOLAN: Thank you, that is very clear. One other question I would put to you on a worst case basis that has not happened but one that some of your remarks seemed to me to touch on. When the South Thames Training and Enterprise Council went into liquidation it was treated, in effect, like any other private company going into liquidation. The Government did not stand behind it so its debts did not help its creditors.

Here, in Scotland, you and your LECs have an unusual relationship. They are, of course, private companies but the staff are Scottish Enterprise staff and your accounts are now consolidated, as would be the case with a parent and its subsidiary companies. Do you undertake any kind of legal liability for their obligations if they are in difficulty? Mrs MacFarlane, that is one for you.

RAY MACFARLANE: Yes. Insofar as they have been implementing the operating contract we would honour contracts which they had awarded, which were awarded for the purposes of fulfilling what we have been set up to do. We would accept responsibility for training contracts, and so on, and our staff in situ would continue to operate in the local area, albeit not as the Local Enterprise Company but on behalf of Scottish Enterprise directly.

CRAWFORD BEVERIDGE: Could I also add that another difference is that while, yes, you would expect our natural monitoring to catch anything that was going wrong along the way, one other important difference here is that the Chief Executives of the 13 Local Enterprise Companies and myself meet on a monthly basis. The chairs of the Local Enterprise Companies and the Chairman meet on a quarterly basis. There is a very tight relationship ongoing so that if there were things that were going wrong in the system we would all know about it a long way in advance.

1677. LORD NOLAN: I think in England that lesson has been very well learned and great care has been taken to avoid another incident. You have prepared for the worst case should it ever arise. You have taken also the most stringent measures to ensure that so far as humanly possibly can that it will not arise. Thank you very much indeed. You have been extremely interesting and helpful and we are very grateful to you busy people for the time you have taken, both in preparing your submissions and in coming along this morning.

DONALD MACKAY: Thank you for the opportunity.

1678. LORD NOLAN: Now, a complete change of scene. Scottish Homes, good afternoon and welcome to you. We have Mr Peter McKinlay, the Chief Executive, Mrs Frances McCall, a board member, and Miss Carole Oatway, Head of Registration and Monitoring.

The Committee are very grateful to you for the information that you have already sent in in writing. Before we start on the questions, I thought I should ask you if there is anything you wish to add by way of preliminary statement or are you happy to go straight on with the questions?

PETER MCKINLAY, FRANCES MCCALL, AND CAROLE OATWAY

PETER McKINLAY (Chief Executive, Scottish Homes): We thought we should take up all of the time answering questions rather than making preliminary statements. If the Committee do not mind, perhaps we could field them among the three of us as seems best.

LORD NOLAN: I am grateful and respectfully agree. Once we have read your papers then, unless there was some afterthought, we find it is helpful to pursue the points with you by word of mouth. I will ask Dame Anne Warburton to start off on that process.

1679. ANNE WARBURTON: Can I begin by saying that one aspect of your paper that I particularly enjoyed was that it began and ended with our principles. I liked the way you documented the application of our seven principles to your work. It was very encouraging.

Could I begin by asking a question which is really a very general question. What do you regard as being the distinctive features of housing associations in Scotland against the background that most of what we have heard and talked about so far has been in England?

PETER McKINLAY: There are two crucial differences. One is the relative size of associations in Scotland and the composition of their management committees. They are very largely tenant controlled or with a very high degree of tenant participation and they are community based. We have nothing remotely resembling a Home Housing Association or the North British with 20,000 or 30,000 houses all over England. The only national remits in Scotland tend to be associations that concentrate on some form of special needs housing. So, the actual shape and nature of the movement in Scotland is very different in that respect.

The second difference is the statutory framework within which Scottish Homes has been designed. We are a very different animal from the Housing Corporation in a number of ways. Predominantly, we have far greater flexibility in the kind of things we can do. We have about 16 different grant mechanisms that allow us to intervene in housing situations, not just in the voluntary housing movement but in the private building sector and elsewhere. These are the two critical differences between the movement in England and ourselves.

1680. ANNE WARBURTON: Would you see it as an advantage to Scottish Homes that your organisation units are smaller?

PETER McKINLAY: There is a trade off. By and large, the economies of scale cannot be realised. There is a view that suggests the optimal size for a housing management business might be 5,000 to 7,000 units. Only 6% of all the housing associations and co-ops in Scotland have over 1,000 houses.

Our main concern is that they are viable rather than optimal and we think the fact that they are community based gives us an enormous advantage in terms of assisting community regeneration which we see as predominantly our business. We do not think our business is solely through suppliers assisting in the provision of new and improved housing. This year 9,200 units approved is the best we have ever achieved and if that is all we did then Scottish housing would continue to deteriorate rather than improve.

We think all the other things we are doing, which is about motivating people and trying to lift economies at national, regional and community level, is the most useful thing we can do. So, yes, small, in this case, is beautiful.

FRANCES McCALL (Board Member, Scottish Homes): But I think it is fair to say not too small and, following on from what Peter said, having the two ends of the spectrum is very important for Scottish Homes and the communities, particularly as there is private finance coming in now and other legislation for voluntary members on committees. Smaller associations can be quite vulnerable but, on the other hand, they can survive quite well.

Scottish Homes has already looked at this particular subject, "Early Days" and said that we will start looking at how we make sure that the smaller associations have enough support. For example, a bigger association could have five or six members of staff and a smaller association might have two or three or two and an extra one at stages of development. We are keeping on top of all that. We recognised "Early Days".

There are lots of activities going on in Scotland in the housing association movement with ourselves in trying to keep looking at all these areas in case anything became a problem and catch "Early Days" and advise them for another way forward. The end of the spectrum is that the small one survives well but it depends on where it is in Scotland and what it is trying to do.

1681. ANNE WARBURTON: Do I properly understand that the two *raisons d'être* for the housing associations—first, to make it, as you said, financially viable producing housing and the other to attain certain social objectives—that the smaller units, and, therefore, the general area of activity of Scottish Homes, perhaps gets a better rating on the social objectives than it does on the financial side? Satisfactory for finance but more than satisfactory on the other end, or am I putting it too crudely?

PETER McKINLAY: I would hesitate to try and measure it in these distinct ways. The socio-economic context has to be looked at as a whole and we try to approach it holistically.

One example of output measurement could be that in England and Wales unilaterally housing association grant rates were driven down by the Housing Corporation. This had the effect of pushing rents up and, in some quarters it is argued, pushing standards of quality of housing provided down and actually not achieving the community

regeneration objectives. Certainly, on that measure we would come out badly because our average HAG rate is 72.5%, whereas in England it is nearer 60%. However, when you take all the other grant mechanisms that I described into effect, we would give much lower percentages to the private sector, our average grant rate is about 64%.

We believe that over the piece, the effect that we have in intervention with public money is significantly better than the Housing Corporation is able to achieve in England, but then I would say that, would I not?

1682. ANNE WARBURTON: Ready to document it. Could I turn to your role in Scottish Homes as regulator of the whole network of the area. What are really the key issues which you feel you have to be looking at, perhaps with your hands on, more than in the South?

CAROLE OATWAY (Head of Registration and Monitoring, Scottish Homes): I do not know that the issues differ greatly between Scotland and England in terms of what we are looking at. At the end of the day, both the Housing Corporation and ourselves have set published performance standards which we would expect associations to meet. Those standards encompass things like accountability, like openness, the service that they provide to their customers. But we are also concerned with the financial viability of the organisations and their ability to survive in a fairly competitive environment.

We measure not just the policies, procedures and inputs but, like our counterparts down in the Housing Corporation, we are also looking at the outputs from those associations. We are looking at their financial standing and one of our main reasons for being interested in the finances is because we recognise the importance of these organisations being fit to attract private finance to help achieve the wider housing objectives than simply what can be achieved through Scottish Homes putting in public money.

1683. ANNE WARBURTON: I notice that you put a lot of emphasis on self-monitoring and I rather wondered how that fitted into Scottish Homes monitoring. It is an inflow, is it?

CAROLE OATWAY: It is a double system we have. We do not believe that any association should be left entirely to its own devices when it comes to monitoring and that is clearly stated within our draft strategy for supervision of housing associations. We believe that we have a duty to monitor those organisations by way of a visit by our staff to that organisation to do an in depth, root and branch examination of it on a certain time interval.

What we have said, in terms of our relationship with housing associations, is that the regularity of those visits can be dictated by the performance of the organisation and we assess that in two ways. One way is on the assessment we have made of that organisation at its last visit and, secondly, through a number of desk-top returns which we will receive from those associations on an annual basis, but it requires associations to maintain high standards across both those supervisory techniques in order to avoid our organisation taking a more intrusive approach to the monitoring of that organisation.

The desk-top returns, certainly, we have just introduced fairly recently and we will rely on associations giving us information which we have to take initially at face value. However, we have advised associations that they will be subject to what we call validatory visits whereby, on a random sampling basis, we will check that the association has given us information that can be backed up if we were to go out and ask for the supporting information.

In addition to that, we will look at a series of indicators which we will develop from these desk-top returns and, where an association seems to be wildly awry from what would appear to be the normal approach, we will contact that association and seek an explanation. If that explanation is satisfactory then all is well and good, but if we find that they have difficulty in explaining an unusual indicator then we may again go out and visit to check to see why that is the case.

ANNE WARBURTON: It sounds like very wide-ranging accountability.

CAROLE OATWAY: It is extremely wide-ranging accountability and, having been out and worked in an association myself at one time, they would agree with a number of other people I have heard give evidence today that they feel they are being very intensively monitored.

1684. ANNE WARBURTON: Possibly at this point I should ask about auditing as part of the accountability. Does every housing association have its audit committee to start with and how does that work out?

CAROLE OATWAY: Each association has its own external auditors that will examine the associations's finances for that individual association. Could I just clarify in terms of auditing, do you mean the audit in terms of us going out to have a look at what they are doing or in terms of their own——

ANNE WARBURTON: Not necessarily internal also. Very widely now a board will set up its own audit committee to supervise the internal work and receive the external audit.

CAROLE OATWAY: Right. I understand exactly what you are pointing to now. In Scotland, because of the size of the organisations, there has not been the same move to have their own internal audit committees that there has been, perhaps, in the English housing associations. However, some of our larger associations are beginning to see the advantages of that and we are certainly encouraging that approach. We are also encouraging, through the Scottish Federation of Housing Associations, associations to look at self-monitoring; that is, over and above what we are asking them to give us information on, to set up their own targets, their own output measures against which the committee can control the organisation.

Scottish Homes themselves are feeding into that process through the publication of national performance information. Therefore, information that we collect nationally we are able to feed back to housing associations which will allow committees who are looking at their own performance to ask appropriately informed questions of their staff as to why their organisation does something differently, more expensively or takes longer to do something than, perhaps, another organisation elsewhere in the country.

1685. ANNE WARBURTON: Thank you very much. Perhaps the next point to take up might be the ways in which you can influence the various housing associations. What sort of relationship is there there? Perhaps I should say that I was particularly struck, under the talk about the code of conduct, that Scottish Homes emphasises that the code of conduct is a voluntary code but, on the other hand, it is stated in your paper that Scottish Homes expects that housing associations will observe it. That intrigued me a little bit.

PETER McKINLAY: In terms of influencing, we are in a somewhat difficult position because housing associations are independent, voluntary bodies notwithstanding that something like, for mainstream rented accommodation, 83% of the cost of every unit is borne by us so they clearly need us. We fund them.

We cannot, except in extremis, order them to do things and we would not be prescriptive. We believe, for example, that in the code of conduct area it is much better to suggest to associations, and the Federation of Scottish Housing Associations joins us in this, better ways of doing things and expect them to adopt them. In practice, that is what happens. Certainly, in the long-term, even in the short term, I do not think it would be conducive to improving the performance of the voluntary movement if we resorted to prescription very often.

1686. ANNE WARBURTON: So, there is a significant difference when you use the word "requires" or "expects"?

PETER McKINLAY: Absolutely.

1687. ANNE WARBURTON: What about the membership of the committees of the housing associations? Do you give advice on that? I noted two facts which you gave us in your paper. One was that most of the members of committees are local, which is not the case in England, and the other was that only 40% have ever had any relevant work experience before becoming members. That is one reason why I ask about whether you influence at all the selection of board members.

PETER McKINLAY: Can I ask Mrs McCall to answer that one.

FRANCES McCALL: Can I just explain by being a board member of Scottish Homes, I also live in a housing co-operative and helped to establish it. We are 10 years down the road now so I can answer your question without doubt myself on what happens locally and I think it is important that it is left to carry on to do that.

In the association elections for the committee of management are made at annual general meetings and specifically in some of our newer co-ops each tenant is actually a member of that organisation so every tenant has the democratic right to come along and vote and be on the management committee or not be on it. The success of it has been the fact that it has been local people who have always been there on that committee and have always done the business of the organisation and made sure that things happen in that community. That is very important to that community that it is local people.

From the accountability side of it it is very important to understand that tenants who are on a committee who live in a street, like I do and I am on the committee, you are more accountable to your local neighbours than you are to private organisations or Scottish Homes because you have accountability walking down your own street and at your own front gate to people who are picking you up before you fall down.

It is an important issue, the accountability and all these other issues that we have raised. In locally based associations, the pressure is local more than it is from outside. That is why they have a good track record and that is why Scottish Homes does not have a lot of inquiries and other things. We can pick things up quickly.

I am sorry, I have forgotten the beginning of your question because I changed it around there. I am sorry about that.

ANNE WARBURTON: The work experience was the only other part.

FRANCES McCALL: In the work experience side of it, there is an awful lot of unemployment in Glasgow in particular and the big cities like Edinburgh and Aberdeen. The amount of time you have to spend on the committee you quite often get someone who has not worked for a while, who can give the time and give the experience. If people have a job then they do not have the same time to spend.

Quite often, I have found from a personal basis, not a board basis, that when people come into committees who are local people who have not worked or are not working or they are not specially skilled as they think, once they are in committees the skill comes out that people did not realise was there. I am sitting here as a board member of Scottish Homes and I am a tenant in a housing co-op. I am not professionally trained to be on the board of Scottish Homes. It is a fact to show that people do have skills and they come out in committees rather than just sit on a committee and not pay any attention and learn anything.

The backing of Scottish Homes on the training aspect is very important. You are seeing the Scottish Federation of Housing Associations this afternoon, I believe, and they will be able to tell the link they have there of training for voluntary committee members. A voluntary member now has to be a private secretary and a finance director to make sure that their director is telling them the truth and that things are OK but they still have the fallback position of Scottish Homes being able to come in and help them through phases if they need that and there is no fear of that at the moment.

PETER McKINLAY: Could I add a slight gloss to that. When, in 1989, the housing association movement had to attract private funding there was an enormous reluctance on the part of banks and building societies to lend to tenant controlled institutions because on the board, unlike most of the large English associations, there were no professionally qualified people. You did not have the retired senior civil servant, the banker, the accountant.

That reluctance has dissipated over the past six and a half years. As the lending institutions became familiar with what my colleague, Mrs McCall, has described and it is somewhat salutary that some of the associations in England which have had significant problems of one sort or another were not tenant controlled with the training that Frances has mentioned, backed up by the immediacy of your next-door neighbour complaining if something is not right. The track record of a much smaller, community based movement in Scotland is first-rate.

1688. ANNE WARBURTON: But it sounds as though it is very much associated with the size of the housing association, its geographic spread. We have seen and heard from housing associations in England whose property is very widespread and they can hardly have a local tenant majority in the same way that the ones that you are talking about can.

FRANCES McCALL: I think it is important that there are models. In Scotland, if we were asked by the Government to insist that housing associations were 10,000, 20,000 or whatever—we have been to Canada and other countries and looked at models. You can still have it tenant controlled if you make it a satellite system where there is a top body but there are all these satellites underneath that body.

We have slightly initiated a few groups like that in Scotland to try it out but if the future meant that associations had to be bigger then you would be looking at a satellite otherwise it does not work. There is no use in people moving from one landlord to another landlord, monolithic, that is not what community regeneration is about. It is very important that the associations are deep in their community but you can still link them up to the one big, large organisation but give local control to satellite systems. There are other areas that may have to be tried in the future that we have not tried out yet. At the moment, I think if something works, just leave it alone and let it grow.

ANNE WARBURTON: It does sound as though perhaps you have dealt in a way with the problem of accountability to other communities, other than the financial accountability. You do not have problems with reaching your local communities in the housing associations.

PETER McKINLAY: While I think that is true, we have set up a housing association tenant ombudsman. That has been going for a year and has dealt with just over 100 complaints. Only three eventually ended up with a finding of maladministration or injustice and in all three cases the housing associations concerned took the Ombudsman's advice and put it right. That is not a lot when you think there are probably 75,000 houses owned and managed by the voluntary movement in Scotland, knocking on quarter of a million people. The Ombudsman step was a right one and a good one and it serves the purpose of a long-stop.

1689. ANNE WARBURTON: I thought you must have been rather satisfied with that first report from the Ombudsman. Could I just ask who appoints the Ombudsman?

PETER McKINLAY: We, the Scottish Homes board, appointed the Ombudsman. There was some debate touched on in a different context by Crawford Beveridge in a similar situation. We had to satisfy the Scottish Federation of Housing Associations and everyone else that the Ombudsman, notwithstanding he was appointed by the board and Scottish Homes pay for running the Ombudsman service, that he was indeed an independent creature.

The first appointment, as it happened, was the ex-Deputy Chairman of Scottish Homes board but everyone who knows John Richards knows that he is not a man to be trifled with so he was a quite inspired first appointment and his independence—the Federation may comment this afternoon—is now not questioned. We think we have a system that works and we do not think we need legislation to make him a creature of statute.

ANNE WARBURTON: Thank you very much. I think I should yield at this point.

LORD NOLAN: Professor King.

PROF ANTHONY KING: Let me join Dame Anne in commending the quality of the submission, which I found very helpful, and it was very good of you to write "boards" where you really wanted to write "management committees".

PETER McKINLAY: Can I say, Mrs Oatway takes all the credit.

1690. PROF ANTHONY KING: Can I just pull your leg, or legs, a little bit about paragraph (9) of the submission. Let me suggest that it appears, first, to report the provisions of the pretty tough Section 15 of the Housing Association Act, 1985, and then, in the second part of paragraph (a) to say, in effect, Section 15 is hereby repealed in Scotland.

That is a caricature of what you actually say, of course, but could you say a little bit about the arguments for the justification underlying the—I do not know if the word "resilements" exists but if it does not I will now invent it—from Section 15.

PETER McKINLAY: Like all the best caricatures, you have captured the fundamental elements of what we are trying to do. The reality is that the powers are there and, if necessary, can be used in their full majesty. But the practicality is that we took the view that it would be unreasonable in many cases to debar people in certain situations from access to a housing association house simply because they had a relative on the committee, or whatever.

It seemed to us a balanced and reasonable exposition to put forward that which we have. I noticed that in taking evidence from Anthony Mayer and Peter Cook this point was touched on and they are considering, I think, following our lead in trying to make Section 15 less prescriptive. That links to what I said earlier that I think the more people do it because they know it is the right thing to do and they do not do it because they know it is a wrong thing to do, the better.

1691. PROF ANTHONY KING: So, you would, I infer from what you have just said, on the whole want to recommend these kinds of changes in Wales and England. You might not want to go so far as recommending them but you would be pleased if they were to follow your example.

Can you give me a sense of the circumstances under which you would want these exceptions to be introduced somewhere else; in other words, would it be across the board or would it be to particular kinds of housing associations? What do you have in mind?

FRANCES McCALL: Can I maybe tell you the difficulties? Here I go again, giving the opposite view, but

as a voluntary member, when a committee gets set up it is local people who set it up. You need a core of local people to keep that energy going all the time.

In the old Act these people could not give themselves a house so you had committee members who had steered the group along and when the group got registered the law said they could not give each other a house. Section 15 is a great boost and a great help to have local people living in the area that can be housed by the association. One of the difficulties for local people on the committee is that in communities it is normal that family lives quite near family or they wish to live near family and the restriction on it meant that people who were on a committee were punishing their families because they were sitting on the committee giving other people houses and they could not give their own family a house. It was a terrible restriction.

Now that it is lifted it has made things much better. There is a criterion to go through to allow it to happen in your association so Scottish Homes keeps quite a firm tab on that and it has to be signed legally and we have to say, yes, that is approvable and you can give that person a house, you have followed the Act through properly.

1692. PROF ANTHONY KING: Could I just press a little bit further on this and I may not have phrased my previous question precisely enough. Do you see these kind of exceptions, these relaxations to Section 15, applying only to the kind of housing association you typically have in Scotland or do you see it being desirable that this kind of exception should be applied across the board to all housing associations? In other words, are you really, in effect, recommending the amendment of the statute?

PETER McKINLAY: I do not think we are recommending the amendment of the statute. The way the statute stands is necessary rather than desirable. But it is a general proposition that should apply to all housing associations and co-ops if this particular set of circumstances arises.

1693. PROF ANTHONY KING: Including very big housing associations?

PETER McKINLAY: In very big ones, as they are constituted in England, it is unlikely that you will have on the committee someone who is a tenant in a social rented house and whose relative may be wanting a house near him or her. They tend to be run by people who are not tenants of the association and, indeed, in the majority of cases I would guess are owner/occupiers and people of some personal means. So, in the larger ones the circumstances are unlikely to arise, but were they to I see no reason in principle why this kind of approach should not apply.

1694. PROF ANTHONY KING: Could I ask you a related question which arises out of your paragraph 8(c) where you say—"Given that most board members are local people in Scotland and very often tenants of the association, there could be difficulties if the board had access to information of a confidential or sensitive nature relating to people who are possibly their neighbours. Reports prepared by staff for submission to the board therefore protect confidentiality by avoiding the use of names and addresses. This helps to ensure objectivity in decision making."

My first question is the obvious one. Do not people mostly guess under these circumstances? Is this really ineffective?

FRANCES McCALL: No, it is very effective, very effective indeed. There is no way that you can guess. We could actually send you an example of a report, if the Committee would like that, Lord Nolan, to look at to understand how it is done. There is no way that you would know. It is very important because if you are on a committee and you are committed and fervently go to the meetings and work hard for it and you fall on hard times accidentally it would be a punishment for you if everybody knew about it and it would upset the whole applecart of what people are trying to do.[4]

PROF ANTHONY KING: The anonymity is desirable, I was just questioning whether it was practical.

FRANCES McCALL: It works.

1695. PROF ANTHONY KING: If you think it is, is this something that, again, you would, in an ideal world, like to see extended to housing associations in England and Wales?

PETER McKINLAY: The fact that we do it means we believe in it and it works and, consequently, if anybody were to ask you to emulate us the answer would be "yes" but it would be impertinent, I think, for us to suggest that the Housing Corporation, or anyone else, should do what we do.

PROF ANTHONY KING: They might think it impertinent if we said it.

PETER McKINLAY: That is probably within the remit of the Committee.

PROF ANTHONY KING: That is why I was asking.

FRANCE McCALL: Can we just say we would encourage them to, Lord Nolan.

1696. LORD NOLAN: If we could take up your offer, is this a report on an individual case that you had in mind or a report showing how you handle such cases?

FRANCES McCALL: We could put together an anonymous example for you to look at of how a committee member receives a report to the Finance Committee about rent arrears, which they do on a monthly basis. They are numbered and it would let you see how it is done and how the Housing Officer works that out. The Housing Officer is the only person in the organisation who knows who the person is.

One of the unfortunate things is that you walk out in the street and you meet the neighbour and the neighbour tells you anyway so it is very difficult. No matter how many times you tell the tenant, "I'm sorry but I don't know what you're talking about" they still feel that you do know anyway but the committee definitely does not know who it is.

LORD NOLAN: I am sorry to have interrupted Professor King but perhaps if you would be kind enough to send us some anonymous reports we would be interested to see them.

FRANCES McCALL: Surely.

1697. PROF ANTHONY KING: Just a couple of other questions. You say here, under paragraph 7(c) "Elections are held annually. Each year at least one third of the board must stand down" and so on. Who says?

---

[4] *See* Evidence, pp. 471.

FRANCES McCALL: The rules say.

PROF ANTHONY KING: Whose rules?

CAROLE OATWAY: The association when it is registered has to register under a set of rules and we will only register the organisation when we have looked at those rules and agreed them. Therefore, they cannot change those rules without coming back to us to ask for permission to change them.

PROF ANTHONY KING: So, the answer to my question, who says, is you say?

CAROLE OATWAY: We say.

1668. PROF ANTHONY KING: Suppose a housing association wanted to have biennial elections?

CAROLE OATWAY: It would require a rule change and they would have to come back to us. We would consider the reasons why they were asking for that rule change and, if there was merit in those reasons, then we may well grant it but it is unlikely. There is a fairly standard format which has worked and we see no reason why that should be changed.

1699. PROF ANTHONY KING: Can I again just pull your legs a little bit in line with something that Dame Anne was saying earlier on. You lay great stress in this document on housing associations being self reliant and yet an awful lot else in the document, and a good deal of what Miss Oatway has been saying, does not seem to me to point in the direction of self reliance. It seems to point in the direction of really very close and detailed supervision and, indeed, instructions by Scottish Homes. That may be fine. I am not querying that, but it sits oddly with the emphasis on self reliance which implies a degree of autonomy.

PETER McKINLAY: It is a relationship of creative tension. There is a very difficult balance we are constantly striving to keep between encouraging housing associations and co-ops to be genuinely self reliant, to be wanting within the organisation to become better—however one defines better—leaner, meaner, supplying a quality service, continuous improvement, benchmarking, all of those things. Ultimately, however, since public money is going into them in substantial quantities, there has to be a panoply of regulation around it.

Our ultimate ambition is so to manage the system that we never have to use a Section 28 again and, ultimately, we never have to use a Section 17 appointee either because they will become redundant in that the movement will have developed an ethos backed up by a professional capability which means the statutory panoply will not be needed. It may be a visionary ambition but it is a good one.

PROF ANTHONY KING: I have other questions but the clock up there says it is a little after one.

LORD NOLAN: We are very grateful to you for answering all our questions so clearly, frankly and succinctly. It has been an extremely valuable 40 minutes and we are most obliged to you for coming along and for all your help, both in writing and by word of mouth. Thank you very much.

WEDNESDAY 31 JANUARY 1996
MORNING SESSION

OPENING STATEMENTS

Opening Statement from Renfrewshire Enterprise

Renfrewshire occupies the south bank of the Firth of Clyde with a population of just under 350,000 and includes the principal towns of Paisley and Greenock. Traditional industries such as shipbuilding, heavy engineering and textiles have made for major growth sectors such as electronics, value-added engineering, food and drink and information technology. Renfrewshire produces circa 40% of all of Scotland's manufactured exports and Glasgow International Airport, located within Renfrewshire, is a significant generator of new economic growth.

Renfrewshire Enterprise (RE) with an annual budget of just under £30 million and a professional resource of 50 executives (total staffing—70) emphasises three main thrusts,

— to strengthen local small and medium sized businesses (SMEs) and promote the start of new growth businesses,

— to improve skills flexibility of the labour force,

— to capitalise on physical assets by improving the environment and developing business locations.

We have five key areas of focus or strategic priorities;

Glasgow Airport Initiative
Inward Investment
Business Growth (especially key industrial sectors)
New Firm Formation
Partnership Areas

Particular issues

Accountability and Openness

As well as having a direct relationship with over 300 client companies RE consults or is represented on approximately 50 groups, many of which meet (relatively) frequently (Annex 2). (This should be set in the context of approx. 50 operational executives and 13 non exec Board Members).

As well as professional experience the Members bring their own personal involvement in, and knowledge of, community business and other relevant activities.

RE publishes its strategy (economic plan for the area) and annual report (performance over past year). The annual report for 94/95 contained a list of companies RE has worked with over the year.

The Scottish Enterprise (SE) Network Transparency and Openness Policy now requires that details of grants made by RE will be held available for inspection by the public.

Board appointments

SE has appointed RE to carry out the functions of a LEC under the terms of an annual operating contract. RE is a private company limited by guarantee and as such appoints its own Chairman and the Board of Directors. It is the responsibility of the Board to ensure that the balance of skills provided by Members is appropriate to the business, and satisfies the requirements of the operating contract with SE. In addition to a maximum of 12 directors RE has a Management Committee of 3 Members, also key people of standing in Renfrewshire who cannot vote on Company business but who do participate fully in Board Meetings and in the Working Groups which consider the detail of RE's projects.

The criteria for Board appointments are set by the Company's Memorandum and Articles of Association which reflects the requirements of the SE Operating Contract. The main criterion is that two thirds of the Board Members must be senior businessmen from private sector companies located in the LEC area.

As a private company limited by guarantee it is the responsibility of the RE Board to select its 8 private sector and 4 public sector directors in such a way as to maintain a balance of knowledge and skills in relation to the business activities. The public sector members are drawn from local authorities or educational institute in Renfrewshire. As well as bringing their experience and expertise to the table the public sector members are able to provide considerable local knowledge of the area.

However irrespective of whether directors are drawn from the private or public sector they serve on the Board as individuals and not as representatives of any individual organisation.

The Board maintains a nominations list of people who have expresed an interest in serving on the Board or who have been recommended. This list is compiled from personal knowledge, through the RE executive contacts, by open invitation at public meetings and by liaison with numerous partner bodies e.g Chambers of Commerce and Local Authorities. In considering nominations the Board have regard to potential conflicts of interest e.g. an individual's professional and/or business activities may render them ineligible for Board membership. (See Annex 3 for list of current Board Members and affiliations).

Conflicts of Interest

The Company established Conflicts of Interest Procedures at its inception in 1991. Registers of potential conflicts are maintained by the Company Secretary for both Directors and RE staff.

The Company recognises the importance of this issue and has a policy of disclosing in the Annual Accounts details of all transactions between RE and organisations in which Directors have a potential conflict of interest. This policy goes beyond the Company's Act requirements which requires disclosure of material items only.

Members are advised of the Company's procedures in relation to potential conflicts of interest, and formal induction sessions are held at the SE Network level for new board members. A manual "Guide for Board Members" is provided to assist individuals in their role as LEC Board members and in particular to highlight corporate governance issues.

Complaints Procedure

The RE Complaints Procedure is published in the Customer Care document (copy attached as Annex 4). Complaints are dealt with by the Chief Exec on behalf of the Board. If an individual or company is not satisfied with the response from RE the complaint can be passed to SE.

As staff are secondees from SE all complaints about their behaviour are investigated locally, but SE must be kept advised of such matters, if they are of import/substance. Any disciplinary action is the responsibility of SE.

RE commissions an annual independent customer satisfaction survey and publishes the results.

Contracts

The contracts and agreements which RE has with third parties are performance or output based.

Contracts relating to Property and Environment activities have very specific outputs which, for the majority of projects are agreed with partner organisations.

The awarding of contracts is subject to the Company's delegated authority and competitive tendering procedures. Tenders are invited by RE and assessed by an independent professional adviser (also appointed subject to competitive tendering procedures).

The contract is awarded based on the adviser's recommendation to the RE project manager. A professional adviser will also monitor performance against the contract and report progress to the responsible RE manager and where appropriate the project partners.

In line with our delegated authority procedures all contracts above certain levels are reported regularly to the RE Board. These contracts are also subject to both internal audit and inspection by SE Audit.

Training of young people is no longer delivered through high volume contracts with training providers. Instead, through the Skillseekers programme, RE agrees to provide funding support towards the costs of delivering an individual training plan which has been agreed between a Skillseeker and an employer and, where appropriate, a training provider.

Training plans must be designed to achieve a recognised vocational qualification and payment of funding is released to employers or training providers as the young person progresses against the training plan. A high proportion of the funding support is held back and released on achievement of the full qualification.

RE holds copies of the individual training plan for every Skillseeker in Renfrewshire and the system allows executives to closely monitor performance. Other Skillseeker monitoring activities include Health and Safety audits and the assessment of training providers against the criteria set within the Scottish Quality Management System (SQMS). All training providers must attain the SQMS standard award to participate in the Skillseekers Programme.

Improper behaviour

RE has established an Audit Committee as a sub group of the main Board which is charged with agreeing and approving an appropriate internal audit plan for the Company, and ensuring that the approved audit plan is achieved.

440

The Committee reviews the results of all auditing activity within the Company including both the External Auditors' and Internal Auditors' reports.

SE monitors the Company's compliance with the Operating Contract through SE Internal Audit, and the results of this work is also reviewed by the Committee. In addition RE can be subject to audit by National Audit Office and European Union Auditors.

As a result of a recent review of the monitoring activities in the Network RE is participating in a pilot arrangement whereby 3 LECs share internal audit resources. This shared resource is delivering an integrated audit plan which satisfies both SE and the LECs' audit requirements.

Details of any transactions involving Companies in which Board Members have declared an interest are routinely reported in the Audit Committee.

All complaints received relating to improper behaviour are dealt with in terms of the Company's complaints procedure published in the RE Customer Care Document.

All contracts are let subject to the Company's standard procedures relating to delegated authority, competitive tendering and conflict of interest.

Although all contracts are performance or output based RE monitors the delivery of third party contracts in slightly different ways dependent on the type of activity being provided by the contractor. Property and Environment and Business Development contracts are monitored by both the Company Executives and, where appropriate, professional advisers.

Training Contracts are monitored by Executives and by the Company's Internal Audit and Monitoring Team. As well as reviewing the management information available within RE the Executives and Monitoring Team members undertake visits to training provider and/or employer premises to review the quality of training being delivered and to discuss any performance issues. The visits also allow the staff to interview trainees regarding their progress against the training plan and to discuss any other issues relating to their training which the trainee wishes to raise.

Opening statement from the Highlands & Islands Enterprise Network

Background

The Highlands and Islands Enterprise Network, which started operations in April 1991, comprises the HIE core, based in Inverness, and 10 Local Enterprise Companies. The area covered by the HIE Network comprises half of the land mass of Scotland and 16% of Great Britain, but includes only 7% of the Scottish population. The HIE Network's aim is to enable the people of the Highlands and Islands to realise their full potential, and we pursue this aim by growing businesses, developing people and strengthening communities.

Statement

With a wide combination of powers, including its unique social development remit, the HIE Network has striven since its inception to establish itself as a role model rural development agency within Europe. The Network has consistently sought to ensure in all of its activities the highest level of propriety and maximum accountability, both to the people it serves and, via the Scottish Office, to Parliament.

The key points which will be of particular interest to the Committee are:-

— our experience of setting up and operating 10 very small Local Enterprise Companies in remote and sparsely populated areas

— the high level of local involvement achieved within our Network since 1991, with steady turnover of LEC Board Members (including Chairmen)

— the effectiveness of our pro-active "Accountability through Openness" policy in informing people of our activities and avoiding conflicts of interest

— the positive impact on our operations of the Charter Mark and Investors in People processes.

Opening statement from the Scottish Council for Voluntary Organisations

SCVO is the umbrella body for voluntary organisations in Scotland with a membership of over 800 organisations. Voluntary organisations have been mainstays of Government programmes for unemployed people since the early 1980's, particularly the provision of training for people with special needs. The sector is also playing an increasing role in local economic development in Scotland's most disadvantaged areas.

When the two Enterprise Networks and their parent bodies, HIE and SEN, were launched in 1991, voluntary organisations expressed concern about the impact which the fusion of enterprise and training functions in these new bodies might have on their existing programmes, particularly those targeted at disadvantaged people. Such concerns have proved well-founded over the last five years with continual downward pressure on trainee unit costs and numbers, coupled with a hostile payment regime having a serious impact on the quality of training which SCVO members were able to provide.

Issues about accountability, transparency and representation were also raised by statutory organisations prior to the creation of these new bodies. With hindsight many of these criticisms appear justified. The private status of LEC's seems peculiar in the context of other Scottish bodies; their monopoly position together with the requirement that LEC Boards should be dominated by private sector interests has created an environment of exclusiveness; public interest in LEC's has been sustained through a succession of press stories about inappropriate spending and conflicts of interest, rather than their roles in delivering public services.

In this context SCVO intends to argue that:

— the status of LEC's should be clarified and changed to that of a public sector institution

— LEC Boards should reflect a much broader community of interest and should have improved governance arrangements

— LEC's should be subject to proper regulation within the framework of an authority which ensures appropriate standards

— LEC decisions, minutes, contracts, processes and interests should be openly available for inspection

— relationships between LEC's and their parent bodies and those between SEN and HIE and the Scottish Office should be clear, concise and publicly understood. In this context the policy parameters of LEC's need clear inspection

— spending and major policy decisions should routinely be the subject of consultation with interested parties.

Opening Statement from Scottish Enterprise

Issue: The arrangements LECs make through openness, membership schemes or otherwise to be accountable to their local community.

LECs are required by SE Operating Contract to carry out a range of activities to ensure they are widely accountable.

Since November 1994 all LECs have operated to a standard published Code of Practice to improve the integrity, accountability and openness of the network. The Code is designed to reflect the unique administrative framework of the network and draws on the appropriate sections of the Treasury Code of Practice for Board members of public bodies, the Government's Code of Practice in Openness, relevant sections of the Cadbury Code, and existing requirements of the LEC Operating Contracts.

The development of Best Practice is ongoing and Scottish Enterprise is confident that the network is accountable to local communities as never before.

Summary of LEC Activities to ensure openness and accountability

— Maintain a public register of Directors' interests

— Publish in annual accounts a list of all contracts orawards made in companies in which Directors have an interest

— Operate a policy on Directors' conflicts of interests

— Operate Contract Disclosure Arrangements

— Publish Annual Accounts, and a synopsis of Annual Business and Operating Plan

— Hold at least one public meeting a year

— Publish statement of Charter Standards

— Operate a Complaints System

— Ensure substantial information flows to press and public on a regular and ad hoc basis.

Examples of Good Practice in the Network

In many instances the network had developed practices to ensure openness/transparency and accountability which go beyond the minimum requirements specified. SE welcomes this commitment but accepts that practices in one organisation due to special operational needs may not be appropriate throughout the network. Each organisation must be free to adopt the systems which best suit its individual culture and operational requirements whilst ensuring they meet at least the minimum standards outlined.

Transparency/Openness to the public

To improve the level of openness and transparency all LECs have, from 1 October 1995, maintained records of all grants, loans, payments to providers or investments of £5,000 or over which are awarded to companies or individuals. The information will be available publicly after a lapse of 6 months (the delay is to protect commercial confidentiality).

Membership schemes

Operate in 4 LECs—   Grampian Enterprise
                                Dunbartonshire Enterprise
                                Dumfries & Galloway Enterprise
                                Enterprise Ayrshire

Grampian Enterprise Ltd was one of the first LECs to adopt a membership scheme. The 300 strong membership are consulted each year prior to the development of the strategic and operational plans. They receive a quarterly newsletter, are invited to Members meetings and the Annual General meeting of Grampian Enterprise. The aim of the scheme is to involve the local community as widely as possible in the "enterprise" culture of the area.

Access to LEC Boards:

Since LECs are private companies involved in commercial transactions it is not considered appropriate for them to hold meetings in public or to publish minutes. They are however encouraged to be accessible to the public and to make public announcements about key items considered at Board meetings.

Forth Valley Enterprise hold informal lunches prior to Board meetings to allow interested parties to meet members and discuss issues.

Because of the geographical spread of the Moray Badenoch & Strathspey Enterprise Ltd area the Board operates a policy to hold Board meetings in different locations each month, with local business people and representatives from local groups being invited to attend a pre-Board meeting lunch and discuss issues with members.

LDA Board Members regularly make presentations and hold discussions with a wide range of interest groups.

Local Consultation

In addition to meeting the requirement to hold an annual public meeting LECs have established formal and informal methods of ensuring local consultation to ensure wide awareness and acceptance of LEC policies, projects and programmes.

All LECs meet regularly with local authorities within their area. This is backed up by the evidence of COSLA (*paragraph 73 of Scottish Affairs Committee report on the Enterprise Networks*) in which a survey of local authorities had shown that in over 90% of cases the relationship with LECs was "positive or very positive".

LECs have arrangements in place for consulting other relevant interest groups—Chambers of Commerce, Enterprise Trusts, Industry Representative Bodies, specific interest groups, voluntary sector organisations, local partnership groups, and MPs. The frequency of the meetings varies from monthly, quarterly or on an ad hoc basis.

— Forth Valley Enterprise ensure that, in addition to being invited to submit formal written comments on their business plan, local authorities and other local economic development agencies are engaged early in the business plan process through a series of workshops.

— Several LECs also run events through the year such as mobile "Roadshows" run by both Enterprise Ayrshire and Lothian & Edinburgh Enterprise Ltd to present their strategy and operating plans to a wide audience within the local area.

— To overcome problems of the wide geographical spread of its area Dumfries & Galloway Enterprise (DGE) have established five District Liaison Groups representing local area business interests, sector specific interests and other community groups. These groups were recently offered the opportunity to join the DGE membership scheme and the majority of members chose to accept the offer.

— Scottish Borders Enterprise (SBE) has established a network of area and sectoral advisory groups which provides an excellent means of consulting with local districts and industries on policies and projects.

These groups involve around 150 people in total and meet on average three times a year. The groups play an important role in generating awareness and acceptance of SBE activities.

Openness with press and media

All LECs issue press releases and announcements on key projects of programmes.

Formal press releases after each Board are issued by Forth Valley Enterprise (FVE) and Glasgow Development Agency whilst Scottish Enterprise, Tayside and Dumfries & Galloway Enterprise Ltd hold face to face briefings after each Board.

FVE also issues press releases when key milestones associated with particular projects of programmes are achieved.

Dunbartonshire Enterprise produces a monthly summary of Board activities and provides a quarterly briefing for MPs and other groups.

Magazines—Dunbartonshire Enterprise, Fife Enterprise, Lanarkshire Development Agency, Scottish Enterprise Tayside, Grampian Enterprise Ltd, and Moray Badenoch and Strathspey produce regular magazines or newsletters to publicise their activities locally.

Issue: The advantages and disadvantages of the different approaches to appointments to LECs boards

Whilst LECs operate differently on points of detail SE is satisfied that all comply to the standard Code of Practice adopted by the network which requires

— policies on the rotation of Directors

— appointments are for specified terms with no automatic re-election

— restrictions on length of service

— an established procedure for selection which is understood by anyone who may be interested

— consultation with local groups, as appropriate, when filling a vacancy

In practice most LECs use Board sub-groups as part of the selection process, and all have established procedures involving wide consultation with local stakeholders and interest groups when seeking nominations—most commonly the local Chamber of Commerce and Local Authorities are contacted.

All LECs are required to make an annual statement to SE giving details of their compliance to the Code of Practice.

Specific Examples of Good Practice

Given the wide coverage of Dumfries & Galloway the LEC has developed a policy of Director representation being apportioned on a geographical basis, aligned to existing local government districts. When a vacancy occurs the relevant District Liaison Group brings forward nominations and recommendations for appointment. The expertise and interests of a nominee are considered by the Board and, in consultation with the District Group, an appointment is made.

Grampian Enterprise and Enterprise Ayrshire. All appointments must be ratified by the Company's membership.

Two LECs, Renfrewshire Enterprise and Grampian Enterprise Ltd, operate a system of Advisory Directors who are treated as full Board Members except that they are not allowed to vote. This allows additional expertise to be brought to the Board's deliberations. Whilst such individuals are not automatically appointed in the event of a vacancy a number of such Members have been subsequently appointed to full Board membership. This has the added value that the member is fully informed and can contribute immediately to the work of the Board.

Issue: The differing approaches, within the contracts or licences, to dealing with conflicts of interest of Directors and staff.

Rules governing conflict of interest have always been included in the LEC Operating Contracts. However, following earlier criticisms of the difficulties in understanding different policies throughout the network since April 1994 all LECs have adopted a standard pattern with only small variations in implementation detail.

SE is satisfied that LEC Board members and staff adhere to a rigorous Conflict of Interest Policy, whilst avoiding excessive bureaucracy.

Summary of activities to deal with conflict of interest[5]

— The maintenance of a public register of Directors interests which is subject to ongoing notification of change and a formal annual update.

— Conflict of interest is a standard agenda item at Board meetings, with members with an interest being excluded from further debate in this area of discussion.

---

[5] *See* Evidence, pp.471–472.

— Details of transactions with business and organisations, with which Directors have a declared interest, are published in LEC Annual Report and Accounts.

— Registers of staff interests are maintained.

Specific Examples of Good Practice

Forth Valley Enterprise has established a "Conflict of Interest" Sub-Committee to ensure that, at an early stage, any project development activity involving a potential involvement with any company or organisation with which a Board Member (or employee) is connected is approved "in principle" or all activity ceased. Following on from this initial "in principle" approval the final approval paper must be considered by the Sub-Committee prior to submission to the Board for approval. At the Board the usual rules of non-involvement in the discussion apply.

Applicants for Scottish Borders Enterprise funding are made aware of who is on the Board and can request that individual Board Members are excluded from the discussion of their project if they feel there would be a conflict.

Issue: The approaches to handling complaints about conduct of LEC staff and concerns about the Board.

LECs are required to have a complaints procedure with details publicised under the citizens charter statement.

In practice LECs follow a standard pattern (a copy of the SE procedure is attached in Annex 1 as an example) and SE is confident that the system currently operates well.

It is anticipated that the complaints procedure will be reviewed for potential improvements as part of the current process of applying for Charter mark status.

Issue: The procedures that are in place for non-financial monitoring of compliance with contracts and licenses.

SE has established a number of methods to ensure compliance and monitoring requirements are allocated to a named individual within a department with relevant responsibility for monitoring.

SE maintains a schedule of Compliance Monitoring (including both financial and non financial monitoring) A copy of the current schedule is attached in Annex 2.

Issue: The ability to pick up improper behaviour—both financial and non-financial on the part of either the LEC or those to whom it contracts

Management are responsible for monitoring compliance with the LEC Operating Contracts (as set out above) and for monitoring the delivery of their own projects and programmes, including propriety issues. In addition, the SE Network has in place comprehensive auditing and monitoring arrangements to assist in ensuring proper accountability for public funds. These arrangements should minimise the risk of improper behaviour with SE, LECs or other contractor.

Summary of Key Elements of Auditing and monitoring arrangements.

— Audit Committees established by the Board of SE and the LECs. Audit Committees receive regular reports of audit and monitoring work.

— Network Internal Audit, comprising teams at SE and LECs, to provide assurance on the effectiveness of internal control systems, designed to effect the business of the network in a proper manner and ensure compliance with policies, directives, laws and regulations.

— The SE Internal Audit team's responsibilities include monitoring and reporting on the activities of the LECs, in particular on matters of propriety in the conduct of their business and compliance with the requirements of the Operating Contract.

— The SE Internal Audit team are also responsible for investigating allegations of improper conduct in the Network.

— LEC Financial appraisal and Monitoring of training providers and other contractors to ensure that they comply with the contractual requirements.

— Examination of the Accounts by External Auditors—accountancy firms appointed as auditors of LECs; NAO are auditors of SE and the consolidated accounts. NAO remit extends to propriety and regularity issues.

Annex 1

SCOTTISH ENTERPRISE COMPLAINTS PROCEDURE

Introduction

At Scottish Enterprise (SE) we value complaints as an extremely important form of customer feedback. Complaints allow us to identify areas for improvement in our operation and to identify areas where our service to our customers can be improved.

Procedure

— All complaints are registered.

— All complaints are investigated rigorously, consulting Local Enterprise Company (LEC) Chief Executives and SE Directors as appropriate. In addition, our Internal Audit Department undertake more in depth investigations when appropriate.

— We aim to handle all complaints as quickly as possible. We aim to respond to all complaints within seven working days. Where this cannot be done because further investigation is required, an interim response will be sent and a fuller response will be provided within a further 14 working days.

— The register of complaints is analyzed and reviewed regularly by the Chief Executive to ensure that the views of our customers are given due consideration when planning for the future and to identify areas for improvement in our handling of complaints.

— In order to assist in resolving complaints as quickly as possible, complaints regarding SE should be directed, in the first instance, to the member of staff most directly concerned. However, if a complainant considers the complaint to be more serious or is not satisfied with their response from the member of staff concerned, their complaint should be directed to the Chief Executive of SE.

— Complaints regarding LECs are, in the first instance, directed to the LEC in question. However, if a complainant is not satisfied with their handling by a LEC, the Chief Executive of SE will further consider the complaint.

Finally, as with any other aspect of SE activity, we welcome comments on our complaints procedure and its operation.

WEDNESDAY 31 JANUARY 1996

AFTERNOON SESSION

Members Present:

The Rt Hon Lord Nolan (Chairman)

Professor Anthony King   Dame Anne Warburton DCVO CMG
Sir William Utting CB

Witnesses:

Chris Cunningham, Chair, Rani Dhir, Member Services Committee Convenor, and David Orr, Director, Scottish Federation of Housing Associations
Ade Kearns, Centre for Housing Research and Urban Studies, University of Glasgow
Ed Weeple, Under Secretary, Alan Fraser, Head of Enterprise and Tourism Division, Tom Kelly, Head of Higher Education Division, and John Henderson, Head of Further Education Funding Unit, Scottish Office

1700. LORD NOLAN: Welcome to our final session of this short set of hearings in Edinburgh. This afternoon, we have three groups of witnesses.

First, we shall be hearing from Chris Cunningham, the Chair, Rani Dhir, Member Services Committee Convenor and David Orr, Director of the Scottish Federation of Housing Associations.

They will be followed by Mr Ade Kearns from the Centre for Housing Research and Urban Studies at the University of Glasgow, who is one of the leading academic researchers on the subject of housing associations.

Finally this afternoon, to provide a wide-ranging official view from the Scottish standpoint, we shall be pleased to welcome Mr Ed Weeple, Under Secretary, Mr Alan Fraser, Head of the Enterprise and Tourism Division, Mr Tom Kelly, Head of the Higher Education Division and Mr John Henderson, Head of the Further Education Funding Unit of the Scottish Office. They will be covering all of our interest in this study except for that of housing associations and I hope that we can do justice to the wide range of their interests in the 45 minutes available.

LORD NOLAN: Now, back we come please to Mr Cunningham, Miss Rani Dhir and David Orr and we look forward to hearing from them about the Scottish Federation of Housing Associations. You have been kind enough to supply us with an opening statement which, of course, will form part of the record. Was there anything you wished to add by way of preliminary remarks before we go into the questions?

CHRIS CUNNINGHAM, RANI DHIR, AND DAVID ORR

CHRIS CUNNINGHAM (Chair, Scottish Federation of Housing Associations): I think it would be appropriate to introduce the Federation as such, but can I first of all thank the Committee for giving us the opportunity of giving evidence and I hope that you will appreciate what we have to say.

Can I start by saying that the Federation is the representative body for approximately 200 housing associations and co-operatives in Scotland. We were

formed in 1975. Previously housing associations in Scotland were represented by a Scottish Council of the National Federation in England. The Federation exists to provide representative services for our members, to provide training, to negotiate on their behalf with government, Scottish Homes and other bodies, to provide good practice guidance and to provide a range of services to our members. All of the housing associations and co-operatives in Scotland are members of the Federation.

The Federation has grown substantially since its birth. First, in the late seventies, but more particularly, in the past five years or so. In 1990 we had approximately 140 members who owned approximately 42,000 houses and today we have just over 200 members who own 80,000 houses, so we have seen substantial growth over the past five years.

The movement in Scotland has grown in response to the particular needs and traditions which exist in Scottish housing and in Scottish life and we reflect in that sense the Scottish agenda.

LORD NOLAN: Yes. Thank you very much. We take it in turns to open the questioning and it is Sir William Utting's turn, so I will ask him to begin, if I may.

1701. SIR WILLIAM UTTING: Thank you, Chairman. We had Scottish Homes just before lunch and the first question put to them by one of my colleagues was really to describe the essential and distinctive features of housing associations in Scotland. I would like to put the same question to you, not with a view to exploring any discrepancies between the two answers, but really so that this Committee does register what these essential features are and how they differ from the housing association movement south of the border.

CHRIS CUNNINGHAM: Not with a view to passing the buck, but can I ask the Director of the Federation to respond.

DAVID ORR (Director, Scottish Federation of Housing Associations): Housing associations and co-operatives in Scotland are very conscious of their links with the communities in which they operate. Not exclusively, but very much predominantly, our members are relatively small organisations that operate in clearly defined geographical areas and have been generated very much as a result of the needs and the views of those communities in inner city areas, peripheral estates and rural areas as well.

We have one housing association that has more than 4,000 units in management, but by far the majority have fewer than 1,000. The typical association is perhaps around 500 houses. More than half of the associations and co-operatives in Scotland are run by committees which are either exclusively or predominantly made up of tenants, so it is very much a movement where tenant participation and tenant control is not just a feature, but one of the key objectives. I think housing associations in Scotland see a very clear objective in terms of providing good quality, affordable housing, but they also have objectives which are about community empowerment, about tenant participation and about building confidence in local communities so that the biggest number of houses you can get is not the only objective. We are looking at a much wider range of community based objectives.

The other thing which is particularly important about Scottish housing associations is the extent to which they work in partnership with local authorities and, indeed, with Scottish Homes. The whole culture is one of partnership where associations, local authorities and Scottish Homes believe that there is such a community of interests, that although we do not always agree, we do believe that co-operation is the most appropriate way for meeting our respective agendas and objectives.

WILLIAM UTTING: Good. If I could pursue a few of those points. I am struck by the fact that you always say housing associations and co-operatives, so the co-operative element is obviously a significant one in Scotland.

DAVID ORR: Yes.

1702. WILLIAM UTTING: How many of these bodies would you characterise as co-operatives out of your membership?

DAVID ORR: About a quarter of the membership. Just under 50 are technically co-operative housing associations. Each one of our members is a housing association according to the definition in the 1985 Act, but just under 50 are co-operative associations. As I am sure you know, those are organisations where the membership and tenants are broadly the same, although there are some deviations. It is far more an important part and focus of the movement in Scotland than it is in England.

1703. WILLIAM UTTING: Yes. This extensive tenant participation and management suggests to me that what you have got are associations that are providing and managing housing now, rather than developing new housing for the future. Is that the case? What is the balance between managing existing stock and planning and developing new services?

DAVID ORR: The balance is 80,000 houses in management now and probably somewhere—it depends how you count it—between 8,000 and 10,000 in the development pipeline at the moment.

1704. WILLIAM UTTING: This is new building—it is not just transfers from local authorities?

DAVID ORR: No it is new building and the modernisation of older stock, some of which was transferred from local authorities, but some of which was a part of housing action areas and previously in private ownership.

1705. WILLIAM UTTING: Yes. And is this development to meet community needs across the board in particular geographical areas, or are you heavily into the provision of special needs and social housing?

DAVID ORR: All of those. I think it would be appropriate to characterise the movement by different kinds of communities. There is a community of interests which is about the provision of special needs housing, supported housing, housing where care is a part of the package and that has always been an important feature of the way the provision has developed in Scotland. There are also general housing associations that operate on wider geographical areas and that are much more typical of the kind of association you will have encountered in England and then there are those which are very much more geographically community centred, whether that is in urban or rural areas. The rural housing association programme is very important.

1706. WILLIAM UTTING: Is most of the money that is coming in now actually for the development of social housing?

DAVID ORR: All of the money that is coming in is for the development or renovation of housing, yes.

1707. WILLIAM UTTING: Is there any tension between what might be called special needs housing and the needs of the ordinary community?

RANI DHIR (Member Services Committee Convenor, Scottish Federation of Housing Associations): I think the movement is certainly characterised by small organisations which meet a wide spectrum of needs. You were talking earlier about co-operatives. There are a large number of co-operatives and community based associations, but almost all of them are involved in some way in special needs. Their contribution to the community is to provide a variety of house types for that community and, by its nature, the general population will include those who have disabilities or require special needs or support. They are not providing one type of housing; it is to meet the community need as a whole.

DAVID ORR: I wonder whether behind your suggestion there may be a suggestion that local tenants who are running housing associations or co-operatives might perhaps feel less inclined to run the supported housing?

WILLIAM UTTING: Absolutely—that was going to be my follow up.

DAVID ORR: The Nimby factor up front. The answer is "no". Housing association tenants and committees have a cross-section of the population the same as any other group, but there is a sense that this is a responsibility that is shared across the board. There will be occasions when there will be debates and arguments about the most appropriate form of housing and whether this group should be in this street, but there is no real suggestion that tenant controlled organisations are less likely to accommodate the needs of people who have different kinds of housing and support needs.

1708. WILLIAM UTTING: And no suggestion that they are entirely preoccupied with the needs and problems of today, to the exclusion of the needs of tomorrow?

CHRIS CUNNINGHAM: It would almost be the reverse, that because so many committees are concerned about communities as a whole, they are concerned about the future of those communities. They are concerned about the long-term needs of those communities as much as they are about addressing particular needs which exist at that moment, so in community based associations and co-ops, you will find a long-term concern about what their community is going to look like in the future.

1709. WILLIAM UTTING: What you say suggests that many housing associations are following a kind of equal opportunities policy when it comes to staffing their boards. Are any of these policies explicit, or is this just the culture of the country?

DAVID ORR: They are explicit to the extent that virtually every association will now have a written down equal opportunities policy, but I have to say that I think the policy has followed the practice, rather than vice versa.

WILLIAM UTTING: Yes.

DAVID ORR: There are gaps in the extent to which representation is genuinely open to all sectors of the community, but there is a will to ensure that that is the case. I do not want to characterise every single housing association in exactly the same way, but there is a sense that we are talking about mixed, integrated and properly functioning communities and not just about building houses and collecting rents.

1710. WILLIAM UTTING: Yes. Where do the equal opportunities policies come from? Is it part of your guidance to housing associations?

CHRIS CUNNINGHAM: Yes, it is. And also from Scottish Homes as regulator. It is from both within the movement and externally. To that extent it reflects the concerns that exist today to ensure that there is equal opportunity for everyone.

1711. WILLIAM UTTING: What about Scottish Homes as a regulator? We are told that it has a fairly hands-on approach. Do you find its approach too heavy, too detailed, too prescriptive, just right or perhaps even a bit soft?

LORD NOLAN: Speak frankly!

CHRIS CUNNINGHAM: The level of regulation reflects the fact that Scottish associations and co-operatives are smaller and therefore there probably is a greater involvement from Scottish Homes in aspects of an association's work than might be the case perhaps in England. They are developing a more flexible regime—to use their words rather than ours—where they want to vary the extent of involvement depending upon the needs of individual organisations. There has been a greater continuity between the previous regulatory regime under the Housing Corporation and the regime that Scottish Homes have operated. I think that individual associations have seen less of a difference between the two regimes than is perhaps the case elsewhere.

DAVID ORR: Scottish Homes is reviewing its current monitoring procedures. We have been quite critical of the extent to which they only comment on weaknesses.

WILLIAM UTTING: On things that are wrong?

DAVID ORR: Yes.

WILLIAM UTTING: Yes.

DAVID ORR: A three part monitoring report where you can either have no cause for concern, cause for concern or serious cause for concern does not give any positive messages, however you look at it. So we have commented on that and I think they are looking at that and making changes.

Scottish Homes has talked quite a lot about the need for self-monitoring by housing associations and we very strongly support that, but we mean something slightly different from what Scottish Homes means. What we mean by that is that it is important that an association is clear about its own objectives and has mechanisms in place that allow it to monitor its own progress against them.

That is an overlapping, but different, process from the one where associations, as it were, self-certify for Scottish Homes' benefit, the things that Scottish Homes seeks to monitor.

WILLIAM UTTING: Yes, quite.

DAVID ORR: And sometimes Scottish Homes, when they talk about self-monitoring, mean self-certifying against Scottish Homes' objectives and we have to clarify that those two are not the same.

1712. WILLIAM UTTING: Yes. The kind of self-monitoring you are talking about, in a sense still requires validation on a selective basis perhaps by some external body?

DAVID ORR: Yes. But if I can make one other comment about monitoring. The framework within which monitoring takes place—Performance Standards, which is a published document of which I think you have a copy—is jointly agreed by the Federation and Scottish Homes and we are very happy that that is the case.

1713. WILLIAM UTTING: Yes. That again leads me on to what I wanted to ask you next, which was about the relationship between you and Scottish Homes and whether or not you feel that guidance you are able to offer is picked up by Scottish Homes and implemented. It sounds as though there may be that kind of relationship. Is that right?

CHRIS CUNNINGHAM: I think that would be broadly fair in the day to day work of associations and co-ops and Scottish Homes; one day we will have a good relationship and the next we will have a bad one, but there is a general recognition, certainly from our perspective, that Scottish Homes within their framework will listen and will take on board what we are saying. It is never perfect, but I think it would be fair to say the relationship is a reasonably close one.

1714. WILLIAM UTTING: Sure, but you do bring together in concentrated form the experience of all your members do you not?

DAVID ORR: Yes.

WILLIAM UTTING: You are obviously an authoritative source of information and advice.

DAVID ORR: It is very unusual for Scottish Homes to publish guidance that has not been agreed with us and it is very unusual for us to publish guidance that has not been agreed with Scottish Homes. That does not mean that we always say exactly the same things and sometimes we will agree to differ, but there is an acceptance of this community of interest.

1715. WILLIAM UTTING: Good. You mentioned operating in partnership with local authorities. What is the reality behind this talk of partnership?

CHRIS CUNNINGHAM: Because most of our members are so small, I believe we have a very good relationship with local authorities on an individual basis. We are reliant upon local authorities in a number of ways, whether it is a question of individual transfers of housing stock or land acquisitions, planning, or whatever. My understanding is that the relationship is very close. We work very closely with local authorities and that applies to all our members, right across the board.

1716. WILLIAM UTTING: Yes. Individually would housing associations be operating to conform with a local authority's housing strategy, for example, or to help deliver part of an overall housing strategy?

RANI DHIR: That is certainly the intention. In addition to the local authority strategy, Scottish Homes strategy also comes into that, so there is a tripartite approach to regenerating communities and investment decisions which involve the local community as well, so they too are brought into the discussion. I would certainly say in relation to more practical issues, many associations accept nominations of around 50 per cent from local authorities for allocating houses, and this certainly contributes to meeting the strategic housing plans of local authorities and their very development proposals are formed with reference to the local authority strategic housing plans.

1717. WILLIAM UTTING: Good. And finally, as far as I am concerned, could you say something about your training programme? I have heard it commented on and you mentioned it yourself. Just tell us a bit more about it.

DAVID ORR: It is fairly extensive. It varies from short courses run several times during the year about health and safety regulations or about new procedures or developments in Scottish Homes policy, through to slightly longer, perhaps residential, events for committee members. There is a core package for committee members, training on finance for non-financial people, development for new development officers, induction—a very wide range—in addition to what is now developing into a more extensive programme of management training, designed for people who are already in management posts, which we have not done very much until recently. There are 11 residential conferences, the biggest of which, our annual conference, attracts about 700 delegates which, from a complete membership of 200 is a very intensive involvement of the movement in what we are doing and a good opportunity for people to work hard and enjoy themselves. Most of these events do combine both.

1718. WILLIAM UTTING: The point was made very strongly to us that management committee members do not need to be people from a professional or business background who are already thoroughly steeped in housing issues, but that it is possible to take people without that sort of background and, with training and experience, produce perfectly competent board of management members. You obviously assist that process through your training programme.

DAVID ORR: We do, yes.

CHRIS CUNNINGHAM: I think it is very important as well to recognise that committee members, who perhaps come onto committees without what appears to be particular housing qualifications or skills, bring experience and skills from their own lives and work experience and knowledge of their local communities. It is very important that we do not discount, but on the contrary recognise, that those skills have some significance in the life of the association or the co-op.

I suppose we would ask the question "What is a relevant skill?" and the answer is probably far wider than a direct, particular qualification might suggest. It is important to recognise that when we look at committee members and what they bring to committees.

WILLIAM UTTING: Thank you. That is relevant to a number of the other organisations that we are looking at as well. Thank you, Chairman.

1719. LORD NOLAN: Would this be right, and not unduly mercenary, that one of the main jobs of the committee is to see that the rents are fixed at a fair and appropriate level and also that they are paid? You depend, do you not, to a considerable extent on private finance and naturally those who lend you money want to know that they are going to get their interest and repayment in due course.

As Sir William was saying, we have heard that this does not necessarily require high level city financiers, but that a good board is one which runs the properties well, to the satisfaction of the tenants.

You mentioned in your evidence that some of your associations, although most of them are of a small or medium size, operate across the country. Does that mean that they are large or just scattered, or both.

CHRIS CUNNINGHAM: Both probably.

DAVID ORR: It depends on your definition. There is no large association in Scotland of the scale that is becoming increasingly common in England. I think there are only four housing associations with more than 2,500 houses in management, so they are not huge, but one or two of them are fairly scattered, particularly the specialist associations that provide housing in all parts of the country.

For example, some of you may have visited Margaret Blackwood Housing Association, which focuses on providing wheelchair accessible housing; it does other things as well, but that is very much what it does. It works in every single area in Scotland, but its total number of units is not huge and some of the sheltered housing associations have a very extensive nationwide portfolio, but that is all really.

1720. LORD NOLAN: Yes. I suppose that does present an added complication when you are dealing with local authorities. We certainly found with some of the bigger associations in England, which span four or five counties, that when we say "What about your local authority involvement?", they say, "Which local authority?" and unless they are going to pack their boards with representatives of four or five, there is a problem. Size is a growing problem in England. Are your associations growing at a pace that you find or foresee difficulties in coping with?

CHRIS CUNNINGHAM: They are growing, but not at a pace that would present the kind of difficulties that I think you are referring to in the case of England.

1721. LORD NOLAN: I am concerned a little with the legal side of this in the sense that the responsibility, for example, for housing the homeless is that of the local authority. Certainly in England you get cases where the local authority stock has been run right down—and in some cases wholly transferred to housing associations—and so you have a rather uneasy division between legal liability and actual ability to meet the need. Is that a problem yet in Scotland or not one that you have had any difficulty with?

RANI DHIR: In practice, the local authority has the right within its powers through the nomination process to nominate clients who may be homeless to the association.

LORD NOLAN: I see.

RANI DHIR: Certainly the Scottish Continuous Recording data, which I believe operates in England as well, shows that we are meeting our obligations there. Where associations do co-operate is by giving priority to applicants who may become homeless so that instead of actually being statutorily homeless and dealt with by the local authority, they would be housed before it got to that stage. We would certainly see that as a contribution towards the problem that arises by preventing homelessness in the first place.

LORD NOLAN: Yes.

DAVID ORR: You probably know that there has only been one local authority in Scotland which has transferred all its housing and that is Berwickshire. The question of ensuring an adequate supply of housing for homeless people is not a structural problem. The relationship between local authorities and housing associations generally speaking works reasonably well. The problem is that there is a lack of supply of affordable housing for rent and that is not about the relationship between the associations and the local authorities.

LORD NOLAN: No. Priorities can create a problem if the local authority's statutory obligations cut across the availability of houses in the housing association's possession and their priorities.

CHRIS CUNNINGHAM: That is a problem in theory and I would acknowledge that there is always that potential, but in practice I do not think you could demonstrate in Scotland that that has actually happened. The relationship is close enough and has worked well so that it does not happen.

1722. LORD NOLAN: Yes. We have heard this in a number of fields in Scotland. It comes back to a very large extent to good relations and it is a credit to you that these evidently exist.

What about the private finance initiative? Do you think that that will interfere with your work—the encouragement of private development to take over social housing, or a part of it? Is it too early to say?

CHRIS CUNNINGHAM: Are you referring to housing associations and co-ops raising private finance?

LORD NOLAN: No. I was thinking more of private development companies, of which there is an increasing likelihood, certainly in England, that they will be encouraged to come into the market for low priced housing and compete with the housing associations.

DAVID ORR: The way in which Scottish Homes currently has an availability of what they call "GRO-grant" funding for private developers to address, certainly in theory and usually in practice, a slightly different part of the market to the one that housing associations and co-ops are looking to, has meant that the demand for private developers to get housing association grant does not really exist in Scotland to the same extent.

LORD NOLAN: I see.

DAVID ORR: The whole process has in any event been put further off into the distance by the fact that it no longer appears in the Housing Bill, even in England.

LORD NOLAN: You are ahead of me there. I am interested to hear that.

DAVID ORR: The HAG to private developers is not part of the published Bill, we are all very pleased to say.

1723. LORD NOLAN: Have you had any pressure for the relaxation of the Section 15 requirements? We have heard that in practice there are certain relaxations already operable in Scotland, as in England. Is the present situation satisfactory in that respect as far as you can see?

CHRIS CUNNINGHAM: It is. Broadly speaking we are happy. It has operated in a relaxed or clear framework since, I think, 1990 or 1991. Housing associations and co-ops are satisfied that the protection is there to ensure that rules are bound to but that it is not unduly restrictive or unreasonable in its interpretation. We are satisfied with the way it works.

LORD NOLAN: Thank you very much. We have come to the end of our time and we are all most grateful for your help and co-operation. There were some who feared that by adding housing associations—and for that matter, universities—to the list of bodies that we were going to look at, there was a necessary implication that we thought they were riddled with sleaze. In fact, our task in this part of our study is to shed light as far as we can upon areas which the public know relatively little about and to show the public, with your help, how the money is being spent, by whom it is being spent and what protections there are against conflicts of interest. This has been a most useful and instructive exercise for us; I hope it will be for the public and we are grateful for your assistance.

CHRIS CUNNINGHAM: Thank you very much.

1724. LORD NOLAN: Hello. This is Ade Kearns. Good afternoon and welcome. Thank you very much for coming along to help us. I know that you have had some correspondence with our Secretary, Alan Riddell, and you have kindly supplied us with your paper on the accountability of non-profit housing providers in the United Kingdom.

Is there anything you would like to say by way of an introductory statement before we get down to questions?

ADE KEARNS

ADE KEARNS (Centre for Housing Research and Urban Studies, University of Glasgow): No, not really.

LORD NOLAN: Then let us get straight on with it. I am going to ask Professor King to lead off with the questions please.

1725. PROF ANTHONY KING: You may think my first question is a little bizarre, but the paper you submitted to us was originally given to the ARNOVA Annual Conference in Cleveland, Ohio, last November. What is ARNOVA?

ADE KEARNS: ARNOVA is an American association of researchers who research the non-profit sector in America. It is quite a large area of academia in America, as you know. In fact there are quite a lot of studies of educational institutions done in that body, so that is a conference of about 500 delegates who meet annually to discuss the field.

PROF ANTHONY KING: 500 by American standards is minuscule.

ADE KEARNS: Yes, but compared to the number of people you get in a conference about the non-profit sector in the UK, it is quite enormous.

1726. PROF ANTHONY KING: I am sure. Colleagues who have read the paper will know this, but not everybody may know that in a sense your paper falls into two parts—one is a disquisition on the subject of accountability and the other is based on your research into Scottish housing associations. Can we take them in that order.

You say at one point—"It seems that the term accountability can mean anything to anyone." and I am sure that members of the Committee would agree that that must be so. What does the term "accountability" mean to you?

ADE KEARNS: The reason I said that is I think it is a great virtue to claim to have and it is a great criticism to

levy at anybody that they haven't got it. The way I look at accountability in the paper is to say that I can see three types of accountability operating in the non-profit sector. One is an administrative type of accountability, which of course we have many versions of in the UK, where you are trying to collect information from organisations and to set procedures for them so that you can get them to act in a certain way and perhaps do what you want them to do. We have them in relation to local government to make sure that there is financial probity, administrative propriety, etc. That is one type of accountability that I discuss.

Another is the use of consumerism as a form of accountability in public services—the introduction of consumerism to try to overcome the imbalance between the provider of the service and the user of the service—and try to replicate the sorts of accountability that people claim exists in markets. I think there has been a lot of that in the public services in this country and that has applied in housing.

The third is the type we are probably more familiar with—the political type of accountability. Here, the concept gets more slippery. Accountability as a relationship arises when one party gives a delegated authority or consent to another party to do something and by virtue of that they have the right to remove that consent or authority. The person who acts has a duty either to be answerable or to provide an account of what they do.

Recent discussions in relation to housing governance in England have suggested that you could make this even broader and say that some types of accountability have a sanction and other types of accountability do not, or that the only sanction is that you publicly embarrass somebody, that you are not happy with their explanation or the account that they provide. I am not too happy about the concept being as wide open as that.

1727. PROF ANTHONY KING: Could I just interrupt to ask why you see that notion of accountability as being wide open? It might be thought to be rather tight and closed in the sense that it carries the implication that somebody can be held to account and either, as you say, removed or publicly shamed or shot or whatever.

ADE KEARNS: No. I am saying that there is quite a difference between saying that the account or answers provided have to be satisfactory and, if not, there is something which follows from that, as opposed to saying there is very little that follows from that.

The other area in which I would say that the situation is quite grey is in the relationship between regulation and accountability and the problem I see in an area like housing is that the sector is increasingly regulated from the centre, but we are trying to say more about how organisations should be accountable locally and that is a difficult situation.

1728. PROF ANTHONY KING: Against that background —I will put it in this rather tough language—what charges would you lodge against either housing associations in Scotland or Scottish Homes on the grounds that they do not afford their stakeholders—I will use that term—adequate forms of accountability?

ADE KEARNS: My comments here would apply as much in England as in Scotland. Housing associations are more accountable to government than to anyone else. That may be understandable because the bulk of their funds come from government or from government agencies. They have to be more accountable locally to people affected by or interested in their work and the evidence we have from research shows that they are less interested in that and are interested in accountability centrally through the systems that government has put in place to ensure that.

1729. PROF ANTHONY KING: Could I interrupt again. I want to be clear about this. You say they feel less accountable—to whom, precisely, as compared with government?

ADE KEARNS: To either tenants or to local residents who are not their tenants, or to prospective tenants—people who are looking for their assistance, but who have not yet achieved it. Their preferred means of accountability to all stakeholders is for the regular provision of information, probably more about policies and strategy than on performance, though there is a significant degree of support for performance indicators and their publication. What is interesting about that is that the representative bodies have not really given this idea much support, but when you ask individual associations and their committees, they are really quite interested in performance information. It gives them a handle on how their organisations are performing against others. If you want to get a true view of their preferences, you have to get past the gatekeepers of the representative bodies to find out how much they would really go along with that.

1730. PROF ANTHONY KING: Can we do that. The gatekeepers of the representative bodies are arrayed behind you and are listening to what you say! We have been told that at least in Scotland—and this may be less true in England, I grant that immediately—in fact housing associations are remarkably accountable to their tenants, not least because tenants tend to form a large proportion of or even a majority of the management committees of the associations. Sticking to Scotland for a moment, do you think that that point has been met satisfactorily?

ADE KEARNS: You certainly have more organisations where there are tenant majorities on committee. That is certainly true, so to that extent, what you say is also true and I would agree with you. That is not the same thing as saying whether those people are in a sufficient position of control and know the business well enough to get a good handle on what an organisation is doing. There are many respects in which committees, and particularly those where there are a lot of tenants on committee, feel under pressure and, to some extent, feel confused about their role. I will come on to say a bit about that.

In the first place, the first perception is entirely what you say. It begins to break down a bit when you talk to some of those committees.

1731. PROF ANTHONY KING: Can you have it both ways? If you are going to have tenant dominated committees or committees with a lot of tenants on them, is it reasonable then to complain if they do not have some of the skills that perhaps a committee would have that was dominated by lawyers and accountants?

ADE KEARNS: I would entirely agree with you, but I do not think that the regulatory system takes account of

that. The regulatory system in my view places an over emphasis on the committee being in control and that message is what confuses committees. It is a bit like the myth of ministerial accountability; they tend to believe that to be in control they have to be all knowing—that they have to know everything that goes on in an organisation and committees, any committee, cannot know everything that goes on in an organisation and they take that message the wrong way. Some of them take the message as being "If I have to be in control, I have to actually be an overseer, be in the organisation all the time to see what is going on.". The thrust of regulation that says that a board has to be in control is not sufficiently explaining practice to committees, such as tenant based committees, to know what it should mean for them in practice to be in control. They feel an awful burden as a result and sometimes get the wrong end of the stick from that message.

1732. PROF ANTHONY KING: What about the two other groups you referred to? We keep hearing, in all kinds of contexts, not just the housing association context, that bodies are supposed to be responsible to something called "the local community" or accountable to the local community but somehow do not adequately do that. Do you have any thoughts as to how housing associations might be made more accountable to the local community? And, by the local community, meaning what exactly?

ADE KEARNS: You asked me that question a minute ago and I said I took it to mean local residents who were not tenants as well as residents who were tenants—because that varies quite a bit between organisations—and perspective tenants looking to be assisted.

1733. PROF ANTHONY KING: And it could be councillors?

ADE KEARNS: Yes, it could be interested organisations who have a remit in the area as well. Yes, I do have some thoughts about how they could be more accountable at the local level, which I see as the area where they should be more accountable. The thing to realise is that most housing associations, despite having said that they like providing information, are not very keen that that provision be put on a statutory basis. I do not agree with that. I think it ought to be.

The standards of performance—and I am talking of England here at the moment—for associations on openness are quite loose and need to be tighter and more explicit. I will give you an example. At the moment it says, for housing associations in England, that they should be encouraged to distribute their annual report. That is a pretty easy thing to say you are doing.

They should make available on request committee papers and minutes and allow observers to attend the non-confidential bits of their meetings and it should go much further than that. The Hancock Committee in England made suggestions about openness and the annual publication of information, which are useful and you will know about. In addition, minutes I believe should be sent to a range of interested and representative bodies, such as local authorities, as you have said, and others and more information should be sent to the members of associations. In my view, we have to remember these are membership organisations. Their weakness at the moment is that they are membership organisations who place little emphasis on their members.

My own research suggests that committees of associations and their staff do not see the membership as a route to accountability and it should be and could be.

1734. PROF ANTHONY KING: Who should the members be? You are undoubtedly even more aware than we are of the fact that the different housing associations have a very different conception both of who ought to constitute their members and what the role of the membership should play. Who do you think should ideally be members of housing associations?

ADE KEARNS: There are three broad groups. One is the tenants, another is the local community of residents, as we discussed, and another would be other interested parties who share the ethos and values of the organisation—and I would include local authorities in that group of interested parties. It may involve a range of organisations with which housing associations are working.

We have to remember that shareholding membership is extremely low and does not grow in the same way as the organisations themselves grow. For example, in England, for housing associations that own between 5,000 and 10,000 properties—and of which there are a reasonable number—the average shareholding membership is 150. That probably has not changed very much from the day they started.

Our recent studies in Scotland showed that only three in five organisations actually sent their annual report to their members and these are the members of the organisation—the 100 odd people who have bought in to say they have got an interest. Only one in five had ever sent any other communication to their members to consult them on an issue or to tell them about an issue or a development.

I do not believe, as some commentators do, that opening up the membership is a threat to associations. It has been said that if the membership was more open, you would get more control by factions. I do not believe that that would be the outcome.

1735. PROF ANTHONY KING: Could you say why not because certainly some of our witnesses south of the border said that they had a very real worry that, for example, if a housing association were proposing to put up some housing perhaps for people with social difficulties of one kind or another that you would suddenly get an influx of new members to the association of people who wanted to protect their own local interests.

ADE KEARNS: I do not think that the people who say that have any evidence to suggest that it has ever happened. Some organisations do have fairly open membership policies and I do not think that coups or takeovers by groups have happened.

I am saying that organisations should put more effort into increasing their membership and having more involvement with them, giving them more of a say in what they do, but the powers that go with being a shareholder—and they hold the ultimate power in these organisations—should be balanced with shareholder responsibility. Shareholders should sign up to something which states that they do agree with the aims and values of the organisation, that they share the objectives. They should be expected to take part in the organisation's affairs, either by attending a specified number of general meetings, or by replying to communications from the organisation if opinions were being sought on the matter. There should be something in the rule to remove members if they are found not to take any part in its active life.

1736. PROF ANTHONY KING: Can I be clear, by the way, about your research. I am sorry to have to ask this question. I probably did overlook something. I got the impression that your research was mainly with Scottish associations.

ADE KEARNS: No, one piece of research was, but there are several fairly large pieces of research which I could briefly explain to you. On two occasions I have studied the composition of housing association committees in England—and I have done that twice in Scotland as well, once in the mid eighties and once in the early nineties, which pre- and post-date the changes that took place around 1988—and I undertook a survey on governance issues for voluntary committee members in England when the NFHA had its inquiry. They commissioned me to solicit the views of volunteers who they felt were not going to get through to the inquiry panel. In that case about 200 committees of associations took part in some research of mine, to express their own views on a range of governance issues.

1737. PROF ANTHONY KING: On the back of that, can I ask you a straight question, which I think we all find ourselves asking from time to time in all manner of different contexts. That is simply this: you give the impression, both in what you say and in the tone you use in saying it, that there are big problems out there, there are defects in the system that need to be remedied. Can you give us your sense of how serious you think these problems are? Is this something to which one should be devoting a lot of effort and resources to changing, or are these simply niggles?

ADE KEARNS: Maybe I have given you slightly the wrong impression. I do not believe that housing associations constitute a sector where we ought to be terribly worried about their probity or accountability. I am saying that they could make improvements. The reason they ought to make improvements is really in their own interests because they face a danger of being incorporated into government if they do not. The only way they can resist that is to have a firm foundation upon which to do so. Being viable membership organisations is one way they can do that; otherwise it is very difficult for them to not be seen as public bodies which are the creations of government, which they are not—yet they do not have much of a defence to that claim, or to the pressures they face to do what government wants them to do.

Increasingly we see a range of housing initiatives where government is looking to associations to do what they want them to do and to implement housing policy. Housing associations are the flavour of the month with government and have been during the period in which the current regime has been in power, but they may not always be and they will have to survive after the change of government and have a good means to claim they ought to survive and be as active tomorrow as they are today.

1738. PROF ANTHONY KING: So you want to make sure that housing associations are firmly and deeply entrenched in the voluntary sector?

ADE KEARNS: Yes. It is a mistake to see them as public bodies in the same sense as some of the others that you will have looked at earlier.

1739. PROF ANTHONY KING: Can I ask you a specifically Scottish question because you raised the point in a specifically Scottish context in your paper. You say—

"There is already a cultural and communication problem in Scotland where associations fail to grasp the concept of "self-monitoring" because all the regulator's explanations of it appear to imply the provision of more information more regularly to the national housing agency."

I forbore to put this to Scottish Homes this morning, but could I ask you to spell out what you had in mind when you said that?

ADE KEARNS: Yes. The other piece of research that we have recently completed was commission by the National Housing Agency in Scotland. It was called "Supporting Voluntary Committee Members", during the course of which we interviewed about 80 committee members of 20 organisations. The national housing agency wanted to know how committee members could be assisted to play the role that they wanted them to play. One of the things they want them to do was to become more self-reliant. Committees have received the message that they have to be more self-reliant, so we spoke to committee members about how they understood that term and what they thought the national housing agency meant when they said "We want you to engage in self-monitoring."

The committee members at the time we researched, which was in the summer, did not really have a clue what that word meant because the minute you said the word "monitoring" they saw it as something that was done to them, rather than something that they did, so there was a complete absence of understanding. But since that time, I know the people behind me here—the representative body—have done quite a lot of work with committees to get them to understand that they have a role in self-monitoring.

What they are not currently understanding is how they can monitor the performance of all the different functions within their organisations and how it is their job to do that. Now, it is easy to say committees should do that, but one of the barriers is that the chief officers of the organisation up to now have not themselves found the time to set such a system in place, to put all the mechanisms in place that would provide committees with all that they need to engage in full self-monitoring. There is a problem of time there, but also one of understanding and that is what I meant by the comment.

1740. PROF ANTHONY KING: Finally, a question that does not relate specifically to Scotland. Elsewhere in your paper, you say—

"In the non-profit housing sector, organisational expansion and the esteem that is seen to go with it can, especially when combined with pressures under the current financial arrangements to reduce subsidies, lead boards to exploit or at least pressurise consumers through higher rents and lower standards. The absence of tenant power and influence and shareholder involvement is crucial in such circumstances."

Could I ask you again a scale question. Do you think that there are large numbers of housing associations, the staff or boards of which are so concerned to enlarge the association and build their own empire that they actually treat their existing tenants in this kind of way? Is this a real, common and widespread problem?

ADE KEARNS: Yes, it is a fairly serious problem. I am aware that one of your earlier witnesses said that large associations are the most aware of the need to protect the interests of their tenants. I take that comment with quite a pinch of salt. All the evidence in England shows that in five years, rents for housing association tenants have gone up 40 per cent above the rate of inflation. What I find odd is how the regulatory system permits that to happen and one of the big issues you ought to face is this question of the separation of the regulatory function. It is a real problem that regulation is carried out by the funder because the funder has a keen vested interest in such a thing as rents rising.

The way housing associations are regulated is quite different from the way, say, public utilities are regulated, where they are either regulated in a combination of consumer interest and to foster competition. In this sector, in my view, regulation does not sufficiently take account of consumer interest because price is not in the regulatory regime. The Ombudsman cannot deal with a rent issue; that is defined as outwith his or her area of competence or responsibility and yet we see such a fast rise in rents.

We do not see the quality of the product itself regulated independently. The quality of the product is regulated through the development administration process, the way an organisation gets approval to build a scheme of houses and the design gets looked at by the funding agency, and yet the studies have shown a decline in standards since the introduction of the new regime in 1988 so that the houses are becoming more standard, space standards are falling. We are not saying they are not good quality, but the standard has dropped. Again, regulation has not prevented that drop happening because the Regulator has a vested interest that those sorts of economies are made in order to make this financial system work.

In that sense, there is a good case for saying that the product and rents, the whole regulatory system, should be clearly separate from the organisation or the part of the organisation that funds associations and the development of their houses.

1741. PROF ANTHONY KING: I said finally, but could I just ask one question—at the risk of sounding like the "Today" programme—that invites a very short answer. Do you think that by and large, very big housing associations are a bad thing? It sounds as though you do.

ADE KEARNS: Yes, because it is very difficult for them to either improve their local accountability or sufficiently take into account, as you said earlier, a whole range of local authority interests and those of many different tenants living in different parts of the country. Yes, the gain is that you get economy out of it. What we do not see is any proof that there is a gain to the tenant out of it. Of course there may be marginally more provision, because they can strike cheaper, larger deals to buy land or to buy components, but somebody has to demonstrate that larger is producing a better service to the tenants and that has not been demonstrated.

1742. WILLIAM UTTING: I thought that the rent rises that you spoke about were actually required by government policy. Are you saying that the Housing Corporation is adding an extra dimension of misery in here for its own purposes?

ADE KEARNS: No. I am saying that what is going on is a bit of a shadow game. The Government has legislated to say that rents are negotiated between a tenant and a landlord and has said that those rents must be affordable. You would have to say two things in response to that. First, there is no evidence that any negotiation goes on. Clearly what tends to happen is that a landlord will set a rent and somebody in a very undesirable situation can either take it or leave it—it is not really a negotiation as the legislation says. I am sorry, I have lost my train of thought.

WILLIAM UTTING: I was pursuing the point simply because the question of whether the same body can be both funder and regulator is one that has cropped up in a number of areas of our study, so we are really quite interested in this.

ADE KEARNS: Yes. I have recollected what I was going to say. The funding system is based upon an idea that a rent is affordable. It requires an assumption to be made about what that is, so calculations are made about what an affordable rent is. Those calculations are not publicly available: open government has not reached as far as the agency making those calculations available.

That is very difficult then because it puts associations in a difficult position. They either move in the direction that they feel government wants them to go in, or they take a risk of saying "What is the consequence if I do not do that?" and that is the sort of greyness. The sanction that goes with not complying with the housing agency or with regulation, is clearly stated. Everything is stated in terms of "We encourage you to do this.", "It is recommended that you do that.", and the organisations all know, "There is probably a cost to me if I do not do it that way.". An encouragement can clearly become an instruction.

Experienced committees are able to resist those pressures and newer ones are less able to do so. If the national housing agency says "We want you to push your rents in this direction.", committees have it within their constitutional control to resist that, but some are more or less likely to put up any resistance.

1743. WILLIAM UTTING: If there was more transparency in that process, would that diminish or remove your objection to the funding agency being the regulator as well?

ADE KEARNS: No, because there are other problems as well that we have not gone into here. It is an odd situation to have the regulator as the same body that is fostering the business.

1744. WILLIAM UTTING: Yes. It is just that in other sectors, the question of the funding gets tied up with

questions of overall effectiveness and whether the quality of the service is being provided too. It is rather difficult that it seems to separate these and put them with different bodies.

ADE KEARNS: I would not agree that communication can overcome that barrier, but the other difficulty associations face is that of their relations with local authorities which are not involved in the regulatory process. That is another problem because they are a main player in the housing field in any district. The Government has not given local authorities a regulatory function and they should be involved in it. That would overcome the suspicions of associations and make relations between them and councils better. At the moment, the regulation is done by central government or its agency and local authorities do not really get a grip on associations in the way that they would like to. An involvement in regulation would help those sets of relationships.

WILLIAM UTTING: Good. Thank you very much. We have been dealing with Scotland today, but I would like to acknowledge the value of your work in England as well. We certainly have had a copy of *Going by the Board* and that was extremely useful to us when we were looking at English housing associations. Thank you.

LORD NOLAN: I am sure you will realise how valuable independent work like yours, based on considerable research, is for us in doing our work, so we are all very grateful to you. Thank you very much for coming along and explaining it to us, as well as giving us your written work.

ADE KEARNS: Thank you.

1745. LORD NOLAN: Now we welcome from the Scottish Office, Mr Ed Weeple, the Under Secretary, Mr Alan Fraser, Head of the Enterprise and Tourism Division, Mr Tom Kelly, the Head of the Higher Education Division and Mr John Henderson, the Head of the Further Education Funding Unit of the Scottish Office.

Mr Weeple, could I ask you to identify your colleagues for the benefit of the record?

ED WEEPLE, ALAN FRASER, TOM KELLY, AND JOHN HENDERSON

ED WEEPLE (Under Secretary, the Scottish Office): Certainly Chairman. On my immediate left is Alan Fraser, who is in charge of the Enterprise and Tourism Division and will be able to speak to you about any questions you have on the local enterprise companies. On my immediate right is Tom Kelly, who is the Head of the Higher Education Division and on my far right is John Henderson, who is responsible for the Scottish Further Education Funding Unit within the Further Education Division.

LORD NOLAN: Thank you. We are also very grateful to you for the material with which you have supplied us. Usually in these question and answer sessions, one of us opens the bowling and another then follows up. This afternoon, as we have so much ground to cover in different fields, we propose that Professor King and I shall be the two bowlers and I will take the lead on the first part of the questioning, which will be about the local enterprise companies. Professor King will follow with any questions he has on that and he will then take the lead on the further and higher education aspect of your evidence. I hope that is convenient.

ED WEEPLE: Certainly Chairman, and on local enterprise companies, I will leave all the responses to Alan Fraser.

1746. LORD NOLAN: Good. Thank you. You have told us something about the process of the setting up of the local enterprise companies in Scotland. What has interested us is the difference of approach as between Scotland on the one hand and England and Wales on the other, both in the character of the two bodies—LECs and TECs—and in the structure by which they operate, the two intermediate enterprise boards in Scotland and the absence of anything exactly similar in England and Wales. Was that a historical accident or was there a division of thought between the Scottish Office and the English authorities over this?

ALAN FRASER (Head of Enterprise and Tourism Division, The Scottish Office): There was a fundamental historical difference in where they were when the issue came up. Essentially, in Scotland we had two non-departmental public bodies, the Scottish Development Agency, which was set up in 1975, and the Highlands and Islands Development Board, which was set up in 1965. These had fairly extensive powers for promotion of economic development in their respective areas and between them they covered the whole of Scotland. So when in 1989/90 thought was turned to how these bodies might be developed with one eye on the experience of the PICs,—the private industrial bodies in the United States—that was part of the inspiration, but there was also a desire to develop on the basis which had been set up by these largely integrated existing bodies. It was seen as a sort of incremental development of that to add to their powers and functions the responsibility for training which had previously been with the training agency.

I cannot really speak in detail for the gestation of the TECs, but they were much more training oriented and it was very much a question of where the former training agency powers went in England, whereas in Scotland we had this quite substantial structure built up.

In some senses, the structure which developed was a response to a number of pressures. One was the clear desire by Ministers to see a greater private sector input to the delivery of these services; another was a response to a growing perception that, certainly in the case of the SDA, some of its critics maintained that it was overly focused on urban and central Scotland and particularly west central Scotland and there was insufficient consideration given to the particular interests of the outlying areas of the country.

1747. LORD NOLAN: Yes. Thank you very much. Would it be right to say that we are still in an evolutionary process and that there are developments taking place even now within both the accounting procedures and the organisation of the LECs and their respective boards? I put to you this broad question and I will tell you why in a moment: have you had any anxieties over the structure as it is developing in Scotland or any reason to think it is not working in a satisfactory way—that is the interposition of the two Enterprise Boards over the individual LECs?

ALAN FRASER: I do not think we would question that fundamental structure. To say we are satisfied with it would sound complacent and we are not. It has been a dynamic situation where the institutions continue to evolve.

We began with a sort of operational imperative to get the new bodies and the Local Enterprise Companies up and running and then, once they were up and running and carrying out their main executive functions satisfactorily, we have continued to go back over the process to iron out difficulties, to see what opportunities there are for improvement and, of course, to take account of the perhaps moving or rising requirements in terms of public accountability.

1748. LORD NOLAN: One of the features that has most struck me in hearing about the development of the LECs in Scotland as against the TECs in England, is the amount of local press interest which we hear is quite considerable, particularly when the local press proprietor does not approve of LECs or has real or perceived objections to the way in which they are being run. Has that on the whole been a help or a hindrance?

ALAN FRASER: It depends who you ask and on which day! Overall it has been healthy because it has brought home to the people concerned that it is not sufficient that they observe the proprieties, but in fact they have to be seen to do so. That is the value of it. On an operational basis—I cannot speak for the individual LECs—I am sure that on some days they have all found the press attention pretty unwelcome and a distraction.

1749. LORD NOLAN: But in England my impression is that there is comparatively little and one of the problems on the English side of the border is that the general public knows very little about what happens in TECs. That has its harmful aspects as you know. There is some suspicion; people know that a great deal of public money passes through their hands. They are very unusual organisations—private companies, with public money—and it seemed to me that in this as in other areas of our inquiry, the press and in particular the local press have a very important part to play in, where appropriate, reassuring people and printing the success stories as well as, of course, criticising where it is due.

Apart from individual cases where there has been criticism of apparent nepotism or misuse of expenses by members of the LEC boards, structurally has there been any criticism of the relationship between the LECs and the Enterprise Boards in the press?

ALAN FRASER: There has been some—not so much of the relationship, but of the manner of appointment of LEC members and other organisations have come forward and said that they do not like the way in which that is done and people have made the alternative case for having people there more in a representational capacity than appointed as individuals on their merits.

The Scottish Select Committee in its inquiry finally came to the conclusion, or almost by default did not suggest that any radically different structure was wanted, but simply reflected that a number of bodies had different views about certain adjustments which might be made. I do not think there is a fundamental difficulty there.

1750. LORD NOLAN: There was a good deal in the report about the relationships between the LECs and the local authorities. We have been hearing a good deal, today in particular, about the success generally experienced it seems by those who have spoken to us about co-operation. There is clearly room for improvement, but the degree to which the LECs are lined up with the local authorities in Scotland as distinct from England again seem to us to be impressive.

Throughout our inquiry into what happens in Scotland—and, of course, in Wales—we are looking to see if lessons can be learned from the English point of view and, vice versa, what there is about the English systems that we might helpfully remind you about. This is what lies behind some of my questions.

Do you have a role in the formation of the Enterprise Agencies' contracts with individual LECs? Are you consulted about them?

ALAN FRASER: Not directly. The original form of the contract was drawn up in consultation with the Department. We approved that. Any substantial changes in the format would have to be agreed with us, but the minor adjustments—because, of course, they are slightly different for each individual local enterprise company each year—would not be something we would get involved in. We essentially deal with Scottish Enterprise and it then articulates our requirements in terms of these contracts and agrees these with the local enterprise companies.

1751. LORD NOLAN: What I had in mind in particular was the difficult and sensitive area of people with special needs, from whom we have heard quite a lot, and whether there was a Scottish Office policy or guideline in relation to that, or whether the LECs, no doubt knowing themselves very well and the enterprise agencies of the need to cater for those who are disadvantaged in one way or another unless there is some row or obvious dissatisfaction, we will leave it to them.

ALAN FRASER: It is perhaps misleading to suggest that. The whole question of people with special needs, either in deprived areas or in the training field of people with special needs is covered in that Scottish Enterprise first of all has a set of strategic objectives which in turn have been agreed with us, and within these there is one which is listed as "access to opportunity". Under that, they agree to allocate a certain amount of resources to particular areas of urban deprivation and work in partnership with a number of other authorities on the ground. That is very much with our guidance and approval.

The mechanism we have is not just the approval of the strategy document, which was revised within about the past 18 months, but also on an annual basis, the Secretary of State writes to the Enterprise bodies a letter of strategic guidance, which follows through from his financial allocations. Under the conditions on which these financial allocations are given, there usually is a specific reference to, for example, people with special needs. There is an overall training scheme but it will say that provision will be required to be made for people with special needs at a certain level, perhaps by reference to the previous year's level or whatever.

LORD NOLAN: Yes.

ALAN FRASER: There is that degree of guidance and then Scottish Enterprise has to ensure that this is done on the ground and then translates this into the contract and the targets set out by the requirements of the contract.

1752. LORD NOLAN: Yes and you have the Enterprise Agencies as statutory bodies and, so to speak, underneath them separate private companies linked by contract?

ALAN FRASER: Yes.

1753. LORD NOLAN: It is an unusual set up and you are moving into the consolidation of the accounts of the LECs with two supervisory boards, rather treating them as if they were a group of companies. Is it right that amongst the results that will produce will be greater access by the National Audit Office to the accounts of the LECs and indeed to visits by the National Audit Office to the LECs which will perhaps remove one area of uncertainty which we have heard about in the past. Will that do you think be, I will not say a weight off your mind but another cause for satisfying people that there is no question about the degree of supervision of the individual LECs on the audit level?

ALAN FRASER: It will be helpful in that sense. One can say then that anyone has access all the way down the line. The other side of the coin of course is that there is a counterpoint which is that the sheer weight now of audit activity is pretty heavy and there is that operational weight. You put the question to me whether from the Department's point of view this will be helpful, but from an operational point of view we have to recognise that it is just one more administrative burden to be thought about. We want to try and minimise the burden and make sure that the information that they have to hand and provide is as much as possible aligned so that the requirements of all the auditing bodies will be met by the same data.

1754. LORD NOLAN: Another interesting aspect which we were hearing about this morning was this: it reflects the much closer relationship which exists between the supervisory Enterprise Boards and the LECs than you get between central government and the TECs in England. It came to mind because we were thinking of the South Thames TEC which you will have heard of—an unhappy story in England—which went bust and was left as a company which had gone bust. The Treasury would not come and bail them out. But we understand now that it is accepted that the two Enterprise Agencies have a responsibility for ensuring that their LECs observe their contracts and, as one might hope and expect, they assured us that they are taking very good care indeed to guard against any breaches of contract that might result in dangers to solvency.

ALAN FRASER: Yes.

LORD NOLAN: This again, if I may say so as the outsider, seems reassuring and good.

ALAN FRASER: That is the position—they keep a pretty close eye on it.

1755. LORD NOLAN: Yes. One feature of the English system is this: it is of course very difficult, particularly in the case of small TECs, to get a satisfactory mix of members on the board. In England you may have heard that there is now a "wild card" theory that you can have at any rate one director who does not fit naturally into any of the categories, but who may, in a particular area, occupy a uniquely valuable position. Is there anything of that sort in Scotland as far as you are aware, or do you find that you have to stick strictly to the official categories?

ALAN FRASER: We stay fairly strictly with the official categories; there is no specific wild card provision, nor, indeed, has anybody suggested that there should be. It is open to the LECs—for there is a one third of their membership who are not business people—to bring in anybody whom they wish. If there were a case made for a particular individual or category outwith the rules, we might agree to alter them, but that has not been made. The only thing which has been done recently is that a request was made to amend slightly the rules to make it quite clear that, for example, the owner of quite a small business could still qualify as a business member of a LEC. Also the absolute rule originally was that there should be no retired business people, but as it was found that in the case of chairmen there were quite often people who had not long retired and who were very suitable it seemed silly to exclude them, so we agreed to revise the rules to include people who had held senior business positions but were recently retired and therefore were still eligible on that basis.

1756. LORD NOLAN: Thank you very much. I would like to go back to the response to the Scottish Affairs Committee Report on LECs. It includes now a proposal that an external complaints adjudicator is to be appointed. Has any further progress been made on the type of adjudicator who is likely to be chosen?

ALAN FRASER: No final decision has been taken. The two Enterprise bodies are working up proposals at the moment which they have not yet submitted to us, but should be submitting to us reasonably soon. They are proposals for the sort of person it might be and how it might work in practice. We have had some rather informal discussion about how it would work out, but we have not actually had a detailed discussion. We wait to see their proposals as a starting point for detailed discussion about it.

1757. LORD NOLAN: Thank you. Do you have any role in respect of LEC staff who identify issues of concern in their own organisations, but are reluctant to complain because of fear of repercussions? Have you had, in other words, any call for the introduction of whistle-blowers in the LECs of the kind that are now quite common in the English commercial scene and, indeed, in the Civil Service?

ALAN FRASER: No, that has not been suggested from within the network. So far there have been, to my knowledge, relatively few complaints from employees about what has been going on and this has not been a problem.

1758. LORD NOLAN: I do not complain, it is good to hear, but your answers, like many we have heard in this field are reassuring. There are times when reassuring answers are rather rare. There are a couple more questions I want to ask you before I hand over to Professor King.

As you know, the Government is moving towards three year licences in England for TECs and, as I understand it, the Highlands and Islands Enterprise Agency tends to work on a three year basis, but there seems some hesitation about this in the Scottish Office so far as Scottish Enterprise is concerned. What is the objection?

ALAN FRASER: The objection is probably more technical than real. There is the problem of giving absolute assurance three years in advance of the level of funding one could give to a local enterprise company, but de facto, they are given an indicative budget in advance and what is happening is that Scottish Enterprise in fact is adopting a rather lighter touch now in discussing their business plans. Every three years they plan to have an in depth dialogue with them about their business plans, but in the intervening years, a much lighter touch and requirement in terms of reporting and review or revision of what has been previously submitted.

1759. LORD NOLAN: Has there been the concern about the building up of excessive reserves? Has that been a major problem?

ALAN FRASER: They have got quite substantial reserves built up.

1760. LORD NOLAN: It is the natural tendency of a cautious businessman is it not?

ALAN FRASER: Yes and these reserves are seen by some of the LECs as being important to them and they like to accumulate reserves. Ministers have had to take a view this year when budgeting has been tight that that is a resource which they can call upon as necessary to supplement the plans they have. That has always been the case, but obviously in a harder year, it is a cushion for them.

1761. LORD NOLAN: Lastly, one question we have asked almost all of our witnesses and we would be grateful for the Scottish Office view. It is the old chestnut about the remuneration of board members. Have you any particular view about that? We have had strongly expressed views, pro and con, at various levels in the enterprise area. There are clearly arguments pro and con and many LECs are fortunate enough to be run by people who are in high positions in their companies or other walks of life and do not need the money.

A view has been put to us that there are some who actually have to make considerable financial sacrifices to give the amount of time needed to help operate a LEC and that if it is a one-man business or a small partnership, there is a case for an option of an allowance, not a full loss of earnings allowance, but something comparable to what councillors or jurymen get. Is the Scottish Office in a position to offer a view on that, or would you rather not?

ALAN FRASER: We are not looking at this at the moment, on the basis that the local enterprise companies seem to be able to attract enough people of the right sort of calibre without offering money. One of the downside difficulties of introducing that—and this comes back to what I said in answer to one of your earlier questions—is that if you want to appear not merely to be observing all the proprieties, but to be above suspicion, it helps a great deal for the individuals and for the body collectively to turn round and say "We are all doing this on a purely voluntary basis for no personal reward.".

LORD NOLAN: Yes.

ALAN FRASER: Once you introduce a payment, you have great difficulties as to how you assess just how much you get and, of course, at one stroke, you remove that particular defence of their motives.

LORD NOLAN: Yes, it is a very wide ranging problem. Thank you very much indeed. Professor King.

1762. PROF ANTHONY KING: Mr Fraser, could I just ask you one question of a kind of wrap-up character. The key word, I suppose, in our terms of reference is "propriety" and clearly the Scottish Office, Scottish Enterprise, the various LECs, the HIE have mechanisms for trying to ensure propriety. There have been, as we know, a few horror stories in the Scottish LEC world, as in most such worlds. Suppose I simply asked you to take the totality of the mechanisms now in place to ensure propriety—absence of conflict of interest and so on—and to rate them, Gallup poll fashion, excellent, good, fair, poor. How would you rate them currently, in 1996?

ALAN FRASER: That is a very difficult question.

PROF ANTHONY KING: That is why I asked it!

ALAN FRASER: I would rate them "good" by today's standards, but conscious of two things. You have to keep on reviewing practice. You are only as good as your last disaster or problem, which may reveal a difficulty or a hole in the regulations. You have to be ready to cope with that. You have to have one eye to rising standards—the recommendations of this Committee will obviously cause us to look again at the sort of structures we have. It is a continuing process.

1763. PROF ANTHONY KING: But how do you think we could contribute to that process? What might this Committee do to cause you, when we meet again, to say emphatically, "excellent" rather than "good"?

ALAN FRASER: It is the natural caution on the part of any bureaucrat to go for "excellent" because tomorrow, something will go wrong and demonstrate that it was not excellent, so I would always be wary of that.

But as to what might come from the Committee, I cannot anticipate what the Committee might come out with, but from what the Chairman has already said, there may be examples of good practice, or best practice, elsewhere which no one in our part of the world or the network has actually thought about which might be quite useful. There might be a more efficient or a less onerous way of securing propriety, in which case we would obviously look quite hard at that.

1764. PROF ANTHONY KING: If you go down to the LEC level, are the mechanisms amongst the different LECs themselves sufficiently varied that even within Scotland one LEC might learn from another?

ALAN FRASER: Yes, they are. The network operates as a network. In that sort of area, and indeed in other areas, there is a lot of sharing of experience and approaches and appropriation of good practice.

1765. PROF ANTHONY KING: Apart from osmosis of the kind you describe, is there any conscious effort to secure a broadcasting of good practice, either by yourselves or by Scottish Enterprise and HIE?

ALAN FRASER: By Scottish Enterprise themselves. The LEC Code of Guidance on Good Corporate Practice, following through from the Cadbury rules, was drafted originally by Scottish Enterprise for their local enterprise companies, but was then developed and agreed in dialogue with them, so they were all involved in the process of finalising that document. They all had, in a sense, an opportunity to put in their particular ideas and to have ownership of the final product.

1766. PROF ANTHONY KING: So you think that the present systems are pretty good, but you are not complacent?

ALAN FRASER: Exactly. That is a fair assessment.

1767. PROF ANTHONY KING: Can I turn to Mr Henderson and ask a few questions about further education. The first question is simply an historical one. In England, as I well know, being in the world of further and higher education, you have the Department, you then have funding councils and then the institutions. In Scotland you have simply either stripped out or, more accurately, never put in that middle layer. Do you know historically what the explanation for that is?

JOHN HENDERSON (Head of the Further Education Funding Unit, Scottish Office): At the time of incorporation there had been a history in Scotland of the Department funding the central institutions and the colleges of education. It was interesting, I was sitting in yesterday when Dr Kennedy of Robert Gordon University said the Department had actually been funding his institution since early this century. I did not actually know it was quite as long as that, so it is quite a long history, whereas of course in England, the polytechnic type colleges had been with the local authorities. That different background meant there was experience in the Department to draw upon.

Interestingly, the view again—and this came out yesterday in evidence from the Association—of the sector itself at the time of incorporation was that it did not want the turbulence of dealing with another body, a funding council, but the sector has an open mind on that. To some extent that reflected what the sector itself felt was justifiable and also the background.

The other significant difference between our approach to funding further education in Scotland is that unlike the funding council in England, we actually fund the entire activity of institutions where as the Further Education Funding Council actually funds levels of activity, so it funds sixth form colleges, FE colleges and FE in other bodies, including some of the higher education institutions, so there is that different approach and background.

1768. PROF ANTHONY KING: Do you find that the system you now operate works satisfactorily from your point of view?

JOHN HENDERSON: Again, echoing what Alan was saying, I hesitate to say "excellent". We are not complacent. It is a very new sector. We have really only been in operation for three years and we are still on the learning curve, so there are things we can still learn, but so far, so good. Things have bedded down reasonably well.

1769. PROF ANTHONY KING: One of the issues we keep coming up against in all kinds of sectors is the business of whether the funder should also be the regulator—whether there should be two different bodies established. Sometimes these two functions are bunged together, sometimes they are kept strictly apart. The Scottish Office is the funder of further education in Scotland. Is it also the regulator of further education institutions in Scotland?

JOHN HENDERSON: In a sense, yes, because the Secretary of State, in terms of the legislation is given certain reserved powers. The main power he is given of course is the duty to fund and secure adequate and sufficient further education in Scotland, but he is also given powers, for example, to remove board members in the event of mismanagement. He is also given the power to close or indeed merge colleges of further education as well, so he has a range of powers in terms of legislation.

1770. PROF ANTHONY KING: So you are the regulators, in effect, in so far as anybody is?

JOHN HENDERSON: Yes.

1771. PROF ANTHONY KING: Do you have to use those powers at all frequently?

JOHN HENDERSON: Certainly the power to remove board members because of mismanagement has not been used in Scotland as it was in England with, I think, Derby College. There has not been that type of difficulty in Scotland, so we have been lucky in that respect. There have been no closures of colleges either, so that power has not been used. The Secretary of State has not used his power of direction over colleges on their use of their duties and powers either.

1772. PROF ANTHONY KING: Are you saying in effect that you have the regulatory function, but that you have never, or virtually never, had to exercise it in practice?

JOHN HENDERSON: There is another way of exercising the regulatory function and that has largely been through the funding mechanism and the controls put in place.

PROF ANTHONY KING: Quite so.

1773. LORD NOLAN: Conditions of grant?

JOHN HENDERSON: That is right—conditions of grant and the financial memorandum between the Department and boards of management. That has been the way of regulating the activities of the colleges.

1774. PROF ANTHONY KING: Picking up the issue of making things conditions of grant, are there codes of conduct frequently and universally in place in Scottish further education institutions?

JOHN HENDERSON: Again, when you were absent yesterday, we heard from the Association of Scottish Colleges, which is a fairly new organisation of all the colleges, that they have taken the initiative to put out to their members a code of practice which deals with such things as recommending having registers of interests and also gives their members guidance on matters such as how to go about filling vacancies on boards as they arise. That has been very helpful.

1775. PROF ANTHONY KING: They have taken the initiative; is this something that the Scottish Office would

want to get involved with? Do they show you drafts of the document?

JOHN HENDERSON: We have been involved and discussed it with them, but it has been a case of self regulation in this area. Clearly, as in many other areas, we need to look at how it is actually put into practice with the colleges to see if there are areas of difficulty and it may be, for example, that the recommendations of this Committee come up with issues that the Department and the Association will need to look at again that perhaps are not covered in the code.

1776. PROF ANTHONY KING: One issue I would like to raise with both you and Mr Kelly is one that, again, we keep stumbling across in a variety of different settings and that is simply the person or group of people who should be involved if in a college or a university there is trouble of some kind or another and there has been trouble, certainly in universities as well as colleges south of the border. In English universities—and, I think, Welsh universities—the system of the Visitor, at least in the pre-1992 institutions, is pretty well established. Most of them have them, even if there may be doubts about the way in which they operate. Is the visitor system, Mr Kelly, one that you have in Scotland?

TOM KELLY (Head of Higher Education Division, Scottish Office): No, there is not an exact equivalent of it. We went through some of the documents on our institutions, and we discovered that there is a Visitor to Glasgow School of Art—it is His Royal Highness the Prince of Wales; we are not quite sure what his duties are. Generally speaking, we do not have such an office. There is the rather special office in the oldest universities of Scotland of the Rector, which is historic and was adopted by the University of Dundee when it was set up in the 1960s, though with the slight difference that there, the Rector is not the Chairman of Court. There is no such office generally speaking in the other three sixties universities or the new universities and other HEI's whose governance has been changed since the 1992 legislation.

1777. PROF ANTHONY KING: Am I right in thinking—and I could be wrong—that in the ancient Scottish universities, the post of Rector is mainly concerned with students and their relations with the institution?

TOM KELLY: He is technically the Chairman of Court and there have been examples of investigations carried out by the Rector, obviously assisted by officers of the university, because generally speaking, Rectors elected by the present method are not going to be expert in these matters themselves. But I cannot give you a very general account of the functions of Rectors because they seem to differ according to individuals and the practices of the individual universities.

1778. PROF ANTHONY KING: I know that we are forbidden from asking you questions about HEI policy and all that, but the Visitor system does seem to have worked pretty well and more frequently than a lot of people realise in universities south of the border. Do you think there is a case for that role being established and having somebody in place to play it, whether or not that person is called the Visitor?

TOM KELLY: It has never been suggested to us by students, those who have moved to the Scottish system from England, academics or others. So whether there is an unfulfilled need that a Visitor would actually meet seems to us an open question at the moment. If there is perceived to be such a need, we would not close our minds to the idea that there should be a Visitor, but our way of proceeding would probably be to say "What are the features of a Visitor system" and to suggest to the sector that these are worth considering so that they can make their own proposals or dispositions to deliver whatever it is that you wanted of a Visitor.

We have not gone down that road, we have not, as I say, seen a need or received any representation to the effect that there is such a need.

1779. PROF ANTHONY KING: Would the same be true in the FE sector?

JOHN HENDERSON: I think that is the same position: there is no evidence that there is an unfulfilled need out there.

1780. PROF ANTHONY KING: Would your reaction be the same to any suggestion—and we are not necessarily about to make one—that there be for either the higher education sector or the further education sector or the two together, some kind of ombudsman person?

TOM KELLY: We have used the Further and Higher Education Charter to suggest that all higher education institutions and FE colleges should put in place appropriate machinery for dealing with grievances.

PROF ANTHONY KING: Collectively or individually?

TOM KELLY: Individually.

PROF ANTHONY KING: Yes.

TOM KELLY: One of the suggestions was that they might have their own local charter. We think it is important that institutions should have ownership of these arrangements because it is in their interests to show that they are capable of solving grievances and dealing with difficult cases in a way that carries the respect of their students and staff. On the whole our dealings with the institutions suggest that that is in their minds. They are well aware that the expectation today is that if you have a complaint, it is going to be dealt with, not just impartially, but in a more transparent way than might have been the case, say, 20 or 30 years ago. They have a very distinct interest, we think, in going down this road.

We have tried to nudge and encourage, rather than to prescribe.

1781. PROF ANTHONY KING: Can I ask you a question which I will put under the heading of "audit", but I do not just mean strictly financial audit. I mean, I suppose, financial audits plus performance indicators of various kinds.

One complaint that you frequently get from public sector bodies is the complaint that they are over-audited, over-regulated, over-leaned on, they are told that they are autonomous institutions and should stand on their own two feet one day and the next day get 27 pieces of mail

telling them in detail what they should do and what forms they should fill in. What is your own perception, from where you sit, of whether the Scottish Office is not asking enough of or is perhaps asking too much from, again, both higher education and further education bodies?

TOM KELLY: There have been complaints particularly about the burden of demands made on the institutions by the funding council and by exercises such as the research assessment exercise. The amount of paperwork involved in some of the research assessment exercises for instance is legendary.

PROF ANTHONY KING: I know!

TOM KELLY: Obviously ministers have taken heed of that and are well aware that some simplification of systems would be extremely welcome in the sector.

As to actually reducing the range of things that the various audit and monitoring processes covers, there is no strong demand for that. What is wanted is a lighter touch and an acceptance that there are some lines in the sand between those things which are legitimate for the Funding Council or the Department to intervene about and those matters which really ought to be left to institutions to settle and solve themselves.

We have not had many border disputes, that must be said, and those that seemed likely to become border disputes, we have tried to sort out informally, rather than let them become major issues. So we do not see that there is a great need to change the arrangements there are at the moment. What we cannot dispute is that universities, say, 30 years ago would be receiving a single block of grant with very modest demands of accountability and that today's demands for accountability are considerably more searching than they were then. There were many more rules about disclosure and submission of information than there would have been then. That cannot be disputed.

PROF ANTHONY KING: You say there are very few border disputes. That might be because the institutions you are funding, precisely because you are funding them, tend to retreat in the face of superior force rather than fight some kind of border conflict that they might lose.

TOM KELLY: I prefer to put it the other way—that there is plenty of opportunity for those issues to be resolved. For example, the Funding Council has met with a complete gathering of chairmen of court and principals to discuss some of these issues about jurisdiction and the way oversight is exercised and that has been extremely helpful in reducing areas of possible tension before they become disputes.

1782. PROF ANTHONY KING: Does that echo—I am asking the question in a leading form—roughly the experience in your part of the world as well?

JOHN HENDERSON: There is a slightly different perspective in further education because the Department are directly funding and perhaps more conscious that they need not over burden institutions with requests that sometimes can be conflicting. I will give you one example: the Statistics part of the Department was gathering statistics in a certain way, we were gathering statistics in a certain way for funding purposes. We realised that this was a double burden on colleges, so we are going to combine the two in one exercise and are working with the colleges to streamline that to make it just essential information.

As another example, recently we put out to all the colleges a request under the heading "Towards a better service", "What do you think of your relationship with us, tell us where there are difficulties, where we can improve?". We take account of that and we shall be feeding back to the colleges the sort of things they have been telling us and trying to learn from them.

TOM KELLY: Could I supplement what I have said by mentioning that certainly for the HEIs, in some areas they are their own self-regulators. John has mentioned the collection of statistics. There is the Higher Education Statistics Agency, the Higher Education Quality Council—both UK bodies, but they are owned by the institutions and the institutions determine policy and operation of all that they do. We know that the Higher Education Statistics Agency is starting to look at performance indicators and we are entitled to assume that they will be capable of coming up with a solution to good, publicly available information which does not add unnecessarily to the burdens on institutions to produce data.

PROF ANTHONY KING: I have taken up rather more than my share of the time, for which I apologise.

LORD NOLAN: Not at all. Much as we would like to prolong this discussion at the expense of your time, I am afraid we have to go and catch aeroplanes.

May I just ask you this: you mentioned a report published in April 1995 on a study commissioned by the Scottish Office from Leishman Management Consulting. We had also been told something about it by the Aberdeen College. It sounded as if it could be of great interest to us. Do you think you could let us have a copy?

ED WEEPLE: We certainly can, Chairman.

LORD NOLAN: We would be much obliged. Thank you very much indeed. We saved you till the end and you have been a very helpful body of witnesses indeed, if I may say so, even if Mr Weeple has been much more silent than we would have expected.

ED WEEPLE: I think it is the way the questions were addressed, Chairman. They were addressed to those with the expertise.

LORD NOLAN: We are very grateful to you all for the help you have given us, both in writing and by coming and answering our questions.

That concludes these sessions of oral evidence in Scotland for our study of local public spending bodies.

It has been a short, but concentrated visit and we have gained a great deal of valuable information both in our formal and less formal discussions. All our Scottish witnesses have been frank and thoughtful and we have covered some very important issues. We are very grateful also for the warm welcome we have had from our witnesses and everyone else we have met.

I hope in turn that we shall be able to make recommendations which will be regarded as helpful to the institutions and people of Scotland and not simply as another bureaucratic burden. Thank you.

WEDNESDAY 31 JANUARY 1996

AFTERNOON SESSION

OPENING STATEMENT

Opening Statement from the Scottish Federation of Housing Associations

Housing associations and co-operatives in Scotland differ significantly from the majority of their counterparts in England and Wales. They are small in size with most having less than 1000 houses and the majority are designed to serve a local community. Levels of tenant and member involvement are high, particularly in housing co-operatives where the percentage of tenants who are also members can be close to 100 per cent. This in turn increases the local accountability of associations and co-operatives as committee members are elected from this pool of local members. It should also be noted that all housing associations and co-operatives are subject to regulation by and are thus accountable to Scottish Homes.

The SFHA has noted with interest the results of NFHA's Inquiry into Housing Association Governance, having made a submission to the Inquiry itself. SFHA has also been involved with Scottish Homes Voluntary Committee Member research. Both of these initiatives will result in improved housing association performance. SFHA, for example, will be enhancing its training programme, devising a Code of Governance for Committee Members and commissioning a Committee Member's Handbook for their guidance.

Finally, SFHA will introduce its Service Mark in early 1996. The Mark will be awarded to housing associations in SFHA membership and will also be available to other organisations provided that i) they are registered with Scottish Homes, ii) that they abide by SFHA's Members' Charter and Statement of Common Values, and iii) that they adhere to SFHA's Codes of Conduct. The Mark has been introduced to ensure the maintenance of high standards within housing associations and as a protection to existing and prospective tenants.

THE COMMITTEE ON STANDARDS IN PUBLIC LIFE SUPPLEMENTARY MEMORANDA RELATING TO TRANSCRIPTS OF ORAL EVIDENCE

The principle documents necessary to understand evidence given by witnesses in the transcripts of oral evidence are included at the end of this volume. Copies of all other submissions received by the Committee, relating to local public spending bodies, may be consulted at the Public Records Office at Kew, the Public Record Office of Northern Ireland in Belfast, the Scottish Public Record Office in Edinburgh, and the National Library of Wales in Aberystwyth.

Supplementary Memorandum from the Comptroller and Auditor General

When I gave evidence to the Committee on 5 December, I agreed to provide an additional note on the work that the National Audit Office would undertake if granted enhanced access rights to all local public spending bodies.

I am pleased to enclose the attached note which sets out the practical implications of having full access rights to housing associations and local enterprise companies and training enterprise councils. The note also refers to the extensive work undertaken by the National Audit Office in the education sector where we already have access.

2 February 1996

The National Audit Office's access to local public spending bodies: Supplementary note by the Comptroller and Auditor General

Part 1:   Introduction

1.1 In their first report, the Committee on Standards in Public Life commented that they saw much merit in the Comptroller and Auditor General being granted inspection rights over all public expenditure. The Comptroller and Auditor General's submission to the Committee in November 1995 gave details of the National Audit Office's access to local public spending bodies, and illustrated the gaps.

1.2 As set out in paragraph 2.2 of the C&AG's earlier note on "Local Public Spending Bodies", access rights are required for examining:

— **Regularity:** which is confirmation that expenditure and receipts are in accordance with the legislation authorising them, any applicable designated authority and the rules of Government Accounting; and that any grants have been expended in accordance with grant conditions.

— **Propriety:** which checks to ensure that expenditure and receipts have been dealt with in accordance with Parliament's expectations as to the way in which public business should be conducted, including the conventions agreed with Parliament and in particular the Committee of Public Accounts.

— **Value for money:** which examines the economy, efficiency and effectiveness with which the body has used its resources.

1.3 At present the C&AG does not have access rights to either Housing Associations or Local Enterprise Companies for any of the three criteria. For Training and Enterprise Councils the C&AG has access for regularity and propriety purposes but not value for money.

1.4 Further to the Comptroller and Auditor General's undertaking to the Committee on 5 December 1995, this note sets out the rationale for the National Audit Office to have full access rights to these three types of local public spending bodies; how these rights would be exercised in practice; and the potential resource implications for the National Audit Office.

Part 2:   Housing Associations

2.1 Housing associations are bodies set up to provide social housing. They are currently the Government's chosen instrument for carrying out an important programme. Although only around a fifth of the registered housing associations in England, Scotland and Wales receive development funds at present, others have received public sector capital grants in the past.

2.2 Although lower than in some recent years, the level of public funding for housing associations in England remains high, at £1.2 billion in the current year (1995-96), and it is planned to continue at around £1 billion a year in the next few years. In Wales and Scotland, public funding for 1995-96 is budgeted at £125 million and £266 million respectively. Associations are subject to external scrutiny, provided by external auditors appointed by the associations themselves, but these auditors do not have any responsibility to report to Parliament. Nor are they able to take an overview across the sector, thereby allowing for dissemination of good practice.

2.3 The National Audit Office have been unable to examine directly in housing associations the effectiveness of the Housing Corporation's controls over regularity, or of housing associations' own internal controls, including whether grants paid to housing associations have been spent in ways which comply with any conditions placed upon them. Nor have they been able to examine propriety, that is whether associations have carried out any business funded by Parliament in line with Parliament's expectations concerning the proper conduct of public business.

2.4 On value for money, the National Audit Office have been given limited access to housing associations through an understanding with the Department of the Environment, which provides for consultation with a sample of individual associations to inform value for money studies of the Housing Corporation. This, however, is subject to discussion with the Department in each case, and applies only to associations that agree to be included.

2.5 Strengthened rights to access would allow the National Audit Office to provide useful feedback to individual associations, draw out and disseminate good practice to the housing association movement, and provide valuable assurance to Parliament. In recognition of this gap in the accountability of housing associations, the Public Accounts Committee recommended in their Twentieth report of Session 1993-94 that inspection rights for the National Audit Office should be made a condition of grant to associations which receive a significant part of their resources from public funds or have publicly funded assets.

2.6 Forthcoming legislation on social housing is expected to bring changes in this sector but it is likely that housing associations will have a continuing role as the main new providers of social housing. Future arrangements for National Audit Office access rights will need to take account of these changes. But in advance of legislation it is difficult to assess whether new developments such as opening housing association grant up to competition will deflect significant funding on a regular basis into other bodies as yet to be defined. If so, some of the same arguments for independent examination might also apply to those bodies.

Exercise of access rights

2.7 The Committee raised with the Comptroller and Auditor General a concern that had been expressed to them that, as many housing associations are small voluntary bodies, to bring them within the system of review by the National Audit Office would amount to an excessive degree of regulation. The Committee wished to know whether such review would be confined to the bigger associations, or would extend across the board.

2.8 In practice some 600 of the 2,300 registered housing associations in England are active developers and over 90 per cent of capital grants to housing associations are paid to 275 associations. A similar pattern exists in Scotland and Wales. The National Audit Office would therefore exercise access rights to a selection to these housing associations, with reference to the monitoring information held by the Department of the Environment and the Housing Corporation; the Scottish Office and Scottish Homes; and the Welsh Office and Housing for Wales. Around 15 housing associations would be visited each year nationwide, concentrating on those most actively developing and receiving substantial amounts of public money.

2.9 As regards housing associations other than the large developing associations, the National Audit Office would occasionally need to assess whether these smaller associations presented any additional risks to public money. This would only arise where associations had been, or were currently, in receipt of public funds, and would normally be based on monitoring information (paragraph 2.8 above) or other sources (eg for example, letters from MPs or the public) suggesting grounds for concern.

2.10 This approach would achieve a reasonable balance of coverage without imposing an onerous burden on housing associations. A programme of 15 visits each year (including Scotland and Wales) would cover, over a five-year period, around 20 per cent of the population of associations receiving the bulk of public funds and this would be sufficient to enable representative general conclusions to be drawn. Other associations would be included as necessary, but on an exceptional basis.

2.11 In exercising these access rights, the National Audit Office would in the first instance focus on propriety issues such as conflicts of interest and that contracts have been properly placed. Whilst the scope of the work at any association would depend on the circumstances, a visit should not normally last more than one staff week.

2.12 The results of each visit would be provided to associations' management committees along the lines of the reports provided for the governing bodies of grant maintained schools and further education colleges. Copies would be made available to the Housing Corporation and the Department of the Environment. The reports on individual housing associations would not normally be published. However, a summary of the more significant findings might be reported to Parliament by way of a short report or memorandum for the Public Accounts Committee.

Resource implications

2.13 In the first year any additional work would be absorbed within the National Audit Office's existing resources. Beyond this, the proposed work outlined above would be unlikely to have a significant effect on the National Audit Office budget—most likely up to five additional staff.

Part 3: Training and Enterprise Councils

3.1 Training and Enterprise Councils were set up to manage the local provision of training for young people and unemployed adults in England and Wales. There are 81 Councils, spending over £1 billion of public funds each year. Public funding represents around 90 per cent of their income.

3.2 The Comptroller and Auditor General has inspection rights to Training and Enterprise Councils as part of the contracts between the Councils and their sponsor departments. This takes the form of access to the books and records of Training and Enterprise Councils, their subsidiaries and their providers to whom they sub-contract training, for the purposes of the examination and certification of the accounts of the departments who fund the Councils. These arrangements also provide sufficient scope for the examination of propriety, including corporate governance issues.

3.3 However, access rights for value for money work are restricted to examinations of the economy, efficiency and effectiveness with which the sponsor departments have used their resources. In practice, government have interpreted this remit narrowly, restricting it to cover only reviews which focus on the steps the departments take to manage these contracts, such as the setting of targets, assessing unit costs and reviewing managements fees, rather than direct examinations of the Council's activities and management.

3.4 As in the education sector, strengthened rights to conduct value for money examinations of Training and Enterprise Councils would allow the National Audit Office to draw on their broad perspective across the sector in producing reports to Parliament, specific good practice guides and management reports for the Councils themselves. This work could give practical help to Training and Enterprise Councils in their pursuit of value for money, as well as providing valuable assurance to Parliament.

Exercise of access rights

3.5 The National Audit Office already carry out inspections of Training and Enterprise Councils for the purposes of auditing the sponsor departments' accounts. The Office is visiting 13 Training and Enterprise Councils and 26 providers in support of their audit of the departments' 1995-96 accounts. The main purpose of these visits is to examine the books and records which relate to the disbursement of public funds, to establish whether the departments' payments to the Councils had been made in accordance with Parliament's wishes as set out in the Councils' contracts with the Secretaries of State, and were properly presented in the departments' accounts. In addition to this work on the accounts, the visits to Councils will also examine whether board members and staff have acted with propriety in accordance with contractual conditions laid down by the Secretaries of State, for example on how to deal with conflicts of interest.

3.6 If the National Audit Office were granted access to Training and Enterprise Councils for value for money purposes, these would be used to carry out selective reviews of the economy, efficiency and effectiveness with which these bodies had carried out their functions funded from the public purse. The National Audit Office however are not seeking access to the work the Councils do on their own account, which represents a small proportion of their activity.

3.7 The National Audit Office are conscious of the burden of audit on Training and Enterprise Councils and other bodies and would continue to work to minimise the effect, for example by liaising closely with departments' internal auditors. Wherever possible, the work would be undertaken in conjunction with the National Audit Office's existing programme of visits to the Councils and not in addition to them.

Resource implications

3.8 The main impact of strengthened access rights would be to improve the depth and quality of our value for money work on the training programmes delivered by the Councils. Any value for money work on the Council's operations would initially be absorbed within the National Audit Office's existing resources and in subsequent years any additional work would not have a significant effect on the National Audit Office's budget.

Part 4:   Local Enterprise Companies

4.1 There are 22 Local Enterprise Companies in Scotland delivering training and other industrial and social programmes, funded through contracts with the Scottish enterprise bodies. They receive almost all of their funds, currently some £400 million each year, from these sources. Each operating contract places an obligation on the Local Enterprise Company to comply with financial procedures and accountability arrangements agreed with the enterprise bodies.

4.2 The National Audit Office do not have formal access rights to Local Enterprise Companies. In order to validate the expenditure incurred under contract, the National Audit Office currently place reliance on information obtained through a combination of informal access and documentation supplied via the enterprise bodies themselves. The National Audit Office use this information in order to satisfy themselves about, for example, the regularity of expenditure in areas such as training and environmental grants. The external auditors of Local Enterprise Companies do not examine these and other regularity issues.

4.3 In relation to value for money work the National Audit Office have secured informal access to Local Enterprise Companies for a study of the Scottish and Highlands and Islands Enterprise Bodies, but this is dependent on an agreement between these two bodies and also the Local Enterprise Companies and is not independently assured.

Exercise of access rights

4.4 If the National Audit Office were to have strengthened access rights, they would apply the same criteria as used for housing associations (see paragraphs 2.8-2.10) in deciding which companies to visit. This would probably result in visits to four companies each year.

Resources

4.5 The provision of formal access rights would have minimal resource implications because of the relatively small number of Local Enterprise Companies to be visited each year, and could therefore be absorbed within existing resources.

Part 5: Summary

5.1 This Note has set out the rationale for the National Audit Office access to housing associations and enterprise bodies. It also explains how this access would be exercised in practice, including resource implications.

5.2 The National Audit Office's work in the education sector has provided Parliament with valuable assurance about the sector. In addition, that work has been beneficial in the identification and dissemination of good practice among the grant-maintained schools, further education colleges and higher education institutions. In this work the National Audit Office have been able to assist these institutions without becoming an unwelcome burden. And in the same way the National Audit Office would aim to exercise access rights to housing associations selectively, placing minimal additional burdens on them.

5.3 The National Audit Office's ability to undertake value for money examination at Training and Enterprise Councils is related only to examination of the departments' use of the funds given to the Councils. The scope for the National Audit Office to add value to the sector would be further increased by the provision of full value for money access rights to Training and Enterprise Councils.

5.4 In the case of Local Enterprise Companies access arrangements are informal and ad hoc, and rely on the agreement of the enterprise bodies. Thus the National Audit Office have no formal right to investigate issues of propriety and governance at the companies themselves. Bringing Local Enterprise Companies into line with practice in England and Wales would enable the National Audit Office to undertake work similar to that being undertaken on corporate governance in Training and Enterprise Councils, and to add value to the sector through examining the value for money with which they have used their resources.

5.5 Strengthening of the National Audit Office's access rights to these three types of body would not require a significant increase in the National Audit Office's resources. Any growth is likely to be minimal and gradual. And we would of course act in co-operation with departments and other auditors to assist these bodies rather than impose additional burden of external inspection.

Supplementary Memorandum from the Housing Corporation

I enclose the supplementary note covering the legal advice received by the Corporation on the publication of reports commissioned under Section 28 of the Housing Associations Act 1985 and the publication, both current and planned, of regulatory information. We have confirmed the range of information in our Annual Reports as mentioned by Mr Peter Shore MP during the Committee session (paragraph 13 of our note) but I am also enclosing information on the use of our powers under Section 17 of the same act which was given from memory by Anthony Mayer in the same exchange.

4 January 1996

Publication of regulatory information

A. Introduction

1. This note covers matters on which the Committee requested further information following evidence given by Peter Cooke and Anthony Mayer on behalf of the Housing Corporation on 5 December 1995.

2. The Committee asked for further information on two issues. The first related to the question of publication of Section 28 inquiry reports. The second related to the regulatory information which is presently published and how that might be enhanced given our intention to publish a regulation stewardship report in 1996.

B. Section 28 inquiry reports

3. The Committee requested clarification of the legal advice referred to in para 19 of the Corporation's Supplementary Memorandum dated 24 November.

'The Corporation has taken legal advice on whether it should publish a Section 28 enquiry report. That advice was strongly against publication *not* on grounds of secrecy but essentially on grounds of natural justice. To publish in advance of any appeal to the High Court what is in effect the case for the prosecution could seriously prejudice any challenge of the Corporation's decision. Furthermore, without the protection of absolute privilege a commitment to publication of an inquirer's report would seriously restrict what could be said in the final report given the law of libel'.

4. The advice of Counsel was taken in 1979 on the general question of the status and standing of the reports of the person (or persons) appointed to conduct an inquiry into the affairs of an association under what is now Section 28 of the Housing Associations Act 1985. It is on the basis of Counsel's advice that the Corporation has approached the question of publication when conducting subsequent Section 28 inquiries mindful, however, that in each case and at each stage in the inquiry process, legal advice needs to be taken to ensure that the Corporation is acting properly in its statutory role as regulator.

5. The advice of Counsel makes it clear that the inquirer's task is to provide the Corporation with *information necessary* to decide whether there has been misconduct or mismanagement in the administration of the association. It is for the Corporation to consider the inquirer's report and any representations put to it by parties named in the report and only then to reach a decision on whether there has been misconduct or mismanagement. Only when it has come to that decision may the Corporation exercise its powers under Section 30 and/or 32.

6. Section 30 permits the Corporation to remove any member, officer, agent or employee responsible for or privy to the misconduct or mismanagement or for its perpetration. Anyone so removed has a right of appeal to the High Court. Section 32 allows the Corporation with the Secretary of State's consent to transfer the association's land and property to another association.

7. The inquirer's report is regarded by the Corporation as 'untested' evidence. It is for that reason that any criticisms contained in the report are put to those individuals concerned so they can make any necessary representations to the Corporation before a decision is reached. Should an appeal to the High Court arise there is little doubt that the inquirer's report would form the core of the Corporation's evidence. To publish this information—effectively constituting the case for the prosecution—in advance of any such hearing could seriously prejudice the appellant's challenge of the Corporation's decision to removal.

8. The advice of Counsel also addressed the liability of the inquirer and the Corporation to an action for libel in the event of his/her report being published. While the view was taken that the inquirer probably has qualified privilege, such privilege would not extend to the Corporation if it published the inquirer's report. Given that the Corporation's purpose in commissioning an inquiry is to gather *whatever* information is needed to establish whether or not there has been misconduct or mismanagement, it would not make sense to limit matters covered simply to avoid an action for libel.

9. The Committee is asked to further note that in the most recently conducted and highly charged case relating to Harambee Housing Association the need for confidentiality lay at the heart of the inquirers' approach. Patricia Scotland QC and Nigel Beckhough, who undertook the inquiry, found it essential to gather much of their evidence from a series of interviews conducted with people involved in the running of the association. For their own personal safety, several of these witnesses were only prepared to give evidence on condition that the information they provided would be treated in confidence.

10. In this case, recognising the local and public interest in the affairs of Harambee, the Corporation took steps throughout to ensure that public statements were issued to record and explain the action being taken. Press notices were thus released at the outset of the Section 28 inquiry, at the time of the receipt of the interim inquiry report and initial suspension of two members; at the conclusion of the inquiry and permanent removal of two members; and at the time of the decision to transfer the association's land and property to another association.

C. Annual reporting of regulatory information

11. There are two principal ways in which we report on regulatory information each year:

(a) through our Annual Report submitted to the Secretary of State for the Environment who in turn is required to lay the Report and our Annual Accounts before Parliament.

(b) through a Stewardship (Regulation) Report is presently prepared to meet the requirements of our sponsor division in the Department of the Environment.

12. The Corporation's Annual Report is a public document. Copies are routinely distributed to local authorities, members of Parliament, housing associations, as well as others (eg representative bodies - National Federation of Housing Associations, National Association of Almshouses, etc).

13. The report on regulatory activity in the Annual Report can be categorised in a number of ways:

(a) trends in the development of regulatory policy and procedure;

(b) outcomes of regulation, eg the use made of our statutory powers in relation to supervision of associations, liquidation's and bankruptcies;

(c) statistical information, eg, number of new associations registering, number removed from the register; number of consents issued under Section 9 of the Housing Associations Act 1985 to allow associations to dispose of land; number of annual account submissions from associations and prosecutions for failure to submit accounts.

14. The Regulation Stewardship Report is not presently published. The Committee have a copy of the report for 1994–95. Non-publication is not due to the confidentiality of information referred to rather that it is tailored to meet the specific requirements of our sponsoring division in the Department. Having decided that next year's report should be published we are now considering the best way of making the information available to a wider audience, avoiding unnecessary overlap with the Annual Report. The Committee's views would therefore be most welcome.

15. At this stage we anticipate the published report would cover the following matters:

— description of how the Corporation's regulatory function is organised—clarifying the lines of accountability—and how it is discharged;

— basic information about new registrations and removals; approvals under Approved Landlord arrangements and maintenance of the Public Register;

— numbers of annual returns and annual accounts received and action taken to deal with those associations failing to submit accounts;

— description of the number of associations whose performance has been reviewed in the year;

— overall findings and conclusions from performance review with policy and practice issues drawn out where appropriate;

— account of the issue of guidance and policy direction aimed at prevention of performance failings;

— outline of supervision cases in terms of the failings identified and the remedial action being taken;

— summary analysis of key performance indicators to establish general health of the movement.

16. Finally, the Committee may like to note that each year after the Budget Statement the Corporation publishes a report setting out its overall priorities and targets for each of its main functions. A copy of *Meeting Challenges* issued in February 1995 has been supplied to the Committee. We would be happy to supply a copy of our next report due out at the end of March 1996.

The number of appointments made to Committees under Section 17 of the Housing Associations Act 1985

Year	Appointments made	Appointments ended	Total at the year end
1990/91	6 in 2 associations	17 in 4 associations	34 in 11 associations
1991/92	0	32 in 10 associations	2 in 1 association
1992/93	14 in 2 associations	2 in 1 association	14 in 2 associations
1993/94	0	0	14 in 2 associations
1994/95	9 in 3 associations	0	23 in 5 associations

Letter from National Council for Voluntary Organisations to the Secretary

Representation of the community on further and higher education bodies

When our Chair, Sir Geoffrey Chandler and Chief Executive, Stuart Etherington, gave evidence to the committee they were asked whether they had any intelligence on the representation of community interests on higher and further education bodies. We made a commitment to consult our members and report back to the Committee.

Only a small proportion of our members have experience of, or relationships with, further and higher education bodies. Those that do are largely in the education and training field themselves. The views of organisations who responded to the request for information were very mixed. Most based their views on the experience of working with one or two educational establishments in their area and thus responses will vary according to local experience. A few umbrella body's responding, had wider experience of a range of institutions and therefore more of an overview.

Of the organisations reporting on local relationships with educational bodies they were equally divided between further education and higher education bodies. Half of the organisations who had contact with these bodies were aware of the representation of community interests on boards, half were not. Of those that were aware of community representation responses were evenly divided between whether the arrangements worked well or not. The vast majority of the organisations who responded to our enquiries did believe that further and higher education bodies could be more responsive to local community needs. One organisation commented that although consultation with community interests did occur this was regarded as being a public relations exercise rather than a process that would genuinely influence future policies and plans.

Views from the umbrella bodies gave more of a national perspective on the way that relationships worked. They shared the concern that industrial and commercial interests pre-dominate on boards. In particular, NIACE, the National Institute for Adult Continuing Education were concerned that representation did not meet the concerns of adult learners in the community - who constitute the majority of students enroled on all types of further and higher education courses. Concern was also expressed about the minimal representation of local community education providers, especially LEA services and centres, voluntary organisations and community groups.

It was generally the view that the composition of boards did not reflect the broader make-up of society, whether locally or nationally, and comments were specifically made about the gender balance and the representation of minority ethnic communities on boards. However, it was suggested that further regulation or legislation might be needed to alter the composition of boards.

In conclusion, there is a general perception that boards could, and should, be more responsive to local needs and that representation of a wider range of interests, experience and expertise would help further and higher education bodies to be so. There was also a number of comments that the assumption that representation of commercial interests enabled education bodies to be more efficient and effective had not been proved in reality. There was general support for wider representation of voluntary and community interests, education providers and local authorities as a means to strengthen the governance and practice of these bodies.

4 March 1996

Supplementary Memorandum from Scottish Homes

Please find enclosed a sample of a typical rent arrears report to Committee in my Housing Co-operative, as promised on Wednesday 31 January.

19 February 1996

Sample of rent arrears report from Calvay Housing Co-operative, Glasgow

Please find attached a sample copy of a typical rent arrears report, that would be presented to the Housing Management and Maintenance Sub Committee.

As you can see from the report, reference numbers are used for each case. Only the Housing Management Staff have access to which Tenant each reference number relates to.

Patricia Gallagher, Housing Manager

Report to the Management and Maintenance Sub-Committee of 01/01/01
Item: 1.3

Subject: Arrears in excess of £500   **Prepared by:Housing Manager**   **Date: 5/2/1996**

Case No	Current Arrears Date	NPRP Expiry	Comments	Recommendations
930814	* (£627.89) £381.12	Feb 96	Tenant has arrangement to pay £150 per month. Arrangement broken in Dec 95	Tenant to attend interview with Housing Manager. Arrangement to be reviewed
930816	* (£576.40) £509.42	Case sisted July 95	Arrangement made in Dec 95 to pay £25 per week ie. £18 to rent and £7 to arrears. Adhering to arrangement	Monitor closely
930904	* (£565.77) £868.33		Tenant has made an arrangement to clear arrear in full	Monitor closely
940509	* (£613.39) £275.34	June 96	DSS deductions on top of full Housing Benefit	Monitor
940802	* (£552.23) £350.27	March 96	Tenant now paying £160 by standing order	Monitor closely

*Arrear level when case first reported to Committee

Supplementary Memorandum from Scottish Enterprise

I enclose an extract from the Operating Contract with the Local Enterprise Companies covering our procedures on Conflict of Interest. I believe this should be substituted for the summary in the opening statement as a more accurate description of the position.

29 February 1996

The Conflict of Interest procedure will ensure (in addition to the duties incumbent on Directors under the Companies Acts) that:

(i) Registers of Interests will be maintained by the Company for Directors and for staff. The Registers of Interest will be open for inspection to Scottish Enterprise. The Register of Directors' Interests will be open to public inspection.

(ii) It shall be the duty of Directors and staff to ensure that their respective interests are duly registered and regularly updated. The Registers will be reviewed by the Company at least annually. The Interests to be registered are as specified in the Best Practice Guide.

(iii) In relation to any contract or other matter under consideration by the Company the Board shall decide whether or not there is any Conflict of Interest.

(iv) Where any Conflict of Interest arises the Board shall take such steps as it considers appropriate having regard to the nature of the Interest and the need to maintain the highest standards of integrity and propriety in relation to the conduct of its affairs.

(v) No contracts, business, finance or other award ("Contract") will be made to any Director or any firm, company or other body in which an Interest has been registered by, or a Conflict of Interest concerning, a Director has arisen unless

    (1) the Board shall have consented in writing to that Contract: and either

    (2.1) the Director concerned shall have been excluded from any deliberation of the Contract and shall have no undue influence on the Board's decision; and

    (2.2) the Contract is disclosed by the Company in its Annual Report: or

    (3) the Interest in question does not concern any private financial or beneficial interest and the Board deals with the Interest in accordance with sub-paragraph iv) above;

    provided always, however, that the Board shall minute such decision and the reasons therefore.

(vi) The Company shall take all reasonable steps to ensure that its Conflict of Interest procedure conforms to any agreement reached between Scottish Enterprise, the Company and other Local Enterprise Companies, or a majority of them.

(vii) Suitable arrangements are established to monitor and manage the Conflict of Interest procedure.

6.7.2 The Complaints Procedure and the Conflict of Interest Procedure will be formulated and operated to a standard acceptable to Scottish Enterprise and the Company will provide Scottish Enterprise with any information it may reasonably require to enable it to monitor the operation of these procedures and review their effectiveness.

6.8 Transparency and openness

6.8.1 The Company will on 1st October in each year make available for inspection by the general public details of all

(i) grants,

(ii) loans,

(iii) investments, or

(iv) payments to Training Providers

of £5,000 or over made by the Company in the six month period ending on 31st March of that year.

6.8.2 The Company will on 1st April in each year starting on 1st April 1997 make available for inspection by the general public details of all

(i) grants,

(ii) loans,

(iii) investments, or

(iv) payments to Training Providers

of £5,000 or over made by the Company in the six months period ending on 30th September in the previous year.

6.8.3 Where, in the opinion of the Company, the disclosure of details referred to in Clauses 6.8.1 and 6.8.2 will be prejudicial to the commercial interest of the recipient or be market sensitive, the Company may refrain from making such details available for inspection by the general public.

The following list includes organisations who contributed written evidence.

Universities & Colleges etc.

Aberdeen College
University of Aberdeen
University of Abertay Dundee
Association for Colleges/Colleges' Employers' Forum
Association of Colleges in the Eastern Region
Association of Scottish Colleges
Association of Teachers & Lecturers
Association of University & College Lecturers
Association of University Teachers
Barry College
Basildon College
Birmingham University, Institute of Local Government Studies
Bolton Institute
Boston College
University of Bradford
University of Brighton
University of Bristol
University of Bristol—Convocation
Cardiff Institute of Higher Education
Cardiff Tertiary College
Cheltenham & Gloucester College
Committee of University Chairmen
Committee of Vice Chancellors & Principals
Conference of Higher Education Internal Auditors
Coventry Technical College
Deeside College
De Montfort University
Derby Tertiary College, Wilmorton
University of Dundee
Dundee College
Dunstable College
University of East Anglia
University of Edinburgh
Edinburgh's Telford College
Exeter College
Furness College
Further Education Funding Council
University of Glamorgan
University of Glamorgan Trade Union Alliance
University of Glasgow
Glasgow Caledonian University
Glasgow School of Art
Guildford College
Gwent Tertiary College
Havant College
Heriot-Watt University
University of Hertfordshire
Higher Education Funding Council for England
University of Huddersfield
Huddersfield Technical College
Huntingdonshire Regional College
John Ruskin College
Kendall College
University of Kent at Canterbury
King's College London
Langside College Glasgow
University of Leeds
Leeds Metropolitan University
University of London, Institute of Education
London School of Economics
Coleg Meirion Dwyfor
Middlesex University
Moray House Institute of Education
Napier University Edinburgh

National Association of Schoolmasters Union of Women Teachers
National Association of Teachers in Further Education & Higher Education
New College Durham
Norfolk College of Arts & Technology
North Birmingham College
North East Surrey College of Technology
Nottingham Trent University
Oxford University
University of Paisley
Pembrokeshire College
University of Plymouth
University of Portsmouth
Queen Margaret College
Queen Mary & Westfield College
Reading University Centre for Ombudsman Studies
Robert Gordon University
Royal Holloway University
Royal Scottish Academy of Music & Drama
St Andrew's College
'Save Our College'
Scottish Higher Education Funding Councils
Sheffield College
Sixth Form Colleges' Association
Solihull College
Southampton Institute
South East Essex College
South Thames College
South Tyneside College
Standing Conference of Principals
Stevenson College
University of Strathclyde
Suffolk College
Swansea Institute of Higher Education
Teeside Tertiary College
Trinity College Carmarthen
UNISON Higher Education
United Medical & Dental Schools of Guy's & St Thomas's Hospitals
University & College Lecturers' Union
University & College Lecturers' Union, Hammersmith & West London College
University of Wales, Bangor
University of Wales College of Medicine
University of Wales, Lampeter
University of Wales, Swansea
Walsall College of Arts & Technology
Welsh Funding Councils
University of West of England, Bristol
Yale College

Grant-maintained Schools etc.

Association of Grant Maintained & Aided Schools
Belper School G.M.
Calday Grange Grammar School
Chelmsford County High School for Girls
Chetwood Primary School, The
Funding Agency for Schools
Grant Maintained Schools Advisory Committee
Grant Maintained Schools Foundation
Great Barr Grant Maintained School
Local Schools Information
National Association of Head Teachers
Professional Association of Teachers

St Gregory's Catholic Comprehensive School
Secondary Heads' Association
Teacher Training Agency
Whitefield Schools & Centre
William Farr Church of England Comprehensive
School

*Training & Enterprise Councils and Local
Enterprise Companies etc.*

Association of British Chambers of Commerce
Central England Training & Enterprise Council
Council of Welsh TECs
Forth Valley Enterprise
Hertfordshire Training & Enterprise Council
Highlands & Islands Enterprise
Humberside Training & Enterprise Council
Lincolnshire Training & Enterprise Council
London TEC Council
Manchester Training & Enterprise Council
Northamptonshire Chamber of Commerce Training &
Enterprise
Northumberland Training & Enterprise Council Group
Renfrewshire Enterprise
Scottish Chambers of Commerce
Scottish Enterprise
South London Training & Enterprise Council
TEC National Council
Wales Chamber of Commerce
Walsall Training & Enterprise Council
West Wales Training and Enterprise Council

Housing Associations etc.

Anchor Housing Association
Bedfordshire Pilgrims Housing Association
Bethnal Green & Victoria Park Housing Association
Bramham, Bolton & Collingham Gardens Residents'
Association
Broomleigh Housing Association
Chartered Institute of Housing
Charnwood Forest Housing Association
Circle 33 Area Committee Steering Group
Circle 33 Housing Association
Eastleigh Housing Association
Family Housing Association
Focus Housing Group
Focus Shareholders' Group
Foundation Housing Association
Hanover Housing Association
Home Housing Association
Housing Corporation
Housing for Wales
Hyde Housing Association
Jephson Housing Association Group
Joseph Rowntree Trust
Leicester Newarke Housing Association
Lincolnshire Rural Housing Association
Liverpool Housing Trust
Longhurst Housing Association
Manchester & District Housing Group
Maritime Housing Association
National Federation of Housing Associations
Orwell Housing Association
Peabody Trust
Scottish Federation of Housing Associations
Scottish Homes
Shepherds Bush Housing Association
Swale Housing Association

Shepherds Bush Housing Association Tenants'
Committee
Threshold Tenant Trust Pimlico Residents' Association
UNISON Housing Association Branch
Wales & West Housing Association
Welsh Federation of Housing Associations
Westcountry Housing Association
West Kent Housing Association
William Sutton Trust

Local Government etc.

Angus District Council
Association of Council Secretaries & Solicitors
Association of County Councils
Association of London Government
Association of Metropolitan Authorities
Brent Council
Broadland District Council
Carlisle City Council
Chesterfield Borough Council
Clackmannan District Council
Cleveland County Council
Colchester Borough Council
Commission for Local Administration in England
Convention of Scottish Local Authorities (CoSLA)
City of Coventry Council
Devonshire County Council
Dudley Metropolitan Borough Council
East Ayrshire Council
Forest of Dean District Council
Hertfordshire County Council
Kent County Council
Kingswood Borough Council
Kirklees Metropolitan Council
Liverpool City Council
Local Government Information Unit
National Association of Councillors
Newark & Sherwood District Council
New Forest District Council
North Tyneside Council
Norwich City Council
City of Nottingham Council
Oundle Town Council
Rugby Borough Council
Society of Local Authority Chief Executives
South Northamptonshire Council
Stevenage Borough Council
Tameside Metropolitan Borough Council
Western Isles Islands Council
Windsor & Maidenhead Borough Council

Other Organisations & Groups

Aldbourne Associates
Association of Chief Executives of National Voluntary
Organisations
Audit Commission
Basil Wyatt & Sons Ltd.
Campaign for State Education
Chartered Institute of Public Finance & Accountancy
(CIPFA)
Charter 88
Community Service Volunteers, National Association
for the Care and Resettlement of Offenders
(NACRO) & Rathbone/Community Industry
Comptroller & Auditor General (Sir John Bourn KCB)
Cornerstone Advisory Service
Council for Academic Autonomy

Council for Academic Freedom & Academic Standards
(CAFAS)
DEMOS
Department for Education & Employment
Ember Research
Enfield Voluntary Service Council
Eversheds Solicitors
Firm Choice Ltd
Grant Thornton Chartered Accountants
Guild of Editors
Halifax Building Society
Institute of Public Service Administrators
Kirkstall Valley Campaign
Maldon District Green Party
Manufacturing, Science & Finance Union (MSF)
National Association of Governors & Managers
National Council for Voluntary Organisations
National Training Federation
Oxstalls Action Group
Parents Opposed to Opting-out (POO)
Parliamentary Commissioner for Administration
(Ombudsman)
Public Concern at Work
Redress
Scottish Council for Voluntary Organisations
Scottish Office Education & Industry Department
South Yorkshire Police Authority
Trades Union Congress
UNISON Southern Region

THE COMMITTEE ON STANDARDS IN PUBLIC LIFE
LIST OF MEETINGS AND VISITS UNDERTAKEN BY THE COMMITTEE
AND MEMBERS OF THE SECRETARIAT

The list includes institutions, representative bodies and organisations which Members of the Committee and Secretariat have met or visited during the course of its study into local public spending bodies.

Universities & Colleges etc.

Association for Colleges
Association of Heads of University Administration
Basildon College of Further Education
Cheltenham and Gloucester College of Higher Education
Colleges Employers Forum
Committee of University Chairman
Council for Academic Freedom and Academic Standards
Council for Academic Autonomy
De Montfort University
Further Education Funding Council for England
Higher Education Funding Council for England
Keele University
Leeds Metropolitan University
Scottish Higher Education Funding Council
Sheffield Hallam University
Stockton and Billingham College of Further Education
Teesside Tertiary College
University of Bath
University of Brighton
University of Bristol
University of Durham
University of Leeds
University of Newcastle
University of Northumbria at Newcastle
University of Sheffield
University of Teesside
University of York
Welsh Funding Councils

Grant-maintained schools etc.

Abbey Grange Church of England (GM) High School, Leeds
Action for Governors' Information and Training
Broomfield County Primary School, Essex
Calday Grange Grammar School, Wirral
Funding Agency for Schools
Grant Maintained Schools Advisory Committee
Grant Maintained Schools Centre
Grant Maintained Schools Foundation
Hylands School, Essex
King Edward VI Grammar School, Essex
National Association of Head Teachers
Newlands Spring Primary School, Essex
Our Lady Immaculate RC Primary School, Essex
Mrs Joan Sallis
Sandon School, Essex

Training and Enterprise Councils and Local Enterprise Companies etc.

Association of British Chambers of Commerce
Professor Robert Bennett
Central England TEC
Gwent TEC
Highlands and Islands Enterprise
Humberside TEC
Inverness and Nairn Enterprise
Lanarkshire Development Agency
Northamptonshire Chamber of Commerce, Training and Enterprise

Scottish Enterprise
SOLOTEC, Bromley
Sussex Chamber of Commerce, Training and Enterprise
TEC Assessors Committee
TEC National Council
West London TEC

Housing Associations etc.

Basildon Community Housing Association
Beacon Housing Association, Slough
Bradford & Northern Housing Association
Broomleigh Housing Association, Bromley
Cara Irish Housing Association
Chartered Institute of Housing
Ealing Family Housing Association
Edinvar Housing Association, Edinburgh
Faifley Housing Association, Glasgow
First Choice Housing Association
Glamorgan and Gwent Housing Association
Govanhill Housing Association, Glasgow
Grosvenor Housing Association, St Helens
Harewood Housing Society
Headrow Housing Association, Leeds
Housing Association Ombudsman
Housing Corporation
Link Housing Association, Edinburgh
London & Quadrant Housing Association
Manningham Housing Association Bradford
Margaret Blackwood Housing Association, Edinburgh
Moat Housing Association, Sevenoaks
National Federation of Housing Associations
Newlon Housing Association, East London
Oxford Brookes Housing Association
Oxford Citizens Housing Association
Oxford Spectrum Housing Association
Scottish Homes
St Helens Housing Association
St Lukes Housing Association, Oxford
Swale Housing Association, Sittingbourne
Taff Housing Association
Tai Cymru (Housing for Wales)
Wales and West Housing Association

Other Organisations.

Audit Commission
Bradford City Council
Department for Education and Employment
Department of the Environment
Government Office for Yorkshire
Government Office for West Midlands
Grant Thornton Accountants
National Audit Office
National Audit Office (Edinburgh)
Oxford City Council
Public Concern at Work
Scottish Office
Sevenoaks District Council
South Bucks District Council
Welsh Office

Printed in the United Kingdom for HMSO
Dd 5064867 5/96 C20 65536 351651 17/35250